Intermediate Accounting

SIXTH CANADIAN EDITION

INTERMEDIATE
ACCOUNTING

Donald E. Kieso, PhD, CPA
KPMG Peat Marwick Emeritus Professor of Accounting
Northern Illinois University
DeKalb, Illinois

Jerry J. Weygandt, PhD, CPA
Arthur Andersen Alumni Professor of Accounting
University of Wisconsin
Madison, Wisconsin

Terry D. Warfield, PhD
PricewaterhouseCoopers Research Scholar
University of Wisconsin
Madison, Wisconsin

V. Bruce Irvine, PhD, CPA, CA
University of Saskatchewan
Saskatoon, Saskatchewan

W. Harold Silvester, PhD, CPA, CA
University of Saskatchewan (Emeritus)
Saskatoon, Saskatchewan

Nicola M. Young, MBA, FCA
Saint Mary's University
Halifax, Nova Scotia

Irene M. Wiecek, CA
University of Toronto
Toronto, Ontario

John Wiley & Sons Canada, Ltd.

National Library of Canada Cataloguing in Publication Data

Kieso, Donald E.
        Intermediate accounting

6th Canadian ed./prepared by V. Bruce Irvine... [et al.]
Includes bibliographical references and index.
ISBN 0-471-64635-0 (v. 1).—ISBN 0-471-64636-9 (v. 2)

1. Accounting. I. Weygandt, Jerry J. II. Irvine, V. Bruce
III. Title

HF5635.I 573 2001   657'.044   C2001-902193-3

Production Credits
Publisher: John Horne
Publishing Services Director: Karen Bryan
Editorial Manager: Karen Staudinger
Sr. Marketing Manager: Janine Daoust
New Media Editor: Elsa Passera
Publishing Services/Permissions Co-ordinator: Michelle Marchetti
Design & Typesetting: Quadratone Graphics Ltd.
Cover Design: Interrobang Graphic Design
Cover Photo: Grant V. Faint/Image Bank
Printing & Binding: Tri-Graphic Printing Limited

Printed and bound in Canada
10 9 8 7 6 5 4 3 2 1

John Wiley & Sons Canada, Ltd.
22 Worcester Road
Etobicoke, Ontario M9W 1L1
Visit our website at: www.wiley.com/canada

Dedicated to our husbands

John and George

and to our children

Hilary

Tim

Megan

Nicholas, and

Katherine

for their support, encouragement, and tolerance

throughout the writing of this book.

About the Authors

Canadian Edition

Nicola M. Young, MBA, FCA, teaches accounting in the Frank H. Sobey Faculty of Commerce at Saint Mary's University in Halifax, Nova Scotia where her responsibilities have varied from the introductory offering to final year advanced financial courses to the survey course in the Executive MBA program. She is the recipient of the Commerce Professor of the Year and the university-wide Alumni teaching medal, and contributes to the academic and administrative life of the university through membership on the Board of Governors, the Quality of Teaching and other Committees. Professor Young has been associated with the Atlantic School of Chartered Accountancy for over twenty-five years in a variety of roles. These include program and course development, teaching, and most recently, chairing ASCA's Education Reform Impact Study. In addition to contributions to the accounting profession at the provincial level, Professor Young has served on national boards of the CICA dealing with licensure and education. For the last ten years, she has worked with the CICA's Public Sector Accounting Board as an Associate, as a member and chair of the Board, and as a member and chair of the Task Force on the Senior Government Financial Reporting Model.

Irene M. Wiecek, CA is Associate Director of the Master of Management and Professional Accounting Program (MMPA) at the Joseph L. Rotman School of Management, University of Toronto where she is also a Faculty member, lecturing primarily in Financial Reporting. She has taught in the Executive MBA, MBA, MMPA, B Com and Management Major Programs covering material from Introductory Accounting to Advanced Accounting. Currently focusing on the area of integrated learning, she is involved in redesigning the MMPA program and has developed numerous cases, which examine financial reporting, and its link to other functional area such as finance and strategy. A prolific case writer, Irene has won case competitions for writing and presenting cases as well as leading and coaching student teams. She has had several cases published in accounting journals. At the professional level, Irene is involved in an educational capacity with both the Canadian and Ontario Institutes of Chartered Accountants, as well as the Society of Management Accountants. Prior to working at the University of Toronto, Irene worked for KPMG as a public accountant and as a consultant in private industry. Irene obtained her Chartered Accountancy designation in 1981.

U.S. Edition

Donald E. Kieso, Ph.D., C.P.A., received his bachelor's degree from Aurora University and his doctorate in accounting from the University of Illinois. He has served as chairman of the Department of Accountancy and is currently the KPMG Peat Marwick Emeritus Professor of Accountancy at Northern Illinois University. He has done postdoctorate work as a Visiting Scholar at the University of California at Berkeley and is a recipient of NIU's Teaching Excellence Award and four Golden Apple Teaching Awards. He has served as a member of the Board of Directors of the Illinois CPA Society, the AACSB's Accounting Accreditation Committees, the State of

Illinois Comptroller's Commission, as Secretary-Treasurer of the Federation of Schools of Accountancy, and as Secretary-Treasurer of the American Accounting Association. From 1989 to 1993 he served as a charter member of the national Accounting Education Change Commission. In 1988, he received the Outstanding Accounting Educator Award from the Illinois CPA Society, in 1992 he received the FSA's Joseph A. Silvoso Award of Merit and the NIU Foundation's Humanitarian Award for Service to Higher Education, and in 1995 he received a Distinguished Service Award from the Illinois CPA Society.

Jerry J. Weygandt, Ph.D., C.P.A., is Arthur Andersen Alumni Professor of Accounting at the University of Wisconsin-Madison. He holds a Ph.D. in accounting from the University of Illinois. Articles by Professor Weygandt have appeared in the Accounting Review, Journal of Accounting Research, Accounting Horizons, Journal of Accountancy, and other academic and professional journals. These articles have examined such financial reporting issues as accounting for price-level adjustments, pensions, convertible securities, stock option contracts, and interim reports. He has served on numerous committees of the American Accounting Association and as a member of the editorial board of the Accounting Review; he also has served as President and Secretary-Treasurer of the American Accounting Association. In addition, he has been actively involved with the American Institute of Certified Public Accountants and has been a member of the Accounting Standards Executive Committee (AcSEC) of that organization. He has served on the FASB task force that examined the reporting issues related to accounting for income taxes and is presently a trustee of the Financial Accounting Foundation. Professor Weygandt has received the Chancellor's Award for Excellence in Teaching and the Beta Gamma Sigma Dean's Teaching Award. He is on the board of directors of M & I Bank of Southern Wisconsin and the Dean Foundation. Recently he received the Wisconsin Institute of CPA's Outstanding Educator's Award and the Lifetime Achievement Award.

Terry D. Warfield, Ph.D., is PricewaterhouseCoopers Research Scholar at the University of Wisconsin-Madison. He received a B.S. and M.B.A. from Indiana University and a Ph.D. in accounting from the University of Iowa. Professor Warfield's area of expertise is financial reporting, and prior to his academic career, he worked for five years in the banking industry. He served as the Academic Accounting Fellow in the Office of the Chief Accountant at the U.S. Securities and Exchange Commission in Washington, D.C., from 1995-1996. While on the staff, he worked on projects related to financial instruments and financial institutions, and he helped coordinate a symposium on intangible asset financial reporting. Professor Warfield's primary research interests concern financial accounting standards and disclosure policies. He has published scholarly articles in The Accounting Review, Journal of Accounting and Economics, Research in Accounting Regulation, and Accounting Horizons, and he has served on the editorial boards of The Accounting Review and Accounting Horizons. He has served on the Financial Accounting Standards Committee of the American Accounting Association (past Chair 1995-1996) and on the Association Council, the Nominations Committee, and the AAA-FASB Research Conference Committee. Professor Warfield has taught accounting courses at the introductory, intermediate, and graduate levels. He has received teaching awards at both the University of Iowa and the University of Wisconsin, and he was named to the Teaching Academy at the University of Wisconsin in 1995.

Preface

··

This edition of *Intermediate Accounting* represents an important milestone in the evolution of this textbook. As with the prior editions, in planning this edition we conducted extensive market research to help us focus on how the text should evolve.

Two themes emerged from this research. These themes confirmed development decisions made in recent editions of *Intermediate Accounting* and suggested ways that we could further enhance the usefulness of the text to students and instructors. The first theme is the continuing rapid pace of information technology. Support for this information technology trend is reflected in the introduction in this edition of the Digital Tool.

The Digital Tool provides a comprehensive set of materials that supplement the already-comprehensive coverage of accounting topics in the textbook. Included are "professional tools" related to written communication, working in groups, and ethics. A financial analyst's toolkit contains a comprehensive primer on financial statement analysis and a collection of over 45 real-company financial statements that students can access for financial statement and other research. Also included are expanded discussions and illustrations for topics such as international accounting, and the accounting for securitizations, and additional real-company disclosures for topics introduced in the text. We believe the Digital Tool will be an invaluable resource to students that will help them get the most out of their Intermediate Accounting investment.

The second theme that emerged from our research is the continuing evolution of the accounting profession and accounting education away from knowledge of accounting facts to the development of skills in how to use accounting facts and procedures in various business contexts. Accountants must act as well as think, and we believe that it is important for students to understand the how as well as the why of accounting. The content and focus of many of the elements of the Digital Tool (writing, working in teams, analyst's toolkit) respond to this trend by providing an expanded set of materials that can be used to extend and apply the concepts and methods introduced within the text.

We continue to strive for a balanced discussion of conceptual and procedural presentation so that these elements are mutually reinforcing. In addition, discussions focus on explaining the rationale behind business transactions before addressing the accounting and reporting for those transactions. As in prior editions, we have thoroughly revised and updated the text to include all the latest developments in the accounting profession and practice. Benefiting from the comments and recommendations of adopters of the fifth edition, we have made significant revisions. Explanations have been expanded where necessary; complicated discussions and illustrations have been simplified; realism has been integrated to heighten interest and relevancy; and new topics and coverage have been added to maintain currency. We have deleted selected fifth edition coverage from the text. To provide the instructor with no loss in material coverage and flexibility in use, discussions of less commonly used methods, more complex, or specialized topics have been moved to the Digital Tool.

NEW FEATURES

Based on extensive reviews, focus groups, and interactions with other intermediate accounting instructors and students, we have developed a number of new pedagogical features and content changes designed both to help students learn more effectively and to answer the changing needs of the course.

Digital Tool

As mentioned earlier, a major new resource developed for this edition is the Digital Tool. This CD-ROM includes a comprehensive set of materials that supplement the already-comprehensive coverage of accounting topics in the textbook. When the Digital Tool icon (shown in the margin) appears in the textbook, the student is directed to expanded materials as described below. Major elements of the Digital Tool are:

Analyst's Toolkit

The Analyst's Toolkit contains the following items.

Database of Real Companies. Over 45 annual reports of well-known companies, including several international companies, are provided on the Digital Tool. These annual reports can be used in a variety of ways. For example, they can be used as illustrations of different presentations of financial information or for comparing note disclosures across companies. In addition, these reports can be used to analyse a company's financial condition and compare its prospects with other companies in the same industry. Assignment material provides some examples of different types of analysis that can be performed.

Company Web Links. Each of the companies in the database of real companies is identified by a Web address to facilitate the gathering of additional information, if desired.

Preformatted Excel Worksheets. Worksheets formatted in Excel are available for some assignments on the Digital Tool. For example, students may be asked to calculate key ratios for a certain company (with a digital calculator provided), and to compare these ratios against those of another company. The other company's ratios are provided on a worksheet to expedite the analysis phase of the assignment.

Additional Enrichment Material. A chapter on Financial Statement Analysis is provided, with related assignment material. This chapter can also be used with the database of annual reports of real companies.

Spreadsheet Tools. Present value templates are provided which can be used to solve time value of money problems.

Additional Internet Links. A number of useful links related to financial analysis are provided to expand expertise in this area.

Professional Toolkit

Consistent with expanding beyond technical accounting knowledge, the Digital Tool emphasizes certain skills necessary to become a successful accountant and financial manager.

Writing Materials. A primer on professional communications is provided that will give students a framework for writing professional materials. This primer discusses issues such as the top ten writing problems, strategies for prewriting, how to do revisions, and tips on clarity. This primer has been class tested and is effective in helping students enhance their writing skills.

Group Work Materials. Recent evaluation of accounting education has identified the need to develop more skills in group problem solving. The Digital Tool provides a second primer dealing with the role that groups play in organizations. Information on what makes a successful group, and how students can participate effectively in the group, is included.

Ethics. Expanded materials on the role of ethics in the profession are part of the Digital Tool, including references to speeches and articles on ethics in accounting and codes of ethics for major professional bodies. It also includes additional case studies on ethics.

Career Professional Spotlights. Every student should have a good understanding of the profession that he or she is entering. Various vignettes in the Digital Tool indicate the types of work that accountants do. These vignettes are interviews with accounting and finance professionals who are at various stages of their careers.

Other aspects of the spotlight on careers are also included. As part of the Digital Tool, the following information is provided to help students make successful career choices:

- A résumé builder, to help students prepare a professional-looking résumé.
- Professional Web links—important links to Web sites that can provide useful career information.

Student Toolkit

Expanded Discussions and Illustrations. This section provides additional topics that are not covered in depth in the textbook. The Digital Tool gives the flexibility to discuss these topics of interest in more detail.

Additional topics are as follows:

- Presentation of work sheet using the periodic method.
- Specialized journals and methods of processing accounting data.
- Comprehensive illustration of transfer of receivables without recourse, with accounting entries.
- Discussion of lesser-used amortization methods, such as the retirement and replacement methods.
- Comprehensive earnings per share exercise.
- Discussion of the conceptual aspects of interperiod tax allocation.
- Real estate leases and leveraged leases.
- The T-account approach to preparation of the statement of cash flows.
- Discussion of accounting for changing prices.
- Settlements and curtailments, accrued benefit asset limitation, and termination benefits.
- Present-value-based measurements.
- Technology tools for time value problems.

International Accounting. An expanded discussion of international accounting institutions, the evolution of international accounting standards, and a framework for understanding differences in accounting practice is provided. This discussion is designed to complement the international reporting problems in the textbook.

Learning Style Survey. Research on left brain/right brain differences and also on learning and personality differences suggests that each person has preferred ways to receive and communicate information. After completing this survey, students will be able to pinpoint the study aids in the text that will help them learn the material based on their particular learning styles.

In summary, the Digital Tool is a comprehensive complement to the sixth edition of Intermediate Accounting, providing new materials as well as a new way to communicate that material.

New Chapter Openings

We have revised the chapter openings to increase student interest and to draw readers into the chapter more quickly. These openings feature:

Chapter preview and outline. A chapter preview explains the importance of the chapter topic. A graphic outline presents a visual "roadmap" of the important topics covered in the chapter.

Brief Exercises

New exercises that focus students on one study objective or topic have been added to the end-of-chapter material.

New "Using Your Judgement" Features

In the fifth edition, we introduced a new Using Your Judgement section in the end-of-chapter assignment materials. This section contains assignments that help develop students' analytical, critical thinking, and interpersonal communication skills. These materials met with wide acceptance and praise in the market, and in this edition we have added some new features, which will give instructors even more choice of materials with which to develop student abilities. These include the following:

Financial Statement Analysis Case. Each case introduces a real-world company and discusses how financial transactions affect their financial statements. Often, an assessment of the company's liquidity, solvency, or financial profitability is performed.

Comparative Analysis Case. The statements of two well-known companies are compared in relation to the topic(s) discussed in the chapter.

Research Case. Each research case provides an opportunity for the student to conduct independent research into an accounting topic related to the chapter content. In many cases, the student must access a data base (sometimes involving use of the Internet) to find the necessary information.

International Reporting Case. We have extended the international coverage in the text by introducing a number of international reporting cases that are based on real companies and designed to illustrate international accounting differences. These cases illustrate the importance of adjusting international financial statements to make them comparable across countries. This emphasis reinforces the user orientation of the "Using Your Judgement" element.

Integration of Financial Statement Analysis

By understanding the accounting processes that generate statements and the tools required to analyze these statements, students learn to look beyond the numbers. Financial ratios are covered early in the text in an appendix to Chapter 5 to enhance teaching flexibility and enable instructors who want earlier coverage to have access to it when they need it. Ratio analysis is also woven throughout the text to expose students to the significance of economic events. Many financial analysis tools are also provided on the Digital Tool.

International Insights & IAS Notes

International Insight paragraphs that describe or compare the accounting practices in other countries are provided in the margin. We have continued this feature to help students understand that other countries sometimes use different recognition and measurement principles to report financial information.

IAS Notes also appear in the margins and describe how International Accounting Standards are similar to, or differ from, Canadian standards.

ENHANCED FEATURES

We have continued and enhanced many of the features that were included in the fifth edition of Intermediate Accounting, including:

Using Your Judgement

The "Using Your Judgement" elements (Financial Reporting Problems, Financial Statement Analysis, Comparative Analysis, and Research Cases) at the end of each chapter have been revised and updated. In addition, explicit writing and group assignments have been integrated into the exercises, problems, and cases. Exercises, problems, and cases that are especially suited for group or writing assignments are identified with special icons, as shown here in the margin.

Real-World Emphasis

We believe that one of the goals of the intermediate accounting course is to orient students to the application of accounting principles and techniques in practice. Accordingly, we have continued our practice of using numerous examples from real corporations, now highlighted in blue, throughout the text. Illustrations and exhibits marked by the icon shown here are excerpts from actual financial statements of existing firms. In addition, the 2000 annual report of Canadian Tire, is included in Appendix 5B, and many real-company financial reports appear in the database on the Digital Tool.

Streamlined Presentation

We have continued our efforts to keep the topical coverage of Intermediate Accounting in line with the way instructors are currently teaching the course. Accordingly, we have moved some optional topics into appendices and have omitted altogether some topics that formerly were covered in appendices, moving them to the Digital Tool. Details are noted in the list of specific content changes below.

Currency and Accuracy

Accounting continually changes as its environment changes; an up-to-date book is therefore a necessity. As in past editions, we have strived to make this edition the most up-to-date and accurate text available.

CONTENT CHANGES

The following list outlines the revisions and improvements made in chapters of this volume.

Chapter 14

- New section on the distinction between financial liabilities and those that are non-financial in nature.
- Material on property taxes payable changed to be consistent with Section 1751 on "Interim Financial Statements."
- Short section on rents and royalties added.
- Obligations under guarantee and warranty provisions and for coupons, premiums, rebates and air miles transferred from contingent liabilities to a separate section on estimated liabilities.
- Alternative entries for estimated liabilities provided.
- Introduction of the use of liquidity ratios for analysis.

Chapter 15

- Discussion on debt that may be settled in cash or shares at the option of the issuer included.
- Key financial statement analysis ratios illustrated in presentation and analysis section.
- Material on accounting for troubled debt from both the perspective of the debtor and creditor (*CICA Handbook*, Section 3025) added.

Chapter 16

- Material on treasury shares moved to appendix.

Chapter 17

- Discussion on stock dividends versus splits expanded.
- Section on key ratios added.

Chapter 18

- New material on stock compensation plans (*CICA Handbook* Section 3870) and EPS (*CICA Handbook* Section 3500) added.
- New appendix that deals with derivative financial instruments and incorporates briefly, the material on Financial Instruments from the Joint Working Group of standard setters.

Chapter 19

- Real world illustration of note disclosure for tax losses carried forward.
- New Canadian examples of actual company disclosures related to income taxes now that the *Handbook* section has been in place for a few years.

Chapter 20

- Settlements, curtailments, accrued benefit asset limitation and termination benefits transferred to the Digital Tool.
- Chapter reorganized to include defined contribution plans in the introduction and terminology section of the chapter.
- References updated to use the new *Handbook* section, rather than the *Exposure Draft*.
- Explanation of the corridor approach clarified.
- Rewritten section on disclosure requirements to bring the chapter into line with *Handbook* Section 3461, along with illustrative disclosures where companies changed to comply with the new standards.

Chapter 21

- Illustrations of different leasing arrangements brought into the chapter from the appendix. Appendix on flowcharts removed.
- Sale and leaseback material moved into an appendix.
- Short section on real estate leases and leveraged leases moved to the Digital Tool.
- Illustration of various Canadian airlines' involvement in capital and operating leases added.
- Clarification of direct financing and sales-type lease terminology.
- Separate section on determining current and noncurrent categories of leases assets and liabilities.

Chapter 22

- Improved explanation of comparative statement of retained earnings for a change in accounting policy applied retroactively with restatement.
- Discussion of changes in reporting entity separated from Section 1506 changes.
- Changes in reporting entity limited to business combinations and discontinued operations.
- Actual company disclosures of accounting changes illustrated.
- Separate section added on the income tax effects of accounting changes.

Chapter 23

- Updated to include requirements of newly issued *Handbook* Section 1540.
- T account method moved to the Digital Tool from the appendix. The work sheet method now covered as the last topic in the chapter. Appendix eliminated.
- Reduced discussion of the evolution of the cash flow statement.
- Earlier discussion of direct versus indirect method.
- Continued equal emphasis on the direct and indirect methods.
- In Yoshi Corporation, removed discussion of amortization of premium on bonds payable and referred reader to the applicable EIC pronouncement by footnote. Example is now the more straight-forward discount amortization.
- Added new sections on interpreting the cash flow statement and cash flow per share information.

Chapter 24

- Material on Segmented information (*CICA Handbook* Section 1701), interim financial information (*CICA Handbook* Section 1751) incorporated.
- Discussion on the measurement issues related to related party transactions expanded.

END-OF-CHAPTER ASSIGNMENT MATERIAL

At the end of each chapter we have provided a comprehensive set of review and homework material consisting of brief exercises, exercises, problems, and short cases. For this edition, many of the exercises and problems have been revised or updated. In addition, the Using Your Judgement sections, which include financial reporting problems, ethics cases, financial statement analysis cases, comparative analysis cases, and research cases have all been updated. A number of international reporting cases that are based on real companies are introduced throughout the textbook. All of the assignment materials have been class tested and/or double checked for accuracy and clarity.

The brief exercises are designed for review, self-testing, and classroom discussion purposes as well as homework assignments. Typically, a brief exercise covers one topic, an exercise one or two topics. Exercises require less time and effort to solve than problems and cases. The problems are designed to develop a professional level of achievement and are more challenging and time-consuming to solve than the exercises. The cases generally require essay as opposed to quantitative solutions; they are intended to confront the student with situations calling for conceptual analysis and the exercise of judgement in identifying problems and evaluating alternatives. The Using Your Judgement assignments are designed to develop students' critical thinking, analytical, interpersonal, and communication skills.

Probably no more than one-fourth of the total exercise, problem, and case material must be used to cover the subject matter adequately; consequently, problem assignments may be varied from year to year.

ACKNOWLEDGMENTS

We thank the users of our fifth edition, including the many students who contributed to this revision through their comments and instructive criticism. Special thanks are extended to the reviewers of and contributors to our sixth edition manuscript and supplements.

Manuscript Reviewers were:

Cécile Ashman
Algonquin College

David T. Carter
University of Waterloo

Carolyn J. Davis
Brock University

Carolyn Doni
Cambrian College

David Fleming
George Brown College

Steve Fortin
McGill University

Leo Gallant
St. Francis Xavier University

Mary A. Heisz
University of Western Ontario

Darrell Herauf
Carleton University

Ron Hill
Southern Alberta Institute of Technology

Wayne Irvine
Mount Royal College

G. Selwyn James
Centennial College

Mort Nelson
Wilfrid Laurier University

Bryan Parker
British Columbia Institute of Technology

Stella M. Penner
University of Alberta

Joe Pidutti
Durham College

Wendy Roscoe
Concordia University

Jo-Anne Ryan
Nipissing University

David J. Sale
Kwantlen University College

Appreciation is also extended to colleagues at the Rotman School of Management, University of Toronto and Saint Mary's University who provided input, suggestions and support, especially Joel Amernic and Dick Chesley—who have provided inspiration through many high-spirited debates on financial reporting theory and practice—and Peter Thomas, who has shared many teaching insights over the years!

Many thanks to the staff at John Wiley and Sons Canada, Ltd. who are superb: President Diane Wood and Publisher John Horne who have been so supportive throughout; Karen Bryan, Publishing Services Director, for her incredible efforts; Elsa Passera, New Media Editor who took on the Digital Tool; Michelle Marchetti, Publishing Services/Permissions Coordinator; Carolyn Wells and Darren Lalonde, Sales Managers; Janine Daoust, Sr. Marketing Manager; and of course all the sales representatives who service the front lines. The editorial contributions of Laurel Hyatt and Alan Johnstone were also appreciated. Most of all, however, we are grateful to cool, collected and super-organized Karen Staudinger, Editorial Manager who conducted the whole show!

Because the success of accounting texts is highly dependent on the quality of the text supplements, special thanks are due to Cécile Ashman and Maria Belanger of Algonquin College who developed the Solution Manual. Maria and Cécile in their detailed work with the problem material also contributed significantly as reviewers, making many valuable suggestions. Appreciation is also due to Majidul Islam and Lynn deGrace of Concordia who ably developed the Instructors' Manual; Gabriela H. Schneider of Grant McEwan Community College for the development of the PowerPoint slides; and to Maureen Fizzell of Simon Fraser University for the preparation of the Test Bank materials. Thank you all.

Word-processing and other office related services were ably provided to the authors by Megan Young, Sandra Fougere-Mahoney, and Cathy Golden. Special thanks also to Cheryne Lowe, Anna Beronja, David Schwinghamer, Elizabeth D'Anjou, Adam Zalev Amy Tse and Fang Mu for their contributions to the Digital Tool and research services.

We appreciate the co-operation of the Accounting Standards Board of the Canadian Institute of Chartered Accountants, especially that of its Director, Ron Salole, as well as that of the CICA itself in allowing us to quote from their materials. We thank Canadian Tire Corporation Limited for permitting us to use its 2000 Annual Report for our specimen financial statements.

Finally, we would like to thank Bruce Irvine and Harold Silvester who, through five editions of this text, provided such a strong foundation. Their enthusiasm for intermediate accounting and their sharing of this with so many students sets a standard for the rest of us to follow.

If this book helps teachers instill in their students an appreciation of the challenges, value, and limitations of accounting, if it encourages students to evaluate critically and understand financial accounting theory and practice, and if it prepares students for advanced study, professional examinations, and the successful and ethical pursuit of their careers in accounting or business, then we will have attained our objective.

Suggestions and comments from users of this book will be appreciated. We have striven to produce an error-free text, but if anything has slipped through the variety of checks undertaken, please let us know so that corrections can be made to subsequent printings.

Irene M. Wiecek   Nicola M. Young
Toronto, Ontario   Halifax, Nova Scotia

November 2001

Brief Contents

Contents

Current Financial and Other Liabilities

LEARNING OBJECTIVES

After studying this chapter, you should be able to:

1. Define liabilities and differentiate between financial and other liabilities.

2. Define current liabilities, describe how they are valued, and identify common types of current liabilities.

3. Explain the classification issues of short-term debt expected to be refinanced.

4. Identify and account for the major types of employee-related liabilities.

5. Explain the accounting for common estimated liabilities.

6. Explain the accounting and reporting standards for loss contingencies.

7. Indicate how financial and other current liabilities and contingencies are presented and analysed.

Preview of Chapter 14

The purpose of this chapter is to explain the basic principles regarding accounting and reporting for current liabilities (most of which are financial liabilities) and contingent liabilities. Chapter 15 addresses issues related to long-term financial liabilities. The content and organization of this chapter are as follows:

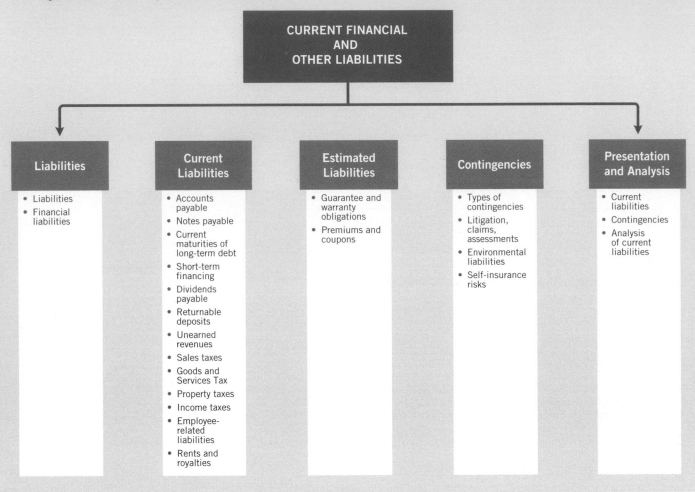

CURRENT FINANCIAL AND OTHER LIABILITIES

Liabilities	Current Liabilities	Estimated Liabilities	Contingencies	Presentation and Analysis
• Liabilities • Financial liabilities	• Accounts payable • Notes payable • Current maturities of long-term debt • Short-term financing • Dividends payable • Returnable deposits • Unearned revenues • Sales taxes • Goods and Services Tax • Property taxes • Income taxes • Employee-related liabilities • Rents and royalties	• Guarantee and warranty obligations • Premiums and coupons	• Types of contingencies • Litigation, claims, assessments • Environmental liabilities • Self-insurance risks	• Current liabilities • Contingencies • Analysis of current liabilities

WHAT IS A LIABILITY?

UNDERLYING CONCEPTS

To determine the appropriate classification of specific financial instruments, proper definitions of assets, liabilities, and equities are needed. The conceptual framework definitions are often used as the basis for resolving controversial classification issues.

The question, "What is a liability?" is not easy to answer. For example, one might ask whether preferred shares are a liability or an ownership claim. The first reaction is to say that preferred shares are in fact an ownership claim and should be reported as part of shareholders' equity. In fact, preferred shares have many elements of debt as well.[1] The issuer (and in some cases the holder) often has the right to call in the shares within a specific period of time, making it similar to a repayment of principal. The

---

[1] This illustration is not just a theoretical exercise. In practice, there are a number of preferred share issues that have all the characteristics of a debt instrument, except that they are called—and legally classified as—preferred shares. In some cases, Canada Customs and Revenue Agency (CCRA) has even permitted the dividend payments to be treated as interest expense for tax purposes.

dividend is often cumulative, making it almost guaranteed and similar to interest. Preferred shares are only one of many financial instruments that are difficult to classify.[2]

Liabilities

To help resolve some of these controversies, the Accounting Standards Board defined liabilities in Section 1000 of the *CICA Handbook* as **"obligations of an enterprise arising from past transactions or events, the settlement of which may result in the transfer of assets, provisions of services or other yielding of economic benefits in the future."**[3] In other words, a liability has three essential characteristics:

> ### OBJECTIVE 1
> Define liabilities and differentiate between financial and other liabilities.

1. It is an obligation to others that entails settlement by future transfer or use of cash or other assets, provision of goods or services on a determinable date, or on the occurrence of some specified event.
2. The entity has little or no opportunity to avoid the obligation.
3. The transaction or other event creating the obligation has already occurred.[4]

Because liabilities involve future disbursements of assets or services, one of the most important features is the date on which they are payable. Currently maturing obligations represent a demand on the enterprise's current assets—a demand that must be satisfied promptly and in the ordinary course of business if operations are to continue. Liabilities with a more distant due date do not, as a rule, represent a claim on the enterprise's current resources and are therefore in a different category. This feature gives rise to the basic division of liabilities into (1) current liabilities and (2) long-term debt.

Financial Liabilities

A distinction is also made between financial liabilities and those that are not financial in nature. Financial liabilities are contractual obligations to deliver cash or other financial assets to another party, or to exchange financial instruments with another party under conditions that are potentially unfavourable.[5] The significance of such a distinction will be greater as the profession moves toward an accounting model where financial assets and financial liabilities are likely to be measured in terms of their fair value rather than historic cost, and for liabilities that are longer term in nature. In this chapter, most current liabilities are financial in nature, although obligations to be met by the delivery of goods or services (e.g., unearned revenue and warranty obligations) are not financial liabilities. Regardless, the difference between fair value and historic cost of **current** liabilities is usually immaterial.

---

[2] As examples of the diversity within preferred shares, companies now issue (1) mandatorily redeemable preferred shares (redeemable at a specified price and time); (2) Dutch auction preferred shares (holders have the right to change the rate at defined intervals through a bidding process); and (3) increasing rate (exploding rate) preferred shares (holder receives an increasing dividend rate each period with the issuer having the right to call the shares at a certain future date). In all three cases, the issuer either has to redeem the shares according to the contract or has to have strong economic reasons for calling the shares. These securities are more like debt than equity. *CICA Handbook* Section 3860, "Financial Instruments," addresses the issues involved in distinguishing between financial liability and equity instruments.

[3] *CICA Handbook*, Section 1000, par. .32.

[4] *Ibid.*, par. .33.

[5] *CICA Handbook*, Section 3860, par. .05(c).

WHAT IS A CURRENT LIABILITY?

OBJECTIVE 2

Define current liabilities, describe how they are valued, and identify common types of current liabilities.

INTERNATIONAL INSIGHT

In France, the balance sheet does not show current liabilities in a separate category. Rather, debts are disclosed separately by maturity in the notes.

The definition of a current liability is directly related to the definition of a current asset. Current assets are cash or other assets that can reasonably be expected to be converted into cash, sold, or consumed in operations within a year from the balance sheet date or within a single operating cycle if a cycle is longer than a year. Current liabilities, although not defined in the *CICA Handbook*, are described as including "**amounts payable within one year from the date of the balance sheet or within the normal operating cycle where this is longer than a year**" and it is specified that "the normal operating cycle should correspond with that used for current assets."[6] This description has gained wide acceptance because it recognizes operating cycles of varying lengths in different industries and takes into consideration the important relationship between current assets and current liabilities.

The operating cycle is the period of time elapsing between the acquisition of goods and services involved in operations (such as the manufacturing process) and the final cash realization resulting from sales and subsequent collections. Industries that manufacture products requiring an ageing process and certain capital-intensive industries have an operating cycle of considerably more than one year. On the other hand, most retail and service establishments have several operating cycles within a year.

There are many different types of current liabilities. The following ones are covered in this section in this order.

1. Accounts payable
2. Notes payable
3. Current maturities of long-term debt
4. Short-term obligations expected to be refinanced
5. Dividends payable
6. Returnable deposits
7. Unearned revenues
8. Sales taxes payable
9. Goods and Services Tax
10. Property taxes payable
11. Income taxes payable
12. Employee-related liabilities
13. Rents and royalties payable

Accounts Payable

Accounts payable, or trade accounts payable, are balances owed to others for goods, supplies, or services purchased on open account. Accounts payable arise because of the time lag between the receipt of services or acquisition of title to assets and the payment for them. This period of extended credit is usually found in the terms of sale (and purchase), for example, 2/10, n/30 or 1/10, E.O.M. and is commonly 30 to 60 days.

Most accounting systems are designed to record liabilities for purchases of goods when the goods are received or, practically, when the invoices are received. Frequently there is some delay in recording the goods and the related liability on the books. If title has passed to the purchaser before the goods are received, the transaction should be recorded at the time of title passage. Attention must be paid to transactions occurring near the end of one accounting period and the beginning of the next to ensure that the record of goods or services received (the inventory or expense) is in agreement with the liability (accounts payable) and that both are recorded in the proper period.

Measuring the amount of an account payable poses no particular difficulty because the invoice received from the creditor specifies the due date and the exact outlay in

---

[6] *CICA Handbook*, Section 1510, par. .03.

money terms that is necessary to settle the account. The only calculation that may be necessary concerns the amount of cash discount. Refer to Chapter 8 for illustrations of entries related to accounts payable and purchase discounts.

Notes Payable

Notes payable are written promises to pay a certain sum of money on a specified future date and may arise from purchases, financing, or other transactions. In some industries, notes (often referred to as trade notes payable are required as part of the sales/purchases transaction in lieu of the normal extension of open account credit. Notes payable to banks or loan companies generally arise from cash loans. Notes may be classified as short-term or long-term, depending on the payment due date. Notes may also be interest-bearing or zero-interest-bearing (i.e., non-interest-bearing).

Interest-Bearing Note Issued

Assume that the Provincial Bank agrees to lend $100,000 on March 1, 2002 to Landscape Corp. if the company signs a $100,000, 12%, four-month note. The entry to record the cash received by Landscape Corp. on March 1 is:

March 1		
Cash	100,000	
Notes Payable		100,000
(To record issuance of 12%, four-month note to Provincial Bank)		

If Landscape Corp. has a December 31 year-end but prepares financial statements semiannually, an adjusting entry is required to recognize interest expense and interest payable of $4,000 ($100,000 × 12% × 4/12) on June 30. The adjusting entry is:

June 30		
Interest Expense	4,000	
Interest Payable		4,000
(To accrue interest for four months on Provincial Bank note)		

If Landscape prepared financial statements monthly, the adjusting entry at the end of each month would be $1,000 ($100,000 × 12% × 1/12).

At maturity (July 1), Landscape Corp. must pay the note's face value of $100,000 plus $4,000 interest ($100,000 × 12% × 4/12).

The entry to record payment of the note and accrued interest is as follows:

July 1		
Notes Payable	100,000	
Interest Payable	4,000	
Cash		104,000
(To record payment of Provincial Bank interest-bearing note and accrued interest at maturity)		

Zero-Interest-Bearing Note Issued

A zero-interest-bearing note may be issued instead of an interest-bearing note. Contrary to its name, a zero-interest-bearing note **does have an interest component**, it is just not added on top of its face or maturity value. Instead, the interest is included in the face amount. It is the difference between the amount of cash received when the note is signed and the face amount payable at maturity. The borrower receives the note's present value in cash and pays back the larger maturity value.

To illustrate, assume that Landscape Corp. issues a $104,000, four-month, zero-interest-bearing note to the Provincial Bank. The note's present value is $100,000.[7] The entry to record this transaction for Landscape Corp. is as follows:

---

[7] The bank discount rate used in this example to find the present value is 11.538%.

March 1		
Cash	100,000	
Discount on Notes Payable	4,000	
Notes Payable		104,000
(To record issuance of four-month, zero-interest-bearing note		
to Provincial Bank)		

The Notes Payable account is credited for the note's face value, which is $4,000 more than the actual cash received. The difference between the cash received and the note's face value is debited to Discount on Notes Payable. Discount on Notes Payable is a contra account to Notes Payable and therefore is subtracted from Notes Payable on the balance sheet. The balance sheet presentation on March 1 is as follows:

ILLUSTRATION 14-1
Balance Sheet Presentation of Discount

Current liabilities		
Notes payable	$104,000	
Less: Discount on notes payable	4,000	$100,000

The amount of the discount, $4,000 in this case, represents the cost of borrowing $100,000 for four months. Accordingly, the discount is charged to interest expense over the life of the note. That is, the debit balance in the Discount on Notes Payable account represents prepaid interest or interest expense chargeable to future periods. Instead of reporting it as a current asset, however, it is reported netted against the Note Payable. Additional accounting issues related to notes payable are discussed in Chapter 15.

Current Maturities of Long-Term Debt

Bonds, mortgage notes, and other long-term indebtedness that mature within 12 months from the balance sheet date—current maturities of long-term debt—are reported as current liabilities. When only part of a long-term debt is to be paid within the next 12 months, as in the case of serial bonds that are to be retired through a series of annual instalments, **the maturing portion of long-term debt is reported as a current liability**, and the balance as long-term debt.

Long-term debts maturing currently should not be included as current liabilities if they are to be:

1. retired by assets accumulated for this purpose that properly have not been shown as current assets;
2. refinanced or retired from the proceeds of a new debt issue (see next topic); or
3. converted into share capital.

In these situations, the use of current assets or the creation of other current liabilities does not occur. Therefore, classification as a current liability is inappropriate. The plan for liquidation of such a debt should be disclosed either parenthetically or by a note to the financial statements.

However, a liability that is **due on demand** (callable by the creditor) or will be due on demand within a year (or operating cycle, if longer) should be classified as a current liability. Liabilities often become callable by the creditor when there is a violation of the debt agreement. For example, most debt agreements specify a given level of equity to debt that must be maintained, or specify that working capital be of a minimum amount. If an agreement is violated, classification of the debt as current is required because it is a reasonable expectation that existing working capital will be used to satisfy the debt. Only if it can be shown that the creditor has lost the right to demand repayment within one year from the balance sheet date, or the debt agreement has a grace period to cure the violation and contractual arrangements are in place that will rectify the violation, can the debt be classified as noncurrent.[8]

---

[8] *EIC-59* "Long-Term Debt with Covenant Violations," November 28, 2000 (CICA).

Short-Term Obligations Expected to Be Refinanced

OBJECTIVE 3

Explain the classification issues of short-term debt expected to be refinanced.

Short-term obligations are those debts that are scheduled to mature within one year after the date of an enterprise's balance sheet or within an enterprise's operating cycle, whichever is longer. Short-term obligations expected to be refinanced on a long-term basis, however, are not expected to require the use of working capital during the next year (or operating cycle).[9]

At one time, the accounting profession generally supported the exclusion of short-term obligations from current liabilities if they were "expected to be refinanced." Because the profession provided no specific guidelines, however, determining whether a short-term obligation was "expected to be refinanced" was usually based solely on management's **intent** to refinance on a long-term basis. A company could obtain a five-year bank loan but, because the bank prefers it, handle the actual financing with 90-day notes, which it keeps turning over or renewing. It was then unclear whether the loan was a long-term or a current liability.

Refinancing Criteria

As a result of these classification problems, the accounting profession requires the exclusion of short-term obligations from current liabilities "to the extent that contractual arrangements have been made for settlement from other than current assets."[10] Professional judgement must be used to determine whether the particular contractual arrangement is adequate to permit classification of the short-term obligation as non-current, with the following conditions generally being required.

1. The entity must **intend to refinance** the obligation on a long-term basis so that the use of working capital will not be required during the following year or operating cycle, if longer.

2. The entity must **demonstrate an ability** to consummate the refinancing. This could be demonstrated by actually refinancing the obligation by issuing a long-term obligation or issuing shares after the balance sheet date but before the financial statements are issued. Alternatively, the entity could enter into a financing agreement that clearly permits the refinancing on a long-term basis on terms that are readily determinable.

If an actual refinancing occurs, the portion of the short-term obligation to be excluded from current liabilities may not exceed the proceeds from the new obligation or equity securities that are applied to retire it. For example, Montavon Winery, with $3 million of short-term debt, issued 100,000 common shares subsequent to the balance sheet date but before the balance sheet was issued, intending to use the proceeds to liquidate the short-term debt at its maturity. If the net proceeds from the sale of the 100,000 shares totalled $2 million, only that amount of the short-term debt could be excluded from current liabilities.

An additional question relates to whether a short-term obligation should be excluded from current liabilities if it is paid off after the balance sheet date and subsequently replaced by long-term debt before the balance sheet is issued. To illustrate, Marquardt Limited pays off short-term debt of $40,000 on January 17, 2003 and issues long-term debt of $100,000 on February 3, 2003. Marquardt's financial statements dated December 31, 2002 are to be issued March 1, 2003. Because repayment of the short-term obligation **before** funds were obtained through long-term financing required the use of **existing** current assets, the profession requires that the short-term obligation be included in current liabilities at the balance sheet date. This is shown graphically below.[11]

---

[9] Refinancing a short-term obligation on a long-term basis means either replacing it with a long-term obligation or with equity securities, or renewing, extending, or replacing it with short-term obligations for an uninterrupted period extending beyond one year (or the operating cycle, if longer) from the date of the enterprise's balance sheet.

[10] *CICA Handbook*, Section 1510, par. .06.

[11] *EIC-122*, "Balance Sheet Classification of Callable Debt Obligations and Debt Obligations Expected to be Refinanced." October 31, 2001 (CICA).

ILLUSTRATION 14-2
Short-Term Debt Paid off after
Balance Sheet Date and Later
Replaced by Long-Term Debt

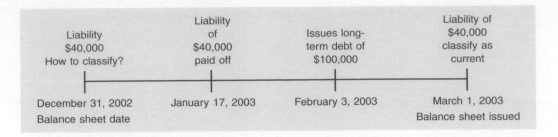

Dividends Payable

A cash dividend payable is an amount owed by a corporation to its shareholders resulting from an authorization by the board of directors. At the dividend declaration date, the corporation assumes a liability that places the shareholders in the position of creditors in the amount of dividends declared. Because cash dividends are normally paid within one year of declaration (generally within three months), they are classified as current liabilities.

Accumulated but undeclared dividends on cumulative preferred shares **are not recognized as a liability** because preferred dividends in arrears are not an obligation until formal action is taken by the board of directors to authorize the earnings' distribution. Nevertheless, the amount of cumulative dividends unpaid is required to be disclosed, usually in a note to the financial statements.

Dividends payable in the form of additional shares **are not recognized as a liability**. Such stock dividends (as discussed in Chapter 17) do not meet the definition of a liability because they do not require future outlays of assets or services. In addition, they are revocable by the board of directors at any time prior to issuance. Undistributed stock dividends are generally reported in the shareholders' equity section because they represent retained earnings in the process of transfer to contributed capital.

**UNDERLYING
CONCEPTS**

Preferred dividends in arrears
represent a probable future
economic sacrifice, but the
expected sacrifice does not
result from a past transaction
or past event. The sacrifice
will result from a future event
(declaration by the board of
directors). Note disclosure
improves the predictive value
of the financial statements.

Returnable Deposits

A company's current liabilities may include returnable cash deposits received from customers and employees. Deposits may be received from customers to guarantee performance of a contract or service or as guarantees to cover payment of expected future obligations. For example, telephone companies often require a deposit when installing a phone. Deposits may also be received from customers as guarantees for possible damage to property left with the customer. Some companies require their employees to make deposits for the return of keys or other company property. The classification of these items as current or noncurrent liabilities is dependent on the time between the date of the deposit and the termination of the relationship that required the deposit.

Unearned Revenues

A magazine publisher such as **Golf Digest** may receive a customer's cheque when magazines are ordered, and an airline company, such as **Air Canada**, often sells tickets for future flights. Restaurants may issue meal tickets that can be exchanged or used for future meals. (Who hasn't received or given a **McDonald's** gift certificate?) Retail stores may issue gift certificates that are redeemable for merchandise. How do these companies account for unearned revenues that are received before goods are delivered or services rendered?

1. When the advance is received, Cash is debited, and a current liability account identifying the source of the unearned revenue is credited.
2. When the revenue is earned, the unearned revenue account is debited, and an earned revenue account is credited.

To illustrate, assume that the Rambeau Football Club sells 5,000 season football tickets at $50 each for its five-game home schedule. The entry for the sales of season tickets is:

Cash	250,000	
Unearned Football Ticket Revenue		250,000
(To record the sale of 5,000 season tickets)		

As each game is completed, the following entry is made:

Unearned Football Ticket Revenue	50,000	
Football Ticket Revenue		50,000
(To record football ticket revenues earned)		

The balance in the Unearned Football Ticket Revenue account, therefore, is unearned revenue and is reported as a current liability in the balance sheet. As revenue is earned, a transfer from unearned revenue to earned revenue occurs. Unearned revenue is material for some companies: In the airline industry, tickets sold for future flights represent a significant portion of total current liabilities. At **Canada 3000,** with an August year end, unearned ticket revenue makes up 34% of current liabilities. Advance ticket sales reported by **Air Canada** and **WestJet Airlines**, both with December 31 year ends, represent 14% and 21%, respectively, of their total current liabilities at that date.

Illustration 14-3 shows specific unearned and earned revenue accounts used in selected types of businesses.

Type of Business	Account Title	
	Unearned Revenue	Earned Revenue
Airline	Unearned Passenger Ticket Revenue	Passenger Revenue
Magazine publisher	Unearned Subscription Revenue	Subscription Revenue
Hotel	Unearned Rental Revenue	Rental Revenue
Auto dealer	Unearned Warranty Revenue	Warranty Revenue

ILLUSTRATION 14-3
Unearned and Earned Revenue Accounts

The balance sheet should report obligations for any commitments that are redeemable in goods and services; the income statement should report revenues earned during the period.

Sales Taxes Payable

Sales taxes on transfers of tangible personal property and on certain services must be collected from customers and remitted to the tax authority. The Sales Taxes Payable account should reflect the liability for sales taxes collected from customers but not yet remitted to the appropriate government.[12] The entry below illustrates the accounting for a sale of $3,000 when a 4% sales tax is in effect.

Cash or Accounts Receivable	3,120	
Sales		3,000
Sales Taxes Payable		120

In some companies, however, the sales tax and the sale amount are not segregated at the time of sale; both are credited to the Sales account. In that case, to reflect the actual sales amount and the correct liability for sales taxes, the Sales account must be reduced (debited) for the amount of the sales taxes due the government on these sales and the Sales Taxes Payable account credited for the same amount. As an illustration, assume that the Sales account balance is $150,000, including sales taxes of 4%. Because the amount recorded in the Sales account is equal to sales plus 4% of sales, or 1.04 times the sales total, the sales are $150,000 divided by 1.04, or $144,230.77. The sales tax liability is $5,769.23 ($144,230.77 × 0.04; or $150,000 − $144,230.77), and the following entry is made to record the amount due the taxing unit.

---

[12] In New Brunswick, Newfoundland and Labrador, and Nova Scotia, the provincial retail sales tax has been combined with the federal Goods and Services Tax and named the Harmonized Sales Tax (HST). The HST is administered for the most part by CCRA and is accounted for on the same basis as the GST for the other provinces.

Sales	5,769.23	
Sales Taxes Payable		5,769.23

Goods and Services Tax

Most businesses in Canada are subject to a Goods and Services Tax (GST). The GST is a tax on the value added by each taxable entity. The amount payable is determined by deducting the amount of GST paid to suppliers on goods and services purchased from the amount of GST collected on sales to customers.

Accounting for GST involves setting up a liability account—GST Payable—to be credited with GST charged on sales and an asset account—GST Recoverable—which is debited for GST paid to suppliers. Normally, the amount collected on sales exceeds the amount paid on purchases so that a net remittance is made. Since GST is also paid on purchases of capital assets, it is possible that the GST Recoverable account will have a larger balance. In these instances, a claim for reimbursement is made to Canada Customs and Revenue Agency (CCRA).

Purchases of taxable goods and services are recorded by debiting the GST Recoverable account for the amount of GST and debiting the appropriate account(s) for the purchase price. Since the amount of GST paid is a recoverable amount, the cost of items acquired should not normally include this tax. As an example, Bateman Limited purchases merchandise for $150,000 plus GST of 7% ($10,500). The entry to record this transaction is as follows.

Merchandise Purchases (or Inventory)	150,000	
GST Recoverable	10,500	
Accounts Payable		160,500

If these goods are sold for $210,000 plus GST of 7% ($14,700), the sale entry is:

Accounts Receivable	224,700	
Sales		210,000
GST Payable		14,700

Because companies are permitted to offset the recoverable and payable amounts, only the net balance of the two accounts is reported on the balance sheet. Until net credit balances are remitted to the Receiver General for Canada, they are reported as a current liability. A net debit balance, on the other hand, is reported as a current asset.

Property Taxes Payable

Local governments generally depend on property taxes as their primary source of revenue. Such taxes are based on the assessed value of both real and personal property and become a lien against property at a date determined by law.[13] The taxes are a liability of the property owner and a cost of the services of such property. The accounting questions that arise from property taxes are:

1. When should the property owner record the liability?
2. To which accounting period should the cost be charged?

The accounting profession, in considering the periods to which property taxes could be charged, contends that generally, the most acceptable basis of providing for property taxes is monthly accrual on the taxpayer's books during the fiscal period of the taxing authority for which the taxes are levied or charged. Charging the taxes in this

---

[13] A lien is the right to have a debt satisfied out of the property belonging to the person owing the debt.

way **relates the expense to the period in which the taxes are used by the government to provide benefits to the property owner**.

Assume that Seaboard Corporation, with a December 31 year end, receives its property tax bill in May each year. The fiscal year for the local municipality is the same as the company's calendar year. Property taxes of $36,000 are levied against Seaboard Corporation for the 2002 calendar year, and become a lien on January 1, 2002. However, notice of taxes is not sent out until May, and taxes are payable in equal instalments on July 1 and September 1. Prior to receiving the tax notice, the company estimates the 2002 taxes at $33,600, or $2,800 per month ($33,600 ÷ 12).

The entries needed throughout 2002 to record the liability, monthly charges, and payments for the 2002 property taxes are illustrated below.

January 31 to April 30, 2002 (monthly expense accrual)		
Property Tax Expense	2,800	
Property Tax Payable/		
Prepaid Property Taxes		2,800

To the end of April, $11,200 (i.e., $2,800 × 4) has been charged to expense and accrued as a liability. When the tax notice for $36,000 is received in May, Seaboard can calculate the correct amount that should have been recognized to date, and the revised amount to charge to expense each month for the remainder of the year.

To the end of May, $15,000 (i.e., 5/12 of $36,000) should be accrued and recognized in expense and the accrual for the rest of the year should be $3,000 per month (i.e., 1/12 of $36,000). The May entry for $3,800 ($15,000 correct accumulated balance less $11,200 accrued to date) includes a "catch-up" adjustment for the first four months. While this is not the treatment accorded a change in estimate in preparing annual financial statements, *Handbook* Section 1751 on "Interim Financial Statements" prefers a catch-up adjustment in the period the estimate is changed.[14]

May 31 (monthly expense accrual and catch-up adjustment)		
Property Tax Expense	3,800	
Property Tax Payable/		
Prepaid Property Taxes		3,800

June 30 (monthly expense accrual)		
Property Tax Expense	3,000	
Property Tax Payable/		
Prepaid Property Taxes		3,000

When the first tax instalment of $18,000 is paid on July 1, the liability account is brought to zero, but it begins to grow again with the July and August accruals. After the August 31 adjustment, the liability balance is $6,000. The September 1 payment of the second and final instalment throws the account into a debit balance, and it will remain in a debit balance until the final accrual on December 31.

As long as this account has a debit balance, it is a **prepaid property tax** account and is reported with current assets.[15]

July 1, 2002 (first tax payment)		
Property Taxes Payable/		
Prepaid Property Taxes	18,000	
Cash		18,000

---

[14] *CICA Handbook*, Section 1751 par. .14(d) requires disclosure of any material changes in estimate affecting amounts reported in prior interim periods or prior fiscal periods.

[15] Some accountants would close out the liability account at this point and separately recognize the prepaid expense in an appropriate asset account, reversing this process when it later becomes a credit balance and later a debit balance again. Such a series of entries tends to confuse and obscure the intent of the entries.

July 31 to August 31, 2002 (monthly expense accrual)		
Property Tax Expense	3,000	
Property Tax Payable/		
Prepaid Property Taxes		3,000

September 1, 2002 (second tax payment)		
Property Taxes Payable/		
Prepaid Property Taxes	18,000	
Cash		18,000

September 30 to December 31, 2002 (monthly expense accrual)		
Property Tax Expense	3,000	
Property Tax Payable/		
Prepaid Property Taxes		3,000

Some accountants advocate accruing property taxes by charges to expense during the fiscal year **ending on the lien date**, rather than during the fiscal year beginning on the lien date (the fiscal year of the tax authority). In such instances, the property tax for the coming fiscal year must be estimated and charged monthly to Property Tax Expense and must be credited to Property Tax Payable. Under this method, the entire amount of the tax is accrued by the lien date and the expense is therefore charged to the fiscal period preceding payment of the tax. Justification for this method exists when the assessment date precedes the lien date by a year or more, as is the case in some taxing units. In such instances, the amount is estimated and accrued by the property owner before receipt of the tax bill.

Recognizing that special circumstances can suggest the use of alternative accrual periods, it is important that the period chosen be consistent from year to year. The selection of any alternative period mentioned is a matter of individual judgement.

Income Taxes Payable

Any federal or provincial income tax varies in proportion to the amount of annual income. Some consider the amount of income tax on annual income as an estimate because the calculation of income (and the tax thereon) is subject to CCRA review and approval. The meaning and application of numerous tax rules, especially new ones, are debatable and often dependent on a court's interpretation. Using the best information and advice available, a business must prepare an income tax return and calculate the income tax payable resulting from the operations of the current period. The taxes payable on a corporation's income, as calculated per the tax return, should be classified as a current liability.

Unlike corporations, proprietorships and partnerships are not taxable entities. Because the individual proprietor and the members of a partnership are subject to personal income taxes on their share of the business's taxable income, income tax liabilities do not appear on the financial statements of proprietorships and partnerships.

Most corporations make periodic tax payments based on estimates of their current year's income tax. As the estimated total tax liability changes, the periodic contributions also change. If in a later year an additional tax is assessed on an earlier year's income, Income Taxes Payable should be credited with the expense charged to current operations.

Differences between taxable income under the tax laws and accounting income under generally accepted accounting principles are common. Because of these differences, the amount of income tax payable to the government in any given year may differ substantially from the income tax expense that relates to income before taxes, as reported on the financial statements. Chapter 19 is devoted solely to the problems of accounting for income tax and presents an extensive discussion of related complex and interesting issues.

Employee-Related Liabilities

Amounts owed to employees for salaries or wages at the end of an accounting period are reported as a current liability. In addition, the following items related to employee compensation are often reported as current liabilities:

OBJECTIVE 4

Identify and account for the major types of employee-related liabilities.

1. payroll deductions,
2. compensated absences, and
3. bonuses.

Payroll Deductions

The most common types of payroll deductions are income taxes, CPP/QPP, employment insurance, and miscellaneous items such as other insurance premiums, employee savings, and union dues. **To the extent the amounts deducted have not been remitted to the proper authority at the end of the accounting period, they should be recognized as current liabilities along with any matching amounts required of the employer.**

Canada (Quebec) Pension Plan (CPP/QPP). The Canada and Quebec pension plans are financed by the imposition of taxes on both the employer and the employee. All employers are required to collect the employee's share of this tax. They deduct it from the employee's gross pay and remit it to the government along with the employer's share. Both the employer and the employee are taxed at the same rate, currently 4.3% each (2001) based on the employee's gross pay up to maximum contributory earnings of $34,800. The maximum annual contribution for each of the employee and employer is $1,496.40 in 2001.

Employment Insurance. Another payroll tax levied by the federal government provides a system of employment insurance. This tax is levied on both employees and employers. Employees must pay a premium of 2.25% (2001) of insurable earnings to an annual maximum contribution of $877.50 while the employer is required to contribute 1.4 times the amount of employee premiums. Insurable earnings are gross wages above a prescribed minimum and below a maximum amount. Both the premium rates and insurable earnings are adjusted periodically.

Income Tax Withholding. Income tax laws require employers to withhold from each employee's pay an amount approximating the applicable income tax due on those wages. The amount of income tax withheld is calculated by the employer according to a government-prescribed formula or a government-provided income tax deduction table and is dependent on the length of the pay period and each employee's wages, marital status, claimed dependents, and other permitted deductions.

Illustration. Assume a weekly payroll of $10,000 entirely subject to CPP (4.3%), employment insurance (2.25%), income tax withholdings of $1,320, and union dues of $88.

The entry to record the wages and salaries paid and the employee payroll deductions is:

Wages and Salaries Expense	10,000	
Employee Income Tax Deductions Payable		1,320
CPP Contributions Payable		430
EI Premiums Payable		225
Union Dues Payable		88
Cash		7,937

The required employer payroll taxes are recognized as compensation-related expenses in the same accounting period as the payroll is recorded. The entry for the required employer contributions follows.

Payroll Tax Expense	745	
CPP Contributions Payable ($430 × 1.0)		430
EI Premiums Payable ($225 × 1.4)		315

The employer is required to remit to the Receiver General for Canada the employees' income tax, CPP, and EI deductions as well as the employer's required contributions for CPP and EI. Until remitted to the government, these amounts are all reported as current liabilities. In a manufacturing enterprise, all payroll costs (wages, payroll taxes, and fringe benefits) are allocated to appropriate cost accounts such as Direct Labour, Indirect Labour, Sales Salaries, Administrative Salaries, and the like. This abbreviated and somewhat simplified discussion of payroll costs and deductions is not indicative of the volume of records and clerical work that are involved in maintaining a sound and accurate payroll system.

Compensated Absences

Compensated absences are absences from employment—such as vacation, illness, and holidays—for which employees will be paid. Employers are required under provincial statutes to give each employee vacation equal to a stipulated number of days or compensation in lieu of the vacation. As a result, employers have an obligation for vacation pay that accrues to the employees. Usually this obligation is satisfied by paying employees their regular salaries for the period that they are absent from work while taking an annual vacation.

Vested rights exist when an employer has an obligation to pay the employee even if his or her employment is terminated; thus, vested rights are not contingent on an employee's future service. Accumulated rights are those that can be carried forward to future periods if not used in the period in which earned. For example, assume that you have earned four days of vacation pay as of December 31, the end of your employer's fiscal year. In a province where vacation pay is prescribed by statute, your employer will have to pay you for these four days even if you terminate your employment. In this situation, your four days of vacation pay are considered vested and should be accrued. Now assume that your vacation days are not vested, but that you can carry the four days over into later periods. Although the rights are not vested, they are accumulated rights for which the employer should provide an accrual, allowing for estimated forfeitures due to turnover.

Entitlement to **sick pay** varies considerably among employers. In some companies, employees are allowed to accumulate unused sick pay and take compensated time off from work even though they are not ill. In other companies, employees receive sick pay only if they are absent because of illness. In the first case, sick pay benefits vest, while in the second case, the benefits do not vest and may or may not accumulate. **When benefits vest, accrual of the estimated liability is recommended.** However, if the sick pay benefits are paid only when employees are absent from work due to illness, accruals are required only if it is likely that the employees will qualify in the future for benefits accrued to the balance sheet date, **and** if the amount can be reasonably estimated. Because of measurement problems, many companies account for non-vesting sick pay on a pay-as-you-go basis.

In summary, the expense and related liability for compensated absences should be recognized in the year in which they are earned by employees whenever a reasonable estimate can be made of amounts expected to be paid out in the future. For example, if new employees receive rights to two weeks' paid vacation at the beginning of their second year of employment, the vacation pay is considered to be earned during the first year's employment.

After the period the employee earned the right is determined, an issue arises as to the rate used to determine the cost of the compensated absence: the current wage rate or an estimated future rate. It is likely that companies will use the current rather than future rate, which is less certain and raises issues concerning the discounting of the future amount.

To illustrate, assume that Amutron Limited began operations on January 1, 2002. The company employed 10 individuals who were paid $480 per week. A total of 20 weeks' vacation was earned by all employees in 2002, but none was used during this year. In 2002, the vacation weeks were used when the current rate of pay was $540 per week for each employee. The entry at December 31, 2002 to accrue the accumulated vacation pay is as follows:

Wages Expense	9,600	
Vacation Wages Payable ($480 × 20)		9,600

At December 31, 2002, the company would report a current liability of $9,600 on its balance sheet. In 2003, the vacation pay earned in 2002 would be recorded as follows:

Vacation Wages Payable	9,600	
Wages Expense	1,200	
Cash ($540 × 20)		10,800

In 2003, the vacation weeks were used and the liability extinguished. Note that the difference between the cash paid and the reduction in the liability account is recorded as an adjustment to Wages Expense in the period when paid. This difference arises because the liability account was accrued at the rates of pay in effect during the period compensated time was earned. The cash paid, however, is based on the rates in effect when the compensated time is used. If the future rates of pay had been estimated correctly and used to calculate the accrual in 2002, then the cash paid in 2003 would be equal to the liability.[16]

Bonus Agreements

For various reasons, many companies give a **bonus** to certain or all officers and employees in addition to their regular salary or wage. Often the bonus amount is dependent on the company's yearly profit. From the enterprise's standpoint, **bonus payments to employees** may be considered additional wages and should be included as a deduction in determining the net income for the year. In a note to its financial statements for the year ending July 31, 2000, **Tesma International Inc.** reports the following:

INTERNATIONAL INSIGHT

In Japan, bonuses to members of the Board of Directors and to the Commercial Code auditors are not treated as expenses. They are considered a distribution of profits and charged against retained earnings.

ILLUSTRATION 14-4
Commitment for Bonuses

> **Tesma International Inc.**
> Note 18 (partial)
>
> The Company's Corporate Constitution requires that a portion of the Company's profits be distributed or used for certain purposes, including but not limited to the following:
>
> - allocation or distribution of 10% of pre-tax profits to employees and/or the Tesma Employee Equity Participation and Profit Sharing Program (including the Tesma International Inc. (Canadian) Deferred Profit Sharing Plan (Tesma DPSP) and the Tesma International of America, Inc. U.S. Employees' Deferred Profit Sharing Plan (Tesma U.S. DPSP) forming part thereof);
>
> - allocation of a minimum of 7% of pre-tax profits to research and development; and
>
> - payment of dividends to shareholders based on a formula of after-tax profits.

To illustrate the entries for an employee bonus, assume a company whose income for 2002 is $100,000 will pay out bonuses of $10,714.29 in January 2003. An adjusting entry dated December 31, 2002, is made to record the bonus as follows.

Employees' Bonus Expense	10,714.29	
Bonus Payable		10,714.29

The expense account appears in the income statement as an operating expense. **The accrued liability, usually payable within a short time period, is generally included as a current liability in the balance sheet.**
In January 2003, when the bonus is paid, the entry is:

Bonus Payable	10,714.29	
Cash		10,714.29

---

[16] Many companies have obligations for benefits payable to employees after they retire. The accounting and reporting standards for post-retirement benefit payments are complex and relate primarily to pensions and post-retirement health care and life insurance benefits. These and other issues of employee future benefits are discussed in Chapter 20.

Care has to be taken in calculating bonus amounts. The bonus formula may specify that the bonus is a given percentage of after-tax income. Because the bonus itself is a tax-deductible expense, simultaneous equations may have to be set up and solved to determine both the bonus and tax amounts.

Rents and Royalties Payable

Similar to bonus arrangements are **contractual agreements covering rents or royalty payments conditional on the amount of revenues earned or the quantity of product produced or extracted**. For example, **SignalGene Inc.**, a Quebec company specializing in genomics research, reported in its 2000 financial statements that "The Company will pay to various university research centers royalties of 1.2% to 7% of sales of licensed products related to a research contract and acquired technology rights and 15% to 20% of sublicensed products related to acquired technology rights."

Conditional expenses based on revenues or units produced are usually less difficult to calculate than bonus arrangements. For example, if a lease calls for a fixed rent payment of $500 per month and 1% of all sales over $300,000 per year, the annual rent obligation amounts to $6,000 plus $0.01 of each dollar of revenue over $300,000. Or a royalty agreement may require the accrual of $1.00 for every tonne of product resulting from the patented process, or the accrual of $0.50 on every barrel of oil extracted to benefit the owner of the mineral rights. As each additional unit of product is produced or extracted, an additional obligation, usually a current liability, is created.

ESTIMATED LIABILITIES

OBJECTIVE 5

Explain the accounting for common estimated liabilities.

Most current liabilities that companies incur can be measured fairly accurately at the amount of cash or the cash equivalent value of other assets likely to be given up to discharge the obligation. However, others don't lend themselves to such certain measurement. Obligations under guarantees and warranties and those that require providing premiums and price reductions in the future, all related to revenue recognized in the current period, usually depend on estimation.

Guarantee and Warranty Obligations

A warranty (**product guarantee**) is a promise made by a seller to a buyer to make good on a product's deficiency of quantity, quality, or performance. It is commonly used by manufacturers as a sales promotion technique. (Automakers, for instance, "hyped" their sales by extending their new-car warranty to seven years or 115,000 km.) For a specified period of time following the date of sale to the consumer, the manufacturer may promise to bear all or part of the cost of replacing defective parts, to perform any necessary repairs or servicing without charge, to refund the purchase price, or even to "double your money back." Warranties and guarantees entail future costs that are sometimes called "after costs" or "post-sale costs," and are often significant.

There are two basic methods of accounting for warranty costs: (1) the cash basis method and (2) the accrual method.

Cash Basis

Under the **cash basis method**, warranty costs are charged to expense as they are incurred. In other words, **warranty costs are charged to the period in which the seller or manufacturer complies with the warranty**. No liability is recognized for future costs arising from warranties, nor is the expense necessarily recognized in the period of the related sale. This method, the only one recognized for income tax purposes, is frequently justified on the basis of expediency when warranty costs are immaterial or when the warranty period is relatively short. The cash basis method is legitimately required when:

1. it is not likely that a liability has been incurred, or
2. the amount of the liability cannot be reasonably estimated.

Accrual Basis—Expense Warranty Approach

Although the future cost is indefinite in amount, due date, and even customer, a liability should be recognized in the accounts if it is likely that future costs will be incurred as a result of sales reported and the amount can be reasonably estimated. The liability amount is an estimate of all the costs that are likely to be incurred after sale and delivery as a result of the warranty provisions. **When the warranty is an integral and inseparable part of the sale** and both recognition criteria are met, the accrual-based expense warranty method must be used. Under this method, warranty costs are charged to operating expense **in the year of sale** and a warranty liability is recognized for the likely claims.

Illustration of Expense Warranty Method. To illustrate the expense warranty method, assume that the Denson Machinery Corporation begins production of a new machine in July 2002, and sells 100 units for $5,000 each by its year end, December 31, 2002. Each machine is under warranty for one year and the company has estimated, from experience with a similar machine, that the warranty cost will probably average $200 per unit. As a result of parts replacements and services rendered in compliance with machinery warranties related to the units of the new machine sold in 2002, the company incurs $4,000 in warranty costs in 2002 and $16,000 in 2003. **One or the other** of the following series of entries is made to record these events.

METHOD A		METHOD B	
1. Sale of 100 machines at $5,000 each, July–December, 2002			
Cash/Accounts Receivable 500,000		Cash/Accounts Receivable 500,000	
Sales	500,000	Sales	500,000
2. Recognition of estimated warranty expense at $200/unit related to 2002 sales			
–No entry–		Warranty Expense 20,000	
		Estimated Liability	
		Under Warranty	20,000
3. Actual warranty costs incurred in 2002			
Warranty Expense 4,000		Estimated Liability	
Cash/Inventory/		Under Warranty 4,000	
Accrued Payroll	4,000	Cash/Inventory/	
		Accrued Payroll	4,000
4. Year-end adjusting entry to accrue outstanding warranty obligations at December 31, 2002			
Warranty Expense 16,000		–No entry–	
Estimated Liability			
Under Warranty	16,000		
5. December 31, 2002 financial statement amounts reported			
Warranty Expense (I/S) $20,000		Warranty Expense (I/S) $20,000	
Estimated Liability		Estimated Liability	
Under Warranty (B/S) $16,000		Under Warranty (B/S) $16,000	
6. Actual warranty costs incurred in 2003			
Warranty Expense 16,000		Estimated Liability	
Cash/Inventory/		Under Warranty 16,000	
Accrued Payroll	16,000	Cash/Inventory/	
		Accrued Payroll	16,000
7. Adjusting entry, December 31, 2003, to adjust liability account to correct balance			
Estimated Liability		–No entry–	
Under Warranty 16,000			
Warranty Expense	16,000		
8. December 31, 2003 financial statement amounts reported			
Warranty Expense (I/S) $–0–		Warranty Expense (I/S) $–0–	
Estimated Liability		Estimated Liability	
Under Warranty (B/S) $–0–		Under Warranty (B/S) $–0–	

ILLUSTRATION 14-5
Warranty Expense and
Liability Entries

Under Method A, the actual warranty costs are charged to expense as incurred. At the end of the accounting period, a further expense and liability are accrued for warranty costs to be incurred in the future relative to current period sales. Alternatively, with Method B the entire expected warranty costs related to current period sales are charged to expense and the related obligation recognized as a liability. As the actual warranty costs are incurred, the liability is reduced. Either series of entries is acceptable: both result in the same reported amounts on the income statement and the balance sheet.

If the cash basis method is applied to the facts in the Denson Machinery Corporation example, $4,000 is recorded as warranty expense in 2002 and $16,000 as warranty expense in 2003, with the total sales being recorded as revenue in 2002. In most instances, application of the cash basis method does not match the warranty expense with the associated revenue derived from such products, therefore violating the matching principle. Where similar warranty policies exist year after year, the differences between the cash and the expense warranty basis on an ongoing basis probably would not be significant, although there would be a mismatch in the early and final years.

Accrual Basis—Sales Warranty Approach

A warranty is sometimes **sold separately from the product**. For example, when you purchase a television set or VCR, you will be entitled to the manufacturer's standard warranty. You will also undoubtedly be offered an extended warranty on the product at an additional cost.[17]

In this case, the seller should account for the warranty costs of the standard warranty included in the product's regular price separately from the sale of the extended warranty. The warranty included in the regular selling price is accounted for under the expense warranty method illustrated above. The extended warranty sold as a separate service is accounted for under a different method: the sales warranty approach. **The revenue on the sale of the extended warranty is deferred** and is generally recognized on a straight-line basis over the life of the contract. Revenue is deferred because the warranty seller has an obligation to perform services over the life of the contract. Only costs that vary with and are directly related to the sale of the contracts (mainly commissions) should be deferred and amortized. Costs such as employees' salaries, advertising, and general and administrative expenses that would have been incurred even if no contracts were sold should be expensed as incurred.

To illustrate, assume you have just purchased a new automobile from Hanlin Auto for $20,000. In addition to the regular warranty on the auto (all repairs will be paid by the manufacturer for the first 60,000 km or three years, whichever comes first), you purchase an extended warranty for $600 that protects you for an additional three years or 60,000 km. The entry to record the automobile sale (with the regular warranty) and the extended warranty sale on January 2, 2002 on Hanlin Auto's books is:

Cash	20,600	
Sales		20,000
Unearned Warranty Revenue		600

The entry to recognize revenue at the end of each of the fourth, fifth, and sixth years (using straight-line amortization) is as follows:

Unearned Warranty Revenue	200	
Warranty Revenue		200

Because the extended warranty contract does not start until after the regular warranty expires, revenue is not recognized until the fourth year. If the costs of performing services under the extended warranty contract are incurred on other than a straight-line basis (as historical evidence might indicate), revenue should be recognized

---

[17] A contract is separately priced if the customer has the option to purchase the services provided under the contract for an expressly stated amount separate from the product price. An extended warranty or product maintenance contract usually meets these conditions.

over the contract period in proportion to the costs expected to be incurred in performing services under the contract.

Premiums, Coupons, Rebates, and Air Miles

Numerous companies offer premiums on either a limited or continuing basis to customers in return for boxtops, certificates, coupons, labels, or wrappers. The **premiums** may be silverware, dishes, a small appliance, toys, other goods or free transportation.[18] Also, **printed coupons** that can be redeemed for a cash discount on items purchased are extremely popular. A more recent marketing innovation is the **cash rebate**, which the buyer can obtain by returning the store receipt, a rebate coupon, and Universal Product Code (UPC label or bar code) to the manufacturer.[19]

These premiums, coupon offers, air miles, and rebates are made to stimulate sales, and their costs **should be charged to expense in the period of the sale** that benefits from the premium plan. This is key to understanding the accounting for the costs associated with these various plans. At the end of the accounting period, many of these premium offers may be outstanding and, when presented for redemption in subsequent periods, require an outflow of company assets. **The number of outstanding premium offers that will be presented for redemption must be estimated in order to reflect the existing current liability and to match costs with revenues.** The cost of premium offers should be charged to Premium Expense, and the outstanding obligations should be credited to an account entitled Estimated Liability for Premiums or Estimated Premium Claims Outstanding.

The following example illustrates the accounting treatment accorded a premium offer. Fluffy Cakemix Corporation offered its customers a large nonbreakable mixing bowl in exchange for $1.00 and 10 boxtops. The mixing bowl costs Fluffy Cakemix Corporation $2.25, and the company estimates that 60% of the boxtops will be redeemed. The premium offer began in June 2002 and resulted in the following transactions and entries during 2002.

1. To record the purchase of 20,000 mixing bowls at $2.25 each:

Inventory of Premium Mixing Bowls	45,000	
Cash		45,000

2. To record sales of 300,000 boxes of cake mix at $1.50:

Cash	450,000	
Sales		450,000

---

[18] Premium plans that have widespread adoption are the frequent flyer programs used by all major airlines. On the basis of mileage accumulated, frequent flyer members are awarded discounted or free airline tickets. Airline customers can earn miles toward free travel by making long-distance phone calls, staying in hotels, and charging gasoline and groceries on a credit card. Those free tickets represent an enormous potential liability because people using them may displace paying passengers.

When airlines first started offering frequent flyer bonuses, everyone assumed that they could accommodate the free ticket holders with otherwise-empty seats. That made the additional cost of the program so minimal that airlines didn't accrue or report the small liability. But, as more and more paying passengers have been crowded off of flights by frequent flyer awardees, the loss of revenue has grown enormously. Although the accounting for this transaction has been studied by the profession, no authoritative guidelines have been issued.

[19] In 2000, 112 million coupons for consumer packaged goods (worth approximately $120 million) were processed in Canada, representing a redemption rate of 4.4%. Most coupons for consumer packaged goods are sent to a plant in Saint John, N.B. where they are scanned and processed. (Source: NCH Promotional Services Ltd.)

UNDERLYING CONCEPTS

Obligations under warranties and coupons meet the definition of a liability. In addition, the matching principle requires that the related expense be reported in the period in which the sale is recognized.

3. To record the redemption of 60,000 boxtops, receipt of $1.00 per 10 boxtops, and delivery of the mixing bowls:

Cash [(60,000 ÷ 10) × $1.00]	6,000	
Premium Expense	7,500	
Inventory of Premium Mixing Bowls		13,500
[Calculation: (60,000 ÷ 10) × $2.25 = $13,500]		

4. To record the end-of-period adjusting entry for the estimated liability for outstanding premiums:

Premium Expense	15,000	
Estimated Liability for Premiums		15,000
Calculation:		
Total boxtops sold in 2002	300,000	
Total estimated redemptions (60%)	180,000	
Boxtops redeemed in 2002	60,000	
Estimated future redemptions	120,000	
Cost of estimated claims outstanding (120,000 ÷ 10) × ($2.25 − $1.00) =	$15,000	

The December 31, 2002 balance sheet of Fluffy Cakemix Corporation will report an Inventory of Premium Mixing Bowls of $31,500 as a current asset and Estimated Liability for Premiums of $15,000 as a current liability. The 2002 income statement will report a $22,500 Premium Expense among the selling expenses.[20]

CONTINGENCIES

Types of Contingencies

IAS NOTE

IAS 37 uses the term "provision" to describe a liability of uncertain timing or amount. The term "contingent" is restricted for liabilities that do not meet the recognition criteria for a provision.

A **contingency** is defined in *CICA Handbook* Section 3290 "as an existing condition or situation involving uncertainty as to possible gain (gain contingency) or loss (loss contingency) to an enterprise that will ultimately be resolved when one or more future events occur or fail to occur."[21] As discussed in Chapter 5, **gain contingencies** are not recorded and are disclosed in the notes only when it is likely that a gain will be realized. As a result, it is unusual to find information about contingent gains in the financial statements and the accompanying notes.

Loss contingencies are existing situations involving uncertainty as to possible loss. A liability incurred as a result of a loss contingency is by definition a **contingent liability**. Contingent liabilities are obligations that are dependent upon the occurrence or nonoccurrence of one or more future events to confirm either its existence or the amount payable.

When a loss contingency exists, the likelihood that the future event or events will confirm the incurrence of a liability can range from highly probable to only slightly probable. The *CICA Handbook* uses the terms **likely, unlikely,** and **not determinable** to identify the range of probability outcomes and assigns the following meanings.

Likely: The chance of occurrence (or nonoccurrence) of the future event is high.

Unlikely: The chance of the occurrence (or nonoccurrence) of the future event is slight.

Not determinable: The chance of the occurrence (or nonoccurrence) of the future event cannot be determined.

---

[20] Note that the series of entries could mirror those of Method B in Illustration 14-5 instead. That is, the estimated full cost of the premium plan associated with the current year's sales and the entire estimated liability could be set up initially. As the premiums are redeemed by customers, the liability is reduced. Both approaches report the same financial statement amounts.

[21] *CICA Handbook*, Section 3290, par. .02.

An estimated loss from a loss contingency should be accrued by a charge to expense and a liability recorded only if both the following conditions are met:[22]

1. information available prior to the issuance of the financial statements indicates that it is likely that a future event will confirm that an asset has been impaired or a liability incurred as of the date of the financial statements and

2. the loss amount can be reasonably estimated.

Neither the exact payee nor the exact date payable need be known to record a liability. **What must be known is whether it is likely that a liability has been incurred**.

The second criterion indicates that an amount for the liability can be reasonably determined; otherwise, it should not be accrued as a liability. Evidence to determine a reasonable estimate of the liability may be based on the company's own experience, experience of other companies in the industry, engineering or research studies, legal advice, or educated guesses by personnel in the best position to know. Often, a range of possible amounts may be determined. If a specific amount within the range is a better estimate than others, this amount should be accrued. If no one amount is more likely than another, the bottom of the range is usually accrued with the amount of the remaining exposure disclosed.

The following table, based on *CICA Handbook* Section 3290, summarizes the accounting and reporting standards for contingencies in a variety of circumstances.

IAS NOTE

In measuring the amount of provision to recognize, IAS 37 uses an "expected value" method whereby the possible outcomes are weighted by their associated probabilities.

Probability	Loss can be reasonably estimated?	
	Yes	No
Likely	Accrue. Report exposure to loss in excess of amount accrued in Notes to Financial Statements*	Report in Notes to Financial Statements*
Not likely	Disclosure not required	Disclosure not required
Not determinable	Report in Notes to Financial Statements*	Report in Notes to Financial Statements*

*Disclose the nature of the contingency and either an estimate of the amount or that an estimate cannot be made.

ILLUSTRATION 14-6
Accounting and Reporting Standards for Loss Contingencies

Illustration 14-7 from the 2000 annual report of **Clearly Canadian Beverage Corporation** is an example of an accrual related to a loss contingency.

ILLUSTRATION 14-7
Disclosure of Accrual Related to a Loss Contingency

> **Clearly Canadian Beverage Corporation**
> Note 15 (partial)
>
> **f) Dispute with D. Bruce Horton and Continental Consulting Ltd.**
>
> In August 1999, a claim was filed against the Company in the Supreme Court of British Columbia by D. Bruce Horton and his company, Continental Consulting Ltd. ("Continental"). Mr. Horton is claiming compensation from the Company for allegedly constuctively dismissing him as an officer of the Company. Continental is claiming compensation from the Company alleging that the Company terminated its management agreement without cause. Mr. Horton and Continental are claiming an aggregate of Cdn $2.4 million plus interest and costs. The Company does not accept Mr. Horton's and Continental's allegations, and has filed statements of defence and has further filed counterclaims against Mr. Horton and Continental for monies owed and damages. The Company has made an accrual based on its expected costs.

Using the terms "likely" and "unlikely" as a basis for determining the accounting for contingencies involves judgement and subjectivity. The items in Illustration 14-8 are examples of loss contingencies and the accounting treatment generally accorded them.

---

[22] Loss contingencies that result in the incurrence of a liability are most relevant to the discussion in this chapter. Loss contingencies that result in the impairment of an asset (e.g., collectibility of receivables or threat of expropriation of assets) are discussed more fully in other chapters of this textbook.

ILLUSTRATION 14-8
Accounting Treatment of Loss Contingencies

Loss Related to	Not Accrued	May Be Accrued*
1. Risk of loss or damage of enterprise property by fire, explosion, or other hazards	X	
2. General or unspecified business risks	X	
3. Risk of loss from catastrophes assumed by property and casualty insurance companies including reinsurance companies	X	
4. Threat of expropriation of assets		X
5. Pending or threatened litigation		X
6. Actual or possible claims and assessments**		X
7. Guarantees of indebtedness of others		X
8. Obligations of commercial banks under "standby letters of credit"		X
9. Agreements to repurchase receivables (or the related property) that have been sold		X

* Should be accrued when both criteria are met (likely and reasonably estimable).
**Estimated amounts of losses incurred prior to the balance sheet date but settled subsequently should be accrued as of the balance sheet date.

INTERNATIONAL INSIGHT

In Germany, company law allows firms to accrue losses for contingencies as long as they are possible and reasonable. Such provisions are one means of smoothing income.

The accounting concepts and procedures relating to contingent items are relatively unsettled. Practising accountants express concern over the diversity that exists in the interpretations of "likely" and "unlikely." Current practice relies heavily on the exact language used in responses received from lawyers, such language being necessarily biased and protective rather than predictive. As a result, accruals and disclosures of contingencies vary considerably in practice. Some of the more common loss contingencies discussed in this chapter are:[23]

1. litigation, claims, and assessments,
2. environmental liabilities, and
3. self-insurance risks

Note that general risk contingencies that are inherent in business operations, such as the possibility of war, strike, uninsurable catastrophes, or a business recession, are not reported in the notes to the financial statements.

Litigation, Claims, and Assessments

The following factors, among others, must be considered in determining whether a liability should be recorded with respect to pending or threatened litigation and actual or possible claims and assessments:

1. the **time period** in which the underlying cause of action occurred,
2. the **probability** of an unfavourable outcome, and
3. the ability to make a **reasonable estimate** of the loss amount.

To report a loss and a liability in the financial statements, the cause for litigation must have occurred on or before the date of the financial statements. It does not matter that the company did not become aware of the existence or possibility of the lawsuit or claims until after the date of the financial statements but before they are issued. To evaluate the likelihood of an unfavourable outcome, consider the nature of the litigation, the progress of the case, the opinion of legal counsel, the experience of the company and others in similar cases, and any management response to the lawsuit.

The outcome of pending litigation, however, can seldom be predicted with any assurance. And, even if the evidence available at the balance sheet date does not favour

---

[23] *Financial Reporting in Canada—2000* states that of the 200 companies surveyed, loss contingencies of the following nature and number were reported: lawsuits, 110; environmental matters, 39; guarantees of the debt of others, 37; possible tax reassessments, 11; and other, 21.

the defendant, it is hardly reasonable to expect the company to publish in its financial statements a dollar estimate of the probable negative outcome. Such specific disclosures could weaken the company's position in the dispute and encourage the plaintiff to intensify its efforts. A typical example of the wording of such a disclosure is the note to the third quarter (March 24, 2001) financial statements of **Danier Leather Inc.**, relating to its litigation concerning a shareholder action, as shown in Illustration 14-9.

Danier Leather Inc.

10. Commitments & Contingencies (thousands of dollars): (in part)

a) Legal proceedings

In the course of its business, the Company from time to time becomes involved in various claims and legal proceedings. In fiscal 1999, the Company and certain of its directors and officers were served with a Statement of Claim under the Ontario Class Proceedings Act. The Claim was filed with the Court by a single individual investor. The plaintiff's claim states that he purchased 5,000 subordinate voting shares at the time of the Company's initial public offering in May 1998. Essentially, the suit seeks rescission of the plaintiff's purchase of shares made in May, 1998, or alternatively, that damages be paid equal to the diminution in value of the shares. In March, 2001, the Court dismissed the plaintiff's claim for rescission. The plaintiff also brought a motion to certify the action as a class action on behalf of investors who purchased shares pursuant to the initial public offering. This motion is anticipated to be heard in July 2001. No amounts have been provided in the accounts of the Company in respect of this matter. The Company strongly believes the suit is wholly without merit and will vigorously defend it.

ILLUSTRATION 14-9
Disclosure of Litigation

With respect to **unfiled suits** and **unasserted claims and assessments**, a company must determine (1) the degree of **probability** that a suit may be filed or a claim or assessment may be asserted and (2) the **probability** of an unfavourable outcome. For example, assume that a company is being investigated by the federal government for possible violations of anti-competition legislation, and that enforcement proceedings have been instituted. Such proceedings may be followed by private claims. In this case, the company must determine the probability of the claims being asserted **and** the likelihood of damages being awarded. If both are likely, if the loss is reasonably estimable, and if the cause for action took place on or before the date of the financial statements, the liability should be accrued.

Environmental Liabilities

Estimates to clean up existing toxic waste sites in Canada run into billions of dollars. In addition, the cost of cleaning up our air and preventing future deterioration of the environment is estimated to cost even more. These costs will increase when one considers the trend to more stringent environmental laws.

CICA Handbook Section 3061 on Property, Plant, and Equipment requires companies to accrue future removal and site restoration costs if the amounts are reasonably determinable.[24] Where the amounts are not reasonably determinable, a contingent liability may exist. At December 31, 2000, **Cominco Limited** reported a liability of $146 million as a provision for reclamation, restoration, and other post-closure costs. The accompanying note to the financial statements explains the company's accounting policy.

Cominco Limited

Site restoration and reclamation obligations

Expenditures related to ongoing environmental and reclamation programs are expensed as incurred, or capitalized and depreciated, depending on the nature of the expenditure.

Provisions for future site restoration and reclamation are charged to earnings over the estimated life of the operating facility, commencing when a reasonably definitive estimate of the cost can be made.

ILLUSTRATION 14-10
Site Restoration and Reclamation Obligations Note—Cominco Limited

---

[24] *Financial Reporting in Canada—2000* reported that 66 of the 200 companies surveyed disclosed the existence of future site removal and restoration costs.

Self-Insurance Risks

UNDERLYING CONCEPTS

Even if the amount of losses is estimable with a high degree of certainty, the losses are not liabilities because they result from a future event and not from a past event.

INTERNATIONAL INSIGHT

In Switzerland, companies may make provisions for general (non-specified) contingencies to the extent allowed by tax regulations.

Uninsured risks may arise in a number of ways, including **noninsurance** of certain risks or **coinsurance** or **deductible clauses** in an insurance contract. But the absence of insurance (often referred to as self-insurance) does not mean that a liability has been incurred at the date of the financial statements. For example, fires, explosions, and other similar events that may cause damage to a company's own property are random in occurrence and unrelated to the company's activities prior to their occurrence. The conditions for accrual stated in *CICA Handbook* Section 3290 are not satisfied prior to the occurrence of the event because, until that time, there is no diminution in the property value. And, unlike an insurance company that has contractual obligations to reimburse policyholders for losses, a company can have no such obligations to itself and hence, **no liability either before or after the occurrence of damage**.

Exposure to **risks of loss resulting from uninsured past injury to others**, however, is an existing condition involving uncertainty about the amount and the timing of losses that may develop, in which case a contingency exists. A company with a fleet of vehicles would have to accrue uninsured losses resulting from injury to others or damage to the property of others that took place prior to the date of the financial statements if it is able to make a reasonable estimate of the liability. However, it should not establish a liability for **expected future injury** to others or damage to the property of others even if the amount of loss is reasonably estimable.

PRESENTATION AND ANALYSIS

Presentation of Current Liabilities

OBJECTIVE 7

Indicate how financial and other current liabilities, and contingencies are presented and analysed.

Theoretically, liabilities should be measured at the present value of the future outlay of cash required to liquidate them. But, in practice, current liabilities are usually recorded in accounting records and reported in financial statements at their full maturity value. Because of the short time periods involved, usually less than one year, the difference between the present value of a current liability and the maturity value is not significant. The slight overstatement of liabilities that results from carrying current liabilities at maturity value is accepted as immaterial.

The current liability accounts are commonly presented as the first classification in the balance sheet's Liabilities and Shareholders' Equity section. In some instances, current liabilities are presented as a group immediately below current assets, with the total of the current liabilities deducted from the total current assets. This is an informative presentation that focuses on the company's investment in working capital.

Within the Current Liability section, the accounts may be listed in order of maturity, in descending order of amount, or in order of liquidation preference. Many companies list "notes payable" first (sometimes called "commercial paper," "bank loans," or "short-term debt"), regardless of relative amount, followed most often with "accounts payable," and end the section with "current portion of long-term debt." Presented in Illustration 14-11 is an excerpt from the December 31, 2000 balance sheet and notes to the financial statements of **Domtar Inc.** that is a representative presentation of the current liabilities found in the reports of large corporations:

ILLUSTRATION 14-11
Balance Sheet Presentation of Current Liabilities

DOMTAR INC.		
(In millions of Canadian dollars)		
	2000	1999
Current liabilities		
Bank indebtedness	$ 47	$ 48
Trade and other payables *(Note 9)*	532	504
Income and other taxes payable	20	39
Long-term debt due within one year *(Note 11)*	41	24
	$640	$615

Note 9. Trade and Other Payables

Trade accounts payable	$272	$215
Accrued salaries, wages and benefits	55	32
Accrued vacation pay	48	48
Accrued interest	30	29
Payables on capital projects	19	23
Provisions for site remediation costs	12	16
Other	96	141
	$532	$504

Go to the Digital Tool for additional disclosures of current liability sections

Detailed and supplemental information concerning current liabilities should be sufficient to provide full disclosure. Separate disclosure is required of the major classes of current liabilities such as bank loans, trade creditors and accrued liabilities, taxes, dividends, deferred revenue, future income taxes, and amounts owing on loans from officers, directors, shareholders, and associated companies. Secured liabilities should be identified clearly, and the related assets pledged as collateral indicated. If the due date of any liability can be extended, the details should be disclosed. Current liabilities should not be offset against assets that are to be applied to their liquidation. Current maturities of long-term debt should be classified as current liabilities.[23]

A major exception exists when a currently maturing obligation is to be paid from assets classified as long-term. For example, if payments to retire a bond payable are made from a bond sinking fund classified as a long-term asset, the bonds payable should be reported in the Long-term Liability section. Presentation of this debt in the Current Liability section would distort the enterprise's working capital position.

Existing commitments that will result in obligations in succeeding periods that are unusual in nature or material in amount may require disclosure. For example, commitments to purchase goods or services, as well as for construction, purchase, or lease of equipment or properties, may require disclosure in the notes to the financial statements.

IAS NOTE

IAS 37 requires more extensive disclosures for provisions and contingent liabilities, including descriptions and reconciliations between opening and closing balances of each class of provisions, and an indication of the uncertainties about the amount or timing of any outflow.

Presentation of Contingencies

As indicated in Illustration 14-6, note disclosure of contingent liabilities is required when:

1. it is likely that a future event will confirm the existence of a loss but the loss cannot be reasonably estimated;
2. a loss has been recognized, but there is an exposure to loss in excess of the amount recorded; and
3. the likelihood of a future confirming event is not determinable.

Certain other contingent liabilities that may be disclosed even though the possibility of loss may be remote include guarantees of indebtedness of others, obligations of commercial banks under "stand-by letters of credit," and guarantees to repurchase receivables (or any related property) that have been sold or assigned. Disclosure should include the nature and amount of the guarantee and, if estimable, the amount that could be recovered from outside parties.

Presented in Illustration 14-12 is a contingencies disclosure note taken from the financial statements of **Four Seasons Hotels Inc.** for the year ended December 31, 2000 that indicates a variety of potential areas of loss.

---

[23] *CICA Handbook*, Section 1510, par. .03 to .08.

ILLUSTRATION 14-12
Contingencies Note

Go to the Digital Tool
for additional disclosures
of contingencies

Four Seasons Hotels Inc.
Note 12 (partial) (in $000)

e) Contingencies:

(i) The Corporation estimates and accrues for the losses, if any, it is likely to incur relating to uninsured contingent liabilities such as guarantees of third party debt, environmental matters, personal injury and property damage at owned or managed hotels, workers' compensation claims, etc. The Corporation's assessment of its potential liability for such matters could change, with the result that the accruals for contingent liabilities recorded in the Corporation's financial statements could increase by a material amount.

(ii) Until 1982, the Corporation held a co-ownership interest in an office building in Toronto. In 1981, the co-owners obtained financing of approximately $22,000 (of which approximately $20,600 plus accrued interest was outstanding as at December 31, 2000) in connection with the property and the Corporation provided a several guarantee with respect to the financing. The Corporation sold its interest in the property to a Canadian insurance company in 1982 for consideration consisting of a cash payment and an assumption by the purchaser of the Corporation's obligations under the mortgage. The Corporation has been advised by the mortgagee that a default has occurred under the mortgage and the mortgagee has commenced a proceeding against the Corporation and another guarantor. The Corporation is vigorously defending the suit and believes that, as a result of, among other things, the sale by the Corporation of its interest in the property and the resulting obligations of the purchaser, obligations of the Corporation, if any, to the mortgagee should be offset by corresponding claims against the purchaser.

(iii) In the ordinary course of its business, the Corporation is named as defendant in legal proceedings resulting from incidents taking place at hotels owned or managed by it. The Corporation maintains comprehensive liability insurance and also requires hotel owners to maintain adequate insurance coverage. The Corporation believes such coverage to be of a nature and amount sufficient to ensure that it is adequately protected from suffering any material financial loss as a result of such claims.

(iv) A number of the Corporation's management contracts are subject to certain performance tests which, if not met, could allow a contract to be terminated prior to its maturity. The Corporation generally has various rights to cure any such defaults to avoid termination. In addition, certain management contracts are terminable by the hotel owner on a defined change of control of FSHI.

(v) The Corporation has guaranteed certain obligations of various directors, officers, and employees in the amount of $941.

Analysis of Current Liabilities

Identifying current liabilities separately from long-term debt is important because it provides information about the company's liquidity. Liquidity refers to a company's ability to convert assets into cash to pay off its current liabilities in the ordinary course of business. The higher the proportion of assets expected to be converted to cash is to the liabilities currently due, the more liquid the company. A company with higher liquidity is better able to withstand financial downturns and has a better chance of taking advantage of investment opportunities that develop.

As indicated in earlier chapters of the text, certain basic ratios such as net cash flow provided by operating activities to current liabilities, and the turnover ratios for receivables and inventory, are useful in assessing liquidity. Two other key ratios are the current ratio and the acid-test ratio.

The **current ratio** is the ratio of total current assets to total current liabilities. The formula is shown below.

ILLUSTRATION 14-13
Formula for Current Ratio

$$\text{Current ratio} = \frac{\text{Current assets}}{\text{Current liabilities}}$$

It is frequently expressed as a coverage of so many times. Sometimes it is called the working capital ratio because working capital is the excess of current assets over current liabilities. The higher the ratio, the more likely the company is able to generate cash to pay its currently maturing liabilities.

A company with a large amount of current assets made up almost entirely of inventory may have a satisfactory current ratio, but may not be very liquid. The current ratio does not indicate that a portion of the current assets may be tied up in slow-moving inventories. With inventories, especially raw materials and work in process, there is a question of how long it will take to transform them into finished product, to sell the finished product, and **then** collect the amounts owed by customers. By eliminating inventories and other non-liquid current assets such as prepaid expenses from the current asset numerator, better information may be provided to assess liquidity. Many analysts favour an acid-test or quick ratio that relates total current liabilities to cash, marketable securities, and receivables. The formula for this ratio is illustrated below.

$$\text{Acid-test ratio} = \frac{\text{Cash} + \text{Marketable securities} + \text{Net receivables}}{\text{Current liabilities}}$$

ILLUSTRATION 14-14
Formula for Acid-test Ratio

To illustrate the calculation of these two ratios, partial balance sheet information for **Derlan Industries Limited**, a fabricating and engineering firm is provided.

ILLUSTRATION 14-15
Current Assets and Liabilities of Derlan Industries Limited

DERLAN INDUSTRIES LIMITED
(Dollars in thousands)

	2000
Current assets	
Cash	$ —
Accounts receivable, net of allowance for doubtful accounts of $557 (1999 – $707)	42,359
Inventories (note 3)	70,110
Prepaid expenses and other	2,879
	$115,348
Current liabilities	
Bank indebtedness	$ 3,293
Accounts payable and accrued liabilities	46,057
Current portion of long-term debt (note 7)	1,190
	$50,540

The calculation of the current and acid-test ratios for Derlan Industries is as follows:

$$\text{Current ratio} = \frac{\text{Current assets}}{\text{Current liabilities}} = \frac{\$115,348}{\$50,540} = 2.3 \text{ times}$$

$$\text{Acid-test ratio} = \frac{\text{Quick assets}}{\text{Current liabilities}} = \frac{\$-0- + \$42,359}{\$50,540} = 0.8 \text{ times}$$

ILLUSTRATION 14-16
Calculation of Current and Acid-test Ratios

While a 2.3 to 1 current ratio and a 0.8 to 1 quick ratio appear adequate, it is difficult to make a conclusive statement about the company's liquidity. Some industries operate in such a way that companies need significant amounts of current and quick assets to current liabilities, while others who generate cash from cash sales (such as Costco, for example), may be very liquid with low current and quick ratios.

SUMMARY OF LEARNING OBJECTIVES
· ·

1 Define liabilities and differentiate between financial and other liabilities. Liabilities are defined as "obligations of an enterprise arising from past transactions or events, the settlement of which may result in the transfer of assets, provision of services or other yielding of economic benefits in the future." Financial liabilities are a subset of liabilities. They are contractual obligations to deliver cash or other financial assets to another party, or to exchange financial instruments with another party under conditions that are potentially unfavourable.

KEY TERMS

accumulated rights, 672

acid-test ratio, 685

bonus, 673

cash dividend payable, 666

compensated absences, 672

contingency, 678

contingent liability, 678

current liabilities, 662

current maturities of long-term debt, 664

current ratio, 684

expense warranty method, 675

financial liabilities, 661

gain contingencies, 678

liabilities, 661

litigation, claims, and assessments, 680

loss contingencies, 678

notes payable, 663

operating cycle, 662

preferred dividends in arrears, 666

premiums, 677

quick ratio, 685

returnable cash deposits, 666

sales warranty approach, 676

self-insurance, 682

short-term obligations expected to be refinanced, 665

trade accounts payable, 662

trade notes payable, 663

unearned revenues, 666

vested rights, 672

warranty, 674

2 Define current liabilities, describe how they are valued, and identify common types of current liabilities. Current liabilities are obligations payable within one year from the balance sheet date or within the operating cycle, where this is longer than a year. The liquidation of a current liability is reasonably expected to require the use of current assets or the creation of other current liabilities. Theoretically, liabilities should be measured at the present value of the future outlay of cash required to liquidate them. In practice, current liabilities are usually recorded in accounting records and reported in financial statements at their full maturity value. There are several types of current liabilities, the most common being accounts and notes payable, along with payroll-related obligations.

3 Explain the classification issues of short-term debt expected to be refinanced. An enterprise is required to exclude a short-term obligation from current liabilities if the following conditions are met: (1) It intends to refinance the obligation on a long-term basis and (2) it demonstrates an ability to consummate the refinancing.

4 Identify and account for the major types of employee-related liabilities. Employee-related liabilities include: (1) payroll deductions; (2) compensated absences; and (3) bonus agreements. Payroll deductions are amounts withheld from employees and the employer's required contributions that have not yet been remitted to the government. Compensated absences earned by employees are company obligations that should be recognized as the employees earn the entitlement to them, provided they can be reasonably measured. Bonuses based on income should be accrued as an expense and liability as the income is earned.

5 Explain the accounting for common estimated liabilities. Some liabilities cannot be measured precisely. Where companies have obligations to provide goods or services in the future related to current period sales, for example, the obligation is reported as a liability and the related expense is matched with the associated revenue. When the company actually incurs the cost (or the reduced revenue) in future periods, the liability is reduced.

6 Explain the accounting and reporting standards for loss contingencies. A loss contingency should be accrued by a charge to expense and a credit to a liability if information available prior to the issuance of the financial statements indicates that it is likely that a liability has been incurred at the date of the financial statements, and the loss amount can be reasonably estimated. If the existence of a liability is likely but not measurable, or if its existence is not determinable, it should be reported in a note to the financial statements.

7 Indicate how financial and other current liabilities and contingencies are presented and analysed. The current liability accounts are commonly presented as the first classification in the liabilities and shareholders' equity section of the balance sheet. Within the current liability section, the accounts may be listed in order of maturity, in descending order of amount, or in order of liquidation preference. Detail and supplemental information concerning current liabilities should be sufficient to meet the requirement of full disclosure. Loss contingencies that are likely but not measurable, or whose outcome is not determinable, should be disclosed in notes to the financial statements. The nature of the contingency and an estimate of the possible loss should be reported. Two common ratios used to analyse liquidity are the current and acid-test ratios.

BRIEF EXERCISES

••

BE14-1 Condo Corporation uses a periodic inventory system and the gross method of accounting for purchase discounts. On July 1, Condo purchased $40,000 of inventory, terms 2/10, n/30, FOB shipping point. Condo paid freight costs of $1,200. On July 3, Condo returned damaged goods and received credit of $6,000. On July 10, Condo paid for the goods. Prepare all necessary journal entries for Condo.

BE14-2   Storm Limited borrowed $50,000 on November 1, 2002 by signing a $50,000, 9%, three-month note. Prepare Storm's November 1, 2002 entry, the December 31, 2002 annual adjusting entry, and the February 1, 2003 entry.

BE14-3   Kawaski Corporation borrowed $50,000 on November 1, 2002 by signing a $51,125, three-month, zero-interest-bearing note. Prepare Kawaski's November 1, 2002 entry, the December 31, 2002 annual adjusting entry, and the February 1, 2003 entry.

BE14-4   At December 31, 2002, Fifa Corporation owes $500,000 on a note payable due February 15, 2003. (a) If Fifa refinances the obligation by issuing a long-term note on February 14 and uses the proceeds to pay off the note due February 15, how much of the $500,000 should be reported as a current liability at December 31, 2002? (b) If Fifa pays off the note on February 15, 2003 and then borrows $1 million on a long-term basis on March 1, how much of the $500,000 should be reported as a current liability at December 31, 2002?

BE14-5   Game Pro Magazine Ltd. sold 10,000 annual subscriptions on August 1, 2002 for $18 each. Prepare Game Pro's August 1, 2002 journal entry and the December 31, 2002 annual adjusting entry.

BE14-6   Flint Corporation made credit sales of $30,000, that are subject to 6% sales tax. The corporation also made cash sales that totalled $19,610 including the 6% sales tax. (a) Prepare the entry to record Flint's credit sales. (b) Prepare the entry to record Flints' cash sales.

BE14-7   Nixil Limited conducts all its business in a province which has a 5% sales tax as well as the 7% GST, both applied on the value of the product or service sold. Assume all Nixil's sales attract both types of tax. Prepare the summary journal entry to record the company's sales for the month of July in which customers purchased $45,500 of goods on account.

BE14-8   Refer to Nixil Limited in BE14-7. During July, Nixil purchased $28,800 of merchandise inventory on which 7% GST was levied. Nixil uses the periodic inventory system. Prepare the summary entry to record the purchases for July and the subsequent entry to record the payment of any GST owing for July to the government.

BE14-9   Fantasy Inc. receives its property tax bill from Jidoor County in March each year. The county uses the tax receipts to provide services for the calendar year. The tax payment is due May 1. At January 31 and February 28, the company recorded property tax expense and property taxes payable of $1,000 (based on 1/12 of $12,000, the taxes levied in 2001). In March 2002, Fantasy received a tax bill of $14,760 for 2002. Prepare Fantasy's March 31 and April 30 accrual entries and the May 1 entry to record the payment of the taxes.

BE14-10   Zone Corporation's weekly payroll of $23,000 included employee income taxes withheld of $3,426, CPP withheld of $990, EI withheld of $920, and health insurance premiums withheld of $250. Prepare the journal entries to record Zone's payroll.

BE14-11   Tale Spin Inc. provides paid vacations to its employees. At December 31, 2002, 30 employees have each earned two weeks of vacation time. The employees' average salary is $600 per week. Prepare Tale Spin's December 31, 2002 adjusting entry.

BE14-12   Gargoyle Corporation provides its officers with bonuses based on income. For 2002, the bonuses total $450,000 and are paid on February 15, 2003. Prepare Gargoyle's December 31, 2002 adjusting entry and the February 15, 2003 entry.

BE14-13   Justice Inc. is involved in a lawsuit at December 31, 2002. (a) Prepare the December 31 entry assuming it is likely that Justice will be liable for $700,000 as a result of this suit. (b) Prepare the December 31 entry, if any, assuming it is not likely that Justice will be liable for any payment as a result of this suit.

BE14-14   Kohlbeck Corp. recently was sued by a competitor for patent infringement. Lawyers have determined that it is likely that Kohlbeck will lose the case and that a reasonable estimate of damages to be paid by Kohlbeck is $200,000. In light of this case, Kohlbeck is considering establishing a $100,000 self-insurance allowance. What entry(ies), if any, should Kohlbeck record to recognize this loss contingency?

BE14-15 Frantic Corp. provides a two-year warranty with one of its products, which was first sold in 2002. In that year, Frantic spent $70,000 servicing warranty claims. At year end, Frantic estimates that an additional $500,000 will be spent in the future to service warranty claims related to 2002 sales. Prepare Frantic's journal entry to record the $70,000 expenditure, and the December 31 adjusting entry.

BE14-16 Refer to Frantic Corp. in BE14–15. Prepare entries for the warranty that recognize the full obligation at the time of sale, the $70,000 expenditure for servicing the warranty during 2002, and the adjusting entry required at year end, if any.

BE14-17 Zwei Corporation sells VCRs. The corporation also offers its customers a two-year warranty contract. During 2002, Zwei sold 15,000 warranty contracts at $99 each. The corporation spent $180,000 servicing warranties during 2002, and it estimates that an additional $900,000 will be spent in the future to service the warranties. Prepare Zwei's journal entries for (a) the sale of contracts, (b) the cost of servicing the warranties, and (c) the recognition of warranty revenue.

BE14-18 Klax Corp. offers a set of building blocks to customers who send in three UPC codes from Klax cereal, along with 50¢. The block sets cost Klax $1.10 each to purchase and 60¢ each to mail to customers. During 2002, Klax sold 1 million cereal boxes. The company expects 30% of the UPC codes to be sent in. During 2002, 120,000 UPC codes were redeemed. Prepare Klax's December 31, 2002 adjusting entry.

EXERCISES

E14-1 **(Balance Sheet Classification of Various Liabilities)** How would each of the following items be reported on the balance sheet? For any identified as a liability, indicate whether it is a financial liability.

  (a) accrued vacation pay
  (b) estimated taxes payable
  (c) service warranties on appliance sales
  (d) bank overdraft
  (e) employee payroll deductions unremitted
  (f) unpaid bonus to officers
  (g) deposit received from customer to guarantee performance of a contract
  (h) sales taxes payable
  (i) gift certificates sold to customers but not yet redeemed
  (j) premium offers outstanding
  (k) discount on notes payable
  (l) personal injury claim pending
  (m) current maturities of long-term debts to be paid from current assets
  (n) cash dividends declared but unpaid
  (o) dividends in arrears on preferred shares
  (p) loans from officers

E14-2 **(Accounts and Notes Payable)** The following are selected 2002 transactions of Astin Corporation:

Sept. 1 Purchased inventory from Encino Company on account for $50,000. Astin records purchases gross and uses a periodic inventory system.
Oct. 1 Issued a $50,000, 12-month, 12% note to Encino in payment of account.
Oct. 1 Borrowed $50,000 from the bank by signing a 12-month, non-interest-bearing $56,000 note.

Instructions

  (a) Prepare journal entries for the transactions above.
  (b) Prepare adjusting entries at December 31.
  (c) Calculate the total net liability to be reported on the December 31 balance sheet for:
    1. the interest-bearing note and
    2. the non-interest-bearing note.

E14-3 **(Refinancing of Short-Term Debt)** On December 31, 2002, Hattie Corporation had $1.2 million of short-term debt in the form of notes payable due February 2, 2003. On January 21, 2003, the company issued 25,000 common shares for $38 per share, receiving $950,000 proceeds after brokerage fees and other costs of issuance. On February 2, 2003, the proceeds from the sale of the shares, supplemented by an additional $250,000 cash, are used to liquidate the $1.2 million debt. The December 31, 2002 balance sheet is issued on February 23, 2003.

Instructions

Show how the $1.2 million of short-term debt should be presented on the December 31, 2002 balance sheet, including note disclosure.

E14-4 **(Refinancing of Short-Term Debt)**   On December 31, 2002, Atkins Corporation has $7 million of short-term debt in the form of notes payable to Provincial Bank due periodically in 2003. On January 28, 2003, Atkins enters into a refinancing agreement with the bank that will permit it to borrow up to 60% of the gross amount of its accounts receivable. Receivables are expected to range between a low of $6 million in May to a high of $8 million in October during the year 2003. The interest cost of the maturing short-term debt is 15%, and the new agreement calls for a fluctuating interest rate at 1% above the prime rate on notes due in 2007. Atkin's December 31, 2002 balance sheet is issued on February 15, 2003.

Instructions

Prepare a partial balance sheet for Atkins at December 31, 2002, showing how its $7 million of short-term debt should be presented, including footnote disclosures.

E14-5 **(Compensated Absences)**   Mostel Limited began operations on January 2, 2001. It employs nine individuals who work eight-hour days and are paid hourly. Each employee earns 10 paid vacation days and 6 paid sick days annually. Vacation days may be taken after January 15 of the year following the year in which they are earned. Sick days may be taken as soon as they are earned; unused sick days accumulate. Additional information is as follows:

Actual Hourly Wage Rate		Vacation Days Used by Each Employee		Sick Days Used by Each Employee	
2001	2002	2001	2002	2001	2002
$10	$11	0	9	4	5

Mostel Limited has chosen to accrue the cost of compensated absences at rates of pay in effect during the period when earned and to accrue sick pay when earned.

Instructions

(a) Prepare journal entries to record transactions related to compensated absences during 2001 and 2002.
(b) Calculate the amounts of any liability for compensated absences that should be reported on the balance sheet at December 31, 2001 and 2002.

E14-6 **(Compensated Absences)**   Assume the facts in the preceding exercise, except that Mostel Limited has chosen not to recognize paid sick leave until used, and has chosen to accrue vacation time at expected future rates of pay without discounting. The company used the following projected rates to accrue vacation time:

Year in Which Vacation Time Was Earned	Projected Future Pay Rates Used to Accrue Vacation Pay
2001	$10.75
2002	$11.60

Instructions

(a) Prepare journal entries to record transactions related to compensated absences during 2001 and 2002.
(b) Calculate the amounts of any liability for compensated absences that should be reported on the balance sheet at December 31, 2001 and 2002.

E14-7 **(Adjusting Entry for Sales Tax)**   During the month of June, Borough Boutique Ltd. had cash sales of $233,200 and credit sales of $153,700, both of which include the 6% sales tax and the 7% GST that must be remitted to the government by July 15. Assume both taxes are applied on the selling price of the goods sold.

Instructions

Prepare the adjusting entry that should be recorded to fairly present the June 30 financial statements.

E14-8 **(Payroll Tax Entries)** The payroll of Auber Corp. for September 2002 is as follows:

Total payroll was $495,000, of which $120,000 represents amounts paid in excess of the maximum pensionable (CPP) and insurable (EI) earnings of certain employees. Income taxes in the amount of $90,000 are withheld, as is $9,000 in union dues. The employment insurance tax rate is 2.25% for employees and 3.15% for employers and the CPP rate is 4.3% for employees and 4.3% for employers.

Instructions

(a) Prepare the necessary journal entries to record the payroll if the wages and salaries paid and the employer payroll taxes are recorded separately.

(b) Prepare the entry to record the payment of all required amounts to Canada Customs and Revenue Agency.

E14-9 **(Payroll Tax Entries)** Green Day Hardware Corp.'s payroll for November 2002 is summarized below.

			Amount Subject to Payroll Taxes	
Payroll	Wages Due	Income Tax Withheld	CPP	EI
Factory	$120,000	$14,500	$120,000	$40,000
Sales	44,000	6,000	32,000	14,000
Administrative	36,000	7,500	36,000	4,000
Total	$200,000	$28,000	$188,000	$58,000

At this point in the year, some employees have already received wages in excess of those to which payroll taxes apply. Assume that the employment insurance rate for employees is 2.25% and for employers is 3.15%. The CPP rate is 4.3% for both the employee and the employer.

Instructions

(a) Prepare a schedule showing the employer's total cost of wages for November by function. (Round all calculations to nearest dollar.)

(b) Prepare the journal entries to record the factory, sales, and administrative payrolls including the employer's payroll taxes.

(c) For every dollar of wages and salaries that Green Day Hardware commits to pay, what is the actual payroll cost to the company?

(d) Prepare the entry to record the payment of the required amounts to Canada Customs and Revenue Agency.

E14-10 **(Warranties)** Soundgarden Corporation sold 200 copymaking machines in 2002 for $4,000 apiece, together with a one-year warranty. Maintenance on each machine during the warranty period averages $330.

Instructions

(a) Prepare entries to record the machine sale and the related warranty costs, assuming that the accrual method is used. Actual warranty costs incurred in 2002 were $17,000.

(b) Based on the data above, prepare the appropriate entries, assuming that the cash basis method is used.

E14-11 **(Warranties)** Crow Equipment Limited sold 500 Rollomatics during 2002 at $6,000 each. During 2002, Crow spent $20,000 servicing the two-year warranties that accompany the Rollomatic. All applicable transactions are on a cash basis.

Instructions

(a) Prepare 2002 entries for Crow using the expense warranty approach. Assume that Crow estimates the total cost of servicing the warranties will be $120,000 for two years.

(b) Prepare 2002 entries for Crow assuming that the warranties are not an integral part of the sale. Assume that of the sales total, $150,000 relates to sales of warranty contracts. Crow estimates the total cost of servicing the warranties will be $120,000 for two years. Estimate revenues earned on the basis of costs incurred relative to total estimated costs.

E14-12 **(Liability for Returnable Containers)** Candlebox Corp. sells its products in expensive, reusable containers. The customer is charged a deposit for each container delivered and receives a refund for each container returned within two years after the year of delivery. Candlebox accounts for the containers not returned within the time limit as being sold at the deposit amount. Information for 2002 is as follows:

Containers held by customers at December 31, 2001

from deliveries in:			
	2000	$170,000	
	2001	480,000	$650,000
Containers delivered in 2002			860,000
Containers returned in 2002 from deliveries in:	2000	$115,000	
	2001	280,000	
	2002	314,000	709,000

Instructions

(a) Prepare all journal entries required for Candlebox Corp. during 2002 for the returnable containers.

(b) Calculate the total amount Candlebox should report as a liability for returnable containers at December 31, 2002.

(c) Should the liability calculated in (b) above be reported as current or long-term?

(AICPA adapted)

E14-13 **(Premium Entries)** Yanni Corporation includes one coupon in each box of soap powder that it packs, and 10 coupons are redeemable for a premium (a kitchen utensil). In 2002, Yanni Corporation purchased 8,800 premiums at 80 cents each and sold 110,000 boxes of soap powder at $3.30 per box; 44,000 coupons were presented for redemption in 2002. It is estimated that 60% of the coupons will eventually be presented for redemption.

Instructions

Prepare all the entries that would be made relative to sales of soap powder and to the premium plan in 2002.

E14-14 **(Contingencies)** Presented below are three independent situations. Answer the question at the end of each situation.

1. During 2002, Salt-n-Pepa Inc. became involved in a tax dispute with Canada Customs and Revenue Agency (CCRA). Salt-n-Pepa's lawyers have indicated that they believe it is probable that Salt-n-Pepa will lose this dispute. They also believe that Salt-n-Pepa will have to pay CCRA between $900,000 and $1.4 million. After the 2002 financial statements were issued, the case was settled with the CCRA for $1.2 million. What amount, if any, should be reported as a liability for this contingency as of December 31, 2002?

2. On October 1, 2002, Jackson Chemical Inc. was identified as a potentially responsible party by the provincial environment ministry. Jackson's management, along with its counsel, have concluded that it is probable that Jackson will be responsible for damages, and a reasonable estimate of these damages is $5 million. Jackson's insurance policy of $9 million has a deductible clause of $500,000. How should Jackson Chemical report this information in its financial statements at December 31, 2002?

3. Etheridge Inc. had a manufacturing plant in Bosnia, which was destroyed in the civil war. It is not certain who will compensate Etheridge for this destruction, but Etheridge has been assured by Bosnian governmental officials that it will receive a definite amount for this plant. The compensation amount will be less than the plant's fair value, but more than its book value. How should the contingency be reported in the financial statements of Etheridge Inc.?

E14-15 **(Premiums)** Presented below are two independent situations.

1. In packages of its products, ITSS Inc. includes coupons that may be presented at retail stores to obtain discounts on other ITSS products. Retailers are reimbursed for the face amount of coupons redeemed plus 10% of that amount for handling costs. ITSS honours requests for coupon redemption by retailers up to three months after the consumer expiration date. ITSS estimates that 60% of all coupons issued will ultimately be redeemed. Information relating to coupons issued by ITSS during 2002 is as follows:

Consumer expiration date	12/31/02
Total face amount of coupons issued	$800,000
Total payments to retailers as of 12/31/02	330,000

(a) What amount should ITSS report as a liability for unredeemed coupons at December 31, 2002?

(b) What amount of premium expense should ITSS report on its 2002 income statement?

2. Baylor Corp. sold 700,000 boxes of pie mix under a new sales promotional program. Each box contains one coupon, which when submitted with $4.00 entitles the customer to a baking pan. Baylor pays $6.00 per pan and $0.50 for handling and shipping. Baylor estimates that 70% of the coupons will be redeemed, even though only 250,000 coupons had been processed during 2002.

(a) What amount should Baylor report as a liability for unredeemed coupons at December 31, 2002?

(b) What amount of expense will Baylor report on its 2002 income statement as a result of the promotional program?

(AICPA adapted)

E14-16 **(Financial Statement Impact of Liability Transactions)** Presented below is a list of possible transactions.

1. Purchased inventory for $80,000 on account (assume perpetual system is used).
2. Issued an $80,000 note payable in payment on account (see item 1 above).
3. Recorded accrued interest on the note from item 2 above.
4. Borrowed $100,000 from the bank by signing a six-month, $112,000, non-interest-bearing note.
5. Recognized four months' interest expense on the note from item 4 above.
6. Recorded cash sales of $75,260, which includes 6% sales tax.
7. Recorded wage expense of $35,000. The cash paid was $25,000; the difference was due to various amounts withheld.
8. Recorded employer's payroll taxes.
9. Accrued accumulated vacation pay.
10. Recorded accrued property taxes payable.
11. Recorded bonuses due to employees.
12. Recorded a contingent loss on a lawsuit that the company will probably lose.
13. Accrued warranty expense (assume expense warranty approach).
14. Paid warranty costs that were accrued in item 13 above.
15. Recorded sales of product and separately sold warranties (assume sales warranty approach).
16. Paid warranty costs under contracts from item 15 above.
17. Recognized warranty revenue (see item 15 above).
18. Recorded estimated liability for premium claims outstanding.
19. Recorded the receipt of a cash down payment on services to be performed in the next accounting period.
20. Received the remainder of the contracted amount and performed the services related to item 19 above.

Instructions

Set up a table using the format shown below and analyse the effect of the 20 transactions on the financial statement categories indicated.

#	Assets	Liabilities	Owners' Equity	Net Income
1				

Use the following code:

I: Increase   D: Decrease   NE: No net effect

E14-17 **(Ratio Calculations and Discussion)** Sprague Corporation has been operating for several years, and on December 31, 2002, presented the following balance sheet:

SPRAGUE CORPORATION
Balance Sheet
December 31, 2002

Cash	$ 40,000	Accounts payable	$ 80,000
Receivables	75,000	Mortgage payable	140,000
Inventories	95,000	Common shares (no par)	150,000
Plant assets (net)	220,000	Retained earnings	60,000
	$430,000		$430,000

The net income for 2002 was $25,000. Assume that total assets are the same in 2001 and 2002.

Instructions

Calculate each of the following ratios. For each of the four, indicate the manner in which it is calculated and its significance as a tool in the analysis of the financial soundness of the company.

(a) current ratio

(b) acid-test ratio

(c) debt to total assets

(d) rate of return on assets

E14-18 (**Ratio Calculations and Analysis**) Hood Limited's condensed financial statements provide the following information:

HOOD LIMITED
Balance Sheet

	Dec. 31, 2002	Dec. 31, 2001
Cash	$ 52,000	$ 60,000
Accounts receivable (net)	198,000	80,000
Marketable securities (short-term)	80,000	40,000
Inventories	440,000	360,000
Prepaid expenses	3,000	7,000
Total current assets	$ 773,000	$ 547,000
Property, plant, and equipment (net)	857,000	853,000
Total assets	$1,630,000	$1,400,000
Current liabilities	240,000	160,000
Bonds payable	400,000	400,000
Common shareholders' equity	990,000	840,000
Total liabilities and shareholders' equity	$1,630,000	$1,400,000

INCOME STATEMENT
For the Year Ended December 31, 2002

Sales	$1,640,000
Cost of goods sold	(800,000)
Gross profit	840,000
Selling and administrative expense	(440,000)
Interest expense	(40,000)
Net income	$ 360,000

Instructions

(a) Determine the following:
   1. Current ratio at December 31, 2002.
   2. Acid-test ratio at December 31, 2002.
   3. Accounts receivable turnover for 2002.
   4. Inventory turnover for 2002.
   5. Rate of return on assets for 2002.
   6. Profit margin on sales.

(b) Prepare a brief evaluation of the financial condition of Hood Limited and of the adequacy of its profits.

E14-19 (**Ratio Calculations and Effect of Transactions**) Presented below is information related to Carver Inc.:

CARVER INC.
Balance Sheet
December 31, 2002

Cash		$ 45,000	Notes payable (short-term)	$ 50,000
Receivables	$110,000		Accounts payable	32,000
Less: Allowance	15,000	95,000	Accrued liabilities	5,000
Inventories		170,000	Share capital (52,000 shares)	260,000
Prepaid insurance		8,000	Retained Earnings	141,000
Land		20,000		
Equipment (net)		150,000		
		$488,000		$488,000

Income Statement
For the Year Ended December 31, 2002

Sales		$1,400,000
Cost of goods sold		
Inventory, Jan. 1, 2002	$200,000	
Purchases	790,000	
Cost of goods available for sale	990,000	
Inventory, Dec. 31, 2002	170,000	
Cost of goods sold		820,000
Gross profit on sales		580,000
Operating expenses		170,000
Net income		$ 410,000

Instructions

(a) Calculate the following ratios or relationships of Carver Inc. Assume that the ending account balances are representative unless the information provided indicates differently.

1. Current ratio
2. Inventory turnover
3. Receivables turnover
4. Earnings per share
5. Profit margin on sales
6. Rate of return on assets for 2002

(b) Indicate for each of the following transactions whether the transaction would improve, weaken, or have no effect on the current ratio of Carver Inc. at December 31, 2002.

1. Write off an uncollectible account receivable, $2,200.
2. Receive a $20,000 down payment on services to be performed in 2003.
3. Pay $40,000 on notes payable (short-term).
4. Collect $23,000 on accounts receivable.
5. Buy equipment on account.
6. Give an existing creditor a short-term note in settlement of account.

E14-20 **(Bonus Calculation and Income Statement Preparation)** The incomplete income statement of Pippen Corp. appears below:

PIPPEN CORP.
Income Statement
For the Year 2002

Revenue		$10,000,000
Cost of goods sold		7,000,000
Gross profit		3,000,000
Administrative and selling expenses	$1,000,000	
Profit-sharing bonus to employees	?	?
Income before income taxes		?
Income taxes		?
Net income		$?

The employee profit-sharing plan requires that 20% of all profits remaining after the deduction of the bonus and income taxes be distributed to the employees by the first day of the fourth month following each year end. The income tax rate is 45%, and the bonus is tax-deductible.

Instructions

Complete the condensed income statement of Pippen Corp. for the year 2002. You will need to develop two simultaneous equations to solve for the bonus amount, one for the bonus and one for the tax.

PROBLEMS

P14-1   Described below are certain transactions of Edwards Corporation.

1. On February 2, the corporation purchased goods from Haley Limited for $50,000 subject to cash discount terms of 2/10, n/30. Purchases and accounts payable are recorded by the corporation, using the periodic system, at net amounts after cash discounts. The invoice was paid on February 26.
2. On April 1, the corporation bought a truck for $40,000 from Smith Motors Limited, paying $4,000 in cash and signing a one-year, 12% note for the balance of the purchase price.
3. On May 1, the corporation borrowed $80,000 from Second Provincial Bank by signing a $92,000 non-interest-bearing note due one year from May 1.
4. On August 14, the board of directors declared a $300,000 cash dividend that was payable on September 10 to shareholders of record on August 31.

Instructions

(a) Make all the journal entries necessary to record the transactions above using appropriate dates.
(b) Edwards Corporation's year end is December 31. Assuming that no adjusting entries relative to the transactions above have been recorded, prepare any adjusting journal entries concerning interest that are necessary to present fair financial statements at December 31.

P14-2   Listed below are selected transactions of Kobe Department Store Ltd. for the current year ending December 31.

1. On December 5, the store received $500 from Jackson Corp. as a deposit to be returned after certain furniture to be used in their stage production was returned on January 15.
2. During December, cash sales totalled $834,750, which includes the 5% sales tax and 7% GST that must be remitted by the 15th day of the following month. Both taxes are levied on the sale amount to the customer.
3. On December 10, the store purchased for cash three delivery trucks for $99,000. A 5% sales tax and 7% GST were charged on the purchase price by the supplier.
4. The store follows a practice of amortizing its property taxes over the 12 months subsequent to their lien date. Property taxes of $66,000 became a lien on May 1 and were paid in two equal instalments on July 1 and October 1.

Instructions

(a) Prepare all the journal entries necessary to record the transactions noted above as they occurred and any adjusting journal entries relative to the transactions that would be required to present fair financial statements at December 31. Date each entry.
(b) Prepare the adjusting journal entries for transactions 2 and 3 above if the 5% sales tax is applied on the purchase or sale amount *plus* the GST.

P14-3   Starr Company Limited pays its office employees weekly. Below is a partial list of employees and their payroll data for August. Because August is the vacation period, vacation pay is also listed.

Employee	Earnings to July 31	Weekly Pay	Vacation Pay to Be Received in August
Mark Hamud	$14,200	$ 480	——
Carrie Frisher	13,500	450	$ 900
Harry Fyord	2,700	110	220
Alexa Guinner	7,400	250	——
Peter Cash	38,000	1,250	2,500

Assume that the income tax withheld is 10% of wages. Union dues withheld are 1% of wages. Vacations are taken the second and third weeks of August by Frisher, Fyord, and Cash. The employment insurance rate is 2.25% for employees (to a maximum of $877.50 per employee per year) and 1.4 times that for employers. The CPP rate is 4.3% for employee and employer on an annual maximum of $34,800 income per employee.

Instructions

Make the journal entries necessary for each of the four August payrolls. The entries for the payroll and for the company's liability are made separately. Also make the entry to record the monthly payment of accrued payroll liabilities.

P14-4 Below is a payroll sheet for Empire Import Corporation for the month of September 2002. The employment insurance rate is 2.25%, and the maximum annual amount per employee is $877.50. The employer's obligation for employment insurance is 1.4 times the amount of the employee deduction. Assume a 10% income tax rate for all employees, and a 4.3% CPP premium charged on both employee and employer to an annual maximum of $1,496.40 per employee. Union dues are 1% of earnings.

Name	Earnings to Aug. 31	September Earnings	Income Tax Withholding	CPP	EI	Union Dues
B.D. Williams	$ 6,800	$ 800				
D. Prowse	6,300	700				
K. Baker	7,600	1,100				
F. Oz	13,600	1,900				
A. Daniels	105,000	15,000				
P. Mayhew	112,000	16,000				

Instructions

(a) Complete the payroll sheet and make the necessary entry to record the payment of the payroll.
(b) Make the entry to record the employer's payroll tax expenses.
(c) Make the entry to record the payment of the payroll liabilities created. Assume that the company pays all payroll liabilities at the end of each month.
(d) What is the total expense the company will report in September 2002 relative to employee compensation?

P14-5 Davey Corporation sells portable computers under a two-year warranty contract that requires the corporation to replace defective parts and provide the necessary repair labour. During 2002, the corporation sells for cash 300 computers at a unit price of $3,500. On the basis of past experience, the two-year warranty costs are estimated to be $155 for parts and $185 for labour per unit. (For simplicity, assume that all sales occurred on December 31, 2002.) The warranty is not sold separately from the computer.

Instructions

(a) Record any necessary journal entries in 2002, applying the cash basis method.
(b) Record any necessary journal entries in 2002, applying the expense warranty accrual method.
(c) What liability relative to these transactions would appear on the December 31, 2002 balance sheet and how would it be classified if the cash basis method is applied?
(d) What liability relative to these transactions would appear on the December 31, 2002 balance sheet and how would it be classified if the expense warranty accrual method is applied?

In 2003, the actual warranty costs incurred by Davey Corporation were $21,400 for parts and $24,900 for labour.

(e) Record any necessary journal entries in 2003, applying the cash basis method.
(f) Record any necessary journal entries in 2003, applying the expense warranty accrual method.

P14-6 Perriman Corporation sells televisions at an average price of $750 and also offers to each customer a separate three-year warranty contract for $75 that requires the company to perform periodic services and replace defective parts. During 2002, the company sold 300 televisions and 270 warranty contracts for cash. It estimates the three-year warranty costs as $20 for parts and $40 for labour and accounts for warranties separately. Assume sales occurred on December 31, 2002, income is recognized on the warranties, and straight-line recognition of warranty revenues occurs.

Instructions

(a) Record any necessary journal entries in 2002.
(b) What liability relative to these transactions would appear on the December 31, 2002 balance sheet and how would it be classified?

In 2003, Perriman Company incurred actual costs relative to 2002 television warranty sales of $2,000 for parts and $3,000 for labour.

(c) Record any necessary journal entries in 2003 relative to 2002 television warranties.
(d) What amounts relative to the 2002 television warranties would appear on the December 31, 2003 balance sheet and how would they be classified?

P14-7 Belle Limited sells a machine for $7,400 with a 12-month warranty agreement that requires the company to replace all defective parts and to provide the repair labour at no cost to the customers. With sales being made evenly throughout the year, the company sells 650 machines in 2002. As a result of product testing, the company estimates that the warranty cost will be $370 per machine ($170 parts and $200 labour). The actual warranty costs were incurred half in 2002 and half in 2003.

Instructions

Assuming that actual warranty costs are incurred exactly as estimated, what journal entries would be made
  (a) under application of the expense warranty accrual method for:
    1. sale of machinery in 2002?
    2. warranty costs incurred in 2002?
    3. warranty expense charged against 2002 revenues?
    4. warranty costs incurred in 2003?
  (b) under application of the cash basis method for:
    1. sale of machinery in 2002?
    2. warranty costs incurred in 2002?
    3. warranty expense charged against 2002 revenues?
    4. warranty costs incurred in 2003?
  (c) What amount, if any, is disclosed in the balance sheet as a liability for future warranty costs as of December 31, 2002 and December 31, 2003 under each method?
  (d) Which method best reflects the income in 2002 and 2003 of Belle Limited? Why?

P14-8 To stimulate the sales of its Alladin breakfast cereal, the Khamsah Corporation places one coupon in each box. Five coupons are redeemable for a premium consisting of a children's hand puppet. In 2003, the company purchases 40,000 puppets at $1.50 each and sells 440,000 boxes of Alladin at $3.75 a box. From its experience with other similar premium offers, the company estimates that 40% of the coupons issued will be mailed back for redemption. During 2003, 105,000 coupons are presented for redemption.

Instructions

  (a) Prepare the journal entries that should be recorded in 2003 relative to the premium plan, assuming the company follows a policy of charging the cost of coupons redeemed to expense as they are redeemed and adjusting the liability account at year end.
  (b) Prepare the journal entries that should be recorded in 2003 relative to the premium plan, assuming the company follows a policy of charging the full estimated cost of the premium plan to expense when the sales are recognized.

P14-9 The Hernandez Candy Corporation offers a CD single as a premium for every five chocolate bar wrappers presented by customers together with $2.00. The chocolate bars are sold by the company to distributors for 30 cents each. The purchase price of each CD to the company is $1.80; in addition it costs 50 cents to mail each CD. The results of the premium plan for the years 2002 and 2003 are as follows (all purchases and sales are for cash):

	2002	2003
CDs purchased	250,000	330,000
Chocolate bars sold	2,895,400	2,743,600
Wrappers redeemed	1,200,000	1,500,000
2002 wrappers expected to be redeemed in 2003	290,000	
2003 wrappers expected to be redeemed in 2004		350,000

Instructions

  (a) Prepare the journal entries that should be made in 2002 and 2003 to record the transactions related to the premium plan of the Hernandez Candy Corporation.
  (b) Indicate the account names, amounts, and classifications of the items related to the premium plan that would appear on the balance sheet and the income statement at the end of 2002 and 2003.
  (c) For any liabilities identified in (b), indicate whether the account is a financial liability. Explain.

P14-10 On November 24, 2002, 26 passengers on Paris Airlines Flight No. 901 were injured upon landing when the plane skidded off the runway. Personal injury suits for damages totalling $5 million were filed on January 11, 2003 against the airline by 18 injured passengers. The airline carries no insurance. Legal counsel has studied each suit and advised Paris that it can reasonably expect to pay 60% of the damages claimed. The financial statements for the year ended December 31, 2002 were issued February 27, 2003.

Instructions

(a) Prepare any disclosures and journal entries required by GAAP for the airline in preparation of the December 31, 2002 financial statements.

(b) Ignoring the November 24, 2002 accident, what liability due to the risk of loss from lack of insurance coverage should Paris Airlines record or disclose? During the past decade, the company has experienced at least one accident per year and incurred average damages of $3.2 million. Discuss fully.

P14-11 Shoyo Corporation, in preparing its December 31, 2002 financial statements, is attempting to determine the proper accounting treatment for each of the following situations:

1. As a result of uninsured accidents during the year, personal injury suits for $350,000 and $60,000 have been filed against the company. It is the judgement of Shoyo's legal counsel that an unfavourable outcome is unlikely in the $60,000 case but that an unfavourable verdict approximating $225,000 will probably result in the $350,000 case.

2. Shoyo Corporation owns a subsidiary in a foreign country that has a book value of $5,725,000 and an estimated fair value of $8.7 million. The foreign government has communicated to Shoyo its intention to expropriate the assets and business of all foreign investors. On the basis of settlements other firms have received from this same country, Shoyo expects to receive 40% of the fair value of its properties as final settlement.

3. Shoyo's chemical product division, consisting of five plants, is uninsurable because of the special risk of injury to employees and losses due to fire and explosion. The year 2002 is considered one of the safest (luckiest) in the division's history because no loss due to injury or casualty was suffered. Having suffered an average of three casualties a year during the rest of the past decade (ranging from $60,000 to $700,000), management is certain that next year the company will probably not be so fortunate.

Instructions

(a) Prepare the journal entries that should be recorded as of December 31, 2002 to recognize each of the situations above.

(b) Indicate what should be reported relative to each situation in the financial statements and accompanying notes. Explain why.

P14-12 Mosaic Music Limited (MML) carries a wide variety of musical instruments, sound reproduction equipment, recorded music, and sheet music. MML uses two sales promotion techniques—warranties and premiums—to attract customers.

Musical instruments and sound equipment are sold with a one-year warranty for replacement of parts and labour. The estimated warranty cost, based on past experience, is 2% of sales.

The premium is offered on the recorded and sheet music. Customers receive a coupon for each dollar spent on recorded music or sheet music. Customers may exchange 200 coupons and $20 for a CD player. MML pays $34 for each CD player and estimates that 60% of the coupons given to customers will be redeemed.

MML's total sales for 2002 were $7.2 million—$5.4 million from musical instruments and sound reproduction equipment and $1.8 million from recorded music and sheet music. Replacement parts and labour for warranty work totalled $164,000 during 2002. A total of 6,500 CD players used in the premium program were purchased during the year and there were 1.2 million coupons redeemed in 2002.

The accrual method is used by MML to account for the warranty and premium costs for financial reporting purposes. The balances in the accounts related to warranties and premiums on January 1, 2002 were as shown below.

Inventory of Premium CD Players	$ 39,950
Estimated Premium Claims Outstanding	44,800
Estimated Liability for Warranties	136,000

Instructions

MML is preparing its financial statements for the year ended December 31, 2002. Determine the amounts that will be shown on the 2002 financial statements for the following:

1. Warranty Expense
2. Estimated Liability for Warranties
3. Premium Expense

4. Inventory of Premium CD Players
5. Estimated Premium Claims Outstanding

(CMA adapted)

P14-13 You are the independent auditor engaged to audit ProVision Corporation's December 31, 2002 financial statements. ProVision manufactures household appliances. During the course of your audit, you discover the following contingent liabilities:

1. ProVision began production on a new dishwasher in June 2002, and by December 31, 2002, sold 100,000 to various retailers for $500 each. Each dishwasher is sold with a one-year warranty included. The company estimates that its warranty expense per dishwasher will amount to $25. At year end, the company had already paid out $1 million in warranty expenditures. ProVision's income statement shows warranty expenses of $1 million for 2002. ProVision accounts for warranty costs on the accrual basis.

2. ProVision's lawyer, Robert Dowski, QC, has informed you that ProVision has been cited for dumping toxic waste into the Salmon River. Clean-up costs and fines amount to $3,330,000. Although the case is still being contested, Dowski is certain that ProVision will most probably have to pay the fine and clean-up costs. No disclosure of this situation was found in the financial statements.

3. ProVision is the defendant in a patent infringement lawsuit by Heidi Golder over ProVision's use of a hydraulic compressor in several of its products. Dowski claims that, if the suit goes against ProVision, the loss may be as much as $5 million; however, Dowski advises that he has insufficient information at this point to determine what might happen as a result of this action. Again, no mention of this suit occurs in the financial statements.

As presented, these liabilities and contingencies are not reported in accordance with GAAP, which may create problems in issuing an unqualified audit report. You feel the need to note these problems in the work papers.

Instructions

Heading each page with the name of the company, balance sheet date, and a brief description of the problem, write a brief narrative for each of the above issues in the form of a memorandum to be incorporated in the audit work papers. Explain what led to the discovery of each problem, what the problem really is, and what you advise your client to do (along with any appropriate journal entries) in order to bring the financial statements in accordance with GAAP.

P14-14 Rodriguez Inc., a publishing company, is preparing its December 31, 2002 financial statements 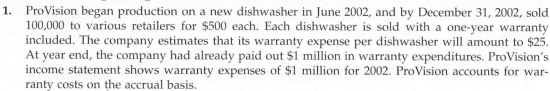 and must determine the proper accounting treatment for the following situations; it has retained your group to assist it in this task.

(a) Rodriguez sells subscriptions to several magazines for a one-year, two-year, or three-year period. Cash receipts from subscribers are credited to magazine subscriptions collected in advance, and this account had a balance of $2.3 million at December 31, 2002. Outstanding subscriptions at December 31, 2002, expire as follows:

During 2003 — $600,000
During 2004 — 500,000
During 2005 — 800,000

(b) On January 2, 2002, Rodriguez discontinued collision, fire, and theft coverage on its delivery vehicles and became self-insured for these risks. Actual losses of $50,000 during 2002 were charged to delivery expense. The 2001 premium for the discontinued coverage amounted to $80,000 and the controller wants to set up a reserve for self-insurance by a debit to delivery expense of $30,000 and a credit to the reserve for self-insurance of $30,000.

(c) A suit for breach of contract seeking damages of $1 million was filed by an author against Rodriguez on July 1, 2002. The company's legal counsel believes that an unfavourable outcome is likely. A reasonable estimate of the court's award to the plaintiff is in the range between $300,000 and $700,000. No amount within this range is a better estimate of potential damages than any other amount.

(d) During December 2002, a competitor company filed suit against Rodriguez for industrial espionage claiming $1.5 million in damages. In the opinion of management and company counsel, it is reasonably possible that damages will be awarded to the plaintiff. However, the amount of potential damages awarded to the plaintiff cannot be reasonably estimated.

Instructions

For each of the above situations, provide the journal entry that should be recorded as of December 31, 2002, or explain why an entry should not be recorded. For each situation, identify what disclosures are required, if any.

(AICPA adapted)

P14-15 Henrik Inc. has a contract with its president, Ms. Sarrat, to pay her a bonus during each of the years 2002, 2003, and 2004. Assume a corporate income tax rate of 40% during the three years. The profit before deductions for bonus and income taxes was $250,000 in 2002, $308,000 in 2003, and $350,000 in 2004. The president's bonus of 12% is deductible for tax purposes in each year and is to be calculated as follows:

(a) In 2002, the bonus is to be based on profit before deductions for bonus and income tax.
(b) In 2003, the bonus is to be based on profit after deduction of bonus but before deduction of income tax.
(c) In 2004, the bonus is to be based on profit before deduction of bonus but after deduction of income tax.

Instructions

Calculate the amounts of the bonus and the income tax for each of the three years.

P14-16 Vittorio Corporation must make calculations and adjusting entries for the following independent situations at December 31, 2002:

1. Its line of amplifiers carries a three-year warranty against defects. Based on past experience, the estimated warranty costs related to dollar sales are: first year after sale—2% of sales; second year after sale—3% of sales; and third year after sale—4% of sales. Sales and actual warranty expenditures for the first three years of business were:

	Sales	Warranty Expenditures
2000	$ 800,000	$ 6,500
2001	1,100,000	17,200
2002	1,200,000	62,000

Instructions

Calculate the amount that Vittorio Corporation should report as warranty expense on its 2002 income statement and as a warranty liability on its December 31, 2002 balance sheet. Assume that all sales are made evenly throughout each year with warranty expenditures also evenly spaced relative to the rates above.

2. With some of its products, Vittorio Corporation includes coupons that are redeemable in merchandise. The coupons have no expiration date and, in the company's experience, 40% of them are redeemed. The liability for unredeemed coupons at December 31, 2001 was $9,000. During 2002, coupons worth $25,000 were issued, and merchandise worth $8,000 was distributed in exchange for coupons redeemed.

Instructions

Calculate the amount of the liability that should appear on the December 31, 2002 balance sheet and the amount of promotional expense that should appear on the 2002 income statement.

(AICPA adapted)

P14-17 Haida Corp. has manufactured a broad range of quality products since 1982. The following information is available for the company's fiscal year ended February 28, 2003.

1. The company has $4 million of bonds payable outstanding at February 28, 2003 that were issued at par in 1995. The bonds carry an interest rate of 7% payable semi-annually each June 1 and December 1.
2. Haida has several notes payable outstanding with its primary banking institution at February 28, 2003 as follows. In each case, the annual interest is due on the anniversary date of the note each year (same as the due dates listed).

Due Date	Amount Due	Interest Rate
April 1, 2003	$150,000	8%
January 31, 2004	200,000	9%
March 15, 2004	500,000	7%
October 30, 2005	250,000	8%

3. Haida has a two-year warranty on selected products, with an estimated cost of 1% of sales being returned in the 12 months following the sale, and a cost of 1.5% of sales being returned in months 13 to 24 following sale. The warranty liability outstanding at February 28, 2002 was $5,700. Sales of warranteed products in the year ended February 28, 2003 were $154,000. Actual warranty costs incurred during the current fiscal year are as follows:

Warranty claims honoured on 2001–2002 sales	$4,900
Warranty claims honoured on 2002–2003 sales	1,100
	$6,000

4. Regular trade payables for supplies and purchases of goods and services on open account are $414,000 at February 28, 2003.
5. The following information relates to Haida's payroll for the month of February 2003. The company's required contribution for EI is 1.4 times that of the employee contribution and for CPP is 1.0 times that of the employee contribution.

Salaries and wages outstanding at February 28, 2003	$220,000
EI withheld from employees	9,500
CPP withheld from employees	16,900
Income taxes withheld from employees	48,700
Union dues withheld from employees	21,500

6. Haida regularly pays GST owing to the government on the 15th of the month following the charging of GST to customers and by suppliers. During February 2003, purchases attracted $28,000 of GST, while the GST charged on invoices to customers totalled $39,900. At Jan. 31, 2003 the balances in the GST Recoverable and GST Payable accounts were $34,000 and $60,000 respectively.
7. Other miscellaneous liabilities included $50,000 of dividends payable on March 15, 2003; $25,000 of bonuses payable to company executives (75% payable in September, 2003 and 25% payable the following March); $75,000 accrued audit fee covering the year ended February 28, 2003; and $330,000 of unearned revenue, one-third of which will be earned in July of each of the next three years.

Instructions

(a) Prepare the current liability section of the February 28, 2003 balance sheet of Haida Corp. Identify any amounts that require separate presentation or disclosure under GAAP.
(b) For each item included as a current liability, identify whether the item is a financial liability. Explain.
(c) If you have excluded any items from the presentation of current liabilities, explain why you have done so.

CONCEPTUAL CASES

C14-1 Presented below is the current liabilities section of Nizami Corporation.

	($000)	
	2002	2001
Current Liabilities		
Notes payable	$ 68,713	$ 7,700
Accounts payable	179,496	101,379
Compensation to employees	60,312	31,649
Accrued liabilities	158,198	77,621
Income taxes payable	10,486	26,491
Current maturities of long-term debt	16,592	6,649
Total current liabilities	$493,797	$251,489

Instructions
Answer the following questions.

(a) What are the essential characteristics that make an item a liability?
(b) How does one distinguish between a current liability and a long-term liability?
(c) How does one distinguish between a financial and a non-financial liability?
(d) What are accrued liabilities? Give three examples of accrued liabilities that Nizami might have.

(e) What is the theoretically correct way to value liabilities? How are current liabilities usually valued?

(f) Why are notes payable often reported first in the current liability section?

(g) What items may comprise Nizami's liability for "Compensation to employees"?

C14-2 D'Annunzio Corporation includes the following items in its liabilities at December 31, 2002:

1. Notes payable, $25 million, due June 30, 2003.
2. Deposits from customers on equipment ordered by them from D'Annunzio, $6,250,000.
3. Salaries payable, $3,750,000, due January 14, 2003.

Instructions

Indicate in what circumstances, if any, each of the three liabilities above would be excluded from current liabilities.

C14-3 The following items are listed as liabilities on the balance sheet of Eleutherios Corporation on December 31, 2002:

Accounts payable	$ 420,000
Notes payable	750,000
Bonds payable	2,250,000

The accounts payable represent obligations to suppliers that are due in January 2003. The notes payable mature on various dates during 2003. The bonds payable mature on July 1, 2003.

These liabilities must be reported on the balance sheet in accordance with generally accepted accounting principles governing the classification of liabilities as current and noncurrent.

Instructions

(a) What is the general rule for determining whether a liability is classified as current or noncurrent?

(b) Under what conditions would any of Eleutherios Corporation's liabilities be classified as noncurrent? Explain your answer.

(CMA adapted)

C14-4 Eshkol Corporation reports in the current liability section of its balance sheet at December 31, 2002 (its year end), short-term obligations of $15,000,000, which includes the current portion of 12% long-term debt in the amount of $11,000,000 that matures in March 2003. Management has stated its intention to refinance the 12% debt whereby no portion of it will mature during 2003. The financial statements are issued on March 25, 2003.

Instructions

(a) Is management's intent enough to support long-term classification of the obligation in this situation?

(b) Assume that Eshkol Corporation issues $13 million of 10-year debentures to the public in January 2003 and that management intends to use the proceeds to liquidate the $11 million debt maturing in March 2003. Furthermore, assume that the debt maturing in March 2003 is paid from these proceeds prior to the issuance of the financial statements. Will this have any impact on the balance sheet classification at December 31, 2002? Explain your answer.

(c) Assume that Eshkol Corporation issues common shares to the public in January and that management intends to entirely liquidate the $11 million debt maturing in March 2003 with the proceeds of this equity securities issue. In light of these events, should the $11 million debt maturing in March 2003 be included in current liabilities at December 31, 2002?

(d) Assume that Eshkol Corporation, on February 15, 2003, entered into a financing agreement with a commercial bank that permits Eshkol Corporation to borrow at any time through 2004 up to $15 million at the bank's prime rate of interest. Borrowings under the financing agreement mature three years after the loan date. The agreement is not cancellable except for violation of a provision with which compliance is objectively determinable. No violation of any provision exists at the financial statements' date of issuance. Assume further that the current portion of long-term debt does not mature until August 2003. In addition, management intends to refinance the $11 million obligation under the terms of the financial agreement with the bank, which is expected to be financially capable of honouring the agreement.

1. Given these facts, should the $11,000,000 be classified as current on the balance sheet at December 31, 2002?

2. Is disclosure of the refinancing method required?

C14-5 Meddev Inc. issued $10 million of short-term commercial paper during the year 2002 to finance plant construction. At December 31, 2002, the corporation's year end, Meddev intends to refinance the commercial paper by issuing long-term debt. However, because the corporation temporarily has excess cash, in January 2003 it liquidates $4 million of the commercial paper as the paper matures. In February 2003, Meddev completes an $18 million long-term debt offering. Later during the month of February, it issues its December 31, 2002 financial statements. The proceeds of the long-term debt offering are to be used to replenish $4 million in working capital, to pay $6 million of commercial paper as it matures in March 2003, and to pay $8 million of construction costs expected to be incurred later that year to complete the plant.

Instructions

(a) What is commercial paper?

(b) How should the $10 million of commercial paper be classified on the December 31, 2002, January 31, 2003, and February 28, 2003 balance sheets? Give support for your answer, including a consideration of the cash element.

(c) What would your answer be if, instead of a refinancing at the financial statements' issue date, a financing agreement existed at that date?

C14-6 Animaniacs Corporation is a toy manufacturer. During the year, the following situations arose:

1. A safety hazard related to one of its toy products was discovered. It is considered probable that liabilities have been incurred. Based on past experience, a reasonable estimate of the loss amount can be made.

2. One of its small warehouses is located on the river bank and could no longer be insured against flood losses. No flood losses have occurred after the date that the insurance became unavailable.

3. This year, Animaniacs began promoting a new toy by including a coupon, redeemable for a movie ticket, in each toy's carton. The movie ticket, which cost Animaniacs $3, is purchased in advance and then mailed to the customer when the coupon is received by Animaniacs. Animaniacs estimated, based on past experience, that 60% of the coupons would be redeemed. Forty-five percent of the coupons were actually redeemed this year, and the remaining 15% of the coupons are expected to be redeemed next year.

Instructions

(a) How should Animaniacs report the safety hazard? Why? Do not discuss future income tax implications.

(b) How should Animaniacs report the noninsurable flood risk? Why?

(c) How should Animaniacs account for the toy promotion campaign in this year?

C14-7 On February 1, 2003, one of the huge storage tanks of Magen Manufacturing Limited exploded. Windows in houses and other buildings within a one-kilometre radius of the explosion were severely damaged, and a number of people were injured. As of February 15, 2003 (when the December 31, 2002 financial statements were completed and sent for printing and public distribution), no suits had been filed or claims asserted against the company as a consequence of the explosion. The company fully anticipates that suits will be filed and claims asserted for injuries and damages. Because the casualty was uninsured and the company considered at fault, Magen Manufacturing will have to cover the damages from its own resources.

Instructions

Discuss fully the accounting treatment and disclosures that should be accorded the casualty and related contingent losses in the financial statements dated December 31, 2002.

C14-8 Presented below is a note disclosure for Frank Corporation:

Litigation and Environmental: The Company has been notified, or is a named or a potentially responsible party in a number of governmental (federal, provincial, and local) and private actions associated with environmental matters, such as those relating to hazardous wastes, including certain Canadian sites. These actions seek clean-up costs, penalties and/or damages for personal injury or to property or natural resources.

In 2002, the Company recorded a pre-tax charge of $56,229,000, included in the "Other Expense (Income)—Net" caption of the Company's Consolidated Statement of Income, as an additional provision for environmental matters. These expenditures are expected to take place over the next several years and are indicative of the company's commitment to improve and maintain the environment in which it operates. At December 31, 2002, environmental accruals amounted to $69,931,000, of which $61,535,000 are considered noncurrent and are included in the "Deferred Credits and Other Liabilities" caption of the Company's Consolidated Balance Sheets.

While it is impossible at this time to determine with certainty the ultimate outcome of environmental matters, it is management's opinion, based in part on the advice of independent counsel (after taking into account accruals and insurance coverage applicable to such actions) that when the costs are finally determined they will not have a material adverse effect on the financial position of the Company.

Instructions
Answer the following questions.
  (a) What conditions must exist before a loss contingency must be recorded in the accounts?
  (b) Suppose that Frank Corporation could not reasonably estimate the amount of the loss, although it could establish with a high degree of probability the minimum and maximum loss possible. How should this information be reported in the financial statements?
  (c) If the loss amount is uncertain, how would the loss contingency be reported in the financial statements?
  (d) If the likelihood of any loss resulting from the litigation is unknown, how would the loss contingency be reported in the financial statements?

C14-9 The following three independent sets of facts relate to (1) the possible accrual or (2) the possible disclosure of an expense or loss.

Situation I
After the date of a set of financial statements, but before they are issued, a company enters into a contract that will probably result in a significant loss to the company. The loss amount can be reasonably estimated.

Situation II
A company offers a one-year warranty for the product that it manufactures. A history of warranty claims has been compiled and the probable amount of claims related to sales for a given period can be determined.

Situation III
A company has adopted a policy of recording self-insurance for any possible losses resulting from injury to others by the company's vehicles. The premium for an insurance policy for the same risk from an independent insurance company would have an annual cost of $4,000. During the period covered by the financial statements, there were no accidents involving the company's vehicles that resulted in injury to others.

Instructions
Discuss the accrual or type of disclosure necessary (if any) and the reason(s) why such disclosure is appropriate for each of the three independent sets of facts above.

(AICPA adapted)

C14-10 The following two independent situations involve liabilities and contingent liabilities:

Part 1
Clarke Corporation sells two products, J-10 and H-44. Each carries a one-year warranty.
  1. Product J-10—Product warranty costs, based on past experience, will normally be 1% of sales.
  2. Product H-44—Product warranty costs cannot be reasonably estimated because this is a new product line. However, the chief engineer believes that product warranty costs are likely to be incurred.

Instructions
How should Clarke report the estimated product warranty costs for each of the two types of merchandise above? Discuss the rationale for your answer. Do not discuss future income tax implications, or disclosures that should be made in Clarke's financial statements or notes.

Part 2
Morrison Inc. is being sued for $4 million for an injury caused to a child as a result of alleged negligence while the child was visiting the Morrison Inc. plant in March 2002. The suit was filed in July 2002. Morrison's lawyer states that it is likely that Morrison will lose the suit and be found liable for a judgement costing anywhere from $400,000 to $2 million. However, the lawyer states that the most probable judgement is $800,000.

Instructions
How should Morrison report the suit in its 2002 financial statements? Discuss the rationale for your answer. Include in your answer disclosures, if any, that should be made in Morrison's financial statements or notes.

(AICPA adapted)

Using Your Judgement

FINANCIAL REPORTING PROBLEM:
CANADIAN TIRE CORPORATION, LIMITED (A)

Instructions

Refer to the financial statements and other documents of **Canadian Tire Corporation, Limited** presented in Appendix 5B and answer the following questions:

(a) What makes up Canadian Tire's current liabilities? Suggest at least five different types of liabilities that are likely included in "Accounts payable and other."

(b) What was Canadian Tire's working capital, acid-test ratio, and current ratio for the two latest years provided? How do these results compare with the measures for five years ago? Comment on the company's current liquidity as well as relative to five years ago. What role do the inventory and accounts receivable turnovers have in assessing a company's liquidity? Discuss relative to Canadian Tire.

(c) What is the current portion of long-term debt? Explain clearly what makes up this amount. If the company's long-term debt does not increase, how much would you expect to see on the 2001 balance sheet as the current portion of long-term debt? Explain clearly what would make up this amount.

(d) What types of commitments and contingencies has Canadian Tire reported in its financial statements? Identify which items are commitments and which are contingencies. What is management's reaction to the contingencies?

CANADIAN TIRE CORPORATION, LIMITED (B)

Canadian Tire Corporation, Limited's 2000 Annual Report states that "*Canadian Tire 'Money'* has the highest participation rate of any other loyalty program in Canada." It also indicates that "In September 2000, Financial Services [one of the company's business segments] re-launched 2.4 million Canadian Tire MasterCard and retail cards with a new and improved loyalty program…one more closely aligned with our famous *Canadian Tire 'Money.'* Customers using our branded credit cards now get even higher rewards with instant 'Money' on the Card for every purchase they make at Associate Stores and Petroleum gas bars."

Customers who pay cash or use their bank debit card for their purchases at Canadian Tire stores receive Canadian Tire "money" equal to 3% of their purchases that can be used as cash to pay for subsequent purchases. The program works in a similar way for the branded credit cards. In addition to "money" the following rewards are also available:

- for gas bar purchases—discounts of up to 70% off selected in-store products, 26 times per year
- through flyers and in-store—special discount coupons giving 2-10 times the base reward on gasoline
- at the pump—automatic "multiplier" discounts for swiped Canadian Tire credit card purchases

Instructions

(a) Does Canadian Tire disclose its accounting policies for its customer loyalty programs as part of its financial statements?

(b) The independent Canadian Tire stores purchase "CT Money" from Canadian Tire Corporation, Limited on a dollar-for-dollar basis. Prepare skeleton journal entries that are likely made by the independent stores as they purchase "CT Money" from head office, as they make cash and CT credit card sales, and as the "CT Cash" is redeemed for merchandise.

(c) Write a brief report on how you think the other rewards described above would be accounted for.

FINANCIAL STATEMENT ANALYSIS CASE

Northland Cranberries

Despite being a publicly traded company only since 1987, Northland Cranberries is one of the world's largest cranberry growers. Despite its short life as a publicly traded corporation, it has engaged in an aggressive growth strategy. As a consequence, the company has taken on significant amounts of both short-term and long-term debt. The following information is taken from recent company annual reports.

	Current Year	Prior Year
Current assets	$ 6,745,759	$ 5,598,054
Total assets	107,744,751	83,074,339
Current liabilities	10,168,685	4,484,687
Total liabilities	73,118,204	49,948,787
Shareholders' equity	34,626,547	33,125,552
Net sales	21,783,966	18,051,355
Cost of goods sold	13,057,275	8,751,220
Interest expense	3,654,006	2,393,792
Income tax expense	1,051,000	1,917,000
Net income	1,581,707	2,942,954

Instructions

(a) Evaluate the company's liquidity by calculating and analysing working capital and the current ratio.

(b) The company provided the following discussion of its liquidity in the Management Discussion and Analysis section of its annual report. Comment on whether you agree with management's statements, and what might be done to remedy the situation.

"The lower comparative current ratio in the current year was due to $3 million of short-term borrowing then outstanding which was incurred to fund the Yellow River Marsh acquisitions last year. As a result of the extreme seasonality of its business, the Company does not believe that its current ratio or its underlying stated working capital at the current fiscal year end is a meaningful indication of the Company's liquidity. As of March 31 of each fiscal year, the Company has historically carried no significant amounts of inventories and by such date all of the Company's accounts receivable from its crop sold for processing under the supply agreements have been paid in cash, with the resulting cash received from such payments used to reduce indebtedness. The Company utilizes its revolving bank credit facility, together with cash generated from operations, to fund its working capital requirements throughout its growing season."

COMPARATIVE ANALYSIS CASES

Case 1   Danier Leather Inc. versus Costco Wholesale Corporation

The current asset and current liability sections of the 2000 and 1999 balance sheets of Danier Leather Inc. and Costco Wholesale Corporation are reproduced below. Danier Leather is a vertically integrated designer, manufacturer, and retailer (primarily at shopping mall, street-front, and power centre locations) of fashion leather and suede clothing and accessories for men, women, and children. Costco sells a limited selection of items in a wide variety of product groups at close to cost prices in stripped down big box stores. It conducts an all-cash business for businesses and individuals, with the goal of selling very large volumes of merchandise and achieving a high inventory turnover.

DANIER LEATHER INC.
(thousands of dollars)

	June 24, 2000	June 26, 1999
Assets		
Current Assets		
Cash and short-term deposits	$ 775	$ 1,628
Accounts receivable	762	369
Inventories (Note 2)	35,124	22,659
Prepaid expenses	197	242
Current portion of future income tax asset (Note 9)	1,163	918
	$ 38,021	$ 25,816
Liabilities		
Current Liabilities		
Accounts payable and accrued liabilities	$ 13,208	$ 6,336
Income taxes payable	3,251	1,473
Current portion of long-term debt (Note 6)	270	247
	$ 16,729	$ 8,056
Other information		
Revenue	$143,011	$108,977
Cost of sales	69,865	56,313

COSTCO WHOLESALE CORPORATION
(thousands of dollars)

	Sept. 3, 2000	Aug. 29, 1999
Current Assets		
Cash and cash equivalents	$ 524,505	$ 440,586
Short-term investments	48,026	256,688
Receivables, net	174,375	168,648
Merchandise inventories, net	2,490,088	2,210,475
Other current assets	233,124	239,516
Total current assets	$ 3,470,118	$ 3,315,913
Current Liabilities		
Short-term borrowings	$ 9,500	$ —
Accounts payable	2,197,139	1,912,632
Accrued salaries and benefits	422,264	414,276
Accrued sales and other taxes	159,717	122,932
Deferred membership income	262,249	225,903
Other current liabilities	353,490	190,490
Total current liabilities	$ 3,404,359	$ 2,866,233
Other information		
Revenue, net sales	$31,620,723	$26,976,453
Cost of sales	28,322,170	24,170,199

Instructions

1. Calculate the current and quick ratios for Danier Leather and Costco at their 1999 and 2000 year ends. Which company appears to have better liquidity? Explain why this is so.

2. Draw a timeline setting out the cash to cash operating cycle of both companies. Include estimates of the number of days each stage in the operating cycle takes. The cycle should include the following stages: from receipt of goods from suppliers to payment to suppliers (accounts payable turnover in days—use COGS/average accounts payable); from receipt of goods from suppliers to sale of merchandise (inventory turnover in days); from sale of goods to collection of cash from customers (accounts receivable turnover). What do these measures tell you about the companies' cash flow?

3. Which company do you think is more liquid? Why?

Case 2 Loblaw Companies Limited versus Sobeys Inc.

Instructions

Go to the Digital Tool, and using **Loblaw Companies Limited** and **Sobeys Inc.** annual report information, answer the following questions:

(a) Calculate the current ratio and acid-test ratio for both companies at the end of the two most recent years reported. Comment generally on the size of the ratios calculated. Is there anything about the industry these companies operate in that might support ratios of this level?

(b) Calculate both companies' (a) current cash debt coverage ratio, (b) cash debt coverage ratio, (c) receivable turnover ratio, and (d) inventory turnover ratio for the most recent year reported. Comment on each company's overall liquidity.

(c) What specifically makes up the current portion of long-term debt at each company's most recently reported fiscal year end? Does either company have long-term debt maturing in the next five years that will require significant cash flows to meet? Explain.

RESEARCH CASE

This chapter makes reference to airlines and their obligations for providing frequent flyers with benefits such as free or reduced-fare travel. Railways also have similar types of programs.

Instructions

Gain access to the financial statements of at least five airlines or railway companies that have such reward programs, using both Canadian and U.S. carriers, if necessary. Prepare a report on the accounting policies and any other disclosures related to their reward programs.

INTERNATIONAL REPORTING CASE

An important difference between North American (Canadian and U.S.) and international accounting standards is the accounting for liabilities related to provisions. Due in part to differences in tax laws, accounting standards in some countries and the standards issued by the International Accounting Standards Committee (IASC) allow recognition of liabilities for items that would not meet the definition of a liability under Canadian or U.S. GAAP. The following note disclosure for liabilities related to provisions was provided by **Hoechst A.G.**, a leading German drug company, in its 1998 annual report. Hoechst prepared its statements in accordance with IASC standards.

Other provisions		
	Dec. 31, 1998	Dec. 31, 1997
	(in DM millions)	
Taxes	2,350	2,349
Restructuring	709	1,109
Damage and product liability claims	795	553
Environmental protection	869	814
Self-insurance loss provisions	631	870
Employee-related commitments	1,123	1,243
Other	2,274	2,538
Total	8,751	9,476
Current portion thereof	(5,013)	(5,679)

Hoechst reported the following additional items in its 1998 annual report. Data for **Merck & Co.**, a large North American drug company, are provided for comparison.

	Hoechst (DM millions)	Merck (US$ millions)
Current assets	20,528	10,229
Average current liabilities	5,346	5,819
Liquid assets	391	3,356
Receivables (net)	14,362	3,374
Cash flow from operations	4,628	5,328

Instructions

(a) Calculate the following ratios for Hoechst and Merck: current ratio, acid-test ratio, and the current cash debt coverage ratio. Compare the liquidity of these two drug companies based on these ratios.

(b) Identify items in Hoechst's provision disclosure that likely would not be recognized as liabilities under Canadian GAAP.

(c) Discuss how the items identified in (b) would affect the comparative analysis in part (a). What adjustments would you make in your analysis? Assume that 75% of the provisions for restructuring and self-insurance are current liabilities.

ETHICS CASES

Case 1

The Ray Corporation, owner of Bleacher Mall, charges Creighton Appliances a rental fee of $6,000 per month plus 5% of yearly profits over $500,000. Harry Creighton, the store owner, directs his accountant, Burt Wilson, to increase the estimate of bad debt expense and warranty costs in order to keep profits at $475,000.

Instructions
Answer the following questions:

(a) Should Wilson follow his boss's directive?

(b) Who is harmed if the estimates are increased?

(c) Is Creighton's directive ethical?

Case 2

Conduit Corporation has a bonus arrangement that grants the financial vice-president and other executives a $15,000 cash bonus if net income exceeds the previous year's by $1 million. Noting that the current financial statements report an increase of $950,000 in net income, Charles Dickinson, the VP Finance, meets with Don Street, the controller, to see what can be done.

Dickinson suggests to Street that the estimate of warranty expense could be reduced by $25,000 and still be a reasonable estimate as the current $500,000 warranty expense that has been recognized is known to be a fairly "soft" estimate. In addition, he suggests instead of recognizing the $250,000 "most likely" estimate of a contingent loss that has already been recorded in relation to outstanding litigation, that the loss be adjusted to $150,000, the lower number in the range of possible outcomes. Because of the uncertainty in estimating the extent of the expected loss, Conduit would disclose in a note the amount recognized and the total additional exposure to loss.

Instructions

(a) Should Street lower his estimate of the warranty liability?

(b) Should Street lower the amount of contingent loss that has been recognized?

(c) What ethical issue is at stake? Is anyone harmed?

(d) Is Dickinson acting ethically?

Case 3

In early 2002, Steel City Incorporated received notice from the provincial environment ministry that a site the company had been using to dispose of waste was considered toxic, and that Steel City would be held responsible for its clean-up under provincial legislation. The vice-president, engineering and the vice-president, finance discussed the situation over coffee. The engineer stated that it would take up to three years to determine the best way to remediate the site and that the cost would be considerable, perhaps as much as $500,000 to $2 million or more.

The engineering vice-president advocates recognizing at least the minimum estimate of $500,000 in the current year's financial statements, while the financial vice-president advocates just disclosing the situation and the inability to estimate the cost in a note to the financial statements.

Instructions

(a) What is the appropriate manner of reporting?

(b) Is there an ethical issue involved in this discussion?

CHAPTER 15

LONG-TERM FINANCIAL LIABILITIES

After studying this chapter, you should be able to:

1. Describe the formal procedures associated with issuing long-term debt.
2. Identify various types of bond issues.
3. Describe the accounting valuation for bonds at date of issuance.
4. Apply the methods of bond discount and premium amortization.
5. Describe the accounting procedures for extinguishment of debt.
6. Explain the accounting procedures for long-term notes payable.
7. Explain the reporting of off-balance-sheet financing arrangements.
8. Indicate how long-term debt is presented and analysed.

Preview of Chapter 15

Long-term debt and financial liabilities continue to play an important role in our capital markets because companies and governments need large amounts of capital to finance their growth. In many cases, the most effective way to obtain capital is through issuing long-term debt. This chapter's purpose is to explain the accounting issues related to long-term debt and financial liabilities. The content and organization of the chapter are as follows.

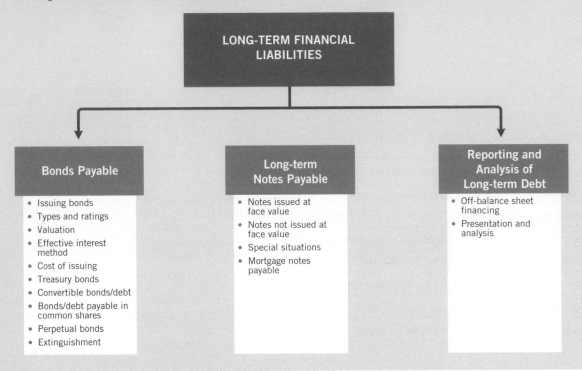

BONDS PAYABLE

OBJECTIVE 1

Describe the formal procedures associated with issuing long-term debt.

Long-term debt consists of probable future sacrifices of economic benefits arising from present obligations that are not payable within a year or the operating cycle of the business, whichever is longer. Bonds payable, long-term notes payable, mortgages payable, pension liabilities, and lease liabilities are examples of long-term debt or liabilities.[1]

Incurring long-term debt is often accompanied by considerable formality. For example, corporations' bylaws usually require approval by the board of directors and the shareholders before bonds can be issued or other long-term debt arrangements can be contracted.

Generally, long-term debt has various **covenants or restrictions** which protect both lenders and borrowers. The covenants and other terms of the agreement between the borrower and the lender are stated in a bond indenture or note agreement. Other terms often included in the indenture or agreement include the amounts authorized to be issued, interest rate, due date or dates, call provisions, property pledged as security, sinking fund requirements, working capital and dividend restrictions, and limitations concerning the assumption of additional debt. Whenever these stipulations are important to completely understand the financial position and the results of operations, they should be described in the body of the financial statements or the notes thereto.

---

[1] Long-term debt/liabilities meet the definition of financial liability as noted in *CICA Handbook*, Section 3860 in that they are a contractual obligation to deliver cash. The terms will be used interchangeably throughout the text.

Although covenants are meant to provide adequate protection to the long-term debt holder, many debtholders suffer considerable losses when additional debt is added to the capital structure, thus increasing solvency risk. Consider what happened to bondholders in the leveraged buyout[2] of **RJR Nabisco**. Solidly rated 9⅜% bonds due in 2016 plunged 20% in value when management announced the leveraged buyout. Such a loss in value occured because the additional debt added to the capital structure increased the likelihood of default. Although bondholders have covenants to protect them, the covenants are often written in a manner that can be interpreted (or misinterpreted) in a number of different ways. Covenants normally incorporate references to certain financial tests/ratios which must be met or the debt will become payable. Thus most companies must ensure that these tests are met or face the consequences (i.e., be prepared to repay the debt). Ratio analysis will be revisited at the end of the chapter.

Issuing Bonds

Bonds are the most common type of long-term debt reported on a company's balance sheet. The main purpose of bonds is to borrow for the long term when the amount of capital needed is too large for one lender to supply. By issuing bonds in $100, $1,000, or $10,000 denominations, a large amount of long-term indebtedness can be divided into many small investing units, thus enabling more than one lender to participate in the loan.

A bond arises from a contract known as a bond indenture and represents a promise to pay: (1) a sum of money at a designated maturity date, plus (2) periodic interest at a specified rate on the maturity amount (face value). Individual bonds are evidenced by a paper certificate and typically have a $1,000 face value. Bond interest payments usually are made semiannually, although the interest rate is generally expressed as an annual rate.

An entire bond issue may be sold to an investment banker who acts as a selling agent when marketing the bonds. In such arrangements, investment bankers may either underwrite the entire issue by guaranteeing a certain sum to the corporation, thus taking the risk of selling the bonds for whatever price they can get (firm underwriting), or they may sell the bond issue for a commission to be deducted from the proceeds of the sale (best efforts underwriting). Alternatively, the issuing company may choose to place (privately) a bond issue by selling the bonds directly to a large institution, financial or otherwise, without the aid of an underwriter **(private placement)**.

Types and Ratings of Bonds

The following are some of the more common types of bonds found in practice.

> **OBJECTIVE 2**
>
> Identify various types of bond issues.

Secured and Unsecured Bonds. Secured bonds are backed by a pledge of some sort of collateral. **Mortgage** bonds are secured by a claim on real estate. **Collateral trust** bonds are secured by shares and bonds of other corporations. Bonds not backed by collateral are **unsecured**. A debenture bond is unsecured. A "**junk bond**" is unsecured and also very risky, and therefore pays a high interest rate. These bonds are often used to finance leveraged buyouts.

Term, Serial Bonds, and Callable Bonds. Bond issues that mature on a single date are called term bonds, and issues that mature in instalments are called serial bonds. Serially maturing bonds are frequently used by schools, municipalities, and provincial or federal governments. Callable bonds give the issuer the right to call and retire the bonds prior to maturity.

Convertible, Commodity-Backed, and Deep Discount Bonds. If bonds are convertible into other securities of the corporation for a specified time after issuance, they are called convertible bonds. Accounting for bond conversions is discussed in Chapter 18. Two

---

[2] A leveraged buyout occurs when a group of individuals, often management, purchases the company. Debt is used to finance the acquisition and it is repaid from cash flows of the company.

new types of bonds have been developed in an attempt to attract capital in a tight money market: commodity-backed bonds and deep discounts.

Commodity-backed bonds (also called asset-linked bonds) are redeemable in measures of a commodity, such as barrels of oil, tons of coal, or ounces of rare metal. Deep discount bonds, also referred to as zero-interest debenture bonds, are sold at a discount that provides the buyer's total interest payoff at maturity.

Registered and Bearer (Coupon) Bonds. Bonds issued in the owner's name are registered bonds and require surrender of the certificate and issuance of a new certificate to complete a sale. A bearer or coupon bond, however, is not recorded in the owner's name and may be transferred from one owner to another by mere delivery.

Income and Revenue Bonds. Income bonds pay no interest unless the issuing company is profitable. Revenue bonds are so called because the interest on them is paid from a specified revenue source.

Three major investment publication companies, **DBRS, Moody's Investors Service,** and **Standard & Poor's Corporation,** issue quality ratings on every public bond issue. The bond quality designations and rating symbols of these firms are as follows in Illustration 15-1.

ILLUSTRATION 15-1
Bond Quality Ratings

	Symbols		
Quality	DBRS	Moody's	Standard & Poor's
Prime	AAA	Aaa	AAA
Excellent	AA	Aa	AA
Upper medium	A	A	A
Lower medium	BBB	Baa	BBB
Marginally speculative	BB	Ba	BB
Very speculative	B	B, Caa	B

A quality rating is assigned to each new public bond issue and is a current assessment of the company's ability to pay with respect to a specific borrowing. The rating may be changed up or down during the issue's outstanding life because the quality is constantly monitored. The debt rating is not a recommendation to purchase, sell, or hold a security, because it does not comment on market prices or suitability for particular investors.

Valuation of Bonds Payable—Discount and Premium

OBJECTIVE 3
....
Describe the accounting valuation for bonds at date of issuance.

IAS NOTE
IAS 39 agrees that all liabilities should be initially recorded at cost and not remeasured to FV unless they are derivatives or liabilities held for trading. The Joint Working Group of standard setters Draft Standard on Financial Instruments proposes fair value however.

The issuance and marketing of bonds to the public does not happen overnight. It usually takes weeks or even months. **Underwriters** must be arranged, **Securities Commission approval** must be obtained, **audits and issuance of a prospectus** may be required, and **certificates must be printed**. Frequently, the terms in a bond indenture are established well in advance of the bond sale. **Between the time the terms are set and the bonds are issued**, the market conditions and the issuing corporation's financial position may **change significantly**. Such changes affect the bonds' marketability and thus their selling price.

A bond issue's selling price is set by **supply and demand** of buyers and sellers, relative **risk**, **market conditions**, and the **state of the economy**. The investment community values a bond at the **present value of its future cash flows**, which consist of (1) interest and (2) principal. The rate used to calculate the present value of these cash flows is the interest rate that provides an **acceptable return on an investment** commensurate with the issuer's **risk** characteristics.

The interest rate written in the terms of the bond indenture (and ordinarily printed on the bond certificate) is known as the stated, coupon, or nominal rate. This rate, which is set by the bond issuer is expressed as a percentage of the bonds' face value, also called the par value, principal amount, or maturity value. If the rate employed by the investment community (buyers) differs from the stated rate, the bonds' present value calculated by the buyers (and the current purchase price) will differ from their face value. The difference between the face value and the bonds' present value is either a *discount* or *premium*.[3] If the bonds sell for less than face value, they are sold at a discount. If the bonds sell for more than face value, they are sold at a premium.

The interest rate actually earned by the bondholders is called the effective yield, or market rate. If bonds sell at a **discount**, the **effective yield is higher than the stated rate**. Conversely, if bonds sell at a **premium**, the **effective yield is lower than the stated rate**. While the bond is outstanding, its price is affected by several variables, most notably the market rate of interest. There is an **inverse relationship** between the market interest rate and the bond price.

To illustrate the calculation of the present value of a bond issue, consider ServiceMaster, which issues $100,000 in bonds, due in five years with 9% interest payable annually at year end. At the time of issue, the market rate for such bonds is 11%. The following time diagram depicts both the interest and the principal cash flows.

INTERNATIONAL INSIGHT

Valuation of long-term debt varies internationally. In Canada and the U.S., discount and premium are booked and amortized over the life of the debt. In some countries (e.g., Sweden, Japan, Belgium), it is permissible to write off the discount and premium immediately.

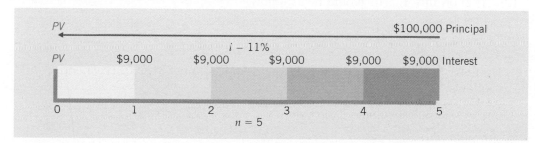

ILLUSTRATION 15-2

Present Value Calculation of Bond Selling at a Discount

The actual principal and interest **cash flows** are discounted at an 11% rate for five periods as follows.

Present value of the principal: $100,000 × .59345	$59,345
Present value of the interest payments: $9,000 × 3.69590	33,263
Present value (selling price) of the bonds	$92,608

By paying $92,608 at the date of issue, the investors will realize an **effective rate or yield** of 11% over the five-year term of the bonds. These bonds would sell at a discount of $7,392 ($100,000 − $92,608). The price at which the bonds sell is typically stated as a **percentage of their face or par value**. For example, the ServiceMaster bonds sold for 92.6 (92.6% of par). If ServiceMaster had received $102,000, we would say the bonds sold for 102 (102% of par).

When bonds sell **below face value**, it means that investors demand a rate of interest higher than the stated rate. The investors are not satisfied with the stated rate because they can earn a greater rate on alternative investments of equal risk. They cannot change the stated rate, so they refuse to pay face value for the bonds. Thus, **by changing the amount invested they alter the effective rate of interest**. The investors receive interest at the stated rate calculated on the face value, but they are earning at **an effective rate that is higher than the stated rate because they paid less than face value for the bonds**. (An illustration of a bond that sells at a premium is shown in Illustrations 15-6 and 15-7.)

---

[3] Until the 1950s, it was common for corporations to issue bonds with low, even-percent coupons (such as 4%) to demonstrate their financial solidarity. Frequently, the result was larger discounts. More recently, it has become acceptable to set the stated rate of interest on bonds in more precise terms, e.g. 10 7/8%. Companies usually attempt to align the stated rate as closely as possible with the market or effective rate at the time of issue. While discounts and premiums continue to occur, their absolute magnitude tends to be much smaller; many times it is immaterial. Professor Bill N. Schwartz (Virginia Commonwealth University) studied the 685 new debt offerings in the U.S. in 1985. Of these, none were issued at a premium. Approximately 95% were issued either with no discount or at a price above 98. Now, however, zero-interest (deep discount) bonds are more popular, which cause substantial discounts.

Bonds Issued at Par on Interest Date

When bonds are issued on an interest payment date at **par (face value)**, no interest has accrued and no premium or discount exists. The accounting entry is made simply for the cash proceeds and the bonds' face value. To illustrate, if 10-year term bonds with a par value of $800,000, dated January 1, 2001, and bearing interest at an annual rate of 10% payable semiannually on January 1 and July 1, are issued on January 1 at par, the entry on the books of the issuing corporation would be:

Cash	800,000	
Bonds Payable		800,000

The entry to record the first semiannual interest payment of $40,000 ($800,000 × 0.10 × 1/2) on July 1, 2001 would be as follows:

Bond Interest Expense	40,000	
Cash		40,000

The entry to record accrued interest expense at December 31, 2001 (year end) would be as follows:

Bond Interest Expense	40,000	
Bond Interest Payable		40,000

Bonds Issued at Discount or Premium on Interest Date

OBJECTIVE 4

Apply the methods of bond discount and premium amortization.

If the $800,000 of bonds illustrated above were issued on January 1, 2001 at 97 (meaning 97% of par), the issuance would be recorded as follows:

Cash ($800,000 × 0.97)	776,000	
Discount on Bonds Payable	24,000	
Bonds Payable		800,000

Because of its relation to interest, as previously discussed, **the discount is amortized and charged to interest expense over the period of time that the bonds are outstanding. Under the** straight-line method,[4] the amount amortized each year is constant. For example, using the bond discount above of $24,000, the amount amortized to interest expense each year for 10 years is $2,400 ($24,000 × 10 years) and, if amortization is recorded annually, it is recorded as follows:

Bond Interest Expense	2,400	
Discount on Bonds Payable		2,400

At the end of the first year, 2001, as a result of the amortization entry above, the unamortized balance in Discount on Bonds Payable is $21,600, ($24,000 − $2,400).

If the bonds were dated and sold on October 1, 2001, and if the corporation's fiscal year ended on December 31, the discount amortized during 2001 would be only 3/12 of 1/10 of $24,000, or $600. Three months of accrued interest must also be recorded on December 31.

Premium on Bonds Payable is accounted for in a manner similar to that for Discount on Bonds Payable. If the 10-year bonds of a par value of $800,000 are dated and sold on January 1, 2001, at 103, the following entry is made to record the issuance:

---

[4] Although the effective interest method is often used for amortization of discount or premium, the straight-line method has been used here. This latter method is popular due to its simplicity. Either method is acceptable since the *CICA Handbook,* Section 3050 allows for any systematic method when bonds are owned as an investment. Section 3860 (Financial Instruments) requires only that the effective interest rate be **disclosed**. The Joint Working Group draft standard on Financial Instruments proposes the use of fair value to measure all financial instruments and therefore, the whole issue of amortization method which results from the use of amortized cost may be a moot point in future.

Cash ($800,000 × 1.03)	824,000	
Premium on Bonds Payable		24,000
Bonds Payable		800,000

At the end of 2001 and for each year the bonds are outstanding, the entry to amortize the premium on a straight-line basis is:

Premium on Bonds Payable	2,400	
Bond Interest Expense		2,400

Bond interest expense is increased by amortizing a discount and decreased by amortizing a premium. Amortization of a discount or premium under the effective interest method is discussed later in this chapter.

Some bonds are **callable** by the issuer after a certain date at a stated price so that the issuing corporation may have the opportunity to reduce its bonded indebtedness or take advantage of lower interest rates. **Whether callable or not, any premium or discount must be amortized over the life to maturity date because early redemption (call of the bond) is uncertain.**

Bonds Issued Between Interest Dates

Bond interest payments are usually made semiannually on dates specified in the bond indenture. When bonds are issued on other than the interest payment dates, **bond buyers will pay the seller the interest accrued from the last interest payment date to the date of issue.** The purchasers of the bonds, in effect, pay the bond issuer in advance for that portion of the full six-months' interest payment to which they are not entitled, not having held the bonds during that period. **The purchasers will receive the full six-months' interest payment on the next semiannual interest payment date.**

To illustrate, if 10-year bonds of a par value of $800,000, dated January 1, 2001, and bearing interest at an annual rate of 10% payable semiannually on January 1 and July 1, are issued on March 1, 2001 at **par plus accrued interest**, the entry on the books of the issuing corporation is:

Cash	813,333	
Bonds Payable		800,000
Bond Interest Expense ($800,000 × 0.10 × 2/12)		13,333
(Interest Payable might be credited instead)		

The purchaser advances two months' interest, because on July 1, 2001, four months after the date of purchase, six months' interest will be received from the issuing company. The company makes the following entry on July 1, 2001:

Bond Interest Expense	40,000	
Cash		40,000

The expense account now contains a debit balance of $26,667, which represents the proper amount of interest expense, four months at 10% on $800,000.

The illustration above was simplified by having the January 1, 2001, bonds issued on March 1, 2001 at par. If, however, the 10% bonds were issued at 102, the entry on March 1 on the issuing corporation's books would be:

Cash [($800,000 × 1.02) + ($800,000 × 0.10 × 2/12)]	829,333	
Bonds Payable		800,000
Premium on Bonds Payable ($800,000 × 16,000)		16,000
Bond Interest Expense		13,333

The premium would be amortized **from the date of sale**, March 1, 2001, not from the date of the bonds, January 1, 2001.

Effective Interest Method

A common method for amortizing of a discount or premium is the effective interest method. Under the effective interest method:

1. Bond interest expense is calculated first by multiplying the carrying value[5] of the bonds at the beginning of the period by the effective interest rate.
2. The bond discount or premium amortization is then determined by comparing the bond interest expense with the interest to be paid.

The calculation of the amortization is depicted graphically as follows:

ILLUSTRATION 15-3
Bond Discount and Premium
Amortization Calculation

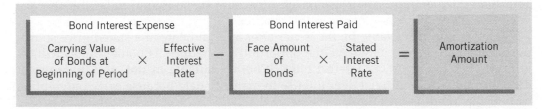

The effective interest method produces a periodic interest expense equal to a **constant percentage of the bonds' carrying value**. Since the percentage is the effective interest rate of interest incurred by the borrower at the time of issuance, the **effective interest method** results in a better **matching** of expenses with revenues than the **straight-line method**.

Both the effective interest and straight-line methods result in the **same total amount of interest expense over the term of the bonds**, and the annual amounts of interest expense are generally quite similar.

Bonds Issued at a Discount

To illustrate amortization of a discount, Evermaster Corporation issued $100,000 of 8% term bonds on January 1, 2001, due on January 1, 2006, with interest payable each July 1 and January 1. Because the investors required an effective interest rate of 10%, they paid $92,278 for the $100,000 of bonds, creating a $7,722 discount. The $7,722 discount is calculated as follows:[6]

ILLUSTRATION 15-4
Calculation of Discount on
Bonds Payable

Maturity of bonds payable		$100,000
Present value of $100,000 due in 5 years at 10%, interest payable semiannually $100,000 × 0.61391	$61,391	
Present value of $4,000 interest payable semiannually for 5 years at 10% annually $4,000 × 7.72173	30,887	
Proceeds from sale of bonds		92,278
Discount on bonds payable		$ 7,722

The five-year amortization schedule appears in Illustration 15-5.

---

[5] The book value, also called the carrying value, equals the face amount minus any unamortized discount or plus any unamortized premium.

[6] Because interest is paid semiannually, the interest rate used is 5% (10% × 6/12). The number of periods is 10 (5 years × 2)

SCHEDULE OF BOND DISCOUNT AMORTIZATION
Effective Interest Method—Semiannual Interest Payments
5-Year, 8% Bonds Sold to Yield 10%

ILLUSTRATION 15-5
Bond Discount Amortization
Schedule

Date	Cash Paid	Interest Expense	Discount Amortized	Carrying Amount of Bonds
1/1/01				$ 92,278
7/1/01	$ 4,000a	$ 4,614b	$ 614c	92,892d
1/1/02	4,000	4,645	645	93,537
7/1/02	4,000	4,677	677	94,214
1/1/03	4,000	4,711	711	94,925
7/1/03	4,000	4,746	746	95,671
1/1/04	4,000	4,783	783	96,454
7/1/04	4,000	4,823	823	97,277
1/1/05	4,000	4,864	864	98,141
7/1/05	4,000	4,907	907	99,048
1/1/06	4,000	4,952	952	100,000
	$40,000	$47,722	$7,722	

a$4,000 = $100,000 × .08 × 6/12   c$614 = $4,614 − $4,000
b$4,614 = $92,278 × .10 × 6/12   d$92,892 = $92,278 + $614

Present Value of Bonds:
[For Excel choose Insert/Function/Financial/PV]

Calculator	Inputs	Spreadsheet
N	10	Nper
I	5/.05	Rate
PV	?(I)	Type
PMT	−4,000	Pmt
FV	−100,000	FV
	92,278	Answer

The entry to record the issuance of Evermaster Corporation's bonds at a discount on January 1, 2001, is:

Cash	92,278	
Discount on Bonds Payable	7,722	
Bonds Payable		100,000

The journal entry to record the first interest payment on July 1, 2001 and amortization of the discount is:

Bond Interest Expense	4,614	
Discount on Bonds Payable		614
Cash		4,000

The journal entry to record the interest expense accrued at December 31, 2001 (year end) and amortization of the discount is:

Bond Interest Expense	4,645	
Bond Interest Payable		4,000
Discount on Bonds Payable		645

Bonds Issued at Premium

If the market had been such that the investors were willing to accept an effective interest rate of 6% on the bond issue described above, they would have paid $108,530 or a premium of $8,530, calculated as follows:

ILLUSTRATION 15-6
Calculation of Premium on
Bonds Payable

Maturity value of bonds payable	$100,000
Present value of $100,000 due in 5 years at 6%, interest payable semiannually $100,000 × 0.74409	$74,409
Present value of $4,000 interest payable semiannually for 5 years at 6% annually $4,000 × 8.53020	34,121
Proceeds from sale of bonds	108,530
Premium on bonds payable	$ 8,530

The five-year amortization schedule appears in Illustration 15-7.

ILLUSTRATION 15-7
Bond Premium Amortization
Schedule

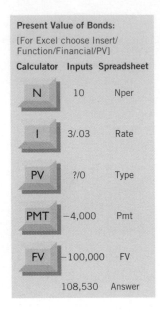

Present Value of Bonds:

[For Excel choose Insert/
Function/Financial/PV]

Calculator	Inputs	Spreadsheet
N	10	Nper
I	3/.03	Rate
PV	?/0	Type
PMT	−4,000	Pmt
FV	−100,000	FV
	108,530	Answer

SCHEDULE OF BOND PREMIUM AMORTIZATION
Effective Interest Method—Semiannual Interest Payments
5-Year, 8% Bonds Sold to Yield 6%

Date	Cash Paid	Interest Expense	Premium Amortized	Carrying Amount of Bonds
1/1/01				$108,530
7/1/01	$ 4,000[a]	$ 3,256[b]	$ 744[c]	107,786[d]
1/1/02	4,000	3,234	766	107,020
7/1/02	4,000	3,211	789	106,231
1/1/03	4,000	3,187	813	105,418
7/1/03	4,000	3,162	838	104,580
1/1/04	4,000	3,137	863	103,717
7/1/04	4,000	3,112	888	102,829
1/1/05	4,000	3,085	915	101,914
7/1/05	4,000	3,057	943	100,971
1/1/06	4,000	3,029	971	100,000
	$40,000	$31,470	$8,530	

[a]$4,000 = $100,000 × 0.08 × 6/12   [c]$744 = $4,000 − $3,256
[b]$3,256 = $108,530 × 0.06 × 6/12   [d]$107,786 = $108,530 − $744

The entry to record the issuance of Evermaster bonds at a premium on January 1, 2001, is:

Cash	108,530	
Premium on Bonds Payable		8,530
Bonds Payable		100,000

The journal entry to record the first interest payment on July 1, 2001 and amortization of the premium is:

Bond Interest Expense	3,256	
Premium on Bonds Payable	744	
Cash		4,000

The discount or premium should be amortized as an adjustment to interest expense over the life of the bond such that it results in a **constant interest rate** when applied to the carrying amount of debt outstanding at the beginning of any given period.

Accruing Interest

In our previous examples, the interest payment dates and the date the financial statements were issued were the same. For example, when Evermaster sold bonds at a premium, the two interest payment dates coincided with the financial reporting dates. However, what happens if Evermaster wishes to report financial statements at the end of February 2001? In this case, the premium is prorated by the appropriate number of months to arrive at the proper interest expense as follows.

ILLUSTRATION 15-8
Calculation of Interest Expense

Interest accrual ($4,000 × 2/6)	$1,333.33
Premium amortized ($744 × 2/6)	(248.00)
Interest expense (Jan. − Feb.)	$1,085.33

The journal entry to record this accrual is as follows:

Bond Interest Expense	1,085	
Premium on Bonds Payable	248	
Bond Interest Payable		1,333

If the company prepares financial statements six months later, the same procedure is followed; that is, the premium amortized would be as follows:

ILLUSTRATION 15-9
Calculation of Premium,
Amortization

Premium amortized (March–June) ($744 × $^4/_6$)	$496.00
Premium amortized (July–August) ($766 × $^2/_6$)	255.33
Premium amortized (March–August, 2001)	$751.33

The calculation is much simpler if the straight-line method is employed. For example, in the Evermaster situation, the total premium is $8,530, which is allocated evenly over the five-year period. Thus, premium amortization per month is $142 ($8,530/60 months).

Classification of Discount and Premium

Conceptually, Discount on Bonds Payable is **not an asset** because it does not provide any **future economic benefit**. The enterprise has the use of the borrowed funds, but for that use it must pay interest. A bond discount means that the company borrowed less than the bond's face or maturity value and therefore is faced with an actual (effective) interest rate higher than the stated (nominal) rate. Conceptually, discount on bonds payable is a **liability valuation account**; that is, it is a reduction of the face or maturity amount of the related liability. This account is referred to as a **contra** account.

Premium on bonds payable has no existence apart from the related debt. The lower interest cost results because the proceeds of borrowing exceed the debt's face or maturity amount. Conceptually, premium on bonds payable is a liability valuation account; that is, it is an addition to the face or maturity amount of the related liability. This account is referred to as an **adjunct** account. In practice, the unamortized portion of discount is frequently shown on the balance sheet as Deferred Charges under assets.[7] Correspondingly, unamortized premium is frequently shown as a deferred credit under liabilities. This is conceptually less appealing for the above noted reasons.

Costs of Issuing Bonds

The issuance of bonds involves engraving and printing costs, legal and accounting fees, commissions, promotion costs, and other similar charges. These items may be debited to a **deferred charge**[8] and amortized over the life of the debt, in a manner similar to that used for discount on bonds.[9]

IAS NOTE
IAS 23 establishes requirements concerning recognition and disclosure of borrowing costs.

To illustrate the accounting for costs of issuing bonds, assume that Microchip Corporation sold $20 million of 10-year debenture bonds for $20,795,000 on January 1, 2002 (also the date of the bonds). Costs of issuing the bonds were $245,000. The entries at January 1, 2002 and December 31, 2002 for issuing of the bonds and amortizing of the bond issue costs would be as follows:

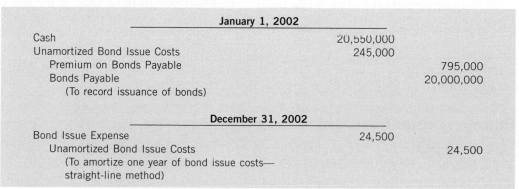

January 1, 2002		
Cash	20,550,000	
Unamortized Bond Issue Costs	245,000	
Premium on Bonds Payable		795,000
Bonds Payable		20,000,000
(To record issuance of bonds)		

December 31, 2002		
Bond Issue Expense	24,500	
Unamortized Bond Issue Costs		24,500
(To amortize one year of bond issue costs— straight-line method)		

---

[7] *CICA Handbook*, Section 3070, par. .02 makes reference to this treatment.

[8] Ibid.

[9] *APB Opinion No. 21* mirrors this approach; however, FASB, in Concepts Statement No. 3, takes the position that debt issue cost can be treated as either an expense (deferred cost) or a reduction of the related debt liability. This is the same issue as with the premium/discount. Debt issue cost is not considered an asset because it provides no future economic benefit. The cost of issuing bonds in effect reduces the proceeds of the bonds issued and increases the effective interest rate and thus may be accounted for the same as the unamortized discount. Thus, presentation is a matter of judgement.

While the bond issue costs could be amortized using the effective interest method, the straight-line method may also be used because it is easier and the results are not materially different.

Treasury Bonds

UNDERLYING CONCEPTS

The use of straight-line amortization versus the effective interest method due to ease is an application of the cost-benefit concept.

Bonds payable that have been reacquired by the issuing corporation or its agent or trustee and have not been cancelled are known as treasury bonds. They should be shown on the balance sheet as a deduction from the bonds payable issued to arrive at a net figure representing bonds payable outstanding.[10] When they are sold or cancelled, the Treasury Bonds account should be credited.

Convertible Debt

Convertible debt allows the holder the option of converting the debt to equity. This added feature allows the holder to participate in increases in value of the company's common shares while retaining the security of a "guaranteed" stream of interest and return of principal. Normally investors will pay more for these instruments and therefore there is some value attachable to the embedded option to acquire the shares. GAAP requires that the issue price be allocated to the two components or elements of the convertible debt (i.e., part to debt, part to equity).[11] This will be discussed in greater depth in Chapter 18.

Bonds Which May Be Settled in Common Shares

IAS NOTE

IAS 32 deals with presentations of financial liabilities including financial liabilities that may be settled by payment of the company's shares. The IAS notes that these instruments are classified as debt.

Sometimes, bonds or other financial instruments are issued such that the issuer has the option to repay/settle the principal in either cash or common shares. Since there is no obligation to deliver cash, the principal portion of the bond does not meet the definition of a liability and is recorded as equity.[12] The obligation to pay interest, however, does meet the definition of an obligation. This raises a measurement issue, i.e., how much is allocated to debt and how much is allocated to equity? The PV of the interest stream may be used to measure the debt portion and thus the remainder is allocated to equity.

Perpetual Bonds

One last point on calculating the present values of a bond issue relates to bonds that have unusually long terms i.e., 100 years or more. These are often referred to as century, millenium or **perpetual bonds**. Some have argued that due to the length of the term, these bonds are more like **equity**. A guick calculation of the present value of 100 year bonds would show that the PV of the principal is negligable while the PV of the interest comprises the bulk of the value attributed to the bond. Since the interest represents a contractual obligation to pay cash, the bond is a **financial liability**. Arguably, a very small portion (i.e., the PV of the principal) could be classified as equity).[13]

Extinguishment of Debt

OBJECTIVE 5

Describe the accounting procedures for extinguishment of debt.

How is the payment of debt—often referred to as extinguishment of debt—recorded? If the bonds (or any other form of debt security) are held to maturity, the answer is straightforward—**no gain or loss is calculated**. Any premium or discount and any issue costs will be fully amortized at the date the bonds mature. As a result, the carrying amount will be equal to the bond's maturity (face) value. As the maturity or face value is also equal to the bond's market value at that time, no gain or loss exists.

---

[10] *CICA Handbook*, Section 3210, par. .05

[11] *CICA Handbook*, Section 3860, par. .24

[12] *CICA Handbook*, EIC Abstract #71.

[13] *CICA Handbook*, Section 3860, A19.

In some cases, debt is extinguished before its maturity date.[14] The amount paid on extinguishment or redemption before maturity, including any call premium and expense of reacquisition, is called the **reacquisition price**. On any specified date, the bonds' **net carrying amount** is the amount payable at maturity, adjusted for unamortized premium or discount, and cost of issuance. Any excess of the net carrying amount over the reacquisition price is a **gain from extinguishment**, whereas the excess of the reacquisition price over the net carrying amount is a **loss from extinguishment**. At the time of reacquisition, the **unamortized premium or discount, and any costs of issue applicable to the bonds, must be amortized up to the reacquisition date**.

To illustrate, assume that on January 1, 1991, General Bell Corp. issued bonds with a par value of $800,000 at 97, due in 20 years. Bond issue costs totalling $16,000 were incurred. Eight years after the issue date, the entire issue is called at 101 and cancelled.[15] The loss on redemption (extinguishment) is calculated as follows (straight-line amortization is used for simplicity):

Reacquisition price ($800,000 × 1.01)		$808,000
Net carrying amount of bonds redeemed:		
Face value	$800,000	
Unamortized discount ($24,000* × 12/20)	(14,400)	
Unamortized issue costs ($16,000 × 12/20)		
(both amortized using straight-line basis)	(9,600)	776,000
Loss on redemption		$ 32,000
*[$800,000 × (1 − 0.97)]		

ILLUSTRATION 15-10
Calculation of Loss on Redemption of Bonds

The entry to record the reacquisition and cancellation of the bonds is:

Bonds Payable	800,000	
Loss on Redemption of Bonds	32,000	
Discount on Bonds Payable		14,400
Unamortized Bond Issue Costs		9,600
Cash		808,000

Note that it is often advantageous for the issuing corporation to acquire the entire outstanding bond issue and replace it with a new bond issue bearing a lower rate of interest. As an example, in June of 2001, **Aliant Telecom Inc.** redeemed its 10.25% First Mortgage Bonds, Series AC, which were originally due August 2006. The bonds were redeemed at 102% of the principal amount plus $0.28 per $1,000 principal amounts representing accrued interest. The premium of 2% was paid due to the fact that the stated interest rate on the bonds is greater than the current market rate and therefore, holders would need to be induced to part with the bonds.

---

[14] Some companies have attempted to extinguish debt through a process known as **in-substance defeasance**. In-substance defeasance is an arrangement whereby a company provides for future repayment of one or more of its long-term debt issues by placing purchased securities in an irrevocable trust, the principal and interest of which are pledged to pay off the principal and interest of its own debt securities as they mature. The company, however, is not legally released from being the primary obligor under the debt that is still outstanding. In some cases, debt holders are not even aware of the transaction and continue to look to the company for repayment. This practice is generally not considered an extinquishment of debt and therefore the debt should not be derecognized nor any gain or loss recognized (*CICA Handbook*, Section 3860, par. .41 (d)). **Legal defeasance** is different and is seen as extinguishment of debt since under legal defeasance, the creditors give up their claim on the company. The company therefore no longer has an obligation to the creditors. The creditors look to the cash flows from the purchased securities for repayment.

[15] The issuer of callable bonds is generally required to exercise the call on an interest date. Therefore, the amortization of any discount or premium will be up to date and there will be no accrued interest. However, early extinguishments through the purchase of bonds in the open market are more likely to be on a date other than the interest date. If the purchase is not made on an interest date, the discount or premium must be amortized and the interest payable must be accrued from the last interest date to the date of reacquisition.

The replacement of an existing issuance with a new one is called refunding. There are two alternative approaches to accounting for the amount of the difference:

1. Gain/loss—income statement. This supports the view that an **extinguishment** has occurred.
2. Defer and amortize existing deferred credit/debits relating to the old debt (e.g., premiums, discounts etc.) over the life of the new debt. This supports the view that the two bond issuances are **in substance** the same and no extinguishments has occurred; rather, a substitution of one issue for another or a renegotiation has occurred of the original debt. A new interest rate is calculated.

In Canada, professional judgement allows a choice. The choice rests on interpreting the **transaction's substance versus the form**. Does the transaction represent the **settlement** of the old debt and issuance of new substantially differing debt? Alternatively, is it merely a **renegotiation of the old debt**?[16] In the U.S., the first alternative is required. Appendix 15A looks at renegotiated debt in more detail dealing with the scenario where the debt is renegotiated under troubled debt restructuring conditions.

LONG-TERM NOTES PAYABLE

OBJECTIVE 6

Explain the accounting procedures for long-term notes payable.

The difference between **current** notes payable and long-term notes payable is the maturity date. As discussed in Chapter 14, short-term notes payable are expected to be paid within a year or the operating cycle—whichever is longer. Long-term notes are similar in **substance** to bonds in that both have fixed maturity dates and carry either a stated or implicit interest rate. However, notes do not trade as readily as bonds in the organized public securities markets. Unincorporated and small corporate enterprises issue notes as their long-term instruments, whereas larger corporations issue both long-term notes and bonds.

Accounting for notes and bonds is quite similar. **Like a bond, a note is valued at the present value of its future interest and principal cash flows, with any discount or premium being similarly amortized over the life of the note.** Calculating the present value of an interest-bearing note, the recording its issuance, and amortizing any discount or premium and accrual of interest are as shown for bonds.

As you might expect, accounting for long-term notes payable parallels accounting for long-term notes receivable as was presented in Chapter 7.

Notes Issued at Face Value

In Chapter 7, we discussed the recognition of a $10,000, three-year note issued at face value by Scandinavian Imports to Bigelow Corp. In this transaction, the stated rate and the effective rate were both 10%. The time diagram and present value calculation on page 315 of Chapter 7 (see Illustration 7-9) for Bigelow Corp. would be the same for the issuer of the note, Scandinavian Imports, in recognizing a note payable. Because the note's present value and its face value are the same, $10,000, no premium or discount is recognized. The issuance of the note is recorded by Scandinavian Imports as follows:

Cash	10,000	
Notes Payable		10,000

Scandinavian Imports would recognize the interest incurred each year as follows:

Interest Expense	1,000	
Cash		1,000

---

[16] *CICA Handbook, EIC Abstract #88* gives benchmark guidance that assists in this decision considering size of the new debt vis a vis the old, change in currency, change in creditor, change in terms.

Notes Not Issued at Face Value

Zero-Interest-Bearing Notes

If a zero-interest-bearing (noninterest-bearing) note[17] is issued solely for cash, its present value is measured by the cash received by the note's issuer. The implicit interest rate is the **rate that equates the cash received with the present value of the amounts received in the future**. The difference between the face amount and the present value (cash received) is recorded as **a discount and amortized to interest expense over the life of the note**.

To illustrate the entries and the amortization schedule, assume that your company is the one that issued the 3-year, $10,000, zero-interest-bearing note to Jeremiah Company as illustrated on page 316 of Chapter 7 (notes receivable). The implicit rate that equated the total cash to be paid ($10,000 at maturity) to the present value of the future cash flows ($7,721.80 cash proceeds at date of issuance) was 9%. (The present value of $1 for three periods at 9% is $0.77218.) The time diagram depicting the one cash flow is shown below:

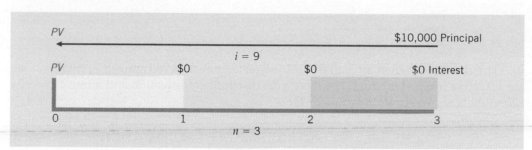

Your entry to record issuance of the note is as follows:

Cash	7,722	
Discount on Notes Payable	2,278	
Notes Payable		10,000

The discount is amortized and interest expense is recognized annually using the **effective interest method**. The three-year discount amortization and interest expense schedule is shown in Illustration 15-11. (This schedule is similar to the note receivable schedule of the company in Illustration 7-11.)

SCHEDULE OF NOTE DISCOUNT AMORTIZATION
Effective Interest Method
0% Note Discounted at 9%

	Cash Paid	Interest Expense	Discount Amortized	Carrying Amount of Bonds
Date of issue				$ 7,721.80
End of year 1	$–0–	$ 694.96[a]	$ 694.96[b]	8,416.76[c]
End of year 2	–0–	757.51	757.51	9,174.27
End of year 3	–0–	825.73[d]	825.73	10,000.00
	$–0–	$2,278.20	$2,278.20	

[a] $7,721.80 × .09 = $694.96   [c] $7,721.80 + $694.96 = $8,416.76
[b] $694.96 − 0 = $694.96   [d] adjustment to compensate for rounding

ILLUSTRATION 15-11
Schedule of Note Discount Amortization

Interest expense at the end of the first year using the effective interest method is recorded as follows:

Interest Expense ($7,722 × 9%)	695	
Discount on Notes Payable		695

---

[17] Although the term "note" is used throughout the discussion, the basic principles and methodology are equally applicable to other long-term debt instruments, such as bonds.

Effective Interest on Note:
[For Excel choose Insert/Function/Financial/Rate]

Calculator	Inputs	Spreadsheet
N	8	Nper
I	?/0	Type
PV	−327	PV
PMT	0	Pmt
FV	1,000	FV
	15	Answer

The total amount of the discount, $2,278 in this case, represents the interest expense to be incurred, and recognized on the note over the three years.

Interest-Bearing Notes

The zero-interest-bearing note above is an example of the extreme difference between the **stated rate** and the **effective rate**. In many cases, the difference between these rates is not so great. Take, for example, the illustration on page 317 Chapter 7 where Marie Co. issued a $10,000, three-year note bearing interest at 10% to Morgan Corp. for cash. The market rate of interest for a note of similar risk is 12%. The time diagram depicting the cash flows and the calculation of the note's present value are shown on page 317 (Illustration 7-12). In this case, because the **effective rate of interest** (12%) is **greater than** the **stated rate** (10%), the note's present value is less than the face value; that is, the note is exchanged at a **discount**. The issuance of the note is recorded by Marie Co. as follows:

Cash	9,520	
Discount on Notes Payable	480	
Notes Payable		10,000

The discount is then amortized and interest expense is recognized annually using the **effective interest method**. The three-year discount amortization and interest expense schedule is shown in Illustration 15-12.

ILLUSTRATION 15-12
Schedule of Note Discount Amortization

SCHEDULE OF NOTE DISCOUNT AMORTIZATION
Effective Interest Method
10% Note Discounted at 12%

	Cash Paid	Interest Expense	Discount Amortized	Carrying Amount of Bonds
Date of issue				$ 9,520
End of year 1	$1,000[a]	$1,142[b]	$142[c]	9,662[d]
End of year 2	1,000	1,159	159	9,821
End of year 3	1,000	1,179	179	10,000
	$3,000	$3,480	$480	

[a]$10,000 × 10% = $1,000   [c]$1,142 − $1,000 = $142
[b]$9,520 × 12% = $1,142   [d]$9,520 + $142 = $9,662

Payment of the annual interest and amortization of the discount for the first year are recorded by Marie Co. as follows (amounts per amortization schedule):

Interest Expense	1,142	
Discount on Bonds Payable		142
Cash		1,000

When the present value exceeds the face value, the note is exchanged at a premium. The premium on a note payable is recorded as a credit and amortized using the effective interest method over the life of the note as annual reductions in the amount of interest expense recognized.

Special Note Payable Situations

The note payable transactions just discussed are the common types of transactions encountered in practice. Three special situations are as follows:

1. notes issued for cash and other rights,
2. notes issued for property, goods, and services, and
3. imputed interest.

Notes Issued for Cash and Other Rights

Sometimes when a note is issued, additional rights or privileges are given to its recipient. For example, a corporation issues at face value a zero-interest-bearing note payable that is to be repaid over five years with no stated interest. In exchange, it agrees to sell merchandise to the lender at less than prevailing prices. In this circumstance, the difference between the present value of the payable and the amount of **cash received should be recorded by the note's issuer (borrower/supplier) simultaneously as a discount (debit) on the note and an unearned revenue (credit) on the future sales**. The discount should be amortized as a charge to interest expense over the life of the note. The unearned revenue, equal in amount to the discount, reflects a partial prepayment for sales transactions that will occur over the next five years. This unearned revenue should be recognized as revenue when sales are made to the lender over the next five years.

To illustrate, assume that the face or maturity value of a five-year, zero-interest-bearing note is $100,000, that it is issued at face value, and that the appropriate rate of interest is 10%. The note's conditions provide that the recipient (lender/customer) can purchase $500,000 of merchandise from its issuer (borrower/supplier) at something less than regular selling price over the next five years. To record the loan, the note's issuer records a discount of $37,908, the difference between the $100,000 face amount of the loan and its present value of $62,092 ($100,000 × PVF5,10% = $100,000 × .62092); as the supplier of the merchandise, the issuer also records a credit to unearned revenue of $37,908. The issuer's journal entry is:

Cash	100,000	
Discount on Notes Payable	37,908	
Notes Payable		100,000
Unearned Revenue		37,908

The Discount on Notes Payable is subsequently amortized to interest expense using the effective interest method. The Unearned Revenue is recognized as revenue from the sale of merchandise and is prorated on the same basis that each period's sales to the lender-customer bear to the total sales to that customer for the term of the note. In this situation the write-off of the discount and the recognition of the unearned revenue are at different rates.

Notes Issued for Property, Goods, and Services

The second type of situation involves the issuance of a note for some noncash consideration such as property, goods, or services. When the debt instrument is **exchanged** for property, goods, or services in a bargained transaction entered into at **arm's length**, the stated interest rate is presumed to be fair unless:

1. no interest rate is stated, or
2. the stated interest rate is unreasonable, or
3. the stated face amount of the debt instrument is materially different from the current cash sales price for the same or similar items or from current market value of the debt instrument.

In these circumstances, the present value of the debt instrument is measured by the **fair value of the property, goods, or services** or by an amount that reasonably approximates the note's market value.[18] **The interest element other than that evidenced by any stated rate of interest is the difference between the note's face amount and the property's fair value.**

---

[18] *CICA Handbook,* Section 3830, par. .05 on nonmonetary transactions notes that nonmonetary transactions should be valued at the FV of the assets given up unless the FV of the assets received is more clearly determinable. This transaction does not meet the definition of a nonmonetary transaction since the note itself is monetary, however, the issue of measurement is key and the basic principles for nonmonetary transactions may be looked to for guidance.

For example, assume that Scenic Development sold land having a cash sale price of $200,000 to Health Spa, Inc. in exchange for Health Spa's five-year, $293,860, zero-interest-bearing note. The $200,000 cash sale price represents the present value of the $293,860 note discounted at 8% for five years. If the transaction is recorded on the sale date at the face amount of the note, $293,860, by both parties, Health Spa's Land account and Scenic's sales would be overstated by $93,860, because the $93,860 represents the interest for five years at an effective rate of 8%. Interest revenue to Scenic and interest expense to Health Spa for the five-year period correspondingly would be understated by $93,860.

Because the difference between the cash sale price of $200,000 and the face amount of the note, $293,860, represents interest at an effective rate of 8%, the transaction is recorded at the exchange date as follows:

ILLUSTRATION 15-13
Entries for Noncash Note Transaction

Health Spa, Inc. Books			Scenic Development Company Books		
Land	200,000		Notes Receivable	293,860	
Discount on Notes Payable	93,860		Discount on Notes Rec.		93,860
Notes Payable		293,860	Sales		200,000

During the five-year life of the note, Health Spa amortizes annually a portion of the discount of $93,860 as a charge to interest expense. Scenic Development records interest revenue totalling $93,860 over the five-year period by also amortizing the discount. The effective interest method is required, although other approaches to amortization may be used if the results obtained are not materially different from those that result from the effective interest method.

Imputed Interest

In instances when the stated rate is known to be unreasonable, the effective rate must be imputed (as explained in Chapter 7). Whenever the **imputed interest rate** is different from the stated rate at the date the note is issued, a discount or premium must be recognized and amortized in subsequent periods. Using the illustration from Chapter 7 (page 320, Illustration 7-14), assume that on December 31, 2002, Wunderlich Company issued a promissory note to Brown Interiors Company for architectural services. The note has a face value of $550,000, a due date of December 31, 2007, and bears a stated interest rate of 2%, payable at the end of each year. The fair value of the architectural services is not readily determinable, nor is the note readily marketable. On the basis of the credit rating of Wunderlich Company, the absence of collateral, the prime interest rate at that date, and the prevailing interest on Wunderlich's other outstanding debt, an 8% interest rate is imputed as appropriate in this circumstance. The time diagram depicting both cash flows is shown as follows.

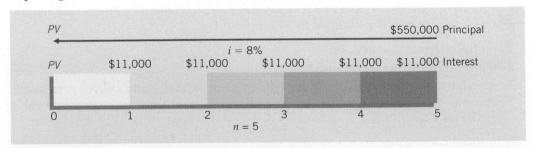

The note's present value of the note and the imputed fair value of the architectural services are determined as follows:

ILLUSTRATION 15-14
Calculation of Imputed Fair Value and Note Discount

Face value of the note		$550,000
Present value of $550,000 due in 5 years at 8% interest payable annually $550,000 × 0.68058	$374,319	
Present value of $11,000 interest payable annually for 5 years at 8%; $11,000 × 3.99271	43,920	
Present value of the note		418,239
Discount on notes payable		$131,761

The issuance of the note and receipt of the architectural services are recorded as follows:

December 31, 2002		
Building (or Construction in Process)	418,239	
Discount on Notes Payable	131,761	
Notes Payable		550,000

The five-year amortization schedule appears below.

ILLUSTRATION 15-15
Schedule of Discount Amortization Using Imputed Interest Rate

SCHEDULE OF NOTE DISCOUNT AMORTIZATION
Effective Interest Method
2% Note Discounted at 8% (Imputed)

Date	Cash Paid (2%)	Interest Expense (8%)	Discount Amortized	Carrying Amount of Note
12/31/02				$418,239
12/31/03	$11,000[a]	$ 33,459[b]	$ 22,459[c]	440,698[d]
12/31/04	11,000	35,256	24,256	464,954
12/31/05	11,000	37,196	26,196	491,150
12/31/06	11,000	39,292	28,292	519,442
12/31/07	11,000	41,558[e]	30,558	550,000
	$55,000	$186,761	$131,761	

[a] $550,000 × 2% = $11,000
[b] $418,239 × 8% = $33,459
[c] $33,459 − $11,000 = $22,459
[d] $418,239 + $22,459 = $440,698
[e] adjustment to compensate for rounding.

Payment of the first year's interest and amortization of the discount is recorded as follows:

December 31, 2003		
Interest Expense	33,459	
Discount on Notes Payable		22,459
Cash		11,000

Mortgage Notes Payable

The most common form of long-term notes payable is a mortgage note payable. A mortgage note payable is a promissory note secured by a document called a mortgage that pledges **title to property** as **security** for the loan. Mortgage notes payable are used more frequently by proprietorships and partnerships than by corporations, as corporations usually find that bond issues offer advantages in obtaining large loans. On the balance sheet, the liability should be reported using a title such as "Mortgage Notes Payable" or "Notes Payable—Secured," with a brief disclosure of the property pledged in notes to the financial statements.

The borrower usually receives cash in the face amount of the mortgage note. In that case, the note's face amount is the true liability and **no discount or premium is involved**. When "points" are assessed by the lender, however, the total amount paid by the borrower exceeds the face amount of the note.[19] Points raise the effective interest rate above the rate specified in the note. A point is 1% of the face of the note. For example, assume that a 20-year mortgage note in the amount of $100,000 with a stated interest rate of 10.75% is given by you as part of the financing of your new house. If the financial institution demands four points to close the financing, you will receive 4% less than $100,000— or $96,000—but you will be obligated to repay the entire $100,000 at the rate of $1,015 per month. Because you received only $96,000, and must repay 100,000, your effective interest rate is increased to approximately 11.3% on the money you actually borrowed.

---

[19] Points in mortgage financing are analogous to the discount on bonds (when originally issued).

Mortgages may be payable in full at maturity or in instalments over the life of the loan. If payable at maturity, the mortgage payable is shown as a long-term liability on the balance sheet until such time as the approaching maturity date warrants showing it as a current liability. If it is payable in instalments, the current instalments due are shown as current liabilities, with the remainder shown as a long-term liability.

Because of unusually high, unstable interest rates and a tight money supply, the traditional **fixed-rate mortgage** recently has been partially supplanted with new and unique mortgage arrangements. Most lenders offer **variable-rate mortgages** (also called floating-rate or adjustable rate mortgages) featuring interest rates tied to changes in the fluctuating market rate. Generally the variable-rate lenders adjust the interest rate at either 1- or 3-year intervals, pegging the adjustments to changes in the prime rate or the Government Treasury bond rate.

REPORTING AND ANALYSIS OF LONG-TERM DEBT

Reporting of long-term debt is one of the most controversial areas in financial reporting. Because long-term debt has a significant impact on the company cash flow, reporting requirements must be substantive and informative. One problem is that the definition of a liability and the recognition criteria as established in the *Handbook* (Section 1000) are sufficiently imprecise that arguments can still be made that certain obligations need not be reported as debt.

Off-Balance-Sheet Financing

OBJECTIVE 7

Explain the reporting of off-balance-sheet financing arrangements.

Off-balance-sheet financing is an attempt to borrow monies in such a way that the obligations are not recorded. It is an issue of extreme importance to accountants (as well as general management). As one writer noted, "The basic drives of humans are few: to get enough food, to find shelter, and to keep debt off the balance sheet."

Illustration

One form of off-balance-sheet financing occurs with project financing arrangements. These arrangements arise when (1) two or more entities form a new entity to construct an operating plant that will be used by both parties; (2) the new entity borrows funds to construct the project and repays the debt from the proceeds received from the project; (3) payment of the debt is guaranteed by the companies that formed the new entity. The advantage of such an arrangement is that **the companies that formed the new entity do not have to report the liability on their books**. To illustrate, assume that Dow Chemical and Exxon Mobil each put up $1 million and form a separate company to build a chemical plant to be used by both companies. The newly formed company borrows $48 million to construct the plant. The arrangement is illustrated below:

ILLUSTRATION 15-16
Project Financing Arrangement

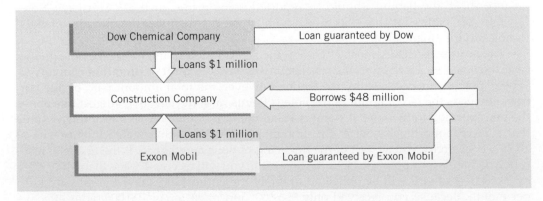

Accounting Question: Which company(ies) report(s) the liability? The answer is a matter of professional judgement. The loan guarantee represents a contractual obligation that the company may choose to disclose. Under contingency accounting, a liability would only be recorded if it were likely that the construction company would default on the loan.[20]

In some cases, project-financing arrangements become more formalized through the use of a variety of contracts. In a simple take-or-pay contract, a purchaser of goods signs an agreement with a seller to pay specified amounts periodically in return for an option to receive products. The purchaser must make specified minimum payments even if delivery of the contracted products is not taken. Often these take-or-pay contracts are associated with project financing arrangements. For example, in Illustration 15-16, Dow Chemical and Exxon Mobil might sign an agreement that they will purchase products from this new plant and that they will make certain minimum payments **even if they do not take delivery of the goods**. Does a liability exist? Again, professional judgement would be needed to analyse the issue. On the one hand, one could argue that a liability does exist since the companies will owe the certain minimum payments one way or another. On the other hand, one might argue that assuming the companies do indeed buy the product, the liability only arises when the product is received. The take-or-pay contract is a contingency

Throughput agreements are similar in concept to take-or-pay contracts, except that a service instead of a product is provided by the asset under construction. Assume that Dow and Exxon Mobil become involved in a project financing arrangement to build a pipeline to transport their various products. They sign an agreement that requires them to pay specified amounts in return for transporting of the product. In addition, these companies are required to make cash payments **even if they do not provide the minimum quantities to be transported**.

Inconsistent methods have been used in practice to account for and disclose the unconditional obligation in a take-or-pay or throughput contract involved in a project financing arrangement. In general, most companies have attempted to develop these types of contracts to get the debt off the balance sheet.

Rationale

Companies attempt to arrange off-balance-sheet financing for several reasons. First, many believe that **removing debt enhances the quality of the balance sheet** and permits credit to be obtained more readily and at less cost.

Second, loan covenants often impose a limitation on the amount of debt a company may have. As a result, off-balance-sheet financing is used because **these types of commitments might not be considered in calculating the debt limitation**.

Third, it is argued by some that the asset side of the balance sheet is severely understated. For example, companies that use LIFO costing for inventories and amortize assets on an accelerated basis will often have carrying amounts for inventories and property, plant, and equipment that are much lower than their current values. As an offset to these lower values, some managements believe that part of the debt does not have to be reported. In other words, **if assets were reported at current values**, less pressure would undoubtedly exist for off-balance-sheet financing arrangements. This is a weak argument.

Whether the arguments above have merit is debatable. The general idea "out of sight, out of mind" may not be true in accounting. Many users of financial statements indicate that they factor these off-balance-sheet financing arrangements into their calculations when assessing **debt to equity relationships**. Similarly, many loan covenants also attempt to take these complex arrangements into account. Nevertheless, many companies still believe that benefits will accrue if certain obligations are not reported on the balance sheet.

The profession's response to these off-balance-sheet financing arrangements has been **increased disclosure (note) requirements**. This response is consistent with an **"efficient markets"** philosophy: the important question is not whether the presentation

---

[20] *CICA Handbook*, Section 3290, par. .12. Alternately, if the business relationship is one that results in joint control over Construction Company, both **Dow** and **Exxon** would have to account for the combined company as a joint venture and proportionately consolidate the assets, liabilities, revenues and expenses of Construction Company. This would result in the debt being at least partially recorded on the books of **Dow** or **Exxon**.

is off-balance sheet or not, but whether the items are disclosed at all.[21] The authors believe that financial reporting would be enhanced if more obligations were recorded on the balance sheet instead of merely described in the notes to the financial statements.[22]

Presentation and Analysis of Long-Term Debt

Presentation of Long-term Debt

OBJECTIVE 8

Indicate how long-term debt is presented and analysed.

Companies that have large amounts and numerous issues of long-term debt frequently report only one amount in the balance sheet and support this with comments and schedules in the accompanying notes. Long-term debt that **matures within one year** should be reported as a **current liability**, unless retirement is to be accomplished with other than current assets. If the debt is to be refinanced, converted into shares, or is to be retired from a bond retirement fund, it should continue to be reported as noncurrent and accompanied with a note explaining the method to be used in its liquidation.[23]

Note disclosures generally indicate the nature of the liabilities, maturity dates, interest rates, call provisions, conversion privileges, restrictions imposed by the creditors, and assets designated or pledged as security. Any assets pledged as security for the debt should be shown in the assets section of the balance sheet. The fair value of the long-term debt should also be disclosed if it is practical to estimate fair value. Finally, disclosure is required of future payments for sinking fund requirements and maturity amounts of long-term debt during each of the next five years.[24] The purpose of these disclosures is to **aid financial statement users in evaluating the amounts and timing of future cash flows**. An example of the type of information provided is shown in the following illustration.

ILLUSTRATION 15-17

Presentation and Disclosure of Long-term Financial Liabilities—MDS Inc.

LIABILITIES AND SHAREHOLDERS' EQUITY

Current		
Bank Indebtedness (note 8)	$ 33.2	$ 40.3
Accounts payable and accrued liabilities	362.9	231.7
Deferred income	67.9	22.6
Income taxes payable	52.0	36.3
Future tax liabilities	—	0.6
Current portion of long-term debt (note 8)	10.0	13.8
	526.0	345.3
Long-term debt (note 8)	540.6	199.2
Deferred income and other (notes 7b and 9)	154.8	58.7
Future tax liabilities	6.1	10.8
Minority interest	19.4	15.9
	$1,246.9	$ 629.9
(Commitments and contingencies—note 17)		
Shareholders' equity		
Share capital (note 10)	782.3	339.4
Retained earnings	405.4	324.1
Cumulative translation adjustment (note 19)	(2.4)	5.8
	1,185.3	669.3
Total liabilities and shareholders' equity	$2,432.2	$1,299.2

---

[21] It is unlikely that the accounting profession will be able to stop all types of off-balance-sheet transactions. Developing new financial instruments and arrangements to sell and market to customers is profitable for investment banking firms and there is a demand for them.

[22] The recent draft standard issued by the Joint Working Group on Financial Instruments is a major step forward in this area. It requires full recognition of all Financial liabilities.

[23] *CICA Handbook*, Section 1510, par. .06.

[24] *CICA Handbook*, Sections 3210 and 3860.

8. Credit Facilities

	Maturity	2000	1999
Long-term credit facilities	2003	$467.5	$144.5
Other	2001 to 2015	83.1	68.5
Total long-term debt		550.6	213.0
Current portion		(10.0)	(13.8)
		$540.6	$199.2

The Company has established long-term credit facilities comprising revolving five-year term loan, a $150 million 364-day extendible revolving credit with a five-year term option, and a $350 million 364-day revolving credit which can be converted to a one-year term loan. Amounts borrowed under these facilities bear interest at floating rates to a maximum of prime and are unsecured. Long-term credit facilities at October 31, 2000 include US$125.7 million of borrowings denominated in US currency (1999—US$67.8).

Other available long-term credit facilities amounting to $62.6 million were assumed as a result of the purchase of Phoenix and are secured against certain assets of the acquired business.

Other long-term debt includes a government loan with a carrying value of $51.0 million (1999—39.3) discounted at an effective interest rate of 7.0%. A long-term investment has been pledged as security for the repayment of this debt (note 5). The remaining debt, amounting to $32.1 million (1999—$29.2), bears interest at annual variable rates tied to bank prime.

Principal repayments of long-term debt are required as follows:

2001	$10.0
2002	15.8
2003	471.7
2004	7.8
2005	7.2
Thereafter	38.1
	$550.6

The Company has operating lines of credit totalling $165.0 million. Specific charges on accounts receivable, inventories, and capital assets have been pledged as security for operating lines of credit totalling $65.0 million. As at October 31, 2000, the Company has borrowed $33.2 million (1999—$40.3) related to these credit facilities.

Under the terms of its operating and term credit agreements, the Company is able to make use of bankers' acceptances to borrow at effective interest rates which are, from time to time, lower than bank prime. As the majority of the long-term debt of the Company is represented by bankers' acceptances or similar short-term credit vehicles for pricing purposes, the carrying value of such debt at October 31, 2000 is a reasonable estimate of its fair value.

Note that if the company has any unconditional long-term obligations (such as project financing arrangements) that are not reported in the balance sheet, extensive note disclosure should be provided.

Analysis of Long-term Debt

Long-term creditors and shareholders are interested in a company's long-run **solvency**, particularly its ability to pay interest as it comes due and to repay the debt's face value at maturity. As mentioned at the beginning of the chapter, many debt agreements include covenants that stipulate that certain ratios be met or the debt will become immediately due. **Debt-to-total-asset** and **times interest earned** are two ratios that provide information about debt-paying ability and long-run solvency. Companies have a vested interest in assuring that debt levels are managed so as not to degrade the company's solvency position.

The debt-to-total-asset ratio measures the percentage of the total assets provided by creditors.[25] It is calculated as shown in the following formula by dividing total debt (both current and long-term liabilities) by total assets:

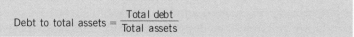

$$\text{Debt to total assets} = \frac{\text{Total debt}}{\text{Total assets}}$$

The **higher the percentage** of debt to total assets, the **greater the risk** that the company may be unable to meet its maturing obligations.

UNDERLYING CONCEPTS

Full disclosure would necessitate disclosure of off balance sheet liabilities.

ILLUSTRATION 15-18
Calculation of Debt-to-Total-Asset Ratio

---

[25] This ratio is sometimes calculated as the debt to equity ratio. Both relationships look at the amount of debt financing.

ILLUSTRATION 15-19
Calculation of Times Interest
Earned Ratio

The times interest earned ratio indicates the company's ability to meet interest payments as they come due. It is calculated by dividing income before interest expense and income taxes by interest expense:

$$\text{Times interest earned} = \frac{\text{Income before income taxes and interest expense}}{\text{Interest expense}}$$

To illustrate these ratios, we will use data from Talisman Energy Inc.'s 2000 Annual Report, which disclosed total liabilities of $5012.1 million, total assets of $8,675.7 million, interest of $135.9 million, income taxes of $679.6 million, and net income of $906.3 million. Talisman's debt-to-total-assets ratio is calculated as follows:

$$\text{Debt to total assets} = \$5012.1/8675.7 = 57.8\%$$

Talisman's times interest earned ratio is calculated as follows:

$$\text{Times interest earned} = 1721.80/135.9 = 12.7 \text{ times}$$

Even though Talisman has a relatively high debt-to-total asset percentage of 57.8%, its interest coverage of 12.7 times appears very safe. Note that when capitalized interest is included, the ratio drops to 10.4.

SUMMARY OF LEARNING OBJECTIVES

KEY TERMS

Asset-linked bond, 714

bearer bond, 714

bond indenture, 713

callable bond, 713

carrying value, 718

commodity-backed bond, 714

convertible bond, 713

coupon bond, 714

debenture bond, 713

debt-to-total-asset ratio, 733

deep discount bond, 714

discount, 715

effective interest method, 718

effective yield, 715

extinguishment of debt, 722

face, par, principal, or maturity value, 714

imputed interest rate, 728

income bond, 714

long-term debt, 712

long-term notes payable, 724

market rate, 715

mortgage notes payable, 729

1 Describe the formal procedures associated with issuing long-term debt. Incurring long-term debt is often a formal procedure. Corporation bylaws usually require approval by the board of directors and the shareholders before bonds can be issued or other long-term debt arrangements can be contracted. Generally, long-term debt has various covenants or restrictions. The covenants and other terms of the agreement between the borrower and the lender are stated in the bond indenture or note agreement.

2 Identify various types of bond issues. (1) *Secured and unsecured bonds.* (2) *Term, serial bonds, and callable bonds.* (3) *Convertible, commodity-backed, and deep discount bonds.* (4) *Registered and bearer (coupon) bonds.* (5) *Income and revenue bonds.* The variety in the types of bonds is a result of attempts to attract capital from different investors and risk takers and to satisfy the issuers' cash flow needs.

3 Describe the accounting valuation for bonds at date of issuance. The investment community values a bond at the present value of its future cash flows, which consist of interest and principal. The rate used to calculate the present value of these cash flows is the interest rate that provides an acceptable return on an investment commensurate with the issuer's risk characteristics. The interest rate written in the terms of the bond indenture and ordinarily appearing on the bond certificate is the stated, coupon, or nominal rate. This rate, which is set by the issuer of the bonds, is expressed as a percentage of the bonds' face value, also called the par value, principal amount, or maturity value. If the rate employed by the buyers differs from the stated rate, the bonds' present value calculated by the buyers will differ from the bonds' face value. The difference between the bonds' face value and the present value is either a discount or premium.

4 Apply the methods of bond discount and premium amortization. The discount (premium) is amortized and charged (credited) to interest expense over the period of time that the bonds are outstanding. Bond interest expense is increased by amortization of a discount and decreased by amortization of a premium. The profession's preferred procedure for amortization of a discount or premium is the effective interest method. Under the effective interest method, (1) bond interest expense is calculated by multiplying the bonds' carrying value at the beginning of the period by the effective interest rate, and (2) the bond discount or premium amortization is then determined by comparing the bond interest expense with the interest to be paid.

5 Describe the accounting procedures for extinguishment of debt. At the time of reacquisition, the unamortized premium or discount and any costs of issue applicable to the debt must be amortized up to the reacquisition date. The amount paid on extinguishment or redemption before maturity, including any call premium and expense of reacquisition, is the reacquisition price. On any specified date, the debt's net carrying amount of the debt is the amount payable at maturity, adjusted for unamortized premium or discount, and cost of issuance. Any excess of the net carrying amount over the reacquisition price is a gain from extinguishment, whereas the excess of the reacquisition price over the net carrying amount is a loss from extinguishment.

6 Explain the accounting procedures for long-term notes payable. Accounting procedures for notes and bonds are quite similar. Like a bond, a note is valued at the present value of its future interest and principal cash flows, with any discount or premium being similarly amortized over the life of the note. Whenever the note's face amount does not reasonably represent the present value of the consideration given or received in the exchange, the entire arrangement must be evaluated to properly record the exchange and the subsequent interest.

7 Explain the reporting of off-balance-sheet financing arrangements. Off-balance-sheet financing is an attempt to borrow funds in such a way that the obligations are not recorded. One type of off-balance-sheet financing occurs with project financing arrangements that may take the form of take-or-pay contracts or throughput agreements.

8 Indicate how long-term debt is presented and analysed. Companies that have large amounts and numerous issues of long-term debt frequently report only one amount in the balance sheet and support this with comments and schedules in the accompanying notes. Any assets pledged as security for the debt should be shown in the assets section of the balance sheet. Long-term debt that matures within one year should be reported as a current liability, unless retirement is to be accomplished with other than current assets. If the debt is to be refinanced, converted into shares, or is to be retired from a bond retirement fund, it should continue to be reported as noncurrent and accompanied with a note explaining the method to be used in its liquidation. Disclosure is required of future payments for sinking fund requirements and maturity amounts of long-term debt during each of the next five years. Debt-to-total-asset and times interest earned are two ratios that provide information about debt-paying ability and long-run solvency.

APPENDIX 15A

Accounting for Troubled Debt

During periods of depressed economic conditions or other financial hardship, some debtors have difficulty meeting their financial obligations. During the late 1980s bad energy loans and the rescheduling of loans between "less developed countries," such as Argentina, Brazil, and Mexico, and major banks created considerable uncertainty in the banking industry. Many companies had to restructure their debts or in some other way be bailed out of negative cash flow situations.

Accounting Issues

The major accounting issues related to troubled debt situations involve **recognition and measurement**. In other words, when should a loss be recognized and at what amount?

To illustrate the major issue related to recognition, assume that Citybank has a $10 million, five-year, 10% loan to Brazil with interest receivable annually. At the end of the third year, Citybank has determined that it probably will be able to collect the annual interest, but only $7 million of this loan at maturity. Should it wait until the loan becomes uncollectible, or should it record a loss immediately? The general recognition principle is: Losses should be recorded immediately if it is **likely** (probable) that the loss will occur and the loss is **measurable**.

Assuming that Citybank decides to record a loss, at what amount should the loss be recorded? Three alternatives are:

1. **Aggregate Cash Flows.** Some argue that a loss should not be recorded unless the aggregate cash flows from the loan are less than its carrying amount. In the Citybank example, the aggregate cash flows expected are $7 million of principal and $2 million of interest ($10 million × 10% × 2), for a total of $9 million. Thus, a loss of only $1 million ($10 million − 9 million) would be reported.

   Advocates of this position argue that Citybank will recover $9 million of the $10 million and, therefore, its loss is only $1 million. Others disagree, noting that this approach ignores present values. That is, the present value of the future cash flows is much less than $9 million and, therefore, the loss is much greater than $1 million.

2. **Present Value—Historical Effective Rate.** Those who argue for the use of present value, however, disagree about the interest rate to use to discount the expected future cash flows. The two rates discussed are the historical (original) effective rate and the **market rate** at the time the loan is recognized as troubled. Those who favour the historical effective rate believe that losses should reflect only a deterioration in credit quality. When the historical effective loan rate is used, the investment's value will change only if some of the legally contracted cash flows are reduced. A loss in this case is recognized because the expected future cash flows have changed. Interest rate changes caused by current economic events that affect the loan's fair value are ignored. This makes the loan valuation consistent with other loans recorded on the balance sheet.

2. **Present Value—Market Rate.** Others believe that expected future cash flows of a troubled loan should be discounted at market interest rates, which reflect current economic events and conditions that are commensurate with the risks involved. The historical effective interest rate reflects the risk characteristics of the loan at the time it was originated or acquired, but not at the time it is troubled. In short, proponents of the market rate believe that a fair value measure should be used.

This appendix addresses issues concerning the accounting by debtors and creditors for troubled debt. Two different types of situations result with troubled debt:

1. Impairments
2. Restructurings
   (a) Settlements
   (b) Modification of terms

In a troubled debt situation, the creditor usually first recognizes a loss on impairment. Subsequently, either the loan terms are modified or the loan is settled on terms unfavourable to the creditor. In unusual cases, the creditor forces the debtor into bankruptcy in order to ensure the highest possible collection on the loan. Illustration 15A-1 shows this continuum:

ILLUSTRATION 15A-1
Usual Progression in Troubled Debt Situations

| Loan Origination | Loan Impairment | Modification of Terms | Bankruptcy |

Impairments

A loan is considered impaired (an impairment) when the "lender no longer has reasonable assurance of timely collection of the full amount of the principal and interest."[26] Creditors should apply their normal review procedures[27] in making the judgement as to the probability of collection. Deterioration of creditworthiness might be determined by review of the following evidence:[28]

- financial statements evidencing liquidity problems
- independent credit reports
- current default on payment
- failure to meet debt covenants
- downgrading of credit status
- decline in market value of traded debt.

If a company is in receivership, bankruptcy or liquidation, this may confirm the deterioration. More general factors such as the state of the economy overall or in a specific industry sector should also be considered.

Once loans are determined to be **impaired**, they should be **measured** at **estimated realizable amounts,** which generally means **discounting the expected future cash flows at the effective interest rate** inherent in the loans (the historical rate).[29] This approach is fine as long as the estimated cash flows are **determinable,** both in amount and timing. If this is not the case, the loan is measured at either:

(a) the FV of any security underlying the loan or,
(b) observable market price for the loan.[30]

Illustration of Loss on Impairment

On December 31, 2001, Prospect Inc. issued a $500,000, five-year, zero-interest-bearing note to Community Bank. The note was issued to yield 10% annual interest. As a result, Prospect received and Community Bank paid $310,460 ($500,000 × 0.62092) on December 31, 2001.[31] A time diagram illustrates the factors involved:

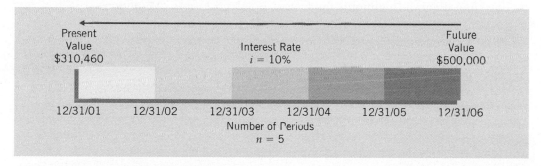

The entries to record this transaction on the books of Community Bank (creditor) and Prospect Inc. (debtor) are as follows:

---

[26] *CICA Handbook,* Section 3025, par. .03.

[27] According to *CICA Handbook* Section 3025, this would include assessing impairment on a loan-by-loan basis as well as a total portfolio basis where there is evidence of systemic risk. Impairment might also be evidenced by payment delays or shortfalls.

[28] *CICA Handbook,* Section 3025, par. .07.

[29] *CICA Handbook,* Section 3025, par. .15. The JWG Draft Standard *Financial Instruments and Similar items* espouses the use of market prices including market interest rates (par. .12).

[30] *CICA Handbook,* Section 3025, par. .14.

[31] PV of $500,000 due in 5 years at 10%, annual compounding = $500,000 × .62092.

ILLUSTRATION 15A-2
Creditor and Debtor Entries to
Record Note

	December 31, 2001			
Community Bank (Creditor)			**Prospect Inc. (Debtor)**	
Notes Receivable	500,000		Cash	310,460
Discount on Notes Receivable		189,540	Discount on Notes	
Cash		310,460	Payable	189,540
			Notes Payable	500,000

Assuming that Community Bank and Prospect Inc. use the effective interest method to amortize discounts, Illustration 15A-3 shows the amortization of the discount and the increase in the note's amount over its life.

ILLUSTRATION 15A-3
Schedule of Interest and
Discount Amortization
(Before Impairment)

COMMUNITY BANK

Date	Cash Received (0%)	Interest Revenue (10%)	Discount Amortized	Carrying Amount of Note
12/31/01				$310,460
12/31/02	$0	$ 31,046[a]	$31,046	341,506[b]
12/31/03	0	34,151	34,151	375,657
12/31/04	0	37,566	37,566	413,223
12/31/05	0	41,322	41,322	454,545
12/31/06	0	45,455	45,455	500,000
Total	$0	$189,540	$189,540	

[a]$31,046 = $310,460 \times 0.10$
[b]$341,506 = $310,460 + $31,046$

Unfortunately, during 2003, Prospect's business deteriorated due to increased competition and a faltering regional economy. After reviewing all available evidence at December 31, 2003, Community Bank determined that it was probable that Prospect would pay back only $300,000 of the principal at maturity. As a result, Community Bank decided that the loan was impaired, and that a loss should be recorded immediately.

To determine the loss, first calculate the **present value of the expected cash flows discounted at the historical effective rate of interest**. This amount is $225,396. The following time diagram highlights the factors involved in this calculation.

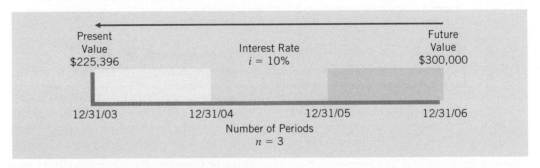

The loss due to impairment is equal to the difference between the present value of the expected future cash flows and the recorded carrying amount of the investment in the loan. The calculation of the loss is shown in Illustration 15A-4.

ILLUSTRATION 15A-4
Calculation of Loss Due
to Impairment

Carrying amount of investment (12/31/03)—Illustration 15A-3	$375,657
Less: Present value of $300,000 due in 3 years at 10% interest compounded annually	
$300,000 × .75132	225,396
Loss due to impairment	$150,261

The loss due to the impairment is $150,261, not $200,000 ($500,000 − $300,000), the loss is measured at a present value amount, not an undiscounted amount, at the time the loss is recorded.

The entry to record the loss is as follows:

December 31, 2003

Community Bank (Creditor)		Prospect Inc. (Debtor)
Bad Debt Expense	150,261	No entry
Allowance for Doubtful Accounts	150,261	

Community Bank (creditor) debits Bad Debt Expense for the expected loss. At the same time, it reduces the overall value of its loan receivable by crediting Allowance for Doubtful Accounts.[32] Interest would be recognized using the effective interest method at 10% (historical rate) based on the $225,396 carrying value. Prospect Inc. (debtor) makes no entry because it still legally owes $500,000.

COMMUNITY BANK

Date	Cash Received (0%)	Interest Revenue (10%)	Discount Amortized	Carrying Amount of None
12/31/03				$225,396
12/31/04	$-0-	$22,540a	$22,540	247,936b
12/31/05	-0-	24,794	24,794	272,730
12/31/06	-0-	27,273	27,273	300,000c
Total	$-0-	$74,607	$74,607	

a   22,539 = $225,396 × 0.10
b   247,936 = $225,396 + 22,540
c   rounding

The entry to record the interest in 2003 would be as follows:

Discount on Notes Receivable	22,540	
Interest Income		22,540

At December 31, 2006, the following entry would be booked.

Allowance for Doubtful Accounts	150,261	
Cash	300,000	
Discount on Note Receivable*	49,739	
Note Receivable		500,000

* $189,540 − 31,046 − 34,151 − 74,607 = 49,736 (rounding)

Troubled Debt Restructurings

A troubled debt restructuring occurs when a creditor "for economic or legal reasons related to the debtor's financial difficulties grants a concession to the debtor that it would not otherwise consider."[33]

A troubled debt restructuring involves one of two basic types of transactions:

1. **settlement** of debt at less than its carrying amount, and
2. **continuation** of debt with a **modification** of terms.

---

[32] In the event that the loan is written off, the loss is charged against the Allowance account. In subsequent periods, if the estimated expected cash flows are revised based on new information, the Allowance account and Bad Debt Expense account are adjusted (either increased or decreased depending whether the conditions improved or worsened) in the same fashion as the original impairment. The terms "loss" and "bad debt expense" are used interchangeably throughout the discussion. Losses related to receivables transactions should be charged to Bad Debt Expense or the related Allowance for Doubtful Accounts because these are the accounts used to recognize changes in values affecting receivables.

[33] "Accounting by Debtors and Creditors for Troubled Debt Restructuring," *FASB Statement No. 15* (Norwalk, Conn.: FASB, June, 1977), par. 1.

Settlement of Debt

A transfer of noncash assets (real estate, receivables, or other assets) or the issuance of the debtor's shares can be used to settle a debt obligation in a troubled debt restructuring. In these situations, **the noncash assets or equity interest given should be accounted for at their fair value**.[34] The debtor is required to determine the excess of the carrying amount of the payable over the fair value of the assets or equity transferred (gain). Likewise, the creditor is required to determine the excess of the receivable over the fair value of those same assets or equity interests transferred (loss). The debtor recognizes a gain equal to the amount of the excess, and the creditor normally would charge the excess (loss) to the income statement. In addition, the debtor recognizes a gain or loss on disposition of assets to the extent that the fair value of those assets differs from their carrying amount (book value).

To illustrate a transfer of assets, assume that Nova Scotia City Bank has loaned $20 million to Union Trust. Union Trust in turn has invested these monies in residential apartment buildings, but because of low occupancy rates it cannot meet its loan obligations. Nova Scotia City Bank agrees to accept from Union Trust real estate with a fair value of $16 million in full settlement of the $20 million loan obligation. The real estate has a recorded value of $21 milion on the books of Union Trust. Assume that no prior allowance for doubtful accounts has been set up. The entry to record this transaction on the books of Nova Scotia City Bank (creditor) is as follows:

Real Estate	16,000,000	
Loss on Loan Impairment	4,000,000	
Note Receivable		20,000,000

The real estate is recorded at fair value, and a charge is made to the Income Statement to reflect the loss.[35]

The entry to record this transaction on the books of Union Trust (debtor) is as follows:

Note Payable	20,000,000	
Loss on Loan Impairment	5,000,000	
Real Estate		21,000,000
Gain on Restructuring of Debt		4,000,000

Union Trust has a loss on the disposition of real estate in the amount of $5 million (the difference between the $21 million book value and the $16 million fair value). In addition, it has a gain on restructuring of debt of $4 million (the difference between the $20 million carrying amount of the note payable and the $16 million fair market value of the real estate).

To illustrate the granting of an equity interest, assume that Nova Scotia City Bank had agreed to accept from Union Trust 320,000 of Union's common shares that have a market value of $16 million, in full settlement of the $20 million loan obligation. The entry to record this transaction on the books of Nova Scotia City Bank (creditor) is as follows:

Investment	16,000,000	
Allowance for Doubtful Accounts	4,000,000	
Note Receivable		20,000,000

The shares received by Nova Scotia City Bank are recorded as an investment at the market value at the date of restructure.

The entry to record this transaction on the books of Union Trust(debtor) is as follows:

Note Payable	20,000,000	
Common Shares		16,000,000
Gain		4,000,000

---

[34] There is currently no specific GAAP in Canada that addresses troubled debt restructurings except for *CICA Handbook* Section 3025 on Impaired Loans which only looks at the creditor's side. Professional judgement would therefore be used, including looking to U.S. GAAP for guidance.

[35] *CICA Handbook*, Section 3025, par. .38.

Modification of Terms

In some cases, a debtor will have serious short-run cash flow problems that lead it to request one or a combination of the following modifications:

1. reduction of the stated interest rate,
2. extension of the maturity date of the debt's face amount,
3. reduction of the debt's face amount, and
4. reduction or deferral of any accrued interest.

In Canada, the accounting for the transaction revolves around whether the economic substance of the debt renegotiation is considered a **settlement** or a **modification/exchange regarding the old debt**.[36]

Where the economic substance is a **settlement**, the old liability is eliminated and a new liability is assumed. Consistent with the view, the new liability is measured at the PV of the revised future cash flows discounted at the currently prevailing market interest rate (consistent with the initial recording of a bond).[37] The gain is therefore the difference between the current PV of the revised cash flows and the old debt carrying value.

Where the economic substance is considered a **modification or exchange**, i.e., the old debt still exists, all existing deferred debits and credits (e.g., debt discounts and premiums, deferred financing costs and deferred foreign exchange) would continue to be deferred and amortized over the remaining debt. A new effective interest rate would be determined based on the carrying amount of the original debt and the revised cash flows.

Illustration

On December 31, 2001, Manitoba National Bank enters into a debt restructuring agreement with Resorts Development Corp., which is experiencing financial difficulties. The bank restructures a $10,500,000 loan receivable issued at par (interest paid to date) by:

1. reducing the principal obligation from $10.5 million to $9 million,
2. extending the maturity date from December 31, 2001, to December 31, 2005, and
3. reducing the interest rate from 12% to 8%. (Market rate currently 9%)

Is this a settlement or a modification? Has a substantial change in the debt occurred (normally evidenced by a change in creditor, currency or cash flows; i.e., by more than 10%). In this case, the creditor is the same and so is the currency and therefore the test to establish whether this is a settlement or not revolves around the cash flows. The PV of both cash flow streams are calculated using the **historic rate** as the discount rate (for consistency and comparability):

> Old debt: PV = $10,500,000 (since the debt is currently due)
> New debt: PV = $9,000,000 (0.6355) + $720,000 (3.0374) = $7,906,600

The new debt's PV differs by >10% of the old debt's PV and therefore the renegotiated debt would be considered a **settlement** and a **gain** would be recorded as evidenced by the following journal entry:

Note Payable—Old	10,500,000	
Note Payable—New		8,708,400
Gain		1,791,600

The new debt would be recorded at the PV of the new cash flows at the market interest rate ($9,000,000 × 0.7084) + ($720,000 × 3.24). This treatment is also supported by the fact that the old debt had expired.

---

[36] *CICA Handbook, EIC Abstract #88*. The Abstract uses a threefold test and if one of the three criteria is met, there is a substantial change and the debt is considered settled. The three criteria are (a) the PV of the new cash flows discounted at the old interest rate are >10% different from the PV of the old cash flows at the historic interest rate, or (b) there is a change in borrowing currency, or (c) there is a change in creditor.

[37] *Ibid.*, Section A.

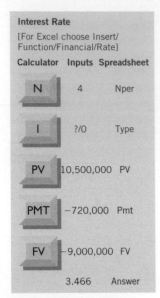

Interest Rate

[For Excel choose Insert/
Function/Financial/Rate]

Calculator	Inputs	Spreadsheet
N	4	Nper
I	?/0	Type
PV	10,500,000	PV
PMT	−720,000	Pmt
FV	−9,000,000	FV
	3.466	Answer

ILLUSTRATION 15A-7
Schedule Showing Reduction of
Carrying Amount of Note

Manitoba National Bank would record any loss on the same basis as an impaired loan (discussed earlier). That is the recorded amount of the loan receivable would be reduced to the amount of the net cash flows receivable (but under the modified terms) discounted at the effective interest rate inherent in the loan at the time the loan was recognized as impaired.

If the test was not met and the debt was considered **modified or exchanged**, the debt would remain on the books at $10.5 million and no gain or loss recognized. As a result, no entry would be made by Resorts Development Corp. (debtor) at the date of restructuring. **A new effective interest rate would be calculated** however, by the debtor in order to record interest expense in future periods. The new effective interest rate equates the present value of the future cash flows specified by the new terms with the pre-restructuring carrying amount of the debt. In this case, the new rate is calculated by relating the pre-restructure carrying amount ($10.5 million) to the total future cash flow ($11,880,000). The rate necessary to discount the total future cash flow ($11,880,000) to a present value equal to the remaining balance ($10.5 million) is 3.466%.[38]

On the basis of the effective rate of 3.466%, the schedule shown in Illustration 15A-7 is prepared.

RESORTS DEVELOPMENT CORP. (DEBTOR)

Date	Interest Paid (8%)	Interest Expense (3.46613%)	Reduction of Carrying Amount	Carrying Amount of Note
12/31/01				$10,500,000
12/31/02	$ 720,000[a]	$ 363,944[b]	$ 356,056[c]	10,143,944
12/31/03	720,000	351,602	368,398	9,775,546
12/31/04	720,000	338,833	381,167	9,394,379
12/31/05	720,000	325,621	394,379	9,000,000
	$2,880,000	$1,380,000	$1,500,000	

[a]$720,000 = $9,000,000 × 0.08
[b]$363,944 = $10,500,000 × 3.46613%
[c]$356,056 = $720,000 − $363,944

Thus, on December 31, 2002 (date of first interest payment after restructure), the debtor makes the following entry:

December 31, 2002		
Notes Payable	356,056	
Interest Expense	363,944	
Cash		720,000

A similar entry (except for different amounts for debits to Notes Payable and Interest Expense) is made each year until maturity. At maturity, the following entry is made:

December 31, 2005		
Notes Payable	9,000,000	
Cash		9,000,000

Manitoba National Bank would again account for the restructuring as an impaired loan.

---

[38] An accurate interest rate (i) can be found by using the formulas on the PV table to set up the following equation:

$$\$10,500,000 = 1/(1 + i)^4 \times \$9,000,000 + [1 - (1/(1 + i)^4]/i \times \$720,000$$

Summary of Learning Objective for Appendix 15A

●●●

9 Distinguish between and account for (1) a loss on loan impairment, (2) a troubled debt restructuring that results in the settlement of a debt, and (3) a troubled debt restructuring that results in a continuation of debt with modification of terms. An impairment loan loss is based on the difference between the present value of the future cash flows and the note's carrying amount. When the debt is considered settled, a gain or loss is recorded. When the new debt is considered to represent a continuation of the old debt (modification or exchange) no gain or loss is recognized and a new effective interest rate is established that equates the carrying value of the old debt with the cash flows under the new arrangements.

Note: All **asterisked** Questions, Brief Exercises, Exercises, Problems, and Conceptual Cases relate to material contained in the appendix to the chapter.

BRIEF EXERCISES

●●●

BE15-1   Branzei Corporation issues $300,000 of 9% bonds, due in 10 years, with interest payable semi-annually. At the time of issue, the market rate for such bonds is 10%. Calculate the bonds' issue price.

BE15-2   Gandhi Limited issued $200,000 of 10% bonds on January 1, 2002. The bonds are due January 1, 2007, with interest payable each July 1 and January 1. The bonds are issued at face value. Prepare the company's journal entries for (a) the January issuance, (b) the July 1 interest payment, and (c) the December 31 adjusting entry.

BE15-3   Assume the bonds in BE15-2 were issued at 98. Prepare the journal entries for (a) January 1, (b) July 1, and (c) December 31. Assume the company records straight-line amortization annually on December 31.

BE15-4   Assume the bonds in BE15-2 were issued at 103. Prepare the journal entries for (a) January 1, (b) July 1, and (c) December 31. Assume Godfrey Inc. records straight-line amortization annually on December 31.

BE15-5   Story Corporation issued $500,000 of 12% bonds on May 1, 2002. The bonds were dated January 1, 2002 and mature January 1, 2007, with interest payable July 1 and January 1. The bonds were issued at face value plus accrued interest. Prepare the company's journal entries for (a) the May 1 issuance, (b) the July 1 interest payment, and (c) the December 31 adjusting entry.

BE15-6   On January 1, 2002, Qix Corporation issued $400,000 of 7% bonds, due in 10 years. The bonds were issued for $372,816 and pay interest each July 1 and January 1. The company uses the effective interest method. Prepare the company's journal entries for (a) the January 1 issuance, (b) the July 1 interest payment, and (c) the December 31 adjusting entry. Assume an effective interest rate of 8%.

BE15-7   Assume the bonds in BE15-6 were issued for $429,757 and the effective interest rate is 6%. Prepare the company's journal entries for (a) the January 1 issuance, (b) the July 1 interest payment, and (c) the December 31 adjusting entry.

BE15-8   Izzy Corporation issued $400,000 of 7% bonds on November 1, 2002 for $429,757. The bonds were dated November 1, 2002 and mature in 10 years, with interest payable each May 1 and November 1. The company uses the effective interest method with an effective rate of 6%. Prepare the company's December 31, 2002, adjusting entry.

BE15-9   At December 31, 2002, Land Corporation has the following account balances:

Bonds payable, due January 1, 2010	$2,000,000
Discount on bonds payable	98,000
Bond interest payable	80,000

Show how the above accounts should be presented on the December 31, 2002 balance sheet, including the proper classifications.

BE15-10 Charyk Corporation issued 10-year bonds on January 1, 2002. Costs associated with the bond issuance were $180,000. Charyk uses the straight-line method to amortize bond issue costs. Prepare the December 31, 2002, entry to record 1999 bond issue cost amortization.

BE15-11 On January 1, 2002, Uzbalis Corporation retired $600,000 of bonds at 99. At the time of retirement, the unamortized premium was $15,000 and unamortized bond issue costs were $5,250. Prepare the corporation's journal entry to record the reacquisition of the bonds.

BE15-12 Capriati, Inc. issued a $100,000, four-year, 11% note at face value to Forest Bank on January 1, 2002 and received $100,000 cash. The note requires annual interest payments each December 31. Prepare Capriati's journal entries to record (a) the note issuance and (b) the December 31 interest payment.

BE15-13 Montana Corporation issued a four-year, $50,000, zero-interest-bearing note to Madden Corp. on January 1, 2002 and received cash of $31,776. The implicit interest rate is 12%. Prepare Montana's journal entries for (a) the January 1 issuance and (b) the December 31 recognition of interest.

BE15-14 Boitano Corporation issued a four-year, $50,000, 5% note to Johnson Corp. on January 1, 2002 and received a computer that normally sells for $39,369. The note requires annual interest payments each December 31. The market interest rate for a note of similar risk is 12%. Prepare Boitano's journal entries for (a) the January 1 issuance and (b) the December 31 interest.

BE15-15 Kwanza Corporation issued a four-year, $50,000, zero-interest-bearing note to Salmon Corp. on January 1, 2002 and received cash of $50,000. In addition, the company agreed to sell merchandise to Salmon at an amount less than regular selling price over the fours-year period. The market interest rate for similar notes is 12%. Prepare Kwanza's January 1 journal entry.

EXERCISES

E15-1 (Classification of Liabilities) Presented below are various account balances of Lang Inc.
1. Unamortized premium on bonds payable, of which $3,000 will be amortized during the next year.
2. Bank loans payable of a winery, due March 10, 2005 (The product requires ageing for five years before sale.)
3. Serial bonds payable, $1 million, of which $200,000 is due each July 31.
4. Amounts withheld from employees' wages for income taxes.
5. Notes payable due January 15, 2004.
6. Credit balances in customers' accounts arising from returns and allowances after collection in full of account.
7. Bonds payable of $2 million maturing June 30, 2003.
8. Overdraft of $1,000 in a bank account. (No other balances are carried at this bank.)
9. Deposits made by customers who have ordered goods.

Instructions
Indicate whether each of the items above should be classified on December 31, 2002 as a current liability, a long-term liability, or under some other classification. Consider each one independently from all others; that is, do not assume that all of them relate to one particular business. If the classification of some of the items is doubtful, explain why in each case.

E15-2 (Classification) The following items are found in the financial statements:
1. Discount on bonds payable
2. Interest expense (credit balance)
3. Unamortized bond issue costs
4. Gain on repurchase of debt
5. Mortgage payable (payable in equal amounts over next three years)
6. Debenture bonds payable (maturing in five years)
7. Notes payable (due in four years)
8. Premium on bonds payable
9. Treasury bonds
10. Income bonds payable (due in three years)

Instructions
Indicate how each of these items should be classified in the financial statements.

E15-3 **(Entries for Bond Transactions)**   Presented below are two independent situations:

1. On January 1, 2001, Simon Limited issued $200,000 of 9%, 10-year bonds at par. Interest is payable quarterly on April 1, July 1, October 1, and January 1.
2. On June 1, 2001, Graceland Inc. issued $100,000 of 12%, 10-year bonds dated January 1 at par plus accrued interest. Interest is payable semiannually on July 1 and January 1.

Instructions

For each of these two independent situations, prepare journal entries to record:
  (a) The issuance of the bonds.
  (b) The payment of interest on July 1.
  (c) The accrual of interest on December 31.

E15-4 **(Entries for Bond Transactions—Straight-line)**   Dion Inc. issued $600,000 of 10%, 20-year bonds on January 1, 2002 at 102. Interest is payable semiannually on July 1 and January 1. The company uses the straight-line method of amortization for bond premium or discount.

Instructions

Prepare the journal entries to record:
  (a) The issuance of the bonds.
  (b) The payment of interest and the related amortization on July 1, 2002.
  (c) The accrual of interest and the related amortization on December 31, 2002.

E15-5 **(Entries for Bond Transactions—Effective Interest)**   Assume the same information as in E15-4, except that the company uses the effective interest method of amortization for bond premium or discount. Assume an effective yield of 9.75%. (*NB:* With a market rate of 9.75%, the issue price would be slightly higher. Ignore this for simplicity sake).

Instructions

Prepare the journal entries to record the following. (Round to the nearest dollar.)
  (a) The issuance of the bonds.
  (b) The payment of interest and related amortization on July 1, 2002.
  (c) The accrual of interest and the related amortization on December 31, 2002.

E15-6 **(Amortization Schedules—Straight-line)**   Majerle Inc. sells 10% bonds having a maturity value of $2 million for $1,855,816. The bonds are dated January 1, 2001, and mature January 1, 2006. Interest is payable annually on January 1.

Instructions

Set up a schedule of interest expense and discount amortization under the straight-line method.

E15-7 **(Amortization Schedule—Effective Interest)**   Assume the same information as E15-6.

Instructions

Set up a schedule of interest expense and discount amortization under the effective interest method. (Hint: the effective interest rate must be calculated.)

E15-8 **(Determine Proper Amounts in Account Balances)**   Presented below are three independent situations:

1. Winans Corporation incurred the following costs in connection with the issuance of bonds: (1) printing and engraving costs, $12,000; (2) legal fees, $49,000, and (3) commissions paid to underwriter, $60,000. What amount should be reported as Unamortized Bond Issue Costs, and where should this amount be reported on the balance sheet?
2. Gershwin Inc. sold $2 million of 10%, 10-year bonds at 104 on January 1, 2001. The bonds were dated January 1, 2001, and pay interest on July 1 and January 1. If Gershwin uses the straight-line method to amortize bond premium or discount, determine the amount of interest expense to be reported on July 1, 2001 and December 31, 2001.
3. Kenoly Inc. issued $600,000 of 9%, 10-year bonds on June 30, 2001 for $562,500. This price provided a yield of 10% on the bonds. Interest is payable semiannually on December 31 and June 30. If Kenoly uses the effective interest method, determine the amount of interest expense to record if financial statements are issued on October 31, 2001.

E15-9 **(Entries and Questions for Bond Transactions)**   On June 30, 2002, Mischa Limited issued $4 million face value of 13%, 20-year bonds at $4,300,920, a yield of 12%. The company uses the effective interest method to amortize bond premium or discount. The bonds pay semiannual interest on June 30 and December 31.

Instructions

   (a) Prepare the journal entries to record the following transactions.

      1. The issuance of the bonds on June 30, 2002.

      2. The payment of interest and the amortization of the premium on December 31, 2002.

      3. The payment of interest and the amortization of the premium on June 30, 2003.

      4. The payment of interest and the amortization of the premium on December 31, 2003.

   (b) Show the proper balance sheet presentation for the liability for bonds payable on the December 31, 2003, balance sheet.

   (c) Answer the following questions.

      1. What amount of interest expense is reported for 2003?

      2. Will the bond interest expense reported in 2003 be the same as, greater than, or less than the amount that would be reported if the straight-line method of amortization were used?

      3. Determine the total cost of borrowing over the life of the bond.

      4. Will the total bond interest expense for the life of the bond be greater than, the same as, or less than the total interest expense if the straight-line method of amortization were used?

E15-10 **(Entries for Bond Transactions)** On January 1, 2001, Aumont Inc. sold 12% bonds having a maturity value of $500,000 for $537,907.37, which provides the bondholders with a 10% yield. The bonds are dated January 1, 2001, and mature January 1, 2006, with interest payable December 31 of each year. The company allocates interest and unamortized discount or premium on the effective interest basis.

Instructions

   (a) Prepare the journal entry at the date of issue.

   (b) Prepare a schedule of interest expense and bond amortization for 2001–2003.

   (c) Prepare the journal entry to record the interest payment and the amortization for 2001.

   (d) Prepare the journal entry to record the interest payment and the amortization for 2003.

E15-11 **(Information Related to Various Bond Issues)** Austin Inc. has issued three types of debt on January 1, 2001, the start of the company's fiscal year.

   1. $10 million, 10-year, 15% unsecured bonds, interest payable quarterly. Bonds were priced to yield 12%.

   2. $25 million par of 10-year, zero-coupon bonds at a price to yield 12% per year.

   3. $20 million, 10-year, 10% mortgage bonds, interest payable annually to yield 12%.

Instructions

Prepare a schedule that identifies the following items for each bond: (1) maturity value, (2) number of interest periods over life of bond, (3) stated rate per each interest period, (4) effective interest rate per each interest period, (5) payment amount per period, and (6) present value of bonds at date of issue.

E15-12 **(Entry for Retirement of Bond; Bond Issue Costs)** On January 2, 1996, Banno Corporation issued $1.5 million of 10% bonds at 97 due December 31, 2005. Legal and other costs of $24,000 were incurred in connection with the issue. Interest on the bonds is payable annually each December 31. The $24,000 issue costs are being deferred and amortized on a straight-line basis over the 10-year term of the bonds. The discount on the bonds is also being amortized on a straight-line basis over the 10 years. (Straight-line is not materially different in effect from the preferable "interest method.")

    The bonds are callable at 101 (i.e., at 101% of face amount), and on January 2, 2001, the company called $900,000 face amount of the bonds and retired them.

Instructions

Ignoring income taxes, calculate the amount of loss, if any, to be recognized by the company as a result of retiring the $900,000 of bonds in 2001 and prepare the journal entry to record the retirement.

(AICPA adapted)

E15-13 **(Entries for Retirement and Issuance of Bonds)** Hagman, Inc. had outstanding $6 million of 11% bonds (interest payable July 31 and January 31) due in 10 years. On July 1, it issued $9 million of 10%, 15-year bonds (interest payable July 1 and January 1) at 98. A portion of the proceeds was used to call the 11% bonds at 102 on August 1. Unamortized bond discount and issue cost applicable to the 11% bonds were $120,000 and $30,000, respectively.

Instructions

Prepare the journal entries necessary to record issue of the new bonds and the refunding of the bonds.

E15-14 (Entries for Retirement and Issuance of Bonds)   On June 30, 1993, Autry Limited issued 12% bonds with a par value of $800,000 due in 20 years. They were issued at 98 and were callable at 104 at any date after June 30, 2001. Because of lower interest rates and a significant change in the company's credit rating, it was decided to call the entire issue on June 30, 2002, and to issue new bonds. New 10% bonds were sold in the amount of $1 million at 102; they mature in 20 years. The company uses straight-line amortization. Interest payment dates are December 31 and June 30.

Instructions
(a) Prepare journal entries to record the retirement of the old issue and the sale of the new issue on June 30, 2002.
(b) Prepare the entry required on December 31, 2002 to record the payment of the first six months' interest and the amortization of premium on the bonds.

E15-15 (Entries for Retirement and Issuance of Bonds)   George Inc. had bonds outstanding with a maturity value of $300,000. On April 30, 2002, when these bonds had an unamortized discount of $10,000, they were called in at 104. To pay for these bonds, the company had issued other bonds a month earlier bearing a lower interest rate. The newly issued bonds had a life of 10 years. The new bonds were issued at 103 (face value $300,000). Issue costs related to the new bonds were $3,000.

Instructions
Ignoring interest, calculate the gain or loss and record this refunding transaction.

(AICPA adapted)

E15-16 (Entries for Non-Interest-Bearing Debt)   On January 1, 2002, Greene Inc. makes the following acquisitions:
1. Purchases land having a fair market value of $200,000 by issuing a five-year, non-interest-bearing promissory note in the face amount of $337,012.
2. Purchases equipment by issuing a 6%, eight-year promissory note having a maturity value of $250,000 (interest payable annually).

The company has to pay 11% interest for funds from its bank.

Instructions
(a) Record the two journal entries that should be recorded by the company for the two purchases on January 1, 2002.
(b) Record the interest at the end of the first year on both notes using the effective interest method.

E15-17 (Imputation of Interest)   Presented below are two independent situations.
1. On January 1, 2002, Wright Inc. purchased land that had an assessed value of $350,000 at the time of purchase. A $550,000, non-interest-bearing note due January 1, 2005 was given in exchange. There was no established exchange price for the land, nor a ready market value for the note. The interest rate charged on a note of this type is 12%. Determine at what amount the land should be recorded at January 1, 2002 and the interest expense to be reported in 2002 related to this transaction.
2. On January 1, 2002, Field Furniture Ltd. borrowed $5, million (face value) from Sinise Inc., a major customer, through a non-interest-bearing note due in four years. Because the note was non-interest-bearing, Field Furniture agreed to sell furniture to this customer at lower than market price. A 10% rate of interest is normally charged on this type of loan. Prepare the journal entry to record this transaction and determine the amount of interest expense to report for 2002.

E15-18 (Imputation of Interest with Right)   On January 1, 2000, Avery Inc. borrowed and received $400,000 from a major customer evidenced by a non-interest-bearing note due in three years. As consideration for the non-interest-bearing feature, Avery agrees to supply the customer's inventory needs for the loan period at lower than the market price. The appropriate rate at which to impute interest is 12%.

Instructions
(a) Prepare the journal entry to record the initial transaction on January 1, 2000. (Round all calculations to the nearest dollar.)
(b) Prepare the journal entry to record any adjusting entries needed at December 31, 2000. Assume that the sales of the company's product to this customer occur evenly over the 3-year period.

E15-19 (Long-Term Debt Disclosure)   At December 31, 2002, Reddy Inc. has outstanding three long-term debt issues. The first is a $2 million note payable, which matures June 30, 2005. The second is a $6 million bond issue, which matures September 30, 2006. The third is a $17,500,000 sinking fund debenture with annual sinking fund payments of $3.5 million in each of the years 2004 through 2008.

Instructions

Prepare the note disclosure required for the long-term debt at December 31, 2002.

*E15-20 (Settlement of Debt) Nieland Inc. owes $200,000 plus $18,000 of accrued interest to First Bank. The debt is a 10-year, 10% note. During 2001, Nieland's business deteriorated due to a faltering regional economy. On December 31, 2001, the bank agrees to accept an old machine and cancel the entire debt. The machine has a cost of $390,000, accumulated amortization of $221,000, and a fair market value of $190,000.

Instructions

    (a) Prepare journal entries for Nieland Inc. and First Bank to record this debt settlement.

    (b) How should Nieland report the gain or loss on the disposition of machine and on restructuring of debt in its 2001 income statement?

    (c) Assume that, instead of transferring the machine, Nieland decides to grant 15,000 of its common shares, which have a fair market value of $190,000 in full settlement of the loan obligation. If First Bank treats Nieland's shares as temporary investments, prepare the entries to record the transaction for both parties.

*E15-21 (Term Modification—Debtor's Entries) On December 31, 2001, the Firstar Bank enters into a debt restructuring agreement with Bradtke Inc., which is now experiencing financial trouble. The bank agrees to restructure a 12%, issued at par, $2 million note receivable by the following modifications:

    1. Reducing the principal obligation from $2 million to $1.9 million.

    2. Extending the maturity date from December 31, 2001 to December 31, 2004.

    3. Reducing the interest rate from 12% to 10%.

Bradtke pays interest at the end of each year. On January 1, 2005, Bradtke Inc. pays $1.9 million in cash to Firstar Bank.

Instructions

    (a) Discuss whether Bradtke should record a gain or not.

    (b) Calculate the rate of interest that Bradtke should use to compute interest expense in future periods.

    (c) Prepare the interest payment entry for Bradtke on December 31, 2003.

    (d) What entry should Bradtke make on January 1, 2005?

*E15-22 (Term Modification—Creditor's Entries) Using the same information as in E15-21 above, answer the following questions related to Firstar Bank (creditor).

Instructions

    (a) What interest rate should Firstar Bank use to calculate the loss on the debt restructuring?

    (b) Calculate the loss that Firstar Bank will suffer from the debt restructuring. Prepare the journal entry to record the loss.

    (c) Prepare the amortization schedule for Firstar Bank after the debt restructuring.

    (d) Prepare the interest receipt entry for Firstar Bank on December 31, 2003.

    (e) What entry should Firstar Bank make on January 1, 2005?

*E15-23 (Settlement—Debtor's Entries) Use the same information as in E15-21 above except that Firstar Bank reduced the principal to $1.6 million rather than $1.9 million. On January 1, 2005, Bradtke pays $1.6 million in cash to Firstar Bank for the principal.

Instructions

    (a) Can Bradtke record a gain under this term modification? If yes, calculate the gain for Bradtke.

    (b) Prepare the journal entries to record the gain on Bradtke's books.

    (c) What interest rate should Bradtke use to calculate its interest expense in future periods? Will your answer be the same as in E14-21 above? Why or why not?

    (d) Prepare the amortization schedule of the note for Bradtke after the debt restructuring.

    (e) Prepare the interest payment entries for Bradtke on December 31 of 2002, 2003, and 2004.

    (f) What entry should Bradtke make on January 1, 2005?

*E15-24 (Settlement—Creditor's Entries) Using the same information as in E15-21 and E15-23 above, answer the following questions related to Firstar Bank (creditor).

Instructions

    (a) What interest should Firstar Bank use to calculate the loss on the debt restructuring?

    (b) Calculate the loss Firstar Bank will suffer under this new term modification. Prepare the journal entry to record the loss on Firstar's books.

(c) Prepare the amortization schedule for Firstar Bank after the debt restructuring.

(d) Prepare the interest receipt entry for Firstar Bank on December 31, 2002, 2003, and 2004.

(e) What entry should Firstar Bank make on January 1, 2005?

*E15-25 (Debtor/Creditor Entries for Settlement of Troubled Debt) Langrova Limited owes $199,800 to Fernandez Inc. The debt is a 10-year, 11% note. Because Langrova is in financial trouble, Fernandez Inc. agrees to accept some property and cancel the entire debt. The property has a book value of $80,000 and a fair market value of $120,000.

Instructions

(a) Prepare the journal entry on Langrova's books for debt restructure.

(b) Prepare the journal entry on Fernandez's books for debt restructure.

*E15-26 (Impairments) On December 31, 2000, Majoli Inc. borrowed $62,092 from Paris Bank, signing a five-year, $100,000 non-interest-bearing note. The note was issued to yield 10% interest. Unfortunately, during 2002, Majoli began to experience financial difficulty. As a result, at December 31, 2002, Paris Bank determined that it was probable that it would receive back only $75,000 at maturity. The market rate of interest on loans of this nature is now 11%.

Instructions

(a) Prepare the entry to record the issuance of the loan by Paris Bank on December 31, 2000.

(b) Prepare the entry (if any) to record the impairment of the loan on December 31, 2002 by Paris Bank.

(c) Prepare the entry (if any) to record the impairment of the loan on December 31, 2002 by Majoli.

*E15-27 (Impairments) On December 31, 1999, Conchita Inc. signed a $1 million note to Sauk City Bank. The market interest rate at that time was 12%. The stated interest rate on the note was 10%, payable annually. The note matures in five years. Unfortunately, because of lower sales, Conchita's financial situation worsened. On December 31, 2001, Sauk City Bank determined that it was probable that the company would pay back only $600,000 of the principal at maturity. However, it was considered likely that interest would continue to be paid, based on the $1 million loan.

Instructions

(a) Determine the amount of cash Conchita received from the loan on December 31, 1999.

(b) Prepare a note amortization schedule for Sauk City Bank up to December 31, 2001.

(c) Determine the loss on impairment that Sauk City Bank should recognize on December 31, 2001.

PROGLEMS

P15-1 The following amortization and interest schedule reflects the issuance of 10-year bonds by Brandon Corporation on January 1, 1994 and the subsequent interest payments and charges. The company's year end is December 31 and financial statements are prepared once yearly.

Amortization Schedule

Year	Cash	Interest	Amount Unamortized	Book Value
1/1/94			$5,651	$ 94,349
1994	$11,000	$11,322	$5,329	$ 94,671
1995	$11,000	$11,361	$4,968	$ 95,032
1996	$11,000	$11,404	$4,564	$ 95,436
1997	$11,000	$11,452	$4,112	$ 95,888
1998	$11,000	$11,507	$3,605	$ 96,395
1999	$11,000	$11,567	$3,038	$ 96,962
2000	$11,000	$11,635	$2,403	$ 97,597
2001	$11,000	$11,712	$1,691	$ 98,309
2002	$11,000	$11,797	$ 894	$ 99,106
2003	$11,000	$11,894	–0–	$100,000

Instructions

(a) Indicate whether the bonds were issued at a premium or a discount and how you can determine this fact from the schedule.

(b) Indicate whether the amortization schedule is based on the straight-line method or the effective interest method and how you can determine which method is used.

(c) Determine the stated interest rate and the effective interest rate.

(d) On the basis of the schedule above, prepare the journal entry to record the issuance of the bonds on January 1, 1994.

(e) On the basis of the schedule above, prepare the journal entry or entries to reflect the bond transactions and accruals for 1994. (Interest is paid January 1.)

(f) On the basis of the schedule above, prepare the journal entry or entries to reflect the bond transactions and accruals for 2001. Brandon Corporation does not use reversing entries.

P15-2 Sam Inc. is building a new hockey arena at a cost of $2 million. It received a down payment of $500,000 from local businesses to support the project, and now needs to borrow $1.5 million to complete the project. It therefore decides to issue $1.5 million of 10.5%, 10-year bonds. These bonds were issued on January 1, 1999, and pay interest annually on each January 1. The bonds yield 10%. The company paid $50,000 in bond issue costs related to the bond sale.

Instructions

(a) Prepare the journal entry to record the issuance of the bonds and the related bond issue costs incurred on January 1, 1999.

(b) Prepare a bond amortization schedule up to and including January 1, 2003, using the effective interest method.

(c) Assume that on July 1, 2002, the company retires half of the bonds at a cost of $800,000 plus accrued interest. Prepare the journal entry to record this retirement.

P15-3 Sales Inc. developed a new sales gimmick to help sell its inventory of new automobiles. Because many new car buyers need financing, the company offered a low down payment and low car payments for the first year after purchase. It believes that this promotion will bring in some new buyers.

On January 1, 2001, a customer purchased a new $25,000 automobile, making a down payment of $1,000. The customer signed a note indicating that the annual interest rate would be 8% and that quarterly payments would be made over three years. For the first year, the company required a $300 quarterly payment to be made on April 1, July 1, October 1, and January 1, 2002. After this one-year period, the customer was required to make regular quarterly payments that would pay off the loan as of January 1, 2004.

Instructions

(a) Prepare a note amortization schedule for the first year.

(b) Indicate the amount the customer owes on the contract at the end of the first year.

(c) Calculate the amount of the new quarterly payments.

(d) Prepare a note amortization schedule for these new payments for the next two years.

(e) What do you think of the new sales promotion used by Sales Inc.?

P15-4 Mills Inc. issued its 9%, 25-year mortgage bonds in the principal amount of $5 million on January 2, 1987, at a discount of $250,000, which it proceeded to amortize by charges to expense over the life of the issue on a straight-line basis. The indenture securing the issue provided that the bonds could be called for redemption in total but not in part at any time before maturity at 104% of the principal amount, but it did not provide for any sinking fund. On December 18, 2001, the company issued its 11%, 20-year debenture bonds in the principal amount of $6 million at 102 and the proceeds were used to redeem the 9%, 25-year mortgage bonds on January 2, 2002. The indenture securing the new issue did not provide for any sinking fund or for retirement before maturity.

Instructions

(a) Prepare journal entries to record the issuance of the 11% bonds and the retirement of the 9% bonds.

(b) Indicate the income statement treatment of the gain or loss from retirement and the note disclosure required. Assume 2002 income from operations of $3.2 million, a weighted number of shares outstanding of 1.5 million, and an income tax rate of 40%.

P15-5 In each of the following independent cases the company closes its books on December 31.

1. Ferry Inc. sells $250,000 of 10% bonds on March 1, 2001. The bonds pay interest on September 1 and March 1. The bonds' due date is September 1, 2004. The bonds yield 12%. Give entries through December 31, 2002.

2. Dougherty Ltd. sells $600,000 of 12% bonds on June 1, 2001. The bonds pay interest on December 1 and June 1. The bonds' due date is June 1, 2005. The bonds yield 10%. On October 1, 2002, Dougherty buys back $120,000 worth of bonds for $126,000 (includes accrued interest). Give entries through December 1, 2003.

Instructions

(Round to the nearest dollar.)

For the two cases above, prepare all of the relevant journal entries from the time of sale until the date indicated. Use the effective interest method for discount and premium amortization (construct amortization tables where applicable). Amortize premium or discount on interest dates and at year end. (Assume that no reversing entries were made.)

P15-6 Presented below are selected transactions on the books of Powerglide Corporation.

May 1, 2001	Bonds payable with a par value of $700,000, which are dated January 1, 2001, are sold at 106 plus accrued interest. They are coupon bonds, bear interest at 12% (payable annually at January 1), and mature January 1, 2011. (Use interest expense account for accrued interest.)
Dec. 31	Adjusting entries are made to record the accrued interest on the bonds, and the amortization of the proper amount of premium. (Use straight-line amortization.)
Jan. 1, 2002	Interest on the bonds is paid.
April 1	Bonds of par value of $420,000 are purchased at 102 plus accrued interest and retired. (Bond premium is to be amortized only at the end of each year.)
Dec. 31	Adjusting entries are made to record the accrued interest on the bonds, and the proper amount of premium amortized.

Instructions

Prepare journal entries for the transactions above.

P15-7 On April 1, 2002, Fontenot Corp. sold 12,000 of its 11%, 15-year, $1,000 face value bonds at 97. Interest payment dates are April 1 and October 1, and the company uses the straight-line method of bond discount amortization. On March 1, 2003, Fontenot took advantage of its favourable share prices shares to extinguish 3,000 of the bonds by issuing 100,000 shares. At this time, the accrued interest was paid in cash. The company's shares were selling for $31 per share on March 1, 2003.

Instructions

Prepare the journal entries needed on the company books to record the following:

(a) April 1, 2002: issuance of the bonds.
(b) October 1, 2002: payment of semiannual interest
(c) December 31, 2002: accrual of interest expense.
(d) March 1, 2003: extinguishment of 3,000 bonds. (No reversing entries made.)

P15-8 On December 31, 2002, Luis Limited acquired a computer from Cuevas Corporation by issuing a $400,000 non-interest-bearing note, payable in full on December 31, 2006. Luis' credit rating permits it to borrow funds from its several lines of credit at 10%. The computer is expected to have a five-year life and a $50,000 salvage value.

Instructions

(a) Prepare the journal entry for the purchase on December 31, 2002.
(b) Prepare any necessary adjusting entries relative to amortization for the asset (use straight-line) and amortization related to the bond (use effective interest method) on December 31, 2003.
(c) Prepare any necessary adjusting entries relative to amortization of the computer and amortization related to the bond on December 31, 2004.

P15-9 Yat-sen Cosmetics Inc. purchased machinery on December 31, 2001, paying $40,000 down and agreeing to pay the balance in four equal instalments of $30,000 payable each December 31. An assumed interest of 12% is implicit in the purchase price.

Instructions

Prepare the journal entries that would be recorded for the purchase and for the payments and interest on the following dates:

(a) December 31, 2001.
(b) December 31, 2002.
(c) December 31, 2003.

(d) December 31, 2004.
(e) December 31, 2005.

P15-10 Presented below are four independent situations:

1. On March 1, 2002, Heide Inc. issued at 103 plus accrued interest $3 million, 9% bonds. The bonds are dated January 1, 2002, and pay interest semiannually on July 1 and January 1. In addition, Heide incurred $27,000 of bond issuance costs. Calculate the net amount of cash received by Heide as a result of the issuance of these bonds.

2. On January 1, 2001, Reymont Ltd. issued 9% bonds with a face value of $500,000 for $469,280 to yield 10%. The bonds are dated January 1, 2001, and pay interest annually. What amount is reported for interest expense in 2001 related to these bonds, assuming that Reymont used the effective interest method for amortizing bond premium and discount?

3. Czeslaw Building Inc. has a number of long-term bonds outstanding at December 31, 2002. These long-term bonds have the following sinking fund requirements and maturities for the next six years.

	Sinking Fund	Maturities
2003	$300,000	$100,000
2004	$100,000	$250,000
2005	$100,000	$100,000
2006	$200,000	—
2007	$200,000	$150,000
2008	$200,000	$100,000

Indicate how this information should be reported in the financial statements at December 31, 2002.

4. In the long-term debt structure of Curie Inc., the following three bonds were reported: mortgage bonds payable $10 million; collateral trust bonds $5 million; bonds maturing in instalments, secured by plant equipment $4 million. Determine the total amount, if any, of debenture bonds outstanding.

P15-11 Balzac Inc. has been producing quality children's apparel for more than 25 years. The company's fiscal year runs from April 1 to March 31. The following information relates to the obligations of Balzac as of March 31, 2002.

Bonds Payable

Balzac issued $5 million of 11% bonds on July 1, 1996 at 96, which yielded proceeds of $4.8 million. The bonds will mature on July 1, 2006. Interest is paid semiannually on July 1 and January 1. Balzac uses the straight-line method to amortize the bond discount.

Notes Payable

Balzac has signed several long-term notes with financial institutions and insurance companies. The maturities of these notes are given in the schedule below. The total unpaid interest for all of these notes amounts to $210,000 on March 31, 2002.

Due Date	Amount Due
April 1, 2002	$ 200,000
July 1, 2002	$ 300,000
October 1, 2002	$ 150,000
January 1, 2003	$ 150,000
April 1, 2003 – March 31, 2004	$ 600,000
April 1, 2004 – March 31, 2005	$ 500,000
April 1, 2005 – March 31, 2006	$ 700,000
April 1, 2006 – March 31, 2007	$ 400,000
April 1, 2007 – March 31, 2008	$ 500,000
	$3,500,000

Estimated Warranties

Balzac has a one-year product warranty on some selected items in its product line. The estimated warranty liability on sales made during the 2000–01 fiscal year and still outstanding as of March 31, 2001 amounted to $84,000. The warranty costs on sales made from April 1, 2001 through March 31, 2002 are estimated at $210,000. The actual warranty costs incurred during the current 2001–02 fiscal year are as follows:

Warranty claims honoured on 2000–01 sales	$ 84,000
Warranty claims honoured on 2001–02 sales	95,000
Total warranty claims honoured	$179,000

Other Information

1. *Trade payables.* Accounts payable for supplies, goods and services purchased on open account amount to $370,000 as of March 31, 2002.
2. *Payroll related items.* Outstanding obligations related to Balzac's payroll as of March 31, 2002 are:

Accrued salaries and wages	$150,000
Income taxes withheld from employees	$ 25,000
Other payroll deductions	$ 27,000

3. *Taxes.* The following taxes incurred but not due until the next fiscal year are:

Income taxes	$310,000
Property taxes	$125,000
Sales taxes	$182,000

4. *Miscellaneous accruals.* Other accruals not separately classified amount to $75,000 as of March 31, 2002.
5. *Dividends.* On March 15, 2002, Balzac's board of directors declared a cash dividend of $.40 per common share and a 10% common stock dividend. Both dividends were to be distributed on April 12, 2002 to the common shareholders of record at the close of business on March 31, 2002. Data regarding Balzac common shares are as follows:

Number of shares issued and outstanding 3 million shares

Market values of common shares:

March 15, 2002	$22.00 per share
March 31, 2002	$21.50 per share
April 12, 2002	$22.50 per share

Instructions

Prepare the balance sheet's liabilities section and appropriate notes to the statement for Balzac Inc. as of March 31, 2002, as they should appear in its annual report to the shareholders.

(CMA adapted)

P15-12 Mathilda B. Reichenbacher, an intermediate accounting student, is having difficulty amortizing bond premiums and discounts using the effective interest method. She has come to you with the following problem, looking for help.

On June 30, 2000, Elbert Inc. issued $3 million face value of 13%, 20-year bonds at $3,225,690, a yield of 12%. The company uses the effective interest method to amortize bond premiums or discounts. The bonds pay semiannual interest on June 30 and December 31. Calculate the amortization schedule for four periods.

Instructions

Using the data above for illustrative purposes, write a short memo (1–1.5 pages double-spaced) to Mathilda, explaining what the effective interest method is, why many might consider it preferable, and how it is calculated. (Do not forget to include an amortization schedule, referring to it whenever necessary.)

*P15-13 On January 1, 2001, Bostan Limited issued a $1.2 million, five-year, zero-interest-bearing note to National Organization Bank. The note was issued to yield 8% annual interest. Unfortunately, during 2002, Bostan fell into financial trouble due to increased competition. After reviewing all available evidence on December 31, 2002, National Organization Bank decided that the loan was impaired. Bostan will probably pay back only $800,000 of the principal at maturity.

Instructions

(a) Prepare journal entries for both Bostan and National Organization Bank to record the issuance of the note on January 1, 2001. (Round to the nearest $10.)
(b) Assuming that both Bostan and National Organization Bank use the effective interest method to amortize the discount, prepare the amortization schedule for the note.
(c) Under what circumstances might National Organization Bank consider Bostan's note to be "impaired"?
(d) Estimate the loss National Organization Bank will suffer from Bostan's financial distress on December 31, 2002. What journal entries should be made to record this loss?

*P15-14 Jeremy Hillary is the sole shareholder of Hillary Inc., which is currently under protection of bankruptcy court. As a "debtor in possession," he has negotiated the following revised loan agreement with Valley Bank. Hillary Inc.'s $400,000, 12%, 10-year note was refinanced with a $400,000, 5%, 10-year note.

Instructions

    (a) What is the accounting nature of this transaction?

    (b) Prepare the journal entry to record this refinancing:

        1. On the books of Hillary Inc.

        2. On the books of Valley Bank.

    (c) Discuss whether generally accepted accounting principles provide the proper information useful to managers and investors in this situation.

*P15-15 Sandro Corporation is having financial difficulty and therefore has asked Botticelli National Bank to restructure its $3 million note outstanding. The present note has three years remaining and pays a current interest rate of 10%. The present market rate for a loan of this nature is 12%. The note was issued at its face value.

Instructions

Presented below are four independent situations. Prepare the journal entry that Sandro and Botticelli National Bank would make for each of these restructurings.

    (a) Botticelli National Bank agrees to take an equity interest in Sandro by accepting common shares valued at $2.2 million in exchange for relinquishing its claim on this note.

    (b) Botticelli National Bank agrees to accept land in exchange for relinquishing its claim on this note. The land has a book value of $1,950,000 and a fair value of $2.4 million.

    (c) Botticelli National Bank agrees to modify the terms of the note, indicating that Sandro does not have to pay any interest on the note over the three-year period.

    (d) Botticelli National Bank agrees to reduce the principal balance down to $2.5 million and require interest only in the second and third year at a rate of 10%.

*P15-16 Dionysus Inc. owes Solomos Bank a 10-year, 15% note in the amount of $250,000. The note is due today, December 31, 2001. Because Dionysus Inc. is in financial trouble, Solomos agrees to accept 60,000 shares of Dionysus's common shares, which are selling for $1.40, reduce the note's face amount to $150,000, extend the maturity date to 12/31/05, and reduce the interest rate to 6%. Interest will continue to be due on December 31 each year. (Interest is still outstanding as at December 31, 2001)

Instructions

    (a) Prepare all the necessary journal entries on the books of Dionysus Inc. from restructure through maturity.

    (b) Prepare all the necessary journal entries on the books of Solomos Bank from restructure through maturity.

*P15-17 At December 31, 2000, Sioux Manufacturing Limited had outstanding a $300,000, 12% note payable to Teton National Bank. Dated January 1, 1998, the note was due December 31, 2001, with interest payable each December 31. During 2001, Sioux notified Teton that it might be unable to meet the scheduled December 31, 2001, payment of principal and interest because of financial difficulties. On September 30, 2001, Teton sold the note, including interest accrued since December 31, 2000, for $280,000 to Osage Foundry, one of Sioux's oldest and largest customers. On December 31, 2000, Osage agreed to accept inventory costing $240,000 and worth $315,000 from Sioux in full settlement of the note.

Instructions

    (a) Prepare the journal entry to record the September 30, 2001 transaction on the books of Teton, Sioux, and Osage. For each, indicate whether the transaction is a troubled debt restructuring.

    (b) Prepare the journal entries to record the December 31, 2001 transaction on the books of Sioux and Osage. For each, indicate whether the transaction is a troubled debt restructuring.

*P15-18 Mildred Corp. owes Taylor Corp. a 10-year, 10% note in the amount of $110,000 plus $11,000 of accrued interest. The note is due today, December 31, 2001. Because Mildred Corp. is in financial trouble, Taylor Corp. agrees to forgive the accrued interest, $10,000 of the principal, and to extend the maturity date to December 31, 2004. Interest at 10% of revised principal will continue to be due on 12/31 each year.

Instructions

    (a) Calculate the new effective interest rate for Mildred Corp. following restructure. (Hint: Use a financial calculator or Excel spreadsheet)

    (b) Prepare a schedule of debt reduction and interest expense for the years 2001 through 2004.

(c) Calculate the gain or loss for Taylor Corp. and prepare a schedule of receivable reduction and interest revenue for the years 2001 through 2004.

(d) Prepare all the necessary journal entries on the books of Mildred Corp. for the years 2001, 2002, and 2003.

(e) Prepare all the necessary journal entries on the books of Taylor Corp. for the years 2001, 2002, and 2003.

CONCEPTUAL CASES

C15-1 On January 1, 2002, Branagh Limited issued for $1,075,230 its 20-year, 13% bonds that have a maturity value of $1 million and pay interest semiannually on January 1 and July 1. Bond issue costs were not material in amount. Below are three presentations of the balance sheet's long-term liability section that might be used for these bonds at the issue date:

1.	Bonds payable (maturing January 1, 2022)	$1,000,000
	Unamortized premium on bonds payable	$ 75,230
	Total bond liability	$1,075,230
2.	Bonds payable—principal	
	(face value $1,000,000 maturing January 1, 2022)	$ 97,220 a
	Bonds payable—interest (semiannual payment 65,000)	$ 978,010 b
	Total bond liability	$1,075,230
3.	Bonds payable—principal (maturing January 1, 2022)	$1,000,000
	Bonds payable—interest ($65,000 per period for 40 periods)	$2,600,000
	Total bond liability	$3,600,000

(a) The present value of $1 million due at the end of 40 (six-month) periods at the yield rate of 6% per period.

(b) The present value of $65,000 per period for 40 (six-month) periods at the yield rate of 6% per period.

Instructions

(a) Discuss the conceptual merit(s) of each of the date-of-issue balance sheet presentations shown above for these bonds.

(b) Explain why investors would pay $1,075,230 for bonds that have a maturity value of only $1 million.

(c) Assuming that a discount rate is needed to calculate the carrying value of the obligations arising from a bond issue at any date during the life of the bonds, discuss the conceptual merit(s) of using for this purpose:

(a) the coupon or nominal rate.

(b) the effective or yield rate at date of issue.

(d) If the obligations arising from these bonds are to be carried at their present value calculated by means of the current market rate of interest, how would the bond valuation at dates subsequent to the date of issue be affected by an increase or a decrease in the market rate of interest?

(AICPA adapted)

C15-2 Thompson Limited has completed a number of transactions during 2001. In January the company purchased under contract a machine at a total price of $1.2 million, payable over five years with instalments of $240,000 per year. The seller has considered the transaction as an instalment sale with the title transferring to Thompson at the time of the final payment.

On March 1, 2001, Thompson issued $10 million of general revenue bonds priced at 99 with a coupon of 10% payable July 1 and January 1 of each of the next 10 years. The July 1 interest was paid and on December 30 the company transferred $1 million to the trustee, Holly Trust Limited, for payment of the January 1, 2002 interest.

Due to the depressed market for the company's shares, Thompson purchased $500,000 par value of their 6% convertible bonds for a price of $455,000. It expects to resell the bonds when the price of its common shares has recovered.

As Thompson's accountant, you have prepared the balance sheet as of December 31, 2001 and have presented it to the company president. You are asked the following questions about it:

1. Why has amortization been charged on equipment being purchased under contract? Title has not passed to the company as yet and, therefore, they are not our assets. Why should the company not show on the left side of the balance sheet only the amount paid to date instead of showing the full contract price on the left side and the unpaid portion on the right side? After all, the seller considers the transaction an instalment sale.
2. What is bond discount? As a debit balance, why is it not classified among the assets?
3. Bond interest is shown as a current liability. Did we not pay our trustee, Holly Trust Limited, the full amount of interest due this period?
4. Treasury bonds are shown as a deduction from bonds payable issued. Why should they not be shown as an asset, since they can be sold again? Are they the same as bonds of other companies that we hold as investments?

Instructions

Outline your answers to these questions by writing a brief paragraph that will justify your treatment.

C15-3 On March 1, 2002, Norris Inc. sold its five-year, $1,000 face value, 9% bonds dated March 1, 2002 at an effective annual interest rate (yield) of 11%. Interest is payable semiannually, and the first interest payment date is September 1, 2002. Norris uses the interest method of amortization. Bond issue costs were incurred in preparing and selling the bond issue. The bonds can be called by Norris at 101 at any time on or after March 1, 2003.

Instructions

(a) 1. How would the bond's selling price be determined?
  2. Specify how all items related to the bonds would be presented in a balance sheet prepared immediately after the bond issue was sold.
(b) What items related to the bond issue would be included in Norris' 2002 income statement, and how would each be determined?
(c) Would the amount of bond discount amortization using the effective interest method of amortization be lower in the second or third year of the life of the bond issue? Why?
(d) Assuming that the bonds were called in and retired on March 1, 2003, how should Norris report the retirement of the bonds on the 2003 income statement?

(AICPA adapted)

C15-4 **Part I.** The appropriate method of amortizing a premium or discount on issuance of bonds is the effective interest method.

Instructions

(a) What is the effective interest method of amortization and how is it different from and similar to the straight-line method of amortization?
(b) How is amortization calculated using the effective interest method. Why and how do amounts obtained using the effective interest method differ from amounts calculated under the straight-line method?

Part II. Gains or losses from the early extinguishment of debt that is refunded can theoretically be accounted for in three ways:

1. Amortized over remaining life of old debt.
2. Amortized over the life of the new debt issue.
3. Recognized in the period of extinguishment.

Instructions

(a) Develop supporting arguments for each of the three theoretical methods of accounting for gains and losses from the early extinguishment of debt.
(b) Which of the methods above is generally accepted as the appropriate amount of gain or loss to be shown in a company's financial statements?

(AICPA adapted)

C15-5 Pitt Corporation is interested in building its own pop can manufacturing plant adjacent to its existing plant in Montreal. The objective would be to ensure a steady supply of cans at a stable price and to minimize transportation costs. However, the company has been experiencing some financial problems and has been reluctant to borrow any additional cash to fund the project. The company is not concerned with the cash flow problems of making payments, but rather with the impact of adding additional long-term debt to their balance sheet.

The president of Pitt, Aidan Quinn, approached the president of the Aluminum Can Corp. (ACC), its major supplier, to see if some agreement could be reached. ACC was anxious to work out an arrangement, since it seemed inevitable that Pitt would begin its own can production. ACC could not afford to lose the account.

After some discussion a two-part plan was worked out. First ACC was to construct the plant on Pitt's land adjacent to the existing plant. Second, Pitt would sign a 20-year purchase agreement. Under the purchase agreement, Pitt would express its intention to buy all of its cans from ACC, paying a unit price, which at normal capacity would cover labour and material, an operating management fee, and the debt service requirements on the plant. The expected unit price, if transportation costs are taken into consideration, is lower than current market. If Pitt did not take enough production in any one year and if the excess cans could not be sold at a high enough price on the open market, Pitt agrees to make up any cash shortfall so that ACC could make the payments on its debt. The bank will be willing to make a 20-year loan for the plant, taking the plant and the purchase agreement as collateral. At the end of 20 years the plant is to become Pitt's property.

Instructions

    (a) What are project financing arrangements?
    (b) What are take-or-pay contracts?
    (c) Should Pitt record the plant as an asset together with the related obligation?
    (d) If not, should Pitt record an asset relating to the future commitment?
    (e) What is meant by off-balance-sheet financing?

Using Your Judgement

FINANCIAL REPORTING PROBLEM 1:
AT HOME CORPORATION (EXCITE@HOME)

Below is an excerpt from the December 31, 2000 financial statements of **At Home Corporation**, alternatively known as Excite@Home.

Excerpt from note to 2000 financial statements:

9. Convertible Debt and Other Liabilities

Convertible Debt

On December 28, 1998, we issued $437 million principal amount of convertible subordinated debentures in a private offering within the United States to qualified institutional investors. The issue price was 52.464% of the $437 million principal amount due at maturity and issuance costs were $6.9 million, resulting in net proceeds to us of $222.4 million. The carrying amount, including accretion of original issue discount, of these convertible debentures was $243.5 million and $236.3 million as of December 31, 2000 and 1999, respectively.

The debentures mature on December 28, 2018, and interest on the debentures at the rate of 0.5246% per annum on the $437 million principal amount due at maturity is payable semi-annually commencing on June 28, 1999. The effective annual interest rate on the debentures, including accretion of original issuance discount and amortization of issuance costs, is approximately 4%. Each $1,000 debenture is convertible at the option of the holder at any time prior to maturity, unless redeemed or otherwise purchased, into 13.1 shares of our Series A common stock. No conversions of these debentures have occurred through December 31, 2000. At our option, we may redeem the debentures beginning in December 2003 for cash equal to the issue price plus accrued original issue discount and accrued interest.

On December 15, 1999, we issued $500 million principal amount of convertible subordinated notes in a private offering within the United States to qualified institutional investors. The net proceeds from this issuance were $485.7 million after deduction of issuance costs of $14.3 million. The notes mature on December 15, 2006 and bear interest at an annual rate of 4.75%. Each $1,000 note is convertible into our Series A common stock at a conversion price of $56.52 per share. No conversions of these notes have occurred through December 31, 2000.

We may redeem these notes beginning in December 2002 for cash equal to a redemption price that decreases ratably from 102.7% of the principal balance in December 2003 to 100% of the principal balance in December 2006, plus accrued interest.

Issuance costs related to our convertible debt were recorded as other assets and are being amortized by charges to interest expense ratably over the term of the debt.

Instructions

(a) Discuss the nature of the company's business. How does the company earn income?

(b) Assess the company's financial situation by looking at liquidity and solvency.

(c) What type of debt was issued on December 28, 1998 above? Why do you suppose that the company would issue the debt such that it receives proceeds of only 52.5% of the debt face value?

(d) Propose a journal entry to record the debt. Assuming no debt was repaid the following year, propose the journal entry to record interest. For simplicity purposes, assume that no value is attributable to the conversion option.

FINANCIAL REPORTING PROBLEM 2:
AT HOME CORPORATION

Following is an excerpt from the company's second quarter report. Note that on August 27, 2001, the company announced that it had received a written notice from two of its holders of Convertible Notes demanding payment of $50 million on the basis that the company breached certain representations made on issuance. According to the company, if the notes were paid in cash, it would have a materially adverse impact on the company's liquidity and the ability to fund its operations.

Excerpt from notes to 2Q financial statements:
5. Financing Transactions—Convertible Note Financing

On June 8, 2001 we issued convertible notes and entered into related agreements with third party investors under which we received $100 million in cash financing. The notes do not bear interest and none of the conversion features discussed below resulted in an initial beneficial conversion feature requiring accounting treatment as a discount and amortization to interest expense. However, we incurred approximately $2 million of debt issuance costs that are being amortized to interest expense over the stated 5-year term of the notes through June 8, 2006. The notes are convertible at any time into shares of our Series A common stock at a rate of $4.38 per share, based on 110% of the weighted-average price of our Series A common stock on June 8, 2001. This conversion rate is subject to reduction as specified in the agreements upon the issuance of common stock in future equity transactions. The holders of these notes may elect to convert the notes at the original issuance price on each anniversary of the date of issuance starting on June 8, 2002, and therefore we have included the principal amount in current liabilities. The notes are also redeemable by us on the second, third and fourth anniversary of the date of issuance. At each such conversion or redemption date, as well as at maturity, we have the option of delivering the par amount in cash or Series A common stock at a rate of 95% of the average of the volume-weighted trading price of the common stock over the 10 trading days prior to each date of issuance, and the shares would be issued in eight equal instalments over an 80-day period. However, if we have not met specified conditions for redeeming the notes in stock, we may be obligated to pay cash rather than stock to satisfy these redemption obligations. In addition, we may elect to pay cash if redeeming the notes in stock results in an unacceptable level of dilution to our stockholders.

We are required to register the resale of the shares issuable upon conversion of the notes in accordance with timeframes specified in our registration rights agreement with the note holders. We are also required to maintain the listing of our Series A common stock on either the New York Stock Exchange, the Nasdaq National Market or the American Stock Exchange. We do not currently meet the Nasdaq continued listing requirement because our net tangible assets and stockholders equity are below the minimum thresholds and the bid price of our Series A common stock is currently less than the minimum $3.00 bid price required when such thresholds are not met. If we do not meet the continued listing requirements of one of these stock markets at any time after receiving a redemption notice from a note holder, if our Series A common stock were delisted, or if we fail to meet other specified conditions in our agreements with the note holders, the notes provide for acceleration of repayment in cash at that time. Our stockholders have approved a reverse stock split which would, if our board of directors elects to implement it, increase the trading price of our Series A common stock above $3.00, but we cannot assure you that this would result in a sustained increase above the minimum bid price requirements. In addition, events of default include failure to meet our payment obligations under these notes or our other outstanding debt obligations, failure to meet material provisions of the notes for a period of 30 days after receiving notice, or filing for bankruptcy. A default under these notes could result in the acceleration of the amounts due under our other outstanding convertible subordinated notes and debentures.

We have granted holders of these notes a security interest in $100 million of our assets that are not otherwise secured, as collateral for the outstanding amounts due under the notes. These notes are senior to our outstanding subordinated notes and debentures.

Instructions

Discuss any financial reporting issues raised by the initial issue and the subsequent call to repay by the note holders.

FINANCIAL STATEMENT ANALYSIS

Canadian Tire Corporation, Limited

Refer to the financial statements and other documents of **Canadian Tire Corporation, Limited** presented in Appendix 5B.

Instructions

Prepare an assessment of its solvency and financial flexibility using ratio and other analysis.

COMPARATIVE ANALYSIS CASE

Sears Canada Inc. versus Hudson's Bay Company

Instructions

Go to the Digital Tool and using the financial information for both companies, answer the following questions.

(a) Calculate the debt-to-total asset ratio and the times interest earned ratio for these two companies. Comment on the quality of these two ratios for both companies.

(b) What financial ratios do both companies use (look in the annual reports) to monitor and portray their financial condition? Do both companies use the same ratios? Are the ratios calculated the same way?

RESEARCH CASES

DBRS

DBRS is a large bond-rating agency in Canada.

Instructions

Access its website at www.dbrs.com and answer the following:

(a) How does DBRS rate the debt of merchandising companies; i.e., what is its methodology?

(b) Which ratios are important in its analysis?

(c) What rating has been assigned to Hudson's Bay and Sears Canada?

(d) Comment on why the ratings in (c) might have been assigned.

(e) Is it possible to have different ratings on different debt instruments within the same company? Explain. (Hint: look at the DBRS list of rated companies or the S&P list of ratings).

ETHICS CASE

Roland Carlson is the president, founder, and majority owner of Thebeau Medical Corporation, an emerging medical technology products company. Thebeau is in dire need of additional capital to keep operating and to bring several promising products to final development, testing, and production. Roland, as owner of 51% of the outstanding common shares, manages the company's operations. He places heavy emphasis on research and development and long-term growth. The other principal shareholder is Jana Kingston who, as a nonemployee investor, owns 40% of the shares. Jana would like to de-emphasize the R & D functions and emphasize the marketing function to maximize short-run sales and profits from existing products. She believes this strategy would raise the market price of Thebeau's shares.

All of Roland's personal capital and borrowing power is tied up in his 51% investment. He knows that any offering of additional shares will dilute his controlling interest because he won't be able to participate in such an issuance. But Jana has money and would likely buy enough shares to gain control of Thebeau. She then would dictate the company's future direction, even if it meant replacing Roland as president and CEO.

The company already has considerable debt. Raising additional debt will be costly, will adversely affect Thebeau's credit rating, and will increase the company's reported losses due to the growth in interest expense. Jana and the other minority shareholders express opposition to the assumption of additional debt, fearing the company will be pushed to the brink of bankruptcy. Wanting to maintain his control and to preserve the direction of "his" company, Roland is doing everything to avoid a share issuance and is contemplating a large issuance of bonds, even if it means the bonds are issued with a high effective-interest rate.

Instructions

(a) Who are the stakeholders in this situation?

(b) What are the ethical issues in this case?

(c) What would you do if you were Roland?

Shareholders' Equity: Contributed Capital

LEARNING OBJECTIVES

After studying this chapter, you should be able to:

1. Discuss the characteristics of the corporate form of organization.
2. Identify the rights of shareholders.
3. Explain the key components of shareholders' equity.
4. Explain the accounting procedures for issuing shares.
5. Identify the major reasons for repurchasing shares.
6. Explain the accounting procedures for reacquiring, retiring, and cancelling shares.
7. Describe the major features of preferred shares.
8. Distinguish between debt and equity.
9. Identify items reported as contributed surplus.
10. Identify the major disclosure requirements.

Preview of Chapter 16

Capital markets are of substantial importance in any economy that functions based on private (versus government) ownership. They provide a forum where prices are established to serve as signals and incentives to guide the allocation of the economy's financial resources. An increasing number of individuals and entities are investing in the capital marketplace (which includes among other "arenas" stock markets and exchanges). This chapter's purpose is to explain the various accounting issues related to different types of shares or equity instruments[1] that corporations issue to raise funds in capital markets. The content and organization of this chapter are as follows:

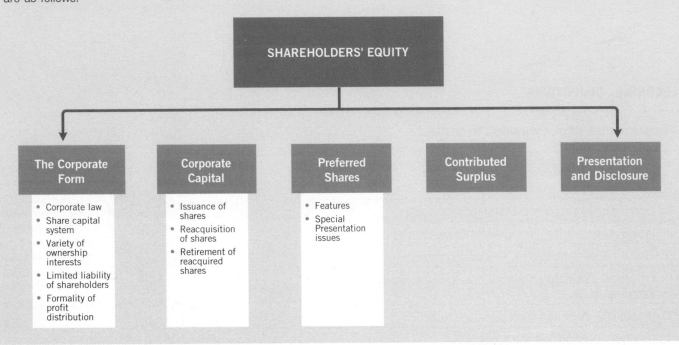

THE CORPORATE FORM

OBJECTIVE 1

Discuss the characteristics of the corporate form of organization.

Of the three **primary forms of business organization—the proprietorship, the partnership, and the corporation**—the dominant form of business is the corporate form. Although the corporate form has a number of advantages (as well as disadvantages) over the other two forms, its principal advantage is that a corporation is a **separate legal entity** and therefore, the entity's owners have **greater legal protection** against lawsuits. An additional important advantage is that incorporation involves the issue of shares, which allows **access to capital markets** for those companies who choose to raise funds in that manner.

Corporations may be classified by the nature of ownership as follows.

1. **Public sector corporations:** governmental units or business operations owned by government units
   (a) **Government units** such as municipalities, cities

---

[1] As defined in Chapter 10, an equity instrument is "any contract that evidences a residual interest in the assets of an entity after deducting its liabilities" per *CICA Handbook*, Section 3860, par. 05 (d). Most shares (including common and preferred shares) may be considered equity instruments however, some preferred shares with debt-like features may be classified as financial liabilities. The latter will be dealt with later in the Chapter.

(b) **Government business enterprises** such as Canada Post and liquor control boards (sometimes referred to as crown corporations)

2. **Private sector corporations:**

(a) **Not-for-profit:** companies whose main objective is something other than profit (such as churches, charities, and colleges). No shares are issued for not-for-profit companies.

(b) **For profit**: companies whose main objective is to increase shareholder value and maximize profit. Shares are issued.

Private companies: shares held by a few shareholders and not available for public purchase. These entities are governed by shareholder agreements, which dictate who may hold the shares and how shareholder interests may or may not be transferred or disposed of. There are numerous private companies in Canada ranging from small businesses to large corporate entities such as McCain Foods and Maple Lodge Farms.

Public companies: shares available for purchase by the general public, normally through a stock exchange such as the Toronto Stock Exchange or stock market such as the CDNX.[2] Public companies must abide by GAAP,[3] securities laws as established by provincial securities commissions, corporations law, and finally by rules established by the exchanges and markets that the companies trade on.

UNDERLYING CONCEPTS

For these companies, the costs of complying with these requirements is high; however, the **benefits** of having access to significant pools of capital as well as limiting liability outweigh those benefits.

This book focuses on the **for profit** type of corporation operating in the **private sector**. Public sector entities and not-for-profit entities are generally covered in advanced accounting courses.

Among the special characteristics of the corporate form that affect accounting are:

1. Influence of **corporate law**
2. Use of a **share capital system**
3. Development of a **variety of ownership interests**
4. **Limited liability** of shareholders
5. Formality of **profit distribution**

Corporate Law

Anyone who wishes to establish a corporation must submit **articles of incorporation** to the provincial or federal government depending on whether the person wishes to carry on business in a specific province or across Canada. Assuming the requirements are properly fulfilled, the corporation **charter** is issued, and the corporation is recognized as a **legal entity** subject to the relevant Business Corporations Act. While the provisions of most provincial business corporations acts are reasonably similar, differences do exist. Consequently, the Canada Business Corporations Act (CBCA) will be the focal point in this chapter when discussing legal aspects.[4]

INTERNATIONAL INSIGHT

In Canada and the United States, shareholders are treated equally regarding access to financial information. That is not always the case in other countries. For example, in Mexico, foreign investors as well as minority investors often have difficulty obtaining financial data. These restrictions are rooted in the habits of companies that for many years have been tightly controlled by a few shareholders and managers.

---

[2] An "exchange" is a more formal marketplace that is more heavily regulated and uses a specific mechanism for pricing shares. Companies must meet certain requirements to be initially "listed" on the exchange and subsequently must continue to meet ongoing requirements to remain listed. These requirements include numerous financial tests such as asset and revenue levels. Stock "markets" use a different share pricing mechanism and are generally less heavily regulated. There is a wide range of types of stock markets. At the more formal end of the range is NASDAQ and at the less formal range are Alternate Trading Systems (ATS), which are very unstructured, Internet-based platforms or marketplaces where interested buyers and sellers may meet and trade shares.

[3] As required under corporations law as discussed in Chapter 1. This gives GAAP legal status.

[4] According to *Financial Reporting in Canada, 2000,* (CICA; Toronto, 2000), 106 out of 200 publicly traded companies were incorporated under the CBCA; 39 were incorporated under the Ontario Business Corporations Act, which is very similar to the CBCA (p. 3).

The articles of incorporation specify such things as the **company name,**[5] place of **registered office**, **classes and maximum numbers of shares authorized**, restrictions of **rights to transfer shares**, number of **directors**, and any restrictions on the **corporation's business**. Once incorporated, share certificates are prepared and issued to shareholders.

Share Capital System

OBJECTIVE 2

Identify the rights of shareholders.

A corporation's share capital is generally made up of a large number of units or shares. These shares may be organized into groups or "**classes**" such as Class A shares versus Class B shares. Within a given class, each share is exactly equal to every other share. The number of shares possessed determines each owner's interest. If a company has but one class of shares divided into 1,000 shares, a person owning 500 shares has one-half of the corporation's ownership interest; one holding 10 shares has a one-hundredth interest.

Each share has certain rights and privileges that can be restricted only by provisions in the articles of incorporation. In the absence of restrictive provisions, each share carries the following basic or inherent rights:

1. To share proportionately in **profits and losses**.
2. To share proportionately in management (the **right to vote** for directors).
3. To share proportionately in corporate **assets upon liquidation**.

The CBCA allows a corporation to assign a fourth right which is the right to share proportionately in any new issues of share of the same class. This right is known as a preemptive right.

The first three rights are to be expected in the ownership of any business; the last may be used in a corporation to protect each shareholder's proportional interest in the enterprise. **The preemptive right protects an existing shareholder from involuntary dilution of ownership interest**. Without this right, shareholders with a given percentage interest might find their interest reduced by the issuance of additional shares without their knowledge and at prices that were not favourable to them. Because the preemptive right that attaches to existing shares makes it inconvenient for corporations to make large issuances of additional shares, as they frequently do in acquiring other companies, many corporations have eliminated it.

INTERNATIONAL INSIGHT

The American and British systems of corporate governance and finance depend to a large extent on equity financing and the widely dispersed ownership of shares traded in highly liquid markets. The German and Japanese systems have relied more on debt financing, interlocking share ownership, banker/directors, and worker/shareholder rights.

The great advantage of the share system is the ease with which an interest in the business may be transferred from one individual to another. Individuals owning shares in a corporation may **sell** them to others **at any time** and **at any price** without obtaining the consent of the company or other shareholders. Each share is the personal property of the owner and may be disposed of at will.[6] All that is required of the corporation is that it maintain a list or **subsidiary ledger of shareholders** as a guide to dividend payments, issuance of share rights, voting proxies, and the like. Because shares are freely and frequently transferred, the corporation must **revise** the subsidiary ledger of shareholders periodically, generally in advance of every dividend payment or shareholders' meeting. Major stock exchanges require controls over record keeping that the typical corporation finds costly to provide. Thus companies generally **outsource** the task to **registrars and transfer agents** who specialize in providing services for recording and transferring shares.

Variety of Ownership Interests

In every corporation, one class of share must represent the basic ownership interest. That class is called common shares. Common shares represent the **residual ownership**

---

[5] Under the CBCA, the name must include the words "Incorporated," "Limited," or "Corporation" or their respective short forms (in English or in French).

[6] The company issuing the shares records a journal entry only when it first issues and sells the shares and when/if it buys the shares back. When shareholders buy and sell shares from each other, this does not get recorded by the company.

interest in the company, and bear the ultimate **risks** of loss and receive the **benefits** of success. A common shareholder is guaranteed **neither** annual dividends **nor** assets upon dissolution. However, common shareholders generally **control** the corporation management through the **voting rights** attached to the shares.[7] They tend to profit most if the company is successful. In the event that a corporation has only one authorized issue of capital shares, that issue is by definition common shares, whether so designated in the charter or not.

In an effort to appeal to all types of investors, corporations may offer two or more classes of shares, each with **different rights or privileges**. In the preceding section it was pointed out that each share of a given issue has the same rights as other shares of the same issue and that there are three rights inherent in every share. By special contracts between the corporation and its shareholders, **certain of these rights may be sacrificed by the shareholder in return for other special rights or privileges**. Thus special classes of shares are created. Because they have certain preferential rights, they are usually called preferred shares. In return for any special preference, the preferred shareholder is always called on to sacrifice some of the inherent rights of common share interests.

A common type of preference is to give the preferred shareholders a **prior claim on earnings**. They are assured a dividend, usually at a stated rate, before any amount may be distributed to the common shareholders. In return for this preference, the preferred share may sacrifice the right to a voice in management or the right to share in profits beyond the stated rate.

A company may accomplish much the same thing by issuing two classes of shares, Class A shares and Class B shares. In this case, one of the issues is the common share and the other issue has some preference or restriction of basic rights. Illustration 16-1 is an excerpt from the notes to the financial statements of **Four Seasons Hotels Inc.**

UNDERLYING CONCEPTS

Because shareholders bear the risks of loss and receive the benefits of success, these shareholders are said to have the risks and rewards of ownership and the shares are treated as assets by the shareholders.

> **(a) Capital stock:**
> **Authorized: 3,986,872**
> Variable Multiple Voting Shares ("VMVS"), entitling the holder to that number of votes that results in the aggregate votes attaching to the VMVS representing approximately 66% of the votes attaching to the VMVS and the Limited Voting Shares ("LVS"), in aggregate, which, at December 31, 2000 was 15.09 votes (1999 – 14.91 votes) per VMVS. Changes in the number of votes attaching to the VMVS necessary to maintain this level will occur concurrently with the issue of additional LVS.
>
> The VMVS rank equally with the LVS as to distributions on liquidation, dissolution or winding-up of FSHI. Dividends declared and paid on the VMVS are in amounts per share equal to 50% of the dividends per share declared and paid on the LVS, regardless of whether the number of votes attaching to the VMVS is further increased.
>
> VMVS are convertible into LVS on a one-for-one basis at the option of the holder. The shares automatically convert into LVS upon any transfer outside of the family of Isadore Sharp, except a transfer of a majority of the shares to a purchaser who makes an equivalent offer to purchase all outstanding VMVS and LVS.
>
> **Unlimited**
> LVS, voting (one vote per share) and ranking equally with the VMVS as to distributions on liquidation, dissolution or winding-up of FSHI.

ILLUSTRATION 16-1
Excerpt from the Notes to the Financial Statements of Four Seasons Hotels Inc.

For these shares, the existence of the VMVS allows the Sharpe family to retain control of the company, as it will always have 66% of the votes.

Limited Liability of Shareholders

Those who "own" a corporation, i.e., the shareholders, contribute either property or services to the enterprise in return for ownership shares. **The property or service invested in the enterprise is the extent of a shareholder's possible loss**. That is, if the corporation sustains losses to such an extent that remaining assets are insufficient to pay creditors, **no recourse** can be had by the creditors against personal assets of the individual

---

[7] Shareholders who have voting rights will elect a board of directors to make major company decisions.

shareholders. In a partnership or proprietorship, owners' personal assets can be accessed to satisfy unpaid claims against the enterprise. Ownership interests in a corporation are legally protected against such a contingency. The shareholders have limited liability— they may lose their investment but they cannot lose **more** than their investment.

While the corporate form of the organization grants the protective feature of limited liability to the shareholders, it also requires that withdrawal of the amount of share-holders' investment represented in share capital accounts not occur unless all prior claims on corporate assets have been paid. The corporation **must maintain this capital until dissolution**. Upon dissolution, it must satisfy all prior claims before distributing any amounts to the shareholders. In a proprietorship or partnership, the owners or partners may withdraw amounts at will because all their personal assets may be called upon to protect creditors from loss.

Under the CBCA, shares must be **without a nominal or par value**. This simply means that all proceeds from the issuance of the shares must be credited to the appro-priate share capital account and become part of the "shareholders' investment" referred to above. In some provinces and in the U.S., shares that have a fixed per-share amount printed on each share certificate are called par value shares.[8] Par value has but one real significance: it establishes the **maximum responsibility of a shareholder in the event of insolvency** (i.e., in jurisdictions where the concept of par value is legally allowed) or other involuntary dissolution. Par value is thus not "value" in the ordinary sense of the word. It is merely an amount per share determined by the incorporators of the company and stated in the corporation charter or certificate of incorporation. Par value establishes the nominal value per share and is the minimum amount that must be paid in by each shareholder if the share is to be fully paid when issued. A corporation may, however, issue its capital share either above or below par, in which case the share is said to be issued at a **premium or a discount**, respectively.

Formality of Profit Distribution

An enterprise's owners determine what is to be done with profits realized through operations. Profits may be **left in the business** to permit expansion or merely to provide a margin of safety, or they may be **withdrawn and divided among the owners**. In a proprietorship or partnership this decision is made by the owner or owners informally and requires no specific action. In a partnership, the partnership agreement would usually articulate how profits/losses are to be shared. In a corporation, however, profit distribution is controlled by certain **legal restrictions**.

First, no amounts may be distributed among the owners unless the **corporate capital is maintained intact**. This reflects the presumption that sufficient net assets or security must be left in the corporation to satisfy the liability holders after any assets have been distributed to shareholders as dividends. Various tests of **corporate solvency** have been used over the years. Under the CBCA, dividends may not be declared or paid if there are reasonable grounds for believing that (1) the corporation is, or would be after the dividend, unable to pay its liabilities as they become due; or (2) the realizable value of the corporation's assets would, as a result of the dividend, be less than the total of its liabilities and stated or legal capital for all classes of shares.

Second, distributions to shareholders must be **formally approved by the board of directors** and recorded in the minutes of their meetings. As the top executive body in the corporation, the board of directors must make certain that no distributions are made to shareholders that are not justified by profits, and directors are generally held per-sonally liable to creditors if liabilities cannot be paid because company assets have been illegally paid out to shareholders.

---

[8] *Accounting Trends and Techniques*—1999 indicates that its 600 surveyed companies reported 654 issues of outstanding common share, 571 par value issues, and 59 no-par issues; 13 of the no-par issues were shown at their stated (assigned) values. However, According to *Financial Reporting in Canada, 2000* (p. 343), only 2 out of 200 companies surveyed used par value.

Third, dividends must be in **full agreement with the capital share contracts as to preferences**. Once the corporation has entered into contracts with various classes of shareholders, the stipulations of such contracts must be observed.

CORPORATE CAPITAL

Owner's equity in a corporation is defined as shareholders' equity or corporate capital. The following three categories normally appear as part of shareholders' equity:

1. common and or preferred shares
2. contributed surplus
3. retained earnings

The first two categories, **shares and contributed surplus**, constitute contributed (paid-in) capital. The third category, retained earnings, represents the enterprise's **earned capital**. Contributed capital is the total amount provided by shareholders to the corporation for use in the business. Earned capital is the capital that develops if the business operates profitably. It consists of all undistributed income that remains invested in the enterprise.

The distinction between paid-in capital and earned capital is important from both legal and economic points of view. Legally, there are restrictions on **dividend payouts** as previously mentioned. Economically, management, shareholders, and others look to earnings for the **corporation's continued existence and growth**.

Shareholders' **equity** is the difference between the enterprise's **assets** and **liabilities** as articulated in the accounting equation:

$$\text{Assets} - \text{liabilities} = \text{equities}$$

Therefore, the owners' or shareholders' interest in a business enterprise is a **residual interest**. Shareholders' (owners') equity represents the cumulative net contributions by shareholders plus earnings that have been retained. As a **residual interest**, shareholders' equity has no existence apart from the enterprise's assets and liabilities—shareholders' equity equals **net assets**. Shareholders' equity is not a claim to specific assets but a claim against a portion of the total assets. Its amount is not specified or fixed; it depends on the enterprise's cumulative profitability. Shareholders' equity grows if the enterprise is profitable, and it shrinks or may disappear entirely if the enterprise is unprofitable.

A final comment: many different meanings are attached to the word "**capital**" because the word is often construed differently by various user groups. In corporate **finance**, for example, capital commonly refers to **sources of financing**. In **law**, capital is considered that portion of shareholders' equity that is required by statute to be **retained in the business for the protection of creditors**. Accountants use the word "capital" when referring not only to shareholder's equity but also to long-term assets (capital assets) or when referring to whether an expenditure should be treated as an asset (capitalized) or expensed. Care should be taken to **observe the context** within which the term is used.

Issuance of Shares

In issuing shares, the following procedures are followed: First, the shares must be **authorized**, as previously mentioned; next, shares are **offered for sale** and contracts to sell shares are entered into; then, amounts to be received for the shares are **collected** and the **shares issued**.

The accounting problems involved in the issuance of shares are discussed under the following topics:

1. Share issue—basic
2. Shares sold on a subscription basis

OBJECTIVE 3

Explain the key components of shareholders' equity.

OBJECTIVE 4

Explain the accounting procedures for issuing shares.

3. Shares issued in combination with other securities (lump sum sales)
4. Shares issued in nonmonetary transactions
5. Costs of issuing shares

Share Issue—Basic

Shares are sold for the price that they will bring in the marketplace. Normally the company will hire specialists (e.g., investment banking firms, underwriters) to **value the shares** and help **promote and sell them**. As payment for their services, the underwriters take a percentage of the total share consideration received from investors as commission. The **net** amount received by the company represents the credit to common or preferred shares. For example, Video Electronics Corporation is organized with 10,000 authorized common shares. No entry, other than a memorandum entry, need be made for the authorization inasmuch as no amount is involved. If 500 shares are then issued for cash at $10 per share, the entry should be:

Cash	5,000	
Common Shares		5,000

If another 500 shares are issued for $11 per share, the entry should be:

Cash	5,500	
Common Shares		5,500

Entries for preferred shares are the same as for common shares as long as the preferred shares are classified as equity. As par value shares are relatively uncommon in Canada, the unique issues associated with these are covered in Appendix 16A.

Shares Sold on a Subscription Basis

The preceding discussion assumed that the share was sold for cash, but shares may also be sold on a subscription basis. Sale of subscribed shares generally occurs when new, small companies "go public" or when corporations offer shares to employees to obtain employee participation in the business ownership. When a share is sold on a subscription basis, its full price is not received initially. Normally only a **partial payment** is made, and the share is not issued until the full subscription price is received.

Accounting for Subscribed Shares. Two new accounts are used when shares are sold on a subscription basis. The first, **Common or Preferred Shares Subscribed**, indicates the corporation's obligation to issue shares upon payment of final subscription balances by those who have subscribed for shares. This account thus signifies a commitment against the unissued shares. Once the subscription price is fully paid, the Common or Preferred Share Subscribed account is debited and the Common or Preferred Shares account is credited. Common or Preferred Shares Subscribed should be presented in the shareholders' equity section below Common or Preferred Shares.

UNDERLYING CONCEPT

Subscriptions Receivable would appear to fulfill all the requirements for an asset. As a result of a past transaction, the company expects to receive a future economic benefit. An Allowance for Doubtful Accounts would disclose the collection risk in the same manner as for Accounts Receivable.

The second account, **Subscriptions Receivable**, indicates the amount yet to be collected before subscribed share will be issued. Controversy exists concerning the presentation of Subscriptions Receivable on the balance sheet. Some argue that Subscriptions Receivable should be reported in the current assets section (assuming, of course, that payment on the receivable will be received within the operating cycle or one year, whichever is longer). They note that it is similar to trade accounts receivable. Trade accounts receivable grow out of sales transactions in the ordinary course of business; subscriptions receivable relate to the issuance of a concern's own share and in a sense represent funds (capital contributions) not yet paid the corporation.

Others argue that Subscriptions Receivable should be reported as **a deduction from shareholders' equity**. Their reasoning is based on a concern that doing otherwise may result in the financial statements users misunderstanding the share capital accounts (i.e., not realizing that some shares are only partially paid for), and that subscribers cannot be forced to pay the unpaid balance of a subscription receivable.

There is no correct answer, although in the U.S., the SEC requires companies to use the contra equity approach.[9] For example, in the prospectus of **Morlan International, Inc.**, as shown in Illustration 16-2, its subscriptions receivable was reported as a contra equity in the following manner (common share subscribed is included in Common Share rather than shown separately).

ILLUSTRATION 16-2
Treatment of Subscriptions Receivable

MORLAN INTERNATIONAL, INC.

Shareholders' equity	
Common stock, par value $.01 a share:	
Authorized 9,000,000 shares	
Issued 3,547,638 shares	$ 35,500
Additional capital	2,146,700
Retained earnings	3,878,600
Less: Subscriptions receivable	(148,500)
Total shareholders' equity	$5,912,300

The journal entries for handling shares sold on a subscription basis are illustrated by the following example. Lubradite Corp. offers shares on a subscription basis to selected individuals, giving them the right to purchase 10 common shares at a price of $20 per share. Fifty individuals accept the company's offer and agree to pay 50% down and to pay the remaining 50% at the end of six months.

At date of issuance		
Subscriptions Receivable (10 × $20 × 50)	10,000	
Common Shares Subscribed		10,000
(To record receipt of subscriptions for 500 shares)		
Cash	5,000	
Subscriptions Receivable		5,000
(To record receipt of first instalment representing 50% of total due on subscribed share)		

When the final payment is received and the share is issued, the entries are:

Six months later		
Cash	5,000	
Subscriptions Receivable		5,000
(To record receipt of final instalment on subscribed share)		
Common Shares Subscribed	10,000	
Common Shares		10,000
(To record issuance of 500 shares upon receipt of final instalment from subscribers)		

Defaulted Subscription Accounts. Sometimes a subscriber is unable to pay all instalments and defaults on the agreement. The question is what to do with the balance of the subscription account as well as the amount already paid in. The answer is a function of the subscription contract, corporate policy, and any applicable law of the jurisdiction of incorporation. The possibilities include returning the amount already paid by the subscriber (possibly after deducting some expenses), treating the amount paid as forfeited and therefore transferred to the Contributed Surplus account, or issuing shares to the subscriber equivalent to the number of that previous subscription payments would have paid in full.

For example, assume that a subscriber to 50 Lubradite common shares defaulted on the final payment. If the subscription contract stated that amounts paid by the defaulting subscriber would be refunded, Lubradite would make the following entry when the default occurs, assuming that the refund was to be paid at a later date:

---

[9] The SEC has specified that subscriptions receivable may be shown as an asset only if collected prior to the publication of the financial statements.

Common Shares Subscribed	1,000	
Subscriptions Receivable		500
Accounts Payable		500
(To record default on 50 shares subscribed for $20 each and on which 50% had been paid.)		

If the amount paid by the subscriber were forfeited, there would be a $500 credit to Contributed Surplus as this is a **capital transaction**.

Shares Issued with Other Securities (Lump Sum Sales)

Generally, corporations sell **classes of shares** separately from one another so that the proceeds relative to each class, and ordinarily even relative to each lot, are known. Occasionally, two or more classes of securities are issued for a single payment or **lump sum**. It is not uncommon, for example, for more than one type or class of security to be issued in the acquisition of another company. The accounting problem in such lump sum sales is the allocation of the proceeds among the several classes of securities, or how to **measure** the separate classes of shares. Two possible measurement techniques are (1) the proportional method and (2) the incremental method. These measurement techniques are often used in accounting, even for issues other than lump sum share issues.

Proportional Method. If the fair value or other sound basis for determining relative value is available for each class of security, the lump sum received is **allocated** among the classes of securities on a **proportional basis**, that is, the ratio that each is to the total. For instance, if 1,000 common shares having a market value of $20 a share and 1,000 preferred shares having a market value of $12 a share are issued for a lump sum of $30,000, the allocation of the $30,000 to the two classes would be as shown below.

ILLUSTRATION 16-3

Allocation in Lump Sum Securities Issuance— Proportional Method

Market value of common (1,000 × $20)	=	$20,000
Market value of preferred (1,000 × $12)	=	12,000
Aggregate market value		$32,000
Allocated to common: $20,000/32,000 × $30,000	=	$18,750
Allocated to preferred: $12,000/32,000 × $30,000	=	11,250
Total allocation		$30,000

Incremental Method. In instances where the fair value of all classes of securities is not determinable, the **incremental method** may be used. The securities' fair value is used as a basis for those classes that are known and the remainder of the lump sum is allocated to the class for which the fair value is not known. For instance, if 1,000 common shares having a market value of $20 and 1,000 preferred shares having no established market value are issued for a lump sum of $30,000, the allocation of the $30,000 to the two classes would be as follows:

ILLUSTRATION 16-4

Allocation in Lump Sum Securities Issuance— Incremental Method

Lump sum receipt		$30,000
Allocated to common (1,000 × $20)	=	20,000
Balance allocated to preferred		$10,000

If no fair value is determinable for any of the classes of shares involved in a lump sum exchange, an expert's appraisal may be used.

Share Issued in Nonmonetary[10] Transactions

Accounting for the issuance of shares for property or services involves an issue of **valuation** or **measurement**. Shares issued for services or property **other than monetary**

---

[10] Note that exchanges are defined to be nonmonetary according to *CICA Handbook*, Section 3830, par. .04 (e) when little or no consideration is involved. If the fair value of the monetary consideration is less than 10% of the fair value of the total consideration given up or received, the transaction is considered nonmonetary.

consideration should be recorded at the **fair value** of the shares **issued** or the **fair value** of the consideration **received**, if the latter is more clearly determinable.[11]

If both are **readily determinable** and the transaction is the result of an **arm's-length exchange**, there will probably be little difference in their fair values by definition since the parties involved in the deal would strike a price that reflects fair value and would only give up consideration equal to the value of the item received. If the fair values of the shares being issued and the property or services being received are not readily determinable, the value to be assigned would be an estimate of fair value and would generally be established by the board of directors or management at an amount that was not controverted by available evidence. **Independent appraisals** usually serve as dependable bases.

The following series of transactions illustrates the procedure for recording the issuance of 10,000 common shares for a patent, in various circumstances:

1. The patent's fair value is not readily determinable but the shares' fair market value is known to be $140,000.

Patent	140,000	
Common Shares		140,000

2. The shares' fair value is not readily determinable, but the patent's fair value is determined to be $150,000.

Patent	150,000	
Common Shares		150,000

3. Neither the shares' nor the patent's market value is readily determinable. An independent consultant values the patent at $125,000, and the board of directors agrees with that valuation.

Patent	125,000	
Common Shares		125,000

In corporate law, the board of directors is granted the **power to set the value** of nonmonetary transactions. Many stakeholders feel that this power has been abused. The issuance of shares for property or services has resulted in cases of overstated corporate capital through intentional overvaluation of the property or services received. The overvaluation of the shareholders' equity resulting from inflated asset values creates what is referred to as **watered shares**. The "water" can be eliminated from the corporate structure by simply writing down the overvalued assets.

If as a result of the issuance of shares for property or services the recorded assets are undervalued, **secret reserves** are created. Secret reserves may also be created by other methods: excessive amortization charges, expensing capital expenditures, excessive writedowns of inventories or receivables, or any other understatement of assets or overstatement of liabilities. An example of a liability overstatement is an excessive provision for estimated product warranties that ultimately results in an understatement of owners' equity, thereby creating a secret reserve.

Costs of Issuing Shares

Direct costs incurred to sell shares, such as underwriting costs, accounting and legal fees, printing costs, and taxes, should be reported as a reduction of the amounts paid in. **Issue costs** are therefore debited to Share Capital because they are **capital transactions** as opposed to **operating transactions**.

Management salaries and other **indirect costs** related to the share issue should be expensed as incurred because it is difficult to establish a relationship between these costs and the proceeds received upon sale. In addition, corporations annually incur costs for maintaining the shareholders' records and handling ownership transfers.

---

[11] *CICA Handbook*, Section 3830, par. .05.

These recurring costs, primarily registrar and transfer agents' fees, are normally charged to expense in the period in which incurred.

Reacquisition of Shares

It is not unusual for companies to buy back their own shares. In fact, share buybacks now exceed dividends as a form of distribution to shareholders.[12] **Merrill Lynch & Co.** estimated that in a recent year more than 1,400 U.S. corporations announced buyback programs totalling over $80 billion and 2.4 billion shares. Two of the biggest share buyback programs were **General Motors'** purchase of 20% (64 million shares) of its shares for $4.8 billion and **Santa Fe Southern Pacific's** buyback of 38% (60 million shares) of its shares for $3.4 billion in the mid-1990s. Data on recent corporate buybacks indicate that companies are continuing to spend millions of dollars to repurchase shares, as shown in the following table.

ILLUSTRATION 16-5
Recent Corporate Buybacks

Company	Year	Amount of Buyback (millions)	Percent of Shares
BankAmerica	1997	$2,025	4.6%
Coca-Cola	1998	445	3.5
Eli Lilly & Co.	1998	2,000	2.6
Gillette	1998	1,119	1.9
Hewlett-Packard	1998	1,292	2.0
Torchmark	1998	126	2.6
XL Capital LTD	1998	255	2.5

Below is a reproduction of a portion of a bid by **Methanex Corporation** (Methanex) to repurchase shares.

ILLUSTRATION 16-6
Issuer bid by Methanex to Repurchase Shares

OFFER BY METHANEX CORPORATION
To Purchase for US$175,000,000 in Cash up to 29,166,666
of its Common Shares for Not More Than US$7.50
and Not Less Than US$6.00 Per Share

Methanex Corporation ("Methanex" or the "Corporation") invites its shareholders ("Shareholders") to deposit common shares (the "Shares") of Methanex pursuant to (i) auction tenders at prices specified by the depositing Shareholders of not more than US$7.50 and not less than US$6.00 per Share (approximately Cdn.$11.51 to Cdn.$9.20 based on the noon rate of exchange quoted by the Bank of Canada on August 7, 2001) ("Auction Tenders") or (ii) purchase price tenders ("Purchase Price Tenders"), in either case upon the terms and subject to the conditions set forth in this offer (the "Offer"). Under a Purchase Price Tender, a depositing Shareholder does not specify a price but rather agrees to have the Shareholder's Shares purchased at the Purchase Price determined as provided herein. Shareholders who tender Shares without making a valid Auction Tender or Purchase Price Tender will be deemed to have made a Purchase Price Tender.

The Offer expires at 6:00 p.m., Toronto time, on September 13, 2001, unless extended. Methanex reserves the right to withdraw the Offer and not take up and pay for any Shares deposited under the Offer unless certain conditions are satisfied. See Section 5 of the Offer, **"CONDITIONS OF THE OFFER."** Methanex will determine a single price per Share (that is not more than US$7.50 or less than US$6.00 per Share) (the "Purchase Price") that it will pay for Shares properly deposited pursuant to the Offer, taking into account the number of Shares deposited pursuant to Auction Tenders and Purchase Price Tenders, the prices specified by Shareholders making Auction Tenders and the price at which Shares deposited pursuant to Purchase Price Tenders are considered to have been deposited. Shares deposited by Shareholders pursuant to Auction Tenders will not be purchased by Methanex pursuant to the Offer if the price specified by Shareholders is greater than the Purchase Price determined by the Corporation. Shareholders who wish to deposit Shares, but who do not wish to specify a price at which such Shares may be purchased by the Corporation, should make a Purchase Price Tender. Shares deposited pursuant to Purchase Price Tenders will be deemed to have been deposited at a price of US$6.00 per Share.

---

[12] At the beginning of the 1990s the situation was just the opposite; that is, share buybacks were less than half the level of dividends. Companies are extremely reluctant to reduce or eliminate their dividends, because they believe that this action would be viewed negatively by the market. On the other hand, many companies are no longer raising their dividends per share at the same percentage rate as increases in earnings per share, thus effectively reducing the dividend payout over time.

The Purchase Price will be the lowest price between US$6.00 and US$7.50 per Share that will enable Methanex to purchase the largest number of tendered Shares having an aggregate purchase price not exceeding US$175,000,000. Each Shareholder who has properly deposited pursuant to an Auction Tender at or below the Purchase Price or pursuant to a Purchase Price Tender and who has not withdrawn Shares will receive the Purchase Price, payable in cash (subject to applicable withholding taxes), for all Shares purchased upon the terms and subject to the conditions of the Offer, including the provisions relating to proration described below.

Since Methanex had approximately 160 million shares outstanding as per its December 31, 2000 financial statements, this bid represents an offer to repurchase approximately 18% of the company's shares. Although the company offers to buy back the shares for a price between $6 and $7.50, not all shares tendered will be bought by the company. The company will start buying the cheapest shares and stop buying when it has acquired the 29 million shares that it set out to repurchase. Therefore, shareholders who tender their shares for sale at a higher price may find that the company has already purchased a sufficient number of shares at a lower price.

The reasons corporations purchase their outstanding share are varied. Some major reasons are:

1. **To increase earnings per share and return on equity.** By reducing shares outstanding and by reducing shareholders' equity, certain performance ratios such as EPS and return on equity are often enhanced.

OBJECTIVE 5

Identify the major reasons for repurchasing shares.

2. **To provide shares for employee share compensation contracts or to meet potential merger needs.** Honeywell Inc. reported that part of its purchase of one million common shares was to be used for employee share option contracts. Other companies acquire shares to have them available for business acquisitions.

3. **To thwart takeover attempts or to reduce the number of shareholders.** By reducing the number of shares held by the public, existing owners and managements can keep "outsiders" from gaining control or significant influence. When Ted Turner attempted to acquire CBS, CBS started a substantial buyback of its shares. Share purchases may also be used to eliminate dissident shareholders.

4. **To make a market in the share.** By purchasing shares in the marketplace, a demand is created that may stabilize the share price or, in fact, increase it. Over the period 1997–2001, Nexfor Inc., a large North American producer of building materials repurchased and cancelled 15.5 million shares for $122 million (representing 10% of the company's shares). The company commented that the shares were undervalued and represented a good deal.

5. **To return cash to shareholders.** In the Methanex example above, Pierre Choquette, President and CEO of Methanex commented, "These planned share repurchases are part of our commitment to return excess cash to shareholders. Our low-cost production facilities and leading market position combined with strong methanol pricing allowed us to generate almost US$400 million in cash from operations over the past year. Our cash balance is currently in excess of US$450 million and we have an undrawn US$291 million credit facility."

Some publicly held corporations have chosen to "go private;" that is, to eliminate public (outside) ownership entirely by purchasing their entire float of outstanding shares. Such a procedure is often accomplished through a **leveraged buyout (LBO)**, in which management or another employee group purchases the company shares and finances the purchase by using the company assets as collateral.

Once shares are reacquired, they may either be **retired** or held in the treasury for **reissue**. If not retired, such shares are referred to as **treasury shares**. Technically, a treasury share is a corporation's own share that has been reacquired after having been issued and fully paid. In Canada, the CBCA, with minor exceptions, requires that purchased shares be **cancelled** and, if the articles limit the number of authorized shares, be restored to the status of authorized but unissued shares. Some provincial jurisdictions allow

UNDERLYING CONCEPTS

When a company reacquires its shares, is this an **asset**? Treasury shares do not give the corporation the right to vote, to exercise preemptive rights as a shareholder, to receive cash dividends, or to receive assets upon corporate liquidation. Therefore, this is not an asset and is presented instead as a contra equity account.

treasury shares to exist; however, treasury shares are relatively uncommon in Canada.[13] In the U.S., many companies hold treasury shares.[14] As a result, Appendix 16A reviews briefly, the accounting for these shares.

Retirement of Reacquired Shares

OBJECTIVE 6
....

Explain the accounting procedures for reacquiring, retiring, and canceling shares.

When shares are purchased or redeemed by the issuing corporation, it is likely that the price paid will differ from the amount received for the shares when they are issued. As this is a **capital transaction**, any gains or losses are booked through equity (versus the income statement).

If the acquisition cost is greater than the original cost, then the acquisition cost should be allocated as follows:

(a) To **share capital**, in an amount equal to par, stated or assigned value of the shares;

(b) Any excess, to **contributed surplus**, to the extent that contributed surplus was created by a net excess of proceeds over cost on cancellation or resale of shares of the same class;

(c) Any excess, to **contributed surplus** in an amount equal to the pro-rata share of the portion of contributed surplus that arose from transactions, other than those in (b) above, in the same class of shares;

(d) Any excess, to **retained earnings.**[15]

If the acquisition cost is less than the original cost, then the acquisition cost should be allocated as follows:

(a) To **share capital**, in an amount equal to the par, stated, or assigned value of the shares;

(b) The difference, to **contributed surplus.**[16]

For shares with **no par value** (most shares in Canada), the assigned value is equal to the **average per share amount** in the account for that class of shares at the transaction date.[17] The difference between the stated or assigned value and the lower cost of acquisition is credited to contributed surplus and is seen as a contribution by the original shareholders that now accrues to the remaining shareholders.[18]

Applying the formulas noted above, in cases where the acquisition **cost is greater than the assigned cost**, this would normally result in debiting share capital (step (a)) and retained earnings (step (b)). Contributed Surplus would only be adjusted if there were a **prior balance** in the Contributed Surplus account that related to the shares being acquired.

To illustrate, assume that Cooke Corporation has the following in its' shareholders' equity accounts:

Share capital:	
Class A, 10,500 shares issued and outstanding	$ 63,000
Class B, 50,000 shares issued and outstanding	100,000
Total share capital	$163,000
Retained earnings	300,000
Total shareholders' equity	$463,000

[13] According to *Financial Reporting in Canada, 2000* (CICA; Toronto, 2000), out of 200 companies, only 3 reported treasury shares (p. 345).

[14] *Accounting Trends and Techniques*—1999 reported that out of 600 companies surveyed, 392 disclosed treasury share but none classified it as an asset.

[15] *CICA Handbook*, Section 3240, par. .15.

[16] *Ibid.*, par. .17.

[17] *Ibid.*, par. .18.

[18] *CICA Handbook*, Section 3240, par. .16.

On January 30, 2002, Cooke purchased and cancelled 500 Class A shares at a cost of $4 per share. The required entry is:

Class A Shares [500($63,000/10,500)]	3,000	
Cash		2,000
Contributed Surplus (1)		1,000

(1) Average per share amount (assigned value) = $63,000/10,500 = $6. Excess of assigned value over reacquisition cost = 6 − 4 = 2 per share for 500 shares.

On September 10, 2002, the company purchased and cancelled an additional 1,000 Class A shares. The purchase cost was $8 per share. The transaction is recorded as follows:

Class A shares [1,000($60,000/10,000)]	6,000	
Contributed Surplus (1)	1,000	
Retained Earnings	1,000	
Cash		8,000

(1) Equals the whole amount of the excess under step (b)

PREFERRED SHARES

Preferred shares are included in a special class of shares that is designated "preferred" because it possesses certain preferences or features not possessed by common shares.[19] The following features are those most often associated with preferred share issues: preference as to dividends, preference as to assets in the event of liquidation, convertible into common shares, callable/redeemable at the option of the corporation, and nonvoting.

The features that distinguish preferred from common share may be of a more restrictive and negative nature than preferences; for example, the preferred share may be nonvoting, noncumulative, and nonparticipating.

Preferred shares may be issued with a dividend preference being expressed as a **percentage of the par value or issue price**. Thus, holders of 8% preferred share issued at $100 are entitled to an annual dividend of $8 per share. This share is commonly referred to as 8% preferred share. In the case of no-par preferred share, a dividend preference is expressed as a **specific dollar amount** per share; for example, $7 per share. This share is commonly referred to as $7 preferred share. A preference as to dividends is not assurance that dividends will be paid; it is merely assurance that the stated dividend rate or amount applicable to the preferred share must be paid before any dividends can be paid on the common share.

Features of Preferred Shares

A corporation may attach whatever preferences or restrictions in whatever combination it desires to a preferred share issue so long as it does not specifically violate its incorporation law, and it may issue more than one class of preferred share. The most common features attributed to preferred share were noted above. Some of these as well as less common features are discussed in greater detail below.

> **OBJECTIVE 7**
> ····································
> Describe the major features of preferred shares.

1. **Cumulative Preferred Shares.** Dividends not paid in any year must be made up in a later year before any profits can be distributed to common shareholders. If the directors fail to declare a dividend at the normal date for dividend action, the dividend is said to have been "passed." Any passed dividend on cumulative preferred share constitutes a **dividend in arrears**. Because no liability exists until the board of directors declares a dividend, a dividend in arrears is **not recorded as a**

---

[19] Companies are issuing an increasing number of different classes of shares that have the attributes of both common and preferred shares. *Financial Reporting in Canada, 2000* (Toronto, CICA) defines preferred shares as shares with no voting rights and in its survey of 200 companies, found that 75 companies disclosed the presence of these shares.

liability but is disclosed in a note to the financial statements. (At common law, if the corporate charter is silent about the cumulative feature, the preferred share is considered cumulative.) Noncumulative preferred share is seldom issued because a passed dividend is lost forever to the preferred shareholder and so this share issue would be less marketable.

2. **Participating Preferred Shares.** Holders of **participating** preferred shares share ratably with the common shareholders in any profit distributions beyond the prescribed rate. That is, a 5% preferred share, if fully participating, will receive not only its 5% return, but also dividends at the same rates as those paid to common shareholders if amounts in excess of 5% of par or stated value are paid to common shareholders. Also, participating preferred shares may not always be **fully participating** as described, but partially participating. For example, provision may be made that 5% preferred share will be participating up to a maximum total rate of 10%, after which it ceases to participate in additional profit distributions; or 5% preferred share may participate only in additional profit distributions that are in excess of a 9% dividend rate on the common share. Participating preferreds are not used extensively.

3. **Convertible Preferred Shares.** The shareholders may at their option **exchange preferred shares for common shares** at a predetermined ratio. The convertible preferred shareholder not only enjoys a preferred claim on dividends but also has the option of converting into a common shareholder with unlimited participation in earnings.

4. **Callable/Redeemable Preferred Shares.** The issuing corporation can **"call"** or **redeem** at its option the outstanding preferred shares at specified future dates and at stipulated prices. Many preferred issues are callable. The call or redemption price is ordinarily set slightly above the original issuance price and is commonly stated in terms related to the par value. The callable feature permits the corporation to use the capital obtained through the issuance of such share until the need has passed or it is no longer advantageous. The existence of a call price or prices tends to set a ceiling on the market value of the preferred shares unless they are convertible into common shares. When a preferred share is called for redemption, any dividends in arrears must be paid.

5. **Retractable Preferred Shares.** The holder of the shares can **"put"** their shares to the company—normally with sufficient notice—and the company must pay the holder for the shares. The retraction option makes this instrument more attractive to the holder as it gives them more choice.

Preferred shares are often issued instead of debt because a company's debt-to-equity ratio has become too high. Issuances may also be made through **private placements**.[20]

Special Presentation Issues

Preferred shares generally have no maturity date, and therefore no legal **obligation** exists to pay the preferred shareholder. As a result, preferred shares have historically been classified as part of **shareholders' equity**. Recently, more and more issuances of preferred share have features that make the security more like a **debt instrument** (legal obligation to pay) than an **equity instrument**. For example, consider preferred shares with a mandatory redemption feature (**mandatorily redeemable/callable shares** or **term preferred shares**). These shares result in the shares being redeemed by the issuer within a prespecified time frame.

In these cases, the company has given to the holder a right to receive future company cash flows and the company has taken on the **obligation to deliver cash** (the

---

[20] The term "private placement" refers to a scenario whereby the shares are only offered privately to a select group of interested investors. In other words, they are not floated for sale on the stock exchange or markets. Private placements are often directed at large institutional or individual investors.

definition of a **financial liability**). Therefore, these types of instruments are presented as **debt** rather than equity and excluded from the shareholders' equity section.[21]

Retractable shares also create an issue since the **holder may require the company to repay the shares**. Thus the company may have to pay out cash or another financial asset and the definition of a financial liability may be met since the payout is beyond the control of the issuer.[22] Note that if the issuer has the option to settle in cash or common shares, the definition of a financial liability is no longer met (i.e., no obligation to pay cash) and the shares may be presented as equity.[23]

Compound financial instruments such as **convertible debt** also create presentation issues. These instruments are called "compound" because they have **both** a **debt** component and an **equity** component. These will be dealt with in Chapter 18.

UNDERLYING CONCEPTS

This is a good example of economic substance over legal form. The legal form of the instrument is that it is equity, i.e., preferred shares, yet the economic substance of the contract is that it creates a liability.

CONTRIBUTED SURPLUS

The term "surplus" is used in an accounting sense to designate the excess of net assets over the total paid-in par or stated value of a corporation's shares.[24] As previously mentioned, this surplus is further divided between "earned" surplus (retained earnings) and "contributed" surplus. Contributed surplus may be derived from a variety of transactions or events noted in Illustration 16-7.

OBJECTIVE 9

Identify items reported as contributed surplus.

ILLUSTRATION 16-7
Transactions that May Affect Contributed Surplus

- Par value shares—issue, retirement (see Appendix 16A)
- Capital donations
- No par shares—repurchase/retirement (see Appendix 16A)
- Liquidating dividends (Chapter 17)
- Financial reorganizations (Chapter 17)
- Stock rights and warrants (Chapter 18)
- Issue of convertible debt (Chapter 18)
- Share subscriptions forfeited

PRESENTATION AND DISCLOSURE

Preferred shares are generally reported as the first item in the shareholders' equity section of a company's balance sheet. **Common shares** are reported next, followed by **Contributed Surplus**. For Contributed Surplus, **only one amount need appear** to summarize all of the possible transactions. A subsidiary ledger or separate general ledger accounts may be kept of the different sources of additional paid-in capital.

Special **presentation** issues relating to preferred shares as well as reacquired shares have already been dealt with in this Chapter. Various **disclosures** are required under the *CICA Handbook*.[25] For example, basic disclosures include authorized share capital, issued share capital and changes in capital since the last balance sheet date. The following would normally be disclosed in note form:

1. Authorized number of shares or a statement noting that this is unlimited,
2. Existence of unique rights (e.g., dividend preference and amount of such dividends, redemption and/or retraction privileges, conversion rights, whether or not they are cumulative),

INTERNATIONAL INSIGHT

In Switzerland, there are no specific disclosure requirements for shareholders' equity. However, companies typically disclose separate categories of capital on the balance sheet.

OBJECTIVE 10

Identify the major disclosure requirements.

---

[21] According to *CICA Handbook*, Section 3860, par. .22, the existence of preferred shares that provide for **mandatory redemption** for a fixed or determinable amount at a fixed or determinable date or where the instrument gives the **holder the right to require the issuer to redeem the shares** after a particular date, for a fixed amount, create a liability. Shares that have terms that make redemption **highly likely or certain** may also create a liability.

[22] *CICA Handbook*, EIC Abstract 13 and Section 3860, par. A20.

[23] *CICA Handbook*, Section 3860, par. A20.

[24] *CICA Handbook*, Section 3250, par. .01.

[25] *CICA Handbook*, Section 3240, pars. .02 -.05.

3. Number of shares issued and amount received,

4. Whether par value or no par value,

5. Amount of any dividends in arrears, and

6. Details of changes during the year.

Section 3860 of the *Handbook* requires additional disclosures of any significant terms and conditions of equity instruments that might affect the amount timing and uncertainty of future cash flows.[26]

Presented below is the shareholders' equity section of **Teleglobe Inc.**

ILLUSTRATION 16-8
Shareholders' Equity Section

CONSOLIDATED FINANCIAL STATEMENTS TELEGLOBE INC.
Consolidated Balance Sheets (Note 2a)

Commitments and contingencies (Note 22)		
Shareholders' equity		
Preferred shares		
Third series, no par value, unlimited shares authorized, 5,000,000 issued and outstanding	81.3	81.3
Fourth series, no par value, 25,000,000 shares authorized, 4,000,000 issued and outstanding	100.0	—
Common shares		
Common shares, no par value, unlimited shares authorized, 255,219,489 issued at December 31, 2000 (253,819,044 at December 31, 1999)	3,956.7	3,941.0
Contributed surplus	1,764.0	—
Retained earnings (Deficit)	(340.7)	30.9
Loan receivable from an officer	—	(2.9)
Cumulative translation adjustment	(7.0)	9.4
	5,554.3	4,059.7
	8,802.1	6,585.7

SUMMARY OF LEARNING OBJECTIVES

1 Discuss the characteristics of the corporate form of organization. Among the specific characteristics of the corporate form that affect accounting are: (1) influence of corporate law; (2) use of the share capital system; (3) development of a variety of ownership interests; (4) limited liability of shareholders; and (5) formality of profit distribution.

2 Identify the rights of shareholders. In the absence of restrictive provisions, each share of share carries the following rights: (1) to share proportionately in profits and losses; (2) to share proportionately in management (the right to vote for directors); (3) to share proportionately in corporate assets upon liquidation. An additional right to share proportionately in any new issues of share of the same class (called the preemptive right), may also be attached to the share.

3 Explain the key components of shareholders' equity. Shareholders' or owners' equity is classified into two categories: contributed capital and earned capital. Contributed capital is composed of share capital and contributed surplus and is the amount advanced by shareholders to the corporation for use in the business. Earned capital (retained earnings) is the capital that develops if the business operates profitably; it consists of all undistributed income that remains invested in the enterprise.

4 Explain the accounting procedures for issuing shares. Accounts required to be kept for different types of shares are: (1) No-par share: common share or common share and contributed surplus, if stated value used. (2) Shares sold on a subscription basis: (a)

---

[26] *CICA Handbook*, Section 3860, par. .52.

KEY TERMS

common or preferred shares subscribed and (b) subscriptions receivable. For shares issued in combination with other securities (lump sum sales), there are two ways to allocate the issue price between securities: (a) the proportional method and (b) the incremental method. For shares issued in nonmonetary transactions the shares are recorded at the fair value of the shares issued or the fair market value of the noncash consideration received, if the latter is more clearly determinable.

5 Identify the major reasons for repurchasing shares. The reasons corporations purchase their outstanding share are varied. Some major reasons are: (1) to increase earnings per share and return on equity; (2) to provide shares for employee share compensation contracts or to meet potential merger needs; (3) to thwart takeover attempts or to reduce the number of shareholders; and (4) to make a market in the shares or (5) to return excess cash to shareholders.

6 Explain the accounting for reacquisition/retirement/cancellation of shares. If the acquisition cost of the shares is greater than the original cost, the difference is allocated to share capital, then contributed surplus, then retained earnings. If the cost is less, the cost is allocated to share capital (to stated or assigned cost) and to the contributed surplus.

7 Describe the major features of preferred shares. Preferred shares are a special class of share that possess certain preferences or features not possessed by the common share. The features that are most often associated with preferred share issues are: (1) preference as to dividends; (2) preference as to assets in the event of liquidation; (3) convertible into common shares; (4) callable/redeemable/retractable at the option of the corporation or holder; and (5) nonvoting. Other features exist such as participating dividends.

8 Distinguish between debt and equity. With the right combination of features (i.e., fixed return, no vote, redeemable), a preferred shareholder may possess more of the characteristics of a creditor than those of an owner. The shares' economic substance must be reviewed to determine whether they meet the definition of a financial liability.

9 Identify items reported as contributed surplus. Contributed surplus may be derived from share issue, repurchase, retirement/cancellation, capital donations, financial reorganizations, issue of stock rights or warrants, issuance of convertible debt, etc.

10 Identify the major disclosure requirements. Significant disclosures are required for shareholder's equity.

APPENDIX 16A

Both par value shares and treasury shares are not allowed under the CBCA. As mentioned in the chapter, however, these two are allowed under certain provincial business corporations acts and are prevalent in the United States. Therefore, these are discussed in greater detail in the Appendix.

Par Value Shares

The par value of a share has no relationship to its fair market value. At present, the par value associated with most capital share issuances is very low ($1, $5, $10).

> **OBJECTIVE 11**
> ....
> Explain accounting for par value shares.

To show the required information for issuance of par value share, accounts must be kept for each class of share as follows:

1. **Preferred or Common Shares.** Reflects the par value of the corporation's issued shares. These accounts are credited when the shares are originally issued. No additional entries are made in these accounts unless additional shares are issued or shares are retired.

2. **Contributed Surplus (Paid-in Capital in Excess of Par or Additional Paid-in Capital in the U.S.).** Indicates any excess over par value paid in by shareholders in return for the shares issued to them. Once paid in, the excess over par becomes a part of the corporation's paid-in capital, and the individual shareholder has no greater claim on the excess paid in than all other holders of the same class of shares.

To illustrate how these accounts are used, assume that Colonial Corporation sold, for $1,100, 100 shares of share with a par value of $5 per share. The entry to record the issuance is:

Cash	1,100	
Common Shares		500
Contributed Surplus		600

When the shares are repurchased and cancelled, the same procedure is followed as outlined in the body of the chapter.

Treasury Shares

OBJECTIVE 12

Explain accounting for treasury shares.

Treasury shares occur when a company repurchases its own shares but does not cancel them. As previously mentioned, this is not allowed under the CBCA, however, it is allowed in the U.S. and in certain provinces and therefore will be covered briefly here. Treasury shares may be resold. The *CICA Handbook* notes that the single transaction method should be used to account for treasury shares. The method treats the repurchase and resale as a single transaction. In essence, the repurchase of treasury shares is the initiation of a transaction that is consummated when shares are resold. Consequently, the holding of treasury shares is viewed as a transition phase between the beginning and end of a single activity.

When shares are purchased, the total cost is debited to Treasury Shares on the balance sheet. This account is shown as a deduction from the total of the components of shareholders' equity in the balance sheet. An example of such disclosure follows:

ILLUSTRATION 16A–1

Treasury Share presentation

Shareholders' equity:	
Common shares, no par value; authorized 24,000,000	
Shares; issued 19,045,870 shares, of which 209,750	
are in treasury	$ 27,686,000
Retained earnings	253,265,000
	$280,951,000
Less: Cost of treasury shares	(7,527,000)
Total shareholders' equity	$273,424,000

When the shares are sold, the Treasury Shares account is credited for their cost. If they are sold at more than their cost, the excess is credited to Contributed Surplus. If they are sold at less, the difference is debited to Contributed Surplus (if related to the same class of shares) and then to Retained Earnings. If the shares are subsequently retired, the journal entries as noted in the body of the chapter would be followed.

SUMMARY OF LEARNING OBJECTIVES FOR APPENDIX 16A

11 Explain accounting for par value shares. These shares may only be valued at par value in the common or preferred share accounts. The excess goes to contributed surplus. On repurchase/cancellation, par value is removed from the common or preferred share accounts with the excess or deficit being booked to contributed surplus or retained earnings as discussed for no par shares.

12 Explain accounting for treasury shares. Treasury shares occur when a company repurchases its own shares and does not cancel or retire them at the same time, i.e., they remain outstanding. The single-transaction method is used when Treasury Shares are purchased. This method treats the purchase and subsequent resale or cancellation as part of the same transaction.

Note: All asterisked Brief Exercises, Exercises, Problems, and Conceptual Cases relate to material contained in the appendix to the chapter.

BRIEF EXERCISES

BE16-1 Viking Corporation issued 300 common shares for $4,100. Prepare the journal entry for the share issue.

*BE16-2 Turbo Inc. issued 200 shares of $5 par value common shares for $1,050. Prepare the journal entry for the share issue.

*BE16-3 Shinobi Limited issued 600 shares of no par value common shares for $10,200. Prepare Shinobi's journal entry if (a) the stock has no par value, and (b) the stock has a par value of $2 per share.

BE16-4 Rambo Inc. sells 300 common shares on a subscription basis at $45 per share. On June 1, Rambo accepts a 40% down payment. On December 1, Rambo collects the remaining 60% and issues the shares. Prepare the company's journal entries.

BE16-5 Lufia Corporation has the following account balances at December 31, 2001:

Common shares subscribed	$ 180,000
Common shares, no par value	210,000
Subscriptions receivable	90,000
Retained earnings	2,340,000
Contributed Surplus	1,320,000

Prepare the December 31, 2001 shareholders' equity section.

BE16-6 Primal Corporation issued 300 no par value common shares and 100 preferred shares for a lump sum of $14,200. The common shares have a market value of $20 per share, and the preferred shares have a market value of $90 per share. Prepare the journal entry to record the issuance.

BE16-7 On February 1, 2001, Ang Corporation issued 2,000 common shares for land worth $31,000. Prepare the February 1, 2001, journal entry.

BE16-8 Powerdrive Corporation issued 2,000 shares of its common shares for $70,000. The company also incurred $1,500 of costs associated with issuing the shares. Prepare the journal entry to record the issuance of the company's share.

BE16-9 Maverick Inc. has 10,000 common shares outstanding. The shares have an average cost of $10 per share. On July 1, 2001, Maverick reacquired 100 shares at $85 per share and retired them. Prepare journal entries to record these transactions.

BE16-10 Rangers Corporation has 20,000 common shares outstanding with an average value of $5. On August 1, 2001, the company reacquired and cancelled 200 shares at $75 per share. Contributed Surplus of $5 per share existed at the time of the reacquisition. Prepare the journal entries to record these transactions.

*BE16-11 Nene Inc. is holding 500 shares of its own common shares as treasury stock. The shares were originally issued at $13 per share and were reacquired at $14 per share. Prepare the necessary journal entry if Mickey Mouse formally retires the treasury share.

BE16-12 Peso Corporation issued 450 preferred shares for $61,500. Prepare the required journal entry to record the issue.

EXERCISES

E16-1 (Recording the Issuances of Common Shares) During its first year of operation, Moylan Corporation had the following transactions pertaining to its common share.

Jan.	10	Issued 80,000 shares for cash at $6 per share.
Mar.	1	Issued 5,000 shares to lawyers in payment of a bill for $35,000 for services rendered in helping the company to incorporate.
July	1	Issued 30,000 shares for cash at $8 per share.
Sept.	1	Issued 60,000 shares for cash at $10 per share.

Instructions
(a) Prepare the journal entries for these transactions.
(b) Calculate the average share value.

E16-2 (Recording the Issuance of Common and Preferred Share) Battle Corporation was organized on January 1, 2001. It is authorized to issue 10,000 preferred shares with an $8 dividend, and 500,000 common shares. The following share transactions were completed during the first year.

Jan.	10	Issued 80,000 common shares for cash at $5 per share.
Mar.	1	Issued 5,000 preferred shares for cash at $108 per share.
Apr.	1	Issued 24,000 common shares for land. The land's asking price was $90,000; its fair value of the land was $80,000.
May	1	Issued 80,000 common shares for cash at $7 per share.
Aug.	1	Issued 10,000 common shares to lawyers in payment of their bill of $50,000 for services rendered in helping the company organize.
Sept.	1	Issued 10,000 common shares for cash at $9 per share.
Nov.	1	Issued 1,000 preferred shares for cash at $112 per share.

Instructions
Prepare the journal entries to record the above transactions.

E16-3 (Subscribed Shares) Galway Inc. intends to sell shares to raise additional capital to allow for expansion in the rapidly growing service industry. The corporation decides to sell these shares through a subscription basis and publicly notifies the investment world. 30,000 shares are offered at $25 a share. The terms of the subscription are 40% down and the balance at the end of six months. All shares are subscribed for during the offering period.

Instructions
Give the journal entry for the original subscription, the collection of the down payments, the collection of the balance of the subscription price, and the issuance of the shares.

E16-4 (Shares Issued for Nonmonetary Assets) Hill Products, Inc., was formed to operate a manufacturing plant in Brockville. The events for the formation of the corporation include the following:
1. 5,000 common shares were issued to investors at $22 per share.
2. 8,000 shares were issued to acquire used equipment that has a net book value to the seller of $140,000.

Instructions
Prepare journal entries for the transactions above.

E16-5 (Shares Issued for Land)   Twenty-five thousand shares were exchanged for undeveloped land that has an appraised value of $1.7 million. At the time of the exchange, the common share was trading at $62 per share on an organized exchange.

Instructions

   (a) Briefly identify the possible alternatives (including those that are totally (unacceptable) for quantifying the cost of the land and briefly support your choice.
   (b) Select the most appropriate alternative and prepare the journal entry.

E16-6 (Lump Sum Sale of Share with Bonds)   Li Corporation is a regional company that is an OSC registrant. The corporation's securities are thinly traded through CDNX. Recently, Li has issued 10,000 units. Each unit consists of a $500 par, 12% subordinated debenture and 10 common shares. The investment banker has retained 400 units as the underwriting fee. The other 9,600 units were sold to outside investors for cash at $880 per unit. Prior to this sale the two-week ask price of common shares was $40 per share. Twelve percent is a reasonable market yield for the debentures.

Instructions

   (a) Prepare the journal entry to record the transaction above:
      1. employing the incremental method assuming the interest rate on the debentures is the best market measure.
      2. employing the proportional method using the recent price quotes on the common share.
   (b) Briefly explain which method is, in your opinion, the better method.

E16-7 (Lump Sum Sales of Common Shares with Preferred Shares)   Dotto Inc. issues 500 common shares and 100 preferred shares for a lump sum of $100,000.

Instructions

   (a) Prepare the journal entry for the issuance when the market value of the common shares is $165 each and market value of the preferred is $230 each.
   (b) Prepare the journal entry for the issuance when only the market value of the common share is known and it is $170 per share.

E16-8 (Lump Sum Sale of Common Shares with Preferreds)   Lauper Limited was organized with 50,000 shares of 9% preferred shares and 100,000 shares of common shares without par value. During the first year, 1,000 shares of preferred and 1,000 shares of common were issued for a lump sum price of $180,000.

Instructions

What entry should be made to record this transaction under each of the following independent conditions?
   (a) Shortly after the transaction described above, 500 shares of preferred shares were sold at $116.
   (b) The directors have established a stated value of $75 a share for the common shares.
   (c) At the date of issuance, the preferred shares had a market price of $140 per share and the common shares had a market price of $40 per share.

E16-9 (Share Issuances and Repurchase)   Kao Corporation is authorized to issue 50,000 shares of common shares. During 2001, the company took part in the following selected transactions:
   1. Issued 5,000 shares at $45 per share, less costs related to the issuance of the shares totalling $7,000.
   2. Issued 1,000 shares for land appraised at $50,000. The shares were actively traded on a national stock exchange at approximately $46 per share on the date of issuance.
   3. Purchased and retired 500 of the company's shares at $43 per share. The shares purchased were originally issued in 2000 at $40 per share.

Instructions

   (a) Prepare a journal entry to record item 1.
   (b) Prepare a journal entry to record item 2.
   (c) Prepare a journal entry to record item 3.

E16-10 (Shares Reacquired and Retired) Dumars Corp. has outstanding 40,000 common shares, which had been issued at $30 per share. The company repurchased 5,000 shares at $45 per share. At year end, the shares were still outstanding.

Instructions

Use the following code to indicate the effect each transaction has on the financial statement categories listed in the table below. (I = Increase; D = Decrease; NE = No effect). Explain your reasoning for each financial statement element.

Assets	Liabilities	Shareholders' Equity	Contributed Surplus	Retained Earnings	Net Income

E16-11 (Preferred Share Entries and Dividends) Dumering Corporation has 10,000 preferred shares (which pay an $8 dividend per share) and 50,000 common shares outstanding at December 31, 2001.

Instructions

Answer the questions in each of the following independent situations.

(a) If the preferred shares are cumulative and dividends were last paid on the preferred shares on December 31, 1998, what are the dividends in arrears that should be reported on the December 31, 2001, balance sheet? How should these dividends be reported?

(b) If the preferred shares are convertible into seven common shares and 4,000 shares are converted, what entry is required for the conversion, assuming the preferred shares were issued for $100 each?

(c) If the preferred shares were issued at $107 per share, how should the preferred shares be reported in the shareholders' equity section?

*E16-12 (Shareholders' Equity Section) Radler Corporation's charter authorized 100,000 shares of $10 par value common shares, and 30,000 shares of 6% cumulative and nonparticipating preferred shares, par value $100 per share. The corporation engaged in the following share transactions through December 31, 2001: 30,000 common shares were issued for $350,000 and 12,000 preferred shares were issued for machinery valued at $1,475,000. Subscriptions for 4,500 common shares have been taken, and 40% of the subscription price of $16 per share has been collected. The shares will be issued upon collection of the subscription price in full. 1,000 common shares have been purchased for $15 and retired. The Retained Earnings balance is $180,000.

Instructions

Prepare the shareholders' equity section of the balance sheet in good form.

E16-13 (Correcting Entries for Equity Transactions) Rae Inc. recently hired a new accountant with extensive experience in accounting for partnerships. Because of the pressure of the new job, the accountant was unable to review what he had learned earlier about corporation accounting. During the first month, he made the following entries for the corporation's capital shares.

May	2	Cash	192,000	
		Common Shares		192,000
		(Issued 12,000 common shares at $16 per share)		
	10	Cash	600,000	
		Common Shares		600,000
		(Issued 10,000 preferred shares at $60 per share)		
	15	Common Shares	15,000	
		Cash		15,000
		(Purchased and retired 1,000 common shares at $15 per share)		
	31	Cash	8,500	
		Common Shares		5,000
		Gain on Sale of Shares		3,500
		(Issued 500 shares at $17 per share)		

Instructions

On the basis of the explanation for each entry, prepare the entries that should have been made for the capital share transactions. Explain your reasoning.

*E16-14 **(Analysis of Equity Data and Equity Section Preparation)** For a recent two-year period, the balance sheet of Santana Corp. showed the following shareholders' equity data in millions.

	2002	2001
Contributed Surplus	$ 931	$ 817
Common shares—par value	545	540
Retained earnings	7,167	5,226
Treasury share	(1,564)	(918)
Total shareholders' equity	$7,079	$5,665
Common share shares issued	218	216
Common share shares authorized	500	500
Treasury shares	34	27

Instructions
(a) Answer the following questions.
  1. What is the par value of the common share?
  2. Was the cost per share of acquiring treasury share higher in 2002 or in 2001?
(b) Prepare the shareholders' equity section for 2002.

PROBLEMS

P16-1 Nells Corp. had the following shareholders' equity on January 1, 2002.

Common shares, 200,000 shares authorized, 100,000 shares issued and outstanding,	$ 200,000
Contributed Surplus	2,300,000
Retained earnings	1,800,000
Total shareholders' equity	$4,300,000

The following transactions occurred, in the order given, during 2002:
  1. Subscriptions were sold for 10,000 common shares at $28 per share. The first payment was for $13 per share.
  2. The second payment was for $15 per share. All payments were received on the second payment except for 1,000 shares.
  3. Per the subscription contract, which requires that defaulting subscribers have all their payments refunded, the company sends a refund cheque to the defaulting subscribers. At this point, common shares are issued to subscribers that have fully paid on the contract.
  4. 10,000 common were repurchased at $20 per share. They were then retired.
  5. 2,000 preferred shares and 3,000 common shares were sold together for $290,000. The common shares had a market value of $27 per share.

Instructions
Prepare the journal entries to record the transactions for the company for 2002.

P16-2 On January 5, 2001, Drabek Corporation received a charter granting the right to issue 5,000 shares of cumulative and non-participating preferred shares carrying an $8 dividend and 50,000 common shares. It then completed these transactions:

Jan.	11	Accepted subscriptions to 20,000 common shares at $16 per share; 40% down payments accompanied the subscription.
Feb.	1	Issued 4,000 preferred shares for the following assets: machinery with a fair value of $50,000; a factory building with a fair value of $110,000; and land with an appraised value of $270,000.
Apr.	15	Collected the balance of the subscription price on the common shares and issued the shares.
July	29	Repurchased 1,800 common shares at $19 per share.
Dec.	31	Declared a $0.25 per share cash dividend on the common shares and declared the preferred dividend.
Dec.	31	Closed the Income Summary account. Net Income was $175,700.

Instructions
(a) Record the journal entries for the transactions listed above.
(b) Prepare the shareholders' equity section of the balance sheet as of December 31, 2001.

P16-3 Amado Limited has two classes of shares outstanding: preferred ($5 dividend) and common. At December 31, 2001, the following accounts were included in shareholders' equity:

Preferred Shares, 150,000 shares issued (authorized, 1 million shares)	$ 3,000,000
Common Shares, 2,000,000 shares (authorized, unlimited)	10,000,000
Contributed Surplus—Preferred	200,000
Contributed Surplus—Common	27,000,000
Retained Earnings	4,500,000

The following transactions affected shareholders' equity during 2002:

Jan.	1	25,000 preferred shares issued at $22 per share.
Feb.	1	40,000 common shares issued at $20 per share.
June	1	2-for-1 stock split (common shares).
July	1	30,000 common shares purchased and retired at $9 per share.
Dec.	31	Net income is $2,100,000.
Dec.	31	The preferred dividend is declared, and a common dividend of 50¢ per share is declared.

Instructions

Prepare the shareholders' equity section for the company at December 31, 2002. Show all supporting calculations.

P16-4 Shikai Corporation's charter authorized issuance of 100,000 common shares and 50,000 preferred shares. The following transactions involving the issuance of shares were completed. Each transaction is independent of the others.

1. Issued a $10,000, 9% bond payable at par and gave as a bonus one preferred share, which at that time was selling for $106 a share.
2. Issued 500 common shares for machinery. The machinery had been appraised at $7,100; the seller's book value was $6,200. The common shares' most recent market price is $15 a share.
3. Voted a $10 dividend on both the 10,000 shares of outstanding common and the 1,000 shares of outstanding preferred. The dividend was paid in full.
4. Issued 375 shares of common and 100 shares of preferred for a lump sum amounting to $11,300. The common had been selling at $14 and the preferred at $65.
5. Issued 200 shares of common and 50 shares of preferred for furniture and fixtures. The common had a fair market value of $16 per share and the furniture and fixtures were appraised at $6,200.

Instructions

Record the transactions listed above in journal entry form.

P16-5 Before Polska Corporation engages in the share transactions listed below, its general ledger reflects, among others, the following account balances (average cost of its share is $30 per share). The Contributed Surplus relates to the common shares.

Contributed Surplus	Common Shares	Retained Earnings
Balance $9,000	Balance $270,000	Balance $80,000

Instructions

Record the journal entries for the transactions noted below:

(a) Bought and cancelled 380 shares at $39 per share.
(b) Bought and cancelled 300 shares at $43 per share.
(c) Sold 3,500 shares at $42 per share.
(d) Sold 1,200 shares at $48 per share.
(e) Bought and cancelled 1,000 shares at $60.

*P16-6 Alberta Inc. is a closely held toy manufacturer. You have been engaged as the independent public accountant to perform the first audit of Alberta. It is agreed that only current-year (2002) financial statements will be audited.

The following shareholders' equity information has been developed from Alberta records on December 31, 2001:

Common shares, no par value; no stated value;	
authorized 30,000 shares; issued 9,000 shares	$405,000
Retained earnings	180,000

The following share transactions took place during 2002:

1. On March 15, Alberta issued 7,000 common shares for $63 per share.
2. On March 31, Alberta reacquired 4,000 common shares from (Alberta's founding shareholder) for $74 per share. These shares were cancelled and retired upon receipt.

For the year 2002, Alberta reported net income of $125,000.

Instructions

(a) How should the shareholders' equity information be reported in the Indiana financial statements for the year ended December 31, 2002?
(b) How would your answer in part (a) have been altered if Alberta had treated the reacquired shares as treasury shares carried at cost rather than retired?

*P16-7 Heinrich Corporation had the following shareholders' equity at January 1, 2002:

Preferred shares, 8%, $100 par value, 10,000 shares authorized,	
4,000 shares issued	$ 400,000
Common shares, $2 par value, 200,000 shares authorized,	
80,000 shares issued	160,000
Common shares subscribed, 10,000 shares	20,000
Contributed Surplus—preferred	20,000
Contributed Surplus—common	940,000
Retained earnings	780,000
	2,320,000
Less: Common share subscriptions receivable	40,000
Total shareholders' equity	$2,280,000

During 2002, the following transactions occurred:

1. 100 shares of common share were exchanged for equipment. The share's market value on the exchange date was $12 per share.
2. 1,000 shares of common share and 100 shares of preferred share were sold for the lump sum price of $24,500. The common shares had a market price of $14 at the time of the sale.
3. 2,000 shares of preferred share were sold for cash at $102 per share.
4. All of the subscribers paid their subscription prices into the firm.
5. The common shares were issued.
6. 1,000 common shares were repurchased and retired by the corporation at $15 per share.
7. Income for 2002 was $246,000.

Instructions

Prepare the shareholder's equity section for the company as of December 31, 2002. (The use of T accounts may help you organize the material.)

*P16-8 Constantine Corp. has the following owners' equity accounts at December 31, 2000:

Common Shares—authorized 8,000 shares (issued, 4800 shares)	$480,000
Retained Earnings	294,000

Instructions

(a) Prepare entries in journal form to record the following transactions, which took place during 2001.
   1. 240 shares were purchased for $97 each.
   2. A $20 per share cash dividend was declared.
   3. The dividend declared in No. 2 above was paid.
   4. The treasury shares purchased in No. 1 above were retired.
   5. 500 shares were purchased at 103 and retired.
   6. 120 shares were purchased at 106 and retired.
(b) Prepare the shareholders' equity section of the company's balance sheet after giving effect to these transactions, assuming that the net income for 2001 was $94,000.

P16-9 The following information relates to Altoona Industries, Inc.

ALTOONA INDUSTRIES, INC.

	2002	2001
	($000)	
Series A first preferred share—subject to mandatory redemption ($4,062,000 liquidation value in 2002 and 2001); authorized 100,000 shares; issued 40,625 shares in 2002 and 2001 (note 6)	$ 4,062	$ 4,062
Common shareholders' equity:		
Common shares, authorized 20,000,000 shares; issued 5,522,602 shares in 2002 and 5,280,602 in 2001	552	528
Contributed Surplus	10,463	6,014
Retained earnings	25,286	17,110
Common shareholders' equity	36,301	23,652

Notes to Consolidated Financial Statements

Note 6: Redeemable Preferred Shares. The Company's preferred shares consist of 250,000 authorized shares of First Preferred Shares of which 40,620 shares of Series A First Preferred Shares were outstanding at December 31, 2002. The Series A First Preferred Shares, which are not convertible, have a carrying value of $80.00 per share representing fair value at date of issuance based upon an independent appraisal and sales to third parties. The shares are entitled to cumulative dividends of $12.70 annually ($3.175 per quarter) per share and must be redeemed at 10% per year commencing on December 31, 2005 at $100.00 per share plus accrued and unpaid dividends. The Company, at its option, may redeem at that price in each year in which mandatory redemption is required an additional number of shares not exceeding the mandatory redemption and may redeem all or any part of the shares at that price plus a premium amounting to $3.55 in 2003 and declining proportionately thereafter through 2011, after which there will be no premium.

Altoona had total debt of $85,979 in 2002. A restrictive covenant on some of the debt prohibits Altoona from additional borrowing if the debt/equity ratio exceeds 2.5 or if retained earnings falls below $17,000.

Instructions

Prepare responses to the following questions based on the above information.

   (a) Do the Series A preferred shares have characteristics more like common share or like debt? Explain.
   (b) What are the present GAAP requirements for redeemable preferred share?
   (c) Is Altoona in violation of its debt covenants in 2002, based upon the reported numbers above? Would your answer change if Altoona classifies the redeemable share as debt?

P16-10 Transactions of Kalila Corporation are as follows:

   1. The company is granted a charter that authorizes issuance of 15,000 preferred shares and 15,000 common shares without par value.
   2. 8,000 common shares are issued to founders of the corporation for land valued by the board of directors at $210,000.
   3. 4,200 preferred shares are sold for cash at $110 each.
   4. 600 common shares are sold to an officer of the corporation for $42 a share.
   5. 300 shares of outstanding preferred share are repurchased and cancelled for cash at $100 each.
   6. 400 preferred shares are repurchased and cancelled for cash at $98 each.
   7. 500 shares of the outstanding common share issued in No. 2 above are repurchased and cancelled at $49 a share.
   8. 2,100 preferred shares are issued at $99 each.

Instructions

   (a) Prepare entries in journal form to record the transactions listed above. No other transactions affecting the capital share accounts have occurred.
   (b) Assuming that the company has retained earnings from operations of $132,000, prepare the shareholders' equity section of its balance sheet after considering all the transactions given.

CONCEPTUAL CASES

....

C16-1 Alvarado Computer Corporation is a small, closely held corporation. Alan Alvarado, President, holds 80% of the shares. Of the remainder, 10% is held by members of his family and 10% by Shaunda Janietsky, a former officer who is now retired. The company's balance sheet at June 30, 2001 was substantially as shown below:

Assets		Liabilities and Shareholders' Equity	
Cash	$ 22,000	Current liabilities	$ 50,000
Other	450,000	Common shares	250,000
	$472,000	Retained earnings	172,000
			$472,000

Additional authorized capital share had never been issued. To strengthen its cash position, the company issued common shares for $100,000 cash to Alan. At the next shareholders' meeting, Janietsky objected and claimed that her interests had been injured.

Instructions

(a) Which shareholder's right was ignored in the issue of shares to Alan Alvarado?

(b) How may the damage to Janietsky's interests be repaired most simply?

(c) If Alan offered Janietsky a personal cash settlement and they agreed to employ you as an impartial arbitrator to determine the amount, what settlement would you propose? Present your calculations with sufficient explanation to satisfy both parties.

C16-2 Algonquin Corporation sold 50,000 common shares on a subscription basis for $40 per share. By December 31, 2001, collections on these subscriptions totalled $1.3 million. No subscriptions have yet been paid in full.

Instructions

(a) Discuss the meaning of the account Common Share Subscribed and indicate how it is reported in the financial statements.

(b) Discuss the arguments in favour of reporting Subscriptions Receivable as a current asset.

(c) Discuss the arguments in favour of reporting Subscriptions Receivable as a contra equity account.

(d) Indicate how these 50,000 shares would be presented on Algonquin's December 31, 2001 balance sheet under the method discussed in (c) above.

C16-3 Haida Corporation is planning to issue 3,000 common shares for two hectares of land to be used as a building site.

Instructions
Discuss any financial reporting issues.

C16-4 Iroquois Corporation purchased $175,000 worth of equipment in 2002 for $100,000 cash and a promise to deliver an indeterminate number of common shares, with a market value of $25,000 on January 1 of each year for the next 4 years. Hence $100,000 in "market value" of shares will be required to discharge the $75,000 balance due on the equipment.

Instructions
Discuss any financial reporting issues.

C16-5 It has been said that (1) the use of the LIFO inventory method during an extended period of rising prices and (2) the expensing of all human resource costs are among the accepted accounting practices that help create "secret reserves."

Instructions
Discuss.

C16-6 The following is an excerpt from a press release issued by **BC Gas Utility Ltd.** regarding 7.10% Cumulative, Redeemable, Retractable First Preference Shares:

> The Directors of BC Gas Utility Ltd. have declared a quarterly dividend of $0.44375 (Canadian) per share on the issued and outstanding 7.10% Cumulative Redeemable Retractable First Preference Shares of BC Gas Utility Ltd. payable on the 30th day of September, 1999 to Shareholders of record at the close of business on the 15th day of September, 1999.
>
> BC Gas Utility Ltd. also announced that, pursuant to the terms of the 7.10% Cumulative Redeemable Retractable First Preference Shares, it is redeeming all of the 3,000,000 issued and outstanding 7.10% First Preference Shares on September 30,1999 at a price of $25.00 per share.

The following is an excerpt from the notes to the financial statements:

NOTE 3 CAPITAL STOCK
6.32% Cumulative Redeemable First Preference Shares
These shares are redeemable at the option of the Company at $25 per share on or after October 31, 2000, and are exchangeable at the option of the Company on or after October 31, 2000 for common shares of the Company's parent, BC Gas Inc., at a price equal to the greater of $3 and 95% of the weighted average trading price of the common shares at that time.

The shares are exchangeable at the option of the holder on or after January 31, 2001 for common shares of BC Gas Inc. at a price equal to the greater of $3 and 95% of the weighted average trading price of the common shares at that time, subject to the right of the Company to redeem the shares for cash or to find substitute purchasers for the preference shares.

Instructions
Discuss any financial reporting issues, relating to the 6.32% and 7.10% shares.

C16-7 The following is a copy of a press release from **Imperial Ginseng Products Limited**:

Private Placement of Preferred Shares
Imperial Ginseng Products Ltd. ("Imperial" or the "Company") has completed, subject to regulatory approval, a private placement of Preferred Shares in the amount of $163,000, pursuant to the Confidential Offering Memorandum of Imperial dated January 25, 1999 and amended March 25, 1999. The Offering Memorandum provides for the issuance, including any conversion of bonds, of up to $20 million of Preferred Shares.

Terms of the Preferred Shares
The Preferred Shares are units consisting of Class "A" Preferred Shares of Imperial and Royalty Participation Units. The total of 163,000 Class "A" Preferred Shares are non-voting, convertible shares issued with an average dividend rate of approximately 12.5% at a price of $1 per share. The Class "A" Preferred Shares are convertible to common shares of the Company at a price of $1.53 per common share, with such conversion price increasing at $0.25 per common share on January 31 of each year starting January 31, 2000. Common shares of Imperial issued as a result of any conversion of the Preferred Shares would be subject to a one-year hold period expiring June 30, 2000.

The 163,000 Royalty Participation Units issued as part of the units, on a one for one basis with the Class "A" Preferred Shares, carry a royalty entitlement consisting of the proceeds from one-half acre of ginseng from each of the 2003, 2004, 2005, and 2006 harvests per 1 million Royalty Participation Units.

The Preferred Shares, subject to certain restrictions and penalties are, after December 31, 1999, retractable at the option of the holder and are redeemable by Imperial. Dividends on the Class "A" Preferred Shares are cumulative and, like the royalty due on the Royalty Participation Units, can be paid, at the option of Imperial, in cash or common shares of Imperial priced at their then current price.

Imperial will pay a commission of 8% as well as other fees on the conversion and private placement and will reimburse management and administrative costs for services with respect to this private placement and conversions to Preferred Shares.

Imperial trades on the Vancouver Stock Exchange Senior Board under the symbol IGP and on NASDAQ's OTC Bulletin Board.

Instructions
Discuss any financial reporting issues.

Using Your Judgement

FINANCIAL REPORTING PROBLEM 1:
CANADIAN TIRE CORPORATION, LIMITED

Instructions
Refer to the financial statements and accompanying notes and discussion of **Canadian Tire Corporation, Limited** presented in Appendix 5B and answer the following questions.

(a) What percentage of the company's authorized common and Class A shares are issued and outstanding?

(b) What was the average issue price of the Class A shares during 2000?

(c) Read the MDA and determine to whom the company is issuing new Class A shares. How is this furthering the success of their business? How many shares were issued and what was the issue cost?

(d) The company has repurchased a significant number of Class A shares this year and last. What is the purpose of repurchasing these shares? How many shares were repurchased and what was the repurchase price?

(e) During 1999, the company changed its accounting policy for accounting for repurchased shares. Review the *Handbook* requirements and assess GAAP compliance.

FINANCIAL REPORTING PROBLEM 2:
AON CORPORATION

The following is an excerpt from the financial statements of **Aon Corporation**, an insurance company:

Redeemable Preferred Stock
At December 31, 2000, 1 million shares of redeemable preferred stock are outstanding. Dividends are cumulative at an annual rate of $2.55 per share. The shares of redeemable preferred stock will be redeemable at the option of Aon or the holders, in whole or in part, at $50.00 per share beginning one year after the occurrence of certain future events.

Capital Securities
In January 1997, Aon created Aon Capital A, a wholly-owned statutory business trust, for the purpose of issuing mandatorily redeemable preferred capital securities (Capital Securities). The sole asset of Aon Capital A is an $824 million aggregate principal amount of Aon's 8.205% Junior Subordinated Deferrable Interest Debentures due January 1, 2027. The back-up guarantees, in the aggregate, provide a full and unconditional guarantee of the Trust's obligations under the Capital Securities.

Aon Capital A issued $800 million of 8.205% capital securities in January 1997. The proceeds from the issuance of the Capital Securities were used to finance a portion of the A&A acquisition. The Capital Securities are subject to mandatory redemption on January 1, 2027 or are redeemable in whole, but not in part, at the option of Aon upon the occurrence of certain events. Interest is payable semi-annually on the Capital Securities. The Capital Securities are categorized in the consolidated statements of financial position as "Company-Obligated Mandatorily Redeemable Preferred Capital Securities of Subsidiary Trust Holding Solely the Company's Junior Subordinated Debentures." The after-tax interest incurred on the Capital Securities is reported as minority interest in the consolidated statements of income.

Instructions:
Discuss any financial reporting issues.

(NB—the shares are presented between liabilities and shareholders' equity as a separate line item).

FINANCIAL REPORTING PROBLEM 3: HUDSON'S BAY COMPANY

The **Hudson's Bay Company** financial statements may be found on the Digital Tool. Note 13 of the statements discusses specific instruments issued by the company called Equity Subordinated Debentures. These instruments are presented as equity on the balance sheet.

Instructions

Discuss the financial reporting issues relating to these instruments.

FINANCIAL STATEMENT ANALYSIS CASE

Hudson's Bay Company

The **Hudson's Bay Company** 2001 financial statements may be found on the Digital Tool.

Instructions

(a) The company had numerous share transactions over the past two years. In both years, the company repurchased shares under normal course issuer bids. Calculate the average price per share for the years ended 1999, 2000, and 2001.

(b) Recreate the journal entry required to repurchase and cancel the shares in 1999 and 2000. What price were the shares repurchased at?

(c) Explain how earnings per share might be affected by these repurchase transactions.

(d) What percentage of Contributed Surplus was created by these two transactions?

COMPARATIVE ANALYSIS CASE

Bank of Montreal versus Royal Bank of Canada

The **Bank of Montreal** and **Royal Bank of Canada** financial statements may be found on the Digital Tool.

Instructions

Go to the Digital Tool and, using the information found there for these companies, answer the following questions.

(a) What is the average cost of the respective company common shares? Compare with market prices.

(b) What is the authorized share capital of each company?

(c) Comment on the different presentations afforded common shares and shareholders' equity by each company.

(d) Describe the changes in the respective companies' common share accounts (number of shares and price) over the past three years. What is the general trend? What types of activities are contributing to the change?

RESEARCH CASES

Case 1

Instructions

Use SEDAR to obtain the most recent proxy statement (Management Proxy—Information Circular) for Air Canada.

(a) On what matters are the shareholders being asked to vote?

(b) Where is the annual meeting being held? Must a shareholder attend the annual meeting in order to vote?

(c) For each of the matters up for vote, what information is included in the proxy statement to aid shareholders in making their decisions?

(d) The proxy statement is generally the best source for identifying how company management is compensated. Examine the executive compensation section of the proxy statement and list the types of compensation received.

Case 2

The September 4, 1995, issue of *Fortune* includes an article by Richard D. Hylton entitled "Share Buybacks Are Hot—Here's How You Can Cash In."

Instructions

Read the article and answer the following questions.

(a) What was the total amount of announced intentions to repurchase shares of share in 1994? What was this figure during the first six months of 1995?

(b) The goal of many of these repurchase programs was to increase the price of the remaining outstanding shares. Identify the three factors that will determine the impact of repurchases on share price.

(c) What did Microsoft do with the shares it repurchased? Why might they use repurchased shares for this purpose rather than issuing new shares?

ETHICS CASE

Jean Loptien, president of Sycamore Corporation, is concerned about several large shareholders who have been very vocal lately in their criticisms of her leadership. She thinks they might mount a campaign to have her removed as the corporation's CEO. She decides that buying them out by purchasing their shares could eliminate them as opponents, and she is confident they would accept a "good" offer. Loptien knows the corporation's cash position is decent, so it has the cash to complete the transaction. She also knows the purchase of these shares will increase earnings per share, which should make other investors quite happy.

Instructions

Answer the following questions:

(a) Who are the stakeholders in this situation?

(b) What are the ethical issues involved?

(c) Should Loptien authorize the transaction?

Shareholders' Equity: Retained Earnings

LEARNING OBJECTIVES

....

After studying this chapter, you should be able to:

1. Describe the policies used in distributing dividends.

2. Identify the various forms of dividend distributions.

3. Explain the accounting for stock dividends.

4. Distinguish between stock dividends and stock splits.

5. Explain the effect of different types of preferred stock dividends.

6. Identify the reasons for appropriating retained earnings.

7. Explain accounting and reporting for appropriated retained earnings.

8. Indicate how shareholders' equity is presented and analysed.

Preview of Chapter 17

Companies use stock splits and stock dividends to send positive signals to their shareholders. In addition, many companies provide other types of dividend distributions. This chapter's purpose is to discuss these and other transactions that affect retained earnings. The content and organization of the chapter are as follows:

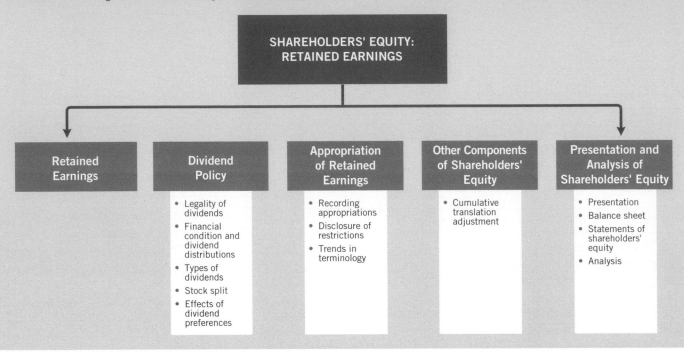

RETAINED EARNINGS

The basic source of **retained earnings**—earnings retained for use in the business—is income from operations. Shareholders assume the greatest **risk** in enterprise operations bearing any losses. In return, they also reap the **rewards**, sharing in any profits resulting from enterprise activities. Any income not distributed among the shareholders becomes additional shareholders' equity. Net income includes a considerable variety of income sources. These include the enterprise's main operation (such as manufacturing and selling a given product), plus any ancillary activities (such as disposing of scrap or renting out unused space), plus the results of extraordinary and unusual items. All give rise to net income that increases retained earnings. The more common items that either increase or decrease retained earnings are expressed in account form below.

ILLUSTRATION 17-1
Transactions that Affect Retained Earnings

RETAINED EARNINGS	
1. Net loss	1. Net income
2. Prior period adjustments (error corrections) and certain changes in accounting principle	2. Prior period adjustments (error corrections) and certain changes in accounting principle
3. Cash or scrip dividends	3. Adjustments due to financial reorganization
4. Stock dividends	
5. Property dividends	
6. Some treasury stock transactions	

Chapter 4 pointed out that the results of irregular transactions should be reported in the income statement, not the retained earnings statement. However, error corrections should be reported as adjustments to beginning retained earnings, bypassing completely the current income statement.

DIVIDEND POLICY

Determining the proper amount of dividends to pay is a difficult financial management decision. Companies that are paying dividends are extremely reluctant to reduce or eliminate their dividend, because they believe that this action could be viewed negatively by the securities market. As a consequence, companies that have been paying cash dividends will make every effort to continue to do so. In addition, the type of shareholder the company has (e.g., retail or institutional investor) plays a large role in determining dividend policy. As indicated in chapter 16, more companies are becoming involved in share buyback programs and are either not starting or not increasing their present dividend program significantly.

> **OBJECTIVE 1**
> ....
> Describe the policies used in distributing dividends.

Very few companies pay dividends in amounts equal to their legally available retained earnings. The major reasons are as follows.

1. Agreements (bond covenants) with specific creditors to retain all or a portion of the earnings, in the form of assets, to build up additional protection against possible loss.
2. Desire to retain assets that would otherwise be paid out as dividends, to finance growth or expansion. This is sometimes called internal financing, reinvesting earnings, or "plowing" the profits back into the business.
3. Desire to smooth out dividend payments from year to year by accumulating earnings in good years and using such accumulated earnings as a basis for dividends in bad years.
4. Desire to build up a cushion or buffer against possible losses or errors in the calculation of profits.

If a company is considering declaring a dividend, two preliminary questions must be asked:

1. Is the corporation's condition such that a dividend is **legally** permissible?
2. Is the corporation's condition such that a dividend is **economically** sound?

Legality of Dividends

A dividend's legality can be determined only by reviewing the applicable law. Distributions to shareholders are generally allowed as long as the corporation is not insolvent. **Insolvency** is defined as the inability to pay debts as they come due in the normal course of business. The CBCA prohibits declaring or paying dividends if there are reasonable grounds for believing that such an action would make the company insolvent, that is (1) result in the corporation being unable to pay its liabilities when they become due or (2) result in the realizable value of the corporation's assets being less than the total of its liabilities and legal capital of all share classes.

Unfortunately, current financial statement disclosures do not include basic information such as: whether a corporation is in compliance with legal requirements; the corporation's capacity to make distributions; or, what legal restrictions exist regarding distributions to shareholders.

Financial Condition and Dividend Distributions

Good business management requires attention to more than the legality of dividend distributions. Consideration must be given to **economic conditions**; most importantly, liquidity. Assume an extreme situation as follows.

ILLUSTRATION 17-2
Balance Sheet, Showing a
Lack of Liquidity

Balance Sheet			
Plant assets	$500,000	Share capital	$400,000
	$500,000	Retained earnings	100,000
			$500,000

The depicted company has a retained earnings credit balance and generally, unless it is restricted, can declare a dividend of $100,000. But because all its assets are plant assets and used in operations, paying a cash dividend of $100,000 would require selling plant assets or borrowing.

Even if we assume a balance sheet showing current assets, the question remains as to whether those cash assets are needed for other purposes.

ILLUSTRATION 17-3
Balance Sheet, Showing Cash
but Minimal Working Capital

Balance Sheet				
Cash	$100,000	Current liabilities		$ 60,000
Plant assets	460,000	Share capital	$400,000	
	$560,000	Retained earnings	100,000	500,000
				$560,000

The existence of current liabilities implies very strongly that some of the cash is needed to meet current debts as they mature. In addition, day-by-day cash requirements for payrolls and other expenditures not included in current liabilities also require cash.

Thus, before a dividend is declared, management must consider **availability of funds to pay the dividend**. Other demands for cash should perhaps be investigated by preparing a **cash forecast**. A dividend should not be paid unless both the present and future financial position appear to warrant the distribution.

Directors must also consider the effect of inflation and replacement costs before making a dividend commitment. During a period of significant inflation, some costs charged to expense under historical cost accounting are understated in terms of **comparative purchasing power**. Income is thereby **overstated** because certain costs have not been adjusted for inflation. For example, **St. Regis Paper Company** reported historical cost net income of $179 million, but when it was adjusted for general inflation, net income was only $68 million. Yet St. Regis paid cash dividends of $72 million. Were cash dividends in excess of what the company could really afford?[1]

Note also that non-payment of dividends may significantly impact the company as well. For instance **Torstar Corporation** has Class B shares that are normally non-voting. However, if the company does not pay dividends for eight consecutive quarters, the shares then have voting rights.

Not all shares carry the right to receive dividends. For example, the **Saskatchewan Wheat Pool** has two classes of shares. Class B shares trade on the TSE and have dividend rights while Class A voting shares are held by farmer-members and are not eligible for dividends. This is presumably due to the fact that the farmers receive other benefits from the Wheat Pool, which is operated as a co-op.

Types of Dividends

OBJECTIVE 2

Identify the various forms of
dividend distributions.

Dividend distributions generally are based either on accumulated profits; that is, retained earnings, or on some other capital item such as contributed surplus. The natural expectation of any shareholder who receives a dividend is that the corporation has operated successfully and that he or she is receiving a share of its profits. A liquidating dividend—that is, a dividend not based on retained earnings—should be adequately described in the accompanying message to the shareholders so that there will be no

---

[1] The notion of ensuring that a company maintain its capital base before paying out dividends is referred to as capital maintenance. Capital maintenance theory is also used as an alternative means of measuring economic income. The idea is that a company should only recognize income (and pay dividends) out of capital in excess of invested capital, otherwise the capital base is eroded and the company is worse off.

misunderstanding about its source. This type of dividend will be discussed in greater depth later in the chapter. Dividends are of the following types:

1. Cash dividends
2. Property dividends
3. Scrip dividends
4. Liquidating dividends
5. Stock dividends.

Dividends are commonly paid in cash but occasionally are paid in shares, scrip, or some other asset.[2] **All dividends, except for stock dividends, reduce the total shareholders' equity in the corporation**, because the equity is reduced either through an immediate or promised future distribution of assets. When a stock dividend is declared, the corporation does not pay out assets or incur a liability. It issues additional shares to each shareholder and nothing more.

Cash Dividends

The board of directors votes on the declaration of cash dividends and if the resolution is properly approved, the dividend is declared. Before it is paid, a current list of shareholders must be prepared. For this reason, there is usually a time lag between declaration and payment. A resolution approved at the January 10 (**date of declaration**) meeting of the board of directors might be declared payable February 5 (**date of payment**) to all shareholders of record January 25 (**date of record**).[3]

The period from January 10 to January 25 gives time for any transfers in process to be completed and registered with the transfer agent. The time from January 25 to February 5 provides an opportunity for the transfer agent or accounting department, depending on who does this work, to prepare a list of shareholders as of January 25 and to prepare and mail dividend cheques.

A declared cash dividend is a liability and, because payment is generally required very soon, is usually a current liability. The following entries are required to record the declaration and payment of an ordinary dividend payable in cash. For example, Rajah Corp. on June 10 declared a cash dividend of 50 cents a share on 1.8 million shares payable July 16 to all shareholders of record June 24.

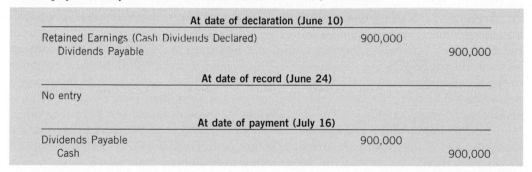

At date of declaration (June 10)		
Retained Earnings (Cash Dividends Declared)	900,000	
Dividends Payable		900,000
At date of record (June 24)		
No entry		
At date of payment (July 16)		
Dividends Payable	900,000	
Cash		900,000

To set up a ledger account that shows the amount of dividends declared during the year, Cash Dividends Declared might be debited instead of Retained Earnings at

---

[2] *Accounting Trends and Techniques—1999* reported that of its 600 surveyed companies, 435 paid a cash dividend on common share, 83 paid a cash dividend on preferred share, 9 issued stock dividends, and 10 issued or paid dividends in kind. Some companies declare more than one type of dividend in a given year.

[3] Theoretically, the ex-dividend date is the day after the date of record. However, to allow time for transfer of the shares, the stock exchanges generally advance the ex-dividend date two to four days. Therefore, the party who owns the shares on the day prior to the expressed ex-dividend date receives the dividends, and the party who buys the stock on and after the ex-dividend date does not receive the dividend. Between the declarations date and the ex-dividend date, the market price of the shares includes the dividend.

the time of declaration. This account is then closed to Retained Earnings at year end. Note that companies with preferred shares that are considered **financial liabilities** in substance should debit Dividends Declared for these shares to a separate account that is given the same accounting treatment as interest on long-term debt.[4]

Dividends may be declared either as a certain percent of par or stated value, such as a 6% dividend on preferred shares, or as an amount per share, such as 60 cents per share on no-par common shares. In the first case, the rate is multiplied by the par or stated value of outstanding shares to get the total dividend; in the second, the amount per share is multiplied by the number of shares outstanding. **Cash dividends are not declared and paid on treasury shares.**

Dividend policies vary among corporations. Some older, well-established firms take pride in a long, unbroken string of quarterly dividend payments.[5] They would lower or pass on the dividend only if forced to do so by a sustained decline in earnings or a critical shortage of cash.

"Growth" companies, on the other hand, pay little or no cash dividends because their policy is to expand as rapidly as internal and external financing permit. Investors in these companies hope that their share price will appreciate in value and that they will realize a profit when they sell their shares (capital appreciation).

Property Dividends

Dividends payable in corporation assets other than cash are called property dividends or **dividends in kind**. Property dividends may be merchandise, real estate, or investments, or whatever form the board of directors designates. Because of the obvious difficulties of dividing units and delivering to shareholders, the usual property dividend is in the form of securities of other companies that the distributing corporation holds as an investment.

For example, when **DuPont's** 23% investment in **General Motors** was held by the U.S. Supreme Court to be in violation of antitrust laws, DuPont was ordered to divest itself of the GM shares within 10 years. The shares represented 63 million shares of GM's 281 million shares then outstanding. DuPont couldn't sell the shares in one block of 63 million, nor could it sell 6 million shares annually for the next 10 years without severely depressing the value of the GM shares. At that time the entire yearly trading volume in GM shares did not exceed 6 million shares. DuPont solved its problem by declaring a property dividend and distributing the GM shares as a dividend to its own shareholders.

A property dividend is a nonreciprocal transfer[6] of nonmonetary assets between an enterprise and its owners. These dividends should be measured at the fair value of the asset given up[7] unless they are considered to represent a spin-off or other form of restructuring or liquidation, in which case, they should be recorded at the carrying value of the non-monetary assets or liabilities transferred.[8] No gain or loss would be recorded in the second instance. The property dividend is seen as another form of dividend (and should therefore be recorded at fair value) unless it represents some sort of restructuring.

The **fair value** of the nonmonetary asset distributed is measured by the amount that would be realizable in an outright sale at or near the time of the distribution. Such an amount should be determined by referring to estimated realizable values in cash transactions of the same or similar assets, quoted market prices, independent appraisals, and other available evidence.

INTERNATIONAL INSIGHT

As a less preferred but still allowable treatment, international accounting standards permit firms to reduce equity by the amount of proposed dividends prior to their legal declaration.

UNDERLYING CONCEPTS

The rationale for this treatment for **spin-off transactions** is that there has been no change in **economic substance** even though there has been a change in legal form. The shareholders own the property directly now whereas they owned it indirectly prior to the transfer.

---

[4] *CICA Handbook,* Section 3860, par. .31. This is for consistency purposes. If the economic substance of the instrument is debt, then regardless of its legal form, the related payments (ie dividends) would be treated as interest for financial reporting purposes.

[5] The Bank of Montreal and the Bank of Nova Scotia have been paying dividends since 1829 and 1833 respectively!

[6] A nonreciprocal transfer of assets or services is a transfer in one direction only, either from or to an enterprise.

[7] *CICA Handbook,* Section 3830, par. .05.

[8] Ibid. par. .11.

The failure to recognize the fair value of nonmonetary assets transferred may both misstate the dividend and fail to recognize gains and losses on nonmonetary assets that have already been earned or incurred by the enterprise. Recording the dividend at fair value permits future comparisons of dividend rates. If cash must be distributed to shareholders in place of the nonmonetary asset, determining the amount to be distributed is simplified.

When the property dividend is declared, the corporation should **restate at fair value the property to be distributed, recognizing any gain or loss** as the difference between the property's fair value and carrying value at date of declaration.[9] The declared dividend may then be recorded as a debit to Retained Earnings (or Property Dividends Declared) and a credit to Property Dividends Payable at an amount equal to the fair value of the property to be distributed. Upon distribution of the dividend, Property Dividends Payable is debited, and the account containing the distributed asset (restated at fair value) is credited.

For example, Trendler, Inc. transferred to shareholders some of its investments in marketable securities costing $1,250,000 by declaring a property dividend on December 28, 2001 to be distributed on January 30, 2002 to shareholders of record on January 15, 2002. At the date of declaration the securities have a market value of $2 million. The entries are as follows:

At date of declaration (December 28, 2001)		
Investments in Securities	750,000	
Gain on Appreciation of Securities		750,000
Retained Earnings (Property Dividends Declared)	2,000,000	
Property Dividends Payable		2,000,000

At date of distribution (January 30, 2002)		
Property Dividends Payable	2,000,000	
Investments in Securities		2,000,000

Scrip Dividends

A scrip dividend—dividend payable in scrip—means that instead of paying the dividend now, the corporation has elected to pay it at some later date. **The scrip issued to shareholders as a dividend is merely a special form of note payable.** For example, at one time the **Bank of Puerto Rico** issued a $9 million note as a dividend that matured 10 years later, at which time each holder of the corporation's 3 million common shares received $3 a share. Scrip dividends may be declared when the corporation has a sufficient retained earnings balance but is short of cash. The recipient of the scrip dividend may hold it until the due date, if one is specified, and collect the dividend or may sell it to obtain immediate cash.

When a scrip dividend is declared, the corporation debits Retained Earnings (or Scrip Dividend Declared) and credits Scrip Dividend Payable or Notes Payable to Shareholders, **reporting the payable as a liability** on the balance sheet. Upon payment, Scrip Dividend Payable is debited and Cash credited. If the scrip bears interest, the interest portion of the cash payment should be debited to Interest Expense and not treated as part of the dividend. For example, Berg Canning Corp. avoided missing its 84th consecutive quarterly dividend by declaring on May 27 a scrip dividend in the form of two-month promissory notes amounting to 80 cents a share on 2,545,000 shares outstanding and payable at the date of record, June 5. The notes paid interest of 10% per annum and matured on July 27. The entries are as follows.

At date of declaration (May 27)		
Retained Earnings (Scrip Dividend Declared)	2,036,000	
Notes Payable to Shareholders ($.80 × 2,545,000)		2,036,000

---

[9] Alternatively, any gain could be recorded on actual payment date since technically, the disposition of the asset is on the date of distribution of the dividend.

At date of payment (July 27)		
Notes Payable to Shareholders	2,036,000	
Interest Expense ($2,036,000 × 2/12 × .10)ᵃ	33,933	
Cash		2,069,933

ᵃ The interest runs from the date of declaration to the date of payment.

Liquidating Dividends

Some corporations use contributed surplus as a basis for dividends. Without proper disclosure of this fact, shareholders may erroneously believe the corporation has been paying dividends out of profits. This misconception can be avoided by requiring that a clear statement of the source of every dividend accompany the dividend cheque.

Dividends based on other than retained earnings are sometimes described as liquidating dividends, thus implying that they are a return of the shareholder's investment rather than of profits. In other words, **any dividend not based on earnings is a reduction of corporate contributed capital and, to that extent, it is a liquidating dividend**. We noted in Chapter 12 that companies in the extractive industries may pay dividends equal to the total of accumulated income and depletion. The portion of these dividends in excess of accumulated income represents a return of part of the shareholder's investment.

For example, McChesney Mines Inc. issued a dividend to its common shareholders of $1.2 million. The cash dividend announcement noted that $900,000 should be considered income and the remainder a return of capital. The entries are:

At date of declaration		
Retained Earnings	900,000	
Contributed Surplus	300,000	
Dividends payable		1,200,000

At date of payment		
Dividends payable	1,200,000	
Cash		1,200,000

In some cases, management may simply decide to cease business and declare a liquidating dividend. In these cases, liquidation may take place over a number of years to ensure an orderly and fair sale of assets. For example, when **Overseas National Airways** was dissolved, it agreed to pay a liquidating dividend to its shareholders over a period of years equivalent to $8.60 per share. Each liquidating dividend payment in such cases reduces Contributed Surplus.

Stock Dividends

OBJECTIVE 3

Explain the accounting for stock dividends.

If the management wishes to "capitalize" part of the earnings (i.e., reclassify amounts from earned to contributed capital) and thus retain earnings in the business on a permanent basis, it may issue a stock dividend. In this case, **no assets are distributed**, and each shareholder has exactly the same proportionate interest in the corporation and the same total book value after the stock dividend was issued as before it was declared. The book value per share is lower because an increased number of shares are held.

There is no clear guidance as to how to account for stock dividends. The big picture issue is whether they are to be treated in the same manner as other dividends or not.[10] On the one hand, as a dividend they should be **recognized** as such and therefore Retained Earnings should be debited and Share Capital credited. If booked as a dividend, how should the transaction be **measured**? One option is to measure at the **par value** of the shares issued as a dividend. Another option is to measure at the **fair value**

---

[10] From a tax perspective CCRA treats stock dividends received the same as other dividends. The dividends are measured at paid up capital (legal capital, which is equal to fair value at the date of dividend declaration for no par shares).

of the shares issued—its market value at the declaration date.[11] On the other hand, an argument exists not to treat stock dividends as a dividend but more like a stock split. This will be discussed in the following sections.

Notwithstanding the foregoing, the CBCA states that for stock dividends, the declared amount of the dividend shall be added to the stated capital account. The CBCA does not allow shares to be issued until they are fully paid for in an amount not less than the fair equivalent of money that the corporation would have received had the shares been issued for cash. Therefore, fair value should be used for companies incorporated under the CBCA, as the legal requirement would limit the choice of accounting.

Ordinarily, the fair value to be used is the shares' market price on the date of the dividend declaration. This is reasonable, given the assumption that the market price will not change materially as a result of the stock dividend. When the market price is significantly affected (e.g., when a relatively large number of shares is being issued) it would be more appropriate to account for the event as a stock split (as discussed later) even though the legal form may be a stock dividend.[12]

To illustrate a stock dividend, assume that a corporation has outstanding 1,000 common shares and retained earnings of $50,000. If the corporation declares a 10% stock dividend, it issues 100 additional shares to current shareholders. If it is assumed that the shares' fair value at the time of the stock dividend is $130 per share and that the shareholders had the option to take the dividend in cash but chose not to, the entry is:

At date of declaration		
Retained Earnings (Stock Dividend Declared)	13,000	
Common Stock Dividend Distributable		13,000

Note that no asset or liability has been affected. The entry merely reflects a reclassification of shareholders' equity. If a balance sheet is prepared between the dates of declaration and distribution, the Common Stock Dividend Distributable should be shown in the shareholders' equity section as an addition to Common Shares (whereas cash or property dividends payable are shown as current liabilities).

When the shares are issued, the entry is:

At date of distribution		
Common Stock Dividend Distributable	13,000	
Common Shares		13,000

No matter what the fair value is at the time of the stock dividend, each shareholder retains the same proportionate interest in the corporation.

Before dividend:	
Common shares, 1,000 shares	$100,000
Retained earnings	50,000
Total shareholders' equity	$150,000

INTERNATIONAL INSIGHT

Revaluation of assets is likely to result in revaluation of capital. Such capital is available as the basis for **stock dividends** in some countries and for cash dividends in others. Some countries require the accumulation of such capital but do not permit it to be used as the basis for either form of dividend.

ILLUSTRATION 17-4
Effects of a Stock Dividend

---

[11] The CICA requires that nonmonetary, non-reciprocal transfers (which include dividends in kind and stock dividends where the shareholder has the option of receiving cash or shares) be recorded at the fair value of the assets given up (*CICA Handbook,* Section 3830, pars. .04 and .05.). However, where the stock dividends are non-optional or where there is a stock split, these transactions are not considered **non-reciprocal transfers** and therefore presumably these transactions are not bound by requirement to measure at fair value. The decision appears to hinge upon whether the dividends may be paid in cash or not. If they may, then they are more "cash-like" and therefore should be recorded the same way as a cash dividend. If not, then an alternative measurement must be used or perhaps no journal entry need be booked at all. This will be further discussed in the following sections.

[12] When the stock dividend is less than 20–25% of the common shares outstanding at the time of the dividend declaration, the accounting profession in the U.S. requires that the **fair market value** of the shares issued be transferred from retained earnings. Stock dividends of less than 20–25% are often referred to as small (ordinary) stock dividends in the U.S.

Shareholders' interests:
A. 400 shares, 40% interest, book value $ 60,000
B. 500 shares, 50% interest, book value   75,000
C. 100 shares, 10% interest, book value   15,000
                                      $150,000

After declaration but before distribution of 10% stock dividend:
If fair value ($130) is used as basis for entry
   Common shares, 1,000 shares $100,000
   Common shares distributable, 100 shares   13,000
   Retained earnings ($50,000 − $13,000)   37,000
      Total shareholders' equity $150,000

After declaration and distribution of 10% stock dividend:
If fair value ($130) is used as basis for entry
   Common shares, 1,100 shares $113,000
   Retained earnings ($50,000 − $13,000)   37,000
      Total shareholders' equity $150,000

Shareholders' interest:
A. 440 shares, 40% interest, book value $ 60,000
B. 550 shares, 50% interest, book value   75,000
C. 110 shares, 10% interest, book value   15,000
                                        $150,000

To continue with our example of the stock dividend's effect, note in Illustration 17-4 that the total shareholders' equity has not changed as a result of the share dividend. Also note that the proportion of the total shares outstanding held by each shareholder is unchanged.

Stock Split

If a company has undistributed earnings over several years and a sizeable balance in retained earnings has accumulated, the market value of its outstanding shares is likely to increase. Shares that were issued at prices less than $50 a share can easily attain a market value in excess of $200 a share. The higher the share's market price, the less readily it can be purchased by some investors. The managements of many corporations believe that for better public relations, wider ownership of the corporation's shares is desirable. They wish, therefore, to have a market price sufficiently low to be within range of the majority of potential investors. To reduce the market value of shares, the common device of a stock split is employed.[13] For example, after its share price increased by 25-fold during 1999, **Qualcomm Inc.** split its shares 4-for-1. Qualcomm's shares had risen above $500 per share, raising concerns that Qualcomm could not meet an analyst target of $1,000 per share. The split reduced the analysts' target to $250, which could better be met with wider distribution of shares at lower trading prices.[14]

---

[13] *The DH&S Review*, May 12, 1986, page 7, listed the following as reasons behind a stock split:
1. To adjust the market price of the company's shares to a level where more individuals can afford to invest in the shares.
2. To spread the shareholder base by increasing the number of shares outstanding and making them more marketable.
3. To benefit existing shareholders by allowing them to take advantage of an imperfect market adjustment following the split.

[14] Some companies use reverse stock splits. A **reverse stock split** reduces the number of shares outstanding and increases the per share price. This technique is used when the share price is unusually low or when management wishes to take control of the company. For example, two officers of **Metropolitan Maintenance Co.** took their company private by forcing a 1-for-3,000 reverse stock split on their shareholders. For every 3,000 old shares, one new share was issued. But anyone who had fewer than 3,000 shares received only cash for his or her stock. Only the two officers owned more than 3,000 shares, so they now own all the stock. *Forbes*, November 19, 1984, p. 54.

From an accounting standpoint, **no entry is recorded for a stock split**; a memorandum note, however, is made to indicate that the number of shares has increased. The lack of change in shareholders' equity is portrayed in Illustration 17-5 of a 2-for-1 stock split on 1,000 shares.

ILLUSTRATION 17-5
Effects of a Stock Split

Shareholders' Equity before 2-for-1 Split		Shareholders' Equity after 2-for-1 Split	
Common shares, 1,000 shares	$100,000	Common shares, 2,000 shares	$100,000
Retained earnings	50,000	Retained earnings	50,000
	$150,000		$150,000

Stock Split and Stock Dividend Differentiated

From a **legal** standpoint a **stock split** is distinguished from a **stock dividend**, because a stock split results in an increase in the number of shares outstanding with no change in the share capital or the retained earnings amounts. A **stock dividend,** results in an increase in both the number of shares outstanding and the share capital while reducing the retained earnings (assuming it is accounted for based on its legal form).

OBJECTIVE 4
....
Distinguish between stock dividends and stock splits.

The reasons for issuing a stock dividend are numerous and varied. Stock dividends can be more of a publicity gesture, because they are considered by many as dividends and, consequently, the corporation is not criticized for retention of profits.

A stock dividend, like a stock split, also may be used to increase the share's marketability, although marketability is often a secondary consideration. If the stock dividend is large, it has the same effect on market price as a stock split. In the U.S., the profession has taken the position that whenever additional shares are issued for the purpose of reducing the unit market price, then the distribution more closely resembles a stock split than a stock dividend. **This effect usually results only if the number of shares issued is more than 20–25% of the number of shares previously outstanding.**[15] A stock dividend of more than 20–25% of the number of shares previously outstanding is called a large stock dividend.[16]

To illustrate a large stock dividend (often referred to as a "stock split-up effected in the form of a dividend"), Rockland Steel, Inc. declared a 30% stock dividend on November 20, payable December 29 to shareholders of record December 12. At the date of declaration, 1 million shares are outstanding (fair market value of $200 per share and carrying value $10 per share). The entries are:

At date of declaration (November 20)		
Retained Earnings[17]	3,000,000	
Common Stock Dividend Distributable		3,000,000
Calculation:		
1,000,000 shares	300,000 Additional shares	
× 30%	× $10 Carrying value	
300,000	$3,000,000	

At date of distribution (December 29)		
Common Stock Dividend Distributable	3,000,000	
Common Shares		3,000,000

Illustration 17-6 summarizes and compares the effects of various types of dividends and stock splits on various elements of the financial statements.

---

[15] *Accounting Research and Terminology Bulletin* No. 43, par. 13.

[16] The SEC has added more precision to the 20–25% rule. Specifically, the SEC indicates that distributions of 25% or more should be considered a "split-up effected in the form of a dividend." Distributions of less than 25% should be accounted for as a stock dividend. The SEC more precisely defined GAAP here, and as a result the SEC rule is followed by public companies.

[17] Often, a split-up effected in the form of a dividend is debited to paid-in capital instead of retained earnings to indicate that this transaction should affect only paid-in capital accounts. No reduction of retained earnings is required except as indicated by legal requirements. See, for example, Taylor W. Foster III and Edmund Scribner, "Accounting for Stock Dividends and Stock Splits: Corrections to Textbook Coverage," *Issues in Accounting Education*, February 1998.

ILLUSTRATION 17-6
Effects of Dividends and Stock Splits on Financial Statement Elements

Effect on:	Declaration of Cash Dividend	Payment of Cash Dividend	Declaration and Distribution of		
			"Small" Stock Dividend	"Large" Stock Dividend	Stock Split
Retained earnings	Decrease	–0–	Decrease[a]	Decrease[b]	–0–
Common shares	–0–	–0–	Increase	Increase	–0–
Contributed surplus	–0–	–0–	–0–	–0–	–0–
Total shareholders' equity	Decrease	–0–	–0–	–0–	–0–
Working capital	Decrease	–0–	–0–	–0–	–0–
Total assets	–0–	Decrease	–0–	–0–	–0–
Number of shares outstanding	–0–	–0–	Increase	Increase	Increase

[a] Generally equal to market value of shares.

[b] May be equal to par stated value of shares or market value. Note that some companies may choose to interpret GAAP such that another account, such as contributed surplus, is debited or that the dividend be treated as a stock split. Legal requirements regarding stated legal capital would also influence the entries for stock dividends.

Effects of Dividend Preferences

OBJECTIVE 5

Explain the effect of different types of preferred stock dividends.

The examples given below illustrate the **effects of** various **dividend preferences** on dividend distributions to common and preferred shareholders. Assume that in a given year, $50,000 is to be distributed as cash dividends, outstanding common shares have a value of $400,000, and 1,000 $6 preferred shares are outstanding at $100,000. Dividends would be distributed to each class as shown below, employing the assumptions given.

1. If the preferred shares are noncumulative and nonparticipating:

ILLUSTRATION 17-7
Dividend Distribution, Noncumulative and Nonparticipating Preferred

	Preferred	Common	Total
$6 × 1000	$6,000		$ 6,000
The remainder to common	0	$44,000	44,000
Totals	$6,000	$44,000	$50,000

2. If the preferred shares are cumulative and nonparticipating, and dividends were not paid on the preferred shares in the preceding two years:

ILLUSTRATION 17-8
Dividend Distribution, Cumulative and Nonparticipating Preferred, with Dividends in Arrears

	Preferred	Common	Total
Dividends in arrears, $6 × 1000 for 2 years	$12,000		$12,000
Current year's dividend, $6 × 1000	6,000		6,000
The remainder to common		$32,000	32,000
Totals	$18,000	$32,000	$50,000

3. If the preferred shares are noncumulative and are fully participating:[18]

ILLUSTRATION 17-9
Dividend Distribution, Noncumulative and Fully Participating Preferred

	Preferred	Common	Total
Current year's dividend, $6	$ 6,000	$24,000	$ 30,000
Participating dividend—pro rata	4,000	16,000	20,000
Totals	$10,000	$40,000	$ 50,000

---

[18] When preferred shares are participating, there may be different agreements as to how the participation feature is to be executed. However, in the absence of any specific agreement the following procedure is recommended:
   a. After the preferred shares are assigned their current year's dividend, the common shares will receive a "like" percentage. In example (3), this amounts to 6% of $400,000.
   b. If there is a remainder of declared dividends for participation by the preferred and common shares, this remainder will be shared in proportion to the carrying value in each share class. In example (3) this proportion is:

Preferred $100,000/500,000 × $20,000 = $4,000

Common $400,000/500,000 × $20,000 = $16,000

The participating dividend was determined as follows:
Current year's dividend:
    Preferred, $6 × 1000 = $ 6,000
    Common, 6% of $400,000 = 24,000 (= a "like amount") $ 30,000
NB the 6% represents $6,000 on pref shares/ $100,000
Amount available for participation
    ($50,000 − $30,000) $ 20,000
Carrying value of shares that are to participate
    ($100,000 + $400,000) $500,000
Rate of participation
    ($20,000/$500,000)   4%
Participating dividend:
    Preferred, (4% of $100,000) $ 4,000
    Common, (4% of $400,000)   16,000
        $ 20,000

4. If the preferred shares are cumulative and fully participating, and if dividends were not paid on the preferred shares in the preceding two years (the same procedure as described in example (3) is used in this example to effect the participation feature):

	Preferred	Common	Total
Dividends in arrears,			
$6 × 1000 for 2 years	$12,000		$12,000
Current year's dividend, $6	6,000	$24,000	30,000
Participating dividend, 1.6%			
($8,000/$500,000)	1,600	$6,400	8,000
Totals	$19,600	$30,400	$50,000

ILLUSTRATION 17-10
Dividend Distribution, Cumulative and Fully Participating Preferred, with Dividends in Arrears

APPROPRIATION OF RETAINED EARNINGS

The act of appropriating retained earnings is a policy matter requiring approval by the board of directors.

Appropriation of retained earnings is nothing more than reclassification of retained earnings for a specific purpose. An appropriation does not set aside cash: It discloses that management **does not intend to distribute assets as a dividend** up to the amount of the appropriation because these assets are needed by the corporation for a specified purpose. The unappropriated retained earnings is debited (reduced) by the amount of the appropriation, and a new account for the specific purpose is established and credited for the transferred amount. When the appropriation is no longer necessary, either because the specific purpose has been accomplished or the loss has occurred or because it no longer appears as a possibility, the appropriation should be returned to unappropriated retained earnings. Various reasons are advanced for appropriations of retained earnings. These include:

1. **Contractual restrictions.** Bond indentures frequently contain a requirement that retained earnings in specified amounts be appropriated each year during the life of the bonds. The appropriation created under such a provision is commonly called Appropriation for Sinking Fund or Appropriation for Bonded Indebtedness.

2. **Existence of possible or expected loss.** Appropriations might be established for estimated losses due to lawsuits, unfavourable contractual obligations, self-insurance, and/or other contingencies.

3. **Protection of working capital position.** The board of directors may authorize the creation of an "Appropriation for Working Capital" out of retained earnings in order to indicate that the amount specified is not available for dividends because it is desirable to maintain a strong current position. Another example involves a decision made to finance a building program by internal financing. An "Appropriation for Plant Expansion" is created to indicate that retained earnings in the amount appropriated will not be considered by the directors as available for dividends.

OBJECTIVE 6

Identify the reasons for appropriating retained earnings.

INTERNATIONAL INSIGHT

In some nations, companies are legally required to create reserves (appropriations) for creditor protection. They must allocate profits to reserves at a specified annual rate until the amount of the required reserve is accumulated.

OBJECTIVE 7

Explain accounting and reporting for appropriated retained earnings.

Some corporations establish appropriations for general contingencies or appropriate retained earnings for unspecified purposes. In some cases this is justified by statutory or contractual restrictions. In other cases no adequate explanation for such actions is available.

Recording Appropriation of Retained Earnings

When a company records an appropriation in the accounts, the unappropriated retained earnings must be reduced by the amount of the appropriation and a new account must be established to receive the amount transferred. The new account Appropriated Retained Earnings is simply a subclassification of total retained earnings. If the appropriation merely augments a previously established amount, the account already in use should receive the credit. The appropriation is recorded as a debit to Retained Earnings and a credit to an appropriately named account that itself is just a subdivision of retained earnings. For example:

1. An Appropriation for Plant Expansion is to be created by transfer from Retained Earnings of $400,000 a year for five years. The entry for each year would be:

Retained Earnings	400,000	
Retained Earnings Appropriated for Plant Expansion		400,000

2. At the end of five years the appropriation would have a balance of $2 million. If we assume that the expansion plan has been completed, the appropriation is no longer required and can be returned to retained earnings.

Retained Earnings Appropriated for Plant Expansion	2,000,000	
Retained Earnings		2,000,000

Return of such an appropriation to retained earnings has the effect of increasing unappropriated retained earnings considerably without affecting the assets or current position. In effect, over the five years, the company has expanded by reinvesting assets acquired through the earnings process.

Disclosure of Restrictions on Retained Earnings

In many corporations, restrictions on retained earnings or dividends exist, but no formal journal entries are made. Such restrictions are best **disclosed by note**. Parenthetical notations are sometimes used, but restrictions imposed by bond indentures and loan agreements commonly require an extended explanation; notes provide a medium for more complete explanations and free the financial statements from abbreviated notations. The note disclosure should reveal the source of the restriction, pertinent provisions, and the amount of retained earnings subject to restriction, or the amount not restricted.[19]

Restrictions may be based on the retention of a certain retained earnings balance, the corporation's ability to observe certain working capital requirements, additional borrowing, and on other considerations. The following example from the annual report of **Methanex Corporation** illustrates a note disclosing potential restrictions on retained earnings and dividends.

ILLUSTRATION 17-11
Disclosure of Restrictions on Retained Earnings and Dividends

9. Capital stock:

(a) The authorized share capital of the Company is comprised as follows:
25,000,000 preferred shares without nominal or par value; and Unlimited number of common shares without nominal or par value.

(b) Under covenants set out in certain debt instruments, the Company can pay cash dividends or make other shareholder distributions to the extent that shareholders' equity is equal to or greater than $850 million.

[19] *CICA Handbook*, Section 3250, par. .10.

Trends in Terminology

As discussed in Chapter 5, the profession's recommendations relating to changes in terminology have been directed primarily to the balance sheet presentation of shareholders' equity so that words or phrases used will more accurately describe the nature of the amounts shown.

The accounting profession has suggested the term "surplus" not be used in financial statements. Substitute terminology is recommended because the term "surplus" connotes a residual or "something not needed." The use of the term is gradually decreasing. "**Retained earnings**" or some similar phrase has generally replaced "earned surplus." Consensus regarding the terminology to replace "contributed surplus" has not yet been reached, inasmuch as this term still appears in most financial statements where there is surplus in excess of retained earnings.[20]

Formerly, the term "reserve" was used in accounting to describe such diverse items as accumulated amortization, allowances for doubtful accounts, current liabilities, and segregations of retained earnings. **The profession recommends that use of the word "reserve" be confined to appropriations of retained earnings if it is to be used at all.**

OTHER COMPONENTS OF SHAREHOLDERS' EQUITY

Cumulative Translation Adjustment

When corporations consolidate the financial statements of a self-sustaining foreign subsidiary with those of the parent company, all accounting elements must be remeasured in Canadian dollars.[21] As the exchange rate changes from period to period, the Canadian dollar equivalent of the subsidiary's net assets changes as well. The accumulated adjustment, which can be either a debit or credit balance, is disclosed in the parent company's Shareholders' Equity section as a separate line item often called Cumulative Translation Adjustment or Foreign Currency Translation Adjustment. Consistent with other shareholders' equity items, companies are required to disclose the significant elements giving rise to changes in the exchange gains and losses accumulated in this account during the period.

PRESENTATION AND ANALYSIS OF SHAREHOLDERS' EQUITY

Presentation

The following three categories normally appear as part of shareholders' equity:

1. Common and preferred shares
2. Contributed surplus
3. Retained earnings or deficit

> **OBJECTIVE 8**
>
> Indicate how shareholders' equity is presented and analysed.

The first two categories, share capital and contributed surplus, constitute contributed (or paid-in) capital; retained earnings represents the enterprise's earned capital. These three categories are reported in summarized form in all enterprises' balance sheets. More detail of additions and deductions to specific shareholders' equity accounts are frequently reported in a separate statement of shareholders' equity.

---

[20] *Financial Reporting in Canada, 2000* (CICA; Toronto, 2000) indicates that out of 200 companies surveyed, 53 had contributed surplus. Of that, 45 used the term "contributed surplus" and the rest used the terms "paid in surplus" or "other surplus."

[21] A self-sustaining foreign operation is one where the parent company's exposure to risk of loss (or gain) from changes in the exchange rate is limited to its investment in the subsidiary's net assets. Further discussion of this is deferred to an advanced accounting course.

Balance Sheet

The presentation below is an example of a shareholders' equity section taken from a balance sheet that includes most of the equity items discussed in Chapters 16 and 17.

ILLUSTRATION 17-12

Shareholders' Equity Presentation

FROST CORPORATION Shareholders' Equity December 31, 2001		
Share Capital		
Preferred shares, $7 cumulative, 100,000 shares authorized, 30,000 shares issued and outstanding		$ 3,000,000
Common shares, no par, stated value $10 per share, 500,000 shares authorized, 400,000 shares issued		4,000,000
Common shares dividend distributable, 20,000 shares		200,000
Total share capital		7,200,000
Contributed surplus		990,000
Total paid-in capital		8,190,000
Retained earnings		
Appropriated for plant expansion	2,200,000	
Unappropriated	2,160,000	4,360,000
Total shareholders' equity		$12,550,000

A company should disclose the pertinent rights and privileges of the various securities outstanding.[22]

Statements of Shareholders' Equity

Statements of shareholders' equity are frequently presented in the following basic format:

1. Balance at the beginning of the period
2. Additions
3. Deductions
4. Balance at the end of the period

The disclosure of changes in the separate accounts comprising shareholders' equity is required to make the financial statements sufficiently informative.[23] Disclosure of such changes may take the form of separate statements or may be made in the basic financial statements or notes thereto. A **columnar format** for the presentation of changes in shareholders' equity items in published annual reports is gaining in popularity.

Analysis

Several ratios use shareholders' equity related amounts to evaluate a company's profitability and long-term solvency. The following four ratios are discussed and illustrated below: (1) rate of return on common shareholders' equity, (2) payout ratio, (3) price earnings ratio, and (4) book value per share.

Rate of Return on Common Shareholders' Equity

A widely used ratio that measures profitability from the common shareholders' viewpoint is rate of return on common shareholders' equity. This ratio shows how many dollars of net income were earned for each dollar invested by the owners. It is calculated

---

[22] *CICA Handbook*, Section 3240.

[23] *Ibid*. par. .05.

by dividing net income less preferred dividends by average common shareholders' equity. For example, assume that Garber's Inc. had net income of $360,000, declared and paid preferred dividends of $54,000, and average common shareholders' equity of $2,550,000. Garber's ratio is calculated in this manner:

$$\text{Rate of return on common shareholders' equity} = \frac{\text{Net income} - \text{preferred dividends}}{\text{Average common shareholders' equity}}$$

$$= \frac{\$360,000 - 54,000}{\$2,550,000}$$

$$= 12\%$$

ILLUSTRATION 17-13
Calculation of Rate of Return on Common Shareholders' Equity

As evidenced above, because preferred shares are present, preferred dividends are deducted from net income to calculate income available to common shareholders. Similarly the carrying value of preferred shares is deducted from total shareholders' equity to arrive at the amount of common shareholders' equity used in this ratio.

When the rate of return on total assets is lower than the rate of return on the common shareholders investment, the company is said to be trading on the equity at a gain. Trading on the equity describes the practice of using borrowed money at fixed interest rates or issuing preferred shares with constant dividend rates in hopes of obtaining a higher rate of return on the money used (sometimes also referred to as **leverage**). These debt issues must be given a prior claim on some or all of the corporate assets. Thus, the advantage to common shareholders of trading on the equity must come from borrowing at a lower rate of interest than the rate of return obtained on the assets borrowed. If this can be done, the capital obtained from bondholders or preferred shareholders earns enough to pay the interest or preferred dividends and to leave a margin for the common shareholders. When this condition exists, trading on the equity is profitable.

Payout Ratio

Another measure of profitability is the payout ratio, which is the ratio of cash dividends to net income. If preferred shares are outstanding, this ratio is calculated for common shareholders by dividing cash dividends paid to common shareholders by net income available to common shareholders. Assuming that Troy Corp. has cash dividends of $100,000 and net income of $500,000, and no preferred shares outstanding, the payout ratio is calculated in the following manner.

$$\text{Payout Ratio} = \frac{\text{Cash Dividends}}{\text{Net income} - \text{Preferred dividends}}$$

$$= \frac{\$100,000}{500,000}$$

$$= 20\%$$

ILLUSTRATION 17-14
Calculation of Payout Ratio

It is important to some investors that the payout be sufficiently high to provide a good yield on the shares.[24] However, payout ratios have declined for many companies because many investors view appreciation in the share value as more important than the dividend amount.

Price Earnings Ratio

The price earnings (P/E) ratio is an oft-quoted statistic used by analysts in discussing the investment possibility of a given enterprise. It is calculated by dividing the share's market price by its earnings per share. For example, Soreson Corp. has a market price of $50 and earnings per share of $4. Its price earnings ratio is calculated as follows.

---

[24] Another closely watched ratio is the dividend yield, the cash dividend per share divided by the share's market price. This ratio affords investors some idea of the rate of return that will be received in cash dividends from their investment.

ILLUSTRATION 17-15
Calculation of Price
Earnings Ratio

$$\text{Price Earnings Ratio} = \frac{\text{Market price of share}}{\text{Earnings per share}}$$

$$= \$50/4$$

$$= 12.5$$

The average price earnings ratio for the 30 shares that constitute the Dow Jones Industrial Average in January 2000 was 31.7. A steady drop in a company's price earnings ratio indicates that investors are wary of the firm's growth potential. Some companies have high P/E ratios (also called "multiples"), while others have low multiples. For instance, **Home Depot** in 2000 enjoyed a P/E ratio of 53, while **Ford Motor Co.** had a low P/E ratio of 7.3. The reason for this difference is linked to several factors: relative risk, stability of earnings, trends in earnings, the market's perception of the company's growth potential and quality of earnings.

Book Value Per Share

A much-used basis for evaluating net worth is found in the **book value** or **equity value per share**. Book value per share is the amount each share would receive if the company were liquidated **on the basis of amounts reported on the balance sheet.** However, the figure loses much of its relevance if the valuations on the balance sheet do not approximate fair market value of the assets. Book value per share is calculated by dividing common shareholders' equity by number of outstanding common shares. Assuming that Chen Corporation's common shareholders' equity is $1 million and it has 100,000 shares outstanding, its book value per share is calculated as follows:

ILLUSTRATION 17-16
Calculation of Book Value
Per Share

$$\text{Book Value Per Share} = \frac{\text{Common shareholders' equity}}{\text{number of outstanding shares}}$$

$$= \frac{\$1,000,000}{100,000}$$

$$= \$10 \text{ per share}$$

When preferred shares are present, an analysis of the covenants involving the preferred shares should be studied. If preferred dividends are in arrears, the preferred shares are participating, or if preferred shares have a redemption or liquidating value higher than their carrying amount, retained earnings must be allocated between the preferred and common shareholders in calcualting book value.

To illustrate, assume that the following situation exists:

ILLUSTRATION 17-17
Calculation of Book Value Per
Share—No Dividends in Arrears

Shareholders' equity	Preferred	Common
Preferred shares, 5%	$300,000	
Common shares		$400,000
Contributed surplus		37,500
Retained earnings	0	162,582
Totals	$300,000	$600,082
Shares outstanding		4,000
Book value per share		$150.02

In the preceding calculation, it is assumed that no preferred dividends are in arrears and that the preferred is not participating. Now assume that the same facts exist except that the 5% preferred is cumulative, participating up to 8%, and that dividends for three years before the current year are in arrears. The common shares' book value is then calculated as follows, assuming that no action has yet been taken concerning dividends for the current year.

Shareholders' equity	Preferred	Common
Preferred shares, 5%	$300,000	
Common shares		$400,000
Contributed surplus		37,500
Retained earnings:		
Dividends in arrears (3 years at 5% a year)	45,000	
Current year requirement at 5%	15,000	20,000
Participating—additional 3%	9,000	12,000
Remainder to common	0	61,582
Totals	$369,000	$531,082
Shares outstanding		4,000
Book value per share		$132.77

ILLUSTRATION 17-18
Calculation of Book Value Per Share—With Dividends in Arrears

In connection with the book value calculation, the analyst must know how to handle the following items: the number of authorized and unissued shares; the number of treasury shares on hand; any commitments with respect to the issuance of unissued shares or the reissuance of treasury shares; and the relative rights and privileges of the various types of shares authorized.

SUMMARY OF LEARNING OBJECTIVES

1 Describe the policies used in distributing dividends. The incorporation laws normally provide information concerning the legal restrictions related to the payment of dividends. Corporations rarely pay dividends in an amount equal to the legal limit. This is due, in part, to the fact that assets represented by undistributed earnings are used to finance future business operations. If a company is considering declaring a dividend, two preliminary questions must be asked: (1) Is the condition of the corporation such that the dividend is legally permissible? (2) Is the condition of the corporation such that a dividend is economically sound?

2 Identify the various forms of dividend distributions. Dividends are of the following types: (1) cash dividends, (2) property dividends, (3) scrip dividends (instead of paying a dividend now, the corporation has elected to pay it at some later date; the scrip issued to shareholders as a dividend is merely a special form of note payable), (4) liquidating dividends (dividends based on other than retained earnings are sometimes described as liquidating dividends), and (5) stock dividends (the nonreciprocal issuance by a corporation of its own shares to its shareholders on a pro rata basis).

3 Explain the accounting for stock dividends. Generally accepted accounting principles are not firm; however, for stock dividends that are relatively small (less than 20 or 25%) and where the shareholder has the option to be paid in cash, the transaction is measured at the fair market value of the shares issued. When a stock dividend is declared, Retained Earnings is debited at the fair market value of the shares to be distributed. The entry includes a credit to Common Stock Dividend Distributable at fair value times the number of shares. Common Stock Dividend Distributable is reported in the shareholders' equity section between the declaration date and the date of issuance. If the number of shares issued exceeds 20 or 25% of the shares outstanding (large stock dividend), Retained Earnings may be debited at carrying value or fair value or not at all. Note that legal requirements would take precedence (e.g., the CBCA).

4 Distinguish between stock dividends and stock splits. A stock dividend is a capitalization of retained earnings that generally results in a reduction in retained earnings and a corresponding increase in certain contributed capital accounts. The total shareholders' equity remains unchanged with a stock dividend. Also, all shareholders retain their same proportionate share of ownership in the corporation. A stock split results in an increase or decrease in the number of shares outstanding. However, no accounting

KEY TERMS

appropriation of retained earnings, 807
book value per share, 812
cash dividends, 799
capital maintenance, 798
large stock dividend, 805
liquidating dividends, 802
payout ratio, 811
price earnings ratio, 811
property dividends, 800
rate of return on common shareholders' equity, 810
retained earnings, 796
scrip dividend, 801
small (ordinary) stock dividend, 803
statements of shareholders' equity, 810
stock dividend, 802
stock split, 804
trading on the equity, 811

entry is required. Similar to a stock dividend, the total dollar amount of all shareholders' equity accounts remains unchanged. A stock split is usually intended to improve the shares' marketability by reducing the market price of the shares being split. Large stock dividends have the same impact on the markets as stock splits, i.e., the market price of the share declines and therefore, whether these should be treated as a stock split or dividend for accounting purposes is a matter of professional judgement. Care should be taken to ensure that legal requirements for stated legal capital are met.

5 Explain the effect of different types of preferred stock dividends. Dividends paid to shareholders are affected by the dividend preferences of the preferred shares. Preferred shares can be: (1) cumulative or noncumulative, and (2) fully participating, partially participating, or nonparticipating.

6 Identify the reasons for appropriating retained earnings. An appropriation of retained earnings serves to restrict for a specific purpose the payout of retained earnings. In general, the reason for retained earnings appropriations is the corporation's desire to reduce the basis upon which dividends are declared (unappropriated credit balance in retained earnings).

7 Explain accounting and reporting for appropriated retained earnings. To establish an appropriation of retained earnings, a corporation prepares a journal entry, debiting unappropriated retained earnings and crediting a specific appropriations account (for example, Retained Earnings Appropriated for Sinking Fund). The entry is confined to shareholders' equity accounts and does not directly affect corporate assets or liabilities. The only way to dispose of an appropriation of retained earnings is to reverse the entry that created the appropriation. Appropriations of retained earnings are frequently disclosed in the notes to the financial statements as an alternative to making a formal entry against retained earnings.

8 Indicate how shareholders' equity is presented and analysed. The shareholders' equity section of a balance sheet includes share capital, contributed surplus, and retained earnings. It may also include Treasury shares, and/or cumulative translation adjustments. A statement of shareholders' equity is often provided. Common ratios used in this area are: rate of return on common shareholders' equity, payout ratio, price earnings ratio, and book value per share.

APPENDIX 17A

Financial Reorganization

OBJECTIVE 9

After studying Appendix 17A, you should be able to: Describe the accounting for a financial reorganization.

A corporation that consistently suffers net losses accumulates negative retained earnings, or a deficit. The general presumption of shareholders is that dividends are paid out of profits and retained earnings. In addition, certain laws in some jurisdictions provide that no dividends may be declared and paid so long as a corporation's paid-in capital has been reduced by a deficit. In these cases, a corporation with a debit balance of retained earnings must accumulate sufficient profits to offset the deficit before dividends may be paid.

This situation may be a real hardship on a corporation and its shareholders. A company that has operated unsuccessfully for several years and accumulated a deficit may have finally "turned the corner." Development of new products and new markets, a new management group, or improved economic conditions may point to much improved operating results. But, if the law prohibits dividends until the deficit has been replaced by earnings, the shareholders must wait until such profits have been earned, which may take a considerable period of time. Furthermore, future success may depend on obtaining additional funds through the sale of shares. If no dividends can be paid for some time, the market price of any new share issue is likely to be low, if such shares can be marketed at all.

Thus, a company with excellent prospects may be prevented from accomplishing its plans because of a deficit, although present management may have had nothing whatever to do with the years over which the deficit was accumulated. To permit the corporation to proceed with its plans might well be to the advantage of all interests in the enterprise; to require it to eliminate the deficit through profits might actually force it to liquidate.

A procedure that enables a company that has gone through financial difficulty to proceed with its plans without the encumbrance of having to recover from a deficit is called a **financial reorganization**. A financial reorganization is defined as a substantial realignment of an enterprise's equity and non-equity interests such that the holders of one or more of the significant classes of non-equity interests and the holders of all of the significant classes of equity interests give up some (or all) of their rights and claims upon the enterprise.[25]

A financial reorganization results from negotiation and culminates with an eventual agreement between non-equity and equity holders in the corporation. These negotiations may take place under the provisions of a legal act (e.g., Companies' Creditors Arrangement Act) or a less formal process.[26] The result gives the companies a "fresh start" and the accounting is often referred to as **fresh start accounting**.

ACCOUNTING APPROACHES

When a financial reorganization occurs, where the same party does not control the company both before and after the reorganization, and where new costs are reasonably determinable, the company's assets and liabilities should undergo a **comprehensive revaluation**.[27] This entails three steps:

1. The deficit balance (retained earnings) is brought to zero. Any asset writedowns or impairments that existed prior to the reorganization should be recorded first. The deficit is reclassified to Share Capital, Contributed Surplus, or a separately identified account within Shareholders' Equity.
2. The changes in debt and equity as negotiated are recorded. Often debt is exchanged for equity reflecting a change in control.
3. The assets and liabilities are comprehensively revalued. This step assigns appropriate going concern values to all assets and liabilities as per the negotiations. The difference between the carrying values prior to the reorganization and the new values after is known as a revaluation adjustment. The **revaluation adjustment** and any costs incurred to carry out the financial reorganization are accounted for as capital transactions and are closed to Share Capital, Contributed Surplus, or a separately identified account within Shareholders' Equity. Note that the new costs of the identifiable assets and liabilities must not exceed the entity's fair value if known.[28]

---

[25] *CICA Handbook*, Section 1625, par. .03.

[26] *Ibid*. par. .15.

[27] *Ibid*. pars. .04 and .05.

[28] *Ibid*. pars. .39 to .49.

Entries Illustrated

The series of entries shown below illustrates the accounting procedures applied in a financial reorganization. Assume New Horizons Inc. shows a deficit of $1 million before the reorganization is effected on June 30, 2001. Under the terms of the negotiation the creditors are giving up rights to payment for the $150,000 debt in return for 100% of the common shares. The original shareholders agree to give up their shares.

1. **Restate impairments of assets that existed prior to the reorganization**

Deficit	750,000	
Inventories (loss on writedown)		225,000
Intangible Assets (loss on writedown)		525,000

Elimination of deficit against contributed surplus

Common shares	1,750,000	
Deficit		1,750,000

2. and 3. **Restatement of assets and liabilities to recognize unrecorded gains and losses and to record the negotiated change in control**

Plant Assets (gain on write-up)	400,000	
Long-term Liabilities (gain on writedown)	150,000	
Common shares		550,000

Note that where there is no change in control, GAAP does not allow a comprehensive revaluation.

Disclosure

When a financial reorganization is effected, the following requirements must be fulfilled:

1. The proposed reorganization should receive the **approval** of the corporation's shareholders before it is put into effect.
2. The new asset and liability valuations should be **fair** and not deliberately understate or overstate assets, liabilities, and earnings.
3. After the reorganization the corporation must have a **zero balance of retained earnings**, although it may have contributed surplus arising from the reorganization.
4. In the period of the reorganization, the following must be **disclosed**:
   (a) The date of the reorganization
   (b) A description of the reorganization
   (c) The amount of the change in each major class of assets, liability of description and shareholders' equity resulting from the reorganization
5. In subsequent reports for a period of at least three years from the reorganization date, the following must be **disclosed**:
   (a) The date of the reorganization
   (b) The revaluation adjustment amount and the shareholders' equity account in which it was recorded
   (c) The amount of the deficit that was reclassified and the account to which it was reclassified
   (d) The measurement bases for the assets and liabilities that were revalued

SUMMARY OF LEARNING OBJECTIVE FOR APPENDIX 17A

●●●

9 Describe the accounting for a financial reorganization. A corporation that has accumulated a large debit balance (deficit) in retained earnings may enter into a process known as a financial reorganization. During a reorganization, creditors and shareholders negotiate a deal to put the company on a new footing. This generally involves a **change in control** and a **comprehensive revaluation** of assets and liabilities. The procedure consists of the following steps: (1) The deficit is reclassified such that the ending balance in Retained Earnings is zero. (2) The change in control is recorded. (3) All assets and liabilities are comprehensively revalued at current values so the company will not be burdened with excessive inventory or fixed asset valuations in following years.

KEY TERMS APPENDIX

comprehensive
  revaluation, 815
financial reorganization,
  815
fresh start accounting, 815
revaluation adjustment,
  815

Note: All asterisked Brief Exercises, Exercises, Problems, and Conceptual Cases relate to material contained in the appendix to the chapter.

BRIEF EXERCISES

●●●

BE17-1 Machines Inc. declared a cash dividend of $1.50 per share on its 2 million outstanding shares. The dividend was declared on August 1, payable on September 9 to all shareholders of record on August 15. Prepare all journal entries necessary on those three dates.

BE17-2 Ren Inc. owns shares of Stahl Corporation that are classified as temporary investment. At December 31, 2001, the securities were carried in Ren's accounting records at their cost of $875,000, which equals their market value. On September 21, 2002 when the securities' market value was $1.4 million, Ren declared a property dividend whereby the Stahl securities are to be distributed on October 23, 2002, to shareholders of record on October 8, 2002. Prepare all journal entries necessary on those three dates.

BE17-3 Might and Magic Inc. declared a scrip dividend of $3.00 per share on its 100,000 outstanding shares. The dividend was declared on January 30 and is payable with interest, at a 12% annual rate, on October 31. Prepare all journal entries necessary on those two dates.

BE17-4 Rex Mining Corp. declared, on April 20, a dividend of $700,000 payable on June 1. Of this amount, $125,000 is a return of capital. Prepare the April 20 and June 1 entries for Rex.

BE17-5 Holmgren Football Corporation has outstanding 200,000 common shares. The corporation declares a 5% stock dividend when the shares' fair value is $65 per share (carrying value is $40 per share). Prepare the journal entries for Holmgren Football Corporation for both the date of declaration and the date of distribution.

BE17-6 Use the information from BE17-5, but assume Holmgren Football Corporation declared a 100% stock dividend rather than a 5% stock dividend. Prepare the journal entries for both the date of declaration and the date of distribution.

BE17-7 Piggs Corporation has outstanding 300,000 common shares with a carrying value of $10 per share. Piggs declares a 3-for-1 stock split. How many shares are outstanding after the split? What is the carrying value per share after the split? What is the total carrying value after the split? What journal entry is necessary to record the split?

BE17-8 Pocahontas Inc. has retained earnings of $2.1 million at December 31, 2001. On that date the board of directors decides to appropriate $800,000 of retained earnings for a legal contingency. Prepare the entry to record the appropriation. Indicate the amount reported as total retained earnings after the appropriation.

*BE17-9 Truck Corporation went through a financial reorganization by writing down plant assets by $125,000 and eliminating its deficit, which was $250,000 prior to the reorganization. As part of the reorganization, the creditors agreed to take back 51% of the common shares in lieu of payment of the debt of $300,000. Prepare the entries to record the financial reorganization.

EXERCISES

E17-1 (Equity Items on the Balance Sheet) The following are selected transactions that may affect shareholders' equity.

1. Recorded accrued interest earned on a note receivable.
2. Declared a cash dividend.
3. Declared and distributed a stock split.
4. Recorded a retained earnings appropriation.
5. Recorded the expiration of insurance coverage that was previously recorded as prepaid insurance.
6. Paid the cash dividend declared in item 2 above.
7. Recorded accrued interest expense on a note payable.
8. Recorded an increase in value of an investment that will be distributed as a property dividend.
9. Declared a property dividend (see item 8 above).
10. Distributed the investment to shareholders (see items 8 and 9 above).
11. Declared a stock dividend.
12. Distributed the stock dividend declared in item 11.

Instructions

In the table below, indicate the effect each of the 12 transactions has on the financial statement elements listed. Use the following code:

I = Increase   D = Decrease   NE = No effect

Item	Assets	Liabilities	Shareholders' Equity	Share Capital	Retained Earnings	Net Income

E17-2 (Classification of Equity Items) Shareholders' equity on the balance sheet of Cherese Corp. is composed of three major sections: A. Share Capital, B. Contributed Surplus, and C. Retained Earnings.

Instructions

Classify each of the following items as affecting one of the three sections above or as D, an item not to be included in shareholders' equity.

1. Net income
2. Dividends payable
3. Stock split
4. Property dividends declared
5. Preferred shares
6. Common shares subscribed
7. Retained earnings appropriated
8. Sinking fund

E17-3 **(Cash Dividend and Liquidating Dividend)** Lotoya Corporation has 10 million common shares issued and outstanding. On June 1 the board of directors voted an 80 cents per share cash dividend to shareholders of record as of June 14, payable June 30.

Instructions

(a) Prepare the journal entry for each of the dates above assuming the dividend represents a distribution of earnings.

(b) How would the entry differ if the dividend were a liquidating dividend?

(c) Assume the company holds 300,000 common shares in the treasury and as a matter of administrative convenience dividends are paid on treasury shares. How should this cash receipt be recorded?

E17-4 **(Preferred Dividends)** The outstanding share capital of Millay Corporation consists of 2,000 shares of preferred and 5,000 common shares for which $250,000 was received. The preferred shares carry a dividend of $8 per share and have $100 stated value.

Instructions

Assuming that the company has retained earnings of $90,000, all of which is to be paid out in dividends, and that preferred dividends were not paid during the two years preceding the current year, state how much each class of shares should receive under each of the following conditions:

(a) The preferred shares are noncumulative and nonparticipating.

(b) The preferred shares are cumulative and nonparticipating.

(c) The preferred shares are cumulative and participating.

E17-5 **(Preferred Dividends)** MacLeish Limited's ledger shows the following balances on December 31, 2002.

Preferred shares—outstanding 20,000 shares	$ 200,000
Common shares—outstanding 30,000 shares	3,000,000
Retained earnings	630,000

Instructions

Assuming that the directors decide to declare total dividends in the amount of $366,000, determine how much each class of shares should receive under each of the conditions stated below. One year's dividends are in arrears on the preferred shares, which pay a dividend of $0.70 per share.

(a) The preferred shares are cumulative and fully participating.

(b) The preferred shares are noncumulative and nonparticipating.

(c) The preferred shares are noncumulative and are participating in distributions in excess of a 10% dividend rate on the common shares.

E17-6 **(Stock Split and Stock Dividend)** The common shares of Hamilton Inc. are currently selling at $120 per share. The directors wish to reduce the share price and increase share volume prior to a new issue. The per share carrying value is $70. Nine million shares are issued and outstanding.

Instructions

Prepare the necessary journal entries assuming:

(a) The board votes a 2-for-1 stock split.

(b) The board votes a 100% stock dividend.

(c) Briefly discuss the accounting and securities market differences between these two methods of increasing the number of shares outstanding.

E17-7 **(Stock Dividends)** Hudson Inc. has 5 million shares issued and outstanding. The book value is $32 per share and market value is $40 per share.

Instructions

Prepare the necessary journal entry for the date of declaration and date of issue assuming:

(a) A 10% stock dividend is declared.

(b) A 50% stock dividend is declared.

(c) If Hudson has 500,000 shares of treasury stock, should the stock dividend be applied to the treasury shares? Explain.

(d) What is the amount of the corporation's liability for the period from the declaration date to the distribution date?

E17-8 (Entries for Stock Dividends and Stock Splits) The shareholders' equity accounts of Chesterton Inc. have the following balances on December 31, 2002:

Common shares, 300,000 shares issued and outstanding	$3,000,000
Contributed surplus	1,200,000
Retained earnings	5,600,000

Common shares are currently selling on the Prairie Stock Exchange at $37.

Instructions

Prepare the appropriate journal entries for each of the following cases:

  (a) A stock dividend of 5% is declared and issued.
  (b) A stock dividend of 100% is declared and issued.
  (c) A 2-for-1 stock split is declared and issued.

E17-9 (Dividend Entries) The following data were taken from the balance sheet accounts of Masefield Corporation on December 31, 2001.

Current assets	$540,000
Investments	624,000
Common shares (no par value, no authorized limit,	
50,000 shares issued and outstanding)	500,000
Contributed surplus	150,000
Retained earnings	840,000

Instructions

Prepare the required journal entries for the following unrelated items:

  (a) A 5% stock dividend is declared and distributed at a time when the shares' market value is $39 per share.
  (b) A scrip dividend of $80,000 is declared.
  (c) A 5-for-1 stock split is effected.
  (d) A dividend in kind is declared January 5, 2002 and paid January 25, 2002, in bonds held as a long-term investment; the bonds have a book value of $100,000 and a fair market value of $135,000.

E17-10 (Calculation of Retained Earnings) The following information has been taken from the ledger accounts of Scotia Corporation.

Total income since incorporation	$317,000
Total cash dividends paid	60,000
Proceeds from sale of donated shares	40,000
Total value of stock dividends distributed	30,000
Unamortized discount on bonds payable	32,000
Appropriated for plant expansion	70,000

Instructions

Determine the current balance of unappropriated retained earnings.

E17-11 (Retained Earnings Appropriations and Disclosures) At December 31, 2001, the retained earnings account of Ellington Inc. had a balance of $320,000. There was no appropriation at this time. During 2002, net income was $235,000. Cash dividends declared during the year were $50,000 on preferred shares and $70,000 on common shares. A stock dividend on common shares resulted in an $88,000 charge to retained earnings. At December 31, 2002, the board of directors decided to create an appropriation for contingencies of $125,000 because of an outstanding lawsuit that does not meet the criteria for accrual.

Instructions

  (a) Prepare the journal entry to record the appropriation at December 31, 2002.
  (b) Prepare a statement of unappropriated retained earnings for 2002.
  (c) Prepare the retained earnings section of the December 31, 2002, balance sheet.
  (d) Assume that in May 2003, the lawsuit is settled and the company agrees to pay $113,000. At this time, the board of directors also decides to eliminate the appropriation. Prepare all necessary entries.
  (e) Return to item 1, but assume that the company decided to disclose the appropriation through a footnote at December 31, 2002, instead of preparing a formal journal entry. Prepare the necessary footnote.

E17-12 **(Shareholders' Equity Section)** Bruno Corporation's post-closing trial balance at December 31, 2001, was as follows.

BRUNO CORPORATION
Post-Closing Trial Balance
December 31, 2001

	Dr.	Cr.
Accounts payable		$ 310,000
Accounts receivable	$ 480,000	
Accumulated amortization—building and equipment		185,000
Contributed surplus—common		1,460,000
Allowance for doubtful accounts		30,000
Bonds payable		300,000
Building and equipment	1,450,000	
Cash	190,000	
Common shares		200,000
Dividends payable on preferred shares—cash		4,000
Inventories	560,000	
Land	400,000	
Preferred shares		500,000
Prepaid expenses	40,000	
Retained earnings		131,000
Totals	$3,290,000	$3,290,000

At December 31, 2001, Bruno had the following number of common and preferred shares:

	Common	Preferred
Authorized	600,000	60,000
Issued	200,000	10,000
Outstanding	190,000	10,000

The dividends on preferred shares are $4 cumulative. In addition, the preferred shares have a preference in liquidation of $50 per share.

Instructions

Prepare the shareholders' equity section of Bruno's balance sheet at December 31, 2001.

(AICPA adapted)

E17-13 **(Participating Preferred and Stock Dividend)** The following is the shareholders' equity section of Sakamoto Corp. at December 31, 2001.

Preferred shares,* authorized 100,000 shares; issued 15,000 shares	$ 750,000
Common shares, authorized 200,000 shares; issued 90,000 shares	1,800,000
Contributed surplus	3,150,000
Total paid-in capital	5,700,000
Retained earnings	4,470,500
Total shareholders' equity	$10,170,500

* The preferred shares have a $6 dividend rate, are cumulative, and are participating in distributions in excess of a $3 dividend on the common shares.

Instructions

(a) No dividends have been paid in 1999 or 2000. On December 31, 2001, Seymour wants to pay a cash dividend of $4 a share to common shareholders. How much cash would be needed for the total amount paid to preferred and common shareholders?

(b) Instead, the company will declare a 15% stock dividend on the outstanding common shares. The shares' market value is $103 per share. Prepare the entry on the date of declaration.

(c) Instead, the company will acquire and cancel 7,500 common shares. The current market value is $103 per share. Prepare the entry to record the retirement, assuming contributed surplus arose from previous cancellations of common shares.

E17-14 (Dividends and Shareholders' Equity Section)   Cleves Corp. reported the following amounts in the shareholders' equity section of its December 31, 2001 balance sheet.

Preferred shares, $10 dividend (10,000 shares authorized, 2,000 shares issued)	$200,000
Common shares, (100,000 shares authorized, 20,000 shares issued)	100,000
Contributed surplus	125,000
Retained earnings	450,000
Total	$875,000

During 2002, the company took part in the following transactions concerning shareholders' equity.

1. Paid the annual 2001 $10 per share dividend on preferred shares and a $2 per share dividend on common shares. These dividends had been declared on December 31, 2001.
2. Purchased 1,700 shares of its own outstanding common shares for $40 per share and cancelled them.
3. Issued 500 shares of preferred shares at $105 per share.
4. Declared a 10% stock dividend on the outstanding common shares when the shares are selling for $45 per share.
5. Issued the stock dividend.
6. Declared the annual 2002 $10 per share dividend on preferred shares and the $2 per share dividend on common shares. These dividends are payable in 2003.
7. Appropriated retained earnings for plant expansion, $200,000.

Instructions

(a) Prepare journal entries to record the transactions described above.

(b) Prepare the December 31, 2002 shareholders' equity section. Assume 2002 net income was $330,000.

E17-15 (Comparison of Alternative Forms of Financing)   Shown below is the liabilities and shareholders' equity section of the balance sheet for Kingston Corp. and Benson Corp. Each has assets totalling $4.2 million.

Kingston Corp.		Benson Corp.	
Current liabilities	$ 300,000	Current liabilities	$ 600,000
Long-term debt, 10%	1,200,000	Common shares	2,900,000
Common shares (100,000 shares issued)	2,000,000	(145,000 shares issued)	
Retained earnings		Retained earnings	
(Cash dividends, $220,000)	700,000	(Cash dividends, $328,000)	700,000
	$4,200,000		$4,200,000

For the year, each company has earned the same income before interest and taxes.

	Kingston Corp.	Benson Corp.
Income before interest and taxes	$1,200,000	$1,200,000
Interest expense	120,000	–0–
	1,080,000	1,200,000
Income taxes (45%)	486,000	540,000
Net income	$ 594,000	$ 660,000

At year end, the market price of Kingston's shares was $101 per share and Benson's was $63.50.

Instructions

(a) Which company is more profitable in terms of return on total assets?

(b) Which company is more profitable in terms of return on shareholders' equity?

(c) Which company has the greater net income per share? Neither company issued nor reacquired shares during the year.

(d) From the point of view of income, is it advantageous to Kingston's shareholders to have the long-term debt outstanding? Why?

(e) What is each company's price earnings ratio?

(f) What is the book value per share for each company?

E17-16 **(Trading on the Equity Analysis)** Presented below is information from the annual report of Emporia Inc.

Operating income	$532,150
Bond interest expense	135,000
	397,150
Income taxes	183,432
Net income	$213,718
Bonds payable	$1,000,000
Common shares	875,000
Appropriation for contingencies	75,000
Retained earnings, unappropriated	300,000

Instructions
Is the company trading on the equity successfully? Explain.

E17-17 **(Calculation of Book Value per Share)** Sondgeroth Inc. began operations in January 1999 and reported the following results for each of its three years of operations.

1999 $260,000 net loss   2000 $40,000 net loss   2001 $800,000 net income

At December 31, 2001, the company's capital accounts were as follows:

Cumulative preferred shares, $8 dividends; authorized, issued, and outstanding 5,000 shares	$500,000
Common shares, authorized 1,000,000 shares; issued and outstanding 750,000 shares	$750,000

The company has never paid a cash or stock dividend. There has been no change in the capital accounts since Sondgeroth began operations. The provincial law permits dividends only from retained earnings.

Instructions
(a) Calculate the common shares' book value at December 31, 2001.
(b) Calculate the common shares' book value at December 31, 2001, assuming that the preferred shares have a liquidating value of $106 per share.

E17-18 **(Financial Reorganization)** The following account balances are available from the ledger of Glamorgan Corporation on December 31, 2000.

Common Shares—20,000 shares authorized and outstanding	$1,000,000
Retained Earnings (deficit)	(190,000)

As of January 2, 2001, the corporation gave effect to a shareholder-approved reorganization by agreeing to pass the common shares over to the creditors in full payment of the $250,000 debt, writing up plant assets by $85,600, and eliminating the deficit.

Instructions
Prepare the required journal entries for the financial reorganization of Glamorgan Corporation.

E17-19 **(Financial Reorganization)** The condensed balance sheets of Regina Limited immediately before and one year after it had completed a financial reorganization appear below.

	Before Reorg	One Year After		Before Reorg	One Year After
Current assets	$ 300,000	$ 420,000	Common shares	$2,400,000	$1,550,000
Plant assets (net)	1,700,000	1,290,000	Contributed Surplus	220,000	
			Retained earnings	(620,000)	160,000
	$2,000,000	$1,710,000		$2,000,000)	$1,710,000

For the year following the financial reorganization, the company reported net income of $190,000, amortization expense of $80,000, and paid a cash dividend of $30,000. As part of the reorganization, the company wrote down inventories by $120,000 in order to reflect circumstances that existed prior to the reorganization. Also, the deficit and any revaluation adjustment was accounted for by charging amounts against contributed surplus until it was eliminated, with any remaining amount being charged against common shares. The common shares are widely held and there is no controlling interest. No purchases or sales of plant assets and no share transactions occurred in the year following the reorganization.

Instructions

Prepare all the journal entries made at the time of the reorganization.

*E17-20 (Financial Reorganization) Sudbury Corporation is under protection of the bankruptcy court and has the following account balances at June 30, 2002.

Cash	$ (5,000)	Accounts payable	$ 450,000
Accounts receivable	320,000	Notes payable	605,000
Inventory	450,000	Taxes and wages	60,000
Equipment	860,000	Mortgage payable	150,000
Accumulated amortization	(525,000)	Common shares	50,000
Intangibles	80,000	Retained earnings	(135,000)
Total	$1,180,000	Total	$1,180,000

The court has accepted the following proposed settlement of the company's affairs. Write down the assets by the following amounts:

Accounts receivable	$140,000
Inventory	$160,000
Intangibles	$ 80,000

Equipment will be written up by $100,000 to reflect fair value.

The trade creditors (accounts payable) will reduce their claim by 30%, will accept one-year notes for 50% of their claim, and retain their current claim for the remaining 20%. The tax, wage, and mortgage claims will remain unchanged. The current common shares will be surrendered to the corporation and cancelled. In consideration thereof, the current shareholders shall be held harmless from any possible personal liability. The current holder of the note payable shall receive 1,000 common shares in full satisfaction of the note payable. After these adjustments have been made, the retained earnings shall be raised to zero.

Instructions

(a) Prepare a balance sheet at June 30, 2002 that reflects the events listed above.
(b) Briefly discuss the nature of a financial reorganization.

PROBLEMS

P17-1 As the newly appointed controller for Farooq Limited, you are interested in analysing the company's "Additional Capital" account in order to present an accurate balance sheet. Your assistant, Dan Ross, who has analysed the account from the company's inception, submits the following summary:

	Debits	Credits
Cash dividends—preferred	$ 114,000	
Cash dividends—common	340,000	
Net income		780,000
Contra to appraisal increase of land*		400,000
Additional assessments of prior years' income taxes	91,000	
Extraordinary gain		22,500
Extraordinary loss	118,500	
Correction of a prior period error	55,000	
	718,500	1,202,500
Credit balance of additional capital account	484,000	0
	$1,202,500	$1,202,500

* appropriately recognized prior to 1990.

Instructions

(a) Prepare a journal entry to close the single "Additional Capital" account now used and to establish appropriately classified accounts. Indicate how you derive the balance of each new account.
(b) If generally accepted accounting principles had been followed, what amount should have been shown as total net income?

P17-2 The balance sheet of Bajor Inc. shows $400,000 common shares consisting of 4,000 shares and retained earnings of $144,000. As company controller, you find that Ro Laren, the assistant treasurer, is $83,000 short in her accounts and had concealed this shortage by adding the amount to the inventory. She owns 750 shares of the company's common shares and, in settlement of the shortage, offers these shares at their book value. The offer is accepted; the company pays her the excess value and distributes the 750 shares thus acquired to the other shareholders.

Instructions

(a) What amount should Bajor Inc. pay the assistant treasurer?
(b) By what journal entries should the foregoing transactions be recorded?
(c) What is the total shareholders' equity after the distribution noted above?

P17-3 Monie Inc. began operations in January 1998 and had the following reported net income or loss for each of its five years of operations:

1998	$225,000 loss
1999	$140,000 loss
2000	$180,000 loss
2001	$422,500 income
2002	$1,535,000 income

At December 31, 2002, the company's capital accounts were as follows:

Common shares, authorized 200,000 shares;	
issued and outstanding 50,000 shares	$1,750,000
$8 nonparticipating noncumulative preferred shares,	
authorized, issued, and outstanding 5,000 shares	500,000
$5 fully participating cumulative preferred shares,	
authorized, issued, and outstanding 10,000 shares	1,500,000

The company has never paid a cash or stock dividend. There has been no change in the capital accounts since the company began operations. The appropriate provincial law permits dividends only from retained earnings.

Instructions

Prepare a work sheet showing the maximum amount available for cash dividends on December 31, 2002, and how it would be distributable to the holders of the common shares and each of the preferred shares. Show supporting calculations in good form.

(AICPA adapted)

P17-4 The board of directors of Ferber Corporation on December 1, 2002 declared a 4% stock dividend on the corporation's common shares, payable on December 28, 2002, only to the holders of record at the close of business December 15, 2002. The directors stipulated that cash dividends were to be paid in lieu of issuing any fractional shares. They also directed that the amount to be charged against retained earnings should be an amount equal to the shares' market value on the record date multiplied by the total of (a) the number of shares issued as a stock dividend, and (b) the number of shares on which cash is paid in place of the issuance of fractional shares. The following facts are given.

1. At the dividend record date:

(a) Shares of Ferber common issued	3,048,750
(b) Shares of Ferber common held in treasury (waiting to be cancelled)	1,100
(c) Shares of Ferber common included in item 1 above held by persons who will receive cash in lieu of fractional shares	222,750

2. Values of Ferber common were:

Market value at December 1 and 15	$21
Book value at December 1 and 15	$14

Instructions

Prepare entries and explanations to record the dividend payment.

(AICPA adapted)

P17-5 The books of Passos Corporation carried the following account balances as of December 31, 2001.

Cash	$1,195,000
Preferred shares, $3 cumulative dividend, nonparticipating,	
15,000 shares issued	750,000
Common shares, no par value, 300,000 shares issued	1,500,000
Contributed surplus (preferred)	150,000
Retained earnings	105,000

The preferred shares have dividends in arrears for the past year (2001).

The board of directors, at its annual meeting on December 21, 2002, declared the following: "The current year dividends shall be $3 on the preferred and $0.30 per share on the common; the dividends in arrears shall be paid by issuing one share of common shares for each 10 shares of preferred held."

The preferred is currently selling at $80 per share and the common at $8 per share. Net income for 2002 is estimated at $77,000.

Instructions

(a) Prepare the journal entries required for the dividend declaration and payment, assuming that they occur simultaneously.

(b) Could the company give the preferred shareholders two years' dividends and common shareholders a 30 cent per share dividend, all in cash?

P17-6 Cajun Corp. has outstanding 2,500 preferred shares, no par value, $6 dividend, which were issued for $250,000 and 15,000 shares of no par value common, for which $150,000 was received. The schedule below shows the amount of dividends paid out over the last four years.

Instructions

Allocate the dividends to each type of shares under assumptions (a) and (b). Express your answers in per-share amounts using the following format.

		Assumptions			
		(a) Preferred, noncumulative, and nonparticipating		(b) Preferred, cumulative, and fully participating	
Year	Paid-out	Preferred	Common	Preferred	Common
1999	$13,000				
2000	$26,000				
2001	$57,000				
2002	$76,000				

P17-7 Guo Limited provides you with the following condensed balance sheet information.

Assets		Liabilities and Shareholders' Equity		
Current assets	$ 40,000	Current and long-term liabilities		$100,000
Investments in ABC		Shareholders' equity		
(10,000 shares at cost)	60,000	Common shares*	$ 20,000	
Equipment (net)	250,000	Contributed surplus	110,000	
Intangibles	60,000	Retained earnings	180,000	310,000
Total assets	$410,000	Total liabilities and		
		shareholders' equity		$410,000

* 10,000 shares issued and outstanding.

Instructions

For each transaction below, indicate the dollar impact (if any) on the following five items: (1) total assets, (2) common shares, (3) contributed surplus, (4) retained earnings, and (5) shareholders' equity. (Each situation is independent.)

(a) The company declares and pays a $0.50 per share dividend.

(b) The company declares and issues a 10% stock dividend when the shares' market price is $14 per share.

(c) The company declares and issues a 40% stock dividend when the shares' market price is $15 per share.

(d) The company declares and distributes a property dividend. The company gives one share of ABC shares for every two shares of company shares held. ABC is selling for $10 per share on the date the property dividend is declared.

(e) The company declares a 2-for-1 stock split and issues new shares.

P17-8 Some of the account balances of Vai Limited at December 31, 2001 are shown below.

$6 Preferred shares (no par, 2,000 shares authorized, 2000 shares issued and outstanding)	$520,000
Common shares (no par, 100,000 shares authorized, 50,000 shares issued and outstanding)	500,000
Contributed surplus	103,000
Unappropriated Retained Earnings	304,000
Retained Earnings Appropriated for Contingencies	75,000
Retained Earnings Appropriated for Fire Insurance	95,000

The price of the company's common shares has been increasing steadily on the market; it was $21 on January 1, 2002, advanced to $24 by July 1, and to $27 at the end of the year 2002. The preferred shares are not openly traded but were appraised at $120 per share during 2002.

Instructions

Give the proper journal entries for each of the following:

(a) The company incurred a fire loss of $71,000 to its warehouse.

(b) The company declared a property dividend on April 1. Each common shareholder was to receive one share of Waterloo Corp. for every 10 shares outstanding. Vai had 8,000 shares of Waterloo (2% of total outstanding shares), which was purchased in 1999 for $68,400. The market value of Waterloo shares was $16 per share on April 1. Record appreciation only on the shares distributed.

(c) On July 1, the company declared a 5% stock dividend to the common (outstanding) shareholders.

(d) The city of Windsor, in an effort to persuade Vai to expand into that city, donated to the company a plot of land with an appraised value of $42,000.

(e) At the annual board of directors meeting, the board decided to "Set up an appropriation in retained earnings for the future construction of a new plant. Such appropriation to be for $125,000 per year. Also, to increase the appropriation for contingencies by $25,000 and to eliminate the appropriation for fire insurance and begin purchasing such insurance from London Insurance Company."

P17-9 The shareholders' equity section of Girod Limited balance sheet on January 1 of the current year is as follows:

Share capital		
Common shares, no par, 20,000 shares authorized, 10,000 shares issued	$1,000,000	
Contributed surplus	400,000	
Total paid-in capital		$1,400,000
Retained earnings		
Unappropriated	328,800	
Appropriated for plant expansion	120,000	
Appropriated for company share buy back	61,200	
Total retained earnings		510,000
Total shareholders' equity		$1,910,000

The following selected transactions occurred during the year.

1. Paid cash dividends of $1.25 per share on the common shares. The dividend had been properly recorded when declared last year.

2. Declared a 10% stock dividend on the common shares when the shares were selling at $113 each in the market.

3. Made a prior period adjustment to correct an error of $70,000, which overstated net income in the previous year. The error was the result of an overstatement of ending inventory.

4. Issued the certificates for the stock dividend.

5. The board appropriated $40,000 of retained earnings for plant expansion, eliminated the appropriation for company share buy back, and declared a cash dividend of $1.65 per share on the common shares.

6. The company reported net income of $235,000 for the year.

Instructions

(a) Prepare journal entries for the selected transactions above (ignore income taxes).

(b) Calculate the unappropriated retained earnings balance at December 31.

P17-10 On December 15, 2001, the directors of Laforge Corporation voted to appropriate $90,000 of retained earnings and to retain in the business assets equal to the appropriation for use in expanding the corporation's factory building. This was the fourth such appropriation; after it was recorded, the shareholders' equity section of Laforge's balance sheet appeared as follows.

Shareholders' equity		
Common shares, no par value, 300,000 shares		
authorized, 200,000 shares issued and outstanding		$2,000,000
Contributed surplus		3,600,000
Total paid-in capital		5,600,000
Retained earnings		
Unappropriated	$1,800,000	
Appropriated for plant expansion	360,000	
Total retained earnings		2,160,000
Total shareholders' equity		$7,760,000

On January 9, 2002, the corporation entered into a contract for the construction of the factory addition for which the retained earnings were appropriated. On November 1, 2002, the addition was completed and the contractor was paid the contract price of $330,000.

On December 14, 2002, the board of directors voted to return the balance of the Retained Earnings Appropriated for Plant Expansion account to Unappropriated Retained Earnings. They also voted a 25,000 share stock dividend distributable on January 23, 2003, to the January 15, 2003 shareholders of record. The stock dividend was paid per the board's resolution. The corporation's shares were selling at $47 in the market on December 14, 2002. Laforge reported net income of $530,000 for 2001 and $600,000 for 2002.

Instructions

(a) Prepare the appropriate journal entries for Laforge Corporation for the information above (December 15, 2001 to January 23, 2003, inclusive).

(b) Prepare the shareholders' equity section of the balance sheet for Laforge at December 31, 2002 in proper accounting form.

P17-11 The following is a summary of all relevant transactions of Jadzia Corporation since it was organized in 1999.

In 1999, 15,000 shares were authorized and 7,000 shares of common shares (no par value) were issued at a price of $57. In 2000, 1,000 shares were issued as a stock dividend when the shares were selling for $62. Three hundred shares of common were bought in 2001 at a cost of $66 per share and cancelled.

In 2000, 10,000 preferred shares were authorized and the company issued 4,000 of them at $113.

The corporation has earned a total of $610,000 in net income after income taxes and paid out a total of $312,600 in cash dividends since incorporation. An appropriation was made in 2001 by the board of directors from retained earnings in the amount of $75,000 for Fixed Asset Replacements.

Instructions

Prepare the shareholders' equity section of the company's balance sheet in proper form as of December 31, 2001.

P17-12 Ducat Corporation has outstanding 2 million common shares of no par value which were issued at $10 each. The balance in its retained earnings account at January 1, 2001, was $24 million and in its contributed surplus account was $5 million. During 2001, the company's net income was $5.7 million. A cash dividend of 60 cents a share was paid June 30, 2001 and a 6% stock dividend was distributed to shareholders of record at the close of business on December 31, 2001. You have been asked to advise on the proper accounting treatment of the stock dividend.

The existing company shares are quoted on a national stock exchange. The shares' market price has been as follows:

October 31, 2001	$31
November 30, 2001	33
December 31, 2001	38
Average price over the two-month period	35

Instructions

(a) Prepare a journal entry to record the cash dividend.

(b) Prepare a journal entry to record the stock dividend.

(c) Prepare the shareholders' equity section (including schedule of retained earnings) of the company balance sheet for the year 2001 on the basis of the foregoing information. Draft a note to the financial statements setting forth the basis of the accounting for the stock dividend and add separately appropriate comments or explanations regarding the basis chosen.

P17-13 Okanagan Inc. was formed on July 1, 1998. It was authorized to issue 300,000 shares of no par value common shares and 100,000 shares of cumulative and nonparticipating preferred stock carrying a $2 dividend. The company has a July 1–June 30 fiscal year.

The following information relates to the company's shareholders' equity account.

Common Shares

Prior to the 2000–01 fiscal year, the company had 110,000 shares of outstanding common issued as follows.

1. 95,000 shares were issued for cash on July 1, 1998 at $31 per share.
2. On July 24, 1998, 5,000 shares were exchanged for a plot of land, which cost the seller $70,000 in 1992 and had an estimated market value of $220,000 on July 24, 1998.
3. 10,000 shares were issued on March 1, 2000; the shares had been subscribed for $42 per share on October 31, 1999.

During the 2000–01 fiscal year, the following transactions regarding common shares took place:

October 1, 2000	Subscriptions were received for 10,000 shares at $46 per share. Cash of $92,000 was received in full payment for 2,000 shares and share certificates were issued. The remaining subscription for 8,000 shares was to be paid in full by September 30, 2001, at which time the certificates were to be issued.
November 30, 2000	The company purchased 2,000 shares of its own common on the open market at $39 per share. These shares were restored to the status of authorized but unissued shares.
December 15, 2000	The company declared a 5% stock dividend for shareholders of record on January 15, 2001, to be issued on January 31, 2001. The company was having a liquidity problem and could not afford a cash dividend at the time. The company's common shares were selling at $52 per share on December 15, 2000.
June 20, 2001	The company sold 500 shares of its own common for $21,000.

Preferred Shares

The company issued 50,000 shares of preferred at $44 per share on July 1, 1999.

Cash Dividends

The company has followed a schedule of declaring cash dividends in December and June with payment being made to shareholders of record in the following month. The cash dividends, which have been declared since the company's inception through June 30, 2001, are shown below:

Declaration Date	Common Shares	Preferred Shares
12/15/99	$0.30 per share	$3.00 per share
6/15/00	$0.30 per share	$1.00 per share
12/15/00	—	$1.00 per share

No cash dividends were declared during June 2001 due to the company's liquidity problems.

Retained Earnings

As of June 30, 2000, the company's retained earnings account had a balance of $690,000. For the fiscal year ending June 30, 2001, the company reported net income of $40,000.

In March of 2000, the company received a term loan from Manitoba Bank. The bank requires the company to establish a sinking fund and restrict retained earnings for an amount equal to the sinking fund deposit. The annual sinking fund payment of $50,000 is due on April 30 each year; the first payment was made on schedule on April 30, 2001.

Instructions

Prepare the shareholders' equity section of the company's balance sheet, including appropriate notes, as of June 30, 2001, as it should appear in its annual report to the shareholders.

(CMA adapted)

P17-14 Durdil Inc. is selling its common shares for $120 per share. Five million shares are currently issued and outstanding. The board of directors wishes to stimulate interest in Durdil common before a forthcoming share issue but does not wish to distribute capital at this time. The board also believes that too many adjustments to the Shareholders' Equity section, especially Retained Earnings, might discourage potential investors.

The board has considered three options for stimulating interest in the shares:

1. A 20% stock dividend
2. A 100% stock dividend
3. A 2-for-1 stock split.

Instructions

Acting as financial advisor to the board, you have been asked to report briefly on each option and, considering the board's wishes, make a recommendation. Discuss the effects of each of the foregoing options.

CONCEPTUAL CASES

···

C17-1 *CICA Handbook* Section 1000 defines various elements of financial statements.

Instructions

Answer the following questions based on Section 1000.

(a) Define and discuss the term "equity."
(b) What transactions or events change owners' equity?
(c) What are examples of changes within owners' equity that do not change the total amount of owners' equity?

C17-2 The directors of Amman Corporation are considering issuing a stock dividend. They have asked you to discuss the proposed action by answering the following questions.

Instructions

(a) What is a stock dividend? How is a stock dividend distinguished from a stock split: (a) From a legal standpoint? (b) From an accounting standpoint?
(b) For what reasons does a corporation usually declare a stock dividend? A stock split?
(c) Discuss the amount, if any, of retained earnings to be capitalized in connection with a stock dividend.

(AICPA adapted)

C17-3 Kitakyushu Inc., a client, is considering authorizing a 10% common stock dividend to common shareholders. Kitakyushu's financial vice-president wishes to discuss the accounting implications of such an authorization with you before the next meeting of the board of directors.

Instructions

(a) The first topic the vice-president wishes to discuss is the nature of the stock dividend to the recipient. Discuss the case against considering the stock dividend as income to the recipient.
(b) The other topic for discussion is the propriety of issuing the stock dividend to all "shareholders of record" or to "shareholders of record exclusive of shares held in the name of the corporation as treasury shares." Discuss the case against issuing stock dividends on treasury shares.

(AICPA adapted)

*C17-4 Henning Inc, a medium-sized manufacturer, has been experiencing losses for the five years that it has been doing business. Although the operations for the year just ended resulted in a loss, several important changes resulted in a profitable fourth quarter, and the company's future operations are expected to be profitable. The treasurer, Peter Henning, suggests that there be a financial reorganization to eliminate the accumulated deficit of $650,000.

Instructions

(a) What are the characteristics of a financial reorganization? In other words, what does it consist of?
(b) List the conditions under which a financial reorganization generally is justified.
(c) Discuss the propriety of the treasurer's proposals to eliminate the deficit of $650,000.

(AICPA adapted)

*C17-5 After operating several years, Lewis Corporation showed a net worth of $1.5 million, of which $300,000 was represented by 3,000 common shares, and $1.2 million by retained earnings. Subsequently, three additional shares were issued for each share held, which made the common shares $1.2 million and retained earnings $300,000. The operations of later years showed an aggregate loss of $840,000, leaving a deficit of $540,000.

Instructions

Write a memorandum giving your opinion of these transactions; disregard their legal aspects.

Using Your Judgement

FINANCIAL REPORTING PROBLEM 1:
CANADIAN TIRE CORPORATION, LIMITED

Instructions
Refer to the financial statements and accompanying notes and discussion of **Canadian Tire Corporation, Limited**, presented in Appendix 5B and answer the following questions.

(a) What amount of cash dividends per share was declared by the company in 2000? What was the dollar amount effect of the cash dividends on shareholders' equity?

(b) What is the company's rate of return on common share equity for 2000 and 1999?

(c) What is the company's payout ratio for 2000 and 1999?

(d) What is the company's book value per share at December 30, 2000 and January 1, 2000?

(e) Does the company have any treasury shares? How are these presented on the balance sheet? How are transactions related to these shares accounted for?

(f) What was the market price range (high/low) of the company's common shares during the quarter ended December 30, 2000?

(g) Using the high price per share in the fourth quarter of 2000, what was the company's price earnings ratio?

FINANCIAL REPORTING PROBLEM 2:
MDS INC.

Below is an excerpt from note 10 to financial statements of **MDS Inc.**

Share Capital
Effective September 26, 2000, the Company declared a one-for-one stock dividend which has essentially the same impact as a two-for-one stock split. Information contained in this note pertaining to dividends, share repurchases, the stock option plan, the stock dividend and share purchase plan and the employee share ownership plan, has been adjusted to reflect the impact of the stock dividend. The tables contained in note 10 a) presents the number of shares issued, repurchased and converted based on the date of the actual transaction.

	Common	
(number of shares in thousands)	Number	Amount
Issued on conversion of Class A to Common	12,945	$ 22.2
Issued on conversion of Class B to Common	47,254	$317.9
Issued subsequent to conversions	9,676	442.6
Stock dividend	69,711	—
Repurchases	(116)	(0.4)
Balance—October 31, 2000	139,470	$782.3

The Statement of Retained Earnings is noted below:

Years Ended October 31 (millions of Canadian dollars) (restated—note 2)	2000	1999	1998
Retained earnings, beginning of year	$324.1	$262.7	$237.6
Net income	110.3	81.9	44.3
Repurchase of shares and options (note 10)	(18.7)	(12.4)	(12.2)
Dividends	(10.3)	(8.1)	(7.0)
Retained earnings, end of year	$405.4	$324.1	$262.7

Instructions
Discuss the financial reporting issues surrounding the stock dividend.

FINANCIAL STATEMENT ANALYSIS CASE

Nortel Networks

On July 29, 1999, **Nortel Networks** announced a 2-for-1 stock split after its shares had risen in value by 70% in 1999. The company was among several others in the industry that had recently split its shares, such as **Lucent Technologies, Cisco Systems,** and **JDS Uniphase.**

Instructions

(a) Why might Nortel have declared a stock split?

(b) What impact did the stock split have on (1) total shareholders' equity; (2) total book value; (3) number of outstanding shares, and (4) book value per share?

(c) What impact did the split have on the shares' market value? What has since happened to the market price?

COMPARATIVE ANALYSIS CASE

The Royal Bank of Canada versus the Bank of Montreal

Instructions

Go to the Digital Tool and, using the annual report information for the above noted companies, answer the following questions.

(a) What amounts of cash dividends per share were declared by each company? What were the dollar amount effects of the cash dividends on each company's shareholders' equity?

(b) What are the respective rates of return on common shareholders' equity for 2000 and 1999? Which company gets the higher return on the equity of its shareholders?

(c) What are the payout ratios for 2000?

(d) What was the market price range (high/low) for the common shares of both companies during the fourth quarter of 2000? Which company's share price increased more (percentage-wise) during 2000?

(e) What was the price earnings ratio at year end for both companies?

RESEARCH CASE

The October 3, 1994, issue of *Barron's* includes an article by Shirley A. Lazo entitled "Split Decision: One Way To Lift Shares."

Instructions

(a) Read the article and answer the following questions.

(b) Why might a stock dividend/split have a positive effect on shareholder wealth?

(c) Why might a stock dividend/split have a negative effect on shareholder wealth?

(d) According to the study described in the article, what happens to the stock prices of banks during the month following a stock dividend/split?

(e) What conclusion was drawn from the study?

ETHICS CASES

*Case 1

"You can't write up assets," said Nick Toby, internal audit director of Paula Nofftz International Inc., to his boss, Jim Coffin, vice-president and chief financial officer. "Nonsense," said Jim, "I can do this as part of a quasi-reorganization of our company." For the last three years, Paula Nofftz International, a farm equipment manufacturing firm, has experienced a downturn in its profits resulting from stiff competition with overseas firms and increasing direct labour costs. Though the prospects are still gloomy, the company is hoping to turn a profit by modernizing its property, plant, and equipment (PP&E). This will require Paula Nofftz International to raise a lot of money.

Over the past few months, Jim tried to raise funds from various financial institutions. They are unwilling to consider lending capital, however, because the company's net book value of fixed assets on the balance sheet, based on historic cost, was not ample to sustain major funding. Jim attempted to explain to bankers and investors that these assets were more valuable than their recorded amounts, given that the company used accelerated amortization methods and tended to underestimate the useful lives of assets. Jim also believes that the company's land and buildings are substantially undervalued because of rising real estate prices over the past several years.

Jim's idea is a simple one: First, declare a large dividend to company shareholders such that Retained Earnings would have a large debit balance. Then, write up the fixed assets of Paula Nofftz International to an amount equal to the deficit in the Retained Earnings account.

Instructions

(a) What are the ethical implications of Jim Coffin's creative accounting scheme?

(b) Who could be harmed if the accounting reorganization were implemented and Paula Nofftz International Inc. received additional funding?

(c) Why can't a company write up assets when their fair value exceeds their original cost?

Case 2

Donald Young, controller for Centre Corporation, wants to discuss with the company president, Rhonda Santo, the possibility of paying a stock dividend. Young knows the company does not have an abundance of cash, yet he is certain Santo would like to give the shareholders something of value this year since it has been a few years since the company has paid any dividends. Young also is concerned that their cash position will not improve significantly in the near future. He feels that shareholders look to retained earnings and, if they see a large balance, believe (erroneously, of course) that the company can pay a cash dividend.

Young wants to propose that the company pay a 100% stock dividend as opposed to a cash dividend or a 2-for-1 stock split. He reasons (1) that the shareholders will receive something of value, other than cash, and (2) that retained earnings will be reduced by the stock dividend (as opposed to a split, which does not affect retained earnings) so shareholders will be less likely to expect cash dividends in the near future.

Instructions
Answer the following questions.

(a) What are the ethical issues involved?

(b) Do you agree with Young's reasoning?

Dilutive Securities and Earnings per Share

LEARNING OBJECTIVES

After studying this chapter, you should be able to:

1. Describe the accounting for the issuance, conversion, and retirement of convertible securities.

2. Explain the accounting for convertible preferred shares.

3. Contrast the accounting for stock warrants and stock warrants issued with other securities.

4. Describe the accounting for stock compensation plans under generally accepted accounting principles.

5. Explain the controversy involving stock compensation plans.

6. Calculate earnings per share in a simple capital structure.

7. Calculate earnings per share in a complex capital structure.

PREVIEW OF CHAPTER 18

The widespread use of dilutive securities has led the accounting profession to examine the area closely. Specifically, the profession has directed its attention to recognizing the dilutive components of these securities at date of issuance and to their impact on earnings per share. The first section of this chapter discusses convertible securities, warrants, stock options, and contingent shares. The second section indicates how these securities are used in earnings per share calculations. The content and organization of the chapter are as follows:

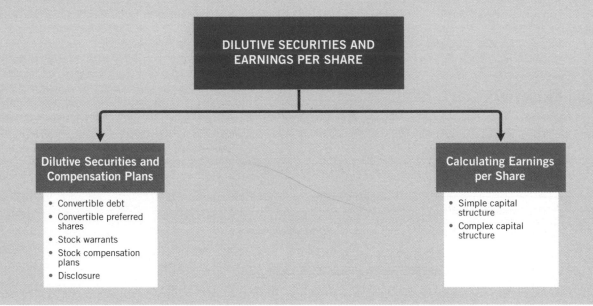

SECTION 1 — Dilutive Securities and Compensation Plans

A **dilutive security** is an instrument or contract that may entitle its holder to obtain a common share. Thus the existence of dilutive securities may cause existing shareholder holdings to become diluted if additional common shares are issued. Dilutive securities are also referred to as potential common shares.

Accounting for Convertible Debt

OBJECTIVE 1

Describe the accounting for the issuance, conversion, and retirement of convertible securities.

If bonds can be converted into other corporate securities during some specified period of time after issuance, they are called **convertible bonds**. A **convertible bond** combines the **benefits** of a bond with the **privilege** of exchanging it for common shares at the holder's option. It is purchased by investors who desire the **security** of a bond holding—**guaranteed interest**—plus the added option of conversion if the common shares' value appreciates significantly.

Corporations issue convertibles for two main reasons. One is the **desire to raise equity capital without giving up more ownership control than necessary**. To illustrate, assume that a company wants to raise $1 million at a time when its common shares are selling at $45 per share. Such an issue would require selling 22,222 shares (ignoring issue costs). By selling 1,000 bonds at $1,000 par, each convertible into 20 common shares, the enterprise may raise $1 million by committing only 20,000 common shares.[1]

A second reason why companies issue convertible securities is to **obtain debt financing at cheaper rates**. Many enterprises would have to issue debt at higher interest rates unless a convertible feature was attached. The conversion privilege entices the investor to accept a lower interest rate than would normally be the case on a straight debt issue. For example, **Amazon.com** recently issued convertible bonds that pay interest at an effective yield of 4.75%, which is much lower than Amazon.com would have to pay if it issued straight debt. For this lower interest rate, the investor receives the right to buy Amazon.com's common shares at a fixed price until maturity.[2]

Accounting for convertible debt involves reporting issues at the time of (1) issuance, (2) conversion, and (3) retirement.

At Time of Issuance

Convertible bonds are compound financial instruments. **Compound financial instruments** have both an equity component and a liability component and are sometimes referred to as hybrid instruments because they have the attributes of both debt and equity. The conversion feature on a convertible bond makes the instrument more valuable to an investor, and therefore, the option feature itself has value i.e. as previously mentioned, an investor is willing to accept lower interest or pay a premium for the convertible bond. The obligation to deliver cash under the bond represents a **financial liability**[3] and the right to acquire the company's common shares represents an **equity instrument**.[4]

Compound instruments must be split into their components and **presented** separately in the financial statements. Since the embedded option to convert to common shares is an **equity instrument**, that part of the debt is presented as **equity**. The remaining component is presented as a **liability**.[5]

If the **economic substance** is to be reflected appropriately in the statements, the debt and equity components need to be **measured and recognized separately**. The issue then becomes one of **measurement**: how much should be allocated toward the equity option? Various alternatives exist to measure these items and there is no prescribed way to measure the individual components. Two options are as follows.

1. Determine the market values of similar straight **debt** (i.e., no conversion feature) and tradable **options**. This would be facilitated if markets existed for both these instruments as separate items. Measurement of the debt portion may be done by a PV calculation, discounting at the market rate for similar debt. Measurement of

UNDERLYING CONCEPT

Even though the instrument's legal form may be debt, the economic substance is that it has both a debt component and an equity component.

INTERNATIONAL INSIGHT

International accounting standards require that the issuer of convertible debt record the liability and equity components separately. However, in the U.S., convertible debt is recorded as a liability only.

---

[1] In fact, the bonds might even sell at a premium due to the embedded stock option.

[2] As with any investment, a buyer has to be careful. For example, **Wherehouse Entertainment Inc.**, which had 6¼% convertibles outstanding, was taken private in a leveraged buyout. As a result, the convertible was suddenly as risky as a junk bond of a highly leveraged company with a coupon of only 6¼%. As one holder of the convertibles noted, "What's even worse is that the company will be so loaded down with debt that it probably won't have enough cash flow to make its interest payments. And the convertible debt we hold is subordinated to the rest of Wherehouse's debt." These types of situations have made convertibles less attractive and have led to the introduction of takeover protection covenants in some convertible bond offerings.

[3] Recall from prior chapters that financial liability is defined by *CICA Handbook* Section 3860, par. .05 as any liability that is a contractual obligation to deliver cash to another party or to exchange financial instruments with another party under conditions that are potentially unfavourable.

[4] Recall also from earlier chapters that an equity instrument is defined by the *CICA Handbook* Section 3860, par. .05 as any contract that evidences a residual interest in an entity's assets after deducting all of its liabilities. This may not appear to necessarily include options and warrants since they are only rights to obtain a residual interest in the company; however, the Appendix to the *Handbook* Section 3860, par. A7 specifically includes warrants and options as examples of equity instruments.

[5] *CICA Handbook*, Section 3860, par. .24.

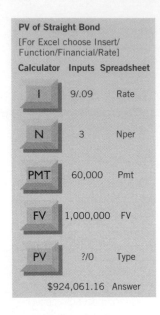

PV of Straight Bond

[For Excel choose Insert/
Function/Financial/Rate]

Calculator	Inputs	Spreadsheet
I	9/.09	Rate
N	3	Nper
PMT	60,000	Pmt
FV	1,000,000	FV
PV	?/0	Type

$924,061.16 Answer

the option portion may be done using an options pricing model.[6] The components are then assigned these values. If the total is greater than or less than the instrument's issue price, the difference is prorated based on respective market or fair values and allocated to the components. This is sometimes referred to as the **proportional** method of allocation.

2. Value only one component (the one that is easier to value—often debt). The other component is valued at whatever is left. This is sometimes called the **incremental** or **residual** method.[7]

For example, assume that Bond Corp. offers three year 6% convertible bonds (par $1,000). Each $1,000 bond may be converted into 250 common shares, which are currently trading at $3. Similar straight bonds carry an interest rate of 9%.

Incremental or residual method. Allocating the proceeds to the liability and equity components under this method involves valuing one component first (i.e., the bond) and then allocating the rest of the value to the other component (i.e., the equity component). The bond may be measured at the PV of the stream of interest payments ($1 million × 6% for three years) plus the PV of the bond itself ($1 million) all discounted at 9% which is the market rate of interest. The remainder of the proceeds is then allocated to the option.[8] The allocation is shown in Illustration 18-1.

ILLUSTRATION 18-1

Incremental Allocation of Proceeds Between Liability and Equity Components

Total proceeds at par	$1,000,000
Less:	
Value of bonds (PV annuity 3 years, 9%, 60,000 + PV $1,000,000, in 3 years, 9%)	(924,061)
Incremental value of option	75,939

Proportional or options pricing model method. To place a value on the two securities using this technique, one would determine (1) the value of bonds (as in the prior method) and (2) the value of the options perhaps using an option pricing model such as the Black-Scholes model.

The allocation between the bonds and options using the proportional method of allocation is shown in Illustration 18-2.

ILLUSTRATION 18-2

Proportional Allocation of Proceeds Between Liability and Equity Components

Value of bonds (PV annuity 3 years, 9%, 60,000 + PV $1,000,000, in 3 years, 9%) = $ 924,061		92.7%
Fair value of option using an option pricing model[9] = 72,341		7.3%
Aggregate fair market value $ 996,402		100.0%

The difference between the proceeds and the calculated fair value is then allocated back to the components based on their respective percentage values. The liability component would be valued at $1 million × 92.7% = 927,000 and the equity component would be valued at $1 million × 7.3% = $73,000.

---

[6] Although the *CICA Handbook* and Canadian GAAP do not mandate specific measurement techniques, Section 3860, par. A25 refers to two possible ways to value the equity components: **residual valuation** (like the **incremental method** above) and **option pricing valuation** (like the **proportional method** above). The *Handbook* presumes that the liability component may generally be valued with little measurement uncertainty using discounting techniques and readily available information about interest (discount) rates.

[7] These measurement techniques are not specific to convertible debt or compound instrument and may be used any time an element's total value needs to be allocated to its individual components.

[8] Note that one could use the market price of a similar bond instead if there were a market for such bonds, although any market price would presumably be similar to the discounted amount, as the market would factor in market interest, stated interest, term and par value.

[9] Calculation of this amount using an options pricing model is beyond the scope of this course and would generally be covered in a finance course. Further explanation of the model may also be found in the *Handbook* Section 3860, A25.

The journal entry to record the issuance would be as follows:

Cash	1,000,000	
Discount on Bonds Payable	73,000	
Bonds Payable		1,000,000
Contributed Surplus—Stock Options		73,000

At Time of Conversion

If bonds are converted into other securities, the principal accounting problem is to determine the amount at which to record the securities exchanged for the bond. Assume holders of the convertible debt of Bond Corp. decide to convert their convertible bonds before the bonds mature. The bond discount will be partially amortized at this point. Assume that the unamortized portion is $14,058. The entry to record the conversion would be as follows:

Bonds Payable	1,000,000	
Contributed Surplus—Stock Options	73,000	
Discount on Bonds Payable		14,058
Common Shares		1,058,942

This method referred to as the **book value method** of recording the bond conversion is the method most commonly used in practice even though there is no GAAP that specifically deals with measurement of the transaction. Support for the book value approach is based on the argument that an agreement was established at the date of the issuance either to pay a stated amount of cash at maturity or to issue a stated number of shares of equity securities. Therefore, when the debt is converted to equity in accordance with the preexisting contract terms, no gain or loss would be recognized upon conversion.[10]

Induced conversions. Sometimes the issuer wishes to induce prompt conversion of its convertible debt-to-equity securities in order to reduce interest costs or to improve its debt-to-equity ratio. As a result, the issuer may offer some form of additional consideration (such as cash or common shares), called a "sweetener." This would be referred to as an induced conversion. The sweetener should be reported as an expense of the current period at an amount equal to the fair value of the additional securities or other consideration given.

Assume that Bond Corp. wishes to reduce interest costs at some point during the life of the debt. It may offer an additional premium to the bondholders to convert. The additional amount is recorded **as an expense of the current period** and not as a reduction of equity. Some argue that the cost of a conversion inducement is a cost of obtaining equity capital. As a result, they contend, it should be recognized as a cost or reduction of the equity capital acquired and not as an expense. In Canada, there is no specific guidance; however, in the U.S., the position is that when an additional payment is needed to make bondholders convert, the payment is for a service (bondholders converting at a given time) and should be reported as an expense.[11]

UNDERLYING CONCEPTS

Both the issues of measurement of common shares on conversion and induced conversion costs deal with determining the economic substance of the transaction. Is the company paying off debt or issuing shares?

---

[10] An alternative approach that has some conceptual merit uses the market value to record the conversion. Under this method, the common shares would be recorded at market value (their market value or the market value of the bonds), the Contributed Surplus, Bonds Payable, and Discount amounts would be zeroed out, and a gain/credit or loss/debit would result. Since the CBCA requires shares to be recorded at their cash equivalent value, legal requirements would tend to support this approach. The interesting question is whether the resulting gain/credit or loss/debit would be treated as an operating or capital transaction. If it was seen as arising from debt extinguishment, it would be an operating item (gain or loss) and recognized through the income statement. If it was seen as part of the process of issuing shares, it should be booked through equity.

[11] "Induced Conversions of Convertible Debt," Statement of Financial Accounting Standards No. 84 (Stamford, Conn.: FASB, 1985).

Retirement of Convertible Debt

The retirement of the liability component of convertible debt (repayment) is treated the same way as non-convertible bonds as explained in Chapter 15. A gain or loss would result if the amount to retire the bonds differed from the carrying value. The equity component would remain in Contributed Surplus.

Convertible Preferred Shares

OBJECTIVE 2

Explain the accounting for convertible preferred shares.

The major difference in accounting for a convertible bond and a convertible preferred share at the date of issue is that convertible bonds have a liability component, whereas the convertible preferreds are considered equity (unless they are found to be financial liabilities in substance, i.e., mandatorily redeemable preferred shares).

When convertible preferred shares are exercised, Preferred Shares, along with any related Contributed Surplus, is debited; Common Shares is credited.

Assume Host Enterprises issued 1,000 shares of common upon conversion of 1,000 shares of preferred that was originally issued for a $200 premium. The entry would be:

Preferred Shares	1,200	
Common Shares		1,200

If part of the original issue price of the preferred shares had been credited to the other Shareholders' Equity accounts such as Contributed Surplus, then these accounts would be debited in the entry to record the conversion.

Stock Warrants

OBJECTIVE 3

Contrast the accounting for stock warrants and stock warrants issued with other securities.

Warrants are certificates entitling the holder to acquire shares at a certain price within a stated period. This right is similar to the **conversion privilege**[12] because warrants, if exercised, become common shares and usually have a dilutive effect (reduce earnings per share) similar to that of the conversion of convertible securities. However, a substantial difference between convertible securities and stock warrants is that upon exercise of the warrants, the holder has to pay a certain amount of money to obtain the shares.

The issuance of warrants or options to buy additional shares normally arises under three situations:

1. When issuing different types of securities, such as bonds or preferred shares, warrants are often included to make the **security more attractive**—to provide an "equity kicker."
2. Upon the issuance of additional common shares, existing shareholders may be given a **preemptive right to purchase common shares** first. Warrants may be issued to evidence that right.
3. Warrants, often referred to as stock options, are given as **compensation to executives and employees**.

The problems in accounting for stock warrants are complex and present many difficulties, some of which remain unresolved.

Stock Warrants Issued with Other Securities

Warrants issued with other securities are basically long-term options to buy common shares at a fixed price. Although some perpetual warrants are traded, generally their life is 5 years, occasionally 10.

Tenneco, Inc. offered a unit comprising one share and one detachable warrant exercisable at $24.25 per share and good for five years. The unit sold for 22¾ ($22.75) and since the price of the common shares the day before the sale was 19⅞ ($19.88), the difference suggests a price of 2⅞ ($2.87) for the warrants.

In this situation, the warrants had an apparent value of 2⅞ ($2.87), even though it would not be profitable at present for the purchaser to exercise the warrant and buy

---

[12] In fact, the convertible securities are seen to have an embedded option or warrant.

the shares, because the share price is much below the exercise price of $24.25. The investor pays for the warrant to receive a **possible future call** on the shares at a fixed price when the price has risen significantly. For example, if the share price rises to $30, the investor has gained $2.88 ($30 minus $24.25 minus $2.87) on an investment of $2.87, a 100% increase. If the price never rises, the investor loses the full $2.87.

The proceeds from the sale of debt with detachable stock warrants should be allocated between the two securities[13] similar to convertible debt. Unlike convertible debt, this instrument includes two distinct and separable components; that is, (1) a bond and (2) a warrant giving the holder the right to purchase common shares at a certain price. Warrants that are detachable can be traded separately from the debt and, therefore, a market value can be determined. As with the convertible debt, the issue is one of how to **measure** the separate components. Similar measurement techniques may be used as for the convertible debt.

Rights to Subscribe to Additional Shares

If a corporation's directors of a corporation decide to issue new shares, the old shareholders may have the right (preemptive privilege) to purchase newly issued shares in proportion to their holdings. The privilege, referred to as a stock right, saves existing shareholders from suffering a dilution of voting rights without their consent, and it may allow them to purchase shares somewhat below their market value. The warrants issued in these situations are of short duration, unlike the warrants issued with other securities.

The certificate representing the stock right states the number of shares the rights holder may purchase, as well as the price at which the new shares may be purchased. Each share owned ordinarily gives the owner one stock right. The price is normally less than the current market value of such shares, which gives the rights a value in themselves. From the time they are issued until they expire, they may be purchased and sold like any other security.

No entry is required when rights are issued to existing shareholders. Only a memorandum entry is needed to indicate the number of rights issued to existing shareholders and to ensure that the company has additional unissued shares registered for issuance in case the rights are exercised. No formal entry is made at this time because no shares have been issued and no cash has been received.

If the rights are exercised, usually a cash payment of some type is involved. An entry crediting Common Shares is made.

Stock Compensation Plans

Another form of warrant arises in stock compensation plans used to pay and motivate employees. This warrant is a stock option, which gives selected employees the option to purchase common shares at a given price over an extended period of time. Stock options are very popular because they meet the objectives of an **effective compensation program**.

Effective compensation has been a subject of considerable interest lately. A consensus of opinion is that effective compensation programs are ones that (1) **motivate employees** to high levels of performance, (2) help **retain executives** and allow for recruitment of new talent, (3) base compensation on employee and company **performance**, (4) maximize the employee's **after-tax benefit** and minimize the employer's **after-tax cost**, and (5) use performance criteria over which the **employee has control**. Although straight cash compensation plans (salary and, perhaps, bonus) are an important part of any compensation program, they are oriented to the **short run**. Many companies recognize that a more **long-run** compensation plan is often needed in addition to a cash component.

Long-term compensation plans attempt to develop in the executive a strong loyalty toward the company. An effective way to accomplish this goal is to give the employees an equity interest based on changes in long-term measures such as increases in earnings per share, **revenues, share price, or market share**. These plans, generally referred to as stock option plans, come in many different forms. Essentially, they

---

[13] A detachable warrant means that the warrant can sell separately from the bond.

($000)	1998 Salary and Bonus	Long-Term Compensation (Options)	Total Pay
1. Michael Eisner **Walt Disney**	$5,764	$569,828	$575,592
2. Mel Karmazin **CBS**	4,000	197,934	201,934
3. Sanford Weill **Citigroup**	7,430	159,663	167,093
4. Stephen Case **America Online**	1,177	158,057	159,233
5. Craig Barrett **Intel**	2,280	114,232	116,511
6. John Welch **General Electric**	10,105	73,559	83,664
7. Henry Schacht **Lucent Technologies**	2,020	65,016	67,037
8. L. Dennis Kozlowski **Tyco International**	3,750	61,514	65,264
9. Henry Silverman **Cendant**	2,818	61,063	63,882
10. M. Douglas Ivester **Coca-Cola**	2,750	54,572	57,322

Top-Paid CEOs

Source: Based on Jennifer Rheingold and Ronald Grover, "Special Report: Executive Pay," *Business Week*, April 19, 1999.

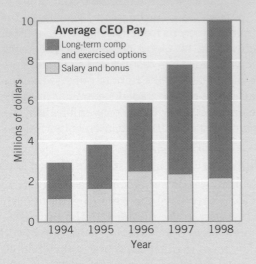

Averages for All 365 Companies Surveyed

Data: *Business Week* Annual Executive Pay Survey

ILLUSTRATION 18-3

Executive Option Compensation

provide the executive with the opportunity to receive shares or cash in the future if the company's performance is satisfactory.

Stock options are the fastest-growing segment of executive pay. Executives want stock option contracts because options can make them instant millionaires if the company is successful. For example, for 365 of the largest U.S. companies, long-term compensation was mostly from exercised stock options. Illustration 18-3 provides an example of some of the higher awards and average compensation for all companies surveyed in 1998.

The Major Accounting Issue

To illustrate the most contentious accounting issue related to stock option plans, suppose that you are an employee of Hurdle Inc. and you are granted options to purchase 10,000 shares of the firm's common shares as part of your compensation. The date you receive the options is referred to as the grant date. The options are good for 10 years; the shares' **market price** and **exercise price** are both $20 at the grant date. What is the value of the compensation you just received?

Some believe you have not received anything; that is, the difference between the **market price** and the **exercise price** is zero and therefore no compensation results. Others argue these options have value: if the share price goes above $20 any time over the next 10 years and you exercise these options, substantial compensation results. For example, if at the end of the fourth year, the shares' market price is $30 and you exercise your options, you will have earned $100,000 [10,000 options × ($30 − $20)], ignoring income taxes.

How should the granting of these options be reported by Hurdle Inc.? In Canada, no previous GAAP existed on this topic and practice was widespread. The CICA has recently approved a new *Handbook* Section that will help provide guidance in this area[14] (along the lines of the U.S. standard[15]).

The new standard allows companies to account for stock compensation plans using either the **intrinsic value method** or the **fair value method** although use of the latter is encouraged. The intrinsic value method requires that compensation cost be meas-

---

[14] At the time of printing of this book the new *Handbook* Section 3870, "Stock-Based Compensation and Other Stock-Based Payments" had been approved.

[15] "Accounting for Stock-Based Compensation," Statement of Financial Accounting Standards No. 123 (Norwalk, Conn.: FASB, 1995).

ured by the **excess of the shares' market price over their exercise price** at the grant date. This approach is referred to as the intrinsic value method because the calculation is not dependent on external circumstances: **it is the difference between the market price of the shares and the exercise price of the options at the grant date**. Hurdle would therefore not recognize any compensation expense related to your options because at the grant date, the market price and exercise price were the same.

The other option is to measure the value of the plan at its fair value—known as the fair value method. Clearly the plan has value since many employees accept the stock options in lieu of salary or bonus. The value, as previously mentioned, lies in the potential for future gain. The use of options pricing models to value the option helps measure what the option is truly worth.

The principle underlying the new standard is as follows: the cost of employee services should be based on the **value of compensation paid** which reflects the value of services provided. Accordingly, the compensation cost arising from employee stock options should be **measured** and **recognized** as the services are provided.[16]

When the corresponding standard was issued in 1995 in the U.S., FASB met with considerable resistance when it proposed **requiring** the fair value method for recognizing the costs of stock options in the financial statements. As a result, under the final standard, a company may **choose** to use **either** the **intrinsic value method or fair value method** when accounting for compensation cost on the income statement. Canada followed suit to promote **international harmonization** of accounting standards, even though the use of the fair value method is more theoretically sound.

If a company uses the **intrinsic value method** to recognize compensation costs for employee stock options, it must provide **expanded disclosures in the notes** on these costs. Specifically, companies that choose the intrinsic value method are required to disclose in a note to the financial statements pro-forma net income and earnings per share (if presented by the company), as if it had used the fair value method. The following sections discuss the accounting for stock options under both the intrinsic and fair value methods as well as the political debate surrounding stock compensation accounting.

OBJECTIVE 4

Describe the accounting for stock compensation plans under generally accepted accounting principles.

Accounting for Stock Compensation

The **CICA encourages adoption of the fair value method**, however the discussion in this section illustrates both methods. Stock option plans involve two main accounting issues:

1. How should compensation expense be determined (**measurement**)?
2. Over what periods should compensation expense be allocated (**recognition**)?

Determining Expense

Using the **fair value method**, total compensation expense is calculated based on the fair value of the options expected to vest[17] on the date the options are granted to the employee(s) (the **grant date**). Fair value for public companies is to be estimated using an **option pricing model**, with some adjustments for the unique factors of employee stock options. No adjustments are made after the grant date in response to subsequent changes in the share price, either up or down. The options pricing model incorporates numerous input measures.[18]

Under the **intrinsic value method** (which has historically been used in Canada), total compensation cost is calculated as the **excess of the market price of the shares over the option price** on the date when both the number of shares to which employees are entitled and the option or purchase price for those shares are known (the measurement date).

---

[16] Stock options issued to non-employees in exchange for other goods or services must be measured according to fair value as nonmonetary transactions.

[17] Vested means "to earn the rights to." An employee's award becomes vested at the date that the employee's right to receive or retain shares of stock or cash under the award is no longer contingent on remaining in the employer 's service.

[18] These factors include the volatility of the underlying stock, the expected life of the options, the risk-free rate during the option life, and expected dividends during the option life.

For many plans, this measurement date is the **grant date**. However, the measurement date may be later for plans with variable terms (either number of shares and/or option price are not known) that depend on events after the date of grant. For such variable plans, compensation expense may have to be estimated based on assumptions as to the final number of shares and the option price (usually at the **exercise date**).

Allocating Compensation Expense

In general, under both the fair and intrinsic value methods, compensation expense is recognized in the periods in which the employee performs the service (the service period). Unless otherwise specified, the service period is the **vesting period**: the time between the **grant date** and the **vesting date**. Thus, total compensation cost is determined at the **grant date** and allocated to the periods benefited by the employees' services.

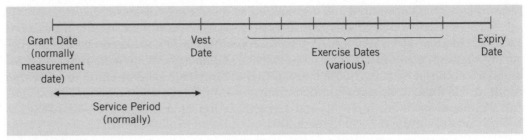

Illustration

To illustrate the accounting for a stock option plan, assume that on November 1, 2000, the shareholders of Chen Corp. approve a plan that grants the company's five executives options to purchase 2,000 shares each of the company's common shares. The options are granted on January 1, 2001, and may be exercised at any time within the next 10 years. The option price per share is $60, and the shares' market price at the date of grant is $70 per share. Using the **intrinsic value method**, the total compensation expense is calculated below.

Market value of 10,000 shares at date of grant ($70 per share)	$700,000
Option price of 10,000 shares at date of grant ($60 per share)	600,000
Total compensation expense (intrinsic value)	$100,000

Using the **fair value method**, total compensation expense is calculated by applying an acceptable fair value option pricing model (such as the Black-Scholes model). To keep this illustration simple, we will assume that the fair value option pricing model determines total compensation expense to be $220,000.

Basic Entries.   The options' value under either method is **recognized** as an expense in the periods in which the employee **performs services**. In the case of Chen Corp., assume that the documents associated with issuance of the options indicate that the expected period of benefit is two years, starting with the **grant date**. The journal entries to record the transactions related to this option contract using both the **intrinsic value** and **fair value method** are shown in Illustration 18-4.

ILLUSTRATION 18-4
Comparison of Entries for Option Contract—Intrinsic Value and Fair Value Methods

Intrinsic Value		Fair Value	
At date of grant (January 1, 2001):			
No entry		No entry	
To record compensation expense for 2001 (December 31, 2001):			
Compensation Expense 50,000		Compensation Expense 110,000	
Contributed Surplus—	50,000	Contributed Surplus—	110,000
Stock Options ($100,000 ÷ 2)		Stock Options ($220,000 / 2)	
To record compensation expense for 2002 (December 31, 2002):			
Compensation Expense 50,000		Compensation Expense 110,000	
Contributed Surplus—		Contributed Surplus—	
Stock Options	50,000	Stock Options	110,000

Under both methods, compensation expense is allocated evenly over the two-year service period. The only difference between the two methods is the **amount of compensation recognized**.

Exercise. If 20% or 2,000 of the 10,000 options were exercised on June 1, 2004 (three years and five months after date of grant), the following journal entry would be recorded using the **intrinsic value method**:

June 1, 2004		
Cash (2,000 × $60)	120,000	
Contributed Surplus—Stock Options (20% × $100,000)		20,000
Common Shares		140,000

Using the **fair value approach**, the entry would be:

June 1, 2004		
Cash (2,000 × $60)	120,000	
Contributed Surplus—Stock Options (20% × $220,000)		44,000
Common Shares		164,000

Expiration. If the remaining stock options are not exercised before their **expiration date**, the balance in the Contributed Surplus account would remain. If the company kept several Contributed Surplus accounts, the balance would be shifted to a Contributed Surplus account indicating that the options had expired. The entry to record this transaction at the date of expiration is shown in Illustration 18-5.

Intrinsic Value		Fair Value	
January 1, 2011 (Expiration date):			
Contributed Surplus—		Contributed Surplus—	
Stock Options	80,000	Stock Options	176,000
Contributed Surplus—		Contributed Surplus—	
Expired Stock Options		Expired Stock Options	
(80% × $100,000)	80,000	(80% × $220,000)	176,000

ILLUSTRATION 18-5
Comparison of Entries for Stock Option Expiration—Intrinsic Value and Fair Value Methods

Adjustment. The fact that a stock option is not exercised does not nullify the propriety of recording the costs of services received from executives and attributable to the stock option plan. However, if a stock option is forfeited because an employee fails to satisfy a service requirement (i.e., leaves employment), the estimate of Compensation Expense recorded should be adjusted as a change in estimate (credit Compensation Expense and debit Contributed Surplus).

Types of Plans

Many different types of plans are used to compensate key executives. In all these plans, the reward amount depends upon future events. Consequently, continued employment is a necessary element in almost all types of plans. The popularity of a given plan usually depends on prospects in the stock market and tax considerations. For example, if it appears that appreciation will occur in a company's shares, a plan that offers the option to purchase shares is attractive to an executive. Conversely, if it appears that price appreciation is unlikely, then compensation might be tied to some performance measure such as an increase in book value or earnings per share.

Three common compensation plans that illustrate different objectives are:

1. Stock option plans.
2. Stock appreciation rights plans.
3. Performance-type plans.

Most plans follow the general guideline for reporting established in the previous sections. A more detailed discussion of Stock Appreciation Rights and Performance-type plans is presented in Appendix 18A.

See additional disclosures of employee stock options.

Noncompensatory Plans

In some companies, stock purchase plans permit **all** employees to purchase shares at a discounted price for a short period of time. These plans are usually classified as **noncompensatory**. Noncompensatory means that the plan's primary purpose is not to compensate the employees but, to enable the employer to secure equity capital or to induce widespread ownership of an enterprise's common shares among employees. Thus, compensation expense is not reported for these plans. Noncompensatory plans have the following characteristics:

1. The plan incorporates no option features other than:
   (a) employees are permitted a short period of time (less than 31 days) to enroll in the plan.
   (b) the purchase price is based solely on market price at date of purchase.
2. The discount from market is small.
3. Substantially all full-time employees may participate.

For example, Mohican Limited had a stock purchase plan under which employees who meet minimal employment qualifications are entitled to purchase Mohican shares at a 5% reduction from market price for a short period of time. The reduction from market price is not considered compensatory because the per share amount of the costs avoided by not having to raise the cash in a public offering is equal to 5%. **Plans that do not possess all of the above-mentioned characteristics are classified as compensatory**.

Disclosure of Compensation Plans

Companies offering stock-based compensation plans must **determine** the fair value of the options. Companies must then decide whether to **use** the fair value method and recognize expense in the income statement, or to use the intrinsic value approach and disclose in the notes the pro forma impact on net income and earnings per share (if presented), as if the fair value method had been used.

Regardless of whether the intrinsic value or fair value method is used, **full disclosure** should be made regarding:

- the accounting policy used
- a description of the plans
- pro forma net income and earnings per share if a method other than the fair value based method is used. The pro forma should reflect the difference in compensation expense due to using the different method.

The following disclosures are also required according to the *CICA Handbook* Section 3870:

> ### Disclosure
>
> .66   An enterprise with one or more stock-based compensation plans should provide a description of the plan(s), including the general terms of awards under the plan(s), such as vesting requirements, the maximum term of options granted, and the number of shares authorized for grants of options or other equity instruments. An enterprise that uses equity instruments to acquire goods or services other than employee services should provide disclosures similar to those required by this paragraph and paragraphs .67–.70 to the extent that those disclosures are important in understanding the effects of those transactions on the financial statements.
>
> .67   The following information should be disclosed:
> (a) The number and weighted average exercise prices of options for each of the following groups of options:
>   (i)   those outstanding at the beginning of the year;
>   (ii)   those outstanding at the end of the year;
>   (iii)   those exercisable at the end of the year;
>   (iv)   those granted during the year;

(v)   those exercised during the year;

(vi) those forfeited during the year; and

(vii) those expired during the year.

(b) The weighted average grant-date fair value of options granted during the year. If the exercise prices of some options differ from the market price of the stock on the grant date, weighted average exercise prices and weighted average fair values of options should be disclosed separately for options whose exercise price:

(i)   equals;

(ii)   exceeds; or

(iii) is less than the market price of the stock on the grant date.

(c) The number and weighted average grant-date fair value of equity instruments other than options, for example, shares of non-vested stock, granted during the year.

(d) A description of the method and significant assumptions used during the year to estimate the fair values of options, including the following weighted average information:

(i)   risk-free interest rate;

(ii)   expected life;

(iii) expected volatility; and

(iv)   expected dividends.

(e) Total compensation cost recognized in income for stock-based employee compensation awards.

(f) Amounts charged or credited to contributed surplus in respect of stock-based employee compensation awards (see SURPLUS, Section 3250).

(g) Amounts credited to share capital in respect of stock-based employee compensation awards (see SHARE CAPITAL, Section 3240).

(h) Amounts receivable from employees in respect of stock-based employee compensation awards that are reflected as assets.

(i) The terms of significant modifications of outstanding awards.

.68   An enterprise that grants options under multiple stock-based employee compensation plans should provide the information required by paragraph .67 separately for different types of awards to the extent that the differences in the characteristics of the awards make separate disclosure important to an understanding of the enterprise's use of stock-based compensation.

.70   For options outstanding at the balance sheet date, the range of exercise prices (as well as the weighted average exercise price) and the weighted average remaining contractual life should be disclosed. If the range of exercise prices is wide (for example, the highest exercise price exceeds approximately 150 percent of the lowest exercise price), the exercise prices should be segregated into ranges that are meaningful for assessing the number and timing of additional shares that may be issued and the cash that may be received as a result of option exercises. The following information should be disclosed for each range:

(a) The number, weighted average exercise price, and weighted average remaining contractual life of options outstanding.

(b) The number and weighted average exercise price of options currently exercisable.

Illustration 18-6 provides the disclosure by **Gateway 2000, Inc.,** which accounts for its stock options using the intrinsic value method.

GATEWAY 2000, INC.

ILLUSTRATION 18-6
Disclosure of Stock Option Plans by Gateway 2000, Inc.

Note 6: Stock Option Plans. The Company maintains various stock option plans for its employees. Employee options are generally granted at the fair market value of the related common stock at the date of grant. These options generally vest over a four-year period from the date of grant or the employee's initial date of employment. In addition, these options expire, if not exercised, ten years from the date of grant. The Company also maintains option plans for non-employee directors. Option grants to non-employee directors generally have an exercise price equal to the fair market value of the related common stock on the date of grant. These options generally vest over one to three-year periods and expire, if not exercised, ten years from the date of grant.

For all of the Company's stock option plans, options for 1,283,000, 2,582,000 and 2,728,000 shares of common stock were exercisable at December 31, 1996, 1997 and 1998 with a weighted average exercise price of $4.28, $9.86 and $17.42, respectively. In addition, options for 672,000, 556,000 and 280,000 shares of Class A common stock were exercisable at December 31, 1996, 1997 and 1998 with a weighted average exercise price of $2.06, $2.01 and $1.93, respectively. Class

A common stock may be converted into an equal number of shares of common stock at any time. There were 12,309,000, 8,328,000 and 11,265,000 shares of common stock available for grant under the plans at December 31, 1996, 1997 and 1998, respectively.

The following table summarizes activity under the stock option plans for 1996, 1997 and 1998 (in thousands, except per share amounts):

	Common Stock	Weighted-Average Price	Class A Common Stock	Weighted-Average Price
Outstanding, December 31, 1995	(8,739)	$ 3.16	(962)	$2.14
Granted	3,260	15.75	—	—
Exercised	(6,305)	1.43	(241)	2.13
Forfeited	(254)	14.15	(8)	3.25
Outstanding, December 31, 1996	(5,440)	12.20	(713)	2.12
Granted	(5,253)	36.08	—	—
Exercised	(463)	11.56	(153)	2.50
Forfeited	(775)	23.69	—	—
Outstanding, December 31, 1997	(9,455)	22.98	(560)	2.02
Granted	6,118	45.17	—	—
Exercised	(2,143)	16.59	(280)	2.10
Forfeited	(1,103)	32.76	—	—
Outstanding, December 31, 1998	(12,327)	$34.19	(280)	$1.93

The following table summarizes information about the Company's Common Stock options outstanding at December 31, 1998 (in thousands, except per share amounts):

	Options Outstanding			Options Exercisable	
Range of Exercise Prices	Number Outstanding at 12/31/98	Weighted-Average Remaining Contractual Life	Weighted-Average Price	Number Exercisable at 12/31/98	Weighted-Average Price
$ 1.19–13.38	1,928	5.57	$ 9.01	1,259	$ 6.76
13.44–29.07	2,287	7.65	22.93	939	20.01
29.31–33.75	2,405	8.87	33.06	267	32.35
34.00–44.75	2,811	8.94	39.55	262	43.88
45.06–62.50	2,896	9.68	55.56	1	61.75

The weighted average fair value per share of options granted during 1996, 1997 and 1998 was $9.65, $21.61 and $27.33, respectively. The fair value of these options was estimated on the date of grant using the Black-Scholes option pricing model with the following weighted-average assumptions used for all grants in 1996, 1997 and 1998: dividend yield of zero percent; expected volatility of 60 percent; risk-free interest rates ranging from 4.7 to 7.2 percent; and expected lives of the options of three and one-half years from the date of vesting.

Since all stock options have been granted with exercise prices equal to the fair market value of the related common stock at the date of grant, no compensation expense has been recognized under the Company's stock option plans. Had compensation cost under the plans been determined based on the estimated fair value of the stock options granted in 1996, 1997 and 1998, net income and net income per share would have been reduced to the pro forma amounts indicated below:

	1996	1997	1998
	(in thousands, except per share amounts)		
Net income—as reported	$250,679	$109,797	$346,399
Net income—pro forma	$241,729	$ 85,804	$297,470
Net income per share—as reported			
Basic	$ 1.64	$ .71	$ 2.23
Diluted	$ 1.60	$ .70	$ 2.18
Net income per share—pro forma			
Basic	$ 1.58	$ .56	$ 1.91
Diluted	$ 1.55	$ .55	$ 1.87

The pro forma effect on net income for 1996, 1997 and 1998 is not fully representative of the pro forma effect on net income in future years because it does not take into consideration pro forma compensation expense related to the vesting of grants made prior to 1995.

Debate over Stock Option Accounting

In general, use of the **fair value approach** results in greater compensation costs relative to the intrinsic value model. For example, a recent study of the companies in the Standard & Poor's 500 stock index documented that on average, earnings in 1998 were overstated by 5% through the use of the intrinsic value method.

It is an understatement to say that corporations were unhappy with the initial requirement to record compensation expense for these plans. Many small high-technology companies were particularly vocal in their opposition, arguing that only through offering stock options can they attract top professional management. They contend that if they are forced to recognize large amounts of compensation expense under these plans, they will be at a competitive disadvantage with larger companies that can withstand higher compensation charges.

A chronology of events related to the development of this standard in the U.S. demonstrates the difficulty in standard setting when various stakeholders believe they are adversely affected.

1. *In June 1993, the FASB issued an exposure draft on stock options.* The recommendations were that the value of stock options issued to employees is compensation that should be recognized in the financial statements. Nonrecognition of these costs results in financial statements that are neither credible nor **representationally faithful**. The draft recommended that option pricing models be used to estimate the value of stock options. In addition, disclosures related to these plans would be enhanced.

2. *The exposure draft met a blizzard of opposition from the business community.* Some argued stock option plans were not compensation expense (**economic substance**); some contended that it was impossible to develop appropriate option pricing models (**measurability**); others said that these standards would be disastrous to American business (**economic consequence**). The economic consequences argument was used extensively. In mid-1993, Congresswoman Anna Eshoo (California) submitted a congressional resolution calling for the FASB not to change its current accounting rules. Eshoo stated that the FASB proposal "poses a threat to economic recovery and entrepreneurship in the United States. . . . (it) hurts low- and mid-level employees and stunts the growth of new-growth sectors, such as high technology which relies heavily on entrepreneurship."

3. *On June 30, 1993, the Equity Expansion Act of 1993 was introduced by Senator Joseph Lieberman (Connecticut).* The bill mandates that the SEC require that no compensation expense be reported on the income statement for stock option plans. Senator Lieberman's bill could have forced the FASB to bend to political pressure and thereby set a precedent for interfering in the Board's operations.

4. *During the latter part of 1993, the FASB looked for political support but found few supporters.* The SEC commissioners all expressed reservations about the FASB's proposed ruling. However, the SEC's chief accountant spoke in opposition to much of the lobbying effort directed against the FASB.

5. *In early 1994, a group of senators wrote to the SEC.* They expressed concern "that the credibility of the financial reporting process may be harmed significantly if Congress, in order to further economic or political goals, either discourages the FASB from revising what the FASB believes to be a deficient standard or overrules the FASB by writing an accounting standard directly into the Federal securities laws."

6. *In late 1994, the FASB decided to encourage, rather than require, recognition of compensation cost based on the fair value method and require expanded disclosures.* The FASB adopted the **disclosure approach** because they were concerned that the "divisiveness of the debate" could threaten the future of accounting standard setting in the private sector. The final standard was issued in October 1995.

OBJECTIVE 5

Explain the controversy involving stock compensation plans.

UNDERLYING CONCEPT

The stock option controversy involves **economic consequence** issues. The accounting profession believes the **neutrality** concept should be followed; others disagree, noting that factors other than accounting theory should be considered.

The stock option saga is a classic example of the difficulty the accounting profession faces in issuing an accounting standard. In this case, many powerful interests aligned against the standard setters; even some who initially appeared to support FASB's actions later reversed themselves. The whole incident is troubling because the debate for the most part is not about the **proper accounting** but more about the standards' **economic consequences**. One of the hallmarks of accounting standards is **neutrality** and therefore, economic consequences should not enter into the debate.

SECTION 2 — Calculating Earnings Per Share

INTERNATIONAL INSIGHT

In many nations (e.g., Switzerland, Sweden, Spain, and Mexico) there is no legal requirement to disclose earnings per share.

Earnings per share data are frequently reported in the financial press and are widely used by shareholders and potential investors in evaluating a company's profitability. **Earnings per share** indicates the income earned by each common share. Thus, **earnings per share is reported only for common shares**. For example, if Osaka Limited has net income of $300,000 and a weighted average number of 100,000 common shares outstanding for the year, earnings per share is $3 ($300,000 ÷ 100,000).

Because of the importance of earnings per share information, most companies are required to report this information on the face of the income statement.[20] The exception is nonpublic companies; because of cost-benefit considerations they do not have to report this information.[21] Generally, earnings per share information is reported below net income in the income statement. For Osaka Limited, the presentation would be as follows.

ILLUSTRATION 18-7
Income Statement Presentation of EPS

Net income	$300,000
Earnings per share	$3.00

When the income statement contains intermediate components of income, earnings per share should be disclosed for each component.[22] The EPS numbers related to these other components may be disclosed on the face of the statement or in the notes. The following is representative assuming that the EPS numbers for discontinued operations and extraordinary items are presented on the face of the income statement.

ILLUSTRATION 18-8
Income Statement Presentation of EPS Components

Earnings per share:	
Income from continuing operations	$4.00
Loss from discontinued operations, net of tax	(.60)
Extraordinary gain, net of tax	1.00
Net income	$4.40

These disclosures enable the financial statements user to recognize the effects of income from continuing operations on EPS, as distinguished from income or loss from irregular items.

---

[20] *CICA Handbook*, Section 3500, par. .60.

[21] A nonpublic enterprise is an enterprise other than (1) one whose debt or equity securities are traded in a public market on a foreign or domestic stock exchange or in the over-the-counter market (including securities quoted locally or regionally) or (2) one that has made a filing or is in the process of making a filing with a securities commission in preparation for the sale of those securities (*CICA Handbook*, Section 3500, par. .02).

[22] *CICA Handbook*, Section 3500, par. .61.

Earnings Per Share—Simple Capital Structure

A corporation's capital structure is simple if it consists only of common shares or includes no potential common shares. A potential common share is a security or other contract that upon conversion or exercise could dilute earnings per common share.[23] (A capital structure is **complex** if it includes securities that could have a dilutive effect on earnings per common share.) The calculation of earnings per share for a simple capital structure involves two items (other than net income): dividends on senior equity instruments[24] (such as preferred shares) and weighted average number of common shares outstanding.

Dividends on Senior Equity Instruments

As indicated earlier, earnings per share relates to earnings per common share. When a company has both common and senior equity instruments outstanding, **the dividends for the current year on these senior equity instruments are subtracted from net income to arrive at income available to common shareholders**. The formula for calculating earnings per share is then as follows.

OBJECTIVE 6

Calculate earnings per share in a simple capital structure.

$$\frac{(\text{Net Income} - \text{Dividends on Senior Equity Instruments})}{\text{Weighted Average Number of Shares Outstanding}} = \text{Earnings Per Share}$$

ILLUSTRATION 18-9
Formula for Calculating Earnings per Share

In reporting earnings per share information, dividends on preferred shares should be subtracted from income from continuing operations and from net income to arrive at income available to common shareholders. If dividends on preferred shares are declared and a net loss occurs, **the preferred dividend is added to the loss** for purposes of calculating the loss per share. If the preferred shares are cumulative and the dividend is not declared in the current year, **an amount equal to the dividend that should have been declared for the current year only** should be subtracted from net income or added to the net loss. Dividends in arrears for previous years should have been included in the previous years' calculations.

Weighted Average Number of Shares Outstanding

In all calculations of earnings per share, the weighted average number of shares outstanding during the period constitutes the basis for the per share amounts reported. Shares issued or purchased during the period affect the amount outstanding and must be **weighted by the fraction of the period they are outstanding**. The rationale for this approach is that the income was generated on the issue proceeds for only part of the year. Accordingly, the number of shares outstanding should be weighted by the same factor. To illustrate, assume that Salomski Inc. has the following changes in its common shares outstanding for the period.

INTERNATIONAL INSIGHT

Where EPS disclosure is prevalent, it is usually based on the weighted average of shares outstanding. Some countries such as Australia, France, Japan, and Mexico use the number of shares outstanding at year end.

ILLUSTRATION 18-10
Shares Outstanding, Ending Balance—Salomski Inc.

Date	Share Changes	Shares Outstanding
January 1	Beginning balance	90,000
April 1	Issued 30,000 shares for cash	30,000
		120,000
July 1	Purchased 39,000 shares	39,000
		81,000
November 1	Issued 60,000 shares for cash	60,000
December 31	Ending balance	141,000

---

[23] *CICA Handbook*, Section 3500, par. .05 defines a potential common share as a security or other contract that may entitle its holder to obtain a common share during the reporting period or after the end of the reporting period. Examples given are debt instruments and preferred shares that are convertible into common shares, warrants, options, and contingently issuable shares.

[24] Senior equity instruments are defined in the *Handbook* as preferred shares and other financial instruments that provide their holders with claims on earnings prior to those of the common shareholders, and are classified as equity. Historically, this has meant only preferred shares but more recently, this definition has been expanded to include other instruments that may have a different legal form but are nonetheless considered senior equity instruments in substance.

To calculate the weighted average number of shares outstanding, the following calculation is made.

ILLUSTRATION 18-11
Weighted Average Number of Shares Outstanding

Dates Outstanding	(A) Shares Outstanding	(B) Fraction of Year	(C) Weighted Shares (A × B)
Jan. 1–Apr. 1	90,000	3/12	22,500
Apr. 1–July 1	120,000	3/12	30,000
July 1–Nov. 1	81,000	4/12	27,000
Nov. 1–Dec. 31	141,000	2/12	23,500
Weighted average number of shares outstanding			103,000

As illustrated, 90,000 shares were outstanding for three months, which translates to 22,500 whole shares for the entire year. Because additional shares were issued on April 1, the shares outstanding change and these shares must be weighted for the time outstanding. When 39,000 shares were purchased on July 1, the shares outstanding were reduced and again a new calculation must be made to determine the proper weighted shares outstanding.

Stock Dividends and Stock Splits

When **stock dividends** or stock splits occur, calculation of the weighted average number of shares requires restatement of the shares outstanding before the stock dividend or split.[25] For example, assume that a corporation had 100,000 shares outstanding on January 1 and issued a 25% stock dividend on June 30. For purposes of calculating a weighted average for the current year, the additional 25,000 shares outstanding as a result of the stock dividend are assumed to have been **outstanding since the beginning of the year**. Thus the weighted average for the year would be 125,000 shares.

The issuance of a stock dividend or stock split requires a restatement (applied retroactively), but the issuance or repurchase of shares for cash is not. Why? The reason is that stock splits and stock dividends do not increase or decrease the net enterprise's assets; only additional shares are issued and, therefore, the weighted average shares must be restated. By restating, valid comparisons of earnings per share can be made between periods before and after the stock split or stock dividend. Conversely, the issuance or purchase of shares for cash changes the amount of net assets. As a result, the company either earns more or less in the future as a result of this change in net assets. Stated another way, a **stock dividend or split does not change the shareholders' total investment**—it only increases (unless it is a reverse stock split) the number of common shares representing this investment.

To illustrate how a stock dividend affects the calculation of the weighted average number of shares outstanding, assume that Baiye Limited has the following changes in its common shares during the year.

ILLUSTRATION 18-12
Shares Outstanding, Ending Balance—Baiye Limited

Date	Share Changes	Shares Outstanding
January 1	Beginning balance	100,000
March 1	Issued 20,000 shares for cash	20,000
		120,000
June 1	60,000 additional shares (50% stock dividend)	60,000
		180,000
November 1	Issued 30,000 shares for cash	30,000
December 31	Ending balance	210,000

---

[25] *CICA Handbook*, Section 3500, par. .58.

The calculation of the weighted average number of shares outstanding would be as follows:

Dates Outstanding	(A) Shares Outstanding	(B) Restatement	(C) Fraction of Year	(D) Weighted Shares (A × B × C)
Jan. 1—Mar. 1	100,000	1.50	2/12	25,000
Mar. 1—June 1	120,000	1.50	3/12	45,000
June 1—Nov. 1	180,000		5/12	75,000
Nov. 1—Dec. 31	210,000		2/12	35,000
Weighted average number of shares outstanding				180,000

ILLUSTRATION 18-13
Weighted Average Number of Shares Outstanding—Share Issue and Stock Dividend

The shares outstanding prior to the stock dividend must be restated. The shares outstanding from January 1 to June 1 are adjusted for the stock dividend so that these shares are stated on the same basis as shares issued subsequent to the stock dividend. Shares issued after the stock dividend do not have to be restated because they are on the new basis. The stock dividend simply restates existing shares. The same type of treatment occurs for a **stock split**.

If a stock dividend or stock split occurs **after the end of the year**, but before the financial statements are issued, the weighted average number of shares outstanding for the year (and any other years presented in comparative form) must be restated.[26] For example, assume that Hendricks Corp. calculates its weighted average number of shares to be 100,000 for the year ended December 31, 2001. On January 15, 2002, before the financial statements are issued, the company splits its shares 3 for 1. In this case, the weighted average number of shares used in calculating earnings per share for 2001 would be 300,000 shares. If earnings per share information for 2000 is provided as **comparative information**, it also must be adjusted for the stock split.

Comprehensive Illustration

Leung Corporation has income before extraordinary item of $580,000 and an extraordinary gain, net of tax, of $240,000. In addition, it has declared preferred dividends of $1 per share on 100,000 preferred shares outstanding. Leung Corporation also has the following changes in its common shares outstanding during 2001.

Dates	Share Changes	Shares Outstanding
January 1	Beginning balance	180,000
May 1	Purchased 30,000 shares	30,000
		150,000
July 1	300,000 additional shares issued (3 for 1 stock split)	300,000
		450,000
December 31	Issued 50,000 shares for cash	50,000
December 31	Ending balance	500,000

ILLUSTRATION 18-14
Shares Outstanding, Ending Balance—Leung Corp.

To calculate the earnings per share information, the weighted average number of shares outstanding is determined as follows.

Dates Outstanding	(A) Shares Outstanding	(B) Restatement	(C) Fraction of Year	(D) Weighted Shares (A × B × C)
Jan. 1–May 1	180,000	3	4/12	180,000
May 1–Dec. 31	150,000	3	8/12	300,000
Weighted average number of shares outstanding				480,000

ILLUSTRATION 18-15
Weighted Average Number of Shares Outstanding

---

[26] *CICA Handbook*, Section 3500, par. .58.

In calculating the weighted average number of shares, the shares sold on December 31, 2001 are ignored because they have not been outstanding during the year. The weighted average number of shares is then divided into income before discontinued and extraordinary items and net income to determine earnings per share. Leung Corporation's preferred dividends of $100,000 are subtracted from income before discontinued and extraordinary items ($580,000) to arrive at income before discontinued and extraordinary items available to common shareholders of $480,000 ($580,000 − $100,000). Deducting the preferred dividends from the income before discontinued and extraordinary items has the effect of also reducing net income without affecting the amount of the extraordinary item. The final amount is referred to as income available to common shareholders.

ILLUSTRATION 18-16
Calculation of Income Available to Common Shareholders

	(A) Income Information	(B) Weighted Shares	(C) Earnings per Share (A ÷ B)
Income before discontinued operations and extraordinary items available to common shareholders	$480,000 *	480,000	$1.00
Extraordinary gain (net of tax)	240,000	480,000	.50
Income available to common shareholders	$720,000	480,000	$1.50

*$580,000 − $100,000

Disclosure of the per share amount for the extraordinary item (net of tax) must be reported either on the face of the income statement or in the notes to the financial statements. Income and per share information reported would be as follows.

ILLUSTRATION 18-17
Earnings per Share, with Extraordinary Item

Income before extraordinary item	$580,000
Extraordinary gain, net of tax	240,000
Net income	$820,000
Earnings per share:	
Income before extraordinary item	$1.00
Extraordinary item, net of tax	.50
Net income	$1.50

Earnings Per Share—Complex Capital Structure

OBJECTIVE 7

Calculate earnings per share in a complex capital structure.

One problem with a basic EPS calculation is that it fails to recognize the potentially dilutive impact on outstanding shares when a corporation has dilutive securities in its capital structure. Dilutive securities present a serious problem because conversion or exercise often has an adverse effect on earnings per share. This adverse effect can be significant and, more important, unexpected unless financial statements call attention to the potential dilutive effect in some manner.

A complex capital structure exists when a corporation has convertible securities, options, warrants, or other rights that upon conversion or exercise could dilute earnings per share. Therefore when a company has a complex capital structure, both **basic** and **diluted earnings per share** are generally reported.

The calculation of diluted EPS is similar to the calculation of basic EPS. The difference is that diluted EPS includes the effect of all dilutive **potential common shares** that were outstanding during the period. The formula in Illustration 18-18 shows the relationship between basic EPS and diluted EPS.

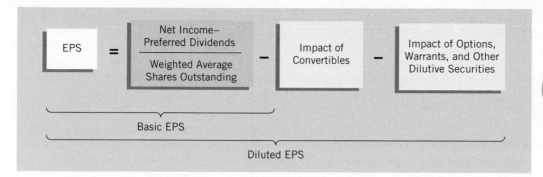

ILLUSTRATION 18-18
Relation between Basic and
Diluted EPS

**INTERNATIONAL
INSIGHT**

The provisions in Canadian and
U.S. GAAP are substantially the
same as those in International
Accounting Standard No. 33,
Earnings per Share, recently
issued by the IASC. The FASB
and IASC worked together on
this standard to achieve
international comparability
related to EPS presentations.

Note that companies with complex capital structures will not report diluted EPS if the securities in their capital structure are antidilutive. Antidilutive securities are securities, that upon conversion or exercise increase earnings per share (or reduce the loss per share). The dual presentation's purpose is to inform financial statement users of situations that will likely occur and to provide "worst case" dilutive situations. If the securities are antidilutive, the likelihood of conversion or exercise is considered remote. Thus, companies that have only antidilutive securities are not permitted to increase earnings per share and are required to report only the basic EPS number.[27]

The calculation of basic EPS was illustrated in the prior section. The discussion in the following sections addresses the effects of convertible and other dilutive securities on EPS calculations.

Diluted EPS—Convertible Securities

At conversion, convertible securities are exchanged for common shares. The method used to measure the dilutive effects of potential conversion on EPS is called the if-converted method. The if-converted method for a convertible bond assumes (1) the conversion of the convertible securities at the beginning of the period (or at the time of the security issuance, if issued during the period),[28] and (2) the elimination of related interest, net of tax. Thus the **denominator**—the weighted average number of shares outstanding—is increased by the additional shares assumed issued. The **numerator**—net income—is increased by the amount of interest expense, net of tax associated with those **potential common shares**.

Comprehensive Illustration—It-Converted Method

As an example, Field Corporation has net income for the year of $210,000 and a weighted average number of common shares outstanding during the period of 100,000 shares. The basic earnings per share is, therefore, $2.10 ($210,000 / 100,000). The company has two convertible debenture bond issues outstanding.[29] One is a 6% issue sold at 100 (total $1,000,000) in a prior year and convertible into 20,000 common shares. The other is a 10% issue sold at 100 (total $1,000,000) on April 1 of the current year and convertible into 32,000 common shares. The tax rate is 40%.

As shown in Illustration 18-19, to determine the numerator, we add back the interest on the if-converted securities less the related tax effect. Because the if-converted method assumes conversion as of the beginning of the year, no interest on the convertibles is assumed to be paid during the year. The interest on the 6% convertibles is $60,000 for the year ($1,000,000 × 6%). The increased tax expense is $24,000 ($60,000 ×

---

[27] *CICA Handbook,* Section 3500, par. .30.

[28] *CICA Handbook,* Section 3500, par. .35.

[29] To simplify, the consequences of measuring and presenting the debt and equity components of the convertible debentures separately have been ignored for this example. As previously noted in the chapter, part of the proceeds would be allocated to the equity component. The interest expense would be calculated using the market interest rate for straight debt, i.e., without the conversion feature.

.40), and the interest added back net of taxes is $36,000 [$60,000 − $24,000 or simply $60,000 × (1 − .40)].

Because 10% convertibles are issued subsequent to the beginning of the year, the shares assumed to have been issued on that date, April 1, are weighted as outstanding from April 1 to the end of the year. In addition, the interest adjustment to the numerator for these bonds would only reflect the interest for nine months. Thus the interest added back on the 10% convertible would be $45,000 [$1,000,000 × 10% × 9/12 year × (1 − .40)]. The calculation of earnings (the numerator) for diluted earnings per share is shown in Illustration 18-19.

ILLUSTRATION 18-19
Calculation of Adjusted Net Income

Net income for the year	$210,000
Add: Adjustment for interest (net of tax)	
6% debentures ($60,000 × [1 − .40])	36,000
10% debentures ($100,000 × 9/12 × [1 − .40])	45,000
Adjusted net income	$291,000

The calculation for shares adjusted for dilutive securities (the denominator) for diluted earnings per share is shown in Illustration 18-20:

ILLUSTRATION 18-20
Calculation of Weighted Average Number of Shares

Weighted average number of shares outstanding	100,000
Add: Shares assumed to be issued:	
6% debentures (as of beginning of year)	20,000
10% debentures (as of date of issue, April 1; 9/12 × 32,000)	24,000
Weighted average number of shares adjusted for dilutive securities	144,000

Field would then report earnings per share based on a dual presentation on the face of the income statement; basic and diluted earnings per share are reported.[30] The presentation is shown in Illustration 18-21.

ILLUSTRATION 18-21
Earnings per Share Disclosure

Net income for the year	$210,000
Earnings per Share (Note X)	
Basic earnings per share ($210,000 ÷ 100,000)	$2.10
Diluted earnings per share ($291,000 ÷ 144,000)	$2.02

Other Factors

The example above assumed that Field's bonds were sold at the face amount. If the bonds are sold at a premium or discount, interest expense must be adjusted each period to account for this occurrence. Therefore, the amount of interest expense added back, net of tax, to net income is the interest expense reported on the income statement, not the interest paid in cash during the period. Likewise, given that convertible debentures are compound instruments, a portion of the proceeds would actually be allocated to the equity component and the discount rate on the debt would be the market interest rate on straight debt.

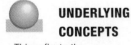

UNDERLYING CONCEPTS

This reflects the conservatism principle.

In addition, the conversion rate on a dilutive security may change over the period the dilutive security is outstanding. In this situation, for the diluted EPS calculation, the **most advantageous conversion rate available to the holder is used**.[31] For example, assume that a convertible bond was issued January 1, 2000, with a conversion rate of 10 common shares for each bond starting January 1, 2002; beginning January 1, 2005, the conversion rate is 12 common shares for each bond; and beginning January 1, 2009, it is 15 common shares for each bond. In calculating diluted EPS in 2000, the conversion rate of 15 shares to one bond is used.

---

[30] Conversion of bonds is dilutive because EPS with conversion ($2.02) is less than basic EPS ($2.10).

[31] *CICA Handbook*, Section 3500, par. .27.

Finally, if the 6% convertible debentures were instead 6% convertible preferred shares, the convertible preferred would also be considered **potential common shares** and included in shares outstanding in diluted EPS calculations. Preferred dividends would not be subtracted from net income in calculating the numerator because it would be assumed that the convertible preferreds were converted and outstanding as common shares for purposes of calculating EPS. Net income would be used as the numerator— no tax effect is calculated because preferred dividends generally are not deductible for tax purposes.

Diluted EPS—Options and Warrants

Stock options and warrants outstanding (whether or not presently exercisable) are included in diluted earnings per share unless they are **antidilutive**. Options and warrants and their equivalents are included in earnings per share calculations through the treasury stock method.

The treasury stock method assumes that the options or warrants are **exercised at the beginning of the year** (or date of issue if later) and the **proceeds** from the exercise of options and warrants are used to **purchase common shares** for the treasury. If the shares' exercise price is lower than the market price, then the proceeds from exercise are not sufficient to buy back all the shares. The **incremental shares remaining** are added to the weighted average number of shares outstanding for purposes of calculating diluted earnings per share.

Assume 1,500 options outstanding at an exercise price of $30 for a common share and a common share market price per share of $50. By applying the treasury stock method, there would be 600 incremental shares outstanding, calculated as follows:[32]

Proceeds from exercise of 1,500 options (1,500 × $30)	$45,000
Shares issued upon exercise of options	1,500
Treasury shares purchasable with proceeds ($45,000 ÷ $50)	900
Incremental shares outstanding (potential common shares)	600

ILLUSTRATION 18-22
Calculation of Incremental Shares

Thus, if the exercise price of the option or warrant is **lower** than the shares' market price, dilution occurs. If the exercise price of the option or warrant is **higher** than the shares' market price, common shares are reduced. In this case, the options or warrants are **antidilutive** because their assumed exercise leads to an increase in earnings per share.

For both options and warrants, **exercise is not assumed unless the average shares' market price is above the exercise price** during the period being reported i.e., the options/warranty are "in the money."[33] As a practical matter, a simple average of the weekly or monthly prices is adequate, so long as the prices do not fluctuate significantly.

Comprehensive Illustration—Treasury Stock Method

To illustrate application of the treasury stock method, assume that Kubitz Industries, Inc. has net income for the period of $220,000. The average number of shares outstanding for the period was 100,000 shares. Hence, basic EPS—ignoring all dilutive securities—is $2.20. The average number of shares under outstanding options (although not exercisable at this time) at an option price of $20 per share is 5,000 shares. The common shares' average market price during the year was $28. The calculation is shown below.

---

[32] The incremental number of shares may be more simply calculated:
  (Market price − option price)/market price × Number of Options = Number of Shares
  ($50 − $30)/$50 × 1,500 options = 600 shares

[33] It might be noted that options and warrants have essentially the same assumptions and calculational problems, although the warrants may allow or require the tendering of some other security such as debt in lieu of cash upon exercise. In such situations, the accounting becomes quite complex.

ILLUSTRATION 18-23
Calculation of Earnings per Share—Treasury Stock Method

	Basic Earnings per Share	Diluted Earnings per Share
Average number of shares under option outstanding:		5000
Option price per share		× $20
Proceeds upon exercise of options		$100,000
Average market price of common shares		$28
Treasury shares that could be repurchased with proceeds ($100,000 ÷ $28)		3,571
Excess of shares under option over the treasury shares that could be repurchased (5,000 − 3,571)— Potential common incremental shares		1,429
Average number of common shares outstanding	$100,000	$100,000
Total average number of common shares outstanding and potential common shares	$100,000 (A)	$101,429 (C)
Net income for the year	$220,000 (B)	$220,000 (D)
Earnings per share	$2.20 (B ÷ A)	$2.17 (D ÷ C)

Contingent Issue Agreement

In certain business transactions, a company may promise to issue common shares if a certain future event happens. For instance, in business combinations, the acquirer may promise to issue additional shares—referred to as **contingently issuable shares**—if certain conditions are met. If these shares are issuable upon the mere passage of time, they are not considered contingently issuable as the passage of time is a certainty.[34] These shares would be considered outstanding for both basic and diluted EPS calculations.

If the shares are issuable upon attaining a certain earnings or market price level for instance, **and this level is met** at the end of the year, they should be considered as outstanding for the calculation of diluted earnings per share.[35] If the conditions have not been met, the diluted EPS may still be affected. The number of contingently issuable shares included in the diluted EPS calculation would be based on the number of shares (if any) that would be issuable if the end of the reporting period were the end of the contingency period and if the impact were dilutive.[36]

For example, assume that Walz Corporation purchased Cardella Limited and agreed to give the shareholders of Cardella 20,000 additional shares in 2004 if Cardella's net income in 2003 is $90,000; in 2002, Cardella's net income is $100,000. Because the 2003 stipulated earnings of $90,000 are already being attained, diluted earnings per share of Walz for 2002 would include the 20,000 contingent shares in the shares outstanding calculation.

Antidilution Revisited

In calculating diluted EPS, the aggregate of all dilutive securities must be considered. But first we must determine which **potentially dilutive securities** are in fact **individually** dilutive and which are antidilutive. Any security that is antidilutive should be **excluded** and cannot be used to offset dilutive securities.

Recall that antidilutive securities are securities whose inclusion in earnings per share calculations would **increase** earnings per share (or reduce net loss per share). Convertible debt is antidilutive if the addition to income of the interest (net of tax) causes a greater percentage increase in income (numerator) than conversion of the

---

[34] *CICA Handbook,* Section 3500, par. .21.

[35] *CICA Handbook,* Section 3500, par. .49. In addition to contingent issuances of stock, other types of situations that might lead to dilution are the issuance of participating securities and two-class common shares. The reporting of these types of securities in EPS calculations is beyond the scope of this textbook.

[36] *Ibid.*

bonds causes a percentage increase in common and potentially dilutive shares (denominator). In other words, convertible debt is antidilutive if conversion of the security causes common share earnings to increase by a greater amount per additional common share than earnings per share was before the conversion.

To illustrate, assume that Kohl Corporation has a 6%, $1 million debt issue that is convertible into 10,000 common shares. Net income for the year is $210,000, the weighted average number of common shares outstanding is 100,000 shares, and the tax rate is 40%. In this case, assumed conversion of the debt into common shares at the beginning of the year requires the following adjustments of net income and the weighted average number of shares outstanding.

Net income for the year	$210,000	Average number of shares outstanding	100,000
Add: Adjustment for interest (net of tax) on 6%[37] debentures $60,000 × (1 − .40)	36,000	Add: Shares issued upon assumed conversion of debt	10,000
Adjusted net income	$246,000	Average number of common and potential common shares	110,000

Basic EPS = $210,000 ÷ 100,000 = $2.10
Diluted EPS = $246,000 ÷ 110,000 = $2.24 = **Antidilutive**

ILLUSTRATION 18-24
Test for Antidilution

As a shortcut, the convertible debt also can be identified as antidilutive by comparing the EPS resulting from conversion, $3.60 ($36,000 additional earnings ÷ 10,000 additional shares), with EPS before inclusion of the convertible debt, $2.10.

With options or warrants, whenever the exercise price is higher than the market price, the security is antidilutive. **Antidilutive securities should be ignored in all calculations and should not be considered in calculating diluted earnings per share.** This approach is reasonable because the profession's intent was to inform the investor of the **possible dilution** that might occur in reported earnings per share and not to be concerned with securities that, if converted or exercised, would result in an increase in earnings per share.

See the Digital Tool for an expanded example.

EPS Presentation and Disclosure

If a corporation's capital structure is complex, the earnings per share presentation would be as follows:

Earnings per common share	
Basic earnings per share	$3.30
Diluted earnings per share	$2.70

ILLUSTRATION 18-25
EPS Presentation—Complex Capital Structure

When a period's earnings include irregular items, per share amounts (where applicable) should be shown for income from continuing operations (i.e., before discontinued operations or Extraordinary items) and net income. Companies that report a discontinued operation or an extraordinary item should present per share amounts for those line items either on the face of the income statement or in the notes to the financial statements. A presentation reporting extraordinary items only is presented in Illustration 18-26.

Basic earnings per share	
Income before extraordinary item	$3.80
Extraordinary item	.80
Net income	$3.00
Diluted earnings per share	
Income before extraordinary item	$3.35
Extraordinary item	.65
Net income	$2.70

ILLUSTRATION 18-26
EPS Presentation, with Extraordinary Item

---

[37] Once again, for simplicity's sake, ignore the impact of splitting out the equity component for the compound instrument.

Earnings per share amounts must be shown for all periods presented and all prior period earnings per share amounts presented should be restated for stock dividends and stock splits. If diluted EPS data are reported for at least one period, they should be reported for all periods presented, even if they are the same as basic EPS. When results of operations of a prior period have been restated as a result of a prior period adjustment, the earnings per share data shown for the prior periods should also be restated. The restatement's effect should be disclosed in the year of the restatement.

Complex capital structures and dual presentation of earnings require the following additional disclosures in note form.

1. adjustments to income before discontinued operations and extraordinary items for returns on senior equity instruments in arriving at income available to common shareholders,

2. a reconciliation of the numerators and denominators of basic and diluted per share calculations for income before discontinued operations and extraordinary items (including individual income and share amount each class of securities that affect EPS), and

3. securities that could potentially dilute basic EPS in the future but were not included in the calculations due to antidilutive features.

Illustration 18-27 presents the reconciliation and the related disclosure that is needed to meet this standard's disclosure requirements.

ILLUSTRATION 18-27
Reconciliation for Basic and Diluted EPS

	For the Year Ended 2002		
	Income (Numerator)	Shares (Denominator)	Per-Share Amount
Income before extraordinary item and accounting change	$7,500,000		
Less: Preferred stock dividends	(45,000)		
Basic EPS			
Income available to common shareholders	7,455,000	3,991,666	$1.87
Warrants		30,768	
Convertible preferred shares	45,000	308,333	
4% convertible bonds (net of tax)	60,000	50,000	
Diluted EPS			
Income available to common shareholders + assumed conversions	$7,560,000	4,380,767	$1.73

Stock options to purchase 1,000,000 shares of common shares at $85 per share were outstanding during the second half of 2002 but were not included in the calculation of diluted EPS because the options' exercise price was greater than the average market price of the common shares. The options were still outstanding at the end of year 2002 and expire on June 30, 2012.

Summary

Calculating earnings per share is a complex issue. It is a controversial area because many securities, although technically not common shares, have many of common shares' basic characteristics. Some companies have issued these types of securities rather than common shares in order to avoid an adverse dilutive effect on earnings per share.

Illustration 18-28 displays the basic points of calculating earnings per share in a simple capital structure.

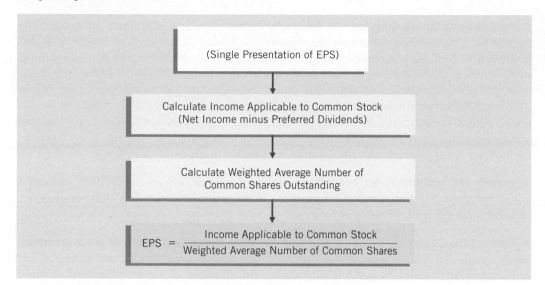

ILLUSTRATION 18-28
Calculating EPS, Simple Capital Structure

Illustration 18-29 shows the calculation of earnings per share for a complex capital structure.

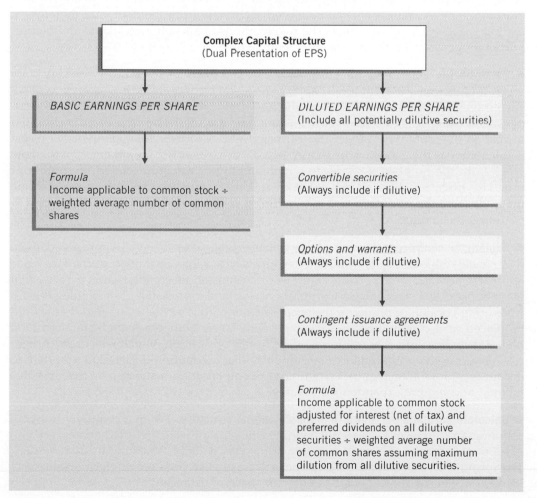

ILLUSTRATION 18-29
Calculating EPS, Complex Capital Structure

SUMMARY OF LEARNING OBJECTIVES

1 Describe the accounting for the issuance, conversion, and retirement of convertible securities. The method for recording convertible bonds at the date of issuance is different from that used to record straight debt issues. As the instrument is a **compound instrument** and contains both debt and equity components, these must be measured separately and presented as debt and equity respectively. Any discount or premium that results from the issuance of convertible bonds is amortized assuming the bonds will be held to maturity. If bonds are converted into other securities, the principal accounting problem is to determine the amount at which to record the securities exchanged for the bond. The book value method is often used in practice.

2 Explain the accounting for convertible preferred shares. When convertible preferred shares are converted, Preferred Shares, along with any related Contributed Surplus, are debited, and Common Shares is credited.

3 Contrast the accounting for stock warrants and stock warrants issued with other securities. Stock rights: No entry is required when rights are issued to existing shareholders. Only a memorandum entry is needed to indicate the number of rights issued to existing shareholders and to ensure that the company has additional unissued shares registered for issuance in case the rights are exercised. Stock warrants: The proceeds from the sale of debt with detachable stock warrants should be allocated between the two securities. Warrants that are detachable can be traded separately from the debt, and therefore, a market value can be determined. The two methods of allocation available are the proportional method and the incremental method.

4 Describe the accounting for stock compensation plans under GAAP. Companies are given a choice in the recognition approach to stock compensation; however, GAAP encourages adoption of the fair value method. Using the fair value method, total compensation expense is calculated based on the fair value of the options that are expected to vest on the grant date. Under the intrinsic value approach, total compensation cost is calculated as the excess of the shares' market price over the option price on the date when both the number of shares to which employees are entitled and the option or purchase price for those shares are known. Under both the fair and intrinsic value methods, compensation expense is recognized in the periods in which the employee performs the services.

5 Explain the controversy involving stock compensation plans. When first proposed, there was considerable opposition to the recognition provisions contained in the fair value approach, because that approach could result in substantial compensation expense that was not previously recognized. Corporations, particularly small high-technology firms, were quite vocal in opposing to the proposed standard. They believed that they would be placed at a competitive disadvantage with larger companies that can withstand higher compensation charges. In response to this opposition, which was based primarily on economic consequences arguments, the accounting profession decided to encourage, rather than require, recognition of compensation cost based on the fair value method and require expanded disclosures.

6 Calculate earnings per share in a simple capital structure. When a company has both common and preferred shares outstanding, the current year preferred share dividend is subtracted from net income to arrive at income available to common shareholders. The formula for calculating earnings per share is net income less preferred share dividends divided by the weighted average of shares outstanding.

7 Calculate earnings per share in a complex capital structure. A complex capital structure requires a dual presentation of earnings per share, each with equal prominence on the face of the income statement. These two presentations are referred to as basic earnings per share and diluted earnings per share. Basic earnings per share is based on the number of weighted average common shares outstanding. Diluted earnings per share indicates the dilution of earnings per share that would have occurred if all potential issuances of common shares that would have reduced earnings per share had taken place.

APPENDIX 18A

Stock Compensation Plans— Additional Complications

Determining Compensation Expense

Two common plans (beyond the stock option plans discussed in the chapter) that illustrate different accounting issues are:

1. Stock appreciation rights plans.
2. Performance-type plans.

> **OBJECTIVE 8**
> ....
> After studying Appendix 18A, you should be able to: Discuss the reporting issues surrounding other compensation plans.

Stock Appreciation Rights

One of the main drawbacks of compensatory stock option plans is that in order to realize the stock options' benefit, the employees must exercise the options and then sell the shares. This creates transactions costs and perhaps financial hardship. One solution to this problem was the creation of stock appreciation rights (SARs). In this type of plan, the executive is given the right to receive compensation equal to the share appreciation, which is defined as the excess of the market price of the shares at the date of exercise over a pre-established price. This share appreciation may be paid in cash, shares, or a combination of both. The major advantage of SARs is that the executive often does not have to make a cash outlay at the date of exercise, but receives a payment for the share appreciation. Unlike shares acquired under a stock option plan, the shares that constitute the basis for calculating the appreciation in a SARs plan are not issued. The executive is awarded only cash or shares having a market value equivalent to the appreciation.

SARs, like other stock-based compensation plans would be accounted for using either the **fair value method** or the **intrinsic value method**. The added complexity with the SAR occurs when the payout is cash or some combination of cash and shares. This creates a **measurement** issue since the company will not know the extent of the liability to pay cash until the **exercise date**.

Assuming that the compensation is ultimately payable in shares, this is an **equity instrument**. Under the fair value method, the value would be **measured** at the **grant date** using an option pricing model and recognized over the service period like other stock based compensation plans.

If the compensation is payable in cash, this creates a **liability** and must be continually remeasured since at exercise, the company will have to actually pay out cash and therefore uses the best estimate of the liability (fair value of shares minus stated price) and **remeasures** each period.

Under the intrinsic value method, the same measurement issue presents itself whether the shares are payable in cash or shares. This is due to the way the compensation cost is measured under this method i.e.,

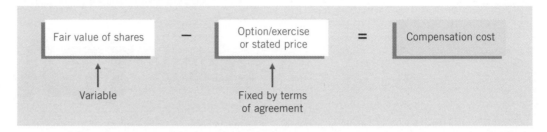

Because the fair value of the shares will continually change, the compensation cost will continually change over the service period (which is normally the vesting period). Therefore, regardless whether the compensation is ultimately payable in cash or shares, it is variable and must be remeasured each period.

How then should compensation expense be recorded during the interim periods from the date of grant to the date of exercise? Such a determination is not easy because it is impossible to know what total compensation cost will be until the date of exercise, and the service period will probably not coincide with the exercise date. The best estimate of the plan's total compensation cost at any interim period is the difference between the stock's current market price and the option price multiplied by the number of stock appreciation rights outstanding. This total estimated compensation cost is then allocated over the service period, to record an expense (or a decrease in expense if market price falls) in each period.[38] At the end of each interim period, total compensation expense reported to date should equal the percentage of the total service period that has elapsed multiplied by the estimated compensation cost.

For example, if at the end of an interim period the service period is 40% complete and total estimated compensation is $100,000, then cumulative compensation expense reported to date should equal $40,000 ($100,000 × .40). As another illustration, in the first year of a four-year plan, the company charges one-fourth of the appreciation to date. In the second year, it charges off two-fourths or 50% of the appreciation to date less the amount already recognized in the first year. In the third year, it charges off three-fourths of the appreciation to date less the amount recognized previously, and in the fourth year it charges off the remaining compensation expense. We will refer to this method as the *percentage approach* for allocating compensation expense.

A special problem arises when the exercise date is later than the service period. In the previous example, if the SARs were not exercised at the end of four years, it would be necessary to account for the difference in the market price and the option price in the fifth year. In this case, compensation expense is adjusted whenever a change in the stock's market price **occurs in subsequent reporting periods until the rights expire or are exercised, whichever comes first**.

Increases or decreases in the market value of those shares between the date of grant and the exercise date, therefore, result in a change in the measure of compensation. Some periods will have credits to compensation expense if the stock's quoted market

---

[38] "Accounting for Stock Appreciation Rights and Other Variable Stock Option or Award Plans," FASB Interpretation No. 28 (Stamford, Conn.: FASB, 1978), par. 2.

price falls from one period to the next; the credit to compensation expense, however, cannot exceed previously recognized compensation expense. In other words, cumulative compensation expense cannot be negative.

To illustrate, assume that Hotels, Inc. establishes a SAR program on January 1, 2001, which entitles executives to receive cash at the date of exercise (anytime in the next five years) for the difference between the shares' market price and the preestablished or stated price of $10 on 10,000 SARs. The shares' market price on December 31, 2001 is $13 and the service period runs for two years (2001–2002). Illustration 18A-1 indicates the amount of compensation expense to be recorded each period, assuming that the executives hold the SARs for three years, at which time the rights are exercised.

ILLUSTRATION 18A-1
Compensation Expense, Stock Appreciation Rights

STOCK APPRECIATION RIGHTS
Schedule of Compensation Expense

(1)	(2)	(3)	(4)	(5)	(6)			
Date	Market Price	Pre-established Price (10,000 SARs)	Cumulative Compensation Recognizable[a]	Percentage Accrued[b]	Cumulative Compensation Accrued to Date	Expense 2001	Expense 2002	Expense 2003
12/31/01	$13	$10	$30,000	50%	$(15,000)	$15,000		
					$(55,000)		$55,000	
12/31/02	$17	$10	$70,000	100%	$(70,000)			
					$(20,000)			$(20,000)
12/31/03	$15	$10	$50,000	100%	$(50,000)			

[a]Cumulative compensation for unexercised SARs to be allocated to periods of service.
[b]The percentage accrued is based on a two-year service period (2001–2002).

In 2001 Hotels would record compensation expense of $15,000 because 50% of the $30,000 total of compensation cost estimated at December 31, 2001 is allocable to 2001.

In 2002, the market price increased to $17 per share; therefore, the additional compensation expense of $55,000 ($70,000 minus $15,000) was recorded. The SARs were held through 2003, during which time the shares decreased to $15. The decrease is recognized by recording a $20,000 credit to compensation expense and a debit to Liability under Stock Appreciation Plan. Note that after the service period ends, since the rights are still outstanding, the rights are adjusted to market at December 31, 2003. Any such credit to compensation expense cannot exceed previous charges to expense attributable to that plan.

As the compensation expense is recorded each period, the corresponding credit should be to a liability account if the stock appreciation is to be paid in cash. If shares are to be issued, then a more appropriate credit would be to Contributed Surplus. The entry to record compensation expense in the first year, assuming that the SARs ultimately will be paid in cash, is as follows:

UNDERLYING CONCEPTS

A requirement to issue shares under a SAR plan does not create a liability, since it is not an obligation to deliver cash.

Compensation Expense	15,000	
Liability under Stock Appreciation Plan		15,000

The liability account would be credited again in 2002 for $55,000 and debited for $20,000 in 2003 when the negative compensation expense is recorded. The entry to record the negative compensation expense is as follows:

Liability under Stock Appreciation Plan	20,000	
Compensation Expense		20,000

At December 31, 2003, the executives receive $50,000; the entry removing the liability is as follows:

Liability under Stock Appreciation Plan	50,000	
Cash		50,000

Compensation expense can therefore increase or decrease substantially from one period to the next.

In general, where the employee has the option to elect to be paid out in shares or cash, assume that they will elect cash. If the employer has the choice, the most likely scenario would be selected.

For this reason, companies with substantial stock appreciation rights plans may choose to use the fair value method because the total compensation expense is determined at the date of grant. Subsequent changes in market price are therefore ignored.

SARs are often issued in combination with compensatory stock options (referred to as tandem or combination plans and the executive must then select which of the two sets of terms to exercise, thereby cancelling the other. The existence of alternative plans running concurrently poses additional problems. You must determine, on the basis of the facts available each period, which of the two plans has the higher probability of exercise and then account for this plan and ignore the other.

Performance-Type Plans

Some executives have become disenchanted with stock compensation plans whose ultimate payment depends on an increase in the common shares' market price. They do not like having their compensation and judgement of performance at the mercy of the stock market's erratic behaviour. As a result, there has been a substantial increase in the use of plans whereby executives receive common shares (or cash) if specified performance criteria are attained during the performance period (generally three to five years). Many large companies now have some type of plan that does not rely on share price appreciation.

The **performance criteria** employed usually are increases in return on assets or equity, growth in sales, growth in earnings per share (EPS), or a combination of these factors. A good illustration of this type of plan is that of **Atlantic Richfield**, which at one time offered performance units valued in excess of $700,000 to the chairman of the board. These performance units are payable in five years, contingent upon the company's meeting certain levels of return on shareholders' equity and cash dividends.

As another example, **Honeywell** uses growth in EPS as its performance criterion. When certain levels of EPS are achieved, executives receive shares. If the company achieves an average annual EPS growth of 13%, the executive will earn 100% of the shares. The maximum allowable is 130%, which would require a 17% growth rate; below 9%, the executives receive nothing.

A performance-type plan's measurement date is the date of exercise because the number of shares that will be issued or the cash that will be paid out when performance is achieved are not known at the date of grant. The company must use its best estimates to measure the compensation cost prior to the date of exercise. The compensation cost is allocated to the periods involved in the same manner as with stock appreciation rights; that is, the percentage approach is used.

Tandem or combination awards are popular with these plans. The executive has the choice of selecting between a performance or stock option award. Companies such as **General Electric** and **Xerox** have adopted plans of this nature. In these cases the executive has the best of both worlds: if either the share price increases or the performance goal is achieved, the executive gains. Sometimes, the executive receives both types of plans, so that the monies received from the performance plan can finance the exercise price on the stock option plan.

Summary of Compensation Plans

A summary of compensation plans and their major characteristics is provided in Illustration 18A-2.

Type of Plan	Measurement Date	Measurement of Compensation	Allocation Period (3)	Allocation Method
Compensatory stock option				
Intrinsic value method	Grant	Market price less exercise price	N/A (generally no compensation expense since FV of shares < option price)	N/A (no compensation expense)
Fair value method	Grant	Option pricing model	Service	Straight-line (since recognition of the cost, once measured is a function of time —the service period)
Stock appreciation rights				
Intrinsic value method	Exercise	Market price less exercise price	Service	Percentage approach for service period, then mark to market
Fair value method	Grant (1)	Option pricing model (2)	Service	Straight-line for service period and then mark to market for those settled in cash
Performance-type plan				
Intrinsic value method	Exercise	Market value of shares issued	Service	Percentage approach for service period, then mark to market
Fair value method	Exercise	Market value of shares issued	Service	Percentage approach for service period, then mark to market

(1) Unless the SAR is payable in cash—then exercise date
(2) Unless payable in cash and then fair value of shares minus stated price (equals best estimate of liability)
(3) Generally vesting period unless total cost is variable beyond that date—must continue to remeasure and accrue (intrinsic value method and all contracts that will be settled in cash)

Summary of Learning Objective for Appendix 18A

8 Discuss the reporting issues surrounding other compensation plans.

1. *Stock appreciation rights:* These compensation plans pose different problems where they are payable in cash or where the intrinsic value method is used to measure the compensation cost. In these instances, the cost must be continually remeasured.

2. *Performance-type plan:* Compensation is measured by the market value of shares issued on the exercise date. Compensation expense is allocated by the percentage approach over the service period, then marked to market.

**APPENDIX 18A
KEY TERMS**

date of exercise, 863
percentage approach, 864
share appreciation, 863
stock appreciation rights (SARs), 863
tandem (combination) plan, 866

APPENDIX 18B

Accounting for Derivatives

BACKGROUND

Companies currently operate in an environment of constant flux caused by volatile markets, new technology, and deregulation. This increases **business risk** including **financial risk**. The response from the financial community has been to develop products to manage some of these risks, hence the rise of derivatives.

Risk management is a very interesting area. Managers of successful companies have always managed risks to **minimize adverse financial consequences**; however, historically, the main **vehicle** for managing risk has been insurance and the main **adverse financial consequences** have been seen as resulting from loss due to fire, theft, damages, and lawsuits. More companies are now looking at managing risk in a more holistic sense, attempting to manage any situations that cause uncertainty. While managing risk **reduces uncertainty** to an acceptable level (which may differ depending on the stakeholders), it also has its **costs**. There are usually **transaction costs** to enter into contracts such as insurance and derivative contracts, which help companies reduce or at least manage risk. Furthermore, managing risk often results in **limiting the potential for gain**.

Derivatives are useful for financial risk management because these instruments' fair values or cash flows can be used to offset the changes in fair values or cash flows of the assets that are at risk, thus reducing or eliminating losses due to adverse financial consequences. The growth in use of derivatives has been aided by the development of powerful calculating and communication technology, which provides new ways to analyse information about markets as well as the power to process high volumes of payments.

UNDERSTANDING DERIVATIVES

Financial instruments may be either primary instruments such as receivables and payables or derivative instruments such as forwards, futures, and options. Most primary financial instruments are **recognized** in the financial statements since they are **traditional** types of assets and liabilities whereas historically, many derivative instruments have **not been recognized** on the balance sheet nor income statement. Primary financial instruments as well as some derivatives have been discussed throughout the text. The more complex instruments and their relationship to risk management will be discussed here.

Increasingly, the accounting profession is moving toward full **recognition** of these instruments in order to provide more **useful information** about the **risks** that a company is exposed to and how it **manages these risks**.

Derivatives are defined as financial instruments, which **create rights and obligations** that have the effect of **transferring** between parties to the instrument one or more of the **financial risks** inherent in an underlying primary instrument.[39] Financial risks

---

[39] *CICA Handbook*, Section 3860, par. .10.

include **price** risk, **credit** risk, **liquidity** risk, and **cash flow** risk. These are briefly defined as follows:[40]

1. Price risk: the risks that an instrument's price or value will change. The price or value may change due to change in currency (**currency** risk), interest rate changes (**interest rate** risk) and market forces (**market** risk). An example of market price risk is the value of a temporary investment in common shares of another company.

2. Credit risk: the risk that one of the parties to the contract will fail to fulfill its obligation under the contract and cause the other party loss e.g., credit risk is usually associated with collection (e.g., accounts receivable have credit risk associated with them).

3. Liquidity risk: the risk that the company itself will not be able to honour the contract and fulfill its obligation. The more debt a company has, the greater the risk that it will not be able to repay the debt and the higher the liquidity risk. All debt increases liquidity risk.

4. Cash flow risk: the risk that cash flows related to a contract (monetary financial instrument) will change over time. An example of this is a debt instrument with a variable interest rate. The variable interest rate will cause the interest payments to change when interest rates change.

Derivatives are so named because they **derive** their value from the underlying primary instrument. For example, a **stock option** to purchase shares of The Hudson's Bay Company is a derivative instrument. It derives its value from the share price of the underlying Hudson's Bay share price. If the share price goes up, the option is worth more. If it goes down, the option may become worthless.

Note that the derivative, in this case the option, allows the holder to participate in increases in the share value without having to hold the actual shares themselves (the options allow the holder the **right to increases in share value**). Thus derivative instruments generally do not result in the transfer of the underlying primary instrument at the contract's inception and perhaps not even upon its maturity.

A forward contract is another type of derivative. Under a forward contract, the parties to the contract each commit upfront to do something in the future, e.g., one party to buy and the other to sell the Hudson's Bay shares at a certain Canadian price amount. The price is locked in under the contract as is the time period. A forward contract not only transfers to the holder the **right to increases in value** of the underlying primary instrument (in this case, the shares), it also creates an **obligation** (to pay a fixed amount at a certain date). The option, on the other hand, creates a **right but not an obligation,** i.e., the holder may choose to exercise the option but need not. The forward contract transfers to the holder the **price risk** regarding the shares. There is also a **credit risk,** i.e., that at the culmination of the contract, the counterparty (the other party to the contract) will not deliver the shares.

For both the forward contract and the option contract, the **delivery** of the underlying instrument was for a **future** date and the contact's value was based on the underlying asset—the Hudson's Bay shares. A forward is often more tailored to the needs of the parties entering into the contract and includes nonstandard terms.

Futures contracts, another popular type of derivative, are the same as forwards except they are standardized and trade on stock markets and exchanges. Futures are often settled on a **net basis**, meaning that the parties do not take delivery of the goods at culmination; rather, they value the contract and determine which party owes the other based on the fair values of the items to be transferred. Moreover, they usually are settled in cash, daily, a feature calling marking to market.

Derivatives have been the focus of some very negative publicity in the past few years with companies suffering significant losses and perhaps even going bankrupt due to derivative instruments. This is partially due to the complexity of these contracts and the fact that they are not well understood by many who use them. One key complexity is the presence of **leverage**. Many derivative instruments use the principle of leverage,

---

[40] *Ibid.* par. .44.

which magnifies the potential gain or loss. Therefore, while the cost to enter into the contract may be relatively low, the potential for gain or loss is exponentially great and has in the past decade forced long-established companies such as Barings Bank and even governments (Orange County in the United States) into bankruptcy.

In this chapter, we will discuss the accounting for three different types of derivatives:

1. Financial forwards or financial futures
2. Options
3. Swaps

WHO USES DERIVATIVES?

Derivatives may be used to **reduce** risk (normally referred to as hedging) or **expose** a company to risks (speculative). Usually, as previously mentioned, derivatives are used to **manage risks** whether these risks are caused by changes in interest rates, the weather, stock prices, oil prices, or foreign currencies.

Producers and Consumers

OBJECTIVE 9

Explain who uses derivatives and why they are used.

McCain Foods Limited is a large producer of potatoes for the consumer market. Assume that McCain believes the present price for potatoes is excellent, but unfortunately it will take two months to harvest its potatoes and deliver them to the market. Because the company is concerned that the price of potatoes will drop, it signs a contract in which it agrees to sell its potatoes today and locks in a market price for delivery in two months (a forward contract).

Who would buy this contract? Suppose on the other side of the contract is **McDonald's Corporation** which wants to have potatoes (for French fries) in two months and is worried that prices will increase.[41] McDonald's is therefore agreeable to delivery in two months at current prices because it knows that it will need potatoes in two months and that it can make an acceptable profit at this price level.

In this situation, if the price of potatoes increases before delivery, you might conclude that McCain loses and McDonald's wins. Conversely, if prices decrease, McCain wins and McDonald's loses. However, the objective is not to gamble on the outcome. In other words, regardless of which way the price moves, both companies should be pleased because both have received a price at which an **acceptable profit** is obtained. In this case, McCain is a **producer** and McDonald's is a **consumer**. Both companies are often referred to as **hedgers** because they are hedging their positions to ensure an acceptable financial result.

Commodity prices are volatile and depend on weather, crop disasters, and general economic conditions. For the producer and the consumer to plan effectively, it makes good sense to lock in specific future revenues or costs in order to run their businesses successfully.

Speculators and Arbitrageurs

In some cases, instead of McDonald's taking a position in the forward contract, a speculator may purchase the contract from McCain. The **speculator** is betting that the price of potatoes will increase and therefore the value of the forward contract will increase. The speculator, who may be in the market for only a few hours, will then sell the forward contract to another speculator or to a company like McDonald's. Thus these types of contracts are often **readily marketable**.

Another user of derivatives is **arbitrageurs**. These market players attempt to exploit inefficiencies in different markets. They seek to lock in profits by simultaneously entering into transactions in two or more markets. For example, an arbitrageur might trade

---

[41] Why would one party think that prices will rise and the other that they will fall? The same information is rarely available to all parties and in most contract negotiations, there is information asymmetry such that the parties expect different outcomes.

in a futures contract and at the same time in the commodity underlying the futures contract, hoping to achieve small price gains on the difference between the two. Arbitrageurs exist because there is information asymmetry in different markets. Some markets are more efficient than others. The arbitrageurs force the markets to move towards each other since they create demand and supply where it previously might not have existed, thus driving the prices either up or down.

Speculators and arbitrageurs are very important to markets because they keep the market liquid on a daily basis.

WHY USE DERIVATIVES?

In the previous illustrations, we explained why McCain (the producer) and McDonald's (the consumer) would become involved in a derivative contract. Consider other types of situations that companies face.

1. Airlines, such as **Air Canada**, are affected by changes in the price of jet fuel.
2. Financial institutions, such as the **Royal Bank, Bank of Montreal**, and **TD CanadaTrust**, are involved in borrowing and lending funds that are affected by changes in interest rates.
3. Multinational corporations, such as **Cisco Systems, Coca-Cola**, and **General Electric**, are subject to changes in foreign exchange rates.

It is not surprising therefore that you find most corporations involved in some form of derivatives transactions.

Many corporations therefore use derivatives extensively and successfully. However, derivatives can be dangerous, and it is critical that all parties involved understand the risks and rewards associated with these contracts.[42]

BASIC PRINCIPLES IN ACCOUNTING FOR DERIVATIVES

In Canada, at present, **there are no recognition and measurement principles for derivatives**.[43] As a result, many derivatives are **not recognized** in the financial statements. However, the accounting profession, as previously mentioned, appears to be reaching some consensus about recognizing and measuring these instruments.[44] To date, that consensus involves the following:

(a) **measurement** of financial instruments at **fair value** (including liabilities),

(b) **recognition** of virtually all gains and losses resulting from changes in fair value in income,

(c) **preclusion of special accounting** for financial instruments used in hedging relationships, and

(d) other recommendations including increased **disclosures**.

> **OBJECTIVE 10**
> ....
> Understand the basic guidelines for accounting for derivatives.

---

[42] There are some well-publicized examples of companies that have suffered considerable losses using derivatives. For example, companies such as **Showa Shell Sekiyu** (Japan), **Metallgesellschaft** (Germany), **Proctor & Gamble** (U.S.), and **Air Products & Chemicals** (U.S.) have incurred significant losses from investments in derivative instruments.

[43] The primary source of GAAP is the *Handbook* Section 3860, which looks at presentations and disclosure only.

[44] The Joint Working Group JWG) of Standard Setters, which includes representatives from Canada, the United States, United Kingdom, Australia, France, Germany, Japan, New Zealand, and Nordic countries, produced a draft Standard on Financial Instruments in December 2000. At present, in a move toward international harmonization, the professional accounting bodies from the constituent countries are seeking feedback in their own countries. The next step will be for the CICA to issue an Exposure Draft.

Fair value is an estimate of the price an enterprise would have received if it had sold the asset or would have paid, if it had been relieved of the liability, on the measurement date in an arm's-length exchange motivated by normal business considerations.[45] The profession believes that fair value will provide statement users the best information about derivative financial instruments. Relying on some other basis of valuation for derivatives, such as historical cost, does not make sense because many derivatives have a historical cost of zero. Furthermore, given the **well-developed markets** for derivatives and for the assets from which derivatives derive their value, the profession believes that **reliable** fair value amounts can be determined for derivative instruments.

On the income statement, any unrealized gain or loss should be **recognized in income**. This allows the income statement to reflect the underlying reality of the risks and how the risks are being managed and therefore, net income represents a **higher quality of earnings**.

Speculation—Illustration of Derivative Financial Instrument

OBJECTIVE 11

Describe the accounting for derivative financial instruments.

To illustrate the measurement and reporting of a derivative financial instrument for **speculative purposes**, we examine a derivative whose value is related to the market price of Laredo Inc. common shares. As in the previous example, you could realize a gain from the Laredo shares' increase in value with the use of a derivative financial instrument, such as a call option.[46] A **call option** gives the holder the right, but not the obligation to buy shares at a preset price (often referred to as the **strike price** or the **exercise price**). For this right to be exposed to the upside potential, the purchaser of an option pays a cost.

For example, assume you enter into a **call option contract** with Baird Investment Corp., which gives you the option to purchase Laredo shares at $100 per share.[47] If the price of Laredo share increases above $100, you can exercise this option and purchase the shares for $100 per share. If Laredo's share never increases above $100 per share, the call option is worthless and you recognize a loss equal to the initial price of the call option.

Accounting Entries

To illustrate the accounting for a call option, assume that you purchased a call option contract on January 2, 2002, when Laredo shares are trading at $100 per share. The terms of the contract give you the option to purchase 1,000 shares of Laredo stock at an option price of $100 per share (the exercise or strike price); the option expires on April 30, 2002. You purchase the call option for $400 and make the following entry:

January 2, 2002		
Temporary investment—Call Option	400	
Cash		400

This payment (referred to as the **option premium**) is generally much less than the cost of purchasing the shares directly. The option premium is comprised of two amounts: (1) intrinsic value and (2) time value. The formula to calculate the option premium is as follows:

ILLUSTRATION 18B-1
Option Price Formula

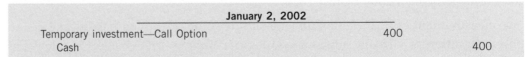
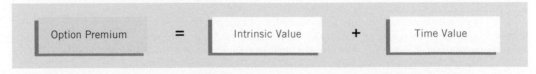

---

[45] *JWG Financial Instruments and Similar Items—Draft Standard* (December 2000), par. .70.

[46] You could use a different type of option contract—a **put option**—to realize a gain if you speculate that the Laredo shares will decline in value. A put option gives the holder the option to **sell** shares at a present price. Thus, a put option **increases** in value when the underlying asset **decreases** in value.

[47]Baird Investment Corp. is referred to as the counterparty. Counterparties frequently are investment bankers or other entities that hold inventories of financial instruments.

Intrinsic value is the difference between the market price and the preset strike price at any point in time. It represents the amount realized by the option holder if the option were exercised immediately. On January 2, 2002, the intrinsic value is zero because the market price is equal to the preset strike price.

Time value refers to the option's value over and above its intrinsic value. Time value reflects the possibility that the option has a fair value greater than zero because there is some **expectation** that the price of Laredo shares will increase above the strike price during the option term. As indicated, the option's value is $400.[48]

On March 31, 2002, the price of Laredo shares has increased to $120 per share and the intrinsic value of the call option contract is now $20,000. That is, you could exercise the call option and purchase 1,000 shares from Baird for $100 per share and then sell the shares in the market for $120 per share. This gives you a gain of $20,000 ($120,000 − $100,000) on the option contract.[49] The entry to record the increase in the **option's intrinsic value**[50] is as follows:

March 31, 2002		
Temporary Investment—Call Option	20,000	
Unrealized Holding Gain or Loss—Income		20,000

A market appraisal indicates that the **option's time value** at March 31, 2002 is $100.[51] The entry to record this change in value of the option is as follows:

March 31, 2002		
Unrealized Holding Gain or Loss—Income	300	
Temporary investment—Call Option ($400 − $100)		300

At March 31, 2002, the call option is reported in your balance sheet at fair value of $20,100.[52] The unrealized holding gain increases net income for the period, while the loss on the option's time value decreases net income.

On April 1, 2002, the entry to record the settlement of the call option contract with Baird is as follows:

April 1, 2002		
Cash	20,000	
Loss on Settlement of Call Option	100	
Temporary Investment—Call Option		20,100

Illustration 18B-2 summarizes the effects of the call option contract on your net income.

Date	Transaction	Income (Loss) Effect
March 31, 2002	Net increase in value of call option ($20,000 − $300)	$19,700
April 1, 2002	Settle call option	(100)
	Total net income	$19,600

ILLUSTRATION 18B-2
Effect on Income—Derivative Financial Instrument

---

[48] The value is estimated using option pricing models, such as the Black-Scholes model. The fair value estimate is affected by the volatility of the underlying stock, the expected life of the option, the risk-free rate of interest, and expected dividends on the underlying shares during the option term.

[49] In practice, you generally do not have to actually buy and sell the **shares** to settle the option and realize the gain. You can settle net. This is referred to as the net settlement feature of option contracts.

[50] Note that at present, this increase in value to market would not be recorded, but under the JWG paper, as previously mentioned, fair value accounting will be used for these instruments in the future.

[51] The decline in value reflects both the decreased likelihood that the Laredo shares will continue to increase in value over the option period and the shorter time to maturity of the option contract.

[52] As indicated earlier, the option's total value at any point in time is equal to the intrinsic value plus the time value.

The accounting summarized in Illustration 18B-2 is in accord with SFAS No. 133 in the United States and JWG Draft Standard on Financial Instruments and Similar Items. Because the call option meets the definition of an asset, it is **recognized** in the balance sheet on March 31, 2002. Furthermore, the call option is **measured** at **fair value** with any gains or losses reported in **income**. Under current accounting, the option would be recorded at initial cost ($400) and written down for a decline in value only. The full gain of $19,600 would only be recognized on April 2, 2002.

To make the initial investment in Laredo shares (traditional financial instrument), you would have to pay the full cost of this share. If you purchase the Laredo shares and the price increases, you could profit. But you also are at risk for a loss if the Laredo shares decline in value. In contrast, derivatives require **little initial investment** i.e., $400, and most derivatives do **not expose the holder to all risks associated with ownership in the underlying financial instrument**. For example, the call option contract can only increase in value. The holder would not lose more than the premium paid. That is, if the price of Laredo shares falls below $100 per share, you would not exercise the option.

Finally, unlike the situation with a traditional financial instrument, you could realize a profit on the call option (related to the price of the Laredo shares) **without ever having to take possession** of the shares. These distinctions between traditional and derivative financial instruments explain in part the popularity of derivatives.

Derivatives Used for Hedging

Companies that are **already exposed to financial risks** because of transactions they have already entered into for strategic purposes, may choose to protect themselves or manage and reduce those risks. For example, most public companies borrow and lend substantial amounts in credit markets and are therefore exposed to significant **financial risks**. That is, they face substantial risk that the fair values or cash flows of interest-sensitive assets or liabilities will change if interest rates increase or decrease **(interest rate risk)**. These same companies often also have significant international operations and are exposed to **exchange rate risk**—the risk that changes in foreign currency exchange rates will negatively impact the profitability of their international businesses. The borrowing creates liquidity risk and lending-credit risk.

Because the value and/or cash flows of derivative financial instruments can vary according to changes in interest rates or foreign currency exchange rates, **derivatives** can be used to **offset the risks** that a firm's fair values or cash flows will be negatively impacted by these market forces. This use of derivatives to offset risks is referred to as hedging. Thus, while **speculation** generally exposes the company to some type of risk or potential for change in value, **hedging** reduces or limits these uncertainties.

Historically, hedging has been afforded special accounting treatment[53] however, the Draft Standard proposed by the JWG, states that hedging should not have special accounting treatment.[54] There are many types of instruments and many ways to reduce risks. Below is an illustration of a fair value hedge.

Fair Value Hedge

In a fair value hedge, a derivative is used to hedge or offset the exposure to changes in the fair value of a **recognized** asset or liability or of an unrecognized firm commit-

---

[53] Under *CICA Handbook*, Section 1650.54, an exchange gain/loss related to a financial instrument which is hedged by a nonmonetary item may be deferred in order to match the offsetting exchange gain/loss. Furthermore, par. .52 dictates that costs associated with a hedge of a purchase or sale commitment are to be included in the price of the purchase or sale. Thus the hedge establishes the cost of purchase or value of the sale.

[54] This may be due to the fact that traditional hedge accounting often involves deferral of related costs which may leave the financial statements open to more bias than desirable. As we will see, the need for special hedge accounting disappears for fair value hedges if all instruments are recognized, measured at fair value and gains/losses are recorded in net income. This is so, since gains offset losses in the income statement.

ment, i.e., reduce **price risk**. In a perfectly hedged position, the gain or loss on the fair value of the derivative and that of the hedged asset or liability should be **equal and offsetting**. A common type of fair value hedge is the use of **interest rate swaps** (discussed below) to hedge the risk that changes in interest rates will impact the fair value of debt obligations. Another typical fair value hedge is the use of **put options** (options to sell the shares at a preset price) to hedge the risk that an equity investment will decline in value.

Interest Rate Swap—A Fair Value Hedge   When a company has repeated, similiar transactions that it wishes to hedge, a swap contract may be used. A swap is a transaction between two parties in which the first party promises to make a series of payments to the second party. Similarly the second party promises to make simultaneous payments to the first party. The parties "swap" payments. Swap contracts are entered into because one party prefers the terms of another party's existing contract and so they agree to swap or trade the terms. Under the swap, each looks after the other's contract terms. The most common type of swap is the interest rate swap, in which one party makes payments based on a fixed or floating rate and the second party does just the opposite. In most cases, financial institutions and other intermediaries find the two parties bring them together and handle the flow of payments between the two parties, as shown below.

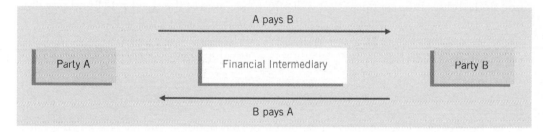

ILLUSTRATION 18B-3
Swap Transaction

Accounting Entries   To illustrate the accounting for a fair value hedge, assume that Jones Corporation issues $1 million of 5-year, 8% fixed-rate bonds on January 2, 2001. The entry to record this transaction is as follows:

January 2, 2001		
Cash	1,000,000	
Bonds Payable		1,000,000

A fixed interest rate was offered to appeal to investors, but Jones is concerned that if market interest rates decline, the liability's fair value will increase and the company will suffer an economic loss.[55] To protect against the risk of loss, Jones decides to **hedge** the risk of a decline in interest rates by entering into a five-year **interest rate swap.** Under the terms of the swap contract:

1. Jones will **receive** fixed payments at 8% (based on the $1 million amount) from a counterparty, and
2. Jones will **pay** variable rates, based on the market rate in effect throughout the life of the swap contract to the counterparty.

As depicted in Illustration 18B-4, by using this swap Jones can change the interest on the bonds payable from a fixed rate to a variable rate. Jones swaps the fixed rate for a variable rate.

---

[55] This economic loss arises because Jones is locked in the 8% interest payments even if rates decline.

ILLUSTRATION 18B-4

Interest Rate Swap

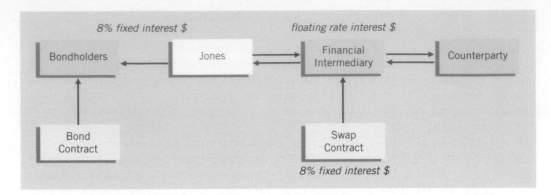

The settlement dates for the swap correspond to the interest payment dates on the debt (December 31). On each interest payment (settlement date), Jones and the counterparty will calculate the difference between current market interest rates and the fixed rate of 8% and determine the value of the swap.[56] As a result, if interest rates decline, the value of the swap contract to Jones increases (Jones has a gain), while at the same time Jones's fixed-rate debt obligation increases (Jones has an economic loss). The swap is an **effective risk-management tool** in this setting because its value is related to the same underlying (interest rates) that will affect the value of the fixed-rate bond payable. Thus, if the swap's value goes up, it offsets the loss related to the debt obligation.

Assuming that the swap was entered into on January 2, 2001 (the same date as the issuance of the debt), the swap at this time has no value; therefore no entry is necessary.

January 2, 2001
No entry required. Memorandum to indicate that the swap contract is signed.

At the end of 2001, the interest payment on the bonds is made. The journal entry to record this transaction is as follows:

December 31, 2001		
Interest Expense	80,000	
Cash (8% × $1,000,000)		80,000

At the end of 2001, market interest rates have declined substantially and therefore the value of the swap contract has increased. Recall (see Illustration 18B-4) that in the swap, Jones is to receive a fixed rate of 8%, or $80,000 ($1 million × 8%), and pay a variable rate (which in this case is 6.8%), or $68,000. Jones therefore receives $12,000 ($80,000 − $68,000) as a settlement payment on the swap contract on the first interest payment date. The entry to record this transaction is as follows:

December 31, 2001		
Cash	12,000	
Interest Expense		12,000

In addition, a market appraisal indicates that the value of the interest rate swap has increased $40,000. This increase in value is recorded as follows:[57]

December 31, 2001		
Other Assets—Swap Contract	40,000	
Unrealized Holding Gain or Loss—Income		40,000

---

[56] The foundation for an interest rate swap is some index of market interest rates. The most commonly used index is the London Interbank Offer Rate, or LIBOR. In this example, we assumed the LIBOR is 6.8%.

[57] Theoretically, this fair value change reflects the present value of expected future differences in variable and fixed interest rates.

This swap contract is reported in the balance sheet[58], and the gain on the hedging transaction is reported in the income statement. Recall that under the JWG Exposure Draft, financial liabilities are also marked to market. The fixed rate debt dollar value has increased by $40,000 due to the decline in interest rate (i.e., the liability is greater). Because interest rates have declined, the company records a loss and a related increase in its liability as follows:

December 31, 2001		
Unrealized Holding Gain or Loss—Income	40,000	
Bonds Payable		40,000

The loss on the hedging activity is reported in net income, and bonds payable in the balance sheet is adjusted to fair value. Note that as long as all financial instruments are recognized, measured at fair value and resulting gains/losses recognized in the income statements, there is no need for special hedge accounting for fair value hedges.

Financial Statement Presentation   Illustration 18B-5 indicates how the asset and liability related to this hedging transaction may be reported on the balance sheet.

JONES CORPORATION
Balance Sheet (partial)
December 31, 2001

Other assets	
Swap contract	$40,000
Long-term liabilities	
Bonds payable	$1,040,000

ILLUSTRATION 18B-5
Balance Sheet Presentation of Fair Value Hedge

The effect on the Jones Company balance sheet is the addition of the swap asset and an increase in the carrying value of the bonds payable. Illustration 18B-6 indicates how the effects of this swap transaction are reported in the income statement.

JONES CORPORATION
Income Statement (partial)
For the Year Ended December 31, 2001

Interest expense ($80,000 − $12,000)		$68,000
Other income		
Unrealized holding gain—swap contract	$40,000	
Unrealized holding loss bonds payable	(40,000)	
Net gain (loss)		$0

ILLUSTRATION 18B-6
Income Statement Presentation of Fair Value Hedge

On the income statement, interest expense of $68,000 is reported. Jones has effectively changed the debt's interest rate from fixed to variable (economic substance). That is, by receiving a fixed rate and paying a variable rate on the swap, the fixed rate on the bond payable is converted to variable, which results in an effective interest rate of 6.8% in 2001.[59] Also, the gain on the swap offsets the loss related to the debt obligation, and therefore the net gain or loss on the hedging activity is zero.

In summary, the accounting for fair value hedges (as illustrated in the Jones example) **records the derivative at its fair value in the balance sheet with any gains**

---

[58] This assumes that the principles established by the JWG are accepted, i.e., full recognition and fair value measurement with gains and losses going through the income statement. At the time this book went to press, practice varied widely, with the tendency toward non-recognition unless cash is paid out or received.

[59] Similar accounting and measurement will be applied at future interest payment dates. Thus, if interest rates increase, Jones will continue to receive 8% on the swap (records a loss) but will also be locked into the fixed payments to the bondholders at an 8% rate (records a gain).

and losses recorded in income. Thus, the gain on the swap **offsets** or **hedges** the loss on the bond payable due to the decline in interest rates.

Hedge of Purchase Commitments

A company may be exposed to a future cash flow commitment which is not yet captured in the financial statements. Assume Lander Inc. signs a contract to buy a machine from LaCroix Limited (a U.S. based company). Under the contract Lander Inc. will take delivery of the machine next year and pay $100,000 U.S. Lander now has a foreign currency risk.

Lander may wish to cover this risk by entering into a forward contract to buy $100,000 U.S. at a fixed rate (say $150,000 Canadian). When the machine is delivered, Lander will settle the forward, take the $100,000 U.S. and pay LaCroix.

An accounting issue arises since the purchase commitment would not be recognized in the financial statements (even under the JWG guidelines—as it is an anticipated transaction and therefore not covered by the JWG guidelines). If the forward contract is recognized and revalued to market (under the JWG guidelines as a financial instrument), then, the resulting gains/losses would be recognized in net income without the offsetting gain or loss on the purchase commitment. Lack of specific hedge accounting creates a mismatch. If the purchase commitment is perfectly hedged (as it is since the amount of the contract is the same as the forward as is the timing of delivery of the U.S.$) there will be no economic loss or gain. Therefore, recognizing a loss or gain on the income statement is misleading.

If the forward contract is not recognized (as under current GAAP), better matching occurs and the cost of the machine is fixed by the forward contract.[60] The machine would be recorded at $150,000 upon delivery.

OTHER REPORTING ISSUES

Disclosure Provisions

OBJECTIVE 12

Describe the disclosure requirements for traditional and derivative financial instruments.

Current disclosure provisions for all financial instruments are significant and focus on risks, including:

1. terms and conditions of instrument
2. interest rate risk
3. credit risk including significant concentrations
4. fair value of all financial instruments both recognized and unrecognized
5. hedges of anticipated future transactions—description of hedge and instrument used.[61]

While these additional disclosures of fair value provide useful information to financial statement users, they are generally provided as supplemental information only. The balance sheet continues to rely primarily on historical cost. Exceptions to this general rule are the fair value requirements where fair value is less than cost. Note 13 to the financial statements of Canadian Tire Corporation on page 218, Vol. 1, illustrates typical disclosures for financial instruments at the present time under *Handbook* Section 3860.

Controversy and Concluding Remarks

The JWG's proposed standards represent the accounting profession's effort to develop accounting guidance for derivatives. Many believe that these new rules are needed to properly measure and report derivatives in financial statements. Others argue that

---

[60] *CICA Handbook*, Section 1650, par. .52.

[61] *CICA Handbook*, Section 3860, pars. .43–.95.

reporting derivatives at fair value results in unrealized gains and losses that are difficult to interpret. Concerns also were raised about the complexity and cost of implementing the standard, since prior to these new proposed standards, many derivatives were not recognized in financial statements.

The profession, as part of its due process, worked to respond to these concerns, holding numerous meetings and receiving comments from hundreds of constituents or constituent groups. The authors believe that the long-term benefits of this standard will far outweigh any short-term implementation costs. As the volume and complexity of derivatives and hedging transactions continues to grow, the risk that investors and creditors will be exposed to unexpected losses arising from derivative transactions also increases. Without this standard, statement readers do not have comprehensive information in financial statements concerning many derivative financial instruments and the effects of hedging transactions using derivatives.

SUMMARY OF LEARNING OBJECTIVES FOR APPENDIX 18B

9 Explain who uses derivatives and why they are used. Any company or individual wanting to ensure against different types of business risks often uses derivative contracts to achieve this objective. In general, where the intent is to manage and reduce risk, these transactions involve some type of hedge. Speculators also are in the market, attempting to find an enhanced return. Speculators are very important to the market because they keep the market liquid on a daily basis. Arbitrageurs also are in the market and attempt to exploit inefficiencies in various derivative contracts. Derivatives are used primarily hedge a company's exposure to fluctuations in interest rates, foreign currency exchange rates, and commodity prices.

10 Understand the basic guidelines for accounting for derivatives. Derivatives should be recognized in the financial statements as assets and liabilities and reported at fair value. Gains and losses resulting from speculation should be recognized immediately in income.

11 Describe the accounting for derivative financial instruments. Derivative financial instruments are reported in the balance sheet and recorded at fair value. Realized and unrealized gains and losses on derivative financial instruments are recorded in income as they arise. Options, swaps, futures, and forwards are common types of derivatives that are recognized, measured at fair value, and disclosed in the notes. Hedges are not afforded special treatment even though some hedge transactions are entered into to hedge future transactions.

12 Describe the disclosure requirements for traditional and derivative financial instruments. Currently, companies must provide information about the terms and conditions, interest rate risks, credit risks, fair values of items recognized and not recognized on the balance sheet, and information about hedging activities. This disclosure will increase with the proposed accounting standards.

APPENDIX 18B KEY TERMS

call option, 872
cash flow risk, 869
counterparty, 869
credit risk, 869
derivative instrument, 868
fair value, 872
fair value hedge, 874
forward contract, 869
futures contract, 869
hedging, 870
interest rate swap, 875
intrinsic value, 873
liquidity risk, 869
net settlement, 873
option premium, 872
price risk, 869
primary instrument, 868
put option, 872
risk management, 868
speculative, 870
strike (exercise) price, 872
swap, 875
time value, 873

Note: All **asterisked** Brief Exercises, Exercises, Problems, and Conceptual Cases relate to material contained in the appendix to the chapter.

BRIEF EXERCISES

BE18-1 Verbitsky Corporation has outstanding 1,000 $1,000 bonds, each convertible into 50 common shares. The bonds are converted on December 31, 2002, when the unamortized discount is $30,000, and the shares' market price is $21 per share. Record the conversion using the market value approach.

BE18-2 Use the information for Verbitsky Corporation given in BE18-1. Record the conversion using the book value approach.

BE18-3 Sealy Corporation issued 2,000 common shares upon conversion of 1,000 shares of preferred shares. The preferred shares were originally issued at $55 per share. The common shares are trading at $26 per share at the time of conversion. Record the conversion of the preferred shares.

BE18-4 Divac Corporation issued 1,000 $1,000 bonds at 101. Each bond was issued with one detachable stock warrant. After issuance, the bonds were selling in the market at 98, and the warrants had a market value of $40. Use the proportional method to record the issuance of the bonds and warrants.

BE18-5 Ceballos Corporation issued 1,000 $1,000 bonds at 101. Each bond was issued with one detachable stock warrant. After issuance, the bonds were selling separately at 98. The warrant's market price without the bonds cannot be determined. Use the incremental method to record the issuance of the bonds and warrants.

BE18-6 On January 1, 2002, Johnson Corporation granted 5,000 options to executives. Each option entitles the holder to purchase one share of Johnson's common shares at $50 per share at any time during the next five years. The shares' market price is $65 per share on the date of grant. The period of benefit is two years. Prepare Johnson's journal entries for January 1, 2002 and December 31, 2002 and 2003, using the intrinsic value method.

BE18-7 Use the information given for Johnson Corporation in BE18-6. Assume the fair value option pricing model determines that total compensation expense is $140,000. Prepare Johnson's journal entries for January 1, 2002 and December 31, 2002 and 2003, using the fair value method.

BE18-8 Haley Corporation had 2002 net income of $1.2 million. During 2002, Haley paid a dividend of $2 per share on 100,000 preferred shares. During 2002, Haley had outstanding 250,000 common shares. Calculate Haley's 2002 earnings per share.

BE18-9 Barkley Corporation had 120,000 common shares outstanding on January 1, 2002. On May 1, 2002, Barkley issued 45,000 shares. On July 1, Barkley purchased and cancelled 10,000 shares. Calculate Barkley's weighted average number of shares outstanding for the year ended December 31, 2002.

BE18-10 Green Corporation had 200,000 common shares outstanding on January 1, 2002. On May 1, Green issued 30,000 shares.
1. Calculate the weighted average number of shares outstanding for the year ended December 31, 2002 if the 30,000 shares were issued for cash.
2. Calculate the weighted average number of shares outstanding for the year ended December 31, 2002 if the 30,000 shares were issued in a stock dividend.

BE18-11 Strickland Corporation earned net income of $300,000 in 2002 and had 100,000 shares of common outstanding throughout the year. Also outstanding all year was $400,000 of 10% bonds, which are convertible into 16,000 shares of common. Strickland's tax rate is 40%. Calculate Strickland's 2002 diluted earnings per share.

BE18-12 Sabonis Corporation reported net income of $400,000 in 2002 and had 50,000 shares of common outstanding throughout the year. Also outstanding all year were 5,000 shares of cumulative preferred shares, each convertible into two shares of common. The preferred shares pay an annual dividend of $5 per share. Sabonis' tax rate is 40%. Calculate Sabonis' 2002 diluted earnings per share.

BE18-13 Sarunas Corporation reported net income of $300,000 in 2002 and had 200,000 shares of common outstanding throughout the year. Also outstanding all year were 30,000 options to purchase common shares at $10 per share. The shares' average market during the year was $15. Calculate diluted earnings per share.

BE18-14 The 2002 income statement of Schrempf Corporation showed net income of $480,000 and an extraordinary loss of $120,000. Schrempf had 50,000 common shares outstanding all year. Prepare Schrempf's income statement presentation of earnings per share.

*BE18-15 Perkins, Inc. established a stock appreciation rights (SAR) program on January 1, 2001, which entitles executives to receive cash at the date of exercise for the difference between the shares' market price and the preestablished price of $20 on 5,000 SARs. The required service period is two years. The shares' market price is $22 on December 31, 2001, and $29 on December 31, 2002. The SARs are exercised on January 1, 2003. Calculate Perkins' compensation expense for 2001 and 2002.

EXERCISES

E18-1 (Issuance and Conversion of Bonds)

Instructions

For each of the unrelated transactions described below, present the entry(ies) required to record each transaction.

(a) Grand Corp. issued $20 million par value 10% convertible bonds at 99. If the bonds had not been convertible, the company's investment banker estimates they would have been sold at 95. Expenses of issuing the bonds were $70,000.

(b) Hussein Limited issued $20 million par value 10% bonds at 98. One detachable stock purchase warrant was issued with each $100 par value bond. At the time of issuance, the warrants were selling for $4.

(c) On July 1, 2001, Tien Limited called its 11% convertible debentures for conversion. The $10 million par value bonds were converted into 1 million common shares. On July 1, there was $55,000 of unamortized discount applicable to the bonds, and the company paid an additional $75,000 to the bondholders to induce conversion of all the bonds. The company records the conversion using the book value method. The balance in the account Contributed Surplus-Conversion Rights was $200,000 at the time of conversion.

E18-2 (Conversion of Bonds) Aubrey Inc. issued $4 million of 10%, 10-year convertible bonds on June 1, 2001 at 98 plus accrued interest. The bonds were dated April 1, 2001, with interest payable April 1 and October 1. Bond discount is amortized semiannually on a straight-line basis. Bonds without conversion privileges would have sold at 97 plus accrued interest.

On April 1, 2002, $1.5 million of these bonds were converted into 30,000 common shares. Accrued interest was paid in cash at the time of conversion.

Instructions

(a) Prepare the entry to record the interest expense at October 1, 2001. Assume that accrued interest payable was credited when the bonds were issued. (Round to nearest dollar.)

(b) Prepare the entry(ies) to record the conversion on April 1, 2002. (Book value method is used.) Assume that the entry to record amortization of the bond discount and interest payment has been made.

E18-3 (Conversion of Bonds) Vargo Limited has bonds payable outstanding in the amount of $500,000 and the Premium on Bonds Payable account has a balance of $7,500. Each $1,000 bond is convertible into 20 preferred shares. All bonds are converted into preferred shares. The Contributed Surplus-Conversion Rights account has a balance of $4,000.

Instructions

(a) Assuming that the book value method was used, what entry would be made?

(b) Assuming that the bonds are quoted on the market at 102 and that the preferred shares may be sold on the market at $51.50, make the entry to record the conversion of the bonds to preferred shares. (Use the market value approach.)

E18-4 **(Conversion of Bonds)** On January 1, 2000, when its common shares were selling for $80 per share, Plato Corp. issued $10 million of 8% convertible debentures due in 20 years. The conversion option allowed the holder of each $1,000 bond to convert the bond into five common shares. The debentures were issued for $10.8 million. The bond payments' present value of the at the time of issuance was $8.5 million and the corporation believes the difference between the present value and the amount paid is attributable to the conversion feature. On January 1, 2001, the corporation's common shares were split 2 for 1, and the conversion rate for the bonds was adjusted accordingly. On January 1, 2002, when the corporation's common shares were selling for $135 per share, holders of 30% of the convertible debentures exercised their conversion options. The corporation uses the straight-line method for amortizing any bond discounts or premiums.

Instructions

(a) Prepare in general journal form the entry to record the original issuance of the convertible debentures.

(b) Prepare in general journal form the entry to record the exercise of the conversion option, using the book value method. Show supporting calculations in good form.

E18-5 **(Conversion of Bonds)** An excerpt from the December 31, 2001, balance sheet of Kepler Corp. shows the following balances:

10% Callable, Convertible Bonds Payable (semiannual interest dates April 30 and October 31; convertible into six common shares per $1,000 of bond principal; maturity date April 30, 2007)	$500,000	
Discount on Bonds Payable	10,240	$489,760
Contributed Surplus-Conversion Rights		$9,000

On March 5, 2002, Kepler Corp. called all of the bonds as of April 30 for the principal plus interest through April 30. By April 30, all bondholders had exercised their conversion to common shares as of the interest payment date. Consequently, on April 30, Kepler Corp. paid the semiannual interest and issued common shares for the bonds. The discount is amortized on a straight-line basis. Kepler uses the book value method.

Instructions

Prepare the entry(ies) to record the interest expense and conversion on April 30, 2002. Reversing entries were made on January 1, 2002. (Round to the nearest dollar.)

E18-6 **(Conversion of Bonds)** On January 1, 2001, Gottlieb Corporation issued $4 million of 10-year, 8% convertible debentures at 104. Investment bankers believe that the debenture would have sold at 102 without the conversion privilege. Interest is to be paid semiannually on June 30 and December 31. Each $1,000 debenture can be converted into eight common shares of Gottlieb Corporation after December 31, 2002.

On January 1, 2003, $400,000 of debentures are converted into common shares, which are then selling at $110. An additional $400,000 of debentures are converted on March 31, 2003. The common shares' market price is then $115. Accrued interest at March 31 will be paid on the next interest date. Bond premium is amortized on a straight-line basis.

Instructions

Make the necessary journal entries for:

(a) December 31, 2002 (c) March 31, 2003

(b) January 1, 2003 (d) June 30, 2003

Record the conversions using the book value method.

E18-7 **(Issuance of Bonds with Warrants)** Illiad Inc. has decided to raise additional capital by issuing $170,000 face value of bonds with a coupon rate of 10%. In discussions with their investment bankers, it was determined that to help the sale of the bonds, detachable stock warrants should be issued at the rate of one warrant for each $100 bond sold. The bonds' value without the warrants is considered to be $136,000, and the warrants' value in the market is $24,000. The bonds sold in the market at issuance for $152,000.

Instructions

(a) What entry should be made at the time of the issuance of the bonds and warrants?

(b) If the warrants were nondetachable, would the entries be different? Discuss.

E18-8 **(Issuance of Bonds with Detachable Warrants)** On September 1, 2001, Sands Corp. sold at 104 (plus accrued interest) 4,000 of its 9%, 10-year, $1,000 face value, nonconvertible bonds with detachable stock warrants. Each bond carried two detachable warrants; each warrant was for one common share at a specified option price of $15 per share. Shortly after issuance, the warrants were quoted on the market for $3 each. No market value can be determined for the bonds above. Interest is payable on December 1 and June 1. Bond issue costs of $30,000 were incurred.

Instructions

Prepare in general journal format the entry to record the issuance of the bonds.

(AICPA adapted)

E18-9 **(Issuance of Bonds with Stock Warrants)** On May 1, 2001, Farhad Limited issued 2,000 $1,000 bonds at 102. Each bond was issued with one detachable stock warrant. Shortly after issuance, the bonds were selling at 98, but the warrants' market value cannot be determined.

Instructions

(a) Prepare the entry to record the issuance of the bonds and warrants.

(b) Assume the same facts as part 1., except that the warrants had a fair value of $30. Prepare the entry to record the issuance of the bonds and warrants.

E18-10 **(Issuance and Exercise of Stock Options)** On November 1, 2001, Columbo Corp. adopted a stock option plan that granted options to key executives to purchase 30,000 common shares. The options were granted on January 2, 2002 and were exercisable two years after the date of grant if the grantee was still a company employee; the options expired six years from date of grant. The option price was set at $40 and using an option pricing model to value the options, the total compensation expense is estimated to be $450,000.

All of the options were exercised during the year 2004; 20,000 on January 3 when the market price was $67, and 10,000 on May 1 when the market price was $77 a share. On April 1, 2003, 2000 options were terminated when the employees resigned from the company. The market value of the shares at that date was $35.

Instructions

Prepare journal entries relating to the stock option plan for the years 2002, 2003, and 2004 under the fair value method. Assume that the employee performs services equally in 2002 and 2003, and that the year-end is December 31.

E18-11 **(Issuance, Exercise, and Termination of Stock Options)** On January 1, 2002, Titania Inc. granted stock options to officers and key employees to buy 20,000 of the company's common shares at $25 per share. The options were exercisable within a five-year period beginning January 1, 2004 by grantees still employed by the company, and expiring December 31, 2008. The service period for this award is two years. Assume that using an option pricing model, the total compensation expense is estimated to be $350,000.

On March 31, 2004, 12,000 option shares were exercised when the common shares' market value was $40 per share.

Instructions

Prepare journal entries using the fair value method to record issuance of the stock options, termination of the stock options, exercise of the stock options, and charges to compensation expense, for the years ended December 31, 2002, 2003, and 2004.

E18-12 **(Issuance, Exercise, and Termination of Stock Options)** On January 1, 2000, Nichols Corporation granted 10,000 options to key executives. Each option allows the executive to purchase one share of Nichols' common shares at a price of $20 per share. The options were exercisable within a two-year period beginning January 1, 2002 if the grantee is still employed by the company at the time of the exercise. On the grant date, Nichols' shares were trading at $25 per share, and a fair value option pricing model determines total compensation to be $400,000.

On May 1, 2002, 8,000 options were exercised when the market price of Nichols' shares was $30 per share. The remaining options lapsed in 2004 because executives decided not to exercise their options.

Instructions

Prepare the necessary journal entries related to the stock option plan for the years ended December 31, 2000 through 2004. Nichols uses the fair value approach to account for stock options.

*E18-13 (Stock Appreciation Rights) On December 31, 1997 (year-end), Beckford Limited issues 150,000 stock appreciation rights to its officers, entitling them to receive cash for the difference between the market price of its stock and a preestablished price of $10. The market price fluctuates as follows: 12/31/98—$14; 12/31/99—$8; 12/31/00—$20; 12/31/01—$19. The service period is four years and the exercise period is seven years. The company recognizes the SAR in its financial statements.

Instructions

(a) Prepare a schedule that shows the amount of compensation expense allocable to each year affected by the stock appreciation rights plan.
(b) Prepare the entry at December 31, 2001 to record compensation expense, if any, in 2001.
(c) Prepare the entry on December 31, 2001, assuming that all 150,000 SARs are exercised.

*E18-14 (Stock Appreciation Rights) Chiu Limited establishes a stock appreciation rights program that entitles its new president Ben Dan to receive cash for the difference between the shares' market price and a preestablished price of $30 (also market price) on December 31, 1998 on 30,000 SARs. The date of grant is December 31, 1998 and the required employment (service) period is four years. The president exercises all of the SARs in 2004. The shares' market value fluctuates as follows: 12/31/99—$36; 12/31/00—$39; 12/31/01—$45; 12/31/02—$36; 12/31/03—$48. The company recognizes the SAR in its financial statements.

Instructions

(a) Prepare a five-year (1999–2003) schedule of compensation expense pertaining to the 30,000 SARs granted President Dan.
(b) Prepare the journal entry for compensation expense in 1999, 2002, and 2003 relative to the 30,000 SARs.

E18-15 (Weighted Average Number of Shares) Newton Inc. uses a calendar year for financial reporting. The company is authorized to issue 9 million common shares. At no time has Newton issued any potentially dilutive securities. Listed below is a summary of Newton's common share activities.

Number of common shares issued and outstanding at December 31, 1999	2,000,000
Shares issued as a result of a 10% stock dividend on September 30, 2000	200,000
Shares issued for cash on March 31, 2001	2,000,000
Number of common shares issued and outstanding at December 31, 2001	4,200,000

A 2-for-1 stock split of Newton's common shares took place on March 31, 2002.

Instructions

(a) Calculate the weighted average number of common shares used in calculating earnings per common share for 2000 on the 2001 comparative income statement.
(b) Calculate the weighted average number of common shares used in calculating earnings per common share for 2001 on the 2001 comparative income statement.
(c) Calculate the weighted average number of common shares to be used in calculating earnings per common share for 2001 on the 2002 comparative income statement.
(d) Calculate the weighted average number of common shares to be used in calculating earnings per common share for 2002 on the 2002 comparative income statement.

(CMA adapted)

E18-16 (EPS: Simple Capital Structure) On January 1, 2002, Wilke Corp. had 480,000 common shares outstanding. During 2002, it had the following transactions that affected the common share account.

February 1	Issued 120,000 shares
March 1	Issued a 10% stock dividend
May 1	Acquired 100,000 common shares (and retired them)
June 1	Issued a 3-for-1 stock split
October 1	Issued 60,000 shares

The company's year-end is December 31.

Instructions

(a) Determine the weighted average number of shares outstanding as of December 31, 2002.
(b) Assume that Wilke Corp. earned net income of $3,456,000 during 2002. In addition, it had 100,000 shares of 9%, $100 par nonconvertible, noncumulative preferred shares outstanding for the entire year. Because of liquidity considerations, however, the company did not declare and pay a pre-

ferred dividend in 2002. Calculate earnings per share for 2002, using the weighted average number of shares determined in part 1.

(c) Assume the same facts as in part 2., except that the preferred shares were cumulative. Calculate earnings per share for 2002.

(d) Assume the same facts as in part 2., except that net income included an extraordinary gain of $864,000 and a loss from discontinued operations of $432,000. Both items are net of applicable income taxes. Calculate earnings per share for 2002.

E18-17 (EPS: Simple Capital Structure)   Valaderez Inc. had 200,000 common shares outstanding on December 31, 2002. During the year 2003, the company issued 8,000 shares on May 1 and retired 14,000 shares on October 31. For the year 2003, the company reported net income of $249,690 after an extraordinary loss of $40,600 (net of tax).

Instructions
What earnings per share data should be reported at the bottom of Valaderez Inc.'s income statement?

E18-18 (EPS: Simple Capital Structure)   Flagstad Inc. presented the following data:

Net income	$2,500,000
Preferred shares: 50,000 shares outstanding,	
$100 par, 8% cumulative, not convertible	$5,000,000
Common shares: Shares outstanding 1/1	750,000
Issued for cash, 5/1	300,000
Acquired treasury stock for cash, 8/1 (shares cancelled)	150,000
2-for-1 stock split, 10/1	

Instructions
Calculate earnings per share for the year ended December 31.

E18-19 (EPS: Simple Capital Structure)   A portion of the combined statement of income and retained earnings of Seminole Inc. for the current year ended December 31, follows:

Income before extraordinary item		$15,000,000
Extraordinary loss, net of applicable income tax (Note 1)		1,340,000
Net income		13,660,000
Retained earnings at the beginning of the year		83,250,000
		96,910,000
Dividends declared:		
On preferred shares—$6.00 per share	$ 300,000	
On common shares—$1.75 per share	14,875,000	15,175,000
Retained earnings at the end of the year		$81,735,000

Note 1. During the year, Seminole Inc. suffered a loss of $1,340,000 after applicable income tax reduction of $1.2 million. This was booked as an extraordinary item.

At the end of the current year, Seminole Inc. has outstanding 8.5 million common shares and 50,000 shares of 6% preferred.

On April 1 of the current year, Seminole Inc. issued 1 million common shares for $32 per share to help finance the casualty.

Instructions
Calculate the earnings per share on common shares for the current year as it should be reported to shareholders.

E18-20 (EPS: Simple Capital Structure)   On January 1, 2002, Le Phong Limited had shares outstanding as follows:

6% cumulative preferred shares, $100 par value,	
issued and outstanding 10,000 shares	$1,000,000
Common shares issued and outstanding 200,000 shares	2,000,000

To acquire the net assets of three smaller companies, the company authorized the issuance of an additional 160,000 common shares. The acquisitions took place as follows:

Date of Acquisition	Shares Issued
Company A April 1, 2002	50,000
Company B July 1, 2002	80,000
Company C October 1, 2002	30,000

On May 14, 2002, Le Phong realized a $90,000 (before taxes) insurance gain on the expropriation of investments originally purchased in 1991.

On December 31, 2002, the company recorded income of $300,000 before tax and exclusive of the gain.

Instructions

Assuming a 50% tax rate, calculate the earnings per share data that should appear on the company financial statements as of December 31, 2002. Assume that the expropriation is extraordinary.

E18-21 **(EPS: Simple Capital Structure)** At January 1, 2002, Langley Limited's outstanding shares included:

> 280,000 shares of $50 par value, 7% cumulative preferred shares
> 900,000 common shares

Net income for 2002 was $2,530,000. No cash dividends were declared or paid during 2002. On February 15, 2003, however, all preferred dividends in arrears were paid, together with a 5% stock dividend on common shares. There were no dividends in arrears prior to 2002.

On April 1, 2002, 450,000 common shares were sold for $10 per share and on October 1, 2002, 110,000 common shares were purchased for $20 per share.

Instructions

Calculate earnings per share for the year ended December 31, 2002. Assume that financial statements for 2002 were issued in March 2003.

E18-22 **(EPS with Convertible Bonds, Various Situations)** In 2000, Ben Lo Inc. issued, at par, 60 $1,000, 8% bonds, each convertible into 100 common shares. The company had revenues of $17,500 and expenses other than interest and taxes of $8,400 for 2001 (assume that the tax rate is 40%). Throughout 2001, 2,000 common shares were outstanding; none of the bonds was converted or redeemed. (Assume, for simplicity's sake, that the convertible bond's equity element is not recorded.)

Instructions

(a) Calculate diluted earnings per share for the year ended December 31, 2001.

(b) Assume the same facts as those assumed for part (a), except that the 60 bonds were issued on September 1, 2001 (rather than in 2000), and none have been converted or redeemed.

(c) Assume the same facts as assumed for part (a), except that 20 of the 60 bonds were actually converted on July 1, 2001.

E18-23 **(EPS with Convertible Bonds)** On June 1, 1999, Mowbray Corp. and Surrey Limited merged to form Lancaster Inc. A total of 800,000 shares were issued to complete the merger. The new corporation reports on a calendar-year basis.

On April 1, 2001, the company issued an additional 400,000 shares for cash. All 1.2 million shares were outstanding on December 31, 2001. Lancaster Inc. also issued $600,000 of 20-year, 8% convertible bonds at par on July 1, 2001. Each $1,000 bond converts to 40 shares of common at any interest date. None of the bonds have been converted to date. If the bonds had been issued without the conversion feature, the interest rate would have been 10%.

Lancaster Inc. is preparing its annual report for the fiscal year ending December 31, 2001. The annual report will show earnings per share figures based upon a reported after-tax net income of $1,540,000 (the tax rate is 40%).

Instructions

Determine for 2001:

(a) The number of shares to be used for calculating:

1. basic earnings per share
2. diluted earnings per share

(b) The earnings figures to be used for calculating:
  1. basic earnings per share
  2. diluted earnings per share

(CMA adapted)

E18-24 (EPS with Convertible Bonds and Preferred Shares) The Shengru Corporation issued 10-year, $5 million par, 7% callable convertible subordinated debentures on January 2, 2001. The bonds have a par value of $1,000, with interest payable annually. The current conversion ratio is 14:1, and in two years it will increase to 18:1. At the date of issue, the bonds were sold at 98. Bond discount is amortized on a straight-line basis. Shengru's effective tax was 35%. Net income in 2001 was $9.5 million, and the company had 2 million shares outstanding during the entire year. For simplicity sake, ignore the requirement to record the debentures' debt and equity components separately.

Instructions
  (a) Prepare a schedule to calculate both basic and diluted earnings per share for the year ended December 31, 2001.
  (b) Discuss how the schedule would differ if the security were convertible preferred shares.

E18-25 (EPS with Convertible Bonds and Preferred Shares) On January 1, 2001, Sharif Limited issued 10-year, $2 million face value, 6% bonds, at par. Each $1,000 bond is convertible into 15 shares of common. Sharif's net income in 2001 was $300,000, and its tax rate was 40%. The company had 100,000 common shares outstanding throughout 2001. None of the bonds were exercised in 2001. For simplicity's sake, ignore the requirement to record the bonds' debt and equity components separately.

Instructions
  (a) Calculate diluted earnings per share for the year ended December 31, 2001.
  (b) Calculate diluted earnings per share for 2001, assuming the same facts as above, except that $1 million of 6% convertible preferred shares was issued instead of the bonds. Each $100 preferred share is convertible into five shares of common.

E18-26 (EPS with Options, Various Situations) Viens Corp.'s net income for 2001 is $50,000. The only potentially dilutive securities outstanding were 1,000 options issued during 2000, each exercisable for one share at $6. None has been exercised, and 10,000 shares of common were outstanding during 2001. The average market price of the company's shares during 2001 was $20.

Instructions
  (a) Calculate diluted earnings per share for the year ended December 31, 2001 (round to nearest cent).
  (b) Assume the same facts as those assumed for part 1., except that the 1,000 options were issued on October 1, 2001 (rather than in 2000). The average market price during the last three months of 2001 was $20.

E18-27 (EPS with Contingent Issuance Agreement) Winsor Inc. recently purchased Holiday Corp., a large home painting corporation. One of the terms of the merger was that if Holiday's income for 2001 were $110,000 or more, 10,000 additional shares would be issued to Holiday's shareholders in 2002. Holiday's income for 2000 was $120,000.

Instructions
  (a) Would the contingent shares have to be considered in Winsor's 2000 earnings per share calculations?
  (b) Assume the same facts, except that the 10,000 shares are contingent on Holiday's achieving a net income of $130,000 in 2001. Would the contingent shares have to be considered in Winsor's earnings per share calculations for 2000?

E18-28 (EPS with Warrants) Howat Corporation earned $360,000 during a period when it had an average of 100,000 common shares outstanding. The common shares sold at an average market price of $15 per share during the period. Also outstanding were 15,000 warrants that could be exercised to purchase one share of common for $10 for each warrant exercised.

Instructions
  (a) Are the warrants dilutive?
  (b) Calculate basic earnings per share.
  (c) Calculate diluted earnings per share.

*E18-29 **(Derivative Transaction)** On January 2, 2000, Jones Corporation purchases a call option for $300 on Merchant common shares. The call option gives Jones the option to buy 1,000 shares of Merchant at a strike price of $50 per share. The market price of a Merchant share is $50 on January 2, 2000 (the intrinsic value is therefore $0). On March 31, 2000, the market price for Merchant stock is $53 per share, and the time value of the option is $200. Assume the proposed JWG standards are GAAP.

Instructions

(a) Prepare the journal entry to record the purchase of the call option on January 2, 2000.

(b) Prepare the journal entry(ies) to recognize the change in the call option's fair value as of March 31, 2000.

(c) What was the effect on net income of entering into the derivative transaction for the period January 2 to March 31, 2000?

*E18-30 **(Fair Value Hedge)** On January 2, 2001, MacCloud Corp. issued a four-year, $100,000 note at 6% fixed interest, interest payable semiannually. MacCloud now wants to change the note to a variable rate note. As a result, on January 2, 2001, MacCloud Corp. enters into an interest rate swap where it agrees to receive 6% fixed and pay LIBOR (London Interbank Offer Rate) of 5.7% for the first six months on $100,000. At each six-month period, the variable rate will be reset. The variable rate is reset to 6.7% on June 30, 2001. Assume the proposed JWG standards are GAAP.

Instructions

(a) Calculate the net interest expense to be reported for this note and related swap transaction as of June 30, 2001.

(b) Calculate the net interest expense to be reported for this note and related swap transaction as of December 31, 2001.

*E18-31 **(Fair Value Hedge)** On January 2, 2000, Parton Corp. issues a five-year, $10 million note at LIBOR, with interest paid annually. The variable rate is reset at the end of each year. The LIBOR rate for the first year is 5.8%. Parton decides it prefers fixed-rate financing and wants to lock in a rate of 6%. As a result, Parton enters into an interest rate swap to pay 6% fixed and receive LIBOR based on $10 million. The variable rate is reset to 6.6% on January 2, 2001. Assume the proposed JWG standards are GAAP.

Instructions

(a) Calculate the net interest expense to be reported for this note and related swap transactions as of December 31, 2000.

(b) Calculate the net interest expense to be reported for this note and related swap transactions as of December 31, 2001.

*E18-32 **(Fair Value Hedge)** Sarazan Corp. issues a four-year, 7.5% fixed-rate interest only, nonprepayable $1 million note payable on December 31, 2000. It decides to change the interest rate from a fixed rate to variable rate and enters into a swap agreement with M&S Corp. The swap agreement specifies that Sarazan will receive a fixed rate at 7.5% and pay variable with settlement dates that match the interest payments on the debt. Assume that interest rates have declined during 2001 and that Sarazan received $13,000 as an adjustment to interest expense for the settlement at December 31, 2001. The loss related to the debt (due to interest rate changes) was $48,000. The value of the swap contract increased $48,000. Assume the proposed JWG standards are GAAP.

Instructions

(a) Prepare the journal entry to record the payment of interest expense on December 31, 2001.

(b) Prepare the journal entry to record the receipt of the swap settlement on December 31, 2001.

(c) Prepare the journal entry to record the change in the fair value of the swap contract on December 31, 2001.

(d) Prepare the journal entry to record the change in the fair value of the debt on December 31, 2001.

*E18-33 **(Fair Value Hedge)** Using the same information from E18-32, consider the swap's effects on M&S Corp. The $1 million nonprepayable note is classified as a Long-term Investment by M&S Corp. Assume the proposed JWG standards are GAAP.

Instructions

    (a) Prepare the journal entry to record the receipt of interest revenue on December 31, 2001.

    (b) Prepare the journal entry to record the payment of the swap settlement on December 31, 2001.

    (c) Prepare the journal entry to record the change in the fair value of the swap contract on December 31, 2001.

    (d) Prepare the journal entry to record the change in the fair value of the debt security on December 31, 2001.

PROBLEMS

P18-1   The shareholders' equity section of McLean Inc. at the beginning of the current year appears below.

Common shares, authorized 1,000,000 shares,	
300,000 shares issued and outstanding	$3,600,000
Retained earnings	570,000

During the current year the following transactions occurred:

    1. The company issued to the shareholders 100,000 rights. Ten rights are needed to buy one share at $32. The rights were void after 30 days. The shares' market price at this time was $34 per share.

    2. The company sold to the public a $200,000, 10% bond issue at par. The company also issued with each $100 bond one detachable stock purchase warrant, which provided for the purchase of common shares at $30 per share. Shortly after issuance, similar bonds without warrants were selling at 96 and the warrants at $8.

    3. All but 10,000 of the rights issued in part 1 were exercised in 30 days.

    4. At the end of the year, 80% of the warrants in part 2 had been exercised, and the remaining were outstanding and in good standing.

    5. During the current year, the company granted stock options for 5,000 shares of common shares to company executives. The company, using an option pricing model, determines that each option is worth $10. The option price is $30. The options were to expire at year end and were considered compensation for the current year.

    6. All but 1,000 shares related to the stock option plan were exercised by year end. The expiration resulted because one of the executives failed to fulfill an obligation related to the employment contract.

Instructions

    (a) Prepare general journal entries for the current year to record the transactions listed above.

    (b) Prepare the shareholders' equity section of the balance sheet at the end of the current year. Assume that retained earnings at the end of the current year is $750,000.

P18-2   Counter Inc. issued $1.5 million of convertible 10-year bonds on July 1, 2001. The bonds provide for 12% interest payable semiannually on January 1 and July 1. The discount in connection with the issue was $34,000, which is being amortized monthly on a straight-line basis. The bonds are convertible after one year into eight shares of Counter Inc.'s common shares for each $1,000 of bonds.

    On August 1, 2002, $150,000 of bonds were turned in for conversion into common shares. Interest has been accrued monthly and paid as due. At the time of conversion, any accrued interest on bonds being converted is paid in cash. For simplicity's sake, ignore the requirement to record the bonds' debt and equity components separately.

Instructions

(Round to nearest dollar)

Prepare the journal entries to record the conversion, amortization, and interest in connection with the bonds as of:

    (a) August 1, 2002 (assume the book value method is used).

    (b) August 31, 2002.

    (c) December 31, 2002, including closing entries for end-of-year.

                                                           (AICPA adapted)

P18-3 ISU Corp. adopted a stock option plan on November 30, 1999 that provided that 70,000 common shares be designated as available for the granting of options to officers of the corporation at a price of $8 a share. The market value was $12 a share on November 30, 1999.

On January 2, 2000, options to purchase 28,000 shares were granted to president Don Pedro: 15,000 for services to be rendered in 2000 and 13,000 for services to be rendered in 2001. Also on that date, options to purchase 14,000 shares were granted to vice-president Beatrice Leonato: 7,000 for services to be rendered in 2000 and 7,000 for services to be rendered in 2001. The shares' market value was $14 a share on January 2, 2000. The options were exercisable for a period of one year following the year in which the services were rendered.

In 2001, neither the president nor the vice-president exercised their options because the shares' market price was below the exercise price. The shares' market value was $7 a share on December 31, 2001, when the options for 2000 services lapsed.

On December 31, 2002, both president Pedro and vice-president Leonato exercised their options for 13,000 and 7,000 shares, respectively, when the market price was $16 a share. The company's year-end is December 31.

Instructions

Prepare the necessary journal entries in 1999 when the stock option plan was adopted, in 2000 when options were granted, in 2001 when options lapsed, and in 2002 when options were exercised. The company elects to use the intrinsic value method.

P18-4 Diane Leto, controller at Yaeger Pharmaceutical Industries, a public company, is currently preparing the calculation for basic and diluted earnings per share and the related disclosure for Yaeger's external financial statements. Below is selected financial information for the fiscal year ended June 30, 2002.

YAEGER PHARMACEUTICAL INDUSTRIES Selected Statement of Financial Position Information June 30, 2002	
Long-term debt	
Notes payable, 10%	$ 1,000,000
7% convertible bonds payable	5,000,000
10% bonds payable	6,000,000
Total long-term debt	$12,000,000
Shareholders' equity	
Preferred Shares, $4.25 cumulative, 100,000 shares authorized, 25,000 shares issued and outstanding	$ 1,250,000
Common Shares, unlimited number of shares authorized, 1,000,000 shares issued and outstanding	4,500,000
Contributed Surplus-Conversion Rights	500,000
Retained earnings	6,000,000
Total shareholders' equity	$12,250,000

The following transactions have also occurred at Yaeger.

1. Options were granted in 2000 to purchase 100,000 shares at $15 per share. Although no options were exercised during 2002, the average price per common share during fiscal year 2002 was $20 per share.
2. Each bond was issued at face value. The 7% convertible debenture will convert into common shares at 50 shares per $1,000 bond. It is exercisable after five years and was issued in 2001. Ignore any requirement to record the bond's debt and equity components separately.
3. The $4.25 preferred shares was issued in 2000.
4. There are no preferred dividends in arrears; however, preferred dividends were not declared in fiscal year 2002.
5. The 1 million shares of common shares were outstanding for the entire 2002 fiscal year.
6. Net income for fiscal year 2002 was $1.5 million, and the average income tax rate is 40%.

Instructions

For the fiscal year ended June 30, 2002, calculate Yaeger Pharmaceutical Industries':

(a) basic earnings per share
(b) diluted earnings per share

P18-5 As auditor for Banquo & Associates, you have been assigned to check Duncan Corporation's calculation of earnings per share for the current year. The controller, Mac Beth, has supplied you with the following calculations:

Net income	$3,374,960
Common shares issued and outstanding:	
Beginning of year	1,285,000
End of year	1,200,000
Average	1,242,500

Earnings per share

$$\frac{\$3,347,960}{1,242,500} = \$2.72 \text{ per share}$$

You have developed the following additional information:

1. There are no other equity securities in addition to the common shares.
2. There are no options or warrants outstanding to purchase common shares.
3. There are no convertible debt securities.
4. Activity in common shares during the year was as follows:

Outstanding, Jan. 1	1,285,000
Shares acquired, Oct. 1	(250,000)
	1,035,000
Shares issued, Dec. 1	165,000
Outstanding, Dec. 31	1,200,000

Instructions

(a) Based on the information above, do you agree with the controller's calculation of earnings per share for the year? If you disagree, prepare a revised calculation of earnings per share.

(b) Assume the same facts as those in (a), except that options had been issued to purchase 140,000 shares of common shares at $10 per share. These options were outstanding at the beginning of the year and none had been exercised or cancelled during the year. The average market price of the common shares during the year was $25 and the ending market price was $35. Prepare a calculation of earnings per share.

P18-6 Hillel Corporation is preparing the comparative financial statements for the annual report to its shareholders for fiscal years ended May 31, 2000 and May 31, 2001. The income from operations for each year was $1.8 million and $2.5 million, respectively. In both years, the company incurred a 10% interest expense on $2.4 million of debt, an obligation that requires interest only payments for five years. The company experienced a loss of $500,000 from a fire in its Scotsland facility in February 2001, which was determined to be an extraordinary loss. The company uses a 40% effective tax rate for income taxes.

The capital structure of Hillel Corporation on June 1, 1999, consisted of 2 million shares of common shares outstanding and 20,000 shares of $50 par value, 8%, cumulative preferred shares. There were no preferred dividends in arrears, and the company had not issued any convertible securities, options, or warrants.

On October 1, 1999, Hillel sold an additional 500,000 shares of the common shares at $20 per share. Hillel distributed a 20% stock dividend on the common shares outstanding on January 1, 2000. On December 1, 2000, Hillel was able to sell an additional 800,000 shares of the common shares at $22 per share. These were the only common share transactions that occurred during the two fiscal years.

Instructions

(a) Identify whether the capital structure at Hillel Corporation is a simple or complex capital structure, and explain why.

(b) Determine the weighted average number of shares that Hillel Corporation would use in calculating earnings per share for the fiscal year ended
1. May 31, 2000.
2. May 31, 2001.

(c) Prepare, in good form, a comparative income statement, beginning with income from operations, for Hillel Corporation for the fiscal years ended May 31, 2000 and May 31, 2001. This statement will be included in Hillel's annual report and should display the appropriate earnings per share presentations.

(CMA adapted)

P18-7 Edmund Halvor of the controller's office of East Aurora Corporation was given the assignment of determining the basic and diluted earnings per share values for the year ending December 31, 2001. Halvor has compiled the information listed below.

1. The company is authorized to issue 8 million common shares. As of December 31, 2000, 3 million shares had been issued and were outstanding.

2. The per share market prices of the common shares on selected dates were as follows:

	Price per Share
July 1, 2000	$20.00
January 1, 2001	21.00
April 1, 2001	25.00
July 1, 2001	11.00
August 1, 2001	10.50
November 1, 2001	9.00
December 31, 2001	10.00

3. A total of 700,000 shares of an authorized 1.2 million shares of convertible preferred shares had been issued on July 1, 2000. The shares were issued at $25, and have a cumulative dividend of $3 per share. The shares are convertible into common shares at the rate of one share of convertible preferred for one share of common. The rate of conversion is to be automatically adjusted for stock splits and stock dividends. Dividends are paid quarterly on September 30, December 31, March 31, and June 30.

4. East Aurora Corporation is subject to a 40% income tax rate.

5. The after-tax net income for the year ended December 31, 2001 was $13,550,000.

The following specific activities took place during 2001.

1. January 1—A 5% common stock dividend was issued. The dividend had been declared on December 1, 2000 to all shareholders of record on December 29, 2000.

2. April 1—A total of 200,000 shares of the $3 convertible preferred shares was converted into common shares. The company issued new common shares and retired the preferred shares. This was the only conversion of the preferred shares during 2001.

3. July 1—A 2-for-1 split of the common shares became effective on this date. The Board of Directors had authorized the split on June 1.

4. August 1—A total of 300,000 shares of common shares were issued to acquire a factory building.

5. November 1—A total of 24,000 shares of common shares were purchased on the open market at $9 per share and cancelled.

6. Common share cash dividends—Cash dividends to common shareholders were declared and paid as follows:

   April 15—$0.30 per share
   October 15—$0.20 per share.

7. Preferred share cash dividends—Cash dividends to preferred shareholders were declared and paid as scheduled.

Instructions

(a) Determine the number of shares used to calculate basic earnings per share for the year ended December 31, 2001.

(b) Determine the number of shares used to calculate diluted earnings per share for the year ended December 31, 2001.

(c) Calculate the adjusted net income to be used as the numerator in the basic earnings per share calculation for the year ended December 31, 2001.

P18-8 The following information pertains to Prancer Limited for 2001:

Net income for the year	$1,200,000
8% convertible bonds issued at par ($1,000 per bond).	
Each bond is convertible into 40 common shares.	2,000,000
6% convertible, cumulative preferred shares, $100 par value.	
Each share is convertible into 3 common shares.	3,000,000
Common shares (600,000 shares outstanding)	6,000,000
Stock options (granted in a prior year) to purchase 50,000	
of common shares at $20 per share	500,000
Tax rate for 2001	40%
Average market price of common shares	$25 per share

There were no changes during 2001 in the number of common shares, preferred shares, or convertible bonds outstanding. To simplify, ignore the requirement to book the convertible bonds' equity portion separately.

Instructions

(a) Calculate basic earnings per share for 2001.
(b) Calculate diluted earnings per share for 2001.

P18-9 Cordelia Corporation is preparing the comparative financial statements to be included in the annual report to shareholders. Cordelia employs a fiscal year ending May 31.

Income from operations before income taxes for Cordelia was $1.4 million and $660,000, respectively, for fiscal years ended May 31, 2001 and 2000. Cordelia experienced an extraordinary loss of $500,000 because of an earthquake on March 3, 2001. A 40% combined income tax rate pertains to any and all of Cordelia Corporation's profits, gains, and losses.

Cordelia's capital structure consists of preferred shares and common shares. The company has not issued any convertible securities or warrants and there are no outstanding stock options.

Cordelia issued 50,000 shares of $100 par value, 6% cumulative preferred shares in 1997. All of these shares are outstanding, and no preferred dividends are in arrears.

There were 1.5 million common shares outstanding on June 1, 1999. On September 1, 1999, Cordelia sold an additional 400,000 common shares at $17 per share. Cordelia distributed a 20% stock dividend on the common shares outstanding on December 1, 2000. These were the only common share transactions during the past two fiscal years.

Instructions

(a) Determine the weighted average number of common shares that would be used in calculating earnings per share on the current comparative income statement for:
  1. The year ended May 31, 2001
  2. The year ended May 31, 2001
(b) Starting with income from operations before income taxes, prepare a comparative income statement for the years ended May 31, 2001 and 2000. The statement will be part of Cordelia Corporation's annual report to shareholders and should include appropriate earnings per share presentation.
(c) A corporation's capital structure is the result of its past financing decisions. Furthermore, the earnings per share data presented on a corporation's financial statements are dependent upon the capital structure.
  1. Explain why Cordelia Corporation is considered to have a simple capital structure.
  2. Describe how earnings per share data would be presented for a corporation that has a complex capital structure.

(CMA adapted)

*P18-10 The treasurer of Miller Corp. has read on the Internet that the stock price of Ewing Inc. is about to take off. In order to profit from this potential development, Miller purchased a call option on Ewing common shares on July 7, 2000 for $240. The call option is for 200 shares (notional value), and the strike price is $70. The option expires on January 31, 2001. The following data are available with respect to the call option:

Date	Market Price of Ewing Shares	Time Value of Call Option
September 30, 2000	$77 per share	$180
December 31, 2000	$75 per share	65
January 4, 2001	$76 per share	30

Assume the proposed JWG standards are GAAP.

Instructions

Prepare the journal entries for Miller for the following dates:

(a) July 7, 2000—Investment in call option on Ewing shares.
(b) September 30, 2000—Miller prepares financial statements.
(c) December 31, 2000—Miller prepares financial statements.
(d) January 4, 2001—Miller settles the call option on the Ewing shares.

*P18-11   Johnstone Corp. purchased a put option on Ewing common shares on July 7, 2000 for $240. The put option is for 200 shares, and the strike price is $70. The option expires on January 31, 2001. The following data are available with respect to the put option:

Date	Market Price of Ewing Shares	Time Value of Put Option
September 30, 2000	$77 per share	$125
December 31, 2000	$75 per share	50
January 31, 2001	$78 per share	0

Assume the proposed JWG standards are GAAP.

Instructions

Prepare the journal entries for Johnstone Corp. for the following dates:
  (a) January 7, 2000—Investment in put option on Ewing shares.
  (b) September 30, 2000—Johnstone prepares financial statements.
  (c) December 31, 2000—Johnstone prepares financial statements.
  (d) January 31, 2001—Put option expires.

*P18-12   Warren Corp. purchased a put option on Echo common shares on January 7, 2001, for $360. The put option is for 400 shares, and the strike price is $85. The option expires on July 31, 2001. The following data are available with respect to the put option:

Date	Market Price of Echo Shares	Time Value of Put Option
March 31, 2001	$80 per share	$200
June 30, 2001	$82 per share	90
July 6, 2001	$77 per share	25

Assume the proposed JWG standards are GAAP.

Instructions

Prepare the journal entries for Warren Corp. for the following dates:
  (a) January 7, 2001—Investment in put option on Echo shares.
  (b) March 31, 2001—Warren prepares financial statements.
  (c) June 30, 2001—Warren prepares financial statements.
  (d) July 6, 2001—Warren settles the call option on the Echo shares.

*P18-13   On December 31, 2000, Mercantile Corp. had a $10 million 8% fixed rate note outstanding, payable in two years. It decides to enter into a two-year swap with First Bank to convert the fixed-rate debt to variable-rate debt. The terms of the swap indicate that Mercantile will receive interest at a fixed rate of 8.0% and will pay a variable rate equal to the six-month LIBOR rate, based on the $10 million amount. The LIBOR rate on December 31, 2000, is 7%. The LIBOR rate will be reset every six months and will be used to determine the variable rate to be paid for the following six-month period.

Mercantile Corp. designates the swap as a fair value hedge. Assume that the hedging relationship meets all the conditions necessary for hedge accounting. The six -month LIBOR rate and the swap and debt fair values are as follows:

Date	6-Month LIBOR Rate	Swap Fair Value	Debt Fair Value
December 31, 2000	7.0%	—	$10,000,000
June 30, 2001	7.5%	(200,000)	9,800,000
December 31, 2001	6.0%	60,000	10,060,000

Assume the proposed JWG standards are GAAP.

Instructions

  (a) Present the journal entries to record the following transactions:
   1. The entry, if any, to record the swap on December 31, 2000.
   2. The entry to record the semiannual debt interest payment on June 30, 2001.
   3. The entry to record the settlement of the semiannual swap amount receivable at 8%, less amount payable at LIBOR, 7%.
   4. The entry to record the change in the debt's fair value on June 30, 2001.
   5. The entry to record the change in the swap's fair value at June 30, 2001.

(b) Indicate the amount(s) reported on the balance sheet and income statement related to the debt and swap on December 31, 2000.

(c) Indicate the amount(s) reported on the balance sheet and income statement related to the debt and swap on June 30, 2001.

(d) Indicate the amount(s) reported on the balance sheet and income statement related to the debt and swap on December 31, 2001.

*P18-14 LEW Jewellery Corp. uses gold in the manufacture of its products. LEW anticipates that it will need to purchase 500 ounces of gold in October 2000 for jewellery that will be shipped for the holiday shopping season. However, if the price of gold increases, LEW's cost to produce its jewellery will increase, which could reduce its profit margins.

To hedge the risk of increased gold prices, on April 1, 2000, LEW enters into a gold futures contract and designates this futures contract as a cash flow hedge of the anticipated gold purchase. The notional amount of the contract is 500 ounces, and the terms of the contract give LEW the option to purchase gold at a price of $300 per ounce. The price will be good until the contract expires on October 31, 2000. Assume the following data with respect to the price of the call options and the gold inventory purchase:

Date	Spot Price for October Delivery
April 1, 2000	$300 per ounce
June 30, 2000	$310 per ounce
September 30, 2000	$315 per ounce

Assume the proposed JWG standards are GAAP.

Instructions

Prepare the journal entries for the following transactions:

(a) April 1, 2000—Inception of the futures contract, no premium paid.

(b) June 30, 2000—LEW prepares financial statements.

(c) September 30, 2000—LEW prepares financial statements.

(d) October 10, 2000—LEW purchases 500 ounces of gold at $315 per ounce and settles the futures contract.

(e) December 20, 2000—LEW sells jewellery containing gold purchased in October 2000 for $350,000. The cost of the finished goods inventory is $200,000.

(f) Indicate the amount(s) reported on the balance sheet and income statement related to the futures contract on June 30, 2000.

(g) Indicate the amount(s) reported in the income statement related to the futures contract and the inventory transactions on December 31, 2000.

*P18-15 On November 3, 2001, Sprinkle Corp. invested $200,000 in 4,000 shares of the common stock of Johnstone Corp. Sprinkle classified this investment as a long-term investment. Sprinkle Corp. is considering making a more significant investment in Johnstone Corp. at some point in the future but has decided to wait and see how the stock does over the next several quarters.

To hedge against potential declines in the value of Johnstone stock during this period, Sprinkle also purchased a put option on the Johnstone stock. Sprinkle paid an option premium of $600 for the put option, which gives Sprinkle the option to sell 4,000 Johnstone shares at a strike price of $50 per share; the option expires on July 31, 2002. The following data are available with respect to the values of the Johnstone stock and the put option:

Date	Market Price of Johnstone Shares	Time Value of Put Option
December 31, 2001	$50 per share	$375
March 31, 2002	$45 per share	175
June 30, 2002	$43 per share	40

Assume the proposed JWG standards are GAAP.

Instructions

(a) Prepare the journal entries for Sprinkle Corp. for the following dates:

    1. November 3, 2001—Investment in Johnstone stock and the put option on Johnstone shares.

    2. December 31, 2001—Sprinkle Corp. prepares financial statements.

    3. March 31, 2002—Sprinkle prepares financial statements.

    4. June 30, 2002—Sprinkle prepares financial statements.

    5. July 1, 2002—Sprinkle settles the put option and sells the Johnstone shares for $43 per share.

(b) Indicate the amount(s) reported on the balance sheet and income statement related to the Johnstone investment and the put option on December 31, 2001.

(c) Indicate the amount(s) reported on the balance sheet and income statement related to the Johnstone investment and the put option on June 30, 2002.

CONCEPTUAL CASES

C18-1 Incurring long-term debt with an arrangement whereby lenders receive an option to buy common shares during all or a portion of the time the debt is outstanding is a frequent corporate financing practice. In some situations, the result is achieved through the issuance of convertible bonds; in others, the debt instruments and the warrants to buy shares are separate.

Instructions

(a) Discuss whether convertible bonds and bonds with detachable warrants should receive different accounting treatment.

(b) At the start of the year, Biron Corp. issued $18 million of 12% notes along with warrants to buy 1.2 million common shares at $18 per share. The notes mature over the next 10 years starting one year from date of issuance with annual maturities of $1.8 million. At the time, Biron had 9.6 million common shares outstanding and the market price was $23 per share. The company received $20,040,000 for the notes and the warrants. For Biron, 12% was a relatively low borrowing rate. If offered alone, at this time, the notes would have been issued at a 22% discount. Prepare the journal entry (or entries) for the issuance of the notes and warrants for the cash consideration received.

(AICPA adapted)

C18-2 On February 1, 1998, Parsons Inc. sold its five-year, $1,000 par value, 8% bonds, which were convertible at the investor's option into Parsons Inc. common shares at a ratio of 10 common shares for each bond. The convertible bonds were sold by Parsons at a discount. Interest is payable annually each February 1. On February 1, 2001, Wong Corp., an investor in the Parsons Inc. convertible bonds, tendered 1,000 bonds for conversion into 10,000 shares of Parsons Inc. common shares that had a market value of $120 per share at the date of the conversion.

Instructions

How should Parsons account for the conversion of the convertible bonds into common shares under both the book value and market value methods? Discuss the rationale for each method.

(AICPA adapted)

C18-3 For various reasons, a corporation may issue warrants to purchase shares of its common shares at specified prices that, depending on the circumstances, may be less than, equal to, or greater than the current market price. For example, warrants may be issued:

1. To existing shareholders on a pro rata basis.
2. To certain key employees under an incentive stock option plan.
3. To purchasers of the corporation's bonds.

Instructions

For each of the three examples of how stock warrants are used:

(a) Explain why they are used.

(b) Discuss the significance of the price (or prices) at which the warrants are issued (or granted) in relation to (1) the current market price of the company's shares, and (2) the length of time over which they can be exercised.

(c) Describe the information that should be disclosed in financial statements, or notes thereto, that are prepared when stock warrants are outstanding in the hands of the three groups listed above.

(AICPA adapted)

*C18-4 In 1999, Sanford Corp. adopted a plan to give additional incentive compensation to its dealers to sell its principal product, fire extinguishers. Under the plan, Sanford transferred 9,000 of its common shares to a trust with the provision that Sanford would have to forfeit interest in the trust and no part of the trust fund could ever revert to Sanford. Shares were to be distributed to dealers on the basis of their shares of fire extinguisher purchases from Sanford (above certain minimum levels) over the three-year period ending June 30, 2002.

In 1999 the shares were closely held. The shares' book value was $7.90 per share as of June 30, 1999, and in 1999 additional shares were sold to existing shareholders for $8 per share. Based on information, the shares' market value was determined to be $8 per share.

In 1999 when the shares were transferred to the trust, Sanford charged Deferred Costs for $72,000 ($8 per share market value) and credited Common shares for the same amount. The deferred cost was charged to operations over a three-year period ended June 30, 2002. Sanford sold a substantial number of shares to the public in 2001 at $60 per share.

In July 2002 all shares in the trust were distributed to the dealers. The shares' market value at their date of distribution from the trust had risen to $110 per share.

Instructions

(a) How much should be reported as selling expense in each of the years noted above, assuming that the company uses the intrinsic value model?

(b) Sanford is also considering other types of option plans. One such plan is a stock appreciation right (SAR) plan. What is a stock appreciation right plan? What is a potential disadvantage of a SAR plan from the company's viewpoint?

C18-5 Presented below is an excerpt from a speech given by SEC Commissioner J. Carter Beese, Jr.

"I believe investors will be far better off if the value of stock options is reported in a footnote rather than on the face of the income statement. By allowing footnote disclosures, we will protect shareholders' current and future investments by not raising the cost of capital for the innovative, growth companies that depend on stock options to attract and retain key employees. I've said it before and I'll say it again: the stock option accounting debate essentially boils down to one thing—the cost of capital. And as long as we can adequately protect investors without raising the cost of capital to such a vital segment of our economy, why would we want to do it any other way?

The FASB has made the assertion that when it comes to public policy, they lack the competence to weigh various national goals. I also agree with the sentiment that, as a general matter, Congress should not be in the business of writing accounting standards.

But the SEC has the experience and the capability to determine exactly where to draw the regulatory lines to best serve investors and our capital markets. That is our mandate, and that is what we do, day in and day out.

But we may have to act sooner rather than later. As we speak, the FASB's proposals are raising the cost of venture capital. That's because venture capitalists are pricing deals based on their exit strategies, which usually include cashing out in public offerings. The FASB's proposals, however, provide incentives for companies to stay private longer—they are able to use options more freely to attract and retain key employees, and they avoid the earnings hit that going public would entail. Even worse, as venture capital deals become less profitable because of the FASB's proposed actions, venture capitalists are starting to look overseas for alternative investment opportunities that lack the investment drag now associated with certain American ventures.

I acknowledge that the FASB deserves some degree of freedom to determine what they believe is the best accounting approach. At the same time, however, I cannot stand by idly for long and watch venture capital increase in price or even flee this country because of a myopic search for an accounting holy grail. At some point, I believe that the SEC must inject itself into this debate, and help the FASB determine what accounting approach is ultimately in the best interests of investors as a whole.

We owe it to shareholders, issuers and all market participants, and indeed our country, to make the best decision in accordance with the public good, not just technical accounting theory."

Instructions

Write a response to Commissioner Beese, defending the use of the concept of neutrality in financial accounting and reporting.

C18-6 "Earnings per share" (EPS) is the most featured single financial statistic about modern corporations. Daily published quotations of share prices have recently been expanded to include for many securities a "times earnings" figure that is based on EPS. Stock analysts often focus their discussions on the EPS of the corporations they study.

Instructions

(a) Explain how dividends or dividend requirements on any class of preferred shares that may be outstanding affect the calculation of EPS.

(b) One of the technical procedures applicable in EPS calculations is the "treasury stock method." Briefly describe the circumstances under which it might be appropriate to apply the treasury stock method.

(c) Convertible debentures are considered potentially dilutive common shares. Explain how convertible debentures are handled for purposes of EPS calculations.

(AICPA adapted)

C18-7 Fernandez Corporation, a new audit client of yours, has not reported earnings per share data in its annual reports to shareholders in the past. The treasurer, Angelo Balthazar, requested that you furnish information about the reporting of earnings per share data in the current year's annual report in accordance with generally accepted accounting principles.

Instructions

(a) Define the term "earnings per share" as it applies to a corporation with a capitalization structure composed of only one class of common shares and explain how earnings per share should be calculated and how the information should be disclosed in the corporation's financial statements.

(b) Discuss the treatment, if any, that should be given to each of the following items in calculating earnings per share of common shares for financial statement reporting.

1. Outstanding preferred shares issued at a premium with a par value liquidation right.

2. The exercise at a price below market value but above book value of a common stock option issued during the current fiscal year to officers of the corporation.

3. The replacement of a machine immediately prior to the close of the current fiscal year at a cost 20% above the original cost of the replaced machine. The new machine will perform the same function as the old machine that was sold for its book value.

4. The declaration of current dividends on cumulative preferred shares.

5. The acquisition of some of the corporation's outstanding common shares during the current fiscal year. The shares were classified as treasury stock.

6. A 2-for-1 stock split of common shares during the current fiscal year.

7. A provision created out of retained earnings for a contingent liability from a possible lawsuit.

C18-8 Matt Kacskos, a shareholder of Howat Corporation, has asked you, the firm's accountant, to explain why his stock warrants were not included in diluted EPS. In order to explain this situation, you must briefly explain what dilutive securities are, why they are included in the EPS calculation, and why some securities are antidilutive and thus not included in this calculation.

Instructions

Write Mr. Kacskos a 1–1.5 page letter explaining why the warrants are not included in the calculation. Use the following data to help you explain this situation.

Howat Corporation earned $228,000 during the period, when it had an average of 100,000 shares of common shares outstanding. The common shares sold at an average market price of $25 per share during the period. Also outstanding were 15,000 warrants that could be exercised to purchase one share of common shares at $30 per warrant.

Using Your Judgement

FINANCIAL REPORTING PROBLEM 1: CANADIAN TIRE CORPORATION, LIMITED

Instructions

Refer to the financial statements and accompanying notes and discussion of **Canadian Tire Corporation, Limited** presented in Appendix 5B and answer the following questions.

(a) The company has five separate stock-based compensation plans. Compare and contrast these plans noting such things as who is eligible, whether they have to buy shares to access any benefit, what the benefit orcompensation is based on (profits or stock price) etc. Prepare a chart.

(b) Review the financial statements and discuss how these plans are accounted for.

(c) Comment on any professional judgement used in accounting for the plans.

(d) Comment on the impact of the above on quality of earnings—does the financial reporting of the plans contribute to higher or lower quality of earnings?

FINANCIAL REPORTING PROBLEM 2: ROYAL GROUP TECHNOLOGIES LTD.

Stock-based compensation plans award managers for assisting the company in achieving higher stock prices and are therefore seen as a form of performance-based compensation. The nature of these arrangements *may* allow companies to record less compensation expense than would have been recorded had the compensation been straight salary and/or salary and bonus. The following case provides an example of a company in an increasingly competitive industry that is using a stock-based compensation plan.

By the mid 1990s, big box stores had taken a dominant position in the Canadian retail market. Stores such as the hardware giant Home Depot had captured a huge portion of Canadian consumers' expenditures on hardware goods and renovation supplies. Prior to **Home Depot's** entry, the hardware goods market in Canada was characterized by many small retail outlets supported by a network of somewhat larger, wholesale distributors. The big box store changed this, effectively consolidating the wholesale and retail market and forcing many smaller businesses to shut down. Because of its size, Home Depot was able to target both individual and commercial customers.

The changes that occurred in the retail sector cascaded through the industry, forcing the suppliers of hardware products to change as well. The big box retailer needed to be supported by a group of suppliers that could produce in large volumes so that national distribution demands could be met. As competition within the manufacturing sector became more intense and profit margins were driven lower, many manufacturers were forced to either consolidate their operations with their competitors or risk being driven out of business. Stock-based compensation plans were seen as an attractive and competitive method to assist in motivating management to achieve corporate objectives and, serve as a means to reduce cash outlays on compensation expense.

Royal Group Technologies Ltd. (Royal) is one such manufacturer. Royal's operations are located primarily in Canada and the United States. It is a manufacturer of technologically advanced, polymer-based home improvement, consumer, and construction products. One of its major customers is Home Depot, which sells Royal products ranging from PVC based fencing, decking, and siding to window profiles and residential doors.

As described in the notes to Royal's financial statements: "The Company has a stock option plan. No compensation expense is recognized for this plan when stock or stock options are issued to management and key operating personnel. Any consideration paid by management and key personnel on exercise of stock options or purchase of stock is credited to capital stock."

As per note 10 of the financial statements, on any block of options granted, one-half become exercisable after three years; the balance may be exercised after six years. All options expire nine years after their issuance. As at September 30, 2000, 9,794,654 stock options were outstanding at a weighted average exercise price of $24.34. Due to the aforementioned restrictions on exercising, only 1,409,572 were exercisable at September 30. The weighted average exercise price of the exercisable options was $27.11. During the year, 732,500 options were granted and 130,400 were exercised. On September 30, 2000 Royal traded on the TSE for approximately $31.00 per share.

Instructions

Discuss the various accounting issues that arise as a result of Royal's stock-based compensation plan. Specifically, what are the financial reporting alternatives with respect to measurement, recognition, and presentation?

(This case was prepared by Adam Zalev, Class 2002, Rotman Master of Management and Professional Accounting program, University of Toronto)

FINANCIAL REPORTING PROBLEM 3:
AIR CANADA

Air Canada is Canada's largest domestic and international airline, providing scheduled and charter air transportation for passengers and cargo. As of December 31, 2000 the airline served 150 destinations, including 68 cities in Canada, 46 cities in the United States, and 36 other international destinations.

Recently, the airline industry has suffered many difficulties and financial setbacks. The high costs associated with operating an airline have claimed many victims, including Canadian Airlines, which was recently purchased by Air Canada in a highly publicized takeover battle. One of the largest cost components on Air Canada's income statement is aircraft fuel. As per the 2000 financial statements, the company spent $1.37 million on fuel for its aircraft during the year. This amounts to more than 15% of the airline's total expenses.

Since aircraft fuel is a commodity good, its price is subject to significant fluctuations. The cost of a barrel of aircraft fuel is determined by demand/supply relationships and other global economic conditions that impact production. As a result, Air Canada, like all other airlines, faces a great deal of uncertainty with respect to the cost it will be required to pay for aircraft fuel. In order to reduce the uncertainty and attempt to limit exposure, Air Canada employs a fuel hedging strategy. Note 15 in the company's 2000 financial statements describes the Airline's method for accounting for its fuel hedging strategy and provides additional disclosure as follows:

The Corporation enters into contracts with certain financial intermediaries, not exceeding two years, to manage its exposure to jet fuel price volatility. Gains and losses resulting from fuel hedging transactions are recognized as a component of fuel expense. As at December 31, 2000 the Corporation had effectively hedged approximately 26% of its projected 2001 fuel requirements. As at December 31, 2000 the fair value of fuel contracts was $25,000,000 in favour of the counterparties.

The company also refers to its aircraft fuel hedging operations in its disclosures of significant accounting policies. Specifically, it states that "Resulting gains and losses [from fuel contracts] are recorded as adjustments to fuel expense **as fuel is purchased**. Premiums and discounts are recorded over the term of the contracts."

Instructions

Discuss the various accounting issues that arise as a result of Air Canada's aircraft fuel hedging strategy. Specifically, what are the financial reporting alternatives with respect to measurement, recognition, and presentation?

(This case was prepared by Adam Zalev, Class 2002, Rotman Master of Management and Professional Accounting program, University of Toronto)

COMPARATIVE ANALYSIS CASE

Hudson's Bay Company versus Sears Canada Inc.

Instructions

Go to the Digital Tool and, using the respective annual reports for these two companies, answer the following questions.

(a) Comment on the capital structure of each company (simple or complex) and why it exists. List the dilutive securities for each. Which one in more complex?

(b) How significant are the dilutive securities in terms of potential dilution?

(c) What employee stock option compensation plans are offered by both companies?

(d) Compare the exercise price of the option plans to the company share price at year end. Comment on the likelihood of the options expiring or being exercised based on this information.

(e) How have the companies accounted for these plans?

(f) Compare EPS with diluted EPS for each company and comment on the differences between the two.

RESEARCH CASE

The TSE 35 Index is made up of 35 of Canada's largest public companies. All of these companies have shares that trade on the TSE and they represent a cross section of various industries. (*Hint:* Search the TSE for "TSE35".)

Instructions

(a) Prepare a list of the companies, that are included in the TSE 35 index.

(b) What criteria must these companies meet in order to be included in this index

(c) What does the index represent?

(d) Identify which industry each of these companies is in. (Hint: look up in the SEDAR database at www.sedar.com).

(e) Which of these companies recorded diluted EPS as well as EPS in the most recently issued financial statements?

(f) Which of these companies have stock option plans?

INTERNATIONAL REPORTING CASE

Clearly Canadian Beverage is a Canadian company that manufactures and distributes its Clearly Canadian line of carbonated mineral water and natural fruit-flavoured sparkling beverages, non-carbonated beverages, and bottled water. Its shares are traded on the NASDAQ exchange. Because its shares trade on a U.S. exchange, Clearly Canadian Beverage must either prepare its financial statements in accordance with U.S. GAAP or prepare a reconciliation of its financial statements (based on Canadian standards) to how they would be reported under U.S. GAAP. As a result of this requirement, Clearly Canadian presented the following information in its financial statements to meet the U.S. GAAP reconciliation requirement.

Instructions

Use the information in the Clearly Canadian disclosure to respond to the following questions.

(a) What are the major differences between earnings reported by Clearly Canadian Beverage and earnings under U.S. GAAP?

(b) What do you think are some reasons why Clearly Canadian Beverage might not want to prepare its financial statements in accordance with U.S. GAAP?

(c) What is the impact of SFAS 123 accounting on Clearly Canadian's profit?

(d) Why isn't this adjustment reflected in the reconciliation schedule?

CLEARLY CANADIAN BEVERAGE

Reconciliation to Accounting Principles Generally Accepted in the United States of America
Differences in generally accepted accounting principles (GAAP) between Canada and the United States as they pertain to these consolidated financial statements are as follows:

	1998 $	1997 $
Net earnings (loss) under Canadian GAAP	310	(12,266)
Foreign currency adjustments—see note A	—	(408)
Earnings (loss) under U.S. GAAP	310	(12,674)
Unrealized holding gains (losses)—see note B	(1,044)	1,742
Foreign currency translation adjustments	(1,983)	—
Comprehensive loss—see note C	(2,717)	(10,932)
Basic earnings (loss) per post-consolidated share before comprehensive income (loss) adjustments (expressed in dollars)	0.05	(2.26)

Note A: Change in reporting currency. Under U.S. GAAP, a change in reporting currency would require a restatement of prior years' financial statements using a weighted average exchange rate for each year in the statement of operations, and current and historical rates for monetary and non-monetary assets and liabilities on the balance sheet.

Note B: Unrealized holding gains (losses). Under U.S. GAAP, the long-term investments in publicly traded companies would be shown at fair market value.

Note C: Comprehensive income (loss). U.S. GAAP requires disclosure of comprehensive income (loss), which is intended to reflect all changes in equity except those resulting from contributions to owners.

In addition, Clearly Canadian provided the following disclosure related to its stock compensation plans: Under a stock option plan, as amended and restated June 27, 1997, the Company may grant options to eligible employees of the Company, provided that the number of shares issuable does not exceed 941,176 post-consolidated common shares of the Company. Options may be issued under the stock option plan as determined at the sole discretion of the Company's board of directors. Options may be issued for a term of up to 10 years at an exercise price to be determined by the Company's board of directors, provided that the exercise price is not less than the average closing price of the Company's shares traded through the facilities of The Toronto Stock Exchange for the 10 trading days preceding the date on which the options are granted.

The Company applies APB Opinion 25, "Accounting for Stock Issued to Employees," and related Interpretations in accounting for the plan. Under APB Opinion 25, because the exercise price of the Company's employee stock options equals the market price of the underlying stock on the date of grant, no compensation cost is recognized.

Statement of Financial Accounting Standards No. 123, "Accounting for Stock-Based Compensation" (SFAS 123), requires the Company to provide pro forma information regarding net income and earnings per share as if compensation cost for the Company's stock option plans had been determined in accordance with the fair value based method prescribed in SFAS 123. The Company estimates the fair value of each stock option at the grant date by using the Black-Scholes option-pricing model with the following weighted-average assumptions used for grants in 1998: dividend yield of $nil (1997—$nil); expected volatility of 70% (1997—70%); risk-free interest rate of 4.7% (1997—4.54%); and expected life to nine years (1997—nine years).

Under the accounting provisions of SFAS 123, the Company's U.S. GAAP profit of $310,000 would have been decreased to a loss of $288,000.

ETHICS CASE

The executive officers of Coach Corporation have a performance-based compensation plan with performance criteria linked to growth in earnings per share. When annual EPS growth is 12%, the Coach executives earn 100% of the shares; if growth is 16%, they earn 125%. If EPS growth is lower than 8%, the executives receive no additional compensation.

In 2000, Joanna Becker, the controller of Coach, reviews year-end estimates of bad debt expense and warranty expense. She calculates the EPS growth at 15%. Peter Reiser, a member of the executive group, remarks over lunch one day that the estimate of bad debt expense might be decreased, increasing EPS growth to 16.1%. Becker is not sure she should do this because she believes that the current estimate of bad debts is sound. On the other hand, she recognizes that a great deal of subjectivity is involved in the calculation.

Instructions

Answer the following questions:

(a) What, if any, is the ethical dilemma for Becker?

(b) Should Becker's knowledge of the compensation plan be a factor that influences her estimate?

(c) How should Becker respond to Reiser's request?

CHAPTER 19

Income Taxes

LEARNING OBJECTIVES

After studying this chapter, you should be able to:

1. Explain the difference between accounting income and taxable income.

2. Explain what a taxable temporary difference is and why a future tax liability is recognized.

3. Explain what a deductible temporary difference is and why a future tax asset is recognized.

4. Differentiate between timing, temporary, and permanent differences.

5. Prepare analyses and related journal entries to record income tax expense when there are multiple temporary differences.

6. Explain the effect of various tax rates and tax rate changes on future income tax accounts.

7. Apply accounting procedures for a tax loss carryback.

8. Apply accounting procedures and disclosure requirements for a tax loss carryforward.

9. Explain why the future income tax asset account is reassessed at the balance sheet date.

10. Explain the need for and be able to apply intraperiod tax allocation.

11. Identify the reporting and disclosure requirements for corporate income taxes.

12. Describe key aspects of the asset-liability (liability) method and identify outstanding issues with this method.

Preview of Chapter 19

As part of prudent management, companies are expected to manage all costs in order to maximize shareholder value. For example, good managers look for the best prices for raw materials and supplies that go into making their products, and are expected to be savvy bargainers in negotiating labour and other service contracts to minimize the overall cost of doing business. Other costs that companies manage are those related to taxes. For example, by using accelerated amortization methods for capital assets, companies can defer paying taxes. With faster tax write-offs on plant and equipment, companies report lower taxable income and pay lower taxes in the early years of the assets' lives, thereby managing tax costs. Money has time value!

Income taxes are a major cost of business to most corporations. As a result, companies spend a considerable amount of time and effort to minimize their tax payments. This chapter discusses the standards that companies follow in reporting income taxes. The chapter's content and organization are as follows:

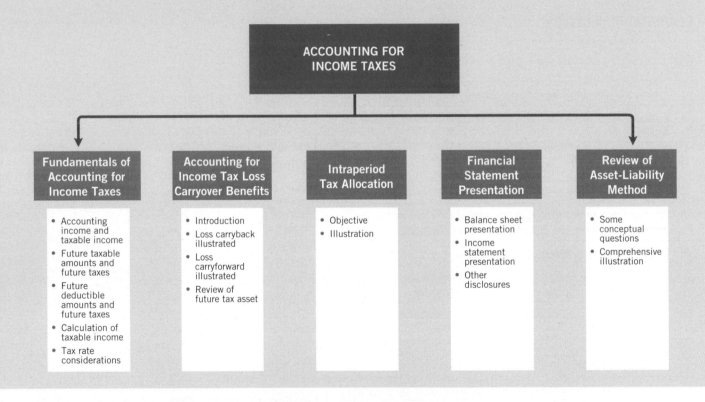

FUNDAMENTALS OF ACCOUNTING FOR INCOME TAXES

Up to this point, you have learned the basic principles that corporations use to report information to investors and creditors. You also recognize that corporations must file income tax returns following the *Income Tax Act* (and related provincial legislation) administered by the Canada Customs and Revenue Agency or CCRA.[1] Because GAAP and tax regulations are different in a number of ways, pretax income on the financial statements (accounting income) and taxable income frequently differ. Consequently, the amount that a company reports as income tax expense will differ from the amount of income taxes payable to the CCRA. Illustration 19-1 highlights these differences.

---

[1] Proprietorships and partnerships are not subject to income taxes as separate legal entities. Instead, their income is taxable in the hands of the proprietor or partners as individuals.

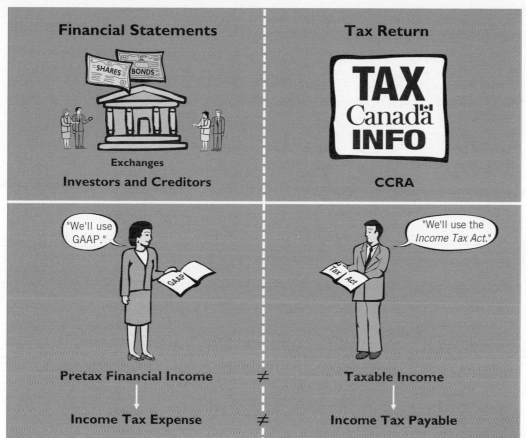

ILLUSTRATION 19-1
Fundamental Differences
between Financial and
Tax Reporting

This chapter explains the application of GAAP in accounting for income taxes—the asset-liability method (or liability method).

IAS NOTE
The IAS, through its Standard #12, also requires application of the liability method.

Accounting Income and Taxable Income

Accounting income is a financial reporting term often referred to as income before taxes, income for financial reporting purposes, or income for book purposes. In this chapter, it is a pre-tax concept. Accounting income is determined according to GAAP and is measured with the objective of providing useful information to investors and creditors. Taxable income (income for tax purposes) is a tax accounting term used to indicate the amount on which income tax payable is calculated. Taxable income is determined according to the *Income Tax Act* and *Regulations*, which is designed to raise money to support government operations.

OBJECTIVE 1
....
Explain the difference between accounting income and taxable income.

To illustrate how differences in GAAP and tax rules affect financial reporting and taxable income, assume that Chelsea Inc. reported revenues of $130,000 and expenses of $60,000 in each of its first three years of operation. Illustration 19-2 shows the (partial) income statements over these three years.

ILLUSTRATION 19-2
Accounting Income

CHELSEA INC. GAAP Reporting				
	2002	2003	2004	Total
Revenues	$130,000	$130,000	$130,000	
Expenses	60,000	60,000	60,000	
Accounting income	**$ 70,000**	**$ 70,000**	**$ 70,000**	**$210,000**
Income tax expense (40%)	$ 28,000	$ 28,000	$ 28,000	$ 84,000

For tax purposes (following tax regulations), Chelsea reported the same expenses to the CCRA in each of the years, but taxable revenues were $100,000 in 2002, $150,000 in 2003, and $140,000 in 2004, as shown in Illustration 19-3.

ILLUSTRATION 19-3
Taxable Income

CHELSEA INC.
Tax Reporting

	2002	2003	2004	Total
Revenues	$100,000	$150,000	$140,000	
Expenses	60,000	60,000	60,000	
Taxable income	**$ 40,000**	**$ 90,000**	**$ 80,000**	**$210,000**
Income tax payable (40%)	$ 16,000	$ 36,000	$ 32,000	$ 84,000

In reality, companies do not submit revised income statements for the tax return, listing only taxable revenues and deductible expenses. Instead they prepare a schedule that begins with the accounting income and then adjusts for each area of difference between GAAP income and taxable income, ending with taxable income. Chelsea's schedules would appear as in Illustration 19-4.

ILLUSTRATION 19-4
Schedule to Reconcile Accounting Income to Taxable Income

CHELSEA INC.

	2002	2003	2004
Accounting income	$70,000	$70,000	$70,000
Less revenue taxable in a future period	(30,000)		
Add revenue recognized in previous period, taxable in current period		20,000	10,000
Taxable income	$40,000	$90,000	$80,000
Taxes payable (40%)	$16,000	$36,000	$32,000

Income tax expense and income tax payable (a 40% tax rate is assumed) differ in each of the three years but in total are the same, as shown in Illustration 19-5.

ILLUSTRATION 19-5
Comparison of Income Tax Expense to Income Tax Payable

CHELSEA INC.
Income Tax Expense and
Income Tax Payable

	2002	2003	2004	Total
Income tax expense	$28,000	$28,000	$28,000	$84,000
Income tax payable	16,000	36,000	32,000	84,000
Difference	$12,000	($ 8,000)	($ 4,000)	$ 0

INTERNATIONAL INSIGHT

In some countries, taxable income and accounting income are the same. As a consequence, accounting for differences between tax and book income is not an issue.

The differences between income tax expense and income tax payable arise because the full accrual method is used to report revenues for financial reporting, whereas, in some areas, a method closer to a modified cash basis is used for tax purposes.[2] As a result, Chelsea reports accounting income of $70,000 and income tax expense of $28,000 for each of the three years. Taxable income, however, fluctuates. For example, in 2002, taxable income is only $40,000, which means that just $16,000 is owed to the CCRA that year.

As indicated in Illustration 19-5, the $12,000 ($28,000 − $16,000) difference between income tax expense and income tax payable in 2002 reflects taxes that will become payable

---

[2] At the risk of oversimplification, the *Income Tax Act* follows a principle of having the tax follow the cash flow. While taxable income is based primarily on income reported under GAAP, in cases where the timing of cash flows differs significantly from the timing of GAAP recognition, revenues tend to be taxable as they are received in cash and expenses are allowable as deductions when paid.

in future periods. This $12,000 difference is often referred to as a deferred—or future—tax amount. In this case it is a future tax liability. In cases where taxes will be lower in the future, Chelsea would record a deferred—or future—tax asset. The measurement of and accounting for future tax liabilities and assets are explained in the following sections.

Future Taxable Amounts and Future Taxes

The example summarized in Illustration 19-5 shows how income tax payable can differ from income tax expense. This happens when there are temporary differences between the amounts reported for tax purposes and those reported in the accounts. A **temporary difference** is the difference between the tax basis of an asset or liability and its reported (carrying or book) amount in the balance sheet that will result in taxable amounts or deductible amounts in future years.[3] **Taxable amounts** or **taxable temporary differences** will increase taxable income in future years, and **deductible amounts** or **deductible temporary differences** will decrease taxable income in future years.

> **OBJECTIVE 2**
>
> Explain what a taxable temporary difference is and why a future tax liability is recognized.

In Chelsea Inc.'s situation, the only difference between the book basis and tax basis of the assets and liabilities relates to accounts receivable that arose from revenue recognized for book purposes. Illustration 19-6 indicates that accounts receivable are reported at $30,000 in the December 31, 2002 GAAP-basis balance sheet, but the receivables have a zero tax basis. They have a zero tax value because all revenues reported in taxable income have been received.

Carrying value	12/31/02	Tax Basis	12/31/02
Accounts receivable	$30,000	Accounts receivable	$-0-

ILLUSTRATION 19-6
Temporary Difference, Sales Revenue

What will happen to this $30,000 temporary difference that originated in 2002 for Chelsea Inc.? Assuming that Chelsea expects to collect $20,000 of the receivables in 2003 and $10,000 in 2004, this will result in taxable amounts of $20,000 in 2003 and $10,000 in 2004. These future taxable amounts will cause taxable income to exceed accounting income in both 2003 and 2004.

In the Accounting Standards Board's view, an assumption inherent in a company's GAAP balance sheet is that the assets and liabilities will be recovered and settled, respectively, at their reported amounts (carrying amounts). This assumption creates a requirement under accrual accounting to recognize the future tax consequences of temporary differences in the current year; that is, the amount of income taxes that will be payable (or refundable) when the assets' reported amounts are recovered or the liabilities are settled. The following diagram illustrates the reversal or turnaround of the temporary difference described in Illustration 19-6 and the resulting taxable amounts in future periods.

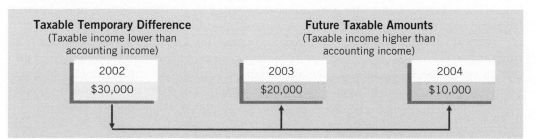

ILLUSTRATION 19-7
Reversal of Temporary Difference, Chelsea Inc.

We have assumed that Chelsea will collect the accounts receivable and report the $30,000 collection as taxable revenues in future tax returns. A payment of income tax will occur in both 2003 and 2004 related to the collection. We therefore should record in Chelsea's books in 2002 the future tax consequences of the revenue and related receivables reflected in the 2002 financial statements. This means we have to recognize a future tax liability at the end of 2002.

---

[3] *CICA Handbook*, Section 3465 par. .09(c).

Future Income Tax Liability

A future income tax liability is the future tax consequences associated with taxable temporary differences. In other words, a future tax liability represents the increase in taxes payable in future years as a result of taxable temporary differences existing at the end of the current year. Recall from the Chelsea example that income tax payable is $16,000 ($40,000 × 40%) in 2002 (Illustrations 19-3 and 4). In addition, a temporary difference exists at year-end because the revenue and related accounts receivable are reported differently for book and tax purposes. The book basis of accounts receivable is $30,000 and the tax basis is zero. Thus, the total future tax liability at the end of 2002 is $12,000, calculated as follows:

ILLUSTRATION 19-8
Calculation of Future Tax Liability, End of 2002

Book basis of accounts receivable	$30,000
Tax basis of accounts receivable	–0–
Taxable temporary difference at the end of 2002	30,000
Tax rate	40%
Future income tax liability at the end of 2002	$12,000

Another way to calculate the future tax liability is to prepare a schedule that indicates the taxable amounts scheduled for the future as a result of existing temporary differences. Such a schedule is needed when the tax rates in future years are different and the calculations become more complex.

ILLUSTRATION 19-9
Schedule of Future Taxable Amounts

	Future Years		
	2003	2004	Total
Future taxable amounts	$20,000	$10,000	$30,000
Tax rate	40%	40%	
Future income tax liability at the end of 2002	$ 8,000	$ 4,000	$12,000

Because it is the first year of operation for Chelsea, there is no future tax liability at the beginning of the year. The income tax expense for 2002 is calculated as follows:

ILLUSTRATION 19-10
Calculation of Income Tax Expense, 2002

Current tax expense, 2002		
Taxable income × tax rate ($40,000 × 40%)		$16,000
Future tax expense, 2002		
Future tax liability, end of 2002	$12,000	
Future tax liability, beginning of 2002	–0–	12,000
Income tax expense (total) for 2002		$28,000

This calculation indicates that income tax expense has two components: current tax expense (which is the amount of income tax payable or refundable for the period) and future tax expense. Future tax expense is the change in the future tax liability balance from the beginning to the end of the accounting period.

Taxes due and payable are credited to Income Tax Payable, while the increase in future taxes is credited to Future Tax Liability. These tax entries could be combined into one entry. However, because disclosure is required of the two components, using two entries makes it easier to keep track of the current tax expense and the future tax expense. For Chelsea Inc., the following entries are made at the end of 2002:

Current Income Tax Expense	16,000	
Income Tax Payable		16,000
Future Income Tax Expense	12,000	
Future Income Tax Liability		12,000

At the end of 2003 (the second year), the difference between the accounts receivable book basis and tax basis is $10,000. This difference is multiplied by the applicable tax rate to arrive at the future tax liability of $4,000 ($10,000 × 40%) to be reported at the end of 2003. Income tax expense for 2003 is calculated as follows:

ILLUSTRATION 19-11
Calculation of Income Tax
Expense, 2003

Current tax expense, 2003		
Taxable income × tax rate ($90,000 × 40%)		$36,000
Future tax expense, 2003		
Future tax liability, end of 2003	$ 4,000	
Future tax liability, beginning of 2003	12,000	(8,000)
Income tax expense (total) for 2003		$28,000

The journal entries to record income taxes for 2003 are as follows:

Current Income Tax Expense	36,000	
Income Tax Payable		36,000
Future Income Tax Liability	8,000	
Future Income Tax Expense/Benefit		8,000

In the entry to record future income taxes **at the end of 2004**, the Future Income Tax Liability, is reduced by another $4,000. This account appears as follows at the end of 2004:

ILLUSTRATION 19-12
Future Income Tax Liability
Account after Reversals

Future Income Tax Liability

		2002	12,000
2003	8,000		
2004	4,000		
		Balance	–0–

The Future Income Tax Liability account has a zero balance at the end of 2004.

Some analysts dismiss future tax liabilities when assessing a company's financial strength.[4] But the AcSB indicates that the future income tax liability meets the definition of a liability established in *CICA Handbook* Section 1000 "Financial Statement Concepts" because:

1. *It results from a past transaction.* In the Chelsea example, services were performed for customers and revenue was recognized in 2002 for financial reporting purposes but was deferred for tax purposes.

2. *It is a present obligation.* Taxable income in future periods will be higher than accounting income as a result of this temporary difference. Thus, a present obligation exists.

3. *It presents a future sacrifice.* Taxable income and taxes due in future periods will result from events that have already occurred. Paying these taxes when they come due will require the transfer or use of assets in the future.

Also note that the balance sheet at the end of each accounting period reports the ultimate cash impact of recovering the account receivable's carrying value. The following table illustrates the relationship between the future economic benefits accruing to Chelsea and the net assets reported on the balance sheet.

	End of 2002	End of 2003
As carrying amount is recovered:		
Future cash to be collected on the receivable	$30,000	$10,000
Future cash outflow for related income tax	12,000	4,000
Net future cash inflow	$18,000	$ 6,000
Reported on the balance sheet:		
Account receivable (in assets)	$30,000	$10,000
Future income tax liability (in liabilities)	12,000	4,000
Net amount reported	$18,000	$ 6,000

---

[4] A study by D. Givoly and C. Hayn, "The Valuation of the Deferred Tax Liability: Evidence from the Stock Market," *The Accounting Review*, April 1992, provides evidence that the stock market views deferred tax liabilities arising from temporary differences as similar to other liabilities. More recently, a study by B. Ayers, "Deferred Tax Accounting Under SFAS No. 109: An Empirical Investigation of its Incremental Value-Relevance Relative to APB No. 11," *The Accounting Review*, April 1998, indicates that SFAS No. 109 increased the usefulness of future tax amounts in financial statements. *CICA Handbook* Section 3465 requirements are almost identical to those of SFAS 109.

If the future tax liability was not recognized at the end of 2002, assets of $30,000 would be reported on the balance sheet, which would generate only $18,000 of future economic benefits. At the end of 2003, net assets would be overstated by $4,000.

Summary of Income Tax Accounting Objectives

One objective of accounting for income taxes is to recognize the amount of taxes payable or refundable for the current year. In Chelsea's case, income tax payable is $16,000 for 2002.

A **second objective** is that of interperiod tax allocation, to recognize future tax liabilities and assets for the future tax consequences of events that have already been recognized in the financial statements or tax returns. Chelsea sold services to customers that resulted in accounts receivable of $30,000 in 2002; the $30,000 was reported on the 2002 income statement—it was not reported on the tax return as income. It will appear on future tax returns as income when it is collected. As a result, a $30,000 temporary difference exists at the end of 2002 that will cause future taxable amounts. A future income tax liability of $12,000 is reported on the balance sheet at the end of 2002, which represents the increase in taxes payable in future years ($8,000 in 2003 and $4,000 in 2004) as a result of a temporary difference existing at the end of the current year. The related future income tax liability is reduced by $8,000 at the end of 2003 and by another $4,000 at the end of 2004. Accounting for the effect of future income taxes on the balance sheet in this way is the basis of the asset-liability method.

In addition to affecting the balance sheet, future taxes affect income tax expense in each of the three years. In 2002, taxable income ($40,000) is less than accounting income ($70,000). Income tax payable for 2002, based on taxable income, is therefore $16,000. Future income tax expense of $12,000 is caused by the increase in the Future Income Tax Liability account on the balance sheet. Income tax expense in total then is $28,000 for 2002.

In 2003 and 2004, taxable income will be more than accounting income due to the reversal of the temporary difference ($20,000 in 2003 and $10,000 in 2004). Income taxes payable will therefore be higher than income tax expense in 2003 and 2004. The Future Income Tax Liability account will be reduced by $8,000 in 2003 and $4,000 in 2004, resulting in credits for these amounts in future income tax expense on the income statement. A **future income tax expense with a credit balance** is often referred to as a **future income tax benefit**.

INTERNATIONAL INSIGHT

In Japan and Korea, future taxes are not recognized; in Sweden, they are generally recognized only through consolidation.

Future Deductible Amounts and Future Taxes

OBJECTIVE 3

Explain what a deductible temporary difference is and why a future tax asset is recognized.

Assume that during 2002, Cunningham Inc. estimated its warranty expense related to the sale of microwave ovens to be $500,000 and that $300,000 of these costs will be incurred in 2003 and $200,000 in 2004. For book purposes, Cunningham reports warranty expense and a related estimated liability for warranties of $500,000 in its 2002 financial statements. **For tax purposes, no deduction is permitted for warranty expense until the costs are actually incurred**; therefore, no warranty liability is recognized on a tax basis balance sheet. Thus, the balance sheet difference at the end of 2002 is as follows:

ILLUSTRATION 19-13
Temporary Difference, Warranty Liability

Carrying value	12/31/02	Tax Basis	12/31/02
Estimated liability for warranties	$500,000	Estimated liability for warranties	$–0–

When the warranty liability is paid, an expense (deductible amount) will be reported for tax purposes. Because of this temporary difference, Cunningham Inc. should recognize in 2002 the tax benefits (positive tax consequences) for the tax deductions that will result from the liability's future settlement. This future tax benefit is reported in the December 31, 2002 balance sheet as a future income tax asset.

Another way to think about this situation is as follows: Deductions will be allowed on future tax returns. These **future deductible amounts** will cause taxable income to be less than accounting income in the future as a result of an existing temporary difference. Cunningham's temporary difference originates (arises) in one period (2002) and reverses over two periods (2003 and 2004). This situation is diagramed as follows:

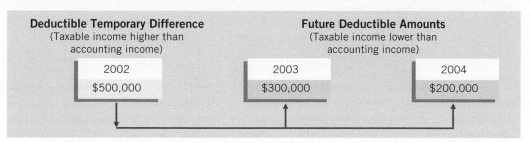

ILLUSTRATION 19-14
Reversal of Temporary
Difference, Cunningham Inc.

Future Income Tax Asset

A future income tax asset is the future tax consequence due to deductible temporary differences. In other words, a future income tax asset represents the reduction in taxes payable or increase in taxes refundable in future years as a result of deductible temporary differences existing at the end of the current year.[5] **Future income tax assets should be recognized only to the extent that it is more likely than not that the future tax asset will be realized**. This is contingent on earning sufficient taxable income in the future against which the temporary differences can be deducted. Section 3465 defines more likely than not as a probability of greater than 50%.[6]

To illustrate the calculation and recognition of the future income tax asset and income tax benefit, the Cunningham example is continued. The warranty liability accrued and expense recognized on the income statement in 2002 is not deductible for tax purposes until the period the actual warranty costs are incurred, expected to be $300,000 in 2003 and $200,000 in 2004. As a result, a deduction will be allowed for tax purposes in 2003 and again in 2004 as the Estimated Liability for Warranties is settled, causing taxable income in those years to be lower than accounting income. The calculation of the future income tax asset at the end of 2002 (assuming a 40% tax rate for 2003 and 2004) is as follows:

Book basis of warranty liability	$500,000
Tax basis of warranty liability	–0–
Deductible temporary difference at the end of 2002	500,000
Tax rate	40%
Future income tax asset at the end of 2002	$200,000

ILLUSTRATION 19-15
Calculation of Future Income Tax
Asset, End of 2002

Another way to calculate the future tax asset is to prepare a schedule that indicates the deductible amounts scheduled for the future as a result of deductible temporary differences. This schedule is shown in Illustration 19-16.

	Future Years		
	2003	2004	Total
Future deductible amounts	$300,000	$200,000	$500,000
Tax rate	40%	40%	
Future income tax asset at the end of 2002	$120,000	$ 80,000	$200,000

ILLUSTRATION 19-16
Schedule of Future Deductible
Amounts

Assuming that 2002 is the company's first year of operations and that income tax payable is $600,000, income tax expense is calculated as follows:

---

[5] *CICA Handbook* Section 3465, par. .09(d) indicates that future income tax assets also include the income tax benefits that arise in respect of the carryforward of unused tax losses and unused income tax reductions, excluding investment tax credits. These are discussed later in the chapter.

[6] *Ibid.*, par. .09(i).

ILLUSTRATION 19-17
Calculation of Income Tax
Expense, 2002

Current tax expense, 2002		
Taxable income × tax rate (given)		$600,000
Future tax expense/benefit, 2002		
Future tax asset, end of 2002	$200,000	
Future tax asset, beginning of 2002	–0–	(200,000)
Income tax expense (total) for 2002		$400,000

The future income tax benefit results from the increase in the future tax asset from the beginning to the end of the accounting period. The future tax benefit captures the warranty costs' future tax deductibility and recognizes this in the current period when the expense was reported for financial reporting purposes. The total income tax expense of $400,000 on the income statement for 2002 is therefore composed of two elements: current tax expense of $600,000 and the future tax benefit of $200,000. For Cunningham Inc., the following journal entries are made at the end of 2002 to recognize income taxes.

Current Income Tax Expense	600,000	
Income Tax Payable		600,000
Future Income Tax Asset	200,000	
Future Income Tax Expense/Benefit		200,000

At the end of the second year, 2003, the difference between the carrying value of the Estimated Liability for Warranties of $200,000 and its tax basis of zero is $200,000. Therefore, the future tax asset at this date is 40% of $200,000, or $80,000. Assuming income tax payable for 2003 is $440,000, the calculation of income tax expense for 2003 is as shown below.

ILLUSTRATION 19-18
Calculation of Income Tax
Expense, 2003

Current tax expense, 2003		
Taxable income × tax rate (given)		$440,000
Future tax expense/benefit, 2003		
Future tax asset, end of 2003	$ 80,000	
Future tax asset, beginning of 2003	200,000	120,000
Income tax expense (total) for 2003		$560,000

As expected, a reduction in the tax asset account, as with assets in general, results in an increase in the expense recognized. The journal entries to record income taxes in 2003 follow.

Current Income Tax Expense	440,000	
Income Tax Payable		440,000
Future Income Tax Expense	120,000	
Future Income Tax Asset		120,000

The total income tax expense of $560,000 on the income statement for 2003 is composed of two elements: current tax expense of $440,000 and future tax expense of $120,000.

Note that the future income tax expense of $120,000 recognized in 2003 **is not related to future events at all**. It represents the using up or reversal of a future income tax benefit recognized at the end of the preceding year. While a third component of income tax expense for the current year, such as Utilization of Previously Recognized Future Tax Assets or Reduction in Future Income Tax Assets, could be given separate recognition, the authors have chosen to incorporate this as a component of future income tax expense or benefit. **In all cases, the future income tax expense or benefit measures the change in the future income tax liability or asset account over the period.** As such, it is a combination of increased future tax liabilities, reversals of taxable temporary differences, recognition of future tax assets, and the use of future tax benefits recognized in the past.

At the end of 2004, the Future Income Tax Asset is further reduced by $80,000, as shown in the T account in Illustration 19-19. Future income tax expense in 2004 is $80,000.

ILLUSTRATION 19-19
Future Income Tax Asset Account
after Reversals

Future Income Tax Asset			
2002	200,000		
		2003	120,000
		2004	80,000
Balance	–0–		

A key issue in accounting for income taxes is whether a future tax asset should be recognized in the accounts. The future income tax asset account has all three aspects of the definition of an asset as found in *CICA Handbook* Section 1000 and therefore should be accorded asset recognition:

1. *It will contribute to future net cash flows.* Taxable income is higher than accounting income in the current year (2002). However, in the next year the opposite occurs, with taxable income lower than income reported for financial statement purposes. Because the deductible temporary difference reduces taxes payable in the future, a future benefit exists at the end of the year.

2. *Access to the benefits are controlled by the entity.* Cunningham has the ability to obtain the benefit of existing deductible temporary differences by reducing its taxes payable in the future. The company has the exclusive right to that benefit and can control others' access to it.

3. *It results from a past transaction or event.* In the Cunningham example, the sale of the product with the two-year warranty is the past event that gives rise to a future deductible temporary difference.

Note that when the future tax asset is recognized, the balance sheet at the end of each accounting period reports the economic resources needed to settle the warranty liability. The following table illustrates this relationship.

	End of 2002	End of 2003
Economic resources needed to settle the obligation:		
Future resources needed to settle the liability	$500,000	$200,000
Future tax savings as liability is settled	200,000	80,000
Net future economic resources needed	$300,000	$120,000
Reported on the balance sheet:		
Warranty liability (in liabilities)	$500,000	$200,000
Future income tax asset (in assets)	200,000	80,000
Net amount reported	$300,000	$120,000

In the absence of interperiod tax allocation (that is, if the future income tax asset is not recognized at the end of 2002), liabilities of $500,000 would be reported on the balance sheet, which require only $300,000 of economic resources to settle. Similarly, the $200,000 liability at the end of 2003 would also be overstated.

Calculation of Taxable Income

Temporary and Permanent Differences

To calculate income taxes currently payable, companies must first determine taxable income. As indicated previously, rather than drawing up a tax income statement of taxable revenues and deductible expenses, companies begin with the income reported on the income statement and then make whatever adjustments are necessary to convert it to the amount that is taxable.

The major reasons for differences between accounting and taxable income, most of which result in or affect the amount of a temporary difference, are provided below.

A. Revenues or gains are taxable after they are recognized in accounting income. An asset, such as a receivable, may be recognized on the balance sheet as revenues or gains are rec-

OBJECTIVE 4
....
Differentiate between timing, temporary, and permanent differences.

ognized on the income statement; however, these amounts may not be included in taxable income until future years when the asset is recovered or realized. Examples include:

- instalment sales accounted for on the accrual basis for financial reporting purposes and on the cash basis for tax purposes, and
- contracts accounted for under the percentage-of-completion method for financial reporting purposes with some or all of the related gross profit deferred for tax purposes.

B. Expenses or losses are deductible after they are recognized in accounting income. A liability (or contra asset) may be recognized on the balance sheet when expenses or losses are recognized for financial reporting purposes; however, amounts are not deductible in calculating taxable income until future periods when the liability is settled. Examples include:

- product warranty liabilities
- estimated losses and liabilities related to discontinued operations and restructurings
- litigation accruals, and
- accrued pension costs.

C. Revenues or gains are taxable before they are recognized in accounting income. A liability (e.g., unearned revenue) may be recognized for an advance payment for goods or services to be provided in future years. For tax purposes, the advance payment may be included in taxable income on the receipt of cash. When the entity recognizes revenue in the future as the goods or services are provided that settle the liability, these amounts are then deductible in calculating taxable income. Examples include:

- subscriptions, royalties, and rentals received in advance, and
- sales and leasebacks, including the deferral of profit on the sale for financial reporting purposes, but reported as realized for tax purposes.

D. Expenses or losses are deductible before they are recognized in accounting income. An asset's cost may be deducted faster for tax purposes than expensed for financial reporting purposes. If future amounts received as the asset is realized are equal to the asset's carrying value, the amounts recovered in excess of the tax value result in taxable amounts in future years. Examples include:

- depreciable property and depletable resources
- deductible pension funding exceeding pension expense recognized, and
- prepaid expenses that are deducted in calculating taxable income in the period paid.

E. Permanent differences. Some differences between taxable income and accounting income are permanent. Permanent differences are caused by items that (1) enter into accounting income but never into taxable income; or (2) enter into taxable income but never into accounting income. Since permanent differences affect only the period in which they occur, **they do not give rise to future taxable or deductible amounts**. As a result, **there are no future tax consequences to be recognized**. Examples of permanent differences include:

- Items that enter into accounting income but never into taxable income. Examples are non-tax-deductible expenses such as fines and penalties, golf and social club dues, and expenses related to the earning of non-taxable revenue; and non-taxable revenue, such as dividends from taxable Canadian corporations, and proceeds on life insurance policies carried by the company on key officers or employees.
- Items that enter into taxable income but never into accounting income, such as depletion allowance of natural resources in excess of their cost.

The differences identified in A to D above are known as timing differences. Their accounting treatment and tax treatment is the same, but the timing of when they are included in accounting income and when they are included in taxable income differs. Timing differences cause the balance of a temporary difference to change. **Timing** differences relate to income, whereas **temporary** differences relate to balance sheet values and cumulative effects. An originating timing difference is the cause of the initial difference between the carrying value and the tax basis of an asset or liability, or of an increase in the temporary difference, regardless of whether the asset or liability's tax basis exceeds or is exceeded by its carrying amount. A reversing timing difference, on the other hand, causes a temporary difference at the beginning of the period to decrease, and the related tax effect is removed from the future income tax account.

For example, assume that Sharp Corp. deducts amortization for tax purposes (CCA) in excess of accounting amortization of $2,000 in each of 1999, 2000, and 2001, and that accounting amortization exceeds CCA of $3,000 in 2002 and in 2003 for the same asset. Assuming a tax rate of 30% for all years involved, the Future Income Tax Liability account would reflect the following activity.

ILLUSTRATION 19-20
Example of Originating and Reversing Differences

Future Income Tax Liability				
		1999	600	Tax effects of originating differences
		2000	600	
		2001	600	
2002	900			Tax effects of reversing differences
2003	900			

The originating differences for Sharp in each of the first three years is $2,000, and the related tax effect of each originating difference is $600. The reversing differences in 2002 and 2003 are each $3,000, and the related tax effect of each is $900.

Multiple Differences Illustrated

To illustrate the calculations when multiple differences exist, assume that the Bio-Tech Corporation reports accounting income of $200,000 in each of the years 2001, 2002, and 2003. The company is subject to a 30% tax rate that is expected to continue into the future, and has the following differences between income reported on the financial statements and taxable income:

OBJECTIVE 5
Prepare analyses and related journal entries to record income tax expense when there are multiple temporary differences.

1. An instalment sale of $18,000 in 2001 is reported for tax purposes over an 18-month period at a constant amount each month as it is collected, beginning January 1, 2002. The entire sale and related profit is recognized for financial reporting purposes in 2001.

2. Premium paid for life insurance carried by the company on key officers is $5,000 in 2002 and 2003. This is not deductible for tax purposes, but is expensed for accounting purposes.

3. A warranty was provided on sales in 2001 and an associated expense of $30,000 was recognized in the same year. It was expected that $20,000 of the warranty work would be performed in 2002 and $10,000 in 2003.

The first and third items result in temporary differences. The second item is a permanent difference with no future tax consequences. The reconciliation of Bio-Tech's accounting income to taxable income and the calculation of income tax payable for each year is as follows.

ILLUSTRATION 19-21
Calculation of Taxable Income and Income Tax Payable

	2001	2002	2003
Accounting income	$200,000	$200,000	$200,000
Adjustments:			
Instalment sale	(18,000)	12,000	6,000
Warranty expense	30,000	(20,000)	(10,000)
Nondeductible expense	—	5,000	5,000
Taxable income	$212,000	$197,000	$201,000
Tax rate	30%	30%	30%
Income tax payable	$ 63,600	$ 59,100	$ 60,300

Note that the calculations always work **from** what has been reported on the financial statements **to** the taxable amount; therefore, revenue items not taxable until a future period are deducted, and expenses not deductible in the year are added back. Conversely, revenue items not included in accounting income but taxable in the period must be added and expenses not included in accounting income but deductible in the year for tax purposes are subtracted.

All differences between accounting income and taxable income are considered in reconciling the income reported on the financial statements to taxable income. Only those resulting in temporary differences, however, are considered when calculating future income tax amounts for the balance sheet. When multiple differences exist, a schedule should be prepared of the balance sheet accounts that have a carrying value and tax basis that differ. Bio-Tech Corporation's analysis and calculation of net temporary differences, the net future income tax asset or liability, and the future income tax expense or benefit for 2001 is shown below. Because the same tax rate is assumed for all periods, calculating the future tax asset and liability is simplified. If the tax rate in future years had been legislated at different rates, a schedule is needed of the tax effects as the timing differences reverse.

ILLUSTRATION 19-22

Calculation of Future Income Tax Asset/Liability and Future Tax Expense—2001

	Carrying Amount	Tax Basis	Taxable (Deductible) Temporary Differences
Assets			
Accounts receivable	$18,000	–0–	$18,000
Liabilities			
Liability for warranties	$30,000	–0–	(30,000)
Net deductible temporary difference			$(12,000)
Future income tax liability $18,000 at 30%			$ 5,400
Future income tax asset $30,000 at 30%			(9,000)
Net future income tax asset, December 31, 2001			(3,600)
Less opening balance, net future income tax asset/liability			–0–
Future income tax expense (benefit)—2001			$ (3,600)

In 2001, Bio-Tech has two originating differences that result in temporary differences. The journal entries to record income taxes for 2001 based on the above analyses are:

Current Income Tax Expense	63,600	
Income Tax Payable (see Illustration 19-21)		63,600
Future Income Tax Asset	3,600	
Future Income Tax Benefit		3,600

At the end of 2002, the following analysis is made of the temporary differences. The two types of temporary differences that originated in 2001 have begun to reverse. Again, the future tax expense or benefit is determined by the change in the future tax asset or liability account on the balance sheet.

ILLUSTRATION 19-23

Calculation of Future Income Tax Asset/Liability and Future Tax Expense—2002

	Carrying Amount	Tax Basis	Taxable (Deductible) Temporary Differences
Assets			
Accounts receivable	$ 6,000	–0–	$ 6,000
Liabilities			
Liability for warranties	$10,000	–0–	(10,000)
Net deductible temporary difference			$(4,000)
Future income tax liability $6,000 at 30%			$ 1,800
Future income tax asset $10,000 at 30%			(3,000)
Net future income tax asset, December 31, 2002			(1,200)
Less opening balance, net future income tax asset			(3,600)
Future income tax expense (benefit)—2002			$ 2,400

The journal entries to record income taxes at December 31, 2002 are:

Current Income Tax Expense	59,100	
Income Tax Payable (see Illustration 19-21)		59,100
Future Income Tax Expense	2,400	
Future Income Tax Asset		2,400

At the end of 2003, all temporary differences have reversed, leaving no temporary differences between balance sheet amounts and tax values.

	Carrying Amount	Tax Basis	Taxable (Deductible) Temporary Differences
Assets			
Accounts receivable	$ –0–	$ –0–	$ –0–
Liabilities			
Liability for warranties	$ 0	$ –0–	–0–
Net taxable (deductible) temporary difference			$ –0–
Net future income tax liability (asset), December 31, 2003			$ –0–
Less opening balance, net future income tax asset			(1,200)
Future income tax expense (benefit)—2003			$ 1,200

ILLUSTRATION 19-24
Calculation of Future Income Tax Asset/Liability and Future Tax Expense—2003

The journal entries at December 31, 2003 reduce the Future Income Tax Asset account to zero and recognize $1,200 future income tax expense for 2003.

Current Income Tax Expense	60,300	
Income Tax Payable (see Illustration 19-21)		60,300
Future Income Tax Expense	1,200	
Future Income Tax Asset		1,200

Illustration 19-25 provides a summary of the bottom portion of the income statements for Bio-Tech for each of the three years.

BIO-TECH CORPORATION
Income Statements (Partial)
for the Years Ending

	2001	2002	2003
Income before income tax expense	$200,000	$200,000	$200,000
Less: income tax expense			
Current expense	63,600	59,100	60,300
Future expense (benefit)	(3,600)	2,400	1,200
	60,000	61,500	61,500
Net income	$140,000	$138,500	$138,500

ILLUSTRATION 19-25
Bio-Tech Corporation Income Statements—2001, 2002, and 2003

Total income tax expense reported in 2001, 2002, and 2003 is $60,000, $61,500, and $61,500, respectively. Although the statutory (enacted) rate of 30% applies for all three years, the effective rate is 30% for 2001 ($60,000/$200,000 = 30%) and 30.75% for 2002 and 2003 ($61,500/$200,000 = 30.75%). The **effective tax rate** is calculated by dividing total income tax expense for the period by the pretax income reported on the financial statements. The difference between the enacted and effective rates in this case is caused by the non-deductible insurance expense.

OBJECTIVE 6
Explain the effect of various tax rates and tax rate changes on future income tax accounts.

Tax Rate Considerations

In the previous illustrations, the enacted tax rate did not change from one year to the next. Therefore, to calculate the future tax amount to be reported on the balance sheet, the temporary difference is simply multiplied by the current tax rate that is expected to apply to future years as well.

Future Tax Rates

What happens if tax rates are different for future years? *CICA Handbook* Section 3465 takes the position that the income tax rates that are expected to apply when the tax liabilities are settled or tax assets are realized should be used. These would normally be those enacted at the balance sheet date.[7] The accounting standard does recognize, however, that situations may exist where a substantively enacted rate may be more appropriate.[8] The rates expected to apply are used in measuring future tax assets and liabilities. For example, assume that Warlen Corp. at the end of 2001 has the following temporary difference of $300,000, calculated as follows.

ILLUSTRATION 19-26
Calculation of Temporary Difference

Book basis of depreciable assets (net book value)	$1,000,000
Tax basis of depreciable assets (UCC)	700,000
Temporary difference	$ 300,000

Furthermore, assume that the $300,000 will reverse and result in taxable amounts in the following years when the tax rates expected to apply are as follows.

ILLUSTRATION 19-27
Future Tax Liability Based on Future Rates

	2002	2003	2004	2005	2006	Total
Future taxable amounts	$80,000	$70,000	$60,000	$50,000	$40,000	$300,000
Tax rate	40%	40%	35%	30%	30%	
Future tax liability	$32,000	$28,000	$21,000	$15,000	$12,000	$108,000

As indicated, the future income tax liability at the end of 2001 is $108,000.

Because the Canadian tax system provides incentives in the form of reductions in the income tax rates applied to taxable income, it is recommended that the tax rate used to calculate the future tax amounts incorporate the tax rate reductions, provided it is more likely than not that the company will qualify for the rate reductions in the periods of reversal.[9] The general principle is to use the expected average or effective tax rate of the period in which the temporary differences are expected to reverse, provided it is based on rates enacted or substantively enacted at the balance sheet date.

Section 3465, consistent with the U.S. standard, prohibits the discounting of future income tax assets and liabilities.[10] The issue of discounting remains a contentious one that requires resolution on a broader level.

Revision of Future Tax Rates

When a change in the tax rate is enacted (or substantively enacted) into law, **its effect on the existing future income tax asset and liability accounts should be recorded immediately as an adjustment to income tax expense in the period of the change**. Assume that on December 10, 2002, a new income tax rate is enacted that lowers the corporate rate from 40% to 35%, effective January 1, 2004. If Hostel Corp. has one temporary difference at the beginning of 2002 related to $3 million of excess capital cost allowance, then it has a Future Income Tax Liability account with a balance of $1.2

---

[7] *Ibid.*, par. .56. Note that this covers changes in tax laws as well as tax rates.

[8] *Ibid.*, par. .58. Use of a substantively enacted rate would require persuasive evidence that the government is able and committed to enacting the proposed change in the foreseeable future. This would usually require that the legislation or regulation has been drafted in an appropriate form and tabled in parliament or presented in Council. *EIC-111* provides more detailed guidance.

[9] Examples of tax incentives include the small business deduction, the manufacturing and processing profits deduction, and the resource allowance deduction.

[10] *CICA Handbook*, Section 3465, par. .57.

million ($3,000,000 × 40%) at January 1, 2002. If taxable amounts related to this difference are scheduled to increase taxable income equally in 2003, 2004, and 2005, the future tax liability at the end of 2002 is $1.1 million, as calculated below.

	2003	2004	2005	Total
Future taxable amounts	$1,000,000	$1,000,000	$1,000,000	$3,000,000
Tax rate	40%	35%	35%	
Future tax liability	$ 400,000	$ 350,000	$ 350,000	$1,100,000

ILLUSTRATION 19-28
Schedule of Future Taxable Amounts and Related Tax Rates

An entry is made at the end of 2002 to recognize the decrease of $100,000 ($1,200,000 − $1,100,000) in the future tax liability.

Future Income Tax Liability	100,000	
Future Income Tax Benefit		100,000

Separate disclosure of this component of future income tax expense is suggested, but not required by Section 3465.

Basic corporate tax rates do not change often and, therefore, the current rate will normally be used. However, provincial rates, foreign tax rates, and surcharges on all levels of income affect the effective rate and may require adjustments to the future tax accounts.

ACCOUNTING FOR INCOME TAX LOSS CARRYOVER BENEFITS

Introduction to Loss Carryback and Carryforward

A loss for income tax purposes or tax loss occurs in a year when tax-deductible expenses and losses exceed taxable revenues and gains. An inequitable tax burden would result if companies were taxed during profitable periods without receiving any tax relief during periods of losses. Therefore, a company pays no income tax for a year in which it incurs a tax loss. In addition, the tax laws permit taxpayers to use a tax loss of one year to offset taxable income of other years. This is accomplished through the tax loss carryback and carryforward provisions of income tax legislation, which allow taxpayers to benefit from tax losses either by recovering taxes previously paid or by reducing taxes that will otherwise be payable in the future.

A corporation may elect to carry a tax loss back against taxable income of the immediately preceding three years, which is a loss carryback. Alternatively, it may elect to carry it forward to the seven years that immediately follow the loss, which is a loss carryforward.[11] Or, it may elect to do both. The following diagram illustrates the carryover periods, assuming a tax loss is incurred in 2002.

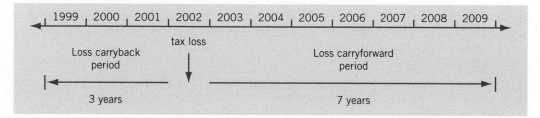

ILLUSTRATION 19-29
Loss Carryback and Carryforward Procedure

If a loss is carried back, it must be applied against the earliest available income—1999 in the example above. The benefit from a loss carryback is the recovery of some or all of the taxes paid in those years. The tax returns for the preceding years are refiled, the current year tax loss is deducted from the previously reported taxable income, and a revised amount of income tax payable for each year is determined. This is compared with the taxes paid for each applicable preceding year, and the government is asked to refund the difference.

[11] The references in this chapter to tax losses is limited to non-capital losses. Special rules apply to capital losses.

If a corporation elects to carry the loss forward instead, or if the full amount of the loss could not be absorbed in the carryback period, the tax loss can be used to offset taxable income in the future, thereby reducing or eliminating taxes that would otherwise be payable in those years.

The decision on how to use a tax loss will depend on factors such as its size, results of the previous years' operations, past and anticipated future tax rates, and other factors in which management sees the greatest tax advantage.

Operating losses are relatively common and can be substantial.[12] Companies that have suffered substantial losses are often attractive merger candidates because, in certain cases, the acquirer may use these losses to reduce its taxable income and, therefore, its income taxes. In a sense, a company that has suffered substantial losses may find itself worth more "dead" than "alive" because of the economic value related to the tax benefit that may be derived from its losses by another company.

The following sections discuss the accounting treatment of loss carrybacks and carryforwards recommended in *CICA Handbook* Section 3465.

OBJECTIVE 7

Apply accounting procedures for a tax loss carryback.

Loss Carryback Illustrated

ILLUSTRATION 19-30
Income and Loss Data—Groh Inc.

To illustrate the accounting procedures for a tax loss carryback, assume that Groh Inc. has no temporary or permanent differences. Groh experiences the following.

Year	Taxable Income or Loss	Tax Rate	Tax Paid
1998	$ 75,000	30%	$22,500
1999	50,000	35%	17,500
2000	100,000	30%	30,000
2001	200,000	40%	80,000
2002	(500,000)	—	–0–

In 2002, Groh Inc. incurs a tax loss that it elects to carry back. The carryback is applied first to 1999, the third year preceding the loss year. Any unused loss is then carried back to 2000 and then to 2001. Accordingly, Groh would file amended tax returns for each of the years 1999, 2000, and 2001, receiving refunds for the $127,500 ($17,500 + $30,000 + $80,000) of taxes paid in those years.

For accounting purposes, the $127,500 represents the **tax benefit of the loss carryback**. This tax effect should be recognized in 2002, the loss year, since the tax loss gives rise to a refund (an asset) that is both measurable and currently realizable.

The following journal entry is appropriate for 2002:

Income Tax Refund Receivable	127,500	
Current Income Tax Benefit		127,500

The Income Tax Refund Receivable is reported on the balance sheet as a current asset at December 31, 2002. The tax benefit is reported on the income statement for 2002 as follows:

ILLUSTRATION 19-31
Recognition of Benefit of the Loss Carryback in the Loss Year

GROH INC. Income Statement (partial) for 2002	
Loss before income taxes	$(500,000)
Income tax benefit	
Current benefit due to loss carryback	127,500
Net loss	$(372,500)

---

[12] *Financial Reporting in Canada—2000* (CICA) indicates that of the 200 companies surveyed from 1996 to 1999, between 25 and 42 companies each year disclosed tax recoveries from the carryback of current year's losses. As well, for each of these years, between 56 and 62 companies disclosed the realization or recognition of previously unrecorded loss carryforward benefits.

If the tax loss carried back to the three preceding years is less than the taxable incomes of those three years, the only entry required is similar to the one indicated above. In the Groh Inc. example, however, the $500,000 tax loss for 2002 exceeds the $350,000 total taxable income from the three preceding years; the remaining $150,000 loss remains to be carried forward.

Loss Carryforward Illustrated

If a net operating loss is not fully absorbed through a carryback or if the company decides not to carry the loss back, then it can be carried forward for up to seven years. Because carryforwards are used to offset future taxable income, the tax benefit associated with a loss carryforward is represented by future tax savings—reductions in taxes in the future that would otherwise be payable. Realization of the future tax benefit depends upon the existence of future taxable income, the prospect of which may be highly uncertain.

> **OBJECTIVE 8**
>
> Apply accounting procedures and disclosure requirements for a tax loss carryforward.

The accounting issue, then, is whether the tax effect of a loss carryforward should be recognized in the loss year when the potential benefits arise, or in future years when the benefits are actually realized. The AcSB, in Section 3465, takes the position that the potential benefit associated with unused tax losses meets the definition of an asset and that the benefit should be recognized **to the extent that it is more likely than not** that future taxable income will be available against which the losses and reductions can be applied.

When a tax loss carryforward is more likely than not to result in future economic benefits, it should be accounted for in the same manner as a deductible temporary difference: a future income tax asset should be recognized that is equal to the expected benefit.

Future Taxable Income More Likely Than Not

To illustrate the accounting for an income tax loss carryforward, the Groh Inc. example is continued. In 2002, after carrying back as much of the loss as possible to the three preceding years, the company has a $150,000 tax loss available to carry forward. Assuming the company determines it is more likely than not to generate sufficient taxable income in the future so that the benefit of the loss can be realized, Groh records a future tax asset to recognize the benefit of the loss. If a rate of 40% is expected to apply to future years, the amount of the asset recognized is $60,000 ($150,000 × 40%). The journal entries to record the benefits of the carryback and the carryforward in 2002 are as follows:

To recognize benefit of loss carryback		
Income Tax Refund Receivable	127,500	
Current Income Tax Benefit		127,500

To recognize benefit of loss carryforward		
Future Income Tax Asset	60,000	
Future Income Tax Benefit		60,000

The income tax refund receivable of $127,500 will be realized immediately as a refund of taxes paid in the past. The Future Income Tax Asset account measures the benefit of the future tax savings. The two accounts credited are contra income tax expense items, which appear on the 2002 income statement as follows.

GROH INC. Income Statement (partial) for 2002		
Loss before income taxes		$(500,000)
Income tax benefit		
Current benefit due to loss carryback	$127,500	
Future benefit due to loss carryforward	60,000	187,500
Net loss		$(312,500)

ILLUSTRATION 19-32
Recognition of the Benefit of the Loss Carryback and Carryforward in the Loss Year

The $60,000 **future tax benefit** for the year results from an increase in the future tax asset account.

For 2003, assume that Groh Inc. returns to profitability and has taxable income of $200,000 from the year's operations, subject to a 40% tax rate. In 2003, Groh Inc. **realizes** the benefits of the entire $150,000 tax loss carryforward, which was **recognized** for accounting purposes in 2002. The income tax payable for 2003 is calculated as follows.

ILLUSTRATION 19-33

Calculation of Income Tax Payable in Year the Loss Carryforward Is Realized

Taxable income before loss carryforward	$200,000
Loss carryforward deduction	(150,000)
Taxable income for 2003	50,000
Tax rate	40%
Income tax payable for 2003	$ 20,000

The journal entries to record income taxes in 2003 are as follows:

Current Income Tax Expense	20,000	
Income Tax Payable ($50,000 × 40%)		20,000
Future Income Tax Expense	60,000	
Future Income Tax Asset ($150,000 × 40%)		60,000

The first entry records the income taxes payable for 2003 and, therefore, current income tax expense. The second entry records the using up of the future income tax asset.

The 2003 income statement below illustrates that the 2003 total income tax expense is based on 2003's reported income. The benefit of the tax loss is not reported in 2003; the benefit was previously reported in 2002.

ILLUSTRATION 19-34

Presentation of the Benefit of Loss Carryforward Realized in 2003, Recognized in 2002

GROH INC.
Income Statement (partial) for 2003

Income before income taxes		$200,000
Income tax expense		
Current	$20,000	
Future	60,000	80,000
Net income		$120,000

Future Taxable Income Not Likely

Return to the Groh Inc. example and 2002. A tax asset (Income Tax Refund Receivable) was recognized in 2002 because the ability to carry back the loss and recover income taxes paid in the past provides evidence that benefits related to $350,000 of the loss will be realized. Assume now that the company's future is uncertain and it is determined at December 31, 2002 that there is insufficient evidence about the possibility of future taxable income to recognize an income tax asset and benefit related to the remaining $150,000 of income tax losses. In this case, the only 2002 income tax entry is:

Income Tax Refund Receivable	127,500	
Current Income Tax Benefit		127,500

The presentation in the following income statement indicates that **only the benefit related to the loss carryback is recognized**. The unrecognized potential tax benefit and related unrecognized future income tax asset associated with the remaining $150,000 of tax losses is relevant information for financial statement readers. Therefore the amounts and expiry dates of unrecognized income tax assets related to the carryforward of unused tax losses must be disclosed. Such information is useful as it makes readers aware of the possibility of future benefits (reduced future income tax outflows) from the loss, even though the likelihood of realizing these benefits is not sufficient to accord them formal recognition in the body of the statements.

ILLUSTRATION 19-35
Recognition of Benefit of Loss Carryback Only

GROH INC. Income Statement (partial) for 2002	
Loss before income taxes	$(500,000)
Income tax benefit	
Current benefit due to loss carryback	127,500
Net loss	$(372,500)

In 2003, assume the company performs better than expected, generating taxable income of $200,000 from its annual operations. After applying the $150,000 loss carryforward, tax is payable on only $50,000 income. With a tax rate of 40%, the following entry is made:

Current Income Tax Expense	20,000	
Income Tax Payable ($50,000 × 40%)		20,000

This entry recognizes the taxes currently payable in the year. Because the potential tax benefit associated with the loss carryforward was not recognized in 2002 as an asset, the tax benefit is recognized in 2003, the year it is realized. The $20,000 current tax expense is made up of two components: income taxes of $80,000 accrued on the 2003 income of $200,000, and a $60,000 tax benefit due to realization of the unrecorded loss carryforward. Separate disclosure of these components is suggested by Section 3465, but is not required.

The 2003 income statement reporting the components of current income tax expense is illustrated below.

ILLUSTRATION 19-36
Recognition of Benefit of Loss Carryforward when Realized

GROH INC. Income Statement (partial) for 2003		
Income before income taxes		$200,000
Income tax expense		
Current expense	$80,000	
Current benefit due to loss carryforward	(60,000)	20,000
Net income		$180,000

If 2003's taxable income had been less than $150,000, only a portion of the unrecorded and unused tax loss could have been applied. The entry to record 2003 income taxes would have been similar to the entry above. A note to the financial statements would be provided to disclose the remaining amount and expiry date of the unused loss.

Review of Future Income Tax Asset Account

Section 3465 recommends recognizing a future income tax asset for all deductible temporary differences and for the carryforward of unused tax losses and income tax reductions, **to the extent that it is more likely than not that the future income tax asset will be realized, i.e., that taxable income will be available against which the deductible temporary differences, unused tax losses, or income tax reductions can be applied**. Consistent with the reporting for all assets, the Future Income Tax Asset account must be reviewed to ensure that the carrying amount is appropriate.

Where it is more likely than not that not enough taxable income will be generated in the future to allow the benefit of the future tax asset to be realized, the future tax asset must be recalculated based on a judgement about the extent to which it will be realized. The account's carrying value is then written down.[13] This "affirmative judge-

OBJECTIVE 9

Explain why the future income tax asset account is reassessed at the balance sheet date.

---

[13] *CICA Handbook*, Section 3465, par. .31(a).

ment" approach differs from the "impairment approach" recommended by FAS 109, which requires recognition of a future income tax asset for all deductible temporary differences, unused tax losses and income tax reductions **offset by an impairment allowance** for the portion of the asset deemed more likely than not to not be realized (a *valuation allowance*). Because there is no substantive difference between the results of applying the two approaches, Section 3465 permits the use of the valuation allowance approach.[14] The approach preferred by the AcSB, however, recognizes only assets that are expected to be realized and eliminates the complexity of valuation of the asset and separate allowance, particularly where the tax rates and laws for the periods of realization are required.

Assume Jensen Corp. has a deductible temporary difference or loss carryforward of $1 million at the end of its first year of operations. Its tax rate is 40% and a future tax asset of $400,000 ($1,000,000 × 40%) is recognized on the basis that it is more likely than not that sufficient taxable income will be generated in the future. The journal entry to record the future income tax benefit and the change in the future tax asset is:

Future Income Tax Asset	400,000	
Future Income Tax Benefit		400,000

If, at the end of the next period, the deductible temporary difference or loss carryforward remains at $1 million but now only $750,000 is more likely than not to be used, the future tax asset expected to be realized is recalculated to be 40% of $750,000, or $300,000. The following entry is made to adjust the asset account.

Future Income Tax Expense	100,000	
Future Income Tax Asset		100,000

Guidance is provided in the *Handbook* on how to determine if it is more likely than not that future taxable income will be available, and the need to exercise judgement in weighing the impact of evidence is emphasized. All available evidence, both positive and negative, should be carefully considered in determining the appropriate value for the future tax account. The following **possible sources of taxable income may be available under the tax law to realize a tax benefit** for deductible temporary differences and tax loss carryovers:

1. future reversals of existing taxable temporary differences
2. future taxable income exclusive of reversing temporary differences and loss carryforwards
3. taxable income in prior carryback years and
4. tax-planning strategies that would, if necessary, be implemented to realize a future income tax asset. Tax strategies are actions that are prudent, feasible, and that would be applied.[15]

Forming a conclusion to recognize a future tax asset is difficult when there is negative evidence such as cumulative losses in recent years. Other examples of **negative evidence** include:

- a history of tax losses or income tax reductions expiring unused
- losses expected in early future years (by a presently profitable entity)
- unsettled circumstances that, if unfavourably resolved, would adversely affect future operations and profit levels on a continuing basis in future years, and
- a carryback, carryforward period that is so brief that it would limit realization of tax benefits, particularly if the enterprise operates in a traditionally cyclical business.[16]

---

[14] *Ibid.*, par. .30.

[15] *Ibid.*, par. .25.

[16] *Ibid.*, par. .27.

Examples of **positive evidence** that might support a conclusion to recognize a future tax asset when there is negative evidence include:

- sufficient existing taxable temporary differences that would result in taxable amounts against which tax losses or reductions can be applied
- existing contracts or firm sales backlog that will produce more than enough taxable income to realize the future tax asset based on existing sale prices and cost structures
- an excess of fair value over the tax basis of the entity's net assets in an amount sufficient to realize the future tax asset, and
- A strong earnings history exclusive of the loss that created the future deductible amount coupled with evidence indicating that the loss is an aberration rather than a continuing condition.[17]

Section 3465 also recommends that the future tax asset account be reviewed to determine whether conditions have changed such that it is now reasonable to **recognize a future tax asset that was previously unrecognized**. If so, a future income tax asset should be recognized to the extent it is more likely than not to be realized.[18] The associated tax benefit is recognized in the income statement of the same period.

Merit Industries Inc. reports its losses available for carryforward in Note 12 to its financial statements for the year ended August 31, 2000.

ILLUSTRATION 19-37
Loss Carryforward Note

MERIT INDUSTRIES INC.
(formerly Harben Industries Ltd.)
Notes to the Consolidated Financial Statements
August 31, 2000

12. Income taxes (in part)

For tax purposes the Company has non-capital losses carry forward, capital losses carry forward, and share issue costs, the future benefits of which have not been recorded in these financial statements as follows:

	Year Ended August 31, 2000	Seven Months Ended August 31, 1999
Future tax benefit of non-capital losses carryforward	$804,275	$—
Future tax benefit of capital losses carryforward	21,263	—
Allowance for future tax benefit of tax losses carryforward	(825,538)	—
Future tax benefit of share issue costs	28,035	—
Allowance for future tax benefit of share issue costs	(28,035)	—
	$ —	$—

The Company's capital losses carryforward of $69,945 can be carried forward indefinitely but only used to offset future taxable capital gains. The Company's non-capital losses carryforward of $1,763,760 expire as follows:

2001	$134,621
2002	176,219
2003	414,027
2004	569,456
2005	332,482
2006	54,870
2007	82,085

In this case, Merit indicates the future tax asset amount and the 100% allowance against the asset value. The effect is the same as not recognizing the future tax asset at all.

---

[17] *Ibid.*, par. .28.

[18] *Ibid.*, par. .31(b).

INTRAPERIOD TAX ALLOCATION

Objective

Another objective of accounting for income taxes is identified in *Handbook* Section 3465.07: **to reflect the cost or benefit related to income tax assets and liabilities in a manner consistent with the transaction or event giving rise to the asset or liability.** In general, this refers to the fact that the current and future income tax expense (benefit) of the current period related to discontinued operations, extraordinary items, adjustments reported in retained earnings, and capital transactions should be reported with the item to which it relates. This approach to allocating taxes *within* the financial statements of the current period is referred to as intraperiod tax allocation. **Interperiod tax allocation**, on the other hand, reflects the appropriate allocation of taxes *between years*.

To illustrate, assume that Copy Doctor Inc. has an ordinary loss from continuing operations of $500,000. The tax rate is 35%. In addition, the company has an extraordinary gain of $900,000, of which $210,000 is not taxable. Accounting and taxable income and income taxes payable are calculated below.

ILLUSTRATION 19-38
Tax Calculations with Extraordinary Item

	Ordinary Income (Loss)	Extraordinary Gain (Loss)	Total
Accounting income (loss)	($500,000)	$900,000	$400,000
Less nontaxable gain	—	(210,000)	(210,000)
Taxable income (loss)	($500,000)	$690,000	$190,000
Tax rate	35%	35%	
Income tax payable	($175,000)	$241,500	$66,500

Whenever income tax is required to be separately reported with a particular component of the income statement, prepare your analysis as indicated throughout the chapter, but set up a separate column for each component as illustrated above. The income tax amounts can then be taken directly from the analysis and reported in the income statement as shown below.

ILLUSTRATION 19-39
Income Statement Presentation—Extraordinary Item

Loss before income taxes and extraordinary item	($500,000)
Current income tax benefit from operating loss	175,000
Loss before extraordinary item	(325,000)
Extraordinary gain ($900,000 less income tax of $241,500)	658,500
Net income	$333,500

FINANCIAL STATEMENT PRESENTATION

Balance Sheet Presentation

Income tax assets and liabilities are required to be reported separately from other assets and liabilities on the balance sheet, and current tax assets and liabilities are reported separately from future tax assets and liabilities.[19]

Where an entity differentiates between current and noncurrent assets and liabilities on its balance sheet, future income tax assets and liabilities, in general, should be classified and reported as **one net current amount** and **one net noncurrent amount**. *The classification of an individual future tax liability or asset as current or noncurrent is determined by the classification of the related asset or liability for financial reporting purposes.*[20]

Most companies engage in a large number of transactions that give rise to future income taxes. The balances in the future income tax accounts should be analysed and

---

[19] *Ibid.*, par. .86.

[20] *Ibid.*, par. .87 and .88.

classified on the balance sheet in two categories: one for current amounts, and one for noncurrent amounts. This procedure is summarized as follows.

1. *Classify the amounts as current or noncurrent.* If they are related to a specific asset or liability, they should be classified in the same manner as the related asset or liability. If not so related, they should be classified on the basis of the expected reversal date.

2. *Determine the net current amount* by summing the various future tax assets and liabilities classified as current. If the net result is an asset, report on the balance sheet as a current asset; if a liability, report as a current liability.

3. *Determine the net noncurrent amount* by summing the various future tax assets and liabilities classified as noncurrent. If the net result is an asset, report on the balance sheet as a noncurrent asset included with "Other Assets;" if a liability, report as a long-term liability.

IAS NOTE

IAS 12 requires that all future (deferred) tax assets and liabilities be reported outside of current assets and liabilities.

To illustrate, assume that K. Scoffi Limited has four future tax items at December 31, 2002. An analysis reveals the following.

ILLUSTRATION 19-40
Classification of Temporary Differences as Current or Noncurrent

Temporary Difference	Resulting Future Tax Asset	Liability	Related Balance Sheet Account	Classification
1. Rent collected in advance: recognized when earned for accounting purposes and when received for tax purposes.	$42,000		Unearned Rent	Current
2. Use of straight-line amortization for accounting purposes and accelerated amortization for tax purposes.		$214,000	Equipment	Noncurrent
3. Recognition of profits on instalment sales during period of sale for accounting purposes and during period of collection for tax purposes.		45,000	Instalment Accounts Receivable	Current
4. Warranty liabilities: recognized for accounting purposes at time of sale; for tax purposes at time paid.	12,000		Estimated Liability under Warranties	Current
Totals	$54,000	$259,000		

The future taxes to be classified as current net to a $9,000 asset ($42,000 + $12,000 − $45,000), and the future taxes to be classified as noncurrent net to a $214,000 liability. Consequently, future income taxes appear on the December 31, 2002 balance sheet as indicated below.

Current assets	
Future income tax asset	$9,000
Long-term liabilities	
Future income tax liability	$214,000

ILLUSTRATION 19-41
Balance Sheet Presentation of Future Income Taxes

As indicated earlier, a future tax asset or liability **may not be related** to an asset or liability for financial reporting purposes. One example is research costs that are recognized as expenses when incurred for financial reporting purposes, but that may be deferred and deducted in later years for tax purposes. Another example is a realizable tax loss carryforward. In both cases, a future tax asset is recorded, but there is no related, identifiable asset or liability for financial reporting purposes. In these situations, future income taxes should be classified according to the expected reversal date of the temporary difference or the date the tax benefit is expected to be realized.[21] That is, the tax effect of the temporary differences expected to reverse or be realized in the next fiscal year should be classified as current and the remainder should be reported as noncurrent.

---

[21] *Ibid.*

Income tax payable is reported as a current liability on the balance sheet. Because corporations are required to make instalment payments to Canada Customs and Revenue Agency (CCRA) through the year, a debit balance may result in this account. This is reported as a current asset called Prepaid Income Taxes. Income Tax Refund Receivable, resulting from carrying the current year's tax loss back against previous years' taxable income, is also reported as a current asset. Current income tax liabilities and current income tax assets would ordinarily be netted.[22]

Income Statement Presentation

In addition to requiring the total income tax expense related to income or loss before discontinued operations and extraordinary items to be presented on the face of the income statement, the following items require separate disclosure:

1. current income tax expense, and the future income tax expense related to income or loss before discontinued operations and extraordinary items; and
2. income tax expense related to discontinued operations and to extraordinary items.[23]

Disclosure of major components of income tax expense included in income or loss before discontinued operations and extraordinary items may be useful to financial statement readers, but is not required. This might include the amount of future tax expense related to a change in income tax rates or the reduction in tax expense due to recognition of a previously unrecorded tax loss, for example.

IAS NOTE

In identified situations, IAS 12 requires companies to disclose the nature of the evidence supporting the recognition of a deferred (future) tax asset.

Other Disclosures

For all entities, separate disclosure is required of the cost of current and future income taxes related to items charged or credited to equity, the amount and expiry date of unused tax losses and reductions, and the amount of deductible temporary differences for which no future tax asset has been recognized.[24] Refer to Illustration 19-37 for an example of this type of disclosure.

For public and other specified companies, the following additional disclosures are required:

1. the nature and tax effect of the temporary differences, unused tax losses, and unused tax reductions that give rise to future income tax assets and future income tax liabilities, with disclosure of significant offsetting items included in the future tax asset and liability balances;
2. the major components of income tax expense included in determining net income or loss for the period before discontinued operations and extraordinary items; and
3. a reconciliation of the income tax expense related to net income or loss for the period before discontinued operations and extraordinary items, to the statutory income tax rate or dollar amount, including the nature and amount using percentages or dollar amounts of each significant reconciling item. Significant offsetting items should be disclosed even if there is no variation from the statutory rate.[25]

These latter disclosures are required for several reasons, some of which are discussed below.

---

[22] *Ibid.*, par. .88. Offsetting is permitted only if they relate to the same taxable entity and the same taxation authority. This issue has greater significance for consolidated financial statements.

[23] *Ibid.*, par. .85 and .93.

[24] *Ibid.*, par. .91.

[25] *Ibid.*, par. .92. These additional disclosures are required of entities with debt or equity securities traded in a public market (a stock exchange or over-the-counter market) that are required to file financial statements with a securities commission, entities that provide financial statements in connection with the issue of securities in a public market, life insurance companies, deposit-taking institutions, and cooperative business enterprises.

Assessment of Quality of Earnings. Many investors seeking to assess the quality of a company's earnings are interested in the reconciliation of accounting income to taxable income. Earnings that are enhanced by a favourable tax effect should be examined carefully, particularly if the tax effect is nonrecurring. For example, one year **Wang Laboratories** reported net income of $3.3 million, or 82 cents a share, versus $3.1 million, or 77 cents a share, in the preceding period. The entire increase in net income and then some resulted from a lower effective tax rate.

Better Predictions of Future Cash Flows. Examining the future portion of income tax expense provides information as to whether taxes payable are likely to be higher or lower in the future. A close examination may disclose the company's policy regarding capitalization of costs, recognition of revenue, and other policies giving rise to a difference between income reported on the financial statements and taxable income. As a result, it may be possible to predict upcoming reductions in future tax liabilities leading to a loss of liquidity because actual tax payments will be higher than the tax expense reported on the income statement.[26]

Helpful in Setting Governmental Policy. Understanding the amount companies currently pay and the effective tax rate is helpful to government policymakers. In the early 1970s, when the oil companies were believed to have earned excess profits, many politicians and other interested parties attempted to determine their effective tax rates. Unfortunately, at that time such information was not available in published annual reports.

The recommendations included in *Handbook* Section 3465, which became effective in 2000 for public companies, represent a significant change in approach and terminology from the requirements of the superceded sections. Companies were required to apply the new standards on a retroactive basis, and, although restatement of prior years' financial statements was encouraged, it was not compulsory. Excerpts from the 2000 financial statements of **Canfor Corporation** are provided below to illustrate the extensive disclosures relative to corporate income taxes.

CANFOR CORPORATION
Year ended December 31
(thousands of dollars)

Included on the Balance Sheet	2000	1999
In current assets		
Income taxes recoverable	$ 2,972	—
Future income taxes (Note 13)	27,983	—
In current liabilities		
Income taxes payable	—	$ 88,828
In noncurrent liabilities		
Future income taxes (net) (Note 13)	363,858	139,058
Included on the Income Statement		
Income tax expense (Note 13)	$ 83,756	$ 75,996

NOTES TO THE CONSOLIDATED FINANCIAL STATEMENTS
1. Accounting Policies (in part)
Changes in accounting policies
The change in accounting for income taxes, which has been applied retroactively without restatement of prior periods, reflects the tax effect of differences between the book and tax basis of assets and liabilities based on enacted tax rates. Previously, deferred income taxes reflected the tax effect, based on historical tax rates, of revenue and expense items reported for accounting purposes in periods different than for tax purposes. The cumulative effect, as at January 1, 2000, of adopting this new accounting policy was to increase fixed assets by $126.4 million, increase future income tax liabilities (previously described as deferred income taxes) by $185.5 million and reduce retained earnings by $59.1 million.

ILLUSTRATION 19-42
Disclosure of Income
Taxes—Canfor Corporation

Go to the Digital Tool for
additional examples of future
tax disclosures.

---

[26] An article by R. P. Weber and J. E. Wheeler, "Using Income Tax Disclosures to Explore Significant Economic Transactions," *Accounting Horizons*, September 1992, discusses how deferred tax disclosures can be used to assess the quality of earnings and to predict future cash flows.

✓ **Income Taxes**

Canfor accounts for income taxes using the liability method. Under this method, future income tax assets and liabilities are determined based on the temporary differences between the accounting basis and the tax basis of assets and liabilities. These temporary differences are measured using the current tax rates and laws expected to apply when these differences reverse. Future tax benefits, such as capital loss carry-forwards, are recognized to the extent that realization of such benefits is considered more likely than not. The effect on future tax assets and liabilities of a change in income tax rates is recognized in earnings in the period that includes the substantive enactment date.

13. Income Taxes

The tax effects of the significant components of temporary differences that give rise to future income tax assets and liabilities are as follows:

(thousands of dollars)	2000 Current	2000 Long Term
Future income tax assets		
Capital loss carry forward	$ —	$33,741
Accruals not currently deductible	25,038	15,972
Post employment benefits	—	8,454
Other	2,945	2,918
	$27,983	$61,085
Future income tax liabilities		
Depreciable capital assets	$ —	$(401,148)
Deferred pension costs	—	(23,589)
Other	—	(206)
	—	$(424,943)
Future income taxes, net	$27,983	$(363,858)

The components of income tax expense are as follows:

(thousands of dollars)	2000	1999
Current	$70,896	$60,924
Future	12,664	11,642
Affiliates	196	3,430
	$83,756	$75,996

The reconciliation of income taxes calculated at the statutory rate to the actual income tax provision is as follows:

(thousands of dollars)	2000*	1999*
Accounting net earnings before income taxes	$209,332	$182,907
Income tax expense at statutory tax rate	82,686	72,248
Large corporation tax	2,796	2,317
Amounts not deductible for tax purposes and other tax adjustments	(1,726)	1,431
Income tax expense	$83,756	$75,996
Effective income tax rate	40.0%	41.5%

The 1999 figures were calculated using the tax allocation method (deferred taxes).
The 2000 figures have been prepared using the liability method (future taxes) (Note 1).

REVIEW OF THE ASSET-LIABILITY METHOD

OBJECTIVE 12

Describe key aspects of the asset-liability (liability) method and identify outstanding issues with this method.

North American standard setters believe that the asset-liability method (sometimes referred to as the liability approach) is the most consistent method of accounting for income taxes. One objective of this approach is to recognize the amount of taxes payable or refundable for the current year. A second objective is to recognize future tax liabilities and assets for the future tax consequences of events that have been recognized in the financial statements or tax returns.

To implement the objectives, the following basic principles are applied in accounting for income taxes at the date of the financial statements:

1. A current tax liability or asset is recognized for the estimated taxes payable or refundable on the tax return for the current year.

2. A future tax liability or asset is recognized for the estimated future tax effects attributable to temporary differences and carryforwards.

3. The measurement of current and future tax liabilities and assets is based on the income tax rates and laws expected to apply when the liability is settled or asset is realized, normally those enacted at the balance sheet date.

4. The measurement of future tax assets is reduced, if necessary, by the amount of any tax benefits that, based on available evidence, are not expected to be realized.

The procedures for determining the future income tax amounts are shown graphically in Illustration 19-43.

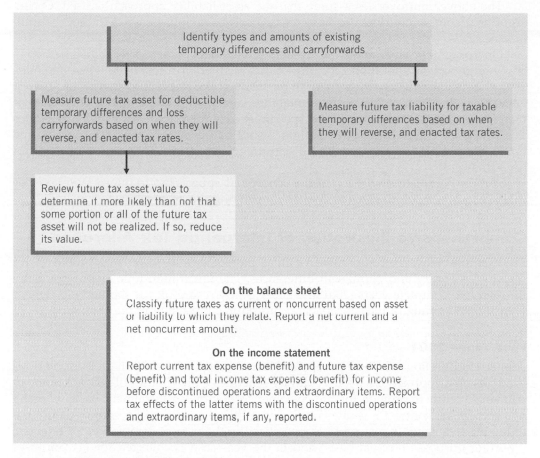

INTERNATIONAL INSIGHT

Nations that recognize future taxes using the liability method include, among others, Australia, Germany, the U.K., and Spain. The European Directives do not specify the accounting for future taxes.

ILLUSTRATION 19-43
Procedures for Calculating and Reporting Future Income Taxes

Some Conceptual Questions

The asset-liability method is the approach that the AcSB deemed most appropriate to record future income taxes. However, some conceptual questions remain. Presented below are three important issues.

1. *Failure to discount.* Without discounting the asset or liability (that is, failing to consider its present value), financial statements do not indicate the appropriate benefit of tax deferral or the burden of tax prepayment. Thus, comparability of the financial statements is impaired because a dollar related to short-term deferral appears to be of the same value as a dollar of longer-term deferral.

2. *Classification issue.* The standards call for future tax assets and liabilities to be classified on the balance sheet based on the classification of the underlying asset or liability that caused the temporary difference. Many take the position that future taxes should be classified relative to when the difference will reverse and therefore disagree with the present requirements.

3. *Dual criteria for recognition of future tax asset.* Many believe that future deductible amounts arising from net operating loss carryforwards are different

from future deductible amounts arising from normal operations. One rationale provided is that a future tax asset arising from normal operations results in a tax prepayment—a prepaid tax asset. In the case of loss carryforwards, no tax prepayment has been made.

Others argue that realization of a loss carryforward is less likely—and thus should require a more severe test—than for a net deductible amount arising from normal operations. Some have suggested that the test be changed from "more likely than not" to "probable" realization. Still others have indicated that because of the nature of net operating losses, future tax assets should never be established for these items.

The above controversies assume that the asset-liability approach is used. Others argue that completely different types of approaches should be used to report future income taxes.

Go to the Digital Tool for a discussion of other conceptual approaches to interperiod tax allocation.

On a pragmatic level, many think that the complexity of the asset-liability method—and interperiod tax allocation generally—is not justified on a cost-benefit basis. In mid-2001, the AcSB issued an exposure draft on "Differential Reporting" that would permit enterprises that have no public accountability (and with the unanimous consensus of their shareholders) to use a number of specific, less complex accounting methods. Under this proposal, the taxes payable method would be permitted to account for income taxes, along with selective required disclosures.[27] As of late 2001, this issue had not been finalized.

A more complete discussion of the conceptual approaches to interperiod tax allocation is available on the Digital Tool accompanying this text.

Comprehensive Illustration of Interperiod Tax Allocation

The example below is a comprehensive illustration of a future income tax problem with several temporary and permanent differences. The illustration follows one company through two complete years (2001 and 2002). Study it carefully. It should help cement your understanding of the concepts and procedures presented in the chapter.

First Year—2001

Allman Corporation, which began operations at the beginning of 2001, produces various products on a contract basis. Each contract generates a gross profit of $80,000. Some of Allman's contracts provide for the customer to pay on an instalment basis whereby one-fifth of the contract revenue is collected in the year of the sale and in each of the following four years. Gross profit is recognized in the year of completion for financial reporting purposes (accrual basis) and in the year cash is collected for tax purposes (instalment basis).

Presented below is information related to Allman's operations for 2001:

1. In 2001, the company completed seven contracts that allow for the customer to pay on an instalment basis. The related gross profit of $560,000 on instalment sales of $1.5 million (to be collected at $300,000 per year beginning in 2001) is recognized for financial reporting purposes, whereas only $112,000 of gross profit on instalment sales was reported on the 2001 tax return. Future collections on the related instalment receivables are expected to result in taxable amounts of $112,000 in each of the next four years.

2. At the beginning of 2001, Allman Corporation purchased depreciable assets with a cost of $540,000. For financial reporting purposes, Allman amortizes these assets using the straight-line method over a six-year service life. For tax purposes, the assets fall into capital cost allowance (CCA) Class 8, permitting a 20% rate, and for the first year the half-year rule is applied. The amortization and net value schedules for both financial reporting and tax purposes follow:

---

[27] *CICA Exposure Draft* "Differential Reporting," July 2001. The taxes payable method recognizes only the current tax expense (benefit) based on tax legislation.

	Accounting			Tax	
Year	Amortization	Carrying Value End of Year		CCA	Undepreciated Capital Cost, End of Year
2001	$ 90,000	$450,000		$ 54,000	$486,000
2002	90,000	360,000		97,200	388,800
2003	90,000	270,000		77,760	311,040
2004	90,000	180,000		62,208	248,832
2005	90,000	90,000		49,766	199,066
2006+	90,000	—		199,066	—
	$540,000			$540,000	

3. The company guarantees its product for two years from the contract completion date. During 2001 the product warranty liability accrued for financial reporting purposes was $200,000, and the amount paid to satisfy the warranty liability was $44,000. The remaining $156,000 is expected to be settled by expenditures of $56,000 in 2002 and $100,000 in 2003.

4. At December 31, 2001, the company accrued non-taxable dividends receivable of $28,000, the only dividend revenue reported for the year.

5. During 2001, non-deductible fines and penalties of $26,000 were paid.

6. Accounting income for 2001 (before the provision for income taxes) amounts to $412,000.

7. The enacted tax rate for 2001 is 50%, and for 2002 and future years is 40%.

8. Allman Corporation has a December 31 year end.

9. The company is expected to have taxable income in all future years.

Taxable Income, Income Tax Payable, Current Income Tax Expense—2001. The first step in determining the company's income tax payable for 2001 is to calculate its taxable income. The calculation—which starts with the income reported on the income statement—is reconciled to taxable income. The taxes levied on the taxable amount are the taxes payable and the current income tax expense for the year.

Accounting income for 2001	$412,000
Permanent differences:	
Nontaxable revenue—dividends	(28,000)
Nondeductible expenses—fines and penalties	26,000
Timing differences:	
Excess gross profit per books ($560,000 – $112,000)	(448,000)
Excess amortization per books ($90,000 – $54,000)	36,000
Excess warranty expense per books ($200,000 – $44,000)	156,000
Taxable income for 2001	$154,000
Income tax payable (current income tax expense) for 2001:	
$154,000 × 50%	$ 77,000

ILLUSTRATION 19-44
Calculation of Taxable Income and Taxes Payable—2001

Future Income Tax Assets and Liabilities at December 31, 2001, and 2001 Future Income Tax Expense. Because future income tax expense is the difference between the opening and closing balance of the net future income tax asset or liability account, the next step is to calculate the future tax asset and liability amounts. These represent the tax effects of the temporary differences at December 31, 2001. The following schedule is helpful in summarizing the temporary differences, the resulting future taxable and deductible amounts, and the correct balance of the future income tax liability or asset account at December 31, 2001.

ILLUSTRATION 19-45
Future Taxable/Deductible
Amounts and Future Tax Liability,
December 31, 2001

	2002	2003	2004	2005	2006+	Total
Future taxable (deductible) amounts						
Instalment sales	$112,000	$112,000	$112,000	$112,000		$448,000
Amortization	(7,200)	12,240	27,792	40,234	(109,066)	(36,000)
Warranty costs	(56,000)	(100,000)				(156,000)
Net taxable (deductible) amount	$48,800	$24,240	$139,792	$152,234	$(109,066)	$256,000
Tax rate enacted for year	40%	40%	40%	40%	40%	
Net future tax liability (asset)	$19,520	$9,696	$55,917	$60,894	$(43,627)	$102,400

The temporary difference caused by the use of the accrual method for financial reporting purposes and the instalment method for tax purposes results in future taxable amounts; hence, a future tax liability exists. Because of the instalment contracts completed in 2001, a temporary difference of $448,000 originates that will reverse in equal amounts over the next four years.

The $36,000 **less CCA** than amortization in 2001 means that in the future, there will be $36,000 **more CCA** deductible for tax purposes than amortization taken on the books. Comparing the CCA and amortization schedule over the next few years illustrates that in some years (2002 and 2006+), excess CCA will be claimed while in others (2003, 2004, and 2005), less CCA than amortization will be claimed. These net out to $36,000 more CCA than amortization in the future. The effects must be assigned to the specific years so the tax effect in each specific year can be determined.

The third temporary difference, caused by different methods of accounting for warranties, will result in deductible amounts in each of 2002 and 2003 as this difference reverses. In summary, if taxable income in a future period is increased, this is a future taxable amount; if taxable income is reduced in the future, it is a deductible amount.

The tax effect is determined year-by-year by applying the enacted rate for each specific year. In this case, because the future tax rates are identical, the future tax liability could have been calculated by simply applying the 40% rate to the net taxable amount at the end of 2001 of $256,000. Note that it is only the **net** future tax liability that has been calculated. **Some may prefer to calculate separately the future tax asset and the future tax liability balances as indicated in the following schedule** along with the determination of the future income tax expense for the year.

ILLUSTRATION 19-46
Determination of Future Income
Tax Expense—2001

		Tax Rate (All future periods)	Future Income Tax Asset	Future Income Tax Liability
Future taxable amounts				
Instalment sales	$448,000	40%		$179,200
Future deductible amounts				
Amortization	$ 36,000	40%	$14,400	
Warranty costs	$156,000	40%	62,400	
			$76,800	$179,200
Future income tax liability, Dec. 31/01				$179,200
Less future income tax asset, Dec. 31/01				76,800
Net future income tax liability, Dec. 31/01				$102,400
Net future income tax liability, opening balance				–0–
Increase in liability account = future income tax expense				$102,400

Income Tax Accounting Entries—2001. The entries to record current and future income taxes for 2001 are as follows:

Current Income Tax Expense	77,000	
Income Tax Payable (Illustration 19-44)		77,000
Future Income Tax Expense	102,400	
Future Income Tax Liability[28]		102,400

Financial Statement Presentation—2001. Future tax assets and liabilities are classified as current and noncurrent on the balance sheet based on the classifications of related assets and liabilities that underlie the temporary differences. They are then summarized into one net current and one net noncurrent amount. The classification of Allman's future tax account at the end of 2001 is shown below.

Balance Sheet Account	Temporary Difference	Resulting Future Tax (Asset)	Liability	Related Account Classification
Instalment receivables	$448,000		$179,200	Current
Depreciable assets	(36,000)	(14,400)		Noncurrent
Liability for warranties	(156,000)	(62,400)		Current
		$(76,800)	$179,200	

ILLUSTRATION 19-47
Classification of Future Tax Asset/Liability Account

For the first temporary difference, the related asset on the balance sheet is the instalment accounts receivable. That asset is classified as a current asset because the company has a trade practice of selling to customers on an instalment basis; hence, the resulting future tax liability is classified as a current liability. The plant assets are classified as noncurrent; therefore, the resulting future tax asset is classified as noncurrent. Since Allman's operating cycle is at least four years in length, the entire $156,000 warranty obligation is classified as a current liability and the related future tax asset of $62,400 is classified as current.[29]

The balance sheet at the end of 2001 reports the following amounts.

BALANCE SHEET, DECEMBER 31, 2001 (partial)

Other (noncurrent) assets		
Future income tax asset		$14,400
Current liabilities		
Income tax payable		$77,000
Future income tax liability ($179,200 − $62,400)		116,800

ILLUSTRATION 19-48
Financial Statement Presentation—2001

INCOME STATEMENT, YEAR ENDED DECEMBER 31, 2001 (partial)

Income before income tax		$412,000
Income tax expense		
Current	$ 77,000	
Future	102,400	179,400
Net income		$232,600

---

[28] Two accounts could have been used here: a debit to a Future Income Tax Asset of $76,800 and a credit to a Future Income Tax Liability of $179,200. The entry given above assumes that only one "control" account is used with the details about the individual temporary differences kept separately in subsidiary accounts or in a file outside the ledger accounts.

[29] If Allman's operating cycle was less than one year in length and the instalment receivables and warranty obligation were classified on the balance sheet partially as current and partially as noncurrent items, then the future tax amounts would have to be allocated between current and noncurrent. A reasonable basis on which to allocate the future tax amounts is to recognize as current assets and liabilities the tax effects of that portion of the temporary differences that will reverse in the next year. The remainder is considered noncurrent. For example, in Allman's case, since $112,000 of the temporary difference related to the instalment receivables is expected to reverse in 2002, the current portion of the related future tax liability is $112,000 × 40% = $44,800; and the noncurrent portion is $179,200 − $44,800 = $134,400. Alternatively, the allocation could be based on the proportion of the asset or liability classified as current and long-term. In this case, $300,000/$1,200,000 or ¼ of $179,200 = $44,800 would be classified as current, the same as the alternative suggested above. Different amounts would result where the temporary differences reverse on a basis different than the method used for the balance sheet classification of the asset or liability.

Second Year—2002

1. During 2002, the company collected one-fifth of the sales price from customers for the receivables arising from contracts completed in 2001. Recovery of the remaining receivables is still expected to result in taxable amounts of $112,000 in each of the following three years.

2. In 2002, the company completed four new contracts with a total selling price of $1 million (to be paid in five equal instalments beginning in 2002) and gross profit of $320,000. For financial reporting purposes, the full $320,000 is recognized in 2002, whereas for tax purposes the gross profit is deferred and taken into taxable income as the cash is received; that is, one-fifth or $64,000 in 2002 and one-fifth in each of 2003 to 2006.

3. During 2002, Allman continued to amortize the assets acquired in 2001 according to the amortization and CCA schedules that appear on page 935. Therefore, amortization expense amounted to $90,000 and CCA of $97,200 was claimed for tax purposes.

4. Information about the product warranty liability account and timing of warranty expenditures at the end of 2002 is reported below.

ILLUSTRATION 19-49
Warranty Liability and Expenditure Information

Balance of liability at beginning of 2002	$156,000
Expense for 2002 income statement purposes	180,000
Amount paid for contracts completed in 2001	(62,000)
Amount paid for contracts completed in 2002	(50,000)
Balance of liability at end of 2002	$224,000
Estimated warranty expenditures:	
$ 94,000 in 2003 due to 2001 contracts	
$ 50,000 in 2003 due to 2002 contracts	
$ 80,000 in 2004 due to 2002 contracts	
$224,000	

5. During 2002, non-taxable dividend revenue was $24,000.

6. A loss of $172,000 was accrued for financial reporting purposes because of pending litigation. This amount is not tax deductible until the period the loss is realized, which is estimated to be 2010.

7. Accounting income for 2002 is $504,800.

8. The tax rate in effect for 2002 is 40%; tax rate increases have been enacted for 2003 and subsequent years at 42%.

Taxable Income, Income Tax Payable, Current Income Tax Expense—2002. The calculation of taxable income, income tax payable, and current income tax expense for 2002 is illustrated below.

ILLUSTRATION 19-50
Calculation of Taxable Income and Taxes Payable—2002

Accounting income for 2002	$504,800
Permanent difference:	
Nontaxable revenue—dividends	(24,000)
Timing differences:	
Collection on 2001 instalment sales	112,000
Excess gross profit per books—2002 contracts ($320,000 − $64,000)	(256,000)
Excess CCA ($97,200 − $90,000)	(7,200)
Payments on warranties from 2001 contracts	(62,000)
Excess warranty expense per books—2002 contracts ($180,000 − $50,000)	130,000
Loss accrual per books	172,000
Taxable income for 2002	$569,600
Income tax payable (current income tax expense) for 2002: $569,600 × 40%	$227,840

Future Income Tax Assets and Liabilities at December 31, 2002, and 2002 Future Income Tax Expense. The next step is to determine the correct balance of the net future income tax asset or liability account at December 31, 2002. The amount required to adjust this account to its correct balance is the future income tax expense/benefit for 2002.

The following schedule is helpful in summarizing the temporary differences existing at the end of 2002 and the resulting future taxable and deductible amounts.

	Future Years				
	2003	2004	2005	2006+	Total
Future taxable (deductible) amounts:					
Instalment sales—2001	$112,000	$112,000	$112,000		$336,000
Instalment sales—2002	64,000	64,000	64,000	$ 64,000	$256,000
Amortization	12,240	27,792	40,234	(109,066)	(28,800)
Warranty costs	(144,000)	(80,000)			(224,000)
Loss accrual				(172,000)	(172,000)
Net taxable (deductible) amount	$ 44,240	$123,792	$216,234	$(217,066)	$167,200
Tax rate enacted for year	42%	42%	42%	42%	
Net future tax liability (asset)	$ 18,581	$ 51,993	$ 90,818	$ (91,168)	$ 70,224

ILLUSTRATION 19-51
Future Taxable/Deductible Amounts and Future Tax Liability, December 31, 2002

The temporary difference caused by the use of the accrual method for financial reporting purposes and the instalment method for tax purposes results in future taxable amounts; hence, a future tax liability exists. A taxable temporary difference of $336,000 remains on the contracts completed in 2001, and $256,000 relates to the 2002 contracts.

To the end of 2002, $28,800 less CCA has been claimed than amortization. In the future there will be $28,800 **more CCA deductible for tax purposes** than amortization taken on the books. The temporary difference due to warranty costs will result in deductible amounts in each of 2003 and 2004 as this difference reverses, and the $172,000 loss not deductible for tax purposes this year will be deductible in the future.

Again, because the future tax rates are identical, the future tax liability could have been calculated by simply applying the 42% rate to the net taxable amount at the end of 2002 of $167,200. For those who prefer to calculate the future tax asset and the future tax liability balances separately, the calculations are shown on the following schedule along with the determination of the future income tax expense for the year.

		Tax Rate (All future periods)	Future Income Tax Asset	Future Income Tax Liability
Future taxable amounts				
2001 instalment sales	$336,000	42%		$141,120
2002 instalment sales	$256,000	42%		107,520
Future deductible amounts				
Amortization	$ 28,800	42%	$ 12,096	
Warranty costs	$224,000	42%	94,080	
Loss accrual	$172,000	42%	72,240	
			$178,416	$248,640
Future income tax liability, Dec. 31/02				$248,640
Less future income tax asset, Dec. 31/02				178,416
Net future income tax liability, Dec. 31/02				$ 70,224
Net future income tax liability, Dec. 31/01				102,400
Decrease in liability account = future income tax benefit				$ (32,176)

ILLUSTRATION 19-52
Determination of Future Income Tax Expense/Benefit—2002

Income Tax Accounting Entries—2002. The entries to record current and future income taxes for 2002 are as follows:

Current Income Tax Expense	227,840	
Income Tax Payable (Illustration 19-50)		227,840
Future Income Tax Liability	32,176	
Future Income Tax Benefit[30]		32,176

---

[30] Refer to footnote 28. Two accounts could have been used here: a debit of $101,616 to a Future Income Tax Asset (i.e., $178,416 − $76,800) and a credit to a Future Income Tax Liability of $69,440 (i.e., $248,640 − $179,200).

Financial Statement Presentation—2002. The classification of Allman's future tax account at the end of 2002 is shown below.

ILLUSTRATION 19-53
Classification of Future Tax Asset/Liability Account

Balance Sheet Account	Temporary Difference	Resulting Future Tax (Asset)	Resulting Future Tax Liability	Related Account Classification
Instalment receivables (total)	$592,000		$248,640	Current
Depreciable assets	(28,800)	(12,096)		Noncurrent
Liability for warranties	(224,000)	(94,080)		Current
Loss accrual	(172,000)	(72,240)		Noncurrent
	$167,200	$(178,416)	$248,640	

The new temporary difference introduced in 2002 due to the litigation loss accrual results in a litigation obligation that is classified as a long-term liability. Therefore, the related future tax asset is noncurrent. The balance sheet at the end of 2002 and the 2002 income statement report the following amounts.

ILLUSTRATION 19-54
Financial Statement Presentation—2002

BALANCE SHEET, DECEMBER 31, 2002 (partial)

Other (noncurrent) assets	
Future income tax asset ($12,096 + $72,240)	$ 84,336
Current liabilities	
Income tax payable	$227,840
Future income tax liability ($248,640 − $94,080)	$154,560

INCOME STATEMENT, YEAR ENDED DECEMBER 31, 2002 (partial)

Income before income tax		$504,800
Income tax expense		
Current	$227,840	
Future	(32,176)*	195,664
Net income		$309,136

*Components may be disclosed

As the major components of income tax expense are required to be disclosed in some cases and are desirable in others, a further analysis can determine how much of the future tax expense is due to a change in the rate of tax used to measure the net future tax liability and how much is due to a change in temporary differences. Because the tax rate for measuring the net future tax liability increased from 40% to 42%, the change in rate results in an increase in the future tax expense. The analysis to explain the $32,176 benefit is as follows.

ILLUSTRATION 19-55
Analysis of Future Income Tax Benefit—2002

Future income tax expense (benefit) due to:		
• Increase in tax rate		
Opening future tax liability at 40%	$102,400	
Opening future tax liability at 42% ($256,000 × .42)	107,520	$5,120
• Originating and reversing timing differences during 2002		
Opening future tax liability at 42%	107,520	
Ending future tax liability at 42%	70,224	
Decrease in net future tax liability		(37,296)
Change in future income tax liability and future income tax expense (benefit) for 2002		$(32,176)

Summary of Learning Objectives

1 Explain the difference between accounting income and taxable income. Accounting income (income reported on the income statement before income taxes) is calculated in accordance with generally accepted accounting principles. Taxable income is calculated in accordance with prescribed tax legislation and regulations. Because tax legislation and GAAP have different objectives, accounting income and taxable income frequently differ.

2 Explain what a taxable temporary difference is and why a future tax liability is recognized. A taxable temporary difference or taxable amount is the difference between the carrying value of an asset or liability and its tax basis such that when the asset is recovered or liability is settled in the future for an amount equal to its carrying value, taxable income of that future period will be increased. Because taxes arise in the future as a result of temporary differences existing at the balance sheet date, the future tax consequences of these taxable amounts must be recognized in the current period as a future tax liability.

3 Explain what a deductible temporary difference is and why a future tax asset is recognized. A deductible temporary difference is the difference between the carrying value of an asset or liability and its tax basis such that when the asset is recovered or a liability is settled in the future for an amount equal to its carrying value, taxable income of that future period will be reduced. Because tax reductions arise in the future as a result of temporary differences existing at the balance sheet date, the future tax consequences of these deductible amounts must be recognized in the current period as a future tax asset.

4 Differentiate between timing, temporary, and permanent differences. Temporary differences are differences between the carrying values of assets and liabilities in the accounts and the values of the same assets and liabilities for tax purposes. The differences originate and change whenever a revenue or expense is recognized in a different accounting period for tax purposes than for financial reporting purposes. In any given year, there are usually differences between income reported on the financial statements and taxable income on the tax return. Those that had no past and have no future tax consequences are known as permanent differences. Their effect is confined to the current period. Those that relate to recognizing revenues and expenses in different periods for book and tax purposes are known as timing differences. Timing differences, therefore, initiate and cause changes in the amount of temporary differences.

5 Prepare analyses and related journal entries to record income tax expense when there are multiple temporary differences. With multiple differences, the following steps should be followed: (1) calculate taxable income and taxes payable; (2) identify all temporary differences between carrying and tax values at the balance sheet date; (3) calculate the net future income tax asset or liability at the end of the period; (4) compare the opening income tax asset or liability with that at the balance sheet date, the difference being the future income tax expense; (5) prepare the journal entries based on the tax payable or receivable (the current income tax expense or benefit) and the change in the amount of the net future tax asset or liability (the future income tax expense or benefit).

6 Explain the effect of various tax rates and tax rate changes on future income tax accounts. Tax rates other than the current rate may be used only when the future tax rates have been enacted into legislation or substantively enacted. When there is a change in the future tax rate, its effect on the future income tax accounts should be recognized immediately. The effects are reported as an adjustment to future income tax expense in the period of the change.

7 Apply accounting procedures for a tax loss carryback. A company may carry a taxable loss back three years and receive refunds to a maximum of the income taxes paid in those years. Because the economic benefits related to the losses carried back are certain,

KEY TERMS

accounting income, 907

asset-liability method, 907

deductible amount, 909

deductible temporary difference, 909

effective tax rate, 919

future income tax asset, 913

future income tax liability, 910

interperiod tax allocation, 912

intraperiod tax allocation, 928

liability method, 907

loss carryback, 921

loss carryforward, 921

loss for income tax purposes, 921

more likely than not, 913

originating timing difference, 917

permanent difference, 916

reversing timing difference, 917

taxable amount, 909

taxable income, 907

taxable temporary difference, 909

tax loss, 921

temporary difference, 909

timing difference, 916

valuation allowance, 926

they are recognized in the period of the loss as a tax benefit on the income statement and as an asset, Income Tax Refund Receivable, on the balance sheet.

8 Apply accounting procedures and disclosure requirements for a tax loss carryforward. A tax loss can be carried forward and applied against the taxable incomes of the succeeding seven years. If the economic benefits related to the tax loss are more likely than not to be realized because of the likelihood of generating sufficient taxable income during the carryforward period, they can be recognized in the period of the loss as a tax benefit in the income statement and as a future tax asset on the balance sheet. If the economic benefits are not more likely than not to be realized, they should not be recognized in the financial statements. Instead, disclosure is required of the amounts of tax loss carryforwards and their expiry dates. If previously unrecorded tax losses are subsequently used to benefit a future period, the benefit is recognized in that future period.

9 Explain why the future income tax asset account is reassessed at the balance sheet date. Consistent with asset valuation principles in general, every asset must be assessed to ensure it is not reported at an amount in excess of the economic benefits expected to be received from the use or sale of the asset. The economic benefit to be received from the future income tax asset is the reduction in future income taxes payable. If it is unlikely that sufficient taxable income will be generated in the future to allow the entity to benefit from future deductible amounts, the income tax asset may have to be written down.

10 Explain the need for and be able to apply intraperiod tax allocation. Because the income statement is classified into income before discontinued operations and extraordinary items, discontinued operations, and extraordinary items, the income taxes associated with each component should be reported with that component. Taxes related to items reported in retained earnings and those associated with share capital should also be reported with the related items in the financial statements.

11 Identify the reporting and disclosure requirements for corporate income taxes. Income taxes currently payable (or receivable) are reported as a current liability (or current asset) on the balance sheet. Future income tax assets and liabilities are classified as one net current and one net noncurrent amount based on the classification of the asset or liability to which the temporary difference relates. If a future tax asset or liability arose from other than an existing balance sheet account, it is classified according to when the temporary differences are expected to reverse. On the income statement, current and future tax expense must be disclosed for income before discontinued operations and extraordinary items. Separate disclosure is required of the amounts and expiry dates of unused tax losses, the amount of deductible temporary differences for which no future tax asset has been recognized, and any tax expense related to items charged or credited to equity. For companies who have outstanding financing from public markets, additional disclosures are required about temporary differences and unused tax losses, about the major components of income tax expense, and the reasons for the difference between the expected statutory tax rate and the effective rate indicated on the income statement.

12 Describe key aspects of the asset-liability (liability) method and identify outstanding issues with this method. The following basic principles are applied in accounting for income taxes at the date of the financial statements: (1) a current tax liability or asset is recognized for the estimated taxes payable or receivable on the tax return for the current year; (2) a future tax liability or asset is recognized for the estimated future tax effects attributable to temporary differences and carryforwards; (3) the measurement of current and future tax liabilities and assets is based on provisions of the enacted tax law; (4) the measurement of future tax assets is reduced, if necessary, by the amount of any tax benefits that, based on available evidence, are not expected to be realized. Those who agree with this method of comprehensive tax allocation are not all agreed on issues related to whether the future tax amounts should be measured at their discounted present values, the basis on which future tax assets and liabilities are classified, and the degree of certainty that should exist before the benefits of future deductible amounts and tax losses should be given accounting recognition.

BRIEF EXERCISES

•••

BE19-1 In 2002, Gonzales Corporation had accounting income of $168,000 and taxable income of $110,000. The difference is due to the use of different amortization methods for tax and accounting purposes. The effective tax rate is 40%. Calculate the amount to be reported as income taxes payable at December 31, 2002.

BE19-2 At December 31, 2002, Thunderforce Inc. owned equipment that had a book value of $80,000 and a tax basis of $48,000 due to the use of different amortization methods for accounting and tax purposes. The enacted tax rate is 35%. Calculate the amount Thunderforce should report as a future tax liability at December 31, 2002.

BE19-3 At December 31, 2001, Serbius Corporation had a future tax liability of $25,000. At December 31, 2002, the future tax liability is $42,000. The corporation's 2002 current tax expense is $43,000. What amount should Serbius report as total 2002 tax expense?

BE19-4 At December 31, 2002, Spacene Corporation had an estimated warranty liability of $125,000 for accounting purposes and $0 for tax purposes. (The warranty costs are not deductible until paid.) The effective tax rate is 40%. Calculate the amount Spacene should report as a future tax asset at December 31, 2002.

BE19-5 At December 31, 2001, Next Inc. had a future tax asset of $35,000. At December 31, 2002, the future tax asset is $59,000. The corporation's 2002 current tax expense is $61,000. What amount should Next report as total 2002 tax expense?

BE19-6 At December 31, 2002, Stargal Corporation has a future tax asset of $200,000. After a careful review of all available evidence, it is determined that it is more likely than not that $80,000 of this future tax asset will not be realized. Prepare the necessary journal entry.

BE19-7 Steagal Corporation had income before income taxes of $175,000 in 2002. Steagal's current income tax expense is $40,000, and future income tax expense is $30,000. Prepare Steagal's 2002 income statement, beginning with income before income taxes.

BE19-8 Jazman Inc. had accounting income of $154,000 in 2002. Included in the calculation of that amount is insurance expense of $4,000, which is not deductible for tax purposes. In addition, the CCA for tax purposes exceeds accounting amortization by $14,000. Prepare Jazman's journal entry to record 2002 taxes, assuming a tax rate of 45%.

BE19-9 Minator Corporation has a taxable temporary difference related to amortization of $630,000 at December 31, 2002. This difference will reverse as follows: 2003, $42,000; 2004, $294,000; and 2005, $294,000. Enacted tax rates are 34% for 2003 and 2004, and 40% for 2005. Calculate the amount Minator should report as a future tax asset or liability at December 31, 2002.

BE19-10 At December 31, 2001, Tick Corporation had a future tax liability of $680,000, resulting from future taxable amounts of $2 million and an enacted tax rate of 34%. In May 2002, new income tax legislation is signed into law that raises the tax rate to 38% for 2002 and future years. Prepare the journal entry for Tick to adjust the future tax liability.

BE19-11 Valquois Corporation had the following tax information:

Year	Taxable Income	Tax Rate	Taxes Paid
1999	$300,000	35%	$105,000
2000	$325,000	30%	$ 97,500
2001	$400,000	30%	$120,000

In 2002, Valquois suffered a net operating loss of $450,000, which it elected to carry back. The 2002 enacted tax rate is 29%. Prepare Valquois' entry to record the effect of the loss carryback.

BE19-12 Zoopler Inc. incurred a net operating loss of $500,000 in 2002. Combined income for 1999, 2000, and 2001 was $400,000. The tax rate for all years is 40%. Prepare the journal entries to record the benefits of the carryback and the carryforward, assuming it is more likely than not that the benefits of the loss carryforward will be realized.

BE19-13 Use the information for Zoopler Inc. given in BE19-12. Assume that it is more likely than not that the entire net operating loss carryforward will not be realized in future years. Prepare all the journal entries necessary at the end of 2002.

BE19-14 Vector Corporation has temporary differences at December 31, 2002 that result in the following balance sheet future tax accounts:

Future tax liability—current	$38,000
Future tax asset—current	$52,000
Future tax liability—noncurrent	$96,000
Future tax asset—noncurrent	$27,000

Indicate how these balances will be presented in Vector's December 31, 2002 balance sheet.

BE19-15 LePage Inc. reported income from continuing operations of $66,000, a loss from discontinued operations of $10,000, and an extraordinary gain of $23,000 in 2003, all before income taxes. All items are fully taxable and deductible for tax purposes. Prepare the bottom of the income statement for LePage Inc. beginning with "income from continuing operations before income taxes and extraordinary items", assuming a tax rate of 40%

EXERCISES

E19-1 **(One Temporary Difference, Future Taxable Amounts, One Rate, No Beginning Future Taxes)** South Shore Corporation has one temporary difference at the end of 2002 that will reverse and cause taxable amounts of $55,000 in 2003, $60,000 in 2004, and $65,000 in 2005. South Shore's accounting income for 2002 is $300,000 and the tax rate is 30% for all years. There are no future tax accounts at the beginning of 2002.

Instructions
  (a) Calculate taxable income and income taxes payable for 2002.
  (b) Prepare the journal entries to record income taxes for 2002.
  (c) Prepare the income tax expense section of the income statement for 2002, beginning with the line "Income before income taxes."

E19-2 **(Two Differences, No Beginning Future Taxes, Tracked through Two Years)** The following information is available for Wenger Corporation for 2002:
  1. Excess of tax amortization over book amortization, $40,000. This $40,000 difference will reverse in equal amounts over the years 2003–2006.
  2. Deferral, for book purposes, of $20,000 of rent received in advance. The rent will be earned in 2003, but is taxable in 2002.
  3. Accounting income, $300,000.
  4. Tax rate for all years, 40%.

Instructions
  (a) Calculate taxable income for 2002.
  (b) Prepare the journal entries to record income taxes for 2002.
  (c) Prepare the journal entries to record income taxes for 2003, assuming taxable income of $325,000 and no temporary differences except those referred to above.

E19-3 **(One Temporary Difference, Future Taxable Amounts, One Rate, Beginning Future Taxes)** Bandibung Corporation began 2002 with a $92,000 balance in the Future Tax Liability account. At the end of 2002, the related temporary difference amounts to $350,000, and it will reverse evenly over the next two years. Accounting income for 2002 is $525,000, the tax rate for all years is 40%, and taxable income for 2002 is $405,000.

Instructions
  (a) Calculate income taxes payable for 2002.
  (b) Prepare the journal entries to record income taxes for 2002.
  (c) Prepare the income tax expense section of the income statement for 2002 beginning with the line "Income before income taxes."

E19-4 **(Three Differences, Calculate Taxable Income, Entry for Taxes)** Geneva Inc. reports accounting income of $70,000 for 2002. The following items cause taxable income to be different than income reported on the financial statements:

1. Amortization on the tax return is greater than amortization on the income statement by $16,000.
2. Rent collected on the tax return is greater than rent earned on the income statement by $22,000.
3. Non-deductible fines for pollution appear as an expense of $11,000 on the income statement.
4. Geneva's tax rate is 30% for all years and the company expects to report taxable income in all future years. There are no future taxes at the beginning of 2002.

Instructions

(a) Calculate taxable income and income taxes payable for 2002.
(b) Prepare the journal entries to record income taxes for 2002.
(c) Prepare the income tax expense section of the income statement for 2002, beginning with the line "Income before income taxes."
(d) Calculate the effective income tax rate for 2002.

E19-5   (Two Temporary Differences, One Rate, Beginning Future Taxes)   The following facts relate to Kumar Corporation:

1. Future tax liability, January 1, 2002, $40,000.
2. Future tax asset, January 1, 2002, $0.
3. Taxable income for 2002, $95,000.
4. Accounting income for 2002, $200,000.
5. Temporary difference at December 31, 2002, giving rise to future taxable amounts, $240,000.
6. Temporary difference at December 31, 2002, giving rise to future deductible amounts, $35,000.
7. Tax rate for all years, 40%.
8. The company is expected to operate profitably in the future.

Instructions

(a) Calculate income taxes payable for 2002.
(b) Prepare the journal entry to record income taxes for 2002.
(c) Prepare the income tax expense section of the income statement for 2002, beginning with the line "Income before income taxes."

E19-6   (Identify Temporary or Permanent Differences)   Listed below are items that are commonly accounted for differently for financial reporting purposes than they are for tax purposes.

Instructions

For each item below, indicate whether it involves:

(a) A timing difference that will result in future deductible amounts and, therefore, will usually give rise to a future income tax asset.
(b) A timing difference that will result in future taxable amounts and, therefore, will usually give rise to a future income tax liability.
(c) A permanent difference.

Use the appropriate letter to indicate your answer for each.

_____ 1. CCA, a declining-balance method, is used for tax purposes, and the straight-line amortization method is used for financial reporting purposes for some plant assets. A 20% rate is used for both. Ignore the half-year rule.
_____ 2. A landlord collects some rents in advance. Rents received are taxable in the period when they are received.
_____ 3. Non-deductible expenses are incurred in obtaining tax-exempt income.
_____ 4. Costs of guarantees and warranties are estimated and accrued for financial reporting purposes.
_____ 5. Instalment sales are accounted for by the accrual method for financial reporting purposes and the cash basis for tax purposes.
_____ 6. For some assets, straight-line amortization is used for both financial reporting purposes and tax purposes but the assets' lives are shorter for tax purposes.
_____ 7. Interest is received on an investment in tax-exempt government bonds.
_____ 8. Proceeds are received from a life insurance company because of the death of a key officer (the company carries a policy on key officers).
_____ 9. The tax return reports no revenue for the dividends received from taxable Canadian corporations. The cost method is used in accounting for the related investments for financial reporting purposes.
_____ 10. Estimated losses on pending lawsuits and claims are accrued for financial reporting purposes. These losses are tax deductible in the period(s) when the related liabilities are settled.

E19-7 (Terminology, Relationships, Calculations, Entries)

Instructions

Complete the following statements by filling in the blanks:

(a) In a period in which a taxable temporary difference reverses, the reversal will cause taxable income to be _____ (less than, greater than) accounting income.

(b) If a $76,000 balance in Future Tax Asset was calculated by use of a 40% rate, the underlying temporary difference amounts to $_____.

(c) Future taxes _____ (are, are not) recorded to account for permanent differences.

(d) If a taxable temporary difference originates in 2002, it causes taxable income of 2002 to be _____ (less than, greater than) accounting income for 2002.

(e) If total tax expense is $50,000 and future tax expense is $65,000, then the current portion of the expense is referred to as current tax _____ (expense, benefit) of $_____.

(f) If a corporation's tax return shows taxable income of $100,000 for Year 2 and a tax rate of 40%, how much will appear on the December 31, Year 2 balance sheet for "Income tax payable" if the company has made estimated tax payments of $36,500 for Year 2? $_____

(g) An increase in the Future Tax Liability account on the balance sheet is recorded by a _____ (debit, credit) to the Future Income Tax Expense account.

(h) An income statement that reports current tax expense of $82,000 and future tax benefit of $23,000 will report total income tax expense of $_____.

(i) A valuation account may be used whenever it is judged to be _____ that a portion of a future tax asset _____ (will be, will not be) realized.

(j) If the tax return shows total taxes due for the period of $75,000 but the income statement shows total income tax expense of $55,000, the difference of $20,000 is referred to as future tax _____ (expense, benefit).

E19-8 (One Temporary Difference through Three Years, One Rate)   Odessa Corporation reports the following amounts in its first three years of operations:

	2002	2003	2004
Taxable income	160,000	139,000	140,000
Accounting income	200,000	120,000	125,000

The difference between taxable income and accounting income is due to one temporary difference. The tax rate is 40% for all years and the company expects to continue with profitable operations in the future.

Instructions

(a) For each year, (1) identify the amount of the temporary difference originating or reversing during that year, and (2) indicate the amount of the temporary difference at the end of the year.

(b) Indicate the balance in the related future tax account at the end of each year and identify it as either a future tax asset or liability.

E19-9 (Carryback and Carryforward of Tax Loss)   The accounting income (or loss) figures for Spangler Corporation are as follows:

1997	$160,000
1998	250,000
1999	80,000
2000	(160,000)
2001	(380,000)
2002	120,000
2003	100,000

Accounting income (or loss) and taxable income (loss) were the same for all years involved. Assume a 45% tax rate for 1997 and 1998 and a 40% tax rate for the remaining years.

Instructions

Prepare the journal entries for the years 1999 to 2003 to record income tax expense and the effects of the tax loss carrybacks and carryforwards assuming Spangler Corporation uses the carryback provision first. All income and losses relate to normal operations.

E19-10 **(Tax Losses, No Temporary Differences)** Rashad Corporation has accounting income (or loss) equal to taxable income (or loss) from 1996 through 2004 as follows:

	Income (Loss)	Tax Rate
1996	$29,000	30%
1997	40,000	30%
1998	17,000	35%
1999	48,000	50%
2000	(150,000)	40%
2001	90,000	40%
2002	30,000	40%
2003	105,000	40%
2004	(60,000)	45%

Accounting income (loss) and taxable income (loss) were the same for all years since Rashad has been in business. Assume the carryback provision is employed to the extent possible. In recording the benefits of a loss carryforward, assume that it is more likely than not that the related benefits will be realized.

Instructions

(a) What entry(ies) for income taxes should be recorded in 2000?
(b) Indicate what the income tax expense portion of the income statement for 2000 should look like. Assume all income (loss) relates to continuing operations.
(c) What entry for income taxes should be recorded in 2001?
(d) How should the income tax expense section of the income statement for 2001 appear?
(e) What entry for income taxes should be recorded in 2004?
(f) How should the income tax expense section of the income statement for 2004 appear?

E19-11 **(Three Differences, Classify Future Taxes)** At December 31, 2002, Surya Corporation had a net future tax liability of $375,000. An explanation of the items that make up this balance follows.

Temporary Differences	Resulting Balances in Future Taxes
1. Excess of tax amortization over book amortization	$200,000
2. Accrual, for book purposes, of estimated loss contingency from pending lawsuit that is expected to be settled in 2003. The loss will be deducted on the tax return when paid.	(50,000)
3. Accrual method used for book purposes and instalment method used for tax purposes for an isolated instalment sale of an investment.	225,000
	$375,000

In analysing the temporary differences, you find that $30,000 of the amortization temporary difference will reverse in 2003 and $120,000 of the temporary difference due to the instalment sale will reverse in 2003. The tax rate for all years is 40%.

Instructions

Indicate the manner in which future taxes should be presented on Surya Corporation's December 31, 2002 balance sheet.

E19-12 **(Two Temporary Differences, One Rate, Beginning Future Taxes)** The following facts relate to Sabrinad Corporation:

1. Future tax liability, January 1, 2002, $60,000.
2. Future tax asset, January 1, 2002, $20,000.
3. Taxable income for 2002, $105,000.
4. Temporary difference at December 31, 2002, giving rise to future taxable amounts, $230,000.
5. Temporary difference at December 31, 2002, giving rise to future deductible amounts, $95,000.
6. Tax rate for all years, 40%. No permanent differences exist.
7. The company is expected to operate profitably in the future.

Instructions

(a) Calculate the amount of accounting income for 2002.
(b) Prepare the journal entries to record income taxes for 2002.
(c) Prepare the income tax expense section of the income statement for 2002, beginning with the line "Income before income taxes."
(d) Calculate the effective tax rate for 2002. Comment.

E19-13 (One Difference, Multiple Rates, Beginning versus No Beginning Future Taxes)   At the end of 2002, McNevil Corporation has $180,000 of temporary differences that will result in reporting future taxable amounts as follows:

2003	$ 60,000
2004	50,000
2005	40,000
2006	30,000
	$180,000

Tax rates enacted as of the beginning of 2001 are:

2001 and 2002	40%
2003 and 2004	30%
2005 and later	25%

McNevil's taxable income for 2002 is $320,000. Taxable income is expected in all future years.

Instructions
- **(a)** Prepare journal entries for McNevil to record income taxes for 2002, assuming that there were no future taxes at the end of 2001.
- **(b)** Prepare journal entries for McNevil to record income taxes for 2002, assuming that there was a balance of $22,000 in a Future Tax Liability account at the end of 2001.

E19-14 (Future Tax Asset—Different Amounts to Be Realized)   Scapriati Corp. had a future tax asset account with a balance of $150,000 at the end of 2001 due to a single temporary difference of $375,000. At the end of 2002, this same temporary difference has increased to $450,000. Taxable income for 2002 is $820,000. The tax rate is 40% for all years.

Instructions
- **(a)** Record income taxes for 2002, assuming that it is more likely than not that the future tax asset will be realized.
- **(b)** Assuming that it is more likely than not that $30,000 of the future tax asset will not be realized, prepare the journal entries to record income taxes for 2002.

E19-15 (Future Tax Liability, Change in Tax Rate)   Notkovich Inc.'s only temporary difference at the beginning and end of 2002 is caused by a $3 million future gain for tax purposes on an instalment sale of a plant asset. The related receivable (only one-half of which is classified as a current asset) is due in equal instalments in 2003 and 2004. The related future tax liability at the beginning of the year is $1.2 million. In the third quarter of 2002, a new tax rate of 34% is enacted into law and is scheduled to become effective for 2004. Taxable income for 2002 is $5 million and taxable income is expected in all future years.

Instructions
- **(a)** Determine the amount reported as a future tax liability at the end of 2002. Indicate proper classification(s).
- **(b)** Prepare the journal entry (if any) necessary to adjust the future tax liability when the new tax rate is enacted into law.
- **(c)** Draft the income tax expense portion of the income statement for 2002. Begin with the line "Income before income taxes." No permanent differences exist.

E19-16 (Two Temporary Differences, Three Years, Multiple Rates)   Taxable income and accounting income would be identical for Anke Corp. except for its treatment of gross profit on instalment sales and estimated costs of warranties. The following income calculations have been prepared:

Taxable income	2001	2002	2003
Excess of revenues over expenses (excluding two timing differences)	$160,000	$210,000	$90,000
Instalment gross profit collected	8,000	8,000	8,000
Expenditures for warranties	(5,000)	(5,000)	(5,000)
Taxable income	$163,000	$213,000	$93,000

Accounting income	2001	2002	2003
Excess of revenues over expenses (excluding two timing differences)	$160,000	$210,000	$90,000
Instalment gross profit earned	24,000	–0–	–0–
Estimated cost of warranties	(15,000)	–0–	–0–
Income before taxes	$169,000	$210,000	$90,000

The tax rates in effect are: 2001, 40%; 2002 and 2003, 45%. All tax rates were enacted into law on January 1, 2001. No future income taxes existed at the beginning of 2001. Taxable income is expected in all future years.

Instructions

Prepare journal entries to record income taxes for 2001, 2002, and 2003.

E19-17 (**Two Differences, Multiple Rates, No Beginning Future Taxes**) In 2001, Wolff Corporation reported amortization expense of $200,000 in its income statement. On its 2001 income tax return, Wolff reported CCA of $320,000. Wolff's income statement also included $80,000 accrued warranty expense that will be deductible for tax purposes when paid. Wolff reported accounting income of $300,000 in 2001. The enacted tax rates are 35% for 2001 and 2002, and 40% for 2003 and subsequent years. The amortization difference and warranty expense will reverse over the next four years as follows:

	Amortization Difference	Warranty Expense
2002	$40,000	$10,000
2003	35,000	15,000
2004	25,000	25,000
2005	20,000	30,000
	$120,000	$80,000

Instructions

(a) Calculate income taxes payable for 2001.
(b) Prepare journal entries to record income taxes for 2001.
(c) Prepare the income tax expense section of the income statement for 2001, beginning with the line "Income before taxes."

E19-18 (**Two Differences, One Rate, Accounting Loss**) McCarther Inc., in its first year of operations, has an accounting loss even though it has taxable income. A reconciliation between these two amounts for the calendar year 2002 is as follows:

Accounting loss	$ (50,000)
Estimated expenses that will be deductible for tax purposes when paid	2,000,000
Excess of CCA over amortization expense	(1,200,000)
Taxable income	$ 750,000

At the end of 2002, the reported amount of McCarther's depreciable assets in the financial statements is $3 million, and the tax basis of these assets is $1.8 million. Future recovery of the depreciable assets will result in $1.2 million of taxable amounts ($300,000 per year in years 2003 to 2006) over the four-year remaining life of the assets. Also, a $2 million estimated liability for litigation expenses has been recognized in the financial statements in 2002, but the related expenses will be deductible on the tax return in 2005 when the liability is expected to be settled. McCarther expects to report taxable income in the next few years.

Instructions

Prepare the journal entries to record income taxes for 2002, assuming a tax rate of 40% for all periods.

E19-19 (**Three Differences, Multiple Rates**) During 2002, Nicole Corp.'s first year of operations, the company reports accounting income of $250,000. Nicole's enacted tax rate is 45% for 2002 and 40% for all later years. Nicole expects to have taxable income in each of the next five years. The effects on future tax returns of temporary differences existing at December 31, 2002 are summarized below:

	Future Years					
	2003	2004	2005	2006	2007	Total
Future taxable (deductible) amounts:						
Instalment sales	$32,000	$32,000	$32,000			$96,000
Amortization	6,000	6,000	6,000	$6,000	$6,000	30,000
Unearned rent	(50,000)	(50,000)				(100,000)

Instructions

(a) Complete the schedule below to calculate future taxes at December 31, 2002.
(b) Calculate taxable income for 2002.
(c) Prepare the journal entries to record income taxes for 2002.

	Future Taxable (Deductible) Amounts	Tax Rate	December 31, 2002	
			Future Tax	
Temporary Difference			Asset	Liability
Instalment sales	$ 96,000			
Amortization	30,000			
Unearned rent	(100,000)			
Totals	$			

E19-20 **(Two Differences, One Rate)** Stone Corp. establishes a $100 million liability at the end of 2002 for the estimated costs of closing two of its manufacturing facilities. All related closing costs will be paid and deducted on the tax return in 2003. Also, at the end of 2002, the company has $50 million of temporary differences due to excess amortization for tax purposes, $7 million of which will reverse in 2003.

The enacted tax rate for all years is 40%, and the company pays taxes of $64 million on $160 million of taxable income in 2002. Stone expects to have taxable income in 2003.

Instructions

(a) Determine the future taxes to be reported at the end of 2002.
(b) Indicate how the future taxes calculated in (a) are to be reported on the balance sheet.
(c) Assuming that the only future tax account at the beginning of 2002 was a future tax liability of $10 million, draft the income tax expense portion of the income statement for 2002 beginning with the line "Income before income taxes." (Hint: You must first calculate (1) the amount of temporary difference underlying the beginning $10 million future tax liability, then (2) the amount of temporary differences originating or reversing during the year, then (3) the amount of accounting income.)

E19-21 **(Two Differences, No Beginning Future Taxes, Multiple Rates)** Hatcherd Inc. has the following differences between the book basis and tax basis of its assets and liabilities at the end of 2002, its first year of operations.

	Book Basis	Tax Basis
Equipment (net)	$400,000	$340,000
Estimated warranty liability	$200,000	$ –0–

It is estimated that the warranty liability will be settled in 2003. The difference in equipment (net) will result in taxable amounts of $20,000 in 2003, $30,000 in 2004, and $10,000 in 2005. The company has taxable income of $520,000 in 2002. As of the beginning of 2002, the enacted tax rate is 34% for 2002 to 2004, and 30% for 2005. Hatcherd expects to report taxable income through 2005.

Instructions

(a) Prepare the journal entries to record income taxes for 2002.
(b) Indicate how future income taxes will be reported on the balance sheet at the end of 2002.

E19-22 **(Amortization, Temporary Difference over Five Years)** Patrician Corp. purchased depreciable assets costing $600,000 on January 2, 2001. For tax purposes, the company uses CCA in a class that has a 40% rate. For financial reporting purposes, the company uses straight-line amortization over five years. The enacted tax rate is 34% for all years. This amortization difference is the only temporary difference the company has. Assume that Patrician has taxable income of $240,000 in each of the years 2001 to 2005 and that all remaining CCA in 2005 can be deducted in that year.

Instructions

Determine the amount of future income taxes and indicate where it should be reported in the balance sheet for each year from 2001 to 2005.

E19-23 **(Two Temporary Differences, Multiple Rates)** Svetland Inc. has two temporary differences at the end of 2002. The first difference stems from instalment sales and the second one results from the accrual of a loss contingency. Svetland's accounting department has developed a schedule of future taxable and deductible amounts related to these temporary differences as follows:

	2003	2004	2005	2006
Taxable amounts	$40,000	$50,000	$60,000	$80,000
Deductible amounts		(15,000)	(19,000)	
	$40,000	$35,000	$41,000	$80,000

As of the beginning of 2002, the enacted tax rate is 34% for 2002 and 2003 and 38% for 2004 to 2007. At the beginning of 2002, the company had no future income taxes on its balance sheet. Taxable income for 2002 is $500,000. Taxable income is expected in all future years.

Instructions

(a) Prepare the journal entries to record income taxes for 2002.

(b) Indicate how future income taxes would be classified on the balance sheet at the end of 2002.

E19-24 **(Two Differences, One Rate, First Year)** The differences between the book basis and tax basis of Castle Corporation's assets and liabilities of at the end of 2002 are presented below.

	Book Basis	Tax Basis
Accounts receivable	$50,000	$-0-
Litigation liability	30,000	-0-

It is estimated that the litigation liability will be settled in 2003. The difference in accounts receivable will result in taxable amounts of $30,000 in 2003 and $20,000 in 2004. The company has taxable income of $350,000 in 2002 and is expected to have taxable income in each of the following two years. Its enacted tax rate is 34% for all years. The company had no temporary differences at the beginning of 2002. The business operating cycle is two years.

Instructions

(a) Prepare the journal entries to record income taxes for 2002.

(b) Indicate how future income taxes will be reported on the balance sheet at the end of 2002.

E19-25 **(Loss Carryback and Carryforward)** Spamela Inc. reports the following pretax income (loss) for both financial reporting purposes and tax purposes:

Year	Accounting Income (Loss)	Tax Rate
2000	$120,000	34%
2001	90,000	34%
2002	(280,000)	38%
2003	220,000	38%

The tax rates listed were all enacted by the beginning of 2000.

Instructions

(a) Prepare the journal entries for the years 2000 to 2003 to record income taxes, assuming the tax loss is first carried back, and that at the end of 2002, the loss carryforward benefits are judged more likely than not to be realized in the future.

(b) Using the assumption in (a), prepare the income tax section of the 2002 income statement beginning with the line "Loss before income taxes."

(c) Prepare the journal entries for 2002 and 2003, assuming that based on the weight of available evidence, it is more likely than not that one-fourth of the carryforward benefits will not be realized.

(d) Using the assumption in (c), prepare the income tax section of the 2002 income statement beginning with the line "Loss before income taxes."

E19-26 **(Loss Carryback)** Beilman Inc. reports the following accounting income (loss) for both book and tax purposes (assume the carryback provision is used where possible):

Year	Accounting Income (Loss)	Tax Rate
2000	$120,000	40%
2001	90,000	40%
2002	(80,000)	45%
2003	(40,000)	45%

The tax rates listed were all enacted by the beginning of 2000.

Instructions

(a) Prepare the journal entries for years 2000 to 2003 to record income taxes.

(b) Prepare the income tax section of the income statements for the years 2000 to 2003 beginning with the line "Income (loss) before income taxes."

E19-27 **(Tax Loss Carryback and Carryforward)** Meyer Inc. reported the following accounting income (loss) for the years 2000 to 2004:

2000	$240,000
2001	350,000
2002	120,000
2003	(570,000)
2004	180,000

Accounting income (loss) and taxable income (loss) were the same for all years involved. The tax rate was 34% for 2000 and 2001, and 40% for 2002 to 2004, all enacted as of March, 2000. Assume the carryback provision is used first for net losses.

Instructions

(a) Prepare the journal entries for the years 2002 to 2004 to record income taxes, assuming that based on the weight of available evidence, it is more likely than not that one-fifth of the carryforward benefits will not be realized.

(b) Prepare the income tax section of the 2002 to 2004 income statements beginning with the line "Income (loss) before income taxes."

E19-28 **(Intraperiod Tax Allocation)** Hamm Corp. had a profitable year on its regular operations in 2003, reporting $435,000 income before income taxes. Unfortunately, a major decision was handed down by the courts in late November 2003, holding Hamm responsible for environmental damage to prime farmland over a 10-year period. Hamm is not insured for such a risk and the company expects it will cost approximately $2.2 million to deal with this problem. Hamm has reported this as an extraordinary item on its 2003 income statement. $150,000 of this estimate is a fine levied by the province and it is not a deductible expense for tax purposes. The remainder is deductible, but not until 2004 when the costs will actually be incurred.

In completing the tax return for 2003, Hamm noted that its accounting income included $100,000 of dividends from taxable Canadian corporations, gross profit of $55,000 that is not taxable until 2005, and golf club dues for top management in the amount of $12,800. There were no future income tax assets or liabilities on the December 31, 2002 financial statements. The tax rate applicable to 2003 and future years is 38%.

Instructions

(a) Calculate income taxes payable and the amount of any future income tax asset or liability at the end of 2003.

(b) Prepare the journal entries to record income taxes for 2003.

(c) Indicate how income taxes would be reported on the income statement for 2003 by drafting the bottom portion of the statement, beginning with "income before taxes and extraordinary items."

PROBLEMS

P19-1 The following information is available for Swanson Corporation for 2002:

1. CCA reported on the tax return exceeded amortization reported on the income statement by $100,000. This difference will reverse in equal amounts of $25,000 over the years 2003 to 2006.
2. Dividends received from taxable Canadian corporations were $10,000.
3. Rent collected in advance on January 1, 2002 totalled $60,000 for a three-year period. Of this amount, $40,000 was reported as unearned at December 31, for book purposes.
4. The tax rates are 40% for 2002 and 35% for 2003 and subsequent years.
5. Income taxes of $360,000 are due per the tax return for 2002.
6. No future taxes existed at the beginning of 2002.

Instructions

(a) Calculate taxable income for 2002.
(b) Calculate accounting income for 2002.
(c) Prepare the journal entries to record income taxes for 2002 and 2003. Assume taxable income was $980,000 in 2003.
(d) Prepare the income tax expense section of the income statement for 2002, beginning with "Income before income taxes."

P19-2 The accounting income of Kristali Corporation differs from its taxable income throughout each of four years as follows:

Year	Accounting Income	Taxable Income	Tax Rate
2002	$280,000	$180,000	35%
2003	320,000	225,000	40%
2004	350,000	270,000	40%
2005	420,000	580,000	40%

Accounting income for each year includes a non-deductible expense of $30,000 (never deductible for tax purposes). The remainder of the difference between accounting income and taxable income in each period is due to one amortization temporary difference. No future income taxes existed at the beginning of 2002.

Instructions

(a) Prepare journal entries to record income taxes in all four years. Assume that the change in the tax rate to 40% was not enacted until the beginning of 2003.
(b) Draft the income tax section of the income statement for 2003.

P19-3 The following information has been obtained for the Kerdyk Corporation.

1. Prior to 2001, taxable income and accounting income were identical.
2. Accounting income is $1.7 million in 2001 and $1.4 million in 2002.
3. On January 1, 2001, equipment costing $1 million is purchased. It is to be amortized on a straight-line basis over eight years for financial reporting purposes, and is a Class 8 – 20% asset for tax purposes.
4. Lottery winnings of $60,000 was won in 2002 on a ticket purchased out of petty cash. This type of windfall is not taxable.
5. Included in 2002 accounting income is an extraordinary gain of $200,000, which is fully taxable.
6. The tax rate is 35% for all periods.
7. Taxable income is expected in all future years.

Instructions

(a) Calculate taxable income and income tax payable for 2002.
(b) Prepare the journal entry(ies) to record 2002 income taxes.
(c) Prepare the bottom portion of Kerdyk's 2002 income statement, beginning with "Income before income taxes and extraordinary item."
(d) Indicate how future income taxes should be presented on the December 31, 2002 balance sheet.

P19-4 Singh Corp.'s reconciliation of its accounting income to its taxable income for 2002 is as follows:

Accounting income	$24,000,000
Litigation accrual for book purposes	8,000,000
Excess amortization for tax purposes	(3,000,000)
Taxable income	$29,000,000

Prior to 2002, Singh reported no temporary differences. As of the beginning of 2002, enacted tax rates are 35% for 2002 and 2003, and 40% for all subsequent years. It is estimated that the litigation accrual will be settled in 2007 and that the temporary difference due to the excess amortization for tax purposes will reverse equally over the three-year period from 2003 to 2005.

Instructions

(a) Determine the income tax payable, future income taxes, and income tax expense to be reported for 2002, assuming that taxable income is expected in all future years.

(b) Classify the future income taxes calculated in (a) into current and noncurrent components. Explain where the future taxes should appear on the balance sheet.

(c) Determine the income tax payable, future income taxes, and income tax expense for 2002, assuming that net operating losses are expected to appear on tax returns for 2003 through 2007 and taxable income is very likely for 2008 and later years.

(d) Classify the future income taxes calculated in (c) into current and noncurrent components. Explain where the future taxes should appear on the balance sheet.

 P19-5 Mearat Inc. reported the following accounting income (loss) and related tax rates during the years 1997 to 2003:

	Accounting Income (Loss)	Tax Rate
1997	$ 40,000	30%
1998	25,000	30%
1999	60,000	30%
2000	80,000	40%
2001	(200,000)	45%
2002	70,000	40%
2003	90,000	35%

Accounting income (loss) and taxable income (loss) were the same for all years since Mearat began business. The tax rates from 2000 to 2003 were enacted in 2000.

Instructions

(a) Prepare the journal entries for the years 2001 to 2003 to record income taxes. Assume that Mearat uses the carryback provision where possible and expects to realize the benefits of any loss carryforward in the year that immediately follows the loss year.

(b) Indicate the effect the 2001 entry(ies) has on the December 31, 2001 balance sheet.

(c) Indicate how the bottom portion of the income statement, starting with "Loss before income taxes," would be reported in 2001.

(d) Indicate how the bottom portion of the income statement, starting with "Income before income taxes," would be reported in 2002.

(e) Prepare the journal entries for the years 2001 to 2003 to record income taxes, assuming that Mearat uses the carryback provision where possible but is uncertain about the ability to realize the benefits of any loss carryforward in the future.

(f) Based on your entries in (e), indicate how the bottom portion of the income statements for 2001 and 2002 would be reported, beginning with "Income (loss) before income taxes."

P19-6 Presented below are two independent situations related to future taxable and deductible amounts resulting from temporary differences existing at December 31, 2002.

1. Pirates Corp. has developed the following schedule of future taxable and deductible amounts:

	2003	2004	2005	2006	2007
Taxable amounts	$300	$300	$300	$ 200	$100
Deductible amount	—	—	—	(1,400)	—

Pirates reported a net future income tax liability of $540 at January 1, 2002.

2. Eagles Corp. has the following schedule of future taxable and deductible amounts:

	2003	2004	2005	2006
Taxable amounts	$300	$300	$ 300	$300
Deductible amount	—	—	(2,000)	—

Eagles Corp. reported a net future tax asset of $600 at January 1, 2002.

Both Pirates Corp. and Eagles Corp. have taxable income of $3,000 in 2002 and expect to have taxable income in all future years. The tax rates enacted as of the beginning of 2002 are 30% for 2002 to 2005 and 35% for years thereafter. All of the underlying temporary differences relate to noncurrent assets and liabilities.

Instructions

(a) For each of these two situations, prepare journal entries to record income taxes for 2002. Show all calculations.

(b) Determine the future income tax assets or liabilities that will be reported on each company's December 31, 2002 balance sheet and indicate their classification.

P19-7 Gators Corp. sold an investment on an instalment basis. The total gain of $60,000 was reported for financial reporting purposes in the period of sale. The company qualifies to use the instalment method for tax purposes. The instalment period is three years; one-third of the sale price is collected in the period of sale. The tax rate was 35% in 2002 and 30% in 2003 and 2004. The 30% tax rate was not enacted in law until 2003. The accounting and tax data for the three years are shown below.

2002 (35% tax rate)

Accounting income	$130,000
Timing difference	40,000
Taxable income	$ 90,000

2003 (30% tax rate)

Accounting income	$ 70,000
Timing difference	20,000
Taxable income	$ 90,000

2004 (30% tax rate)

Accounting income	$ 70,000
Timing difference	20,000
Taxable income	$ 90,000

Instructions

(a) Prepare the journal entries to record income taxes at the end of each year. No future income taxes existed at the beginning of 2002.

(b) Explain how the future taxes will appear on the balance sheet at the end of each year. (Assume the Instalment Accounts Receivable is classified as a current asset.)

(c) Draft the income tax expense section of the income statement for each year, beginning with "Income before income taxes."

P19-8 The following information was disclosed during the audit of Muster Inc.

1.

Year	Amount Due per Tax Return
2001	$140,000
2002	112,000

2. On January 1, 2001, equipment costing $400,000 is purchased. For financial reporting purposes, the company uses straight-line amortization over a five-year life. For tax purposes, the company uses CCA at a 25% rate.

3. In January 2002, $225,000 is collected in advance rental of a building for a three-year period. The entire $225,000 is reported as taxable income in 2002, but $150,000 of the $225,000 is reported as unearned revenue in 2002 for financial reporting purposes. The remaining amount of unearned revenue will be earned equally in 2003 and 2004.

4. The tax rate is 40% in 2001 and all subsequent periods.

5. No temporary differences existed at the end of 2000. Muster expects to report taxable income in each of the next five years.

Instructions

(a) Determine the amount to report for future income taxes at the end of 2001 and indicate how it should be classified on the balance sheet.

(b) Prepare the journal entry(ies) to record income taxes for 2001.

(c) Draft the income tax section of the income statement for 2001 beginning with "Income before income taxes." (Hint: You must calculate taxable income and then combine that with changes in temporary differences to arrive at accounting income.)

    (d) Determine the future income taxes at the end of 2002 and indicate how they should be classified on the balance sheet.

    (e) Prepare the journal entry(ies) to record income taxes for 2002.

    (f) Draft the income tax section of the income statement for 2002 beginning with "Income before income taxes."

P19-9 Kringe Corporation began operations at the beginning of 2002. The following information pertains to this company.

1. Accounting income for 2002 is $100,000.
2. The tax rate enacted for 2002 and future years is 40%.
3. Differences between the 2002 income statement and tax return are listed below:

    (a) Warranty expense accrued for financial reporting purposes amounts to $5,000. Warranty deductions per the tax return amount to $2,000.

    (b) Gross profit on construction contracts using the percentage-of-completion method for book purposes amounts to $92,000. Gross profit on construction contracts for tax purposes amounts to $62,000.

    (c) Amortization of property, plant, and equipment for financial reporting purposes amounts to $60,000. CCA charged on the tax return amounts to $80,000.

    (d) A $3,500 fine paid for violation of pollution laws was deducted in computing accounting income.

    (e) Dividend revenue earned on an investment is tax-exempt and amounts to $1,400.

    (Assume (a) is short-term in nature; assume (b) is long-term in nature.)

4. Taxable income is expected for the next few years.

Instructions

    (a) Calculate taxable income for 2002.

    (b) Calculate the future taxes at December 31, 2002 that relate to the temporary differences described above. Clearly label them as future tax asset or liability.

    (c) Prepare the journal entry to record income taxes for 2002.

    (d) Draft the income tax expense section of the income statement beginning with "Income before income taxes."

P19-10 At December 31, 2001, the Hewlett Corporation had a temporary difference (related to pensions) and reported a related future tax asset of $40,000 on its balance sheet. At December 31, 2002, Hewlett has five temporary differences. An analysis of these reveals the following.

	Future Taxable (Deductible) Amounts		
Temporary Difference	2003	2004	2005+
1. Pension expense as incurred on the books; deductible when funded for tax purposes	($30,000)	($20,000)	($10,000)
2. Royalties collected in advance; recognized when earned for accounting purposes and when received for tax purposes	(76,000)	—	—
3. Various expenses accrued for accounting purposes; recognized for tax purposes when paid	(24,000)	—	—
4. Recognition of profits on instalment sales during the period of sale for accounting purposes and during the period of collection for tax purposes	36,000	36,000	36,000
5. Acquisition of equipment: CCA for tax purposes, straight-line for accounting purposes	90,000	50,000	40,000
	$ (4,000)	$66,000	$66,000

The enacted tax rate has been 40% for many years. In November 2003, the rate was changed to 38% for all periods after January 1, 2004. Assume the company has income taxes of $180,000 due per the tax return for 2002.

Instructions

    (a) Indicate the manner in which future income taxes should be presented on Hewlett Corporation's December 31, 2002 balance sheet.

    (b) Calculate taxable income for 2002.

    (c) Calculate accounting income for 2002.

    (d) Draft the income tax section of the 2002 income statement, beginning with the line "income before income taxes."

CONCEPTUAL CASES

C19-1 The amount of income taxes due to the government for a period of time is rarely the amount reported on the income statement for that period as income tax expense.

Instructions

(a) Explain the objectives of accounting for income taxes in general purpose financial statements.

(b) Explain the basic principles that are applied in accounting for income taxes at the date of the financial statements to meet the objectives discussed in (a).

(c) List the steps in the annual calculation of future tax liabilities and assets.

C19-2 The Majoli Corporation appropriately uses the asset-liability method to record future income taxes. Majoli reports amortization expense for certain machinery purchased this year using CCA for income tax purposes and the straight-line basis for financial reporting purposes. The tax deduction is the larger amount this year.

Majoli received rent revenues in advance this year. These revenues are included in this year's taxable income. However, for financial reporting purposes, these revenues are reported as unearned revenues, a current liability.

Instructions

(a) What are the principles of the asset-liability approach?

(b) How would Majoli account for the temporary differences?

(c) How should Majoli classify the future tax consequences of the temporary differences on its balance sheet?

C19-3 The asset-liability approach for recording future income taxes is now an integral part of generally accepted accounting principles.

Instructions

(a) Indicate whether each of the following independent situations results in a temporary difference or a permanent difference and explain why.

1. Estimated warranty costs (covering a three-year warranty) are expensed for financial reporting purposes at the time of sale but deducted for income tax purposes when paid.

2. Amortization for book and income tax purposes differs because of different bases of carrying the related property, which was acquired in a trade-in. The different bases are a result of different rules used for book and tax purposes to calculate the cost of assets acquired in a trade-in.

3. A company properly uses the equity method to account for its 30% investment in another company. The investee pays non-taxable dividends that are about 10% of its annual earnings.

4. A company reports a contingent loss it expects will result from an ongoing lawsuit. The loss is not reported on the current year's tax return. Half the loss is a penalty it expects to be charged by the courts. This portion of the loss is not a tax deductible expenditure, even when paid.

(b) Discuss the nature of the future income tax accounts and possible classifications in a company's balance sheet. Indicate the manner in which these accounts are to be reported.

C19-4 Listed below are common items that are treated differently for financial reporting purposes than they are for tax purposes.

1. Excess of charge to accounting records (allowance method) over charge to tax return (direct write-off method) for uncollectible receivables.

2. Excess of accrued pension expense over amount paid.

3. Receipt of dividends from a Canadian corporation treated as income for accounting purposes, but which are not subject to tax.

4. Instalment sales are accounted for on the accrual basis for financial reporting purposes and on the cash basis for tax purposes.

5. Expenses incurred in obtaining tax-exempt income.

6. A trademark acquired directly from the government is capitalized and amortized over subsequent periods for accounting purposes and expensed for tax purposes.

7. Prepaid advertising expense deferred for accounting purposes and deducted as an expense for tax purposes.

8. Premiums paid on life insurance of officers (corporation is the beneficiary).

9. Penalty for filing a late tax return.

10. Proceeds of life insurance policies on lives of officers.
11. Estimated future warranty costs are recognized in determining accounting income.
12. Fine for polluting, not tax deductible.
13. Excess of CCA over accounting amortization.
14. Tax-exempt interest revenue.
15. Excess depletion for accounting purposes over amount taken for tax purposes.
16. Estimated gross profit on long-term construction contract is reported in the income statement; some of this gross profit is deferred for tax purposes.

Instructions

For each item above

(a) indicate if it is:
  1. a permanent difference, or
  2. a timing difference resulting in a temporary difference.
(b) indicate if it will:
  1. create future taxable amounts, or
  2. create future deductible amounts, or
  3. not affect any future tax returns.
(b) indicate if it usually will:
  1. result in reporting a future tax liability, or
  2. result in reporting a future tax asset, or
  3. not result in reporting any future taxes.

C19-5

Part A

This year Davenport Corporation has each of the following items in its income statement:

1. Gross profit on instalment sales.
2. Revenues on long-term construction contracts.
3. Estimated costs of product warranty contracts.
4. Premiums on officers' life insurance with Davenport Corporation as beneficiary.

Instructions

(a) Under what conditions would future income taxes need to be reported in the financial statements?
(b) Specify when future income taxes would need to be recognized for each of the items above, and indicate the rationale for such recognition.

Part B

Davenport Corporation's president has heard that future income taxes can be classified in different ways in the balance sheet.

Instructions

Identify the conditions under which future income taxes would be classified as a noncurrent item in the balance sheet. What justification exists for such classification?

(AICPA adapted)

C19-6 At December 31, 2002, Golden Corporation has one temporary difference that will reverse and cause taxable amounts in 2003. In 2002, new tax legislation set taxes equal to 45% for 2002, 40% for 2003, and 34% for 2004 and years thereafter.

Instructions

Explain what circumstances would call for Golden to calculate its future tax liability at the end of 2002 by multiplying the temporary difference by:

(a) 45%.
(b) 40%.
(c) 34%.

C19-7 Joe Ali and Merry Madison are discussing accounting for income taxes. They are currently studying a schedule of taxable and deductible amounts that will arise in the future as a result of existing temporary differences. The schedule is as follows:

	Current Year		Future Years		
	2002	2003	2004	2005	2006
Taxable income	$850,000				
Taxable amounts		$375,000	$375,000	$375,000	$375,000
Deductible amounts				(2,400,000)	
Enacted tax rate	50%	45%	40%	35%	30%

Instructions

(a) Explain the concept of future taxable amounts and future deductible amounts as illustrated in the schedule.

(b) How do the carryback and carryforward provisions affect the reporting of future tax assets and future tax liabilities?

Using Your Judgement

FINANCIAL REPORTING PROBLEM: CANADIAN TIRE CORPORATION, LIMITED

Instructions

Refer to the financial statements and accompanying notes and discussion of **Canadian Tire Corporation, Limited** presented in Appendix 5B and answer the following questions.

(a) Identify all income tax accounts reported on the December 31, 2000 balance sheet or in notes cross-referenced to the balance sheet. Explain clearly what each account represents.

(b) What temporary differences existed that resulted in the future income tax asset or liability at the end of 2000? Is this information required to be provided? Suggest likely causes of the temporary differences.

(c) Identify all income tax accounts reported on the combined statement of income and retained earnings or in notes cross-referenced to this statement, and explain what each represents. Has Canadian Tire applied intraperiod tax allocation in 2000? Explain.

(d) Identify all references to income taxes on the statement of cash flows or in notes cross-referenced to this statement, and explain why these are included on the statement.

(e) What was the effective tax rate for Canadian Tire in 2000? in 1999? What caused the effective rate to differ from the statutory rate? For each reason given, explain whether the effective rate was made higher or lower, and why.

FINANCIAL STATEMENT ANALYSIS CASE

Stelco Inc. is a well known Canadian producer and fabricator of industrial steel products.

Effective January 1, 2000, and in accordance with new *CICA Handbook* Section 3465, Stelco changed from the deferral method to the liability method of accounting for future income taxes. The company's financial statements for the year ended December 31, 2000 reported this event retroactively as a change in accounting policy without restating the financial statements of prior periods.

On June 20, 2001, the *Globe and Mail*'s Report on Business noted that:

> "**Stelco Inc.** is taking a $27-million non-cash charge in the second quarter to reflect lower corporate taxes in Ontario. Stelco said yesterday the income tax charge amounts to about 26 cents a share and will affect the company's earnings..."

Instructions

Through SEDAR (www.sedar.com) or Stelco's website, obtain a copy of Stelco's financial statements for its year ended December 31, 2000. Answer the following questions.

(a) What was the effect on Stelco's financial statements of the retroactive change in accounting policy for income taxes? Was this significant in relation to Stelco's net income? To its net assets?

(b) Did the company have future income tax assets or future tax liabilities at December 31, 2000? What were the balances of any such accounts?

(c) Identify the nature of the temporary differences underlying the future tax accounts on the December 31, 2000 balance sheet. Indicate whether these were taxable or deductible temporary differences.

(d) The June 20, 2001 newspaper article indicated that corporate taxes "in Ontario are being cut by four percentage points between 2002 and 2005." Explain, with reference to the December 31, 2000 future tax accounts, how the enactment of the tax reduction in 2001 would affect the financial statements of Stelco.

(e) Briefly explain why Stelco reported an income tax benefit (recovery) on its 2000 income statement even though the company reported income before taxes of $2 million.

COMPARATIVE ANALYSIS CASE

Loblaw Companies Limited and Sobeys Inc.

Instructions

Go to SEDAR (www.sedar.com), the company web sites or the Digital Tool and, using **Loblaw Companies Limited** financial statements for the year ended December 30, 2000 and **Sobeys Inc.** financial statements for the year ended May 5, 2001, answer the following questions.

(a) Identify all areas where intraperiod tax allocation was used by both companies. This requires a careful reading of some of the notes to the financial statements as well as the main statements themselves. Prepare a schedule of the total income tax provision or recovery for each company, listing where the provision or recovery was reported.

(b) Did both companies report the adoption of the new accounting standard for income taxes in *Handbook* Section 3465 in the same way? Comment.

(c) Compare the two companies' future income tax assets and/or future income tax liabilities, and identify to the extent possible what temporary differences are responsible for these accounts. Would you expect two companies in the same industry to have similar temporary differences? Do they?

(d) Would you expect both companies to be subject to similar income tax legislation and tax rates? Compare the companies' statutory and effective rates and explain why there are differences, if applicable.

RESEARCH CASES

Case 1

The CICA Accounting Standards Board issued revised accounting standards on "Income Taxes," effective for companies with year ends beginning on or after January 1, 2000. The new standards represent a shift from the deferral method of accounting for income taxes to the liability or asset-liability method.

Instructions

(a) Identify the major differences between these two approaches. What would you expect to be the major financial statement changes as a company adopts the liability method? Be specific. (Note: Research this issue using a variety of sources or use the Digital Tool for information on various approaches to accounting for income taxes.)

(b) Obtain the financial statements of four different companies for the period in which they adopted the liability method. In general, how did each account for the change in accounting policy?

(c) For each company in (b), what balance sheet accounts required adjustment as a result of the change in policy? Comment. Were the same accounts affected for all companies? In general, were the companies affected in a positive way? Were the adjustments significant? Did all companies provide the same type and amount of disclosure?

Case 2

The deferred or future tax liability requires special consideration for financial statement readers.

Instructions

Obtain a recent edition of a financial statement analysis textbook, read the section related to the future or deferred income tax liability, and answer the following questions.

(a) What are the major analytical issues associated with future tax liabilities?

(b) What type of adjustments to future tax liabilities do analysts make when examining financial statements?

INTERNATIONAL REPORTING CASE

Tomkins PLC is a British company that operates in four business sectors: industrial and automotive engineering; construction components; food manufacturing; and professional, garden, and leisure products. Tomkins prepares its accounts in accordance with U.K. accounting standards. Like Canadian and U.S. reporting, UK financial reporting is investor-oriented. As a result, British companies report different income amounts for tax and financial reporting purposes. British companies receive different tax treatment for such items as amortization (capital allowances), and they receive tax credits for operating losses. Tomkins reported income of £305 million in 1999 and reported total shareholders' funds of £2,221 million at May 31, 1999. Tomkins provided the following disclosures related to taxes in its May 31, 1999, annual report.

PRINCIPAL ACCOUNTING POLICIES—TAX

The tax charge is based on the profit for the year and takes into account tax deferred due to timing differences between the treatment of certain items for tax and accounting purposes. Deferred tax is calculated under the liability method and it is considered probable that all liabilities will crystallise. Deferred tax assets are not recognised in respect of provisions for post-retirement benefits.

Note 5: Tax on Profit on Ordinary Activities

	1999 £ million	1998 £ million
Corporation tax at 31%	56.6	69.6
Overseas tax	85.5	95.8
Deferred tax – UK (see note 16)	5.1	(7.1)
– Overseas (see note 16)	7.3	9.2
Associated undertakings' tax	0.7	3.0
	155.2	170.5

The tax charge on exceptional items in 1999 and 1998 is £nil.

Note 16: Provisions for Liabilities and Charges

	1999 £ million	1998 £ million
The deferred tax provision comprises:		
Excess of capital allowances over depreciation charged	98.5	102.9
Other timing differences	40.8	25.5
Advance corporation tax recoverable	—	(30.3)
	139.3	98.1

Results under U.S. Accounting Principles

The consolidated financial statements are prepared in conformity with accounting principles generally accepted in the UK (UK GAAP), which differ in certain respects from those generally accepted in the United States (US GAAP). The significant areas of difference affecting the Tomkins consolidated financial statements are described below:

Deferred Income Tax. In Tomkins' consolidated financial statements, deferred tax is calculated under the liability method and it is considered probable that all liabilities will crystallise. Deferred tax assets are not recognised in respect of provision for post-retirement benefits. Under US GAAP, deferred taxes are provided for all temporary differences on a full liability basis. Deferred tax assets are also recognized to the extent that their realisation is more likely than not.

U.S. and current Canadian GAAP relating to income taxes are virtually identical. If Tomkins had used current Canadian GAAP for deferred (future) taxes, its income would have been lower by £8.2 million in 1999 and shareholders' equity at May 31, 1999 would have been £87.5 million higher.

Instructions

Use the information in the Tomkins disclosure to answer the following:

(a) Prepare the journal entry that would be required to reconcile Tomkins' income to current Canadian GAAP for the differences in future taxes under Canadian and UK accounting standards.

(b) Prepare the journal entry that would be required to reconcile Tomkins' shareholders' equity to current Canadian GAAP for the differences in future taxes.

(c) In light of the information disclosed under "Principal Accounting Policies—Tax," explain why you think Tomkins' equity under U.S. and current Canadian GAAP would be higher at May 31, 1999.

(d) Tomkins indicates that "Deferred tax is calculated under the liability method and it is considered probable that all (deferred tax) liabilities will crystallise [be realized]." Does this approach cause any problems in comparing the financial statements of Canadian, U.S., and UK companies? Explain.

ETHICS CASE

Henrietta Aguirre, CGA, is the newly hired director of corporate taxation for Mesa Incorporated, which is a publicly traded corporation. Ms. Aguirre's first job with Mesa was to review the company's accounting practices on future income taxes. In doing her review, she noted differences between tax and book amortization methods that permitted Mesa to recognize a sizeable future tax liability on its balance sheet. As a result, Mesa did not have to report current income tax expenses. Aguirre also discovered that Mesa has an explicit policy of selling off fixed assets before they reversed in the future tax liability account. This policy, coupled with the rapid expansion of its capital asset base, allowed Mesa to "defer" all income taxes payable for several years, at the same time as it reported positive earnings and an increasing EPS. Aguirre checked with the legal department and found the policy to be legal, but she's uncomfortable with the ethics of it.

Instructions
Answer the following questions.

(a) Why would Mesa have an explicit policy of selling assets before they reversed in the future tax liability account?

(b) What are the ethical implications of Mesa's "deferral" of income taxes?

(c) Who could be harmed by Mesa's ability to "defer" income taxes payable for several years, despite positive earnings?

(d) In a situation such as this, what are Ms. Aguirre's professional responsibilities as a CGA?

CHAPTER 20

Pensions and Other Employee Future Benefits

LEARNING OBJECTIVES

....

After studying this chapter, you should be able to:

1. Distinguish between accounting for the employer's pension plan and accounting for the pension fund.

2. Identify types of pension plans and their characteristics.

3. Identify the accounting and disclosure requirements for defined contribution plans.

4. Explain alternative measures for valuing the pension obligation.

5. Identify the components of pension expense.

6. Identify transactions and events that affect the projected benefit obligation.

7. Identify transactions and events that affect the balance of the plan assets.

8. Explain the usefulness of—and be able to complete—a work sheet to support the employer's pension expense entries.

9. Explain the pension accounting treatment of past service costs.

10. Explain the pension accounting treatment of actuarial gains and losses, including corridor amortization.

11. Identify the differences between pensions and post-retirement health care benefits.

12. Identify the financial reporting and disclosure requirements for defined benefit plans.

13. Identify the financial accounting and reporting requirements for defined benefit plans whose benefits do not vest or accumulate.

Preview of Chapter 20

Many business organizations and their employees are increasingly concerned about retirement planning. This has resulted in the establishment of private pension and other benefit plans in companies of all sizes. The majority of employer pension plan assets is held in trusteed pension funds, so named because they are governed by the provisions of a trust agreement. The size of these funds is impressive. By the end of 2000, the market value of assets held in trusteed pension funds in Canada was close to $600 billion, up from $420 billion four years earlier, making this pool of capital second in size only to the financial assets of the chartered banks.[1]

Pensions are a part of the employees' overall compensation package that also includes additional post-retirement and other benefits. The substantial growth of these plans, both in number of employees covered and the dollar amount of benefits, has increased the significance of their costs in relation to a company's financial position, results of operations, and cash flows. This chapter discusses the accounting issues related to these future benefits. The content and organization of the chapter are as follows:

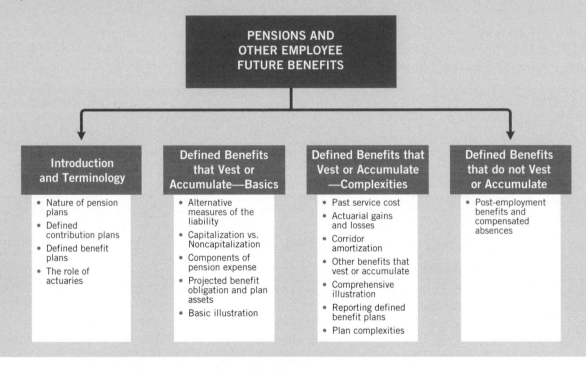

INTRODUCTION AND TERMINOLOGY

This chapter covers a variety of employee future benefits that are "earned by active employees and expected to be provided to them when they are no longer providing active service" and that are usually covered by an organization's benefit policies.[2] It begins by explaining basic terminology and the difference between defined contribution and defined benefit plans. Defined contribution plans have few complexities—the costs are basically recognized as expense as the company makes payments to cover the costs; in effect, a cash basis. The majority of the chapter is devoted to discussing the complex accounting issues related to defined benefit pension and other plans with benefits that vest or accumulate as the employee provides service. The cost of these future benefits is accrued as expense by the company as the employees provide the requisite

---

[1] *The Daily*, Statistics Canada, July 17, 2000 and June 26, 2001.

[2] *CICA Handbook*, Section 3461, par. .005.

service; that is, full accrual accounting is applied. The chapter ends with accounting for situations where employees are entitled to benefits if needed in the future but the benefits received are not a function of their length of service. In this case, as it is impossible to associate the benefits' cost with the service period, the "event accrual" method of accounting is appropriate.

Nature of Pension Plans

A pension plan is an arrangement whereby an employer provides benefits (payments) to employees after they retire for services they provided while they were working. Pension accounting may refer either to **accounting for the employer or accounting for the pension plan**, and it is the former that is the subject of this chapter. The company or employer is the organization sponsoring the pension plan. It incurs the cost and contributes to the pension fund. The fund or plan is the entity that receives the employer contributions, administers the pension assets, and makes the benefit payments to the pension recipients (retired employees). Illustration 20-1 shows the three entities involved in a pension plan and indicates the flow of cash among them.

> **OBJECTIVE 1**
> Distinguish between accounting for the employer's pension plan and accounting for the pension fund.

ILLUSTRATION 20-1
Flow of Cash Among Pension Plan Participants

The pension plan above is being funded;[3] that is, the employer (company) sets funds aside for future pension benefits by making payments to a funding agency that is responsible for accumulating the pension plan assets and for making payments to the recipients as the benefits become due. In an insured plan, the funding agency is an insurance company; in a trust fund plan, the funding agency is a trustee.

In contributory plans, the employees bear part of the stated benefits' cost or voluntarily make payments to increase their benefits, whereas the employer bears the entire cost in noncontributory plans. Companies generally design pension plans in accordance with federal income tax laws that permit deductibility of the employer's and employees' contributions to the pension fund and tax-free status of earnings from pension fund assets. The pension benefits are taxable as received by the pension recipient.

The need for proper administration of and sound accounting for pension funds becomes apparent when one appreciates the size of these funds. Listed below are the pension expense, fund assets, and shareholders' equity of a sample of large Canadian companies.

ILLUSTRATION 20-2
Pension Expense, Pension Fund Assets, and Shareholders' Equity

Company	Year	Pension Expense	Pension Fund Assets	Shareholders' Equity
		$ million	$ million	$ million
Nortel Networks[1]	2000	$96.0	$6,303	$28,760.0
Bombardier	2001	89.5	2,488	3,812.4
Royal Bank of Canada	2000	64.0	4,321	13,541.0
Canadian Pacific	2000	(35.5)	6,135.5	9,555.5

[1] in millions of U.S. dollars

The plan should be a separate legal and accounting entity for which a set of books is maintained and financial statements are prepared. General purpose financial state-

---

[3] When used as a verb, **fund** means to pay to a funding agency (as to fund future pension benefits or to fund pension cost). Used as a noun, it refers to assets accumulated in the hands of a funding agency (trustee) for the purpose of meeting pension benefits when they become due.

IAS NOTE

IAS 19 applies to Employee Benefits, and is not restricted to benefits provided when employees are not providing active service. It covers short-term compensated absences, profit sharing, and bonus plans in addition to post-employment benefits.

OBJECTIVE 2
....
Identify types of pension plans and their characteristics.

OBJECTIVE 3
....
Identify the accounting and disclosure requirements for defined contribution plans.

INTERNATIONAL INSIGHT

Outside Canada and the U.S., private pension plans are less common because many other nations tend to rely on government-sponsored pension plans. Consequently, accounting for defined benefit pension plans is typically a less important issue elsewhere.

ments for pension plans, not covered in this chapter, are prescribed by the *CICA Handbook* in Section 4100. Instead, this chapter is devoted to the pension and other future employee benefit issues **of the employer** as the plan sponsor. The two most common types of pension plan are defined contribution plans and defined benefit plans.

Defined Contribution Plans

A defined contribution plan is a plan that specifies how contributions are determined rather than the benefits the individual is to receive or the method of determining those benefits. The plan also attributes the contributions to specific individuals.[4] The contributions may be a fixed sum, for example, $1,000 per year, or be related to salary, such as 6% of regular plus overtime earnings. Usually, no promise is made regarding the ultimate benefits paid out to the employees.

The amounts contributed are usually turned over to an independent third-party or trustee who acts on behalf of the beneficiaries—the participating employees. The trustee assumes ownership of the pension assets and is accountable for their investment and distribution. The trust is separate and distinct from the employer. The size of the pension benefits that the employee finally collects under the plan depends on the amounts contributed to the pension trust, the income accumulated in the trust, and the treatment of forfeitures of funds caused by early terminations of other employees.

Because the contribution is defined, **the accounting for a defined contribution plan is straightforward**. The employer's annual cost (pension expense) is simply the amount that it is obligated to contribute to the plan. A liability is reported on the employer's balance sheet only if the contribution has not been made in full, and an asset is reported only if more than the required amount has been contributed. The employer generally assumes no further obligation or risk relative to this plan.

When a defined contribution plan is initiated or amended, the employer may be obligated to make contributions for employee services provided prior to the date of the initiation or amendment. This obligation is referred to as **prior or past service cost**. Amounts arising as past service costs are amortized in a rational and systematic manner as part of the annual benefit expense, over the period the organization is expected to benefit from the plan change.[5]

In addition to pension expense, the only disclosure required by the employer under a defined contribution plan is the nature and effect of significant matters affecting comparability from period to period.[6]

Defined Benefit Plans

A defined benefit plan defines the benefits that the employee will receive at the time of retirement. The formula that is typically used provides for the benefits to be a function of the employee's years of service and compensation level when he or she nears retirement. In order to ensure that appropriate resources are available to pay the benefits at retirement, it is usually a requirement that funds be set aside during the service life of the employees. To determine what the contribution should be today to meet the pension benefit commitments that will arise at retirement, many different contribution approaches could be used. Whatever funding method is employed, it should provide enough money at retirement to meet the benefits defined by the plan.

The **employees** are the beneficiaries of a **defined contribution** trust, but the **employer** is the beneficiary of a **defined benefit** trust. The trust's primary purpose

---

[4] *CICA Handbook*, Section 3461, par. .006(f).

[5] *Ibid.*, par. .019.

[6] *Ibid.*, par. .154.

under a defined benefit plan is to safeguard assets and to invest them so that there will be enough to pay the employer's obligation to the employees when they retire. In **form**, the trust is a separate entity; in **substance**, the trust liabilities belong to the employer. That is, **as long as the plan continues, the employer is responsible for paying the defined benefits (without regard to what happens in the trust)**. Any shortfall in the accumulated assets held by the trust must be made up by the employer. Excess assets accumulated in the trust may be able to be recaptured by the employer, either through reduced future funding or through a reversion of funds depending on the trust agreement, plan documents, and provincial legislation.[7]

With a defined benefit plan, the employer assumes the economic risks: the employee is secure because the benefits to be paid upon retirement are predefined, but the employer is at risk because the cost is uncertain. The cost depends on factors such as employee turnover, mortality, length of service, and compensation levels as well as investment returns earned on pension assets, inflation, and other economic conditions over long periods of time.

Because the cost to the company is subject to a wide range of uncertain future variables, **accounting for a defined benefit plan is complex**. Measuring the pension expense and liability to be recognized each period as employees provide services to earn their pension entitlement is not an easy task. In addition, an appropriate funding pattern must be established to assure that enough funds will be available at retirement to provide the benefits promised. **Note that the expense to be recognized each period is not necessarily equal to the cash funding contribution, just as amortization expense recognized on the use of plant and equipment is not defined in terms of how the asset is paid for or financed**.

The accounting issues related to defined benefit plans are complex, but interesting. The discussion in the following sections, therefore, deal primarily with this type of plan.

The Role of Actuaries in Pension Accounting

Because the problems associated with many benefit plans involve complicated actuarial considerations, actuaries are engaged to ensure that the plan is appropriate for the employee group covered. Actuaries are individuals who are trained through a long and rigorous certification program to assign probabilities to future events and their financial effects.[8] The insurance industry employs actuaries to assess risks and to advise on the setting of premiums and other aspects of insurance policies. Employers rely heavily on actuaries for assistance in developing, implementing, and funding pension plans.

Actuaries make predictions, called actuarial assumptions, of mortality rates, employee turnover, interest and earnings rates, early retirement frequency, future salaries, and any other factors necessary to operate a pension plan. They assist by calculating the various measures that affect the financial statements, such as the pension obligation, the annual cost of servicing the plan, and the cost of amendments to the plan. In summary, accounting for defined benefit pension plans is highly reliant upon information and measurements provided by actuaries.

INTERNATIONAL INSIGHT

Japan is the most rapidly aging nation in the developed world, with 24% of the population expected to be over 65 by the year 2015, compared with 17% in Canada and Europe and 15% in the U.S.

---

[7] The ownership of pension fund surpluses has been the subject of much recent litigation. The courts have increasingly determined that pension fund surpluses or a significant portion of them should accrue to the benefit of the employee group. Provincial pension legislation increasingly dictates how pension surpluses are to be dealt with.

[8] An actuary's primary purpose in pension accounting is to ensure that the company has established an appropriate funding pattern to meet its pension obligations. This calculation entails developing a set of assumptions and continued monitoring of these assumptions to assure their realism. That the general public has little understanding of what an actuary does is illustrated by the following excerpt from *The Wall Street Journal*: "A polling organization once asked the general public what an actuary was and received among its more coherent responses the opinion that it was a place where you put dead actors."

PLANS WITH DEFINED BENEFITS THAT VEST OR ACCUMULATE—THE BASICS

The most complex type of benefit plan is one that provides defined benefits that vest in the employee or accumulate to an employee's credit based on length of service. Employees' rights to pension benefits, for example, usually vest after they work a specified number of years, and the benefit amount generally increases with the length of service provided. Vesting occurs when the entitlement to future benefits is no longer contingent on the employee remaining in the entity's service. The rights to most other retirement benefits, such as supplementary health insurance, usually accrue to employees who have been employed for a required length of time and/or who have reached a specified age. Other post-employment benefits and compensated absences vest or accumulate as well. Examples include sick leave that accumulates and is paid out without an illness-related absence and long-term disability that increases with length of service.[9] As stated earlier, accounting for the costs of such benefits follows full accrual accounting in that the expense and liability are recognized over the periods in which the related services are provided in exchange for the benefits.[10] Accounting for defined benefit plans where the benefits vest or accumulate is explained below as it relates to the most common employee future benefit—a defined benefit pension plan.

In accounting for defined benefit pension plans, two primary questions arise: (1) What amount of pension obligation should be reported in the employer's financial statements? (2) What is the pension expense for the period? Attempting to answer the first question has been controversial.

Alternative Measures of the Liability

OBJECTIVE 4

Explain alternative measures for valuing the pension obligation.

Most agree that an employer's **pension obligation** is the deferred compensation obligation it has to its employees for their service under the pension plan terms, but there are alternative ways of measuring this accrued benefit. One measure of the obligation is to base it only on the benefits vested to the employees. Under most pension plans, a specific minimum number of years of service to the employer is required before an employee achieves vested benefits status. The vested benefit obligation is calculated using current salary levels and includes only vested benefits.

Another measure of the obligation is to base the calculation of the deferred compensation amount on all years of service performed by employees under the plan—both vested and nonvested—using current salary levels. This measurement of the pension obligation is called the accumulated benefit obligation.

A third measure bases the calculation of the deferred compensation amount on both vested and nonvested service using future salaries. This measurement of the pension obligation is called the projected benefit obligation. Because future salaries are expected to be higher than current salaries, this approach results in the largest measurement of the pension obligation. Within this method, two different approaches exist. One, the projected benefit method **prorated on salaries**, allocates the cost to each period based on the percentage of total estimated career compensation earned by the employee in that period. Because salaries are expected to increase over time, relatively low amounts are attributed to the employees' early years and large amounts to later years. The projected benefit method **prorated on services** allocates an equal portion of the cost of the total estimated benefit to each year of an employee's service. The result of this method is an accrual of a more equal charge each period.

The choice among these measures is critical because it affects the amount of the pension liability and the annual pension expense reported. The diagram in Illustration 20-3 presents the differences in these three measurements. **Regardless of the approach used, the estimated future benefits to be paid are discounted to present value.**

---

[9] *CICA Handbook*, Section 3461, par. .030.

[10] *Ibid.*, par. .029.

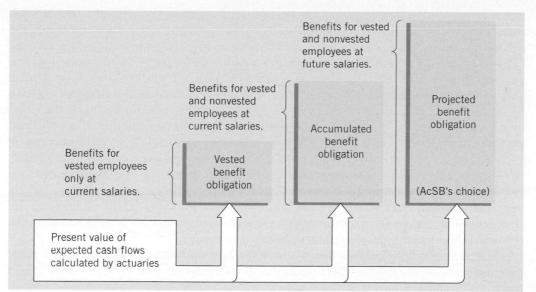

ILLUSTRATION 20-3
Different Measures of the
Pension Obligation

Which of these approaches did the Accounting Standards Board adopt? *Handbook* Section 3461 recommends the projected benefit method, prorated on services.[11] This means that the obligation is the present value of vested and nonvested benefits accrued to date based on employees' future salary levels.[12]

Those critical of the projected benefit obligation argue that using future salary levels is tantamount to adding future obligations to existing ones. Those in favour of the projected benefit obligation contend that a promise by an employer to pay benefits based on a percentage of the employees' future salary is far different from a promise to pay a percentage of their current salary, and such a difference should be reflected in the pension liability and pension expense.

Capitalization versus Noncapitalization

Another fundamental choice in accounting for pensions and other future benefits is whether a capitalization or noncapitalization approach should be taken. The major issue in this case is whether the full obligation should be recognized as a liability (capitalization), or whether the amount recorded should be restricted and related to the amount of expense recognized (noncapitalization).

Under a capitalization approach, pension plan assets and full pension obligations are reported as assets and liabilities on the employer company's balance sheet. This portrays the economic substance of the pension plan arrangement, since the employer has a clear obligation to pay pension benefits for employee services already performed. As the employees work, pension expense is incurred and the employer's liability increases. The pension liability and the pension assets are both reduced through the payment of benefits to retired employees. Funding the plan is recognized on the balance sheet by the transfer of company assets into a separate category of asset set aside for the pension fund, but the funding has no effect on the liability amount.

INTERNATIONAL INSIGHT

Whereas Canadian GAAP requires companies to base pension expense on estimated future compensation levels, Germany and Japan do not.

UNDERLYING CONCEPTS

Recognizing the smaller benefit obligation ignores the going concern concept. A going concern would not expect to settle the obligation today at current salaries and wages. A going concern would expect to settle the obligation based upon future salary levels.

---

[11] *Ibid.*, par. .034. However, if future salary levels or cost escalation do not affect the amount of the future benefits, the accumulated benefit method can be used to determine the accrued benefit obligation.

[12] When the term "present value of benefits" is used throughout this chapter, it really means the actuarial present value of benefits. Actuarial present value is the amount payable adjusted to reflect the time value of money and the probability of payment (by means of decrements for events such as death, disability, withdrawals, or retirement) between the present date and the expected date of payment. For simplicity, we will use the term "present value" instead of "actuarial present value" in our discussion.

A noncapitalization approach, on the other hand, is more consistent with the legal form of pension arrangements whereby the plan is considered a separate legal and accounting entity. Cash and investments set aside to fund pension obligations are considered assets of the pension plan, not of the employer company; therefore, neither the pension assets nor the obligation are recognized on the employer's balance sheet. Under this approach, the employer accrues a pension liability equal to the pension expense recognized, and as long as the employer's contribution to the fund trustee is the same as the pension expense, the balance sheet reports no asset or liability related to the pension plan. If the funding exceeds the expense recognized, a prepaid expense is included on the balance sheet; if the funding is less than the expense, a pension liability is reported. When the trustee pays benefits to retirees, the employer records no entries because the company's recorded assets and liabilities are not reduced. This approach is often referred to as a method of off-balance-sheet financing because the underfunding of the plan itself for which the employer is ultimately responsible is not recognized on the company's balance sheet.

The Accounting Standards Board adopted a noncapitalization approach as a compromise position in *Handbook* Section 3461 and its predecessor section, consistent with the U.S. standard.

Major Components of Pension Expense

OBJECTIVE 5

Identify the components of pension expense.

There is broad agreement that pension costs should be accounted for on the accrual basis and be matched with the accounting periods that benefit from the employees' service. The profession recognizes that accounting for pension plans requires measuring the cost and identifying it with appropriate time periods. Determining pension expense for a particular period, however, is complex. The following illustration summarizes the major components and the effect of each on pension expense.

1. *Service Cost.* The service cost is the cost of the benefits to be provided in exchange for employees' services rendered in the current period. The actuary predicts the additional benefits that must be paid under the plan's benefit formula as a result of the employees' current year's service and then discounts the cost of these benefits to their present value. The service cost component is reduced by any employee contributions to the plan.

ILLUSTRATION 20-4
Components of Pension Expense

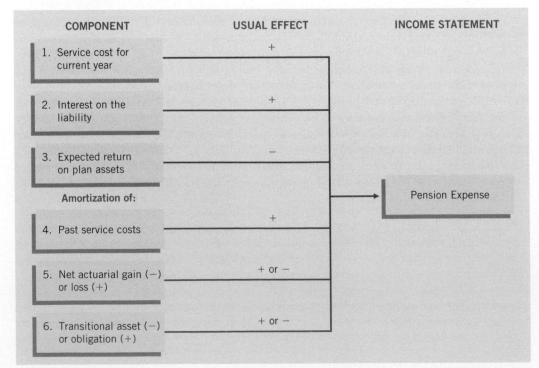

For defined benefit plans where future benefits depend on or are increased by the length of service, the actuary should base his or her calculations on future salary levels and attribute the cost of the future benefits to the accounting periods beginning at the date of hire and ending when the employee obtains full eligibility for benefits. This is known as the attribution period. The obligation to provide benefits is attributed to the periods in which the employee provides the service that gives rise to the benefits. While the date of hire is the most common date for employees to begin earning benefits, it may be a later date, and full eligibility for benefits may occur at a date prior to retirement.[13]

2. *Interest on the Liability.* Because a pension is a deferred compensation arrangement whereby this element of wages is deferred and an obligation is created, the time value of money becomes a factor. Because the obligation is not paid until maturity, it is measured on a discounted basis and interest is accrued with the passage of time. **Interest accrues each year on the projected benefit obligation just as it does on any discounted debt.** It is the interest for the period on the projected benefit obligation outstanding during the period.

What interest rate should be used? Section 3461 requires the use of a current market rate, such as the current yield on high-quality debt instruments or the current settlement rate, the rate implied in an insurance contract that could be purchased to effectively settle the pension obligation. The rate used should be the one determined at the beginning of the period.[14] Note that minor changes in the interest rate used to discount pension benefits can dramatically affect the measurement of the employer's obligation. For example, a 1% decrease in the discount rate could increase pension liabilities 15%. Discount rates used to measure the pension liability are required to be changed at each measurement date to reflect current rates.

3. *Expected Return on Plan Assets.* The return earned by the accumulated pension fund assets in a particular year is relevant in measuring the net cost to the employer of sponsoring an employee pension plan. Pension plan assets are usually investments in shares, bonds, other securities, and real estate that are held to earn a reasonable return, generally at a minimum of risk. The return earned on these assets increases the fund balance and correspondingly reduces the employer's net cost of providing employees' pension benefits. The actual return, composed of changes in the market values of fund assets as well as interest and dividends earned, can be highly variable from one year to the next. For this reason, the expected return, based on the expected long-term rate of return on plan assets applied to the fair value (or market-related value) of the plan assets, is used.

Note that the **expected** rate of return is the same as the **actual** return adjusted for experience gains or losses on the assets in the period; that is, for the difference between what was expected and what was actually experienced. As will be discussed later, the variance between the yearly actual return and the expected return may be included in periodic pension expense, but amortized over future periods.

4. *Amortization of Past Service Costs.* Plan initiation or amendment often includes provisions to recognize or to increase the benefits for service provided in prior years. The present value of the additional future benefits so granted is calculated by the actuary and is known as past service costs. Because plan amendments are granted with the expectation that the employer will realize economic benefits in future periods from continued employee service, the past service cost is generally allocated to pension expense in the future, normally in equal amounts over the expected period to full eligibility of the affected employee group.[15]

UNDERLYING CONCEPTS

The matching concept and the definition of a liability justify accounting for pension cost on the accrual basis. This requires recording an expense when the future benefits are earned by the employees and recognizing an existing obligation to pay pensions later based on current services received.

---

[13] *Ibid.,* par. .038 and .039.

[14] *Ibid.,* par. .050 and .075.

[15] *Ibid.,* par. .079.

5. *Amortization of the Net Actuarial Gain or Loss.* Actuarial gains and losses arise from two sources: (1) a change in actuarial assumptions; that is, assumptions as to the occurrence of future events that affect the measurement of the future benefit costs and obligations; and (2) experience gains and losses—the difference between what has occurred and the previous actuarial assumptions as to what was expected.[16] When assumptions are proven to be inaccurate by later events, adjustments are needed. The net accumulated actuarial gain or loss, if significant, is amortized over future periods using a "corridor approach" described later in the chapter.

6. *Amortization of Transitional Asset or Obligation.* The amendments to the pension accounting standard in the late 1980s and the introduction of Section 3461 in 2000 involved significant changes to the accounting for pensions and other employee future benefits. When companies apply the new requirements for the first time, they must determine the unrecorded excess or deficiency of the projected benefit obligation over the fair value of the plan assets at that time. Where the new standards are applied **prospectively**, the net transitional asset or transitional obligation or liability is amortized to expense rather than given immediate recognition. The transitional balance is amortized in a systematic and rational basis over an appropriate period of time, which normally is the expected average remaining service life of the employee group covered by the plan.[17] The expected average remaining service life of an employee group, known as EARSL, is the total number of years of future service expected to be rendered by that group divided by the number of employees in the group.

Five other components of expense for the period are identified in the accounting standard. These include gains and losses on plan settlements and curtailments, termination benefits, and amounts recognized as a valuation allowance, which are discussed on the Digital Tool.

Go to the Digital Tool for an expanded discussion

Projected Benefit Obligation and Plan Assets

Although not recognized on the employer's balance sheet as liabilities and assets, the projected benefit obligation and plan assets lie at the heart of accounting for pension costs. Understanding the nature of the obligation and fund assets and the transactions and events that affect their measurement helps clarify the study of accounting for benefit plans.

The following illustration summarizes the projected benefit obligation, or PBO, from the perspective of the transactions and events that change it. At any point in time, the PBO represents the actuarial present value of the benefits accumulated by employees for services rendered to date. This increases as employees render further services, as interest is added, and as plans are amended to increase future benefits related to past service. Payments to retirees reduce the liability, and changed assumptions either increase or decrease the liability balance. Actuaries provide most of the necessary measurements related to the PBO.

OBJECTIVE 6

Identify transactions and events that affect the projected benefit obligation.

ILLUSTRATION 20-5
Projected Benefit Obligation—Continuity Schedule

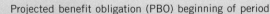

	Projected benefit obligation (PBO) beginning of period
+	Current service cost
+	Interest cost
+	Past service costs of plan amendments during period
−	Benefits paid to retirees
±	Actuarial gains (−) or losses (+) during period on the PBO
=	Projected benefit obligation (PBO) end of period

OBJECTIVE 7

Identify transactions and events that affect the balance of the plan assets.

The plan assets are the other major element. As can be seen from Illustration 20-6, the assets increase as a result of contributions from the employer (and employee, if the plan is contributory) and from the actual return generated on the assets invested. The

---

[16] *Ibid.*, par. .024(e).

[17] *Ibid.*, par. .167.

pool of assets is reduced by payments to retirees. The relationship between the actual and expected return is also illustrated, indicating that the actual return is composed of what was expected and the difference between the expected and the actual return. The plan trustee provides most of this information.

```
        Plan assets, fair value at beginning of period
      + Contributions from employer company, and employees, if applicable
      + Expected return
      + Experience gain on assets  ⎫
                or                 ⎬  or ± Actual return
      − Experience loss on assets  ⎭
      − Benefits paid to retirees
      = Plan assets, fair value at end of period
```

ILLUSTRATION 20-6
Plan Assets—Continuity Schedule

The difference between the projected benefit obligation and the pension assets' fair value at any point in time is known as the plan's funded status. A plan with liabilities that exceed assets is underfunded; a plan with accumulated assets in excess of the related obligation is overfunded.[18]

Before covering the other pension expense components in detail, we will illustrate the basic accounting entries for the first three components: service cost, interest cost, and expected return on plan assets.

Basic Illustration

Essential to the accounting for pensions (and other similar future benefits) under *Handbook* Section 3461 is the fact that it applies a noncapitalization approach. This means that several significant items related to the plan are not recognized in the accounts and on the financial statements of the employer. These include the following items.

1. projected benefit obligation,
2. pension plan assets,
3. unrecognized past service costs,
4. unrecognized net actuarial gain or loss, and
5. unrecognized net transitional asset or liability.

As discussed later, the employer is required to disclose many of these balances in the notes to the financial statements, but the balances are not recognized in the body of the financial statements. Their amounts must be known at all times because they are used to calculate annual pension expense. Therefore, in order to track these off-balance-sheet pension items, supplementary information has to be maintained outside the formal general ledger system. As an example of how this could be done, a work sheet unique to pension accounting will be used to keep track of both the recognized and unrecognized balances and to illustrate the relationship among all the components.[19] The pension work sheet format is shown in Illustration 20-7.

UNDERLYING CONCEPTS

Many plans are underfunded but still quite viable. For example, Loews Corp. had a $159 million shortfall. But Loews at that time had earnings of $594 million and a good net worth. Thus, the going concern assumption permits us to ignore these pension underfundings in many cases because in the long run they are not significant.

	General Journal Entries			Memo Record	
Items	Annual Pension Expense	Cash	Prepaid/ Accrued Cost	Projected Benefit Obligation	Plan Assets

ILLUSTRATION 20-7
Basic Format of Pension Work Sheet

---

[18] When **Algoma Steel Inc.** of Sault Ste. Marie, Ontario was granted protection from its creditors in April 2001 in order to come up with a restructuring plan, the company reported a $625 million shortfall in its pension plan, according to documents filed in court. Algoma's total shareholders' equity at December 31, 2000 was reported at $236 million. The Province of Ontario insurance fund for defined benefit pension plans at this time stood at only $230 million. The Algoma pension shortfall will play a significant role in the future of the company, its employees, and pensioners.

[19] The use of this pension entry work sheet is taken from Paul B. W. Miller, "The New Pension Accounting (Part 2)," *Journal of Accountancy*, February 1987, pp. 86–94.

The left-hand "General Journal Entries" columns of the work sheet underlie entries in the general ledger accounts. The right-hand "Memo Record" columns maintain balances on the unrecognized (noncapitalized) pension items. On the first line of the work sheet, the beginning balances are recorded. Subsequently, transactions and events related to the pension plan are recorded, using debits and credits and using both sets of records as if they were one for recording the entries. For each transaction or event, the debits must equal the credits and the balance in the Prepaid/Accrued Cost column must equal the net balance in the memo record.

2000 Entries and Work Sheet

To illustrate the use of a work sheet and how it helps in accounting for a pension plan, assume that on January 1, 2000, Zarle Corporation adopts *CICA Handbook* Section 3461 to account for its defined benefit pension plan. The following facts apply to the pension plan for the year 2000.

1. Plan assets, January 1, 2000 are $100,000 and at December 31, 2000 are $111,000.
2. Projected benefit obligation, January 1, 2000 is $100,000 and at December 31, 2000 is $112,000.
3. Annual service cost for 2000 is $9,000, accrued as of the end of 2000.
4. Interest (discount) rate on the liability for 2000 is 10%.
5. Expected and actual earnings on plan assets for 2000 is 10%.
6. Contributions (funding) in 2000 are $8,000, remitted at the end of 2000.
7. Benefits paid to retirees during the year are $7,000, paid at the end of 2000.

Using the data presented above, Illustration 20-8 presents the work sheet, including the beginning balances and all of the pension "entries" needed by Zarle Corporation in 2000. The beginning balances of the projected benefit obligation and the pension plan assets are recorded on the work sheet's first line in the memo record. They are not recorded in the general journal and, therefore, are not reported as a liability and an asset in Zarle Corporation's financial statements. These two significant pension items are prime examples of off-balance-sheet amounts that affect pension expense but are not recorded as assets and liabilities in the employer's books.

ILLUSTRATION 20-8
Pension Work Sheet—2000

Items	General Journal Entries			Memo Record	
	Annual Pension Expense	Cash	Prepaid/ Accrued Cost	Projected Benefit Obligation	Plan Assets
Balance, Jan 1, 2000				100,000 Cr.	100,000 Dr.
(a) Service cost	9,000 Dr.			9,000 Cr.	
(b) Interest cost	10,000 Dr.			10,000 Cr.	
(c) Expected return	10,000 Cr.				10,000 Dr.
(d) Contributions		8,000 Cr.			8,000 Dr.
(e) Benefits paid				7,000 Dr.	7,000 Cr.
Expense entry, 2000	9,000 Dr.		9,000 Cr.		
Contribution, 2000		8,000 Dr.	8,000 Dr.		
Balance, Dec. 31, 2000			1,000 Cr.	112,000 Cr.	111,000 Dr.

Entry (a) recognizes the service cost component, which increases pension expense by $9,000 and increases the liability (projected benefit obligation) by $9,000. Entry (b) accrues the interest cost, which increases both the liability and the pension expense by $10,000 (the beginning projected benefit obligation multiplied by the discount rate of 10%). Entry (c) records the expected return on plan assets, which increases the plan assets and decreases the pension expense. Entry (d) reflects Zarle Corporation's contribution (funding) of assets to the pension fund; cash is decreased by $8,000 and plan assets are increased by $8,000. Entry (e) records the benefit payments made to retirees, which results in equal $7,000 decreases to the plan assets and the projected benefit obligation.

The adjusting journal entry on December 31, 2000 to formally record the pension expense for the year is as follows:

Pension Expense	9,000	
Prepaid/Accrued Pension Cost		9,000

When Zarle Corporation issued its $8,000 cheque to the pension fund trustee, the following entry was made:

Prepaid/Accrued Pension Cost	8,000	
Cash		8,000

The credit balance in the Prepaid/Accrued Pension Cost account of $1,000 represents the difference between the 2000 pension expense of $9,000 and the amount funded of $8,000. Because the full amount recognized as expense was not funded, a Prepaid/Accrued Pension Cost account credit balance remains. This account is usually reported as Accrued Pension Cost and is included with long-term liabilities. If the amount funded exceeded the pension expense recognized, the account would have a debit balance, be described as Deferred Pension Expense, and be included as an asset in the balance sheet with the deferred charges.

The Prepaid/Accrued Pension Cost account balance of $1,000 also equals the net of the balances in the memo accounts. A reconciliation of the off-balance-sheet items with the accrued pension cost liability reported in the balance sheet is shown in Illustration 20-9.

Projected benefit obligation (Credit)	$(112,000)
Plan assets at fair value (Debit)	111,000
Funded status—net liability (Credit)	$ (1,000)
Accrued pension cost liability (Credit)	$ (1,000)

ILLUSTRATION 20-9
Pension Reconciliation Schedule—December 31, 2000

If the net of the memo record balances is a credit, the reconciling amount in the prepaid/accrued cost column will be a credit that is equal in amount. If the net of the memo record balances is a debit, the prepaid/accrued cost amount will be a debit that is equal in amount. The work sheet is designed to highlight the relationships among these amounts—information that will be useful later in preparing the notes related to pension disclosures.

PLANS WITH DEFINED BENEFITS THAT VEST OR ACCUMULATE— COMPLEXITIES

Amortization of Unrecognized Past Service Cost (PSC)

When a defined benefit plan is either initiated (adopted) or amended, credit is often given to employees for years of service provided prior to the date of initiation or amendment. As a result of these credits for past services, the actuary remeasures the projected benefit obligation, which is usually greater than it was before. The increase in the projected benefit obligation at the date of initiation or amendment is the cost of the retroactive benefits. This increase is often substantial.

One question that arises is whether the expense and related liability for these past service costs should be fully recognized at the time the plan is initiated or amended. The AcSB has taken the position that no expense for these costs should be recognized at the time of the plan's adoption or amendment. The board's rationale is that the employer would not provide credit for past years of service unless it expected to receive benefits in the future. As a result, *Handbook* Section 3461 specifies that the retroactive benefits' cost should be recognized as an expense on a straight-line basis over the appropriate period benefiting, which normally would be the expected period to full eligibil-

> **OBJECTIVE 9**
> Explain the pension accounting treatment of past service costs.

INTERNATIONAL INSIGHT

In Canada, past service cost is generally amortized over the average period to full eligibility. In Germany, past service cost is recognized immediately. In the Netherlands, prior service cost may either be recognized immediately or directly charged to shareholders' equity.

ity of the employee group covered by the plan.[20] This accounting treatment is consistent with the upper limit of the attribution period (i.e., the expected period to full eligibility) that is used for attributing current service cost to accounting periods. It has the effect of smoothing the amount of pension expense from year to year.

To illustrate the amortization of unrecognized past service cost, assume that Zarle Corporation amends its defined benefit pension plan on January 1, 2001 to grant past service benefits to certain employees. The company's actuaries determine that this causes an increase in the projected benefit obligation of $80,000. The affected employees are grouped according to expected remaining years of service to full eligibility and the expected remaining service period is calculated as follows.

Group	Number of Employees	Expected Remaining Years of Service to Full Eligibility	Total
A	40	1	40
B	20	2	40
C	40	3	120
D	50	4	200
E	20	5	100
	170		500

Expected period to full eligibility = $500 \div 170 = 2.94$

Note: FASB prefers a "years-to-service" amortization method similar to a units-of-production computation. In the first year, for example, 170 service years are worked by employees. Therefore, 170/500 of the past service cost is recognized in the first year.

ILLUSTRATION 20-10
Calculation of Expected Period to Full Eligibility

The amortization of the unrecognized past service cost to be recognized in pension expense each year is $27,211 ($80,000 \div 2.94$) in 2001, $27,211 in 2002, and the remainder of $25,578 in 2003. Note that although the projected benefit obligation is increased as soon as the company amends the plan on January 1, 2001, the expense and associated liability **are recognized on the books of Zarle over a three-year period**, 2001 to 2003. At the end of 2001 and 2002, therefore, a portion of the increased obligation has not been recognized in the financial statements, but is an off-balance-sheet amount.

If full capitalization of all pension plan elements had been adopted, the increase in the company's obligation would have been given accounting recognition immediately as a credit to the liability and a charge (debit) to an intangible asset. The intangible asset treatment assumes that the cost of additional pension benefits increases loyalty and productivity and reduces turnover among the affected employees. This account would be amortized over its useful life.

However, past service cost is accounted for off-balance-sheet initially and may be called unrecognized past service cost. Although not recognized on the balance sheet immediately, past service cost is a factor in calculating pension expense.

IAS NOTE

IAS 19 requires that past service costs be recognized immediately to the extent that the benefits are already vested. Otherwise, they are amortized over the period to when they will be vested.

2001 Entries and Work Sheet

Continuing the Zarle Corporation illustration into 2001, we note that the January 1, 2001 amendment to the pension plan grants to employees past service benefits having a present value of $80,000. The annual amortization of $27,211 for 2001 as calculated in the previous section is carried forward in this illustration. The following facts apply to the pension plan for the year 2001.

1. On January 1, 2001, Zarle Corporation grants past service benefits having a present value of $80,000.
2. Annual service cost for 2001 is $9,500.
3. Interest on the pension obligation (PBO) is 10%.
4. Expected and actual return on plan assets is 10%.

---

[20] *CICA Handbook*, Section 3461, par. .079. Companies could conclude that the benefits are received over a shorter period of time, such as would be the case if it has a history of regular plan amendments.

5. Annual contributions (funding) are $20,000.
6. Benefits paid to retirees in 2001 are $8,000.
7. Amortization of past service cost (PSC) is $27,211.
8. At December 31, 2001, the PBO is $212,700 and plan assets are $134,100.

In all chapter examples and end-of-chapter problem material, unless otherwise specified, **it is assumed that current service cost is credited at year end and that contributions to the fund and benefits paid to retirees are year-end cash flows.**

Illustration 20-11 presents all of the pension "entries" and information used by Zarle Corporation in 2001. The work sheet's first line shows the beginning balances of the Accrued Pension Cost liability account and the memo accounts. Entry (f) records Zarle Corporation's granting of past service benefits by adding $80,000 to the projected benefit obligation and to the unrecognized (noncapitalized) past service cost. Entries (g), (h), (i), (k), and (l) are similar to the corresponding entries in 2000. Entry (j) recognizes the 2001 amortization of unrecognized past service cost by including $27,211 in Pension Expense, reducing the Unrecognized Past Service Cost memo account by the same amount.

ILLUSTRATION 20-11
Pension Work Sheet—2001

	General Journal Entries			Memo Record		
Items	Annual Pension Expense	Cash	Prepaid/ Accrued Cost	Projected Benefit Obligation	Plan Assets	Unrecognized Past Service Cost
Balance, Dec. 31, 2000			1,000 Cr.	112,000 Cr.	111,000 Dr.	
(f) Past service cost				80,000 Cr.		80,000 Dr.
Balance, Jan. 1, 2001			1,000 Cr.	192,000 Cr.	111,000 Dr.	80,000 Dr.
(g) Service cost	9,500 Dr.			9,500 Cr.		
(h) Interest cost	19,200 Dr.			19,200 Cr.		
(i) Expected return	11,100 Cr.				11,100 Dr.	
(j) Amortization of PSC	27,211 Dr.					27,211 Cr.
(k) Contribution		20,000 Cr.			20,000 Dr.	
(l) Benefits paid				8,000 Dr.	8,000 Cr.	
Expense entry, 2001	44,811 Dr.		44,811 Cr.			
Contribution, 2001		20,000 Cr.	20,000 Dr.			
Balance, Dec. 31, 2001			25,811 Cr.	212,700 Cr.	134,100 Dr.	52,789 Dr.

The journal entry on December 31, 2001 to formally record the pension expense for the year is as follows.

Pension Expense	44,811	
Prepaid/Accrued Pension Cost		44,811

When the company made its contributions to the pension fund, the following entry was recorded.

Prepaid/Accrued Pension Cost	20,000	
Cash		20,000

Because the expense exceeds the funding, the Accrued Pension Cost liability account increases by the $24,811 difference ($44,811 less $20,000). In 2001, as in 2000, the balance of the Prepaid/Accrued Pension Cost account ($25,811) is equal to the net of the balances in the memo accounts as shown in the following reconciliation schedule.

ILLUSTRATION 20-12
Pension Reconciliation Schedule—December 31, 2001

Projected benefit obligation (Credit)	$(212,700)
Plan assets at fair value (Debit)	134,100
Funded status—net liability (Credit)	$ (78,600)
Unrecognized past service cost (Debit)	52,789
Accrued pension cost liability (Credit)	$ (25,811)

Actuarial Gains and Losses

Of great concern to companies that have pension plans are the uncontrollable and unexpected swings in pension expense that could be caused by (1) large and sudden changes in the market value of plan assets and (2) changes in actuarial assumptions that affect the amount of the projected benefit obligation. If these gains or losses were to be fully included in pension expense in the period when they occured, substantial fluctuations in pension expense would result. Therefore, the profession decided to reduce the volatility associated with pension expense by using smoothing techniques that dampen and in some cases fully eliminate the fluctuations.

Asset Gains and Losses

The return on plan assets is a component of pension expense that normally reduces the expense amount. A significant change in the actual return could substantially affect pension expense for the year. Assume a company has used 8% as an expected return on plan assets while the actual return experienced is 40%. Should this substantial and perhaps one-time event affect current pension expense?

Actuaries ignore current fluctuations when they develop a funding pattern to pay expected benefits in the future. They develop an expected rate of return and multiply it by an asset value weighted over a reasonable period of time to arrive at an expected return on plan assets. This return is then used to determine the funding pattern.

The board adopted the actuaries' approach in order to avoid recording wide swings that might occur in the actual return: use of the expected return on plan assets is required as a component of pension expense. To achieve this goal, the fair value (or market-related value) of plan assets at the beginning of the year adjusted by additional contributions and payments to retirees during the year is multiplied by the expected long-term rate of return (the actuary's rate). The market-related value of plan assets is a calculated value that recognizes changes in fair value in a systematic and rational manner over no more than five years.[21] Throughout our Zarle Corporation illustrations, market-related value and fair value of plan assets are assumed equal.

The difference between the expected return and the actual return is referred to as an asset experience gain or loss. A gain occurs when the actual return is greater than the expected return and a loss occurs when actual returns are less than expected.

The amount of asset gain or loss is determined at the end of each year by comparing the calculated expected return with the actual return earned. In the preceding example, the expected return on Zarle's pension fund assets for 2001 was $11,100. If the actual return on the plan assets for the year 2001 was $12,000, then an experience gain of $900 ($12,000 − $11,100) exists. Plan assets are increased by $12,000, annual expense is credited with $11,100, and an unrecognized actuarial gain of $900 is included in the memo accounts and combined with unrecognized gains and losses accumulated in prior years.

Liability Gains and Losses

In estimating the projected benefit obligation (the liability), actuaries make assumptions about such variables as mortality rate, retirement rate, turnover rate, disability rate, and salary amounts. Any difference between these assumed rates and amounts and those actually experienced changes the amount of the projected benefit obligation (PBO). Seldom does actual experience coincide exactly with actuarial predictions. Such an unexpected gain or loss that results in a change in the projected benefit obligation is referred to as a liability experience gain or loss. Actuarial gains and losses also arise when the assumptions used by the actuary in calculating the PBO are revised, causing

---

[21] *Ibid.*, par. .076 and .077. Different ways of calculating market-related value may be used for different asset classes. For example, an employer might use fair value for bonds and a five-year moving-average for equities, but the manner of determining market-related value should be applied consistently from year to year for each asset class.

a change in the obligation amount. An example is the effect of a change in the interest rate used to discount the pension cash flows on the obligation calculation. Because experience gains and losses are similar to and affect the PBO in the same way as actuarial gains and losses, both types are referred to as actuarial gains and losses.

To illustrate, assume that the expected projected benefit obligation of Zarle Corporation was $212,700 at December 31, 2001. If the company's actuaries, using December 31, 2001 estimates, calculate a projected benefit obligation of $213,500, then the company has suffered an actuarial loss of $800 ($213,500 − $212,700). If the actuary calculates a reduced obligation, an actuarial gain results. The PBO is adjusted to its correct balance and the difference is included in the memo accounts as an unrecognized actuarial gain or loss.

Corridor Amortization for Net Actuarial Gains and Losses

Because the asset gains and losses and the liability gains and losses can and are expected to offset each other over time, the accumulated unrecognized net gain or loss may not grow very large. In fact, this is the reason given for not including these gains and losses directly in pension expense each year. But it is possible that no offsetting will occur and the balance of the unrecognized net gain or loss will continue to grow. To limit its growth, the corridor approach is used for amortizing the net unrecognized gain or loss. Under this approach, the unrecognized net gain or loss balance is considered too large and must be amortized **only when it exceeds the arbitrarily selected criterion of 10% of the larger of the beginning balance of the projected benefit obligation and the fair value or market-related value of the plan assets**.

To illustrate the corridor approach, assume data on the projected benefit obligation and the plan assets over a six-year period as shown in Illustration 20-13.

ILLUSTRATION 20-13
Calculation of the Corridor

Beginning-of-the-Year Balances	Projected Benefit Obligation	Fair or Market-Related Asset Value	Corridor* +/− 10%
2000	**$1,000,000**	$ 900,000	$100,000
2001	**1,200,000**	1,100,000	120,000
2002	1,300,000	**1,700,000**	170,000
2003	1,500,000	**2,250,000**	225,000
2004	1,700,000	**1,750,000**	175,000
2005	**1,800,000**	1,700,000	180,000

* The corridor becomes 10% of the larger (in boldface) of the projected benefit obligation and the fair or market-related plan asset value.

If the balance of the net unrecognized gain or loss stays within the corridor limits each year, no amortization is required—the unrecognized net gain or loss is carried forward unchanged. This becomes more apparent when the data are portrayed graphically as in Illustration 20-14.

ILLUSTRATION 20-14
Graphic Illustration of the Corridor

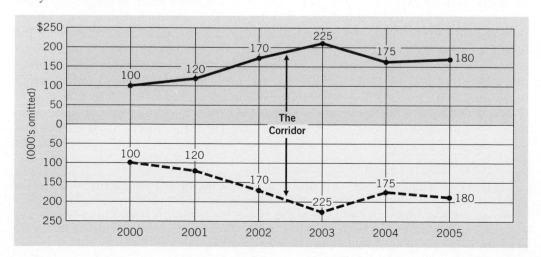

If amortization is required, the minimum amortization is the excess divided by the active employees' average remaining service period.[22] Any systematic method of amortization may be used in lieu of the amount determined under this approach, provided it is greater than the minimum and is used consistently for both gains and losses, and is disclosed.

Illustration

In applying the corridor approach in any particular year, **the calculations are based on beginning-of-the-period balances only**. That is, amortization of the excess unrecognized net gain or loss is included as a component of pension expense only if the unrecognized net gain or loss **at the beginning of the year** exceeded **the beginning-of-the-year corridor**. If no unrecognized net gain or loss exists at the beginning of the period, no recognition of gains or losses can result in the current period.

To illustrate the amortization of unrecognized net gains and losses, assume a company provides the following information.

	2001	2002	2003
Projected benefit obligation, January 1	$2,100,000	$2,600,000	$2,900,000
Fair/market-related asset value, January 1	2,600,000	2,800,000	2,700,000
Net actuarial loss in year	400,000	300,000	–0–

If the employee group's average remaining service life is five and one-half years, the schedule to amortize the unrecognized net loss is as follows.

ILLUSTRATION 20-15
Corridor Test and Gain/Loss Amortization

Year	Projected Benefit Obligation[a]	Plan Assets[a]	Corridor[b]	Beginning of Year Cumulative Unrecognized Net Loss	Minimum Amortization of Loss (For Current Year)
2001	$2,100,000	$2,600,000	$260,000	$ –0–	$ –0–
2002	2,600,000	2,800,000	280,000	400,000	21,818[c]
2003	2,900,000	2,700,000	290,000	678,182[d]	70,579[d]

[a] All as of the beginning of the period.
[b] 10% of the greater of projected benefit obligation or plan assets fair and market-related value.
[c] $400,000 − $280,000 = $120,000; $120,000 ÷ 5.5 = $21,818
[d] $400,000 − $21,818 + $300,000 = $678,182; $678,182 − $290,000 = $388,182; $388,182 ÷ 5.5 = $70,579.

Note that the unrecognized net gain or loss is a cumulative number. At the end of a year, it is the opening balance of the cumulative unrecognized net gain or loss increased or decreased by asset and liability gains and losses attributable to the current year, and reduced by the amortization in the current year, if applicable. This becomes the next year's opening balance.

As indicated in the illustration above, the $400,000 loss at the beginning of 2002 increased pension expense in 2002 by $21,818. This amount is small in comparison with the total loss of $400,000 and indicates that the corridor approach dampens the effects (reduces volatility) of these gains and losses on pension expense. The rationale for the corridor is that gains and losses result from refinements in estimates as well as real changes in economic value and that over time some of these gains and losses will offset one another. It therefore seems reasonable that gains and losses should not be recognized fully as a component of pension expense in the period in which they arise.[23]

Note that these gains and losses are subject to triple smoothing. First, the asset gain or loss is smoothed by using the expected return. Then the unrecognized gain or loss

---

[22] *Ibid.*, par. .088.

[23] However, gains and losses that arise from a single occurrence not directly related to the operation of the pension plan and not in the ordinary course of the employer's business should be recognized immediately. For example, a gain or loss that is directly related to a plant closing, a disposal of a segment, or a similar event that greatly affects the size of the employee work force is recognized as a part of the gain or loss associated with that event.

at the beginning of the year is not amortized unless it is greater than the corridor. Finally, the excess is spread over the remaining service life of existing employees.

2002 Entries and Work Sheet

Continuing the Zarle Corporation illustration into 2002, the following facts apply to the pension plan.

1. Annual service cost for 2002 is $13,000.
2. Interest on accrued benefits is 10%.
3. Expected return on plan assets is 10% or $13,410.
4. Actual return on plan assets is $12,000.
5. Market-related and fair values of plan assets at December 31, 2002 are $159,600.
6. Amortization of past service cost in 2002 is $27,211.
7. Annual contributions (funding) are $24,000.
8. Benefits paid to retirees in 2002 are $10,500.
9. Changes in actuarial assumptions establish the end-of-year PBO at $265,000.

The work sheet in Illustration 20-16 presents all of the pension information needed by Zarle Corporation in 2002. The beginning balances that relate to the pension plan are recorded on the work sheet's first line. In this case, the beginning balances for Zarle Corporation are the ending balances from the 2001 pension work sheet in Illustration 20-11.

ILLUSTRATION 20-16
Pension Work Sheet—2002

| | General Journal Entries | | | Memo Record | | | |
Items	Annual Pension Expense	Cash	Prepaid/ Accrued Cost	Projected Benefit Obligation	Plan Assets	Unrecognized Past Service Cost	Unrecognized Actuarial Gain or Loss
Balance, Dec. 31, 2001			25,811 Cr.	212,700 Cr.	134,100 Dr.	52,789 Dr.	
(m)Service cost	13,000 Dr.			13,000 Cr.			
(n) Interest cost	21,270 Dr.			21,270 Cr.			
(o) Expected return	13,410 Cr.				13,410 Dr.		
(p) Amortization of PSC	27,211 Dr.					27,211 Cr.	
(q) Contributions		24,000 Cr.			24,000 Dr.		
(r) Benefits paid				10,500 Dr.	10,500 Cr.		
(s) Liability loss				28,530 Cr.			28,530 Dr.
(t) Asset loss					1,410 Cr.		1,410 Dr.
Expense entry, 2002	48,071 Dr.		48,071 Cr.				
Contribution, 2002		24,000 Cr.	24,000 Dr.				
Balance, Dec. 31, 2002			49,882 Cr.	265,000 Cr.	159,600 Dr.	25,578 Dr.	29,940 Dr.

Entries (m), (n), (o), (p), (q), and (r) are similar to the corresponding entries explained in 2000 or 2001. Entries (o) and (t) are related. The recording of the expected return in entry (o) has been illustrated in 2000 and 2001. In both these years, it was assumed that the actual return on plan assets was equal to the expected return. In 2002, the expected return of $13,410 (the expected rate of 10% times the beginning-of-the-year fair or market-related value of the plan assets of $134,100) is higher than the actual return of $12,000. The resulting asset loss of $1,410 ($13,410 − $12,000) is not recognized in pension expense in 2002.

Entry (s) records the change in the projected benefit obligation that results from a change in actuarial assumptions. As indicated, the actuary has now calculated the ending balance to be $265,000. Given that the memo record balance at December 31 is $236,470 ($212,700 + $13,000 + $21,270 − $10,500), a difference of $28,530 ($265,000 − $236,470) is indicated. This $28,530 increase in the employer's obligation is an actuarial loss that is deferred by debiting it to the work sheet Unrecognized Actuarial Gain or Loss account. No amortization of the net actuarial loss is recognized in 2002 because the amortization is based on the net actuarial gain or loss that existed at the first of the year, which was $0.

The journal entry on December 31, 2002 to formally record pension expense for the year is as follows.

Pension Expense	48,071	
Prepaid/Accrued Pension Cost		48,071

The company has already recorded the $24,000 contribution during the year as follows.

Prepaid/Accrued Pension Cost	24,000	
Cash		24,000

As illustrated previously for the 2000 and 2001 work sheets, the credit balance of the Prepaid/Accrued Pension Cost account at December 31, 2002 of $49,882 is equal to the net of the balances in the memo accounts as shown below.

ILLUSTRATION 20-17
Pension Reconciliation
Schedule—December 31, 2002

Projected benefit obligation (Credit)	$(265,000)
Plan assets at fair value (Debit)	159,600
Funded status—net liability (Credit)	$(105,400)
Unrecognized past service cost (Debit)	25,578
Unrecognized net actuarial loss (Debit)	29,940
Accrued pension cost liability (Credit)	$ (49,882)

Take a minute to understand what this reconciliation tells you. The plan is under-funded by $105,400, yet on the books, a liability of only $49,882 is reported. This is a discrepancy of $55,518. Over time, as the balance of the unrecognized past service cost and net actuarial loss are amortized to expense (debit Expense, credit Liability) the liability on the books will be increased by $55,518 and there will be no difference between the funded status and the liability recognized on the books.

Other Defined Benefit Plans with Benefits that Vest or Accumulate

Other Post-retirement Benefit Plans

Companies also provide their employees with other post-employment benefits as part of their compensation package. These may include such benefits as health care, pre-scription drugs, life insurance, dental and eye care, legal and tax services, tuition assis-tance, or free or subsidized travel. In the past, companies accounted for the cost of these employee future benefits as an expense in the period the benefits were provided to the retirees, their spouses, dependents, and beneficiaries; that is, on a pay-as-you-go basis.

In 1990, after much study, the FASB issued *Statement No. 106*, "Employers' Account-ing for Post-retirement Benefits Other Than Pensions." This standard required a change from the pay-as-you-go method of accounting for these benefits to an accrual basis. Similar to pension accounting, the accrual basis necessitates measuring the employer's obligation to provide future benefits and accrual of the cost during the years that the employee provides service. When the standard was first applied, the effect on most U.S. companies was significant. For example, **General Motors** announced a U.S. $20.8 billion charge against its 1992 earnings resulting from the adoption of the new stan-dard, and this at a time when the company's net book value prior to the charge was approximately U.S. $28 billion!

The pay-as-you-go basis remained the predominant method for most companies in Canada until the adoption of *Handbook* Section 3461, effective in 2000. This stan-dard requires Canadian companies to account for all defined benefit plans where the benefits vest or accumulate on the same basis as they account for defined benefit pension plans, and on the same basis as *SFAS* No. 106.[24] Some of the larger Canadian

---

[24] The impact of the change in Canada is not as significant as in the U.S. because we have broader universal health care coverage. A Financial Executives Institute Canada (FEI) study esti-mated a total Canadian unreported liability of $52 billion, almost entirely unfunded.

companies with reporting requirements south of the border moved to adopt the FASB standard soon after it was issued.

Unlike pension benefits, companies tend not to prefund their other post-employment benefit plans. One reason is because payments to prefund health care costs, for example, unlike contributions to a pension trust, are not tax deductible. Another reason is that such benefits were once perceived as low-cost employee benefits that could be changed or eliminated at will and, therefore, were not a legal liability. The accounting definition of a liability now goes beyond the notion of a legally enforceable claim to encompass equitable or constructive obligations, making it clear that many future benefit promises are liabilities. In addition, the costs and liabilities are increasing as the population ages and as new expensive drugs and technology lengthen life expectancy.

OBJECTIVE 11

Identify the differences between pensions and post-retirement health care benefits.

Differences Between Pension Benefits and Post-retirement Health Care Benefits

Although these two types of retirement benefits appear similar, there are some significant differences, as shown in the exhibit below.

Item	Pensions	Health Care Benefits
Funding	Generally funded	Generally NOT funded
Benefit	Well defined and level dollar amount	Generally uncapped and great variability
Beneficiary	Retiree (maybe some benefit to surviving spouse)	Retiree, spouse, and other dependants
Benefit Payable	Monthly	As needed and used
Predictability	Variables are reasonably predictable	Utilization difficult to predict; level of cost varies geographically and fluctuates over time

ILLUSTRATION 20-18
Differences Between Pensions and Post-retirement Health Care Benefits

Measuring the net periodic post-retirement benefit cost is involved and complex. Due to the uncertainties in forecasting health care costs, rates of utilization, changes in government health programs, and the differences employed in nonmedical assumptions (discount rate, employee turnover, rate of pre-65 retirement, spouse-age difference, etc.), estimates of post-retirement benefit costs may have a large margin of error. Is the information, therefore, relevant, reliable, or verifiable? The FASB, in adopting *Statement* 106, concluded "that the obligation to provide post-retirement benefits meets the definition of a liability, is representationally faithful, is relevant to financial statement users, and can be measured with sufficient reliability at a justifiable cost."[25] Failure to accrue an obligation and an expense prior to paying benefits is considered an unfaithful representation of what financial statements purport to represent. The Canadian standard setters agreed.

Many companies opposed the requirement warning that the standard would devastate earnings. Others argued that putting "soft" numbers on the balance sheet was inappropriate and, finally, others noted that it would force companies to curtail these benefits to employees.

The authors believe that the standard setters deserve special praise for this standard. Because this issue was addressed, companies now recognize the magnitude of these costs. This recognition has led to efforts to control escalating health care and other post-retirement benefit costs.

The basic concepts, accounting terminology, and measurement methodology applicable to defined benefit pensions are equally applicable to the requirements for other benefits that vest or accumulate on the basis of service provided by employees. The recognition and measurement criteria for the obligation and plan assets are the same, as is the actuarial valuation method, the attribution period, and the calculation of the current cost of benefits.

One area where there is a difference in the variables that affect the calculation of the current expense is the relative size of the transitional amount. If a company first applies the recommendations of Section 3461 **on a prospective basis** to future benefits

---

[25] *FASB Statement No. 106*, par. 163.

such as post-retirement health care and life insurance, a large transitional liability is likely to result. This is caused by significant unrecognized liabilities and negligible plan assets due to the common practice of not funding these plans. The net unrecorded obligation is amortized in a rational and systematic manner, normally over the expected average remaining service life of the active employees covered by the plan.[26] The amortization is a component of the current benefit expense.

Many companies adopted the new accounting policy on a retroactive basis, recognizing the net accrued obligation as a liability and the accumulated cost as an adjustment to opening retained earnings. In other respects, accounting for the benefit costs is similar to that illustrated for defined benefit pensions.

Other Post-employment Benefits and Compensated Absences

Full accrual accounting is appropriate for post-employment benefits and compensated absences where the benefits either vest in the employee or accumulate with the length of service provided. Therefore the same recognition and measurement principles as applied above for pensions and other retirement benefits should be used, subject to the standard recognition caveats that (1) the amount of the liability and expense can be reasonably estimated; and (2) payment of the benefits is probable.

Examples of such benefits include sabbaticals where unrestricted time off with pay is granted for past service, service-related long-term disability benefits, or sick days not used that accumulate and get paid out on retirement.[27] Assume, for example, an employee benefit plan that provides a cash bonus of $500 per year of service on termination of employment or retirement from the company provided the employee has been employed for a minimum of 10 years. Because the right to the benefit is earned by rendering service and the benefit increases with the length of service provided, the cost and related liability should be accrued from the date of employment. The measurement of the obligation and expense would take into consideration the probabilities related to employee turnover. The fact that the benefits do not vest for 10 years does not eliminate the need to recognize the cost and liability over the first 10 years of employment.

Benefits such as sick leave that accumulates with service but that does not vest in the employee should, in theory, be accrued as the employee provides service. In practical terms, the difficulty in determining a reasonable estimate of the amount, coupled with its relative immateriality, means that the cost is often not accrued.

Comprehensive Illustration with a Transitional Balance

Assume that on January 1, 2000, Quest Limited adopted the new accounting standards to account for its retirement health care benefit plan and accounted for the change in accounting policy on a prospective basis. The following facts apply to this plan two years later in 2002.

1. Plan assets at fair value (also market-related value) on January 1, 2002 are $10,000.
2. PBO, January 1, 2002 is $426,000.
3. Unrecognized transition liability at January 1, 2002 is $336,000 (original amount of $368,000; amortization period of 23 years).
4. Unrecognized net actuarial loss at January 1, 2002 is $48,000.
5. Accrued benefit liability at January 1, 2002 is $32,000.
6. Actual return on plan assets in 2002 is $600.

---

[26] Section 3461 gives companies the option of accounting for the change in accounting policy on a retroactive basis. Retroactive adjustment has the effect of charging the net transition cost to the opening balance of retained earnings rather than to current income, as in the U.S. standard, or to current and future income, as under the prospective option.

[27] Sabbaticals where the employee is expected to use the compensated absence to perform research or provide other activities to the benefit of the organization need not be accrued over the period the sabbatical is earned.

7. Expected return on plan assets in 2002 is $800.
8. Discount rate is 8%.
9. Increase in PBO, December 31, 2002 due to change in actuarial assumptions is $20,000.
10. Service cost for 2002 is $26,000.
11. Contributions (funding) to plan in 2002 are $50,000.
12. Benefit payments on behalf of retirees in 2002 are $35,000.
13. Expected average remaining service life (EARSL), January 1, 2002 is 24 years.

Illustration 20-19 presents all of the analysis and information needed by Quest Limited in 2002.

ILLUSTRATION 20-19
Quest Limited Work Sheet—2002

	General Journal Entries			Memo Record			
Items	Annual Expense	Cash	Prepaid/ Accrued Cost	PBO	Plan Assets	Unrecognized Transition Amount	Unrecognized Net Actuarial Gain or Loss
Balance, Jan. 1, 2002			32,000 Cr.	426,000 Cr.	10,000 Dr.	336,000 Dr.	48,000 Dr.
(a) Service cost	26,000 Dr.			26,000 Cr.			
(b) Interest cost	34,080 Dr.			34,080 Cr.			
(c) Expected return	800 Cr.				800 Dr.		
(d) Experience loss					200 Cr.		200 Dr.
(e) Contributions		50,000 Cr.			50,000 Dr.		
(f) Benefits paid				35,000 Dr.	35,000 Cr.		
(g) Amortization: Transition liability	16,000 Dr.					16,000 Cr.	
(h) Inc. in PBO—loss				20,000 Cr.			20,000 Dr.
(i) Amortization: Unrecognized net actuarial loss	225 Dr.						225 Cr.
Expense entry, 2002	75,505 Dr.		75,505 Cr.				
Contribution, 2002		50,000 Cr.	50,000 Dr.				
Balance, Dec. 31, 2002			57,505 Cr.	471,080 Cr.	25,600 Dr.	320,000 Dr.	67,975 Dr.

Entry (a) records the service cost component, which increases the retirement health benefit expense by $26,000 and the liability (PBO) by $26,000. Entry (b) accrues the interest cost, which increases both the liability (PBO) and the expense by $34,080—the weighted-average PBO multiplied by the discount rate of 8%. Because the service cost, benefits paid, and actuarial loss are all assumed to take place at the end of the year, the PBO's weighted-average balance for the year is the opening balance of $426,000.

Entries (c) and (d) are related. The expected return of $800 is higher than the actual return of $600. The expected return is calculated by applying the expected long-term rate of return on plan assets to the weighted-average fair or market-related value of plan assets. The payments on behalf of retirees and contributions received from the employer are assumed to be year-end transactions. The weighted-average value for 2002, therefore, is the opening balance at January 1, 2002. The expected return of $800 is given in this case. The experience loss of $200 ($800 − $600) is deferred by increasing (debiting) the Unrecognized Net Actuarial Loss.

Entry (e) records Quest Limited's contribution (funding) of assets to the retirement health care benefit fund. Entry (f) records the benefit payments made for the benefit of retirees, which results in equal $35,000 decreases to the plan assets and the liability (PBO). Entry (g) records the amortization of the unrecognized transition obligation. It is amortized over the employee group's expected average remaining service life on January 1, 2000 of 23 years. The amortization of $16,000 ($368,000 ÷ 23) increases the expense and decreases the unrecognized costs associated with the transition obligation.[28]

---

[28] If Quest Limited had applied the accounting standard retroactively instead, the net transition obligation would have been given full accounting recognition as a liability with the accumulated costs of $368,000 recognized as an adjustment to the January 1, 2000 balance of retained earnings. As the full transition balance would have been recognized in the accounts, no future amortization is required.

Entry (h) records the change in the PBO that results from a change in actuarial assumptions. This $20,000 increase in the employer's accumulated liability is an actuarial loss that is deferred by increasing (debiting) the unrecognized net actuarial loss.

The last adjustment, entry (i), records the (minimum) amortization of the unrecognized net actuarial loss. The $225 amortization is determined as follows.

Corridor amount—10% of the greater of the January 1, 2002	
balance of the PBO ($426,000) and the fair/market-related	
value of the plan assets ($10,000): $426,000 × 10%	$42,600
Unamortized net actuarial loss, January 1, 2002	$48,000
Excess of unamortized loss over corridor amount,	
January 1, 2002: $48,000 − $42,600	$5,400
Minimum amortization required: $5,400 ÷ 24	$225

Quest Limited could use a different method of amortization, but the minimum amortization in 2002 is $225. This increases the current retirement health care benefit expense and reduces the unrecognized net actuarial loss.

During 2002, Quest Limited recorded the cash disbursement to the benefit fund as follows.

Prepaid/Accrued Retirement Health Cost	50,000	
Cash		50,000

All that remains is to record the December 31, 2002 adjusting journal entry to recognize the annual retirement health benefit expense.

Retirement Health Benefit Expense	75,505	
Prepaid/Accrued Retirement Health Cost		75,505

The balance of the Accrued Retirement Health Cost account at December 31, 2002 of $57,505 is equal to the net of the balances in the memo accounts as shown in the following reconciliation.

ILLUSTRATION 20-20
Reconciliation Schedule—
December 31, 2002

Projected health benefit PBO (Credit)	$(471,080)
Plan assets at fair value (Debit)	25,600
Funded status—net liability (Credit)	$(445,480)
Unrecognized transition amount (Debit)	320,000
Unrecognized net actuarial loss (Debit)	67,975
Accrued retirement health cost liability (Credit)	$ (57,505)

Reporting Defined Benefit Plans in Financial Statements

OBJECTIVE 12

Identify the financial reporting and disclosure requirements for defined benefit plans.

One might suspect that a phenomenon as significant and complex as pensions and other defined benefit plans would involve extensive reporting and disclosure requirements. *Handbook* Section 3461 has considerably expanded the disclosures required over the predecessor section, with the objective of providing better information for users to assess the amounts and likelihood of cash flows associated with future benefits, the relationship between cash flows and pension and other benefits expense, the impact of employee benefits on the income statement, and the reasonableness of the assumptions that underlie the measurement of the liability, fund assets, and current expense. In addition, information about unrecognized amounts informs readers of the extent to which obligations to employees to date will affect future earnings.

Consistent with the profession's interest in differential reporting, two levels of disclosure exist—one for all companies, and an expanded level of disclosure for public enterprises, co-operative organizations, deposit-taking institutions, and life insurance enterprises.

All enterprises are required to disclose information about amounts recorded in the financial statements, the off-balance sheet accounts, and underlying assumptions used.[29]

---

[29] *CICA Handbook*, Section 3461, par. .155.

Amounts recorded in the financial statements: As well as the amount of expense recognized for the period (income statement), the period-end balance of the accrued benefit liability or accrued benefit asset (balance sheet), and the amount of employer and employee contributions (cash flows) must be disclosed.

Off-balance sheet accounts: The actuarially determined accrued benefit obligation (PBO), the fair value of the plan assets, and the resulting plan surplus or deficit at the balance sheet date is required disclosure, along with the amount of benefits paid during the period.

Underlying assumptions: To help in assessing the reasonableness of the amounts reported, the discount rate, the expected long-term rate of return on plan assets, the rate of compensation increase, information about the trends, and rate assumptions used to calculate the cost of health care benefits are all required disclosures.

For financial institutions and enterprises that are widely held, as described above, an additional level of information is required:

(a) reconciliation of the beginning and ending balances of the accrued benefit obligation (PBO);

(b) reconciliation of the beginning and ending balances of the plan assets' fair value, along with the expected return on plan assets for the period;

(c) the unamortized balances of past service costs, net actuarial gains or losses, and the net transitional obligation or asset at the balance sheet date, and the amount of amortization of each for the period.[30]

Additional disclosures related to complex issues not included as part of the chapter discussion are required, and enterprises are encouraged to extend their disclosures beyond this where it will help users to better understand the financial statements.

Companies organize these disclosures in a variety of acceptable ways. **Bombardier Inc.**, whose notes to the financial statements for employee future benefits is reproduced below, reported an Accrued Benefit Asset on its January 31, 2001 balance sheet of $146.6 million as well as an Accrued Benefit Liability of $492.1 million, both of which are reported in more detail in the notes. Because the company has more than one plan and the position of one plan cannot be netted with that of another, the asset and liability are reported separately. Note that the "plans for post-retirement benefits other than pensions are all unfunded." Bombardier changed its accounting for employee future benefits to comply with new Section 3461, effective February 1, 2000. The change was applied retroactively and the change's effect is reported in Note 1 to the financial statements included below.

UNDERLYING CONCEPTS

This represents another compromise between relevance and reliability. The disclosure of the unrecognized items attempts to balance these objectives.

UNDERLYING CONCEPTS

Does it make a difference to users of financial statements whether pension information is recognized in the financial statements or disclosed only in the notes? The standard setters were not sure, so in accordance with the full disclosure principle, they decided to provide extensive pension plan disclosures.

Go to the Digital Tool for more examples of disclosures

NOTES TO CONSOLIDATED FINANCIAL STATEMENTS
For the years ended January 31, 2001 and 2000
(tabular figures in millions of Canadian dollars, except share capital and share option plans)

1. **CHANGES IN ACCOUNTING POLICIES (IN PART)**
Employee Future Benefits
Also, effective February 1, 2000, the Corporation retroactively adopted the new method of accounting for employee future benefits required by the Canadian Institute of Chartered Accountants, without restating prior years. Under the new recommendations, the cost of pension and other post-retirement benefits earned by employees is actuarially determined using the projected benefit method prorated on service and Management's best estimate of expected health care costs. Plan obligations are discounted using current market interest rates. Previously, costs for employee future benefits other than pension were mainly expensed as incurred and pension cost obligations were discounted using the expected long-term rate of return on plan assets.

As a result of this change, the accrued benefit liability increased by $303.1 million, the deferred income tax liability decreased by $92.5 million and retained earnings decreased by $210.6 million as at February 1, 2000.

ILLUSTRATION 20-21
Illustrative Disclosure—
Bombardier Inc.

---

[30] *Ibid.*, par. .157.

20. EMPLOYEE FUTURE BENEFITS

The Corporation sponsors several defined benefit qualified and nonqualified pension plans and other post-retirement benefit plans for its employees.

The significant actuarial assumptions adopted to determine the Corporation's accrued benefit obligations are as follows (weighted-average assumptions as at the December 31, 2000 measurement date):

	2001	
	Pension Benefits	Other Benefits
Discount rate	6.70%	7.09%
Expected long-term rate of return on plan assets	8.00%	—
Rate of compensation increase	4.25%	4.60%
Health care cost trend	—	5.39%

In Canada, a 7.50% annual rate of increase in the per capita cost of covered health care benefits was assumed for the year ending January 31, 2002. This rate is assumed to decrease gradually to 5.50% for fiscal 2004 and to remain at that level thereafter. In other countries, the health care cost trend remains constant.

The following tables provide a reconciliation of the changes in the plans' accrued benefit obligations and fair value of assets over the year ended January 31, 2001, and a statement of the funded status as at January 31:

	2001	
	Pension Benefits	Other Benefits
Accrued benefit obligations		
Obligation at beginning of year	$2,600.8	$214.0
Current service cost	108.8	12.3
Employee contributions	35.6	—
Interest cost	177.6	16.1
Plan amendments	63.6	—
Actuarial loss	59.7	9.2
Benefits paid	(106.4)	(9.8)
Effect of foreign currency exchange rate changes	(52.9)	0.7
Obligation at end of year	$2,886.8	$242.5
Plan assets		
Fair value at beginning of year	$2,531.9	
Actual return on plan assets	12.2	
Employer contributions	63.8	
Employee contributions	35.6	
Benefits paid	(106.4)	
Effect of foreign currency exchange rate changes	(48.4)	
Fair value at end of year	$2,488.7	
Funded status		
Plan deficit	$(398.1)	$(242.5)
Unrecognized amounts	282.8	10.0
Net recognized amount	$(115.3)	$(232.5)

The following table provides the amounts recognized in the balance sheet as at January 31:

	2001	
	Pension Benefits	Other Benefits
Accrued benefit asset	$ 146.6	$ —
Accrued benefit liability	(261.9)	(232.5)
Net amount recognized	$(115.3)	$(232.5)

The accrued benefit obligations and fair value of plan assets, for pension plans with accrued benefit obligations in excess of plan assets, were $2,247.4 million and $1,807.3 million, respectively, as at January 31, 2001. The Corporation's plans for post-retirement benefits other than pensions are all unfunded.

The following table provides components of the net benefit plan cost for the year ended January 31:

	2001	
	Pension Benefits	Other Benefits
Current service cost	$108.8	$12.3
Interest cost	177.6	16.1
Expected return on plan assets	(198.8)	—
Other	1.9	—
Net benefit plan cost	$ 89.5	$28.4

For the year ended January 31, 2000
The present value of accrued pension benefit obligations attributed to services rendered up to the balance sheet dates and the net assets available to provide for these obligations, at market-related values, were as follows as at January 31:

	2000
Pension fund assets	$2,507.5
Accrued pension benefit obligations	$2,077.6

Plan Complexities

This chapter has provided the basics of accounting for employee future benefits. Complexities arise from temporary deviations from the benefit plan, valuation of the accrued benefit asset, obligation settlements, benefits provided for through insurance contracts or other arrangements, plan curtailments, termination benefits, and multi-employer or multiple-employer plans. The Digital Tool briefly discusses issues related to settlements, curtailments, limitations on the valuation of the accrued benefit asset, and termination benefits.

INTERNATIONAL INSIGHT

U.S. GAAP requires recognition of a minimum liability if the accumulated benefit obligation exceeds the fair value of plan assets.

Go to the Digital Tool for expanded discussions.

DEFINED BENEFIT PLANS—BENEFITS DO NOT VEST OR ACCUMULATE

Post-employment Benefits and Compensated Absences

Some post-employment benefits and compensated absences are available to all employees regardless of the length of service provided. Entitlement to these benefits is not dependent on or increased by length of service, nor do the benefits vest or accumulate. Employees are eligible for benefits by virtue of being an employee. Examples of this type of benefit include parental (maternity and paternity) leave and some short-term and long-term disability benefits.

For this type of benefit plan, the AcSB recommends that the liability and expense be recognized only "when the event that obligates the entity occurs."[31] Thus, when an employee applies for parental leave or when an employee becomes disabled, the total estimated liability and expense associated with the event is recognized at that point as follows.

> **OBJECTIVE 13**
>
> Identify the financial accounting and reporting requirements for defined benefit plans whose benefits do not vest or accumulate.

Employee Benefit Expense	xxx	
Parental Leave Benefits Payable		xxx
or		
Estimated Disability Liability		xxx

As the compensated absences are taken and the employee is paid, the liability is reduced:

Parental Leave Benefits Payable	xxx	
or		
Estimated Disability Liability	xxx	
Cash		xxx

---

[31] *Ibid*, par. .029.

In theory, the liability for and cost of the benefits should be accrued as employees provide services. Practical difficulties in measuring the liability and the relative immateriality of the amounts involved lie behind the proposal to defer recognition until an event occurs that obligates the company to provide the benefit. Thus, this method of accounting has been referred to as the "event accrual" method. Similar measurement problems may exist with sick leave that accumulates but does not vest. The "event accrual" method may be appropriate in this circumstance as well.

Concluding Observation

The analysis of issues related to pension plans is often the subject of articles in the financial press. This is hardly surprising given the obligations companies have and the billions of dollars of assets held by Canadian pension funds. *Handbook* Section 3461 imposes uniform treatment for plans with similar characteristics and clarifies many issues. It helps users understand the financial implications of a company's benefit plans on its financial position, results of operations, and cash flows.

Critics still argue, however, that much remains to be done. One issue in particular relates to the delayed recognition of certain events. Changes in pension plan obligations and changes in the value of plan assets are still not recognized immediately but instead are systematically incorporated over subsequent periods through a process of amortization.

Summary of Learning Objectives

1 Distinguish between accounting for the employer's pension plan and accounting for the pension fund. The company or employer is the organization sponsoring the pension plan. It incurs the cost and makes contributions to the pension fund. The fund or plan is the entity that receives the contributions from the employer, administers the pension assets, and makes the benefit payments to the pension recipients (retired employees). The fund should be a separate legal and accounting entity for which a set of books is maintained and financial statements are prepared.

2 Identify types of pension plans and their characteristics. The two most common types of pension arrangements are: (1) Defined contribution plans: the employer agrees to contribute to a pension trust a certain sum each period based on a formula. This formula may consider such factors as age, length of employee service, employer's profits, and compensation level. Only the employer's contribution is defined; no promise is usually made regarding the ultimate benefits paid out to the employees. (2) Defined benefit plans: define the benefits that the employee will receive at the time of retirement. The formula typically used provides for the benefits to be a function of the employee's years of service and compensation level when he or she nears retirement.

3 Identify the accounting and disclosure requirements for defined contribution plans. Defined contribution plans are accounted for on a cash basis. Companies are required to disclose the expense recognized for the period and the nature and effect of significant matters affecting comparability from period to period.

4 Explain alternative measures for valuing the pension obligation. One measure of the pension obligation bases it only on the benefits vested to the employees. Vested benefits are those that the employee is entitled to receive even if the employee is no longer employed. The vested benefits pension obligation is calculated using current salary levels and includes only vested benefits. Another measure of the obligation, called the accumulated benefit obligation, bases the calculation of the deferred compensation amount on all years of service performed by employees under the plan—both vested and nonvested—using current salary levels. A third measure, called the projected benefit obligation, bases the calculation of the deferred compensation amount on both vested and nonvested service using future salaries.

5 Identify the components of pension expense. Pension expense is a function of the following components: (1) service cost; (2) interest on the liability; (3) expected return on plan assets; (4) amortization of past service costs; (5) amortization of the net actuarial gain or loss; and (6) amortization of any transitional asset or obligation.

6 Identify transactions and events that affect the projected benefit obligation. The projected benefit obligation is the actuarial present value of the accumulated pension benefits earned for employee services provided to date based on the pension formula, incorporating expected future salaries. The balance of the PBO is increased by the pension benefits earned by employees for services provided in the current period, by the interest cost on the outstanding obligation, by plan amendments that usually increase employee entitlements for prior services, and by actuarial losses. The balance is reduced by the payment of pension benefits and by actuarial gains. The PBO is also affected by plan settlements and curtailments and by enhanced benefits offered for early retirement.

7 Identify transactions and events that affect the balance of the plan assets. Plan assets are the cash and investments set aside to meet retirement benefit payments when they become due. They are measured at fair value. Plan assets are increased by company contributions and the actual return earned on fund assets (that is, the expected return plus the asset experience gain or minus the asset experience loss), and are reduced by pension benefits paid to retirees.

8 Explain the usefulness of—and be able to complete—a work sheet to support the employer's pension expense entries. A pension work sheet accumulates all the information needed to calculate pension expense, including continuity schedules for the off-balance sheet projected benefit obligation, fund assets, unrecognized past service costs, unrecognized actuarial gains and losses, and unrecognized transition amount. By completing the changes in the off-balance-sheet memo accounts and pulling out information that affects the calculation of pension expense, year-end balances are determined. The balances in the memo accounts reconcile to the reported prepaid or accrued pension cost account on the company's balance sheet.

9 Explain the pension accounting treatment of past service costs. Past service costs arise from giving credit to employees for service provided prior to the date of initiation or amendment of a pension plan and, for defined benefit plans, are measured as the increase in the projected benefit obligation as a result of such change. Because the increased pension benefits are expected to benefit the employer as the employee group covered provides service to the company in the future, past service costs are amortized to pension expense over the expected period to full eligibility of the affected employee group.

10 Explain the pension accounting treatment of actuarial gains and losses, including corridor amortization. Actuarial gains and losses represent the difference between the expected return on plan assets and the actual return earned, the change in the projected benefit obligation due to the difference between expected variables and actual outcomes, and changes in actuarial assumptions. If these changes were taken into pension expense each year in their entirety, reported pension expense would fluctuate widely. Because the actuary uses long-term rates to project amounts necessary to fund the estimated pension obligation, expected long-term rates are used to calculate pension expense. The net actuarial gain or loss is required to be amortized into pension expense only when it grows to an amount in excess of 10% of the greater of the PBO and the fair or market-related value of the fund assets. At a minimum, the excess amount is required to be amortized over the employee group's EARSL.

KEY TERMS

accumulated benefit obligation, 970

actual return, 973

actuarial assumptions, 969

actuarial gains and losses, 974

actuaries, 969

asset experience gain or loss, 980

attribution period, 973

capitalization approach, 971

contributory plans, 967

corridor approach, 981

defined benefit plan, 968

defined contribution plan, 968

EARSL, 974

expected average remaining service life, 974

expected return, 973

experience gains and losses, 974

funded, 967

funded status, 975

liability experience gain or loss, 980

market-related value of plan assets, 980

noncapitalization approach, 972

noncontributory plans, 967

PBO, 974

past service cost (PSC), 973

pension plan, 967

projected benefit obligation, 970

service cost, 972

settlement rate, 973

transitional asset, 974

transitional obligation or liability, 974

unrecognized net gain or loss, 981

unrecognized past service cost, 978

vested benefit obligation, 970

vesting, 970

11 Identify the differences between pensions and post-retirement health care benefits. Post-retirement health care benefits are more difficult to measure than pension benefits due mainly to the uncertainties associated with the changing health care environment and the variability of usage by those eligible for benefits.

12 Identify the financial reporting and disclosure requirements for defined benefit plans. There are two levels of disclosure required by GAAP—all companies are required to report information about amounts recorded in the financial statements, the off-balance sheet accounts and underlying assumptions used; and public companies and others with broad public accountability have additional requirements. These include reconciliations of both the PBO and plan asset balances from one year to the next and additional information about the unamortized balances.

13 Identify the financial accounting and reporting requirements for defined benefit plans whose benefits do not vest or accumulate. In this case, full accrual accounting cannot be applied as there is no specified service period over which to accrue the cost of and liability for the benefits. Instead, the "event accrual" method is applied: when the event obligating the employer to provide the benefit occurs, the total estimated expense and liability are recognized.

BRIEF EXERCISES

BE20-1 The following information is available for Jack Borke Corporation for 2002:

Service cost	$29,000
Interest on PBO	22,000
Expected return on plan assets	20,000
Amortization of unrecognized past service cost	15,200
Amortization of unrecognized net actuarial loss	500

Calculate Borke's 2002 pension expense.

BE20-2 For Becker Corporation, year-end plan assets were $2 million. At the beginning of the year, plan assets were $1,680,000. During the year, contributions to the pension fund were $120,000 while benefits paid were $200,000. Calculate Becker's actual return on plan assets.

BE20-3 At January 1, 2002, Uddin Corporation had plan assets of $250,000 and a projected benefit obligation of the same amount. During 2002, service cost was $27,500, the discount rate was 10%, actual and expected return on plan assets were $25,000, contributions were $20,000, and benefits paid were $17,500. Prepare a pension work sheet for Uddin Corporation for 2002.

BE20-4 For 2002, Potts Corporation had pension expense of $32,000 and contributed $25,000 to the pension fund. Prepare Potts Corporation's journal entries to record pension expense and funding.

BE20-5 Duesbury Corporation amended its pension plan on January 1, 2002 and granted prior service benefits with a cost of $120,000 to its employees. The employees are expected to provide a total of 2,000 service years in the future, with 350 service years in 2002. Calculate past service cost amortization for 2002.

BE20-6 At December 31, 2002, Conway Corporation had a projected benefit obligation of $510,000, plan assets of $322,000, unrecognized past service cost of $127,000, and accrued pension cost of $61,000. Prepare a pension reconciliation schedule for Conway.

BE20-7 Hunt Corporation had a projected benefit obligation of $3.1 million and plan assets of $3.3 million at January 1, 2002. Hunt's unrecognized net actuarial loss was $475,000 at that time. The average remaining service period of Hunt's employees is 7.5 years. Calculate Hunt's minimum amortization of the unrecognized actuarial loss for 2002.

BE20-8 O'Neill Corporation provides the following information at December 31, 2002:

Projected benefit obligation	$2,800,000
Plan assets at fair value	2,000,000
Accrued pension cost	200,000

Calculate the amount of the unrecognized past service cost at December 31, 2002.

BE20-9 At December 31, 2002, Judy Corporation has the following balances:

Projected benefit obligation	$3,400,000
Plan assets at fair value	2,420,000
Unrecognized past service cost	990,000

Determine the account and its balance to be reported on the Judy Corporation December 31, 2002 balance sheet.

BE20-10 Caleb Corporation has the following information available concerning its post-retirement benefit plan for 2002:

Service cost	$40,000
Interest cost	52,400
Expected return on plan assets	26,900
Amortization of unrecognized transition liability	24,600

Calculate Caleb's 2002 post-retirement expense.

BE20-11 For 2002, Benjamin Inc. calculated its annual post-retirement expense as $240,900. Benjamin's contribution to the plan during 2002 was $160,000. Prepare Benjamin's 2002 entry to record post-retirement expense and the entry to record the disbursement for the contribution into the plan.

EXERCISES

E20-1 (Defined Contribution Plan) LinDu Limited provides a defined contribution pension plan for its employees. The plan requires the company to deduct 5% of each employee's gross pay each payroll period as the employee contribution, to be matched by an equal contribution from the company. Both amounts are remitted to the pension trustee within 10 days of the end of each month for the previous month's payrolls. At November 30, 2002, LinDu reported $25,500 of withheld and matched contributions owing to the trustee. During December, LinDu reported gross salaries and wages of $274,300.

Instructions

(a) Prepare the entry to record the December payment to the plan trustee.
(b) What amount of pension expense will the company report for December 2002?
(c) Determine the appropriate pension account and its balance to be reported on the December 31, 2002 balance sheet.

E20-2 (Pension Expense, Journal Entries) The following information is available for the pension plan of Kiley Corporation for the year 2002:

Actual and expected return on plan assets	$12,000
Benefits paid to retirees	40,000
Contributions (funding)	95,000
Discount rate	10%
Past service cost amortization	8,000
Projected benefit obligation, January 1, 2002	500,000
Service cost	60,000

Instructions

(a) Calculate pension expense for 2002.
(b) Prepare the journal entries to record pension expense and the employer's contribution to the pension plan in 2002.

E20-3 **(Calculation of Pension Expense)** Rebek Corporation provides the following information about its defined benefit pension plan for the year 2002:

Service cost	$ 90,000
Contribution to the plan	105,000
Past service cost amortization	10,000
Actual and expected return on plan assets	64,000
Benefits paid	40,000
Accrued pension cost liability at January 1, 2002	10,000
Plan assets at January 1, 2002	640,000
Projected benefit obligation at January 1, 2002	800,000
Unrecognized past service cost balance at January 1, 2002	150,000
Interest/discount (settlement) rate	10%

Instructions

Calculate pension expense for the year 2002.

E20-4 **(Preparation of Pension Work Sheet with Reconciliation)** Using the information in E20-3, prepare a pension work sheet inserting January 1, 2002 balances, showing December 31, 2002 balances and the journal entries recording pension expense and the funding.

E20-5 **(Basic Pension Work Sheet)** The following facts apply to the pension plan of Borke Inc. for the year 2002:

Plan assets, January 1, 2002	$490,000
Projected benefit obligation, January 1, 2002	490,000
Interest and expected earnings rate	8.5%
Annual pension service cost	40,000
Contributions (funding)	30,000
Actual return on plan assets	49,700
Benefits paid to retirees	33,400

Instructions

Using the preceding data, calculate pension expense for the year 2002 and provide the entries to recognize pension expense and the funding for the year.

E20-6 **(Average Remaining Service Life and Amortization)** Valente Company has five employees participating in its defined benefit pension plan. Expected years of future service for these employees at the beginning of 2002 are as follows:

Employee	Future Years of Service
Ed	3
Yasser	4
Mati	6
Suzanne	6
Alikah	6

On January 1, 2002, the company amended its pension plan, increasing its projected benefit obligation by $60,000.

Instructions

Calculate the amount of past service cost amortization for the years 2002 through 2007 using the straight-line method.

E20-7 **(Calculation of Actual Return)** Jamil Importers provides the following pension plan information:

Fair value of pension plan assets, January 1, 2002	$2,300,000
Fair value of pension plan assets, December 31, 2002	2,725,000
Contributions to the plan in 2002	250,000
Benefits paid retirees in 2002	350,000

Instructions

From the data above, calculate the actual return on the plan assets for 2002.

E20-8 **(PBO and Fund Asset Continuity Schedules)** The following defined benefit pension data of Doret Corp. apply to the year 2002:

Projected benefit obligation, 1/1/02 (before amendment)	$560,000
Plan assets, 1/1/02	546,200
Prepaid/accrued pension cost (credit), 1/1/02	13,800
On January 1, 2002, Doret Corp., through plan amendment, grants prior service benefits having a present value of	100,000
Discount rate, and expected return	9%
Annual pension service cost	58,000
Contributions (funding)	55,000
Actual return on plan assets	52,280
Benefits paid to retirees	40,000
Past service cost amortization for 2002	17,000

Instructions

(a) Prepare a continuity schedule for the PBO for 2002.

(b) Prepare a continuity schedule for the plan assets for 2002.

(c) Calculate pension expense for 2002 and prepare the entry to record the expense.

(d) Identify the year-end balances in all pension-related accounts, both those reported on the balance sheet and those that are off-balance sheet accounts.

(e) Prepare a reconciliation of the plan's funded status to the asset or liability reported on the December 31, 2002 balance sheet.

E20-9 **(Application of the Corridor Approach)** Dougherty Corp. has beginning-of-the-year present values for its projected benefit obligation and fair values for its pension plan assets as follows:

	Projected Benefit Obligation	Plan Assets Value
2000	$2,000,000	$1,900,000
2001	2,400,000	2,500,000
2002	2,900,000	2,600,000
2003	3,600,000	3,000,000

The average remaining service life per employee in 2000 and 2001 is 10 years and in 2002 and 2003 is 12 years. The unrecognized net actuarial gain or loss that occurred during each year is as follows: 2000, $280,000 loss, 2001, $90,000 loss; 2002, $10,000 loss; and 2003, $25,000 gain.

Instructions

Using the corridor approach, calculate the minimum amount of net actuarial gain or loss to be amortized and charged to pension expense in each of the four years.

E20-10 **(Pension Calculations and Disclosures)** Mila Enterprises Ltd. provides the following information relative to its defined benefit pension plan:

BALANCES OR VALUES AT DECEMBER 31, 2002

Projected benefit obligation	$2,737,000
Accumulated benefit obligation	1,980,000
Vested benefit obligation	1,645,852
Fair value of plan assets	2,278,329
Unrecognized past service cost	205,000
Unrecognized net actuarial loss (1/1/02 balance, –0–)	45,680
Accrued pension cost liability	207,991
Other pension plan data:	
Service cost for 2002	$ 94,000
Past service cost amortization for 2002	45,000
Actual return on plan assets in 2002	130,000
Expected return on plan assets in 2002	175,680
Interest on January 1, 2002 projected benefit obligation	253,000
Contributions to plan in 2002	92,329
Benefits paid	140,000

Instructions

(a) Prepare the required disclosures for Mila's financial statements for the year ended December 31, 2002, assuming the company is not a public company nor one with broad public accountability.

(b) Prepare the additional disclosures required if Mila's common shares were traded on the Toronto Stock Exchange.

E20-11 **(Pension Expense, Reconciliation Schedule, No Work Sheet)** Vail Corp. sponsors a defined benefit pension plan for its employees. On January 1, 2002, the following balances relate to this plan:

Plan assets	$480,000
Projected benefit obligation	625,000
Prepaid/accrued pension cost (credit)	45,000
Unrecognized past service cost	100,000

As a result of the operation of the plan during 2002, the following additional data are provided by the actuary:

Service cost for 2002	$90,000
Discount or settlement rate	9%
Actual return on plan assets in 2002	57,000
Amortization of past service cost	19,000
Expected return on plan assets	52,000
Unexpected loss from change in projected benefit obligation, due to change in actuarial predictions	76,000
Contributions (plan funding) in 2002	99,000
Benefits paid retirees in 2002	85,000

Instructions

(a) Calculate pension expense for Vail Corp. for the year 2002. Do not use a work sheet.

(b) Prepare the entries to record pension expense and the funding of the plan in the year.

(c) At December 31, 2002, prepare a schedule reconciling the funded status of the plan with the pension amount reported on the balance sheet. Do not use a work sheet to determine the amounts.

E20-12 **(Missing Information)** The following information is available for different companies' defined benefit pension plans for 2002.

	A Corp.	B Corp.	C Corp.
Accrued pension cost/asset	$ –0–	$ 45,000 cr	?
Accumulated benefit obligation	260,000	370,000	190,000
Fair value of plan assets	255,000	?	245,000
Projected benefit obligation	350,000	455,000	220,000
Unrecognized past service cost	?	110,000	22,000

Instructions

Determine the missing amounts.

E20-13 **(Post-retirement Benefit Expense Calculation)** Marvos Corp. provides the following information about its post-retirement benefit plan for the year 2002:

Service cost	$ 90,000
Past service cost amortization	3,000
Contribution to the plan	16,000
Actual and expected return on plan assets	62,000
Benefits paid	40,000
Plan assets at January 1, 2002	710,000
Post-retirement benefit obligation at January 1, 2002	810,000
Unrecognized past service cost balance at January 1, 2002	20,000
Amortization of net transition liability	5,000
Unrecognized net transition liability at January 1, 2002	80,000
Discount rate	9%

Instructions

Calculate the post-retirement benefit expense for 2002.

E20-14 **(Post-retirement Benefit Work Sheet)**

Instructions

(a) Using the information in E20-13, complete a post-retirement work sheet for 2002.

(b) Prepare all required journal entries made by Marvos in 2002.

E20-15 **(Pension Expense, Journal Entries, Disclosure)** Griseta Limited sponsors a defined benefit pension plan for its employees. The following data relate to the operation of the plan for the year 2002.

1. The actuarial present value of future benefits earned by employees for services rendered in 2002 amounted to $56,000.
2. The company's funding policy requires a contribution to the pension trustee of $145,000 for 2002.
3. As of January 1, 2002, the company had a projected benefit obligation of $1 million and an unrecognized past service cost of $400,000. The fair value of pension plan assets amounted to $600,000 at the beginning of the year. The actual and expected return on plan assets was $54,000. The discount rate was 9%.
4. Amortization of unrecognized past service cost was $40,000 in 2002.
5. No benefits were paid in 2002.

Instructions

(a) Determine pension expense that should be recognized by the company in 2002.

(b) Prepare the journal entries to record pension expense and the employer's contribution to the pension trustee in 2002.

(c) Determine the plan's funded status and reconcile this to the prepaid/accrued pension cost on the December 31, 2002 balance sheet.

(d) Assuming Griseta is not a public company and does not have broad public accountability, prepare the required disclosures for the 2002 financial statements.

E20-16 **(Pension Expense, Entries, Statement Presentation)** Altom Corporation received the following selected information from its pension plan trustee concerning the operation of the company's defined benefit pension plan for the year ended December 31, 2002.

	January 1, 2002	December 31, 2002
Projected benefit obligation	$2,000,000	$2,077,000
Market related and fair value of plan assets	800,000	1,130,000
Actuarial gains	–0–	200,000

The service cost component of pension expense for employee services rendered in the current year amounted to $77,000 and the amortization of unrecognized past service cost was $115,000. The company's actual funding (contributions) of the plan in 2002 amounted to $250,000. The expected return on plan assets and the actual rate were both 10%; the discount rate was 10%. No prepaid/accrued pension cost existed on January 1, 2002. Assume no benefits were paid in 2002.

Instructions

(a) Determine the pension expense that should be recognized by the company in 2002.

(b) Prepare the journal entries to record pension expense and the employer's contribution to the pension plan in 2002.

(c) Indicate the pension-related amounts that would be reported on the income statement and the balance sheet for Altom Corporation for the year 2002.

E20-17 **(Calculation of Actual Return, Gains and Losses, Corridor Test, Past Service Cost, Pension Expense, and Reconciliation)** Berstler Limited sponsors a defined benefit pension plan. The corporation's actuary provides the following information about the plan:

	January 1, 2002	December 31, 2002
Vested benefit obligation	$1,500	$1,900
Accumulated benefit obligation	1,900	2,730
Projected benefit obligation	2,800	3,645
Plan assets (fair value)	1,700	2,620
Discount rate and expected rate of return	10%	10%
Prepaid/(accrued) pension cost	–0–	?
Unrecognized past service cost	1,100	?
Service cost for the year 2002		400
Contributions (funding in 2002)		800
Benefits paid in 2002		200

The average remaining service life and period to full eligibility is 20 years.

Instructions

    (a) Calculate the actual return on the plan assets in 2002.

    (b) Calculate the amount of the unrecognized net actuarial gain or loss as of December 31, 2002 (assume the January 1, 2002 balance was zero).

    (c) Calculate the amount of actuarial gain or loss amortization for 2002 using the corridor approach. How will 2003's expense be affected, if at all?

    (d) Calculate the amount of past service cost amortization for 2002.

    (e) Calculate pension expense for 2002.

    (f) Prepare a schedule reconciling the plan's funded status with the amounts reported on the December 31, 2002 balance sheet.

E20-18 **(Work Sheet for E20-17)** Using the information in E20-17 about Berstler Limited's defined benefit pension plan, prepare a 2002 pension work sheet with supplementary schedules of calculations. Prepare the journal entry at December 31, 2002 to record pension expense. Also, prepare a schedule reconciling the plan's funded status with the pension amounts reported in the balance sheet.

E20-19 **(Post-retirement Benefit Reconciliation Schedule)** Presented below is partial information related to Conley Corp. at December 31, 2003:

Accrued post-retirement benefit obligation	$950,000
Plan assets (at fair value)	650,000
Past service cost not yet recognized in post-retirement expense	60,000
Net actuarial gains/losses	–0–
Unrecognized transition liability	100,000

Instructions

    (a) Present the schedule reconciling the funded status with the asset/liability reported on the balance sheet at December 31, 2003.

    (b) Assume the same facts as given above except that Conley Corp. has an unrecognized actuarial gain of $20,000 at December 31, 2003 that arose in the current period.

E20-20 **(Post-retirement Benefit Expense, Funded Status, and Reconciliation)** Rosek Inc. provides the following information related to its post-retirement benefits for the year 2003:

Accrued post-retirement benefit obligation at January 1, 2003	$610,000
Plan assets, January 1, 2003	42,000
Prepaid/accrued post-retirement benefit, January 1, 2003	–0–
Actual and expected return on plan assets, 2003	3,000
Amortization of transition liability, 2003	35,000
Discount rate	10%
Service cost, 2003	57,000
Contributions (funding) during 2003	22,000
Payments on behalf of retirees from plan	6,000
Actuarial loss on accrued benefit obligation, 2003 (end of year)	88,000

The only unrecognized cost related to this plan at January 1, 2003 was the unrecognized transition liability.

Instructions

    (a) Calculate post-retirement benefit expense for 2003.

    (b) Determine the December 31, 2003 balance of the fund assets, the accrued obligation, and the funded status.

    (c) Determine the balance of the prepaid/accrued post-retirement benefit account on the December 31, 2003 balance sheet.

    (d) Reconcile the funded status with the amount reported on the balance sheet.

E20-21 **(Reconciliation and Unrecognized Loss)** Presented below is partial information related to Burr Corporation at December 31, 2002:

Market-related and fair value of plan assets	$700,000
Projected benefit obligation	930,000
Past service cost not yet recognized in pension expense	120,000
Unamortized actuarial gains/losses	–0–

Instructions

(a) Present a schedule reconciling the funded status with the asset/liability reported on the balance sheet.

(b) Assume the same facts as in (a) except that Burr Corporation has an experience loss of $16,000 during 2002.

(c) Explain the rationale for the treatment of the unrecognized loss and the past service cost not yet recognized in pension expense.

E20-22 (Corridor Amortization) The actuary for the pension plan of Brush Inc. calculated the following net gains and losses:

Net Gain or Loss	
Incurred during the Year	(Gain) or Loss
2001	$480,000
2002	300,000
2003	(210,000)
2004	(290,000)

Other information about the company's pension obligation and plan assets is as follows:

As of January 1	Projected Benefit Obligation	Plan Assets
2001	$4,000,000	$2,400,000
2002	$4,520,000	$2,200,000
2003	$4,980,000	$2,600,000
2004	$4,250,000	$3,040,000

Brush Inc. has a stable labour force of 400 employees who are expected to receive benefits under the plan. It is anticipated that their expected average remaining service life is 12 years. The beginning balance of unrecognized net actuarial gain/loss is zero on January 1, 2001. The plan assets' market-related value and fair value are the same for the four-year period.

Instructions

(Round to the nearest dollar)

Prepare a schedule that reflects the minimum amount of amortization of the unrecognized net actuarial gain or loss for each of the years 2001, 2002, 2003, and 2004. Apply the "corridor" approach in determining the amount to be amortized each year.

E20-23 (Pension Expense, Reconciliation, Corridor Approach) Lo Limited sponsors a defined benefit pension plan for its 600 employees. The company's actuary provided the following information about the plan:

	January 1, 2002	December 31, 2002
Projected benefit obligation	$2,800,000	$3,909,000
Plan assets, at fair and market related value	1,700,000	2,370,000
Net actuarial (gain) or loss in the year on the PBO	–0–	401,000
Discount rate		11%
Actual and expected asset return rate		10%
Contributions to fund		500,000

The company anticipates that the employees' expected average remaining service life and expected period to full eligibility is 10.5 years. The service cost component of net periodic pension expense for employee services rendered amounted to $400,000 in 2002. At January 1, 2002, the only unrecognized amounts related to past service costs of $1.1 million. No benefits have been paid.

Instructions

(Round to the nearest dollar)

(a) Calculate pension expense to be reported in 2002.

(b) Prepare continuity schedules for the PBO and the fund assets for 2002.

(c) Reconcile the funded status at December 31, 2002 with the amount recognized on the December 31, 2002 balance sheet.

(d) Calculate the amortization, if any, of the net actuarial gain or loss to be included in pension expense in 2003.

E20-24 **(Maternity Benefits)**   Salim Corporation offers enriched maternity benefits to the women on its staff. While the government provides compensation based on employment insurance legislation for a period of 12 months, Salim increases the amounts received and extends the period of compensation. The benefit program tops up the amount received to 100% of the employee's salary for the first 12 months, and pays the employee 75% of full salary for another six months after the employment insurance payments have ceased.

Jen Hussar, who earns $48,000 per year, announced to her manager in early June 2002 that she was expecting a baby in mid-November. On October 29, 2002, nine weeks before the end of the calendar and Salim's fiscal year, Jen began her 18 month maternity leave. Assume that the employment insurance pays her a maximum of $600 per week for 52 weeks.

Instructions

(Round to the nearest dollar)

   (a) Prepare all entries required to be made by Salim Corporation during its 2002 fiscal year related to the maternity benefits plan. Be sure to include the date of each entry you make.

   (b) Prepare one entry to summarize all entries the company will make in 2003 relative to Jen Hussar's leave.

PROBLEMS

P20-1   On January 1, 2002, Diapeter Corporation has the following defined benefit pension plan balances:

Projected benefit obligation	$4,200,000
Fair value of plan assets	$4,200,000

The interest (settlement) rate applicable to the plan is 10%. On January 1, 2003, the company amends its pension agreement so that prior service costs of $500,000 are created. Other data related to the pension plan are:

	2002	2003
Service costs	$150,000	$180,000
Unrecognized past service costs amortization	–0–	90,000
Contributions (funding) to the plan	140,000	185,000
Benefits paid	200,000	280,000
Actual return on plan assets	252,000	260,000
Expected rate of return on assets	6%	8%

Instructions

   (a) Prepare a pension work sheet for the pension plan for 2002 and 2003.

   (b) As of December 31, 2003, prepare a schedule reconciling the funded status with the reported liability (accrued pension cost).

P20-2   Dayte Corporation reports the following January 1, 2002 balances for its defined benefit pension plan: plan assets, $200,000; projected benefit obligation, $200,000. Other data relating to three years' operation of the plan are as follows:

	2002	2003	2004
Annual service cost	$16,000	$19,000	$26,000
Discount rate and expected rate of return	10%	10%	10%
Actual return on plan assets	17,000	21,900	24,000
Annual funding (contributions)	16,000	40,000	48,000
Benefits paid	14,000	16,400	21,000
Unrecognized past service cost (plan amended, 1/1/03)		160,000	
Amortization of unrecognized past service cost		54,400	41,600
Change in actuarial assumptions establishes a			
December 31, 2004 projected benefit obligation of:			520,000

Instructions

   (a) Prepare a continuity schedule of the projected benefit obligation over the three-year period.

   (b) Prepare a continuity schedule of the fund assets over the three-year period.

   (c) Determine pension expense for 2002, 2003, and 2004.

(d) Prepare the journal entries to reflect the pension plan transactions and events for each year.

(e) Prepare a schedule reconciling the plan's funded status with the pension amounts reported in the financial statements at December 31, 2004.

P20-3 Paolo Corporation sponsors a defined benefit plan for its 100 employees. On January 1, 2002, the company's actuary provided the following information.

Unrecognized past service cost	$150,000
Pension plan assets (fair value)	200,000
Accumulated benefit obligation	260,000
Projected benefit obligation	350,000

The participating employees' average remaining service period to full eligibility is 10.5 years. All employees are expected to receive benefits under the plan. On December 31, 2002, the actuary calculated that the present value of future benefits earned for employee services rendered in the current year amounted to $52,000; the projected benefit obligation was $452,000; fair value of pension assets was $276,000; and the accumulated benefit obligation amounted to $365,000. The expected return on plan assets and the discount rate on the projected benefit obligation were both 10%. The actual return on plan assets is $11,000. The company's current year contribution to the pension plan amounted to $65,000. No benefits were paid during the year.

Instructions

(Round to the nearest dollar)

(a) Determine the components of pension expense that the company will recognize in 2002. (With only one year involved, you need not prepare a work sheet.)

(b) Prepare the journal entries to record pension expense and the company's funding of the pension plan in 2002.

(c) Calculate the amount of the 2002 increase/decrease in unrecognized actuarial gains or losses and the amount to be amortized in 2002 and 2003.

(d) Prepare a schedule reconciling the plan's funded status with the pension amounts reported in the financial statement as of December 31, 2002.

P20-4 Manon Corporation sponsors a defined benefit pension plan. The following information related to the pension plan is available for 2002 and 2003:

	2002	2003
Plan assets (fair value), December 31	$380,000	$465,000
Projected benefit obligation, January 1	600,000	700,000
Prepaid (accrued) pension cost balance, January 1	(40,000)	?
Unrecognized past service cost, January 1	250,000	240,000
Service cost	60,000	90,000
Actual and expected return on plan assets	24,000	30,000
Amortization of past service cost	10,000	12,000
Contributions (funding)	110,000	120,000
Interest/settlement rate	9%	9%

Instructions

(a) Calculate pension expense for 2002 and 2003.

(b) Prepare journal entries to record the pension expense and the company's pension plan funding for both years.

(c) Assuming Manon is not a public company or a company with broad public accountability, prepare the required notes to the financial statements at December 31, 2003.

P20-5 Dubel Toothpaste Corporation initiated a defined benefit pension plan for its 50 employees on January 1, 2001. The insurance company that administers the pension plan provides the following information for the years 2001, 2002, and 2003:

	For Year Ended December 31,		
	2001	2002	2003
Plan assets (fair value)	$50,000	$ 85,000	$170,000
Projected benefit obligation	63,900	?	?
Net actuarial (gain) loss re: PBO	8,900	(24,500)	84,500
Employer's funding contribution (made at end of year)	50,000	60,000	95,000

There were no balances as of January 1, 2001 when the plan was initiated. The actual and expected return on plan assets was 10% over the three-year period but the settlement rate used to discount the company's pension obligation was 13% in 2001, 11% in 2002, and 8% in 2003. The service cost component of net periodic pension expense amounted to the following: 2001, $55,000; 2002, $85,000; and 2003, $119,000. The average remaining service life per employee is 10 years. No benefits were paid in 2001, $30,000 of benefits were paid in 2002, and $18,500 of benefits were paid in 2003 (all benefits paid at end of year).

Instructions

Do either (a), (b), (c), and (e) or (d) and (e), depending on what your instructor assigns. (Round amounts to the nearest dollar.)

(a) Prepare a continuity schedule for the projected benefit obligation over the three-year period.
(b) Prepare a continuity schedule for the plan assets over the three-year period.
(c) Calculate the amount of net periodic pension expense that the company will recognize in 2001, 2002, and 2003.
(d) Prepare and complete a pension work sheet for each of 2001, 2002 and 2003.
(e) Prepare the journal entries to record net periodic pension expense and the employer's funding contributions for the years 2001, 2002, and 2003.

P20-6 Ekedahl Inc. has sponsored a noncontributory-defined benefit pension plan for its employees since 1984. Prior to 2002, cumulative net pension expense recognized equalled cumulative contributions to the plan. Other relevant information about the pension plan on January 1, 2002, is as follows:

1. The company has 200 employees who are expected to receive benefits under the plan. The employees' expected period to full eligibility is 13 years with an EARSL of 16 years.
2. The projected benefit obligation amounted to $5 million and the fair and market-related value of pension plan assets was $3 million. Unrecognized past service cost was $2 million.

On December 31, 2002, the projected benefit obligation was $4,750,000. The fair value of the pension plan assets amounted to $3.9 million at the end of the year. A 10% discount rate and an 8% expected asset return rate was used in the actuarial present value calculations in the pension plan. The present value of benefits attributed by the pension benefit formula to employee service in 2002 amounted to $200,000. The employer's contribution to the plan assets was $575,000 in 2002. No pension benefits were paid to retirees during this period.

Instructions

(Round all amounts to the nearest dollar)

(a) What amount of past service cost will be included as a component of pension expense for 2002, 2003, and 2004?
(b) Calculate pension expense for the year 2002.
(c) Prepare the journal entries required to account for the company's pension plan for 2002.
(d) Determine the amount of any actuarial gains or losses in 2002 and the amount to be amortized to expense in 2002 and 2003.
(e) Prepare a schedule reconciling the plan's funded status with the pension amounts reported in the financial statements as of December 31, 2002.

P20-7 Farrey Corp. sponsors a defined benefit pension plan for its employees. On January 1, 2003, the following balances related to this plan:

Plan assets (fair value)	$520,000
Projected benefit obligation	725,000
Prepaid/accrued pension cost (credit)	33,000
Unrecognized past service cost	81,000
Unrecognized net actuarial gain/loss (debit)	91,000

As a result of the plan's operation during 2003, the actuary provided the following additional data at December 31, 2003:

Service cost for 2003	$108,000
Discount rate, 9%; expected rate of return, 10%	
Actual return on assets in 2003	48,000
Amortization of past service cost	25,000
Contributions in 2003	138,000
Benefits paid retirees in 2003	85,000
Average period to full eligibility of employee group	10 years
Average remaining service life of active employees	13 years

Instructions

Using the preceding data, calculate pension expense for Farrey Corp. for the year 2003 by preparing a pension work sheet that incorporates the journal entry to record pension expense.

P20-8 Glesen Corporation sponsors a defined benefit pension plan for its employees. The following data relate to the operation of the plan for the years 2002 and 2003:

	2002	2003
Projected benefit obligation, January 1	$650,000	
Plan assets (fair value and market related value), January 1	410,000	
Prepaid/accrued pension cost (credit), January 1	80,000	
Unrecognized past service cost, January 1	160,000	
Service cost	40,000	$59,000
Settlement rate (discount rate)	10%	10%
Expected rate of return	9%	9%
Actual return on plan assets	36,000	61,000
Amortization of past service cost	70,000	55,000
Annual contributions	72,000	81,000
Benefits paid retirees	31,500	54,000
Increase in projected benefit obligation due to changes in actuarial assumptions	87,000	–0–
Average service life and period to full eligibility of employees		20 years
Vested benefit obligation at December 31		464,000

Instructions

(a) Prepare a pension work sheet for both 2002 and 2003.

(b) Prepare the employer journal entries to reflect the pension transactions and events for 2002 and 2003.

(c) At December 31, 2003, prepare a schedule reconciling the pension plan's funded status with the pension amounts reported in the financial statements.

P20-9 Connie Harpin was recently promoted to assistant controller of Glomski Corporation, having previously served Glomski as a staff accountant. One of her new responsibilities is to prepare the annual pension accrual. Judy Gralapp, the corporate controller, provided Harpin with last year's working papers and information from the actuary's annual report. The pension work sheet for the prior year is presented below.

	Journal Entry			Memo Records		
	Pension Expense	Cash	Prepaid (Accrued) Cost	Projected Benefit Obligation	Plan Assets	Unrecognized Past Service Cost
June 1, 2001[1]				$ (20,000)	$20,000	
Service cost[1]	$1,800			(1,800)		
Interest[2]	1,200			(1,200)		
Actual return[3]	(1,600)				1,600	
Contribution[1]		$(1,000)			1,000	
Benefits paid[1]				900	(900)	
Past service cost[4]				(2,000)		$2,000
Journal entries	$1,400		$(1,400)			
		$(1,000)	1,000			
May 31, 2002 balance			$ (400)	$(24,100)	$21,700	$2,000

[1] Per actuary's report.

[2] Beginning projected benefit obligation × discount rate of 6%.

[3] Expected return was $1,600 (beginning plan assets × expected return of 8%).

[4] A plan amendment that granted employees retroactive benefits for work performed in earlier periods took effect on May 31, 2002. The amendment increased the May 31, 2002 projected benefit obligation by $2,000. No amortization was recorded in the fiscal year ended May 31, 2002.

Pertinent information from the actuary's report for the year ended May 31, 2003 is presented below. The report indicated no actuarial gains or losses in the fiscal year ended May 31, 2003.

Contribution	$ 425	Actual return on plan assets	$1,736
Service cost	$3,000	Benefits paid	$ 500
Discount rate	6%	Average remaining service life	10 years
Expected return	8%		
Average period to full eligibility	8 years		

Instructions

(a) Prepare the pension work sheet for Glomski Corporation for the year ended May 31, 2003.
(b) Prepare the employer's journal entries required to reflect the accounting for Glomski Corporation's pension plan for the year ended May 31, 2003.

P20-10   RWL Limited provides a long-term disability program for its employees through an insurance company. For an annual premium of $18,000, the insurance company takes on the responsibility for providing salary continuation on a long-term basis after a three-month waiting period, during which time RWL continues to pay the employee at full salary. The employees contribute to the cost of this plan through regular payroll deductions that amount to $6,000 for the year. In late October 2002, Tony Hurst, a department manager earning $5,400 per month, was injured and was not expected to be able to return to work for at least one year.

Instructions

Prepare all entries made by RWL in 2002 in connection with the benefit plan, as well as any entries required in 2003.

P20-11   Hass Foods Inc. sponsors a post-retirement medical and dental benefit plan for its employees. The company adopts the provisions of *Handbook* Section 3461 beginning January 1, 2002. The following balances relate to this plan on January 1, 2002.

Plan assets	$ 200,000
Accrued post-retirement benefit obligation	882,000
No past service costs exist	

As a result of the plan's operation during 2002, the following additional data are provided by the actuary:

Service cost for 2002 is $70,000.
Discount rate is 9%.
Contributions to plan in 2002 are $60,000.
Expected return on plan assets is $9,000.
Actual return on plan assets is $15,000.
Benefits paid on behalf of retirees from plan are $44,000.
Average remaining service to full eligibility is 20 years.
Average remaining service to expected retirement is 22 years.
Transition amount is to be amortized.

Instructions

(a) Using the preceding data, calculate the post-retirement benefit expense for 2002 by preparing a work sheet that shows the journal entry for post-retirement benefit expense and the year-end balances in the related post-retirement benefit memo accounts. Assume that contributions and benefits are paid at the end of the year.
(b) At December 31, 2002, prepare a schedule reconciling the plan's funded status with the post-retirement amount reported on the balance sheet.

CONCEPTUAL CASES

C20-1   Shikkiah Corp. tries to attract the most knowledgeable and creative employees it can find. To help in this regard, it offers to a special group of technology employees the right to a fully paid sabbatical leave after every five years of continuous service. There are no restrictions on the employees as to what they do during the sabbatical year, but it is the company's objective that they come back renewed with fresh ideas.

Shikkiah hired three employees in early 2002 who were entitled to this benefit. Each new hire agreed to a starting salary of $75,000 per year.

Instructions

(a) Explain generally how this employee benefit should be accounted for by Shikkiah Corp.
(b) Assume you are the assistant to the company controller. In response to the controller's request, list all the information you need in order to prepare the adjusting entry required at December 31, 2002 relative to this plan.

(c) Assume that the activities during the sixth (the sabbatical) year are dictated by the company, and the employees must work on research and promotion activities that will benefit the company. Would your answer to (a) change? Explain why or why not.

C20-2 Many business organizations have been concerned with providing for employee retirement since the late 1800s. During recent decades, a marked increase in this concern has resulted in the establishment of private pension and other post-retirement benefit plans in most companies of any size.

   The substantial growth of these plans, both in numbers of employees covered and in the types and amounts of retirement benefits, has increased the significance of the cost of these benefit plans in relation to the financial position, results of operations, and cash flows of many companies. In examining these benefit plans, accountants encounter certain terms. The elements of benefit costs that the terms represent must be dealt with appropriately if generally accepted accounting principles are to be reflected in the financial statements of entities with such plans.

Instructions

(a) Define a private benefit plan. How does a contributory plan differ from a noncontributory plan?
(b) Differentiate between "accounting for the employer" and "accounting for the benefit plan."
(c) Explain the terms "funded" and "benefit liability" as they relate to:
   1. the benefit plan.
   2. the employer.
(d) 1. Discuss the theoretical justification for accrual recognition of future benefit costs.
   2. Discuss the theoretical justification for "event accrual" accounting for future benefit costs.
   3. Discuss the relative objectivity of the measurement process of full accrual versus event accrual versus cash (pay-as-you-go) accounting for annual benefit costs.
(e) Distinguish among the following as they relate to pension plans.
   1. Service cost
   2. Past service costs
   3. Actuarial funding methods
   4. Vested benefits

C20-3 The following items appear on Harth Corporation's financial statements.
   1. Under the caption Assets:
      Prepaid pension cost
   2. Under the caption Liabilities:
      Accrued pension cost
   3. On the income statement:
      Pension expense

Instructions

Explain the significance of each item above on corporate financial statements.

C20-4 In examining the costs of pension plans, an accountant encounters certain terms. The components of pension costs that the terms represent must be dealt with appropriately if generally accepted accounting principles are to be reflected in the financial statements of entities with pension plans.

Instructions

(a) 1. Discuss the theoretical justification for accrual recognition of pension costs.
   2. Discuss the relative objectivity of the measurement process of accrual versus cash (pay-as-you-go) accounting for annual pension costs.
(b) Explain the following terms as they apply to accounting for pension plans:
   1. Market-related asset value
   2. Contributory plan
   3. Actuarial funding methods
   4. Projected benefit obligation
   5. Capitalization approach
   6. Corridor approach
(c) What information should be disclosed about a company's pension plans in its financial statements and its notes? Explain briefly why differential disclosure is permitted.

(AICPA adapted)

C20-5 Helen Ito, president of Ito-Mail Inc., is discussing the possibility of developing a pension plan for company employees with Esther Knox, controller, and Jason Nihles, assistant-controller. Their conversation is as follows:

Helen Ito: If we are going to compete with our competitors, we must have a pension plan to attract good talent.

Esther Knox: I must warn you, Helen, that a pension plan will take a large bite out of our income. The only reason why we have been so profitable is the lack of a pension cost in our income statement. In some of our competitors' cases, pension expense is 30% of pretax income!

Jason Nihles: Why do we have to worry about a pension cost now anyway? Benefits do not vest until after 10 years of service. If they do not vest, then we are not liable. We should not have to report an expense until we are legally liable to provide benefits.

Helen Ito: But, Jason, the employees would want credit for prior service with full vesting 10 years after starting service, not 10 years after starting the plan. How would we allocate the large past service cost?

Jason Nihles: Well, I believe that the past service cost is a cost of providing a pension plan for employees forever. It is an intangible asset that will not diminish in value because it will increase the morale of our present and future employees and provide us with a competitive edge in acquiring future employees.

Helen Ito: I hate to disagree, but I believe the past service cost is a benefit only to the present employees. This prior service is directly related to the composition of the employee group at the time the plan is initiated and is in no way related to any intangible benefit received by the company because of the plan's existence. Therefore, I propose that the past service cost be amortized over the remaining lives of the existing employees.

Esther Knox (somewhat perturbed): But what about the income statement? You two are arguing theory without consideration of our income figure.

Helen Ito: Settle down, Esther.

Esther Knox: Sorry, perhaps Jason's approach to resolving this approach is the best one. I am just not sure.

Instructions

(a) Assuming that Ito-Mail Inc. establishes a pension plan, how should their liability for pensions be calculated in the first year?

(b) How should their liability be calculated in subsequent years?

(c) How should pension expense be calculated each year?

(d) Assuming that the pension fund is set up in a trusteed relationship, should the fund assets be reported on the books of Ito-Mail Inc.?

(e) What interest rate should be used in the present value calculations?

(f) How should actuarial gains and losses be reported?

C20-6 Lyons Corporation is a medium-sized manufacturer of paperboard containers and boxes. The corporation sponsors a noncontributory, defined benefit pension plan that covers its 250 employees. Sam Ling has recently been hired as president of Lyons Corporation. While reviewing last year's financial statements with Siew Secord, controller, Ling expressed confusion about several of the items in the footnote to the financial statements relating to the pension plan. In part, the footnote reads as follows.

> **Note J.** The company has a defined benefit pension plan covering substantially all of its employees. The benefits are based on years of service and the employee's compensation during the last four years of employment. The company's funding policy is to contribute annually the maximum amount allowed under federal tax legislation. Contributions are intended to provide for benefits expected to be earned in the future as well as those earned to date.

Effective for the year ending December 31, 2001, Lyons Corporation adopted the provisions of *CICA Handbook* Section 3461—Employee Future Benefits. The net periodic pension expense on Lyons Corporation's comparative Income Statement was $72,000 in 2002 and $57,680 in 2001.

The following are selected figures from the plan's funded status and amount recognized in the Lyons Corporation's Statement of Financial Position at December 31, 2002 ($000 omitted):

Actuarial present value of benefit obligations:	
Accumulated benefit obligation (including vested benefits of $636)	$ (870)
Projected benefit obligation	$(1,200)
Plan assets at fair value	1,050
Projected benefit obligation in excess of plan assets	$ (150)

Given that Lyons Corporation's work force has been stable for the last six years, Ling could not understand the increase in the net periodic pension expense. Secord explained that the net periodic pension expense consists of several elements, some of which may decrease the net expense.

Instructions

(a) Determining the net periodic pension expense is a function of six major elements. List and briefly describe each element.

(b) Describe the major difference and the major similarity between the accumulated benefit obligation and the projected benefit obligation.

(c) Explain why actuarial gains and losses are not recognized on the income statement in the period in which they arise. Briefly describe how actuarial gains and losses are recognized.

(CMA adapted)

C20-7 Ruth Moore and Carl Nies have to do a class presentation on employee future benefits, particularly those related to pensions and other post-retirement benefits. In developing the class presentation, they decided to provide the class with a series of questions related to these benefits and then to discuss the answers in class. Given that the class has all read *Handbook* Section 3461, they felt this approach would provide a lively discussion. Here are the situations:

1. In an article in *The Globe and Mail* prior to the adoption of Section 3461, it was reported that the discount rates used by the largest 200 companies for pension reporting ranged from 5 to 11%. Does new Section 3461 alleviate this problem?

2. An article indicated that when *Handbook* Section 3461 was issued, it caused a significant increase in the liability for employee future benefits for most companies. Why might this situation have occurred?

3. A recent article noted that while "smoothing" is not necessarily an accounting virtue, pension accounting has long been recognized as an exception—an area of accounting in which at least some dampening of market swings is appropriate. This is because pension funds are managed so that their performance is insulated from the extremes of short-term market swings. A pension expense that reflects the volatility of market swings might, for that reason, convey information of little relevance. Are these statements true?

4. Many companies' funds hold assets twice as large as they need to fund their pension plans. Are these assets necessarily reported on the balance sheets of these companies? If not, where are they reported?

5. Understanding the impact of post-retirement benefit accounting and reporting requires detailed information about a company's benefit plans and an analysis of the relationship of many factors, particularly:

    (a) the transition amount, the date of initial application, and the method of accounting for the change in accounting policy,

    (b) the type of plan(s) and any significant amendments,

    (c) the plan participants,

    (d) the funding status, and

    (e) the actuarial funding method and assumptions currently used.

    What impact does each item have on financial statement presentation?

6. An article noted, "You also need to decide whether to amortize gains and losses using the corridor method, or to use some other systematic method. Under the corridor approach, only gains and losses in excess of 10% of the greater of the projected benefit obligation or the plan assets would have to be amortized." What is the corridor method and what is its purpose?

7. In an exposure draft on pensions, the Financial Accounting Standards Board required a note that discussed the sensitivity of pension expense to changes in the interest rate and the salary progression assumption. This note might read as follows:

    "At December 31, 2001, the weighted-average discount rate and rate of increase in future compensation levels used in determining the actuarial present value of the projected benefit obligation were 9% and 6%, respectively. Those assumptions can have a significant effect on the amounts reported. To illustrate, increasing the discount rate assumption to 10% would have decreased the projected benefit obligation and net periodic pension expense by $340,000 and $50,000, respectively, for the year ended December 31, 2001. Increasing the rate of change of future compensation levels to 7% would have increased the projected benefit obligation and net periodic pension cost by $180,000 and $30,000, respectively, for the year ended December 31, 2001."

    Why do you believe this disclosure was eliminated from the final pronouncement?

Instructions

What answers do you believe Ruth and Carl gave to each of these questions?

C20-8 Rachel Avery, accounting clerk in the personnel office of Clarence G. Avery Corp., has begun to calculate pension expense for 2003 but is not sure whether she should include the amortization of unrecognized actuarial gains and losses. She is currently working with the following beginning-of-the-year present values for the projected benefit obligation and fair values for the pension plan:

	Projected Benefit Obligation	Plan Assets Value
2000	$2,200,000	$1,900,000
2001	2,400,000	2,600,000
2002	2,900,000	2,600,000
2003	3,900,000	3,000,000

The average remaining service life per employee in 2000 and 2001 is 10 years and in 2002 and 2003 is 12 years. The net actuarial gain or loss that occurred during each year is as follows:

2000	$280,000 loss
2001	90,000 loss
2002	12,000 loss
2003	25,000 gain

Instructions

You are the manager in charge of accounting. Write a memo to Rachel Avery, explaining why in some years she must amortize some of the actuarial gains and losses and in other years she does not need to. Explain this situation fully, including a calculation of the amount of actuarial gain or loss that is amortized and charged to pension expense in each of the four years listed above. Include an appropriate amortization schedule, referring to it whenever necessary.

Using Your Judgement

FINANCIAL REPORTING PROBLEM:
CANADIAN TIRE CORPORATION, LIMITED

Instructions

Refer to the financial statements and accompanying notes and discussion of Canadian Tire Corporation, Limited presented in Appendix 5B and answer the following questions.

(a) What kind of post-retirement benefits does Canadian Tire offer its employees?

(b) What method of accounting does the company use to account for this plan in 2000? What method did the company use in prior years?

(c) Does Canadian Tire report a transition asset/liability in connection with the adoption of *Handbook* Section 3461? Why or why not? What was the net effect on opening retained earnings of this change in policy? Why does this differ from the adjustment to the accrued benefit liability? Explain.

(d) What is the funded status of this plan at December 30, 2000? Explain.

(e) How significant is the cost of this plan in 2000 in relation to net income?

FINANCIAL STATEMENT ANALYSIS CASE

Aliant Inc.

Aliant Inc. is the combination of what were previously the Atlantic province telecoms: Bruncor Inc., Island Telecom Inc., Maritime Telephone and Telegraph Company, Limited, and NewTel Enterprises Limited. Aliant reported an accrued benefit **obligation** of $42,063 thousand on its consolidated balance sheet at December 31, 2000 as compared with an accrued benefit **asset** of $83,664 thousand at December 31, 1999. Obtain access to the financial statements of Aliant Inc. for the year ended December 31, 2000 through SEDAR (www.sedar.com).

Instructions

(a) Review the financial statements and provide an explanation for the shift from the significant asset position at the end of 1999 to the significant liability position at the end of 2000.

(b) Identify the amount of the accrued benefit obligation at December 31, 2000 for the company's pension benefit plans and for the other benefit plans. Note their relative size.

(c) Identify the benefits expense recognized in 2000 for the company's pension benefit plans and for the other benefit plans. Note their relative size, and explain why they differ so much from the relative size of the plan obligations identified in (b).

COMPARATIVE ANALYSIS CASE

Cascades Inc. versus Derlan Industries Limited

Cascades Inc. is a Canadian company involved in the production, converting, and marketing of packaging products, fine papers, and tissue papers. Derlan Industries Limited, also a Canadian company, manufactures products for the aerospace and pump industries.

Instructions

Go to the Digital Tool or the SEDAR website and, using Cascades Inc. and Derlan Industries Limited financial statement information for their years ended December 31, 2000, answer the following questions:

(a) What kind of benefit plans do Cascades and Derlan provide for their employees?

(b) Compare the types of transactions and events that caused changes during the 2000 year in the accrued benefit obligation for each company's benefit plans. Identify the similarities and any differences.

(c) Compare the types of transactions and events that caused changes in the plan assets for each company's benefit plans. Identify the similarities and any differences.

(d) Compare the components of benefits expense for each company. Identify the similarities and any differences.

(e) At which company would you prefer to be an employee insofar as the level of certainty related to the ability to pay the future benefits?

(f) Compare the underlying assumptions used in the calculation of amounts related to the benefit plans for the two companies. Which company is more conservative in the assumptions used? Comment.

RESEARCH CASES

Case 1

Instructions

Examine the employee future benefit footnotes of three companies of your choice and answer the following questions.

(a) For each company, identify the following three assumptions: (1) the discount rate, (2) the rate of compensation increase used to measure the projected benefit obligation, and (3) the expected long-run rate of return on plan assets.

(b) Comment on any significant differences between the assumptions used by each firm.

(c) Did any of the companies change their assumptions during the period covered by the footnote? If so, what was the effect on the financial statements?

(d) Identify the types and assumptions underlying any future benefit plans other than pensions. Are these standard among companies? Comment.

Case 2

The December 1995 issue of *Accounting Horizons* includes an article by Alan I. Blankley and Edward P. Swanson entitled "A Longitudinal Study of SFAS 87 Pension Rate Assumptions." The article represents an excellent example of how academic research can address controversial accounting issues.

Instructions

(a) Read the article's "introduction" section and answer the following questions.

(b) According to the business press, firms are manipulating estimates of expected rates of return on plan assets and discount rates. What are the effects of these alleged manipulations?

(c) What was the reaction of the Securities and Exchange Commission?

(d) What is the article's purpose? How did the authors obtain the data used in their study?

(e) What are the authors' major conclusions?

INTERNATIONAL REPORTING CASE

Volvo, a Swedish company in the automotive and transport equipment industry, prepares its financial statements in accordance with Swedish accounting standards. In 1998, Volvo had income of 8,638 million SEK (Swedish Kronor) with assets of 204,426 million SEK at December 31, 1998. Volvo sponsors a pension plan for its employees in Sweden and the U.S. and provided the following disclosure related to its pension provisions in the notes to its financial statements.

VOLVO

Note 22: Provisions for postemployment benefits

	1996	1997	1998
Provisions for pensions	1,937	1,905	1,451
Provisions for other postemployment benefits	1,213	1,391	1,485
Total	3,150	3,296	2,936

The amounts shown for Provisions for postemployment benefits correspond to the actuarially calculated value of obligations not insured with a third party or secured through transfers of funds to pension foundations. The amount of pensions falling due within one year is included. The Swedish Group companies have insured their pension obligations with third parties. Group pension costs in 1998 amounted to 3,567. The greater part of pension costs consist of continuing payments to independent organizations that administer pension plans. Assets in pension foundations at market value exceeded the corresponding pension obligations by 425.

Volvo's shares trade on the NASDAQ in the United States (and on several European stock exchanges as well). As a consequence of listing its shares in the U.S., Volvo provides additional disclosure in its notes on the differences in accounting for its pension plans under U.S. and Swedish accounting standards. If Volvo had applied U.S. GAAP to its pensions, income would have been 313 million SEK higher in 1998, and shareholders' equity would have been 1,548 higher at December 31, 1998. The following excerpt about pension accounting differences between the U.S. and Sweden was taken from Volvo's notes.

Significant differences between Swedish and U.S. accounting principles

Note J: Provision for pensions and other postemployment benefits. The greater part of the Volvo Group's pension commitments are defined contribution plans; that is, they are met through regular payments to independent authorities or organs that administer pension plans. There is no difference between U.S. and Swedish accounting principles in accounting for these pension plans.

Other pension commitments are defined benefit plans; that is, the employee is entitled to receive a certain level of pension, usually related to the employee's final salary. In these cases the annual pension cost is calculated based on the current value of future pension payments. In Volvo's consolidated accounts, provisions for pensions and pension costs for the year in the individual companies are calculated based on local rules and directives. In accordance with U.S. GAAP, provisions for pensions and pension costs for the year should always be calculated as specified in SFAS 87, "Employers Accounting for Pensions." The difference lies primarily in the choice of discount rates and the circumstance that U.S. calculations of capital-valuation, in contrast to the Swedish, are based on salaries calculated at time of retirement.

Instructions

Recognizing that Canadian GAAP for pension benefits mirrors that of the U.S., use the information on Volvo to respond to the following requirements.

(a) What are the key differences in accounting for pensions under Canadian and Swedish standards?

(b) Briefly explain how differences in Canadian and Swedish standards for pensions would affect the amounts reported in the financial statements.

(c) In light of the differences identified above, what are the likely reason(s) that Volvo's income and equity would be higher under U.S. and Canadian GAAP than under Swedish accounting standards?

ETHICS CASE

Philip Regan, Chief Executive Officer of Relief Dynamics Inc., a large defence contracting firm, is considering ways to improve the company's financial position after several years of sharply declining profitability. One way to do this is to reduce or completely eliminate Relief's commitment to present and future retirees who have full prescription and dental benefits coverage. Despite financial problems, Relief still is committed to providing excellent pension benefits.

Instructions
Answer the following questions:

(a) What factors should Regan consider before making his decision to cut post-retirement health benefits?

(b) Does your answer to the above question change if Relief Dynamics were paying Phil Regan, CEO, a salary of $30 million per year?

(c) In your opinion, how do you expect that *Handbook* Section 3461 influenced the commitment of many organizations to its employees?

CHAPTER 21

Leases

LEARNING OBJECTIVES

After studying this chapter, you should be able to:

1. Explain the nature, economic substance, and advantages of lease transactions.

2. Identify and explain the accounting criteria and procedures for capitalizing leases by the lessee.

3. Identify the lessee's disclosure requirements for capital leases.

4. Identify the lessee's accounting and disclosure requirements for an operating lease.

5. Contrast the operating and capitalization methods of recording leases.

6. Calculate the lease payment required for the lessor to earn a given return.

7. Identify the classifications of leases for the lessor.

8. Describe the lessor's accounting for direct financing leases.

9. Describe the lessor's accounting for sales-type leases.

10. Describe the lessor's accounting for operating leases.

11. Identify the lessor's disclosure requirements.

12. Describe the effect of residual values, guaranteed and unguaranteed, on lease accounting.

13. Describe the effect of bargain purchase options on lease accounting.

14. Describe the lessor's accounting treatment for initial direct costs.

After studying Appendix 21A, you should be able to :

15. Describe the lessee's accounting for sale-leaseback transactions.

Preview of Chapter 21

Leasing has grown tremendously in popularity and today is the fastest growing form of capital investment. Instead of borrowing money to buy an airplane, a computer, a nuclear core, or a satellite, a company leases it. Even gambling casinos lease their slot machines. Airlines and railroads lease huge amounts of equipment, many hotel and motel chains lease their facilities, and most retail chains lease the bulk of their retail premises and warehouses. The popularity of leasing is evidenced by the fact that 149 of 200 companies surveyed in *Financial Reporting in Canada—2000* disclosed lease data.[1]

Because of the significance and prevalence of lease arrangements, the need for uniform accounting and complete informative reporting of these transactions has intensified. In this chapter, we will look at the accounting issues related to leasing. The chapter's content and organization are as follows.

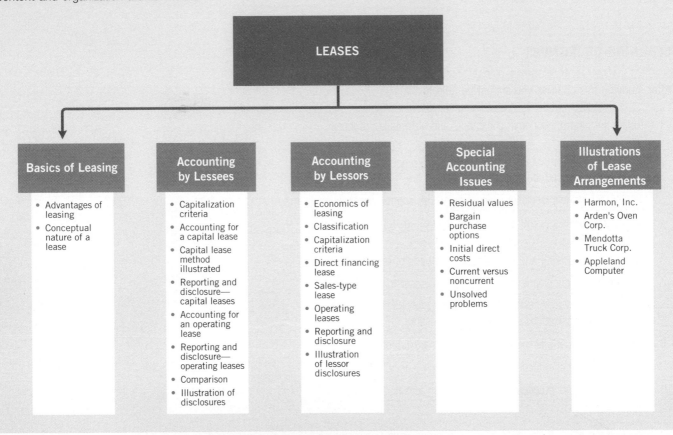

BASICS OF LEASING

OBJECTIVE 1

Explain the nature, economic substance, and advantages of lease transactions.

A **lease** is a contractual agreement between a **lessor** and a **lessee** that gives the lessee the right to use specific property, owned by the lessor, for a specified period of time in return for stipulated, and generally periodic, cash payments (rents). An essential element of the lease agreement is that the lessor conveys less than the total interest in the property. Because of the financial, operating, and risk advantages that the lease arrangement provides, many businesses and other types of organizations lease substantial amounts of property, both real and personal, as an alternative to ownership.

Because a lease is a contract, the provisions agreed to by the lessor and lessee may vary widely and may be limited only by their ingenuity. The lease's duration—lease

---

[1] Clarence Byrd, Ida Chen, Heather Chapman, *Financial Reporting in Canada—2000*, CICA, 2000.

term—may be anything from a short period of time to the entire expected economic life of the asset. The rental payments may be level from year to year, increasing in amount, or decreasing; they may be predetermined or may vary with sales, the prime interest rate, the consumer price index, or some other factor. In most cases the rent is set to enable the lessor to recover the asset's cost plus a fair return over the life of the lease.

The obligations for taxes, insurance, and maintenance (executory costs) may be assumed by either the lessor or the lessee, or they may be divided. Restrictions comparable to those in bond indentures may limit the lessee's activities regarding dividend payments or the incurrence of further debt and lease obligations in order to protect the lessor from default on the rents. The lease contract may be non-cancellable or may grant the right to early termination on payment of a set scale of prices plus a penalty. In case of default, the lessee may be liable for all future payments at once, receiving title to the property in exchange; or the lessor may have the right to sell to a third party and collect from the lessee all or a portion of the difference between the sale price and the lessor's unrecovered cost.

Alternatives open to the lessee at termination of the lease may range from none, to the right to purchase the leased asset at the fair market value, to the right to renew or buy it at a nominal price.

Advantages of Leasing

Although leasing is not without its disadvantages, the growth in its use suggests that it often has a genuine advantage over owning property. Some of the commonly discussed advantages of leasing are:

1. *100% financing at fixed rates.* Leases are often signed without requiring any money down from the lessee, which helps to conserve scarce cash—an especially desirable feature for new and developing companies. In addition, lease payments often remain fixed, which protects the lessee against inflation and increases in the cost of money. The following comment regarding a conventional loan is typical: "Our local bank finally agreed to finance 80% of the purchase price but wouldn't go any higher, and they wanted a floating interest rate. We just couldn't afford the down payment and we needed to lock in a payment we knew we could live with."

   From the lessor's point of view, financial institutions and leasing companies find leasing attractive because it provides competitive interest margins.

2. *Protection against obsolescence.* Leasing equipment reduces risk of obsolescence to the lessee, and in many cases passes the risk of residual value to the lessor. For example, **Syntex Corp.** (a pharmaceutical maker) leases computers. Syntex is permitted under the lease agreement to turn in an old computer for a new model at any time, cancelling the old lease and writing a new one. The cost of the new lease is added to the balance due on the old lease, less the old computer's trade-in value. As the treasurer of Syntex remarked, "Our instinct is to purchase." But when new computers come along in a short time "then leasing is just a heck of a lot more convenient than purchasing."

   On the other hand, the lessor can benefit from the property reversion at the end of the lease term. Residual values can produce very large profits. For example, **Citicorp** at one time assumed that the commercial aircraft it was leasing to the airline industry would have a residual of 5% of its purchase price. It turned out that the planes were worth 150% of their cost—a handsome price appreciation. However, three years later these same planes slumped to 80% of their cost, still a residual value far greater than the projected 5%.

3. *Flexibility.* Lease agreements may contain less restrictive provisions than other debt agreements. Innovative lessors can tailor a lease agreement to the lessee's special needs. For instance, rental payments can be structured to meet the timing of cash revenues generated by the equipment so that payments are made when the equipment is productive.

4. *Less costly financing for lessee, tax incentives for lessor.* Some companies find leasing cheaper than other forms of financing. For example, start-up companies in depressed industries, or companies in low tax brackets may lease as a way of claiming tax benefits that might otherwise be lost. Investment tax credits and capital cost allowance deductions are of no benefit to companies that have little or no taxable income. Through leasing, these tax benefits are used by the leasing companies or financial institutions, which can pass some of these tax benefits back to the asset's user in the form of lower rental payments.

5. *Off-balance-sheet financing.* Certain leases do not add debt on a balance sheet or affect financial ratios, and may add to borrowing capacity.[2] Off-balance-sheet financing is critical to some companies. For example, the airlines use lease arrangements extensively, which results in a great deal of off-balance-sheet financing. Illustration 21-1 indicates that debt levels are understated by a substantial amount for **Air Canada, WestJet Airlines Ltd.,** and **Canada 3000 Inc.**

ILLUSTRATION 21-1
Reported Debt and Unrecognized Operating Lease Obligations

	Air Canada December 31, 2000 ($ millions)	WestJet December 31, 2000 ($ thousands)	Canada 3000 April 30, 2001 ($ thousands)
Long-term liabilities, excluding future income taxes and deferred credits	$4,786	$ 49,472	$ 33,540
Shareholders' equity	$ 316	$181,092	$ 136,328
Unrecognized future minimum lease payments under existing operating leases	$5,761	$ 56,779	$1,178,239

Conceptual Nature of a Lease

If an airline borrows $47 million on a 10-year note from the bank to purchase a Boeing 757 jet plane, it is clear that an asset and related liability should be reported on the company's balance sheet at that amount. If the airline purchases the 757 for $47 million directly from Boeing through an instalment purchase over 10 years, it is equally clear that an asset and related liability should be reported (i.e., the instalment transaction should be "capitalized"). However, if the Boeing 757 is leased for 10 years through a non-cancellable lease transaction with payments of the same amount as the instalment purchase transaction, differences of opinion emerge about how this transaction should be reported. The various views on accounting for leases can be summarized as follows.

Do not capitalize any leased assets. Because the lessee does not own the property, capitalization is considered inappropriate. Furthermore, a lease is an executory contract requiring continuing performance by both parties. Because other executory contracts (such as purchase commitments and employment contracts) are not capitalized, leases should not be capitalized either.

Capitalize leases that are similar to instalment purchases. Accountants should report transactions in accordance with their economic substance; therefore, if instalment purchases are capitalized, so also should leases that have similar characteristics. In the example above, the airline is committed to the same payments over a 10-year period for either a lease or an instalment purchase; lessees simply make rental payments,

---

[2] As demonstrated later in this chapter, certain types of lease arrangements are not capitalized on the balance sheet. The liability section is thereby relieved of large lease commitments that, if recorded, would adversely affect the debt-to-equity ratio. The reluctance to record lease obligations as liabilities is one of the primary reasons capitalized lease accounting is resisted and circumvented by lessees.

whereas owners make mortgage payments. Why shouldn't the financial statements report these transactions in the same manner?

Capitalize all long-term leases. Under this approach, the long-term right to use property justifies its capitalization. This property rights approach capitalizes all long-term leases.[3]

Capitalize firm leases where the penalty for nonperformance is substantial. A final approach is to capitalize only "firm" (non-cancellable) contractual rights and obligations. "Firm" means that it is unlikely that performance under the lease can be avoided without a severe penalty.[4]

In short, the various viewpoints range from no capitalization to capitalization of all leases. The CICA standard is consistent with the approach that capitalizes leases that are similar to an instalment purchase, noting that **a lease that transfers substantially all of the benefits and risks of property ownership should be capitalized**.

This viewpoint implies three basic conclusions: (1) the characteristics that indicate that substantially all of the benefits and risks of ownership have been transferred must be identified; (2) the same characteristics should apply consistently to the lessee and the lessor; and (3) those leases that do **not** transfer substantially all the benefits and risks of ownership should not be capitalized but rather should be accounted for as rental payments and receipts.

By capitalizing the present value of the future rental payments, the *lessee* records an asset and a liability at an amount generally representative of the asset's fair value or purchase price. The *lessor,* having transferred substantially all the benefits and risks of ownership, removes the asset from its balance sheet, replacing it with a receivable. The typical journal entries for the lessee and the lessor, assuming equipment is leased and is capitalized, appear as follows.

Lessee			Lessor		
Leased Equipment	XXX		Lease Receivable (net)	XXX	
Lease Obligation		XXX	Equipment		XXX

ILLUSTRATION 21-2
Journal Entries for Capitalized Lease

Having capitalized the asset, the lessee recognizes the amortization. The lessor and lessee treat the lease rental payments as the receipt and the payment, respectively, of interest and principal.

If the lease is not capitalized, no asset is recorded by the lessee and no asset is removed from the lessor's books. When a lease payment is made, the lessee records rental expense and the lessor recognizes rental revenue.

The remainder of this chapter presents the different types of leases and the specific criteria, accounting rules, and disclosure requirements set out by the CICA in accounting for leases.

ACCOUNTING BY LESSEES

From the lessee's standpoint, all leases are classified for accounting purposes as either an operating lease or a capital lease. Where the risks and benefits of ownership are

OBJECTIVE 2

Identify and explain the accounting criteria and procedures for capitalizing leases by the lessee.

---

[3] The property rights approach was originally recommended in *Accounting Research Study No. 4* (New York: AICPA, 1964), pp. 10–11. Recently, this view has received additional support. See Warren McGregor, "Accounting for Leases: A New Approach," Special Report (Norwalk, Conn.: FASB, 1996) and H. Nailor and A. Lennard, "Capital Leases: Implementation of a New Approach," *Financial Accounting Series No. 206A* (FASB, 2000).

[4] Yuji Ijiri, Recognition of Contractual Rights and Obligations, *Research Report* (Stamford, Conn.: FASB, 1980).

transferred from the lessor to the lessee, the lease must be accounted for as a capital lease (capitalization method); otherwise, it is accounted for as an operating lease (non-capitalization method).[5]

Capitalization Criteria

CICA Handbook Section 3065, par. .06 specifies that if, at the lease's inception, **any one of the following criteria is met**, the risks and benefits of ownership are assumed to be transferred to the lessee, and the lessee should classify and account for the arrangement as a capital lease.

1. There is reasonable assurance that the lessee will obtain ownership of the leased property by the end of the lease term. If there is a bargain purchase option in the lease, it is assumed that the lessee will exercise it and obtain ownership.

2. The lease term is such that the lessee will receive substantially all of the economic benefits expected to be derived from the use of the leased property over its life span. This is usually assumed to occur if the lease term is 75% or more of the leased property's economic life.

3. The lease allows the lessor to recover its investment in the leased property and to earn a return on the investment. This is assumed to occur if the present value of the minimum lease payments (excluding executory costs) is equal to substantially all (usually 90% or more) of the leased property's fair value.

If any one of these criteria is met, the lease must be accounted for as a capital lease. Otherwise, the lease is classified and accounted for by the lessee as an operating lease. The flowchart below illustrates this decision. The capitalization criteria, however, are controversial and can be difficult to apply in practice.

ILLUSTRATION 21-3
Diagram of Lessee's Criteria for Lease Classification

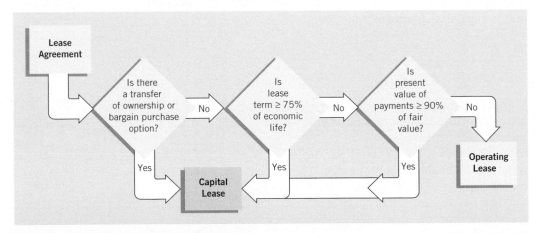

Transfer of Ownership Test

UNDERLYING CONCEPTS

Capitalization of leases illustrates the necessity for good definitions. The lease fits the definition of an asset, as it gives the lessee the economic benefits that flow from the possession or the use of the asset.

If the lease transfers ownership of the asset to the lessee, it is a capital lease. This criterion is not controversial and is easily implemented in practice.

The transfer of ownership may be facilitated at the end of the lease term without additional consideration or through a bargain purchase option. A bargain purchase option is a provision allowing the lessee to purchase the leased property for a price that is significantly lower than the property's expected fair value at the date the option becomes exercisable. At the lease's inception, the difference between the option price

---

[5] What are the risks and benefits (or rewards) of ownership? *Handbook* Section 3065, par. .05 identifies the benefits as "the expectation of profitable operations over the property's economic life and of gain from appreciation in value or realization of a residual value." Alternatively, the risks "include possibilities of losses from idle capacity or technological obsolescence and of variation in return due to changing economic conditions."

and the expected fair value must be large enough to make exercise of the option reasonably assured.[6]

For example, assume that you were to lease a car for $599 per month for 40 months with an option to purchase it for $100 at the end of the 40-month period. If the car's estimated fair value is $3,000 at the end of the 40 months, the $100 option to purchase is clearly a bargain and, therefore, capitalization is required. In other cases, the criterion may not be as easy to apply, and determining now that a certain future price is a bargain can be difficult.

Economic Life Test

If the lease period equals or exceeds 75% of the asset's economic life, it follows that most of the risks and rewards of ownership are transferred to the lessee. However, determining the lease term and asset's economic life may be troublesome.

The lease term is generally considered the fixed, non-cancellable term of the lease. However, this period can be extended if a bargain renewal option is provided in the lease agreement. A bargain renewal option is a provision allowing the lessee to renew the lease for a rental that is lower than the expected fair rental at the date the option becomes exercisable. At the lease's inception, the difference between the renewal rental and the expected fair rental must be great enough to make exercise of the option to renew reasonably assured.

For example, if a computer is leased for two years at a rental of $100 per month and then subsequently can be leased for $10 per month for another two years when the fair rental at that time is $60 per month, it clearly is a bargain renewal option, and the lease term is considered to be four years. However, with bargain renewal options, as with bargain purchase options, it is sometimes difficult to determine what is a bargain.[7]

Determining estimated economic life can also pose problems, especially if the leased item is a specialized item or has been used for a significant period of time. For example, determining the economic life of a nuclear core is extremely difficult because it is subject to much more than normal wear and tear.

INTERNATIONAL INSIGHT

In some nations (e.g., Italy, Japan) accounting principles do not specify criteria for capitalization of leases. In others (e.g., Sweden, Switzerland) such criteria exist, but capitalization of the leases is optional.

Recovery of Investment by Lessor Test

If the minimum lease payments' present value equals or exceeds 90% of the asset's fair value, then the leased asset should be capitalized. The rationale for this test is that if the minimum lease payments' present value is reasonably close to the asset's market price, the lessor is recovering its investment in the asset plus a return on the investment through the lease arrangement and the asset is effectively being purchased by the lessee.

In determining the minimum lease payments' present value, three important concepts are involved: (1) minimum lease payments, (2) executory costs, and (3) the discount rate.

Minimum Lease Payments. In general, the minimum lease payments are those the lessee is obligated to make or can be expected to make in connection with the leased property. Minimum lease payments **from the lessee's point of view** are defined as including:

---

[6] The Emerging Issues Committee of the CICA, in *EIC—30*, concluded that the ultimate test is whether there is reasonable assurance that the lessee will obtain ownership by the end of the lease. A situation, for example, where there is no bargain purchase option but other lease provisions make it probable that the lessee will acquire the leased property for its fair value at the end of the lease term are sufficient to classify the transaction as a capital lease.

[7] The original lease term is also extended for leases having the following: substantial penalties for nonrenewal; periods for which the lessor has the option to renew or extend the lease; renewal periods preceding the date a bargain purchase option becomes exercisable; and renewal periods in which the lessee guarantees the lessor's debt related to the leased property.

1. **Minimum rental payments**—Minimum payments the lessee is obligated to make to the lessor under the lease agreement, excluding executory costs (defined below). The minimum rental payments may be equal to the minimum lease payments. However, the minimum lease payments also include any lessee guaranteed residual value, penalty for failure to renew, or a bargain purchase option, if these are included in the agreement.

2. **Guaranteed residual value**—The residual value is the leased property's estimated fair value at the end of the lease term. The lessor often transfers the risk of loss to the lessee or to a third party by requiring a guarantee of the estimated residual value. The guaranteed residual value is (1) the amount at which the lessor has the right to require the lessee to purchase the asset; or (2) the amount the lessee or the third-party guarantor guarantees the lessor will realize. The unguaranteed residual value, that portion of the residual value that is not guaranteed or is guaranteed solely by a party related to the lessor, is not included in the definition of minimum lease payments. Often, no part of the residual is guaranteed.

3. **Penalty for failure to renew or extend the lease**—The amount payable by the lessee if the agreement specifies that the lease must be extended or renewed and the lessee fails to do so.

4. **Bargain purchase option**—As indicated earlier, an option given to the lessee to purchase the equipment at the end of the lease term at a price that is sufficiently below the expected fair value so that, at the lease's inception, purchase appears to be reasonably assured. Ordinarily, if a bargain purchase option is included in the lease agreement, a guaranteed residual and penalty would not apply.[8]

Executory Costs.   Like most assets, leased tangible assets require the incurrence of insurance, maintenance, and property tax expenses—called executory costs—during their economic life. If the lessor retains responsibility for paying these ownership-type costs, any portion of each lease payment that represents the recovery of executory costs from the lessee **should be excluded** in calculating the minimum lease payments' present value. This portion of the lease payment does not represent payment on or a reduction of the capitalized obligation. If the portion of the lease payment that represents executory costs is not determinable from the provisions of the lease, an estimate of the amount must be made. Many lease agreements, however, specify that executory costs are to be paid to the appropriate third parties directly by the lessee; in these cases, the rental payments can be used without adjustment in the present value calculations.

Discount Rate.   The lessee calculates the present value of the minimum lease payments using the lessee's incremental borrowing rate, which is defined as the interest rate that, at the lease's inception, the lessee would have incurred to borrow, over a similar term and with similar security for the borrowing, the funds necessary to purchase the leased asset.[9] For example, assume that Mortenson Inc. decides to lease computer equipment for a five-year period at a cost of $10,000 a year. To determine whether the payment value is less than 90% of the property's fair market value, the lessee discounts the payments using its incremental borrowing rate. Determining that rate will often require judgement because it is based on a hypothetical property purchase.

There is one exception to the use of this rate. If (1) the lessee knows the implicit interest rate used by the lessor in calculating the amount of the lease payments; and (2) it is less than the lessee's incremental borrowing rate, then the lessee must use the lessor's implicit rate. The interest rate implicit in the lease is the discount rate that corresponds to the lessor's internal rate of return on the lease.[10]

IAS NOTE

IAS 17 requires the lessee to use the interest rate implicit in the lease whenever it is reasonably determinable. Otherwise, the lessee's incremental borrowing rate is used.

---

[8] *CICA Handbook*, Section 3065, par. .03(q).

[9] *Ibid.*, Section 3065, par. .03(p).

[10] *Ibid.*, par. .03(m).

The purpose of this exception is twofold. First, the lessor's implicit rate is generally a more realistic rate to use in determining the amount, if any, to report as the asset and related liability for the lessee. Second, the guideline is provided to ensure that the lessee does not use an artificially high incremental borrowing rate **that would cause the minimum lease payments' present value to be less than 90% of the property's fair value and thus make it possible to avoid capitalization of the asset and related liability!** The lessee may argue that it cannot determine the implicit rate of the lessor and therefore the higher rate should be used. However, in many cases, the implicit rate used by the lessor is disclosed or can be approximated. Determining whether or not a reasonable estimate could be made requires judgement, particularly where the result from using the incremental borrowing rate comes close to meeting the 90% test. Because the leased property cannot be capitalized at more than its fair value, the lessee is prevented from using an excessively low discount rate.

Accounting for a Capital Lease

Asset and Liability Recorded

In a capital lease transaction, the lessee uses the lease as a source of financing. The lessor provides the leased asset to the lessee and finances the transaction by accepting instalment payments. The lessee treats the transaction as if an asset was purchased and a long-term liability was created. Over the life of the property leased, the rental payments made by the lessee to the lessor constitute a repayment of principal plus interest.

The lessee recognizes the asset and liability at the lower of (1) the minimum lease payments' present value as defined above; and (2) the fair value of the leased asset at the lease's inception. The rationale for this approach is that, like all other assets, a leased asset cannot be recorded at more than its fair value.

Amortization Period and Method

One troublesome aspect of accounting for the amortization of the capitalized leased asset relates to the amortization period. For example, if the lease agreement transfers ownership of the asset to the lessee or contains a bargain purchase option (criterion 1), the leased asset is amortized in a manner consistent with the lessee's normal amortization policy for owned assets, **using the asset's economic life**.

On the other hand, if the lease does not transfer ownership or does not contain a bargain purchase option, the leased asset is amortized **over the term of the lease**, because the leased asset reverts to the lessor after this point.

The lessee should amortize the leased asset by applying conventional amortization methods such as straight-line, declining-balance, or units of production methods.

Effective Interest Method

Although the amounts initially capitalized as an asset and recorded as an obligation are calculated at the same present value, **the subsequent amortization of the asset and the discharge of the obligation are independent accounting processes**.

Over the term of the lease, the effective interest method is used to allocate each lease payment between principal and interest. This method produces a periodic interest expense equal to a constant percentage of the obligation's outstanding balance. The discount rate used by the lessee to determine the present value of the minimum lease payments is used by the lessee in applying the effective interest method to capital leases.

Capital Lease Method Illustrated

Lessor Corporation and Lessee Corporation sign a lease agreement dated January 1, 2002, which calls for Lessor Corporation to lease equipment to Lessee Corporation beginning January 1, 2002. The lease agreement's terms and provisions and other pertinent data are as follows.

1. The term of the lease is five years, and the lease agreement is non-cancellable, requiring equal rental payments of $25,981.62 at the beginning of each year (annuity due basis).

2. The equipment has a fair value at the lease's inception of $100,000, an estimated economic life of five years, and no residual value.

3. Lessee Corporation pays all of the executory costs directly to third parties except for the property taxes of $2,000 per year, which are included in the annual payments to the lessor.

4. The lease contains no renewal options, and the equipment reverts to Lessor Corporation at the termination of the lease.

5. Lessee Corporation's incremental borrowing rate is 11% per year.

6. Lessee Corporation amortizes similar equipment it owns on a straight-line basis.

7. Lessor Corporation set the annual rental to earn a rate of return on its investment of 10% per year; this fact is known to Lessee Corporation.

The lease meets the criteria for classification as a capital lease because (1) the lease term of five years, being equal to the equipment's estimated economic life of five years, satisfies the 75% test; or because (2) the minimum lease payments' present value ($100,000 as calculated below) exceeds 90% of the property's fair value ($100,000).

The minimum lease payments are $119,908.10 ($23,981.62 × 5), and the amount capitalized as leased assets is $100,000, the present value of the minimum lease payments determined as follows.

ILLUSTRATION 21-4

Calculation of Capitalized Lease Payments

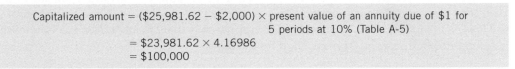

Capitalized amount = ($25,981.62 − $2,000) × present value of an annuity due of $1 for 5 periods at 10% (Table A-5)

= $23,981.62 × 4.16986

= $100,000

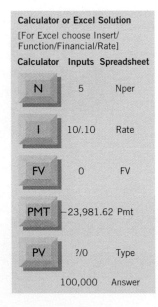

Calculator or Excel Solution

[For Excel choose Insert/ Function/Financial/Rate]

Calculator	Inputs	Spreadsheet
N	5	Nper
I	10/.10	Rate
FV	0	FV
PMT	−23,981.62	Pmt
PV	?/0	Type
	100,000	Answer

The lessor's implicit interest rate of 10% is used instead of the lessee's incremental borrowing rate of 11% because (1) it is lower and (2) the lessee has knowledge of it.[11]

The entry to record the capital lease on Lessee Corporation's books on January 1, 2002 is:

Equipment under Capital Leases	100,000	
Obligations under Capital Leases		100,000

The journal entry to record the first lease payment on January 1, 2002 is:

Property Tax Expense	2,000.00	
Obligations under Capital Leases	23,981.62	
Cash		25,981.62

Each lease payment of $25,981.62 consists of three elements: (1) a reduction in the principal of the lease obligation, (2) a financing cost (interest expense), and (3) executory costs (property taxes). The total financing cost or interest expense over the lease's term is the difference between the lease payments' present value ($100,000) and the actual cash disbursed, net of executory costs ($119,908.10), or $19,908.10. The annual interest expense, applying the effective interest method, is a function of the outstanding obligation, as illustrated below.

---

[11] If Lessee Corporation had an incremental borrowing rate of 9% (lower than the 10% rate used by Lessor Corporation) and it did not know the rate used by Lessor Corporation, the present value calculation would yield a capitalized amount of $101,675.35 ($23,981.62 × 4.23972). Because this amount exceeds the equipment's $100,000 fair value, Lessee Corporation would capitalize the $100,000 and use 10% as its effective rate for amortization of the lease obligation.

ILLUSTRATION 21-5
Lease Amortization Schedule for
Lessee—Annuity Due Basis

LESSEE CORPORATION
Lease Amortization Schedule
(Annuity due basis)

Date	Annual Lease Payment	Interest (10%) on Unpaid Obligation	Reduction of Lease Obligation	Balance of Lease Obligation
	(a)	(b)	(c)	(d)
1/1/02				$100,000.00
1/1/02	$ 23,981.62	$ –0–	$ 23,981.62	76,018.38
1/1/03	23,981.62	7,601.84	16,379.78	59,638.60
1/1/04	23,981.62	5,963.86	18,017.76	41,620.84
1/1/05	23,981.62	4,162.08	19,819.54	21,801.30
1/1/06	23,981.62	2,180.32*	21,801.30	–0–
	$119,908.10	$19,908.10	$100,000.00	

(a) Lease payment as required by lease, excluding executory costs.
(b) Ten percent of the preceding balance of (d) except for 1/1/02; since this is an annuity due, no time has elapsed at the date of the first payment and no interest has accrued.
(c) (a) minus (b).
(d) Preceding balance minus (c).
*Rounded by 19 cents.

At Lessee Corporation's fiscal year end, December 31, 2002, accrued interest is recorded as follows.

Interest Expense	7,601.84	
Interest Payable		7,601.84

Amortization of the leased equipment over its lease term of five years, applying Lessee Corporation's normal amortization policy (straight-line method), results in the following entry on December 31, 2002.

Amortization Expense—Leased Equipment	20,000	
Accumulated Amortization—Leased Equipment		20,000
($100,000 / 5 years)		

At December 31, 2002, the assets recorded under capital leases are separately identified on the lessee's balance sheet, or in a note cross-referenced to the balance sheet. Similarly, the related obligations are separately identified. The principal portion due within one year or the operating cycle, whichever is longer, is classified with current liabilities and the remainder with noncurrent liabilities. For example, the current portion of the December 31, 2002 total obligation of $76,018.38 in the lessee's amortization schedule is the amount of the reduction in the principal of the obligation within the next 12 months, or $16,379.78. The liability section as it relates to lease transactions at December 31, 2002 is as follows.

ILLUSTRATION 21-6
Reporting Current and
Noncurrent Lease Liabilities

Current liabilities	
Interest payable	$ 7,601.84
Obligations under capital leases	16,379.78
Noncurrent liabilities	
Obligations under capital leases	$59,638.60

The journal entry to record the lease payment of January 1, 2003 is as follows.

Property Tax Expense	2,000.00	
Interest Payable[12]	7,601.84	
Obligations under Capital Leases	16,379.78	
Cash		25,981.62

---

[12] This entry assumes the company does not prepare reversing entries. If reversing entries are used, the Interest Expense account would be debited for this amount.

Entries through 2006 follow the pattern above. Other executory costs (insurance and maintenance) assumed by Lessee Corporation would be recorded in a manner similar to that used to record operating costs incurred on other assets owned by Lessee Corporation.

Upon expiration of the lease, the amount capitalized as leased equipment is fully amortized and the lease obligation is fully discharged. If not purchased, the equipment is returned to the lessor, and the leased equipment and related accumulated amortization accounts are removed from the books. If the equipment is purchased for $5,000 at the termination of the lease, and the equipment's estimated total life is changed from five to seven years, the following entry would be made.

Equipment ($100,000 + $5,000)	105,000	
Accumulated Amortization—Leased Equipment	100,000	
Equipment under Capital Leases		100,000
Accumulated Amortization—Equipment		100,000
Cash		5,000

Reporting and Disclosure Requirements—Capital Leases

Consistent with the recognition of property, plant, and equipment and a long-term liability, most of the required disclosures are similar to those required in *Handbook* Sections 3061 and 3210 for property, plant, and equipment and long-term liabilities. *CICA Handbook* Section 3065, pars. .21 to .26, identify the following required disclosures.

1. The gross amount of assets recorded under capital leases and related accumulated amortization.
2. Amortization expense on leased assets. This may be disclosed separately or as part of amortization expense for fixed assets, and the methods and rates of amortization should be disclosed.
3. Separate disclosure of lease obligations from other long-term obligations, with separate disclosure of related details about interest rates, expiry dates, and any significant restrictions imposed as a result of the lease agreements.
4. The current portion, if any, of the lease obligations, as a current liability.
5. Future minimum lease payments, in the aggregate and for each of the five succeeding fiscal years, with a separate deduction for amounts included in the minimum lease payments representing executory costs and imputed interest. (The resulting net amount is the total lease obligation reported on the balance sheet.)
6. Interest expense related to lease obligations, disclosed separately or included in interest on long-term indebtedness.

IAS NOTE

IAS 17 also requires disclosure of renewal options, purchase options, contingent rentals, and other contingencies.

Although not required, it may be appropriate to disclose separately total contingent rentals (rentals based on a factor other than the passage of time) as well as the amount of future minimum rentals receivable from non-cancellable sub-leases.

Accounting for an Operating Lease

Under an operating lease, neither the leased asset nor the obligation to make lease payments is given accounting recognition. Instead, the lease payments are treated as rent expense, assigned to the accounting periods benefiting from the use of the leased asset.[13] Appropriate accruals or deferrals are made if the accounting period ends between cash payment dates.

---

[13] *EIC-21, Accounting for Lease Inducements by the Lessee* (CICA: January 21, 1991) provides guidance on accounting for the benefits of lease inducements such as an upfront cash payment to the lessee, initial rent-free periods, etc. It is recommended that such benefits be taken into income over the lease's term on a straight-line or other basis that is representative of the pattern of benefits from the leased property.

Assume the capital lease illustrated above does not qualify as a capital lease and, by default, is accounted for as an operating lease. The charge to the income statement for rent expense in each year is $25,981.62, the amount of the rental payment. The journal entry to record the payment each January 1 is as follows.

Prepaid Rent	25,981.62	
Cash		25,981.62

At each December 31 fiscal year end, the following entry is made, assuming adjusting entries are prepared only annually.

Rent Expense	25,981.62	
Prepaid Rent		25,981.62

Reporting and Disclosure Requirements—Operating Leases

While disclosure of the amount of operating lease rentals charged against income and other details related to operating lease agreements may be desirable, there are only two required disclosures.

1. The future minimum lease payments, in total and for each of the next five years and
2. A description of the nature of other commitments under such leases.[14]

These disclosures allow readers to assess the impact of such agreements on the organization.

Comparison of Capital Lease with Operating Lease

As indicated above, if the lease had been accounted for as an operating lease, the first-year charge to operations would have been $25,981.62, the amount of the rental payment. Treating the transaction as a capital lease, however, resulted in a first-year charge of $29,601.84: straight-line amortization of $20,000, interest expense of $7,601.84, and executory expenses of $2,000. The schedule below shows that while the **total** charges to operations are the same over the lease term whether the lease is accounted for as a capital lease or as an operating lease, the charges are higher in the earlier years and lower in the later years under the capital lease treatment.[15]

OBJECTIVE 5

Contrast the operating and capitalization methods of recording leases.

LESSEE CORPORATION
Schedule of Charges to Operations
Capital Lease versus Operating Lease

ILLUSTRATION 21-7
Comparison of Charges to Operations—Capital vs. Operating Leases

Year	Capital Lease Amortization	Executory Costs	Interest	Total Charge	Operating Lease Charge	Difference
2002	$ 20,000	$ 2,000	$ 7,601.84	$ 29,601.84	$ 25,981.62	$ 3,620.22
2003	20,000	2,000	5,963.86	27,963.86	25,981.62	1,982.24
2004	20,000	2,000	4,162.08	26,162.08	25,981.62	180.46
2005	20,000	2,000	2,180.32	24,180.32	25,981.62	$(1,801.30)
2006	20,000	2,000	—	22,000.00	25,981.62	(3,981.62)
	$100,000	$10,000	$19,908.10	$129,908.10	$129,908.10	$ –0–

---

[14] *CICA Handbook*, Section 3065, par. .31 to .33.

[15] The higher charges in the early years is one reason lessees are reluctant to classify leases as capital leases. Lessees, especially those of real estate, claim that it is not more costly to operate the leased asset in the early years than in the later years; thus, they advocate an even charge similar to that provided by the operating method.

If an accelerated amortization method is used, the differences between the amounts charged to operations under the two methods would be even larger in the earlier and later years.

In addition, using the capital lease approach results in an asset and related liability of $100,000 initially reported on the balance sheet, whereas no such asset or liability is reported under the operating method. A capital lease therefore has the following effects on the lessee's financial statements.

1. The amount of reported debt (both short-term and long-term) is higher.
2. The amount of total assets (specifically long-lived assets) is higher.
3. Income, and therefore retained earnings, is lower early in the life of the lease.

It is not surprising that the business community resists capitalizing leases as the resulting **higher** debt-to-equity ratio, **reduced** total asset turnover, and **reduced** rate of return on total assets are perceived to have a detrimental effect on the company.

Whether this resistance is well founded is a matter of conjecture. **From a cash flow point of view, the company is in the same position whether the lease is accounted for as an operating or a capital lease.** The reasons managers often give when arguing against capitalization are that it can more easily lead to violation of loan covenants; it can affect the amount of compensation received (for example, a stock compensation plan tied to earnings); and it can lower rates of return and increase debt-to-equity relationships, thus making the company less attractive to present and potential investors.[16]

Illustration of Capital and Operating Lease Disclosures by the Lessee

The following excerpts from the financial statements of **TELUS Corporation** for the year ended December 31, 2000 illustrate the disclosure by a lessee of both capital and operating leases.

ILLUSTRATION 21-8
Capital and Operating Lease Disclosures by a Lessee

Go to the Digital Tool for additional lease disclosures.

TELUS CORPORATION
Consolidated Balance Sheet (in part)
As At December 31
($ millions)

	2000	1999
Capital assets, net (Note 10)	$11,531.0	$5,878.3
Short-term obligations (Note 12)	5,033.3	573.2
Long-term debt (Note 13)	3,047.3	1,555.5
Commitments (Note 15)		

2. **Summary of Significant Accounting Policies (in part)**
   (h) **Leases (in part)**

   Leases are classified as capital or operating depending upon the terms and conditions of the contracts.

   Where the Company is the lessee, asset values recorded under capital leases are amortized on a straight-line basis over the term of the lease. Obligations recorded under capital leases are reduced by lease payments net of imputed interest.

---

[16] One study indicates that management's behaviour did change as a result of the profession's requirements to capitalize certain leases. For example, many companies restructured their leases to avoid capitalization; others increased their purchases of assets instead of leasing; and others, faced with capitalization, postponed their debt offerings or issued stock instead. However, it is interesting to note that the study found no significant effect on stock or bond prices as a result of capitalization of leases. A. Rashad Abdel-khalik, "The Economic Effects on Lessees of *FASB Statement No. 13*, Accounting for Leases," Research Report (Stamford, Conn.: FASB, 1981).

10. Capital Assets, Net

(millions)	Cost	Accumulated Depreciation and Amortization	Net Book Value 2000	Net Book Value 1999
Telecommunications assets	$13,887.6	$ 8,293.2	$ 5,594.4	$4,132.9
Assets leased to customers	416.3	303.4	112.9	51.1
Buildings	1,224.5	649.4	575.1	560.5
Office equipment & furniture	637.4	403.7	233.7	155.6
Assets under capital lease	77.5	40.3	37.2	25.4
Intangible assets:				
Subscriber base	284.1	5.9	278.2	—
Spectrum licenses	3,565.2	18.7	3,546.5	—
Other	861.5	536.9	324.6	382.6
	20,954.1	10,251.5	10,702.6	5,308.1
Land	85.3	—	85.3	82.8
Plant under construction	679.9	—	679.9	443.6
Materials and supplies	63.2	—	63.2	43.8
	$21,782.5	$10,251.5	$11,531.0	$5,878.3

13. Long-term Debt (in part)
(a) Details of Long-term Debt

Capital leases (Note 15d) issued at varying rates of interest up to 11.75% and maturing on various dates up to 2004	26.9	27.4

15. Commitments and Contingent Liabilities (in part)

(d) The Company occupies leased premises in various centers and has land, buildings and equipment under operating leases.

At December 31, 2000, the future minimum lease payments under capital leases and operating leases were:

(millions)	Capital Leases	Operating Leases
2001	$13.6	$115.8
2002	11.0	90.4
2003	4.1	66.1
2004	.6	56.7
2005		44.7
Total future minimum lease payments	29.3	
Less imputed interest	2.4	
Capital lease liability	$26.9	

It is interesting to see the magnitude of the unrecognized operating lease obligations relative to the recorded capital lease obligations reported in Note 15.

ACCOUNTING BY LESSORS

Economics of Leasing

The lessor determines the rental amount basing it on the rate of return—the implicit rate—needed to justify leasing the asset. The key variables considered in establishing the rate of return are the lessee's credit standing, the length of the lease, and the status of the residual value (guaranteed versus unguaranteed). In the Lessor Corporation/Lessee Corporation example that starts on page 1023, the lessor wanted a 10% return, the equipment's fair value was $100,000 (also the lessor's cost), and the estimated residual value was zero. Lessor Corporation determined the amount of the rental payment in the following manner.

> **OBJECTIVE 6**
> Calculate the lease payment required for the lessor to earn a given return.

ILLUSTRATION 21-9
Calculation of Lease Payments

Fair value of leased equipment	$100,000.00
Less: Present value of the amount to be recovered through bargain purchase option or residual value at end of lease term	–0–
Present value of amount to be recovered by lessor through lease payments	$100,000.00
Five beginning-of-the-year lease payments to yield a 10% return ($100,000 ÷ 4.16986a)	$ 23,981.62

aPV of an annuity due (Table A-5); $i = 10\%$, $n = 5$

If a bargain purchase option or other residual value is involved, the lessor does not have to recover as much through the rental payments. Therefore, the present value of such amounts is deducted before determining the lease payment. This is illustrated later in the chapter in more detail.

Classification of Leases by the Lessor

OBJECTIVE 7

Identify the classifications of leases for the lessor.

IAS NOTE

IAS 17 does not differentiate between direct financing and sales-type leases.

From the **lessor's** standpoint, all leases are classified for accounting purposes as one of the following:

(a) Operating lease or
(b) Direct financing lease or sales-type lease.

Similar to the lessee's decision, where the risks and benefits are retained for the most part by the lessor, the lessor accounts for the agreement as an operating lease.[17] Where the risks and benefits of ownership related to the leased property are transferred from the lessor to the lessee, the lessor accounts for the lease as either a direct financing or a sales-type lease.

Whether a lease is a direct financing or a sales-type lease depends on the situation. Some companies enter into lease agreements as a means of selling their products (usually a sales-type lease) while other companies are in business to facilitate the financing of a variety of assets in order to generate financing income (usually a direct financing lease).

Capitalization Criteria

If at the inception of the lease agreement the lease meets *one or more* of the following Group I criteria and *both* of the following Group II criteria, the lessor classifies and accounts for the arrangement as either a direct financing lease or a sales-type lease.[18] Note that the Group I criteria are identical to the criteria that must be met for a lease to be classified as a capital lease by a lessee.

ILLUSTRATION 21-10
Capitalization Criteria for the Lessor

Group I
1. There is reasonable assurance that the lessee will obtain ownership of the leased property by the end of the lease term. If there is a bargain purchase option in the lease, it is assumed that the lessee will exercise it and obtain ownership.
2. The lease term is such that the lessee will receive substantially all of the economic benefits expected to be derived from the use of the leased property over its life span. This is usually assumed to occur if the lease term is 75% or more of the economic life of the leased property.
3. The lease allows the lessor to recover its investment in the leased property and to earn a return on the investment. This is assumed to occur if the present value of the minimum lease payments (excluding executory costs) is equal to substantially all (usually 90% or more) of the fair value of the leased property.

Group II
1. The credit risk associated with the lease is normal when compared with the risk of collection of similar receivables.
2. The amounts of any unreimbursable costs that are likely to be incurred by the lessor under the lease can be reasonably estimated.

[17] *CICA Handbook*, Section 3065, par. .09 and .10.

[18] *Ibid.*, par. .07.

Why the Group II requirements? The answer is that the profession wants to make sure that the lessor has really transferred the risks and benefits of ownership. If collectibility of payments is not reasonably assured or if performance by the lessor is incomplete, then it is inappropriate to remove the leased asset from the lessor's books and recognize revenue. In short, the Group II criteria are standard revenue recognition criteria applied to a lease situation.

Computer leasing companies at one time used to buy IBM equipment, lease it, and remove the leased assets from their balance sheets. In leasing the asset, the computer lessors stated that they would substitute new IBM equipment if obsolescence occurred. However, when IBM introduced a new computer line, IBM refused to sell it to the computer leasing companies. As a result, a number of computer leasing companies could not meet their contracts with their customers and were forced to take back the old equipment. What the computer leasing companies had taken off the books now had to be reinstated. Such a case demonstrates one reason for Group II requirements.

The difference for the lessor between a direct financing lease and a sales-type lease is the presence or absence of a manufacturer's or dealer's profit (or loss). A sales-type lease incorporates a manufacturer's or dealer's profit, but a direct financing lease does not. The profit (or loss) to the lessor is the difference between the fair value of the leased property at the lease's inception, and the lessor's cost or carrying amount (book value). Normally, sales-type leases arise when manufacturers or dealers use leasing as a means of marketing their products. For example, a computer manufacturer will lease its computer equipment to businesses and institutions. Direct financing leases, on the other hand, generally result from arrangements with lessors who are primarily engaged in financing operations, such as lease-finance companies, banks, insurance companies, and pension trusts. However, a lessor need not be a manufacturer or dealer to realize a profit (or loss) at the inception of the lease that requires application of sales-type lease accounting.

All leases that do not qualify as direct financing or sales-type leases are classified and accounted for by the lessors as operating leases. The following flowchart shows the circumstances under which a lease is classified by the lessor as operating, direct financing, or sales-type.

ILLUSTRATION 21-11
Flowchart of Lessor's Criteria for Lease Classification

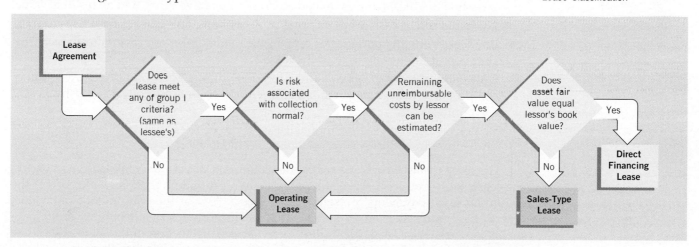

It is possible that a lessor that does not meet both Group II criteria will classify a lease as an **operating** lease while the lessee will classify the same lease as a **capital** lease. In such an event, both the lessor and lessee carry the asset on their books and both amortize the capitalized asset.

Accounting for a Direct Financing Lease

Leases that are in substance the financing of an asset purchase by a lessee require the lessor to remove the asset from its books and replace it with a receivable. The accounts and information needed to record a direct financing lease are as follows.

OBJECTIVE 8
·······························
Describe the lessor's accounting for direct financing leases.

DIRECT FINANCING LEASE TERMS		
Term	Account	Explanation
Gross investment in lease	Lease Payments Receivable	The undiscounted lease payments (excluding executory costs) plus any residual value accruing to the lessor at the end of the lease term or any bargain purchase option.[19]
Unearned finance revenue	Unearned Interest Revenue (contra account to Lease Payments Receivable)	The difference between the undiscounted Lease Payments Receivable and the carrying amount of the leased property.
Net investment in lease		The gross investment (the receivable) less the unearned finance or interest revenue included therein; i.e., the gross investment's present value.

The net investment is the present value of the items making up the gross investment, the difference between these two accounts being the unearned interest. The unearned interest revenue is amortized and taken into income over the lease term by applying the effective interest method. Thus, a constant rate of return is produced on the net investment in the lease.

Illustration of Direct Financing Lease (Annuity Due)

The following presentation, using the data from the preceding Lessor Corporation/Lessee Corporation example beginning on page 1023, illustrates the accounting treatment accorded a direct financing lease. The information relevant to Lessor Corporation in accounting for this lease transaction is repeated as follows.

1. The lease is for a five-year term that begins January 1, 2002, is non-cancellable, and requires equal rental payments of $25,981.62 at the beginning of each year. Payments include $2,000 of executory costs (property taxes).

2. The equipment has a cost of $100,000 to Lessor Corporation, a fair value at the lease's inception of $100,000, an estimated economic life of five years, and no residual value.

3. No initial direct costs were incurred in negotiating and closing the lease contract.

4. The lease contains no renewal options and the equipment reverts to Lessor Corporation at the termination of the lease.

5. Collectibility is reasonably assured and no additional costs (with the exception of the property taxes being reimbursed by the lessee) are to be incurred by Lessor Corporation.

6. Lessor Corporation set the annual lease payments to ensure a rate of return of 10% on its investment, as shown previously in Illustration 21-9.

The lease meets the criteria for classification as a direct financing lease because (1) the lease term exceeds 75% of the equipment's estimated economic life, or (2) the minimum lease payments' present value exceeds 90% of the equipment's fair value, and (3) the credit risk is normal relative to similar receivables (collectibility of the payments is reasonably assured), and (4) there are no further unreimbursable costs to be incurred by Lessor Corporation. It is not a sales-type lease because there is no dealer profit between the equipment's fair value ($100,000) and the lessor's cost ($100,000).

The lease payments receivable (gross investment) is calculated as follows.

---

[19] The *Handbook* defines the gross investment as "the minimum lease payments plus any unguaranteed residual value accruing to the lessor at the end of the lease term." This is often confusing. To make sense of the definition, you have to remember that the definition of "minimum lease payments" for a lessor includes: (a) rental payments (excluding executory costs), (b) any bargain purchase option, (c) any guaranteed residual value, and (d) any penalty for failure to renew.

ILLUSTRATION 21-12
Calculation of Lease Payments
Receivable

Lease payments receivable = Lease payments (excluding executory costs) plus residual value
or bargain purchase option
= [($25,981.62 − $2,000) × 5] + $0
= $119,908.10

The unearned interest revenue is the difference between the lease payments receivable and the lessor's cost or carrying value of the leased asset as shown below.

ILLUSTRATION 21-13
Calculation of Unearned Interest
Revenue

Unearned interest revenue = Lease payments receivable minus asset's cost or carrying value
= $119,908.10 − $100,000
= $19,908.10

The net investment in this direct financing lease is the lease payments' present value of $100,000 or the gross investment of $119,908.10 minus the unearned interest revenue of $19,908.10.

The acquisition of the asset by the lessor, its transfer to the lessee, the resulting receivable, and the unearned interest income are recorded on January 1, 2002 as follows.

Equipment Purchased for Lease	100,000	
Cash[20]		100,000
Lease Payments Receivable	119,908.10	
Equipment Purchased for Lease		100,000.00
Unearned Interest Revenue Leases		19,908.10

The unearned interest revenue is classified on the balance sheet as a contra account to the receivable account. Generally, the lease payments receivable, although **recorded** at the gross investment amount, is **reported** in the balance sheet at the "net investment" amount (gross investment less unearned interest revenue) and entitled "Net investment in capital leases."[21] It is classified either as current or noncurrent, depending on when the net investment is to be recovered.

The leased equipment with a cost of $100,000, representing Lessor Corporation's investment, is replaced with a net lease receivable. In a manner similar to the lessee's treatment of interest, Lessor Corporation applies the effective interest method and recognizes interest revenue as a function of the unrecovered net investment, as shown in Illustration 21-14.

ILLUSTRATION 21-14
Lease Amortization Schedule for
Lessor—Annuity Due Basis

LESSOR CORPORATION
Lease Amortization Schedule
(Annuity due basis)

Date	Annual Lease Payment (a)	Interest (10%) on Net Investment (b)	Net Investment Recovery (c)	Net Investment (d)
1/1/02				$100,000.00
1/1/02	$ 23,981.62	$ −0−	$ 23,981.62	76,018.38
1/1/03	23,981.62	7,601.84	16,379.78	59,638.60
1/1/04	23,981.62	5,963.86	18,017.76	41,620.84
1/1/05	23,981.62	4,162.08	19,819.54	21,801.30
1/1/06	23,981.62	2,180.32*	21,801.30	−0−
	$119,908.10	$19,908.10	$100,000.00	

[20] The lessor probably finances the purchase of this asset over a term generally coinciding with the term of the lease. Because the lessor's cost of capital is lower than the rate implicit in the lease, the lessor earns a profit generated by the interest spread.

[21] While lessees may record and report the lease obligation on a net basis, lessors tend to recognize the gross amount in receivables. Unlike the lessee, lessors may have hundreds or thousands of lease contracts to administer and the amounts to be collected are the gross receivables. Therefore, for administrative simplicity, amounts received are a direct reduction of the receivable and the interest is determined and adjusted for separately.

(a) Annual rental that provides a 10% return on net investment (exclusive of executory costs).
(b) Ten percent of the preceding balance of (d) except for 1/1/02.
(c) (a) minus (b).
(d) Preceding balance minus (c).
*Rounded by 19 cents.

On January 1, 2002, the journal entry to record receipt of the first year's lease payment is as follows.

Cash	25,981.62	
Lease Payments Receivable		23,981.62
Property Tax Expense		2,000.00

On December 31, 2002, the interest revenue earned during the first year is recognized through the following entry.

Unearned Interest Revenue—Leases	7,601.84	
Interest Revenue—Leases		7,601.84

T accounts for the lease receivable and the unearned interest contra account after these entries are posted appear as follows.

ILLUSTRATION 21-15
General Ledger Lease Asset Accounts

	Lease Payments Receivable		Unearned Interest Revenue		Net Investment in Lease
Jan. 1/02	$119,908.10			$19,908.10	$100,000.00
Jan. 1/02		23,981.62			(23,981.62)
	95,926.48			19,908.10	76,018.38
Dec. 31/02			7,601.84		7,601.84
	95,926.48			12,306.26	83,620.22

At December 31, 2002, the net investment under capital leases is reported in the lessor's balance sheet among current assets or noncurrent assets, or both. The portion due within one year or the operating cycle, whichever is longer, is classified as a current asset and the rest with noncurrent assets.

The net investment at December 31, 2002 is $83,620.22, which is the balance at January 1, 2002 of $76,018.38 plus interest receivable for 2002 of $7,601.84. The **current portion** is determined as follows:

Recovery of net investment within 12 months from the balance sheet date	$16,379.78
Interest accrued to the balance sheet date	7,601.84
Current portion of net investment	$23,981.62

The **long-term portion** is the $59,638.60 remainder. Illustration 21-14 indicates this is the net investment remaining to be recovered beyond 12 months from the balance sheet date.

The asset section as it relates to lease transactions to December 31, 2002 appears as follows.

ILLUSTRATION 21-16
Reporting Lease Transactions by Lessor

Current assets	
Net investment in capital leases	$23,981.62
Noncurrent assets (investments)	
Net investment in capital leases	$59,638.60

The following entries record receipt of the second year's lease payment and recognition of the interest earned in 2003.

January 1, 2003		
Cash	25,981.62	
Lease Payments Receivable		23,981.62
Property Tax Expense		2,000.00

December 31, 2003		
Unearned Interest Revenue—Leases	5,963.86	
Interest Revenue—Leases		5,963.86

Journal entries through 2006 follow the same pattern except that no entry is recorded in 2006 (the last year) for earned interest. Because the receivable is fully collected by January 1, 2006, no investment balance is outstanding during 2006 to which Lessor Corporation could attribute any interest. When the lease term is completed, the gross receivable and the unearned interest revenue have been fully written off. Note that **Lessor Corporation recorded no amortization**. If the equipment is sold to Lessee Corporation for $5,000 when the lease expires, Lessor Corporation would recognize the disposition of the equipment as follows.

Cash	5,000	
Gain on Sale of Leased Equipment		5,000

Accounting for a Sales-Type Lease

Accounting for a sales-type lease is very similar to accounting for a direct financing lease. The major difference is that the lessor in the sales-type lease usually has manufactured or otherwise acquired the leased asset for resale and is looking, through the lease agreement, to recover the asset's selling price through the lease payments. The cost or carrying value on the lessor's books is usually less than the asset's fair value to the customer. The lessor, therefore, must record a sale and the cost of goods sold for the asset being "sold."

The same data from the Lessor Corporation/Lessee Corporation example beginning on page 1023 are used to illustrate the accounting for a sales-type lease. There is one exception—instead of the leased asset having a cost of $100,000 to Lessor Corporation, assume that Lessor Corporation manufactured the asset and that it is in Lessor's inventory at a cost of $85,000. Lessor's regular selling price for this asset, its fair value, is $100,000, and it is this amount that the company wants to recover through the lease payments.

The following terms apply for a sales-type lease.

OBJECTIVE 9

Describe the lessor's accounting for sales-type leases.

SALES-TYPE LEASE TERMS

Term	Account	Explanation
Gross investment in lease	Lease Payments Receivable	The undiscounted lease payments (excluding executory costs) plus any residual value accruing to the lessor at the end of the lease term or any bargain purchase option. (same as for a direct financing lease).
Unearned finance revenue	Unearned Interest Revenue (contra account to Lease Payments Receivable)	The difference between the undiscounted Lease Payments Receivable and the fair value of the leased property.
Net investment in lease		The gross investment (the receivable) less the unearned finance or interest revenue included therein; i.e., the present value of the gross investment (same as for a direct financing lease).
Sales price of the asset	Sales	The present value of the lease payments receivable reduced by the present value of any unguaranteed residual.
Cost of the leased asset being sold	Cost of Goods Sold	The cost of the asset to the lessor, reduced by the present value of any unguaranteed residual.

The lessor's accounting entries to record the lease transactions are the same as those illustrated earlier for a direct financing lease with the exception of the entry at the lease's inception. Sales and cost of goods sold must be recorded in a sales-type lease. The entries are as follows.

January 1, 2002		
Lease Payments Receivable	119,908.10	
Unearned Interest Revenue—Leases		19,908.10
Sales		100,000.00
Cost of Goods Sold	85,000.00	
Inventory		85,000.00
Cash	25,981.62	
Lease Payments Receivable		23,981.62
Property Tax Expense		2,000.00
December 31, 2002		
Unearned Interest Revenue—Leases	7,601.84	
Interest Revenue—Leases		7,601.84

Compare the January 1, 2002 entries for the two types of lease. The direct financing lease removes the cost of the leased asset (the net investment the lessor wants to recover) from the lessor's books. The sales-type lease recognizes that what is being recovered is the asset's selling price and therefore records a sale. The cost of the inventory is transferred to cost of goods sold. In this case, the lessor recognizes a **gross profit** from the sale reported **at the lease's inception**, and **interest or finance income over the period of the lease** until the lease payments receivable is no longer outstanding. A lessor with a direct financing lease **reports only financing income over the lease term**.

Operating Leases

OBJECTIVE 10

Describe the lessor's accounting for operating leases.

Under an operating lease, each rental receipt by the lessor is recorded as rental revenue. The leased asset is amortized by the lessor in the normal manner, with the amortization expense of the period matched against the rental revenue. The amount of revenue recognized in each accounting period is a level amount (straight-line basis) regardless of the lease provisions, unless another systematic and rational basis is more representative of the pattern in which benefits are derived from the leased asset. In addition to the amortization charge, maintenance costs and the cost of any other services rendered under the lease provisions that pertain to the current accounting period are charged to expense. Costs paid to independent third parties such as appraisal fees, finder's fees, and costs of credit checks are amortized over the life of the lease.

Illustration of an Operating Lease

To illustrate the accounting for an operating lease, assume that the Lessor Corporation/Lessee Corporation example above does not meet the capitalization criteria and is therefore classified as an operating lease. The entry to record the cash rental receipt, assuming the $2,000 is to cover the lessor's property tax expense, is as follows.

Cash	25,981.62	
Rental Revenue		25,981.62

Amortization is recorded by the lessor as follows (assuming a straight-line method, a cost basis of $100,000, and a five-year life).

Amortization Expense—Leased Equipment	20,000	
Accumulated Amortization—Leased Equipment		20,000

If property taxes, insurance, maintenance, and other operating costs during the year are the lessor's obligation, they are recorded as expenses chargeable against the gross rental revenues.

If the lessor owns plant assets that it uses in addition to those leased to others, the leased equipment and accompanying accumulated amortization are separately classified in an account such as Equipment Leased to Others or Investment in Leased Property. If significant in amount or in terms of activity, the rental revenues and accompanying expenses are separated in the income statement from sales revenue and cost of goods sold.

Reporting and Disclosure Requirements for the Lessor

For direct financing and sales-type leases, the *Handbook* requires lessors to disclose on the balance sheet their net investment in leases, appropriately segregated between current and long-term categories, and to report how the investment in leases has been calculated for purposes of income recognition. In addition, the amount of finance income from these types of lease must be disclosed.[22]

> **OBJECTIVE 11**
> ....
> Identify the lessor's disclosure requirements.

The list of desirable disclosures is longer, with the AcSB suggesting that the total future minimum lease payments receivable, unguaranteed residual values, unearned finance income, executory costs included in minimum lease payments, contingent rentals taken into income, lease terms, and the amounts of minimum lease payments receivable for each of the next five years would be useful information.[23] Few companies report this level of detail.

The objective of the required disclosures for **operating leases** is to enable users to assess the extent of resources committed to this activity and the resulting cash flows generated. For operating leases, lessors must report the cost and related accumulated amortization of property held for leasing purposes and the amount of rental income from such leases. Further disclosure concerning minimum future rentals and contingent rentals included in income is at management's discretion.[24]

Illustration of Lease Disclosures by Lessors

Excerpts from the financial statements of **TELUS Corporation** for its year ended December 31, 2000 are reproduced in Illustration 21-17 to provide a good example of the disclosures provided by a lessor for direct financing or sales-type leases as well as operating leases. TELUS was also used to illustrate the reporting of leases from a lessee's point of view earlier in the chapter.

ILLUSTRATION 21-17
Lease Disclosures by a Lessor

TELUS CORPORATION
Consolidated Balance Sheet (in part)
As At December 31
($ million)

	2000	1999
Current Assets		
Accounts receivable (Note 8)	$ 1,008.5	$ 663.6
Capital assets, net (Note 10)	11,531.0	5,878.3
Other Assets		
Leases receivable	80.5	66.3

2. Summary of Significant Accounting Policies (in part)

(h) Leases (in part)

Leases are classified as capital or operating depending upon the terms and conditions of the contracts.

Where the Company is the lessor, the majority of capital leases are through its subsidiary, Telecom Leasing Canada (TLC) Limited, which acts as a financing intermediary. The long-term leases receivable represent the present value of future lease payments receivable due beyond one year. Finance income derived from these financing leases is recorded so as to produce a constant rate of return over the terms of the leases.

Revenue from operating leases of equipment is recognized when service is rendered to customers. The leased equipment is depreciated in accordance with the Company's depreciation policy.

5. Other Revenues (in part)

(millions)	2000	1999
Rental	$ 79.7	$ 92.7

---

[22] *CICA Handbook*, Section 3065, par. .54.

[23] *Ibid.*

[24] *Ibid.*, par. .57 to .59.

8. Accounts Receivable (in part)

(millions)	2000	1999
Trade receivables	$ 788.3	$544.7
Current portion of leases receivable	64.5	55.1
Other	155.7	63.8
	$1,008.5	$663.6

10. Capital Assets, Net (in part)

(millions)	Cost	Accumulated Depreciation and Amortization	Net Book Value 2000	Net Book Value 1999
Assets leased to customers	416.3	303.4	112.9	51.1

Go to the Digital Tool for additional lease disclosures.

Note 2 (h) explains TELUS' accounting policies as a lessor. For the capitalized leases—**direct financing leases** in this situation—the leases receivable are included on the balance sheet split between current and non-current "Other" assets. It is not clear where the finance income is reported on the income statement, but a reader could assume it is included in "Other" income as the dollar value is relatively minor compared with the company's main operating revenues. For its **operating lease** activities, TELUS discloses the capital assets dedicated to the leasing activity in Note 10 and the rental income on the income statement that corresponds to these assets.

SPECIAL ACCOUNTING ISSUES

Special features of lease arrangements that need to be dealt with are:

1. Residual values
2. Bargain purchase options
3. Initial direct costs of the lessor, and
4. Classification between current and noncurrent.

Residual Values

OBJECTIVE 12

Describe the effect of residual values, guaranteed and unguaranteed, on lease accounting.

Up to this point, we have generally ignored discussion of residual values in order that the basic accounting issues related to lessee and lessor accounting could be developed. Residual values add some complexity to the accounting for leases, but the requirements can be readily explained.

The residual value is the leased asset's estimated fair value at the end of the lease term. Frequently, a significant residual value exists at the end of the lease term, especially when the leased asset's economic life exceeds the lease term. If title does not pass to the lessee and a bargain purchase option does not exist (criterion 1), the lessee returns physical custody of the asset to the lessor at the end of the lease term.[25]

Guaranteed versus Unguaranteed

The residual value may be unguaranteed or guaranteed by the lessee. If the lessee, for example, agrees to make up any deficiency below a stated amount at the end of the lease term, that stated amount is the guaranteed residual value.

The guaranteed residual value is used in lease arrangements for two reasons. The first is a business reason: It protects the lessor against any loss in estimated residual value, thereby ensuring the lessor of the desired rate of return on investment. The

---

[25] When the lease term and the economic life are not the same, the asset's residual value and salvage value will probably differ. Salvage value refers to the estimated value at the end of the asset's economic life and is normally negligible.

second, discussed more fully later in the chapter, relates to how the lease is classified by the lessor and lessee.

Effect on Lease Payments

A guaranteed residual value—by definition—has more assurance of realization than an unguaranteed residual value. As a result, the lessor may reduce the required rate of return, and therefore the rental rate, because the certainty of recovery is increased. It makes no difference from an accounting point of view whether the residual value is guaranteed or unguaranteed as the net investment recorded by the lessor, once the rate is set, will be the same.

Assume the same data as in the continuing Lessee Corporation/Lessor Corporation illustrations except that a residual value of $5,000 is estimated at the end of the five-year lease term. The lessor, whether a sales-type or direct financing lease, wants to recover a net investment of $100,000 and earn a return of 10%.[26] Whether the residual value is guaranteed or unguaranteed, Lessor Corporation calculates the lease payments as follows.

LESSOR'S CALCULATION OF LEASE PAYMENTS (10% ROI) Guaranteed or Unguaranteed Residual Value (Annuity due basis)	
Fair value of leased asset	$100,000.00
To be recovered through residual value, end of year 5:	
Present value of residual value ($5,000 × 0.62092, Table A-2)	3,104.60
Amount to be recovered by lessor through lease payments	$ 96,895.40
Five periodic lease payments ($96,895.40 ÷ 4.16986, Table A-5)	$ 23,237.09

ILLUSTRATION 21-18
Lessor's Calculation of Lease Payments

Contrast this lease payment with the lease payment of $23,981.62 calculated in Illustration 21-9, when no residual value existed. The payments are less because a portion of the lessor's net investment of $100,000 is recovered through the residual value. Because the residual value is not received for five years, its present value is used in the calculation.

Lessee Accounting for Residual Value

Whether the estimated residual value is guaranteed or unguaranteed has both economic and accounting consequence **to the lessee**. The accounting difference is that the lease payments to be capitalized **include the guaranteed residual value** but **exclude an unguaranteed residual value**. Where the residual value is not guaranteed, the lessee assumes no responsibility or obligation for the asset's condition at the end of the lease term, therefore the residual value is not included in the calculation of the lease obligation.

Guaranteed Residual Value. A guaranteed residual value affects the amounts capitalized as a leased asset and a lease obligation by the lessee. In effect, it is an additional lease payment that will be paid in property or cash, or both, at the end of the lease term. Using the rental payments as calculated by the lessor in Illustration 21-18, the "minimum lease payments" are $121,185.45 ([$23,237.09 × 5] + $5,000).[27] The capitalized present value of the minimum lease payments is calculated as follows.

---

[26] Technically the rate of return demanded by the lessor would be different depending upon whether the residual value was guaranteed or unguaranteed. We are ignoring this difference in subsequent sections to simplify the illustrations.

[27] Minimum lease payments for a lessee is defined in *Handbook* Section 3065 as (i) the minimum rental payments excluding executory costs, (ii) the residual guaranteed by the lessee or the amount of bargain purchase option, and (iii) any penalty payable by the lessee at the end of the lease for failure to renew or extend the lease.

ILLUSTRATION 21-19
Calculation of Lessee's
Capitalized Amount—Guaranteed
Residual Value

LESSEE'S CAPITALIZED AMOUNT (10% RATE)
(Annuity due basis; guaranteed residual value)

Present value of five annual rental payments of $23,237.09 ($23,237.09 × 4.16986, Table A-5)	$ 96,895.40
Present value of guaranteed residual value of $5,000 due five years after date of inception: ($5,000 × 0.62092, Table A-2)	3,104.60
Lessee's capitalized amount	$100,000.00

Lessee Corporation's schedule of interest expense and amortization of the $100,000 lease obligation results in a $5,000 guaranteed residual value payment at the end of five years, as shown in Illustration 21-20.

ILLUSTRATION 21-20
Lease Amortization Schedule
for Lessee—Guaranteed
Residual Value

LESSEE CORPORATION
Lease Amortization Schedule
(Annuity due basis, guaranteed residual value)

Date	Lease Payment	Interest (10%) on Unpaid Obligation	Reduction of Lease Obligation	Lease Obligation
	(a)	(b)	(c)	(d)
1/1/02				$100,000.00
1/1/02	$ 23,237.09	$ –0–	$ 23,237.09	76,762.91
1/1/03	23,237.09	7,676.29	15,560.80	61,202.11
1/1/04	23,237.09	6,120.21	17,116.88	44,085.23
1/1/05	23,237.09	4,408.52	18,828.57	25,256.66
1/1/06	23,237.09	2,525.67	20,711.42	4,545.24
12/31/06	5,000.00*	454.76**	4,545.24	–0–
	$121,185.45	$21,185.45	$100,000.00	

(a) Annual lease payment as required by lease, excluding executory costs.
(b) Preceding balance of (d) × 10%, except 1/1/02.   *Represents the guaranteed residual value.
(c) (a) minus (b).   **Rounded by 24 cents.
(d) Preceding balance minus (c).

The journal entries in the first column of Illustration 21-25 to record the leased asset and obligation, amortization, interest, property tax, and lease payments are made on the basis that the residual value is guaranteed. The format of these entries is the same as illustrated earlier, but the amounts are different because of the capitalized residual value. The leased asset is recorded at $100,000 and is amortized over five years. To calculate amortization, the guaranteed residual value is subtracted from the cost of the leased asset. Assuming the straight-line method is used, the amortization expense each year is $19,000 ([$100,000 − $5,000] × 1/5).

At the end of the lease term, before the lessee transfers the asset to the lessor, the leased asset and obligation accounts have the following balances.

ILLUSTRATION 21-21
Account Balances on Lessee's
Books at End of Lease Term—
Guaranteed Residual Value

Equipment under capital leases	$100,000.00	Interest payable	$ 454.76
Less: Accumulated amortization — capital leases	95,000.00	Obligations under capital leases	4,545.24
	$ 5,000.00		$5,000.00

If the leased property's fair value is less than $5,000 at the end of the lease term, Lessee Corporation will record a loss. Assume that Lessee Corporation amortized the leased asset down to its residual value of $5,000 but that the asset's fair value at December 31, 2006 is $3,000. In this case, Lessee Corporation records the following journal entry, assuming cash is paid to make up the residual value deficiency.

Loss on Capital Lease	2,000.00	
Interest Payable	454.76	
Obligations under Capital Leases	4,545.24	
Accumulated Amortization—Capital Leases	95,000.00	
Equipment under Capital Leases		100,000.00
Cash		2,000.00

If the fair value exceeds $5,000, a gain may or may not be recognized. Gains on guaranteed residual values will be apportioned to the lessor and lessee in whatever ratio the parties initially agreed.

If the lessee had amortized the asset's total $100,000 cost instead of $95,000, a misstatement would occur; that is, the asset's carrying amount at the end of the lease term would be zero. Thus, if the asset is worth $5,000, the lessee would report a gain of $5,000 when it transfers the asset back to the lessor. As a result, amortization expense would be overstated and net income understated in 2002–2005, but in the last year, 2006, net income would be overstated.

Unguaranteed Residual Value. An unguaranteed residual value from the lessee's viewpoint is the same as no residual value in terms of its effect on the lessee's calculation of the minimum lease payments and the capitalization of the leased asset and lease obligation. Assume the same facts as those above except that the $5,000 residual value is **unguaranteed**. The annual lease payment is the same ($23,237.09) because whether the residual is guaranteed or unguaranteed, Lessor Corporation's amount to be recovered through lease rentals is the same: $96,895.40. Lessee Corporation's minimum lease payments are $116,185.45 ($23,237.09 × 5), and the company capitalizes the following amount.[28]

LESSEE'S CAPITALIZED AMOUNT (10% RATE)
(Annuity due basis, unguaranteed residual value)

Present value of five annual rental payments of $23,237.09, $i = 10\%$	
$23,237.09 × 4.16986 (Table A-5)	$96,895.40
Present value of unguaranteed residual value of $5,000 (not capitalized by lessee)	–0–
Lessee's capitalized amount	$96,895.40

ILLUSTRATION 21-22
Calculation of Lessee's Capitalized Amount—Unguaranteed Residual Value

Lessee Corporation's schedule of interest expense and amortization of the lease obligation of $96,895.40, assuming an unguaranteed residual value of $5,000 at the end of five years, is provided in Illustration 21-23.

LESSEE CORPORATION
Lease Amortization Schedule (10%)
(Annuity due basis, unguaranteed residual value)

ILLUSTRATION 21-23
Lease Amortization Schedule for Lessee—Unguaranteed Residual Value

Date	Lease Payment	Interest (10%) on Unpaid Obligation	Reduction of Lease Obligation	Lease Obligation
	(a)	(b)	(c)	(d)
1/1/02				$96,895.40
1/1/02	$ 23,237.09	$ –0–	$23,237.09	73,658.31
1/1/03	23,237.09	7,365.83	15,871.26	57,787.05
1/1/04	23,237.09	5,778.71	17,458.38	40,328.67
1/1/05	23,237.09	4,032.87	19,204.22	21,124.45
1/1/06	23,237.09	2,112.64*	21,124.45	–0–
	$116,185.45	$19,290.05	$96,895.40	

(a) Annual lease payment as required by lease, excluding executory costs.
(b) Preceding balance of (d) × 10%, except Jan. 1, 2002.
(c) (a) minus (b).
(d) Preceding balance minus (c).
*Rounded by 19 cents.

---

[28] For a lessee, the definition of "minimum lease payments" excludes an unguaranteed residual.

The journal entries needed to record the leased asset and obligation, amortization, interest, property tax, and payments on the lease obligation on the basis that the residual value is unguaranteed are reported in the right hand column of Illustration 21-25. The format of these entries is the same as illustrated earlier. Note that the leased asset is recorded at $96,895.40 and is amortized over five years. Assuming that the straight-line method is used, the amortization expense each year is $19,379.08 ($96,895.40 ÷ 5). At the end of the lease term, before the lessee transfers the asset to the lessor, the following balances remain in the accounts.

ILLUSTRATION 21-24

Account Balances on Lessee's Books at End of Lease Term—Unguaranteed Residual Value

Equipment under capital leases	$96,895	Obligations under capital leases	$–0–
Less: Accumulated amortization—			
capital leases	96,895		
	$ –0–		

Assuming the asset's fair value at the end of the lease term is $3,000, no entry is required except to remove the asset from the books. No loss is reported.

If the lessee **had** amortized the asset down to its estimated—but unguaranteed—residual value, a misstatement would occur. That is, the carrying amount of the leased asset would be $5,000 at the end of the lease, but the obligation under the capital lease would be zero before the transfer of the asset. Thus, the lessee would end up reporting a loss of $5,000 when it transferred the asset to the lessor. Amortization would be understated and net income overstated in 2002 through 2005, but in 2006, the last year, net income would be understated because of the loss recorded.

Lessee Entries Involving Residual Values. The entries by Lessee Corporation for both a guaranteed and an unguaranteed residual value are shown in Illustration 21-25 in comparative form.

ILLUSTRATION 21-25

Comparative Entries for Guaranteed and Unguaranteed Residual Values, Lessee Corporation

Guaranteed Residual Value			Unguaranteed Residual Value		
Capitalization of Lease 1/1/02:					
Equipment under Capital Leases	100,000.00		Equipment under Capital Leases	96,895.40	
Obligations under Capital Leases		100,000.00	Obligations under Capital Leases		96,895.40
First Payment 1/1/02:					
Property Tax Expense	2,000.00		Property Tax Expense	2,000.00	
Obligations under Capital Leases	23,237.09		Obligations under Capital Leases	23,237.09	
Cash		25,237.09	Cash		25,237.09
Adjusting Entry for Accrued Interest 12/31/02:					
Interest Expense	7,676.29		Interest Expense	7,365.83	
Interest Payable		7,676.29	Interest Payable		7,365.83
Entry to Record Amortization 12/31/02:					
Amortization Expense—Capital Leases	19,000.00		Amortization Expense—Capital Leases	19,379.08	
Accumulated Amortization—			Accumulated Amortization—		
Capital Leases		19,000.00	Capital Leases		19,379.08
([$100,000 − $5,000] ÷ 5 years)			($96,895.40 ÷ 5 years)		
Second Payment 1/1/03:					
Property Tax Expense	2,000.00		Property Tax Expense	2,000.00	
Obligations under Capital Leases	15,560.80		Obligations under Capital Leases	15,871.26	
Interest Payable	7,676.29		Interest Payable	7,365.83	
Cash		25,237.09	Cash		25,237.09

Lessor Accounting for Residual Value

Direct Financing Lease. As indicated earlier, the lessor works on the assumption that the residual value will be realized at the end of the lease term whether guaranteed or unguaranteed. The lease payments required by the lessor to earn a given return on investment are the same ($23,237.09) whether the residual value is guaranteed or not.

Using the Lessee Corporation/Lessor Corporation data and assuming a residual value, either guaranteed or unguaranteed, of $5,000 and classification of the lease as a direct financing lease, the following amounts are calculated.

Gross investment	= ($23,237.09 × 5) + $5,000 = $121,185.45
Net investment:	
PV of lease payments + PV of residual value,	= $23,237.09 × 4.16986 (Table A-5) +
or amount to be recovered	$5,000 × 0.62092 (Table A-2) = $100,000
Unearned interest revenue	= $121,185.45 − $100,000 = $21,185.45

The amortization schedule with a guaranteed or unguaranteed residual value is identical, as shown in Illustration 21-27.

LESSOR CORPORATION
Lease Amortization Schedule
(Annuity due basis, guaranteed or unguaranteed residual value)

Date	Lease Payment	Interest (10%) on Net Investment	Net Investment Recovery	Net Investment
	(a)	(b)	(c)	(d)
1/1/02				$100,000.00
1/1/02	$ 23,237.09	$ –0–	$ 23,237.09	76,762.91
1/1/03	23,237.09	7,676.29	15,560.80	61,202.11
1/1/04	23,237.09	6,120.21	17,116.88	44,085.23
1/1/05	23,237.09	4,408.52	18,828.57	25,256.66
1/1/06	23,237.09	2,525.67	20,711.42	4,545.24
12/31/06	5,000.00*	454.76**	4,545.24	0
	$121,185.45	$21,185.45	$100,000.00	

(a) Lease payment as required by lease, excluding executory costs.
(b) Preceding balance of (d) × 10%, except January 1, 2002.
(c) (a) minus (b).
(d) Preceding balance minus (c).
*Represents the residual value.
**Rounded by 24 cents.

Lessor Corporation's entries during the first year are shown in Illustration 21-28 for this direct financing lease. Note the similarity to the lessee's entries in Illustration 21-25.

Inception of Lease 1/1/02:		
Lease Payments Receivable	121,185.45	
Equipment Purchased for Lease		100,000.00
Unearned Interest Revenue—Leases		21,185.45
First Payment Received 1/1/02:		
Cash	25,237.09	
Lease Payments Receivable		23,237.09
Property Tax Expense		2,000.00
Adjusting Entry for Accrued Interest 12/31/02:		
Unearned Interest Revenue—Leases	7,676.29	
Interest Revenue—Leases		7,676.29

Sales-Type Lease. As already indicated, the primary difference between a direct financing lease and a sales-type lease is the existence of a manufacturer's or dealer's gross profit (or loss). The gross investment and the unearned interest revenue account are the same for both types of leases whether a guaranteed or an unguaranteed residual value is involved.

When recording sales revenue and cost of goods sold, however, there is a difference in accounting for guaranteed and unguaranteed residual values. The guaranteed residual value can be considered part of sales revenue because the lessor knows that the entire amount will be realized. There is less certainty, however, that any unguaranteed residual portion of the asset has been "sold" (i.e., will be realized); therefore, sales and cost of goods sold are recognized only for the portion of the asset for which realization is assured. **The gross profit amount on the asset's sale is the same**, however, whether a guaranteed or unguaranteed residual value is involved as the present value of any unguaranteed residual is withheld from the calculation **of both sales and cost of goods sold amounts**.

To illustrate a sales-type lease with and without a guaranteed residual value, assume the same facts as in the preceding direct financing lease situation (pages 1042–1043). The estimated residual value is $5,000 (the present value of which is $3,104.60), the annual lease payments are $23,237.09 (the present value of which is $96,895.40), and the leased equipment has an $85,000 cost to the manufacturer, Lessor Corporation. At the end of the lease term, assume that the leased asset's fair value is $3,000.

The amounts relevant to a sales-type lease are calculated in Illustration 21-29.

ILLUSTRATION 21-29

Calculation of Lease Amounts by Lessor Corporation—Sales-Type Lease

	Sales-Type Lease	
	Guaranteed Residual Value	Unguaranteed Residual Value
Gross investment	$121,185.45 ([$23,237.09 × 5] + $5,000)	Same
Unearned interest revenue	$21,185.45 ($121,185.45 − [$96,895.40 + $3,104.60])	Same
Sales	$100,000 ($96,895.40 + $3,104.60)	$96,895.40
Cost of goods sold	$85,000	$81,895.40 ($85,000 − $3,104.60)
Gross profit	$15,000 ($100,000 − $85,000)	$15,000 ($96,895.40 − $81,895.40)

The profit recorded by Lessor Corporation at the point of sale is the same, $15,000, whether the residual value is guaranteed or unguaranteed, but the sales revenue and cost of goods sold amounts are different.

The 2002 and 2003 entries and the entry to record the asset's return at the end of the lease term are provided in Illustration 21-30. The only differences pertain to the original entry that recognizes the lease and the final entry to record the leased asset's return.

ILLUSTRATION 21-30

Entries for Guaranteed and Unguaranteed Residual Values, Lessor Corporation—Sales-Type Lease

Guaranteed Residual Value			Unguaranteed Residual Value		
To record sales-type lease at inception (January 1, 2002):					
Cost of Goods Sold	85,000.00		Cost of Goods Sold	81,895.40	
Lease Payments Receivable	121,185.45		Lease Payments Receivable	121,185.45	
Sales Revenue		100,000.00	Sales Revenue		96,895.40
Unearned Interest Revenue		21,185.45	Unearned Interest Revenue		21,185.45
Inventory		85,000.00	Inventory		85,000.00
To record receipt of the first lease payment (January 1, 2002):					
Cash	25,237.09		Cash	25,237.09	
Lease Payments Receivable		23,237.09	Lease Payments Receivable		23,237.09
Property Tax Expense		2,000.00	Property Tax Expense		2,000.00
To recognize interest revenue earned during the first year (December 31, 2002):					
Unearned Interest Revenue	7,676.29		Unearned Interest Revenue	7,676.29	
Interest Revenue		7,676.29	Interest Revenue		7,676.29
(See lease amortization schedule, Illustration 21-27)					
To record receipt of the second lease payment (January 1, 2003):					
Cash	25,237.09		Cash	25,237.09	
Lease Payments Receivable		23,237.09	Lease Payments Receivable		23,237.09
Property Tax Expense		2,000.00	Property Tax Expense		2,000.00
To recognize interest revenue earned during the second year (December 31, 2003):					
Unearned Interest Revenue	6,120.21		Unearned Interest Revenue	6,120.21	
Interest Revenue		6,120.21	Interest Revenue		6,120.21
To record receipt of residual value at end of lease term (December 31, 2006):					
Inventory	3,000		Inventory	3,000	
Cash	2,000		Loss on Capital Lease	2,000	
Lease Payments Receivable		5,000	Lease Payments Receivable		5,000

The estimated unguaranteed residual value in a sales-type lease (and a direct financing-type lease) must be reviewed periodically. If the estimate of the unguaranteed residual value declines, the accounting for the transaction must be revised using the changed estimate. The decline represents a reduction in the lessor's net investment and is recognized as a loss in the period in which the residual estimate is reduced. Upward adjustments in estimated residual value are not recognized.

Bargain Purchase Options

A bargain purchase option allows the lessee to purchase the leased property for a future price that is substantially less than the property's expected future fair value. The price is so favourable at the lease's inception that the future exercise of the option is reasonably assured. If a bargain purchase option exists, the lessee's accounting assumes it will be exercised and the title to the leased property will be transferred to the lessee. Therefore, **the lessee must include the present value of the option price when calculating the minimum lease payments and the amount to capitalize**.

> **OBJECTIVE 13**
> ....
> Describe the effect of bargain purchase options on lease accounting.

For example, assume that Lessee Corporation in the illustration beginning on page 1023 had an option to buy the leased equipment for $5,000 at the end of the five-year lease term when the fair value is expected to be $18,000. The significant difference between the option price and the estimated fair value indicates this is a bargain purchase option, and exercising the option is reasonably assured. The following calculations are affected by a bargain purchase option **in the same way as they were by a guaranteed residual value**.

1. The amount of the five lease payments necessary for the lessor to earn a 10% return on net investment.
2. The amount of the minimum lease payments.
3. The amount capitalized as leased assets and lease obligation.
4. The amortization of the lease obligation.

Therefore, the calculations and amortization schedule necessary for a $5,000 **bargain purchase option** are identical to those shown previously for the $5,000 **guaranteed residual value**.

The only difference between the lessee accounting treatment for a bargain purchase option and a guaranteed residual value of identical amounts and circumstances is in the calculation of the annual amortization. In the case of a guaranteed residual value, the lessee amortizes the asset over the lease term because the asset will revert to the lessor. In the case of a bargain purchase option, the lessee uses the asset's economic life and its estimated residual value at that time because it is assumed that the lessee will acquire title to the asset by exercising the option.

The lessor includes the bargain purchase option price in Lease Payments Receivable and its present value in the net investment in the lease. The accounting is similar to that for a guaranteed residual value, regardless of whether the lease is a direct financing or a sales-type lease.

Initial Direct Costs of the Lessor

Initial direct costs are defined in Section 3065.03(l) of the *CICA Handbook* as:

> **OBJECTIVE 14**
> ....
> Describe the lessor's accounting treatment for initial direct costs.

"those costs incurred by the lessor that are directly associated with negotiating and executing a specific leasing transaction. Such costs include commissions, legal fees and costs of preparing and processing documents for new leases. Such costs do not include supervisory and administrative costs, promotion and lease design costs intended for recurring use, costs incurred in collection activities and provisions for uncollectible rentals."

The costs directly related to an employee's time spent on a specific lease transaction may also be considered initial direct costs.

In a **direct financing lease**, initial direct costs are expensed as incurred and the lessor offsets this expense by taking into income an equal amount of the unearned interest income. At the lease's inception, therefore, the net effect on income is zero; however, the amount of the net investment in the lease (the gross investment less the unearned interest income) is increased as a result.

For example, if the Lease Payments Receivable (gross investment in the lease) account is $600,000 with unearned interest income at the lease's inception of $200,000, the net investment is $400,000. If initial direct costs of $35,000 are incurred and expensed and $35,000 of the unearned interest is recognized as earned, the net investment is increased to $435,000 ($600,000 − [$200,000 − $35,000]).

UNDERLYING CONCEPTS

The accounting treatment for the lessor's initial direct costs is an application of the matching principle.

Because the finance income earned on the net investment should be recognized at a constant rate of return each period, the lessor must recalculate the effective rate (it will be lower) for purposes of amortizing the net investment.[29] In this way, the initial costs are recognized over the lease term in the form of reduced interest income each period.

In a **sales-type lease** transaction, the lessor expenses the initial direct costs in the year of incurrence; that is, they are expensed in the period in which the profit on the sale is recognized.

For **operating leases**, the lessor defers initial direct costs and allocates them over the lease term in proportion to the recognition of rental income.

Classification between Current and Noncurrent

The classification of the lease obligation/net investment was presented earlier in an annuity due situation. As indicated in Illustration 21-6, the lessee's current liability is the reduction in principal of the lease obligation within 12 months from the balance sheet date **plus** interest accrued to the balance sheet date. Coincidentally, the total of these two amounts is equal to the rental payment of $23,981.62 to be made one day later on January 1 of the next year. Similarly, as shown in Illustration 21-16, the lessor's current asset is the amount to be collected ($23,981.62) one day later on January 1, 2003. In both these instances, the balance sheet date is December 31 and the due·date of the lease payment is January 1 (less than one year), so the total of the principal reduction on January 1 and the interest accrued to December 31 is the same as the rental payment ($23,981.62). This will only happen when the payment is due the day following the fiscal year end. This is not common.

Also, what happens if the situation is an ordinary annuity rather than an annuity due and the lease payment dates do not coincide with the company's fiscal year? To illustrate, assume that the lease was signed and effective on September 1, 2002, with the first lease payment to be made September 1, 2003—an ordinary annuity situation. The remaining facts of the Lessee Corporation/Lessor Corporation case, excluding the executory costs, continue to apply. Because the rents are paid at the end of the lease periods instead of the beginning, the five rents are set at $26,379.73 to earn the lessor an interest rate of 10%. The companies have December 31 year ends. Illustration 21-31 provides the appropriate lease amortization schedule for this lease, based on the September 1 anniversary dates of the lease.

---

[29] To calculate the effective or implied rate of interest in a lease when it isn't given, students are referred to page A-11, "Illustration: Calculation of the Interest Rate" in Appendix: Accounting and the Time Value of Money. In short, "*i*" is the internal rate of return. It is a matter of solving for "*i*" when the present value amount, the annuity amount, and "*n*" are all known. The interest rate is the rate that equates the present value amount (in this case the net investment) with the annuity payments. It may have to be calculated using a trial and error method.

ILLUSTRATION 21-31
Lease Amortization Schedule—
Ordinary Annuity Basis, Mid-Year
Lease Date

LESSEE CORPORATION/LESSOR CORPORATION
Lease Amortization Schedule
(Ordinary annuity basis)

Date	Annual Lease Payment	Interest (10%)	Reduction of Principal	Balance of Lease Obligation/ Net Investment
1/9/02				$100,000.00
1/9/03	$ 26,379.73	$10,000.00	$16,379.73	83,620.27
1/9/04	26,379.73	8,362.03	18,017.70	65,602.57
1/9/05	26,379.73	6,560.26	19,819.47	45,783.10
1/9/06	26,379.73	4,578.31	21,801.42	23,981.68
1/9/07	26,379.73	2,398.05 *	23,981.68	–0–
	$131,898.65	$31,898.65	$100,000.00	

*Rounded by 12 cents.

At December 31, 2002, the lease obligation/net investment in the lease is still $100,000. How much should be reported in current liabilities on the December 31, 2002 balance sheet and how much in long-term liabilities? The answer here is the same as in earlier chapters: the current portion is the principal that will be repaid within 12 months from the balance sheet date (i.e., $16,379.73). In addition, any interest accrued to the balance sheet date (i.e., 10% of $100,000 × 4/12 = $3,333) will be reported in current liabilities. The long-term portion of the obligation or net investment is the principal that will not be repaid within 12 months from the balance sheet date, or $83,620.27.

On December 31, 2003, the long-term portion of the lease is $65,602.57. The principal due within 12 months from December 31, 2003, or $18,017.70, is included as a current liability along with interest accrued to December 31, 2003 of $2,787 (10% of $83,620.27 × 4/12).

Lease Accounting—Unsolved Problems

As indicated at the beginning of this chapter, lease accounting is a much abused area in which strenuous efforts are made to circumvent *CICA Handbook* Section 3065. In practice, the accounting rules for capitalizing leases have been rendered partially ineffective by the strong desires of lessees to resist capitalization. Leasing generally involves large dollar amounts that, when capitalized, materially increase reported liabilities and adversely affect the debt-to-equity and other ratios. Lease capitalization is also resisted because charges to expense made in the early years of the lease term are higher when leases are capitalized than when treated as operating leases, frequently without tax benefit. As a consequence, much effort has been devoted to beating the profession's lease capitalization rules.[30]

To avoid asset capitalization, lease agreements are designed, written, and interpreted so that none of the three criteria is satisfied from the lessee's viewpoint. Devising lease agreements in such a way has not been too difficult when the following specifications are met.

1. Make certain that the lease does not specify the transfer of the property title to the lessee and does not include a bargain purchase option.

2. Set the lease term at something less than 75% of the leased property's estimated economic life.

3. Arrange for the minimum lease payments' present value to be less than 90% of the leased property's fair value.

INTERNATIONAL INSIGHT

The U.S. standards for leases are consistent with Handbook Section 3065, but, as is the case with many of the standards, the U.S. rules are much more prescriptive and detailed.

---

[30] Richard Dieter, "Is Lessee Accounting Working?" *The CPA Journal*, August 1979, pp. 13 – 19. This article provides interesting examples of abuses of U.S. *Statement No. 13*, discusses the circumstances that led to the current situation, and proposes a solution.

But the real challenge lies in disqualifying the lease as a capital lease to the lessee while having the same lease qualify as a capital (sales or financing) lease to the lessor. Unlike lessees, lessors try to avoid having lease arrangements classified as operating leases.[31]

Avoiding the first two criteria is relatively simple, but it takes a little ingenuity to avoid the "90% recovery test" for the lessee while satisfying it for the lessor. Two of the factors involved in this effort are (1) the use of the incremental borrowing rate by the lessee when it is higher than the implicit interest rate of the lessor, by making information about the implicit rate unavailable to the lessee; and (2) residual value guarantees.

The lessee's use of the higher interest rate is probably the more popular subterfuge. While lessees are knowledgeable about the fair value of the leased property and, of course, the rental payments, they generally are not aware of the estimated residual value used by the lessor. Therefore the lessee who does not know exactly what the lessor's implicit interest rate is, is free to use its own incremental borrowing rate.

The residual value guarantee is the other popular device used by lessees and lessors. In fact, a whole new industry has emerged to circumvent symmetry between the lessee and the lessor in accounting for leases. The residual value guarantee has spawned numerous companies whose principal function is to guarantee the residual value of leased assets. For a fee, these "third-party guarantors" (insurers) assume the risk of deficiencies in leased asset residual value.

Because the (guaranteed) residual value is included in the minimum lease payments for the lessor, the 90% recovery of fair value test is satisfied and the lease is a nonoperating lease to the lessor. Because the residual value is guaranteed by a third party, the lessee's minimum lease payments do not include the guarantee. Thus, by merely transferring some of the risk to a third party, lessees can alter substantially the accounting treatment by converting what would otherwise be capital leases to operating leases.

Much of this circumvention is encouraged by the nature of the criteria used, and accounting standard-setting bodies, both domestic and international, continue to have poor experience with arbitrary size and percentage criteria, such as "90% of," "75% of," etc.

This situation provided the motivation for further study of the topic and the subsequent publication of papers on new approaches to lease accounting. Some authors have taken an approach that, because all non-cancellable lease contracts result in the lessee acquiring an asset (property rights) and a liability (lease obligation) as defined under the conceptual frameworks of standard-setting bodies in Canada, the U.S., the IASC and others, and because the recognition criteria identified in these conceptual frameworks are met, all finance and most, if not all, operating leases qualify for recognition as assets and liabilities.[32]

ILLUSTRATIONS OF DIFFERENT LEASE ARRANGEMENTS

To illustrate a number of concepts discussed in this chapter, assume that Morgan Bakeries is involved in four different leases as described below. These leases are non-cancellable and in no case does the lease agreement automatically transfer title of the leased properties to the lessee during or at the end of the lease term. All leases start on January 1, 2002, with the first rental due at the beginning of the year. Additional information is provided in Illustration 21-32.

---

[31] The reason is that most lessors are financial institutions and do not want these types of rental assets on their balance sheets. Furthermore, the capital lease transaction from the lessor's standpoint provides higher income flows in the lease's earlier periods.

[32] Warren McGregor, Principal Author, *Accounting for Leases: A New Approach—Recognition by Lessees of Assets and Liabilities Arising under Lease Contracts*, (FASB, 1996) and H. Nailor and A. Lennard, "Capital Leases: Implementation of a New Approach," *Financial Accounting Series No. 206A* (FASB, 2000), both G4+1 Special Reports. See also *Accounting Horizons*, September, 2001 for four commentaries on lease accounting.

	Harmon, Inc.	Arden's Oven Corp.	Mendota Truck Corp.	Appleland Computer
Type of property	Cabinets	Oven	Truck	Computer
Yearly rental	$6,000	$15,000	$5,582.62	$3,557.25
Lease term	20 years	10 years	3 years	3 years
Estimated economic life	30 years	25 years	7 years	5 years
Purchase option	None	$75,000 at end of 10 years $4,000 at end of 15 years	None	$3,000 at end of 3 years, which approximates fair value
Renewal option	None	5-year renewal option at $15,000 per year	None	1 year at $1,500; no penalty for non-renewal; standard renewal clause
Fair value at inception of lease	$60,000	$120,000	$20,000	$10,000
Cost of asset to lessor	$60,000	$120,000	$15,000	$10,000
Residual value				
Guaranteed	–0–	–0–	$7,000	–0–
Unguaranteed	$5,000	–0–	–0–	$3,000
Incremental borrowing rate of lessee	12%	12%	12%	12%
Executory costs paid by	*Lessee* $300 per year	*Lessee* $1,000 per year	*Lessee* $500 per year	*Lessor* Estimated to be $500 per year
Present value of minimum lease payments				
Using incremental borrowing rate of lessee	$50,194.68	$115,153.35	$20,000	$8,224.16
Using implicit rate of lessor	Not known	Not known	Not known	Known by lessee, $8,027.48
Estimated fair value at end of lease	$5,000	$80,000 at end of 10 years $60,000 at end of 15 years	Not available	$3,000
Credit risk of lease	Normal	Normal	Normal	Normal
Lessor's unreimbursable costs can be estimated	Yes	Yes	Yes	Yes

ILLUSTRATION 21-32
Illustrative Lease Situations

Harmon, Inc.

The following is an analysis of the Harmon, Inc. lease.

1. **Transfer of title?** In lease? No. Bargain purchase option? No.
2. **Economic life test (75% test).** The lease term is 20 years and the estimated economic life is 30 years. Thus it does not meet the 75% test.
3. **Recovery of investment test (90% test).**

Fair value	$60,000	Rental payments	$ 6,000
Rate	90%	PV of annuity due for	
90% of fair value	$54,000	20 years at 12%	×8.36578
		PV of rental payments	$50,194.68

Because the minimum lease payments' present value is less than 90% of the fair value, the 90% test is not met either. Both Morgan and Harmon should account for this lease as an operating lease, as indicated by the entries shown below for January 1, 2002.

ILLUSTRATION 21-33
Comparative Entries for
Operating Lease

Morgan Bakeries (Lessee)		Harmon, Inc. (Lessor)	
Rent Expense 6,000		Cash 6,000	
Cash	6,000	Rental Revenue	6,000

Alternatively, Morgan might debit Prepaid Rent (Harmon might credit Unearned Rent Revenue) and charge (credit) the $6,000 to income at $500 per month. Harmon continues to carry the leased cabinets in its books and amortizes them over their economic life.

Arden's Oven Corp.

The following is an analysis of the Arden's Oven Corp. lease.

1. **Transfer of title?** In lease? No. Bargain purchase option? The $75,000 option at the end of 10 years does not appear to be sufficiently less than the expected fair value of $80,000 to make it reasonably assured that it will be exercised. However, the $4,000 at the end of 15 years when the fair value is $60,000 does appear to be a bargain. From the information given, criterion 1 is therefore met. Note that both the guaranteed and the unguaranteed residual values are assigned zero values because the lessor does not expect to repossess the leased asset.

2. **Economic life test (75% test).** Given that a bargain purchase option exists, the lease term is the initial lease period of 10 years plus the 5-year renewal option since it precedes a bargain purchase option. Even though the lease term is now considered to be 15 years, this test is still not met because 15 years represents only 60% of the 25-year economic life.

3. **Recovery of investment test (90% test).**

Fair value	$120,000	Rental payments	$ 15,000.00
Rate	90%	PV of annuity due for	
90% of fair value	$108,000	15 years at 12%	×7.62817
		PV of rental payments	$114,422.55

PV of bargain purchase option: $4,000(PVF_{15,12\%}) = $4,000(.18270) = 730.80

PV of rental payments	$114,422.55
PV of bargain purchase option	730.80
PV of minimum lease payments	$115,153.35

The minimum lease payments' present value is greater than 90% of the fair value; therefore, the 90% test is met. Morgan Bakeries should account for this as a capital lease because at least one of the three criteria is met. Assuming that Arden's implicit rate is the same as Morgan's incremental borrowing rate, the following entries are made on January 1, 2002.

ILLUSTRATION 21-34
Comparative Entries for Capital Lease—Bargain Purchase Option

Morgan Bakeries (Lessee)		Arden's Oven Corp. (Lessor)	
Leased Asset—Oven 115,153.35		Lease Payments	
Obligation under		Receivable 229,000*	
Capital Lease	115,153.35	Unearned Interest	
		Revenue	109,000
		Asset—Oven	120,000
		*([$15,000 × 15] + $4,000)	

Morgan Bakeries amortizes the leased asset over its economic life of 25 years because it is assumed that the lessee will acquire title to the asset through the bargain purchase option. Arden uses the direct financing method and not sales-type lease accounting because the asset's fair value and cost are the same at the lease's inception.

Mendota Truck Corp.

The following is an analysis of the Mendota Truck Corp. lease.

1. **Transfer of title?** In the lease? No. Bargain purchase option? No.

2. **Economic life test (75% test).** The lease term is three years and the estimated economic life is seven years. Thus it does not meet the 75% test.

3. **Recovery of investment test (90% test).**

Fair value	$20,000	Rental payments	$ 5,582.62
Rate	90%	PV of annuity due for	
90% of fair value	$18,000	3 years at 12%	×2.69005
		PV of rental payments	$15,017.54

PV of guaranteed residual value: $7,000(PVF_{3,12\%}) = \$7,000(.71178) = \$4,982.46$

PV of rental payments	$15,017.54
PV of guaranteed residual value	4,982.46
PV of minimum lease payments	$20,000.00

The minimum lease payments' present value is greater than 90% of the fair value; therefore, the 90% test is met. Assuming that Mendota's implicit rate is the same as Morgan's incremental borrowing rate, the following entries are made on January 1, 2002.

ILLUSTRATION 21-35
Comparative Entries for Capital Lease

Morgan Bakeries (Lessee)			Mendota Truck Corp. (Lessor)		
Leased Asset—Truck	20,000.00		Lease Payments		
Obligation under			Receivable	23,747,86*	
Capital Lease		20,000.00	Cost of Goods Sold	15,000.00	
			Inventory—Truck		15,000.00
			Sales		20,000.00
			Unearned Interest		
			Revenue		3,747.86
			*([$5,582.62 × 3] + $7,000)		

The leased asset is amortized by Morgan over three years to its guaranteed residual value.

Appleland Computer

The following is an analysis of the Appleland Computer lease.

1. **Transfer of title?** In lease? No. Bargain purchase option? No. The option to purchase at the end of three years at fair value is clearly not a bargain.

2. **Economic life test (75% test).** The lease term is three years and no bargain renewal period exists. Therefore the 75% test is not met.

3. **Recovery of investment test (90% test).**

Fair value	$10,000		Rental payments	$3,557.25
Rate	90%		Less executory costs	500.00
90% of fair value	$ 9,000			3,057.25
			PV of annuity due factor	
			for 3 years at 12%	×2.69005
			PV of minimum lease payments	
			using incremental	
			borrowing rate	$8,224.16

The minimum lease payments' present value using the incremental borrowing rate is $8,224.16; using the implicit rate, it is $8,027.48 (see Illustration 21-32). The lessor's implicit rate must, therefore, be higher than the lessee's incremental borrowing rate. Given this situation, the lessee uses the $8,224.16 (lower interest rate when discounting) for deciding on criterion 3. Because the minimum lease payments' present value is lower than 90% of the fair value, the recovery of investment test is not met.

The following entries are made on January 1, 2002, indicating an operating lease.

ILLUSTRATION 21-36
Comparative Entries for Operating Lease

Morgan Bakeries (Lessee)			Appleland Computer (Lessor)		
Rent Expense	3,557.25		Cash	3,557.25	
Cash		3,557.25	Rental Revenue		3,557.25

Note: If the lease payments had been $3,557.25 with no executory costs included, this lease would qualify for capital lease accounting treatment. If the renewal option of $1,500 for Year 4 is considered a bargain renewal option, the minimum lease payments' present value (as shown below) is closer, but still below the 90% cut-off, and an operating lease treatment is still appropriate.

PV of minimum lease payments, years 1 to 3 (as above)	$8,224.16
Add PV of beginning of year 4 payment	
$1,500 − $500 = $1,000 × .71178	711.78
PV of minimum lease payments	$8,935.94

Summary of Learning Objectives

....

1 Explain the nature, economic substance, and advantages of lease transactions. A lease is a contract between two parties whereby the lessee is granted the right to use property owned by the lessor. In situations where the lessee obtains the use of the majority of the economic benefits inherent in a leased asset, the transaction is similar in substance to acquiring an asset. Therefore, the lessee recognizes the asset and associated liability and the lessor transfers the asset. The major advantages of leasing for the lessee relate to the cost and flexibility of the financing and protection against obsolescence, and for the lessor to the attractiveness of the finance income.

2 Identify and explain the accounting criteria and procedures for capitalizing leases by the lessee. Where the risks and benefits of owning the leased asset are transferred to the lessee as evidenced by either the transfer of title, the use of the majority of the asset services inherent in the leased asset, or the recovery by the lessor of its investment in the leased asset plus a return on that investment, the asset should be capitalized on the lessee's balance sheet and a liability recognized for the obligation owing to the lessor. The amount capitalized is the present value of the minimum lease payments, an amount based on that for which the lessee has accepted responsibility in the lease agreement. The lessee accounts for the leased asset and lease liability as it would any other capital asset and obligation by recording amortization and interest expense. Lease payments reduce the liability, including any accrued interest.

3 Identify the lessee's disclosure requirements for capital leases. Lessees must disclose information similar to the required disclosures for capital assets and long-term debt in general. In addition, the total future minimum lease payments and those required in each of the next five years must be reported with a separate deduction for executory and interest costs to reconcile the total owing to the obligation reported on the balance sheet.

4 Identify the lessee's accounting and disclosure requirements for an operating lease. A lessee recognizes the lease payments made as rent expense in the period covered by the lease, usually on a time proportion basis. The lessee must disclose the future minimum lease payments in total and for each of the next five years, and the nature of any other commitments under such leases.

5 Contrast the operating and capitalization methods of recording leases. Over the term of a lease, the total amount charged to expense is the same whether the lease has been treated as a capital lease or as an operating lease. The difference relates to the timing of recognition for the expense (more is charged in the early years for a capital lease), the type of expense charged (amortization and interest expense for a capital lease versus rent expense for an operating lease), and the recognition for a capital lease versus non-recognition for an operating lease of the leased asset and obligation on the balance sheet over the term of the lease.

6 Calculate the lease payment required for the lessor to earn a given return. The lessor determines the investment it wants to recover from a leased asset. If the lessor has acquired an asset for the purpose of leasing it, the lessor usually wants to recover the asset's cost. If the lessor participates in leases as a means of selling its product, it is usually the sales price it wants to recover. The lessor's investment in the cost or selling price can be recovered in part through the asset's estimated residual value if it is to be returned to the lessor, or through a bargain purchase price expected to be paid by the lessee, if part of the lease agreement. Other than from these sources, the lessor recovers its investment through the lease payments. The periodic lease payment, therefore, is the annuity amount whose present value exactly equals the amount to be recovered through lease payments.

7 Identify the classifications of leases for the lessor. If a lease in substance transfers the risks and benefits of ownership of the leased asset to the lessee (decided in the same way as for the lessee) and revenue recognition criteria related to collectibility and ability to estimate any remaining costs are met, the lessor accounts for the lease as either a direct financing or a sales-type lease. The existence of a manufacturer's or dealer's profit on the amount to be recovered from the lessee differentiates the sales-type lease from a direct financing lease where the objective is to generate only finance income. If any one of the capitalization or revenue recognition criteria is not met, the lessor accounts for the lease as an operating lease.

8 Describe the lessor's accounting for direct financing leases. The lessor removes the leased asset from its books and replaces it with its net investment in the lease. This is made up of two accounts: (1) the gross investment or lease payments receivable, which captures the dollars to be received through lease payments (excluding executory costs) plus estimated residual values or bargain purchase options, offset by (2) the portion of these amounts that represents unearned interest. The net investment, therefore, represents the present value of the lease payments and the residual value or bargain purchase option amounts. Looked at another way, this also represents the cost of the leased asset to the lessor. As the lease payments are received, the receivable is reduced. As time passes, the unearned interest is taken into income based on the implicit rate of return applied to the net investment.

9 Describe the lessor's accounting for sales-type leases. The lessor records sales revenue offset by the net investment in the lease. Again, the net investment is made up of two accounts: (1) the gross investment or lease payments receivable; and (2) the contra account representing the unearned interest included in the lease payments receivable. In addition, the lessor transfers the cost of the leased asset from inventory to cost of goods sold. In the period of the lease's inception the lessor reports a gross profit on sale and over the lease term recognizes finance income earned based on the outstanding net investment.

10 Describe the lessor's accounting for operating leases. The lessor records the lease payments received from the lessee as rental revenue in the period covered by the lease payment. Because the leased asset remains on the lessor's books, the lessor records amortization expense.

11 Identify the lessor's disclosure requirements. For direct financing and sales-type leases, the lessor must disclose its net investment in the leases, segregated according to current and noncurrent asset categories, and how the investment was calculated for purposes of income recognition. The amount of finance income recognized must also be disclosed. For operating leases, separate disclosure is required of the cost and accumulated amortization of property held for leasing purposes, and the amount of rental income earned.

12 Describe the effect of residual values, guaranteed and unguaranteed, on lease accounting. When a lessee guarantees a residual value, it is obligated to return either the leased asset or cash or a combination of both equal to that guaranteed value. This amount is therefore included in the lease obligation and leased asset value. The lessee amortizes the asset to this value by the end of the lease term. If the residual is unguaranteed, the lessee takes no responsibility for the residual and it is excluded from the lessee's calculations. From the lessor's viewpoint in a direct financing lease, it makes no difference whether or not the residual is guaranteed. The expected residual is included in the lessor's calculations as the best estimate of what will be returned at the end of the lease. In a sales-type lease, the gross investment, net investment, and unearned finance income are not affected by whether or not the residual is guaranteed. The only difference is that when the residual is unguaranteed, the uncertainty associated with whether or not the full sales amount will be realized dictates that sales revenue and cost of goods sold accounts be reduced by the unguaranteed residual's present value. There is no difference, however, in the amount of gross profit recognized on the sales-type lease.

13 Describe the effect of bargain purchase options on lease accounting. In a lease with a bargain purchase option, it is assumed that the lessee will exercise the option and that the title to the leased asset will be transferred to the lessee. The bargain purchase option's present value is therefore included in the amount capitalized as the asset and lease liability. Because the assumption is that the lessee will acquire title, the asset is amortized over its economic life. The lessor, whether a direct financing lease or a sales-type lease, includes the bargain purchase option in the gross investment and its present value in the net investment in the leased asset.

14 Describe the lessor's accounting treatment for initial direct costs. In all cases, the initial direct costs are matched with the revenue generated from the incurrence of the costs. For an operating lease, they are deferred and recognized over the same period as the rental revenue is recognized; for a sales-type lease, they are deducted in the same period as the gross profit on sale is recognized; and for a direct financing lease, they are amortized over the term of the lease.

Go to the Digital Tool for an expanded discussion of real estate leases and leveraged leases.

APPENDIX 21A

Sale-Leaseback Transactions

OBJECTIVE 15

After studying Appendix 21A, you should be able to: Describe the lessee's accounting for sale-leaseback transactions.

Sale-leaseback describes a transaction in which the property owner (the seller-lessee) sells the property to another party (the purchaser-lessor) and simultaneously leases it back from the new owner. The use of the property is generally continued without interruption. This type of transaction is fairly common.[33]

For example, a company buys land, constructs a building to its specifications, sells the property to an investor, and then immediately leases it back. The advantage of a sale and leaseback from the seller's viewpoint usually involves financing considerations. If an equipment purchase has already been financed, a sale-leaseback can allow the seller to refinance at lower rates if rates have decreased, or a sale-leaseback can provide additional working capital when liquidity is tight.

---

[33] *Financial Reporting in Canada—2000* (CICA, 2000) reports that out of 200 companies surveyed, six companies in 1999, three in 1998, seven in 1997 and five in 1996 disclosed information related to sale and leaseback transactions.

To the extent the seller-lessee's use of the asset sold continues after the sale, **the sale-leaseback is really a form of financing only,** and therefore no gain or loss should be recognized on the transaction. In substance, the seller-lessee is simply borrowing funds. On the other hand, if the seller-lessee gives up the right to the use of the asset sold, the transaction is in substance a sale, and gain or loss recognition is appropriate. Trying to ascertain when the lessee has given up the use of the asset is sometimes difficult, however, and complex rules have been formulated to identify this situation.[34] The profession's basic position in this area is that the lease should be accounted for as a capital, direct financing, or operating lease, as appropriate, by the seller-lessee and by the purchaser-lessor.[35]

Lessee Accounting

If the lease meets one of the three criteria for treatment as a capital lease, **the seller-lessee accounts for the transaction as a sale and the lease as a capital lease.** Any profit or loss experienced by the seller-lessee from the sale of the assets that are leased back under a capital lease are deferred and amortized over the lease term (or the economic life if criterion 1 is satisfied) in proportion to the amortization of the leased assets. If the leased asset is land only, the amortization is on a straight-line basis over the lease term.[36] If Lessee, Inc. sells equipment having a book value of $580,000 and a fair value of $623,110 to Lessor, Inc. for $623,110 and leases the equipment back for $50,000 a year for 20 years, the profit of $43,110 (that is, $623,110 − $580,000) is deferred and amortized over the 20-year period at the same rate that the $623,110 leased asset is amortized. The $43,110 is credited originally to "Unearned Profit on Sale-Leaseback."

If not one of the capital lease criteria is satisfied, **the seller-lessee accounts for the transaction as a sale and the lease as an operating lease.** Under an operating lease, such profit or loss is deferred and amortized in proportion to the rental payments over the period of time the assets are expected to be used by the lessee.[37]

The profession requires, however, that when there is a legitimate loss on the sale of the asset—that is, when the asset's fair value **is less than** the book value (carrying amount)—the loss must be recognized immediately.[38] For example, if Lessee, Inc. sells equipment having a book value of $650,000 and a fair value of $623,110, the difference of $26,890 is charged directly to a loss account.[39]

Lessor Accounting

If the lease meets one of the criteria in Group I and both the criteria in Group II (see Illustration 21-10), **the purchaser-lessor records the transaction as a purchase and a direct financing lease.** If the lease does not meet the criteria, the purchaser-lessor records the transaction as a purchase and an operating lease. The criteria for a sales-type lease would not be met in a sale-leaseback transaction.

---

[34] Guidance is provided in *EIC-25* (CICA, April 22, 1991) for situations where the leaseback relates to only a portion of the property sold by the seller-lessee. A discussion of the issues related to these transactions and others such as real estate sale-leaseback transactions are beyond the scope of this textbook.

[35] *CICA Handbook*, Section 3065, par. .66.

[36] *Ibid.*, par. .68.

[37] *Ibid.*, par. .69.

[38] There can be two types of losses in sale-leaseback arrangements. One is a real economic loss that results when the asset's carrying amount is higher than its fair value. In this case, the loss should be recognized. An artificial loss results when the sale price is below the asset's carrying amount but the fair value is above the carrying amount. In this case the loss is more in the form of prepaid rent and should be deferred and amortized in the future.

[39] *Ibid.*, par. .70.

Sale-Leaseback Illustration

To illustrate the accounting treatment accorded a sale-leaseback transaction, assume that Lessee Inc. on January 1, 2002 sells a used Boeing 747 having a carrying amount on its books of $75.5 million, to Lessor Inc. for $80 million and immediately leases the aircraft back under the following conditions:

1. The term of the lease is 15 years, non-cancellable, and requires equal rental payments of $10,487,443 at the beginning of each year.
2. The aircraft has a fair value of $80 million on January 1, 2002, and an estimated economic life of 15 years.
3. Lessee Inc. pays all executory costs.
4. Lessee Inc. amortizes similar aircraft that it owns on a straight-line basis over 15 years.
5. The annual payments assure the lessor a 12% return, the same as Lessee's incremental borrowing rate.
6. The present value of the minimum lease payments is $80 million or $10,487,443 × 7.62817 (Table A-5: $i = 12$, $n = 15$).

This lease is a capital lease to Lessee Inc. because the lease term exceeds 75% of the aircraft's estimated remaining life or because the minimum lease payments' present value exceeds 90% of the aircraft's fair value. Assuming that collectibility of the lease payments is reasonably assured and that no important uncertainties exist in relation to unreimbursable costs yet to be incurred by the lessor, Lessor Inc. should classify this lease as a direct financing lease.

The journal entries to record the transactions related to this lease for both Lessee Inc. and Lessor Inc. for the first year are presented below.

ILLUSTRATION 21A-1
Comparative Entries for Sale-Leaseback for Lessee and Lessor

Lessee Inc.			Lessor Inc.		
Sale of Aircraft by Lessee to Lessor Inc., January 1, 2002, and leaseback transaction:					
Cash	80,000,000		Aircraft	80,000,000	
Aircraft (net)		75,500,000	Cash		80,000,000
Unearned Profit on					
Sale-Leaseback		4,500,000	Lease Payments Receivable	157,311,645	
Aircraft under Capital Leases	80,000,000		Aircraft		80,000,000
Obligations under Capital Leases		80,000,000	Unearned Interest Revenue		77,311,645
			($10,487,443 × 15 = $157,311,645)		
First Lease Payment, January 1, 2002:					
Obligations under			Cash	10,487,443	
Capital Leases	10,487,443		Lease Payments		
Cash		10,487,443	Receivable		10,487,443
Incurrence and Payment of Executory Costs by Lessee Inc. throughout 2002:					
Insurance, Maintenance,			(No entry)		
Taxes, etc. Expense	XXX				
Cash or Accounts Payable		XXX			
Amortization Expense for 2002 on the Aircraft, December 31, 2002:					
Amortization Expense	5,333,333		(No entry)		
Accumulated Amortization—					
Leased Aircraft		5,333,333			
($80,000,000 ÷ 15)					
Amortization of Deferred Profit on Sale-Leaseback by Lessee Inc., December 31, 2002:					
Unearned Profit on			(No entry)		
Sale-Leaseback	300,000				
Amortization Expense		300,000			
($4,500,000 ÷ 15)					
Note: A case might be made for crediting Revenue instead of Amortization Expense.					
Interest for 2002, December 31, 2002:					
Interest Expense	8,341,507[a]		Unearned Interest Revenue	8,341,507	
Interest Payable		8,341,507	Interest Revenue		8,341,507[a]

*Partial Lease Amortization Schedule:

Date	Annual Rental Payment	Interest 12%	Reduction of Balance	Balance
1/1/02				$80,000,000
1/1/02	$10,487,443	$ –0–	$10,487,443	69,512,557
1/1/03	10,487,443	$8,341,507	2,145,936	67,366,621

Although there are no specific disclosure requirements for a sale-leaseback transaction other than those required for leases in general, the following is an example of how **Air Canada** reported such a transaction.

ILLUSTRATION 21A-2
Example of Sale-Leaseback Disclosure

AIR CANADA
Year Ended December 31, 2000
(in $ millions)

- Note 1 to the Consolidated Financial Statements (in part)
  m) Deferred Credits. Gains on sale and leaseback of assets are deferred and amortized to income over the terms of the leases as a reduction in rental expense.

	2000	1999
• Consolidated Statement of Cash Flow		
Investing Cash Flows (in part)		
Proceeds from sale and leaseback of assets	$292	$137
• Note 10 Deferred Credits (in part)		
Gain on sale and leaseback of assets	$350	$255

Summary of Learning Objective for Appendix 21A

15 **Describe the lessee's accounting for sale-leaseback transactions.** A sale and leaseback is accounted for by the lessee as if the two transactions are related. Any gain or loss, with the exception of a "real" loss, must be deferred by the lessee and recognized in income over the lease term. If it is an operating lease, the seller lessee takes the deferred gain or loss into income in proportion to the rental payments made; if it is a capital lease, the deferred gain or loss is taken into income over the same period and basis as the amortization of the leased asset.

KEY TERMS APPENDIX

Sale-leaseback, 1054

Note: All asterisked Brief Exercises, Exercises, Problems, and Conceptual Cases relate to material contained in the chapter appendix.

BRIEF EXERCISES

BE21-1 WarpSpeed Corporation leased equipment from Photon Inc. The lease term is five years and requires equal rental payments of $30,000 at the beginning of each year. The equipment has a fair value at the lease's inception of $138,000, an estimated useful life of eight years, and no residual value. WarpSpeed pays all executory costs directly to third parties. Photon set the annual rental to earn a rate of return of 10%, and this fact is known to WarpSpeed. The lease does not transfer title or contain a bargain purchase option. How should WarpSpeed classify this lease?

BE21-2 Waterworld Corporation leased equipment from Costner Ltd. The lease term is four years and requires equal rental payments of $37,283 at the beginning of each year. The equipment has a fair value at the lease's inception of $130,000, an estimated useful life of four years, and no residual value. Waterworld pays all executory costs directly to third parties. The appropriate interest rate is 10%. Prepare Waterworld's January 1, 2002 journal entries at the inception of the lease.

BE21-3 Beckner Corporation recorded a capital lease at $200,000 on January 1, 2002. The interest rate is 12%. Beckner Corporation made the first lease payment of $35,947 on January 1, 2002. The lease requires eight annual payments. The equipment has a useful life of eight years with no residual value. Prepare Beckner Corporation's December 31, 2002 adjusting entries.

BE21-4 Use the information for Beckner Corporation from BE21-3. Assume that at December 31, 2002, Beckner made an adjusting entry to accrue interest expense of $19,686 on the lease. Prepare Beckner's January 1, 2003 journal entry to record the second lease payment of $35,947. Assume no reversing entries are made.

BE21-5 Jana Corporation enters into a lease on January 1, 2002 that does not transfer ownership or contain a bargain purchase option. It covers three years of the equipment's eight-year useful life, and the minimum lease payments' present value is less than 90% of the fair market value of the asset leased. Prepare Jana's journal entry to record its January 1, 2002 annual lease payment of $37,500.

BE21-6 Fadhil Corporation leased equipment that was carried at a cost of $150,000 to Swander Inc., the lessee. The term of the lease is six years beginning January 1, 2002, with equal rental payments of $30,677 at the beginning of each year. All executory costs are paid by Swander directly to third parties. The equipment's fair value at the lease's inception is $150,000. The equipment has a useful life of six years with no residual value. The lease has an implicit interest rate of 9%, no bargain purchase option, and no transfer of title. Collectibility is reasonably assured with no additional costs to be incurred by Fadhil. Prepare Fadhil Corporation's January 1, 2002 journal entries at the inception of the lease.

BE21-7 Use the information for Fadhil Corporation from BE21-6. Assume the direct financing lease was recorded at a present value of $150,000. Prepare Fadhil's December 31, 2002 entry to record interest.

BE21-8 Sigut Corporation owns equipment that cost $72,000 and has a useful life of eight years with no residual value. On January 1, 2002, Sigut leases the equipment to Havaci Inc. for one year with one rental payment of $15,000 on January 1. Prepare Sigut Corporation's 2002 journal entries.

BE21-9 Estey Corporation enters into a six-year lease of machinery on January 1, 2002 that requires six annual payments of $30,000 each, beginning January 1, 2002. In addition, Estey guarantees the lessor a residual value of $20,000 at lease-end. The machinery has a useful life of six years. Prepare Estey's January 1, 2002 journal entries assuming an interest rate of 10%.

BE21-10 Use the information for Estey Corporation from BE21-9. Assume that for Moxey Corporation, the lessor, collectibility is reasonably predictable, there are no important uncertainties concerning costs, and the machinery's carrying amount is $155,013. Prepare Moxey's January 1, 2002 journal entries.

BE21-11 Arbeau Corporation manufactures replicators. On January 1, 2003, it leased to Barnes Limited a replicator that had cost $110,000 to manufacture. The lease agreement covers the replicator's five-year useful life and requires five equal annual rentals of $45,400 each. The equipment reverts to Arbeau at the end of the lease. There is no residual value guarantee. An interest rate of 12% is implicit in the lease agreement. Collectibility of the rentals is reasonably assured, and there are no important uncertainties concerning costs. Prepare Arbeau's January 1, 2003 journal entries.

*BE21-12 On January 1, 2003, Ryan Animation sold a truck to Coyne Finance for $35,000 and immediately leased it back. The truck was carried on Ryan Animation's books at $28,000. The term of the lease is five years, and title transfers to Ryan Animation at lease-end. The lease requires five equal rental payments of $9,233 at the end of each year. The appropriate rate of interest is 10%, and the truck has a useful life of five years with no salvage value. Prepare Ryan Animation's 2003 journal entries.

EXERCISES

E21-1 **(Lessee Entries; Capital Lease with Unguaranteed Residual Value)** On January 1, 2002, Burke Corporation signed a five-year non-cancellable lease for a machine. The terms of the lease called for Burke to make annual payments of $8,668 at the beginning of each year, starting January 1, 2002. The machine has an estimated useful life of six years and a $5,000 unguaranteed residual value. The machine reverts back to the lessor at the end of the lease term. Burke uses the straight-line method of amortization for all of its plant assets. Burke's incremental borrowing rate is 10%, and the lessor's implicit rate is unknown.

Instructions

(a) What type of lease is this? Explain.

(b) Calculate the present value of the minimum lease payments for the lessee.

(c) Prepare all necessary journal entries for Burke for this lease through January 1, 2003.

E21-2 **(Lessee Calculations and Entries; Capital Lease with Guaranteed Residual Value)** Delaney Corporation leases an automobile with a fair value of $8,725 from Simon Motors, Inc. on the following terms:

1. Non-cancellable term of 50 months.
2. Rental of $200 per month (at end of each month; present value at 1% per month is $7,840).
3. Estimated residual value after 50 months is $1,180 (the present value at 1% per month is $715). Delaney Corporation guarantees the residual value of $1,180.
3. Estimated economic life of the automobile is 60 months.
3. Delaney Corporation's incremental borrowing rate is 12% a year (1% a month). Simon's implicit rate is unknown.

Instructions

(a) What is the nature of this lease to Delaney Corporation?

(b) What is the present value of the minimum lease payments for Delaney?

(c) Record the lease on Delaney Corporation's books at the date of inception.

(d) Record the first month's amortization on Delaney Corporation's books (assume straight-line).

(e) Record the first month's lease payment.

E21-3 **(Lessee Entries; Capital Lease with Executory Costs and Unguaranteed Residual Value)** On January 1, 2002, Lahey Paper Corp. signs a 10-year non-cancellable lease agreement to lease a storage building from Sheffield Storage Corporation. The following information pertains to this lease agreement:

1. The agreement requires equal rental payments of $72,000 beginning on January 1, 2002.
2. The building's fair value on January 1, 2002 is $440,000.
3. The building has an estimated economic life of 12 years, with an unguaranteed residual value of $10,000. Lahey Paper Co. amortizes similar buildings on the straight-line method.
4. The lease is nonrenewable. At the termination of the lease, the building reverts to the lessor.
5. Lahey Paper's incremental borrowing rate is 12% per year. The lessor's implicit rate is not known by Lahey Paper Co.
6. The yearly rental payment includes $2,470.51 of executory costs related to taxes on the property.

Instructions

Prepare the journal entries on the lessee's books to reflect the signing of the lease agreement and to record the payments and expenses related to this lease for the years 2002 and 2003. Lahey Paper's fiscal year end is December 31.

E21-4 **(Lessee Entries; Capital Lease with Executory Costs and Unguaranteed Residual Value, May 31 Year End)**

Instructions

Refer to the data and other information provided in E21-3. Prepare the journal entries on the lessee's books to reflect the lease signing and to record payments and expenses related to this lease for the calendar years 2002 and 2003. Lahey Paper's fiscal year end is May 31. Assume Lahey Paper does not prepare reversing entries.

E21-5 **(Lessor Entries; Direct Financing Lease with Option to Purchase)** Castle Leasing Corporation signs a lease agreement on January 1, 2002 to lease electronic equipment to Jan Wai Corporation. The term of the non-cancellable lease is two years and payments are required at the end of each year. The following information relates to this agreement.

1. Jan Wai Corporation has the option to purchase the equipment for $16,000 upon the termination of the lease.
2. The equipment has a cost and fair value of $160,000 to Castle Leasing Corporation; the useful economic life is two years, with a residual value of $16,000.
3. Jan Wai Corporation is required to pay $5,000 each year to the lessor for executory costs.
4. Castle Leasing Corporation wants to earn a return of 10% on its investment.
5. Collectibility of the payments is reasonably predictable, and there are no important uncertainties surrounding the costs yet to be incurred by the lessor.

Instructions

(a) Prepare the journal entries on Castle Leasing's books to reflect the payments received under the lease and to recognize income for the years 2002 and 2003.

(b) Assuming that Jan Wai Corporation exercises its option to purchase the equipment on December 31, 2003, prepare the journal entry to reflect the sale on Castle's books.

E21-6 **(Type of Lease; Amortization Schedule)** Maroscia Leasing Corporation leases a new machine that has a cost and fair value of $95,000 to Sharrer Corporation on a three-year non-cancellable contract. Sharrer Corporation agrees to assume all risks of normal ownership including such costs as insurance, taxes, and maintenance. The machine has a three-year useful life and no residual value. The lease was signed on January 1, 2002; Maroscia Leasing Corporation expects to earn a 9% return on its investment. The annual rentals are payable on each December 31.

Instructions

(a) Discuss the nature of the lease arrangement and the accounting method that each party to the lease should apply.

(b) Prepare an amortization schedule that would be suitable for both the lessor and the lessee and that covers all the years involved.

E21-7 **(Lessor Entries; Sales-Type Lease)** Crosley Corporation, a machinery dealer, leased a machine to Ernst Corporation on January 1, 2002. The lease is for an eight-year period and requires equal annual payments of $35,013 at the beginning of each year. The first payment is received on January 1, 2002. Crosley had purchased the machine during 2001 for $160,000. Collectibility of lease payments is reasonably predictable, and no important uncertainties exist about costs yet to be incurred by Crosley. Crosley set the annual rental to ensure an 11% rate of return. The machine has an economic life of ten years with no residual value and reverts to Crosley at the termination of the lease.

Instructions

(a) Calculate the amount of each of the following:
  1. Gross investment.
  2. Unearned interest revenue.
  3. Net investment in the lease.

(b) Prepare all necessary journal entries for Crosley for 2002.

E21-8 **(Lessee-Lessor Entries; Sales-Type Lease)** On January 1, 2002, Garcin Corporation leased equipment to Flynn Corporation. The following information pertains to this lease.

  1. The term of the non-cancellable lease is six years, with no renewal option. The equipment reverts to the lessor at the termination of the lease.
  2. Equal rental payments are due on January 1 of each year, beginning in 2002.
  3. The equipment's fair value on January 1, 2002 is $150,000, and its cost to Garcin is $120,000.
  4. The equipment has an economic life of eight years, with an unguaranteed residual value of $10,000. Flynn amortizes all its equipment on a straight-line basis.
  5. Garcin set the annual rental to ensure an 11% rate of return. Flynn's incremental borrowing rate is 12%, and the lessor's implicit rate is unknown to the lessee.
  6. Collectibility of lease payments is reasonably predictable, and no important uncertainties exist about costs yet to be incurred by the lessor.

Instructions

(a) Discuss the nature of this lease to Garcin and Flynn.

(b) Calculate the amount of the annual rental payment.

(c) Prepare all the necessary journal entries for Flynn for 2002.

(d) Prepare all the necessary journal entries for Garcin for 2002.

E21-9 **(Lessee Entries with Bargain Purchase Option)** The following facts pertain to a non-cancellable lease agreement between Hebert Leasing Corporation and Ibrahim Corporation, a lessee.

Inception date	May 1, 2002
Annual lease payment due at the beginning of each year, starting May 1, 2002	$21,227.65
Bargain purchase option price at end of lease term	$ 4,000.00
Lease term	5 years
Economic life of leased equipment	10 years
Lessor's cost	$65,000.00
Fair value of asset at May 1, 2002	$91,000.00
Lessor's implicit rate	10%
Lessee's incremental borrowing rate	10%

The collectibility of the lease payments is reasonably predictable, and there are no important uncertainties about the costs yet to be incurred by the lessor. The lessee assumes responsibility for all executory costs.

Instructions

(Round all numbers to the nearest cent.)

(a) Discuss the nature of this lease to Ibrahim Corporation.

(b) Discuss the nature of this lease to Hebert Corporation.

(c) Prepare a lease amortization schedule for Ibrahim Corporation for the five-year lease term.

(d) Prepare the journal entries on the lessee's books to reflect the signing of the lease agreement and to record the payments and expenses related to this lease for the years 2002 and 2003. Ibrahim's annual accounting period ends on December 31. Reversing entries are not used by Ibrahim.

E21-10 **(Lessor Entries with Bargain Purchase Option)** A lease agreement between Hebert Leasing Corporation and Ibrahim Corporation is described in E21-9.

Instructions

(Round all numbers to the nearest cent.)

Refer to the data in E21-9 and provide the following for the lessor.

(a) Calculate the amount of gross investment at the lease's inception.

(b) Calculate the amount of net investment at the inception of the lease.

(c) Prepare a lease amortization schedule for Hebert Leasing Corporation for the five-year lease term.

(d) Prepare the journal entries to reflect the signing of the lease agreement and to record the receipts and income related to this lease for the years 2002, 2003, and 2004. The lessor's accounting period ends on December 31. Reversing entries are not used by Hebert.

E21-11 **(Calculation of Rental; Journal Entries for Lessor)** Jamil Leasing Corporation signs an agreement on January 1, 2002 to lease equipment to Irvine Limited. The following information relates to this agreement.

1. The term of the non-cancellable lease is six years with no renewal option. The equipment has an estimated economic life of six years.

2. The asset's cost to the lessor is $245,000. The asset's fair value at January 1, 2002 is $245,000.

3. The asset will revert to the lessor at the end of the lease term, at which time the asset is expected to have a residual value of $43,622, none of which is guaranteed.

4. Irvine Limited assumes direct responsibility for all executory costs.

5. The agreement requires equal annual rental payments, beginning on January 1, 2002.

6. Collectibility of the lease payments is reasonably predictable. There are no important uncertainties about costs yet to be incurred by the lessor.

Instructions

(Round all numbers in parts (b) and (c) to the nearest cent.)

(a) Assuming the lessor desires a 10% rate of return on its investment, calculate the amount of the annual rental payment required. Round to the nearest dollar.

(b) Prepare an amortization schedule that would be suitable for the lessor for the lease term.

(c) Prepare all of the journal entries for the lessor for 2002 and 2003 to record the lease agreement, the receipt of lease payments, and the recognition of income. Assume the lessor's annual accounting period ends on December 31.

E21-12 **(Amortization Schedule and Journal Entries for Lessee)** Jodrey Leasing Corporation signs an agreement on January 1, 2002, to lease equipment to LeBlanc Limited. The following information relates to this agreement.

1. The term of the non-cancellable lease is five years with no renewal option. The equipment has an estimated economic life of five years.

2. The asset's fair value at January 1, 2002 is $80,000.

3. The asset will revert to the lessor at the end of the lease term, at which time the asset is expected to have a residual value of $7,000, none of which is guaranteed.

4. LeBlanc Limited assumes direct responsibility for all executory costs, which include the following annual amounts: (1) $900 to Rocky Mountain Insurance Corporation for insurance; (2) $1,600 to Laclede County for property taxes.

5. The agreement requires equal annual rental payments of $18,142.95 to the lessor, beginning on January 1, 2002.

6. The lessee's incremental borrowing rate is 12%. The lessor's implicit rate is 10% and is known to the lessee.
7. LeBlanc Limited uses the straight-line amortization method for all equipment.
8. LeBlanc uses reversing entries when appropriate.

Instructions

(Round all numbers to the nearest cent.)

(a) Prepare an amortization schedule that would be suitable for the lessee for the lease term.
(b) Prepare all of the lessee's journal entries for 2002 and 2003 to record the lease agreement, the lease payments, and all expenses related to this lease. Assume the lessee's annual accounting period ends on December 31.

E21-13   (Accounting for an Operating Lease)   On January 1, 2002, Novac Corp. leased a building to Wisen Inc. The relevant information related to the lease is as follows:

1. The lease arrangement is for 10 years.
2. The leased building cost $4,500,000 and was purchased for cash on January 1, 2002.
3. The building is amortized on a straight-line basis. Its estimated economic life is 50 years.
4. Lease payments are $275,000 per year and are made at the end of the year.
5. Property tax expense of $85,000 and insurance expense of $10,000 on the building were incurred by Novac in the first year. Payment on these two items was made at the end of the year.
6. Both the lessor and the lessee are on a calendar-year basis.

Instructions

(a) Prepare the journal entries that Novac Corp. should make in 2002.
(b) Prepare the journal entries that Wisen Inc. should make in 2002.
(c) If Novac paid $30,000 to a real estate broker on January 1, 2002 as a fee for finding the lessee, how much should be reported as an expense for this item in 2002 by Novac Corp.?

E21-14   (Accounting and Disclosure for an Operating Lease)   On January 1, 2002, a machine was purchased for $900,000 by Pomeroy Corp. The machine is expected to have an eight-year life with no salvage value. It is to be amortized on a straight-line basis. The machine was leased to St. Leger Inc. on January 1, 2002 at an annual rental of $210,000. Other relevant information is as follows.

1. The lease term is three years.
2. Pomeroy Corp. incurred maintenance and other executory costs of $25,000 in 2002 related to this lease.
3. The machine could have been sold by Pomeroy Corp. for $940,000 instead of leasing it.
4. St. Leger is required to pay a rent security deposit of $35,000 and to prepay the last month's rent of $17,500.

Instructions

(a) How much should Pomeroy Corp. report as income before income tax on this lease for 2002?
(b) What amount should St. Leger Inc. report for rent expense for 2002 on this lease?
(c) What financial statement disclosures are required for both companies' December 31, 2002 year ends relative to this lease?

E21-15   (Operating Lease for Lessee and Lessor)   On February 20, 2002, Sigouin Inc. purchased a machine for $1.5 million for the purpose of leasing it. The machine is expected to have a 10-year life, no residual value, and will be amortized on the straight-line basis. The machine was leased to Roudy Corporation on March 1, 2002 for a four-year period at a monthly rental of $19,500. There is no provision for the renewal of the lease or purchase of the machine by the lessee at the expiration of the lease term. Sigouin paid $30,000 of commissions associated with negotiating the lease in February 2002:

Instructions

(a) What expense should Roudy Corporation record as a result of the facts above for the year ended December 31, 2002? Show supporting calculations in good form.
(b) What income or loss before income taxes should Sigouin record as a result of the facts above for the year ended December 31, 2002?

(AICPA adapted)

E21-16   (Lessor Entries, Determine Type of Lease, Calculate Lease Payment, Spreadsheet Application, Financial Statement Amounts)   Cadette Corp. leases a car to Jaimme DeLory on June 1, 2002. The term of the non-cancellable lease is 48 months. The following information is provided about the lease.

1. The lessee is given an option to purchase the automobile at the end of the lease term for $5,000.
2. The automobile's fair value on June 1, 2002 is $29,500. It is carried in Cadette's inventory at $21,200.
3. The car has an economic life of seven years, with a $1,000 residual value at that time. The car's estimated fair value is $10,000 after four years, $7,000 after five years and $2,500 after six years.
4. Cadette wants to earn a 12% rate of return (1% per month) on any financing transactions.
5. Jaimme DeLory represents a reasonable credit risk and no future costs are anticipated in relation to this lease.
6. The lease agreement calls for a $1,000 down payment on June 1, 2002 and 48 equal monthly payments on the first of each month beginning June 1, 2002.

Instructions

(a) Determine the amount of the monthly lease payment.
(b) What type of lease is this to Cadette Corp.? Explain.
(c) Using a computer spreadsheet program, prepare a lease amortization schedule for the 48 month lease term.
(d) Prepare entries, if any, that are required on December 31, 2002, Cadette's fiscal year end.
(e) How much income will Cadette report on its 2002 income statement relative to this lease?
(f) What is the net investment in the lease to be reported on the December 31, 2002 balance sheet? How much is reported in current assets? In non-current assets?

*E21-17 (Sale and Leaseback) On January 1, 2002, Hein Do Corporation sells a computer system to Liquidity Finance Corp. for $680,000 and immediately leases the computer back. The relevant information is as follows.

1. The computer system was carried on Hein Do's books at a value of $600,000.
2. The term of the non-cancellable lease is 10 years; title will transfer to Hein Do.
3. The lease agreement requires equal rental payments of $110,666.81 at the end of each year.
4. The incremental borrowing rate of Hein Do Corporation is 12%. Hein Do is aware that Liquidity Finance Corp. set the annual rental to ensure a rate of return of 10%.
5. The computer has a fair value of $680,000 on January 1, 2002 and an estimated economic life of 10 years with no residual value at that time.
6. Hein Do pays executory costs of $9,000 per year.

Instructions

Prepare the journal entries for both the lessee and the lessor for 2002 to reflect the sale and leaseback agreement. No uncertainties exist, and collectibility is reasonably certain.

*E21-18 (Lessee-Lessor, Sale-Leaseback) Presented below are four independent situations.

(a) On December 31, 2002, Zarle Inc. sold equipment to Daniell Corp. and immediately leased it back for 10 years. The equipment's sales price was $520,000, its carrying amount $400,000, and its estimated remaining economic life 12 years. Determine the amount of deferred revenue to be reported by Zarle Inc. from the equipment sale on December 31, 2002.
(b) On December 31, 2002, Wasicsko Corp. sold a machine to Cross Ltd. and simultaneously leased it back for one year. The machine's sale price was $480,000, the carrying amount $420,000, and it had an estimated remaining useful life of 14 years. The rental payments' present value for the one year is $35,000. At December 31, 2002, how much should Wasicsko report as deferred revenue from the sale of the machine?
(c) On January 1, 2002, McKane Corp. sold an airplane with an estimated useful life of 10 years. At the same time, McKane leased back the plane for 10 years. The airplane's sales price was $500,000, the carrying amount $379,000, and the annual rental $73,975.22. McKane Corp. intends to amortize the leased asset using the sum-of-the-years'-digits amortization method. Discuss how the gain on the sale should be reported at the end of 2002 in the financial statements.
(d) On January 1, 2002, Sondgeroth Corp. sold equipment with an estimated useful life of five years. At the same time, Sondgeroth leased back the equipment for two years under a lease classified as an operating lease. The equipment's sales price (fair value) was $212,700, the carrying amount was $300,000, the monthly rental under the lease $6,000, and the rental payments' present value $115,753. For the year ended December 31, 2002, identify the items that would be reported on Sondgeroth's income statement for the sale-leaseback transaction.

PROBLEMS

P21-1 Stine Leasing Corporation agrees to lease machinery to Potter Corporation on January 1, 2002. The following information relates to the lease agreement.

1. The lease's term is seven years with no renewal option, and the machinery has an estimated economic life of nine years.
2. The machinery's cost is $420,000, and the asset's fair value on 1/1/02 is $560,000.
3. At the end of the lease term, the asset reverts to the lessor. At this time the asset is expected to have a residual value of $80,000 and this value is guaranteed by Potter. Potter amortizes all of its equipment on a straight-line basis.
4. The lease agreement requires equal annual rental payments, beginning on January 1, 2002.
5. The collectibility of the lease payments is reasonably predictable and there are no important uncertainties about costs yet to be incurred by the lessor.
6. Stine desires a 10% rate of return on its investments. Potter's incremental borrowing rate is 11%, and the lessor's implicit rate is unknown.

Instructions

(a) Discuss the nature of this lease for both the lessee and the lessor.
(b) Calculate the amount of the annual rental payment required.
(c) Calculate the present value of the minimum lease payments for the lessee, and for the lessor.
(d) Prepare the journal entries Potter would make in 2002 and 2003 related to the lease arrangement.
(e) Prepare the journal entries Stine would make in 2002 and 2003.

P21-2 Synergetics Inc. leased a new crane to Gumowski Construction under a five-year non-cancellable contract starting January 1, 2002. Terms of the lease require payments of $22,000 each January 1, starting January 1, 2002. Synergetics will pay insurance, taxes, and maintenance charges on the crane, which has an estimated life of 12 years, a fair value of $160,000, and a cost to Synergetics of $160,000. The crane's estimated fair value is expected to be $45,000 at the end of the lease term. No bargain purchase or renewal options are included in the contract. Both Synergetics and Gumowski adjust and close books annually at December 31. Collectibility of the lease payments is reasonably certain and no uncertainties exist relative to unreimbursable lessor costs. Gumowski's incremental borrowing rate is 10% and Synergetics' implicit interest rate of 9% is known to Gumowski.

Instructions

(a) Identify the type of lease involved and give reasons for your classification. Discuss the accounting treatment that should be applied by both the lessee and the lessor.
(b) Prepare all the entries related to the lease contract and leased asset for the year 2002 for the lessee and lessor, assuming the following executory costs: insurance, $500; taxes, $2,000; and maintenance, $650. Straight-line amortization should be used for the leased asset. It is expected to have a salvage value of $10,000 at the end of its useful life.
(c) Identify what should be presented in the balance sheet and income statement and related notes of both the lessee and the lessor at December 31, 2002.

P21-3 Cascade Industries and Hardy Inc. enter into an agreement that requires Hardy Inc. to build three diesel-electric engines to Cascade's specifications. Upon completion of the engines, Cascade has agreed to lease them for a period of 10 years and to assume all costs and risks of ownership. The lease is non-cancellable, becomes effective on January 1, 2002, and requires annual rental payments of $620,956 each January 1, starting January 1, 2002.

Cascade's incremental borrowing rate is 10% and the implicit interest rate used by Hardy Inc. and known to Cascade is 8%. The total cost of building the three engines is $3.9 million. The engines' economic life is estimated to be 10 years, with residual value expected to be zero. Cascade amortizes similar equipment on a straight-line basis. At the end of the lease, Cascade assumes title to the engines. Collectibility of the lease payments is reasonably certain and no uncertainties exist relative to unreimbursable lessor costs.

Instructions

(Round all numbers to the nearest dollar.)

(a) Discuss the nature of this lease transaction from the viewpoints of both lessee and lessor.
(b) Prepare the journal entry or entries to record the transactions on January 1, 2002 on the books of Cascade Industries.

(c) Prepare the journal entry or entries to record the transactions on January 1, 2002 on the books of Hardy Inc.

(d) Prepare the journal entries for both the lessee and lessor to record interest expense (revenue) at December 31, 2002. (Prepare a lease amortization schedule for two years.)

(e) Show the items and amounts that would be reported on the balance sheet (not notes) at December 31, 2002 for both the lessee and the lessor.

(f) Identify how the lease transactions would be reported on each company's cash flow statement in 2002.

P21-4 The following facts pertain to a non-cancellable lease agreement between Alschuler Leasing Corporation and McKee Electronics, a lessee, for a computer system.

Inception date	October 1, 2002
Lease term	6 years
Economic life of leased equipment	6 years
Fair value of asset at October 1, 2002	$200,255
Residual value at end of lease term	–0–
Lessor's implicit rate	10%
Lessee's incremental borrowing rate	10%
Annual lease payment due at the beginning of each year, beginning with October 1, 2002	$41,800

The collectibility of the lease payments is reasonably predictable, and there are no important uncertainties about costs yet to be incurred by the lessor. The lessee assumes responsibility for all executory costs, which amount to $5,500 per year and are to be paid each October 1, beginning October 1, 2002. (This $5,500 is not included in the rental payment of $41,800.) The asset will revert to the lessor at the end of the lease term. The straight-line amortization method is used for all equipment.

The following amortization schedule has been prepared correctly for use by both the lessor and the lessee in accounting for this lease. The lease is to be accounted for properly as a capital lease by the lessee and as a direct financing lease by the lessor.

Date	Annual Lease Payment/ Receipt	Interest (10%) on Unpaid Obligation/ Net Investment	Reduction of Lease Obligation/ Net Investment	Balance of Lease Obligation/ Net Investment
10/01/02				$200,255
10/01/02	$ 41,800	–0–	$ 41,800	158,455
10/01/03	41,800	$15,846	25,954	132,501
10/01/04	41,800	13,250	28,550	103,951
10/01/05	41,800	10,395	31,405	72,546
10/01/06	41,800	7,255	34,545	38,001
10/01/07	41,800	3,799 *	38,001	–0–
	$250,800	$50,545	$200,255	

*Rounding error is $1.

Instructions

(Round all numbers to the nearest dollar.)

(a) Assuming the lessee's accounting period ends on September 30, answer the following questions with respect to this lease agreement.

1. What items and amounts will appear on the lessee's income statement for the year ending September 30, 2003?
2. What items and amounts will appear on the lessee's balance sheet at September 30, 2003?
3. What items and amounts will appear on the lessee's income statement for the year ending September 30, 2004?
4. What items and amounts will appear on the lessee's balance sheet at September 30, 2004?

(b) Assuming the lessee's accounting period ends on December 31, answer the following questions with respect to this lease agreement.

1. What items and amounts will appear on the lessee's income statement for the year ending December 31, 2002?
2. What items and amounts will appear on the lessee's balance sheet at December 31, 2002?
3. What items and amounts will appear on the lessee's income statement for the year ending December 31, 2003?
4. What items and amounts will appear on the lessee's balance sheet at December 31, 2003?

P21-5 Assume the same information as in P21-4.

Instructions
(Round all numbers to the nearest dollar.)
(a) Assuming the lessor's accounting period ends on September 30, answer the following questions with respect to this lease agreement:
1. What items and amounts will appear on the lessor's income statement for the year ending September 30, 2003?
2. What items and amounts will appear on the lessor's balance sheet at September 30, 2003?
3. What items and amounts will appear on the lessor's income statement for the year ending September 30, 2004?
4. What items and amounts will appear on the lessor's balance sheet at September 30, 2004?

(b) Assuming the lessor's accounting period ends on December 31, answer the following questions with respect to this lease agreement.
1. What items and amounts will appear on the lessor's income statement for the year ending December 31, 2002?
2. What items and amounts will appear on the lessor's balance sheet at December 31, 2002?
3. What items and amounts will appear on the lessor's income statement for the year ending December 31, 2003?
4. What items and amounts will appear on the lessor's balance sheet at December 31, 2003?

P21-6 The following facts pertain to a non-cancellable lease agreement between Voris Leasing Corporation and Zarle Corporation, a lessee.

Inception date	January 1, 2002
Annual lease payment due at the beginning of each year, beginning with January 1, 2002	$81,365
Residual value of equipment at end of lease term, guaranteed by the lessee	$50,000
Lease term	6 years
Economic life of leased equipment	6 years
Fair value of asset at January 1, 2002	$400,000
Lessor's implicit rate	12%
Lessee's incremental borrowing rate	12%

The lessee assumes responsibility for all executory costs, which are expected to amount to $4,000 per year. The asset will revert to the lessor at the end of the lease term. The lessee uses the straight-line amortization method for all equipment.

Instructions
(Round all numbers to the nearest dollar.)
(a) Provide proof that the lessor's implicit interest rate is 12%.
(b) Prepare an amortization schedule for the lessee covering the lease term.
(c) Prepare all of the journal entries for the lessee for 2002 and 2003 to record the lease agreement, the lease payments, and all expenses related to this lease. Assume the lessee's annual accounting period ends on December 31 and reversing entries are used when appropriate.

 P21-7 Hilary Steel Corporation, as lessee, signed a lease agreement for equipment for five years, beginning December 31, 2001. Annual rental payments of $32,000 are to be made at the beginning of each lease year (December 31). The taxes, insurance, and the maintenance costs are the lessee's obligation. The interest rate used by the lessor in setting the payment schedule is 10%; Hilary's incremental borrowing rate is 12%. Hilary is unaware of the rate being used by the lessor. At the end of the lease, Hilary has the option to buy the equipment for $1, considerably below its estimated fair value at that time. The equipment has an estimated useful life of seven years with no residual value. Hilary uses the straight-line method of amortization on similar owned equipment.

Instructions
(Round all numbers to the nearest dollar.)
(a) Prepare the journal entry or entries, with explanations, that should be recorded on December 31, 2001 by Hilary.
(b) Prepare the journal entry or entries, with explanations, that should be recorded on December 31, 2002 by Hilary. (Prepare the lease amortization schedule for all five payments.)

(c) Prepare the journal entry or entries, with explanations, that should be recorded on December 31, 2003 by Hilary.

(d) What amounts would appear on Hilary's December 31, 2003 balance sheet relative to the lease arrangement?

(e) What amounts would appear on Hilary's cash flow statement for 2001 relative to the lease arrangement? Where would the amounts be reported?

P21-8 On January 1, 2002, Doss Corporation contracts to lease equipment for five years, agreeing to make a payment of $94,732 (including the executory costs of $6,000) at the beginning of each year, starting January 1, 2002. The taxes, insurance, and maintenance, estimated at $6,000 a year, are the lessee's obligations. The leased equipment is to be capitalized at $370,000. The asset is to be amortized on a double-declining-balance basis and the obligation is to be reduced on an effective-interest basis. Doss's incremental borrowing rate is 12%, and the implicit rate in the lease is 10%, which is known by Doss. Title to the equipment transfers to Doss when the lease expires. The asset has an estimated useful life of five years and no residual value.

Instructions

(Round all numbers to the nearest dollar.)

(a) Explain the probable relationship of the $370,000 amount to the lease arrangement.

(b) Prepare the journal entry or entries that should be recorded on January 1, 2002, by Doss Corporation.

(c) Prepare the journal entry to record amortization of the leased asset for the year 2002.

(d) Prepare the journal entry to record the interest expense for the year 2002.

(e) Prepare the journal entry to record the lease payment of January 1, 2003, assuming reversing entries are not made.

(f) What amounts will appear on the lessee's December 31, 2002 balance sheet and cash flow statement relative to the lease contract?

P21-9 Roesch Inc. was incorporated in 2000 to operate as a computer software service firm with a fiscal year ending August 31. Roesch's primary product is a sophisticated on-line inventory-control system; its customers pay a fixed fee plus a usage charge for using the system.

Roesch has leased a large, Alpha-3 computer system from the manufacturer. The lease calls for a monthly rental of $50,000 for the 144 months (12 years) of the lease term. The system's estimated useful life is 15 years.

Each scheduled monthly rental payment includes $4,000 for full-service maintenance on the computer to be performed by the manufacturer. All rentals are payable on the first day of the month beginning with August 1, 2001, the date the system was installed and the lease agreement was signed.

The lease is non-cancellable for its 12-year term, and it is secured only by the manufacturer's chattel lien on the Alpha-3 system. Roesch can purchase the Alpha-3 system from the manufacturer at the end of the 12 year lease term for 75% of the computer's fair value at that time.

This lease is accounted for as a capital lease by Roesch, and the equipment is amortized by the straight-line method with no expected residual value. Borrowed funds for this type of transaction would cost Roesch 12% per year (1% per month). Following is a schedule of the present value of $1 for selected periods discounted at 1% per period when payments are made at the beginning of each period.

Periods (months)	Present Value of $1 per Period Discounted at 1% per Period
1	1.000
2	1.990
3	2.970
143	76.658
144	76.899

Instructions

Prepare, in general journal form, all entries Roesch should make in its accounting records during August 2001 relating to this lease. Give full explanations and show supporting calculations for each entry. Remember, August 31, 2001 is the end of Roesch's fiscal accounting period and it will be preparing financial statements on that date. Do not prepare closing entries.

(AICPA adapted)

P21-10 Thomash Corporation manufactures specialty equipment with an estimated economic life of 12 years and leases it to Provincial Airlines Corp. for a period of 10 years. The equipment's normal selling price is $210,482 and its unguaranteed residual value at the end of the lease term is estimated to be $20,000.

Provincial will pay annual payments of $30,000 at the beginning of each year and all maintenance, insurance, and taxes. Thomash incurred costs of $135,000 in manufacturing the equipment and $4,000 in negotiating and closing the lease. Thomash has determined that the collectibility of the lease payments is reasonably predictable, that no additional costs will be incurred, and that the implicit interest rate is 10%.

Instructions

(Round all numbers to the nearest dollar.)

(a) Discuss the nature of this lease in relation to the lessor and calculate the amount of each of the following items:

1. Gross investment.
2. Unearned interest revenue.
3. Sales price.
4. Cost of sales.

(b) Prepare a 10-year lease amortization schedule.

(c) Prepare all of the lessor's journal entries for the first year of the lease, assuming the lessor's fiscal year end is five months into the lease. Reversing entries are not used.

(d) Determine the current and noncurrent portion of the net investment five months into the lease at the lessor's fiscal year end.

(e) Assume the $20,000 residual value is guaranteed by the lessee. Identify the changes necessary to parts (a) to (d).

P21-11   Assume the same data as in P21-10 with Provincial Airlines Corp. having an incremental borrowing rate of 10%.

Instructions

(Round all numbers to the nearest dollar.)

(a) Discuss the nature of this lease in relation to the lessee and calculate the amount of the initial obligation under capital leases.

(b) Prepare a 10-year lease amortization schedule.

(c) Prepare all of the lessee's journal entries for the first year, assuming the lease year and Provincial's fiscal year are the same.

P21-12   During 2002, Lau Leasing Ltd. began leasing equipment to small manufacturers. Below is information regarding the leasing arrangements.

1. Lau Leasing Ltd. leases equipment with terms from three to five years depending on the equipment's useful life. At the lease expiration, the equipment is sold to the lessee at 10% of the lessor's cost, the equipment's expected residual value.

2. The amount of the lessee's monthly payment is calculated by multiplying the lessor's cost of the equipment by the payment factor applicable to the term of the lease.

Term of Lease	Payment Factor
3 years	3.32%
4 years	2.63%
5 years	2.22%

3. The excess of the gross contract receivable for equipment rentals over the cost (reduced by the estimated residual value at the termination of the lease) is recognized as revenue over the term of the lease under the straight-line method.

4. The following leases were entered into during 2002.

Machine	Dates of Lease	Period of Lease	Machine Cost
Die	7/1/02–6/30/06	4 years	$150,000
Press	9/1/02–8/31/05	3 years	$120,000

Instructions

(a) Prepare a schedule of gross contracts receivable for equipment rentals at the dates of the lease for the die and press machines.

(b) Prepare a schedule of unearned lease income at December 31, 2002 for each machine lease.

(c) Prepare a schedule calculating the present dollar value of lease payments receivable (gross investment) for equipment rentals at December 31, 2002. (The present dollar value of the "lease receivables for equipment rentals" is the outstanding amount of the gross lease receivables less the unearned lease income included therein.) Without prejudice to your solution to part (b), assume that the unearned lease income at December 31, 2002 was $68,000.

(AICPA adapted)

P21-13 In 1999, Yin Trucking Corporation negotiated and closed a long-term lease contract for newly constructed truck terminals and freight storage facilities. The buildings were erected to the company's specifications on land owned by the company. On January 1, 2000, Yin Trucking Corporation took possession of the lease properties. On January 1, 2000 and 2001, the company made cash payments of $1,048,000 that were recorded as rental expenses.

Although the terminals have a composite useful life of 40 years, the non-cancellable lease runs for 20 years from January 1, 2000, with a purchase option available upon expiration of the lease.

The 20-year lease is effective for the period January 1, 2000 through December 31, 2019. Advance rental payments of $900,000 are payable to the lessor on January 1 of each of the first 10 years of the lease term. Advance rental payments of $320,000 are due on January 1 for each of the last 10 years of the lease. The company has an option to purchase all of these leased facilities for $1 on December 31, 2019. It also must make annual payments to the lessor of $125,000 for property taxes and $23,000 for insurance. The lease was negotiated to assure the lessor a 6% rate of return.

Instructions

(Round all numbers to the nearest dollar.)

(a) Prepare a schedule to calculate for Yin Trucking Corporation the discounted present value of the terminal facilities and related obligation at January 1, 2000.

(b) Assuming that the discounted present value of terminal facilities and related obligation at January 1, 2000 was $8.4 million, prepare journal entries for Yin Trucking Corporation to record the:

1. Cash payment to the lessor on January 1, 2002.
2. Amortization of the cost of the leased properties for 2002 using the straight-line method and assuming a zero residual value.
3. Accrual of interest expense at December 31, 2002.

Selected present value factors are as follows.

Periods	For an Ordinary Annuity of $1 at 6%	For $1 at 6%
1	0.943396	.943396
2	1.833393	.889996
8	6.209794	.627412
9	6.801692	.591898
10	7.360087	.558395
19	11.158117	.330513
20	11.469921	.311805

(AICPA adapted)

P21-14 Jennings Inc. manufactures an X-ray machine with an estimated life of 12 years and leases it to Gocker Medical Centre for a period of 10 years. The machine's normal selling price is $343,734, and its guaranteed (by the lessee) residual value at the end of the lease term is estimated to be $15,000. The hospital will pay rents of $50,000 at the beginning of each year and all maintenance, insurance, and taxes. Jennings Inc. incurred costs of $210,000 in manufacturing the machine and $14,000 in negotiating and closing the lease. Jennings Inc. has determined that the collectibility of the lease payments is reasonably predictable, that there will be no additional costs incurred, and that the implicit interest rate is 10%.

Instructions

(Round all numbers to the nearest dollar.)

(a) Discuss the nature of this lease in relation to the lessor and calculate the amount of each of the following items:

1. Gross investment.
2. Unearned interest revenue.
3. Sales price.
4. Cost of sales.

(b) Prepare a 10-year lease amortization schedule.

(c) Prepare all of the lessor's journal entries for the first year.

(d) Identify the balance sheet, income statement and cash flow amounts to be reported on Jennings' first balance sheet, income statement, and statement of cash flows, and prepare any required note disclosures.

(e) Assume instead that the residual value is not guaranteed. Identify what changes are necessary in parts (a) to (d) to reflect this situation.

P21-15 Assume the same data as in P21-14 and that Gocker Medical Centre has an incremental borrowing rate of 10%.

Instructions

(Round all numbers to the nearest dollar.)

(a) Discuss the nature of this lease in relation to the lessee and calculate the amount of the initial obligation under capital leases.

(b) Prepare a 10-year lease amortization schedule.

(c) Prepare all of the lessee's journal entries for the first year.

(d) Prepare any note disclosures required at the end of Year 1 and determine the balance sheet and income statement amounts that will be reported at the end of the first year.

P21-16 You are auditing the December 31, 2002 financial statements of Shamess, Inc., manufacturer of novelties and party favours. During your inspection of the company garage, you discovered that a 2001 Shirk automobile not listed in the equipment subsidiary ledger is parked in the company garage. You ask the plant manager about the vehicle, and she tells you that the company did not list the automobile because the company was only leasing it. The lease agreement was entered into on January 1, 2002, with Yablon New and Used Cars.

You decide to review the lease agreement to ensure that the lease should be afforded operating lease treatment, and you discover the following lease terms:

1. Non-cancellable term of 50 months.
2. Rental of $180 per month (at the end of each month; present value at 1% per month is $7,055).
3. Estimated residual value after 50 months is $1,100 (the present value at 1% per month is $699). Shamess guarantees the residual value of $1,100.
4. Estimated economic life of the automobile is 60 months.
5. Shamess's incremental borrowing rate is 12% per year (1% per month).

Instructions

You are a senior auditor writing a memo to your supervisor, the audit partner in charge of this audit, to discuss the above situation. Be sure to include (a) why you inspected the lease agreement, (b) what you determined about the lease, and (c) how you advised your client to account for this lease. Explain every journal entry that you believe is necessary to record this lease properly on the client's books.

P21-17 Lanier Dairy Ltd. leases its milking equipment from Zeff Finance Corporation under the following lease terms.

1. The lease term is 10 years, non-cancellable, and requires equal rental payments of $25,250 due at the beginning of each year starting January 1, 2002.
2. The equipment has a fair value and cost at the inception of the lease (January 1, 2002) of $185,078, an estimated economic life of 10 years, and a residual value (which is guaranteed by Lanier Dairy) of $20,000.
3. The lease contains no renewal options and the equipment reverts to Zeff Finance Corporation on termination of the lease.
4. Lanier Dairy's incremental borrowing rate is 9% per year; the implicit rate is also 9%.
5. Lanier Dairy amortizes similar equipment that it owns on a straight-line basis.
6. Collectibility of the payments is reasonably predictable, and there are no important uncertainties about the costs yet to be incurred by the lessor.

Instructions

(a) Describe the nature of the lease and, in general, discuss how the lessee and lessor should account for the lease transaction.

(b) Prepare the journal entries for the lessee and lessor at January 1, 2002 and December 31, 2002 (the lessee's and lessor's year end).

(c) Prepare the journal entries at January 1, 2003 for the lessor and lessee. Assume no reversing entries.

(d) What would have been the amount capitalized by the lessee upon the inception of the lease if:

1. The residual value of $20,000 had been guaranteed by a third party, not the lessee?
2. The residual value of $20,000 had not been guaranteed at all?

(e) On the lessor's books, what would be the amount recorded as the net investment at the inception of the lease, assuming:

1. Zeff Finance had incurred $1,200 of direct costs in processing the lease?
2. The residual value of $20,000 had been guaranteed by a third party?
3. The residual value of $20,000 had not been guaranteed at all?

(f) Suppose the milking equipment's useful life is 20 years. How large would the residual value have to be at the end of 10 years in order for the lessee to qualify for the operating method? (Assume that the residual value would be guaranteed by a third party.) (Hint: The lessee's annual payments will be appropriately reduced as the residual value increases.)

*P21-18 The head office and main branch of the North Central Credit Union has operated in the central business district for almost 50 years. In 1986, new offices were constructed on the same site at a cost of $9.5 million. The new building was opened on January 4, 1987 and was expected to be used for 35 years, at which time it would have a value of approximately $2 million.

In 2002, as the conventional banks began to reconsider merger strategies among themselves, North Central felt the time was right to expand the number of its community branches throughout the province. The development and construction of more branches required significant financing, and North Central looked into selling the building that housed its head office and main branch as a source of cash. On June 29, 2002, Rural Life Insurance Company Ltd. purchased the building (but not the land) for $8 million and immediately entered into a 20-year lease with North Central to lease back the space occupied.

The terms of the lease were as follows.

1. Non-cancellable, with an option to purchase the building at the end of the lease for $1,000,000.
2. An annual rental of $838,380, payable on June 29 each year beginning on June 29, 2002.
3. Rural Life expects to earn a return of 10% on its net investment in the lease, the same as North Central's incremental borrowing rate.
4. North Central is responsible for maintenance, insurance, and property taxes.
5. Estimates of useful life and residual value have not changed appreciably since 1987.

Instructions

(a) Prepare all entries for North Central Credit Union from June 29, 2002 to December 31, 2003. North Central has a calendar year fiscal period.
(b) Assume instead that there was no option to purchase, that $8 million represents the building's fair value on June 29, 2002, and that the lease term was 12 years. Prepare all entries for North Central from June 29, 2002 to December 31, 2003.

CONCEPTUAL CASES

C21-1 On January 1, 2002, Quach Corporation entered into a non-cancellable lease for a machine to be used in its manufacturing operations. The lease transfers ownership of the machine to Quach by the end of the lease term. The term of the lease is eight years. The lease payment made by Quach on January 1, 2002 was one of eight equal annual payments. At the inception of the lease, the criteria established for classification as a capital lease by the lessee were met.

Instructions

(a) What is the theoretical basis for the accounting standard that requires certain long-term leases to be capitalized by the lessee? Do not discuss the specific criteria for classifying a specific lease as a capital lease.
(b) How should Quach account for this lease at its inception and determine the amount to be recorded?
(c) What expenses related to this lease will Quach incur during the first year of the lease, and how will they be determined?
(d) How should Quach report the lease transaction on its December 31, 2002 balance sheet?

C21-2 Novkovic Inc. entered into a lease arrangement with Morgan Leasing Corporation for a particular machine. Morgan's primary business is leasing and it is not a manufacturer or dealer. Novkovic will lease the machine for a period of three years, which is 50% of the machine's economic life. Morgan will take possession of the machine at the end of the initial three-year lease and lease it to another, smaller company that does not need the most current version of the machine. Novkovic does not guarantee any residual value for the machine and will not purchase the machine at the end of the lease term.

Novkovic's incremental borrowing rate is 15%, and the implicit rate in the lease is 14%. Novkovic has no way of knowing the implicit rate used by Morgan. Using either rate, the minimum lease payments' present value is between 90% and 100% of the machine's fair value at the date of the lease agreement.

Novkovic has agreed to pay all executory costs directly and no allowance for these costs is included in the lease payments.

Morgan is reasonably certain that Novkovic will pay all lease payments, and, because Novkovic has agreed to pay all executory costs, there are no important uncertainties regarding costs to be incurred by Morgan. Assume that no indirect costs are involved.

Instructions

(a) With respect to Novkovic (the lessee), answer the following.
   1. What type of lease has been entered into? Explain the reason for your answer.
   2. How should Novkovic calculate the appropriate amount to be recorded for the lease or asset acquired?
   3. What accounts will be created or affected by this transaction and how will the lease or asset and other costs related to the transaction be matched with earnings?
   4. What disclosures must Novkovic make regarding this leased asset?

(b) With respect to Morgan (the lessor), answer the following.
   1. What type of leasing arrangement has been entered into? Explain the reason for your answer.
   2. How should this lease be recorded by Morgan, and how are the appropriate amounts determined?
   3. How should Morgan determine the appropriate amount of earnings to be recognized from each lease payment?
   4. What disclosures must Morgan make regarding this lease?

(AICPA adapted)

C21-3 On January 1, Shinault Corporation, a lessee, entered into three non-cancellable leases for brand-new equipment, Lease L, Lease M, and Lease N. None of the three leases transfers ownership of the equipment to Shinault at the end of the lease term. For each of the three leases, the present value at the beginning of the lease term of the minimum lease payments, excluding that portion of the payments representing executory costs such as insurance, maintenance, and taxes to be paid by the lessor, is 75% of the equipment's fair value.

The following information is peculiar to each lease:
1. Lease L does not contain a bargain purchase option; the lease term is equal to 80% of the equipment's estimated economic life.
2. Lease M contains a bargain purchase option; the lease term is equal to 50% of the equipment's estimated economic life.
3. Lease N does not contain a bargain purchase option; the lease term is equal to 50% of the equipment's estimated economic life.

Instructions

(a) How should Shinault Corporation classify each of the three leases above, and why? Discuss the rationale for your answer.
(b) What amount, if any, should Shinault record as a liability at the lease's inception for each of the leases?
(c) Assuming that the rental payments are made on a straight-line basis, how should Shinault record each rental payment for each of the leases?

(AICPA adapted)

C21-4
Part 1 Capital leases and operating leases are the two classifications of leases described in *CICA Handbook* Section 3065 from the lessee's standpoint.

Instructions

(a) Describe how a capital lease would be accounted for by the lessee both at the inception of the lease and during the first year of the lease, assuming the lease transfers ownership of the property to the lessee by the end of the lease.
(b) Describe how an operating lease would be accounted for by the lessee both at the inception of the lease and during the first year of the lease, assuming equal monthly payments are made by the lessee at the beginning of each month of the lease. Describe the change in accounting, if any, when rental payments are not made on a straight-line basis.

Do not discuss the criteria for distinguishing between capital leases and operating leases.

Part 2 Sales-type leases and direct financing leases are two of the classifications of leases described in *CICA Handbook* Section 3065 from the lessor's standpoint.

Instructions

Compare and contrast a sales-type lease with a direct financing lease as follows:
(a) Gross investment in the lease.
(b) Amortization of unearned interest revenue.

(c) Manufacturer's or dealer's profit.

(d) Initial direct costs.

Do not discuss the criteria for distinguishing between the leases described above and operating leases.

(AICPA adapted)

C21-5 Brayes Corporation is a diversified company with nationwide interests in commercial real estate developments, banking, copper mining, and metal fabrication. The company has offices and operating locations in major cities throughout Canada. Corporate headquarters for Brayes Corporation is located in a metropolitan area of a western province, and executives connected with various phases of company operations travel extensively. Corporate management is currently evaluating the feasibility of acquiring a business aircraft that can be used by company executives to expedite business travel to areas not adequately served by commercial airlines. Proposals for either leasing or purchasing a suitable aircraft have been analysed, and the leasing proposal was considered to be more desirable.

The proposed lease agreement involves a twin-engine turboprop Viking that has a fair value of $1 million. This plane would be leased for a period of 10 years beginning January 1, 2002. The lease agreement is cancellable only upon accidental destruction of the plane. An annual lease payment of $141,700 is due on January 1 of each year; the first payment is to be made on January 1, 2002. Maintenance operations are strictly scheduled by the lessor, and Brayes Corporation will pay for these services as they are performed. Estimated annual maintenance costs are $6,900. The lessor will pay all insurance premiums and local property taxes, which amount to a combined total of $4,000 annually and are included in the annual lease payment of $141,780. Upon expiration of the 10-year lease, Brayes Corporation can purchase the Viking for $44,440. The plane's estimated useful life is 15 years, and its value in the used plane market is estimated to be $100,000 after 10 years. The residual value probably will never be less than $75,000 if the engines are overhauled and maintained as prescribed by the manufacturer. If the purchase option is not exercised, possession of the plane will revert to the lessor, and there is no provision for renewing the lease agreement beyond its termination on December 31, 2011.

Brayes Corporation can borrow $1 million under a 10-year term loan agreement at an annual interest rate of 12%. The lessor's implicit interest rate is not expressly stated in the lease agreement, but this rate appears to be approximately 8% based on 10 net rental payments of $137,780 per year and the initial market value of $1 million for the plane. On January 1, 2002, the present value of all net rental payments and the purchase option of $44,440 is $888,890 using the 12% interest rate. The present value of all net rental payments and the $44,440 purchase option on January 1, 2002 is $1,022,226 using the 8% interest rate implicit in the lease agreement. The financial vice-president of Brayes Corporation has established that this lease agreement is a capital lease as defined in *CICA Handbook* Section 3065 on "Leases."

Instructions

(a) What is the appropriate amount that Brayes Corporation should recognize for the leased aircraft on its balance sheet after the lease is signed?

(b) Without prejudice to your answer in part (a), assume that the annual lease payment is $141,780 as stated in the question, that the appropriate capitalized amount for the leased aircraft is $1 million on January 1, 2002, and that the interest rate is 9%. How will the lease be reported in the December 31, 2002 balance sheet and related income statement? (Ignore any income tax implications.)

(CMA adapted)

*C21-6 On January 1, 2002, Dyer Corporation sold equipment for cash and leased it back. As seller-lessee, Dyer retained the right to substantially all of the remaining use of the equipment.

The term of the lease is eight years. There is a gain on the sale portion of the transaction. The lease portion is classified appropriately as a capital lease.

Instructions

(a) What is the theoretical basis for requiring lessees to capitalize certain long-term leases? Do not discuss the specific criteria for classifying a lease as a capital lease.

(b) 1. How should Dyer account for the sale portion of the sale-leaseback transaction at January 1, 2002?

2. How should Dyer account for the leaseback portion of the sale-leaseback transaction at January 1, 2002?

(c) How should Dyer account for the gain on the sale portion of the sale-leaseback transaction during the first year of the lease? Why?

(AICPA adapted)

*C21-7 On December 31, 2001, Truttman Corp. sold six-month-old equipment at fair value and leased it back. There was a loss on the sale. Truttman pays all insurance, maintenance, and taxes on the equipment. The lease provides for eight equal annual payments, beginning December 31, 2002, with a present value equal to 85% of the equipment's fair value and sales price. The lease's term is equal to 80% of the equipment's useful life. There is no provision for Truttman to reacquire ownership of the equipment at the end of the lease term.

Instructions

(a) 1. Why is it important to compare an equipment's fair value with the present value of the lease payments and its useful life to the lease term?
   2. Evaluate Truttman's leaseback of the equipment in terms of each of the three criteria for determining a capital lease.

(b) How should Truttman account for the sale portion of the sale-leaseback transaction at December 31, 2001?

(c) How should Truttman report the leaseback portion of the sale-leaseback transaction on its December 31, 2002 balance sheet?

Using Your Judgement

··

FINANCIAL REPORTING PROBLEM: MARK'S WORK WEARHOUSE LTD.

Instructions

Through the SEDAR website (www.sedar.com) or other source of your choosing, access the financial statements of Mark's Work Wearhouse Ltd. (MWWL) for its year ended January 27, 2001. Refer to the financial statements and notes to the financial statements and answer the following questions.

(a) Identify all lease arrangements indicated in the company's financial statements and notes. Indicate whether MWWL is the lessor or the lessee. For each separate lease arrangement, indicate the title and balances of the related lease accounts included on the financial statements.

(b) Has MWWL provided all the lease disclosures as required by the accounting standards?

(c) Calculate the following ratios for MWWL based on the 2001 published financial statements:

    1. debt-to-equity ratio

    2. capital asset turnover ratio

    3. total asset turnover ratio

    4. return on investment (net income to total assets)

(d) Assume you would like to compare MWWL's financial statements with those of competitors who purchase the buildings in which their businesses are housed and who acquire all necessary equipment outright. To do this, you will need to capitalize the operating lease obligations reported by MWWL.

    1. What information do you need to capitalize operating lease commitments?

    2. Provide an estimate of the amount that would have to be capitalized for MWWL, stating your assumptions.

    3. Recalculate the ratios in (c) above.

    4. Compare the recalculated ratios with the original results and comment on the differences.

COMPARATIVE ANALYSIS CASE

Air Canada versus Canada 3000 Inc.

The accounting for operating leases is a controversial issue. Many contend that firms employing operating leases are using significantly more assets and are more highly leveraged than indicated by the balance sheet alone. As a result, analysts often use footnote disclosures to "constructively capitalize" operating lease obligations. One way to do so is to increase a firm's assets and liabilities by the present value of all future minimum rental payments.

Instructions

Go to the Digital Tool and/or SEDAR website (www.sedar.com) and using the most recent Air Canada and Canada 3000 Inc. financial statements, answer the following questions.

(a) What types of leases are used by Air Canada and Canada 3000 and what assets are leased?

(b) How long-term are these leases?

(c) What amount did each company report as its future minimum annual rental commitments under capital leases? operating leases?

(d) What does "leveraged" mean in the opening paragraph above?

(e) Calculate the capital asset turnover and debt-to-equity ratios for Canada 3000 and Air Canada at the most recent year end based on the balance sheets provided.

(f) Using an 8% discount rate, estimate the capitalized value of the off-balance-sheet operating leases for each company.

(g) Incorporate the capitalized values from part (f) and recalculate the ratios in part (e). Comment on the results.

RESEARCH CASES

Case 1

Instructions

Contact an automobile dealership and obtain all information necessary about the out-of-pocket costs of purchasing a specific model of car assuming you were to pay cash for the purchase. Also acquire details of the costs associated with leasing the same model car. Answer the following questions:

(a) What terms and conditions are associated with the lease—that is, lease term, residual values and whether they are guaranteed by the lessee or not, the lessor's implicit interest rate, purchase options, etc.?

(b) What cash flows are associated with the lease?

(c) Which do you think is the better deal? Briefly explain.

Case 2

Present day U.S. and Canadian accounting standards for leases were developed prior to agreement on the conceptual frameworks adopted in the two countries and as set out in *CICA Handbook* Section 1000. Recently there has been a call for new lease standards based on asset and liability definitions agreed upon in these frameworks. In 1996, the FASB and other G4+1 organizations published a Special Report, *Accounting for Leases: A New Approach*, authored principally by Warren McGregor of Australia. This report called for the capitalization of all non-cancellable leases with a term longer than one year.

Dennis Monson, in *Accounting Horizons* (September 2001), provides a commentary on "The Conceptual Framework and Accounting for Leases."

Instructions

(a) Identify *Handbook* Section 1000 definitions of assets and liabilities.

(b) Read Dennis Monson's commentary and respond to the following questions:

1. What is the difference between a "financial components" approach and a "whole asset" approach?

2. What general method does Monson use in trying to decide which approach is preferred?

3. Which method does Monson support? Explain.

INTERNATIONAL REPORTING CASE

As discussed in the chapter, U.S. and Canadian GAAP for leases allow companies to use off-balance-sheet financing for the purchase of operating assets. International accounting standards are similar to North American GAAP in that under these rules, companies can keep leased assets and obligations off their balance sheets. However, under *International Accounting Standard No. 17 (IAS 17)*, leases are capitalized based on the subjective evaluation of whether the risks and rewards of ownership are transferred in the lease. In Japan, virtually all leases are treated as operating leases. Furthermore, unlike U.S., Canadian, and IAS standards, the Japanese rules do not require disclosure of future minimum lease payments.

Presented are financial data for three major airlines that lease some part of their aircraft fleet. American Airlines prepares its financial statements under U.S. GAAP and leases approximately 27% of its fleet. KLM Royal Dutch Airlines and Japan Airlines (JAL) present their statements in accordance with their home country GAAP (Netherlands and Japan respectively). KLM leases about 22% of its aircraft, and JAL leases approximately 50% of its fleet.

Financial Statement Data	American Airlines (millions of U.S. dollars)	KLM Royal Dutch Airlines (millions of guilders)	Japan Airlines (millions of yen)
As reported			
Assets	20,915	19,205	2,042,761
Liabilities	14,699	13,837	1,857,800
Income	985	606	4,619
Estimated impact of capitalizing operating leases on:[1]			
Assets	5,897	1,812	244,063
Liabilities	6,886	1,776	265,103
Income	(143)	24	(9,598)

[1] Based on *Apples to Apples: Global Airlines: Flight to Quality* (New York: N.Y.: Morgan Stanley Dean Witter, October 1998).

Instructions

(a) Using the "as reported" data for each airline, calculate the rate of return on assets and the debt-to-assets ratio. Compare these companies on the basis of this analysis.

(b) Adjust the "as reported" numbers of the three companies for the effects of non-capitalization of leases and then redo the analysis in part (a).

(c) The following statement was overheard in the library: "Non-capitalization of operating leases is not that big a deal for profitability analysis based on rate of return on assets, since the operating lease payments (under operating lease accounting) are about the same as the sum of the interest and amortization expense under capital lease treatment." Do you agree? Explain.

(d) Since the accounting for leases worldwide is similar, does your analysis above suggest there is a need for an improved accounting standard for leases? (Hint: Reflect on comparability of information about these companies' leasing activities, when leasing is more prevalent in one country than in others.)

ETHICS CASE

Cuby Corporation entered into a lease agreement for 10 photocopy machines for its corporate headquarters. The lease agreement qualifies as an operating lease in all terms except there is a bargain purchase option. After the five-year lease term, the corporation can purchase each copier for $1,000, when the anticipated market value is $2,500.

Glenn Beckert, the financial vice-president, thinks the financial statements must recognize the lease agreement as a capital lease because of the bargain purchase agreement. The controller, Tareek Kessinger, disagrees: "Although I don't know much about the copiers themselves, there is a way to avoid recording the lease liability." She argues that the corporation might claim that copier technology advances rapidly and that by the end of the lease term the machines will most likely not be worth the $1,000 bargain price.

Instructions

Answer the following questions:

(a) What ethical issue is at stake?

(b) Should the controller's argument be accepted if she does not really know much about copier technology? Would it make a difference if the controller were knowledgeable about the pace of change in copier technology?

(c) What should Beckert do?

CHAPTER 22

Accounting Changes and Error Analysis

LEARNING OBJECTIVES

After studying this chapter, you should be able to:

1. Identify the types of accounting changes.

2. Describe a change in accounting policy.

3. Understand how to account for retroactive-with-restatement type of accounting changes.

4. Understand how to account for retroactive-without-restatement type of accounting changes.

5. Understand how to account for prospective-type accounting changes.

6. Describe the accounting for changes in estimates.

7. Describe the accounting for correction of errors.

8. Identify changes in a reporting entity.

9. Identify economic motives for changing accounting methods.

10. Analyse the effect of errors.

Preview of Chapter 22

This chapter discusses various types of accounting changes and error corrections and how they are reported in financial statements. In addition, it provides a framework for the analysis and calculations required for correcting errors. The chapter's content and organization are as follows:

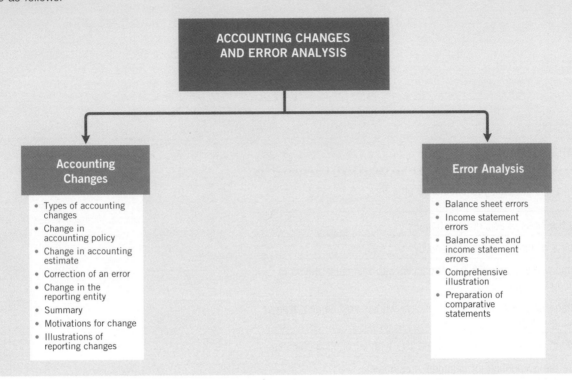

ACCOUNTING CHANGES AND ERROR ANALYSIS

Accounting Changes
- Types of accounting changes
- Change in accounting policy
- Change in accounting estimate
- Correction of an error
- Change in the reporting entity
- Summary
- Motivations for change
- Illustrations of reporting changes

Error Analysis
- Balance sheet errors
- Income statement errors
- Balance sheet and income statement errors
- Comprehensive illustration
- Preparation of comparative statements

ACCOUNTING CHANGES

Financial press readers regularly see headlines about companies that report accounting changes and related events. Why do these accounting changes occur? First, the accounting profession may mandate a new accounting method or standard. For example, major revisions to the accounting standards for income taxes and employee future benefits became effective in 2000. Second, changing economic conditions may cause a company to change its methods of accounting. Third, changes in technology and in operations may require a company to revise the service lives, amortization method, or expected residual value of amortizable assets. Most Canadian telecommunications companies recently changed their estimates of useful lives as well as their amortization methods due to changes in the competitive (regulatory) environment and in technology.

The accountant must also make changes when accounting errors are discovered. How should such errors be corrected and disclosed so that the financial information's usefulness is enhanced?

Before *CICA Handbook* Section 1506, "Accounting Changes," was issued in 1980, companies had considerable flexibility and were able to use alternative accounting treatments for essentially equivalent situations. When steel companies changed their methods of amortizing plant assets from accelerated to a straight-line basis, the change's effect was presented in many different ways. The cumulative difference between the amortization charges that had been recorded and those that would have been recorded under the new method could have been reported in the income statement of the period of the change. Or the change could have been ignored, and the unamortized asset balance simply amortized on a straight-line basis in the future. Or companies could simply have restated the prior periods on the basis that the straight-line approach had always been used. When alternative methods exist to account for similar events, comparability of the statements between periods and between companies is diminished and useful historical trend data are obscured.

Types of Accounting Changes

The profession has established categories for the different types of changes that occur in practice. The three types of accounting changes identified in Section 1506 of the *CICA Handbook* on "Accounting Changes" are:

1. **Change in an accounting policy.** A change from one generally accepted accounting principle to another generally accepted accounting principle: for example, a change in the method of amortization from a double-declining to a straight-line method for plant assets.

2. **Change in an accounting estimate.** A change that occurs as the result of new information or as additional experience is acquired. An example is a change in the estimate of the service lives of assets subject to amortization.

3. **Correction of an error in prior period financial statements.** Errors occur as a result of mathematical mistakes, mistakes in applying accounting principles, or oversight or misuse of facts that existed at the time financial statements were prepared. An example is the incorrect application of the retail inventory method for determining the final inventory value.

In addition, *Handbook* Sections 1581 on "Business Combinations" and 3475 on "Discontinued Operations" require specific accounting and reporting when the components making up the reporting entity change.

4. **Change in reporting entity.** A change resulting from a business combination or the disposal or discontinuation of a distinguishable component of an entity making up a line of business: for example, the acquisition of a subsidiary.

Changes are classified into these four categories because the individual characteristics of each category necessitate different methods of recognition in the financial statements. Each of these items is discussed separately to investigate its unusual characteristics, to determine how each should be accounted for, and show how the information should be reported in comparative statements.[1]

Change in an Accounting Policy

A change in accounting policy involves a change **from one generally accepted accounting principle or the methods used in their application to another**. For example, a company might change the basis of inventory costing from average cost to FIFO. Or it might change the method of amortization on plant assets from accelerated to straight-line, or vice versa. Another change might be from a policy of not capitalizing interest on self-constructed assets to one where interest is capitalized.

Each circumstance must be carefully examined to ensure that a change in policy has actually occurred. **A change in accounting policy does not result from the adop-**

> **OBJECTIVE 1**
> ....
> Identify the types of accounting changes.

UNDERLYING CONCEPTS
While the qualitative characteristic of usefulness may be enhanced by changes in accounting, the characteristics of comparability and consistency may be adversely affected.

> **OBJECTIVE 2**
> ....
> Describe a change in accounting policy.

[1] Clarence Byrd, Ida Chen and Heather Chapman report in *Financial Reporting in Canada—2000* [CICA] that 87 of the 200 surveyed companies in 1999 reported a change in accounting policy. Although a change in accounting estimate is not required to be disclosed, 3 of the 200 companies reported such a change. The correction of an error is rare, with only one of the survey companies in the 1996 to 1999 period reporting this type of accounting change. Business combinations were reported by 102 companies and discontinued operations by 44 of the surveyed companies in 1999.

tion of a new policy that recognizes events that have occurred for the first time or that were previously immaterial. For example, when an amortization method that is adopted for newly acquired plant assets is different from the method or methods used for previously recorded assets of a similar type, a change in accounting policy has not occurred. Certain marketing expenditures that were previously immaterial and expensed in the period incurred may become material and acceptably deferred and amortized without a change in accounting policy occurring.

Adopting a different policy necessitated by events or transactions clearly different in substance from those previously occurring would also not be considered a change in accounting policy. For example, if a company changes from the direct write-off method to the allowance method of accounting for bad debts because of changing from primarily cash-based sales to sales on account, this would not be recognized as a change in accounting policy. The method used previously was appropriate for the circumstances that existed then; the new policy is appropriate for the changed circumstances.

Finally, if the accounting policy previously followed was not acceptable, or if the policy was applied incorrectly, the change to a generally accepted accounting policy is considered a correction of an error. A switch from the cash basis of accounting to the accrual basis is considered an error correction. If a company (incorrectly) deducted residual values when calculating double-declining amortization on tangible capital assets and later recalculates the amortization without deducting the estimated residual value, the change is considered an error correction.

Three approaches have been suggested for reporting changes in accounting policies in the accounts:

INTERNATIONAL INSIGHT

In the U.S., the current or "catch-up" method is used to account for changes in accounting principles. The cumulative effect is recognized on the income statement between extraordinary items and net income.

1. **Retroactively.** Retroactive treatment requires calculating the new method's cumulative effect on the financial statements at the beginning of the period as if it had always been used. A retroactive adjustment of the financial statements is then made, recasting prior years' financial statements on a basis consistent with the newly adopted policy. Advocates of this position argue that only by restating prior periods can changes in accounting principles and methods lead to comparable financial statements. If this approach is not used, the year previous to the change will be on the old method; the year of the change will report the entire cumulative adjustment in income; and the year following will present financial statements on the new basis without the change's cumulative effect. Consistency is considered essential in providing meaningful earnings-trend data and other financial relationships necessary to evaluate the business.

2. **Currently.** The new method's cumulative effect on the financial statements at the beginning of the period is calculated. This adjustment is then reported in the current year's income statement, most likely as a special item between the captions "Extraordinary items" and "Net income." Advocates of this position argue that restating financial statements for prior years results in a loss of confidence by investors in financial reports. How will a present or prospective investor react when told that the earnings reported five years ago are now entirely different? Restatement, if permitted, also might upset many contractual and other arrangements that were based on the old figures. For example, profit-sharing arrangements based on the old policy might have to be recalculated and completely new distributions made, which might create numerous legal problems. Many practical difficulties also exist: the cost of restatement may be excessive, or restatement may be impossible based on data available.

3. **Prospectively.** (in the future). With prospective treatment, previously reported results remain; no change is made. Opening balances are not adjusted, and no attempt is made to allocate charges or credits to past periods. Instead, the new policy is adopted for the current and future periods only. Advocates of this position argue that once management presents financial statements based on acceptable accounting principles and methods, they are final; management cannot change

prior periods by adopting new principles and methods. According to this line of reasoning, the cumulative adjustment in the current year is not appropriate, because such an approach includes amounts that have little or no relationship to the current year's income or economic events.

Handbook Section 1506 settled the question of which approach is best for a change in accounting policy by requiring retroactive treatment, except in circumstances where the amount of the retroactive adjustment cannot be reasonably determined.

Retroactive-with-Restatement Accounting Method

The general requirement when there is a choice of two or more appropriate principles or methods used in their application, and a change is made, is the **retroactive method with restatement of prior periods**. This is applied as follows:

1. The newly adopted accounting policy is applied retroactively, along with any income tax effects.

2. Financial statement amounts for prior periods included for comparative purposes are restated to give effect to the new accounting policy.

3. A description of the change and its effect on the current and prior periods' financial statements is disclosed.

Illustration: To illustrate the retroactive-with-restatement method, assume that Lang Ltd. decided at the beginning of 2003 to change from the declining balance tax (CCA) method of amortization to the straight-line method for financial reporting on its plant and equipment. Lang has been using the same method of amortization as permitted by the *Income Tax Act* (Class 8, 20% rate), but has decided to switch to the straight-line method used by 90% of the companies in its industry. The assets originally cost $120,000 in 2001 and have an estimated useful life of 10 years and a residual value of $10,000. The data assumed for this example are provided in Illustration 22-1.

Year	CCA Amortization	Straight-Line Amortization	Difference	Tax Effect 40%	Effect on Income (net of tax)
2001	$12,000	$11,000	$1,000	$400	$600
2002	21,600	$11,000	$10,600	$4,240	$6,360
Cumulative effect			$11,600	$4,640	$6,960
2003	$17,280	$11,000	$6,280	$2,512	$3,768

The entry made to record this change in accounting policy in 2003 is:

Accumulated Amortization	11,600	
Future Income Tax Liability		4,640
Retained Earnings—Cumulative Effect of Change in Accounting Policy		6,960

The debit of $11,600 to Accumulated Amortization is the excess of the CCA amortization over the straight-line amortization for the years preceding the current year. The credit of $4,640 to the Future Income Tax Liability reflects the interperiod tax allocation adjustment for the difference between the tax and book values of the plant and equipment assets at the end of 2002. The cumulative effect on Retained Earnings is the difference between the reduced amortization expenses for 2001 and 2002 ($11,600) and the increase in income tax expense recognized ($4,640) because of the increase in the reported incomes for the same two years.

The information presented in the **original** income statements and statements of retained earnings prior to the changes for 2001 and 2002 is provided in Illustration 22-2.

ILLUSTRATION 22-2
Summarized Statements Originally
Issued for 2001 and 2002

	2002	2001
Income before extraordinary item (assumed)	$120,000	$111,000
Extraordinary item (assumed)	(30,000)	–0–
Net income	$90,000	$111,000
Earnings per share		
Basic earnings per share (100,000 shares)		
Income before extraordinary item	$1.20	$1.11
Extraordinary item	(0.30)	–0–
Net income	$0.90	$1.11
Retained earnings, opening	$450,000	$389,000
Add: net income	90,000	111,000
	540,000	500,000
Less: dividends (assumed)	56,200	50,000
Retained earnings, ending	$483,800	$450,000

When Lang issues its 2003 financial statements with comparative numbers for 2002, the 2002 financial statements must reflect the straight-line amortization as if Lang had always used the straight-line method. The comparative income and retained earnings statements issued in 2003 would appear as follows.

ILLUSTRATION 22-3
Summarized Statements Issued
for 2003 and 2002 with 2002
Restated

	2003	2002 (restated)
Income before extraordinary item	$135,000	$126,360*
Extraordinary item	–0–	(30,000)
Net income	$135,000	$ 96,360
Earnings per share		
Basic earnings per share (100,000 shares)		
Income before extraordinary item	$1.35	$1.26
Extraordinary item	–0–	(0.30)
Net income	$1.35	$0.96

	2003	2002 (restated)
Retained Earnings:		
Balance at beginning of year		
As previously reported	$483,800	$450,000
Retroactive change in accounting policy (Note 1)	6,960	600
As restated	490,760	450,600
Net income	135,000	96,360
	625,760	546,960
Dividends	63,000	56,200
Balance at end of year	$562,760	$490,760

Note 1—Change in Amortization Method for Plant Assets. In 2003, amortization of plant and equipment is calculated by use of the straight-line method. In prior years, beginning in 2001, amortization of plant and equipment was calculated by the declining-balance method. The straight-line method has been applied retroactively to equipment acquisitions of prior years. The effect of the change in 2003 was to increase net income by $3,768 (or 3.8 cents per share). The 2002 comparative income statement has been retroactively restated to reflect the change's effect on 2002 net income (an increase of $6,360, or approximately six cents per share). Income for 2002 and prior periods would have been increased by $6,960 or seven cents per share.

*restated ($120,000 + $6,360)

The **restated** 2002 income statement reports $10,600 less amortization expense and $4,240 more income tax expense than previously reported for 2002, resulting in an income $6,360 higher than originally reported in 2002. Earnings per share are also restated.

The adjustments to the statement of retained earnings are more complex. For 2002 (restated), the previously reported opening retained earnings balance must be adjusted for the effects on income **prior to January 1, 2002**. In this case, the cumulative adjustment relating to periods prior to January 1, 2002 is limited to $600, the after-tax effect on 2001 income. In some situations, the cumulative effect relates to many prior years. The restated opening retained earnings for 2002 of $450,600 is, therefore, the balance that would have been reported if Lang had used the straight-line method originally. The revised net income for 2002 is added to this and the 2002 dividends are deducted to give the adjusted retained earnings at the end of 2002.

For the 2003 statement of retained earnings, the previously reported opening retained earnings balance (i.e., 2002 ending balance) must be adjusted for the effects on income (and therefore retained earnings) prior to January 1, 2003. The cumulative adjustment at this date is $6,960.

Note that only the financial statements presented for comparison purposes are restated to show the change's effect and that any change attributable to those periods prior to the earliest comparative period presented is shown as an adjustment to beginning retained earnings. Other balance sheet accounts affected by the change should also be restated.

Retroactive-without-Restatement Accounting Method

Retroactively restating individual prior years' financial statements requires information that may, in many cases, be unreasonably difficult to obtain, even though the cumulative effect can be determined. For example, assume a company changed its method of accounting for post-retirement benefits other than pensions as a result of new accounting standards introduced for 2000. Although newly issued recommendations should not be considered of retroactive effect, retroactive adjustment may be appropriate and is often encouraged. Assume that in the past, the company recognized payments made for medical premiums for retirees as expense as the payments were made—a pay-as-you-go method. Under the new standard, the expense is required to be estimated and charged to the period in which the employees earn the entitlement to the future benefit. This is an accrual approach.

The company may wish to apply this change in principle retroactively. While this new standard's cumulative effect can be calculated, the effect on individual prior periods may not be reasonably determined. In such cases, the *Handbook* permits retroactive adjustment without restating prior periods' financial statements.

Illustration: To illustrate the retroactive-without-restatement method, assume that Denson Corporation has accounted for its pensioner medical benefits on a pay-as-you-go basis. In 2000, the company changed to the accrual method required under the new accounting standards in *Handbook* Section 3461. The cumulative accrued medical benefits earned by employees but unrecognized in the accounts to December 31, 1999 were $220,000. For tax purposes (assume a 40% rate), only expenditures made for the medical premiums are tax deductible. Illustration 22-4 sets out the information for analysis.

Year	Cost of Medical Benefits Earned by Employees (accrual method)	Premiums Paid for Medicine Benefits (Pay-as-you-go-method)	Difference	Tax Effect 40%	Effect on Net Incomes
Prior to 2000	$220,000	$75,000	$145,000	$58,000	$87,000
In 2000	$ 32,000	$15,000	$ 17,000	$ 6,800	$10,200

OBJECTIVE 4
Understand how to account for retroactive-without-restatement type of accounting changes.

ILLUSTRATION 22-4
Effect of Change in Accounting Policy to Comply with Section 3461

The entry to record the change in 2000 is:

Future Income Tax Asset	58,000	
Retained Earnings—Change in Accounting Policy	87,000	
Accrued Post-retirement Medical Benefits Liability		145,000

The Accrued Post-retirement Medical Benefits Liability account is recognized effective January 1, 2000, representing the accrued but previously unrecognized obligation and expense. The Future Income Tax Asset account is used to recognize interperiod tax allocation because as the medical premiums are paid in the future, Denson can deduct these amounts in calculating taxable income. If the company had used the accrual method from the beginning in accounting for this employee benefit, retained earnings would have been $87,000 less than the amounts reported in its financial statements at January 1, 2000.

Because it was not practicable to determine this policy change's effect on each previous year, the change's cumulative effect is reported only as an adjustment to the opening balance of Retained Earnings for the current year, along with the related income tax effect, as illustrated below.

ILLUSTRATION 22-5
Reporting a Change in
Accounting Policy without
Restatement

Statement of Retained Earnings

	2000	1999
Opening balance, as previously reported (assumed)	$1,696,000	$1,600,000
Less: Adjustment for the cumulative effect on prior periods of the change in accounting policy, net of income tax of $58,000 (Note A)	87,000	—
Opening balance, as restated	1,609,000	1,600,000
Net income (assumed)	120,000	96,000
Balance, end-of-year	$1,729,000	$1,696,000

Note A—Change in Accounting Policy: Effective January 1, 2000, the Company changed its method of accounting for post-retirement medical benefits for its employees to comply with new *CICA Handbook* Section 3461. The costs of medical benefits are now accrued as earned by employees. Prior period financial statements have not been restated for the $87,000 after-tax additional costs recognized. The effect of the change in accounting policy on 2000 net income is a reduction of $10,200 net of tax.

IAS NOTE

IAS 8, unlike the Canadian standard, requires disclosure of the reason for a change in accounting policy.

Note that this example is similar to the case involving restatement of prior periods' financial statements. The journal entries to record the accounting change are similar since the change's cumulative effect on retained earnings is recorded as an adjustment to beginning Retained Earnings. The only difference between retroactive adjustment **with restatement** and **without restatement** is in the financial statements for prior periods issued for comparative purposes. **Restatement** provides financial statement readers with amounts for prior periods that would have been reported had the new policy been in effect originally. On the other hand, retroactive adjustment **without restatement** leaves the comparative financial statements as originally reported and presents the change's cumulative effect as an adjustment to beginning Retained Earnings. In both examples, as required by Section 1506 of the *Handbook*, the change's effect on the current year's income is disclosed in the notes.

Prospective Accounting Method

OBJECTIVE 5

Understand how to account for prospective-type accounting changes.

Retroactively applying an accounting policy change may not be possible in some cases because it would be extremely difficult to obtain the necessary financial data. This situation could arise, for example, when adopting a new *Handbook* recommendation or legislative requirement of such a nature that the necessary accounting change's cumulative effect could not be determined without incurring unreasonable cost or using imprecise data. In these rare circumstances, it is permissible to make the required or desired accounting change in the current year without restating the beginning Retained Earnings.

As an example, suppose that a company changes its policy on capitalization of interest to begin capitalizing interest on certain long-term construction projects. Companies would find it extremely difficult to determine the adjusted cost and accumulated amortization necessary to apply the method retroactively. In these cases, the *Handbook* permits prospective application of the accounting change. That is, the new accounting policy would be applied in the current and future years.

Change in an Accounting Estimate

To prepare financial statements, you must estimate the effects of future conditions and events. Future conditions and events and their effects cannot be perceived with certainty; therefore, estimating requires the exercise of judgement. Accounting estimates will change as new events occur, as more experience is acquired, or as additional information is obtained. The following are examples of items that require estimates:

OBJECTIVE 6

Describe the accounting for changes in estimates.

1. uncollectible receivables
2. inventory obsolescence
3. useful lives and residual values of assets
4. periods benefited by deferred costs
5. liabilities for warranty costs and income taxes
6. recoverable mineral reserves

The effects of changes in estimates are handled prospectively.[2] That is, no changes are made to previously reported results. Changes in estimates are viewed as **normal recurring corrections and adjustments**—the natural result of the accounting process—and retroactive treatment is prohibited. Opening balances are not adjusted, and no attempt is made to "catch up" for prior periods. Financial statements of prior periods are not restated. Instead, the effects of all changes in estimate are accounted for in (1) the period of change if the change affects that period only or (2) the period of change and future periods if the change affects both.

The circumstances related to a change in estimate are different from those related to a change in accounting policy. If changes in estimates were handled on a retroactive or catch-up basis, continual adjustments of prior years' incomes would occur. It seems proper to accept the view that because new conditions or circumstances exist, the revision fits the new situation and should be handled in the current and future periods.

IAS NOTE

IAS 8 and Section 1506 agree on the accounting treatment for changes in estimates, but IAS 8 requires disclosing the change's nature and amount, if material.

Illustration.   To illustrate the accounting for a change in estimate, Underwriter Labs Inc. purchased a building for $300,000 that was originally estimated to have a useful life of 15 years and no residual value. Amortization has been recorded for five years on a straight-line basis. On January 1, 2003, the useful life estimate is revised so that the asset is considered to have a total life of 25 years. For simplicity, assume the useful life for financial reporting and tax purposes is the same. The accounts at the beginning of the sixth year are as follows:

Building	$300,000
Less: Accumulated amortization—building (5 × $20,000)	100,000
Book value of building, January 1, 2003	$200,000

ILLUSTRATION 22-6
Book Value after Five Years' Amortization

The entry to record amortization for 2003 is:

Amortization Expense	10,000	
Accumulated Amortization—Building		10,000

The $10,000 amortization charge is calculated as follows:

$$\text{Amortization charge} = \frac{\text{Book value of asset} - \text{residual value}}{\text{Remaining service life}} = \frac{\$200,000 - \$\text{-}0\text{-}}{25 \text{ years} - 5 \text{ years}} = \$10,000$$

ILLUSTRATION 22-7
Amortization after Change in Estimate

Because changes in estimates are considered normal and recurring events in the accounting process, there are no disclosure requirements for such changes.

It is sometimes difficult to differentiate between a change in an estimate and a change in an accounting policy. Assume that a company changes from deferring and amortizing certain marketing costs to recording them as an expense as incurred because

INTERNATIONAL INSIGHT

In most nations, changes in accounting estimates are treated prospectively. International differences occur in the degree of disclosure required.

---

[2] *CICA Handbook*, Section 1506, par. .25.

future benefits of these costs have become doubtful. Is this a change in policy or a change in estimate? **In cases when it is unclear whether a change in policy or a change in estimate has occurred, the change should be considered a change in estimate.** The *CICA Handbook* suggests that a change attributed to "changed circumstances, experience or new information" should be treated as a change in estimate.[3]

Correction of an Error in Prior Period Financial Statements

> **OBJECTIVE 7**
> ....
> Describe the accounting for correction of errors.

Handbook Section 1506 also discusses how a correction of an error should be handled in the financial statements. No business, large or small, is immune from errors. The risk of material errors, however, may be reduced through installing good internal controls and applying sound accounting procedures.

The following are examples of accounting errors.

1. A change from an accounting policy that is not generally accepted to an accounting policy that is acceptable. The rationale adopted is that the prior periods were incorrectly presented because an improper accounting policy was applied. Example: a change from the cash basis of accounting to the accrual basis.

2. Mathematical mistakes that result from adding, subtracting, and so on. Example: the incorrect totalling of the inventory count sheets in calculating the inventory value.

3. Changes in estimates that occur because of a misinterpretation or misrepresentation of information. Example: correcting for the previous adoption of a clearly unrealistic amortization rate.

4. An oversight, such as failing to accrue or defer certain expenses and revenues at the end of the period or failing to use residual value in calculating the amortization base for the straight-line approach.

5. A misappropriation of assets. Example: correcting previous years' financial statements because inventory theft was discovered.

IAS NOTE

IAS 8 permits an alternative, usually where a company's comparative statements are required to agree with those previously issued. In this case, a current year adjustment is made to income, with additional disclosures required.

As soon as they are discovered, errors must be corrected by proper entries in the accounts and reflection in the financial statements. **The profession requires that corrections of errors in prior period financial statements be accounted for retroactively in the year in which the error is discovered, and be reported in the financial statements as an adjustment to the beginning balance of retained earnings.** If comparative statements are presented, the prior statements affected should be restated to correct the error. The disclosures need not be repeated in the financial statements of subsequent periods.

Illustration: In 2002, the bookkeeper for Selectric Corporation discovered that in 2001 the company failed to record in the accounts $20,000 of amortization expense on a newly constructed building. Capital cost allowance was correctly included in the tax return. Because of this timing difference, reported net income for 2001 was $150,000 and taxable income was $130,000. The following entries were made for income taxes in 2001, assuming a 40% tax rate.

Current Income Tax Expense	52,000	
Income Tax Payable		52,000
Future Income Tax Expense	8,000	
Future Income Tax Liability		8,000

As a result of the $20,000 amortization error in 2001:

Amortization expense (2001) was understated	$20,000
Accumulated amortization is understated	20,000
Income tax expense (2001) was overstated	
($20,000 × 40%)	8,000
Net income (2001) was overstated	12,000
Future income tax liability is overstated	
($20,000 × 40%)	8,000

---

[3] *Ibid.*, par. .23.

The entry made in 2002 to correct for the omission of $20,000 of amortization in 2001, assuming the books for 2001 have been closed, is:

Retained Earnings	12,000	
Future Income Tax Liability	8,000	
Accumulated Amortization—Buildings		20,000

The journal entry to record the error correction is the same whether single-period or comparative financial statements are prepared; however, presentation on the financial statements will differ. If single-period financial statements are presented, the error is reported as an adjustment to the opening balance of retained earnings of the period in which the error is discovered, as reported in Illustration 22-8.

ILLUSTRATION 22-8
Reporting an Error—Single-Period Financial Statements

Retained earnings, January 1, 2002		
As previously reported		$350,000
Correction of an error (amortization)	$20,000	
Less: Applicable income tax reduction	8,000	(12,000)
Restated balance of retained earnings, January 1, 2002		338,000
Add: Net income 2002		400,000
Retained earnings, December 31, 2002		$738,000

If comparative financial statements are prepared, adjustments are made to correct the amounts for all affected accounts reported in the statements for all periods reported. The data for each year being presented should be restated to the correct basis, and any cumulative adjustment should be made to the opening balance of retained earnings for the earliest period being reported. This is exactly the same as the previously illustrated retroactive-with-restatement treatment for a change in accounting policy. For example, in the case of Selectric Corporation, the error of omitting the amortization of $20,000 in 2001, which was discovered in 2002, results in restating the 2001 financial statements when presented in comparison with those of 2002. The following accounts in the 2001 financial statements (presented in comparison with those of 2002) will be restated:

ILLUSTRATION 22-9
Reporting an Error—Comparative Financial Statements

In the December 31, 2001 balance sheet:	
Accumulated amortization—buildings	$ 20,000 increase
Future income tax liability	$ 8,000 decrease
Retained earnings, Dec. 31, 2001	$12,000 decrease
In the 2001 income statement:	
Amortization expense—buildings	$ 20,000 increase
Income tax expense	$ 8,000 decrease
Net income	$12,000 decrease
In the 2001 retained earnings statement:	
2001 net income added in	$12,000 decrease
Retained earnings, Dec. 31, 2001 balance	
(due to lower net income for the period)	$12,000 decrease

The 2002 financial statements in comparative form with those of 2001 are prepared as if the error had not occurred, with the exception of correcting the opening balance of the previously reported opening retained earnings amount. The Statement of Retained Earnings would be identical to the statement in Illustration 22-8. In addition, a note to the 2002 financial statements is included, describing the error and disclosing the correction's effect on the current and prior years' financial statements and the fact that prior statements have been restated.

A problem may arise in differentiating between an error and a change in estimate. How do we determine whether the information was overlooked in earlier periods (an error) or whether it results from new information, more experience, or subsequent developments (change in estimate)? A proper determination is important because a different accounting treatment is applied if it is an error correction (retroactive) than if it is a change in estimate (prospective). The general rule is that careful estimates that later prove to be incorrect should be considered changes in estimate. Only when the estimate was obviously calculated incorrectly because of lack of expertise or in bad faith should the adjustment be considered an error. There is no clear demarcation here, and good judgement must be used in light of all the circumstances.

Change in the Reporting Entity

Circumstances often arise such that the entity's financial statements for the current period actually represent the activities of a different operation from that reported on in the prior period, or that the entity going forward into the subsequent year will differ from that operating currently. For example, when the reporting entity merges with or acquires the operations of other businesses during the year, the underlying activities and operations of the entity change from those reported on in previous periods. Similarly, when major segments of a company's operations are discontinued, the operations underlying the reporting entity's financial statements in the future also change. Such circumstances are collectively referred to as a change in reporting entity.[4]

When there has been a business combination during the period, the reporting entity should disclose sufficient information to allow readers to assess the effect of the acquisition(s) on the entity's financial position. The most important of these disclosures are:

1. A description of the enterprise acquired, including the percentage of voting shares acquired, if applicable.
2. The date from which income of the acquired business is included in the reporting entity's income.
3. The purchase's cost and how it was allocated to major classes of assets acquired and liabilities assumed.[5]

It may also be desirable to provide limited pro-forma supplemental information on revenues, extraordinary items, net income, and EPS as if the acquisition had taken place at the first of the period.

Prior to the release of *Handbook* Section 1581 in 2001, companies had the limited option of accounting for some business combinations as poolings-of-interest. Such combinations were required to be accounted for on a retroactive basis. New Section 1581 permits only the purchase method of accounting for business combinations. Applying this method is consistent with accounting for the purchase of any new asset: the results from operating that asset are included in income only from the date of acquisition—a prospective approach.

When a reporting entity sells, abandons, shuts down, or otherwise disposes of a business segment (or has a formal plan of disposal), the entity's operations and net assets are composed of operations and net assets of continuing operations (in which investors and others have a keen interest) and those of the discontinued operations. Much more useful information is presented if each type of operation's results and position is reported separately.

Therefore, when a reporting entity has discontinued or formally plans to discontinue a business segment, specific reporting and disclosures are required so that financial statement users can determine the likely effect on the results of future operations. The major disclosures required include:

1. Separate reporting on the income statement of the results (including total revenue and income taxes) of continuing and discontinued operations **for the current and prior periods reported**.
2. A description of the segment being discontinued, and the date, or expected date, of disposal.

---

[4] The *CICA Handbook* does not define a change in reporting entity. However, Sections 1581, 1590, 1600, and 3050 prescribe the reporting and disclosure requirements for business combinations, long-term investments, and consolidations, and Section 3475 prescribes the requirements for discontinued operations.

[5] *CICA Handbook* Section 1581, par. .55.

3. A description and the carrying value on the balance sheet date of the major classes of assets and liabilities of the discontinued segment.[6]

In summary, although there is no change in the bottom line of previous periods, the presentation of prior years' results provided for comparison purposes are reconfigured into the results of operations that will continue into the future and those that will not. This provides users with better information for prediction purposes.

Summary of Accounting Changes

Developing recommendations for reporting accounting changes has helped resolve several significant and long-standing accounting problems. Yet, because of diversity in situations and characteristics of the items encountered in practice, applying professional judgement is still of paramount importance. The primary objective is to serve the user of the financial statements. Achieving this requires full disclosure and an absence of misleading inferences. The principal distinction and treatments presented in the earlier discussion are summarized in Illustration 22-10.

Changes in accounting policies are considered appropriate only when the enterprise demonstrates that the alternative generally accepted accounting policy or its method of application that is adopted is **preferable** to the existing one. Preferability among accounting policies should be determined based on whether the new policy constitutes an **improvement in financial reporting**, not on its effect on income and taxes alone. But it is not always easy to determine what is an improvement in financial reporting. **How does one measure preferability or improvement?** One enterprise might argue that a change in accounting policy from FIFO to LIFO inventory valuation better matches current costs and current revenues. Conversely, another enterprise might change from LIFO to FIFO because it wishes to report a more realistic ending inventory. How do you determine which is the better of these two arguments? It appears that the auditor should have some "standard" or "objective" as a basis for determining the preferred method. Because no universal standard or objective is generally accepted, the problem of determining preferability continues to be a difficult one.

UNDERLYING CONCEPTS

This is an excellent example of the qualitative characteristic of relevance: providing information with predictive value.

CHANGE IN ACCOUNTING POLICY

General Rule. Use the retroactive-with-restatement approach by:
1. Reporting current and future results on the new basis.
2. Restating all prior period financial statements presented for comparison.
3. Providing note disclosures that describes the change and its effect on the current period's financial statements, and the effect on the prior periods.

Exceptions. Use the retroactive-without-restatement approach by:
1. Reporting the current and future results on the new basis.
2. Reporting the adjustment's cumulative effect in the statement of retained earnings as an adjustment to the beginning balance, and disclosing that prior period financial statements have not been restated.
3. Describing the change and its effect on the current year's net income.

CHANGE IN ACCOUNTING ESTIMATE

Use the prospective approach by:
1. Reporting current and future results on the new basis.
2. Presenting prior period financial statements as previously reported.
3. Making no adjustment to current period opening balances and no catch-up provisions.

CORRECTION OF AN ERROR

Use the retroactive-with-restatement approach by:
1. Correcting all prior period statements presented.
2. Restating the beginning balance of retained earnings for the first period presented when the error effects extend to a period prior to that one.
3. Providing a note that describes the error, its effect on the current and prior year financial statements, and that prior-period financial statements have been restated.

ILLUSTRATION 22-10
Summary of Accounting Changes

---

[6] *Ibid.*, Section 3475, par. .06 to .13.

CHANGE IN REPORTING ENTITY

Use the prospective treatment and disclosure by:
1. Taking into account the results of operations of acquired enterprises from the date of acquisition only.
2. Providing information useful for assessing the effect of an acquisition on the entity's financial position.
3. Reporting discontinued operations from the date of disposal or a formal plan of disposal only.
4. Restating current and prior period income statements provided for comparison purposes into continuing and discontinued operations with no change in bottom-line net income.

Motivations for Change

OBJECTIVE 9

Identify economic motives for changing accounting methods.

Difficult as it is to determine which accounting standards have the strongest conceptual support, other complications make the process even more complex. These complications stem from the fact that managers (and others) have a self-interest in how the financial statements make the company look. Managers naturally wish to show their financial performance in the best light. A favourable profit picture can influence investors, and a strong liquidity position can influence creditors. Too favourable a profit picture, however, can provide union negotiators with ammunition during bargaining talks. Also, if the federal government has established price controls, managers might believe that lower-trending profits might persuade the regulatory authorities to grant their company a price increase. Hence, managers might have varying profit motives depending on economic times and whom they seek to impress.

Research has provided additional insights into why companies may prefer certain accounting methods. Some of these reasons are as follows.

1. **Political costs.** As companies become larger and more politically visible, politicians and regulators devote more attention to them. Many suggest that these politicians and regulators can "feather their own nests" by imposing regulations on these organizations for the benefit of their own constituents. Thus the larger the firm, the more likely it is to become subject to regulation such as anti-competition regulation and the more likely it is required to pay higher taxes. Therefore, companies that are politically visible may attempt to report income numbers that are low, to avoid the scrutiny of regulators. By reporting low income numbers, companies hope to reduce their exposure to the perception of monopoly power. In addition, other constituents such as labour unions may be less willing to ask for wage increases if reported income is low. Thus, researchers have found that the larger the company, the more likely it is to adopt approaches that decrease income when selecting accounting methods.[7]

2. **Capital structure.** A number of studies have indicated that a company's capital structure can affect the selection of accounting methods. For example, a company with a high debt-to-equity ratio is more likely to be constrained by debt covenants. That is, a company may have a debt covenant that indicates that it cannot pay any dividends if retained earnings fall below a certain level. As a result, this type of company is more likely to select accounting methods that will increase net income. For example, one group of writers indicated that a company's capital structure affected its decision whether to expense or capitalize interest.[8] Others indicated that full cost accounting was selected instead of successful efforts by companies that have high debt-to-equity ratios.[9]

---

[7] Ross Watts and Jerold Zimmerman, "Towards a Positive Theory of the Determination of Accounting Standards," *The Accounting Review*, January 1978.

[8] R. M. Bowen, E. W. Noreen, and J. M. Lacy, "Determinants of the Corporate Decision to Capitalize Interest," *Journal of Accounting and Economics*, August 1981.

[9] See, for example, Dan S. Dhaliwal, "The Effect of the Firm's Capital Structure on the Choice of Accounting Methods," *The Accounting Review*, January 1980; and W. Bruce Johnson and Ramachandran Ramanan, "Discretionary Accounting Changes from 'Successful Efforts' to 'Full Cost' Methods: 1970–1976," *The Accounting Review*, January 1988. The latter study found that firms that changed to full cost were more likely to exhibit higher levels of financial risk (leverage) than firms that retained successful efforts.

3. **Bonus payments.** If bonus payments paid to management are tied to income, it has been found that management will select accounting methods that maximize their bonus payments. Thus, in selecting accounting methods, management does concern itself with the effect of accounting income changes on their compensation plans.[10]

4. **Smooth earnings.** Substantial increases in earnings attract the attention of politicians, regulators, and competitors. In addition, large increases in income create problems for management because the same results are difficult to achieve the following year. Compensation plans may adjust to these higher numbers as a baseline and make it difficult for management to achieve its profit goals and receive its bonus compensation the following year. Conversely, large decreases in earnings might be viewed as a signal that the company is in financial trouble. Furthermore, substantial decreases in income raise concerns on the part of shareholders, lenders, and other interested parties about management's competency. Thus, companies have an incentive to manage or smooth earnings. Management typically believes that a steady growth of 10% per year is much better than 30% growth one year followed by a 10% decline the next.[11] In other words, management usually prefers a gradually increasing income report (often referred to as income smoothers) and sometimes changes accounting methods to ensure such a result.

Management pays careful attention to the accounting it follows and often changes accounting methods not for conceptual reasons, but rather for economic reasons. As indicated throughout this textbook, such arguments have come to be known as "economic consequences" arguments, since they focus on the supposed impact of accounting on the behaviour of investors, creditors, competitors, governments, and the managers of the reporting companies themselves, rather than address the conceptual justification for accounting standards.[12]

To counter these pressures, standard setters have declared, as part of their conceptual framework, that they will assess the merits of proposed standards from a position of neutrality. That is, the soundness of standards should not be evaluated on the grounds of their possible impact on behaviour. It is not the Accounting Standards Board's place to choose standards according to the kinds of behaviour they wish to promote and the kinds they wish to discourage. At the same time, it must be admitted that some standards **will** often have the effect of influencing behaviour. Yet their justification should be conceptual, not behavioural.

Illustrations of Reporting Changes

West Fraser Timber Co. Ltd. reported a number of accounting changes in its financial statements for the year ended December 31, 2000. The company identifies three changes in accounting policy in 2000 as well as acquisitions in both its 2000 and 1999 fiscal periods.

---

[10] See, for example, Mark Zmijewski and Robert Hagerman, "An Income Strategy Approach to the Positive Theory of Accounting Standard Setting/Choice," *Journal of Accounting and Economics*, 1985.

[11] O. Douglas Moses, "Income Smoothing and Incentives: Empirical Tests Using Accounting Changes," *The Accounting Review,* April 1987. Findings provide evidence that smoothers are associated with firm size, the existence of bonus plans, and the divergence of actual earnings from expectations.

[12] Economic consequences arguments—and there are many of them—are manipulation through the use of lobbying and other forms of pressure brought on standard setters. We have seen examples of these arguments in the oil and gas industry about successful efforts versus full cost, in the technology area with the issue of mandatory expensing of research and most development costs, and so on.

ILLUSTRATION 22-11
Examples of Reporting
Accounting Changes

WEST FRASER TIMBER CO. LTD.

Earnings per common share (notes 2 and 17)	2000	1999
Basic	$4.23	$4.93
Diluted	$4.14	$4.82
RETAINED EARNINGS ($000)		
Balance—beginning of year	$681,494	$550,257
Change in accounting for future income taxes (note 2)	(13,054)	—
	668,440	550,257
Net earnings	131,458	147,421
	799,898	697,678
Convertible obligation (note 11b)	(2,280)	(1,510)
Cancellation of shares (note 10)	2,213	2,149
Dividends		
Preferred shares	—	(615)
Common shares	(16,989)	(16,208)
Balance—end of year	$782,842	$681,494

NOTES TO CONSOLIDATED FINANCIAL STATEMENTS
(Figures in tables are in thousands of Canadian dollars, except where indicated)

2. CHANGE IN ACCOUNTING POLICIES
Future income taxes
Effective January 1, 2000, the company adopted the liability method of accounting for income taxes in accordance with the recommendations of the Canadian Institute of Chartered Accountants ("CICA"). Under this method, future tax assets and liabilities are based upon differences between financial reporting and tax bases of assets and liabilities measured using current income tax rates. The company has adopted the new recommendations retroactively without restating prior years' financial statements. The cumulative effect of adopting the liability method of accounting for income taxes at January 1, 2000 was to increase capital assets by $119 million, decrease retained earnings by $13 million and increase future income taxes (previously described as deferred income taxes) by $132 million. Net earnings and earnings per share for 1999 remain unchanged. Prior to January 1, 2000, income taxes were accounted for by the deferral method.

Earnings per share
Effective December 31, 2000, the company changed its method of calculating earnings per share in accordance with the recommendations of the CICA. The company has adopted the new recommendations retroactively and has restated prior years' financial statements. The effect of adopting the new recommendations on the prior year's financial statements is as follows:

	1999 (Restated)	1999
Basic earnings per share (dollars)	$4.93	$4.88
Diluted earnings per share (dollars)	$4.82	$4.75

Employee benefit plans
Effective January 1, 2000, the company changed its policy for accounting for employee future benefits in accordance with the recommendations of the CICA, on a prospective basis. Prior to adoption of the new recommendations, post-retirement benefits other than pensions were accounted for on a cash basis.

The company accrues its obligations under employee benefit plans and related costs, net of plan assets. The cost of pensions and other post-retirement benefits earned by employees is determined actuarially, using the projected benefit method prorated on length of service and management's best estimate of expected investment performance, salary escalation, retirement age of employees and expected health care costs and premiums.

Defined benefit pension plan assets are reported at market values. The discount rate used to determine the accrued benefit obligation was determined by reference to market yields. Adjustments and transitional amounts are amortized on a straight-line basis over the average service period of the employee groups, which is estimated to be 13 years.

3. ACQUISITIONS
2000
a) Effective December 15, 2000, the company acquired two sawmills in the southern United States and entered into a long-term timber supply contract with the seller.

The acquisition has been accounted for by the purchase method and the results of operations have been included with those of the company from the effective date.

Net assets acquired at fair values:

Non-cash working capital	$ 16,997
Timber deposits	3,689
Capital assets	91,174
Cash consideration	$111,860

b) Effective November 1, 2000, the company acquired a 50% interest in a sawmill and timber rights located in Alberta.

The company's share of the cash consideration for the purchase amounted to $5,685,000.

1999

Effective November 3, 1999, the company acquired the forest products business and assets of Zeidler Forest Industries Ltd., consisting of plywood and veneer plants and related timber rights.

The acquisition has been accounted for by the purchase method and the results of operations have been included with those of the company from the effective date.

Net assets acquired at fair values:

Non-cash working capital	$20,550
Capital assets	69,053
Reforestation obligation assumed	(15,200)
Cash consideration	$74,403

Go to the Digital Tool for additional disclosures.

All three of the changes in accounting policy relate to changes in the accounting standards comprising GAAP. *Handbook* Section 1506 assigns priority to other *Handbook* sections in determining the preferred treatment for a change in policy to conform to new *Handbook* recommendations. The introduction to the *Handbook* states that new recommendations **need** not, but **may be**, retroactively applied. Whenever new standards and recommendations are issued, the standard will identify whether retroactive or prospective treatment is preferred under its transitional provisions. Sometimes it is left up to the individual company to determine which to use, although specific disclosures are generally prescribed.

ERROR ANALYSIS

As indicated earlier, material errors are unusual in large corporations because internal control procedures coupled with the diligence of the accounting staff are ordinarily sufficient to find any major errors in the system. Smaller businesses may face a different problem. These enterprises may not be able to afford an internal audit staff or to implement the necessary control procedures to ensure that accounting data are always recorded accurately.[13]

In practice, firms do not correct for errors discovered that do not have a significant effect on the financial statements. For example, the failure to record accrued wages of $5,000 when the total payroll for the year is $1,750,000 and net income is $940,000 is not considered significant, and no correction is made. Obviously, defining materiality is difficult, and experience and judgement must be used to determine whether adjustment is necessary for a given error. All errors discussed in this section are assumed to be material and to require adjustment. The tax effects are ignored initially to simplify and allow you to zero in on the direct effects of the errors themselves.

The accountant must answer three questions in error analysis:

1. What type of error is involved?
2. What entries are needed to correct the error?
3. How are financial statements to be restated once the error is discovered?

As indicated earlier, the profession requires that errors be treated retroactively with restatement and reported in the current year as adjustments to the beginning balance of Retained Earnings, net of income tax effects. If comparative statements are presented, the prior statements affected are restated to correct the error.

OBJECTIVE 10

Analyse the effect of errors.

---

[13] See Mark L. DeFord and James Jiambalvo, "Incidence and Circumstances of Accounting Errors," *The Accounting Review,* July 1991, for examples of different types of errors and why these errors might have occurred.

Three types of errors can occur. Because each type has its own peculiarities, it is important to differentiate among them.

Balance Sheet Errors

These errors affect only the presentation of an asset, liability, or shareholders' equity account. Examples are classifying a short-term receivable as part of the investment section; a note payable as an account payable; and plant assets as inventory. Reclassification of the item to its proper position is needed when the error is discovered. If comparative statements that include the error year are prepared, the balance sheet for the error year is restated correctly.

Income Statement Errors

These errors affect only the presentation of the nominal accounts in the income statement. Errors involve the improper classification of revenues or expenses, such as recording interest revenue as part of sales, purchases as bad debt expense, and amortization expense as interest expense. An income statement classification error has no effect on the balance sheet or on net income. A reclassification entry is needed when the error is discovered, if it is discovered in the year it is made. If the error occurred in prior periods, no entry is needed at the date of discovery because the accounts for the year of the misclassification are closed and the current year is correctly stated. If comparative statements that include the error year are prepared, the income statement for the error year is restated correctly.

Balance Sheet and Income Statement Errors

The third type of error involves both the balance sheet and income statement. For example, assume that accrued wages payable were overlooked by the bookkeeper at the end of the accounting period. The error's effect is to understate expenses and liabilities, and overstate net income for that accounting period. This type of error affects both the balance sheet and the income statement and is classified in one of two ways—counterbalancing or noncounterbalancing.

Counterbalancing errors are errors that will be offset or self-corrected over two periods. In the previous illustration, the failure to record accrued wages is considered a counterbalancing error because over a two-year period, the error will no longer be present. In other words, failing to record accrued wages in the previous period means: (1) wages expense for the first period is understated, (2) net income for the first period is overstated, (3) accrued wages payable (a liability) at the end of the first period is understated, and (4) retained earnings at the end of the first period is overstated. In the next period, wages expense is overstated, and net income is understated, but both accrued wages payable (a liability) and retained earnings at the end of the second period are now correct. **For the two years combined**, both wages expense and net income are correct, as are the ending balance sheet amounts of wages payable and retained earnings. Most errors in accounting that affect both the balance sheet and income statement are counterbalancing errors.

Noncounterbalancing errors are errors that are not offset in the next accounting period; for example, the failure to capitalize equipment that has a useful life of five years. If we expense this asset immediately, expenses will be overstated in the first period but understated in the next four periods. At the end of the second period, the error's effect is not fully offset. Net income is correct in the aggregate only at the end of five years, because the asset would have been fully amortized at this point. Thus, **noncounterbalancing errors are those that take longer than two periods to correct themselves**.

Only in rare instances is an error never reversed; for example, when land is initially expensed. Because land is not subject to amortization, the error is not offset until the land is sold.

Counterbalancing Errors

The usual types of counterbalancing errors are illustrated on the following pages. In studying these illustrations, a number of points should be remembered. First, and this is key, **the entries will differ depending on whether or not the books have been closed for the period in which the error is found**.

1. **The books have been closed.**

   (a) If the error is already counterbalanced, no entry is necessary.

   (b) If the error is not yet counterbalanced, an entry is necessary to adjust the present balance of retained earnings and the other balance sheet account(s) affected.

2. **The books have not been closed.**

   (a) If the error is already counterbalanced and the company is in the second year, an entry is necessary to correct the current period income statement account(s) and to adjust the beginning balance of Retained Earnings.

   (b) If the error is not yet counterbalanced, an entry is necessary to adjust the beginning balance of Retained Earnings, and correct the current period income statement account(s) and balance sheet account(s) affected.

Second, if comparative statements are presented, it is necessary to restate the amounts for comparative purposes. **Restatement is necessary even if a correcting journal entry is not required**. To illustrate, assume that Sanford Cement Ltd. failed to accrue revenue in 2000 when earned, but recorded the revenue in 2001 when received. The error is discovered in 2003. No entry is necessary to correct for this error because the effects have been counterbalanced by the time the error is discovered in 2003. However, if comparative financial statements for 2000 through 2003 are presented, the accounts and related amounts for the years 2000 and 2001 should be restated correctly for financial reporting purposes.

The following are examples of counterbalancing errors. Income tax effects have been ignored.

1. **Failure to record accrued wages.** On December 31, 2002, accrued wages of $1,500 were not recognized. The entry in 2003 to correct this error, assuming that the books have not been closed for 2003, is:

Retained Earnings	1,500	
Wages Expense		1,500

   The rationale for this entry is as follows: (1) When the accrued wages of 2002 are paid in 2003, an additional debit of $1,500 is made to 2003 Wages Expense. (2) Wages Expense—2003 is overstated by $1,500. (3) Because 2002 accrued wages were not recorded as Wages Expense—2002, the net income for 2002 was overstated by $1,500. (4) Because 2002 net income is overstated by $1,500, the Retained Earnings account is overstated by $1,500 because net income is closed to Retained Earnings.

   If the books have been closed for 2003, no entry is made because the error is counterbalanced.

2. **Failure to record prepaid expenses.** In January 2002, a two-year insurance policy costing $1,000 was purchased; Insurance Expense was debited, and Cash was credited. No adjusting entries were made at the end of 2002.

   The entry on December 31, 2003 to correct this error, assuming that the books have not been closed for 2003, is:

Insurance Expense	500	
Retained Earnings		500

   If the books are closed for 2003, no entry is made because the error is counterbalanced.

3. **Understatement of unearned revenue.** On December 31, 2002, cash of $50,000 was received as a prepayment for renting certain office space for the following year. The entry made when the rent payment was received was a debit to Cash and a credit to Rent Revenue. No adjusting entry was made as of December 31, 2002. The entry on December 31, 2003 to correct this error, assuming that the books have not been closed for 2003, is:

Retained Earnings	50,000	
Rent Revenue		50,000

If the books are closed for 2003, no entry is made because the error is counterbalanced.

4. **Overstatement of accrued revenue.** On December 31, 2002, interest revenue of $8,000 was accrued that applied to 2003. The entry made on December 31, 2002 was to debit Interest Receivable and credit Interest Revenue. The entry on December 31, 2003 to correct this error, assuming that the books have not been closed for 2003, is:

Retained Earnings	8,000	
Interest Revenue		8,000

If the books have been closed for 2003, no entry is made because the error is counterbalanced.

5. **Overstatement of purchases.** The accountant recorded a purchase of merchandise for $9,000 in 2002 that applied to 2003. The physical inventory for 2002 was correctly stated. The company uses the periodic inventory method. The entry on December 31, 2003 to correct this error, assuming that the books have not been closed for 2003, is:

Purchases	9,000	
Retained Earnings		9,000

If the 2003 books have been closed, no entry is made because the error is counterbalanced.

6. **Understatement of ending inventory.** On December 31, 2002, the physical inventory count was understated by $25,000 because the inventory crew failed to count one section of a merchandise warehouse. The entry on December 31, 2003 to correct this error, assuming the 2003 books have not yet been closed, is:

Inventory (beginning)	25,000	
Retained Earnings		25,000

If the books are closed for 2003, no entry would be made because the error has been counterbalanced.

7. **Overstatement of purchases and inventories.** Sometimes, both the physical inventory and the purchases are incorrectly stated. Assume that purchases for 2002 were overstated by $9,000 and that inventory was overstated by the same amount. The entry on December 31, 2003 to correct this error before the 2003 books are closed is:

Purchases	9,000	
Inventory (beginning)		9,000

The net income for 2002 is correct because the overstatement of purchases was offset by the overstatement of ending inventory in cost of goods sold. As with the other examples of counterbalancing errors, no entry is required if the 2003 books have already been closed.

Noncounterbalancing Errors

Because such errors do not counterbalance over a two-year period, the entries for non-counterbalancing errors are more complex and correcting entries are needed, even if the books have been closed. The best approach is to identify what the relevant account balances **are** in the accounts, what they **should be**, and then bring them to the correct balances through correcting entries.

1. **Failure to record amortization.** Assume that a machine with an estimated five-year useful life was purchased on January 1, 2002 for $10,000. The accountant incorrectly expensed this machine in 2002 and the error was discovered in 2003. If we assume that the company uses straight-line amortization on similar assets, the entry on December 31, 2003 to correct this error, given that the 2003 books are not yet closed, is:

Machinery	10,000	
Amortization Expense (2003)	2,000	
Retained Earnings		8,000
Accumulated Amortization		4,000

Retained Earnings		
Expense reported in 2002	$10,000	
Correct amortization for 2002 (20% × $10,000)	(2,000)	
Retained earnings understated as of Dec. 31, 2002 by	$ 8,000	

Accumulated Amortization	
Accumulated amortization (20% × $10,000 × 2)	$ 4,000

If the books are closed for 2003, the entry is:

Machinery	10,000	
Retained Earnings		6,000
Accumulated Amortization		4,000

Retained Earnings		
Retained earnings understated as of Dec. 31, 2002 by	$ 8,000	
Correct amortization for 2003 (20% × $10,000)	(2,000)	
Retained earnings understated as of Dec. 31, 2003 by	$ 6,000	

2. **Failure to adjust for bad debts.** Assume a company has inappropriately been using the direct write-off method when the allowance method should have been applied. For example, assume that the following bad debt expense has been recognized as the debts have actually become uncollectible:

	2002	2003
From 2002 sales	$550	$690
From 2003 sales		700

The company estimates that an additional $1,400 will be written off in 2004, of which $300 is applicable to 2002 sales and $1,100 to 2003 sales. The entry on December 31, 2003 to correct the accounts for bad debt expense, assuming that the books have not been closed for 2003, is:

Bad Debt Expense	410	
Retained Earnings	990	
Allowance for Doubtful Accounts		1,400

Allowance for doubtful accounts:
Additional $300 for 2002 sales and $1,100 for 2003 sales.

Bad debts and retained earnings balance:	2002	2003
Bad debt expense charged ($550 + $690 = $1,240)	$1,240	$ 700
Additional bad debts anticipated	300	1,100
Correct amount of bad debt expense	1,540	1,800
Charges currently included in each period	(550)	(1,390)
Bad debt expense adjustment	$ 990	$ 410

If the books have been closed for 2003, the entry is:

Retained Earnings	1,400	
Allowance for Doubtful Accounts		1,400

Income Tax Effects

As previously indicated, the income tax effects have not been reported with the above correcting entries to allow you to focus on the effects of the errors themselves. Once you understand the correcting entries, you can add the income tax effects.

If a correction **increases a previous year's income** (either by an increase in revenue or a decrease in expense), the income tax expense for that period will usually be increased—more income, more tax. If the correction **reduces a previous year's income** (either by a decrease in revenue or an increase in expense), the income tax expense for that period will usually be reduced—less income, less tax. The net correction to Retained Earnings, therefore, is net-of-tax. Note that for counterbalancing errors, the income tax effects also offset each other over the two-year period, assuming tax rates have not changed.

Because the tax return for the previous period has already been filed, any adjustment of the previous year's balance sheet accounts and income for financial reporting purposes will create a temporary difference between tax values and the corrected book values. The tax effect, therefore, is captured in the Future Income Tax Asset/Liability account.

Illustration 22-12 identifies the correcting entries required, including the tax effects for the counterbalancing and noncounterbalancing examples provided on pages 1097 to 1099. A constant 40% income tax rate is assumed.

ILLUSTRATION 22-12
Correcting Entries with Income Tax Effects

	BOOKS FOR 2003		
Error	Not Closed		Closed
COUNTERBALANCING ERRORS			
1. Accrued Wages			
Retained Earnings	900		–No Entry–
Future Income Tax			
Asset/Liability	600		
Wages Expense		1500	
2. Prepaid expenses			
Insurance Expense	500		–No Entry–
Retained Earnings		300	
Future Income Tax			
Asset/Liability		200	
3. Unearned Revenue			
Retained Earnings	30,000		–No Entry–
Future Income Tax			
Asset/Liability	20,000		
Rent Revenue		50,000	
4. Accrued Revenue			
Retained Earnings	4,800		–No Entry–
Future Income Tax			
Asset/Liability	3,200		
Interest Revenue		8,000	
5. Overstatement of Purchases			
Purchases	9,000		No Entry–
Retained Earnings		5,400	
Future Income Tax			
Asset/Liability		3,600	
6. Understatement of Ending Inventory			
Inventory (beginning)	25,000		–No Entry–
Retained Earnings		15,000	
Future Income Tax			
Asset/Liability		10,000	
7. Overstatement of Purchases and Inventories			
Purchases	9,000		–No Entry–
Inventory (beginning)		9,000	

NONCOUNTERBALANCING ERRORS

1. Amortization

Machinery	10,000		Machinery	10,000		
Amortization Expense	2,000		Accumulated Amortization		4,000	
Accumulated Amortization		4,000	Retained Earnings		3,600	
Retained Earnings		4,800	Future Income Tax			
Future Income Tax			Asset/Liability		2,400	
Asset/Liability		3,200				

2. Bad Debts

Bad Debt Expense	410		Retained Earnings	840		
Retained Earnings	594		Future Income Tax			
Future Income Tax			Asset/Liability	560		
Asset/Liability	396		Allowance for Doubtful		1,400	
Allowance for Doubtful		1,400	Accounts			
Accounts						

Comprehensive Illustration: Numerous Errors

In some circumstances, a combination of errors occurs. A work sheet is therefore prepared to facilitate the analysis. To demonstrate the use of a work sheet, the following problem is presented for solution. The mechanics of the work sheet preparation should be apparent from the solution format. The tax effects are omitted.

The income statements of the Hudson Corporation for the three years ended December 31, 2001, 2002, and 2003 indicate the following net incomes.

2001	$17,400
2002	20,200
2003	11,300

An examination of the company's accounting records for these years indicates that several errors were made in arriving at the net incomes reported. The following errors were discovered.

1. Wages earned by workers but not paid at December 31 were consistently omitted from the records. The amounts omitted were:

December 31, 2000	$1,000
December 31, 2001	$1,400
December 31, 2002	$1,600

These amounts were recorded as expenses when paid in the year following that in which they were earned by employees.

2. The merchandise inventory on December 31, 2001 was overstated by $1,900 as the result of errors made in the footings and extensions on the inventory sheets.

3. Insurance of $1,200, applicable to 2003, was expensed on December 31, 2002.

4. Interest receivable in the amount of $240 was not recorded on December 31, 2002.

5. On January 2, 2002, a piece of equipment costing $3,900 was sold for $1,800. At the date of sale, the equipment had accumulated amortization of $2,400. The cash received was recorded as Miscellaneous Income in 2002. In addition, amortization was recorded for this equipment in both 2002 and 2003 at the rate of 10% of cost.

The first step in preparing the work sheet is to prepare a schedule showing the corrected net income amounts for the years ended December 31, 2001, 2002, and 2003. Each correction of the amount originally reported is clearly labelled. The next step is to indicate the balance sheet accounts affected as of December 31, 2003. The completed work sheet for Hudson Corporation is provided in Illustration 22-13.

HUDSON CORPORATION
Work Sheet to Correct Income and Balance Sheet Errors

	Work Sheet Analysis of Changes in Net Income				Balance Sheet Correction at December 31, 2003		
	2001	2002	2003	Totals	Debit	Credit	Account
Net income as reported	$17,400	$20,200	$11,300	$48,900			
Wages unpaid, 12/31/01	(1,000)	1,000		–0–			
Wages unpaid, 12/31/02		(1,400)	1,400	–0–			
Wages unpaid, 12/31/03			(1,600)	(1,600)		$1,600	Wages Payable
Inventory overstatement, 12/31/01	(1,900)	1,900		–0–			
Unexpired insurance, 12/31/02		1,200	(1,200)	–0–			
Interest receivable, 12/31/02		240	(240)	–0–			
Correction for entry made on sale of equipment, 1/2/02ª		(1,500)		(1,500)	$2,400	3,900	Accumulated Amortization Machinery
Overcharge of amortization, 2002		390		390	390		Accumulated Amortization
Overcharge of amortization, 2003			390	390	390		Accumulated Amortization
Corrected net income	$14,500	$22,030	$10,050	$46,580			

ªCost	$ 3,900
Accumulated amortization	2,400
Book value	1,500
Proceeds from sale	1,800
Gain on sale	300
Income reported	(1,800)
Adjustment	$ (1,500)

ILLUSTRATION 22-13
Work Sheet to Correct Income and Balance Sheet Errors

Correcting entries **if the books have not been closed for 2003** are:

Retained Earnings	1,400	
Wages Expense		1,400

(To correct wages expense charged to 2003 that should have been charged to prior year.)

Wages Expense	1,600	
Wages Payable		1,600

(To record proper wages expense and accrual for wages at 2003 year end.)

Insurance Expense	1,200	
Retained Earnings		1,200

(To correct insurance expense charged to 2002 that should have been charged to 2003.)

Interest Revenue	240	
Retained Earnings		240

(To correct interest revenue recognized in 2003 that should have been reported in 2002.)

Retained Earnings	1,500	
Accumulated Amortization	2,400	
Machinery		3,900

(To record write-off of machinery and the correction of the gain reported in 2002.)

Accumulated Amortization	780	
Amortization Expense		390
Retained Earnings		390

(To correct for improper charges to amortization expense in 2002 and 2003.)

If the books have been closed for 2003, the correcting entries are:

Retained Earnings	1,600	
Wages Payable		1,600

(To correct for the cumulative effect of accrued wages errors to December 31, 2003.)

Retained Earnings	1,500	
Accumulated Amortization	2,400	
Machinery		3,900

(To record write-off of machinery and the correction of the gain reported in 2002.)

Accumulated Amortization	780	
Retained Earnings		780

(To correct for improper charges to amortization expense in 2002 and 2003.)

Preparation of Comparative Financial Statements

Up to now, our discussion of error analysis has been concerned with identifying the type of error involved and accounting for its correction in the accounting records. The error correction should be presented on comparative financial statements. In addition, 5 or 10-year summaries are often provided for the interested financial statement reader. Illustration 22-14 shows how a typical year's financial statements are restated given many different errors.

Dick & Wally's Outlet Ltd. is a small retail outlet in the town of Priestly Sound. Lacking expertise in accounting, they do not keep adequate records. As a result, numerous errors occurred in recording accounting information. The errors are listed below.

1. The bookkeeper inadvertently failed to record a cash receipt of $1,000 on the sale of merchandise in 2003.

2. Accrued wages expense at the end of 2002 was $2,500; at the end of 2003, $3,200. The company does not accrue for wages; all wages are charged to administrative expense.

3. The beginning inventory was understated by $5,400 because goods in transit at the end of last year were not counted. The proper purchase entry had been made.

4. No allowance had been set up for estimated uncollectible receivables. Dick and Wally decided to set up such an allowance for the estimated probable losses as of December 31, 2003 for 2002 accounts of $700, and for 2003 accounts of $1,500. They also decided to correct the charge against each year so that it shows the losses (actual and estimated) relating to that year's sales. Accounts have been written off to bad debt expense (selling expense) as follows:

	In 2002	In 2003
2002 accounts	$400	$2,000
2003 accounts		1,600

5. Unexpired insurance not recorded at the end of 2002 was $600, and at the end of 2003, $400. All insurance is charged to Administrative Expense.

6. An account payable of $6,000 should have been a note payable.

7. During 2002, an asset that cost $10,000 and had a book value of $4,000 was sold for $7,000. At the time of sale, Cash was debited and Miscellaneous Revenue was credited for $7,000.

8. As a result of the last transaction, the company overstated amortization expense (an administrative expense) in 2002 by $800 and in 2003 by $1,200.

9. In a physical count, the company determined the final inventory to be $40,000.

Presented below is a work sheet that begins with the unadjusted trial balance of Dick & Wally's Outlet; the correcting entries and their effect on the financial statements can be determined by examining the work sheet.

DICK & WALLY'S OUTLET
Work Sheet Analysis to Adjust Financial Statements for the Year 2003

	Trial Balance Unadjusted		Adjustments		Income Statement Adjusted		Balance Sheet Adjusted	
	Debit	Credit	Debit	Credit	Debit	Credit	Debit	Credit
Cash	3,100		(1) 1,000				4,100	
Accounts Receivable	17,600						17,600	
Notes Receivable	8,500						8,500	
Inventory, Jan. 1, 2003	34,000		(3) 5,400		39,400			
Property, Plant and Equipment	112,000			(7) 10,000a			102,000	
Accumulated Amortization		83,500	(7) 6,000a					75,500
			(8) 2,000					
Investments	24,300						24,300	
Accounts Payable		14,500	(6) 6,000					8,500
Notes Payable		10,000		(6) 6,000				16,000
Capital Stock		43,500						43,500
Retained Earnings		20,000	(4) 2,700b	(3) 5,400				
			(7) 4,000a	(5) 600				
			(2) 2,500	(8) 800				17,600
Sales		94,000		(1) 1,000		95,000		
Purchases	21,000				21,000			
Selling Expenses	22,000			(4) 500b	21,500			
Administrative Expenses	23,000		(2) 700	(5) 400	22,700			
			(5) 600	(8) 1,200				
Totals	265,500	265,500						
Wages Payable				(2) 3,200				3,200
Allowance for Doubtful Accounts				(4) 2,200b				2,200
Unexpired Insurance			(5) 400				400	
Inventory, Dec. 31, 2003						(9) 40,000	(9) 40,000	
Net Income					30,400			30,400
Totals			31,300	31,300	135,000	135,000	196,900	196,900

Calculations:

			For Sales in	
aMachinery		bBad Debts	2002	2003
Proceeds from sale	$7,000	Bad debts charged	$2,400	$1,600
Book value of machinery	4,000	Additional bad debts anticipated	700	1,500
Gain on sale	3,000		3,100	3,100
Income credited	7,000	Charges currently made to each year	(400)	(3,600)
Retained earnings adjustment	$4,000	Bad debt adjustment	$2,700	$ (500)

ILLUSTRATION 22-14
Work Sheet to Adjust Financial Statements

SUMMARY OF LEARNING OBJECTIVES

1 Identify the types of accounting changes. Four different types of accounting changes are: (1) Change in accounting policy: a change from one generally accepted accounting principle or method used in its application to another generally accepted accounting principle or method. (2) Change in an accounting estimate: a change that occurs as the result of new information or as additional experience is acquired. (3) Correction of a prior period error: a change that occurs because of an error discovered in a prior period's financial statements. (4) Change in reporting entity: a significant change in a reporting entity's financial position and operations due to business acquisitions or the discontinuation of a business segment.

2 Describe a change in accounting policy. A change in accounting policy involves a change from one generally accepted accounting principle or its method of application to another generally accepted principle or method. A change in accounting principle does not result from the adoption of a new principle in recognition of events that have occurred for the first time or that were previously immaterial or a policy change brought about because of circumstances that are clearly different in substance from those previously existing. If the accounting principle previously followed was not acceptable, or if the principle was applied incorrectly, a change to a generally accepted accounting principle is considered an error correction.

3 Understand how to account for retroactive-with-restatement type of accounting changes. The general requirement for changes in accounting policy is that the change's cumulative effect (net of tax) be shown as an adjustment to the beginning retained earnings. Income statements of the affected prior periods presented for comparison purposes are restated to show, on a retroactive basis, the effects of the new accounting policy.

4 Understand how to account for retroactive-without-restatement type of accounting changes. When a change in accounting policy's effects on particular prior periods cannot be readily determined, the cumulative effect of the change (net of tax) is shown as an adjustment to the beginning retained earnings. Comparative financial statements of prior periods presented for comparison are not restated.

5 Understand how to account for prospective-type accounting changes. Accounting changes given prospective treatment affect only the current and future fiscal periods. There is no adjustment of current year opening balances.

6 Describe the accounting for changes in estimates. Changes in estimates must be handled prospectively; that is, no changes should be made in previously reported results. Opening balances are not adjusted, and no attempt is made to "catch up" for prior periods. Financial statements of prior periods are not restated.

7 Describe the accounting for correction of errors. As soon as they are discovered, errors must be corrected by proper entries in the accounts and reported in the financial statements. The profession requires that error corrections be accorded retroactive-with-restatement treatment. The correction is recorded in the year in which the error is discovered, and is reported in the financial statements as an adjustment to the beginning balance of retained earnings. If comparative statements are presented, the prior statements affected should be restated to correct the error. The disclosures need not be repeated in the financial statements of subsequent periods.

8 Identify changes in a reporting entity. A change in an entity's net assets due to an acquisition of another business or the discontinuation of a significant segment of the business is required to be disclosed. This is relevant information for users who want to determine what the basis is for future operations.

9 Identify economic motives for changing accounting methods. Managers might have varying motives underlying the change in an accounting method, depending on economic times and circumstances. Some of the aspects that affect decisions about changing accounting methods are: (1) political costs, (2) capital structure, (3) bonus payments, and (4) the desire to smooth earnings.

10 Analyse the effect of errors. Three types of errors can occur: (1) Balance sheet errors: affect only the presentation of an asset, liability, or shareholders' equity account. (2) Income statement errors: affect only the presentation of the nominal accounts in the income statement. (3) Errors that affect both the balance sheet and income statement. This last type of error is classified into two types: (1) Counterbalancing errors: the effects will be offset or corrected over two periods. (2) Noncounterbalancing errors: the effects are not offset in the next accounting period but take longer than two periods to correct themselves.

KEY TERMS

changes in estimate, 1087

change in accounting policy, 1081

change in reporting entity, 1090

correction of an error, 1088

counterbalancing errors, 1096

noncounterbalancing errors, 1096

prospective treatment, 1082

retroactive treatment, 1082

retroactive-with-restatement method,1083

retroactive-without-restatement method, 1085

BRIEF EXERCISES

BE22-1 Beaulieu Corporation decided at the beginning of 2002 to change from the capital cost allowance method of amortizing its capital assets to straight-line amortization. The company will continue to use the capital cost allowance method for tax purposes. For years prior to 2002, total amortization expense under the two methods is as follows: capital cost allowance $128,000 and straight line $80,000. The tax rate is 35%. Prepare Beaulieu's 2002 journal entry to record the change in accounting policy.

BE22-2 Bickner Corp. changed amortization methods in 2002 from straight line to double-declining balance. The assets involved were acquired early in 1999 for $175,000 and had an estimated useful life of eight years with no residual value. The 2002 income using the straight-line method was $250,000. Bickner had 10,000 common shares outstanding all year. What is the accounting change's effect on the reported income and EPS for 2002? Ignore income taxes.

BE22-3 Boey, Inc. changed from the average cost flow assumption to the FIFO cost flow assumption in 2003. The increase in the prior years' income before taxes as a result of this change is $525,000. The tax rate is 40%. Prepare Boey's 2003 journal entry to record the change in accounting principle.

BE22-4 Castle Corporation purchased a computer system for $60,000 on January 1, 2001. It was amortized based on a seven-year life and an $18,000 residual value. On January 1, 2003, Castle revised these estimates to a total useful life of four years and a residual value of $10,000. Prepare Castle's entry to record 2003 amortization expense.

BE22-5 In 2003, Hiatt Corporation discovered that equipment purchased on January 1, 2001 for $75,000 was expensed in error at that time. The equipment should have been amortized over five years, with no residual value. The effective tax rate is 30%. Prepare Hiatt's 2003 journal entry to correct the error and record 2003 amortization.

BE22-6 At January 1, 2003, Monat Corp. reported retained earnings of $2 million. In 2003, Monat discovered that 2002 amortization expense was understated in error by $500,000. In 2003, net income was $900,000 and dividends declared were $250,000. The tax rate is 40%. Prepare a 2003 retained earnings statement for Monat Corp.

BE22-7 Indicate the effect—Understate, Overstate, No Effect—that each of the following errors has on 2002 net income and 2003 net income:

	2002	2003
(a) Wages payable were not recorded at 12/31/02.	___	___
(b) Equipment purchased in 2001 was expensed.	___	___
(c) Equipment purchased in 2002 was expensed.	___	___
(d) 2002 ending inventory was overstated.	___	___
(e) Patent amortization was not recorded in 2003.	___	___

EXERCISES

E22-1 **(Error and Change in Policy—Amortization)** Cunningham Ltd. purchased a machine on January 1, 2000 for $550,000. At that time, it was estimated that the machine would have a 10-year life and no residual value. On December 31, 2003, the firm's accountant found that the entry for amortization expense had been omitted in 2001. In addition, management informed the accountant that it planned to switch to straight-line amortization, starting with the year 2003. At present, the company uses the double-declining balance method for amortizing equipment.

Instructions

Assuming this is a change in accounting policy, prepare the general journal entries the accountant should make at December 31, 2003 (ignore tax effects).

E22-2 **(Change in Policy and Change in Estimate—Amortization)** Kato Inc. acquired the following assets in January 1999:

Equipment: estimated service life, 5 years; residual value, $15,000	$525,000
Building: estimated service life, 30 years; no residual value	$693,000

The equipment has been amortized using the double-declining balance method for the first three years for financial reporting purposes. In 2002, the company decided to change the method of calculating amortization to the straight-line method for the equipment, but no change was made in the estimated service life or residual value. It was also decided to change the building's total estimated service life from 30 years to 40 years, with no change in the estimated residual value. The building is amortized on the straight-line method.

The company has 100,000 common shares outstanding. Results of operations for 2002 and 2001 are shown below:

	2002	2001
Net income (amortization for 2002 has been calculated on the straight-line basis for both the equipment and building[a])	$385,000	$380,000
Income per share	$3.85	$3.80

[a] Note that the calculation for amortization expense for 2002 and 2001 for the building was based on the original estimate of a 30 year service life.

Instructions

(a) Calculate the effect of the change in accounting principle to be reported in the restated statement of retained earnings for 2002, and prepare the journal entry to record the change. (Ignore tax effects.)
(b) Calculate the amount of income and EPS reported on the comparative financial statements presented in 2002. (Ignore tax effects.)

E22-3 **(Change in Policy, Change in Accounting Estimate)** On January 1, 1998, Zhang Corporation purchased a building and equipment that have the following useful lives, residual values, and costs:

Building: 40-year estimated useful life, $50,000 residual value, $800,000 cost
Equipment: 12-year estimated useful life, $10,000 residual value, $100,000 cost

The building and equipment have been amortized under the double-declining balance method through 2001. In 2002, the company decided to switch to the straight-line method of amortization. In 2003, Zhang decided to change the equipment's total useful life to nine years, with a residual value of $5,000 at the end of that time. You may ignore income taxes.

Instructions

(a) What is the amount of the adjustment to opening retained earnings as of January 1, 2002?
(b) What is the amount of the adjustment to opening retained earnings as of January 1, 2001 for purposes of the comparative statements?
(c) Prepare the journal entry(ies) necessary to record the changes made in 2002.
(d) Calculate amortization expense on the equipment for 2003.

E22-4 **(Change in Estimate—Amortization)** Peterell Corp. purchased equipment for $510,000 that was estimated to have a useful life of 10 years with a residual value of $10,000. Amortization has been entered for seven years on a straight-line basis. In 2002, it is determined that the total estimated life should be 15 years with a residual value of $5,000.

Instructions

(a) Prepare the entry (if any) to correct the prior years' amortization.
(b) Prepare the entry to record amortization for 2002.

E22-5 **(Change in Policy—Amortization)** Englehart Industries Ltd. changed from the straight-line method to the double-declining balance method in 2002 on all its plant assets. The appropriate information related to this change is as follows:

Year	Double-Declining Balance Amortization	Straight-Line Amortization	Difference
2000	$250,000	$125,000	$125,000
2001	225,000	125,000	100,000
2002	202,500	125,000	77,500

Net income for 2001 was reported at $270,000; net income for 2002 would be reported at $300,000 if based on the straight-line method.

Instructions

(a) Assuming a tax rate of 30%, what is the amount of the adjustment to opening retained earnings as of January 1, 2002?

(b) What is the adjustment amount to opening retained earnings as of January 1, 2001, assuming Englehart uses the retroactive-with-restatement method of accounting for this change?

(c) Prepare the journal entry(ies) to record the adjustment in the accounting records, assuming the accounting records for 2002 are not yet closed.

E22-6 (Change in Policy—Amortization) At the end of fiscal 2002, management of Dibec Manufacturing Corporation decided to change its amortization method from the straight-line method to the double-declining balance method for financial reporting purposes. For federal income taxes, the company must continue to use the CCA method. The income tax rate for all years is 30%. At the end of fiscal 2002, the company has 200,000 common shares issued and outstanding. Information regarding amortization expense and income after income taxes is as follows:

Amortization expense to date under:

	Straight Line	Double-Declining Balance
Pre-2001	$400,000	$950,000
2001	150,000	260,000
2002	140,000	250,000

Reported income after income taxes (straight line method):

2001	$1,200,000
2002	$1,400,000

Reported retained earnings:

December 31, 2001	$6,500,000
December 31, 2000	$5,900,000

Instructions

(a) Prepare the journal entries to record the change in accounting policy in 2002 and indicate how the change in amortization method would be reported in the income statement of 2002. Also indicate how earnings per share would be disclosed. (Hint: don't forget the income tax effects.)

(b) Assuming the retroactive-with-restatement method is used to account for this change, what correction needs to be made to the January 1, 2001 retained earnings balance on the comparative statement of retained earnings?

(c) What amortization expense amount will be reported in 2002?

E22-7 (Change in Policy—Long-term Contracts) Erikson Construction Company Ltd. changed from the completed-contract to the percentage-of-completion method of accounting for long-term construction contracts during 2003. For tax purposes, the company employs the completed-contract method and will continue this approach in the future. The appropriate information related to this change is as follows:

	Pretax Income from:		
	Percentage-of-Completion	Completed-Contract	Difference
2002	$780,000	$590,000	$190,000
2003	700,000	480,000	220,000

Instructions

(a) Assuming that the change qualifies as a change in accounting policy and that the tax rate is 35%, what is the amount of net income that will be reported in 2003?

(b) What entry(ies) are necessary to adjust the accounting records for the change in accounting policy?

(c) If this change was made to reflect changed circumstances, how should the change be accounted for?

E22-8 **(Various Changes in Policy—Inventory Methods)** Below is the net income of Anita Instrument Corp., calculated under three different inventory methods using a periodic system. Anita Instrument began operations on January 1, 1999.

	FIFO	Average Cost	LIFO
1999	$26,000	$24,000	$20,000
2000	30,000	25,000	21,000
2001	28,000	27,000	24,000
2002	34,000	30,000	26,000

Instructions

(Ignore tax considerations)

(a) Assume that in 2002, Anita decided to change from the average cost method to the FIFO method of costing inventories. Prepare the journal entry necessary for the change that took place during 2002, and show all the appropriate information needed for reporting on a comparative basis.

(b) Assume that in 2002, Anita, which had been using the FIFO method since incorporation in 1999, changed to the LIFO method of costing inventories in order to be consistent with the U.S. parent company that acquired Anita in 2002. Prepare the journal entry necessary for the change, and show all the appropriate information needed for reporting on a comparative basis.

E22-9 **(Change in Policy—Inventory Methods)** Garneau Corporation began operations on January 1, 1999 and uses the average cost method of pricing inventory. Management is contemplating a change in inventory methods for 2002. Garneau uses a periodic inventory system. The following information is available for the years 1999 to 2001:

	Net Income Calculated Using		
	Average Cost Method	FIFO Method	Specific Identification
1999	$15,000	$20,000	$16,000
2000	18,000	24,000	17,000
2001	20,000	27,000	22,000

Instructions

(Ignore tax considerations)

(a) If Garneau changes from the average cost method to the FIFO method in 2002, what is the required adjustment to retained earnings at January 1, 2002?

(b) If Garneau changes from the specific identification method to the average cost method in 2002, what is the required adjustment to retained earnings at January 1, 2001 on the comparative financial statements?

(c) Assume Garneau used the FIFO method during the years 1999 to 2001. In 2002, Garneau changed to the specific identification method. Prepare the journal entry necessary to record the change in policy.

E22-10 **(Error Correction Entries)** The first audit of the books of Gensing Limited was made for the year ended December 31, 2002. In examining the books, the auditor found that certain items had been overlooked or incorrectly handled in the last three years. These items are:

1. At the beginning of 2000, the company purchased a machine for $510,000 (residual value of $51,000) that had a useful life of six years. The bookkeeper used straight-line amortization, but failed to deduct the residual value in calculating the amortization base for the three years.

2. At the end of 2001, the company accrued sales salaries of $45,000 in excess of the correct amount.

3. A tax lawsuit that involved the year 2000 was settled late in 2002. It was determined that the company owed an additional $85,000 in taxes related to 2000. The company did not record a liability in 2000 or 2001 because the possibility of losing was considered remote. The company charged the $85,000 to retained earnings in 2002 as a correction of a prior year's error.

4. Gensing purchased another company early in 2000 and recorded goodwill of $450,000. Gensing amortized goodwill in 2000 ($22,500), in 2001 ($45,000), and in 2002 ($45,000). *Handbook* Section 3062 specifies that goodwill acquired prior to July 1, 2001 should not be amortized after January 1, 2002.

5. In 2002, the company changed its basis of inventory costing from FIFO to weighted average cost. The change's cumulative effect was to decrease net income of prior years by $71,000. The company debited this cumulative effect to Retained Earnings. The average cost method was used in calculating income for 2002.

6. In 2002, the company wrote off $87,000 of inventory stolen from one of its warehouses in 2001, but not uncovered until 2002. This loss was charged to a loss account in 2002.

Instructions

Prepare the journal entries in 2002 to correct the books where necessary, assuming that the 2002 books have not been closed. Disregard effects of corrections on income tax.

E22-11 **(Change in Principle and Error; Financial Statements)** Presented below are the comparative statements for Habbe Inc.

	2002	2001
Sales	$340,000	$270,000
Cost of sales	200,000	142,000
Gross profit	140,000	128,000
Expenses	88,000	50,000
Net income	$ 52,000	$ 78,000
Retained earnings (Jan. 1)	$125,000	$ 72,000
Net income	52,000	78,000
Dividends	(30,000)	(25,000)
Retained earnings (Dec. 31)	$147,000	$125,000

The following additional information is provided:

1. In 2002, Habbe Inc. decided to change its amortization method from sum of the years' digits to the straight-line method. The differences in the two amortization methods for the assets involved are:

	2002	2001
Sum of the years' digits	$30,000[a]	$40,000
Straight line	25,000	25,000

[a]The 2002 income statement contains amortization expense of $30,000.

2. In 2002, the company discovered that the ending inventory for 2001 was overstated by $24,000; ending inventory for 2002 is correctly stated.

Instructions

(a) Prepare the revised income and retained earnings statements for 2001 and 2002, assuming retroactive-with-restatement treatment (ignore income tax effects). Do not prepare footnotes.
(b) Prepare the revised income and retained earnings statements for 2001 and 2002, assuming retroactive-without-restatement treatment (ignore income tax effects). Do not prepare footnotes.

E22-12 **(Error Analysis and Correcting Entry)** You have been engaged to review the financial statements of Linette Corporation. In the course of your examination, you conclude that the bookkeeper hired during the current year is not doing a good job. You notice a number of irregularities as follows:

1. Year-end wages payable of $3,400 were not recorded because the bookkeeper thought that "they were immaterial."
2. Accrued vacation pay for the year of $31,100 was not recorded because the bookkeeper "never heard that you had to do it."
3. Insurance for a 12-month period purchased on November 1 of this year was charged to insurance expense in the amount of $2,640 because "the amount of the cheque is about the same every year."
4. Reported sales revenue for the year is $2,120,000. This includes all sales taxes collected for the year. The sales tax rate is 6%. Because the sales tax is forwarded to the provincial minister of revenue, the Sales Tax Expense account is debited because the bookkeeper thought that "the sales tax is a selling expense." At the end of the current year, the balance in the Sales Tax Expense account is $103,400.

Instructions

Prepare the necessary correcting entries, assuming that Linette uses a calendar-year basis and that the books for the current year are not yet closed.

E22-13 **(Error Analysis and Correcting Entry)** The reported net incomes for the first two years of Gustafson Products, Inc., were as follows: 2001—$147,000; 2002—$185,000. Early in 2003, the following errors were discovered:

1. Amortization of equipment for 2001 was understated $17,000.
2. Amortization of equipment for 2002 was overstated $38,500.
3. December 31, 2001 inventory was understated $50,000.
4. December 31, 2002 inventory was overstated $16,200.

Instructions

Prepare the correcting entry necessary when these errors are discovered. Assume that the books for 2002 are closed. Ignore income tax considerations.

E22-14 **(Error Analysis)** Henning Tool Corporation's December 31 year-end financial statements contained the following errors:

	December 31, 2001	December 31, 2002
Ending inventory	$9,600 overstated	$8,100 understated
Amortization expense	$2,300 overstated	—

An insurance premium of $66,000 was prepaid in 2001 covering the years 2001, 2002, and 2003. The entire amount was charged to expense in 2001. In addition, on December 31, 2002, fully amortized machinery was sold for $15,000 cash, but the entry was not recorded until 2003. There were no other errors during 2001 or 2002, and no corrections have been made for any of the errors. Ignore income tax considerations.

Instructions

(a) Calculate the errors' total effect on 2002 net income.
(b) Calculate the errors' total effect on the amount of Henning's working capital at December 31, 2002.
(c) Calculate the errors' total effect on the balance of Henning's retained earnings at December 31, 2002.

E22-15 **(Error Analysis; Correcting Entries)** A partial trial balance of Hartsack Corporation is as follows on December 31, 2002:

	Dr.	Cr.
Supplies on hand	$ 2,700	
Accrued salaries and wages		$ 1,500
Interest receivable on investments	5,100	
Prepaid insurance	90,000	
Unearned rent		–0–
Accrued interest payable		15,000

Additional adjusting data:
1. A physical count of supplies on hand on December 31, 2002 totalled $1,100. Through oversight, the Accrued Salaries and Wages account was not changed during 2002. Accrued salaries and wages on December 31, 2002 amounted to $4,400.
2. The Interest Receivable on Investments account was also left unchanged during 2002. Accrued interest on investments amounts to $4,350 on December 31, 2002.
3. The unexpired portions of the insurance policies totalled $65,000 as of December 31, 2002.
4. $28,000 was received on January 1, 2002 for the rent of a building for both 2002 and 2003. The entire amount was credited to rental income.
5. Amortization for the year was erroneously recorded as $5,000 rather than the correct figure of $50,000.
6. A further review of prior years' amortization calculations revealed that amortization of $7,200 was not recorded in error. It was decided that this oversight should be corrected by adjusting prior years' income.

Instructions

(a) Assuming that the books have not been closed, what are the adjusting entries necessary at December 31, 2002? Ignore income tax considerations.
(b) Assuming that the books have been closed, what are the adjusting entries necessary at December 31, 2002? Ignore income tax considerations.

E22-16 **(Error Analysis)** The before-tax income for Lonnie Holland Corp. for 2001 was $101,000 and $77,400 for 2002. However, the accountant noted that the following errors had been made:
1. Sales for 2001 included amounts of $38,200 that had been received in cash during 2001, but for which the related products were delivered in 2002. Title did not pass to the purchaser until 2002.
2. The inventory on December 31, 2001 was understated by $8,640.
3. The bookkeeper, in recording interest expense for both 2001 and 2002 on bonds payable, made the following entry on an annual basis:

Interest Expense	15,000	
Cash		15,000

The bonds have a face value of $250,000 and pay a stated interest rate of 6%. They were issued at a discount of $15,000 on January 1, 2001, to yield an effective interest rate of 7%. (The effective yield method should be used.)

4. Ordinary repairs to equipment had been erroneously charged to the Equipment account during 2001 and 2002. Repairs in the amount of $8,500 in 2001 and $9,400 in 2002 were so charged. The company applies a rate of 10% to the balance in the Equipment account at year end in determining its amortization charges.

Instructions

Prepare a schedule showing the calculation of corrected income before taxes for 2001 and 2002.

E22-17 **(Error Analysis)** When the records of Haida Corporation were reviewed at the close of 2002, the errors listed below were discovered. For each item, indicate by a check mark in the appropriate column whether the error resulted in an overstatement, an understatement, or had no effect on net income for the years 2001 and 2002.

	2001			2002		
	Over-statement	Under-statement	No Effect	Over-statement	Under-statement	No Effect
1. Failure to record amortization of patent in 2002						
2. Failure to record the correct amount of ending 2001 inventory, the amount was understated because of a calculation error						
3. Failure to record merchandise purchased in 2001 (it was also omitted from ending inventory in 2001 but was not yet sold)						
4. Failure to record accrued interest on notes payable in 2001 (amount was recorded when paid in 2002)						
5. Failure to reflect supplies on hand on balance sheet at end of 2001						

E22-18 **(Accounting for Accounting Changes)** Listed below are various types of accounting changes.

_____ 1. Change in a plant asset's residual value
_____ 2. Change due to overstatement of inventory
_____ 3. Change from sum of the years' digits to straight-line method of amortization
_____ 4. Change from consolidated financial statements covering three subsidiaries to consolidated financial statements reflecting the net assets and results of five subsidiaries due to the acquisition of two more subsidiaries
_____ 5. Change from weighted average cost to FIFO inventory method
_____ 6. Change in the rate used to calculate warranty costs
_____ 7. Change from an unacceptable accounting principle to an acceptable accounting principle
_____ 8. Change in a patent's amortization period
_____ 9. Change from completed-contract to percentage-of-completion method on construction contracts because of increased ability to estimate costs to complete and percentage complete
_____ 10. Recognition of additional income taxes owing from three years ago as a result of improper calculations by the accountant who wasn't familiar with income tax legislation and income tax returns

Instructions

For each change or error, indicate how it would be accounted for using the following code letters:

(a) Accounted for in the current year only
(b) Accounted for prospectively
(c) Accounted for retroactively
(d) None of the above

PROFBLEMS

P22-1 Siew Kim Enterprises Ltd. reported income before income taxes of $176,000, $180,000, and $198,000 in each of the past three years—2000, 2001, and 2002 respectively. The following information is also available.

1. Siew Kim lost a court case in which it was the defendant, relating to a patent infringement suit. Siew Kim is required to pay a competitor $35,000 to settle the suit. No previous entries had been recorded in the books relative to this case as Siew Kim management felt they would win.

2. A review of the company's provision for uncollectible accounts during 2002 resulted in a determination that 1% of sales is the appropriate amount of bad debt expense to be charged to operations, rather than the 1½% used for the preceding two years. Bad debt expense recognized in 2001 and 2000 was $25,000 and $17,500 respectively. The company would have recorded $22,500 bad debt expense under the old rate for 2002. No entry has yet been made in 2002 for bad debt expense.

3. Siew Kim acquired land on January 1, 1999 at a cost of $45,000. The land was charged to the equipment account in error and has been amortized since then on the basis of a five-year life with no residual value.

4. During 2002, the company changed from the double-declining balance method of amortization for its building to the straight-line method. Both methods were equally acceptable, and Siew Kim changed to the straight-line method as it was the most widely used method in the industry in Canada. Total amortization under both methods for the past three years is as follows:

	Straight-line	Declining-balance
2000	$32,000	$60,000
2001	32,000	57,000
2002	32,000	54,150

5. Early in 2002, Siew Kim determined that a piece of specialized equipment purchased in January, 1999 at a cost of $54,000 with an estimated life of five years and residual value of $4,000 is now estimated to continue in use until the end of 2006 with a $2,000 residual value. The company has been using straight-line amortization for this equipment.

Instructions

(a) For each of the foregoing accounting changes, errors, or transactions, present the journal entry(ies) Siew Kim needs to make to correct or adjust the accounts, assuming the accounts for 2002 have not yet been closed. If no entry is required, write "none" and briefly explain why. Ignore income tax considerations.

(b) Prepare the entries required in (a) above assuming an income tax rate of 25% throughout the fiscal periods identified.

P22-2 Roland Corporation is having its financial statements audited for the first time as of December 31, 2002. The auditor has found the following items that occurred in previous years:

1. Roland purchased equipment on January 2, 1999 for $65,000. At that time, the equipment had an estimated useful life of 10 years with a $5,000 residual value. The equipment is amortized on a straight-line basis. On January 2, 2002, as a result of additional information, the company determined that the equipment had a total useful life of seven years with a $3,000 residual value.

2. During 2002, Roland changed from the double-declining balance method for its building to the straight-line method. The auditor provided the following calculations, which present amortization on both bases:

	2002	2001	2000
Straight line	$27,000	$27,000	$27,000
Declining-balance	48,600	54,000	60,000

3. Roland purchased a machine on July 1, 1999, at a cost of $80,000. The machine has a residual value of $8,000 and a useful life of eight years. Roland's bookkeeper recorded straight-line amortization during each year but failed to consider the residual value.

Instructions

(a) Prepare the necessary journal entries to record each of the preceding changes or errors. The books for 2002 have not been closed.

(b) Calculate the 2002 amortization expense on the equipment.

(c) Calculate the comparative net incomes for 2001 and 2002, starting with income before the effects of any of the changes identified above. Income before amortization expense was $300,000 in 2002 and $210,000 in 2001.

P22-3 On December 31, 2002, before the books were closed, the management and accountant of Keltner Inc. made the following determinations about three amortizable assets:

1. Capital asset A was purchased January 2, 1999. It originally cost $495,000 and the straight-line method was chosen for amortization purposes. The asset was originally expected to be useful for 10 years and have a zero residual value. In 2002, the decision was made to change the amortization method from straight line to double-declining balance, and the estimates relating to useful life and residual value remained unchanged (assume a change in policy).

2. Capital asset B was purchased January 3, 1998. It originally cost $120,000 and the straight-line method was chosen for amortization purposes. The asset was expected to be useful for 15 years and have a zero residual value. In 2002, the decision was made to shorten this asset's total life to nine years and to estimate the residual value at $3,000.

3. Capital asset C was purchased January 5, 1998. The asset's original cost was $140,000 and this amount was entirely expensed in 1998 in error. This particular asset has a 10-year useful life and no residual value. The straight-line method is appropriate.

Additional data:

1. Income in 2002 before amortization expense amounted to $400,000.
2. Amortization expense on assets other than A, B, and C totalled $55,000 in 2002.
3. Income in 2001 was reported at $370,000.
4. Ignore all income tax effects.
5. 100,000 common shares were outstanding in 2001 and 2002. No dividends were declared in either year.

Instructions

(a) Prepare all necessary entries in 2002 to record these determinations.
(b) Calculate the adjusted net income and earnings per share for 2001 and 2002.
(c) Prepare comparative retained earnings statements for Keltner Inc. for 2001 and 2002. The company reported retained earnings of $200,000 at December 31, 2000.

P22-4 Kandu Inc. was organized in late 1999 to manufacture and sell hosiery. The company has been fairly successful, as indicated by the following reported net incomes.

1999	$140,000a	2001	$205,000
2000	160,000b	2002	276,000

aIncludes a $12,000 decrease because of change in bad debt experience rate.
bIncludes an extraordinary gain of $40,000.

The company has decided to expand operations and has applied for a sizeable bank loan. The bank officer has indicated that the records should be audited and comparative statements should be presented to facilitate analysis by the bank. Kandu Inc., therefore, hired the auditing firm of Check & Doublecheck Co. and has provided the following additional information.

1. In early 2000, Kandu Inc. changed its estimate from 1% to 2% on the amount of bad debt expense to be charged to operations. Bad debt expense for 1999 using a 2% rate is $24,000. The company, therefore, restated its net income for 1999.

2. In 2002, the auditor discovered that the company had changed its method of inventory costing from average cost to FIFO. The effect on the income statements for the previous years is as follows:

	1999	2000	2001	2002
Net income unadjusted, average cost basis	$140,000	$160,000	$205,000	$276,000
Net income unadjusted, FIFO basis	155,000	165,000	215,000	260,000
	$ 15,000	$ 5,000	$ 10,000	($ 16,000)

3. In 2000, the company changed its method of amortization from the straight-line method to the accelerated approach. The company used the accelerated method in 2000. The effect on the income statement for the previous year is as follows:

	1999
Net income unadjusted—accelerated method	$133,000
Net income unadjusted—straight-line method	140,000
	$ 7,000

4. In 2002, the auditor discovered that:

(a) The company incorrectly understated the ending inventory by $11,000 in 2001.

(b) A dispute developed in 2000 with the Canada Customs and Revenue Agency over the deductibility of entertainment expenses. In 1999, the company was not permitted these deductions, but a tax settlement was reached in 2002 that allowed these expenses. As a result of the court's finding, tax expenses in 2002 were reduced by $60,000.

Instructions

(a) Indicate how each of these changes or corrections should be handled in the accounting records. Ignore income tax considerations.

(b) Calculate the amount of net income to be reported on comparative income statements for the years 1999 to 2002.

P22-5   The management of Kreiter Instrument Corporation had concluded, with the concurrence of its independent auditors, that results of operations would be more fairly presented if Kreiter changed its method of costing inventory from FIFO to average cost in 2002. Given below is the five-year summary of income and a schedule of what the inventories might have been if stated on the average cost method.

KREITER INSTRUMENT CORPORATION
Statement of Income and Retained Earnings for the Years Ended May 31

	1998	1999	2000	2001	2002
Sales—net	$13,964	$15,506	$16,673	$18,221	$18,898
Cost of goods sold					
Beginning inventory	1,000	1,100	1,000	1,115	1,237
Purchases	13,000	13,900	15,000	15,900	17,100
Ending inventory	(1,100)	(1,000)	(1,115)	(1,237)	(1,369)
Total	12,900	14,000	14,885	15,778	16,968
Gross profit	1,064	1,506	1,788	2,443	1,930
Administrative expenses	700	763	832	907	989
Income before taxes	364	743	956	1,536	941
Income taxes (50%)	182	372	478	768	471
Net income	182	371	478	768	470
Retained earnings—beginning	1,206	1,388	1,759	2,237	3,005
Retained earnings—ending	$ 1,388	$ 1,759	$ 2,237	$ 3,005	$ 3,475
Earnings per share	$ 1.82	$ 3.71	$ 4.78	$ 7.68	$ 4.70

SCHEDULE OF INVENTORY BALANCES USING AVERAGE COST METHOD
Year Ended May 31

1997	1998	1999	2000	2001	2002
$950	$1,124	$1,091	$1,270	$1,480	$1,699

Instructions

(a) Prepare comparative statements for the five years, assuming that Kreiter changed its inventory costing method to average cost. Indicate the effects on net income and earnings per share for the years involved. (All amounts except EPS are rounded up to the nearest dollar.)

(b) Prepare the statement of retained earnings for 2002 with a comparative statement for 2001 to be issued to shareholders, assuming retroactive-with-restatement treatment.

P22-6   McInnes Corporation has decided that in preparing its 2002 financial statements, two changes should be made from the methods used in prior years:

1. **Amortization.** McInnes has always used the CCA method for tax and financial reporting purposes but has decided to change during 2002 to the straight-line method for financial reporting only. The effect of this change is as follows:

	Excess of CCA over Straight-line Amortization
Prior to 2001	$1,365,000
2001	106,050
2002	103,950
	$1,575,000

Amortization is charged to cost of sales and to selling, general, and administrative expenses on the basis of 75% and 25%, respectively.

2. **Bad debt expense.** In the past, McInnes recognized bad debt expense equal to 1.5% of net sales. After careful review, it has been decided that a rate of 1.75% is more appropriate for 2002. Bad debt expense is charged to selling, general, and administrative expenses.

The following information is taken from preliminary financial statements, prepared before giving effect to the two changes:

MCINNES CORPORATION
Condensed Balance Sheet
December 31, 2002

	2002	2001
Assets		
Current assets	$43,561,000	$43,900,000
Plant assets, at cost	45,792,000	43,974,000
Less: Accumulated amortization	23,761,000	22,946,000
	$65,592,000	$64,928,000
Liabilities and Shareholders' Equity		
Current liabilities	$21,124,000	$23,650,000
Long-term debt	15,154,000	14,097,000
Share capital	11,620,000	11,620,000
Retained earnings	17,694,000	15,561,000
	$65,592,000	$64,928,000

MCINNES CORPORATION
Income Statement
for the Year Ended December 31, 2002

	2002	2001
Net sales	$80,520,000	$78,920,000
Cost of goods sold	54,847,000	53,074,000
	25,673,000	25,846,000
Selling, general, and administrative expenses	19,540,000	18,411,000
	6,133,000	7,435,000
Other income (expense), net	(1,198,000)	(1,079,000)
Income before income taxes	4,935,000	6,356,000
Income taxes	2,220,750	2,860,200
Net income	$ 2,714,250	$ 3,495,800

There have been no temporary differences between any book and tax items prior to the changes above. The effective tax rate is 45%.

Instructions

(a) For the items listed below, calculate the amounts that would appear on the comparative (2002 and 2001) financial statements of McInnes Corporation after adjustment for the two accounting changes. Show amounts for both 2002 and 2001, and prepare supporting schedules as necessary.

1. Accumulated amortization
2. Future tax asset/liability
3. Selling, general, and administrative expenses
4. Current portion of income tax expense
5. Future portion of income tax expense

(b) Prepare the comparative financial statements that will be issued to shareholders for McInnes' year ended December 31, 2002.

P22-7 You have been assigned to examine the financial statements of Lemke Corporation for the year ended December 31, 2002. You discover the following situations:

1. Amortization of $3,200 for 2002 on delivery vehicles was not recorded.

2. The physical inventory count on December 31, 2001, improperly excluded merchandise costing $19,000 that had been temporarily stored in a public warehouse. Lemke uses a periodic inventory system.

3. The physical inventory count on December 31, 2002, improperly included merchandise with a cost of $8,500 that had been recorded as a sale on December 27, 2002 and held for the customer to pick up on January 4, 2003.

4. A collection of $5,600 on account from a customer received on December 31, 2002 was not recorded until January 2, 2003.

5. In 2002, the company sold for $3,700 fully amortized equipment that originally cost $22,000. The company credited the proceeds from the sale to the Equipment account.

6. During November 2002, a competitor company filed a patent-infringement suit against Lemke, claiming damages of $220,000. The company's legal counsel has indicated that an unfavourable verdict is probable and a reasonable estimate of the court's award to the competitor is $125,000. The company has not reflected or disclosed this situation in the financial statements.

7. Lemke has a portfolio of temporary investments reported as short-term investments at the lower of cost and market. No entry has been made in 2002 to adjust to market. Information on cost and market value is as follows:

	Cost	Market
December 31, 2001	$95,000	$95,000
December 31, 2002	$84,000	$82,000

8. At December 31, 2002, an analysis of payroll information shows accrued salaries of $12,200. The Accrued Salaries Payable account had a balance of $16,000 at December 31, 2002, which was unchanged from its balance at December 31, 2001.

9. A large piece of equipment was purchased on January 3, 2002 for $32,000 and was charged in error to Repairs Expense. The equipment is estimated to have a service life of eight years and no residual value. Lemke normally uses the straight-line amortization method for this type of equipment.

10. A $15,000 insurance premium paid on July 1, 2001 for a policy that expires on June 30, 2004 was charged to insurance expense.

11. A trademark was acquired at the beginning of 2001 for $50,000. Through an oversight, no amortization has been recorded since its acquisition. Lemke expected the trademark to benefit the company for a total of approximately 15 years.

Instructions

Assume the trial balance has been prepared but the books have not been closed for 2002. Assuming all amounts are material, prepare journal entries showing the adjustments that are required. Ignore income tax considerations.

P22-8 Voga Company is adjusting and correcting its books at the end of 2002. In reviewing its records, the following information is compiled.

1. Voga has failed to accrue sales commissions payable at the end of each of the last three years, as follows:

December 31, 2000	$11,300
December 31, 2001	$4,000
December 31, 2002	$2,500

2. In reviewing the December 31, 2002 inventory, Voga discovered errors in its inventory-taking procedures that have caused inventories for the last three years to be incorrect, as follows:

December 31, 2000	Overstated	$16,000
December 31, 2001	Understated	$21,000
December 31, 2002	Overstated	$6,700

Voga has already made an entry that established the incorrect December 31, 2002 inventory amount.

3. At December 31, 2002, Voga decided to change the amortization method on its office equipment from double-declining balance to straight line. Assume that tax amortization is higher than the double-declining amortization taken for each period. The following information is available (the tax rate is 40%):

	Double-Declining Balance	Straight Line	Pretax Difference	Tax Effect	Difference, Net of Tax
Prior to 2002	$70,000	$40,000	$30,000	$12,000	$18,000
2002	12,000	10,000	2,000	800	1,200

Voga has already recorded the 2002 amortization expense using the double-declining balance method.

4. Before 2002, Voga accounted for its income from long-term construction contracts on the completed contract basis because it was unable to reliably measure the degree of completion nor the estimated costs to complete. Early in 2002, Voga's growth permitted the company to hire an experienced cost accountant and the company changed to the percentage-of-completion basis for financial accounting purposes. The completed contract method will continue to be used for tax purposes. Income for 2002 has been recorded using the percentage-of-completion method. The income tax rate is 40%. The following information is available:

	Pretax Income	
	Percentage of Completion	Completed Contract
Prior to 2002	$150,000	$95,000
2002	60,000	20,000

Instructions

(a) Prepare the journal entries necessary at December 31, 2002 to record the above corrections and changes as appropriate. The books are still open for 2002. Voga has not yet recorded its 2002 income tax expense and payable amounts so current year tax effects may be ignored. Prior year tax effects must be considered in items 3 and 4.

(b) If there are alternative methods of accounting for any items listed above, explain what the options are and how you determined the method chosen.

P22-9 On May 5, 2003, you were hired by Hollenbeck Inc., a closely held company, as a staff member of its newly created internal auditing department. While reviewing the company's records for 2001 and 2002, you discover that no adjustments have yet been made for the items listed below.

Items

1. Interest income of $14,100 was not accrued at the end of 2001. It was recorded when received in February 2002.
2. A computer costing $8,000 was expensed when purchased on July 1, 2001. It is expected to have a four-year life with no residual value. The company typically uses straight-line amortization for all fixed assets.
3. Research costs of $33,000 were incurred early in 2001. They were capitalized and were to be amortized over a three-year period. Amortization of $11,000 was recorded for 2001 and $11,000 for 2002. For tax purposes, the research costs were expensed as incurred.
4. On January 2, 2001, Hollenbeck leased a building for five years at a monthly rental of $8,000. On that date, the company paid the following amounts, which were expensed when paid for both financial reporting and tax purposes.

Security deposit	$25,000
First month's rent	8,000
Last month's rent	8,000
	$41,000

5. The company received $30,000 from a customer at the beginning of 2001 for services that it is to perform evenly over a three-year period beginning in 2001. None of the amount received was reported as unearned revenue at the end of 2001. The $30,000 was included in taxable income in 2001.
6. Merchandise inventory costing $18,200 was in the warehouse at December 31, 2001, but was incorrectly omitted from the physical count at that date. The company uses the periodic inventory method.

Instructions

Indicate the effect of any errors on the net income figure reported on the income statement for the year ending December 31, 2001, and the retained earnings figure reported on the balance sheet at December 31, 2002. Assume all amounts are material and an income tax rate of 25% is appropriate for all years. Using the following format, enter the appropriate dollar amounts in the appropriate columns. Assume each item is independent of the other items. It is not necessary to total the columns on the grid.

	Net Income for 2001		Retained Earnings at 12/31/02	
Item	Understated	Overstated	Understated	Overstated

(CIA adapted)

P22-10   Kipawa Corporation has used the accrual basis of accounting for several years. A review of the records, however, indicates that some expenses and revenues have been handled on a cash basis because of errors made by an inexperienced bookkeeper. Income statements prepared by the bookkeeper reported $29,000 net income for 2001 and $37,000 net income for 2002. Further examination of the records reveals that the following items were handled improperly.

1. Rent was received from a tenant in December 2001; the amount, $1,300, was recorded as income at that time even though the rental pertained to 2002.

2. Wages payable on December 31 have been consistently omitted from the records of that date and have been entered as expenses when paid in the following year. The amounts of the accruals recorded in this manner were:

December 31, 2000	$1,100
December 31, 2001	1,500
December 31, 2002	940

3. Invoices for office supplies purchased have been charged to expense accounts when received. Inventories of supplies on hand at the end of each year have been ignored, and no entry has been made for them.

December 31, 2000	$1,300
December 31, 2001	740
December 31, 2002	1,420

Instructions

Prepare a schedule that will show the corrected net income for the years 2001 and 2002. All items listed should be labelled clearly. Ignore income tax considerations.

P22-11   Kolb Corporation is in the process of negotiating a loan for expansion purposes. Kolb's books and records have never been audited and the bank has requested that an audit be performed. Kolb has prepared the following comparative financial statements for the years ended December 31, 2002 and 2001:

KOLB CORPORATION
Balance Sheet
as of December 31, 2002 and 2001

	2002	2001
Assets		
Current assets		
Cash	$163,000	$ 82,000
Accounts receivable	392,000	296,000
Allowance for doubtful accounts	(37,000)	(18,000)
Temporary investments, at cost	78,000	78,000
Merchandise inventory	207,000	202,000
Total current assets	803,000	640,000
Plant assets		
Property, plant, and equipment	167,000	169,500
Accumulated amortization	(121,600)	(106,400)
Plant assets (net)	45,400	63,100
Total assets	$848,400	$703,100

Liabilities and Shareholders' Equity

Liabilities		
Accounts payable	$121,400	$196,100

Shareholders' equity		
Common shares, no par value, authorized 50,000 shares, issued and outstanding 20,000 shares	260,000	260,000
Retained earnings	467,000	247,000
Total shareholders' equity	727,000	507,000
Total liabilities and shareholders' equity	$848,400	$703,100

KOLB CORPORATION
Statement of Income
for the Years Ended December 31, 2002 and 2001

	2002	2001
Sales	$1,000,000	$900,000
Cost of sales	430,000	395,000
Gross profit	570,000	505,000
Operating expenses	210,000	205,000
Administrative expenses	140,000	105,000
	350,000	310,000
Net income	$ 220,000	$195,000

During the audit, the following additional facts were determined:

1. An analysis of collections and losses on accounts receivable during the past two years indicates a drop in anticipated bad debts losses. After consulting with management, it was agreed that the loss experience rate on sales should be reduced from the recorded 2% to 1½%, beginning with the year ended December 31, 2002.

2. An analysis of temporary investments revealed that the total market valuation for these investments as of the end of each year was as follows:

December 31, 2001	$82,000
December 31, 2002	$65,000

3. The merchandise inventory at December 31, 2001 was overstated by $8,900 and the merchandise inventory at December 31, 2002 was overstated by $13,600.

4. On January 2, 2001, equipment costing $30,000 (estimated useful life of 10 years and residual value of $5,000) was incorrectly charged to operating expenses. Kolb records amortization on the straight-line method. In 2002, fully amortized equipment (with no residual value) that originally cost $17,500 was sold as scrap for $2,800. Kolb credited the proceeds of $2,800 to the equipment account.

5. An analysis of 2001 operating expenses revealed that Kolb charged to expense a four-year insurance premium of $4,700 on January 15, 2001.

Instructions

(a) Prepare the journal entries to correct the books at December 31, 2002. The books for 2002 have not been closed. Ignore income taxes.

(b) Prepare a schedule showing the calculation of corrected net income for the years ended December 31, 2002 and 2001, assuming that any adjustments are to be reported on comparative statements for the two years. The first items on your schedule should be the net income for each year. Ignore income taxes. (Do not prepare financial statements.)

(AICPA adapted)

P22-12 You have been asked by a client to review the records of Ashok Corporation, a small manufacturer of precision tools and machines. Your client is interested in buying the business, and arrangements have been made for you to review the accounting records.

Your examination reveals the following:

1. Ashok Corporation commenced business on April 1, 1999, and has been reporting on a fiscal year ending March 31. The company has never been audited, but the annual statements prepared by the bookkeeper reflect the following income before closing and before deducting income taxes:

Year Ended March 31	Income Before Taxes
2000	$ 71,600
2001	111,400
2002	103,580

2. A relatively small number of machines has been shipped on consignment. These transactions have been recorded as ordinary sales and billed as such with the gross profit on sale recognized as shipped. On March 31 of each year, machines billed and in the hands of consignees amounted to:

2000	$6,500
2001	none
2002	5,590

Sales price was determined by adding 30% to cost. Assume that the consigned machines are sold the following year.

3. On March 30, 2001, two machines were shipped to a customer on a C.O.D. basis. The sale was not entered until April 5, 2001 when cash was received for $6,100. The machines were not included in the inventory at March 31, 2001. (Title passed on March 30, 2001.)

4. All machines are sold subject to a five-year warranty. It is estimated that the expense ultimately to be incurred in connection with the warranty will amount to ½ of 1% of sales. The company has charged an expense account for actual warranty costs incurred. Sales per books and warranty costs were:

Year Ended March 31	Sales	Actual Warranty Costs Incurred for Sales Made in			
		2000	2001	2002	Total
2000	$ 940,000	$760			$ 760
2001	1,010,000	360	$1,310		1,670
2002	1,795,000	320	1,620	$1,910	3,850

5. A review of the corporate minutes reveals the manager is entitled to a bonus of ½ of 1% of the income before deducting income taxes and the bonus. The bonuses have never been recorded or paid.

6. Bad debts have been recorded on a direct write-off basis. Experience of similar enterprises indicates that losses will approximate ¼ of 1% of sales. Bad debts written off and expensed were:

	Bad Debts Incurred on Sales Made in			
	2000	2001	2002	Total
2000	$750			$ 750
2001	800	$ 520		1,320
2002	350	1,800	$1,700	3,850

7. The bank deducts 6% on all contracts financed. Of this amount, ½% is placed in a reserve to the credit of Ashok Corporation that is refunded to Ashok as finance contracts are paid in full. The reserve established by the bank has not been reflected in Ashok's books. The excess of credits over debits (net increase) to the reserve account with Ashok on the books of the bank for each fiscal year were as follows:

2000	$ 3,000
2001	3,900
2002	5,100
	$12,000

8. Commissions on sales have been entered when paid. Commissions payable on March 31 of each year were:

2000	$1,400
2001	800
2002	1,120

Instructions

(a) Present a schedule showing the revised income before income taxes for each of the years ended March 31, 2000, 2001, and 2002. Make calculations to the nearest whole dollar.

(b) Prepare the journal entry or entries you would give the bookkeeper to correct the books. Assume the books have not yet been closed for the fiscal year ended March 31, 2002. Disregard correction of income taxes.

(AICPA adapted)

CONCEPTUAL CASES

C22-1 Cranmore Inc. has recently hired a new independent auditor, Jodie Larson, who says she wants "to get everything straightened out." Consequently, she has proposed the following accounting changes in connection with Cranmore Inc.'s 2002 financial statements:

1. At December 31, 2001, Cranmore had a receivable of $820,000 from Michael Inc. on its balance sheet. Michael Inc. has been declared bankrupt, and no recovery is expected. Cranmore proposes to write off the receivable against retained earnings as a prior period item.

2. Cranmore proposes the following changes in amortization policies:

   (a) For office furniture and fixtures, it proposes to change from a 10-year useful life to an 8-year life. If this change had been made in prior years, retained earnings at December 31, 2001 would have been $250,000 less. The effect of the change on 2002 income alone is a reduction of $60,000.

   (b) For its manufacturing assets, Cranmore proposes to change from double-declining balance amortization to straight line. If straight-line amortization had been used for all prior periods, retained earnings would have been $380,800 greater at December 31, 2001. The change's effect on 2002 income alone is a reduction of $48,800.

   (c) For its equipment in the leasing division, Cranmore proposes to adopt the sum-of-the-years'-digits amortization method. The company had never used SYD before. The first year the company operated a leasing division was 2002. If straight-line amortization were used, 2002 income would be $110,000 greater.

3. In preparing its 2001 statements, one of Cranmore's bookkeepers overstated ending inventory by $235,000 because of a mathematical error. The company proposes to treat this item as a prior period adjustment.

4. In the past, the company has spread preproduction costs in its furniture division over five years. Because its latest furniture is of the "fad" type, it appears that the largest volume of sales will occur during the first two years after introduction. Consequently, the company proposes to amortize preproduction costs on a per-unit basis, which will result in expensing most of such costs during the first two years after the furniture's introduction. If the new accounting method had been used prior to 2002, retained earnings at December 31, 2001 would have been $375,000 less.

5. For the nursery division, Cranmore proposes to switch from FIFO to average cost inventories because it believes that average cost will provide a better matching of current costs with revenues. The effect of making this change on 2002 earnings will be an increase of $320,000. Cranmore says that the change's effect on December 31, 2001 retained earnings cannot be determined.

6. To achieve a better matching of revenues and expenses in its building construction division, the company proposes to switch from the completed-contract method of accounting to the percentage-of-completion method. Had the percentage-of-completion method been employed in all prior years, retained earnings at December 31, 2001 would have been $1,175,000 greater.

Instructions

(a) For each of the changes described above decide whether:

   1. the change involves an accounting policy, accounting estimate, or error correction.

   2. restatement of opening retained earnings is required.

(b) What would be the proper adjustment to the December 31, 2001, retained earnings? What would be the new policies' effect on the 2002 income statement?

C22-2 Various types of accounting changes can affect the financial statements of a business enterprise differently. Assume that the following list describes changes that have a material effect on the financial statements for the current year of your business enterprise.

1. a change from the completed-contract method to the percentage-of-completion method of accounting for long-term construction-type contracts because of increased sophistication of your costing department

2. a change in the estimated useful life of previously recorded capital assets as a result of newly acquired information

3. a change from deferring and amortizing preproduction costs to recording such costs as an expense when incurred because the costs' future benefits have become doubtful (the new accounting method was adopted in recognition of the change in estimated future benefits)

4. a change from including the employer share of CPP premiums with Payroll Tax Expenses to including it with "Retirement Benefits" on the income statement

5. correction of a mathematical error in inventory costing made in a prior period

6. cessation of production and sale of plant and equipment of the manufacturing operations considered a business segment

7. a change from direct costing to full absorption costing for inventory valuation
8. a change from presenting unconsolidated statements to presenting consolidated statements for the company and its two long-held subsidiaries
9. a change in the method of accounting for leases for tax purposes to conform with the financial accounting method; as a result, both future and current taxes payable changed substantially
10. the acquisition of a new subsidiary
11. a change from the FIFO method of inventory costing to the average cost method of inventory costing

Instructions

Identify the type of change that is described in each item above and indicate whether the prior year's financial statements should be restated when presented in comparative form with the current year's statements.

C22-3 Listed below are three independent, unrelated sets of facts relating to accounting changes.

Situation 1

Millhouse Corp. is in the process of having its first audit. The company's policy on recognizing revenue is to use the instalment method. However, *Handbook* Section 3400 permits the use of the instalment method of revenue recognition only in circumstances that are not present here. Millhouse president A. G. Shumway is willing to change to an acceptable method.

Situation 2

Nestor Corp. decides in January 2002 to adopt the straight-line method of amortization for plant equipment. The straight-line method will be used for new acquisitions as well as for previously acquired plant equipment for which amortization had been provided on an accelerated basis.

Situation 3

Ozmon Ltd. determined that its capital assets' depreciable lives are too long to fairly match the assets' cost with the revenue produced. The company decided at the beginning of the current year to reduce the useful lives of all of its existing capital assets by five years.

Instructions

For each situation described, provide the information indicated below.

    (a) type of accounting change
    (b) manner of reporting the change under current generally accepted accounting principles including a discussion, where applicable, of how amounts are calculated
    (c) the change's effect on the balance sheet and income statement

C22-4 Ali Reiners, controller of Luftsa Corp., is aware that there is a *Handbook* section on accounting changes. After reading the section, she is confused about what action to take on the following items related to Luftsa Corp. for the year 2002.

1. In 2002, Luftsa decided to change its policy on accounting for certain marketing costs. Previously, the company had chosen to defer and amortize all marketing costs over at least five years because Luftsa believed that a return on these expenditures did not occur immediately. Recently, however, the time differential has considerably shortened, and Luftsa is now expensing the marketing costs as incurred.
2. In 2002, the company examined its entire policy relating to the amortization of plant equipment. Plant equipment had normally been amortized over a 15-year period, but recent experience has indicated that the company was incorrect in its estimates and that the assets should be amortized over a 20-year period.
3. One division of Luftsa Corp., Rosentiel Co., has consistently shown an increasing net income from period to period. On closer examination of its operating statement, it is noted that bad debt expense and inventory obsolescence charges are much lower than in other divisions. In discussing this with the division's controller, it has been learned that the controller has increased his net income each period by knowingly making low estimates related to the write-off of receivables and inventory.
4. In 2002, the company purchased new machinery that should increase production dramatically. The company has decided to amortize this machinery on an accelerated basis, even though other machinery is amortized on a straight-line basis.
5. All equipment sold by Luftsa is subject to a three-year warranty. It has been estimated that the expense ultimately to be incurred on these machines is 1% of sales. In 2002, because of a production breakthrough, it is now estimated that ½ of 1% of sales is sufficient. In 2000 and 2001, warranty expense was calculated as $64,000 and $70,000, respectively. The company now believes that these warranty costs should be reduced by 50%.

6. In 2002, the company decided to change its method of inventory pricing from average cost to the FIFO method. The change's effect on prior years is to increase 2000 income by $65,000 and increase 2001 income by $20,000.

Instructions

Ali Reiners has come to you, her accountant, for advice about the situations above. Prepare a memorandum to Reiners, indicating the appropriate accounting treatment that should be given each of these situations.

C22-5 Rydell Manufacturing Ltd. is preparing its year-end financial statements. The controller, Thea Kimbria, is confronted with several decisions about statement presentation with regard to the following items:

1. The vice-president of sales had indicated that one product line has lost its customer appeal and will be phased out over the next three years. Therefore, a decision has been made to lower the estimated lives on related production equipment from the remaining five years to three years.
2. Estimating the lives of new products in the Leisure Products Division has become very difficult because of the highly competitive conditions in this market. Therefore, the practice of deferring and amortizing preproduction costs has been abandoned in favour of expensing such costs as they are incurred.
3. The Hightone Building was converted from a sales office to offices for the accounting department at the beginning of this year. Therefore, the expense related to this building will now appear as an administrative expense rather than a selling expense on the current year's income statement.
4. When the year-end physical inventory adjustment was made for the current year, the controller discovered that the prior year's physical inventory sheets for an entire section of warehouse were mislaid and excluded from last year's count.
5. The method of accounting used for financial reporting purposes for certain receivables has been approved for tax purposes during the current tax year by the CCRA. This change for tax purposes will cause both current taxes payable and future tax liabilities to change substantially.
6. Management has decided to switch from the FIFO inventory valuation method to the average cost inventory valuation method for all inventories.
7. Rydell's Custom Division manufactures large-scale, custom-designed machinery on a contract basis. Management decided to switch from the completed-contract method to the percentage-of-completion method of accounting for long-term contracts.

Instructions

(a) *CICA Handbook* Section 1506, "Accounting Changes," identifies three types of accounting changes: changes in accounting policy, changes in accounting estimates, and corrections of errors of prior periods. For each of the three types of accounting change:
   1. Define the type of change.
   2. Explain the general accounting treatment required according to *Handbook* Section 1506 with respect to the current year and prior years' financial statements.

(b) For each of the seven changes Rydell Manufacturing Ltd. has made in the current year, identify and explain whether the change is a change in accounting policy, in estimate, or due to error. If any of the changes is not one of these three types, explain why.

(CMA adapted)

C22-6 As a professional accountant, you have been contacted by Ben Teiken, CEO of Sports-Pro Athletics, Inc., a manufacturer of a variety of athletic equipment. He has asked you how to account for the following changes.

1. Sports-Pro appropriately changed its amortization method for its production machinery from the double-declining balance method to the production method effective January 1, 2002.
2. Effective January 1, 2002, Sports-Pro appropriately changed the residual values used in calculating amortization for its office equipment.
3. In December 2002, Sports-Pro formalized its plan to discontinue a major segment of its business early in 2003.

Instructions

Write a one to one-and-a-half page letter to Ben Teiken explaining how each of the above changes should be presented in the December 31, 2002 financial statements.

Using Your Judgement

FINANCIAL REPORTING PROBLEM:
CANADIAN TIRE CORPORATION, LIMITED

Instructions

Refer to the financial statements and accompanying notes and discussion of Canadian Tire Corporation, Limited presented in Appendix 5B and answer the following questions or instructions.

(a) Identify the changes in accounting policy reported by Canadian Tire during the two years covered by its income statements for 1999 and 2000. Indicate the year of change and describe the nature of the changes.

(b) For each change in accounting policy, identify, if possible, the cumulative effect on prior years and the effect on operating results in the year of change.

(c) Prepare the journal entries likely made by Canadian Tire to recognize the changes in policy.

(d) What alternative methods could Canadian Tire have chosen to report these changes? What would have been the effect on the financial statements actually reported for 1999 and 2000 if the alternative method(s) had been applied?

COMPARATIVE ANALYSIS CASE

Falconbridge Limited, Inco Limited, and Noranda Inc.

Instructions

From the SEDAR website (www.sedar.com) or other source, obtain the 2000 financial statements of Falconbridge Limited, Inco Limited, and Noranda Inc., three companies in the metals and minerals industry. Answer the following questions or instructions.

(a) Identify the changes in accounting principles reported by these companies in their 2000 fiscal year. Were similar changes accounted for and reported in the same way by all three? Compare the extent of the disclosures by each company.

(b) Would you expect these changes to have a similar effect on all three companies? Did they? Were the changes equally significant to all companies?

(c) Do the companies report what the effect is on the current year's income of these changes? Comment.

RESEARCH CASES

Case 1

In July 2001, the CICA released its new recommendations on accounting for goodwill and other intangibles. Section 3062, entitled "Goodwill and Other Intangible Assets," effective for fiscal years beginning on or after January 2002 for public companies, includes very specific transitional provisions for the accounting and reporting of this revised accounting policy, or accounting change.

Instructions

(a) Investigate what the accounting requirements are for this change in accounting policy.

(b) Suggest reasons why the Accounting Standards Board might have decided on this treatment.

(c) What disclosures are required when companies adopt the new recommendations?

Case 2

The reporting of errors in previous years' financial statements is not a common event. In May 1998, **Philip Services Corp.** re-released its 1997 financial statements with restatements for the 1995, 1996, and 1997 fiscal years for errors relating to these previous years' financial statements.

Instructions

(a) Obtain a copy of the revised 1997 financial statements. These are available on the SEDAR website (www.sedar.com). Identify the nature of the errors reported, and the effect of each on the financial statements of each year, if possible.

(b) How significant were these errors relative to the results of operations reported for each of the years?

(c) The Philip Services Corp. situation was widely reported in the financial press. What can you determine was the cause of such errors?

Case 3

Instructions

The March 25, 1996 issue of Forbes includes a brief article entitled "Super Slipup." Read the article and answer the following questions.

(a) What error was made with respect to the financial statements of **Baby Superstore, Inc.**?

(b) To what did the company attribute the error?

(c) What happened to the company's share price upon discovery of the error?

(d) What negative effects did the error have on investors' perceptions of Baby Superstore? Are these concerns legitimate?

ETHICS CASE

Andy Frain is an audit senior of a large public accounting firm who has just been assigned to the Usher Corporation's annual audit engagement. Usher has been a client of Frain's firm for many years. Usher is a fast-growing business in the commercial construction industry. In reviewing the capital asset ledger, Frain discovered a series of unusual accounting changes, in which the useful lives of assets, amortized using the straight-line method, were substantially lowered near the midpoint of the original estimate. For example, the useful life of one dump truck was changed from 10 to 6 years during its fifth year of service. Upon further investigation, Andy was told by Vince Lloyd, Usher's accounting manager, "I don't really see your problem. After all, it's perfectly legal to change an accounting estimate. Besides, our CEO likes to see big earnings!"

Instructions

Answer the following questions:

(a) What are the ethical issues concerning Usher's practice of changing the useful lives of capital assets?

(b) Who could be harmed by Usher's unusual accounting changes?

(c) What should Frain do in this situation?

CHAPTER 23

Statement of Cash Flows

LEARNING OBJECTIVES

After studying this chapter, you should be able to:

1. Describe the purpose and uses of the statement of cash flows.

2. Define cash and cash equivalents.

3. Identify the major classifications of cash flows and explain the significance of each.

4. Contrast the direct and indirect methods of calculating net cash flow from operating activities.

5. Differentiate between net income and net cash flows from operating activities.

6. Prepare a statement of cash flows.

7. Read and interpret a statement of cash flows.

8. Identify the financial reporting and disclosure requirements for the statement of cash flows.

9. Use a work sheet to prepare a statement of cash flows.

Preview of Chapter 23

Examining a company's income statement may provide insights into its profitability, but it does not provide much information about its liquidity and financial flexibility. This chapter's purpose is to explain the main components of a statement of cash flows, the types of information it provides, and how to read, prepare, and interpret such a statement. The chapter's content and organization are as follows:

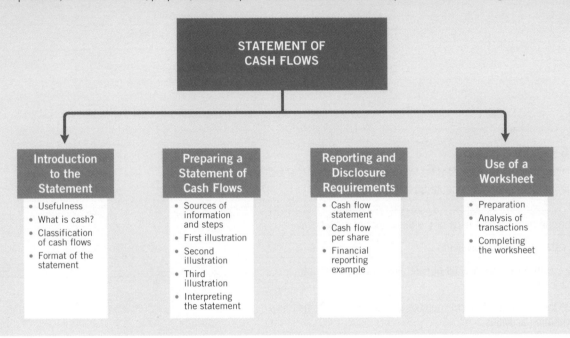

INTRODUCTION TO THE STATEMENT OF CASH FLOWS

OBJECTIVE 1

Describe the purpose and uses of the statement of cash flows.

Will the company be able to continue to pay dividends? Where did the cash come from to invest in acquiring the subsidiary this year? Will the company have sufficient cash to meet the significant debt maturing next year? How did cash increase when there was a net loss for the period? How were the bond issue proceeds used? How was the expansion in plant and equipment financed? These questions cannot be answered by reviewing the balance sheet and income statement. A cash flow statement is needed.

The primary purpose of the statement of cash flows is to provide information about an entity's cash receipts and cash payments during a period. A secondary objective is to provide information on a cash basis about its operating, investing, and financing activities. The statement of cash flows therefore reports cash receipts, cash payments, and net change in cash resulting from an enterprise's operating, investing, and financing activities during a period, in a format that reconciles the beginning and ending cash balances.

Usefulness of the Statement of Cash Flows

The information in a statement of cash flows should help investors, creditors, and others assess the following:

1. **The liquidity and solvency of an entity—its capacity to generate cash and its needs for cash resources.** The timing and degree of certainty of expected cash inflows need to be determined in light of the entity's requirements for cash to pay maturing debt, maintain and increase productive capacity, and distribute a return to owners.[1]

---

[1] *CICA Handbook*, Section 1540, par. .01.

2. **The amounts, timing, and uncertainty of future cash flows.** Historical cash flows are often useful in helping to predict future cash flows. By examining relationships between items such as sales and net cash flow from operating activities, or net cash flow from operating activities and increases or decreases in cash, it is possible to make better predictions of the amounts, timing, and uncertainty of future cash flows than is possible using accrual basis data.

3. **The reasons for the difference between net income and net cash flow from operating activities.** The net income number is important, because it provides information on a business enterprise's success or failure from one period to another. But some people are critical of accrual basis net income because estimates must be made to arrive at it. As a result, the number's reliability is often challenged. Such is not the case with cash. Readers of the financial statements benefit from knowing the reasons for the difference between net income and net cash flow from operating activities. Then they can assess for themselves the income number's reliability.

UNDERLYING CONCEPTS

The statement of cash flows is another example of relevant information— information that is useful in assessing and predicting future cash flows.

What Is Cash?

As part of a company's cash management system, short-term investments are often held instead of cash, thereby allowing the company to earn a return on cash balances in excess of its immediate needs. Also, it is common for an organization to have an agreement with the bank that permits the account to fluctuate between a positive balance and an overdraft. Because an entity's cash activity and position are more appropriately described by including these other cash management activities, the AcSB recommends that cash flows be defined as inflows and outflows of cash and cash equivalents.

Cash is defined as cash on hand and demand deposits. Cash equivalents are short-term, highly liquid investments that are readily convertible to known amounts of cash and are subject to an insignificant risk of change in value.[2] **Nonequity** investments acquired with short maturities and bank overdrafts repayable on demand, both of which result from and are an integral part of an organization's cash management policies, are included in cash and cash equivalents.[3]

Throughout the discussion and illustrations in this chapter, the use of the term "cash" should be interpreted to mean "cash and cash equivalents."

OBJECTIVE 2

Define cash and cash equivalents.

Classification of Cash Flows

The statement of cash flows classifies cash receipts and cash payments according to whether they were a result of an operating, investing, or a financing activity. Transactions and other events characteristic of each kind of activity and the significance of each type of cash flow are as follows:

1. Operating activities are the enterprise's principal revenue-producing activities and other activities that are not investing or financing activities.[4] Operating flows generally involve the cash effects of transactions that determine net income, such as collections from customers on accounts receivable; and payments to suppliers on accounts payable, CCRA on income taxes payable, and employees on salaries and wages payable.

The level of cash provided from or used in operations is key information for financial statement users. Like blood flowing through the veins and arteries of our

OBJECTIVE 3

Identify the major classifications of cash flows and explain the significance of each.

---

[2] *Ibid.*, par. .06(a), (b) and (c).

[3] *Ibid.*, par. .08 suggests a maturity "of, say three months or less from the date of acquisition." Examples of cash equivalents are treasury bills, commercial paper, and money market funds purchased with cash that is in excess of immediate needs.

[4] *Ibid.*, par. .06(d).

bodies, operating cash flows—derived mainly from receipts from customers—are needed to maintain the organization's systems: to meet payrolls, to pay suppliers, to cover rentals and insurance, and to pay taxes. In addition, surplus flows from operations are needed to repay loans, to take advantage of new investment opportunities, and to pay dividends without having to seek new external financing.

2. Investing activities cover the acquisition and disposal of long-term assets and other investments not included in cash equivalents.[5] They include (a) making and collecting loans and (b) acquiring and disposing of investments and productive long-lived assets.

   The use of cash in investment activities tells the financial statement reader whether the entity is ploughing cash back into additional long-term assets that will generate profits and increased cash flows in the future, or whether the stock of long-term productive assets is being decreased by conversion into cash.

3. Financing activities result in changes in the size and composition of the enterprise's equity capital and borrowings.[6] They include (a) obtaining cash through the issuance of debt and repaying the amounts borrowed and (b) obtaining capital from owners and providing them with a return on, and a return of, their investment.

   Details of the cash flows related to financing activities allow readers to assess the potential for future claims to the organization's cash and to identify major changes in the form of financing, especially between debt and equity.

Illustration 23-1 identifies a business enterprise's typical cash receipts and payments and classifies them according to whether they are operating, investing, or financing activities. **Note that the operating cash flows are related almost entirely to working capital (current asset and current liability) accounts, the investing cash flows generally involve long-term asset items, and the financing flows are derived principally from changes in long-term liability and equity accounts.**

ILLUSTRATION 23-1
Classification of Typical Cash
Inflows and Outflows

Operating
    Cash inflows
        From cash sales and collections from customers
           on account
        From returns on loans (interest) and equity securities
           (dividends)
        From receipts for royalties, rents, and fees
    Cash outflows
        To suppliers on account
        To employees for services
        To government for taxes
        To lenders for interest
        To others for expenses

Generally Non-Cash Current Asset and Current Liability Items

Investing
    Cash inflows
        From sale of property, plant, and equipment
        From sale of debt or equity securities of other entities
        From collection of principal on loans to other entities
    Cash outflows
        To purchase property, plant, and equipment
        To purchase debt or equity securities of other entities.
        To make loans to other entities

Generally Long-Term Asset Items

---

[5] *Ibid.*, par. .06(e).

[6] *Ibid.*, par. .06(f).

Financing
Cash inflows
From issuance of equity securities
From issuance of debt (bonds and notes)
Cash outflows
To shareholders as dividends
To redeem long-term debt or reacquire share capital
To reduce capital lease obligations

Generally
Long-Term
Liability
and Equity
Items

Some cash flows related to investing or financing activities are classified as operating activities. For example, **dividends and interest received and paid and included when determining net income** are classified as operating activities. Any **dividends or interest paid that are charged against retained earnings** are included as financing flows.[7]

Other items, although reported on the income statement, relate directly to investing and financing activities. For example, cash received from the sale of property, plant, and equipment is properly classified as an investing cash inflow. The amount of the gain or loss reported in the income statement, however, must be excluded in determining cash flows from operating activities. Similarly, a gain or loss on the repayment (extinguishment) of debt is not an operating cash flow. The cash outflow to redeem the debt, not the amount of the gain or loss, is the actual cash flow and the repayment is clearly a financing activity.

Outflows and proceeds on the sale of securities and loans acquired specifically for resale (trading securities) are treated similar to flows related to inventories acquired for resale—as operating cash flows.

Income taxes present another complexity. While income tax expense can be identified with specific operating, investing, and financing transactions, the related cash payments for taxes usually cannot be. For this reason, income tax payments are classified as operating cash flows unless they can be specifically identified with financing and investing activities.[8]

How should significant noncash transactions that affect an organization's asset and capital structure be handled? Examples of such noncash transactions are:

1. acquisition of assets by assuming liabilities (including capital lease obligations) or by issuing equity securities
2. exchanges of nonmonetary assets
3. conversion of debt or preferred shares to common shares, and
4. issuance of equity securities to retire debt.

Because the cash flow statement reports only activities' effects in terms of cash flows, significant investing and financing transactions that do not affect cash **are excluded from the statement** and are required to be disclosed elsewhere in the financial statements.[9]

Format of the Statement of Cash Flows

The three activities discussed in the preceding section constitute the general format of the statement of cash flows. The operating activities section almost always appears first, followed by the investing and financing activities sections. The individual inflows and

IAS NOTE

IAS 7 permits interest and dividends received and paid to be reported as either operating, investing, or financing flows, but requires consistency from period to period.

UNDERLYING CONCEPTS

By rejecting the requirement to allocate taxes to the various activities, the Accounting Standards Board invoked the cost-benefit constraint. The information would be beneficial, but the cost of providing such information would exceed the benefits of providing the information.

---

[7] Dividend payments recognized in the income statement relate to equity securities that are determined to be liabilities in substance, and interest payments charged to retained earnings relate to debt securities that are judged to be equity instruments in substance. The statement of cash flows, therefore, treats returns to in-substance equity holders as financing outflows and to those designated as creditors as operating outflows.

[8] *CICA Handbook*, Section 1540, par. .38.

[9] *Ibid.*, par. .46.

outflows from investing and financing activities are reported separately; that is, they are reported gross, not netted against one another. Thus, cash outflow from the purchase of property is reported separately from the cash inflow from the sale of property. Similarly, the cash inflow from the issuance of debt is reported separately from the cash outflow for debt retirement. Not reporting them separately obscures the enterprise's investing and financing activities and makes it more difficult to assess future cash flows.[10]

The skeleton format of a statement of cash flows is provided in Illustration 23-2. Note that it reconciles the beginning and ending cash balances as reported in the comparative balance sheets.

ILLUSTRATION 23-2
Format of the Statement of Cash Flows

COMPANY NAME Statement of Cash Flows Period Covered		
Cash flows from operating activities		
Net income		XXX
Adjustments to reconcile net income to net cash provided by (used in) operating activities: (List of individual items)	XX	XX
Net cash provided by (used in) operating activities		XXX
Cash flows from investing activities		
(List of individual inflows and outflows)	XX	
Net cash provided by (used in) investing activities		XXX
Cash flows from financing activities		
(List of individual inflows and outflows)	XX	
Net cash provided by (used in) financing activities		XXX
Net increase (decrease) in cash		XXX
Cash at beginning of period		XXX
Cash at end of period		XXX

OBJECTIVE 4

Contrast the direct and indirect methods of calculating net cash flow from operating activities.

Illustration 23-2 derives the net cash flow from operating activities indirectly by making the necessary adjustments to the net income reported on the income statement. This is referred to as the **indirect method** (or reconciliation method). The cash flow from operating activities could be calculated directly by identifying the sources of the cash receipts and payments. This approach is referred to as the **direct method** and is illustrated below.

ILLUSTRATION 23-3
Cash Flows from Operating Activities—Direct Method

Cash flows from operating activities	
Cash receipts from customers	XX
Cash receipts from other revenue sources	XX
Cash payments to suppliers for goods and services	(XX)
Cash payments to and on behalf of employees	(XX)
Cash payments of income taxes	(XX)
Net cash flow provided by (used in) operating activities	XX

There has been considerable controversy about which method should be recommended for use. The AcSB encourages use of the direct method because it provides additional information, but its use is not mandatory.[11]

---

[10] Netting is permitted in limited circumstances. See *Handbook* Section 1540, par. .25 to .27.

[11] Unfortunately, use of the direct method is rare in Canada. Prior to the AcSB stating a preference for the direct method in 1997, *Financial Reporting in Canada—1995* reported that 1 of 300 surveyed companies in 1994 used the direct method. In 1999, two companies out of 200 surveyed used the direct method.

Direct Versus Indirect

In general, reporting companies tend to prefer the indirect method, although commercial lending officers and other investors tend to express a strong preference for the direct method because of the additional information it provides.

In Favour of the Direct Method. The direct method's principal advantage is that it shows operating cash receipts and payments. That is, it is more consistent with the objective of a statement of cash flows—to provide information about cash receipts and cash payments—than the indirect method, which does not report operating cash receipts and payments.

Supporters of the direct method contend that knowing the specific sources of operating cash receipts and the purposes for which operating cash payments were made in past periods is useful in estimating future operating cash flows. Furthermore, information about amounts of major classes of operating cash receipts and payments is more useful than information only about their arithmetic sum (the net cash flow from operating activities). Such information is more revealing of an enterprise's ability to (1) generate sufficient cash from operating activities to pay its debts, (2) reinvest in its operations, and (3) make distributions to its owners.[12]

Many corporate providers of financial statements say that they do not currently collect information in a manner that allows them to determine amounts, such as cash received from customers or cash paid to suppliers. But supporters of the direct method contend that the incremental cost of assimilating such operating cash receipts and payments data is not significant.

In Favour of the Indirect Method. The indirect method's principal advantage is that it focuses on the differences between net income and net cash flow from operating activities. That is, it provides a useful link between the statement of cash flows and the income statement and balance sheet.

Many providers of financial statements contend that it is less costly to adjust net income to net cash flow from operating activities (indirect) than it is to report gross operating cash receipts and payments (direct). Supporters of the indirect method also state that the direct method, which effectively reports income statement information on a cash rather than an accrual basis, may erroneously suggest that net cash flow from operating activities is as good as, or better than, net income as a measure of performance.

As the indirect method has been used almost exclusively in the past, both preparers and users are more familiar with it and this helps perpetuate its use. Each method provides different but useful information. The best solution may lie in mandating the direct method, which comes closer to meeting the statement's stated objectives, and requiring disclosure of the differences between net income and cash flow from operations.

INTERNATIONAL INSIGHT

FASB also encourages the use of the direct method over the indirect. If the direct method is used, there is a requirement to provide a reconciliation between net income and cash flow from operating activities.

PREPARING A STATEMENT OF CASH FLOWS

Sources of Information and Steps in the Process

The statement of cash flows was previously called the Statement of Changes in Financial Position for good reason.[13] By analysing the changes in all noncash accounts on the statement of financial position, or balance sheet, from one period to the next, the sources of all cash receipts and all cash disbursements can be identified and summarized. Illustration 23-4 explains why this is so.

---

[12] "The Statement of Cash Flows," *Statement of Financial Accounting Standards No. 95* (Stamford, Conn.: FASB, 1987), par. 107 and 111.

[13] Prior to the existing standard on cash flows, significant noncash transactions were included in the statement because of their effect on the entity's asset and capital structure. This difference illustrates the change in focus from a statement of changes in financial position (old terminology) to a statement of cash flows (new terminology).

ILLUSTRATION 23-4
Relationship of Changes in Cash
to Other Balance Sheet Accounts

$$A = L + OE$$
$$\Delta A = \Delta(L + OE)$$
$$\Delta A = \Delta L + \Delta OE$$
$$\Delta(Cash + noncash\ A) = \Delta L + \Delta OE$$
$$\Delta Cash + \Delta noncash\ A = \Delta L + \Delta OE$$
$$\Delta Cash = \Delta L + \Delta OE - \Delta noncash\ A$$

Note: Δ is a symbol meaning "change in."

Therefore, unlike the other major financial statements that are prepared from the adjusted trial balance, the statement of cash flows is prepared by analysing the changes in the balance sheet accounts over the accounting period. Information to prepare this statement usually comes from the following three sources.

Comparative balance sheets provide the amount of the change in each asset, liability and equity account from the period's beginning to end.

The current income statement provides details about the change in the balance sheet retained earnings account, and information to help determine the amount of cash provided by, or used in, operations during the period.

Selected transaction data from the general ledger provide additional detailed information needed to determine how cash was provided or used during the period.

Preparing the statement of cash flows from the data sources above involves three major steps.

Step 1. Determine the change in cash. This procedure is straightforward because the difference between the beginning and ending cash and cash equivalents balances can easily be calculated by examining the comparative balance sheets. Explaining this change is the objective of the subsequent analysis.

OBJECTIVE 5
....
Differentiate between net
income and net cash flows
from operating activities.

Step 2. Record information from the income statement on the statement of cash flows. This is the starting point for calculating cash flows from operating activities. **Whenever subsequent analyses indicate that the operating cash flow and the amount reported on the income statement differ, the income statement numbers originally recognized are adjusted.**

Most adjustments fit into one of three categories.

Category 1. Amounts reported as revenue and expense on the income statement are not the same as cash received from customers and cash paid to the suppliers of goods and services. Companies receive cash from customers for revenue reported in a previous year, and do not receive cash for all the revenue reported as earned in the current period. Similarly, cash payments are made in the current period to suppliers for goods and services acquired, used, and recognized as expense in a preceding period. In addition, not all amounts recognized as expenses in the current year are paid for by year end. Most of these adjustments are related to receivables, payables, and other working capital accounts.

Category 2. Some expenses, such as amortization, represent deferred costs incurred and paid for in a previous period. While there was a cash flow associated with the original acquisition of the asset (an investing flow), there is no cash flow associated with the amortization of these assets over their period of use.

Category 3. Amounts reported as gains or losses on the income statement are not usually the same as the cash flow from the transaction and, in many cases, the underlying activity is not an operating transaction. For example, gains and losses on the disposal of long-term assets and the early retirement of long-term debt are reported on the income statement. These result, respectively, from an investing and a financing transaction and the cash flow amounts are the proceeds on disposal of the asset and the payment to retire the debt, not the amount of the reported gain or loss.

Step 3. Analyse the change in each balance sheet account, identify all cash flows associated with changes in the account balance, and record the effect on the statement of cash flows. This analysis identifies all investing and financing cash flows, and all adjustments needed to convert income reported on the income statement to cash flows from operations. Analyse the balance sheet accounts one at a time until all the changes in each account have been explained and the related cash flows identified.

Step 4. Complete the statement of cash flows. Calculate subtotals for operating, investing, and financing activities and ensure the change in cash thus determined is equal to the actual change in cash for the period.[14]

On the following pages we work through these four steps in the process of preparing the statement of cash flows for three different companies of increasing complexity.

First Illustration—Tax Consultants Inc.

To illustrate the basic steps in preparing a statement of cash flows, we will use the first year of operations for Tax Consultants Inc. The company started on January 1, 2002, when it issued 60,000 common shares for $60,000 cash. The company rented its office space and furniture and equipment and performed tax consulting services throughout the first year. The comparative balance sheets at the beginning and end of 2002 and the income statement and additional information for 2002 are reproduced in Illustrations 23-5 and 23-6 respectively.

> **OBJECTIVE 6**
> ....
> Prepare a statement of cash flows.

COMPARATIVE BALANCE SHEETS

Assets	Dec. 31, 2002	Jan. 1, 2002	Change Increase/Decrease
Cash	$49,000	$-0-	$49,000 Increase
Accounts receivable	36,000	-0-	36,000 Increase
Total	$85,000	$ 0	
Liabilities and Shareholders' Equity			
Accounts payable	$ 5,000	$-0-	5,000 Increase
Common shares	60,000	-0-	60,000 Increase
Retained earnings	20,000	-0-	20,000 Increase
Total	$85,000	$-0-	

ILLUSTRATION 23-5
Comparative Balance Sheets, Tax Consultants Inc., 2002

INCOME STATEMENT
For the Year Ended December 31, 2002

Revenues	$125,000
Operating expenses	85,000
Income before income taxes	40,000
Income tax expense	6,000
Net income	$ 34,000

Additional Information
Examination of selected data indicates that a dividend of $14,000 was declared during the year.

ILLUSTRATION 23-6
Income Statement, Tax Consultants Inc., 2002

Step 1: Determine the change in cash. The first step in preparing a statement of cash flows—determining the change in cash—is a simple calculation. Tax Consultants Inc. had no cash on hand at the beginning of 2002, and $49,000 was on hand at the end of 2002; thus, the change in cash for 2002 was an increase of $49,000. The next steps are more complex and involve additional analysis.

---

[14] On occasion, even experienced accountants get to this step and find the statement does not balance! Don't despair. Determine the amount of your error and review your analysis until found.

Step 2: Record information from the income statement on the statement of cash flows.
As the bulk of the cash activity in any organization is related to operating cash flows, the second step takes information from the statement of operations (the income statement) and reports it on the cash flow statement under the heading "Cash flows from operating activities." The specific information taken from the income statement and reported on the cash flow statement in this step depends on whether the indirect or the direct approach is used. Regardless of the approach used, this information will be converted from the accrual to the cash basis through adjustments identified in Step 3.

Indirect Method. To determine the amount of cash generated by or used in operations, the indirect approach begins by transferring the amount of net income reported on the income statement to the operating section of the cash flow statement, as indicated in Illustration 23-7. Whenever the analysis in Step 3 indicates an operating cash inflow or outflow that differs from the amount of revenue or expense captured in the net income figure, an adjustment is made to the net income number to "correct" it to the operating cash impact.

ILLUSTRATION 23-7
Indirect Approach

INDIRECT APPROACH	
Cash flows from operating activities	
Net income	+34,000
Adjustments:	
Cash flows from investing activities	
Cash flows from financing activities	

Direct Method. Under this approach, skeleton headings similar to those identified in Illustration 23-3 are set up under "Cash flows from operating activities." The number and description of these headings may vary from company to company. Amounts reported on the income statement are then transferred on a line-by-line basis to the heading that comes closest to representing the type of cash flow, until all components of net income have been transferred.

Illustration 23-8 indicates that three headings are appropriate initially for Tax Consultants Inc. Because all income statement amounts are transferred to the Operating Activities section of the statement of cash flows, the amount transferred is equal to net income, the same amount as under the indirect approach.

ILLUSTRATION 23-8
Direct Approach

DIRECT APPROACH	
Cash flows from operating activities	
Cash receipts from customers	+125,000
Cash payments to suppliers	− 85,000
Cash payments of income taxes	− 6,000
	+ 34,000
Cash flows from investing activities	
Cash flows from financing activities	

In Step 3 using the direct approach, adjustments are made to the appropriate line item within the Operating Cash Flow section whenever the analysis indicates an operating cash flow that is not equal in amount to the revenue or expense reported on the income statement. Revenues of $125,000 will be converted into the amount of cash received from customers; operating expenses of $85,000 will be adjusted to the amount of cash payments made to suppliers; and income tax expense of $6,000 will become income tax payments remitted to the government. Under this approach, the specific revenue and expense lines are adjusted. Under the indirect method discussed above, it is only the bottom-line net income number that is adjusted.

Step 3. Analyse the change in each balance sheet account, identify any cash flows associated with a change in the account balance, and record the effect on the statement of cash flows. By analysing the change in each balance sheet account, transactions that involve cash can be identified and the effects recorded on the cash flow statement.

Because the change in each balance sheet account has to be explained, **begin with the first noncash asset and work down through each asset, liability, and equity account in turn**. The results of Step 3 are provided in Illustration 23-9, where each item is referenced to the analysis below.

ILLUSTRATION 23-9
Preparation of Cash Flow Statement, Tax Consultants Inc.

Cash flows from operating activities

INDIRECT METHOD

Net income	+34,000
Adjustments: Increase in accounts receivable	−36,000 (a)
Increase in accounts payable	+ 5,000 (b)
	+ 3,000

DIRECT METHOD

Cash receipts from customers	+125,000	−36,000 (a)	+89,000
Cash payments to suppliers	− 85,000	+ 5,000 (b)	−80,000
Cash payments of income taxes	− 6,000		− 6,000
	+ 34,000		+ 3,000

Cash flows from investing activities —0—

Cash flows from financing activities

Proceeds from issue of common shares	+60,000 (c)
Dividends paid	−14,000 (d)
	+46,000
Increase in cash	+49,000

(a) **Accounts Receivable.** During the year, Tax Consultants' receivables increased by $36,000. Because the Accounts Receivable account is increased by the amount of revenue recognized and decreased by the cash received from customers, the cash received from customers must have been $36,000 less than the revenue reported on the 2002 income statement. An adjustment is needed, therefore, to the income statement numbers in the Operating Activities section of the cash flow statement. Under the indirect method, $36,000 is deducted from the net income number because $36,000 less cash came in than is included in the revenue component of the net income reported. Using the direct method, the revenue number is reduced directly.

(b) **Accounts Payable.** Accounts Payable is increased by purchases of goods and services on account and decreased by payments on account. Tax Consultants' purchases must have exceeded cash payments by $5,000 during 2002. An adjustment of $5,000 is required to convert the purchases included in net income to the amount paid to suppliers.

 Under the indirect method, $5,000 is added back to net income to reflect the fact that the amounts previously deducted as expense did not use an equivalent amount of cash. Under the direct approach, the $5,000 adjustment is made to the operating expense line where the cost of the goods and services purchased were charged.

(c) **Common Shares.** The increase in this account resulted from the issue of shares:

Cash	60,000	
Common Shares		60,000

The $60,000 inflow of cash is a financing inflow that is reported on the statement of cash flows.

(d) **Retained Earnings.** $34,000 of the increase in this account is explained by net income. This has been recognized on the statement already as the starting point in calculating cash flows from operations. The remaining change in the account is explained by the entry:

Retained Earnings	14,000	
Cash		14,000

The cash outflow of $14,000 for paying dividends is reported as a financing outflow. The entire dividend must have been paid in cash because the company does not report a Dividends Payable account that increased.

The changes in all balance sheet accounts have been explained and their cash effects have been reported appropriately on the statement of cash flows. The statement can now be completed.

Step 4. Complete the statement of cash flows.   Calculate subtotals for each of the operating, investing, and financing sections of the statement, and then the change in cash for the year. This should agree with the change identified in Step 1. The $49,000 increase in Tax Consultants' cash balance during 2002 has been explained.

The completed statement illustrating both the indirect and the direct method is provided in Illustration 23-10.

ILLUSTRATION 23-10
Completed Statement of Cash Flows, Tax Consultants Inc.

STATEMENT OF CASH FLOWS
Year Ended December 31, 2002

Indirect Method			Direct Method		
Cash flows from operations			Cash flows from operations		
Net income	$34,000		Cash received from customers		$89,000
Less: Increase in			Less cash payments:		
accounts receivable	(36,000)		To suppliers	$80,000	
Add: Increase in accounts payable	5,000		For income taxes	6,000	86,000
	3,000				3,000
Cash flows from investing activities	–0–		Cash flows from investing activities		–0–
Cash flows from financing activities			Cash flows from financing activities		
Proceeds on issue of common shares	60,000		Proceeds on issue of common shares		60,000
Payment of dividends	(14,000)		Payment of dividends		(14,000)
	46,000				46,000
Increase in cash during year	49,000		Increase in cash during year		49,000
Opening cash balance	–0–		Opening cash balance		–0–
Cash, December 31, 2002	$49,000		Cash, December 31, 2002		$49,000

The $49,000 increase in cash was generated by a combination of net operating inflows of $3,000 and net financing inflows (primarily from the sale of common shares) of $46,000. Note that net cash provided by operating activities is the same whether the direct or indirect method is used. The indirect method explains how the company could report a healthy income of $34,000 yet have an operating inflow of cash of only $3,000. The main reason is that $36,000 of the revenue reported has not yet been collected. The direct method provides different insights into operating cash flows. The reason for the $3,000 contribution to cash from operations is because cash collections from customers ($89,000) were marginally more than the operating cash outflows to suppliers (of $80,000) and the government for taxes (of $6,000).

Second Illustration—Eastern Window Products Limited (EWPL)

To illustrate the preparation of a more complex statement of cash flows, we will use the operations of Eastern Window Products Limited (EWPL) for its 2003 year. EWPL has been operating for a number of years, and the company's comparative balance sheets at December 31, 2003 and 2002, its statement of income and retained earnings for the year ended December 31, 2003, and other information are provided in Illustration 23-11.

BALANCE SHEETS—DECEMBER 31

ILLUSTRATION 23-11
Comparative Balance Sheets, Statement of Income and Retained Earnings, EWPL

	2003 $	2002 $	Change Increase/Decrease $
Cash	37,000	59,000	22,000 Decrease
Accounts receivable	46,000	56,000	10,000 Decrease
Inventory	82,000	73,000	9,000 Increase
Prepaid expense	6,000	7,500	1,500 Decrease
Land	70,000	—	70,000 Increase
Building	200,000	—	200,000 Increase
Accumulated amortization—building	(6,000)	—	6,000 Increase
Equipment	68,000	63,000	5,000 Increase
Accumulated amortization—equipment	(19,000)	(10,000)	9,000 Increase
	484,000	248,500	
Accounts payable	70,000	59,100	10,900 Increase
Income taxes payable	4,000	1,000	3,000 Increase
Wages payable	2,000	2,700	700 Decrease
Mortgage payable	152,400	—	152,400 Increase
Bonds payable	50,000	40,000	10,000 Increase
Common shares	80,000	72,000	8,000 Increase
Retained earnings	125,600	73,700	51,900 Increase
	484,000	248,500	

STATEMENT OF INCOME AND RETAINED EARNINGS
Year Ended December 31, 2003

Sales revenue		$592,000
Less: Cost of goods sold		355,000
Gross profit		237,000
Salaries and wages expense	$55,000	
Interest expense	16,200	
Amortization expense	15,000	
Other operating expenses	51,000	137,200
Income before income tax		99,800
Income tax expense		39,900
Net income		59,900
Retained earnings, January 1		73,700
Dividends declared		(8,000)
Retained earnings, December 31		$125,600

Additional Information
The company assumed a mortgage of $155,000 on acquiring land and building during 2003.

Step 1. Determine the change in cash. Cash decreased by $22,000 from a balance of $59,000 at the first of the year to $37,000 at the end of the year.

Step 2. Record information from the income statement on the statement of cash flows. Under the **indirect approach**, record the $59,900 net income in the Operating Activities section of the cash flow statement.

Under the **direct approach**, set up skeleton headings for the types of operating cash flows involved. Illustration 23-12 indicates that six headings are likely to be appropriate for EWPL, including an "Other expenses/losses" section that includes items such as amortization expense that do not fall under the other headings. Because all income statement amounts are transferred to the Operating Activities section, the amount transferred is equal to net income, the same amount as under the indirect approach.

As you proceed through Step 3 using the direct approach, sales revenue of $592,000 will be converted into cash received from customers; cost of goods sold of $355,000 and other operating expenses of $51,000 will be adjusted to an amount that represents cash payments to suppliers for goods and services acquired; salaries and wages expense of $55,000 will become cash payments made to and on behalf of employees; interest expense of $16,200 becomes interest payments made; and income tax expense of $39,900 becomes income tax payments remitted to the government.

Step 3. Analyse the change in each balance sheet account, identify any cash flows associated with a change in the account balance, and record the effect on the statement of cash flows. The results of this step are provided in Illustration 23-12, where each item is referenced to the analysis below.

ILLUSTRATION 23-12
Statement of Cash Flows
Working Paper, EWPL

CASH FLOWS FROM OPERATING ACTIVITIES
Indirect Method

Net income		+59,900
Adjustments: Decrease in accounts receivable		+10,000 (a)
Increase in inventory		− 9,000 (b)
Decrease in prepaid expenses		+ 1,500 (c)
Amortization expense, building		+ 6,000 (e)
Amortization expense, equipment		+ 9,000 (g)
Increase in accounts payable		+10,900 (h)
Increase in income taxes payable		+ 3,000 (i)
Decrease in wages payable		− 700 (j)
Net income		+90,600

Direct Method

Cash receipts from customers	+592,000	+10,000 (a)	+602,000
Cash payments to suppliers for goods and services	−355,000	− 9,000 (b)	
	− 51,000	+ 1,500 (c)	−402,600
		+10,900 (h)	
Cash payments to employees	− 55,000	− 700 (j)	− 55,700
Cash interest payments	− 16,200		− 16,200
Cash payments of income taxes	− 39,900	+ 3,000 (i)	− 36,900
Other expenses/losses—amortization	− 15,000	+ 6,000 (e)	—
		+ 9,000 (g)	
	+ 59,900		+ 90,600

CASH FLOWS FROM INVESTING ACTIVITIES

Purchase of land and building	−115,000 (d)
Purchase of equipment	− 5,000 (f)
	−120,000

CASH FLOWS FROM FINANCING ACTIVITIES

Mortgage payable	− 2,600 (k)
Bonds issued	+ 10,000 (l)
Shares issued	+ 8,000 (m)
Dividends paid	− 8,000 (n)
	+ 7,400
CHANGE IN CASH	− 22,000

(a) **Accounts Receivable.** During the year, EWPL's receivables decreased by $10,000. Because the Accounts Receivable account is increased by the amount of revenue recognized and decreased by cash received from customers, the cash inflow from customers must have been $10,000 greater than the revenue reported on the 2003 income statement. Under the indirect method, $10,000 is added to the net income number because $10,000 more cash came in than is included in the revenue component of the net income reported. Under the direct method, the revenue number is increased directly.

(b) **Inventory.** Inventory increased by $9,000 in 2003. Because the Inventory account is increased by the purchase of goods and is reduced by transferring costs to cost of goods sold, EWPL must have purchased $9,000 more inventory than it sold and, therefore, $9,000 more than the costs included in cost of goods sold on the income statement. The first part of this analysis does not tell us how much cash was paid for the purchases, but merely converts cost of goods sold to the cost of purchases in the year. The analysis of accounts payable (see item (h) below) converts the amount purchased to the cash payments to suppliers.

Cost of goods sold of $355,000 was deducted on the income statement in calculating net income. Under the indirect method, net income must be further reduced by $9,000 to adjust for the additional $9,000 of goods purchased, but not yet sold. Under the direct method, the $9,000 adjustment is made to cost of goods sold directly to adjust it to the cost of goods purchased.

(c) **Prepaid Expenses.** Prepaid expenses decreased by $1,500 during 2003. Because this account is increased by the acquisition of goods and services in advance of use and decreased by transferring the cost of the goods and services used up to expense—the same as for inventory—EWPL must have recognized $1,500 more expense than the amount purchased. The expenses reported on the income statement, therefore, must be reduced by $1,500 to adjust them to the cost of goods and services purchased. Under the indirect method, $1,500 is added back to the income reported. Under the direct method, the appropriate expense is reduced directly for the $1,500. When the Accounts Payable account is analysed below, the purchases will be adjusted to cash payments to suppliers.

(d) **Land, Building.** The balance sheets indicate an increase in land of $70,000 and an increase in building of $200,000, suggesting an investing cash outflow of $270,000. The investment in real property, however, is often financed by assuming a mortgage note payable that results in a lower net cash outflow. As a review of the records indicates that EWPL assumed a $155,000 mortgage in acquiring the land and building, the actual investing cash outflow is only $115,000 (the $270,000 cost of the land and building less the financing provided by the mortgage of $155,000).

It is often useful to prepare the underlying journal entry.

Land	70,000	
Building	200,000	
Mortgage Payable		155,000
Cash		115,000

This entry explains the change in the Land and the Building accounts on the balance sheet; it explains part of the change in the Mortgage Payable account (see item (k) below); and it identifies the actual outflow of cash of $115,000. This is reported as an investing cash flow on the statement.

(e) **Accumulated Amortization, Building.** The $6,000 increase in this account is due entirely to the recognition of amortization expense for the year.

Amortization expense	6,000	
Accumulated amortization, building		6,000

The entry records a noncash event. Under the indirect approach, $6,000 is added back to net income because amortization expense did not require the use of cash. Under the direct approach, amortization expense is adjusted directly.

(f) **Equipment.** EWPL purchased $5,000 of equipment during 2003. This resulted in an investing outflow of cash of $5,000.

(g) **Accumulated Amortization, Equipment.** The $9,000 increase in this account is due to amortization expense for the year. As explained in item (e), the statement's operating activities section must be adjusted for this noncash expense.

(h) **Accounts Payable.** The Accounts Payable account is increased by the cost of purchases and decreased by payments on account. EWPL's cash payments to suppliers, therefore, must have been $10,900 less than the goods and services purchased during 2003. In steps (b) and (c) above, cost of goods sold and other expenses were adjusted to convert them to the cost of goods and services purchased during the year. A further adjustment of $10,900 is required to adjust the purchases to the amount of the cash outflow.

Under the indirect method, $10,900 is added back to net income to reflect the fact that the amounts deducted for purchases did not use an equivalent amount of cash. Under the direct approach, the $10,900 adjustment reduces the cost of goods and services purchased to the cash outflow for these purchases.

(i) **Income Taxes Payable.** This liability account is increased by the current income tax expense reported and decreased by payments to the government. Income tax expense, therefore, exceeded payments by $3,000. Under the indirect method, the $3,000 difference is added back to net income. The direct method adjustment is to the income tax expense line.

(j) **Wages Payable.** Similar to other current payables, this account is increased by amounts recognized as expense and decreased by payments, in this case, to employees. The $700 decrease in this account indicates that cash outflows were $700 greater than wages expense. Under the indirect method, an additional $700 is deducted from the reported income. Salaries and wages expense is adjusted under the direct approach.[15]

(k) **Mortgage Payable.** The cash flow associated with part of the change in this account was identified above in item (d). If the account increased by $155,000 on the assumption of the mortgage, principal payments of $2,600 must have been made to reduce the balance to $152,400. The entry underlying this transaction is:

Mortgage Payable	2,600	
Cash		2,600

The outflow of $2,600 is a financing activity.

(l) **Bonds Payable.** The increase in this account is explained by the following entry.

Cash	10,000	
Bonds Payable		10,000

The $10,000 inflow of cash from the bond issue is a financing cash flow.

(m) **Common Shares.** The $8,000 increase in this account resulted from the issue of shares:

Cash	8,000	
Common shares		8,000

The $8,000 inflow of cash is a financing flow.

(n) **Retained Earnings.** $59,900 of the increase in retained earnings is explained by net income. This has been recognized on the cash flow statement already as the starting point in calculating cash flows from operations. The remainder of the change is explained by the entry for dividends:

Retained Earnings	8,000	
Cash		8,000

The payment of dividends charged to retained earnings is a financing flow.

The changes in all balance sheet accounts have now been explained, all information required to prepare the statement of cash flows has been identified, and the statement can be completed.

---

[15] For all current asset and current liability account changes that adjust accrual basis net income to cash flows from operations, a simple check can be made. The adjustment for all increases in current asset accounts should have the same effect within the Operating Activities section of the cash flow statement. All decreases in current asset accounts should have the same effect. All increases and decreases in current liability accounts should have the opposite effect of increases and decreases, respectively, in current asset accounts. This is a useful mechanical procedure to double-check your adjustments.

Step 4. Complete the statement of cash flows. Subtotals are calculated for each section of the statement and the change in cash indicated is compared with the change calculated in Step 1. Both indicate a $22,000 decrease in EWPL's cash balance during 2003.

A statement in good form is then prepared from the working paper developed in Illustration 23-12, using more appropriate descriptions and explanations. Illustration 23-13 indicates what the final statement might look like if the indirect method is chosen. The additional disclosures provided are discussed in a later section of the chapter.

ILLUSTRATION 23-13
EWPL Statement of Cash Flows, 2003—Indirect Method

EASTERN WINDOW PRODUCTS LIMITED
Statement of Cash Flows
Year Ended December 31, 2003

Cash provided by (used in) operations:

Net income		$59,900
Add back noncash expense—amortization		15,000
Add (deduct) changes in noncash working capital*—		
accounts receivable	$10,000	
inventory	(9,000)	
prepaid expenses	1,500	
accounts payable	10,900	
income taxes payable	3,000	
wages payable	(700)	15,700
		90,600

Cash provided by (used in) investing activities:

Purchase of property, plant, and equipment		(120,000)

Cash provided by (used in) financing activities:

Payment on mortgage payable	(2,600)	
Proceeds on issue of bonds	10,000	
Dividends paid	(8,000)	
Proceeds on issue of common shares	8,000	7,400
Decrease in cash		(22,000)
Cash balance, beginning of year		59,000
Cash balance, end of year		$37,000

Notes: 1. Cash consists of cash on hand and balances with banks.
  2. Cash outflows during the year for interest and income taxes were $16,200 and $36,000, respectively.
  3. During the year, property was acquired at a total cost of $275,000 (land $70,000; building $200,000; equipment $5,000) of which $155,000 was financed directly by the assumption of a mortgage.

*Many companies provide only the subtotal on the statement of cash flows and report the details in a note to the financial statements.

Where the direct method is preferred, the Operating Activities section of the cash flow statement would appear as follows.

ILLUSTRATION 23-14
Operating Activities Section, EWPL, Direct Method

Cash provided by (used in) operations	
Received from customers	$602,000
Payments to suppliers	(402,600)
Payments to and on behalf of employees	(55,700)
Interest payments	(16,200)
Income taxes paid	(36,900)
	$90,600

Third Illustration—Yoshi Corporation

The next step is to see how the same principles are applied to more complex situations. Some of these complexities are illustrated below for Yoshi Corporation, using the same approach as in the previous examples. Those who prefer a more structured method of accumulating the information for the cash flow statement should refer to the work sheet approach later in the chapter or the T-account method illustrated on the Digital Tool.

The comparative balance sheets of Yoshi Corporation at December 31, 2003 and 2002, the statement of income and retained earnings for the year ended December 31, 2003, and selected additional information are provided in Illustrations 23-15, 23-16, and 23-17.

ILLUSTRATION 23-15
Comparative Balance Sheets—
Yoshi Corporation

YOSHI CORPORATION
Comparative Balance Sheets
December 31, 2003 and 2002

	2003 $	2002 $	Change Increase/Decrease $
Asset			
Cash	20,000	32,000	12,000 Decrease
Short-term investments	39,000	34,000	5,000 Increase
Accounts receivable	106,500	52,700	53,800 Increase
Allowance for doubtful accounts	(2,500)	(1,700)	800 Increase
Inventories	303,000	311,000	8,000 Decrease
Prepaid expenses	16,500	17,000	500 Decrease
Investment in shares of Porter Corp.	18,500	15,000	3,500 Increase
Deferred development costs	190,000	30,000	160,000 Increase
Land	131,500	82,000	49,500 Increase
Equipment	187,000	142,000	45,000 Increase
Accumulated amortization, equipment	(29,000)	(31,000)	2,000 Decrease
Buildings	262,000	262,000	—
Accumulated amortization, buildings	(74,100)	(71,000)	3,100 Increase
Goodwill	7,600	10,000	2,400 Decrease
Total Assets	1,176,000	884,000	
Liabilities			
Accounts payable	130,000	131,000	1,000 Decrease
Dividends payable, term preferred shares	2,000	—	2,000 Increase
Accrued liabilities	43,000	39,000	4,000 Increase
Income taxes payable	3,000	16,000	13,000 Decrease
Bonds payable	100,000	100,000	—
Discount on bonds payable	(2,200)	(2,500)	300 Decrease
Term preferred shares	60,000	—	60,000 Increase
Future income tax liability	9,000	6,000	3,000 Increase
Total Liabilities	344,800	289,500	
Shareholders' Equity			
Common shares	247,000	88,000	159,000 Increase
Retained earnings	601,200	506,500	94,700 Increase
Treasury shares	(17,000)	—	17,000 Increase
Total Shareholders' Equity	831,200	594,500	
Liabilities and Shareholders' Equity	1,176,000	884,000	

ILLUSTRATION 23-16
Statement of Income and
Retained Earnings—Yoshi
Corporation

YOSHI CORPORATION
Statement of Income and Retained Earnings
Year Ended December 31, 2003

Net sales		$924,500
Equity in earnings of Porter Corp.		5,500
		930,000
Expenses		
Cost of goods sold	$395,400	
Salaries and wages	200,000	
Selling and administrative	134,600	
Amortization	14,600	
Interest and dividend expense	11,300	
Impairment loss—Goodwill	2,400	
Other expenses and losses	12,000	770,300
Income before income tax and extraordinary item		159,700
Income tax: Current	47,000	
Future	3,000	50,000
Income before extraordinary item		109,700

Extraordinary item: Gain on expropriation of land, net of tax of $2,500		8,000
Net income		117,700
Retained earnings, January 1		506,500
Less: Cash dividends, common shares	6,000	
Stock dividends, common shares	15,000	
Excess of cost of treasury shares over reissue price	2,000	23,000
Retained earnings, December 31		$601,200

YOSHI CORPORATION
Additional Information

ILLUSTRATION 23-17
Additional Information—
Yoshi Corporation

1. Short-term investments represent temporary holdings of money market instruments.

2. During 2003, bad debts written off amounted to $1,450.

3. Yoshi accounts for its 22% interest in Porter Corp. using the equity method. Porter Corp. paid a dividend in 2003.

4. During 2003, Yoshi incurred $200,000 of market development costs, which met the criteria for deferral. $40,000 of deferred costs were amortized in the year.

5. Land in the amount of $54,000 was purchased through the issue of term preferred shares. In addition, the municipality expropriated a parcel of land resulting in a gain of $10,500 before tax.

6. An analysis of the Equipment account and related accumulated amortization indicates the following:

Equipment:	Balance, January 1, 2003	$142,000
	Cost of equipment purchased	53,000
	Cost of equipment sold (sold at a loss of $1,500)	(8,000)
	Balance, December 31, 2003	$187,000

Accumulated amortization:	
Balance, January 1, 2003	$ 31,000
Accumulated amortization on equipment sold	(2,500)
Amortization expense, 2003	11,500
Major repair charged to accumulated amortization	(11,000)
Balance, December 31, 2003	$ 29,000

7. An analysis of the common shares account discloses the following:

Balance, January 1, 2003	$ 88,000
Issuance of a 2% stock dividend	15,000
Sale of shares for cash	144,000
Balance, December 31, 2003	$247,000

8. During 2003, Yoshi purchased its own common shares in the market at a cost of $34,000, holding them as treasury shares.

   Later in the year, half of these shares were reissued for proceeds of $15,000.

9. Changes in other balance sheet accounts resulted from usual transactions and events.

Step 1. Determine the change in cash. Because Yoshi's cash and cash equivalents include temporary holdings of money market instruments as well as cash balances, the change in cash to be explained is a decrease of $7,000. This is the difference between the opening cash and cash equivalents of $66,000 ($32,000 + $34,000) and the ending cash and cash equivalents of $59,000 ($20,000 + $39,000).

Step 2. Record information from the income statement on the statement of cash flows. Under the **indirect method**, the net income of $117,700 is "slotted in" as the starting point, as indicated in Illustration 23-18.

Using the **direct method**, skeleton headings that cover each type of cash flow—from customer receipts to the extraordinary gain—are set up within the Operating Activities section of the cash flow statement, as shown in Illustration 23-18. The description of each line may differ from situation to situation, but the income statement provides clues as to the types of operating cash flows and how they should be described. For example, the equity basis income from the investment in Porter Corp. is not a cash flow, but it will be replaced after adjustment with any dividends received from the investment.

Each amount making up the net income of $117,700 is transferred to the most appropriate skeleton heading on the cash flow statement work sheet. Amounts reported as cost of goods sold, selling and administrative expense, and other expenses and losses form the base for what will eventually be "cash paid to suppliers for goods and services." Income tax expense on ordinary income and on the extraordinary gain are both included on the line that will be adjusted to income taxes paid. The extraordinary item must be handled on a before-tax basis since the tax is reported separately.

ILLUSTRATION 23-18
Statement of Cash Flows
Working Paper—Yoshi Corporation

CASH FLOWS FROM OPERATING ACTIVITIES

Indirect Method

Net income		+117,700
Adjustments:	Increase in accounts receivable, net of write-offs	− 55,250 (a)
	Bad debt expense	+ 2,250 (b)
	Decrease in inventories	+ 8,000 (c)
	Decrease in prepaid expenses	+ 500 (d)
	Equity method investment income	− 5,500 (e)
	Dividend from equity method investment	+ 2,000 (e)
	Amortization of market development costs	+ 40,000 (f)
	Extraordinary gain on expropriation of land	− 10,500 (g)
	Loss on disposal of equipment	+ 1,500 (h)
	Amortization expense, equipment	+ 11,500 (h)
	Amortization expense, buildings	+ 3,100 (i)
	Impairment loss, goodwill	+ 2,400 (j)
	Decrease in accounts payable	− 1,000 (k)
	Increase in dividends payable on term preferred shares	+ 2,000 (l)
	Increase in accrued liabilities	+ 4,000 (m)
	Decrease in income taxes payable	− 13,000 (n)
	Amortization of bond discount	+ 300 (o)
	Increase in future income tax liability	+ 3,000 (q)
		+113,000

Direct Method

Receipts from customers	+924,500	−55,250 (a)	+869,250
Received from investment in Porter Corp.	+ 5,500	− 5,500 (e)	+ 2,000
		+ 2,000 (e)	
Payments for goods and services	−395,400	+ 2,250 (b)	
	−134,600	+ 8,000 (c)	
	− 12,000	+ 500 (d)	
		+40,000 (e)	−490,750
		+ 1,500 (h)	
		− 1,000 (k)	
Payments to employees	−200,000	+ 4,000 (m)	−196,000
Interest and dividend payments	− 11,300	+ 2,000 (l)	− 9,000
		+ 300 (o)	
Income taxes paid	− 50,000	−13,000 (n)	− 62,500
	− 2,500	+ 3,000 (q)	
Other items:			
Amortization expense	− 14,600	+11,500 (h)	—
		+ 3,100 (i)	
Impairment loss	− 2,400	+ 2,400 (j)	—
Extraordinary gain, before tax	+ 10,500	−10,500 (g)	—
	+117,700		+113,000

CASH FLOWS FROM INVESTING ACTIVITIES

Market development costs incurred	−200,000 (f)
Proceeds on expropriation of land (extraordinary item)	+ 15,000 (g)
Purchase of equipment	− 53,000 (h)
Proceeds on sale of equipment	+ 4,000 (h)
Major repair costs incurred	− 11,000 (h)
	−245,000

CASH FLOWS FROM FINANCING ACTIVITIES

Proceeds on issue of term preferred shares	+ 6,000 (p)
Proceeds on issue of common shares	+144,000 (r)
Dividends paid on common shares	− 6,000 (s)
Proceeds on reissue of treasury shares	+ 15,000 (s)
Payment to acquire treasury shares	− 34,000 (t)
	+125,000

CHANGE IN CASH	−7,000

Step 3. Analyse the change in each balance sheet account, identify any cash flows associated with a change in the account balance, and record the effect on the statement of cash flows. The analysis begins with accounts receivable because the short-term investments are considered cash equivalents.

(a) **Accounts Receivable.** Unlike the previous illustrations, Yoshi reports both the receivable and its contra allowance account. The receivable control account is increased by sales on account and reduced by the total of cash received from customers and accounts written off. During 2003, the receivable account increased by $53,800, indicating that the sales reported on the income statement exceeded the total of cash received on account and the accounts written off by $53,800. Because accounts written off explain $1,450 of the difference, the actual cash inflow from customers must have been $55,250 less than the sales revenue reported (i.e., $53,800 plus $1,450). Prepare a T account to verify this reasoning:

Accounts Receivable			
Jan.1	52,700		
Sales	924,500	1,450	Accounts written off (given)
		?	Cash receipts
Dec. 31	106,500		

The cash receipts must have been $869,250, an amount $55,250 less than the revenue reported on the income statement. Using the indirect approach, $55,250 is deducted from the net income reported because the cash received from customers was less than the revenue reported in net income. Under the direct method, the revenue of $924,500 is adjusted directly to convert it to cash received from customers.

(b) **Allowance for Doubtful Accounts.** This account had an opening balance of $1,700, was increased by bad debt expense, reduced by accounts written off, and ended the year at $2,500. With accounts written off of $1,450, bad debt expense must have been $2,250 ($1,700 + bad debt expense − $1,450 = $2,500; or prepare a T account to determine this). Because bad debt expense does not require the use of cash, the net income number in the Operating Activities section must be adjusted.

Under the indirect method, $2,250 is added back to net income. Under the direct method, the $2,250 adjustment reduces the expense line that includes bad debt expense. In this example, it is assumed to be in selling expenses.

The only time it is necessary to analyse the Accounts Receivable and the Allowance account separately is when the direct method is used. This is because two adjustments are needed: one to adjust the revenue reported ($55,250) and the other to adjust the noncash bad debt expense ($2,250). When the indirect method is used, both adjustments correct the net income number. The analysis is easier, therefore, if you zero in on the change in the **net accounts receivable** and make one adjustment to the net income number.[16]

(c) **Inventories.** Because the Inventory account is increased by the cost of goods purchased and decreased by the transfer of costs to cost of goods sold, the $8,000 decrease in the Inventory account indicates that cost of goods sold exceeded purchases by $8,000. Using the indirect approach, $8,000 is added back to the net income number because the cost of goods sold that was deducted to determine net income was higher than the purchases made in the year. The direct approach adjusts cost of goods sold directly to convert it to the cost of goods purchased. The analysis of Accounts Payable in step (k) will convert the purchases to cash paid to suppliers.

(d) **Prepaid Expenses.** The $500 decrease in this account resulted because the costs charged to the income statement were $500 greater than the costs of acquiring

---

[16] For Yoshi Corporation, net receivables increased $53,000, from $51,000 ($52,700 − $1,700) at the beginning of the year to $104,000 ($106,500 − $2,500) at year end. The increase means that $53,000 of income was recognized that did not result in a corresponding cash flow. On the cash flow statement under the indirect method, one adjustment to reduce net income by $53,000 is all that is needed.

prepaid goods and services in the year. For reasons similar to the inventory analysis in step (c), $500 is either added back to net income under the indirect approach, or adjusts the expense line associated with the prepaid expense under the direct approach. It is assumed in this case that the prepaid expenses were charged to selling and administrative expenses when they were used.

(e) **Investment in Shares of Porter Corp.**   The journal entries that explain the increase of $3,500 in this account are:

Investment in Porter Corp.	5,500	
Equity in earnings of Porter Corp.		5,500
(To record investment income in Porter Corp.		
using the equity method.)		
Cash	2,000	
Investment in Porter Corp.		2,000
(To record the dividend received from Porter Corp.)		

The investment income amount is given on the income statement and the dividend amount is deduced from the change in the account balance. There was no cash flow as a result of the investment income; therefore, an adjustment is needed to reduce net income. Under the indirect method, the $5,500 is deducted to offset the $5,500 included in net income; under the direct approach, the $5,500 adjustment is made to the specific revenue line.

The second entry indicates an operating cash inflow of $2,000. An adjustment is needed to the net income number reported because it does not include the dividend amount. Using the indirect method, $2,000 is added to net income; under the direct approach, $2,000 is added to the same line as the $5,500 deduction above to complete the adjustment of equity-basis income to cash received from the investment in Porter.

(f) **Deferred Development Costs.**   Two types of transactions affected this account in the current year, summarized in the following journal entries.

Deferred development costs	200,000	
Cash		200,000
(To record capitalized development costs.)		
Market development expenses	40,000	
Deferred development costs		40,000
(To record the amortization of deferred		
development costs.)		

The first entry indicates a cash outflow of $200,000. This is an investing cash outflow and is recognized in the cash flow statement's investing activities section.

The second entry did not affect cash. As explained earlier, it is important to be alert to noncash amounts included in net income. This $40,000 expense did not require the use of cash; an adjustment to the net income number is therefore needed under the indirect approach. Under the direct method, the adjustment is made to the specific expense: in this case, to the selling and administrative expense line.

(g) **Land.**   The Land account increased by $49,500 during 2003. Because you know that land was purchased at a cost of $54,000 during the year, there must have been a disposal of land that cost $4,500. The entries that affect this account in 2003, therefore, were as follows.

Land	54,000	
Term preferred shares		54,000
(To record the purchase of land through		
the issue of term preferred shares.)		
Cash	15,000	
Land		4,500
Gain on disposal of land		10,500
(To record the appropriation of land		
costing $4,500 by the municipality.)		

The first entry indicates that there were no cash flows associated with this transaction. Although this investment and financing transaction is not reported on the statement of cash flows, information about such noncash transactions is required to be disclosed elsewhere in the financial statements.

The second transaction entry identifies a cash inflow of $15,000 on land disposal. This is an investing inflow because it affects the stock of noncurrent assets in which the company has invested. It is included on the cash flow statement and is separately disclosed as the cash effect of an extraordinary item.

The second transaction also results in a gain on the income statement of $10,500. By including "net income" in the statement's Operating Cash Flow section initially in Step 2, the $10,500 gain is included in income as if the gain had generated $10,500 of operating cash flows. This is incorrect for two reasons. First, the cash inflow was $15,000, not $10,500. Second, the cash flow was an investing, not an operating, flow. An adjustment is needed, therefore, to deduct $10,500 from the income reported using the indirect method or from the extraordinary item if the direct method is used.

(h) **Equipment and Accumulated Amortization, Equipment.**   All information needed to replicate the entries made to both these accounts in 2003 is provided.

Equipment	53,000	
Cash		53,000
Cash	4,000	
Loss on disposal of equipment	1,500	
Accumulated amortization, equipment	2,500	
Equipment		8,000
Amortization expense	11,500	
Accumulated amortization		11,500
Accumulated amortization, equipment	11,000	
Cash		11,000

The first entry explains a cash outflow of $53,000 due to the purchase of equipment, an investing activity.

The second entry records the disposal of an asset that cost $8,000 with accumulated amortization of $2,500; that is, a book value of $5,500. To be sold at a loss of $1,500, the proceeds on disposal must have been $4,000. The analysis of this item is similar to the analysis of the land disposal in step (g). The cash impact is an inflow of $4,000. This is an investing inflow because it affects the stock of investment in noncurrent assets. The transaction results in a loss of $1,500 that is reported on the 2003 income statement. Because an outflow of $1,500 was not the cash effect (it was an inflow of $4,000) and because this was not an operating flow (it was an investing flow), an adjustment is needed in the Operating Cash Flow section. The $1,500 loss is added back to net income under the indirect method, or to the appropriate line (other expenses and losses) under the direct approach.

The third entry reflects the annual amortization expense. Amortization does not require the use of cash, so an adjustment adding back this amount to net income is needed. Under the direct method, the amortization line itself is corrected.

The fourth entry records the payment of $11,000 for major repairs.[17] The $11,000 cash outflow results from an investing activity.

(i) **Buildings and Accumulated Amortization, Buildings.**   There was no change in the asset account during the year and, in the absence of additional information, the increase in the accumulated amortization account must have been due entirely to the amortization expense recorded for the year. The $3,100 noncash expense is an adjustment in the Operating Activities section.

---

[17] Because the repairs result in "recouping" past amortization, the company charged them to accumulated amortization instead of to the asset account.

(j) **Goodwill.** The $2,400 decrease in Goodwill is the result of the following entry.

Impairment Loss—Goodwill	2,400	
Goodwill		2,400

Recognizing the loss did not affect cash. Under the indirect method, $2,400 is added back to net income; under the direct approach, the impairment loss line itself is reduced.

(k) **Accounts Payable.** Because the Accounts Payable account is increased by purchases on account for operations and decreased by payments to suppliers, cash outflows to suppliers must have exceeded purchases by $1,000 in 2003. Previous cash flow statement adjustments, such as those in (c) and (d), converted expenses reported on the income statement to the amount of purchases of goods and services. The analysis of accounts payable completes this by converting the purchases amount to the cash paid for purchases. The indirect method adjustment deducts an additional $1,000 from the net income reported, while the direct method adjusts the expense line.

(l) **Dividends Payable on Term Preferred Shares.** The $2,000 increase in this account indicates that dividends paid were $2,000 less than the dividends declared on these shares. Because the term preferred shares are reported within the balance sheet's Liability section they must be, in substance, a financial liability. The dividends on these shares are treated the same as interest on debt and, in this case, they have been deducted as dividend expense on the income statement. Under the indirect approach, $2,000 is added back to net income because the cash outflow was less than the dividend expense reported. Under the direct approach, the line item that includes the outflow for dividend expense is reduced.

(m) **Accrued Liabilities.** This account is increased by expenses accrued and decreased by payments of the amounts accrued. During 2003, the payments must have been $4,000 less than the expenses reported: $4,000 must therefore be added back to net income under the indirect method. Using the direct approach, you must determine which expenses should be adjusted. If it was interest expense that was accrued and paid, the interest expense line is adjusted; if wages and salaries payable, the salaries and wages expense is adjusted. In Illustration 23-18, it is assumed that the accruals relate to payroll costs accrued.

(n) **Income Taxes Payable.** This account is increased by recognizing current tax expense and decreased by payments to the tax authorities. The $13,000 reduction in this account indicates that the cash outflows were $13,000 greater than the expense recognized. Net income is adjusted downward by $13,000 under the indirect approach and the income tax line is adjusted under the direct method.

(o) **Bonds Payable, and Discount on Bonds Payable.** Although there was no change in the Bonds Payable account, the Discount on Bonds account was reduced through amortization with the following entry.

Interest Expense	300	
Discount on Bonds Payable		300

The entry results in the recognition of an expense with no corresponding use of cash. An adjustment of $300 is added back to net income under the indirect method, or to the interest expense line under the direct.[18]

(p) **Term Preferred Shares.** Term preferred shares of $60,000 were issued during the year, $54,000 of which were issued in exchange for land. This transaction was

---

[18] *EIC-47, Interest Discount or Premium in the Statement of Changes in Financial Position* (CICA, October 15, 1993) explains how debt issued at a premium or discount should be reported on the statement of cash flows at issuance, as amortized and when redeemed. The complexity is beyond intermediate coverage. Those interested should refer to the EIC.

analysed in (g) above. The remaining issue of shares, in the absence of information to the contrary, must have been for cash:

Cash	6,000	
Term preferred shares		6,000

This is reported as a financing inflow.

(q) **Future Income Tax Liability.** The increase in this account's credit balance was a result of the following entry:

Future income tax expense	3,000	
Future income tax liability		3,000

Because this portion of income tax expense did not require the use of cash, $3,000 is added back to net income under the indirect approach and to the income tax expense line under the direct method.

(r) **Common Shares.** The following entries summarize the changes to this account in 2003.

Retained earnings	15,000	
Common shares		15,000
Cash	144,000	
Common shares		144,000

The first entry records the stock dividend, which neither required nor generated cash. The issue of a stock dividend is not a financing and/or investing transaction, and therefore, is not required to be reported. The second entry records a $144,000 inflow of cash as a result of issuing shares, a financing activity. This is reported as a financing inflow on the cash flow statement.

(s) **Retained Earnings.** The statement of income and retained earnings explains the $94,700 change in this account. The $117,700 increase due to net income and the cash flows associated with it already have been included in the Operating Activities section of the cash flow statement. The $6,000 decrease due to dividends paid on the common shares is reported as a financing outflow. The $15,000 decrease due to the stock dividend was analysed above as having no cash flow implications.

The remaining $2,000 decrease due to the excess of cost of treasury shares over the issue price needs to be examined more closely. The entry underlying this transaction is:

Cash	15,000	
Retained earnings	2,000	
Treasury shares ($34,000 × ½)		17,000

This indicates there was a cash inflow of $15,000 on the reissue of treasury shares, which is reported as a financing activity.

(t) **Treasury Shares.** The $17,000 increase in this account during the year resulted from the company's purchase of its common shares as recorded in the entry below, and the subsequent sale of treasury shares as analysed in step (s) above.

Treasury shares	34,000	
Cash		34,000

The purchase is a $34,000 financing outflow of cash. The cash inflow from the reissue of half these shares has been recognized on the cash flow statement already.

The changes in all balance sheet accounts have now been analysed and those with cash implications have been recorded on the cash flow statement working paper. **The following general statements summarize the approach to the analysis.**

1. For most current asset and current liability accounts, zero in on what increases and what decreases each account. Compare the impact on the income statement with the amount of the related cash flow and adjust the income number(s) in the operating activities section of the cash flow statement to the cash flow effect accordingly.

2. For noncurrent asset and noncurrent liability accounts in general, reconstruct summary journal entries that explain how and why each account changed. Analyse each entry in turn:

   (a) The cash impact is the amount of the debit or credit to cash. Include each cash impact as an investing or financing cash flow on the cash flow statement.

   (b) Identify all debits or credits to income statement accounts where the operating cash impact is not equal to the amount of the revenue, gain, expense, or loss reported. Each of these requires an adjustment to the net income number(s) originally reported in the operating activities classification.

While the transactions entered into by Yoshi Corporation represent a good cross section of common business activities, they do not encompass all possible situations. The general principles and approaches used in the above analyses, however, can be applied to most other transactions and events.

Step 4. Complete the statement of cash flows. Determine subtotals for each major classification of cash flow and ensure that the statement reconciles to the actual change in cash identified in Step 1.

The working paper prepared in Illustration 23-18 should be presented with more appropriate descriptions and complete disclosure to enable readers to better interpret the information and comply with GAAP. Illustration 23-19 presents the completed statement of cash flows, using the direct method to explain the operating flows.

ILLUSTRATION 23-19
Statement of Cash Flows—
Yoshi Corporation (Direct Method)

YOSHI CORPORATION
Statement of Cash Flows
Year Ended December 31, 2003

Cash provided by (used in) operations:

Received from customers		$869,250
Dividends received on long-term equity investments		2,000
Payments to suppliers		(490,750)
Payments to and on behalf of employees		(196,000)
Payments for interest, and dividends on term preferred shares		(9,000)
Income taxes paid		(62,500)
		113,000
Cash provided by (used in) investing activities:		
Investment in development costs	($200,000)	
Purchase of equipment	(53,000)	
Major repairs incurred	(11,000)	
Proceeds on expropriation of land, an extraordinary item	15,000	
Proceeds on sale of equipment	4,000	(245,000)
Cash provided by (used in) financing activities:		
Proceeds on issue of common shares	$144,000	
Proceeds on issue of term preferred shares	6,000	
Purchase of treasury shares	(34,000)	
Proceeds on reissue of treasury shares	15,000	
Dividends paid on common shares	(6,000)	125,000
Decrease in cash and cash equivalents (Note 1)		(7,000)
Cash and cash equivalents, January 1		66,000
Cash and cash equivalents, December 31		$ 59,000

Note 1: Cash and cash equivalents are defined as cash on deposit and money market instruments included as short-term investments.

Note 2: Preferred shares valued at $54,000 were issued during the year as consideration for the purchase of land.

For those who prefer the indirect method of reporting operating cash flows, Illustration 23-20 indicates how the statement's Operating Activities section might look.

Cash provided by (used in) operations:		
Net income		$117,700
Add back noncash expenses:		
Amortization	$14,600	
Impairment loss—goodwill	2,400	
Bad debts	2,250	
Amortization of bond discount	300	
Amortization of development costs	40,000	59,550
Equity in income of Porter Corp. in excess of dividends received		(3,500)
Deduct nonoperating gains (net)		
Extraordinary gain on land	(10,500)	
Loss on disposal of equipment	1,500	(9,000)
Deferral of income tax liability to future periods		3,000
Changes in noncash working capital accounts (see Note A)		(54,750)
		$113,000
Note A—changes in noncash working capital:		
Accounts receivable	($55,250)	
Inventory	8,000	
Prepaid expenses	500	
Accounts payable	(1,000)	
Dividends payable, term preferred shares	2,000	
Accrued liabilities	4,000	
Income taxes payable	(13,000)	
	($54,750)	

Interpreting the Statement

OBJECTIVE 7
Read and interpret a
statement of cash flows.

There is considerable flexibility in how the information is reported in the cash flow statement. The way in which information is summarized and described can enhance the information content and help users interpret and understand the significance of the cash flow data.

The Yoshi Corporation statement in Illustrations 23-19 and 20 provides valuable information to financial statement readers. Cash receipts from customers and dividends from investments generated $113,000 more cash than needed to pay operating costs (direct method). Although $59,550 of noncash expenses were deducted in calculating net income, the growth in accounts receivable held operating cash flows to almost the same level as the income reported (indirect method).

The $113,000 of excess operating cash flows allowed Yoshi to internally finance almost half of its investment activities during the year of $245,000, most of it spent on developmental activities. The remainder of cash required for investment was generated mainly through financing activities, eating into existing cash balances only marginally to the extent of $7,000. The majority of new financing was achieved through the issue of common equity. This is reasonable given that the funds were invested in development costs—assets often difficult to finance through debt.

Users must exercise care in interpreting cash flow statements. Companies in a growth or development stage will generally use more cash in their operating activities than they receive from customers, a situation that should reverse as the business life cycle matures. Users of financial statements should also look beyond the amount of cash generated or used in operations, and analyse the reasons for the operating cash flows. Were collections on accounts receivable at an all-time high and accounts payable stretched to their limits? If so, the operating cash flows in the period under review are probably not indicative of replicable operating cash flows.

Details of cash flows related to financing activities allow readers to assess the potential for future claims to the organization's cash and to identify major changes in the form of financing, especially between debt and equity. Companies in a growth stage

INTERNATIONAL INSIGHT

Consolidated statements of cash flows may be of limited use to analysts evaluating multinational companies. Without disaggregation, users of such statements are not able to determine "where in the world" the funds are sourced and used.

will usually report significant amounts of cash generated from financing activities—financing that is needed to handle the significant investment activity. As growth levels off and operations begin to generate positive cash flows, financing flows tend to reverse as debt is repaid and, if appropriate, shares are redeemed.

REPORTING AND DISCLOSURE REQUIREMENTS

Cash Flow Statements

> **OBJECTIVE 8**
>
> Identify the financial reporting and disclosure requirements for the statement of cash flows.

In addition to requiring that cash flows be reported according to operating, investing, and financing classifications, *Handbook* Section 1540 requires separate disclosure of the following.

1. cash flows (before tax) associated with extraordinary items, classified as operating, investing, or financing, as appropriate
2. cash outflows for interest and dividends paid and included as a component of net income (as operating flows), as well as those charged to retained earnings (as financing flows)
3. cash flows related to income taxes, classified as operating cash flows unless specifically identifiable with investing or financing activities
4. cash flows and other specified information from business combinations and disposals of business units (both as investing flows)
5. the policy for determining cash and cash equivalents; the components of cash and cash equivalents, with a reconciliation of the amounts reported on the cash flow statement with the amounts reported on the balance sheet; and the amount of cash and cash equivalents whose use is restricted[19]

The recommendations leave the choice between the direct and indirect method up to the preparer, although the AcSB encourages reporting operating cash flows under the direct approach. The recommendations also require the reporting of gross cash inflows and outflows from investing and financing activities rather than netted amounts, and separate disclosure elsewhere in the financial statements about investing and financing transactions that did not generate or use cash resources. Other requirements related to financial institutions, foreign currency cash flows, and business combinations and disposals are left to a course in advanced financial accounting.

Cash Flow per Share Information

IAS NOTE

There is no IAS standard dealing with cash flow per share.

Because a number of companies report cash flow per share data in their financial statements, the Accounting Standards Board issued *EIC-34* in 1991 to ensure that readers were adequately informed about this statistic. The Emerging Issues Committee concluded that when companies provide cash flow per share data, they should be reported as part of the statement of cash flows, and not the income statement where it might be given more prominence than the earnings per share. The committee did not specify how cash flow per share should be measured, but took the approach that companies should disclose information so that readers can determine how the numbers reported are determined.

In late 2000, the AcSB approved a project to develop guidance on calculating and presenting cash flow per share information in financial statements. As of November 2001, an *Exposure Draft* is in process proposing limited amendments to Section 1540 that address presentation of cash flow per share information.

Go to the Digital Tool for additional examples of cash flow statements.

Financial Reporting Example

The Consolidated Cash Flow Statement of **Canfor Corporation** for its year ended December 31, 2000 is provided in Illustration 23-21. Much of the additional information required is presented on the face of the statement itself, although most companies

---

[19] *CICA Handbook*, Section 1540, pars. .32 - .50.

tend to provide it in notes to the financial statements. It is also interesting to note that the company had a negative cash balance at December 31, 2000. Review the statement for the considerable differences in cash activity from one year to the next.

Consolidated Cash Flow Statement

ILLUSTRATION 23-21
Cash Flow Statement—Canfor Corporation

Year ended December 31 (thousands of dollars)	2000	1999
Cash generated from (used in)		
Operating activities		
Net income from continuing operations	$ 125,576	$ 106,911
Items not affecting cash:		
Depreciation, depletion and amortization	112,691	70,166
Future income taxes	12,664	11,642
Other	(8,814)	(10,111)
Non-cash working capital changes (see below)	(141,353)	32,327
	100,764	210,935
Financing activities		
Proceeds from issue of common shares (Note 9)	96	239,490
Proceeds from acquisition bank loan	—	150,000
Repayment of acquisition bank loan	(20,000)	(100,000)
Repayment of long-term debt and capital leases	(30,734)	(30,536)
Dividends paid to common shareholders	(21,083)	—
Premium on stock options issued	(156)	—
Interest on convertible debentures, net of taxes	(4,686)	—
	(76,563)	258,954
Investing activities		
Purchase of investment (Note 2)	—	(433,223)
Purchase of property, plant, equipment and timber	(121,802)	(119,856)
Proceeds from sale of property, plant, equipment, investments and other	2,373	13,527
	(119,429)	(539,552)
Increase (decrease) in net cash (short-term indebtedness)		
From continuing operations	(95,228)	(69,663)
From discontinued operations (Note 2)	—	13,787
Net cash at beginning of year	30,191	86,067
Net cash (short-term indebtedness) at end of year	$ (65,037)	$ 30,191
Net cash (short-term indebtedness) comprises		
Cash	$ 16,693	$ 18,313
Temporary investments	—	56,613
Unpresented cheques	(41,452)	(42,401)
Operating bank loans	(40,278)	(2,334)
	$ (65,037)	$ 30,191
Non-cash working capital changes		
Accounts receivable	$ 51,390	$ 10,073
Income taxes	(93,834)	63,104
Future income taxes	13,638	—
Inventories	(1,143)	(28,580)
Prepaid expenses	(2,123)	1,411
Accounts payable and accrued liabilities	(109,281)	(13,681)
	$ (141,353)	$ 32,327

Interest paid by continuing operations in 2000 was $61,343 (1999 - $38,817)
and income taxes paid were $159,984 (1999 - income taxes recovered $6,844)

USE OF A WORK SHEET

When numerous adjustments are necessary, or other complicating factors are present, **a work sheet is often used to assemble and classify the data that will appear on the statement of cash flows**. The work sheet (a "spreadsheet" when using computer software) is merely a device that aids in the preparation of the statement; its use is optional. The skeleton format of the work sheet for preparing the statement of cash flows using the indirect method is shown in Illustration 23-22.

ILLUSTRATION 23-22
Format of Work Sheet for Preparing Statement of Cash Flows

STATEMENT OF CASH FLOWS FOR THE YEAR ENDED...

Balance Sheet Accounts	End of Last Year Balances	Reconciling Items Debits	Reconciling Items Credits	End of Current Year Balances
Debit balance accounts	XX	XX	XX	XX
	XX	XX	XX	XX
Totals	XX			XXX
Credit balance accounts	XX	XX	XX	XX
	XX	XX	XX	XX
Totals	XX			XXX
Cash Flows				
Operating activities				
Net income		XX		
Adjustments		XX	XX	
Investing activities				
Receipts (dr.) and payments (cr.)		XX	XX	
Financing activities				
Receipts (dr.) and payments (cr.)		XX	XX	
Totals		XXX	XXX	
Increase (decrease) in cash		(XX)	XX	
Totals		XXX	XXX	

The following guidelines are important in using a work sheet:

1. In the Balance Sheet Accounts section, accounts with debit balances are listed separately from those with credit balances. This means, for example, that Accumulated Amortization is listed under credit balances and not as a contra account under debit balances. The beginning and ending balances of each account are entered. As the analysis proceeds, each line pertaining to a balance sheet account should balance. That is, the beginning balance plus or minus the reconciling item(s) must equal the ending balance. When this agreement exists for all balance sheet accounts, all changes in account balances have been identified and reconciled.

2. The bottom portion of the work sheet consists of an area to record the operating, investing, and financing cash flows. This section provides the detail for the change in the cash balance during the period—information used to prepare the formal statement of cash flows. Inflows of cash are entered as debits in the reconciling columns and outflows of cash are entered as credits in the reconciling columns. Thus, in this section, the sale of equipment for cash at book value is entered as a debit under inflows of cash from investing activities. Similarly, the purchase of land for cash is entered as a credit under outflows of cash from investing activities.

3. The reconciling items shown in the work sheet are not entered in any journal or posted to any account. They do not represent either adjustments or corrections of the balance sheet accounts. They are used only to facilitate the preparation of the statement of cash flows.

Preparing the Work Sheet

The preparation of a work sheet involves a series of prescribed steps. The steps in this case are:

Step 1. Enter the balance sheet accounts and their beginning and ending balances in the appropriate Balance Sheet Accounts section.

Step 2. Enter the debits and credits from the summary entries that explain the changes in each balance sheet account (other than cash), identify all that affect cash, and enter these amounts in the reconciling columns at the bottom of the work sheet.

Step 3. After the analysis is complete and the changes in all balance sheet accounts have been explained, enter the increase or decrease in cash on the balance sheet cash line (or lines, if cash equivalents) and at the bottom of the work sheet. The totals of the reconciling columns should balance.

Go to the Digital Tool for a discussion of the T-account approach to preparing the Statement of Cash Flows.

To illustrate procedures for preparing the work sheet, the same comprehensive illustration used earlier for Yoshi Corporation is presented. The indirect method serves initially as the basis for calculating net cash provided by operating activities. An illustration of the direct method is also provided. The financial statements and other data related to Yoshi Corporation for its year ended December 31, 2003 are presented in Illustrations 23-15, 16, and 17. Most of the analysis was discussed earlier in the chapter and additional explanations related to the work sheet are provided throughout the discussion that follows.

Analysis of Transactions

Before the analysis begins, Yoshi's balance sheet accounts are transferred to the work sheet opening and ending balance columns. The following discussion explains the individual adjustments that appear on the work sheet in Illustration 23-23. It assumes you are familiar with the analysis of the Yoshi illustration earlier in the chapter.

ILLUSTRATION 23-23
Work Sheet for Preparation of Statement of Cash Flows— Yoshi Corporation

WORK SHEET FOR PREPARATION OF STATEMENT OF CASH FLOWS
Year Ended December 31, 2003

	Balance 12/31/02	Reconciling Items–2003 Debits		Reconciling Items–2003 Credits		Balance 12/31/03
Debits						
Cash	32,000			(23)	12,000	20,000
Short-term investments	34,000	(23)	5,000			39,000
Accounts receivable	52,700	(2)	55,250	(2)	1,450	106,500
Inventories	311,000			(3)	8,000	303,000
Prepaid expenses	17,000			(4)	500	16,500
Investment in shares of Porter Corp.	15,000	(5)	5,500	(5)	2,000	18,500
Deferred development costs	30,000	(6)	200,000	(6)	40,000	190,000
Land	82,000	(7)	54,000	(7)	4,500	131,500
Equipment	142,000	(8)	53,000	(8)	8,000	187,000
Buildings	262,000					262,000
Goodwill	10,000			(9)	2,400	7,600
Discount on bonds payable	2,500			(10)	300	2,200
Treasury shares	—	(11)	34,000	(11)	17,000	17,000
Total debits	990,200					1,300,800
Credits						
Allowance for doubtful accounts	1,700	(2)	1,450	(12)	2,250	2,500
Accumulated amortization, equipment	31,000	(8)	2,500	(13)	11,500	29,000
Accumulated amortization, buildings	71,000	(13)	11,000	(14)	3,100	74,100
Accounts payable	131,000	(15)	1,000			130,000
Dividends payable, term preferred shares	—			(16)	2,000	2,000

WORK SHEET FOR PREPARATION OF STATEMENT OF CASH FLOWS
Year Ended December 31, 2003 (continued)

	Balance 12/31/02	Reconciling Items–2003 Debits		Reconciling Items–2003 Credits		Balance 12/31/03
Accrued liabilities	39,000			(17)	4,000	43,000
Income taxes payable	16,000	(18)	13,000			3,000
Bonds payable	100,000					100,000
Term preferred shares	—			(7)	54,000	60,000
				(19)	6,000	
Future income tax liability	6,000			(20)	3,000	9,000
Common shares	88,000			(21)	15,000	247,000
				(21)	144,000	
Retained earnings	506,500	(11)	2,000	(1)	117,700	601,200
		(21)	15,000			
		(22)	6,000			
Total credits	990,200					1,300,800

Cash Flows

Operating activities:

		Debits		Credits	
Net income		(1)	117,700		
Increase in accounts receivable				(2)	55,250
Decrease in inventories		(3)	8,000		
Decrease in prepaid expenses		(4)	500		
Equity in earnings of Porter Corp.				(5)	5,500
Dividend from Porter Corp.		(5)	2,000		
Amortization, deferred development costs		(6)	40,000		
Gain on expropriation of land				(7)	10,500
Loss on disposal of equipment		(8)	1,500		
Impairment loss, goodwill		(9)	2,400		
Amortization of bond discount		(10)	300		
Bad debt expense		(12)	2,250		
Amortization expense, equipment		(13)	11,500		
Amortization expense, buildings		(14)	3,100		
Decrease in accounts payable				(15)	1,000
Dividend, term preferred shares		(16)	2,000		
Increase in accrued liabilities		(17)	4,000		
Decrease in income taxes payable				(18)	13,000
Future income tax liability		(20)	3,000		

Investing activities:

		Debits		Credits	
Development costs incurred				(6)	200,000
Proceeds on disposal of land		(7)	15,000		
Purchase of equipment				(8)	53,000
Proceeds on sale of equipment		(8)	4,000		
Major repair costs incurred				(13)	11,000

Financing activities:

		Debits		Credits	
Purchase of treasury shares				(11)	34,000
Proceeds on reissue of treasury shares		(11)	15,000		
Proceeds on issue of term preferred shares		(19)	6,000		
Proceeds on sale of common shares		(21)	144,000		
Dividend on common shares				(22)	6,000
			840,950		847,950
Decrease in cash		(23)	7,000		
			847,950		847,950

1. **Net income.** Because so much of the analysis requires adjustments to convert accrual basis income to the cash basis, the net income number is usually the first reconciling item put in the work sheet. The entry to reflect this and the balance sheet account affected is:

Net income (operating cash inflow)	117,700	
Retained earnings		117,700

The credit to retained earnings explains part of the change in that account. We know that net income did not generate $117,700 of cash, so this number is considered a tentative one that will be adjusted whenever the subsequent analysis identifies revenues and expenses whose cash impact differs from the revenue and expense amounts incorporated in the net income number. It is a starting point only.[20]

2. **Accounts receivable.** Because the entire bottom of the work sheet when completed will explain the change in cash and cash equivalents (defined as cash and short-term investments in this illustration), and because all balance sheet accounts have to be analysed, accounts receivable is a logical starting point. The following two entries summarize the net change in this account and identify the other accounts affected.

Accounts receivable	55,250	
Revenue		55,250
Allowance for doubtful accounts	1,450	
Accounts receivable		1,450

Accounts receivable increased by $53,800 during the year after writing off accounts totalling $1,450. The increase due to reporting revenue in excess of cash receipts therefore must have been $55,250. This requires an adjustment to the net income reported in the work sheet's Operating Activities section. The other entry explains changes in two balance sheet accounts with no cash impact. Enter these on the work sheet.

3. **Inventories.** The entry to explain the net change in the Inventory account is as follows.

Cost of goods sold	8,000	
Inventories		8,000

The credit to inventories explains the change in that account. The debit is an expense of $8,000 that was deducted in calculating net income, but which did not use cash. This requires a debit column adjustment to the net income in the Operating Activities section.[21]

4. **Prepaid expenses.** Assuming the prepaid expenses were selling and administrative in nature, the following entry summarizes the change in this account during the year.

Selling and administrative expense	500	
Prepaid expenses		500

The credit entry explains the change in the Prepaid Expenses account. The debit represents a noncash expense deducted on the income statement and requires an adjustment to the net income reported in the operating activity category.

5. **Investment in shares of Porter Corp.** Entries explaining the change in this account are:

Investment in shares of Porter Corp.	5,500	
Equity in earnings of Porter Corp.		5,500
Cash	2,000	
Investment in shares of Porter Corp.		2,000

[20] Some accountants prefer to slot in "income before extraordinary items" within the Operating Activities section and the "extraordinary item" within the Investing or Financing Activity section, as appropriate. In the Yoshi example, the extraordinary item is an investing activity. Regardless, the transaction underlying the extraordinary item must be revisited in the subsequent analysis and be further adjusted. For this reason, the authors prefer to begin with the net income and adjust for the extraordinary item later in the analysis.

[21] This analysis is consistent with that earlier in the chapter. If $8,000 of cost of goods sold came from a reduction in inventory levels, purchases for the year must have been $8,000 less than cost of goods sold. Therefore the analysis equally well converts cost of goods sold to the level of purchases in the year.

The first entry explains part of the change in the investment account and identifies a noncash revenue included in net income. The entry to adjust net income for this is a $5,500 credit. The second entry credit explains the remainder of the change in the balance sheet account. The debit portion of the entry represents an operating inflow of cash that is not included in net income. The Operating Activities section is adjusted to reflect this $2,000 operating cash inflow.

6. **Deferred development costs.** Noting that the development costs relate to marketing activities, the entries to summarize the changes in this account are as follows.

Deferred development costs	200,000	
Cash		200,000
Selling and administrative expense	40,000	
Deferred development costs		40,000

The first entry identifies an outflow of cash related to investment in this noncurrent asset—an investing flow. The second entry recognizes the amortization of these deferred costs—a noncash expense—reported in net income. The adjustment adds back (debits) $40,000 to the net income number. Remember to enter the transactions that explain changes in the balance sheet accounts as you proceed.

7. **Land.** The entries affecting the Land account are:

Land	54,000	
Term preferred shares		54,000
Cash	15,000	
Land		4,500
Gain on disposal of land (extraordinary item)		10,500

The first entry explains changes in both the Land and Term Preferred Shares accounts—a noncash transaction. The second entry identifies a $15,000 investing inflow of cash, a reduction of $4,500 in the Land account, and a gain reported in net income that does not correspond to the actual cash flow, and which results from an investing transaction. Net income is adjusted.

8. **Equipment.** Entries affecting the Equipment account are reproduced below.

Equipment	53,000	
Cash		53,000
Cash	4,000	
Loss on disposal of equipment	1,500	
Accumulated amortization, equipment	2,500	
Equipment		8,000

The first entry identifies a $53,000 investing outflow of cash. The second entry explains the remainder of the change in the asset account and part of the change in the Accumulated Amortization account, reports a $4,000 investing inflow of cash, and a $1,500 noncash loss reported in net income that needs to be adjusted.

9. **Goodwill.** The decrease in Goodwill is an impairment loss.

Impairment loss—goodwill	2,400	
Goodwill		2,400

The impairment loss is a noncash charge to the income statement. It therefore requires an adjustment to the net income included in the Operating Activities section.

10. **Discount on bonds payable.** The entry to record discount amortization is:

Interest expense	300	
Discount on bonds payable		300

Again, a noncash expense was deducted in determining income and must be adjusted.

11. **Treasury shares.** The change in this account is explained in two entries.

Treasury shares	34,000	
Cash		34,000
Cash	15,000	
Retained earnings	2,000	
Treasury shares ($34,000 × ½)		17,000

The first entry identifies a $34,000 financing outflow of cash to acquire the company's own shares. The second entry explains the remainder of the change in the Treasury Shares account and part of the change in retained earnings, and identifies a $15,000 inflow of cash from the reissue of the shares—a financing transaction.

12. **Allowance for doubtful accounts.** Part of the change in this account was explained previously in item 2 above. The remaining entry to this account recognized bad debt expense.

Bad debt expense	2,250	
Allowance for doubtful accounts		2,250

This completes the explanation of changes to the Allowance account. In addition, it identifies a noncash expense of $2,250, which requires an adjustment to net income in the Operating Activities section.

13. **Accumulated amortization, equipment.** One of the changes in the accumulated Amortization account was explained previously in item 8. The remainder of the entries affecting this account are:

Amortization expense	11,500	
Accumulated amortization, equipment		11,500
Accumulated amortization, equipment	11,000	
Cash		11,000

The first entry identifies an $11,500 noncash expense requiring an adjustment to net income and the cash flows from operations. The second entry explains the remainder of the change in the account—an investing outflow of cash.

14. **Accumulated amortization, buildings.** With no change in the Buildings account during the year, the only entry needed to explain the change in the Accumulated Amortization account is:

Amortization expense	3,100	
Accumulated amortization, buildings		3,100

This $3,100 noncash expense requires an adjustment to the net income number in the Operating Activities section.

15. **Accounts payable.** The summary entry to explain the net change in this account is:

Accounts payable	1,000	
Cash		1,000

The reduction in the payables balance resulted from paying out $1,000 more cash than purchases recorded. Cost of goods sold and other expenses have already been adjusted to represent the goods and services purchased, so a $1,000 credit adjustment is needed to convert the purchases to the amount paid; i.e., to the operating cash outflow.

16. **Dividends payable on term preferred shares.** The summary entry explaining the net change in this account follows.

Dividend expense (income statement expense)	2,000	
Dividends payable on term preferred shares		2,000

The increase in the liability account is due to recognizing more dividends as an expense (these shares are a financial liability in substance) than dividends paid in the year. $2,000 is added back to net income to adjust the operating cash flows to equal cash dividends paid in 2003.

17. **Accrued liabilities.** The $4,000 increase in this account was caused by recognizing $4,000 more expense than payments on accrued liabilities in the year.

Salaries and wages expense (assumed)	4,000	
Accrued liabilities		4,000

To adjust, $4,000 must be added back (debited) to the cash provided by net income as reported.

18. **Income taxes payable.** The decrease in this account occured because Yoshi Corporation paid out more cash than the expense reported.

Income taxes payable	13,000	
Cash		13,000

Because the expense reported has been deducted in determining the income number, an additional $13,000 outflow must be deducted or credited on the work sheet.

19. **Term preferred shares.** $54,000 of the increase in this account has already been analysed. The remaining increase is assumed to have resulted from the following entry, a $6,000 financing inflow.

Cash	6,000	
Term preferred shares		6,000

20. **Future income tax liability.** The increase in this account is due to the deferral of the tax liability to future periods.

Future income tax expense	3,000	
Future income tax liability		3,000

The change in the balance sheet account is explained, and the noncash portion of income tax expense is adjusted by adding back $3,000 to net income.

21. **Common shares.** Two entries explain the change in this account over the year.

Retained earnings	15,000	
Common shares		15,000
Cash	144,000	
Common shares		144,000

The first entry records the stock dividend issued. As discussed earlier, this is a noncash activity that, although explaining the change in two balance sheet accounts, is not part of the cash flow statement. The second entry records the inflow of cash for shares sold—a financing flow.

22. **Retained earnings.** Most of the changes in this account have already been dealt with above. One additional entry is needed to explain the remainder of the change.

Retained earnings (dividends)	6,000	
Cash		6,000

This entry records a financing outflow of cash for dividends on common shares.

Completing the Work Sheet

All that remains to complete the balance sheet portion of the work sheet is to credit the Cash account by $12,000 and debit the Short-Term investments by $5,000, netting to a $7,000 credit or decrease in cash. The $7,000 debit to balance this work sheet entry is inserted at the bottom of the work sheet. The debit and credit reconciling item columns are then totalled and balanced.

If the direct method of determining cash flows from operating activities is preferred, one change is needed to the above procedures. Instead of debiting the net income of $117,700 and using this as the starting point to represent cash inflows from operations, the individual revenues, expenses, gains, and losses (netting to $117,700) are transferred to the Operating Activities section on a line-by-line basis. Where income statement items differ from the actual cash generated or used, adjustments are made to the specific line item involved.

The analysis is simplified if items that will be reported together on the final statement are grouped together, and if all income tax amounts are grouped as well. This step and the adjustments needed in the Operating Activities section are shown in Illustration 23-24. The adjustments in the Operating Activities section are exactly the same as those made using the indirect approach, except that they are made to a specific line item instead of to net income.

ILLUSTRATION 23-24
Operating Activities Work Sheet—Direct Method

DIRECT METHOD

		Debits (inflow)		Credits (outflow)
Cash Flows				
Operating activities:				
Net sales	(1)	924,500	(2)	55,250
Equity in earnings of Porter Corp.	(1)	5,500	(5)	5,500
	(5)	2,000		
Cost of goods sold	(3)	8,000	(1)	395,400
			(15)	1,000
Selling and administrative expense	(4)	500	(1)	134,600
	(6)	40,000		
	(12)	2,250		
Other expenses and losses	(8)	1,500	(1)	12,000
Salaries and wages expense	(17)	4,000	(1)	200,000
	(10)	300		
Interest and dividend expense	(16)	2,000	(1)	11,300
Impairment loss—goodwill	(9)	2,400	(1)	2,400
Income tax expense	(20)	3,000	(1)	50,000
			(1)	2,500
			(18)	13,000
Amortization expense	(13)	11,500	(1)	14,600
	(14)	3,100		
Extraordinary gain, before tax	(1)	10,500	(7)	10,500

The bottom part of the work sheet provides the necessary information to prepare the formal statement of cash flows shown in Illustrations 23-19 (direct method) and 23-20 (indirect method).

Summary of Learning Objectives

1 Describe the purpose and uses of the statement of cash flows. The primary purpose of the statement of cash flows is to provide information about an entity's cash receipts and cash payments during a period. A secondary objective is to report the entity's operating, investing, and financing activities during the period. The statement's objective is to provide information about historical changes in an enterprise's cash so that investors and creditors can assess the amount, timing, and degree of certainty of an entity's future cash flows, as well as the organization's needs for cash and how it will be used.

2 Define cash and cash equivalents. The definition of cash flows is related to an organization's cash management activities. Cash and cash equivalents include cash on hand, demand deposits, and short-term, highly liquid nonequity investments that are convertible to known amounts of cash with insignificant risk of changes in value, reduced by bank overdrafts that are repayable on demand.

3 Identify the major classifications of cash flows and explain the significance of each. Cash flows can be classified into those resulting from operating, investing, and financing activities. A company's ability to generate operating cash flows affects its capacity to pay dividends to shareholders, to take advantage of investment opportunities, to provide internal financing for growth, and to meet obligations when they fall due. The level of cash spent in investing activities affects an organization's potential for future cash flows. Cash invested in increased levels of productive assets forms the basis for future operating cash inflows. Financing cash activities affect the firm's capital structure and, therefore, the requirements for future cash outflows.

4 Contrast the direct and indirect methods of calculating net cash flow from operating activities. Under the direct approach, major classes of operating cash receipts and cash disbursements are determined. The calculations are summarized in a schedule of changes from the accrual to the cash basis income statement. The direct approach of reporting net cash flow from operating activities is presented in a condensed cash basis income statement. The indirect method begins with the net income reported and adjusts this number whenever the cash received and paid out for activities related to operations differs from the revenues, gains, expenses, and losses included in net income.

5 Differentiate between net income and net cash flows from operating activities. The calculation of net income is the direct result of the accrual-based accounting model, which recognizes revenues when earned and matches expenses with those revenues. Cash flow from operations differs from this in three ways: (1) cash inflows from customers and outflows to suppliers do not necessarily fall in the same accounting period as the associated revenues and expenses; (2) some expenses, such as amortization, do not have corresponding operating cash outflows but result instead from investing outflows of previous periods; and (3) net income includes gains and losses on the disposal and retirement of noncurrent assets and liabilities that do not represent the cash flows of the underlying transaction and that are investing and financing rather than operating flows in nature.

6 Prepare a statement of cash flows. Preparing the statement involves determining the change in cash and cash equivalents during the period, slotting in either the net income (indirect method) or line items from the income statement (direct method) as the starting point within the statement's Operating Activities section, and analysing the changes in each balance sheet account to identify all transactions with a cash impact. Transactions with a cash impact are recorded on the cash flow statement. To ensure that all cash flows have been identified, the results recorded on the statement are compared with the change in cash during the period. The formal statement is then prepared, complete with appropriate descriptions and disclosures.

7 Read and interpret a statement of cash flows. The first step is to look at the subtotals for the three classifications of activities and the overall change in cash. This provides a high level summary of the period's cash flows. Next, analyse the items within each section for additional insights.

8 Identify the financial reporting and disclosure requirements for the statement of cash flows. Separate disclosure is required of cash flows associated with extraordinary items, interest and dividends received and paid, the components of cash and cash equivalents reconciled to the amounts reported on the balance sheet, and the amount of and explanation for cash and cash equivalents not available for use. All income tax cash flows should be reported as operating flows unless they can be linked directly to investing or financing flows. Gross amounts should be reported except in specifically permitted circumstances, and noncash investing and financing transactions should be excluded from the cash flow statement with details reported elsewhere on the financial statements.

9 Use a work sheet to prepare a statement of cash flows. A work sheet can be used to organize the analysis and cash flow information needed to prepare a statement of cash flows. This method accounts for all changes in the balances of non-cash balance sheet accounts from the period's beginning to the end, identifying all operating, investing, and financing cash flows in the process. The cash flow statement is prepared from this cash flow information, which is accumulated at the bottom of the work sheet.

BRIEF EXERCISES

BE23-1 Gladhanders Corporation had the following activities in 2002:

Sale of land	$130,000
Purchase of inventory	845,000
Retirement of bonds payable	72,000
Purchase of equipment	415,000
Issue of common shares	320,000
Purchase of long-term investments	59,000

Calculate the amount Gladhanders should report as net cash provided (used) by investing activities in its statement of cash flows.

BE23-2 Chrono Corporation had the following activities in 2002:

Payment of accounts payable	$770,000
Issue of common shares	250,000
Payment of dividends	
(charged to retained earnings)	300,000
Collection of note receivable	100,000
Issue of bonds payable	510,000
Purchase of company's own shares	46,000

Calculate the amount Chrono should report as net cash provided (used) by financing activities in its 2002 statement of cash flows.

BE23-3 Ryker Corporation is preparing its 2003 statement of cash flows, using the indirect method. Presented below is a list of items that may affect the statement. Using the code below, indicate how each item will affect Ryker's 2003 statement of cash flows.

Code Letter	Effect
A	Added to net income in the operating section
D	Deducted from net income in the operating section
R-I	Cash receipt in investing section
P-I	Cash payment in investing section
R F	Cash receipt in financing section
P-F	Cash payment in financing section
N	Noncash investing and/or financing activity

Items

_____ **(a)**   increase in accounts receivable
_____ **(b)**   decrease in accounts receivable
_____ **(c)**   issue of shares
_____ **(d)**   amortization expense
_____ **(e)**   sale of land at book value
_____ **(f)**   sale of land at a gain
_____ **(g)**   payment of dividends charged to retained earnings
_____ **(h)**   purchase of land and building
_____ **(i)**   purchase of long-term portfolio investment
_____ **(j)**   increase in accounts payable
_____ **(k)**   decrease in accounts payable
_____ **(l)**   loan from bank by signing note
_____ **(m)** purchase of equipment using a note
_____ **(n)**   increase in inventory
_____ **(o)**   issue of bonds
_____ **(p)**   retirement of bonds
_____ **(q)**   sale of equipment at a loss
_____ **(r)**   purchase of company's own shares to be held as treasury shares

BE23-4 Azure Corporation had the following 2002 income statement:

Sales	$200,000
Cost of goods sold	120,000
Gross profit	80,000
Operating expenses (includes amortization of $21,000)	50,000
Net income	$ 30,000

The following accounts increased during 2002: accounts receivable, $17,000; inventory, $11,000; accounts payable, $13,000. Prepare the cash flows from operating activities section of Azure's 2002 statement of cash flows using the direct method.

BE23-5 Use the information from BE23-4 for Azure Corporation. Prepare the cash flows from operating activities section of Azure's 2002 statement of cash flows using the indirect method.

BE23-6 At January 1, 2002, Cyberslider Inc. had accounts receivable of $72,000. At December 31, 2002, accounts receivable is $59,000. Sales for 2002 is $420,000. Calculate Cyberslider's 2002 cash receipts from customers.

BE23-7 Ciao Corporation had January 1 and December 31 balances as follows:

	1/1/03	12/31/03
Inventory	$90,000	$113,000
Accounts payable	61,000	69,000

For 2003, cost of goods sold was $500,000. Calculate Ciao's 2003 cash payments to suppliers of merchandise.

BE23-8 In 2002, Fieval Corporation had net cash provided by operating activities of $531,000; net cash used by investing activities of $963,000; and net cash provided by financing activities of $585,000. At January 1, 2002, the cash balance was $333,000. Calculate December 31, 2002 cash.

BE23-9 Tool Time Corporation had the following 2002 income statement:

Revenues	$100,000
Expenses	60,000
	$ 40,000

In 2002, Tool Time had the following activity in selected accounts:

Accounts Receivable					Allowance for Doubtful Account			
1/1/02	20,000						1,200	1/1/02
Revenues	100,000	1,000	Write-offs	Write-offs	1,000		1,540	Bad debt expense
		90,000	Collections					
12/31/02	29,000						1,740	12/31/02

Prepare Tool Time's cash flows from operating activities section of the statement of cash flows using (a) the direct method and (b) the indirect method.

BE23-10 October Corporation reported net income of $50,000 in 2003. Amortization expense was $17,000. The following working capital accounts changed:

Accounts receivable	$11,000	increase
Long-term investments	16,000	increase
Inventory	7,400	increase
Nontrade note payable	15,000	decrease
Accounts payable	9,300	increase

Calculate net cash provided by operating activities.

BE23-11 In 2002, Izzy Corporation reported a net loss of $70,000. Izzy's only net income adjustments were amortization expense, $84,000, and increase in accounts receivable, $8,100. Calculate Izzy's net cash provided (used) by operating activities.

BE23-12 In 2002, Mufosta Inc. issued 1,000 common shares for land worth $50,000.

(a) Prepare Mufosta's journal entry to record the transaction.
(b) Indicate the effect the transaction has on cash.
(c) Indicate how the transaction is reported on the statement of cash flows.

BE23-13 Indicate in general journal form how the items below would be entered in a work sheet to prepare the statement of cash flows.

    (a) Net income is $317,000.
    (b) Cash dividends declared (charged to retained earnings) and paid totalled $120,000.
    (c) Equipment was purchased for $114,000.
    (d) Equipment that originally cost $40,000 and had accumulated amortization of $32,000 was sold for $13,000.

EXERCISES

E23-1 **(Classification of Transactions)** Hot Chili Corp. had the following activity in its most recent year of operations:

(a) purchase of equipment	**(g)** amortization of intangible assets
(b) redemption of bonds	**(h)** purchase of company's own shares
(c) sale of building	**(i)** issue of bonds for land
(d) amortization, equipment	**(j)** payment of dividends on common shares
(e) exchange of equipment for furniture	**(k)** increase in interest receivable on notes receivable
(f) issue of common shares	**(l)** pension expense exceeds amount funded

Instructions

Using the indirect method, classify the items as (1) operating—add to net income; (2) operating—deduct from net income; (3) investing; (4) financing; or (5) significant noncash investing and financing activities.

E23-2 **(Accounting Cycle and Financial Statements)** Listed below are the transactions of Isao Aoki, an interior design consultant, for the month of September, 2002.

Sept.		
	1	Isao Aoki begins business as an interior design consultant, investing $30,000 for 5,000 common shares of the company, I.A. Design Limited.
	2	Purchases furniture and display equipment from Green Jacket Co. for $17,280.
	4	Pays rent for office space for the next three months at $680 per month.
	7	Employs a part-time secretary, Michael Bradley, at $300 per week.
	8	Purchases office supplies on account from Mann Corp. for $1,142.
	9	Receives cash of $1,690 from clients for services performed.
	10	Pays miscellaneous office expenses, $430.
	14	Invoices clients for consulting services, $5,120.
	18	Pays Mann Corp. on account, $600.
	19	Pays a dividend of $1.00 per share on the 5,000 outstanding shares.
	20	Receives $980 from clients on account.
	21	Pays Michael Bradley two weeks' salary, $600.
	28	Invoices clients for consulting services, $2,110.
	29	Pays the September telephone bill of $135 and miscellaneous office expenses of $85.

At September 30, the following information is available:

    1. The furniture and display equipment have a useful life of five years and an estimated residual value of $1,500. Straight-line amortization is appropriate.
    2. One weeks' salary is owing to Michael Bradley.
    3. Office supplies of $825 remain on hand.
    4. Two months' rent has been paid in advance.
    5. The invoice for electricity for September of $195 has been received, but not paid.

Instructions

    (a) Prepare journal entries to record the transaction entries for September. Set up a T account for the Cash account and post all cash transactions to the account. Find the balance of cash at September 30, 2002.
    (b) Prepare any required adjusting entries at September 30, 2002.
    (c) Prepare an adjusted trial balance at September 30, 2002.
    (d) Prepare a balance sheet and income statement for the month ended September 30, 2002.
    (e) Prepare a cash flow statement for the month of September, 2002. Use the indirect method for the cash flows from operating activities.
    (f) Recast the cash flow from operating activities section using the direct method.
    (g) How does the cash flow statement compare to the Cash account prepared in item (a) above?

E23-3 **(Statement Presentation of Transactions—Indirect Method)** Each of the following items must be considered in preparing a statement of cash flows (indirect method) for Sage Inc. for the year ended December 31, 2002.

1. Plant assets that cost $20,000 six years before and were being amortized on a straight-line basis over 10 years with no estimated residual value were sold for $5,300.
2. During the year, 10,000 common shares were issued for $43 cash per share.
3. Uncollectible accounts receivable in the amount of $27,000 were written off against the Allowance for Doubtful Accounts.
4. The company sustained a net loss for the year of $50,000. Amortization amounted to $22,000, and a gain of $9,000 was reported on the sale of land for $39,000 cash.
5. A three-month Canadian treasury bill was purchased for $100,000 on November 13, 2002. The company uses a cash and cash-equivalent basis for its cash flow statement.
6. Patent amortization for the year was $20,000.
7. The company exchanged common shares for a 70% interest in Tabaco Corp. for $900,000.

Instructions

State where each item should be shown in the statement of cash flows, if at all.

E23-4 **(Preparation of Operating Activities Section—Direct Method)** The income statement of Vincus Company is shown below:

VINCUS COMPANY Income Statement for the Year Ended December 31, 2002		
Sales		$6,900,000
Cost of goods sold		
Beginning inventory	$1,900,000	
Purchases	4,400,000	
Goods available for sale	6,300,000	
Ending inventory	1,600,000	
Cost of goods sold		4,700,000
Gross profit		2,200,000
Operating expenses		
Selling expenses	450,000	
Administrative expenses	700,000	1,150,000
Net income		$1,050,000

Additional information:

1. Accounts receivable increased $360,000 during the year.
2. Prepaid expenses increased $170,000 during the year.
3. Accounts payable to suppliers of merchandise decreased $275,000 during the year.
4. Accrued salaries payable increased $10,000 during the year.
5. Administrative expenses include amortization expense of $60,000.
6. Selling expenses include commissions and salaries of $280,000; administrative expenses include salaries of $525,000.

Instructions

Prepare the operating activities section of the statement of cash flows for the year ended December 31, 2002 for Vincus Company using the direct method.

E23-5 **(Preparation of Operating Activities Section—Indirect Method)** Data for the Vincus Company are presented in E23-4.

Instructions

Prepare the operating activities section of the statement of cash flows using the indirect method.

E23-6   (**Preparation of Operating Activities Section—Direct Method**)   Krauss Corp.'s income statement for the year ended December 31, 2002 contained the following condensed information:

Revenue from fees		$840,000
Operating expenses (excluding amortization)	$624,000	
Amortization expense	60,000	
Loss on sale of equipment	26,000	710,000
Income before income taxes		130,000
Income tax expense		40,000
Net income		$ 90,000

Krauss's balance sheet contained the following comparative data at December 31:

	2002	2001
Accounts receivable	$37,000	$54,000
Accounts payable	41,000	31,000
Income taxes payable	4,000	8,500

Instructions

Prepare the operating activities section of the statement of cash flows using the direct method.

E23-7   (**Preparation of Operating Activities Section—Indirect Method**)   Data for Krauss Corp. are presented in E23-6.

Instructions

Prepare the operating activities section of the statement of cash flows using the indirect method.

E23-8   (**Calculation of Operating Activities—Direct and Indirect Methods**)   Presented below are two independent situations:

Situation A

Lennox Corp. reports revenues of $200,000 and operating expenses of $110,000 in its first year of operations, 2003. Accounts receivable and accounts payable at year end were $71,000 and $29,000, respectively. Ignore income taxes.

Instructions

Using first the direct method and then the indirect method, calculate net cash provided by operating activities.

Situation B

The income statement for Bleust Corporation shows cost of goods sold $310,000 and operating expenses of $230,000, including amortization expense of $13,000 and salaries and wages expense of $122,000. The comparative balance sheet for the year shows that inventory increased $26,000, prepaid expenses decreased $8,000, accounts payable decreased $17,000, and accrued wages payable increased $11,000.

Instructions

Calculate (a) cash payments to suppliers of goods and services and (b) cash payments to employees.

E23-9   (**Convert Net Income to Operating Cash Flow—Indirect Method**)   Leung Limited reported net income of $36,500 for its latest year ended March 31, 2003.

Instructions

For each situation below, calculate the cash flow from operations assuming the following balance sheet amounts.

	Accounts Receivable March 31		Inventory March 31		Accounts Payable March 31	
	2003	2002	2003	2002	2003	2002
(a)	$20,000	$21,500	$16,500	$17,900	$ 9,000	$ 9,300
(b)	$23,000	$20,000	$17,300	$20,500	$14,600	$10,200
(c)	$20,000	—	$12,000	—	$ 7,000	—
(d)	$19,500	$21,000	$19,500	$15,600	$10,200	$14,100
(e)	$21,500	$24,000	$12,900	$14,000	$13,300	$11,300

E23-10 (Schedule of Net Cash Flow from Operating Activities—Indirect Method) Ballard Corp. reported $145,000 of net income for 2002. The accountant, in preparing the statement of cash flows, noted several items that might affect cash flows from operating activities. These items are listed below:

1. During 2002, Ballard reported the sale of equipment with a carrying value of $23,500 for $12,000.
2. During 2002, Ballard sold 1,000 Lontel Corporation common shares at $75 per share. The acquisition cost of these shares was $99 per share. This investment was shown on Ballard's December 31, 2001 balance sheet as a long-term portfolio investment.
3. During 2002, Ballard changed from the straight-line method to the double-declining balance method of amortization for its machinery. The debit to opening retained earnings was $14,600.
4. During 2002, Ballard revised its estimate for bad debts. Before 2002, Ballard's bad debt expense was 1% of its net sales. In 2002, this percentage was increased to 2%. Net sales for 2002 were $500,000, and net accounts receivable decreased by $12,000 during 2002.
5. During 2002, Ballard issued 500 common shares for a patent. The shares' market value on the transaction date was $23 per share.
6. Amortization expense for 2002 is $39,000.
7. Ballard Corp. holds 40% of Nirvana Corporation's common shares as a long-term investment. Nirvana reported $27,000 of net income for 2002.
8. Nirvana Company paid a total of $2,000 of cash dividends to all shareholders in 2002.
9. During 2002, Ballard declared a 10% stock dividend. One thousand no par value common shares were distributed. The market price at date of issuance was $20 per share.
10. Ballard Corp. paid $10,000 in dividends: $2,500 of this amount was paid on term preferred shares classified as a long-term liability.

Instructions

Prepare a schedule that shows the net cash flow from operating activities using the indirect method. Assume no items other than those listed above affected the calculation of 2002 net cash flow from operating activities.

E23-11 (Statement of Cash Flows—Direct Method) El Lobos Corp. uses the direct method to prepare its statement of cash flows. El Lobos's trial balances at December 31, 2002 and 2001 are as follows:

	Dec. 31, 2002	Dec. 31, 2001
Debits		
Cash	$ 35,000	$ 32,000
Accounts receivable	33,000	30,000
Inventory	31,000	47,000
Property, plant, and equipment	100,000	95,000
Unamortized bond discount	4,500	5,000
Cost of goods sold	250,000	380,000
Selling expenses	141,500	172,000
General and administrative expenses	137,000	151,300
Interest expense	4,300	2,600
Income tax expense	20,400	61,200
	$756,700	$976,100
Credits		
Allowance for doubtful accounts	$ 1,300	$ 1,100
Accumulated amortization	16,500	15,000
Accounts payable	25,000	15,500
Income taxes payable	21,000	29,100
Future income tax liability	5,300	4,600
8% callable bonds payable	45,000	20,000
Common shares	59,100	47,500
Retained earnings	44,700	64,600
Sales	538,800	778,700
	$756,700	$976,100

Additional information:

1. El Lobos purchased $5,000 of equipment during 2002.
2. El Lobos allocated one-third of its amortization expense to selling expenses and the remainder to general and administrative expenses.
3. Bad debt expense for 2002 was $5,000 and writeoffs of uncollectible accounts totalled $4,800.

Instructions

Determine what amounts El Lobos should report in its statement of cash flows for the year ended December 31, 2002 for the following:

(a) cash collected from customers
(b) cash paid to suppliers of goods and services (excluding interest and income taxes)
(c) cash paid for interest
(d) cash paid for income taxes

E23-12 **(Classification of Transactions)** Following are selected balance sheet accounts of Aliman Corp. at December 31, 2002 and 2001, and the increases or decreases in each account from 2001 to 2002. Also presented is selected income statement information for the year ended December 31, 2002 and additional information.

Selected balance sheet accounts	2002	2001	Increase (Decrease)
Assets			
Accounts receivable	$ 34,000	$ 24,000	$10,000
Property, plant, and equipment	277,000	247,000	30,000
Accumulated amortization	(178,000)	(167,000)	11,000
Liabilities and shareholders' equity			
Bonds payable	49,000	46,000	3,000
Dividends payable	8,000	5,000	3,000
Common shares	31,000	22,000	9,000
Retained earnings	104,000	91,000	13,000

Selected income statement information for the year ended December 31, 2002	
Sales revenue	$155,000
Amortization expense	33,000
Gain on sale of equipment	14,500
Net income	31,000

Additional information:

1. During 2002, equipment costing $45,000 was sold for cash.
2. Accounts receivable relate to sales of merchandise.
3. During 2002, $20,000 of bonds payable were issued in exchange for property, plant, and equipment. There is no discount or premium on any bonds.

Instructions

Determine the category (operating, investing, or financing) and the amount that should be reported in the statement of cash flows for the following items:

(a) payments for purchases of property, plant, and equipment
(b) proceeds from the sale of equipment
(c) cash dividends paid
(d) redemption of bonds payable

E23-13 **(Statement of Cash Flows—Indirect and Direct Method)** Condensed financial data of Quan Limited for 2002 and 2001 are presented below.

QUAN LIMITED Comparative Balance Sheet as of December 31, 2002 and 2001		
	2002	2001
Cash	$1,800	$1,150
Receivables	1,750	1,300
Inventory	1,600	1,900
Plant assets	1,900	1,700
Accumulated amortization	(1,200)	(1,170)
Long-term investments	1,300	1,420
	$7,150	$6,300
Accounts payable	$1,200	$ 900
Accrued liabilities	200	250
Bonds payable	1,400	1,550
Share capital	1,900	1,700
Retained earnings	2,450	1,900
	$7,150	$6,300

QUAN LIMITED
Income Statement
for the Year Ended December 31, 2002

Sales	$6,900
Cost of goods sold	4,700
Gross margin	2,200
Selling and administrative expense	930
Income from operations	1,270
Other revenues and gains	
Gain on sale of investments	80
Income before tax	1,350
Income tax expense	540
Net income	$810

Additional information:

During the year, $70 of common shares were issued in exchange for plant assets. No plant assets were sold in 2002.

Instructions

(a) Prepare a statement of cash flows using the indirect method.

(b) Prepare a statement of cash flows using the direct method.

E23-14 **(Statement of Cash Flows—Direct and Indirect Method)** Condensed financial data of Tyne Corporation for the years ended December 31, 2002 and December 31, 2001 are presented below.

TYNE CORPORATION
Comparative Balance Sheet
as of December 31, 2002 and 2001

	2002	2001
Cash	$160,800	$ 38,400
Receivables	123,200	49,000
Inventories	112,500	57,900
Investments	90,000	101,000
Plant assets	240,000	212,500
	$726,500	$458,800
Accounts payable	$ 90,000	$ 60,200
Salaries payable	10,000	5,000
Mortgage payable	50,000	77,000
Accumulated amortization	30,000	52,000
Common shares	175,000	131,100
Retained earnings	371,500	133,500
	$726,500	$458,800

TYNE CORPORATION
Income Statement
for the Year Ended December 31, 2002

Sales	$440,000	
Interest and other revenue (Includes gain on sale of investments of $5,000)	20,000	$460,000
Less:		
Cost of goods sold	80,000	
Salaries	50,000	
Selling and administrative expenses	10,000	
Amortization	42,000	
Income taxes	5,000	
Interest charges	3,000	
Loss on sale of plant assets	12,000	202,000
Net income		$258,000

Additional information:

New plant assets costing $85,000 were purchased during the year. Common shares were issued in exchange for plant assets with a fair value of $20,000. Investments were sold during the year.

Instructions

(a) Prepare a statement of cash flows using the indirect method.

(b) Prepare the cash flow statement's operating activities section using the direct method.

E23-15 **(Statement of Cash Flows—Direct Method and Indirect Method)** Tuit Inc., a greeting card company, had the following statements prepared as of December 31, 2003.

TUIT INC.
Comparative Balance Sheet
as of December 31, 2003 and 2002

	12/31/03	12/31/02
Cash and cash equivalents	$ 41,000	$ 25,000
Accounts receivable	68,000	51,000
Inventories	40,000	60,000
Prepaid rent	5,000	4,000
Printing equipment	154,000	130,000
Accumulated amortization, equipment	(35,000)	(25,000)
Goodwill	40,000	50,000
Total assets	$313,000	$295,000
Accounts payable	$ 46,000	$ 40,000
Income taxes payable	4,000	6,000
Wages payable	8,000	4,000
Short-term loans payable	8,000	10,000
Long-term loans payable	60,000	69,000
Common shares	130,000	130,000
Retained earnings	57,000	36,000
Total liabilities and equity	$313,000	$295,000

TUIT INC.
Income Statement
for the Year Ending December 31, 2003

Sales		$338,150
Cost of goods sold		165,000
Gross margin		173,150
Operating expenses		120,000
Operating income		53,150
Interest expense	$11,400	
Impairment loss, goodwill	10,000	
Gain on sale of equipment	(2,000)	19,400
Income before tax		33,750
Income tax expense		6,750
Net income		$ 27,000

Additional information:

1. Dividends on common shares in the amount of $6,000 were declared and paid during 2003.
2. Amortization expense is included in operating expenses, as are salaries and wages expense of $69,000.
3. Equipment with a cost of $20,000 and that was 70% amortized was sold during 2003.

Instructions

(a) Prepare a statement of cash flows using the direct method.

(b) Prepare a statement of cash flows using the indirect method.

E23-16 (Statement of Cash Flows—Indirect Method) Presented below are data taken from the records of Antoni Corporation.

	December 31, 2002	December 31, 2001
Cash	$ 15,000	$ 8,000
Current assets other than cash	85,000	60,000
Long-term investments	10,000	53,000
Plant assets	335,000	215,000
	$445,000	$336,000
Accumulated amortization	$ 20,000	$ 40,000
Current liabilities	40,000	22,000
Bonds payable	75,000	–0–
Share capital	254,000	254,000
Retained earnings	56,000	20,000
	$445,000	$336,000

Additional information:

1. Long-term investments carried at a cost of $43,000 on December 31, 2001 were sold in 2002 for $34,000.
2. Plant assets that cost $50,000 and were 80% amortized were sold during 2002 for $8,000.
3. Net income as reported on the income statement for the year was $46,000.
4. Dividends paid amounted to $10,000.
5. Amortization charged for the year was $20,000.

Instructions

Prepare a statement of cash flows for the year 2002 using the indirect method.

E23-17 (Cash Provided by Operating, Investing, and Financing Activities) The balance sheet data of Bruin Corporation at the end of 2002 and 2001 follow:

	2002	2001
Cash	$ 30,000	$ 35,000
Accounts receivable (net)	55,000	45,000
Merchandise inventory	65,000	45,000
Prepaid expenses	15,000	25,000
Equipment	90,000	75,000
Accumulated amortization—equipment	(18,000)	(8,000)
Land	70,000	40,000
Totals	$307,000	$257,000
Accounts payable	$ 65,000	$ 52,000
Accrued expenses	15,000	18,000
Notes payable—bank, long-term	–0–	23,000
Bonds payable	30,000	–0–
Common shares	189,000	159,000
Retained earnings	8,000	5,000
	$307,000	$257,000

Land with a fair value of $30,000 was exchanged for common shares; all equipment purchased was for cash. Equipment costing $10,000 was sold for $3,000; book value of the equipment was $6,000. Cash dividends of $10,000 were declared and paid during the year.

Instructions

Calculate net cash provided (used) by:

(a) operating activities
(b) investing activities
(c) financing activities

E23-18 **(Statement of Cash Flows—Indirect Method and Balance Sheet)** Jobim Inc. had the following condensed balance sheet at the end of operations for 2002.

JOBIM INC. Balance Sheet December 31, 2002			
Cash	$ 8,500	Current liabilities	$15,000
Current assets other than cash	29,000	Long-term notes payable	25,500
Investments	20,000	Bonds payable	25,000
Plant assets (net)	67,500	Share capital	75,000
Land	40,000	Retained earnings	24,500
	$165,000		$165,000

During 2003 the following occurred:

1. A tract of land was purchased for $9,000.
2. Bonds payable in the amount of $15,000 were retired at par.
3. An additional $10,000 of common shares were issued.
4. Dividends totalling $9,375 were paid to shareholders.
5. Net income for 2003 was $35,250 after allowing amortization of $13,500.
6. Land was purchased in exchange for $22,500 in bonds.
7. Jobim Inc. sold part of its investment portfolio for $12,875. This transaction resulted in a gain of $2,000 for the firm. This was not a security the company had acquired for trading purposes.
8. Both current assets (other than cash) and current liabilities remained at the same amount.

Instructions

(a) Prepare a statement of cash flows for 2003 using the indirect method.
(b) Prepare the condensed balance sheet for Jobim Inc. as it would appear at December 31, 2003.

E23-19 **(Partial Statement of Cash Flows—Indirect Method)** The accounts below appear in the ledger of Lazic Limited.

		Retained Earnings	Dr.	Cr.	Bal.
Jan.	1, 2002	Credit balance			$ 42,000
Aug.	15	Dividends (cash)	$15,000		27,000
Dec.	31	Net income for 2002		$40,000	67,000

		Machinery	Dr.	Cr.	Bal.
Jan.	1, 2002	Debit balance			$140,000
Aug.	3	Purchase of machinery	$62,000		202,000
Sept.	10	Cost of machinery constructed	48,000		250,000
Nov.	15	Machinery sold		$56,000	194,000

		Accumulated Amortization—Machinery	Dr.	Cr.	Bal.
Jan.	1, 2002	Credit balance			$ 84,000
Apr.	8	Extraordinary repairs	$21,000		63,000
Nov.	15	Accum. amortization on machinery sold	25,200		37,800
Dec.	31	Amortization for 2002		$16,800	54,600

Instructions

From the postings in the accounts above, indicate how the information is reported on a statement of cash flows by preparing a partial statement of cash flows using the indirect method. The loss on sale of equipment (November 15) was $5,800.

E23-20 **(Work Sheet Analysis of Selected Transactions)** The transactions below took place during the year 2002.

1. Convertible bonds payable with a book value of $300,000 were exchanged for unissued no par value common shares.
2. The net income for the year was $410,000.
3. Amortization charged on the building was $90,000.
4. The Appropriations for Bond Indebtedness in the amount of $300,000 was returned to Retained Earnings during the year because the bonds were retired during the year.

5. Old office equipment was traded in on the purchase of dissimilar office equipment and the following entry was made:

Office Equipment	50,000	
Accum. Amortization—Office Equipment	30,000	
Office Equipment		40,000
Cash		34,000
Gain on Disposal of Plant Assets		6,000

The Gain on Disposal of Plant Assets was credited to current operations as ordinary income.

6. Dividends in the amount of $123,000 were declared. They are payable in January of next year.

Instructions

For each item, indicate by journal entries the adjustments and reconciling items that would be made on a work sheet for a statement of cash flows.

E23-21 **(Work Sheet Preparation)** Below is the comparative balance sheet for McKinley Corporation.

	Dec. 31, 2003	Dec. 31, 2002
Cash	$ 16,500	$ 21,000
Short-term investments	25,000	19,000
Accounts receivable	43,000	45,000
Allowance for doubtful accounts	(1,800)	(2,000)
Prepaid expenses	4,200	2,500
Inventories	81,500	65,000
Land	50,000	50,000
Buildings	125,000	73,500
Accumulated amortization—buildings	(30,000)	(23,000)
Equipment	53,000	46,000
Accumulated amortization—equipment	(19,000)	(15,500)
Delivery equipment	39,000	39,000
Accumulated amortization—delivery equipment	(22,000)	(20,500)
Patents	15,000	–0–
	$379,400	$300,000
Accounts payable	$ 26,000	$ 16,000
Short-term notes payable (trade)	4,000	6,000
Accrued payables	3,000	4,600
Mortgage payable	73,000	53,400
Bonds payable	50,000	62,500
Share capital	150,000	106,000
Retained earnings	73,400	51,500
	$379,400	$300,000

Dividends of $15,000 were declared and paid in 2003.

Instructions

From this information, prepare a work sheet for a statement of cash flows. Make reasonable assumptions as appropriate. The short-term investments are a mix of debt and equity securities and were not purchased for trading purposes.

E23-22 **(Explain Changes in Cash Flow)** Ellwood House, Inc. had the following condensed balance sheet at the end of operations for 2001.

ELLWOOD HOUSE, INC.
Balance Sheet
December 31, 2001

Cash	$ 10,000	Current liabilities	$ 14,500
Current assets (noncash)	34,000	Long-term notes payable	30,000
Long-term investments	40,000	Bonds payable	32,000
Plant assets	57,500	Share capital	80,000
Land	38,500	Retained earnings	23,500
	$180,000		$180,000

During 2002, the following occurred:

1. Ellwood House, Inc. sold part of its investment portfolio for $15,500, resulting in a gain of $500 for the firm. The company rarely sells and buys securities of this nature.

2. Dividends totalling $19,000 were paid to shareholders.
3. A parcel of land was purchased for $5,500.
4. Common shares with a fair value of $20,000 were issued.
5. $10,000 of bonds payable were retired at par.
6. Heavy equipment was purchased through the issuance of $32,000 of bonds.
7. Net income for 2002 was $42,000 after allowing amortization of $13,550.
8. Both current assets (other than cash) and current liabilities remained at the same amount.

Instructions

(a) Prepare a statement of cash flows for 2002 using the indirect method.
(b) Draft a one-page letter to Mr. Gerald Brauer, president of Ellwood House, Inc., briefly explaining the company's cash activities during the year. Refer to your cash flow statement whenever necessary.

E23-23 **(Analysis of Changes in Capital Asset Accounts and Related Cash Flows)** MacAskill Mills Limited engaged in the following activities in 2002.

1. The Land account increased by $50,000 over the year: Land that originally cost $12,000 was exchanged for another parcel of land valued at $30,000 and a lump sum cash receipt of $10,000. Additional land was acquired later in the year in a cash purchase.
2. The Furniture and Fixtures account had a balance of $67,500 at the beginning of the year and $62,000 at the end. The related Accumulated Amortization account decreased over the same period from a balance of $24,000 to $15,200. Fully amortized office furniture that cost $10,000 was sold to employees during the year for $1,000; fixtures that cost $3,000 with a net book value of $700 were written off; and new fixtures were acquired and paid for.
3. A five-year capital lease for specialized machinery was entered into halfway through the year whereby the company agreed to make five annual payments (in advance) of $25,000, after which the machinery will revert to the lessor. The present value of these lease payments at the 10% rate implicit in the lease was $104,247. The first payment was made as agreed.

Instructions

For each situation described above:

(a) Prepare the underlying journal entries made by MacAskill Mills during 2002 to record all information related to the changes in each capital asset and associated accounts over the year.
(b) Identify the amount(s) of the cash flows that result from the transactions and events recorded, and determine the classification of each.
(c) Identify all charges (debits) or credits to the 2002 income statement that did not generate or use identical amounts of operating cash flows and that, therefore, require adjustments to the net income number(s) reported in the Operating Activities section of the cash flow statement.

PROBLEMS

P23-1 The following is Mann Corp.'s comparative balance sheet accounts at December 31, 2002 and 2001, with a column showing the increase (decrease) from 2001 to 2002.

COMPARATIVE BALANCE SHEET

	2002	2001	Increase (Decrease)
Cash	$ 807,500	$ 700,000	$107,500
Accounts receivable	1,128,000	1,168,000	(40,000)
Inventories	1,850,000	1,715,000	135,000
Property, plant, and equipment	3,307,000	2,967,000	340,000
Accumulated amortization	(1,165,000)	(1,040,000)	125,000
Investment in Bligh Corp.	305,000	275,000	30,000
Loan receivable	262,500	—	262,500
Total assets	$6,495,000	$5,785,000	
Accounts payable	$1,015,000	$ 955,000	$ 60,000
Income taxes payable	30,000	50,000	(20,000)
Dividends payable	80,000	100,000	(20,000)
Capital lease obligation	400,000	—	400,000
Share capital, common	2,000,000	2,000,000	—
Retained earnings	2,970,000	2,680,000	290,000
Total liabilities and shareholders' equity	$6,495,000	$5,785,000	

Additional information:

1. On December 31, 2001, Mann acquired 25% of Bligh Corp.'s common shares for $275,000. On that date, the carrying value of Bligh's assets and liabilities, which approximated their fair values, was $1.1 million. Bligh reported income of $120,000 for the year ended December 31, 2002. No dividend was paid on Bligh's common shares during the year.

2. During 2002, Mann loaned $300,000 to TLC Corp., an unrelated company. TLC made the first semi-annual principal repayment of $37,500, plus interest at 10%, on December 31, 2002.

3. On January 2, 2002, Mann sold equipment costing $60,000, with a carrying amount of $35,000, for $40,000 cash.

4. On December 31, 2002, Mann entered into a capital lease for an office building. The present value of the annual rental payments is $400,000, which equals the building's fair value. Mann made the first rental payment of $60,000 when due on January 2, 2003.

5. Net income for 2002 was $370,000.

6. Mann declared and paid cash dividends for 2002 and 2001 as follows:

	2002	2001
Declared	December 15, 2002	December 15, 2001
Paid	February 28, 2003	February 28, 2002
Amount	$80,000	$100,000

Instructions

Prepare a statement of cash flows for Mann Corp. for the year ended December 31, 2002, using the indirect method.

(AICPA adapted)

P23-2 The comparative balance sheets for Tamiskada Corporation show the following information:

	December 31	
	2002	2001
Cash	$ 38,500	$13,000
Accounts receivable	12,250	10,000
Inventory	12,000	9,000
Investments	–0–	3,000
Building	–0–	29,750
Equipment	40,000	20,000
Patent	5,000	6,250
Totals	$107,750	$91,000
Allowance for doubtful accounts	$3,000	$4,500
Accumulated amortization on equipment	2,000	4,500
Accumulated amortization on building	–0–	6,000
Accounts payable	5,000	3,000
Dividends payable	–0–	5,000
Notes payable, short-term (nontrade)	3,000	4,000
Long-term notes payable	31,000	25,000
Common shares	43,000	33,000
Retained earnings	20,750	6,000
	$107,750	$91,000

Additional data related to 2002 are as follows:

1. Equipment that had cost $11,000 and was 30% amortized at time of disposal was sold for $2,500.

2. $10,000 of the long-term note payable was paid by issuing common shares.

3. Cash dividends paid were $5,000.

4. On January 1, 2002, the building was completely destroyed by a flood. Insurance proceeds on the building were $30,000 (net of $2,000 taxes).

5. Investments (trading securities) were sold at $3,700 above their cost. The company has made many similar sales and investments in the past.

6. Cash of $15,000 was paid to acquire equipment.

7. A long-term note for $16,000 was issued to acquire equipment.

8. Interest of $2,000 and income taxes of $6,500 were paid in cash.

Instructions

(a) Prepare a statement of cash flows using the indirect method. Flood damage is infrequent in that part of the country.

(b) Write a brief note to accompany the completed statement, summarizing and commenting on the year's cash activities.

P23-3 Cabanza Corporation has not yet prepared a formal statement of cash flows for the 2002 fiscal year. Comparative balance sheets as of December 31, 2001 and 2002, and a statement of income and retained earnings for the year ended December 31, 2002, are presented below.

CABANZA CORPORATION
Statement of Income and Retained Earnings
Year Ended December 31, 2002
($000)

Sales		$3,800
Expenses		
Cost of goods sold	$1,200	
Salaries and benefits	725	
Heat, light, and power	75	
Amortization, buildings and equipment	80	
Property taxes	19	
Patent amortization	25	
Miscellaneous expenses	10	
Interest	30	2,164
Income before income taxes		1,636
Income taxes		818
Net income		818
Retained earnings—Jan. 1, 2002		310
		1,128
Stock dividend declared and issued		600
Retained earnings—Dec. 31, 2002		$ 528

CABANZA CORPORATION
Comparative Balance Sheet
December 31
($000)

Assets	2002	2001
Current assets		
Cash	$ 383	$ 100
Gov't of Canada T-Bills (60 day)	–0–	50
Accounts receivable	740	500
Inventory	720	560
Total current assets	1,843	1,210
Long-term assets		
Land	150	70
Buildings and equipment	910	600
Accumulated amortization	(200)	(120)
Patents (less amortization)	105	130
Total long-term assets	965	680
Total assets	$2,808	$1,890
Liabilities and Shareholders' Equity		
Current liabilities		
Accounts payable	$ 420	$ 340
Income taxes payable	40	20
Notes payable (trade)	320	320
Total current liabilities	780	680
Long-term notes payable—due 2004	200	200
Total liabilities	980	880
Shareholders' equity		
Common shares outstanding	1,300	700
Retained earnings	528	310
Total shareholders' equity	1,828	1,010
Total liabilities and shareholders' equity	$2,808	$1,890

Instructions

Prepare a statement of cash flows using the direct method.

(CMA adapted)

P23-4 Ashley Limited had the following information available at the end of 2002:

ASHLEY LIMITED
Comparative Balance Sheet
as of December 31, 2002 and 2001

	2002	2001
Cash	$ 15,000	$ –0–
Accounts receivable	17,500	16,950
Short-term working capital investments	20,000	30,000
Inventory	42,000	35,000
Prepaid rent	3,000	12,000
Prepaid insurance	2,100	900
Office supplies	1,000	750
Land	125,000	175,000
Building	350,000	350,000
Accumulated amortization	(105,000)	(87,500)
Equipment	525,000	400,000
Accumulated amortization	(130,000)	(112,000)
Patent	45,000	50,000
Total assets	$910,600	$871,100
Temporary bank overdraft	$ –0–	$ 12,000
Accounts payable	27,000	20,000
Income taxes payable	5,000	4,000
Wages payable	5,000	3,000
Short-term notes payable (trade)	10,000	10,000
Long-term notes payable (non-trade)	60,000	70,000
Bonds payable	400,000	400,000
Common shares	260,000	237,500
Retained earnings	143,600	114,600
Total liabilities and equity	$910,600	$871,100

ASHLEY LIMITED
Income Statement
for the Year Ended December 31, 2002

Sales revenue		$1,160,000
Cost of goods sold		(748,000)
Gross margin		412,000
Operating expenses		
Selling expenses	$ 19,200	
Administrative expenses	124,700	
Salaries and wages expense	92,000	
Amortization expense	40,500	
Total operating expenses		(276,400)
Income from operations		135,600
Other revenues/expenses		
Gain on sale of land	8,000	
Gain on sale of working capital investments	4,000	
Dividend revenue	2,400	
Interest expense	(51,750)	(37,350)
Income before taxes		98,250
Income tax expense		(39,400)
Net income		$ 58,850

Instructions

Prepare a statement of cash flows for Ashley Limited using the direct method, accompanied by a schedule reconciling net income to cash flow from operations.

P23-5 Tang Inc. had the following information available at the end of 2002:

TANG INC.
Comparative Balance Sheet
as of December 31, 2002 and 2001

	2002	2001
Cash	$ 46,000	$ 30,000
Accounts receivable	330,000	296,000
Prepaid insurance	16,000	22,000
Merchandise inventory	400,000	350,000
Office supplies	4,000	7,000
Long-term investments (cost method)	380,000	325,000
Long-term investments (equity method)	775,000	700,000
Land	665,000	500,000
Building	1,300,000	1,300,000
Accumulated amortization—building	(400,000)	(360,000)
Equipment	500,000	550,000
Accumulated amortization—equipment	(155,000)	(135,000)
Goodwill	43,000	65,000
Total assets	$3,904,000	$3,650,000
Accounts payable	$ 95,000	$ 70,000
Income taxes payable	26,000	15,000
Accrued liabilities	47,000	40,000
Dividends payable	–0–	80,000
Long-term notes payable	45,000	50,000
Bonds payable	1,000,000	1,000,000
Discount on bonds payable	(50,750)	(64,630)
Preferred shares	735,000	600,000
Common shares	1,150,000	1,150,000
Retained earnings	876,750	749,630
Treasury stock (common, at cost)	(20,000)	(40,000)
Total liabilities and equity	$3,904,000	$3,650,000

TANG INC.
Income Statement
for the Year Ended December 31, 2002

Sales revenue		$1,007,500
Cost of goods sold		403,000
Gross profit		604,500
Selling/administrative expenses		222,087
Income from operations		382,413
Other revenues/expenses		
Long-term investment income (equity method)	$115,000	
Dividend income (cost method)	15,000	
Gain on sale of equipment	15,000	145,000
Interest expense		(98,880)
Income before taxes		428,533
Income tax expense		(171,413)
Net income		$ 257,120

Additional information:

1. In early January, equipment with a book value of $45,000 was sold for a gain.
2. Long-term investments carried under the equity method: Tang's share of investee income totalled $115,000 in 2002. Tang received dividends from this long-term investment totalling $40,000 during 2002.
3. Cost of goods sold includes $102,000 of direct labour, and selling and administrative expenses include $113,500 of personnel costs.

4. An impairment loss on goodwill of $22,000 was recognized in 2002 and included in selling and administrative expenses.

5. Dividends of $130,000 were declared in 2002.

Instructions

(a) Prepare a statement of cash flows using the indirect method.

(b) Prepare a statement of cash flows using the direct method.

P23-6 You have completed the field work in connection with your audit of Casar Corporation for the year ended December 31, 2002. The following schedule shows the balance sheet accounts at the beginning and end of the year.

	Dec. 31, 2002	Dec. 31, 2001	Increase or (Decrease)
Cash	$ 267,900	$ 298,000	($30,100)
Accounts receivable	479,424	353,000	126,424
Inventory	731,700	610,000	121,700
Prepaid expenses	12,000	8,000	4,000
Investment in Amarill Ltd.	110,500	–0–	110,500
Cash surrender value of life insurance	2,304	1,800	504
Machinery	207,000	190,000	17,000
Buildings	535,200	407,900	127,300
Land	52,500	52,500	–0–
Patents	69,000	64,000	5,000
Goodwill	50,000	50,000	–0–
Bond discount and issue expense	4,502	–0–	4,502
	$2,522,030	$2,035,200	
Income taxes payable	$ 90,250	$ 79,600	$ 10,650
Accounts payable	299,280	280,000	19,280
Dividends payable	70,000	–0–	70,000
Bonds payable—8%	125,000	–0–	125,000
Bonds payable—12%	–0–	100,000	(100,000)
Allowance for doubtful accounts	35,300	40,000	(4,700)
Accumulated amortization—buildings	424,000	400,000	24,000
Accumulated amortization—machinery	173,000	130,000	43,000
Common shares—no par value	1,285,200	1,455,600	(170,400)
Appropriation for plant expansion	10,000	–0–	10,000
Retained earnings—unappropriated	10,000	(450,000)	460,000
	$2,522,030	$2,035,200	

STATEMENT OF RETAINED EARNINGS

January 1, 2002		Balance (deficit)	$(450,000)
March 31, 2002		Net income for first quarter of 2002	25,000
April 1, 2002		Transfer from contributed capital	425,000
		Balance	–0–
December 31, 2002		Net income for last three quarters of 2002	90,000
December 31, 2002		Dividend declared—payable January 21, 2003	(70,000)
December 31, 2002		Appropriation for plant expansion	(10,000)
		Balance	$ 10,000

Your working papers contain the following information:

1. On April 1, 2002, the existing deficit was written off against contributed capital (common shares).

2. On November 1, 2002, new common shares were sold for cash.

3. A patent was purchased for $15,000.

4. During the year, machinery that had a cost basis of $16,400 and on which there was accumulated amortization of $5,200 was sold for $7,000. No other plant assets were sold during the year.

5. The 12%, 20-year bonds were dated and issued on January 2, 1990. Interest was payable on June 30 and December 31. They were sold originally at par. These bonds were retired at 102 plus accrued interest on March 31, 2002.

6. The 8%, 40-year bonds were dated January 1, 2002, and were sold on March 31 at 97 plus accrued interest. Interest is payable semiannually on June 30 and December 31. Expense of issuance was $839.

7. Casar Corporation acquired a 40% interest in Amarill Ltd. on January 2, 2002, for $100,000. The income statement of Amarill Ltd. for 2002 shows a net income of $26,250, and no dividends were paid in the current year. Casar accounts for this investment using the equity method.
8. Extraordinary repairs to buildings of $7,200 were charged to Accumulated Amortization—Buildings.
9. Interest paid in 2002 was $10,500 and income taxes paid were $34,000.

Instructions

From the information above, prepare a statement of cash flows using the indirect method. A work sheet is not necessary, but the principal calculations should be supported by schedules or skeleton ledger accounts.

P23-7 Presented below are the 2002 financial statements of Cymbala Corporation.

CYMBALA CORPORATION
Comparative Balance Sheet

	December 31, 2002	December 31, 2001
	$ in millions	
Assets		
Current assets:		
Cash	$ 20.4	$ 7.5
Receivables (net of allowance for doubtful accounts of $5 million in 2002 and $4.6 million in 2001)	241.6	213.2
Inventories		
Finished goods	83.7	84.7
Raw materials and supplies	115.7	123.8
Prepaid expenses	6.2	6.7
Total current assets	467.6	435.9
Property, plant, and equipment:		
Plant and equipment	2,361.8	2,217.7
Less: Accumulated amortization	(993.4)	(890.1)
	1,368.4	1,327.6
Timberland—net	166.3	169.5
Property, plant, and equipment—net	1,534.7	1,497.1
Other assets	74.7	34.7
Total assets	$2,077.0	$1,967.7
Liabilities and Shareholders' Equity		
Current liabilities:		
Bank overdrafts (temporary)	$ 25.5	$ 20.2
Accounts payable	102.2	91.3
Accrued liabilities		
Payrolls and employee benefits	73.5	73.9
Interest and other expenses	44.3	29.4
Federal and provincial income taxes	17.4	12.7
Current maturities of long-term debt	13.2	10.5
Total current liabilities	276.1	238.0
Long-term liabilities:		
Future income taxes	333.6	280.0
4.75% to 11.25% revenue bonds with maturities to 2022	174.6	193.4
Other revenue bonds at variable rates with maturities to 2029	46.3	26.6
77/8% sinking fund debentures due 2008	19.5	21.0
8.70% sinking fund debentures due 2018	75.0	75.0
91/2% convertible subordinated debentures due 2023	–0–	38.9
93/4% notes due 2005	50.0	50.0
Promissory notes	–0–	60.2
Mortgage debt and miscellaneous obligations	25.7	21.7
Other long-term liabilities	21.8	–0–
Total long-term liabilities	746.5	766.8
Shareholders' equity:		
Common shares (no par value, 60,000,000 shares authorized, 26,661,770 and 25,265,921 shares outstanding as of December 31, 2002 and 2001)	244.4	196.9
Retained earnings	810.0	766.0
Total shareholders' equity	1,054.4	962.9
Total liabilities and shareholders' equity	$2,077.0	$1,967.7

Statement of Income and Retained Earnings

$ in millions, except per share amounts	2002
Income	
Net sales	$2,044.2
Cost of sales	(1,637.8)
Gross margin	406.4
Selling, general, and administrative expense	(182.6)
Provision for reduced operations	(41.0)
Operating income	182.8
Interest on long-term debt	(33.5)
Other income—net	2.2
Pretax income	151.5
Income taxes	(61.2)
Net income	$ 90.3
Earnings per share	$ 3.39
Retained earnings	
Retained earnings at beginning of year	$ 766.0
Add: Net income	90.3
	856.3
Deduct: Dividends on common shares ($1.76 a share in 2002)	46.3
Retained earnings at year end	$ 810.0

Additional information

1. Amortization and cost of timberland harvested was $114.6 million.
2. The provision for reduced operations included a decrease in cash of $15.9 million.
3. Purchases of plant and equipment were $182.5 million, and purchases of other assets were $40 million.
4. Sales of plant and equipment resulted in cash inflows of $5.2 million. All sales were at book value.
5. The changes in long-term liabilities are summarized below:

Increase in future income taxes	$ 53.6
New borrowings	63.2
Debt retired by cash payments	(86.5)
Debt converted into shares	(37.4)
Reclassification of current maturities	(13.2)
Decrease in long-term liabilities	$(20.3)

6. The increase in common shares results from the issuance of shares for debt conversion, $37.4 million, and shares issued for cash, $10.1 million.
7. Interest paid during 2002 was $21.2 million and income tax paid was $2.9 million.

Instructions

(a) Prepare a statement of cash flows for the Cymbala Corporation using the indirect method.
(b) Prepare a brief memo that summarizes the company's cash activities during the year.

P23-8 Comparative balance sheet accounts of Secada Inc. are presented below:

SECADA INC.
Comparative Balance Sheet Accounts
December 31, 2002 and 2001

	December 31	
Debit Accounts	2002	2001
Cash	$ 45,000	$ 33,750
Accounts Receivable	67,500	60,000
Merchandise Inventory	30,000	24,000
Long-term Investments, cost method	22,250	38,500
Machinery	30,000	18,750
Buildings	67,500	56,250
Land	7,500	7,500
Totals	$269,750	$238,750
Credit Accounts		
Allowance for Doubtful Accounts	$ 2,250	$ 1,500
Accumulated Amortization—Machinery	5,625	2,250
Accumulated Amortization—Buildings	13,500	9,000
Accounts Payable	30,000	24,750
Accrued Payables	2,375	1,125
Income Taxes Payable	1,000	1,500
Long-term Note Payable, non-trade	26,000	31,000
Common Shares, no par value	150,000	125,000
Retained Earnings	39,000	42,625
Total	$269,750	$238,750

Additional data:

1. Net income for the year was $42,500.
2. Cash dividends declared during the year were $21,125.
3. A 20% stock dividend was declared during the year. $25,000 of retained earnings was capitalized.
4. Investments that cost $20,000 were sold during the year for $23,750.
5. Machinery that cost $3,750, on which $750 of amortization had accumulated, was sold for $2,200.

Secada's 2002 income statement follows:

Sales		$640,000
Less cost of goods sold		380,000
Gross margin		260,000
Less: Operating expenses (includes $8,625 amortization, and $5,400 bad debts)		180,450
Income from operations		79,550
Other: Gain on sale of investments	$3,750	
Loss on sale of machinery	(800)	2,950
Income before taxes		82,500
Income tax expense		40,000
Net income		$ 42,500

Instructions

(a) Calculate net cash flow from operating activities using the direct method.
(b) Prepare a statement of cash flows using the indirect method.

P23-9 Ivan Inc., a major retailer of bicycles and accessories, operates several stores and is a publicly traded company. The comparative Statement of Financial Position and Income Statement for Ivan as of May 31, 2003 are provided. The company is preparing its Statement of Cash Flows.

IVAN INC.
Comparative Statement of Financial Position
as of May 31, 2003 and May 31, 2002

	2003	2002
Current assets		
Cash	$ 33,250	$ 20,000
Accounts receivable	80,000	58,000
Merchandise inventory	210,000	250,000
Prepaid expenses	9,000	7,000
Total current assets	332,250	335,000
Plant assets		
Plant assets	600,000	502,000
Less: Accumulated amortization	150,000	125,000
Net plant assets	450,000	377,000
Total assets	$782,250	$712,000
Current liabilities		
Accounts payable	$123,000	$115,000
Salaries payable	47,250	72,000
Interest payable	27,000	25,000
Total current liabilities	197,250	212,000
Long-term debt		
Bonds payable	70,000	100,000
Total liabilities	267,250	312,000
Shareholders' equity		
Common shares	370,000	280,000
Retained earnings	145,000	120,000
Total shareholders' equity	515,000	400,000
Total liabilities and shareholders' equity	$782,250	$712,000

IVAN INC.
Income Statement
for the Year Ended May 31, 2003

Sales	$1,255,250
Cost of merchandise sold	722,000
Total gross margin	533,250
Expenses	
Salary expense	252,100
Interest expense	75,000
Other expenses	8,150
Amortization expense	25,000
Total expenses	360,250
Operating income	173,000
Income tax expense	43,000
Net income	$ 130,000

The following is additional information concerning Ivan's transactions during the year ended May 31, 2003.

1. Plant assets costing $98,000 were purchased by paying $48,000 in cash and issuing 5,000 common shares.
2. The "other expenses" relate to prepaid items.
3. In order to supplement its cash, Ivan issued an additional 4,000 common shares.
4. There were no penalties assessed for the retirement of bonds.
5. Cash dividends of $105,000 were declared and paid at the end of the fiscal year.

Instructions

(a) Compare and contrast the direct method and the indirect method for reporting cash flows from operating activities.

(b) Prepare a statement of cash flows for Ivan Inc. for the year ended May 31, 2003, using the direct method. Be sure to support the statement with appropriate calculations.

(c) Using the indirect method, calculate only the net cash flow from operating activities for Ivan Inc. for the year ended May 31, 2003.

P23-10 Comparative balance sheet accounts of Jensen Limited are presented below:

JENSEN LIMITED
Comparative Balance Sheet Accounts
December 31, 2002 and 2001

Debit Balances	2002	2001
Cash	$ 80,000	$ 51,000
Accounts Receivable	145,000	130,000
Merchandise Inventory	75,000	61,000
Long-term Investments, at cost	55,000	85,000
Equipment	70,000	48,000
Buildings	145,000	145,000
Land	40,000	25,000
Totals	$610,000	$545,000
Credit Balances		
Allowance for Doubtful Accounts	$ 10,000	$ 8,000
Accumulated Amortization—Equipment	21,000	14,000
Accumulated Amortization—Building	37,000	28,000
Accounts Payable	70,000	60,000
Income Taxes Payable	12,000	10,000
Long-term Notes Payable	62,000	70,000
Common Shares	310,000	260,000
Retained Earnings	88,000	95,000
Totals	$610,000	$545,000

Jensen's 2002 income statement is as follows:

Sales		$950,000
Less: Cost of goods sold		600,000
Gross profit		350,000
Less: Operating expenses (includes amortization and bad debt expense)		250,000
Income from operations		100,000
Other revenues and expenses		
Gain on sale of investments	$15,000	
Loss on sale of equipment	(3,000)	12,000
Income before taxes		112,000
Income taxes		45,000
Net income		$ 67,000

Additional data:

1. Equipment that cost $10,000 and was 40% amortized was sold in 2002.
2. Cash dividends were declared and paid during the year.
3. Common shares were issued in exchange for land.
4. Investments that cost $35,000 were sold during the year.
5. Cost of goods sold includes $115,000 of direct labour, and operating expenses includes $56,000 of wages.

Instructions

(a) Prepare a statement of cash flows using the indirect method.

(b) Prepare the "cash provided by operating activities" section under the direct method.

(c) Comment on the company's cash activities during the year.

P23-11 Seneca Corporation has contracted with you to prepare a statement of cash flows. The controller has provided the following information.

	December 31	
	2002	2001
Cash	$ 38,500	$13,000
Accounts receivable	12,250	10,000
Inventory	12,000	9,000
Investments	–0–	3,000
Building	–0–	29,750
Equipment	40,000	20,000
Patent	5,000	6,250
	$107,750	$91,000
Allowance for doubtful accounts	$ 3,000	$ 4,500
Accumulated amortization on equipment	2,000	4,500
Accumulated amortization on building	–0–	6,000
Accounts payable	5,000	3,000
Dividends payable	–0–	6,000
Notes payable, short-term (nontrade)	3,000	4,000
Long-term notes payable	31,000	25,000
Share capital	43,000	33,000
Retained earnings	20,750	5,000
	$107,750	$91,000

Additional data related to 2002 are as follows:

1. Equipment that cost $11,000 and was 40% amortized at time of disposal was sold for $2,500.
2. $10,000 of the long-term note payable was paid by issuing common shares.
3. Cash dividends paid were $6,000.
4. On January 1, 2002, the building was completely destroyed by a flood. Insurance proceeds on the building were $33,000 (net of $4,000 taxes).
5. Long-term investments were sold at $2,500 above their cost. It is unusual for the company to make such sales.
6. Cash of $15,000 was paid to acquire equipment.
7. A long-term note for $16,000 was issued to acquire equipment.
8. Interest of $2,000 and income taxes of $5,000 were paid in cash.

Instructions

(a) Use the indirect method to analyse the above information and prepare a statement of cash flows for Seneca. Flood damage is unusual and infrequent in that part of the country.

(b) What would you expect to observe in the operating, investing, and financing sections of a statement of cash flows of:

1. a severely financially troubled company?
2. a recently formed company which is experiencing rapid growth?

CONCEPTUAL CASES

C23-1 The following statement was prepared by Abriendo Corporation's accountant:

ABRIENDO CORPORATION
Statement of Sources and Application of Cash
for the Year Ended September 30, 2002

Sources of cash	
Net income	$ 95,000
Amortization and depletion	70,000
Increase in long-term debt	179,000
Common shares issued under employee option plans	16,000
Changes in current receivables and inventories, less current	
liabilities (excluding current maturities of long-term debt)	14,000
	$374,000

Application of cash	
Cash dividends	$ 60,000
Expenditure for property, plant, and equipment	214,000
Investments and other uses	20,000
Change in cash	80,000
	$374,000

The following additional information relating to Abriendo Corporation is available for the year ended September 30, 2002:

1. The corporation received $16,000 in cash from its employees on its employee stock option plans, and wage and salary expense attributable to the option plans was an additional $22,000.

2.

Expenditures for property, plant, and equipment	$250,000
Proceeds from retirements of property, plant, and equipment	36,000
Net expenditures	$214,000

3. A stock dividend of 10,000 Abriendo common shares was distributed to common shareholders on April 1, 2002, when the per-share market price was $7.

4. On July 1, 2002, when its market price was $6 per share, 16,000 Abriendo Corporation common shares were issued in exchange for 4,000 preferred shares.

5.

Amortization expense	$ 65,000
Depletion expense	5,000
	$ 70,000

6.

Increase in long-term debt	$620,000
Retirement of debt	441,000
Net increase	$179,000

Instructions

(a) In general, what are the objectives of a statement of the type shown above for the Abriendo Corporation? Explain.

(b) Identify the weaknesses in the form and format of the Abriendo Corporation's statement of cash flows without reference to the additional information (assume adoption of the indirect method).

(c) For each of the six items of additional information for the statement of cash flows, indicate the preferred treatment and explain why the suggested treatment is preferable.

(AICPA adapted)

C23-2 George Sundem and Bea Goldfarb are examining the following statement of cash flows for Tropical Clothing Store Ltd.'s first year of operations.

TROPICAL CLOTHING STORE LTD.
Statement of Cash Flows
for the Year Ended January 31, 2003

Sources of cash	
From sales of merchandise	$ 362,000
From sale of common shares	400,000
From sale of investment	120,000
From amortization	80,000
From issuance of note for truck	30,000
From interest on investments	8,000
Total sources of cash	1,000,000
Uses of cash	
For purchase of fixtures and equipment	340,000
For merchandise purchased for resale	253,000
For operating expenses (including amortization)	170,000
For purchase of investment	85,000
For purchase of truck by issuance of note	30,000
For purchase of treasury shares	10,000
For interest on note	3,000
Total uses of cash	891,000
Net increase in cash	$ 109,000

George claims that Tropical's statement of cash flows is an excellent portrayal of a superb first year with cash increasing $109,000. Bea replies that it was not a superb first year, that the year was an operating failure, that the statement was incorrectly presented, and that $109,000 is not the actual increase in cash.

Instructions

(a) With whom do you agree, George or Bea? Explain your position.

(b) Using the data provided, prepare a statement of cash flows in proper indirect method form. The only noncash items in income are amortization and the gain from the sale of the investments.

C23-3 HTM Limited is a young and growing producer of electronic measuring instruments and technical equipment. You have been retained by HTM to advise it in preparing a statement of cash flows using the indirect method. For the fiscal year ended October 31, 2002, you have obtained the following information concerning certain HTM events and transactions.

1. The amount of reported earnings for the fiscal year was $800,000, which included a deduction for an extraordinary loss of $110,000 (see item 5 below).
2. Amortization expense of $315,000 was included in the earnings statement.
3. Uncollectible accounts receivable of $40,000 were written off against the allowance for doubtful accounts. Also, $51,000 of bad debt expense was included in determining income for the fiscal year, and the same amount was added to the allowance for doubtful accounts.
4. A gain of $9,000 was realized on the sale of a machine; it originally cost $75,000, of which $30,000 was unamortized on the date of sale.
5. On April 1, 2002, lightning caused an uninsured building loss of $110,000 ($180,000 loss, less reduction in income taxes of $70,000). This extraordinary loss was included in determining income as indicated in 1 above.
6. On July 3, 2002, building and land were purchased for $700,000; HTM gave in payment $75,000 cash, $200,000 market value of its unissued common shares, and signed a $425,000 mortgage note payable.
7. On August 3, 2002, $800,000 face value of HTM's 10% convertible debentures were converted into common shares. The bonds were originally issued at face value.

Instructions

Explain whether each of the seven numbered items above is a source or use of cash. Explain how each should be disclosed in HTM's statement of cash flows for the fiscal year ended October 31, 2002 using the indirect approach for the operating activities section. If any item is neither a source nor a use of cash, explain why it is not and indicate the disclosure, if any, that should be made of the item in the company's statement of cash flows for the fiscal year ended October 31, 2002.

C23-4 Each of the following items must be considered in preparing a statement of cash flows for JCY Fashions Inc. for the year ended December 31, 2002.

1. Equipment that had cost $20,000 when purchased six and one-half years ago and was being amortized on a 10-year basis, with no estimated residual value, was sold for $5,250.
2. During the year, goodwill of $15,000 was completely written off as an impairment loss.
3. During the year, 500 no par value common shares were issued for $34 a share.
4. The company sustained a net loss for the year of $2,100. Amortization on plant and equipment amounted to $2,000 and patent amortization was $400.
5. An Appropriation for Contingencies in the amount of $80,000 was created by a charge against Retained Earnings.
6. Uncollectible accounts receivable in the amount of $2,000 were written off against the Allowance for Doubtful Accounts.
7. Investments that cost $12,000 when purchased four years earlier were sold for $10,600.
8. Bonds payable with a par value of $24,000 on which there was an unamortized bond premium of $2,000 were redeemed at 103.

Instructions

For each item, state where it is to be shown in the statement and then how you would present the necessary information, including the amount. Consider each item to be independent of the others. Assume that correct entries were made for all transactions as they took place.

C23-5 In 1974, the CICA's Accounting Research Committee issued a replacement to Handbook Section 1540 on the Statement of Source and Application of Funds. The new section expanded the funds statement to include significant noncash exchanges affecting the entity's asset and capital structure. The statement could show either changes in cash, working capital, or quick assets.

In 1985, Section 1540 was revised again. This revision required that changes in cash and cash equivalents be reported. In addition, the statement should present information for operating activities, financing activities, and investing activities.

Most recently, in 1998, new requirements were put in place for Section 1540. These changes completed the move from a statement of changes in financial position to one clearly focussed on cash flows.

Instructions

(a) Identify at least three reasons for developing the statement of cash flows.

(b) Explain the purposes of the cash flow statement.

(c) Identify and describe the three categories of activities that must be reported in the statement of cash flows.

(d) Identify two methods for reporting cash flows from operations. Are both permitted under GAAP? Explain.

(e) Describe the financial reporting requirements for non-cash investing and financing transactions. Include in your description two examples of non-cash investing and financing transactions.

Using Your Judgement

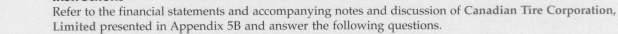

FINANCIAL REPORTING PROBLEM:
CANADIAN TIRE CORPORATION, LIMITED

Instructions

Refer to the financial statements and accompanying notes and discussion of **Canadian Tire Corporation, Limited** presented in Appendix 5B and answer the following questions.

(a) What definition of cash and cash equivalents does Canadian Tire use? Can you reconcile the change in cash to the balance sheet amounts reported?

(b) The company's net income reported for 1999 and 2000 are very close. Does the same hold true for the amount of cash generated from operating activities? If so, why? If not, explain the major reasons for the difference.

(c) Identify what the total investing and financing needs for cash were during 2000. In general, where did the company get the cash to meet these needs?

(d) What were the company's total investing needs for cash in 1999? In general, where did they get the cash to meet these requirements?

(e) Within the operating cash flow section, explain why the "Postretirement benefits" and "Loss on disposals of property and equipment" appear to be sources of cash.

(f) What are the two major investments requiring the use of cash in 2000?

(g) Within the financing activities section, explain, with reference to the four most significant amounts, what the company's financing activities consisted of. How does this compare with the previous year?

(h) Comment briefly on the company's solvency and financial flexibility.

FINANCIAL STATEMENT ANALYSIS CASE

Vermont Teddy Bear Co.

Founded in the early 1980s, the **Vermont Teddy Bear Co.** designs and manufactures teddy bears and markets them primarily as gifts called Bear-Grams or Teddy Bear-Grams. Bear-Grams are personalized teddy bears delivered directly to the recipient for special occasions such as birthdays and anniversaries. The Shelburne, Vermont, company's primary markets are New York, Boston, and Chicago. Sales have jumped dramatically in recent years. Such dramatic growth has significant implications for cash flows. Provided below are the cash flow statements, in U.S. dollars, for the current and prior years for the company.

	Current Year	Prior Year
Cash flows from operating activities:		
Net income	$ 17,523	$ 838,955
Adjustments to reconcile net income to net cash provided by operating activities		
Deferred income taxes	(69,524)	(146,590)
Depreciation and amortization	316,416	181,348
Changes in assets and liabilities:		
Accounts receivable, trade	(38,267)	(25,947)
Inventories	(1,599,014)	(1,289,293)
Prepaid and other current assets	(444,794)	(113,205)
Deposits and other assets	(24,240)	(83,044)
Accounts payable	2,017,059	(284,567)
Accrued expenses	61,321	170,755
Accrued interest payable, debentures	—	(58,219)
Other	—	(8,960)
Income taxes payable	—	117,810

	Current Year	Prior Year
Net cash provided by (used for) operating activities	236,480	(700,957)
Net cash used for investing activities	(2,102,892)	(4,422,953)
Net cash (used for) provided by financing activities	(315,353)	9,685,435
Net change in cash and cash equivalents	$ (2,181,765)	$ 4,561,525

Other information

	Current Year	Prior Year
Current liabilities	$ 4,055,465	$ 1,995,600
Total liabilities	4,620,085	2,184,386
Net sales	20,560,566	17,025,856

Instructions

(a) Note that net income in the current year was only $17,523 compared with prior year income of $838,955, but cash flow from operations was $236,480 in the current year and a negative $700,957 in the prior year. Explain the causes of this apparent paradox.

(b) Evaluate Vermont Teddy Bear's liquidity, solvency, and profitability for the current year using cash flow-based ratios.

AT&T Canada Inc.

AT&T Canada Inc. is engaged primarily in developing and constructing telecommunications networks for providing local, long distance, data, and Internet services in Canada. *The Globe and Mail* "Report on Business" reported on August 6, 2001 that:

"**AT&T Canada Inc.** has closed a deal that is expected to shave its profit margins in the short term but boost the company's cash reserves by about $100 million, as the telephone services firm attempts to deal with its mounting losses and slow revenue growth….The company…said it had reached a deal…that will see AT&T Canada receive cash up front. In exchange, the firm will sell the investor a larger sum of bills that the phone company is owed….The money will be used to 'help fund AT&T Canada's operating and working capital needs.'"

Instructions

From the SEDAR website (www.sedar.com) or the AT&T Canada website, obtain a copy of the AT&T Canada Consolidated Statement of Cash Flows for the year ended December 31, 2000, with comparative statements for 1999 and 1998. Respond to the following questions.

(a) Prepare a summary of the company's total operating, investing, and financing cash flows for the three-year period ending December 31, 2000.

(b) Based on your answer to (a), write a short explanation of why you think AT&T is experiencing cash flow problems.

(c) Write a brief summary of the major ways in which the company has met its cash requirements over the three-year period. Comment particularly on the extent of debt relative to equity financing and the significance of this type of financing to the company for future cash requirements.

(d) Explain why the factoring solution described in the newspaper article can only be a short-term solution.

COMPARATIVE ANALYSIS CASE

AnorMED Inc. versus Biomira Inc.

AnorMED Inc. and Biomira Inc. are both incorporated under the Canada Business Corporations Act and both are engaged in the biotechnology and pharmaceutical industry. AnorMED (British Columbia based) is primarily engaged in discovering and developing innovative small molecule therapeutic products, while Biomira (an Alberta company) researches and develops therapeutic products for the treatment of cancer.

Instructions

From the SEDAR website or the company websites, obtain the comparative financial statements of AnorMED for its year ended March 31, 2001 and of Biomira for its year ended December 31, 2000. Review the financial statements and respond to the following questions.

(a) Compare the companies' income statements and comment on the results of operations of both companies over the past two fiscal periods. What is the major reason for the results reported?

(b) How would you expect companies in this industry and stage of development to be financed? Why? Is this consistent with what is reported on their balance sheets? Comment.

(c) For the two most recent years reported by each company, write a brief explanation of their cash activities at the level of total operating, investing, and financing flows. Note any similarities and differences.

(d) How do the investments that AnorMED and Biomira make differ from the investments made by companies in other industries? Describe the difference in general and then how it affects each of the financial statements.

(e) Are the companies liquid? Explain. On what does the solvency and financial flexibility of companies in this industry depend?

RESEARCH CASE

The March 25, 1996 issue of *Barron's* includes an article by Harry B. Ernst and Jeffrey D. Fotta entitled "Weary Bull."

Instructions

Read the article and answer the following questions.

(a) The article describes a cash flow-based model used by investors. Identify the model and briefly describe its purpose.

(b) How does the model classify a firm's cash flows?

(c) Identify one way in which the cash flow classifications described in the article differ from those under GAAP.

(d) How can the model be used to predict stock prices?

ETHICS CASE

Durocher Guitar Corp. is in the business of manufacturing top-quality, steel-string folk guitars. In recent years the company has experienced working capital problems resulting from the procurement of factory equipment, the unanticipated buildup of receivables and inventories, and the payoff of a balloon mortgage on a new manufacturing facility. The founder and president of the company, Laraine Durocher, has attempted to raise cash from various financial institutions, but to no avail because of the company's poor performance in recent years. In particular, the company's lead bank, First Provincial, is especially concerned about Durocher's inability to maintain a positive cash position. The commercial loan officer from First Provincial told Laraine, "I can't even consider your request for capital financing unless I see that your company is able to generate positive cash flows from operations."

Thinking about the banker's comment, Laraine came up with what she believes is a good plan: with a more attractive statement of cash flows, the bank might be willing to provide long-term financing. To "window dress" cash flows, the company can sell its accounts receivables to factors and liquidate its raw material inventories. These rather costly transactions would generate lots of cash. As the chief accountant for Durocher Guitar, it is your job to tell Laraine what you think of her plan.

Instructions

Answer the following questions:

(a) What are the ethical issues related to Laraine Durocher's idea?

(b) What would you tell Laraine Durocher?

CHAPTER 24

Full Disclosure in Financial Reporting

LEARNING OBJECTIVES

••

After studying this chapter, you should be able to:

1. Review the full disclosure principle and describe problems of implementation.

2. Explain the use of notes in financial statement preparation.

3. Discuss the accounting issues related to special transactions/events

4. Describe the disclosure requirements for major segments of a business.

5. Describe the accounting problems associated with interim reporting.

6. Identify the major disclosures found in the auditor's report.

7. Understand management's responsibilities for financials.

8. Identify issues related to financial forecasts and projections.

9. Describe the profession's response to fraudulent financial reporting.

Preview of Chapter 24

It is very important to read not only the financial statements and related information, but also the president's letter and management discussion and analysis (MD&A). In this chapter we cover several disclosures that must accompany the financial statements so that they are not misleading. The content and organization of the chapter are as follows:

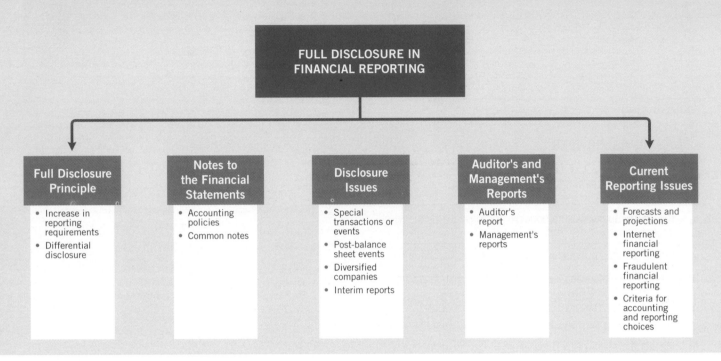

FULL DISCLOSURE IN FINANCIAL REPORTING				
Full Disclosure Principle	**Notes to the Financial Statements**	**Disclosure Issues**	**Auditor's and Management's Reports**	**Current Reporting Issues**
• Increase in reporting requirements • Differential disclosure	• Accounting policies • Common notes	• Special transactions or events • Post-balance sheet events • Diversified companies • Interim reports	• Auditor's report • Management's reports	• Forecasts and projections • Internet financial reporting • Fraudulent financial reporting • Criteria for accounting and reporting choices

FULL DISCLOSURE PRINCIPLE

OBJECTIVE 1

Review the full disclosure principle and describe problems of implementation.

UNDERLYING CONCEPT

Here is a good example of the **trade-off** between the **cost/benefit** constraint and the **full disclosure** principle.

Some useful information is better provided in the financial statements and some is better provided by means of financial reporting other than financial statements. For example, earnings and cash flows are readily available in financial statements, but investors might do better to look at comparisons with other companies in the same industry, found in news articles or brokerage house reports.

Financial statements, notes to the financial statements, and supplementary information are areas directly affected by GAAP. Other types of information found in the annual report, such as management's discussion and analysis, are not subject to GAAP. Illustration 24-1 indicates the types of financial information presented.

As indicated in Chapter 2, the profession has adopted a **full disclosure principle** that calls for financial reporting of **any financial facts significant enough to influence the judgement of an informed reader**. In some situations, the benefits of disclosure may be apparent but the costs uncertain, whereas in other instances the costs may be certain but the benefits of disclosure not as apparent. How much information is enough information? It is a difficult question to answer. While not enough clearly is problematic, sometimes too much, often referred to as **information overload**, is equally as problematic.

Different users want different information, and it becomes exceedingly difficult to develop disclosure policies that meet their varied objectives.

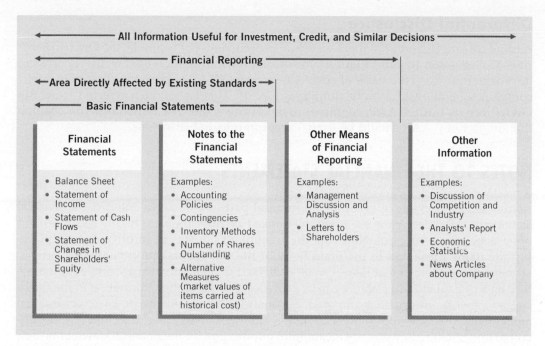

ILLUSTRATION 24-1
Types of Financial Information

Increase in Reporting Requirements

Disclosure requirements have increased substantially over the past several decades. One survey showed that in a sample of 25 large, well-known companies, the average number of pages of notes to the financial statements increased from 9 to 17 and the average number of pages for management's discussion and analysis went from 7 to 12 over a recent 10-year period. This result is not surprising because, as illustrated throughout this textbook, the accounting profession has issued many standards in the last 10 years that have substantial disclosure provisions.[1] The reasons for this increase in disclosure requirements are varied. Some of them are as follows:

Complexity of the Business Environment. The difficulty of distilling economic events into summarized reports has been magnified by the increasing complexity of business operations in such areas as derivatives, leasing, business combinations, pensions, financing arrangements, revenue recognition, and deferred taxes. As a result, **notes to the financial statements** are used extensively to explain these transactions and their future effects.

Necessity for Timely Information. Today, more than ever before, users are demanding information that is current and predictive. For example, more complete **interim data** are required. Published financial forecasts, long avoided and even feared by management, are recommended.

Accounting as a Control and Monitoring Device. The government has recently sought more information and public disclosure of such phenomena as management compensation, environmental pollution, related party transactions, errors and irregularities, and illegal activities.

---

[1] As one writer has noted, rapid growth in additional financial reporting requirements and rapid changes in existing requirements are likely to be permanent features of the financial reporting environment. For the user, the result is a bewildering increase in financial data to interpret. William H. Beaver, *Financial Reporting: An Accounting Revolution,* 2nd ed. (Englewood Cliffs, N.J.: Prentice-Hall, 1989), pp. 1-2. The survey results were taken from Ray J. Groves, "Financial Disclosure: When More Is Not Better," *Financial Executive,* May/June 1994.

Differential Disclosure

A trend toward differential disclosure is also occurring. For example, the Ontario Securities Commission requires that certain substantive information be directly reported to it.[2] Furthermore, on the basis of cost/benefit, the CICA has proposed that non-public companies be allowed a more simplified GAAP[3] This issue, often referred to as **Big GAAP versus Little GAAP**, continues to be controversial. The FASB takes the position that one set of GAAP should be used, except in unusual situations.

NOTES TO THE FINANCIAL STATEMENTS

OBJECTIVE 2

Explain the use of notes in financial statement preparation.

As mentioned previously, notes are an **integral part** of a business enterprise's financial statements. However, they are often overlooked because they are highly technical and often appear in small print. **Notes are the accountant's means of amplifying or explaining the items presented in the main body of the statements**. Information pertinent to specific financial statement items can be explained in qualitative terms, and supplementary data of a quantitative nature can be provided to expand the information in the financial statements. Restrictions imposed by financial arrangements or basic contractual agreements also can be explained in notes. Although notes may be technical and difficult to understand, they provide meaningful information for the financial statements user.

Accounting Policies

Accounting policies of a given entity are the specific accounting principles and methods currently employed and considered most appropriate to present fairly the enterprise's financial statements. Information about the accounting policies adopted and followed by a reporting entity is essential for financial statement users in making economic decisions. The disclosure should be given as the initial note or in a separate Summary of Significant Accounting Policies section preceding the notes to the financial statements. The Summary of Significant Accounting Policies answers such questions as: What method of amortization is used on plant assets? What valuation method is employed on inventories? What amortization policy is followed in regard to intangible assets? How are marketing costs handled for financial reporting purposes?

Refer to Appendix 5B, for an illustration of note disclosure of accounting policies (Note 1) and other notes accompanying the audited financial statements of **Canadian Tire Corporation**.

Analysts examine carefully the summary of accounting policies section to determine whether the company is using conservative or liberal accounting practices. For example, recognizing revenues prior to delivery of products would be considered liberal. On the other hand, using the successful efforts method for an oil and gas company would generally be viewed as following a conservative practice.

Common Notes

Many of the notes to the financial statements have been discussed throughout this textbook. Others will be discussed more fully in this chapter. The more common relate to the following financial statement elements and items.

---

[2] Specifically, the OSC rules require that interim financial statements include a balance sheet, income statement, and statements of retained earnings and cash flows as well as requiring companies to complete an Annual Information Form and specify content for the MD&A.

[3] *CICA Exposure Draft— Differential Reporting, July 2001* would allow non-public companies to be exempt from the following standards: consolidation, certain provisions regarding financial instruments regarding fair value disclosures and presentation of debt versus equity, future income taxes, and others.

Major Disclosures
Inventory
Property, Plant, and Equipment
Liabilities
Equity
Contingencies and Commitments
Taxes, Pensions, and Leases
Changes in Accounting Policies

Go to the Digital Tool for additional examples of many of these disclosures.

The disclosures listed above have been discussed in earlier chapters. Four additional disclosures of significance—**special transactions or events, subsequent events, segment reporting**, and **interim reporting**—are illustrated in the following sections.

DISCLOSURE ISSUES

Disclosure of Special Transactions or Events

Related party transactions, errors and irregularities, and illegal acts pose especially sensitive and difficult problems. The accountant or auditor who has responsibility for reporting on these types of transactions has to be extremely careful that the rights of the reporting company and the needs of financial statement users are properly balanced.

Related party transactions arise when a business enterprise engages in transactions in which one of the transacting parties has the ability to influence significantly the policies of the other, or in which a nontransacting party has the ability to influence the policies of the two transacting parties. Related parties include:

(a) companies or individuals who **control**, or are controlled by, or are under common control with the reporting enterprise,

(b) investors and investees where there is **significant influence** or **joint control**,

(c) company management,

(d) members of immediate family of the above noted,

(e) the other party where a management contract exists, or

(f) other.[4]

Transactions involving related parties cannot be presumed to be carried out at "arm's length" because the requisite conditions of competitive, free-market dealings may not exist. Transactions such as borrowing or lending money at abnormally low or high interest rates, real estate sales at amounts that differ significantly from appraised value, exchanges of **nonmonetary** assets, and transactions involving enterprises that have no economic substance ("shell corporations") suggest that related parties may be involved. Because of the above, there is a **measurement issue**. A basic assumption about financial information is that it is **transactions based** and that the transactions are between **arm's length parties**. Therefore, if this is not the case, these transactions should be at least **disclosed**. Furthermore, special **measurement principles** exist for related party transactions that may require the transaction to be remeasured.

The accountant is expected to report the **economic substance** rather than the legal form of these transactions and to make adequate disclosures. The following disclosures are recommended:[5]

1. the nature of the relationship(s) involved,
2. a description of the transactions,
3. the recorded amounts of transactions,
4. the measurement basis used,
5. amounts due from or to related parties and the terms and conditions related thereto,

---

INTERNATIONAL INSIGHT

In Switzerland, there are no requirements to disclose related party transactions. In Italy and Germany, related parties do not include a company's directors.

OBJECTIVE 3

Discuss the accounting issues related to special transactions/events.

---

[4] *CICA Handbook,* Section 3840, par. .04.

[5] *Ibid,* par. .43.

6. contractual obligations with related parties, and

7. contingencies involving related parties.

Certain related parties must be remeasured to the **carrying amount** of the underlying assets or services exchanged. Carrying amount is defined as the amount of the item transferred as recorded in the books of the transferor. This is the case if the transaction is **not in the normal course of business**, there is **no substantive change in ownership**, and/or the **exchange amount is not supported by independent evidence**. The argument to support remeasurement rests on the premise that if the transaction is not an ordinary transaction for the enterprise, there might not be a reasonable measure of fair value. Furthermore, if there is no change in ownership, no bargaining has taken place and therefore, the price that is arrived at for the exchange may not represent a value that would have been arrived at had the transaction been arm's length.

For transactions that are in the normal course of business, if they do not represent a **culmination of the earnings process**, they must also be remeasured. This argument rests on the premise that if no culmination occurs, there is **no real exchange of risks and rewards of ownership** and therefore, no gain or loss should be recognized. This is only an issue where the transaction is also a **nonmonetary** transaction.

Illustration 24-2 is a decision tree that reflects the judgement involved when determining how to treat related party transactions.

IAS NOTE

IAS 24 does not deal with remeasurement of related party transactions—only disclosure.

ILLUSTRATION 24-2
Related Party Transactions—
Decision Tree[6]

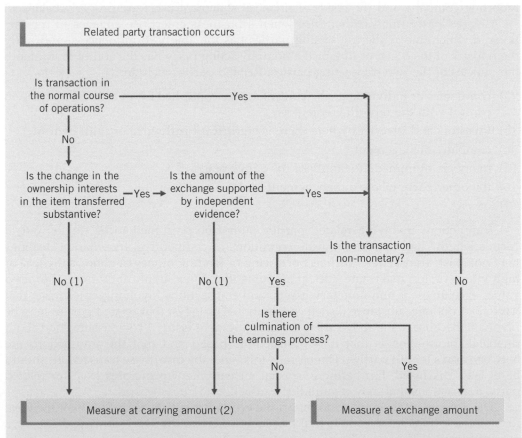

(1) Carrying amount is used for both monetary and non-monetary transactions in these circumstances.
(2) In rare circumstances, when the carrying amount of the item received is not available, a reasonable estimate of the carrying amount, based on the transferor's original cost, may be used to measure the exchange.

---

[6] *CICA Handbook*, Section 3840, Appendix.

Where transactions are **remeasured** to carrying value, the difference between the carrying amounts of the items exchanged is booked as a **charge or credit to equity**.[7] To illustrate, assume that Hudson Limited, a manufacturing company, sells land worth $20,000 to Bay Limited. The companies are related by virtue of the fact that the same shareholder has a 90% equity interest in each company (the rest of the shares are publicly traded). The land has a carrying value of $15,000 on Hudson's books. In exchange, Bay Limited, also a manufacturing company, transfers to Hudson a building that has a net book value of $12,000. This transaction is **not in the ordinary course of business** since both companies are manufacturing companies and would not normally be selling capital assets such as land and buildings. Therefore, the transaction is subject to further analysis.

Looking at the decision tree, the next question is whether there has been a **substantive change in ownership**. Do different parties own the items exchanged before and after the transaction? Since the same controlling shareholder owns both assets before and after the transaction (albeit indirectly, through the companies) there is no substantive change in ownership.[8] Therefore, the transaction would be remeasured to carrying values with the following journal entry on the Hudson books:

Property, plant, and equipment	12,000	
Retained earnings	3,000	
Land		15,000

Bay would record the land at $15,000 and take the building off its books. The resulting credit would be booked to Contributed Surplus. Note that the difference between the carrying value is generally viewed as an **equity contribution or distribution** and is therefore booked through equity.

Accounting errors are defined as unintentional mistakes, whereas irregularities are intentional distortions of financial statements.[9] As indicated in this textbook, when errors are discovered, the financial statements should be corrected. The same treatment should be given to irregularities. The discovery of irregularities, however, gives rise to a whole different set of suspicions, procedures, and responsibilities on the part of the accountant or auditor.[10]

Illegal acts are defined by the CICA as "a violation of a domestic or foreign statutory law or government regulation attributable to the entity…or to management or employees acting on the entity's behalf."[11] The term "illegal act" is not meant to include personal misconduct by the entity's management or employees, which may be unrelated to the enterprise's business activities. In these situations, the accountant or auditor must evaluate the **adequacy of disclosure** in the financial statements and may have to assess whether the item should be recognized in the balance sheet or income statement. For example, if revenue is derived from an illegal act that is considered **material** in relation to the financial statements, this information should be disclosed. Furthermore, if the illegal act creates a liability to pay a fine, this would need to be reflected in the balance sheet and income statement.

---

[7] *Ibid*, par. .09.

[8] As a benchmark, a substantive change in ownership may be deemed to have occurred if an unrelated party has gained or given up >20% interest in the items exchanged (*CICA Handbook*, Section 3840, par. .31). In the example above, if the controlling shareholder only owned say 70% of both companies and the shares were publicly traded (i.e. the different shareholders), then one might argue substantive change in ownership may be evident. This is not so clear-cut, however; since the majority shareholders have controlling interest, no real "bargaining" would have happened between the minority shareholders and the majority shareholder. The resolution of this issue would be a matter of judgement.

[9] "The Auditor's Responsibility to Detect and Report Errors and Irregularities," *Statement on Auditing Standards No. 53* (New York, AICPA, 1988).

[10] The profession became so concerned with certain management frauds that affect financial statements that it established a National Commission on Fraudulent Financial Reporting. The major purpose of this organization was to determine how fraudulent reporting practices can be constrained. Fraudulent financial reporting is discussed later in this chapter.

[11] *CICA Handbook*, Section 5136, par. .03.

Many companies are involved in **related party transaction**. **Errors** and **irregularities** and **illegal acts**, however, are the exception rather than the rule. **Disclosure** plays a very important role in these areas because the transaction or event is more qualitative than quantitative and involves more subjective than objective evaluation. The financial statement users must be provided with some indication of the **existence and nature** of these transactions, where **material**, through disclosures, modifications in the auditor's report, or reports of changes in auditors.

Post-Balance Sheet Events (Subsequent Events)

Notes to the financial statements should explain any significant financial events that took place after the formal balance sheet date, but before it is finally issued. These events are referred to as subsequent events since they occur subsequent to the balance sheet date. The subsequent events period is time-diagrammed as shown in Illustration 24-3.

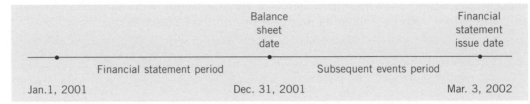

	Balance sheet date	Financial statement issue date
Financial statement period		Subsequent events period
Jan.1, 2001	Dec. 31, 2001	Mar. 3, 2002

A period of several weeks, and sometimes months, may elapse after the end of the year before the financial statements are issued. Taking and pricing the inventory, reconciling subsidiary ledgers with controlling accounts, preparing necessary adjusting entries, assuring that all transactions for the period have been entered, obtaining an audit of the financial statements by independent public accountants, and printing the annual report all take time. During the period between the balance sheet date and its distribution to shareholders and creditors, important transactions or other events may occur that materially affect the company's financial position or operating situation.

Many who read a recent balance sheet believe the balance sheet condition is constant and project it into the future. However, readers must be told if the company has sold one of its plants, acquired a subsidiary, suffered extraordinary losses, settled significant litigation, or experienced any other important event in the post-balance sheet period. Without an explanation in a note, the reader might be misled and draw inappropriate conclusions.

Two types of events or transactions occurring after the balance sheet date may have a material effect on the financial statements or may need to be considered to interpret these statements accurately.

1. **Events that provide additional evidence about conditions that existed at the balance sheet date, affect the estimates used in preparing financial statements, and, therefore, result in needed adjustments:** All information available prior to the issuance of the financial statements is used to evaluate **estimates previously made**. To ignore these subsequent events is to pass up an opportunity to improve the financial statements' accuracy. This first type encompasses information that would have been recorded in the accounts **had it been known** at the balance sheet date.

    For example, if a loss on an account receivable results from a customer's bankruptcy subsequent to the balance sheet date, the financial statements are adjusted before their issuance. The bankruptcy stems from the customer's poor financial health existing at the balance sheet date.

    The same criterion applies to settlements of litigation. The financial statements must be adjusted if the events that gave rise to the litigation, such as personal injury or patent infringement, took place prior to the balance sheet date. If the event giving rise to the claim took place subsequent to the balance sheet date, no adjustment is necessary but disclosure is. To illustrate, a loss resulting from a customer's fire or flood after the balance sheet date is not indicative of conditions existing at that date. Thus, adjustment of the financial statements is not necessary.

2. **Events that provide evidence about conditions that did not exist at the balance sheet date but arise subsequent to that date and do not require adjustment of the financial statements:** Some of these events may have to be disclosed to keep the financial statements from being misleading. These disclosures take the form of notes, supplemental schedules, or even pro forma "as if" financial data prepared as if the event had occurred on the balance sheet date. Below are examples[12] of such events that require disclosure (but do not result in adjustment):

(a) events such as fire or floods that result in a loss,

(b) decline in the market value of investments,

(c) purchase of a business,

(d) commencement of litigation where the cause of action arose subsequent to the balance sheet date,

(e) changes in foreign currency rates, and

(f) issuance of shares or debt.

An example of subsequent events disclosure from the 2000 annual report of Nortel Networks, is presented in Illustration 24-4.

22. Subsequent events

Subsequent to the Company's February 15, 2001 announcement in which the Company provided new guidance for financial performance for the fiscal year and first quarter 2001, the Company and certain of its officers and directors have been named as defendants in a number of putative class action lawsuits. These lawsuits, which have been filed through February 28, 2001 in the United States and Canada on behalf of shareholders who acquired the Company's common shares as early as November 1, 2000 and as late as February 15, 2001, allege violations of United States federal and Canadian provincial securities laws. The Company intends to vigorously defend all such served actions.

On February 13, 2001, the Company acquired JDS Uniphase Corporation's Zurich, Switzerland-based subsidiary (the "Zurich Subsidiary"), as well as related assets in Poughkeepsie, New York (the "New York Related Assets"). The Zurich Subsidiary was a designer and manufacturer of strategic 980 nanometer pump-laser chips, which provide the energy source by which light is strengthened as it is transmitted on fiber between cities or buildings. The acquisition was completed by way of a merger of the Zurich Subsidiary with and into an indirect, wholly owned subsidiary of the Company. Pursuant to the terms of the agreement between the parties, approximately 65.7 million of the Company's common shares were issued to JDS Uniphase Corporation on closing (valued at approximately $1,900 at closing). In addition, up to an additional 16.4 million of the Company's common shares will be payable after December 31, 2003, to the extent Nortel Networks does not meet certain purchase commitments from JDS Uniphase Corporation by that date.

On February 8, 2001, Old Nortel completed completed an offering of $1,500 of 6.125 percent notes which mature on February 15, 2006 (the "Notes"). The Notes will pay interest on a semi-annual basis on February 15 and August 15, beginning on August 15, 2001. The Notes are redeemable, at any time at Old Nortel's option, at a redemption price equal to the principal amount thereof plus accrued and unpaid interest and a make-whole premium.

Many subsequent events or developments are not likely to require either adjustment of or disclosure in the financial statements. Typically, these are nonaccounting events or conditions that managements normally communicate by other means. These events include legislation, product changes, management changes, strikes, unionization, marketing agreements, and loss of important customers.

Reporting for Diversified (Conglomerate) Companies

In the last several decades, business enterprises have had, at times, a tendency to diversify their operations, investing in diverse businesses. As a result of such diversification efforts, investors and investment analysts have sought more information concerning the details behind conglomerate financial statements. Particularly, they want income statement, balance sheet, and cash flow information on the **individual** segments that compose the **total** business income figure.

---

[12] *CICA Handbook*, Section 3820, par. .09.

ILLUSTRATION 24-5
Segmented Information Note—
Torstar Corporation

An illustration of segmented (disaggregated) financial information is presented for **Torstar Corporation** in the following example.

17. Segmented information

Management has determined that the company operates 3 business segments:

Newspapers – Publishing of daily newspapers including The Toronto Star, The Hamilton Spectator and The Kitchener-Waterloo Record, the operations of Metroland (community newspapers), and related ventures;

Book Publishing – Publishing of romance fiction and creation and selling of activity based products for women and children (distributed through retail outlets and by direct mail);

Interactive media – Interactive media businesses of the Newspapers and Book Publishing operations, Toronto Star Television and investments in Interactive media companies.

Segment profit or loss has been defined as operating profit which corresponds to operating profit as presented in the Consolidated Statements of Income. No interest, foreign exchange, goodwill amortization or income taxes are allocated to business or geographic segments.

Summary of Business and Geographic Segments of the company

Business Segments	Operating Revenue		Depreciation and Amortization		Operating Profit	
	2000	1999	2000	1999	2000	1999
Newspapers	$843,066	$765,717	$57,131	$48,991	$111,815	$107,836
Book publishing	579,169	577,013	13,097	13,104	102,300	88,207
Interactive media	22,839	8,646	4,061	1,725	(5,455)	(4,009)
Segment Totals	1,445,074	1,351,376	74,289	63,820	208,660	192,034
Corporate			779	1,243	(9,804)	(6,708)
Consolidated	$1,445,074	$1,351,376	$75,068	$65,063	$198,856	$185,326

	Identifiable Assets		Additions to Capital Assets & Goodwill	
	2000	1999	2000	1999
Newspapers	$966,132	$935,391	$54,552	$417,733
Book publishing	416,162	400,327	6,131	9,313
Interactive media	53,967	52,363	9,087	2,400
Segment Totals	1,436,261	1,388,081	69,770	429,446
Corporate	49,802	54,933	3,933	1,584
			$73,703	$431,030
Investment in associated business	29,091	35,293		
Discontinued operations	240,610	248,095		
Consolidated	$1,755,764	$1,726,402		

Geographic Segments	Operating Revenue		Capital Assets and Goodwill	
	2000	1999	2000	1999
Canada	$879,670	$795,916	$766,658	$779,516
United States	368,324	335,507	98,389	103,114
Other (a)	197,080	219,953	30,070	32,790
Segment Totals	$1,445,074	$1,351,376	$895,117	$915,420

(a) Principally – United Kingdom, Japan, Germany, Australia, Italy and France.

If only the consolidated figures are available to the analyst, much information regarding the composition of these figures is hidden in aggregated totals. There is no way to tell from the consolidated data the extent to which the differing product lines **contribute to the company's profitability, risk, and growth potential**. For example, the newspaper segment returns a 11.5% operating profit (on funds invested in identifiable assets) while the book publishing segment shows a profit of 24.6%. Note that the interactive media segment, although very small, is generating a loss.

Companies have always been somewhat hesitant to disclose segmented data for the reasons listed below.

1. Without a thorough knowledge of the business and an understanding of such important factors as the competitive environment and capital investment requirements, the investor may find the segmented information meaningless or may even draw improper conclusions about the segments' reported earnings.
2. Additional disclosure may harm reporting firms because it may be helpful to competitors, labour unions, suppliers, and certain government regulatory agencies.
3. Additional disclosure may discourage management from taking intelligent business risks because segments reporting losses or unsatisfactory earnings may cause shareholder dissatisfaction with management.
4. The wide variation among firms in the choice of segments, cost allocation, and other accounting problems limits the usefulness of segmented information.
5. The investor is investing in the company as a whole and not in the particular segments, and it should not matter how any single segment is performing if the overall performance is satisfactory.
6. Certain technical problems, such as classification of segments and allocation of segment revenues and costs (especially "common costs"), are formidable.

On the other hand, the advocates of segmented disclosures offer these reasons in support of the practice.

1. Segmented information is needed by the investor to make an intelligent investment decision regarding a diversified company.
   (a) Sales and earnings of individual segments are needed to forecast consolidated profits because of the differences between segments in growth rate, risk, and profitability.
   (b) Segmented reports disclose the nature of a company's businesses and the relative size of the components as an aid in evaluating the company's investment worth.
2. The absence of segmented reporting by a diversified company may put its unsegmented, single product-line competitors at a competitive disadvantage because the conglomerate may obscure information that its competitors must disclose.

The advocates of segmented disclosures appear to have a much stronger case. Many users indicate that segmented data are the most useful financial information provided, aside from the basic financial statements.

Professional Pronouncements

The development of accounting standards for segmented financial information has been a continuing process during the past quarter century. The basic reporting requirements are discussed below.

Objective of Reporting Segmented Information

The objective of reporting segmented financial data is to provide information about the different types of business activities in which an enterprise engages and the different economic environments in which it operates, in order to help users of financial statements.

1. better understand the enterprise's performance,
2. better assess its prospects for future net cash flows, and
3. make more informed judgements about the enterprise as a whole.[13]

Basic Principles

A company might meet the segmented reporting objective by providing complete sets of financial statements that are disaggregated in several ways, for example, by products or services, by geography, by legal entity, or by type of customer. However, it is not feasible to provide all of that information in every set of financial statements. The CICA requires that **general purpose financial statements** include selected information on a single basis of segmentation. The method chosen is referred to as the management approach. The management approach is based on the way the management segments the company for making **operating decisions**. Consequently, the segments are evident from the company's organization structure. It focuses on information about components of the business that management uses to make decisions about operating matters. These components are called **operating segments**.

Identifying Operating Segments

An operating segment is a component of an enterprise:

IAS NOTE

IAS 14 gives guidance on determination of segment. The determination is based on the risks and returns approach i.e., where the segment has different business **risks** and **rewards**.

1. that engages in **business activities** from which it earns revenues and incurs expenses,
2. whose operating results are **regularly reviewed** by the company's chief operating decision-maker to assess segment performance and allocate resources to the segment, and
3. for which **discrete financial information is available**.

Information about two or more operating segments may be aggregated only if the segments have the same basic characteristics in each of the following areas:

1. the nature of the products and services provided,
2. the nature of the production process,
3. the type or class of customer,
4. the methods of product or service distribution, and
5. if applicable, the nature of the regulatory environment.

After the company decides on the segments for possible disclosure, a **quantitative materiality test** is made to determine whether the segment is significant enough to warrant actual disclosure. An operating segment is regarded as significant and therefore identified as a reportable segment if it satisfies **one or more** of the following quantitative thresholds:[14]

1. Its **revenue** (including both sales to external customers and intersegment sales or transfers) is 10% or more of the combined revenue of all the enterprise's operating segments.
2. The absolute amount of its **profit or loss** is 10% or more of the greater, in absolute amount, of
   (a) the combined operating profit of all operating segments that did not incur a loss, or
   (b) the combined loss of all operating segments that did report a loss.
3. Its **assets** are 10% or more of the combined assets of all operating segments.

In applying these tests, two additional factors must be considered. First, segment data must explain a significant portion of the company's business. Specifically, the

---

[13] *CICA Handbook*, Section 1701, par. .02.

[14] *Ibid.* par., .19.

segmented results must equal or exceed 75% of the combined sales to unaffiliated customers for the entire enterprise. This test prevents a company from providing limited information on only a few segments and lumping all the rest into one category.

Second, the profession recognizes that reporting too many segments may overwhelm users with detailed information and has therefore proposed 10 as an upper limit benchmark for the **number of segments** that a company should be required to disclose.

To illustrate these requirements, assume a company has identified six possible reporting segments (000 omitted).

Segments	Total Revenue (Unaffiliated)	Operating Profit (Loss)	Assets
A	$100	$10	$60
B	50	2	30
C	700	40	390
D	300	20	160
E	900	18	280
F	100	(5)	50
	$2,150	$85	$970

ILLUSTRATION 24-6
Data for Different Possible
Reporting Segments

The respective tests may be applied as follows:

Revenue test: 10% × $2,150 = $215; C, D, and E meet this test.

Operating profit (loss) test: 10% × $90 = $9 (note that the $5 loss is ignored); A, C, D, and E meet this test.

Assets tests: 10% × $970 = $97; C, D, and E meet this test.

The segments are therefore A, C, D, and E, assuming that these four segments have enough sales to meet the 75% of combined sales test. The 75% test is calculated as follows:

75% of combined sales test: 75% × $2,150 = $1,612.50; the sales of A, C, D, and E total $2,000 ($100 + $700 + $300 + $900); therefore, the 75% test is met.

Measurement Principles

The accounting principles to be used for segment disclosure need not be the same as the principles used to prepare the consolidated statements. This flexibility may at first appear inconsistent. But, preparing segment information in accordance with generally accepted accounting principles would be difficult because some principles are not expected to apply at a segment level. Examples are accounting for the cost of company-wide employee benefit plans and accounting for income taxes in a company that files one overall tax return.

Allocations of joint, common, or company-wide costs solely for external reporting purposes are not required. Common costs are those incurred for the benefit of more than one segment and whose interrelated nature prevents a completely objective division of costs among segments. For example, the company president's salary is difficult to allocate to various segments. Allocations of common costs are inherently arbitrary and may not be meaningful if they are not used for internal management purposes. There is a presumption that allocations to segments are either **directly attributable** or **reasonably allocable**. Disclosure should be made regarding choices made in measuring segmented information.

Segmented Information Reported

The CICA requires that an enterprise report provides.[15]

1. *General information about its reportable segments.* This includes factors that management considers most significant in determining the company's reportable segments, and the types of products and services from which each operating segment derives its revenues.

---

[15] *CICA Handbook*, Section 1701, pars. .29–.42.

2. *Segment profit and loss, assets, and related information.* Total profit or loss and total assets for each reportable segment. In addition, the following specific information about each reportable segment must be reported if the amounts are regularly reviewed by management:

   (a) revenues from external customers,
   (b) revenues from transactions with other operating segments of the same enterprise,
   (c) interest revenue,
   (d) interest expense,
   (e) amortization of capital assets and goodwill,
   (f) unusual items,
   (g) equity in the net income of investees subject to significant influence,
   (h) income tax expense or benefit,
   (i) extraordinary items, and
   (j) significant noncash items other than amortization expense.
   (k) other

3. *Reconciliations.* An enterprise must provide a reconciliation of the total of the segments' revenues to total revenues, a reconciliation of the total of the operating segments' profits and losses to its income before income taxes, discontinued operations and extraordinary items, and a reconciliation of the total of the operating segments' assets to total assets. Other reconciliations for other significant items disclosed should also be presented and all reconciling items should be separately identified and described for all of the above.

4. *Major customers.* If 10% or more of the revenues is derived from a single customer, the enterprise must disclose the total amount of revenues from each such customer by segment.

5. *Information about geographic areas.* Revenues from external customers (Canada versus foreign), capital assets and goodwill (Canada versus foreign). Disclose foreign information by country if material.

Interim Reports

One further source of information for the investor is interim reports. As noted earlier, interim reports cover periods of less than one year. While at one time, **annual** reporting was considered sufficient in terms of providing timely information, demand quickly grew for **quarterly** information and now capital markets are moving rapidly to even more frequent disclosures. Illustration 24-7 presents the disclosure of selected quarterly data for **Tootsie Roll Industries, Inc.**

ILLUSTRATION 24-7
Disclosure of Selected Quarterly Data

TOOTSIE ROLL INDUSTRIES, INC.
For the Year Ended December 31, 1998
(Thousands of dollars except per share data)

	First	Second	Third	Fourth
Net sales	$69,701	$85,931	$144,230	$88,797
Gross margin	36,966	45,133	73,251	45,692
Net earnings	11,217	13,910	27,216	15,183
Net earnings per share	.23	.29	.57	.32

	Share Prices		
	High	Low	Dividends
1st Qtr	38–13/32	29–27/32	$.0401
2nd Qtr	40–3/4	34–31/32	$.0525
3rd Qtr	47–1/4	33–3/4	$.0525
4th Qtr	42–7/8	34–1/8	$.0525

Because of the short-term nature of the information in these reports, however, there is considerable controversy as to the general approach that should be employed. One group (which holds the discrete view) believes that each interim period should be treated as a separate accounting period; deferrals and accruals would therefore follow the principles employed for annual reports. Accounting transactions should be reported as they occur, and expense recognition should not change with the period of time covered. Another group (which holds the integral view) believes that the interim report is an integral part of the annual report and that deferrals and accruals should take into consideration what will happen for the entire year. In this approach, estimated expenses are assigned to parts of a year on the basis of sales volume or some other activity base. The current *Handbook* section reinforces the **discrete view** with a few exceptions.

One notable exception is in calculating tax expense. Normally a company would prepare its tax return at year end and assess taxes payable and related tax balances. It is neither cost effective nor feasible (since tax rates are often graduated, e.g., increasing with increasing taxable income) to do this for each interim period and therefore annual estimates are made. Specifically, an estimate is made of interim taxable income and temporary differences and then the annual estimated tax rate is applied. Another exception relates to the employer's portion of payroll taxes. Although these may be remitted by the employer early in the year (as they are required to be by law), they are assessed by the government on an annual basis. Therefore, for interim reporting periods, the total estimated annual amount is allocated to the interim periods such that the expense is recognized on an accrual basis as opposed to a cash basis. Exceptions related to inventory are noted below.

UNDERLYING CONCEPT

For information to be **relevant**, it must be available to decision-makers before it loses its capacity to influence their decisions (**timeliness**). Interim reporting is an excellent example of this concept.

Interim Reporting Requirements

The profession indicates that the same accounting principles used for annual reports should be employed for interim reports. Revenues should be recognized in interim periods on the same basis as they are for annual periods. For example, if the instalment sales method is used as the basis for recognizing revenue on an annual basis, then the instalment basis should be applied to interim reports as well. Also, costs directly associated with revenues (product costs), such as materials, labour and related fringe benefits, and manufacturing overhead should be treated in the same manner for interim reports as for annual reports.

Companies generally should use the same inventory pricing methods (FIFO, LIFO, etc.) for interim reports that they use for annual reports. However, the following exceptions are appropriate at interim reporting periods.

1. When LIFO inventories are liquidated at an interim date and are expected to be replaced by year end, cost of goods sold should include the expected cost of replacing the liquidated LIFO base and not give effect to the interim liquidation.
2. Planned variances under a standard cost system that are expected to be absorbed by year end ordinarily should be deferred.[16]

Costs and expenses other than product costs, often referred to as **period costs**, are often charged to the interim period as incurred. But they may be allocated among interim periods based on an estimate of time expired, benefit received, or activity associated with the periods.

At a minimum, the **balance sheet, income statement, statement of retained earnings, statement of cash flows, and notes** are required.[17] The balance sheet should be presented as at the **end of the current interim period** with a **comparative** balance sheet as of the end of the immediately preceding fiscal year. The income statement should be presented for the **current interim period**, interim **year to date** with like **comparatives**.

---

[16] *CICA Handbook*, Section 1751, par. .26.

[17] *CICA Handbook*, Section 1751 par. .10.

IAS NOTE

IAS 34 deals with interim financial reporting.

For the statement of retained earnings, the information should be presented **cumulatively** for the current fiscal year to date with **comparatives**. Finally, for the cash flow statements, information should be presented for the **current interim period**, and **cumulatively** for the current fiscal **year to date** with like **comparatives**.[18] **EPS** information is also required where an enterprise is required to present this information in its annual information.[19]

Regarding **disclosure**, the following interim data should be reported as a minimum.[20]

1. When the statements do not comply with GAAP for the annual statements, so disclose. Disclose also that the statements should be read in conjunction with the annual statements.
2. A statement that the company follows the same accounting policies and methods as the most recent annual financial statements except for any new policy or method, any policies adopted to address the preparation of interim statements only, but where there is no impact on the annual financial statements, any special accounting methods adopted to address temporary costing fluctuations.
3. A description of any seasonality or cyclicality of interim period operations.
4. The nature and amount of changes in estimates.
5. Information about reportable segments.
6. Events subsequent to the interim period.
7. Specific information about business combinations, plans to exit and activity, restructure, integrate or reorganize, discontinued operations, and extraordinary items.
8. Information about contingencies.
9. Any other information required for fair presentation.

Unique Problems of Interim Reporting

Changes in Accounting. What happens if a company decides to change an accounting principle in the third quarter of a fiscal year? Should the cumulative effect adjustment be charged or credited to that quarter? Presentation of a cumulative effect in the third quarter may be misleading because of the inherent subjectivity associated with the first two quarters' reported income. In addition, a question arises as to whether such a change might not be used to manipulate a given quarter's income. **These changes should be reflected by retroactive application to prior interim periods unless the data are not available. The comparable interim periods of prior fiscal years should also be restated**.[21]

Earnings per Share. Interim reporting of earnings per share has all the problems inherent in calculating and presenting annual earnings per share, and then some. If shares are issued in the third period, EPS for the first two periods will not be indicative of year-end EPS. If an extraordinary item is present in one period and new equity shares are sold in another period, the EPS figure for the extraordinary item will change for the year. On an annual basis, only one EPS figure is associated with an extraordinary item and that figure does not change; the interim figure is subject to change. **For purposes of calculating earnings per share and making the required disclosure determinations, each interim period should stand alone. That is, all applicable tests should be made for that single period**.[22]

---

[18] *Ibid.* par., .16.

[19] *Ibid.* par., .12.

[20] *Ibid.* par., .14.

[21] *CICA Handbook,* Section 1751, par. .31.

[22] *Ibid.* B35 and B36.

Seasonality. Seasonality occurs when sales are compressed into one short period of the year while certain costs are fairly evenly spread throughout the year. For example, the natural gas industry has its heavy sales in the winter months, as contrasted with the beverage industry, which has its heavy sales in the summer months.

The problem of seasonality is related to the matching concept in accounting. Expenses should be matched against the revenues they create. In a seasonal business, wide fluctuations in profits occur because off-season sales do not absorb the company's fixed costs (for example, manufacturing, selling, and administrative costs that tend to remain fairly constant regardless of sales or production). Revenues and expenses should be recognized and accrued when they are earned or incurred according to GAAP. This also holds for interim periods. Thus, a company would only defer recognition of costs or revenues if it would be appropriate to do so at year end (i.e., the same tests are applied).

Continuing Controversy. The profession has recently developed the stringent standards noted above for interim reporting and this has alleviated much of the controversy that existed regarding the discrete and integral perspectives.

Controversy remains concerning the independent auditor's involvement in interim reports. Many auditors are reluctant to express an opinion on interim financial information, arguing that the data are too tentative and subjective. Conversely, an increasing number of individuals advocate some type of examination of interim reports. A compromise may be a limited review of interim reports that provides some assurance that an examination has been conducted by an outside party and that the published information appears to be in accord with generally accepted accounting principles.

Analysts want financial information as soon as possible, before it's old news. We may not be far from a continuous database system in which corporate financial records can be accessed by microcomputer. Investors might be able to access a company's financial records via computer whenever they wish and put the information in the format they need. Thus, they could learn about sales slippage, cost increases, or earnings changes as they happen, rather than waiting until after the quarter has ended.[23]

A steady stream of information from the company to the investor could be very positive because it might alleviate management's continual concern with short-run interim numbers. It would also alleviate much of the allocation problems that plague current GAAP.

AUDITOR'S AND MANAGEMENT'S REPORTS

Auditor's Report

Another important source of information that is often overlooked is the auditor's report. An **auditor** is an accounting professional who conducts an independent examination of the accounting data presented by a business enterprise. If the auditor is satisfied that the financial statements present the financial position, results of operations, and cash flows fairly in accordance with generally accepted accounting principles, an unqualified opinion is expressed as shown in Illustration 24-8.

> **OBJECTIVE 6**
> ....
> Identify the major disclosures found in the auditor's report.

---

[23] A step in this direction is the OSC's mandate for companies to file their financial statements electronically. The system, called SEDAR (EDGAR in the United States and required by the SEC) provides interested parties with computer access to financial information such as periodic filings, corporate prospectuses, and proxy materials.

ILLUSTRATION 24-8
Example of Auditor's Report for
Magna International Inc.

Auditor's Report

To the Shareholders of **Magna International Inc.**

We have audited the consolidated balance sheets of Magna International Inc. as at December 31, 2000 and 1999 and the consolidated statements of income and retained earnings and cash flows for the years ended December 31, 2000 and 1999, the five month period ended December 31, 1998 and the year ended July 31, 1998. These financial statements are the responsibility of the Company's management. Our responsibility is to express an opinion on these financial statements based on our audits.

   We conducted our audits in accordance with auditing standards generally accepted in Canada and the United States. Those standards require that we plan and perform an audit to obtain reasonable assurance whether the financial statements are free of material misstatement. An audit includes examining, on a test basis, evidence supporting the amounts and disclosures in the financial statements. An audit also includes assessing the accounting principles used and significant estimates made by management, as well as evaluating the overall financial statement presentation.

   In our opinion, these consolidated financial statements present fairly, in all material respects, the financial position of the Company as at December 31, 2000 and 1999 and the results of its operations and its cash flows for the years ended December 31, 2000 and 1999, the five month period ended December 31, 1998 and the year ended July 31, 1998 in accordance with accounting principles generally accepted in Canada.

/s/ Ernst & Young LLP

Ernst & Young LLP
Chartered Accountants

Toronto, Canada
February 20, 2001

INTERNATIONAL INSIGHT

In Germany, auditors' opinions address whether the statements have been prepared in accordance with German law—a statutory audit.

In preparing this report, the auditor follows these reporting standards in accordance with the reporting standard articulated in the *Handbook* under section 5100, par. .02.

1. The report should **identify the financial statements** (i.e., which company and which reporting period) and distinguish between the responsibilities of management and the responsibilities of the auditor.

2. The report should describe the **scope of the auditor's examination** (i.e., what the auditors did).

3. The report should contain either an expression of **opinion** on the financial statements or an assertion that an opinion cannot be expressed (in which case a reason should be given).

4. Where an opinion is given, it should state whether the financial statements **present fairly, in all material respects, the financial position, results of operations, and cash flows in accordance with an appropriately disclosed basis of accounting, which would normally be GAAP**. If there is a reservation, the report should explain it.

   In most cases, the auditor issues a standard unqualified or clean opinion; that is, the auditor expresses the opinion that the financial statements present fairly, in all material respects, the entity's financial position, results of operations, and cash flows in conformity with generally accepted accounting principles. Certain circumstances, although they do not affect the auditor's unqualified opinion, may require the auditor to add an explanatory paragraph to the audit report.

   In some situations, however, the auditor is required to (1) express a **qualified** opinion, (2) express an **adverse** opinion, or (3) **disclaim** an opinion. A qualified opinion contains an exception to the standard opinion. Ordinarily the exception is not of sufficient magnitude to invalidate the statements as a whole; if it were, an adverse opinion would be rendered. The usual circumstances in which the auditor may deviate from the standard unqualified short-form report on financial statements are as follows.

1. The examination's **scope** is limited or affected by conditions or restrictions. This would be the case where the auditor is not able to complete all the work he/she needs to in order to render an opinion e.g., a firm has destroyed the records.

2. The statements **do not fairly present financial position or results of operations**. This would be evident where GAAP or an appropriate basis of financial reporting is not followed.

If the auditor is confronted with one of the situations noted above, the opinion must be qualified. A qualified opinion states that, except for the effects of the matter to which the qualification relates, the financial statements present fairly, in all material respects, the financial position, results of operations, and cash flows in conformity with generally accepted accounting principles.

An **adverse opinion** is required in any report in which the exceptions to fair presentation are so material that in the independent auditor's judgement a qualified opinion is not justified. In such a case, the financial statements taken as a whole are **not presented in accordance with generally accepted accounting principles**. Adverse opinions are rare, because most enterprises change their accounting to conform to the auditor's desires.

A **disclaimer of an opinion** is appropriate when the auditor has gathered so little information on the financial statements that **no opinion can be expressed**.

The audit report should provide useful information to the investor. One investment banker noted, "Probably the first item to check is the auditor's opinion to see whether or not it is a clean one—'in conformity with generally accepted accounting principles'—or is qualified in regard to differences between the auditor and company management in the accounting treatment of some major item, or in the outcome of some major litigation."

Management's Reports

Management's Discussion and Analysis

Management's discussion and analysis (MD&A) section covers three financial aspects of an enterprise's business—liquidity, capital resources, and results of operations. **It requires management to highlight favourable or unfavourable trends and to identify significant events and uncertainties that affect these three factors**. This approach obviously involves a number of subjective estimates, opinions, and soft data. However, securities commissions have mandated this disclosure, believing the **relevance** of this information exceeds the potential lack of **reliability**.

How this section of the annual report can be made even more effective is the subject of continuing questions such as:

1. Is sufficient forward-looking information being disclosed under current MD&A requirements?
2. Should MD&A disclosures be changed to become more of a risk analysis?
3. Should the MD&A be audited by independent auditors?

Management's Responsibilities for Financial Statements

The accounting profession has for many years attempted to educate the public regarding the fact that a company's management has the primary responsibility for the preparation, integrity, and objectivity of the company's financial statements. Companies now include a statement acknowledging this responsibility in the audited financial statements, often just prior to the audit report. An example of the report is shown in Illustration 24-9.

> **OBJECTIVE 7**
> Understand management's responsibilities for financials.

ILLUSTRATION 24-9
Management Report
Acknowledging Responsibility for
the Financial Statements—Four
Seasons Hotels Inc.

Management's Responsibility for Financial Reporting

The management of Four Seasons Hotels Inc. is responsible for the preparation and integrity of the financial statements and related financial information of the Corporation and the selection of accounting principles appropriate to the Corporation's circumstances. The consolidated financial statements, notes and other financial information included in the Annual Report were prepared in accordance with accounting principles generally accepted in Canada. The statements also include estimated amounts based on informed judgments of current and future events, for items such as the useful lives of capital assets and provisions for impairment in the value of assets. These estimates are made with appropriate consideration of the materiality of the amounts involved. The financial information presented elsewhere in the Annual Report is consistent with that in the financial statements.

Management is also responsible for maintaining a system of internal controls and budgeting procedures which are designed to provide reasonable assurance that assets are safeguarded, transactions are executed and recorded in accordance with management's authorization, and relevant and reliable financial information is produced. To augment the internal control system, the Corporation maintains a program of internal audits covering significant aspects of the operations.

The Corporation's Audit Committee is appointed by the Board of Director's annually. The Committee meets with the internal and independent auditors (who have free access to the Audit Committee) and with management, to satisfy itself that each group is properly discharging its responsibilities, and to review the financial statements, the independent auditor's report and other financial information appearing in the Corporation's Annual Report. The Audit Committee reports its findings to the Board of Director's for its consideration in approving the financial statements for issuance to the shareholders.

KPMG LLP, the independent auditors appointed by the shareholders of the Corporation, have examined the financial statements in accordance with generally accepted auditing standards.

February 15, 2001

ISADORE SHARP (SIGNED)
Chairman and Chief Executive Officer

DOUGLAS L. LUDWIG (SIGNED)
Chief Financial Officer
Executive Vice-President and Treasurer

CURRENT REPORTING ISSUES

Reporting on Financial Forecasts and Projections

OBJECTIVE 8

Identify issues related to financial forecasts and projections.

In recent years, the investing public's demand for more and better information has focused on disclosure of corporate expectations for the future.[24] These disclosures take one of two forms.[25]

Financial forecast. Prospective financial statements that present, to the best of the responsible party's knowledge and belief, an entity's expected financial position, results of operations, and cash flows. A financial forecast is based on the responsible party's assumptions reflecting conditions it expects to exist and the course of action it expects to take.

Financial projection. Prospective financial statements that present, to the best of the responsible party's knowledge and belief, given one or more hypothetical assumptions, an entity's expected financial position, results of operations, and cash flows. A financial projection is based on the responsible party's assumptions reflecting conditions it

---

[24] Some areas in which companies are using financial information about the future are equipment lease-versus-buy analysis, analysis of a company's ability to successfully enter new markets, and examining merger and acquisition opportunities. In addition, forecasts and projections are also prepared for use by third parties in public offering documents (requiring financial forecasts), tax-oriented investments, and financial feasibility studies. Use of forward-looking data has been enhanced by the increased capability of the microcomputer to analyse, compare, and manipulate large quantities of data.

[25] *CICA Handbook*, Section 4250, pars. .03–.05.

expects would exist and the course of action it expects would be taken, given one or more hypothetical assumptions.

The difference between a financial forecast and a financial projection is that a forecast attempts to provide information on what is expected to happen, whereas a projection may provide information on what is not necessarily expected to happen, but might take place.

Financial forecasts are the subject of intensive discussion with journalists, corporate executives, securities commissions, financial analysts, accountants, and others. Predictably, there are strong arguments on either side. Listed below are some of the arguments.

Arguments for requiring published forecasts:

1. Investment decisions are based on future expectations; therefore, information about the future facilitates better decisions.
2. Forecasts are already circulated informally, but are uncontrolled, frequently misleading, and not available equally to all investors. This confused situation should be brought under control.
3. Circumstances now change so rapidly that historical information is no longer adequate for prediction.

Arguments against requiring published forecasts:

1. No one can foretell the future. Therefore forecasts, while conveying an impression of precision about the future, will inevitably be wrong.
2. Organizations will strive only to meet their published forecasts, not to produce results that are in the shareholders' best interest.
3. When forecasts are not proved to be accurate, there will be recriminations and probably legal actions.[26]
4. Disclosure of forecasts will be detrimental to organizations, because it will fully inform not only investors, but also competitors (foreign and domestic).

The CICA has issued a statement on standards for accountants' services on prospective financial information. This statement established procedures and reporting standards for presenting financial forecasts and projections.[27] It requires the following:

1. that **appropriate assumptions** be used,
2. that the **time period** not extend beyond the point in time for which such information can be reasonably estimated,
3. that the information be presented in accordance with the **accounting policies** expected to be used in the historical financial statements,
4. that the statements include at least an **income statement**,
5. that there be a **cautionary note** attached,
6. that the information be **clearly labelled** a forecast or projection and
7. various other disclosures, including assumptions, accounting policies, and the extent to which actual results versus estimated results are incorporated, and others.

To encourage management to disclose this type of information, securities law has a safe harbour rule. This rule provides protection to an enterprise that presents an erroneous forecast as long as the forecast is prepared on a reasonable basis and is disclosed in good faith. However, many companies note that the safe harbour rule does not work in practice, since it does not cover oral statements, nor has it kept them out of court.

---

[26] The issue is serious. Over a recent three-year period, 8% of the companies on the NYSE have been sued because of an alleged lack of financial disclosure. Companies complain that they are subject to lawsuits whenever the stock price drops. As one executive noted: 'You can even be sued if the stock price goes up because you did not disclose the good news fast enough.'

[27] *CICA Handbook*, Section 4250.

Experience in Great Britain

The U.S. has permitted financial forecasts for years, and the results have been fairly successful. Some significant differences exist between the British and the North American business and legal environment,[28] but probably none that could not be overcome if influential interests in Canada cooperated to produce an atmosphere conducive to quality forecasting. A typical British forecast adapted from a construction company's report to support a public offering of shares is as follows.

ILLUSTRATION 24-10
Financial Forecast of a
British Company

Profits have grown substantially over the past 10 years and directors are confident of being able to continue this expansion. . . . While the rate of expansion will be dependent on the level of economic activity in Ireland and England, the group is well structured to avail itself of opportunities as they arise, particularly in the field of property development, which is expected to play an increasingly important role in the group's future expansion.

Profits before taxation for the half year ended 30th June 1999 were £402,000. On the basis of trading experiences since that date and the present level of sales and completions, the directors expect that in the absence of unforeseen circumstances, the group's profits before taxation for the year to 31st December 1999 will be not less than £960,000.

No dividends will be paid in respect of the year December 31, 1999. In a full financial year, on the basis of above forecasts (not including full year profits) it would be the intention of the board, assuming current rates of tax, to recommend dividends totalling 40% (of after-tax profits), of which 15% payable would be as an interest dividend in November 2000 and 25% as a final dividend in June 2001.

Questions of Liability

What happens if a company does not meet its forecasts? Are the company and the auditor going to be sued? If a company, for example, projects an earnings increase of 15% and achieves only 5%, should the shareholder be permitted to have some judicial recourse against the company? One court case involving **Monsanto Chemical Corporation** has provided some guidelines. In this case, Monsanto predicted that sales would increase 8 to 9% and that earnings would rise 4 to 5%. In the last part of the year, the demand for Monsanto's products dropped as a result of a business turndown. Therefore, instead of increasing, the company's earnings declined. The company was sued because the projected earnings figure was erroneous, but the judge dismissed the suit because the forecasts were the best estimates of qualified people whose intents were honest. **Nortel Networks** is currently the subject of litigation for forecasting higher earnings than actually occurred.

Safe harbour rules are intended to protect enterprises that provide good-faith projections. However, much concern exists as to how securities commissions and the courts will interpret such terms as "good faith" and "reasonable assumptions" when erroneous forecasts mislead users of this information.

Internet Financial Reporting

How can companies improve the usefulness of their financial reporting practices? Many companies are using the Internet's power and reach to provide more useful information to financial statement readers. Recent surveys indicate that over 80% of large companies have Internet sites, and a large proportion of these companies' websites contain links to their financial statements and other disclosures.[29] The increased popularity of

---

[28] The British system, for example, does not permit litigation on forecasted information, and the solicitor is not permitted to work on a contingent basis. See "A Case for Forecasting—The British Have Tried it and Find that it Works," *World* (New York: Peat Marwick, Mitchell & Co., Autumn 1978), pp. 10–13.

[29] The FASB has recently issued a report on electronic dissemination of financial reports. This report summarized current practice and research conducted on Internet financial reporting. Business Reporting Research Project, "Electronic Distribution of Business Reporting Information" (Norwalk, Conn.: FASB, 2000).

such reporting is not surprising, since the costs of printing and dissemination of paper reports could be reduced with the use of Internet reporting.

How does Internet financial reporting improve the overall usefulness of a company's financial reports? First, dissemination of reports via the Web can allow firms **to communicate with more users** than is possible with traditional paper reports. In addition, **Internet reporting allows users to take advantage of tools** such as search engines and hyperlinks to quickly find information about the firm and, sometimes, to download the information for analysis, perhaps in computer spreadsheets. Finally, **Internet reporting can help make financial reports more relevant** by allowing companies to report expanded disaggregated data and more timely data than is possible through paper-based reporting. For example, some companies voluntarily report weekly sales data and segment operating data on their websites.

Given these benefits and ever-improving Internet tools, will it be long before electronic reporting replaces paper-based financial disclosure? The main obstacles to achieving complete electronic reporting are related to equality of access to electronic financial reporting and the reliability of the information distributed via the Internet. Although companies may practise Internet financial reporting, they must still prepare traditional paper reports because some investors may not have Internet access. These investors would receive differential (less) information relative to other "wired" investors if companies were to eliminate paper reports. In addition, at present, Internet financial reporting is a voluntary means of reporting. As a result, there are no standards as to the completeness of reports on the Internet, nor is there the requirement that these reports be audited. One concern in this regard is that computer "hackers" could invade a company's website and corrupt the financial information contained therein.

Thus, although Internet financial reporting is gaining in popularity, until issues related to differential access to the Internet and the reliability of information disseminated via the Web are addressed, we will continue to see traditional paper-based reporting.

Fraudulent Financial Reporting

The importance of an effective financial reporting system cannot be underestimated, because it provides the financial information that ensures the proper functioning of the capital and credit markets. Unfortunately, the system does not always work as planned.

The case of **E.S.M. Government Securities, Inc. (E.S.M.)** exemplifies the seriousness of these frauds. E.S.M. was a Florida securities dealer entrusted with monies to invest by municipalities from across the United States.[30] The cities provided the cash to E.S.M. that they thought was collateralized with government securities. Examination of E.S.M.'s balance sheet indicated that the company owed about as much as it expected to collect. Unfortunately, the amount it expected to collect was from insolvent affiliates, which, in effect, meant that E.S.M. was bankrupt. In fact, E.S.M. had been bankrupt for more than six years, and the fraud was discovered only because a customer questioned a note to the balance sheet. More than $300 million of losses had been disguised.

Although frauds such as these are unusual, they do raise questions about the financial reporting process. The accounting profession continues to examine this process to determine whether improvements can be made. Basic issues such as the following must be addressed:

1. How well are accounting practices and disclosures serving the public?
2. Are auditors meeting their obligations to the investing public?
3. What are the effects of the securities commissions' disclosure, compliance, and enforcement policies?

> **OBJECTIVE 9**
>
> Describe the profession's response to fraudulent financial reporting.

---

[30] For an expanded discussion of this case, see Robert J. Sack and Robert Tangreti, "ESM: Implications for the Profession," *Journal of Accountancy*, April 1987.

4. Could the effect of these regulatory accounting policies have contributed to company failures?

5. What legislative proposals, if any, are necessary to address perceived weaknesses in accounting and auditing standards and regulatory procedures?

Many other groups have been studying the financial reporting environment. One such American group, the National Commission on Fraudulent Financial Reporting, chaired by James C. Treadway, Jr. identified causal factors that lead to fraudulent financial reporting and provided steps to reduce its incidence.[31]

The commission defined **fraudulent financial reporting** as "**intentional or reckless conduct, whether act or omission, that results in materially misleading financial statements.**" It also noted that fraudulent reporting can involve gross and deliberate distortion of corporate records (such as inventory count tags), or misapplication of accounting principles (failure to disclose material transactions).[32]

Causes of Fraudulent Financial Reporting

Fraudulent financial reporting usually occurs because of conditions in the internal or external environment.[33] Influences in the internal environment relate to poor systems of internal control, management's poor attitude toward ethics, or perhaps a company's liquidity or profitability. Those in the external environment may relate to industry conditions, overall business environment, or legal and regulatory considerations.

General incentives for fraudulent financial reporting are the desire to obtain a higher share price or debt offering, to avoid default on a loan covenant, or to make a personal gain of some type (additional compensation, promotion). Situational pressures on the company or an individual manager also may lead to fraudulent financial reporting. Examples of these situational pressures include:

1. Sudden decreases in revenue or market share. A single company or an entire industry can experience these decreases.

2. Unrealistic budget pressures, particularly for short-term results. These pressures may occur when headquarters arbitrarily determines profit objectives and budgets without taking actual conditions into account.

3. Financial pressure resulting from bonus plans that depend on short-term economic performance. This pressure is particularly acute when the bonus is a significant component of the individual's total compensation.

Opportunities for fraudulent financial reporting are present in circumstances when the fraud is easy to commit and when detection is difficult. Frequently these opportunities arise from:

1. *The absence of a board of directors or audit committee* that vigilantly oversees the financial reporting process.

2. *Weak or nonexistent internal accounting controls.* This situation can occur, for example, when a company's revenue system is overloaded as a result of a rapid expansion of sales, an acquisition of a new division, or the entry into a new, unfamiliar line of business.

---

[31] Report of the National Commission on Fraudulent Financial Reporting, (Washington D.C., 1987).

[32] *Ibid.*, page 2. Unintentional errors as well as corporate improprieties (such as tax fraud, employee embezzlements, and so on) that do not cause the financial statements to be misleading are excluded from the definition of fraudulent financial reporting.

[33] The discussion in this section is taken from the Report of the National Commission on Fraudulent Financial Reporting, pp. 23–24.

3. *Unusual or complex transactions* such as the consolidation of two companies, the divestiture or closing of a specific operation, and agreements to buy or sell government securities under a repurchase agreement.

4. *Accounting estimates requiring significant subjective judgement* by company management, such as reserves for loan losses and the yearly provision for warranty expense.

5. *Ineffective internal audit staff* resulting from inadequate staff size and severely limited audit scope.

A weak corporate ethical climate contributes to these situations. Opportunities for fraudulent financial reporting also increase dramatically when the accounting principles followed in reporting transactions are nonexistent, evolving, or subject to varying interpretations.

Response of the Profession

The profession is working to find solutions to the problem of fraudulent financial reporting. In Canada, the CICA has created the Risk Management and Governance Board, whose mandate is to develop frameworks and guidance in the area of corporate governance and risk management. The CICA has also partnered with the TSE and CDNX to create the Joint Committee on Corporate Governance. Its mandate is to review the current Canadian environment and compare Canadian and international best practices on corporate governance. These initiatives are just the beginning.

The CICA, in its efforts to harmonize accounting standards with the U.S. and globally, is also tightening up on GAAP.

Some feel that these efforts are not enough. They argue that our current environment, with provincial securities commissions (versus national), GAAP (which allows significant judgement) and our legal system, is conducive to fraudulent reporting. The concern has been raised that without a solid system to safeguard our capital markets and investors, investment will indeed dry up in Canada.[34]

Criteria for Making Accounting and Reporting Choices

Throughout this textbook, we have stressed the need to provide information that is useful to predict the amounts, timing, and uncertainty of future cash flows. To achieve this objective, judicious choices between alternative accounting concepts, methods, and means of disclosure must be made. You are probably surprised by the large number of choices among acceptable alternatives that accountants are required to make.

You should recognize, however, as indicated in Chapter 1, that accounting is greatly influenced by its environment. Because it does not exist in a vacuum, it seems unrealistic to assume that alternative presentations of certain transactions and events will be eliminated entirely. Nevertheless, we are hopeful that the profession, through developing a conceptual framework, will be able to focus on the needs of financial statement users and eliminate diversity where appropriate. The profession must continue its efforts to develop a sound foundation upon which financial standards and practice can be built. As Aristotle said: "The correct beginning is more than half the whole."

---

[34] Al Rosen, " Easy Prey," *(Canadian Business)* April 16, 2001, p. 12.

SUMMARY OF LEARNING OBJECTIVES

1 Review the full disclosure principle and describe problems of implementation. The full disclosure principle calls for financial reporting of any financial facts significant enough to influence the judgement of an informed reader. Implementing the full disclosure principle is difficult, because the cost of disclosure can be substantial and the benefits difficult to assess. Disclosure requirements have increased because of (1) the growing complexity of the business environment, (2) the necessity for timely information, and (3) the use of accounting as a control and monitoring device.

2 Explain the use of notes in financial statement preparation. Notes are the accountant's means of amplifying or explaining the items presented in the main body of the statements. Information pertinent to specific financial statement items can be explained in qualitative terms, and supplementary data of a quantitative nature can be provided to expand the information in the financial statements. Common note disclosures relate to such items as accounting policies; inventories; property, plant, and equipment; credit claims; contingencies and commitments; and subsequent events.

3 Discuss the accounting issues related to special transactions/events. Transactions such as related party and subsequent events pose special accounting issues. Related party transactions may have to be remeasured. Subsequent events might also cause the statements to be remeasured, disclosures are very important in these cases.

4 Describe the disclosure requirements for major segments of a business. If only the consolidated figures are available to the analyst, much information regarding the composition of these figures is hidden in aggregated figures. There is no way to tell from the consolidated data the extent to which the differing product lines contribute to the company's profitability, risk, and growth potential. As a result, segment information is required by the profession in certain situations.

5 Describe the accounting problems associated with interim reporting. Interim reports cover periods of less than one year. Two viewpoints exist regarding interim reports. One view (discrete view) holds that each interim period should be treated as a separate accounting period. Another view (integral view) is that the interim report is an integral part of the annual report and that deferrals and accruals should take into consideration what will happen for the entire year.

The same accounting principles used for annual reports should be employed for interim reports. A number of unique reporting problems exist.

6 Identify the major disclosures found in the auditor's report. If the auditor is satisfied that the financial statements present the financial position, results of operations, and cash flows fairly in accordance with generally accepted accounting principles, an unqualified opinion is expressed. A qualified opinion contains an exception to the standard opinion; ordinarily the exception is not of sufficient magnitude to invalidate the statements as a whole.

An adverse opinion is required in any report in which the exceptions to fair presentation are so material that a qualified opinion is not justified. A disclaimer of an opinion is appropriate when the auditor has gathered so little information on the financial statements that no opinion can be expressed.

7 Understand management's responsibilities for financials. Management's discussion and analysis section covers three financial aspects of an enterprise's business: liquidity, capital resources, and results of operations. Management has primary responsibility for the financial statements and this responsibility is often indicated in a letter to shareholders in the annual report.

8 Identify issues related to financial forecasts and projections. There is a concern that companies will be sued if the forecasts are not met. To encourage management to disclose this type of information, securities commissions have issued "safe harbour" rules. The safe harbour rule generally provides protection to an enterprise that presents an erroneous forecast as long as the projection was prepared on a reasonable basis and was disclosed in good faith. However, the safe harbour rule has not worked well in practice.

9 Describe the profession's response to fraudulent financial reporting. Fraudulent financial reporting is intentional or reckless conduct, whether by act or omission, that results in materially misleading financial statements. Fraudulent financial reporting usually occurs because of poor internal control, management's poor attitude toward ethics, and so on. The profession is working to find solutions.

Note: All **asterisked** Brief Exercises, Exercises, Problems, and Conceptual Cases relate to materials contained in the appendix to the chapter.

BRIEF EXERCISES

BE24-1 An annual report of D. Robillard Industries states: "The company and its subsidiaries have long term leases expiring on various dates after December 31, 2001. Amounts payable under such commitments, without reduction for related rental income, are expected to average approximately $5,711,000 annually for the next three years. Related rental income from certain subleases to others is estimated to average $3,094,000 annually for the next three years." What information is provided by this note?

BE24-2 An annual report of **Ford Motor Company** states: "Net income a share is computed based upon the average number of shares of capital stock of all classes outstanding. Additional shares of common stock may be issued or delivered in the future on conversion of outstanding convertible debentures, exercise of outstanding employee stock options, and for payment of defined supplemental compensation. Had such additional shares been outstanding, net income a share would have been reduced by 10¢ in the current year and 3¢ in the previous year.

"As a result of capital stock transactions by the company during the current year (primarily the purchase of Class A Stock from Ford Foundation), net income a share was increased by 6¢." What information is provided by this note?

BE24-3 Linden Corporation is preparing its December 31, 2000 financial statements. Two events that occurred between December 31, 2000 and March 10, 2001, when the statements were issued, are described below.

1. A liability, estimated at $150,000 at December 31, 2000, was settled on February 26, 2001 at $170,000.
2. A flood loss of $80,000 occurred on March 1, 2001.

What effect do these subsequent events have on 2000 net income?

BE24-4 Bess Marvin, a student of Intermediate Accounting, was heard to remark after a class discussion on diversified reporting: "All this is very confusing to me. First we are told that there is merit in presenting the consolidated results and now we are told that it is better to show segmented results. I wish they would make up their minds." Evaluate this comment.

BE24-5 Psuikoden Corporation has seven industry segments with total revenues as follows:

Genso	600	Sergei	225
Konami	650	Takuhi	200
RPG	250	Nippon	700
Red Moon	375		

Based only on the revenues test, which industry segments are reportable?

BE24-6 Operating profits and losses for the seven industry segments of Psuikoden Corporation are:

Genso	90	Sergei	(20)
Konami	(40)	Takuhi	34
RPG	25	Nippon	100
Red Moon	50		

Based only on the operating profit (loss) test, which industry segments are reportable?

BE24-7 Assets for the seven industry segments of Psuikoden Corporation are:

Genso	500	Sergei	200
Konami	550	Takuhi	150
RPG	400	Nippon	475
Red Moon	400		

Based only on the assets test, which industry segments are reportable?

BE24-8 Aigee Limited purchases land from its president for $100,000. The land was purchased by the president 20 years ago for $50,000. Prepare the journal entry to record the land.

BE24-9 Bing Corp. exchanges computer software (book value $3,000) with Chun Corp (book value of software exchanged: $5,000). The software performs different functions and has a fair value of $10,000. Both companies are 100% owned by the same individual. Discuss how this transaction should be measured and prepare the journal entries for both companies to record the exchange. Explain reasoning.

BE24-10 How would the above transaction be recorded if the transaction were arm's length?

BE24-11 How would the transaction in BE 24-9 be recorded if the individual shareholder only owned 40% of the shares of each company? Discuss and prepare journal entries.

EXERCISES

E24-1 **(Post-Balance Sheet Events)** Madrasah Corporation issued its financial statements for the year ended December 31, 2002 on March 10, 2003. The following events took place early in 2003.
1. On January 10, 10,000 common shares were issued at $66 per share.
2. On March 1, Madrasah determined after negotiations with the Canada Customs and Revenue Agency that income taxes payable for 2002 should be $1.27 million. At December 31, 2002, income taxes payable were recorded at $1.1 million.

Instructions
Discuss how the preceding post-balance sheet events should be reflected in the 2002 financial statements.

E24-2 **(Post-Balance Sheet Events)** For each of the following subsequent (post-balance sheet) events, indicate whether a company should (a) adjust the financial statements, (b) disclose in notes to the financial statements, or (c) neither adjust nor disclose.

_____ 1. Settlement of federal tax case at a cost considerably in excess of the amount expected at year end.
_____ 2. Introduction of a new product line.
_____ 3. Loss of assembly plant due to fire.
_____ 4. Sale of a significant portion of the company's assets.
_____ 5. Retirement of the company president.
_____ 6. Prolonged employee strike.
_____ 7. Loss of a significant customer.
_____ 8. Issuance of a significant number of common shares.
_____ 9. Material loss on a year-end receivable because of a customer's bankruptcy.
_____ 10. Hiring of a new president.
_____ 11. Settlement of prior year's litigation against the company.
_____ 12. Merger with another company of comparable size.

E24-3 **(Segmented Reporting)** Carlton Corp. is involved in four separate industries. The following information is available for each of the four industries:

Operating Segment	Total Revenue	Operating Profit (Loss)	Assets
W	$60,000	$15,000	$167,000
X	10,000	3,000	83,000
Y	23,000	(2,000)	21,000
Z	9,000	1,000	19,000
	$102,000	$17,000	$290,000

Instructions

Determine which of the operating segments are reportable based on the:

(a) revenue test.
(b) operating profit (loss) test.
(c) assets test.

PROBLEMS

P24-1 Your firm has been engaged to examine the financial statements of Sabrina Corporation for the year 2002. The bookkeeper who maintains the financial records has prepared all the unaudited financial statements for the corporation since its organization on January 2, 1996. The client provides you with the information below.

SABRINA CORPORATION
Balance Sheet
As of December 31, 2002

Assets		Liabilities	
Current assets	$1,881,100	Current liabilities	$ 962,400
Other assets	5,171,400	Long-term liabilities	1,439,500
		Capital	4,650,600
	$7,052,500		$7,052,500

An analysis of current assets discloses the following:

Cash (restricted in the amount of $400,000 for plant expansion)	$ 571,000
Investments in land	185,000
Accounts receivable less allowance of $30,000	480,000
Inventories (LIFO flow assumption)	645,100
	$1,881,100

Other assets include:

Prepaid expenses	$ 47,400
Plant and equipment less accumulated amortization of $1,430,000	4,130,000
Cash surrender value of life insurance policy	84,000
Unamortized bond discount	49,500
Notes receivable (short-term)	162,300
Goodwill	252,000
Land	446,200
	$5,171,400

Current liabilities include:

Accounts payable	$ 510,000
Notes payable (due 2004)	157,400
Estimated income taxes payable	145,000
Premium on common shares	150,000
	$ 962,400

Long-term liabilities include:

Unearned revenue	$ 489,500
Dividends payable (cash)	200,000
8% bonds payable (due May 1, 2007)	750,000
	$1,439,500

Capital includes:

Retained earnings	$2,810,600
Common shares; authorized 200,000 shares, 184,000 shares issued	1,840,000
	$4,650,600

The supplementary information below is also provided.

1. On May 1, 2002, the corporation issued at 93.4, $750,000 of bonds to finance plant expansion. The long-term bond agreement provided for the annual payment of interest every May 1. The existing plant was pledged as security for the loan. Use straight-line method for discount amortization.

2. The bookkeeper made the following mistakes:
   (a) In 2000, the ending inventory was overstated by $183,000. The ending inventories for 2001 and 2002 were correctly calculated.
   (b) In 2002, accrued wages in the amount of $275,000 were omitted from the balance sheet and these expenses were not charged on the income statement.
   (c) In 2002, a gain of $175,000 (net of tax) on the sale of certain plant assets was credited directly to retained earnings.
3. A major competitor has introduced a line of products that will compete directly with Sabrina's primary line, now being produced in a specially designed new plant. Because of manufacturing innovations, the competitor's line will be of comparable quality but priced 50% below Sabrina's line. The competitor announced its new line on January 14, 2003. Sabrina indicates that the company will meet the lower prices that are high enough to cover variable manufacturing and selling expenses, but permit recovery of only a portion of fixed costs.
4. You learned on January 28, 2003, prior to completion of the audit, of heavy damage because of a recent fire to one of Sabrina's two plants; the loss will not be reimbursed by insurance. The newspapers described the event in detail.

Instructions

Analyse the above information to prepare a corrected balance sheet for Sabrina in accordance with proper accounting and reporting principles. Prepare a description of any notes that might need to be prepared. The books are closed and adjustments to income are to be made through retained earnings.

P24-2 Friendly Corporation is a diversified company that operates in five different industries: A, B, C, D, and E. The following information relating to each segment is available for 2001. Sales of segments B and C included intersegment sales of $20,000 and $100,000, respectively.

	A	B	C	D	E
Sales	$40,000	$ 80,000	$580,000	$35,000	$55,000
Cost of goods sold	19,000	50,000	270,000	19,000	30,000
Operating expenses	10,000	40,000	235,000	12,000	18,000
Total expenses	29,000	90,000	505,000	31,000	48,000
Operating profit (loss)	$11,000	$(10,000)	$ 75,000	$ 4,000	$ 7,000
Assets	$35,000	$ 60,000	$500,000	$65,000	$50,000

Instructions

(a) Determine which of the segments are reportable based on the:
   1. revenue test.
   2. operating profit (loss) test.
   3. assets test.
(b) Prepare the necessary disclosures.

CONCEPTUAL CASES

C24-1 Lion Corporation is in the process of preparing its annual financial statements for the fiscal year ended April 30, 2001. The company manufactures plastic, glass, and paper containers for sale to food and drink manufacturers and distributors.

Lion Corporation maintains separate control accounts for its raw materials, work-in-process, and finished goods inventories for each of the three types of containers. The inventories are valued at the lower of cost or market.

The company's property, plant, and equipment are classified in the following major categories: land, office buildings, furniture and fixtures, manufacturing facilities, manufacturing equipment, and leasehold improvements. All fixed assets are carried at cost. The depreciation methods employed depend upon the type of asset (its classification) and when it was acquired.

Lion Corporation plans to present the inventory and fixed asset amounts in its April 30, 2001 balance sheet as shown below.

Inventories	$4,814,200
Property, plant, and equipment (net of amortization)	$6,310,000

Instructions

What information regarding inventories and property, plant, and equipment must be disclosed by Lion Corporation in the audited financial statements issued to shareholders, either in the body or the notes, for the 2000–2001 fiscal year?

(CMA adapted)

C24-2 Rem Inc. produces electronic components for sale to manufacturers of radios, television sets, and digital sound systems. In connection with her examination of Rem's financial statements for the year ended December 31, 2001, Maggie Zeen, CA, completed field work two weeks ago. Ms. Zeen now is evaluating the significance of the following items prior to preparing her auditor's report. Except as noted, none of these items have been disclosed in the financial statements or notes.

Item 1

A 10-year loan agreement, which the company entered into three years ago, provides that dividend payments may not exceed net income earned after taxes subsequent to the date of the agreement. The balance of retained earnings at the date of the loan agreement was $420,000. From that date through December 31, 2001, net income after taxes has totalled $570,000 and cash dividends have totalled $320,000. Based on these data the staff auditor assigned to this review concluded that there was no retained earnings restriction at December 31, 2001.

Item 2

Recently Rem interrupted its policy of paying cash dividends quarterly to its shareholders. Dividends were paid regularly through 2000, discontinued for all of 2001 to finance purchase of equipment for the company's new plant, and resumed in the first quarter of 2002. In the annual report, dividend policy is to be discussed in the president's letter to shareholders.

Item 3

A major electronics firm has introduced a line of products that will compete directly with Rem's primary line, now being produced in the specially designed new plant. Because of manufacturing innovations, the competitor's line will be of comparable quality but priced 50% below Rem's line. The competitor announced its new line during the week following completion of field work. Ms. Zeen read the announcement in the newspaper and discussed the situation by telephone with Rem executives. Rem will meet the lower prices that are high enough to cover variable manufacturing and selling expenses but will permit recovery of only a portion of fixed costs.

Item 4

The company's new manufacturing plant building, which cost $2.4 million and has an estimated life of 25 years, is leased from Ancient National Bank at an annual rental of $600,000. The company is obligated to pay property taxes, insurance, and maintenance. At the conclusion of its 10-year non-cancellable lease, the company has the option of purchasing the property for $1.00. In Rem's income statement, the rental payment is reported on a separate line.

Instructions

For each of the items above, discuss any additional disclosures in the financial statements and notes that the auditor should recommend to her client. (The four items' cumulative effect should not be considered.)

C24-3 You have completed your audit of Keesha Inc. and its consolidated subsidiaries for the year ended December 31, 2001, and were satisfied with the results of your examination. You have examined the financial statements of Keesha for the past three years. The corporation is now preparing its annual report to shareholders. The report will include the consolidated financial statements of Keesha and its subsidiaries and your short-form auditor's report. During your audit the following matters came to your attention:

1. A vice-president who is also a shareholder resigned on December 31, 2001, after an argument with the president. The vice-president is soliciting proxies from shareholders and expects to obtain sufficient proxies to gain control of the board of directors so that a new president will be appointed. The president plans to have a note prepared that would include information of the pending proxy fight, management's accomplishments over the years, and an appeal by management for the support of shareholders.

2. The corporation decides in 2001 to adopt the straight-line method of depreciation for plant equipment. The straight-line method will be used for new acquisitions as well as for previously acquired plant equipment for which depreciation had been provided on an accelerated basis.
3. The Canada Customs and Revenue Agency is currently examining the corporation's 1998 federal income tax return and is questioning the amount of a deduction claimed by the corporation's domestic subsidiary for a loss sustained in 1998. The examination is still in process, and any additional tax liability is indeterminable at this time. The corporation's tax counsel believes that there will be no substantial additional tax liability.

Instructions

(a) Prepare the notes, if any, that you would suggest for the items listed above.
(b) State your reasons for not making disclosure by note for each of the listed items for which you did not prepare a note.

(AICPA adapted)

C24-4 Presented below are three independent situations.

Situation 1

A company offers a one-year warranty for the product that it manufactures. A history of warranty claims has been compiled and the probable amounts of claims related to sales for a given period can be determined.

Situation 2

Subsequent to the date of a set of financial statements, but prior to the issuance of the financial statements, a company enters into a contract that will probably result in a significant loss to the company. The loss amount can be reasonably estimated.

Situation 3

A company has adopted a policy of recording self-insurance for any possible losses resulting from injury to others by the company's vehicles. The premium for an insurance policy for the same risk from an independent insurance company would have an annual cost of $4,000. During the period covered by the financial statements, there were no accidents involving the company's vehicles that resulted in injury to others.

Instructions

Discuss the accrual or type of disclosure necessary (if any) and the reason(s) why such disclosure is appropriate for each of the three independent sets of facts above.

(AICPA adapted)

C24-5 At December 31, 2001, Brandt Corp. has assets of $10 million liabilities of $6 million, common shares of $2 million (representing 2 million common shares of $1.00 par), and retained earnings of $2 million. Net sales for the year 2001 were $18 million, and net income was $800,000. As auditors of this company, you are making a review of subsequent events on February 13, 2002, and you find the following.

1. On February 3, 2002, one of Brandt's customers declared bankruptcy. At December 31, 2001, this company owed Brandt $300,000, of which $40,000 was paid in January, 2002.
2. On January 18, 2002, one of the client's three major plants burned.
3. On January 23, 2002, a strike was called at one of Brandt's largest plants, which halted 30% of its production. As of today (February 13) the strike has not been settled.
4. A major electronics enterprise has introduced a line of products that would compete directly with Brandt's primary line, now being produced in a specially designed new plant. Because of manufacturing innovations, the competitor has been able to achieve quality similar to that of Brandt's products, but at a price 50% lower. Brandt officials say they will meet the lower prices, which are high enough to cover variable manufacturing and selling costs but permit recovery of only a portion of fixed costs.
5. Merchandise traded in the open market is recorded in the company's records at $1.40 per unit on December 31, 2001. This price had prevailed for two weeks, after release of an official market report that predicted vastly enlarged supplies; however, no purchases were made at $1.40. The price throughout the preceding year had been about $2.00, which was the level experienced over several years. On January 18, 2002, the price returned to $2.00, after public disclosure of an error in the official calculations of the prior December, correction of which destroyed the expectations of excessive supplies. Inventory at December 31, 2001 was on a lower of cost or market basis.
6. On February 1, 2002, the board of directors adopted a resolution accepting the offer of an investment banker to guarantee the marketing of $1.2 million of preferred shares.

Instructions

State in each case how the 2001 financial statements would be affected, if at all.

C24-6 You are compiling the consolidated financial statements for Vender Corporation International. The corporation's accountant, Vincent Jones, has provided you with the following segment information.

Note 7: Major Segments of Business

VCI conducts funeral service and cemetery operations in the United States and Canada. Substantially all revenues of VCI's major segments of business are from unaffiliated customers. Segment information for fiscal 2001, 2000, and 1999 follows:

	Funeral	Floral	Cemetery	Corporate	Dried Whey	Limousine	Consolidated
				(thousands)			
Revenues:							
2001	$302,000	$10,000	$ 83,000	$ —	$7,000	$14,000	$416,000
2000	245,000	6,000	61,000	—	4,000	8,000	324,000
1999	208,000	3,000	42,000	—	1,000	6,000	260,000
Operating Income:							
2001	$ 79,000	$ 1,500	$ 18,000	$ (36,000)	$ 500	$ 2,000	$ 65,000
2000	64,000	200	12,000	(28,000)	200	400	48,800
1999	54,000	150	6,000	(21,000)	100	350	39,600
Capital Expenditures[a]:							
2001	$ 26,000	$ 1,000	$ 9,000	$ 400	$ 300	$ 1,000	$ 37,700
2000	28,000	2,000	60,000	1,500	100	700	92,300
1999	14,000	25	8,000	600	25	50	22,700
Depreciation and Amortization:							
2001	$ 13,000	$ 100	$ 2,400	$ 1,400	$ 100	$ 200	$ 17,200
2000	10,000	50	1,400	700	50	100	12,300
1999	8,000	25	1,000	600	25	50	9,700
Identifiable Assets:							
2001	$334,000	$ 1,500	$162,000	$114,000	$ 500	$ 8,000	$620,000
2000	322,000	1,000	144,000	52,000	1,000	6,000	526,000
1999	223,000	500	78,000	34,000	500	3,500	339,500

[a]Includes $4,520,000, $111,480,000, and $1,294,000 for the years ended April 30, 2001, 2000, and 1999, respectively, for purchases of businesses.

Instructions

Determine which of the above segments must be reported separately and which can be combined under the category "Other." Then, write a one-page memo to the company's accountant, Vincent Jones, explaining the following:

(a) What segments must be reported separately and what segments can be combined.

(b) What criteria you used to determine reportable segments.

(c) What major items for each must be disclosed.

C24-7 Presented below is an excerpt from the financial statements of **H. J. Heinz Company** segment and geographic data.

The company is engaged principally in one line of business—processed food products—which represents over 90% of consolidated sales. Information about the company business by geographic area is presented in the table below.

There were no material amounts of sales or transfers between geographic areas or between affiliates, and no material amounts of United States export sales.

				Foreign			
(in thousands of U.S. dollars)	Domestic	United Kingdom	Canada	Western Europe	Other	Total	Worldwide
Sales	$2,381,054	$547,527	$216,726	$383,784	$209,354	$1,357,391	$3,738,445
Operating income	246,780	61,282	34,146	29,146	25,111	149,685	396,465
Identifiable assets	1,362,152	265,218	112,620	294,732	143,971	816,541	2,178,693
Capital expenditures	72,712	12,262	13,790	8,253	4,368	38,673	111,385
Depreciation expense	42,279	8,364	3,592	6,355	3,606	21,917	64,196

Instructions

(a) Why does H. J. Heinz not prepare segment information on its products or services?

(b) Why are revenues by geographical area important to disclose?

C24-8 The following article appeared in *The Wall Street Journal.*

WASHINGTON—The Securities and Exchange Commission staff issued guidelines for companies grappling with the problem of dividing up their business into industry segments for their annual reports.

An industry segment is defined by the Financial Accounting Standards Board as a part of an enterprise engaged in providing a product or service or a group of related products or services primarily to unaffiliated customers for a profit.

Although conceding that the process is a "subjective task" that "to a considerable extent, depends on the judgement of management," the SEC staff said companies should consider the nature of the products, the nature of their production and their markets and marketing methods to determine whether products and services should be grouped together or in separate industry segments.

Instructions

(a) What does financial reporting for segments of a business enterprise involve?

(b) Identify the reasons for requiring financial data to be reported by segments.

(c) Identify the possible disadvantages of requiring financial data to be reported by segments.

(d) Identify the accounting difficulties inherent in segment reporting.

C24-9 J. J. Kersee Corporation, a publicly traded company, is preparing the interim financial data that it will issue to its shareholders and the Securities Commission at the end of the first quarter of the 2000–2001 fiscal year. Kersee's financial accounting department has compiled the following summarized revenue and expense data for the first quarter of the year:

Sales	$60,000,000
Cost of goods sold	36,000,000
Variable selling expenses	2,000,000
Fixed selling expenses	3,000,000

Included in the fixed selling expenses was the single lump sum payment of $2 million for television advertisements for the entire year.

Instructions

(a) J. J. Kersee Corporation must issue its quarterly financial statements in accordance with generally accepted accounting principles regarding interim financial reporting.

　1. Explain whether Kersee should report its operating results for the quarter as if the quarter were a separate reporting period in and of itself or as if the quarter were an integral part of the annual reporting period.

　2. State how the sales, cost of goods sold, and fixed selling expenses would be reflected in Kersee Corporation's quarterly report prepared for the first quarter of the 2000–2001 fiscal year. Briefly justify your presentation.

(b) What financial information, as a minimum, must Kersee Corporation disclose to its shareholders in its quarterly reports?

(CMA adapted)

C24-10 The following statement is an excerpt from a document on interim financial reporting:

Interim financial information is essential to provide investors and others with timely information as to the progress of the enterprise. The usefulness of such information rests on the relationship that it has to the annual results of operations. Accordingly, the Board has concluded that each interim period should be viewed primarily as an integral part of an annual period.

In general, the results for each interim period should be based on the accounting principles and practices used by an enterprise in the preparation of its latest annual financial statements unless a change in an accounting practice or policy has been adopted in the current year. The Board has concluded, however, that certain accounting principles and practices followed for annual reporting purposes may require modification at interim reporting dates so that the reported results for the interim period may better relate to the results of operations for the annual period.

Instructions

Listed below are six independent cases on how accounting facts might be reported on an individual company's interim financial reports. For each of these cases, state whether the method proposed to be used for interim reporting would be acceptable under generally accepted accounting principles applicable to interim financial data. Support each answer with a brief explanation.

(a) King Limited takes a physical inventory at year end for annual financial statement purposes. Inventory and cost of sales reported in the interim quarterly statements are based on estimated gross profit rates, because a physical inventory would result in a cessation of operations. The company does have reliable perpetual inventory records.

(b) Florence Limited is planning to report one-fourth of its pension expense each quarter.

(c) Lopez Corp. wrote inventory down to reflect lower of cost or market in the first quarter. At year end, the market exceeds the original acquisition cost of this inventory. Consequently, management plans to write the inventory back up to its original cost as a year-end adjustment.

(d) Witt Corp. realized a large gain on the sale of investments at the beginning of the second quarter. The company wants to report one-third of the gain in each of the remaining quarters.

(e) Marble Limited has estimated its annual audit fee. It plans to prorate this expense equally over all four quarters.

(f) McNeil Inc. was reasonably certain it would have an employee strike in the third quarter. As a result, it shipped heavily during the second quarter but plans to defer the recognition of the sales in excess of the normal sales volume. The deferred sales will be recognized as sales in the third quarter when the strike is in progress. McNeil management thinks this is more nearly representative of normal second- and third-quarter operations.

C24-11 An article in *Barron's* noted:

Okay. Last fall, someone with a long memory and an even longer arm reached into that bureau drawer and came out with a moldy cheese sandwich and the equally moldy notion of corporate forecasts. We tried to find out what happened to the cheese sandwich—but, rats!, even recourse to the Freedom of Information Act didn't help. However, the forecast proposal was dusted off, polished up and found quite serviceable. The SEC, indeed, lost no time in running it up the old flagpole—but no one was very eager to salute. Even after some of the more objectionable features—compulsory corrections and detailed explanations of why the estimates went awry—were peeled off the original proposal.

Seemingly, despite the Commission's smiles and sweet talk, those craven corporations were still afraid that an honest mistake would lead down the primrose path to consent decrees and class action suits. To lay to rest such qualms, the Commission last week approved a "Safe Harbor" rule that, providing the forecasts were made on a reasonable basis and in good faith, protected corporations from litigation should the projections prove wide of the mark (as only about 99% are apt to do).

Instructions

(a) What are the arguments for preparing profit forecasts?

(b) What is the purpose of the "safe harbour" rule?

(c) Why are corporations concerned about presenting profit forecasts?

Using Your Judgement

FINANCIAL REPORTING PROBLEM:
CANADIAN TIRE CORPORATION, LIMITED

In response to the investing public's demand for greater disclosure of corporate expectations for the future, safe harbour rules and legislation have been passed to encourage and protect corporations that issue financial forecasts and projections. Review the company's Management Discussion and Analysis section in Appendix 5B.

Instructions

Refer to the company's financial statements and accompanying notes to answer the following questions.

(a) What general expectation does the company have for the retail industry in the next year? How is Canadian Tire reacting to this expectation?

(b) Give examples of hard data forecasts (if any) that the company discloses for the upcoming year. Give some examples of soft data forecasts. (Hard being defined as concrete and soft being defined as open to judgement, interpretation, or change.)

(c) What caveats or other statements that temper its forecasts does the company make?

(d) What is the difference between a financial forecast and a financial projection?

COMPARATIVE ANALYSIS CASE

Sears Canada Inc. versus Hudson's Bay Company

Instructions

Go to the Digital Tool and, using the annual reports for both companies, answer the following questions.

(a) What specific items do the companies discuss in their Accounting Policies notes (prepare a list of the headings only)?

(b) Note the similarities and differences. Comment and tie into the nature of the businesses.

(c) For what lines of business or segments do the companies present segmented information?

(d) Note and comment on the similarities and differences between the auditors' reports submitted by the independent auditors.

RESEARCH CASES

Case 1

The May/June 1994 issue of *Financial Executive* includes an article by Ray J. Groves, entitled "Financial Disclosure: When More Is Not Better."

Instructions

Read the article and answer the following questions.

(a) What is the author's professional background?

(b) What does the article assert regarding the quantity of disclosure presently required under GAAP?

(c) What specific disclosure requirements does the author find excessive?

(d) As of 1972, how many pages were devoted to the annual report, the footnotes to the financial statements, and the MD&A? What were these figures as of 1982?

(e) What were the author's two major suggestions?

Case 2

Al Rosen, a prominent forensic accountant in Canada, in his article entitled "Easy Prey" (*Canadian Business* April 16, 2001), comments that Canadian investors are being swindled.

Instructions
Read the article and argue for this statement as well as against.

Case 3

In an article entitled "Mind the GAAP," which appeared in *Canadian Business* on May 14, 2001, author Al Rosen argues that generally accepted accounting principles are not generally accepted. In the article he compares the differences between profit and loss for seven companies—Canadian GAAP versus U.S. GAAP.

Instructions
Obtain the financial statements of at least two of the companies and look at the note to the financial statements where the companies reconcile net income under Canadian to net income under U.S. GAAP. What are the major differences? Which earnings number is more useful to users? Why?

ETHICS CASES

Case 1

Patty Gamble, the financial vice-president, and Victoria Maher, the controller, of Castle Manufacturing Corporation are reviewing the company's financial ratios for the years 2000 and 2001. The financial vice-president notes that the profit margin on sales ratio has increased from 6% to 12%, a hefty gain for the two-year period. Gamble is in the process of issuing a media release that emphasizes the efficiency of Castle Manufacturing in controlling cost. Victoria Maher knows that the difference in ratios is due primarily to an earlier company decision to reduce the estimates of warranty and bad debt expense for 2001. The controller, not sure of her supervisor's motives, hesitates to suggest to Gamble that the company's improvement is unrelated to efficiency in controlling cost. To complicate matters, the media release is scheduled in a few days.

Instructions

(a) What, if any, is the ethical dilemma in this situation?
(b) Should Maher, the controller, remain silent? Give reasons.
(c) What stakeholders might be affected by Gamble's media release?
(d) Give your opinion on the following statement and cite reasons: "Because Gamble, the vice-president, is most directly responsible for the media release, Maher has no real responsibility in this matter."

Case 2

In June 2001, the board of directors for Holtzman Enterprises Inc. authorized the sale of $10 million of corporate bonds. Michelle Collins, treasurer for Holtzman Enterprises Inc., is concerned about the date when the bonds are issued. The company really needs the cash, but she is worried that if the bonds are issued before the company's year end (December 31, 2001), the additional liability will have an adverse effect on a number of important ratios. In July, she explains to company president Kenneth Holtzman that if they delay issuing the bonds until after December 31, the bonds will not affect the ratios until December 31, 2002. They will have to report the issuance as a subsequent event, which requires only footnote disclosure. Collins predicts that with expected improved financial performance in 2002, ratios should be better.

Instructions

(a) What are the ethical issues involved?
(b) Should Holtzman agree to the delay?

Accounting and the Time Value of Money

LEARNING OBJECTIVES

. . . .

After studying this appendix, you should be able to:

1. Identify accounting topics where time value of money is relevant.
2. Distinguish between simple and compound interest.
3. Know how to use appropriate compound interest tables.
4. Identify variables fundamental to solving interest problems.
5. Solve future and present value of single sum problems.
6. Solve future value of ordinary and annuity due problems.
7. Solve present value of ordinary and annuity due problems.
8. Use spreadsheet functions to solve time value of money problems.

PREVIEW FOR APPENDIX

The timing of the returns on investments has an important effect on the worth of the investment (asset), and the timing of debt repayments has a similarly important effect on the value of the debt commitment (liability). As a business person, you will be expected to make present and future value measurements and to understand their implications. The purpose of this appendix is to present the tools and techniques that will help you measure the present value of future cash inflows and outflows. The content and organization of the appendix are as follows:

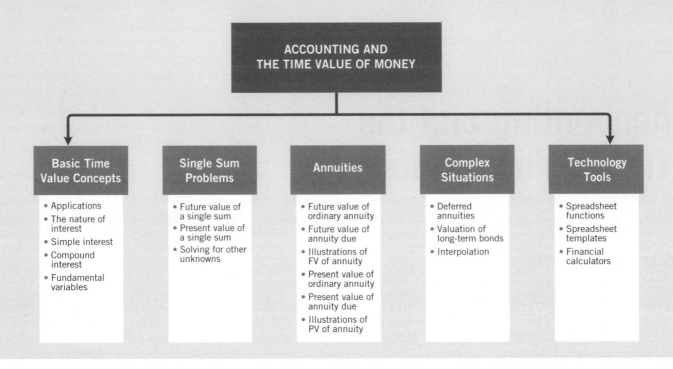

BASIC TIME VALUE CONCEPTS

In accounting (and finance), the term **time value of money** is used to indicate a relationship between time and money—that a dollar received today is worth more than a dollar promised at some time in the future. Why? Because of the opportunity to invest today's dollar and receive interest on the investment. Yet, when you have to decide among various investment or borrowing alternatives, it is essential to be able to compare today's dollar and tomorrow's dollar on the same footing—to "compare apples to apples." We do that by using the concept of **present value**, which has many applications in accounting.

Applications of Time Value Concepts

OBJECTIVE 1

Identify accounting topics where time value of money is relevant.

Compound interest, annuities, and application of present value concepts are relevant to making measurements and disclosures when accounting for various financial statement elements.[1] The following are some examples examined in this book and the chapters in which they appear:

1. **Notes.** Valuing receivables and payables that carry no stated interest rate or a different than market interest rate (Chapters 7 and 15).

2. **Leases.** Valuing assets and obligations to be capitalized under long-term leases, and measuring the amount of the lease payments and annual leasehold amortization (Chapter 21).

3. **Amortization of Premiums and Discounts.** Measuring amortization of premium or discount on both bond investments and bonds payable (Chapters 10 and 15).

4. **Pensions and Other Post-Retirement Benefits.** Measuring service cost components of employers' post-retirement benefits expense and benefit obligations (Chapter 20).

5. **Capital Assets.** Determining the value of assets acquired under deferred-payment contracts (Chapter 11).

6. **Sinking Funds.** Determining the contributions necessary to accumulate a fund for debt retirement (Chapter 15).

7. **Business Combinations.** Determining the value of receivables, payables, liabilities, accruals, goodwill, and commitments acquired or assumed in a "purchase" (Chapters 10 and 13).

8. **Amortization.** Measuring amortization charges under the sinking fund and the annuity methods (Chapter 12).

9. **Instalment Contracts.** Measuring periodic payments on long-term sales or purchase contracts (Chapters 6 and 15).

In addition to their accounting and business applications, compound interest, annuity, and present value concepts are applicable to personal finance and investment decisions. In purchasing a home, planning for retirement, and evaluating alternative investments, you must understand time value of money concepts.

Nature of Interest

Interest **is payment for the use of money.** It is the excess cash received or paid over and above the amount lent or borrowed (principal). For example, if the Toronto Dominion Bank lends you $1,000 with the understanding that you will repay $1,150, the $150 excess over $1,000 represents interest expense to you and interest revenue to the bank.

The amount of interest to be paid is generally stated as a rate over a specific period of time. For example, if you use the $1,000 for one year before repaying $1,150, the rate of interest is 15% per year ($150/$1,000). The custom of expressing interest as a rate is an established business practice.[2]

The interest rate is commonly expressed as it is applied to a one-year time period. Interest of 12% represents a rate of 12% per year, unless otherwise stipulated. The state-

---

[1] J. Alex Milburn, *Incorporating the Time Value of Money Within Financial Accounting* (Toronto: Canadian Institute of Chartered Accountants, 1988), p. 1. This is an excellent study regarding financial accounting and present value measurements. Its objective is to "develop proposals for reflecting the time value of money more fully within the existing financial accounting framework so as to enable a substantive improvement in the usefulness and credibility of financial statements" (p. 1). While we, the authors, accept the basic premise of this study, it is not our intention to examine the model and suggested changes to current financial accounting that are presented. The purpose of this appendix is more basic—to examine the time value of money and show how it can be incorporated in making measurements.

[2] Federal and provincial legislation requires the disclosure of the effective interest rate on an *annual basis* in contracts. That is, instead of, or in addition to, stating the rate as "1% per month," it must be stated as "12% per year" if it is simple interest or "12.68% per year" if it is compounded monthly.

ment that a corporation will pay bond interest of 12%, payable semiannually, means a rate of 6% every six months, not 12% every six months.

How is the *rate* of interest determined? One of the most important factors is the level of **credit risk** (risk of nonpayment). Other factors being equal, the higher the credit risk, the higher the interest rate. Every borrower's risk is evaluated by the lender. A low-risk borrower like Canadian Pacific Ltd. may obtain a loan at or slightly below the going market "prime" rate of interest. You or the neighbourhood delicatessen, however, will probably be charged several percentage points above the prime rate.

Another important factor is **inflation** (change in the general purchasing power of the dollar). Lenders want to protect the purchasing power of the future cash flows to be received (interest payments and return of the principal). If inflation is expected to be significant in the future, lenders will require a higher number of dollars (i.e., a higher interest rate) in order to offset their anticipation that the purchasing power of these dollars will be reduced.

In addition to receiving compensation for risk and expected inflation, lenders also desire a **pure** or **real return** for letting someone else use their money. This real return reflects the amount the lender would charge if there were no possibility of default or expectation of inflation.

The *amount* of interest related to any financing transaction is a function of three variables:

1. **Principal**—the amount borrowed or invested.
2. **Interest Rate**—a percentage of the outstanding principal.
3. **Time**—the number of years or portion of a year that the principal is outstanding.

Simple Interest

Simple interest is calculated on the amount of the principal only. It is the return on (or growth of) the principal for one time period. Simple interest[3] is commonly expressed as:

$$\text{Interest} = p \times i \times n$$

where

$p = \text{principal}$
$i = \text{rate of interest for a single period}$
$n = \text{number of periods}$

To illustrate, if you borrowed $1,000 for a three-year period, with a simple interest rate of 15% per year, the total interest to be paid would be $450, calculated as follows:

$$\begin{aligned}\text{Interest} &= (p)(i)(n) \\ &= (\$1,000)(0.15)(3) \\ &= \$450\end{aligned}$$

Compound Interest

John Maynard Keynes, the legendary English economist, supposedly called it magic. Mayer Rothschild, the founder of the famous European banking firm, is said to have proclaimed it the eighth wonder of the world. Today people continue to extol its wonder and its power.[4] The object of their affection is compound interest.

Compound interest *is calculated on the principal and any interest earned that has not been paid.* To illustrate the difference between simple interest and compound inter-

---

[3] Simple interest is also expressed as i (interest) $= P$(principal) $\times R$(rate) $\times T$(time).

[4] Here is an illustration of the power of time and compounding interest on money. In 1626, Peter Minuit bought Manhatten Island from the Manhattoe Indians for $24 worth of trinkets and beads. If the Indians had taken a boat to Holland, invested the $24 in Dutch securities returning just 6% per year, and kept the money and interest invested at 6%, by 1971 they would have had $13 billion, enough to buy back all the land on the island and still have a couple of billion dollars left (*Forbes*, June 1, 1971). By 1998, 372 years after the trade, the $24 would have grown to approximately $63 billion—$62 trillion had the interest rate been 8%.

est, assume that you deposit $1,000 in the Last Canadian Bank, where it earns simple interest of 9% per year. Assume that you deposit another $1,000 in the First Canadian Bank, where it earns annually compounded interest of 9%. Finally, assume that in both cases you do not withdraw any interest until three years from the date of deposit. The calculation of interest to be received is shown in Illustration A-1.

ILLUSTRATION A-1
Simple vs. Compound Interest

	Last Canadian Bank			First Canadian Bank		
	Simple Interest Calculation	Simple Interest	Accumulated Year-End Balance	Compound Interest Calculation	Compound Interest	Accumulated Year-End Balance
Year 1	$1,000.00 × 9%	$ 90.00	$1,090.00	$1,000.00 × 9%	$ 90.00	$1,090.00
Year 2	1,000.00 × 9%	90.00	1,180.00	1,090.00 × 9%	98.10	1,188.10
Year 3	1,000.00 × 9%	90.00	1,270.00	1,188.10 × 9%	106.93	1,295.03
		$270.00 ←	$25.03 Difference	→ $295.03		

Note that simple interest uses the initial principal of $1,000 to calculate the interest in all three years, while compound interest uses the accumulated balance (principal plus interest to date) at each year end to calculate interest in the succeeding year. Obviously, if you had a choice between investing at simple interest or at compound interest, you would choose compound interest, all other things—especially risk—being equal. In the example, compounding provides $25.03 of additional interest income.

Compound interest is generally applied in business situations. Financial managers view and evaluate their investment opportunities in terms of a series of periodic returns, each of which can be reinvested to yield additional returns. Simple interest is generally applicable only to short-term investments and debts that are due within one year.

Compound Interest Tables

Five different compound interest tables are presented at the end of this appendix (see pages A-27–A-31). These tables are the source for various "interest factors" used to solve problems that involve interest in this appendix and throughout the book. The titles of these five tables and their contents are:

OBJECTIVE 3
Know how to use appropriate compound interest tables.

1. **Future Value of 1.** Contains the amounts to which $1.00 will accumulate if deposited now at a specified rate and left for a specified number of periods (Table A-1).
2. **Present Value of 1.** Contains the amounts that must be deposited now at a specified rate of interest to equal $1.00 at the end of a specified number of periods (Table A-2).
3. **Future Value of an Ordinary Annuity of 1.** Contains the amounts to which periodic rents of $1.00 will accumulate if the rents are invested at the end of each period at a specified rate of interest for a specified number of periods (Table A-3).
4. **Present Value of an Ordinary Annuity of 1.** Contains the amounts that must be deposited now at a specified rate of interest to permit withdrawals of $1.00 at the end of regular periodic intervals for the specified number of periods (Table A-4).
5. **Present Value of an Annuity Due of 1.** Contains the amounts that must be deposited now at a specified rate of interest to permit withdrawals of $1.00 at the beginning of regular periodic intervals for the specified number of periods (Table A-5).

Illustration A-2 shows the general format and content of these tables. It is from Table A-1, "Future Value of 1," which indicates the amount to which a dollar accumulates at the end of each of five periods at three different rates of compound interest.

ILLUSTRATION A-2
Excerpt from Table A-1

	Future Value of 1 at Compounding Interest		
Period	9%	10%	11%
1	1.09000	1.10000	1.11000
2	1.18810	1.21000	1.23210
3	1.29503	1.33100	1.36763
4	1.41158	1.46410	1.51807
5	1.53862	1.61051	1.68506

Interpreting the table, if $1.00 is invested for three periods at a compound interest rate of 9% per period, it will amount to $1.30 (1.29503 × $1.00), the compound future avalue. If $1.00 is invested at 11%, at the end of four periods it amounts to $1.52. If the investment is $1,000 instead of $1.00, it will amount to $1,295.03 ($1,000 × 1.29503) if invested at 9% for three periods, or $1,518.07 if invested at 11% for four periods.

Throughout the foregoing discussion and the discussion that follows, the use of the term *periods* instead of *years* is intentional. While interest is generally expressed as an annual rate, the compounding period is often shorter. Therefore, the annual interest rate must be converted to correspond to the length of the period. To convert the "annual interest rate" into the "compounding period interest rate," *divide the annual rate by the number of compounding periods per year.* In addition, the number of periods is determined by *multiplying the number of years involved by the number of compounding periods per year.*

To illustrate, assume that $1.00 is invested for six years at 8% annual interest compounded quarterly. Using Table A-1, the amount to which this $1.00 will accumulate is determined by reading the factor that appears in the 2% column (8% ÷ 4) on the 24th row (6 years × 4), namely 1.60844, or approximately $1.61.

Because interest is theoretically earned every second of every day, it is possible to calculate continuously compounded interest. As a practical matter, however, most business transactions assume interest is compounded no more frequently than daily.

How often interest is compounded can make a substantial difference to the rate of return achieved. For example, 9% interest compounded daily provides a 9.42% annual yield, or a difference of 0.42%. The 9.42% is referred to as the effective yield or rate,[5] whereas the 9% annual interest rate is called the stated, nominal, coupon, or face rate. When the compounding frequency is greater than once a year, the effective interest rate is higher than the stated rate.

Fundamental Variables

OBJECTIVE 4

Identify variables fundamental to solving interest problems.

The following four variables are fundamental to all compound interest problems:

1. **Rate of Interest.** This rate, unless otherwise stated, is an annual rate that must be adjusted to reflect the length of the compounding period if it is less than a year.
2. **Number of Time Periods.** This is the number of compounding periods for which interest is to be computed.
3. **Future Value.** The value at a future date of a given sum or sums invested, assuming compound interest.
4. **Present Value.** The value now (present time) of a future sum or sums discounted, assuming compound interest.

The relationship of these four variables is depicted in the **time diagram** in Illustration A-3.

---

[5] The formula for calculating the effective annual rate in situations where the compounding frequency (n) is more than once a year is as follows:

$$\text{Effective rate} = (1 + i)^n - 1$$

where i = the interest rate per compounding period, and
n = the number of compounding periods per year

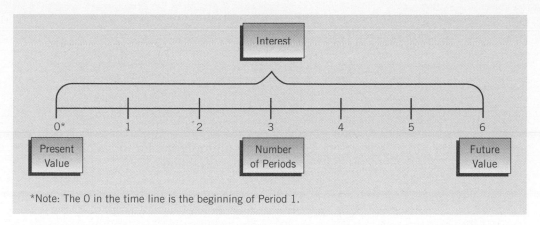

In some cases all four of these variables are known, but in many business situations at least one is unknown. Frequently, the accountant is expected to determine the unknown amount or amounts. To do this, a time diagram can be very helpful in understanding the nature of the problem and finding a solution.

The remainder of the appendix covers the following six major time value of money concepts. Both formula and interest table approaches are used to illustrate how problems may be solved:

1. Future value of a single sum.
2. Present value of a single sum.
3. Future value of an ordinary annuity.
4. Future value of an annuity due.
5. Present value of an ordinary annuity.
6. Present value of an annuity due.

SINGLE SUM PROBLEMS

Many business and investment decisions involve a single amount of money that either exists now or will exist in the future. Single sum problems can generally be classified into one of the following two categories:

1. Determining the *unknown future value* of a known single sum of money that is invested for a specified number of periods at a specified interest rate.
2. Determining the *unknown present value* of a known single sum of money that is discounted for a specified number of periods at a specified interest rate.

Future Value of a Single Sum

The **future value** of a sum of money is the future value of that sum when left to accumulate for a certain number of periods at a specified rate of interest per period.

The amount to which 1 (one) will accumulate may be expressed as a formula:

$$FVF_{n,\,i} = (1 + i)^n$$

where

$FVF_{n,\,i}$ = future value factor for n periods at i interest
i = rate of interest for a single period
n = number of periods

To illustrate, assume that $1.00 is invested at 9% interest compounded annually for three years. The amounts to which the $1.00 will accumulate at the end of each year are:

$$FVF_{1,\,9\%} = (1 + 0.09)^1 \text{ for the end of the first year.}$$
$$FVF_{2,\,9\%} = (1 + 0.09)^2 \text{ for the end of the second year.}$$
$$FVF_{3,\,9\%} = (1 + 0.09)^3 \text{ for the end of the third year.}$$

These compound amounts accumulate as shown in Illustration A-4.

ILLUSTRATION A-4
Accumulation of Compounding
Amounts

Period	Beginning-of-Period Amount	$\times$	Multiplier $(1 + i)$	$=$	End-of-Period Amount*	Formula $(1+i)^n$
1	1.00000		1.09		1.09000	$(1.09)^1$
2	1.09000		1.09		1.18810	$(1.09)^2$
3	1.18810		1.09		1.29503	$(1.09)^3$

*These amounts appear in Table A-1 in the 9% column.

To calculate the *future value of any single amount*, multiply the future value of 1 factor (future value factor) by its present value (principal) as follows:

$$FV = PV(FVF_{n,\,i})$$

where

FV = future value
PV = present value (principal or single sum)
$FVF_{n,\,i}$ = future value factor for n periods at i interest

For example, what is the future value of $50,000 invested for five years at 11% compounded annually? In time-diagram form, this investment situation is indicated in Illustration A-5.

ILLUSTRATION A-5
Time Diagram for Future Value
Calculation

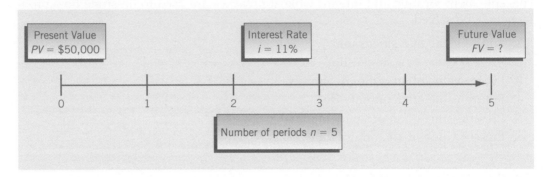

This investment problem is solved as follows.

$$FV = PV(FVF_{n,\,i})$$
$$= \$50,000(FVF_{5,\,11\%})$$
$$= \$50,000\,(1.68506)$$
$$= \$84,253.$$

The future value factor of 1.68506 appears in Table A-1 in the 11% column and 5-period row.

To illustrate a more complex business situation, assume that at the beginning of 2001 Ontario Hydro deposits $250 million in an escrow account with the Royal Bank as a commitment toward a small nuclear power plant to be completed December 31, 2004. How much will be on deposit at the end of four years if interest is compounded semiannually at 10%?

With a known present value of $250 million, a total of eight compounding periods (4 × 2), and an interest rate of 5% per compounding period (10% ÷ 2), this problem can be time-diagrammed and the future value determined as indicated in Illustration A-6.

ILLUSTRATION A-6
Time Diagram for Future Value
Calculation

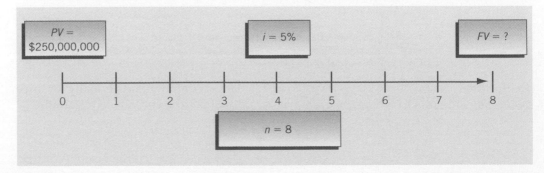

$$FV = \$250{,}000{,}000(FVF_{8,\,5\%})$$
$$= \$250{,}000{,}000(1.47746)$$
$$= \$369{,}365{,}000.$$

The deposit of $250 million will accumulate to $369,365,000 by December 31, 2004. The future value factor is found in Table A-1 (5% column and the 8-period row).

Present Value of a Single Sum

A previous example showed that $50,000 invested at an annually compounded interest rate of 11% will be worth $84,253 at the end of five years. It follows that $84,253 to be received five years from now is presently worth $50,000, given an 11% interest rate (i.e., $50,000 is the present value of this $84,253). The present value is the amount that must be invested now to produce a known future value. The *present value is always a smaller amount than the known future value because interest is earned and accumulated on the present value to the future date.* In determining the future value we move forward in time using a process of accumulation, while in determining present value we move backward in time using the process of discounting.

The present value of 1 (one) (present value factor) may be expressed as a formula:

where
$$PVF_{n,\,i} = \frac{1}{(1 + i)^n}$$

$PVF_{n,\,i}$ = present value factor for n periods at i interest

To illustrate, assume that $1.00 is discounted for three periods at 9%. The present value of the $1.00 is discounted each period as follows.

$$PVF_{1,\,9\%} = 1/(1 + 0.09)^1 \text{ for the first period}$$
$$PVF_{2,\,9\%} = 1/(1 + 0.09)^2 \text{ for the second period}$$
$$PVF_{3,\,9\%} = 1/(1 + 0.09)^3 \text{ for the third period}$$

Therefore, the $1.00 is discounted as shown in Illustration A-7.

Discount Periods	Future Value	÷	Divisor $(1 + i)^n$	=	Present Value*	Formula $1/(1+i)^n$
1	1.00000		1.09		0.91743	$1/(1.09)^1$
2	1.00000		$(1.09)^2$		0.84168	$1/(1.09)^2$
3	1.00000		$(1.09)^3$		0.77218	$1/(1.09)^3$

*These amounts appear in Table A-2 in the 9% column.

ILLUSTRATION A-7
Present Value of $1 Discounted at 9% for Three Periods

Table A-2, "Present Value of 1," shows how much must be invested now at various interest rates to equal 1 at the end of various periods of time.

The present value of *any single future value* is as follows:

where
$$PV = FV(PVF_{n,\,i})$$

PV = present value
FV = future value

$PVF_{n,\,i}$ = present value of 1 for n periods at i interest

To illustrate, assume that your favourite uncle proposes to give you $4,000 for a trip to Europe when you graduate three years from now. He will finance the trip by investing a sum of money now at 8% compound interest that will accumulate to $4,000 upon your graduation. The only conditions are that you graduate and that you tell him how much to invest now.

To impress your uncle, you might set up a time diagram as shown in Illustration A-8 and solve the problem as follows.

ILLUSTRATION A-8
Time Diagram for Present Value
Calculation

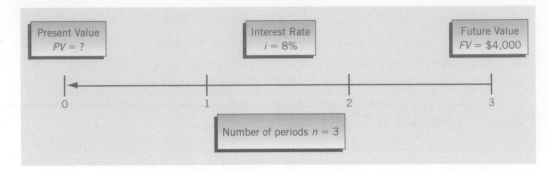

$$PV = \$4,000(PVF_{3,\ 8\%})$$
$$= \$4,000(0.79383)$$
$$= \$3,175.32.$$

Advise your uncle to invest $3,175.32 now to provide you with $4,000 upon graduation. To satisfy your uncle's other condition, you must simply pass this course and many more. Note that the present value factor of 0.79383 is found in Table A-2 (8% column, 3-period row).

Solving for Other Unknowns

In calculating either the future value or the present value in the previous single sum illustrations, both the number of periods and the interest rate were known. In business situations, both the future value and the present value may be known, and either the number of periods or the interest rate may be unknown. The following two illustrations demonstrate how to solve single sum problems when there is either an unknown number of periods (n) or an unknown interest rate (i). These illustrations show that if any three of the four values (future value, FV; present value, PV; number of periods, n; interest rate, i) are known, the one unknown can be derived.

Illustration: Calculation of the Number of Periods. A local charity in Regina wants to accumulate $70,000 for the construction of a day-care centre. If at the beginning of the current year the association is able to deposit $47,811 in a building fund that earns 10% interest compounded annually, how many years will it take for the fund to accumulate to $70,000?

In this situation, the present value ($47,811), future value ($70,000), and interest rate (10%) are known. A time diagram of this investment is shown in Illustration A-9.

ILLUSTRATION A-9
Time Diagram for Number of
Periods Calculation

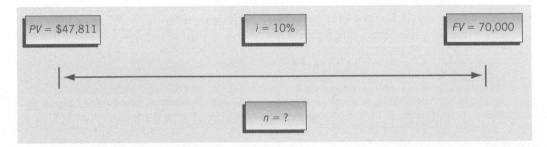

The unknown number of periods can be determined using either the future value or present value approaches, as shown below.

Future Value Approach	Present Value Approach
$FV = PV(FVF_{n,\ 10\%})$	$PV = FV(PVF_{n,\ 10\%})$
$\$70,000 = \$47,811(FVF_{n,\ 10\%})$	$\$47,811 = \$70,000(PVF_{n,\ 10\%})$
$FVF_{n,\ 10\%} = \dfrac{\$70,000}{\$47,811} = 1.46410$	$PVF_{n,\ 10\%} = \dfrac{\$47,811}{\$70,000} = 0.68301$

Using the future value factor of 1.46410, refer to Table A-1 and read down the 10% column to find that factor in the 4-period row. Thus, it will take four years for the $47,811 to accumulate to $70,000. Using the present value factor of 0.68301, refer to Table A-2 and read down the 10% column to also find that factor is in the 4-period row.

Illustration: Calculation of the Interest Rate. The Canadian Academic Accounting Association wants to have $141,000 available five years from now to provide scholarships to individuals who undertake a PhD program. At present, the executive of the CAAA has determined that $80,000 may be invested for this purpose. What rate of interest must be earned on the investments in order to accumulate the $141,000 five years from now?

Illustration A-10 provides a time diagram of this problem.

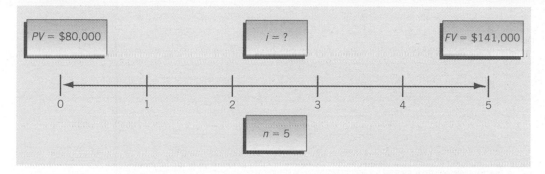

Given that the present value, future value, and number of periods are known, the unknown interest rate can be determined using either the future value or present value approaches, as shown below.

Future Value Approach	Present Value Approach
$FV = PV(FVF_{5,\,i})$	$PV = FV(PVF_{5,\,i})$
$\$141{,}000 = \$80{,}000(FVF_{5,\,i})$	$\$80{,}000 = \$141{,}000(PVF_{5,\,i})$
$FVF_{5,\,i} = \dfrac{\$141{,}000}{\$80{,}000} = 1.7625$	$PVF_{5,\,i} = \dfrac{\$80{,}000}{\$141{,}000} = 0.5674$

Using the future value factor of 1.7625, refer to Table A-1 and read across the 5-period row to find a close match of this future value factor in the 12% column. Thus, the $80,000 must be invested at 12% to accumulate to $141,000 at the end of five years. Using the present value factor of 0.5674 and Table A-2, reading across the 5-period row shows this factor in the 12% column.

ANNUITIES

The preceding discussion involved only the accumulation or discounting of a single principal sum. Accountants frequently encounter situations in which a series of amounts are to be paid or received over time (e.g., when loans or sales are paid in instalments, invested funds are partially recovered at regular intervals, and cost savings are realized repeatedly). When a commitment involves a series of equal payments made at equal intervals of time, it is called an annuity. By definition, an annuity requires that (1) *the periodic payments or receipts* (called *rents*) *always be the same amount*; (2) the *interval between such rents always be the same*; and (3) the *interest be compounded once each interval*.

The future value of an annuity *is the sum of all the rents plus the accumulated compound interest on them*. Rents may, however, occur at either the beginning or the end of the periods. To distinguish annuities under these two alternatives, an annuity is classified as an ordinary annuity *if the rents occur at the end of each period, and as an annuity due if the rents occur at the beginning of each period*.

OBJECTIVE 6
....
Solve future value of ordinary
and annuity due problems.

Future Value of an Ordinary Annuity

One approach to calculating the future value of an annuity is to determine the future value of each rent in the series and then aggregate these individual future values. For example, assume that $1 is deposited at the **end** of each of five years (an ordinary annuity) and earns 12% interest compounded annually. The future value can be calculated as indicated in Illustration A-11 using the "Future Value of 1" for each of the five $1 rents.

ILLUSTRATION A-11
Solving for the Future Value of
an Ordinary Annuity

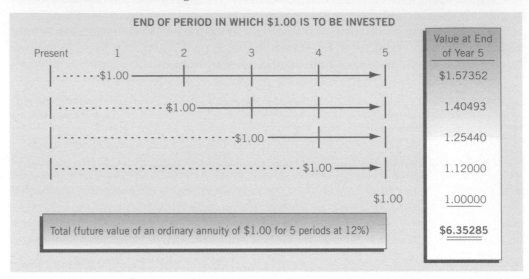

Although the foregoing procedure for computing the future value of an ordinary annuity produces the correct answer, it is cumbersome if the number of rents is large. A more efficient way of determining the future value of an ordinary annuity of 1 is to apply the following formula:

$$FVF - OA_{n, i} = \frac{(1 + i)^n - 1}{i}$$

where

$FVF - OA_{n, i}$ = future value factor of an ordinary annuity
n = number of compounding periods
i = rate of interest per period

Using this formula, Table A-3 has been developed to show the "Future Value of an Ordinary Annuity of 1" for various interest rates and investment periods. Illustration A-12 is an excerpt from this table.

ILLUSTRATION A-12
Excerpt from Table A-3

	Future value of an ordinary annuity of 1		
Period	10%	11%	12%
1	1.00000	1.00000	1.00000
2	2.10000	2.11000	2.12000
3	3.31000	3.34210	3.37440
4	4.64100	4.70973	4.77933
5	6.10510	6.22780	6.35285*

*Note that this factor is the same as the sum of the future values of 1 factors shown in Illustration A-11.

Interpreting the table, if $1.00 is invested at the end of each year for four years at 11% interest compounded annually, the value of the annuity at the end of the fourth year will be $4.71 (4.70973 × $1.00). The $4.71 is made up of $4 of rent payments ($1 at the end of each of the 4 years) and compound interest of $0.71.

The future value of an ordinary annuity is calculated as follows.

$$\text{Future value of an ordinary annuity} = R(FVF - OA_{n, i})$$

where

$FVF - OA_{n, i}$ = future value factor of an ordinary annuity for
n periods at i interest
R = periodic rent

To illustrate, what is the future value of five $5,000 deposits made at the end of each of the next five years, earning interest at 12%? The time diagram is shown in Illustration A-13 and the derivation of the solution for this problem follows.

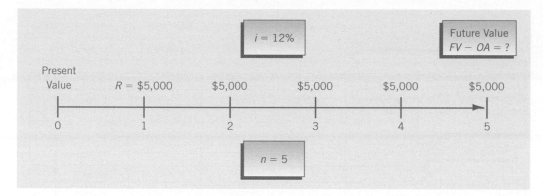

ILLUSTRATION A-13
Time Diagram for Future Value Calculation of an Ordinary Annuity

$$\text{Future value of an ordinary annuity} = R(FVF - OA_{n,\,i})$$
$$= \$5,000(FVF - OA_{5,\,12\%})$$
$$= \$5,000\left(\frac{(1 + 0.12)^5 - 1}{0.12}\right)$$
$$= \$5,000(6.35285)$$
$$= \$31,764.25$$

The future value factor of an ordinary annuity of 6.35285 is found in Table A-3 (12% column, 5-period row).

To illustrate these calculations in a business situation, assume that Lightning Electronics Limited's management decides to deposit $75,000 at the end of each six-month period for the next three years for the purpose of accumulating enough money to meet debts that mature in three years. What is the future value that will be on deposit at the end of three years if the annual interest rate is 10%?

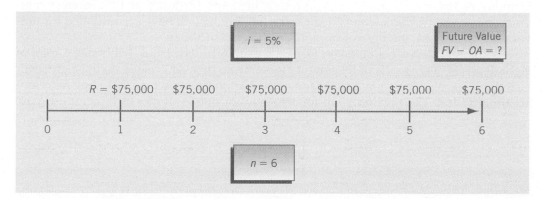

ILLUSTRATION A-14
Time Diagram for Future Value Calculation of an Ordinary Annuity

$$\text{Future value of an ordinary annuity} = R(FVF - OA_{n,\,i})$$
$$= \$75,000(FVF - OA_{6,\,5\%})$$
$$= \$75,000\left(\frac{(1 + 0.05)^6 - 1}{0.05}\right)$$
$$= \$75,000(6.80191)$$
$$= \$510,143.25$$

Thus, six deposits of $75,000 made at the end of every six months and earning 5% per period will grow to $510,143.25 at the time of the last deposit.

Future Value of an Annuity Due

The preceding analysis of an **ordinary annuity** was based on the fact that the periodic rents occur at the **end** of each period. An annuity due is based on the fact that the periodic rents occur at the **beginning** of each period. This means an annuity due will accumulate interest during the first period whereas an ordinary annuity will not. Therefore, the significant difference between the two types of annuities is in the number of interest accumulation periods involved. The distinction is shown graphically in Illustration A-15.

ILLUSTRATION A-15
Comparison of the Future Value of an Ordinary Annuity With that of an Annuity Due

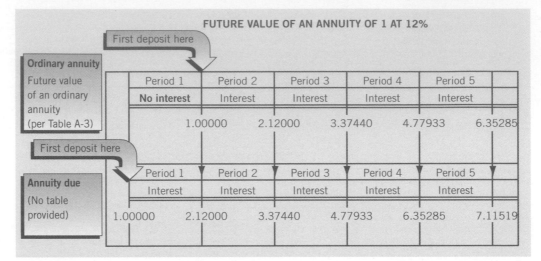

Because the cash flows from the annuity due come exactly one period earlier than for an ordinary annuity, the future value of the annuity due factor is exactly 12% higher than the ordinary annuity factor. Therefore, *to determine the future value of an annuity due factor, multiply the corresponding future value of the ordinary annuity factor by one plus the interest rate.* For example, to determine the future value of an annuity due factor for five periods at 12% compound interest, simply multiply the future value of an ordinary annuity factor for five periods (6.35285) by one plus the interest rate (1 + 0.12) to arrive at the future value of an annuity due, 7.11519 (6.35285 × 1.12).

To illustrate, assume that Hank Lotadough plans to deposit $800 a year on each birthday of his son Howard, starting today, his tenth birthday, at 12% interest compounded annually. Hank wants to know the amount he will have accumulated for university expenses by the time of his son's eighteenth birthday.

As the first deposit is made on his son's tenth birthday, Hank will make a total of eight deposits over the life of the annuity (assume no deposit is made on the eighteenth birthday). Because each deposit is made at the beginning of each period, they represent an annuity due. The time diagram for this annuity due is shown in Illustration A-16.

ILLUSTRATION A-16
Time Diagram for Future Value Calculation of an Annuity Due

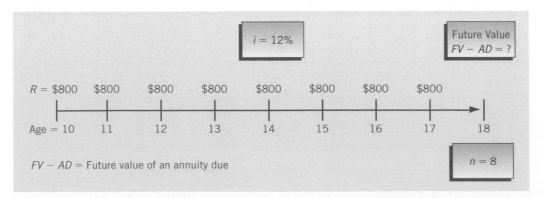

Referring to Table A-3, "Future Value of an Ordinary Annuity of 1," for eight periods at 12%, a factor of 12.29969 is found. This factor is then multiplied by (1 + 0.12) to arrive at the future value of an annuity due factor. As a result, the accumulated amount on his son's eighteenth birthday is calculated as shown in Illustration A-17.

ILLUSTRATION A-17
Calculation of the Future Value
of an Annuity Due

1. Future value of an ordinary annuity of 1 for 8 periods at 12% (Table A-3)	12.29969
2. Factor (1 + 0.12)	× 1.12
3. Future value of an annuity due of 1 for 8 periods at 12%	13.77565
4. Periodic deposit (rent)	× $800
5. Accumulated value on son's eighteenth birthday	$11,020.52

Because expenses to go to university for four years are considerably in excess of $11,000, Howard will likely have to develop his own plan to save additional funds.

Illustrations of Future Value of Annuity Problems

In the previous annuity examples, three values were known (amount of each rent, interest rate, and number of periods) and were used to determine the unknown fourth value (future value). The following illustrations demonstrate how to solve problems when the unknown is (1) the amount of the rents; or (2) the number of rents in ordinary annuity situations.

Illustration: Calculating the Amount of Each Rent. Assume that you wish to accumulate $14,000 for a down payment on a condominium five years from now and that you can earn an annual return of 8% compounded semiannually during the next five years. How much should you deposit at the end of each six-month period?

The $14,000 is the future value of 10 (5 × 2) semiannual end-of-period payments of an unknown amount at an interest rate of 4% (8% ÷ 2). This problem is time-diagrammed in Illustration A-18.

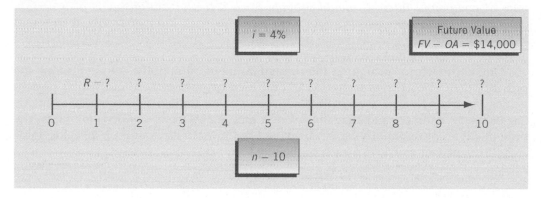

ILLUSTRATION A-18
Time Diagram for Calculating
the Semiannual Payment of an
Ordinary Annuity or Rent

Using the formula for the future value of an ordinary annuity, the amount of each rent is determined as follows.

$$\text{Future value of an ordinary annuity} = R(FVF - OA_{n,\,i})$$
$$\$14,000 = R(FVF - OA_{10,\,4\%})$$
$$\$14,000 = R(12.00611)$$
$$\frac{\$14,000}{12.00611} = R$$
$$R = \$1,166.07$$

Thus, you must make 10 semiannual deposits of $1,166.07 each in order to accumulate $14,000 for your down payment. The future value of an ordinary annuity of 1 factor of 12.00611 is provided in Table A-3 (4% column, 10-period row).

Illustration: Calculating the Number of Periodic Rents. Suppose that your company wants to accumulate $117,332 by making periodic deposits of $20,000 at the end of each year that will earn 8% compounded annually. How many deposits must be made?

The $117,332 represents the future value of $n(?)$ $20,000 deposits at an 8% annual rate of interest. Illustration A-19 provides a time diagram for this problem.

ILLUSTRATION A-19
Time Diagram for Number of
Periods Calculation for an
Ordinary Annuity

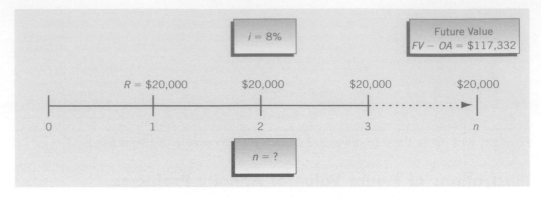

Using the future value of an ordinary annuity formula, the factor is determined as follows.

$$\text{Future value of an ordinary annuity} = R(FVF - OA_{n,\,i})$$
$$\$117{,}332 = \$20{,}000(FVF - OA_{n,\,8\%})$$
$$(FVF - OA_{n,\,8\%}) = \frac{\$117{,}332}{\$20{,}000} = 5.86660$$

Using Table A-3 and reading down the 8% column, 5.86660 is in the 5-period row. Thus, five deposits of $20,000 each must be made.

Present Value of an Ordinary Annuity

OBJECTIVE 7

Solve present value of
ordinary and annuity due
problems.

The *present value of an annuity* *may be viewed as the single amount that, if invested now at compound interest, would provide for a series of withdrawals of a certain amount per period for a specific number of future periods*. In other words, the present value of an ordinary annuity is the present value of a series of rents to be withdrawn at the end of each equal interval.

One approach to calculating the present value of an annuity is to determine the present value of each rent in the series and then aggregate these individual present values. For example, assume that $1.00 is to be received at the *end* of each of five periods (an ordinary annuity) and that the interest rate is 12% compounded annually. The present value of this annuity can be calculated as shown in Illustration A-20 using Table A-2, "Present Value of 1," for each of the five $1 rents.

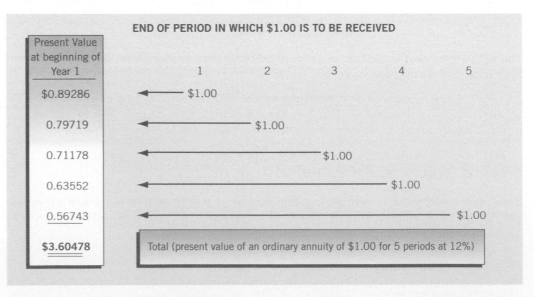

This calculation indicates that if the single sum of $3.60 is invested today at 12% interest, $1.00 can be withdrawn at the end of each period for five periods. This procedure is cumbersome. Using the following formula is a more efficient way to determine the present value of an ordinary annuity of 1:

$$PVF - OA_{n,i} = \frac{1 - \frac{1}{(1+i)^n}}{i}$$

Table A-4, "Present Value of an Ordinary Annuity of 1," is based on this formula. Illustration A-21 is an excerpt from this table.

Present Value of an Ordinary Annuity of 1			
Period	10%	11%	12%
1	0.90909	0.90090	0.89286
2	1.73554	1.71252	1.69005
3	2.48685	2.44371	2.40183
4	3.16986	3.10245	3.03735
5	3.79079	3.69590	3.60478*

*Note that this factor is equal to the sum of the present value of 1 factors shown in the previous schedule.

ILLUSTRATION A-21
Excerpt from Table A-4

The general formula for the present value of any ordinary annuity is as follows.

Present value of an ordinary annuity $= R(PVF - OA_{n,i})$

where

$PVF - OA_{n,i}$ = present value of an ordinary annuity of 1 factor
R = periodic rent (ordinary annuity)

To illustrate, what is the present value of rental receipts of $6,000, each to be received at the end of each of the next five years when discounted at 12%? This problem is time-diagrammed in Illustration A-22 and the solution follows.

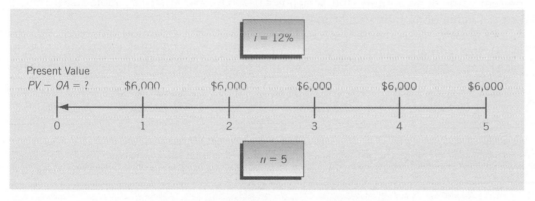

ILLUSTRATION A-22
Time Diagram for Present Value Calculation of an Ordinary Annuity

Present value of an ordinary annuity $= R(PVF - OA_{n,i})$
$= \$6,000(PVF - OA_{5,\,12\%})$
$= \$6,000(3.60478)$
$= \$21,628.68$

The present value of the five ordinary annuity rental receipts of $6,000 each is $21,628.68. The present value of the ordinary annuity factor, 3.60478, is from Table A-4 (12% column, 5-period row).

Present Value of An Annuity Due

In the discussion of the present value of an ordinary annuity, the final rent was discounted back the same number of periods as there were rents. In determining the present value of an annuity due, there is one fewer discount periods. This distinction is shown graphically in Illustration A-23.

ILLUSTRATION A-23

Comparison of the Present Value of an Ordinary Annuity with that of an Annuity Due

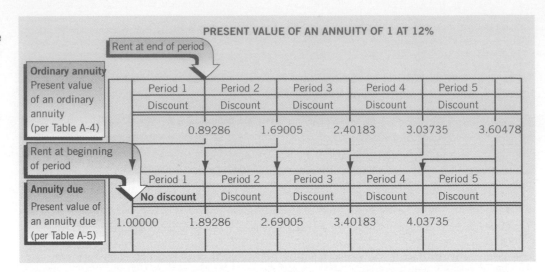

Because each cash flow (rent) comes exactly one period sooner in the present value of an annuity due, the present value of the cash flows is exactly 12% higher than the present value of an ordinary annuity. Thus, *the present value of an annuity due factor can be found by multiplying the present value of an ordinary annuity factor by one plus the interest rate.* For example, to determine the present value of an annuity due factor for five periods at 12% interest, take the present value of an ordinary annuity factor for five periods at 12% interest (3.60478) and multiply it by 1.12 to arrive at the present value of an annuity due, which is 4.03735 (3.60478 × 1.12). Table A-5 provides present value of annuity due factors.

To illustrate, assume that Space Odyssey Inc. rents a communications satellite for four years with annual rental payments of $4.8 million to be made at the beginning of each year. Assuming an annual interest rate of 11%, what is the present value of the rental obligations?

This problem is time-diagrammed in Illustration A-24.

ILLUSTRATION A-24

Time Diagram for Present Value Calculation of an Annuity Due

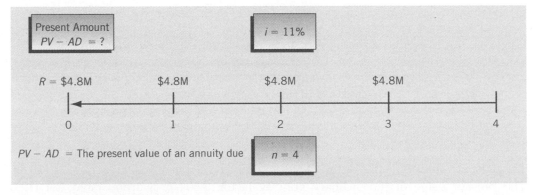

This problem can be solved as shown in Illustration A-25.

ILLUSTRATION A-25

Calculations of Present Value of an Annuity Due

1. Present value factor of an ordinary annuity of 1 for 4 periods at 11% (Table A-4)	3.10245
2. Factor (1 + 0.11)	× 1.11
3. Present value factor of an annuity due of 1 for 4 periods at 11%	3.44371
4. Periodic deposit (rent)	× $4,800,000
5. Present value of payments	$16,529.808

Since Table A-5 gives present value of an annuity due factors, it can be used to obtain the required factor 3.44371 (in the 11% column, 4-period row).

Illustrations of Present Value of Annuity Problems

The following illustrations show how to solve problems when the unknown is (1) the present value; (2) the interest rate; or (3) the amount of each rent for present value of annuity problems.

Illustration: Calculation of the Present Value of an Ordinary Annuity. You have just won Lotto B.C. totalling $4,000,000. You will be paid the amount of $200,000 at the end of each of the next 20 years. What amount have you really won? That is, what is the present value of the $200,000 cheques you will receive over the next 20 years? A time diagram of this enviable situation is shown in Illustration A-26 (assuming an interest rate of 10%).

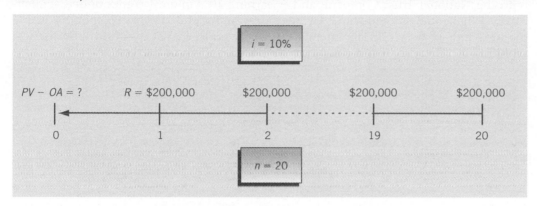

ILLUSTRATION A-26
Time Diagram for Present Value
Calculation of an Annuity Due

The present value is determined as follows:

$$\text{Present value of an ordinary annuity} = R(PVF - OA_{n,\,i})$$
$$= \$200,000(PVF - OA_{20,\,10\%})$$
$$= \$200,000(8.51356)$$
$$= \$1,702,712$$

As a result, if Lotto B.C. deposits $1,702,712 now and earns 10% interest, it can draw $200,000 a year for 20 years to pay you the $4,000,000.

Illustration: Calculation of the Interest Rate. Many shoppers make purchases by using a credit card. When you receive an invoice for payment, you may pay the total amount due or pay the balance in a certain number of payments. For example, if you receive an invoice from VISA with a balance due of $528.77 and are invited to pay it off in 12 equal monthly payments of $50.00 each with the first payment due one month from now, what rate of interest are you paying?

The $528.77 represents the present value of the twelve $50 payments at an unknown rate of interest. This situation is time-diagrammed in Illustration A-27, which is followed by the determination of the interest rate.

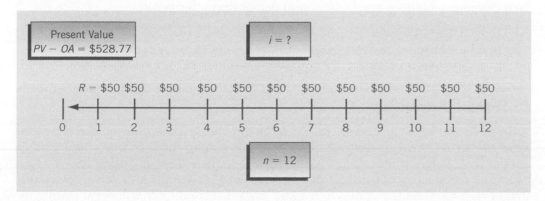

ILLUSTRATION A-27
Time Diagram for Rate of
Interest Calculation of an
Ordinary Annuity

$$\text{Present value of an ordinary annuity} = R(PVF - OA_{n,\,i})$$
$$\$528.77 = \$50(PVF - OA_{12,\,i})$$
$$PVF - OA_{12,\,i} = \frac{\$528.77}{\$50} = 10.57540$$

Referring to Table A-4 and reading across the 12-period row, the 10.57534 factor is in the 2% column. Since 2% is a monthly rate, the nominal annual rate of interest is 24% ($12 \times 2\%$) and the effective annual rate is 26.82413% $[(1 + 0.02)^{12} - 1]$. At such a high rate of interest, you are better off paying the entire bill now if possible.

Illustration: Calculation of a Periodic Rent. Vern and Marilyn have saved $18,000 to finance their daughter Dawn's university education. The money has been deposited with the National Trust Company and is earning 10% interest compounded semiannually. What equal amounts can Dawn withdraw at the end of every six months during the next four years while she attends university and exhaust the fund with the last withdrawal? This problem is time-diagrammed as shown in Illustration A-28.

ILLUSTRATION A-28
Time Diagram for Calculation of the Withdrawal Amount of an Ordinary Annuity

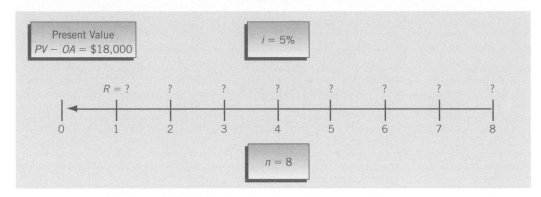

The answer is not determined simply by dividing $18,000 by 8 withdrawals because that ignores the interest earned on the money remaining on deposit. Given that interest is compounded semiannually at 5% ($10\% \div 2$) for eight periods (4 years $\times$ 2) and using the present value of an ordinary annuity formula, the amount of each withdrawal is determined as follows:

$$\text{Present value of an ordinary annuity} = R(PVF - OA_{n,\,i})$$
$$\$18,000 = R(PVF - OA_{8,\,5\%})$$
$$\$18,000 = R(6.46321)$$
$$R = \$2,784.99$$

COMPLEX SITUATIONS

It is often necessary to use more than one table to solve time value of money problems. Two common situations are illustrated to demonstrate this point:

1. Deferred annuities.
2. Bond problems.
3. Interpolation of tables

Deferred Annuities

A deferred annuity *is an annuity in which the rents begin a specified number of periods after the arrangement or contract is made.* For example, "an ordinary annuity of six annual rents deferred four years" means that no rents will occur during the first four years and that the first of the six rents will occur at the end of the fifth year. "An annuity due of six annual rents deferred four years" means that no rents will occur during the first four years, and that the first of six rents will occur at the beginning of the fifth year.

Future Value of a Deferred Annuity. Determining the future value of a deferred annuity is relatively straightforward. Because there is no accumulation or investment on which interest accrues during the deferred periods, the future value of a deferred annuity is the same as the future value of an annuity not deferred.

To illustrate, assume that Sutton Co. Ltd. plans to purchase a land site in six years for the construction of its new corporate headquarters. Because of cash flow problems, Sutton is able to budget deposits of $80,000 only at the end of the fourth, fifth, and sixth years, which are expected to earn 12% annually. What future value will Sutton have accumulated at the end of the sixth year?

Illustration A-29 gives a time diagram of this situation.

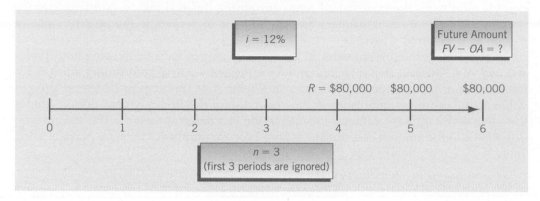

ILLUSTRATION A-29
Time Diagram for Calculation of the Future Value of a Deferred Annuity

The amount accumulated is determined by using the standard formula for the future value of an ordinary annuity:

$$FV - OA = R(FVF - OA_{n,\,i})$$
$$= \$80,000(FVF - OA_{3,\,12\%})$$
$$= \$80,000(3.37440)$$
$$= \$269,952$$

Present Value of a Deferred Annuity. In determining the present value of a deferred annuity, recognition must be given to the facts that no rents occur during the deferral period, and that the future actual rents must be discounted for the entire period.

For example, Shelly Desrosiers has developed and copyrighted a software computer program that is a tutorial for students in introductory accounting. She agrees to sell the copyright to Campus Micro Systems for six annual payments of $5,000 each, the payments to begin five years from today. The annual interest rate is 8%. What is the present value of the six payments?

This situation is an ordinary annuity of six payments deferred four periods as is time-diagrammed in Illustration A-30.

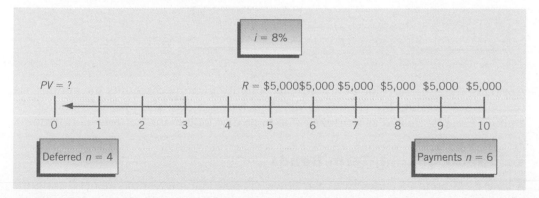

ILLUSTRATION A-30
Time Diagram for Calculation of the Present Value of a Deferred Annuity

Two options are available to solve this problem. The first is by using only Table A-4 and making the calculations shown in Illustration A-31.

ILLUSTRATION A-31
Calculation of the Present Value
of a Deferred Annuity

1. Each periodic rent		$ 5,000
2. Present value factor of an ordinary annuity of 1 for total periods (10) [(number of rents (6) plus number of deferred periods (4)] at 8%	6.71008	
3. Less: Present value factor of an ordinary annuity of 1 for the number of deferred periods (4) at 8%	3.31213	
4. Difference		× 3.39795
5. Present value of 6 rents of $5,000 deferred 4 periods		$16,989.75

The subtraction of the present value factor of an ordinary annuity of 1 for the deferred periods eliminates the nonexistent rents during the deferral period and converts the present value factor of an ordinary annuity of 1 for 10 periods to the present value of 6 rents of 1, deferred 4 periods.

Alternatively, the present value of the six rents may be calculated using both Tables A-2 and A-4. The first step is to determine the present value of an ordinary annuity for the number of rent payments involved using Table A-4. This step provides the present value of the ordinary annuity as at the beginning of the first payment period (this is the same as the present value at the end of the last deferral period). The second step is to discount the amount determined in Step 1 for the number of deferral periods using Table A-2. Application of this approach is as follows.

$$\text{Step 1:} \quad PV - OA = R(PVF - OA_{n,\,i})$$
$$= \$5,000(PVF - OA_{6,\,8\%})$$
$$= \$5,000(4.62288) \quad \text{Table A-4 (Present Value of an Ordinary Annuity)}$$
$$= \$23,114.40$$

$$\text{Step 2:} \quad PV = FV(PVF_{n,\,i})$$
$$= \$23,114.40(PVF_{4,\,8\%})$$
$$= \$23,114.40\,(0.73503) \quad \text{Table A-2 (Present Value of a Single Sum)}$$
$$= \$16,989.75$$

A time diagram reflecting the completion of this two-step approach is shown in Illustration A-32.

ILLUSTRATION A-32
Time Diagram Reflecting
the Two-step Approach for
Present Value Calculation of
a Deferred Annuity

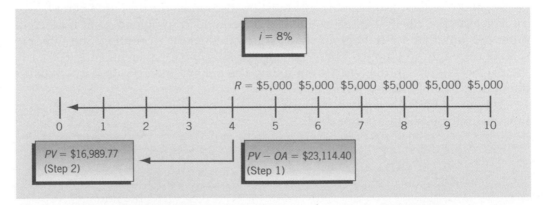

Applying the present value of an ordinary annuity formula discounts the annuity six periods, but because the annuity is deferred four periods, the present value of the annuity must be treated as a future value to be discounted another four periods.

Valuation of Long-Term Bonds

A long-term bond provides two cash flows: (1) periodic interest payments during the life of the bond; and (2) the principal (face value) paid at maturity. At the date of issue, bond buyers determine the present value of these two cash flows using the market rate of interest.

The periodic interest payments represent an annuity while the principal represents a single sum. The current market value of the bonds is the combined present values of the interest annuity and the principal amount.

To illustrate, Servicemaster Inc. issues $100,000 of 9% bonds due in five years with interest payable annually at year end. The current market rate of interest for bonds of similar risk is 11%. What will the buyers pay for this bond issue?

The time diagram depicting both cash flows is shown in Illustration A-33.

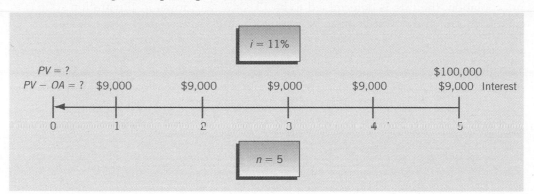

ILLUSTRATION A-33
Time Diagram for Valuation of Long-term Bonds

Illustration A-34 shows how the present value of the two cash flows is calculated.

1. Present value of the principal: $FV(PVF_{5, 11\%})$ – $100,000(.59345)$ – $59,345.00

2. Present value of interest payments: $R(PVF - OA_{5, 11\%}) = \$9,000(3.69590)$ 33,263.10

3. Combined present value (market price) $92,608.10

ILLUSTRATION A-34
Calculation of the Present Value of an Interest Bearing Bond

By paying $92,608.10 at date of issue, the buyers of the bonds will earn an effective yield of 11% over the 5-year term of the bonds.

Interpolation of Tables to Derive Interest Rates

Throughout the previous discussion, the illustrations were designed to produce interest rates and factors that could be found in the tables. Frequently it is necessary to interpolate to derive the exact or required interest rate. Interpolation is used to calculate a particular unknown value that lies between two values given in a table. The following examples illustrate interpolation using Tables A-1 and A-4.

Example 1. If $2,000 accumulates to $5,900 after being invested for 20 years, what is the annual interest rate on the investment?

Dividing the future value of $5,900 by the investment of $2,000 gives 2.95, which is the amount to which $1.00 will grow if invested for 20 years at the unknown interest rate. Using Table A-1 and reading across the 20-period line, the value 2.65330 is found in the 5% column and the value 3.20714 is in the 6% column. The factor 2.95 is between 5% and 6%, which means that the interest rate is also between 5% and 6%. By interpolation, the rate is determined to be 5.536%, as shown in Illustration A-35 ($i =$ unknown rate and $d =$ difference between 5% and i).

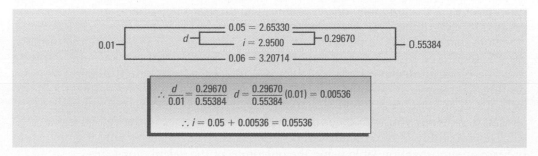

ILLUSTRATION A-35
Interpolating to Derive the Rate of Interest for an Amount

Example 2. You are offered an annuity of $1,000 a year, beginning one year from now for 25 years, for investing $7,000 cash today. What rate of interest is your investment earning?

Dividing the investment of $7,000 by the annuity of $1,000 gives a factor of 7, which is the present value of an ordinary annuity of 1 for 25 years at an unknown interest rate. Using Table A-4 and reading across the 25-period line, the value 7.84314 in the 12% column and the value 6.46415 is in the 15% column. The factor 7 is between 12% and 15%, which means that the unknown interest rate is between 12% and 15%. By interpolation, the rate is determined to be 13.834%, as shown in Illustration A-36 (i = unknown rate and d = difference between 12% and i):

ILLUSTRATION A-36
Interpolating to Derive the Rate of Interest for an Ordinary Annuity

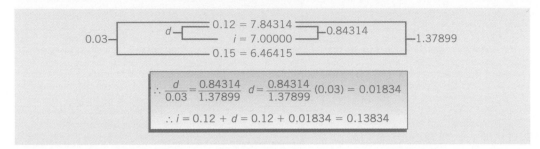

$$\therefore \frac{d}{0.03} = \frac{0.84314}{1.37899} \quad d = \frac{0.84314}{1.37899}(0.03) = 0.01834$$

$$\therefore i = 0.12 + d = 0.12 + 0.01834 = 0.13834$$

Interpolation assumes that the difference between any two values in a table is linear. Although such an assumption is incorrect, the margin of error is generally insignificant if the table value ranges are not too wide.

TECHNOLOGY TOOLS FOR TIME VALUE PROBLEMS

OBJECTIVE 8

Use spreadsheet functions to solve time value of money problems.

Business professionals, once they have mastered the underlying concepts of present and future values, will often use a spreadsheet program or financial calculator to solve time value of money problems instead of using compound interest tables.

Using Spreadsheet Functions

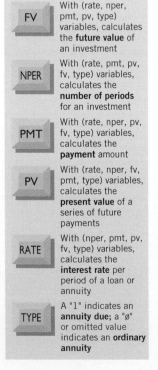

FV With (rate, nper, pmt, pv, type) variables, calculates the **future value** of an investment

NPER With (rate, pmt, pv, fv, type) variables, calculates the **number of periods** for an investment

PMT With (rate, nper, pv, fv, type) variables, calculates the **payment** amount

PV With (rate, nper, fv, pmt, type) variables, calculates the **present value** of a series of future payments

RATE With (nper, pmt, pv, fv, type) variables, calculates the **interest rate** per period of a loan or annuity

TYPE A "1" indicates an **annuity due**; a "ø" or omitted value indicates an **ordinary annuity**

Spreadsheet software programs, such as Excel and Lotus, are commonly used to help formulate and solve business problems. As they become more sophisticated, more functions that are commonly used are built into the options available to the user. Excel, for example, has a variety of functions available to "INSERT" into the spreadsheet. These include such function categories as Financial, Math & Trig, Statistical, Logical, and Database, among others.

Assuming the "Financial" option is chosen, many common functions are available. Function names associated with this appendix and the time value of money are described in the margin note.

To use this capability in Excel, choose the spreadsheet cell where you want the result of the time value calculation to be displayed. Then, from the Menu bar, click on "Insert," and choose the "Financial" function from the drop-down list. The next step depends on which variable you are trying to determine. Refer to the margin note to determine which "Function name" is appropriate. When a "Function name" is chosen, the program provides you with a list of variables needed to determine the value of the function. Insert the amounts, one at a time. The program itself helps you through the process by describing what each term means.

Note that the **FV** is recognized as a positive number as it is a future cash inflow, the **PV** should be preceded with a minus sign as it is a current outflow, and the **Rate** must be typed in decimal form, i.e., 10% is 0.10. "Type" can be left blank if you are dealing with single sums only or with an ordinary annuity, otherwise, insert a "1" to indicate an annuity due. When all variables have been provided, the program calculates and provides you with the missing value, and inserts it in the cell chosen.

This capability of the spreadsheet program is very useful, especially if you wish to prepare an amortization table using the outcomes of the calculations.

Spreadsheet Applications Using Templates

Quite apart from using the built-in functions available, spreadsheets can be used by programming the future and present value formulas discussed in the appendix into the spreadsheet cells. Once programmed, the spreadsheet "template" can then be used to solve time value of money problems repeatedly. Refer to the Digital Tool for an explanation of how this can be done.

Financial Calculators

Financial calculators allow you to solve present and future value problems by entering the time value of money variables into the calculator. Instructions on how to use a financial calculator are provided on the Digital Tool that accompanies this text.

Summary of Learning Objectives

1 Identify accounting topics where the time value of money is relevant. Some of the applications of time value of money measurements to accounting topics are: (1) notes; (2) leases; (3) amortization of premiums and discounts; (4) pensions and other post-retirement benefits; (5) capital assets; (6) sinking funds; (7) business combinations; (8) amortization; and (9) instalment contracts.

2 Distinguish between simple and compound interest. See Fundamental Concepts following this Summary.

3 Know how to use appropriate compound interest tables. In order to identify the appropriate compound interest table to use of the five given, you must identify whether you are solving for (1) the future value of a single sum; (2) the present value of a single sum; (3) the future value of an annuity; or (4) the present value of an annuity. In addition, when an annuity is involved, you must identify whether these amounts are received or paid (1) at the beginning of each period (ordinary annuity); or (2) at the end of each period (annuity due).

4 Identify variables fundamental to solving interest problems. The following four variables are fundamental to all compound interest problems: (1) *Rate of interest:* unless otherwise stated, an annual rate that must be adjusted to reflect the length of the compounding period if less than a year. (2) *Number of time periods:* the number of compounding periods (a period may be equal to or less than a year). (3) *Future value:* the amount at a future date of a given sum or sums invested assuming compound interest. (4) *Present value:* the value now (present time) of a future sum or sums discounted assuming compound interest.

5 Solve future and present value of single sum problems. See Fundamental Concepts following this Summary, items 5(a) and 6(a).

6 Solve future value of ordinary and annuity due problems. See Fundamental Concepts following this Summary, item 5(b).

7 Solve present values of ordinary and annuity due problems. See Fundamental Concepts following this Summary, item 6(b).

8 Use spreadsheet functions to solve time value of money problems. Using spreadsheet functions is only one way of using technology to help with the calculations. Instructions on the use of spreadsheet templates and financial calculators are located on the Digital Tool.

KEY TERMS

accumulation, *A-9*

annuity, *A-11*

annuity due, *A-13*

compound interest, *A-4*

deferred annuity, *A-20*

discounting, *A-9*

effective yield or rate, *A-6*

future value, *A-7*

future value of an
    annuity, *A-11*

interest, *A-3*

interpolation, *A-23*

ordinary annuity, *A-11*

present value, *A-9*

present value of an
    annuity, *A-16*

principal, *A-3*

simple interest, *A-4*

stated, nominal, coupon,
    or face rate, *A-16*

FUNDAMENTAL CONCEPTS

1. **Simple Interest.** Interest is calculated only on the principal, regardless of interest that may have accrued in the past.

2. **Compound Interest.** Interest is calculated on the unpaid interest of past periods, as well as on the principal.

3. **Rate of Interest.** Interest is usually expressed as an annual rate, but when the interest period is shorter than one year, the interest rate for the shorter period must be determined.

4. **Annuity.** A series of payments or receipts (called rents) that occur at equal intervals of time. The types of annuities are:

   (a) **Ordinary Annuity.** Each rent is payable (receivable) at the end of a period.

   (b) **Annuity Due.** Each rent is payable (receivable) at the beginning of a period.

5. **Future Value.** Value at a later date of a given sum that is invested at compound interest.

   (a) **Future Value of 1** (or amount of a given sum). The future value of $1.00 (or a single given sum), a, at the end of n periods at i compound interest rate (Table A-1).

   (b) **Future Value of an Annuity.** The future value of a series of rents invested at compound interest; it is the accumulated total that results from a series of equal deposits at regular intervals invested at compound interest. Both deposits and interest increase the accumulation.

      1. **Future Value of an Ordinary Annuity.** The future value on the date of the last rent (Table A-3).

      2. **Future Value of an Annuity Due.** The future value one period after the date of the last rent. When an annuity due table is not available, use Table A-3 with the following formula:

$$\text{Amount of annuity due of 1 for } n \text{ rents} = \text{Amount of ordinary annuity of 1 for } n \text{ rents} \times (1 + \text{interest rate}).$$

6. **Present Value.** The value at an earlier date (usually now) of a given sum discounted at compound interest.

   (a) **Present Value of 1** (or present value of a single sum). The present value (worth) of $1.00 (or a given sum), p, due n periods hence, discounted at i compound interest (Table A-2).

   (b) **Present Value of an Annuity.** The present value (worth) of a series of rents discounted at compound interest; it is the present sum when invested at compound interest that will permit a series of equal withdrawals at regular intervals.

      1. **Present Value of an Ordinary Annuity.** The value now of $1.00 to be received or paid each period (rents) for n periods, discounted at i compound interest (Table A-4).

      2. **Present Value of an Annuity Due.** The value now of $1.00 to be received or paid at the beginning of each period (rents) for n periods, discounted at i compound interest (Table A-5). To use Table A-4 for an annuity due, apply this formula:

$$\text{Present value of an annuity due of 1 for } n \text{ rents} = \text{Present value of ordinary annuity of 1 for } n \text{ rents} \times (1 + \text{interest rate}).$$

TABLE A-1

FUTURE VALUE OF 1
(FUTURE VALUE OF A SINGLE SUM)

$$FVF_{n,\,i} = (1 + i)^n$$

(n) periods	2%	2½%	3%	4%	5%	6%	8%	9%	10%	11%	12%	15%
1	1.02000	1.02500	1.03000	1.04000	1.05000	1.06000	1.08000	1.09000	1.10000	1.11000	1.12000	1.15000
2	1.04040	1.05063	1.06090	1.08160	1.10250	1.12360	1.16640	1.18810	1.21000	1.23210	1.25440	1.32250
3	1.06121	1.07689	1.09273	1.12486	1.15763	1.19102	1.25971	1.29503	1.33100	1.36763	1.40493	1.52088
4	1.08243	1.10381	1.12551	1.16986	1.21551	1.26248	1.36049	1.41158	1.46410	1.51807	1.57352	1.74901
5	1.10408	1.13141	1.15927	1.21665	1.27628	1.33823	1.46933	1.53862	1.61051	1.68506	1.76234	2.01136
6	1.12616	1.15969	1.19405	1.26532	1.34010	1.41852	1.58687	1.67710	1.77156	1.87041	1.97382	2.31306
7	1.14869	1.18869	1.22987	1.31593	1.40710	1.50363	1.71382	1.82804	1.94872	2.07616	2.21068	2.66002
8	1.17166	1.21840	1.26677	1.36857	1.47746	1.59385	1.85093	1.99256	2.14359	2.30454	2.47596	3.05902
9	1.19509	1.24886	1.30477	1.42331	1.55133	1.68948	1.99900	2.17189	2.35795	2.55803	2.77308	3.51788
10	1.21899	1.28008	1.34392	1.48024	1.62889	1.79085	2.15892	2.36736	2.59374	2.83942	3.10585	4.04556
11	1.24337	1.31209	1.38423	1.53945	1.71034	1.89830	2.33164	2.58043	2.85312	3.15176	3.47855	4.65239
12	1.26824	1.34489	1.42576	1.60103	1.79586	2.01220	2.51817	2.81267	3.13843	3.49845	3.89598	5.35025
13	1.29361	1.37851	1.46853	1.66507	1.88565	2.13293	2.71962	3.06581	3.45227	3.88328	4.36349	6.15279
14	1.31948	1.41297	1.51259	1.73168	1.97993	2.26090	2.93719	3.34173	3.79750	4.31044	4.88711	7.07571
15	1.34587	1.44830	1.55797	1.80094	2.07893	2.39656	3.17217	3.64248	4.17725	4.78459	5.47357	8.13706
16	1.37279	1.48451	1.60471	1.87298	2.18287	2.54035	3.42594	3.97031	4.59497	5.31089	6.13039	9.35762
17	1.40024	1.52162	1.65285	1.94790	2.29202	2.69277	3.70002	4.32763	5.05447	5.89509	6.86604	10.76126
18	1.42825	1.55966	1.70243	2.02582	2.40662	2.85434	3.99602	4.71712	5.55992	6.54355	7.68997	12.37545
19	1.45681	1.59865	1.75351	2.10685	2.52695	3.02560	4.31570	5.14166	6.11591	7.26334	8.61276	14.23177
20	1.48595	1.63862	1.80611	2.19112	2.65330	3.20714	4.66096	5.60441	6.72750	8.06231	9.64629	16.36654
21	1.51567	1.67958	1.86029	2.27877	2.78596	3.39956	5.03383	6.10881	7.40025	8.94917	10.80385	18.82152
22	1.54598	1.72157	1.91610	2.36992	2.92526	3.60354	5.43654	6.65860	8.14028	9.93357	12.10031	21.64475
23	1.57690	1.76461	1.97359	2.46472	3.07152	3.81975	5.87146	7.25787	8.95430	11.02627	13.55235	24.89146
24	1.60844	1.80873	2.03279	2.56330	3.22510	4.04893	6.34118	7.91108	9.84973	12.23916	15.17863	28.62518
25	1.64061	1.85394	2.09378	2.66584	3.38635	4.29187	6.84847	8.62308	10.83471	13.58546	17.00000	32.91895
26	1.67342	1.90029	2.15659	2.77247	3.55567	4.54938	7.39635	9.39916	11.91818	15.07986	19.04007	37.85680
27	1.70689	1.94780	2.22129	2.88337	3.73346	4.82235	7.98806	10.24508	13.10999	16.73865	21.32488	43.53532
28	1.74102	1.99650	2.28793	2.99870	3.92013	5.11169	8.62711	11.16714	14.42099	18.57990	23.88387	50.06561
29	1.77584	2.04641	2.35657	3.11865	4.11614	5.41839	9.31727	12.17218	15.86309	20.62369	26.74993	57.57545
30	1.81136	2.09757	2.42726	3.24340	4.32194	5.74349	10.06266	13.26768	17.44940	22.89230	29.95992	66.21177
31	1.84759	2.15001	2.50008	3.37313	4.53804	6.08810	10.86767	14.46177	19.19434	25.41045	33.55511	76.14354
32	1.88454	2.20376	2.57508	3.50806	4.76494	6.45339	11.73708	15.76333	21.11378	28.20560	37.58173	87.56507
33	1.92223	2.25885	2.65234	3.64838	5.00319	6.84059	12.67605	17.18203	23.22515	31.30821	42.09153	100.69983
34	1.96068	2.31532	2.73191	3.79432	5.25335	7.25103	13.69013	18.72841	25.54767	34.75212	47.14252	115.80480
35	1.99989	2.37321	2.81386	3.94609	5.51602	7.68609	14.78534	20.41397	28.10244	38.57485	52.79962	133.17552
36	2.03989	2.43254	2.88928	4.10393	5.79182	8.14725	15.96817	22.25123	30.91268	42.81808	59.13557	153.15185
37	2.08069	2.49335	2.98523	4.26809	6.08141	8.63609	17.24563	24.25384	34.00395	47.52807	66.23184	176.12463
38	2.12230	2.55568	3.07478	4.43881	6.38548	9.15425	18.62528	26.43668	37.40434	52.75616	74.17966	202.54332
39	2.16474	2.61957	3.16703	4.61637	6.70475	9.70351	20.11530	28.81598	41.14479	58.55934	83.08122	232.92482
40	2.20804	2.68506	3.26204	4.80102	7.03999	10.28572	21.72452	31.40942	45.25926	65.00087	93.05097	267.86355

TABLE A-2

PRESENT VALUE OF 1
(PRESENT VALUE OF A SINGLE SUM)

$$PVF_{n,\,i} = \frac{1}{(1+i)^n} = (1+i)^{-n}$$

(n) periods	2%	2½%	3%	4%	5%	6%	8%	9%	10%	11%	12%	15%
1	.98039	.97561	.97087	.96156	.95238	.94340	.92593	.91743	.90909	.90090	.89286	.86957
2	.96117	.95181	.94260	.92456	.90703	.89000	.85734	.84168	.82645	.81162	.79719	.75614
3	.94232	.92860	.91514	.88900	.86384	.83962	.79383	.77218	.75132	.73119	.71178	.65752
4	.92385	.90595	.88849	.85480	.82270	.79209	.73503	.70843	.68301	.65873	.63552	.57175
5	.90583	.88385	.86261	.82193	.78353	.74726	.68058	.64993	.62092	.59345	.56743	.49718
6	.88797	.86230	.83748	.79031	.74622	.70496	.63017	.59627	.56447	.53464	.50663	.43233
7	.87056	.84127	.81309	.75992	.71068	.66506	.58349	.54703	.51316	.48166	.45235	.37594
8	.85349	.82075	.78941	.73069	.67684	.62741	.54027	.50187	.46651	.43393	.40388	.32690
9	.83676	.80073	.76642	.70259	.64461	.59190	.50025	.46043	.42410	.39092	.36061	.28426
10	.82035	.78120	.74409	.67556	.61391	.55839	.46319	.42241	.38554	.35218	.32197	.24719
11	.80426	.76214	.72242	.64958	.58468	.52679	.42888	.38753	.35049	.31728	.28748	.21494
12	.78849	.74356	.70138	.62460	.55684	.49697	.39711	.35554	.31863	.28584	.25668	.18691
13	.77303	.72542	.68095	.60057	.53032	.46884	.36770	.32618	.28966	.25751	.22917	.16253
14	.75788	.70773	.66112	.57748	.50507	.44230	.34046	.29925	.26333	.23199	.20462	.14133
15	.74301	.69047	.64186	.55526	.48102	.41727	.31524	.27454	.23939	.20900	.18270	.12289
16	.72845	.67362	.62317	.53391	.45811	.39365	.29189	.25187	.21763	.18829	.16312	.10687
17	.71416	.65720	.60502	.51337	.43630	.37136	.27027	.23107	.19785	.16963	.14564	.09293
18	.70016	.64117	.58739	.49363	.41552	.35034	.25025	.21199	.17986	.15282	.13004	.08081
19	.68643	.62553	.57029	.47464	.39573	.33051	.23171	.19449	.16351	.13768	.11611	.07027
20	.67297	.61027	.55368	.45639	.37689	.31180	.21455	.17843	.14864	.12403	.10367	.06110
21	.65978	.59539	.53755	.43883	.35894	.29416	.19866	.16370	.13513	.11174	.09256	.05313
22	.64684	.58086	.52189	.42196	.34185	.27751	.18394	.15018	.12285	.10067	.08264	.04620
23	.63416	.56670	.50669	.40573	.32557	.26180	.17032	.13778	.11168	.09069	.07379	.04017
24	.62172	.55288	.49193	.39012	.31007	.24698	.15770	.12641	.10153	.08170	.06588	.03493
25	.60953	.53939	.47761	.37512	.29530	.23300	.14602	.11597	.09230	.07361	.05882	.03038
26	.59758	.52623	.46369	.36069	.28124	.21981	.13520	.10639	.08391	.06631	.05252	.02642
27	.58586	.51340	.45019	.34682	.26785	.20737	.12519	.09761	.07628	.05974	.04689	.02297
28	.57437	.50088	.43708	.33348	.25509	.19563	.11591	.08955	.06934	.05382	.04187	.01997
29	.56311	.48866	.42435	.32065	.24295	.18456	.10733	.08216	.06304	.04849	.03738	.01737
30	.55207	.47674	.41199	.30832	.23138	.17411	.09938	.07537	.05731	.04368	.03338	.01510
31	.54125	.46511	.39999	.29646	.22036	.16425	.09202	.06915	.05210	.03935	.02980	.01313
32	.53063	.45377	.38834	.28506	.20987	.15496	.08520	.06344	.04736	.03545	.02661	.01142
33	.52023	.44270	.37703	.27409	.19987	.14619	.07889	.05820	.04306	.03194	.02376	.00993
34	.51003	.43191	.36604	.26355	.19035	.13791	.07305	.05340	.03914	.02878	.02121	.00864
35	.50003	.42137	.35538	.25342	.18129	.13011	.06763	.04899	.03558	.02592	.01894	.00751
36	.49022	.41109	.34503	.24367	.17266	.12274	.06262	.04494	.03235	.02335	.01691	.00653
37	.48061	.40107	.33498	.23430	.16444	.11579	.05799	.04123	.02941	.02104	.01510	.00568
38	.47119	.39128	.32523	.22529	.15661	.10924	.05369	.03783	.02674	.01896	.01348	.00494
39	.46195	.38174	.31575	.21662	.14915	.10306	.04971	.03470	.02430	.01708	.01204	.00429
40	.45289	.37243	.30656	.20829	.14205	.09722	.04603	.03184	.02210	.01538	.01075	.00373

TABLE A-3

FUTURE VALUE OF AN ORDINARY ANNUITY OF 1

$$FVF - OA_{n,\,i} = \frac{(1 + i)^n - 1}{i}$$

(n) periods	2%	2½%	3%	4%	5%	6%	8%	9%	10%	11%	12%	15%
1	1.00000	1.00000	1.00000	1.00000	1.00000	1.00000	1.00000	1.00000	1.00000	1.00000	1.00000	1.00000
2	2.02000	2.02500	2.03000	2.04000	2.05000	2.06000	2.08000	2.09000	2.10000	2.11000	2.12000	2.15000
3	3.06040	3.07563	3.09090	3.12160	3.15250	3.18360	3.24640	3.27810	3.31000	3.34210	3.37440	3.47250
4	4.12161	4.15252	4.18363	4.24646	4.31013	4.37462	4.50611	4.57313	4.64100	4.70973	4.77933	4.99338
5	5.20404	5.25633	5.30914	5.41632	5.52563	5.63709	5.86660	5.98471	6.10510	6.22780	6.35285	6.74238
6	6.30812	6.38774	6.46841	6.63298	6.80191	6.97532	7.33592	7.52334	7.71561	7.91286	8.11519	8.75374
7	7.43428	7.54743	7.00240	7.00020	0.14201	0.30301	0.02200	0.20011	9.48717	9.78327	10.08901	11.06680
8	8.58297	8.73612	8.89234	9.21423	9.54911	9.89747	10.63663	11.02847	11.43589	11.85943	12.29969	13.72682
9	9.75463	9.95452	10.15911	10.58280	11.02656	11.49132	12.48756	13.02104	13.57948	14.16397	14.77566	16.78584
10	10.94972	11.20338	11.46338	12.00611	12.57789	13.18079	14.48656	15.19293	15.93743	16.72201	17.54874	20.30372
11	12.16872	12.48347	12.80780	13.48635	14.20679	14.97164	16.64549	17.56029	18.53117	19.56143	20.65458	24.34928
12	13.41209	13.79555	14.19203	15.02581	15.91713	16.86994	18.97713	20.14072	21.38428	22.71319	24.13313	29.00167
13	14.68033	15.14044	15.61779	16.62684	17.71298	18.88214	21.49530	22.95339	24.52271	26.21164	28.02911	34.35192
14	15.97394	16.51895	17.08632	18.29191	19.59863	21.01507	24.21492	26.01919	27.97498	30.09492	32.39260	40.50471
15	17.29342	17.93193	18.59891	20.02359	21.57856	23.27597	27.15211	29.36092	31.77248	34.40536	37.27972	47.58041
16	18.63929	19.38022	20.15688	21.82453	23.65749	25.67253	30.32428	33.00340	35.94973	39.18995	42.75328	55.71747
17	20.01207	20.86473	21.76159	23.69751	25.84037	28.21288	33.75023	36.97371	40.54470	44.50084	48.88367	65.07509
18	21.41231	22.38635	23.41444	25.64541	28.13238	30.90565	37.45024	41.30134	45.59917	50.39593	55.74972	75.83636
19	22.84056	23.94601	25.11687	27.67123	30.53900	33.75999	41.44626	46.01846	51.15909	56.93949	63.43968	88.21181
20	24.29737	25.54466	26.87037	29.77808	33.06595	36.78559	45.76196	51.16012	57.27500	64.20283	72.05244	102.44358
21	25.78332	27.18327	28.67649	31.96920	35.71925	39.99273	50.42292	56.76453	64.00250	72.26514	81.69874	118.81012
22	27.29898	28.86286	30.53670	34.24707	38.50521	43.39229	55.45676	62.87334	71.40275	81.21431	92.50258	137.63164
23	28.84496	30.58443	32.45288	36.61789	41.43048	46.99583	60.89330	69.53194	79.54302	91.14788	104.60289	159.27638
24	30.42186	32.34904	34.42647	39.08260	44.50200	50.81558	66.76476	76.78981	88.49733	102.17415	118.15524	184.16784
25	32.03030	34.15776	36.45926	41.64591	47.72710	54.86451	73.10594	84.70090	98.34706	114.41331	133.33387	212.79302
26	33.67091	36.01171	38.55304	44.31174	51.11345	59.15638	79.95442	93.32398	109.18177	127.99877	150.33393	245.71197
27	35.34432	37.91200	40.70963	47.08421	54.66913	63.70577	87.35077	102.72314	121.09994	143.07864	169.37401	283.56877
28	37.05121	39.85990	42.93092	49.96758	58.40258	68.52811	95.33883	112.96822	134.20994	159.81729	190.69889	327.10408
29	38.79223	41.85630	45.21885	52.96629	62.32271	73.63980	103.96594	124.13536	148.63093	178.39719	214.58275	377.16969
30	40.56808	43.90270	47.57542	56.08494	66.43885	79.05819	113.28321	136.30754	164.49402	199.02088	241.33268	434.74515
31	42.37944	46.00027	50.00268	59.32834	70.76079	84.80168	123.34587	149.57522	181.94343	221.91317	271.29261	500.95692
32	44.22703	48.15028	52.50276	62.70147	75.29883	90.88978	134.21354	164.03699	201.13777	247.32362	304.04772	577.10046
33	46.11157	50.35403	55.07784	66.20953	80.06377	97.34316	145.95062	179.80032	222.25154	275.52922	342.42945	644.66553
34	48.03380	52.61289	57.73018	69.85791	85.06696	104.18376	158.62667	196.98234	245.47670	306.83744	384.52098	765.36535
35	49.99448	54.92821	60.46208	73.65222	90.32031	111.43478	172.31680	215.71076	271.02437	341.58955	431.66350	881.17016
36	51.99437	57.30141	63.27594	77.59831	95.83632	119.12087	187.10215	236.12472	299.12681	380.16441	484.46312	1014.34568
37	54.03425	59.73395	66.17422	81.70225	101.62814	127.26812	203.07032	258.37595	330.03949	422.98249	543.59869	1167.49753
38	56.11494	62.22730	69.15945	85.97034	107.70955	135.90421	220.31595	282.62978	364.04343	470.51056	609.83053	1343.62216
39	58.23724	64.78298	72.23423	90.40915	114.09502	145.05846	238.94122	309.06646	401.44778	523.26673	684.01020	1546.16549
40	60.40198	67.40255	75.40126	95.02552	120.79977	154.76197	259.05652	337.88245	442.59256	581.82607	767.09142	1779.09031

TABLE A-4

PRESENT VALUE OF AN ORDINARY ANNUITY OF 1

$$PVF - OA_{n,\,i} = \frac{1 - \dfrac{1}{(1+i)^n}}{i}$$

(n) periods	2%	2½%	3%	4%	5%	6%	8%	9%	10%	11%	12%	15%
1	.98039	.97561	.97087	.96154	.95238	.94340	.92593	.91743	.90909	.90090	.89286	.86957
2	1.94156	1.92742	1.91347	1.88609	1.85941	1.83339	1.78326	1.75911	1.73554	1.71252	1.69005	1.62571
3	2.88388	2.85602	2.82861	2.77509	2.72325	2.67301	2.57710	2.53130	2.48685	2.44371	2.40183	2.28323
4	3.80773	3.76197	3.71710	3.62990	3.54595	3.46511	3.31213	3.23972	3.16986	3.10245	3.03735	2.85498
5	4.71346	4.64583	4.57971	4.45182	4.32948	4.21236	3.99271	3.88965	3.79079	3.69590	3.60478	3.35216
6	5.60143	5.50813	5.41719	5.24214	5.07569	4.91732	4.62288	4.48592	4.35526	4.23054	4.11141	3.78448
7	6.47199	6.34939	6.23028	6.00205	5.78637	5.58238	5.20637	5.03295	4.86842	4.71220	4.56376	4.16042
8	7.32548	7.17014	7.01969	6.73274	6.46321	6.20979	5.74664	5.53482	5.33493	5.14612	4.96764	4.48732
9	8.16224	7.97087	7.78611	7.43533	7.10782	6.80169	6.24689	5.99525	5.75902	5.53705	5.32825	4.77158
10	8.98259	8.75206	8.53020	8.11090	7.72173	7.36009	6.71008	6.41766	6.14457	5.88923	5.65022	5.01877
11	9.78685	9.51421	9.25262	8.76048	8.30641	7.88687	7.13896	6.80519	6.49506	6.20652	5.93770	5.23371
12	10.57534	10.25776	9.95400	9.38507	8.86325	8.38384	7.53608	7.16073	6.81369	6.49236	6.19437	5.42062
13	11.34837	10.98319	10.63496	9.98565	9.39357	8.85268	7.90378	7.48690	7.10336	6.74987	6.42355	5.58315
14	12.10625	11.69091	11.29607	10.56312	9.89864	9.29498	8.24424	7.78615	7.36669	6.98187	6.62817	5.72448
15	12.84926	12.38138	11.93794	11.11839	10.37966	9.71225	8.55948	8.06069	7.60608	7.19087	6.81086	5.84737
16	13.57771	13.05500	12.56110	11.65230	10.83777	10.10590	8.85137	8.31256	7.82371	7.37916	6.97399	5.95424
17	14.29187	13.71220	13.16612	12.16567	11.27407	10.47726	9.12164	8.54363	8.02155	7.54879	7.11963	6.04716
18	14.99203	14.35336	13.75351	12.65930	11.68959	10.82760	9.37189	8.75563	8.20141	7.70162	7.24967	6.12797
19	15.67846	14.97889	14.32380	13.13394	12.08532	11.15812	9.60360	8.95012	8.36492	7.83929	7.36578	6.19823
20	16.35143	15.58916	14.87747	13.59033	12.46221	11.46992	9.81815	9.12855	8.51356	7.96333	7.46944	6.25933
21	17.01121	16.18455	15.41502	14.02916	12.82115	11.76408	10.01680	9.29224	8.64869	8.07507	7.56200	6.31246
22	17.65805	16.76541	15.93692	14.45112	13.16800	12.04158	10.20074	9.44243	8.77154	8.17574	7.64465	6.35866
23	18.29220	17.33211	16.44361	14.85684	13.48857	12.30338	10.37106	9.58021	8.88322	8.26643	7.71843	6.39884
24	18.91393	17.88499	16.93554	15.24696	13.79864	12.55036	10.52876	9.70661	8.98474	8.34814	7.78432	6.43377
25	19.52346	18.42438	17.41315	15.62208	14.09394	12.78336	10.67478	9.82258	9.07704	8.42174	7.84314	6.46415
26	20.12104	18.95061	17.87684	15.98277	14.37519	13.00317	10.80998	9.92897	9.16095	8.48806	7.89566	6.49056
27	20.70690	19.46401	18.32703	16.32959	14.64303	13.21053	10.93516	10.02658	9.23722	8.45780	7.94255	6.51353
28	21.28127	19.96489	18.76411	16.66306	14.89813	13.40616	11.05108	10.11613	9.30657	8.60162	7.98442	6.53351
29	21.84438	20.45355	19.18845	16.98371	15.14107	13.59072	11.15841	10.19828	9.36961	8.65011	8.02181	6.55088
30	22.39646	20.93029	19.60044	17.29203	15.37245	13.76483	11.25778	10.27365	9.42691	8.69379	8.05518	6.56598
31	22.93770	21.39541	20.00043	17.58849	15.59281	13.92909	11.34980	10.34280	9.47901	8.73315	8.08499	6.57911
32	23.46833	21.84918	20.38877	17.87355	15.80268	14.08404	11.43500	10.40624	9.52638	8.76860	8.11159	6.59053
33	23.98856	22.29188	20.76579	18.14765	16.00255	14.23023	11.51389	10.46444	9.56943	8.80054	8.13535	6.60046
34	24.49859	22.72379	21.13184	18.41120	16.19290	14.36814	11.58693	10.51784	9.60858	8.82932	8.15656	6.60910
35	24.99862	23.14516	21.48722	18.66461	16.37419	14.49825	11.65457	10.56682	9.64416	8.85524	8.17550	6.61661
36	25.48884	23.55625	21.83225	18.90828	16.54685	14.62099	11.71719	10.61176	9.67651	8.87859	8.19241	6.62314
37	25.96945	23.95732	22.16724	19.14258	16.71129	14.73678	11.77518	10.65299	9.70592	8.89963	8.20751	6.62882
38	26.44064	24.34860	22.49246	19.36786	16.86789	14.84602	11.82887	10.69082	9.73265	8.91859	8.22099	6.63375
39	26.90259	24.73034	22.80822	19.58448	17.01704	14.94907	11.87858	10.72552	9.75697	8.93567	8.23303	6.63805
40	27.35548	25.10278	23.11477	19.79277	17.15909	15.04630	11.92461	10.75736	9.77905	8.95105	8.24378	6.64178

TABLE A-5

PRESENT VALUE OF AN ANNUITY DUE OF 1

$$PVF - AD_{n,\,i} = 1 + \frac{1 - \dfrac{1}{(1 + i)^{n-1}}}{i}$$

(n) periods	2%	2¹⁄₂%	3%	4%	5%	6%	8%	9%	10%	11%	12%	15%
1	1.00000	1.00000	1.00000	1.00000	1.00000	1.00000	1.00000	1.00000	1.00000	1.00000	1.00000	1.00000
2	1.98039	1.97561	1.97087	1.96154	1.95238	1.94340	1.92593	1.91743	1.90909	1.90090	1.89286	1.86957
3	2.94156	2.92742	2.91347	2.88609	2.85941	2.83339	2.78326	2.75911	2.73554	2.71252	2.69005	2.62571
4	3.88388	3.85602	3.82861	3.77509	3.72325	3.67301	3.57710	3.53130	3.48685	3.44371	3.40183	3.28323
5	4.80773	4.76197	4.71710	4.62990	4.54595	4.46511	4.31213	4.23972	4.16986	4.10245	4.03735	3.85498
6	5.71346	5.64583	5.57971	5.45182	5.32948	5.21236	4.99271	4.88965	4.79079	4.69590	4.60478	4.35216
7	6.60143	6.50813	6.41719	6.24214	6.07569	5.91732	5.62288	5.48592	5.35526	5.23054	5.11141	4.78448
8	7.47199	7.34939	7.23028	7.00205	6.78637	6.58238	6.20637	6.03295	5.86842	5.71220	5.56376	5.16042
9	8.32548	8.17014	8.01969	7.73274	7.46321	7.20979	6.74664	6.53482	6.33493	6.14612	5.96764	5.48732
10	9.16224	8.97087	8.78611	8.43533	8.10782	7.80169	7.24689	6.99525	6.75902	6.53705	6.32825	5.77158
11	9.98259	9.75206	9.53020	9.11090	8.72173	8.36009	7.71008	7.41766	7.14457	6.88923	6.65022	6.01877
12	10.78685	10.51421	10.25262	9.76048	9.30641	8.88687	8.13896	7.80519	7.49506	7.20652	6.93770	6.23371
13	11.57534	11.25776	10.95400	10.38507	9.86325	9.38384	8.53608	8.16073	7.81369	7.49236	7.19437	6.42062
14	12.34837	11.98319	11.63496	10.98565	10.39357	9.85268	8.90378	8.48690	8.10336	7.74987	7.42355	6.58315
15	13.10625	12.69091	12.29607	11.56312	10.89864	10.29498	9.24424	8.78615	9.36669	7.98187	7.62817	6.72448
16	13.84926	13.38158	12.93794	12.11839	11.37966	10.71225	9.55948	9.06069	8.60608	8.19087	7.81086	6.84737
17	14.57771	14.05500	13.56110	12.65230	11.83777	11.10590	9.85137	9.31256	8.82371	8.37916	7.97399	6.95424
18	15.29187	14.71220	14.16612	13.16567	12.27407	11.47726	10.12164	9.54363	9.02155	8.54879	8.11963	7.04716
19	15.99203	15.35336	14.75351	13.65930	12.68959	11.82760	10.37189	9.75563	9.20141	8.70162	8.24967	7.12797
20	16.67846	15.97889	15.32380	14.13394	13.08532	12.15812	10.60360	9.95012	9.36492	8.83929	8.36578	7.19823
21	17.35143	16.58916	15.87747	14.59033	13.46221	12.46992	10.81815	10.12855	9.51356	8.96333	8.46944	7.25933
22	18.01121	17.18455	16.41502	15.02916	13.82115	12.76408	11.01680	10.29224	9.64869	9.07507	8.56200	7.31246
23	18.65805	17.76541	16.93692	15.45112	14.16300	13.04158	11.20074	10.44243	9.77154	9.17574	8.64465	7.35866
24	19.29220	18.33211	17.44361	15.85684	14.48857	13.30338	11.37106	10.58021	9.88322	9.26643	8.71843	7.39884
25	19.91393	18.88499	17.93554	16.24696	14.79864	13.55036	11.52876	10.70661	9.98474	9.34814	8.78432	7.43377
26	20.52346	19.42438	18.41315	16.62208	15.09394	13.78336	11.67478	10.82258	10.07704	9.42174	8.84314	7.46415
27	21.12104	19.95061	18.87684	16.98277	15.37519	14.00317	11.80998	10.92897	10.16095	9.48806	8.89566	7.49056
28	21.70690	20.46401	19.32703	17.32959	15.64303	14.21053	11.93518	11.02658	10.23722	9.54780	8.94255	7.51353
29	22.28127	20.96489	19.76411	17.66306	15.89813	14.40616	12.05108	11.11613	10.30657	9.60162	8.98442	7.53351
30	22.84430	21.45355	20.18845	17.98371	16.14107	14.59072	12.15841	11.19828	10.36961	9.65011	9.02181	7.55088
31	23.39646	21.93029	20.60044	18.29203	16.37245	14.76483	12.25778	11.27365	10.42691	9.69379	9.05518	7.56598
32	23.93770	22.39541	21.00043	18.58849	16.59281	14.92909	12.34980	11.34280	10.47901	9.73315	9.08499	7.57911
33	24.46833	22.84918	21.38877	18.87355	16.80268	15.08404	12.43500	11.40624	10.52638	9.76860	9.11159	7.59053
34	24.98856	23.29188	21.76579	19.14765	17.00255	15.23023	12.51389	11.46444	10.56943	9.80054	9.13535	7.60046
35	25.49859	23.72379	22.13184	19.41120	17.19290	15.36814	12.58693	11.51784	10.60858	9.82932	9.15656	7.60910
36	25.99862	24.14516	22.48722	19.66461	17.37419	15.49825	12.65457	11.56682	10.64416	9.85524	9.17550	7.61661
37	26.48884	24.55625	22.83225	19.90828	17.54685	15.62099	12.71719	11.61176	10.67651	9.87859	9.19241	7.62314
38	26.96945	24.95732	23.16724	20.14258	17.71129	15.73678	12.77518	11.65299	10.70592	9.89963	9.20751	7.62882
39	27.44064	25.34860	23.49246	20.36786	17.86789	15.84602	12.82887	11.69082	10.73265	9.91859	9.22099	7.63375
40	27.90259	25.73034	23.80822	20.58448	18.01704	15.94907	12.87858	11.72552	10.75697	9.93567	9.23303	7.63805

BRIEF EXERCISES

(Interest rates are per annum unless otherwise indicated.)

BEA-1 Prof. Cheng invested $10,000 today in a fund that earns 8% compounded annually. To what amount will the investment grow in 3 years? To what amount would the investment grow in 3 years if the fund earns 8% annual interest compounded semiannually?

BEA-2 Itzak Lo needs $20,000 in 4 years. What amount must he invest today if his investment earns 12% compounded annually? What amount must he invest if his investment earns 12% annual interest compounded quarterly?

BEA-3 Janet Jack will invest $30,000 today. She needs $222,000 in 21 years. What annual interest rate must she earn?

BEA-4 Webster Corp. will invest $10,000 today in a fund that earns 5% annual interest. How many years will it take for the fund to grow to $13,400?

BEA-5 Boleyn Ltd. will invest $5,000 a year for 20 years in a fund that will earn 12% annual interest. If the first payment into the fund occurs today, what amount will be in the fund in 20 years? If the first payment occurs at year-end, what amount will be in the fund in 20 years?

BEA-6 Williams needs $200,000 in 10 years. How much must he invest at the end of each year, at 11% interest, to meet his needs?

BEA-7 Jack Thompson's lifelong dream is to own his own fishing boat to use in his retirement. Jack has recently come into an inheritance of $400,000. He estimates that the boat he wants will cost $350,000 when he retires in 5 years. How much of his inheritance must he invest at an annual rate of 12% (compounded annually) to buy the boat at retirement?

BEA-8 Refer to the data in BEA-7. Assuming quarterly compounding of amounts invested at 12%, how much of Jack Thompson's inheritance must be invested to have enough at retirement to buy the boat?

BEA-9 Linda Van Esch is investing $12,961 at the end of each year in a fund that earns 10% interest. In how many years will the fund be at $100,000?

BEA-10 Aaron Rana wants to withdraw $20,000 each year for 10 years from a fund that earns 8% interest. How much must he invest today if the first withdrawal is at year-end? How much must he invest today if the first withdrawal takes place immediately?

BEA-11 Mark Link's VISA balance is $1,124.40. He may pay if off in 18 equal end-of-month payments of $75 each. What interest rate is Mark paying?

BEA-12 Corinne Donne is investing $200,000 in a fund that earns 8% interest compounded annually. What equal amounts can Corinne withdraw at the end of each of the next 20 years?

BEA-13 Bayou Inc. will deposit $20,000 in a 12% fund at the end of each year for 8 years beginning December 31, 2002. What amount will be in the fund immediately after the last deposit?

BEA-14 Hollis Sho wants to create a fund today that will enable her to withdraw $20,000 per year for 8 years, with the first withdrawal to take place 5 years from today. If the fund earns 8% interest, how much must Hollis invest today?

BEA-15 Acadian Inc. issues $1,000,000 of 7% bonds due in 10 years with interest payable at year-end. The current market rate of interest for bonds of similar risk is 8%. What amount will Acadian receive when it issues the bonds?

BEA-16 Walt Frazier is settling a $20,000 loan due today by making 6 equal annual payments of $4,864.51. Determine the interest rate on this loan, if the payments begin one year after the loan is signed.

BEA-17 Consider the loan in BEA-16. What payments must Walt Frazier make to settle the loan at the same interest rate but with the 6 payments beginning on the day the loan is signed?

EXERCISES

(Interest rates are per annum unless otherwise indicated.)

EA-1 **(Present Value Problem)** A hockey player was reported to have received an $11 million contract. The terms were a signing bonus of $500,000 in 2000 plus $500,000 in 2010 through the year 2013. In addition, he was to receive a base salary of $300,000 in 2000 that was to increase $100,000 a year to the year 2004; in 2005 he was to receive $1 million a year that would increase $100,000 per year to the year 2009. Assuming that the appropriate interest rate was 9% and that each payment occurred on December 31 of the respective year, calculate the present value of this contract as of December 31, 2000.

EA-2 **(Future Value and Present Value Problems)** Presented below are three unrelated situations:

1. Fishbone Ltd. recently signed a 10-year lease for a new office building. Under the lease agreement, a security deposit of $12,000 was made that would be returned at the expiration of the lease with interest compounded at 10% per year. What amount will the company receive when the lease expires?

2. Stevenson Corporation, having recently issued a $20 million, 15-year bond, is committed to make annual sinking fund deposits of $600,000. The deposits are made on the last day of each year and yield a return of 10%. Will the fund at the end of 15 years be sufficient to retire the bonds? If not, what will the excess or deficiency be?

3. Under the terms of her salary agreement, President Joanie McKaig has an option of receiving either an immediate bonus of $40,000 or a deferred bonus of $70,000, payable in 10 years. Ignoring tax considerations and assuming a relevant interest rate of 8%, which form of settlement should President McKaig accept?

EA-3 **(Calculations for a Retirement Fund)** Greg Parent, a super salesman who is contemplating retirement on his fifty-fifth birthday, plans to create a fund that will earn 8% and enable him to withdraw $20,000 per year on June 30, beginning in 2007 and continuing through 2010. Greg intends to make equal contributions to this fund on June 30 of each of the years 2003–2006.

Instructions

(a) How much must the balance of the fund equal on June 30, 2006 in order for Greg Parent to satisfy his objective?

(b) What is the required amount of each of Greg's contributions to the fund?

EA-4 **(Unknown Rate)** LEW Corporation purchased a machine at a price of $100,000 by signing a note payable, which requires a single payment of $123,210 in 2 years. Assuming annual compounding of interest, what rate of interest is being paid on the loan?

EA-5 **(Unknown Periods and Unknown Interest Rate)**

1. Curtis Joseph wishes to become a millionaire. His money market fund has a balance of $92,296 and has a guaranteed interest rate of 10%.

Instructions

How many years must Curtis leave the balance in the fund in order to get his desired $1,000,000?

2. Oleta Firestone desires to accumulate $1 million in 15 years using her money market fund balance of $182,696.

Instructions

At what interest rate must her investment compound annually?

EA-6 **(Calculation of Bond Prices)** What will you pay for a $50,000 debenture bond that matures in 15 years and pays $5,000 interest at the end of each year if you want to earn a yield of **(a)** 8%? **(b)** 10%? **(c)** 12%?

EA-7 **(Evaluation of Purchase Options)** Hsang Excavating Inc. is purchasing a bulldozer. The equipment has a price of $100,000. The manufacturer has offered a payment plan that would allow Hsang to make 10 equal annual payments of $16,274.53, with the first payment due one year after the purchase.

Instructions

(a) How much interest will Hsang pay on this payment plan?

(b) Hsang could borrow $100,000 from its bank to finance the purchase at an annual rate of 9%. Should Hsang borrow from the bank or use the manufacturer's payment plan to pay for the equipment?

EA-8 **(Calculation of Pension Liability)** Erasure Inc. is a furniture manufacturing company with 50 employees. Recently, after a long negotiation with the local union, the company decided to initiate a pension plan as part of its compensation package. The plan will start on January 1, 2002. Each employee covered by the plan is entitled to a pension payment each year after retirement. As required by accounting standards, the controller of the company needs to report the projected pension obligation (liability). On the basis of a discussion with the supervisor of the Personnel Department and an actuary from an insurance company, the controller develops the following information related to the pension plan:

Average length of time to retirement	15 years
Expected life duration after retirement	10 years
Total pension payment expected each year for all retired employees.	
Payment made at the end of the year.	$700,000/year
The interest rate is 8%.	

Instructions

On the basis of the information given, determine the projected pension obligation.

EA-9 **(Amount Needed to Retire Shares)** Debugit Inc. is a computer software development company. In recent years, it has experienced significant growth in sales. As a result, the Board of Directors has decided to raise funds by issuing redeemable preferred shares to meet cash needs for expansion. On January 1, 2002 the company issued 100,000 redeemable preferred shares with the intent to redeem them on January 1, 2012. The redemption price per share is $25.

As the controller of the company, Kriss Krass is asked to set up a plan to accumulate the funds that will be needed to retire the redeemable preferred shares in 2012. She expects the company to have a surplus of funds of $125,000 each year for the next 10 years, and decides to put these amounts into a sinking fund. Beginning January 1, 2003 the company will deposit $125,000 into the sinking fund annually for 10 years. The sinking fund is expected to earn 10% interest compounded annually. However, the sinking fund will not be sufficient for the redemption of the preferred shares. Therefore, Kriss plans to deposit on January 1, 2007 a single amount into a savings account that is expected to earn 9% interest.

Instructions

What is the amount that must be deposited on January 1, 2007?

EA-10 **(Analysis of Alternatives)** S.O. Simple Ltd., a manufacturer of low-sodium, low-cholesterol T.V. dinners, would like to increase its market share in Atlantic Canada. In order to do so, S.O. Simple has decided to locate a new factory in the Halifax area. S.O. Simple will either buy or lease a building, depending upon which is more advantageous. The site location committee has narrowed down the options to the following three buildings:

Building A: Purchase for a cash price of $600,000, useful life 25 years.

Building B: Lease for 25 years, making annual payments of $69,000 at the beginning of each year.

Building C: Purchase for $650,000 cash. This building is larger than needed; however, the excess space can be sublet for 25 years at a net annual rental of $7,000. Rental payments will be received at the end of each year. S.O. Simple has no aversion to being a landlord.

Instructions

In which building would you recommend that S.O. Simple locate, assuming a 12% interest rate?

EA-11 **(Calculation of Bond Liability)** Wittar Ltd. manufactures skating equipment. Recently the vice president of operations of the company has requested construction of a new plant to meet the increasing needs for the company skates. After a careful evaluation of the request, the board of directors has decided to raise funds for the new plant by issuing $2 million of 11% corporate bonds on March 1, 2002, due on March 1, 2017, with interest payable each March 1 and September 1. At the time of issuance, the market rate of interest for similar financial instruments is 10%.

Instructions
As the controller of the company, determine the selling price of the bonds.

EA-12 (Future Value and Changing Interest Rates) Melanie Doane intends to invest $10,000 in a trust on January 10 of every year, 2002 to 2016, inclusive. She anticipates that interest rates will change during that period of time as follows:

1/10/02–1/09/05	10%
1/10/05–1/09/12	11%
1/10/12–1/09/16	12%

How much will Melanie have in trust on January 10, 2016?

EA-13 (Retirement of Debt) Glen Chan borrowed $70,000 on March 1, 2002. This amount plus accrued interest at 12% compounded semiannually is to be repaid on March 1, 2012. To retire this debt, Glen plans to contribute five equal amounts to a debt retirement fund starting on March 1, 2007 and continuing for the next four years. The fund is expected to earn 10% per annum.

Instructions
How much must Glen Chan contribute each year to provide a fund sufficient to retire the debt on March 1, 2012?

EA-14 (Unknown Rate) On July 17, 2002 Bruce Lendrum borrowed $42,000 from his grandfather to open a clothing store. Starting July 17, 2003 Bruce has to make 10 equal annual payments of $6,500 each to repay the loan.

Instructions
What interest rate is Bruce Lendrum paying? (Interpolation is required.)

EA-15 (Unknown Rate) As the purchaser of a new house, Sandra Pederson signed a mortgage note to pay the Canadian Bank $14,000 every six months for 20 years, at the end of which time she will own the house. At the date the mortgage was signed, the purchase price was $198,000 and Sandra made a down payment of $20,000. The first mortgage payment is to be made six months after the date the mortgage was signed.

Instructions
Calculate the exact rate of interest earned by the bank on the mortgage. (Interpolate if necessary.)

PROBLEMS

PA-1 Answer each of these unrelated questions:
1. On January 1, 2002 Gadget Corporation sold a building that cost $250,000 and had accumulated amortization of $100,000 on the date of sale. Gadget received as consideration a $275,000 noninterest-bearing note due on January 1, 2005. There was no established exchange price for the building and the note had no ready market. The prevailing rate of interest for a note of this type on January 1, 2002 was 9%. At what amount should the gain from the sale of the building be reported?
2. On January 1, 2002 Gadget Corporation purchased 200 of the $1,000 face value, 9%, 10-year bonds of Fox Inc. The bonds mature on January 1, 2012, and pay interest annually beginning January 1, 2003. Gadget Corporation purchased the bonds to yield 11%. How much did Gadget pay for the bonds?
3. Gadget Corporation bought a new machine and agreed to pay for it in equal annual instalments of $4,000 at the end of each of the next 10 years. Assuming an interest rate of 8% applies to this contract, how much should Gadget record as the cost of the machine?
4. Gadget Corporation purchased a tractor on December 31, 2002, paying $20,000 cash on that date and agreeing to pay $5,000 at the end of each of the next eight years. At what amount should the tractor be valued on December 31, 2002, assuming an interest rate of 12%?
5. Gadget Corporation wants to withdraw $100,000 (including principal) from an investment fund at the end of each year for nine years. What is the required initial investment at the beginning of the first year if the fund earns 11%?

PA-2 When Norman Peterson died, he left his wife Vera an insurance policy contract that permitted her to choose any one of the following four options:

1. $55,000 immediate cash.
2. $3,700 every three months, payable at the end of each quarter for five years.
3. $18,000 immediate cash and $1,600 every three months for 10 years, payable at the beginning of each three-month period.
4. $4,000 every three months for three years and $1,200 each quarter for the following 25 quarters, all payments payable at the end of each quarter.

Instructions

If money is worth 2½% per quarter, compounded quarterly, which option will you recommend that Vera choose?

PA-3 Pennywise Inc. has decided to surface and maintain for 10 years a vacant lot next to one of its discount retail outlets to serve as a parking lot for customers. Management is considering the following bids that involve two different qualities of surfacing for a parking area of 12,000 m².

Bid A. A surface that costs $5.25 per square metre. This surface will have to be replaced at the end of five years. The annual maintenance cost on this surface is estimated at 20 cents per square metre for each year except the last of its service. The replacement surface will be similar to the initial surface.

Bid B. A surface that costs $9.50 per square metre. This surface has a probable useful life of 10 years and will require annual maintenance in each year except the last year, at an estimated cost of 9 cents per square metre.

Instructions

Prepare calculations that show which bid should be accepted by Pennywise Inc. You may assume that the cost of capital is 9%, that the annual maintenance expenditures are incurred at the end of each year, and that prices are not expected to change during the next 10 years.

PA-4 Robyn Hood, a bank robber, is worried about her retirement. She decides to start a savings account. Robyn deposits annually her net share of the "loot," which consists of $75,000 per year, for three years beginning January 1, 2002. Robyn is arrested on January 4, 2004 (after making the third deposit) and spends the rest of 2004 and most of 2005 in jail. She escapes in September of 2005 and resumes her savings plan with semiannual deposits of $30,000 each, beginning January 1, 2006. Assume that the bank's interest rate is 9% compounded annually from January 1, 2002 through January 1, 2005, and 12% compounded semiannually thereafter.

Instructions

When Robyn retires on January 1, 2009 (six months after her last deposit), what will be the balance in her savings account?

PA-5 Provide a solution to each of the following situations by calculating the unknowns (use the interest tables):

1. Leslie Rooke invests in a $180,000 annuity insurance policy at 9% compounded annually on February 8, 2002. The first of 20 receipts from the annuity is payable to Leslie 10 years after the annuity is purchased (February 8, 2012). What will be the amount of each of the 20 equal annual receipts?
2. Kevin Tait owes a debt of $30,000 from the purchase of his new sports car. The debt bears interest of 8% payable annually. Kevin wishes to pay the debt and interest in eight annual instalments, beginning one year hence. What equal annual instalments will pay the debt and interest?
3. On January 1, 2002 Mike Myers offers to buy Dan Carbey's used combine for $45,000, payable in 10 equal instalments that include 9% interest on the unpaid balance and a portion of the principal, with the first payment to be made on January 1, 2002. How much will each payment be?

PA-6 During the past year, Leanne Cundall planted a new vineyard on 150 ha of land that she leases for $27,000 a year. She has asked you to assist in determining the value of her vineyard operation.

The vineyard will bear no grapes for the first five years (Years 1–5). In the next five years (Years 6–10), Leanne estimates that the vines will bear grapes that can be sold for $60,000 each year. For the next 20 years (Years 11–30), she expects the harvest to provide annual revenues of $100,000. During the last 10 years (Years 31–40) of the vineyard's life, she estimates that revenues will decline to $80,000 per year.

During the first five years the annual cost of pruning, fertilizing, and caring for the vineyard is estimated at $9,000; during the years of production, Years 6–40, these costs will rise to $10,000 per year. The relevant market rate of interest for the entire period is 12%. Assume that all receipts and payments are made at the end of each year.

Instructions

Tanya McIvor has offered to buy Leanne's vineyard business. On the basis of the present value of the business, what is the minimum price Leanne should accept?

PA-7 Handyman Inc. owns and operates a number of hardware stores on the Prairies. Recently the company has decided to locate another store in a rapidly growing area of Manitoba; the company is trying to decide whether to purchase or lease the building and related facilities.

Purchase. The company can purchase the site, construct the building, and purchase all store fixtures. The cost would be $1,650,000. An immediate down payment of $400,000 is required, and the remaining $1,250,000 would be paid off over five years at $300,000 per year (including interest). The property is expected to have a useful life of 12 years and then it will be sold for $500,000. As the owner of the property, the company will have the following out-of-pocket expenses each period:

Property taxes (to be paid at the end of each year)	$40,000
Insurance (to be paid at the beginning of each year)	$27,000
Other (primarily maintenance, which occurs at the end of each year)	$16,000
	$83,000

Lease. Jensen Corp. Ltd. has agreed to purchase the site, construct the building, and install the appropriate fixtures for Handyman Inc. if Handyman will lease the completed facility for 12 years. The annual costs for the lease will be $240,000. The lease would be a triple-net lease, which means that Handyman will have no responsibility related to the facility over the 12 years. The terms of the lease are that Handyman would be required to make 12 annual payments (the first payment to be made at the time the store opens and then each following year). In addition, a deposit of $100,000 is required when the store is opened that will be returned at the end of the twelfth year, assuming no unusual damage to the building structure or fixtures.

Currently the cost of funds for Handyman Inc. is 10%.

Instructions

Which of the two approaches should Handyman Inc. follow?

PA-8 Presented below are a series of time value of money problems for you to solve.

1. Your client, Kate Greenaway, wishes to provide for the payment of an obligation of $250,000 that is due on July 1, 2008. Kate plans to deposit $20,000 in a special fund each July 1 for eight years, starting July 1, 2001. She also wishes to make a deposit on July 1, 2000 of an amount that, with its accumulated interest, will bring the fund up to $250,000 at the maturity of the obligation. She expects the fund to earn interest at the rate of 4% compounded annually. Calculate the amount to be deposited on July 1, 2000.

2. On January 1, 2000 Keeley Inc. initiated a pension plan under which each of its employees will receive a pension annuity of $10,000 per year beginning one year after retirement and continuing until death. Employee A will retire at the end of 2006 and, according to mortality tables, is expected to live long enough to receive eight pension payments. What is the present value of Keeley Inc.'s pension obligation for employee A at the beginning of 2000 if the interest rate is 10%?

3. McLachlan Ltd. purchases bonds from Rankin Inc. in the amount of $500,000. The bonds are 10-year, 12% bonds that pay interest semiannually. After three years (and receipt of interest for three years), McLachlan needs money and, therefore, sells the bonds to Doyle Corp., which demands interest at 16% compounded semiannually. What is the amount that McLachlan will receive on the sale of the bonds?

PA-9 Answer the following questions related to Gervais Inc.

1. Gervais Inc. has $572,000 to invest. The company is trying to decide between two alternative uses of the funds. One alternative provides $80,000 at the end of each year for 12 years; the other pays a single lump sum of $1,900,000 at the end of 12 years. Which alternative should Gervais select? Assume the interest rate is constant over the entire investment.

2. Gervais Inc. has just purchased a new computer system. The fair market value of the equipment is $824,150. The purchase agreement specified an immediate down payment of $200,000 and semiannual payments of $76,952 that begin at the end of six months for five years. What interest rate, to the nearest percent, was used in discounting this purchase transaction?

3. Gervais Inc. loaned $600,000 to Whistler Corporation. Gervais accepted a note due in seven years at 8% compounded semiannually. After two years (and receipt of interest for two years), Gervais needed money and therefore sold the note to Royal Canadian Bank, which required interest on the note of 10% compounded semi-annually. What amount did Gervais receive from the sale of the note?

4. Gervais Inc. wishes to accumulate $1,300,000 by December 31, 2012 to retire outstanding bonds. The company deposits $300,000 on December 31, 2002, which will earn interest at 10% per year compounded quarterly, to help in the debt retirement. The company wants to know what additional equal amounts should be deposited at the end of each quarter for 10 years to ensure that $1,300,000 is available at the end of 2012. (The quarterly deposits will also earn interest at a rate of 10%, compounded quarterly.) Round to even dollars.

PA-10 Laird Wightman is a financial executive with Marsh Corporation. Although Laird has not had any formal training in finance or accounting, he has a "good sense" for numbers and has helped the company grow from a very small ($500,000 sales) to a large operation ($45 million sales). With the business growing steadily, however, the company needs to make a number of difficult financial decisions that Laird feels are a little "over his head." He has therefore decided to hire a new employee with facility in "numbers" to help him. As a basis for determining whom to employ, he asked each prospective employee to prepare answers to questions relating to the following situations he has encountered recently. Here are the questions that you are asked to answer:

1. In 2000 Marsh Corporation negotiated and closed a long-term lease contract for newly constructed truck terminals and freight storage facilities. The buildings were constructed on land owned by the company. On January 1, 2001 Marsh took possession of the leased property. The 20-year lease is effective for the period January 1, 2001 through December 31, 2020. Rental payments of $800,000 are payable to the lessor (owner of facilities) on January 1 of each of the first 10 years of the lease term. Payments of $300,000 are due on January 1 for each of the last 10 years of the lease term. Marsh has an option to purchase all the leased facilities for $1.00 on December 31, 2020. At the time the lease was negotiated, the fair market value of the truck terminals and freight storage facilities was approximately $7.2 million. If the company had borrowed the money to purchase the facilities, it would have had to pay 10% interest. Should the company have purchased rather than leased the facilities?

2. Last year the company exchanged some land for a noninterest-bearing note. The note was to be paid at the rate of $12,000 per year for nine years, beginning one year from the date of the exchange. The interest rate for the note was 11%. At the time the land was originally purchased, it cost $90,000. What is the fair value of the note?

3. The company has always followed the policy to take any cash discounts offered on goods purchased. Recently the company purchased a large amount of raw materials at a price of $800,000 with terms 2/10, n/30 on which it took the discount. If Marsh's cost of funds was 10%, should the policy of always taking cash discounts be continued?

Company Index

Subject Index